OXFORD HISTORY OF
EARLY MODERN EUROPE

General Editor: R. J. W. EVANS

GERMANY AND THE HOLY ROMAN EMPIRE

Joachim Whaley is Professor of German History and Thought in the Faculty of Modern and Medieval Languages at the University of Cambridge, and a Fellow of Gonville and Caius College.

Praise for GERMANY AND THE HOLY ROMAN EMPIRE VOLUME I

'the most comprehensive work on the subject in recent times and [it] will almost certainly achieve the rank of a standard work...a singular monument of Anglo-Saxon learning...a model of historical scholarship...recommended not only to scholars but also to students and anyone interested in history...Whaley's style makes reading his book a pleasure'

Wolfgang Burgdorf, *Frankfurter Allgemeine Zeitung*

'brilliantly successful...a detailed account of two hundred years of German history. Whaley demonstrates a stupendous knowledge of German history...the most important English-language work on pre-modern German history for at least two decades'

Axel Gotthard, *Sehepunkte*

'scholars...will concur in their debt to Whaley's magnum opus...[it] stands apart as the most authoritative account of the early modern empire'

C. Ingrao, *ChoiceReviews.online*

'[Whaley's] two volumes are exceptionally well written and highly nuanced and reflect the latest scholarship...they represent a huge personal achievement...they will...provide a standard of scholarship against which all future works will be measured'

Alan Sked, *Reviews in History*

'The massive achievement of this superb and authoritative study is to rescue the Holy Roman Empire from the condescension of history...It is hard to overestimate the scale of Whaley's achievement. The Holy Roman Empire was a labyrinth of hundreds of tiny princedoms, duchies, bishoprics and independent city states, each with its own jurisdictions and special patterns of allegiance...Whaley effortlessly weaves them together...The scholarship in this book is profound...yet it is a surprisingly easy read. Above all Whaley has rewritten the course of German history by suggesting that there was nothing about German society, culture or political structure that created the conditions for 20th-century authoritarianism'

Peter Oborne, *Daily Telegraph*

'Whaley's account is one of the best works on early modern German history. From the first page to the last, it shows how German history can be presented as both a history of Emperor and Empire, and a history of a common culture. It will immediately establish itself as a standard guide to its subject'

Georg Schmidt, Friedrich Schiller University, Jena

More praise for GERMANY AND THE HOLY ROMAN EMPIRE VOLUME I

'[Whaley's] work, though different in emphasis and organisation, stands equal with the major German speaking syntheses today existing such as by Horst Rabe, Karl Otmar von Aretin, Heinz Schilling, or Georg Schmidt. His detailed knowledge of the vast relevant research literature, in German or in any other language, on topics ranging from the later fifteenth to the early nineteenth century is breath-taking. As such, this work is a must-read for all students of Early Modern Germany unless they work on specific issues of social and demographic history... The superior quality of Whaley's synthesis is beyond question. This is a masterpiece that demands close attention and respect'

Robert von Friedeburg, *H-Soz-u-Kult*

'Whaley accomplishes his argosy with poise and style. These two volumes, which will undoubtedly become a first point of reference, are a remarkable achievement'

Tom Scott, *English Historical Review*

'an overall account whose methodological reflection, thematic range, and wealth of detail are unparalleled... these two volumes will quickly become standard works ... their particular form, combining sections on historiography and methodology, structural history and the history of events, has no counterpart in the German-language historiography... Whaley presents the development of the Holy Roman Empire from the late Middle Ages to its dissolution, debates older and more recent models of interpretation, identifies thematic priorities, and describes lines of historical development without passing over individual events. The text also presents a wealth of regional features and episodes in context which demonstrates the author's outstanding grasp of the detail of both imperial history and German regional history'

Stefan Ehrenpreis, *German Historical Institute London Bulletin*

'successfully combines an expert's love of detail with a clear view of the large picture... Whaley's work offers the reader a comprehensive view... which pursues a consistent line throughout... a valuable handbook for history teachers, students and journalists... the work is recommended to anyone interested in the historical-political development of Germany in Europe'

Willi Eisele, *AHF-Information*

Germany and the Holy Roman Empire

BY
JOACHIM WHALEY

VOLUME 1
FROM MAXIMILIAN I TO THE PEACE OF
WESTPHALIA 1493–1648

OXFORD
UNIVERSITY PRESS

OXFORD
UNIVERSITY PRESS

Great Clarendon Street, Oxford OX2 6DP

Oxford University Press is a department of the University of Oxford.
It furthers the University's objective of excellence in research, scholarship,
and education by publishing worldwide. Oxford is a registered trade mark of
Oxford University Press in the UK and in certain other countries

First published 2012
First published in paperback 2013

Published in the United States of America by Oxford University Press
198 Madison Avenue, New York, NY 10016, United States of America

ISBN 978–0–19–873101–6 (Hbk)
ISBN 978–0–19–968882–1 (Pbk)

For Alice

Acknowledgements

I have incurred numerous debts during my work on this project and it is my pleasure to record some of them here. The list of institutions may be complete, but I have no doubt that I have overlooked many individuals and I should apologize to them at this point.

The British Academy provided me with a generous Wolfson European Fellowship when I started work, which enabled me to spend time at the Herzog August Bibliothek in Wolfenbüttel. Book and research grants provided by Gonville and Caius College, Cambridge have been invaluable at every stage. The College also generously awarded me an additional grant towards the cost of the index. I am grateful to the Electors of the Tiarks German Scholarship Fund, who kindly agreed to pay for the maps and to help with other costs I incurred in the production of the manuscript. A generous grant from the Newton Trust helped me in the final stages of checking the manuscript for submission and preparing it for publication.

Among the many people who have given me help and encouragement over the years, I should like to thank the following: Geoff Bailey, Derek Beales, Ilya Bercovich, Tim Blanning, Nicholas Boyle, Annabel Brett, Anita Bunyan, Paul Castle, Stephanie Chan, Christopher Clark, Christophe Duhamelle, Richard Duncan-Jones, Richard Evans, Stephen Fennell, Axel Gotthard, the late Trevor Johnson, Andreas Klinger, Charlotte Lee, Neil McKendrick, Ian Maclean, Alison Martin, Sharon Nevill, Barry Nisbet, Sheilagh Ogilvie, William O'Reilly, Roger Paulin, the late Volker Press, Ritchie Robertson, Heinz Schilling, Anton Schindling, Alexander Schmidt, Georg Schmidt, Luise Schorn-Schütte, Brendan Simms, Ingrid Sindermann-Mittmann, Gareth Stedman Jones, Mikuláš Teich, Alice Teichova, Andrew Thompson, Maiken Umbach, Helen Watanabe-O'Kelly, Siegrid Westphal, Peter Wilson, Charlotte Woodford, and Chris Young.

My work would not have been possible without the assistance of the staff of the Cambridge University Library. In particular, David Lowe and Christian Staufenbiel have been absolutely marvellous. I have much appreciated Christian's willingness to respond to (far too many) e-mails marked 'urgent' and the speed with which he has so often made it possible for me to consult a newly acquired book. He and David Lowe together make the University Library surely one of the best places in the world to pursue research in German studies.

At Gonville and Caius College, Yvonne Holmes, Wendy Fox and Louise Mills have provided assistance at crucial points. The combined efforts of Harvey Barker, Maki Lam, Matt Lee, and Richard Pettit in the College Computer Office have ensured that I did not on occasion delete large parts of the text by mistake and they rescued me promptly, and with great good humour, from all too many 'computer crises'. In the Caius library, Mark Statham and Sonia Londero have always been unfailingly helpful.

I am grateful to Philip Stickler and David Watson of the Cambridge University Department of Geography Cartographic Unit for their help in devising the maps which accompany each volume.

At Oxford University Press, I would like to thank my wonderfully helpful Commissioning Editor Stephanie Ireland, and Production Editor Emma Barber. Elizabeth Stone (copy-editor) and Fiona Barry (proofreader) have also been most thorough and efficient.

Robert Evans invited me to undertake this project and he has been constantly supportive ever since. He has also been extremely patient in awaiting the outcome. I am deeply grateful to him for his trust in me and for the care and attention with which he read various sections of the text over the years and then the draft of the whole manuscript in the summer of 2010.

Among many more personal debts, I am grateful to David Theobald and Peter Crabbe for cups of tea and diverting conversations about things other than 'the book', and to the Reverend Margaret Mabbs, who asked every year.

My greatest debt, as the dedication indicates, is to Alice.

Joachim Whaley
Cambridge
31.x.11

Contents

VII. THE THIRTY YEARS WAR, 1618–1648

A Note on Terminology and Usage

Even the question of how to refer to 'Germany' in the early modern period has aroused controversy. I have used a variety of forms as they have seemed appropriate. The term 'German lands' was employed with increasing frequency from about the middle of the fourteenth century. In humanist discourse around 1500, 'Germany' is frequently found. It remained in use in political discourse and in literature. The title *Das Heilige Römische Reich deutscher Nation*, which gained currency around 1500, also underlines the identification of the empire as a specifically German polity. The title of the empire was variously abbreviated, but, increasingly, 'Deutsches Reich', 'das Reich', or simply 'Deutschland' were employed. I have referred to the empire as the 'Reich' throughout and I also frequently refer to the 'German lands' and 'Germany', meaning more or less the same area (including Austria), throughout.

Institutions of the Reich have also been referred to by their German names. I have thus preferred Kreis (plural Kreise) to the awkward English term 'Circles', Reichshofrat to Imperial Aulic Council, and Reichskammergericht to Imperial Chamber Court. These and other German terms are explained in the Glossary.

I have generally used the German forms for the names of people and places, except where that would impede identification of an individual or place well known in English (for example, Frederick the Great). German names have almost invariably been used for places that also have Polish, Czech, or Hungarian names. The use of German names in such cases has, in the past, been the subject of bitter argument, a reflection of the troubled history of the relations between the Germans and their eastern neighbours. The use of German names in this work does not imply any position on those arguments, no more than the implicit inclusion of the Austrians in the term 'German' at many points of the book indicates any sympathy or nostalgia on the part of the author for notions of a 'greater Germany'. The same applies to the preference given in this work to the German names of places in Alsace and elsewhere.

Geographical terms such as Lower Germany and Upper Germany have been given in English. 'Upper' and 'Lower' normally refer to altitude and river flows, though this can be misleading. The Upper Palatinate, for example, originally a possession of the Rhineland Lower Palatinate, became a Bavarian possession from the 1620s, and it is now one of seven administrative regions of the modern *Land* of Bavaria, to the north-east, next to the Czech border. In other cases, 'Upper' and 'Lower' can refer to the major or stem territory of a principality and a minor exclave respectively.

The use of the term 'Calvinist' is problematic, for those Germans who were referred to as 'Calvinists' were really the heirs of Zwingli and Bullinger rather than followers of Calvin, whose impact was greater in France. The term 'Calvinist' was used frequently in the late sixteenth century, but it soon acquired pejorative connotations. The German reformed churches generally referred to themselves as 'Reformed' or, later, 'deutsch-reformiert' (to distinguish themselves from the Huguenot immigrants of the late seventeenth century, who were indeed Calvinist and who were generally known in Germany as 'französisch-reformiert'). I have used 'Calvinist' only in contexts where it seems appropriate, and have otherwise generally preferred the terms 'Reformed' and 'German Reformed'.

The vocabulary of the currency, weights, and measures of early modern Germany is characterized by an almost impossible variety. The Reich used both (gold) gulden and (silver) thaler as main denominations throughout the early modern period, though the thaler came to predominate. Lesser coins varied according to region, or even locality. This is also true of weights and measures, where the same word could denote a wide variety of different actual entities. I have not attempted to standardize or to provide equivalents, either contemporary or modern: that would be a formidable task for a single year, let alone over three centuries. The best guides to this profusion are Fritz Verdenhalven's *Alte Maße, Münzen und Gewichte aus dem deutschen Sprachgebiet* (Neustadt a.d. Aisch, 1968) and Wolfgang Trapp, *Kleines Handbuch der Maße, Zahlen, Gewichte und der Zeitrechnung*, 2nd edn (Stuttgart, 1996).

The most important square measure for this book is the square mile. I have converted German square miles either into English square miles (1 German square mile or 'Quadratmeile' is 21.25 English square miles) or into square kilometres (1 German square mile or 'Quadratmeile' is 55.05 square kilometres).

In general, I have simplified German orthography throughout, especially by usually preferring 'ss' to 'ß'. The German and Latin titles of works that appear in the text are normally accompanied by an English translation, except where the sense of the sentence makes the meaning obvious. Date of birth and death or regnal dates have been given where it seems appropriate.

A Note on Maps and Online Resources

Maps are a serious problem for any historian of the Holy Roman Empire. Only the largest formats, far exceeding what is possible in the average-sized book, are capable of reflecting the complexity of the territorial arrangements in the early modern Reich. Even some regional maps would need to be quite large to show accurately the fragmented nature of many territories or the difference, for example, between the boundaries of prince-bishoprics which a prince-bishop ruled as a prince and the diocese of which he was spiritual head.

The maps contained in this work can only provide a very rough general orientation. An excellent collection of maps with greater detail may be found online in the collection commissioned by the German Historical Institute, Washington DC, entitled German History in Documents and Images (GHDI), at http://germanhistorydocs.ghi-dc.org/about.cfm (accessed 4 May 2011). The relevant sections are: volume 1, 'From the Reformation to the Thirty Years War (1500–1648)', edited by Thomas A. Brady and Ellen Utzy Glebe, and volume 2, 'From Absolutism to Napoleon (1648–1815)', edited by William Hagen.

The best historical atlas in print is probably *Putzger: Historischer Weltatlas*, edited by Ernst Bruckmüller and Peter Claus Hartmann (103rd edn, Berlin, 2001). The indispensable seven-volume handbook on the religious and ecclesiastical history of the German territories between 1500 and 1648, edited by Anton Schindling and Walter Ziegler (cited as Schindling and Ziegler, *Territorien*), provides an area map of *c*.1500 for each territory discussed. The best historical atlas for religious and ecclesiastical history is now *Atlas zur Kirche in Geschichte und Gegenwart: Heiliges Römisches Reich, deutschsprachige Länder*, edited by Erwin Gatz, with Rainald Becker, Clemens Brodkorb, Helmut Flachenecker, and Karsten Bremer (Regensburg, 2009). Other useful maps relating to religious history generally, including the Reichskirche, may also be found in *Atlas zur Kirchengeschichte: Die christlichen Kirchen in Geschichte und Gegenwart*, edited by Hubert Jedin, Kenneth Scott Latourette, and Jochen Martin, 3rd revised edition, edited by Jochen Martin (Freiburg, 2004), pp. 64–94.

The Internet has made a wealth of biographical information accessible. The standard German (*Allgemeine Deutsche Biographie* and *Neue Deutsche Biographie*), Austrian (*Österreichisches Biographisches Lexikon*), and Swiss (*Historisches Lexikon der Schweiz*) biographical dictionaries are searchable via the 'biography portal' at http://www.biographie-portal.eu/about (accessed 4 May 2011). Constantin Wurzbach's *Biographisches Lexikon des Kaiserthums Österreich*, 60 vols (1856–91) may be searched at http://www.literature.at/collection.alo?objid=11104 (accessed 4 May 2011). Friedrich Wilhelm Bautz's invaluable *Biographisch-bibliographisches Kirchenlexikon* is available in updated form at http://www.bautz.de/bbkl/ (accessed 4 May 2011).

Images of places and buildings are now also available online: a simple search using either an English search engine or—often much better for searching a

German term or place name, a German-language search engine, such as via www. altavista.de, can quickly yield an image that gives an excellent sense of place. Many a building described in the literature as influenced by Versailles turned out to bear no likeness at all!

Finally, anyone working on German history, or wishing to find further literature on particular points, should be eternally grateful to the editors of the *Jahresberichte für deutsche Geschichte* at the Berlin-Brandenburgische Akademie der Wissenschaften. Their online bibliography, which includes everything published on German history since 1974 and is updated daily, is, quite simply, incomparable. It can be found at http://www.jdg-online.de (accessed 4 May 2011).

Abbreviations

ADB	*Allgemeine Deutsche Biographie*, 56 vols (Munich and Leipzig, 1875–1902).
BWDG	*Biographisches Wörterbuch zur deutschen Geschichte*, ed. Karl Bosl, Günther Franz, and Hanns Hubert Hofmann, 2nd edn, 3 vols (Munich, 1973–4).
DBE	*Deutsche Biographische Enzyklopädie*, ed. Walther Killy and Rudolf Vierhaus, 13 vols in 15 (Darmstadt, 1995–2003).
DVG	*Deutsche Verwaltungsgeschichte, Band 1: Vom Spätmittelalter bis zum Ende des Reiches*, ed. Kurt G. A. Jeserich, Hans Pohl, and Georg Christoph von Unruh (Stuttgart, 1983).
HBayG	*Handbuch der Bayerischen Geschichte*, ed. Max Spindler, Franz Brunhölzl, and Hans Fischer, 4 vols in 6 (Munich, 1967–75).
HdtBG, i	*Handbuch der deutschen Bildungsgeschichte, Band I: 15. bis 17. Jahrhundert*, ed. Notker Hammerstein (Munich, 1996).
HdtBG, ii	*Handbuch der deutschen Bildungsgeschichte, Band 2: 18. Jahrhundert*, ed. Notker Hammerstein and Ulrich Herrmann (Munich, 2005).
HbDSWG	*Handbuch der Deutschen Wirtschafts- und Sozialgeschichte, Band 1: Von der Frühzeit bis zum Ende des 18. Jahrhunderts*, ed. Herman Aubin and Wolfgang Zorn (Stuttgart, 1978).
HDR	*Handwörterbuch zur Deutschen Rechtsgeschichte*, ed. Adalbert Erler and Ekkehard Kaufmann (Berlin, 1964–).
HLB	http://www.historisches-lexikon-bayerns.de/base/start (last accessed 15 November 2010).
HLS	*Historisches Lexikon der Schweiz*, ed. Marco Jorio (Basle, 2002–).
IPM	Instrumentum Pacis Monasteriense (the Peace of Münster 1648).
IPO	Instrumentum Pacis Osnabrugense (the Peace of Osnabrück 1648).
LdM	*Lexikon des Mittelalters*, 10 vols (Munich, 1980–99).
NDB	*Neue Deutsche Biographie* (Berlin, 1953–).
RGG	*Die Religion in Geschichte und Gegenwart. Handwörterbuch für Theologie und Religionswissenschaft*, ed. Hans Dieter Betz, Don S. Browning, Bernd Janowski, and Eberhard Jürgel, 4th edn, 9 vols (Munich, 1998–2005).
TRE	*Theologische Realenzyklopädie*, ed. Gerhard Krause and Gerhard Müller, 38 vols (Berlin, 1977–2007).

List of Maps

The Holy Roman Empire: 1547 (major territories)

Legend:

Hohenzollern territories
- Brandenburg
- Franconian

Wettin territories
- Albertine Saxony
- Ernestine Saxony

Wittelsbach territories
- Bavarian
- Palatinate

Oldenburg territories
- Schleswig-Holstein
- Oldenburg

- Empire boundary
- Ecclesiastical territories

Habsburg territories
- Austrian
- Spanish

Map labels: Prussia, Poland, Denmark, Bohemia, France, Swiss Confederation, Savoy, Rep. of Venice, Austria, Ottoman Empire

Scale: 0 — 100 kilometres

The Kreise of the Holy Roman Empire c.1512

Kreis

- Empire boundary
- Electoral Rhine
- Upper Rhine
- Burgundian
- Austrian
- Westphalian
- Upper Saxon
- Lower Saxon
- Franconian
- Swabian
- Bavarian

N.B. Hatching denotes regions with large numbers of Imperial Knights.

Prussia

Poland

Denmark

Bohemia (no Kreis)

Rep. of Venice

Swiss Confederation

Savoy

Italian States

France

0   100
kilometres

—

Introduction

NARRATIVES OF EARLY MODERN GERMAN HISTORY

The history of Germany presents the historian with particular difficulties. At every stage the disrupted and often turbulent development of the country since the early nineteenth century has been reflected in the ways that its historians have written about their past. Indeed, to a quite extraordinary degree, the writing of German history since the nineteenth century has been political and informed by ideas about the historical identity of the German people. In the nineteenth century, historians played a central role in defining the nation. In the twentieth century, each rupture or new phase in the nation's history has prompted a re-evaluation of the national past. In the years immediately after 1918, and again in the 1930s, that process produced distinctive variations on the patterns of historical interpretation developed in the nineteenth century.

After 1945, however, the whole of German history was subject to radical revisions that challenged many of the fundamental assumptions on which historical research in Germany had previously been based. This process, differently pursued in the Federal Republic and the former German Democratic Republic (GDR) and with new inflections since the reunification of Germany in 1990, has brought about a transformation in our understanding of the history of the Holy Roman Empire in the early modern era.

These changing perceptions are of central importance to an understanding both of German history as a whole and of the significance and meaning given to particular periods in it. Indeed, it is probably true of German history more than most national histories that it cannot be fully understood without some sense of how it was written by previous generations. Consequently, one of the aims of this book is to show how German historians have understood the history of the later Holy Roman Empire in the context of their national history and to show how their own historical experience has shaped their approach to the early modern period. This introduction will therefore give an account of some of the views that have developed over the past two centuries.

The subject of this work is the evolution of German-speaking Central Europe within the framework of the Holy Roman Empire from the late fifteenth century to the early nineteenth century. Around 1500, the reforms attempted by Holy Roman Emperor Maximilian I resulted in the emergence of a new kind of polity in the Reich. The emperor failed in his financial and military demands. Yet the agreement that was secured on a general peace and on the creation of a higher court of law to protect it, and the continuing negotiations with the Reichstag that ensued, marked a decisive turning point. The polity was set on a new course of development that continued through to the end of the eighteenth century.

The constitutional balance that prevailed in Germany was quite unlike that which characterized the British, French, or Spanish monarchies, though it was similar to the constitutional system of the Polish-Lithuanian Kingdom or to the decentralized commonwealths developed around the same time by the Swiss or somewhat later by the Dutch. In the Holy Roman Empire, the formula *Kaiser und Reich* (Emperor and Reich or Imperial Estates) described a dual system which functioned at two levels, distinct though linked in complex ways. At one level, the Reich developed from a medieval feudal system based on the personal relationship between the king and his noble vassals into something increasingly like a federal system. The essential infrastructure of the king and his fiefs remained in place until the Reich was dissolved in 1806. More than in most other parts of Europe, the authority of the monarch was limited and it was subject to fairly strict and explicit constraints.

It is true that historians of other European countries now see the development of the dynastic state in less absolute terms and emphasize its limitations and weaknesses.[1] The 'composite monarchies' of Britain, France, and Spain were collections of provinces, principalities, or kingdoms which retained, because they clung to them, traditional rights and institutions in defiance of centralizing monarchs and their officials.[2]

The German case is, however, rather different again. For here, at the second level, princes and other subordinate corporations and individuals retained a far greater degree of autonomy from the monarch. It was at this level that many of the essential functions of the state developed: taxation, the regulation of society, the raising of armed forces, and the like. In some of the larger territories, from the late fifteenth century this led to the emergence of structures that have been called states by some German historians. The term may seem appropriate as far as internal function is concerned. Yet the rulers of these territories remained vassals of the emperor. They were overlords of their people, but never sovereigns. Their powers were subject to the laws of the Reich and to the authority of the emperor, to whom their people could appeal as a higher authority.

The nature of this dual system and its effects on the development of the German lands has been understood in different ways by successive generations of historians. In the national tradition of the nineteenth and first half of the twentieth centuries, the early modern period was viewed as an era of decline and decay.[3] On the one hand, romantic notions of a medieval German Christian Reich appeared to reveal a contrast with the divisions of the Holy Roman Empire and its manifest lack of universal influence after the Reformation. For many Catholic scholars of the

---

[1] Bonney, *Dynastic states*, 305–60.
[2] Elliott, 'Composite monarchies'.
[3] Faulenbach, *Ideologie*, 38–42; Eckert and Walther, 'Frühneuzeitforschung'; Puschner, 'Reichsromantik'; Thamer, 'Reich'; Langewiesche, 'Reichsidee'.

nineteenth century, the Reformation represented the end of medieval universalism. On the other hand, nationalist historians bemoaned the decline of a supposedly strong medieval German empire or kingdom into a period of anarchic division and disunity after about 1500. Protestant historians in Prussia and elsewhere in Germany could regard the Reformation as a heroic German achievement. For the rest, however, these historians concurred in the view that the decades around 1500 saw the final degeneration of the Reich. The supposed triumph of the princes over the emperor, and the assertion of particularism, led first to a century of bitter divisions and protracted conflicts over religion.

In the early seventeenth century, those conflicts gained an international dimension, and for thirty years the German lands became a battlefield. The end of the war, according to nationalist tradition, marked the nadir of German unity. The German lands were ravaged and exhausted; German society was shattered and German culture all but extinguished. Amidst the ruins, the German princes allegedly established absolutist states untrammelled by any moderating authority. The Peace of Westphalia, which concluded the hostilities in 1648, was viewed as the Magna Carta of particularism. It enshrined the absolute rights of the princes and codified the impotence of both the emperor and the German people.

For the next one-and-a-half centuries, in the traditional view, the Reich survived only as a decrepit shell: corrupt and moribund, a hollow mockery of the once strong medieval empire with its universal mission. In 1918, a young second-generation American scholar of literature at the University of Minnesota, well versed in the writings of the nineteenth-century German historians, went so far as to conclude that the Reich really 'had no history at all' after 1648 and that 'it continued for a while longer to lead a miserable, meaningless existence because its patient, slow-moving subjects lacked the initiative and in many cases the intelligence to effect its actual dissolution'.[4]

According to the mainstream nationalist tradition, two developments in the eighteenth century paved the way out of the trough. First, the emergence of Brandenburg-Prussia as a strong monarchy capable of leadership laid the foundations for the future unification of Germany. The process was a slow one. Even Frederick the Great was unable to rally the princes in the Fürstenbund of the 1780s. His successors saved Germany in the wars against Napoleon, but even their appeal to the nation proved short-lived, leaving later rulers and statesmen to take up the national cause. Second, the eighteenth century supposedly saw the emergence for the first time of a truly national German culture, unpolitical at first, developing at a distance from the state in cosmopolitan idealism, but politicized by degrees through engagement with the French Revolution and Napoleon. Both strands of development allegedly came together in the German nation state of 1871, which resumed the national history of the Germans that had been interrupted in the late Middle Ages.

---

[4] Zeydel, *Holy Roman Empire*, 15. The volume was republished as late as 1966 and reissued by Columbia University Press in 2009. Zeydel (1893–1973) went on to a distinguished career as Professor of German at Cincinnati from 1926 to 1961.

In varying permutations, with differences of emphasis according to regional (for example, Prussian or south German) or religious (Protestant or Catholic) affiliation, this vision of national history prevailed more or less unchallenged until 1945. It also became the established view of things in the minds of non-German historians, partly through the influence of James Bryce's classic account of the Holy Roman Empire first published in 1864, which drew heavily on the work of Ranke and his contemporaries.[5] Significantly, Bryce devoted just twenty-eight pages, some 16 per cent, of his text to the last three centuries of the Reich. In the sixth expanded and corrected edition of the book in 1906, as much space was devoted to the creation of the new German Empire of the nineteenth century as to the early modern Reich.

Alongside what might be described as the 'official' Prussian-German view of the past, also broadly endorsed by non-Prussian German Protestants, there were of course also alternatives, though they never became dominant. In the first decades after 1815, there was a variety of Catholic and Austrian overviews of German history. Even they shared the general view of the tragedy of German history after 1648, though they tended to emphasize the 'un-German' character of Prussia.[6]

Increasingly, however, Austrian historians focused on their own 'national' history and came to regard the Reich as rather peripheral to that more important narrative.[7] Few persisted in pursuing the wider *gesamtdeutsch* or 'greater German' perspective, which saw early modern Austria as part of the 'Germany' encapsulated in the Holy Roman Empire. Following the collapse of the Austro-Hungarian Empire in 1919, such a perspective became politically controversial in the context of discussions concerning the unification of Germans and Austrians and then of the *Anschluss* in 1938.[8] It is significant that this period saw the production of important work on the early modern Reich by Austrian scholars such as Heinrich von Srbik (1878–1951).[9]

Following the collapse of the Third Reich, Austrian historians once again tended to marginalize the German dimension of their history. The assumption by the last Holy Roman Emperor, Francis II, of the new title of Emperor of Austria in 1804, two years before the Holy Roman Empire was dissolved in 1806, had a crucial effect on Austrian historiography, which has important implications for the historiography of the Reich generally. The search for the prehistory of the Austrian Empire encouraged a focus on the factors that distinguished Austria from the rest of the Reich from the early sixteenth century onwards. The question of whether Austria can be said to have 'left' the Reich at any stage will recur at many points throughout this study.

The development of attitudes to the Holy Roman Empire in other parts of non-Prussian Germany in the decades after its demise in 1806 was not dissimilar.[10] The

---

[5] Bryce, *Holy Roman Empire*. A 14th printing of the 6th edition of 1904 (corrected 1906) appeared as late as 1968.

[6] Brechenmacher, *Geschichtsschreibung*, 209–39.

[7] Fellner, 'Reichsgeschichte'; Gnant, 'Reichsgeschichte'; Klueting, *Reich*, 2–5.

[8] The following provide useful insights: Blänsdorf, 'Staat'; Brechenmacher, 'Österreich'.

[9] Derndarsky, 'Srbik'.

[10] Burgdorf, *Weltbild*, 227–51, 277–83.

crucial point here was the emergence of new sovereign states in the first decade of the nineteenth century. One of the main ambitions of these territories in the years around 1800 was to escape the overlordship of the emperor. When they were able to do so with Napoleon's help in the years after 1801 they acquired extensive additional lands, which formed the basis of their new existence as sovereign states of the German Confederation after 1815. The integration of new lands and new subjects was accompanied by the elaboration of a new historical identity. They removed the imperial eagles and other symbols of the emperor's authority from their public buildings and renamed streets and squares in their towns. They also commissioned histories that emphasized the 'Reich Württemberg' or the 'Reich Bayern', the history of independent states, rather than the history of subordinate territories of the Holy Roman Empire. In the new German states that emerged after 1815, the imperial past was often regarded as nothing but an impediment to their own emergence as modern polities in the German Confederation.

After 1945, following the disaster of the Third Reich, German historiography was characterized by a conscious turn against the traditions of the nation state and by a gradual revision of some of the historical myths of the past.[11] In the view that now began to emerge, the implications of which are still being explored and elaborated today, perceptions of the history of the Holy Roman Empire have undergone substantial transformation.

Belief in the existence of a strong medieval empire between the eleventh and thirteenth centuries has been challenged and largely discredited. Scholars of the late Middle Ages, notably Peter Moraw, have revised the traditional perception of the fourteenth and fifteenth centuries as a period of decay and descent into anarchy.[12] On the contrary, Moraw has argued, this period saw the gradual emergence and consolidation of the infrastructure of the Holy Roman Empire in a protracted process of what he calls an 'intensification' of forms of government and control (*Verdichtungsprozess*). This occurred both at the level of imperial institutions and in the lands of the greater vassals of the Reich. At each level, the process reached a crucial stage by the end of the fifteenth century, culminating in a reform movement in which both Emperor Maximilian I and the German Estates simultaneously pursued separate interests and, more or less, a common cause.

The compromise that emerged from this reform movement around 1500 set the framework for the next three hundred years. Here, again, the re-evaluations of scholars such as Hanns Hubert Hoffmann, Karl Otmar von Aretin, Gerhard Oestreich, F. H. Schubert, Heinrich Lutz, and Volker Press, have resulted in a new view.[13] Instead of regarding the Reich as a static system, as for example described in the great systematic compendia of eighteenth-century lawyers such as Johann Jakob Moser and Stephan Heinrich Pütter, modern historical research

'Reich, Nation und Staat', 215–16; Schulze, *Geschichtswissenschaft*, 160.
The following recent surveys are also helpful: Prietzel, *Reich* and Schubert,
'ssungsgeschichtsschreibung', 146–51; Klueting, *Reich*, 7–17.

has concentrated on the idea of the Reich as a dynamically evolving polity. While retaining both its medieval feudal character and the medieval legacy of the dualism between emperor and Reich (or Imperial Estates), the Reich continued to develop as a constitutional system. Far from stagnating, in other words, the Holy Roman Empire went through a remarkable series of transformations in the last three centuries of its existence.

Paradoxically perhaps, the challenges which previous historians saw as milestones of decline were in fact complex motors of change. The Reformation divided the German lands in religious terms, but it simultaneously promoted the search for a constitutional modus vivendi that would preserve the polity. The inadequacy of the compromise embodied in the Peace of Augsburg in 1555 generated further dissension, but also new forms of coexistence. The Thirty Years War was both a European conflict fought largely on German soil and a constitutional crisis of the Reich exacerbated by the wider struggle. It resulted in the Peace of Westphalia, which renegotiated the constitutional settlement reached in 1555 and provided the framework for the next one-and-a-half centuries. Again, where previous historians saw sclerosis and stagnation leading to terminal paralysis, more recent scholars have seen a system that functioned effectively in many ways, both as the keystone of a European balance of powers and as a stable framework for the German territories and their inhabitants.

It is true that the equilibrium that emerged after 1648 was threatened significantly by the emergence of Brandenburg-Prussia as a major power in the north. The aspirations of successive Hohenzollern princes, above all Frederick the Great between 1740 and 1786, transcended the traditional forms of German territorial government, reaching for sovereignty rather than just overlordship. Yet the challenge to the Reich in fact remained implicit and was never translated into reality. It was matched, moreover, by similar developments in the Austrian lands. Indeed, Joseph II arguably challenged the constitution of the Reich more radically and more openly than Frederick the Great ever did. In the event, the sovereign ambitions of Austria and Prussia did not come to fruition by the efforts of their rulers. The Reich was destroyed by the French revolutionary armies and by Napoleon. In the resulting vacuum, not only Austria and Prussia but also other large territories such as Baden, Bavaria, Hessen, and Württemberg became fully sovereign states.

This final transformation is analysed in the concluding chapters. Several lines of continuity are suggested between the early modern and the modern periods: a variety of ways in which modern Germany emerged from the Holy Roman Empire and was shaped by its institutions and by its historical experience. The very existence of such continuities serves to underline once more the need to discount the negative view of the Reich in its final three centuries that characterized the nationalist tradition in German historiography.

Since the reunification of Germany in 1990, the attention given to four themes has been striking. First, some scholars, notably Georg Schmidt, have argued that the Reich should in fact be regarded as a state, similar in some ways to the 'composite monarchies' of Britain and France, and different in that it manage develop mechanisms to avoid civil war on grounds of religion or revol upheaval.[14] Second, others have preferred to emphasize that German history is European history and are intrigued by the function of the Reich as a system of law and peace at the centre of Europe, or by the idea of the Reich and its Kreise (regional associations) as a kind of precursor of today's European Union.[15] Third, Georg Schmidt and others have also emphasized the national dimension of early modern German history, and have placed new emphasis on the patriotic traditions in the Reich.[16] Fourth, there has been a tendency to emphasize the relative modernity of the early modern Reich in many respects: the achievement, for example, between 1555 and 1648 of a religious peace that endured and that gave individuals, even ordinary subjects, rights over their religious worship and their property; or the devolution of legislative powers to the regions and the development of inter-territorial cooperation in social or economic policy.

These new approaches have often been controversial.[17] Some believe that they strain the concept of 'state' to an almost impossible degree or that they are unhistorical in seeking to portray the Reich as a rather idealized forerunner of the European Union. Others have jibbed at the notion that patriotism or nationalism might have existed in what they believe was a pre-national era. The idea that the Reich was in any sense modern seems inherently absurd to those who believe it was antiquated and anachronistic. Even so, the new approaches have undoubtedly illuminated qualities of the Reich that existed in fact, and were recognized to exist, for example, by many eighteenth-century commentators. Above all, they have caught the imagination of a new generation of scholars, and over the last two decades they have promoted a real boom in research into virtually every aspect of the history of the early modern Reich.

A number of new approaches to the social and economic history of the period have also been crucial to the new view of the Reich's final centuries. There is a long tradition of research in this area, dating back to the nineteenth century, but here, too, the post-1945 reticence with regard to the concepts of nation and state altered the focus of interest. In part, novel perceptions of the development of early modern German society also resulted from the engagement with the arguments put forward by Marxist historians of the GDR after 1949 that Germany experienced a failed 'early bourgeois revolution' around 1500. The Reich played a purely negative role in this idea.[18] When the Reich flourished, universalism and links with the papacy had obstructed the national development of Germany; in its period of post-medieval decline, it allowed the German lands to become a theatre for European wars, while at the same time the reinforcement of the feudal system obstructed the emergence of bourgeois capitalism.

---

[14] Schmidt, 'Reich und die deutsche Kulturnation' and *idem, Geschichte, passim.*

[15] See, for example, Schilling, 'Reich' and Hartmann, 'Heiliges Römisches Reich', 11–12, 21–2.

[16] See, for example, particularly works listed in the bibliography by Horst Dreitzel, Caspar Hirschi, Alexander Schmidt, Georg Schmidt, Joachim Whaley, and Martin Wrede.

[17] For a discussion of some central controversies, see Whaley, 'Old Reich' and Schnettger, 'Reichsverfassungsgeschichtsschreibung', 146–51.

[18] Dorpalen, *German history*, 99–186; Vogler, 'Konzept'.

In this context, the Reformation was seen as the expression of a general crisis of society (*gesamtgesellschaftliche Krise*). Luther's protest was both anti-Roman and above all anti-feudal. The frustration of his challenge and the defeat of the peasant uprising ushered in the re-feudalization of German society. The triumph of the princes and their involvement in the politics of the religious conflict and in the European power struggle led to the disaster of the Thirty Years War. In the ruins of devastated Germany, the princes came to the fore again in the rise of absolutism: the last pre-modern permutation of the feudal order. Only in the eighteenth century, it was argued, did the economic and social preconditions for capitalism begin to develop very gradually. The progressive, anti-feudal ideology of the *Aufklärung* (Enlightenment) challenged the old order but did not overcome it. The absence of a French-style revolution in Germany at the end of the eighteenth century, it was argued, was to have fateful consequences for the future in that it facilitated the emergence of a particularly aggressive form of capitalism and imperialism.

On the one hand, in its blunt doctrinaire form, the theory of a failed 'early bourgeois revolution', with all of its supposed long-term consequences, did not make a significant impact on the interpretation of early modern German history. On the other hand, it provided an important stimulus to the study of the social and economic dimensions. Furthermore, parallel to it, often stimulated by it, and evolving in critical engagement with it, there was a renewed interest in social and economic history in the Federal Republic from the early 1960s. The main pre-occupations here were: the study of the economic foundations of German society; the social structure of the German territories, their courts, and administrations; the development and role of towns and cities, and the role played by non-noble groups (especially the theologically or legally trained, educated *Bürger*); and, not least, the question of whether the 'common man' was the passive victim of a failed revolution or rather as active a participant as the *Bürger*, noble, or prince in shaping the development of the German lands.

Two recent works draw on these strands of social and economic history and relate them to the larger narratives of German history. Peter Blickle's history of freedom in Germany from the late Middle Ages to the early nineteenth century, published in 2003, combines decades of research on peasant resistance with insights into early modern discourses of liberty and conceptions of government and society.[19] Thomas Brady's history of Germany between 1400 and 1650 appeared just as this present work was completed. His central focus is the Reformation and its implications for German society and politics. The starting point of 1400 is significant, for it emphasizes the long social and religious prehistory of the Reformation. The terminal date of 1650 reflects the view that the options that had been so open during the first half of the sixteenth century were now firmly closed.[20]

If the early modern Reich was once a rather neglected period of German history, it is now one of the boom areas. What has emerged overall is a more differentiated view of early modern Germany. The conventional picture of a backward, repressed,

---

[19] Blickle, *Leibeigenschaft*.   [20] Brady, *German histories*.

and stultified society has been questioned by challenging the criteria by which backwardness is defined. There were undoubtedly backwaters, territories where little or nothing changed, whose administrations were characterized by incompetence and tyrannical harshness. However, the fact that the German lands did not develop a nation state or experience a revolutionary transformation is now no longer perceived as necessarily a sign of general backwardness.

The elaboration of the intellectual and cultural dimensions of this period has proved much more problematic. To some extent, this has reflected the gulf between disciplines such as history, theology, philosophy, and literary studies that has characterized the German academic system, like that of Britain. It is, however, also the result of the persistence of traditional historical narratives within those disciplines. Overall, these emphasized the significance of the Reformation period and of the eighteenth century while seriously undervaluing the one-and-a-half centuries in between. Only in the last two decades or so have more modern surveys begun to delineate the outlines of new narratives.

In theological studies, the achievements of Luther and his contemporaries were long perceived to have overshadowed everything until the age of the *Aufklärung*. The monumental history of Pietism edited by Martin Brecht and others has filled a major gap in a comprehensive fashion.[21] The contributions to this multi-volume handbook illuminate both the numerous sixteenth-century and early seventeenth-century origins of the phenomenon and its myriad ramifications for the development of Protestantism in Germany and elsewhere in the later seventeenth and eighteenth centuries.

Academic philosophers rarely deemed the pre-Kantian period to be worthy of study, while many doubted whether there was such a thing as German political and social thought at all. Siegfried Wollgast's remarkable survey of German philosophy 1550–1650, published in the GDR in 1988, long remained an isolated and rather neglected work.[22] It is only recently that scholars such as Howard Hotson and Martin Mulsow have begun to re-map the terrain in novel ways that promise to provide an alternative to the old master-narratives that focused on the great texts by the canonical thinkers.[23] An indispensable foundation for any further study has now also been provided by the handbooks on seventeenth-century German thought published as part of the new edition of Friedrich Ueberweg's three-volume nineteenth-century classic, the *Grundriss der Geschichte der Philosophie* (1863–6).[24]

In literary and cultural studies, too, there has traditionally been a concentration on the *Aufklärung* and the age of Goethe, the beginnings of German literary modernity. The early modern period is often viewed as a beginning and an end with no middle; a brilliant humanist culture in the first half of the sixteenth century that gradually faded away, leaving a void that was only filled in the middle decades

---

[21] *Geschichte des Pietismus*, i and ii.

[22] Wollgast, *Philosophie*; Mulsow, *Moderne*.

[23] Hotson, *Commonplace Learning*; Mulsow, *Moderne*; essays in Mulsow, *Spätrenaissance-Philosophie*.

[24] See Holzhey, Schmidt-Biggemann and Mudroch, *Philosophie* and Schobinger, *Philosophie*.

of the eighteenth century by the literary revival of which Goethe became the Olympian symbol and figurehead. Even the renewed interest in baroque literature that has been evident during the past two or three decades has done little to dispel the image of the seventeenth century as the *saeculum obscurum* in German history.[25]

Much has been done since 1945 to map out the development of German political ideas in this period. The work of scholars such as Leonard Krieger in the 1950s and Hans Maier in the 1960s was vital in establishing a new understanding of the fundamental difference between the German tradition and that of the west.[26] This had hitherto been rather crudely depicted as the difference between a conservative, if not authoritarian, conception of the state and society on the one hand and a Western tradition of rights on the other.

More recent work has been concerned with tracing the evolution of the theory of the Reich and the development of notions of government more all-embracing than those found in, say, the French or English traditions. Gerald Strauss has illuminated the political and social implications of the reception of Roman law in the sixteenth century.[27] Robert von Friedeburg has demonstrated the significance of the idea of self-defence against an unjust monarch in sixteenth-century Germany for the development of ideas of justified resistance to authority in England between 1550 and 1680.[28] The significance in the German context of the ideas of thinkers such as Pufendorf, often considered exclusively as a contributor to a European tradition of natural law, has become clearer.[29] Horst Dreitzel has analysed concepts of monarchy and princely rule from the early sixteenth century to the early nineteenth century.[30] Michael Stolleis has explored the implications for the political theory of both the Reich and the territories of the German tradition of public law.[31]

The challenge remains, however, of reconciling this research into theology, philosophy, literature, and ideas with the new thinking about the history of the Holy Roman Empire. Above all, and of particular significance for the aims of this volume, little of this literature is widely known to English-speaking students or to scholars other than specialists in the period.[32] Treatment of the Holy Roman Empire in the current English-language surveys of European history is generally cursory and rarely includes names such as Melchior von Osse, Dietrich Reinkingk, and Veit Ludwig von Seckendorff, to name but three significant German political theorists of the sixteenth and seventeenth centuries.

Clearly, it is not possible in a study such as this to discuss in detail all the implications of the constitutional, social and economic, intellectual and cultural narratives sketched out here. Two broad questions, however, inform the structure

---

[25] Most recently: Meid, *Literatur*. Meid's extensive bibliography is not included in the printed book but may be found at http://www.chbeck.de/downloads/Bibliographie%20Autoren_Anonyme%20Werke.pdf (accessed 4 May 2011).

[26] Krieger, *Idea*; Maier, *Staats- und Verwaltungslehre*.

[27] Strauss, *Law*.

[28] Friedeburg, *Self-defence*.

[29] Dreitzel, 'Zehn Jahre', 383–95; Dreitzel, 'Pufendorf'; Hammerstein, 'Pufendorf'.

[30] Dreitzel, *Monarchiebegriffe*.

[31] Stolleis, *Öffentliches Recht*, i and ii.

[32] A notable exception is Wilson, *Reich*, which deals with important aspects of the period 1558–1806.

and argument of the work as a whole. One question concerns political traditions; the other concerns wider aspects of collective historical experience and identity.

The first question may be formulated as a modern version of the traditional theme of the differences between Germany and the West. This theme has a long pedigree, whether as a source of national pride to many German scholars before 1945 or as a source of the long-term problems of German history in the eyes of many non-German scholars writing before 1945 and both Germans and non-Germans since. A rather different, and more fruitful, perspective is gained if one focuses on the fact that there was no revolution in the German lands at the end of the eighteenth century. This question has more often than not seemed to be of fundamental significance to historians of nineteenth- and twentieth-century Germany. Hans Ulrich Wehler, for example, launched his monumental history of modern Germany with the assertion: 'In the beginning, there was no revolution.'[33] In his work, as in that of many others on modern Germany, the implications are largely negative. The early modern period, by consequence, is viewed as one of failure. The Reich and its territories are perceived to have obstructed modernizing change. Society and economy failed to develop in such a way as to generate a viable challenge to the old order, either in the Reformation or in the eighteenth century. Nor did such a challenge emerge from any intellectual or cultural traditions.

The absence of a revolution does not, however, necessarily equate with a lack of movement, and change by means of evolution is not necessarily conservative or unpolitical. For while there was no revolution in pre-modern Germany, there was reform. Indeed, the unity of the early modern period is underlined by the fact that it is characterized by a remarkably persistent sequence of phases of reform at the level of both Reich and territories. The dates 1517, 1555, 1648, 1700, 1740–50, and finally 1789, around which the sections of this book are organized, all mark watersheds in this process. To emphasize the continuity between these movements is to emphasize in particular that 1648 was not the great watershed in German history, as many have continued to assume. Volker Press's 1996 study of Germany in the seventeenth century and Georg Schmidt's 1999 study of the Reich from 1495 to 1806 are among the few major works that have explicitly challenged this *idée fixe* in German historiography.[34]

Each reform phase from the late fifteenth to the late eighteenth century was accompanied by a challenge, complex and multi-causal in nature, to the status quo. Each crisis was broadly resolved, or at least accommodated, in ways that cannot be adequately described as conservative. Indeed, the process generated a variety of unique phenomena that may, on the contrary, be seen as progressive: an imperial framework that ultimately facilitated the peaceful coexistence of the major Christian denominations; an imperial system which preserved the independent existence of even the smallest subsidiary unit against the predatory inclinations and ambitions of the largest ones, and which provided mechanisms whereby the subjects of all of them could appeal against their overlords through the imperial courts; systems

---

[33] Wehler, *Gesellschaftsgeschichte*, i, 35. [34] Press, *Kriege*; Schmidt, *Geschichte*.

of government within many territories capable of pursuing more all-embracing legal, social, and welfare aims than many of the supposedly more progressive Western monarchies. These are but some of the distinctive products of German history after 1500.

Of course, early modern administrations in the German lands were subject to the same kind of limitations as any other early modern state. It is now generally accepted, for example, that absolutism was far from absolute. The fact that legislation was both frequently reiterated and frequently amended is undoubtedly evidence for its relative ineffectiveness. The aspirations of princes and magistrates were perennially frustrated by the wayward behaviour of individuals and groups, by the stubborn resistance of society to regulation imposed from above. Yet although government was ineffective, its aims and actions nonetheless shaped the development of societies in distinctive ways. Resistance from below, the participation of the *gemeiner Mann* (the common man) in the governmental process, was undoubtedly an important feature of early modern German society, and was recognized as such by those who governed, whether as princes or magistrates. The infinite variety of such forms of participation and resistance helped shape the evolving governmental framework of society and its ethos.

A similar point applies to the Reich. It is customary in cursory surveys of the Holy Roman Empire to cite some of the many critical voices of the eighteenth century which bemoaned or derided it as monstrous, sclerotic, or simply absurd. Yet these are easily matched by more positive assessments, which emphatically denied that the Germans were backward, and which praised 'German liberty' as the characteristic of a unique historically evolved German *Rechtsordnung* (comprehensive system of law). Indeed, most German commentators of the later eighteenth century, and even those who wrote in 1805 or 1806, insisted that the Reich was a state, a limited monarchy, albeit with individual traditions that distinguished it from its neighbours.

To draw attention to these positive evaluations of the German situation towards the end of the eighteenth century is not to indulge in nostalgia for the old Reich. Nor is it to deny that the Reich was both in need of reform and apparently incapable of it. What it permits, however, is a more wide-ranging view of how it functioned as a polity, and of the intellectual, religious, and cultural forces that shaped its development as the national framework for the German territories. The first main theme of this work, therefore, proceeds from the question of how the Reich worked. That question informs the treatment of ideas and culture in what follows, just as it determines the way that society and economy have been approached.

Ideas and culture are also important for the second broad theme addressed by this work, namely collective historical experience and identity. Much of the work on this period by German historians after 1945 was characterized by the studious avoidance of terms such as state and nation. In a sense their endeavours, rather ironically, mirrored those of their nationalist predecessors. The early modern period is perceived as one of disunity, even of deficiency, which a 'delayed nation' had to make up in the nineteenth century.[35]

Such a general view might seem to be reinforced by glaring historical truths. The Reich had no capital city. It was fragmented into several hundred units represented in the Reichstag (405 in 1521; 314 in 1780), not including over a thousand other, often minuscule, entities that had no representation there. Indeed, the sheer variety often seems to defy any generalization at all. Gerhard Köbler's *Historisches Lexikon der deutschen Länder*, for example, contains entries on over 5,000 entities that have had legal existence since the Middle Ages. The overwhelming majority of them existed at some point during the period 1500–1800.[36] Moreover, the Reich included an extraordinary variety of landscapes, economies, social conditions, and cultural regions between the Rhine and the Oder, the Baltic and the Alps. Finally, the German lands were also divided by religion, an unbridgeable gulf created by the Reformation and never healed.

All of this seems to justify the commonplace that the Germans developed an identity anchored on the locality, city, or territory in which they happened to live. The word *Vaterland* (fatherland) often describes the immediate local or regional context, rather than the 'national' framework. Yet *Vaterland* did often refer to the Reich and there is ample evidence for a strong sense of identification with the Reich throughout the early modern period.[37]

A tendency to associate national identity with modern nationhood has hampered appreciation of a sense of identity in the German lands which pre-dated modern nationalism. It is, of course, difficult to say precisely just how the Reich was perceived by the common man at any stage. Even at this level, though, there is evidence that during the course of the early modern period there was a growing awareness of the Reich as a German Reich, and as a legal order equipped with institutions to which even peasants had access. Furthermore, the wars in which the Reich was involved, especially those against the Turks and the French, also generated patriotic responses that reinforced solidarity in the Reich and a sense of a common identity and destiny.

Such sentiments are inevitably more explicit in the thinking of educated groups. They are evident in the desire for reform of the Reich around 1500. They are present, too, in the reflections of those legally trained politicians of the later sixteenth century who sought compromise after the conflict generated by the Reformation. They were expressed clearly in the writings of early seventeenth-century figures such as Melchior Goldast von Haiminsfeld. They are found with increasing frequency from the late seventeenth century. They come to assume a particular significance in the eighteenth century in the reflections of individuals such as Johann Christoph Gottsched or Johann Gottfried Herder as they pondered

---

[35] The phrase, much used in debates about modern German history over the last sixty years, originated in the title of the second, 1959, edition of Helmuth Plessner's *Die verspätete Nation: Über die politische Verführbarkeit bürgerlichen Geistes*, first published as *Das Schicksal deutschen Geistes in seiner bürgerlichen Epoche* in 1935.

[36] Köbler, *Lexikon*, viii.

[37] Whaley, '*Reich*', *passim*.

the differences between the 'national' characteristics of the Germans and the French, or in the vast compendia of imperial constitutions and laws produced by the likes of Johann Jakob Moser or Stephan Heinrich Pütter.

These attitudes are frequently misrepresented as frustrated expressions of German nationalism. In particular, the humanists' rediscovery of Tacitus's *Germania* and the construction of the mythology of the Germanic origins of the Germans have often been viewed as the prehistory of modern nationalist ideology.[38] To study these traditions in the light of the uses to which they were put in the late nineteenth and early twentieth centuries is, however, to distort their early modern meaning. To examine them in context, without the disfiguring shadows of hindsight, renders such clichés as the frustrated nationalist of *c*.1500 or the apolitical cultural hero of *c*.1800 anachronistic.

What emerges instead is an equally distinctive, but in no way sinister, German 'ideology' that had no use for ideas of nation states and the like: an awareness of varying levels of identification, from locality to Reich, a multiplicity of interlocking and overlapping 'fatherlands' expressed in the contemporary formula of 'unity in diversity'.[39] This sense, moreover, a commonplace in discussions of 'Germany' and German identity between 1750 and 1830, specifically reflected the collective historical experience of the German lands since about 1450. For all the emphasis placed by some scholars on the medieval origins of the sense of German identity, the experience on which this continuing and pervasive national patriotic discourse was based, together with the legal, cultural, and religious traditions that shaped it, was the experience of the early modern Reich.

If the history of the German lands in the period is the history of localities and territories, it is also the history of the union of those entities. It is the history of their survival as a legal and cultural community in the face of challenges from the Reformation onwards that might have been expected to destroy any such thing. It is the history of their solidarity in the face of perennial external threats. Not least, it is the history of a Central European polity that played a key role in the politics of early modern Europe as a whole. Perhaps inevitably, a work such as this might seem to emphasize union, if not unity. The discussion of general trends will inevitably appear to ignore many of the exceptions to every rule. Yet variety and, at times, the appearance of incoherence are fundamental to any understanding of early modern German history. Indeed, the essence of the system was the preservation of individuality and difference.

---

[38] Krebs, 'Dangerous book'.   [39] Whaley, 'Kulturelle Toleranz', 201, 216–24.

I

GERMANY AND THE HOLY ROMAN EMPIRE IN 1500

1
Origins and Frontiers

To speak of Germany in 1500 raises fundamental questions about the history of the early modern Holy Roman Empire. The term 'Germany' is itself deeply problematic. In the late fifteenth century there was undoubtedly a growing sense of what was German. This was based on language and on awareness of a common ethnic identity and historical experience. It was reinforced by the sense, in some German-speaking territories, of common political interests that needed to be defended and hence expressed in legal and institutional forms. During the fifteenth century the terms 'German lands' and 'German nation' were increasingly employed to convey this community of interests; in 1474 the Reich was first referred to in a document as the Holy Roman Empire of the German Nation, and this nomenclature was formally established in 1512.[1] The link between Reich and 'Nation' which it expressed was not, however, defined in precise terms.

Indeed, neither the Reich nor the 'German nation' can be easily defined at this time. The Reich's origins lay in the translation of the inheritance of the Roman Empire northwards by Charlemagne and the gradual assumption of the imperial title by the German kings after Otto I (912–973), who succeeded as king of Germany in 936, subjugated Italy, and became king of the Lombards in 951–2, and was crowned emperor in 962.[2] The idea of a *translatio imperii* was fundamental to the ethos of the Reich: the prestige of the emperor was immeasurably enhanced by the notion that he held supreme power inherited from the emperors in Rome. Henry IV (1050–1106) had added the title *Rex Romanorum*, thereafter given to the elected king (known as the *römisch-deutscher König*) before his coronation as emperor.[3] The epithet 'Holy' was added by the Hohenstaufen Emperor Frederick I in 1157, reflecting his ambition to dominate Italy and the papacy, as well as the areas north of the Alps.

The disparate origins and multifaceted character of the Reich are reflected in the titles and coronation rites of its rulers. The fact that the German monarchy remained an elective system undoubtedly contributed to the perpetuation of an

[1] The term 'Reich' will be used for empire throughout, since this is the term used most frequently in contemporary sources. On the evolution of the nomenclature, see Nonn, 'Heiliges Römisches Reich'.
[2] The following passages are based on the studies by Boockmann, *Stauferzeit*, Leuschner, *Deutschland*, and Herbers and Neuhaus, *Reich*, 1–127. A good survey in English is Du Boulay, *Germany*.
[3] On the assumption of the title *Rex Romanorum* by the German kings, see *LdM*, v, 1304–9 and vii, 777–8.

itinerant court and the lack of a clear geographical centre or capital city. Yet the Reich's titles themselves were vague and not geographically specific: *Imperium Romanum, Imperium Christianum, Imperium mundi*—Roman, Christian, and universal. In so far as there were geographical fixed points, they lay in places of little significance from the point of view of government. The coronation of the ruler as German king (with the title King of the Romans) took place in Aachen from the reign of Charlemagne until 1531; after the coronation of Ferdinand I in that year, the ceremony took place in Frankfurt, or sometimes simply in the same place as the election had occurred. Throughout the Middle Ages, the king's subsequent coronation as emperor took place in St Peter's in Rome at the hands of the pope. The first emperor not crowned in this way was Maximilian who, in 1508, simply declared himself *Erwählter Römischer Kaiser* (Elected Roman Emperor). The last papal coronation was that of Charles V, which took place in Bologna in 1530. In between coronations the imperial insignia, in theory located in Aachen, were moved from place to place until 1424, when the most important objects (including the crown, sceptre, orb, sword, and the holy lance) were located in Nuremberg.[4]

Successive German dynasties had elaborated the geographical implications of the imperial titles, bringing large parts of Eastern Europe into the constellation, in addition to the mass of lands north and south of the Alps. The Luxemburg emperors Charles IV (r. 1347–78), Wenzel (r. 1378–1400), and Sigismund (r. 1411–37) attempted to secure Bohemia, Silesia, Lusatia, the Mark of Brandenburg, and above all, but outside the Reich, Hungary as stem lands. At no stage was their dominion over these lands secure or stable. On the contrary, it was punctuated by rebellions and the periodic emergence of successful rival claimants. Yet by virtue of marriage and inheritance strategies, the Luxemburg emperors generated a catalogue of potential claims which were inherited by the Habsburg dynasty when Sigismund died in 1437, leaving as his heiress his daughter Elizabeth, who had married Albert V of Habsburg in 1421. Albert's election as emperor in 1438 combined the Bohemian, Hungarian, and German crowns for the first time. By then, however, the Kingdom of Burgundy had been irrevocably lost: the last German emperor crowned King of Burgundy was Charles IV in 1356; on his death in 1378 the kingdom was dissolved and largely absorbed into France. By then, the emperors had also effectively lost control over much of what remained of the Kingdom of Italy.

Luxemburg ambitions had focused on the east. In a sense the Luxemburg rulers had thus marginalized the German territories, allowing the new Burgundian rulers from the house of Valois (Dukes of Burgundy from 1363) to consolidate and exploit discontent amongst the German princes. As a result, their Habsburg heirs were almost immediately obliged to turn their attentions to the west. They responded to the challenge of the Burgundian Charles the Bold in turn with rapprochement, with military force, and, ultimately more effectively, with a marriage alliance between Charles's daughter and heiress Maria and Frederick III's heir

---

[4] Conrad, *Rechtsgeschichte*, i, 317–18, 326–7 and ii, 66–74; Rabe, *Geschichte*, 109–11.

Maximilian, which came to fruition in April 1477, shortly after Charles's death. The addition of Burgundy as well as the Franche Comté to the Habsburg patrimony, and hence to the empire, was itself the prelude to more extensive schemes which bore fruit in the establishment, again by marriage, of aspirations to Aragon and Castile. That, in turn, was a response to the growing hostility of France, where Louis XI (r. 1461–83), Charles VIII (r. 1483–98), and Louis XII (r. 1498–1515) successively harboured designs not only on the Burgundian inheritance but also on the imperial position in Italy.

The elaboration of the territorial ambitions of the Luxemburg and Habsburg dynasties, which reached their culmination in the reign of Maximilian I (as king and co-ruler with his father Frederick III after 1486, as sole ruler from 1493, and as emperor from 1508 to 1519), generated insecurity as well as power. The Habsburgs created an empire arguably more universal in potential than any previous imperial dynasty. Yet their need for resources to press their various claims, or to defend them periodically from hostile neighbours such as the kings of France, led them to exert pressure on the German territories. The call on their part for the reform of the Reich, for laws and institutions that would enshrine their rights, was above all a response to that pressure.

The collection of overlordships and territories that Maximilian I inherited, together with those he acquired by marriage and whose overlordship he assumed with the imperial title, dominated the map of Europe. Yet while on paper this area might seem like a monolithic block, it was far from being anything of the kind. The emperor wielded power and influence to very different degrees in different areas. Just as there were jurisdictions of varying age and antiquity, so the real meaning of these jurisdictions, and their value to the emperor as vehicles of potential power, varied considerably. All of them broadly came under the umbrella of the Holy Roman Empire, but in terms of institutional or governmental reality, in terms of imperial kingship, that title meant different things at different times.

Attempts to compile accurate maps of the Reich are hampered by two difficulties. First, there is a perpetual uncertainty over external boundaries. They changed with great frequency, and they are difficult to draw with precision at any point. Second, there is the virtual technical impossibility of reproducing the internal territorial boundaries on the page in such a way that the eye can make sense of their sheer complexity. This latter problem will be discussed in relation to the structure of the imperial system or constitution. First, however, an outline of the extremities *circa* 1500 will illuminate not only questions of geographical extent but also factors that constrained the functioning of the system in certain areas.[5]

In some ways the very question of frontiers in relation to the Holy Roman Empire is anachronistic. They were not fixed or clear. On the contrary, because they arose out of the feudal relationships between king and vassals, they varied as that relationship changed, for example with the extinction of dynasties or noble lines, or by marriage treaties. Furthermore, a noble could be vassal to two overlords

---

[5] A discussion of frontiers may be found in Conrad, *Rechtsgeschichte*, i, 399–43 and ii, 106–11, and Rabe, *Geschichte*, 13–23.

simultaneously, thus creating overlapping lordships and an imponderable nexus of rights, claims, and aspirations. Equally important was the fact that the 'Holy Roman Empire of the German Nation' was more than just a German empire. Within its lands there was a multinational mixture of groups who spoke French, Dutch, Frisian, Sorbian, Czech, Slovenian, Italian, Ladin, and Rhaeto-Romanic. Nor did the empire by any means embrace all German-speaking areas, since it excluded all German-speaking settlements in eastern Europe, the so-called *Sprachinseln* (linguistic islands).[6]

Even so, it is possible to speak of the emergence of a 'German' Reich in the decades around 1500. In theory, the fifteenth-century Reich was composed of three major blocks or groups of territories: Italy, Germany, and Burgundy. In practice, however, only the Kingdom of Germany remained. One of Maximilian's enduring ambitions was to recover the Italian and Burgundian lands that had been lost; at one stage he even tried to reconquer Provence in order to regain the old centre of the Burgundian kingdom at Arles. Yet ultimately these were projects that failed and by the end of his reign the Reich was, more than ever, exclusively centred on the Kingdom of Germany.

Maximilian may have envisaged the three kingdoms as a unity, but neither Italy nor Burgundy could in fact be said to have fully belonged to the early modern Reich in so far as it developed as a bond for the German lands. At the same time, the idea of the Reich as a universal Christian monarchy steadily lost ground. Ultimately, it became more a part of the dynastic mythology of the Habsburgs than a real attribute or aspiration of the system that came to embrace primarily those represented (*Mit Sitz und Stimme*, 'with seat and vote') in the Reichstag or diet.[7] Of the three Imperial Archchancellors (the Archbishops of Mainz, Trier, and Cologne for Germany, Burgundy, and Italy, respectively) only the Archbishop of Mainz actually held a chancellery as *sacri imperii per Germaniam archicancellarius*.

This process of segmentation of the larger Reich, of differentiation between the periphery and the German lands, is most graphically illustrated in the south. The Italian territories, for example, had been a major part of the Hohenstaufen Empire. Some parts, such as Venice at the end of the fifteenth century, went their independent ways. Yet other parts still remained. Savoy, the duchies of Milan, Modena, and Parma, together with the Republics of Genoa, Lucca, Pisa, Florence, and Siena, continued to regard the emperor as their overlord. With the exception of Savoy, however, none was represented at the Reichstag; and none at all was included in any of the regional institutional structures (Reichskreise) developed in the early sixteenth century.[8] The rituals of enfeoffment (often accompanied by substantial monetary tributes and bribes) continued to be played out at the accession of a local dynasty or of an emperor. Even at the end of the eighteenth century *Reichsitalien* extended over some 250–300 fiefs involving some 50–70

---

[6] Neuhaus, *Reich*, 5; see also the comments on language on pp. 51–3.
[7] The term 'Reichstag' will normally be used throughout; the occasional use of 'diet' does not convey any different meaning.
[8] See pp. 35–6.

families.[9] But these territories were not subject to the jurisdiction of the imperial courts and paid no imperial taxes. Johann Jacob Moser, the great eighteenth-century commentator on the law of the Reich, repeatedly stated in his works that Italy unquestionably belonged to the Reich, but that it had no real link with Germany. Furthermore, as an expert on German law, he said, he was unable even to give an explanation of its constitution.[10]

The Italian territories became in effect part of a more narrowly defined Habsburg dynastic patrimony, and formed the basis for the Habsburg claims in Italy into the nineteenth century. While the Archbishop of Cologne retained the title of *sacri imperii per Italiam archicancellarius* until the end of the Reich, imperial interests in Italy were in fact administered by plenipotentiaries appointed in Vienna, such as Leopold of Tuscany during the reign of Joseph II. To all intents and purposes, however, the Italian lands played no active or meaningful role in the early modern Reich and hence are excluded from this study.[11]

A different kind of exclusion applies to the Swiss confederation. A potential rift between the confederation, with its communal traditions, and the essentially aristocratic empire was progressively reinforced during the fifteenth century by their opposition to the territorial claims and aspirations of the Habsburgs. After 1471, the 'eidgenössische Orte' no longer appeared at the Reichstag and held separate communal meetings (Tagsatzungen). A final attempt by Maximilian I to subjugate them failed in 1499; they were then able to have their exemption from the jurisdiction of the empire confirmed. Formally, they remained within the Reich. However, even the Swiss border cities, such as Basle and Schaffhausen, ceased to attend the Reichstag after 1530 and the confederation persisted in asserting and maintaining its traditional autonomy within the empire until its sovereignty was finally recognized in the Peace of Westphalia of 1648.[12]

In the west, the frontier presents a more varied picture. Much of Alsace was dominated by Habsburg territory, while Strassburg and the ten Upper Alsatian Imperial Cities all clearly belonged to the empire. Further north the Dukes of Lorraine were vassals of the emperor, but also of the king of France in respect of the Duchy of Bar, whose link with the Reich was purely nominal.[13] More complex was the situation concerning the Burgundian lands. The County of Burgundy (Freigrafschaft Burgund or Franche Comté), wedged between Lorraine in the north and Savoy in the south, clearly once belonged to the Reich (since the ninth century), though the Imperial City of Besançon formed a significant enclave at its centre. The extent of the county's integration into the Reich was, however, limited by its status as a Habsburg territory which, in 1556, passed into the hands of the Spanish line

[9] Köbler, *Lexikon*, 315–16; Aretin, *Das Reich*, 76–163; Aretin, *Altes Reich*, i, 112–15; Conrad, *Rechtsgeschichte*, ii, 110–11.
[10] Moser, *Grund-Riss*, 75–7, 690–713.
[11] For further information, see Schnettger, *Genua*, 23–38; Schnettger, 'Impero romano'; Aretin, *Altes Reich*, i, 112–15, 201–8, 310–12, ii, 85–96, 128–34, 194–215, 351–80, 458–67, and iii, 63–71, 168–71; Aretin, *Das Reich*, 76–163.
[12] Blickle, 'Eidgenossen'; Stadler, 'Schweiz'.
[13] Monter, *Bewitched duchy*, 21–58.

and played a crucial role in the enduring conflict between Spain and France, to which the county eventually fell in 1674–8.

The northern parts of the Burgundian inheritance in Brabant, Flanders, and the Low Countries remained similarly peripheral to the Reich proper.[14] While those parts of the southern Netherlands that remained in Habsburg hands (Spanish until 1713–14; Austrian thereafter) were formally included in a Burgundian Kreis, they were all exempted from imperial jurisdiction and dues in 1548. Thus the emerging Dutch Republic technically remained part of the empire until 1648. While developments there—political, intellectual, and cultural—came to exert significant influence over the German lands, they cannot in any meaningful sense be regarded as *Reichsstände*, or Estates of the Holy Roman Empire. These territories played a far greater role than the Italian ones, but this above all reflected their greater significance in the power political interests of the Austrian Habsburg dynasty. Like his colleague in Cologne, the Archbishop of Trier found his status inflated in a purely honorific way by virtue of his title as *sacri imperii per Galliam et regnum Arelatense archicancellarius*.[15]

The frontier in the north was perhaps the most clear-cut of all, though it too reveals a peculiarity of considerable significance for the early modern Reich. The Duchy of Holstein belonged to the Reich; Schleswig, by contrast, was Danish. The two were united in the Treaty of Ripen 1460, when Christian I of Denmark inherited the lands of the extinct ducal line of Schaumburg (by virtue of his claims as senior heir of the house of Oldenburg). As a result, the king of Denmark became a vassal of the emperor and subject to the jurisdiction of the Reich in respect of Holstein. This created a situation that was to recur repeatedly in the later history of the Reich; for example, with regard to Saxony and Poland or Hanover and Great Britain. The existence of non-German monarchs as vassals of the emperor and princes of the Reich was one of the factors that made it into something of a keystone of a European state system. At the same time, the fact that these were non-Habsburg monarchs also added to the checks on Habsburg power in the Reich, making transgressions on their part, potentially at least, causes of European wars.

In the north-east, things were less straightforward in a different way. While Pomerania, Brandenburg, and Silesia were imperial fiefs, the extensive lands of the Teutonic Knights (*Deutscher Orden*) were not.[16] These territories, stretching across northern Poland and northwards through Lithuania, Latvia, and Estonia, were the result of thirteenth-century conquests by the religious Teutonic Order as it turned its energies away from the Holy Land towards the conquest and Christianization of the pagan north. They owed loyalty to the emperor under the Golden Bull of Rimini 1226, but their relationship with the Reich developed largely as a result of the threats posed to their conquests by Poland and Russia, which resented the incursions made by the German aggressors. A Polish counter-offensive in the

[14] Mout, 'Niederlande'; Press, 'Niederlande'; Israel, *Dutch Republic 1476–1806*, 9–40, 64, 66, 68–70.

[15] The *Regnum Arelatense* was so called because the Burgundian coronations originally took place in Arles.

[16] Du Boulay, *Germany*, 110–14; Boockmann, *Orden*, 197–224.

fifteenth century resulted in significant territorial losses, which effectively parti-
tioned the Order: the Prussian lands were subject to Poland and the papacy; the
lands of the northern or Lithuanian branch were disputed between Russia and
Poland. While the latter maintained some degree of independence as a result, the
Prussian branch of the Order sought to keep Poland at bay by electing Grand
Masters from German princely houses in 1498 (Frederick of Saxony) and 1511
(Albrecht of Brandenburg-Ansbach). This did not prevent the area becoming the
Duchy of Prussia when the Order was secularized in 1525. However, the fact that it
remained in the hands of the Hohenzollern dynasty ensured the perpetuation of the
ties to the Reich. The lands of the Lithuanian branch of the Order, by contrast,
became the Duchy of Kurland, outside the Reich, in 1561, when it was secularized
by *Landmeister* Gotthard Ketteler.

Immediately to the south of Brandenburg lay a complex of territories attached to
the Kingdom of Bohemia and characterized by special privileges quite different
from those in any other part of the Reich. By about 1500, this complex included, in
addition to Bohemia itself, the Duchy of Silesia, and the Margravates of Moravia
and Upper and Lower Lusatia. These lands came into the direct possession of the
Habsburgs by inheritance in 1526. Unlike the Habsburg Burgundian territories,
however, whose special privileges arose with the accession of the Habsburgs as
overlords, the Bohemian crown had long enjoyed a distinctive position in the
Reich. For one thing, Bohemia was (since 1198) the only subordinate kingdom
in the Reich. The Bohemian king's position as an imperial Elector had been
confirmed by the Golden Bull in 1356, but he did not participate in the deliberations of the Electoral College. Like all Electors, his territories were exempt from
imperial jurisdiction in that subjects could not appeal to imperial appeal courts
(*privilegium de non appellando*) and the imperial lower courts did not operate within
them (*privilegium de non evocando*).[17]

Perhaps even more significant, and of enormous importance later, was the
existence within Bohemia of distinct political and religious traditions. The right of
the Bohemian Estates to elect their king was vigorously reasserted on every occasion.
In 1471, for example, on the death of the Bohemian King George Podiebrady, they
elected the Polish Jagiellonian, Ladislas II. Even when Ferdinand I of Habsburg
gained the crown by inheritance in 1526, the Bohemian Estates insisted on their
right to 'elect' him before he was actually crowned. This tradition of political
independence was reinforced by the survival, in the face of both imperial and Church
opposition and radical Taborite insurrection, of the mainstream Hussite or Utraquist
religion. In Bohemia, therefore, alone among the imperial lands, a 'national' religion
reinforced a 'national' ideology in the Estates. At the end of the sixteenth century, this
constellation was to become the catalyst for the outbreak of the Thirty Years War.[18]

The circle is completed with the Habsburg lands proper in the south-east. With
the exception of Hungary, which came by inheritance (albeit disputed) in 1526
with the death of the last Jagiellonian king of Bohemia and Hungary, the core

---

[17] Conrad, *Rechtsgeschichte*, ii, 160, 164, 168. See also, Begert, *Böhmen, passim*.
[18] See pp. 448–56.

Habsburg lands all belonged to the Reich. The Archduchy of Austria, the Duchies of Styria, Carinthia, and Carniola, along with the Counties of the Tyrol and Görz (on the Adriatic), formed a more or less coherent bloc in the hands of the Habsburg dynasty. Like the other Habsburg lands, they enjoyed exemption and special privileges in the Reich. A further characteristic of this frontier was the way that Habsburg lands straddled it, with Hungary outside the Reich.[19] In northern Italy, the Prince-Bishoprics of Brixen and Trent abutted the Habsburg lands and their rulers were princes of the Reich until 1803, although they played no significant role in imperial politics.

From the 1440s onwards, the need of the dynasty first to secure this kingdom, and indeed the Austrian territories generally, from the Turks and then to defend it involved them, and by extension the Reich, in sporadic and often protracted armed conflict for more than two centuries. The ways in which this both helped to integrate the Reich and, in the long term, underlined the Habsburgs' sense of distinction and even difference from it, will form a central theme of this work. Above all, the fact that the Habsburgs were themselves based on the geographical periphery of the Reich had immense implications for the future development of the system as a whole. While they were undoubtedly the most powerful of all the German dynasties, hegemony perpetually eluded them. A similar power at the geographical centre of the Reich, or even firmly in the north, south, or west, would have created a very different empire, perhaps even a German 'national' monarchy similar to the French.

A survey of the Reich's major frontier areas conveys a sense of the many gradations of imperial rule at the periphery. Direct dynastic government by the Habsburgs in the south-east is matched by semi-autonomous forms in the Swiss cantons, and this in turn contrasts with the informal, but no less significant, non-membership of the lands of the Teutonic Knights (later Prussia) in the north-east. In each area, different dynastic and legal traditions gave rise to differing degrees of imperial jurisdiction, and in some cases distinctions between the jurisdiction of the emperor as Habsburg dynast and the Reich as a legal entity. Some of these areas (Italy, Switzerland, the Low Countries) were gradually falling away from the empire, contributing to a process of consolidation of what remained into a German Reich. In the case of Switzerland and the Low Countries, however, this was by no means obvious at the beginning of the sixteenth century, but the result of a long process over the next hundred years.

The variety on the periphery was matched by variety in the interior. This is perhaps best approached by turning first to the imperial constitution, before surveying the territorial map of the 'German' Reich itself. For the fragmented patchwork that existed there was itself the result of the way that the imperial framework had developed in the later Middle Ages. The culmination of that development in a series of reforms of the imperial system around 1500 placed the seal on the basic features of the territorial map and thus laid the foundations for the further evolution of the Reich in the early modern period.

---

[19] Evans, *Making*, 157–60.

2

The Reich as a Polity

The major difficulty encountered in describing the imperial constitution before 1500 is the fact that it had no systematic written form. Nor was there a clearly defined set of imperial institutions with a continuous history, let alone demonstrable efficacy. The arrangements that prevailed in the fifteenth century had evolved over a period of several centuries, and historians are divided over key aspects of the process. There is debate over whether the privileges granted to the princes were a sign of weakness in the rule of the Hohenstaufen monarchs and their successors. There is disagreement over the extent of imperial government at any stage from the eleventh to the fifteenth centuries, and finally there is disagreement over the motivation and nature of the key reforms carried out in 1495 and 1500. Some argue that the reforms represented a return to a past state, however idealized. Others maintain that they represented a radical new departure, though there is also dispute over the extent to which what emerged actually reflected the aims of the reformers, or whether in reality the outcome was a messy and contradictory compromise. The conclusions reached at the Reichstag in 1495 and 1500 are clearly of prime significance for the early modern period, since they were the point to which all subsequent attempts to define or redefine the imperial constitution referred back. These reforms themselves, however, in a sense articulated developments that had taken place over the previous two or three centuries.

Several things seem certain, whether or not one regards the history of the post-Hohenstaufen monarchy as one of decline. The first is the persistence of Reich as an elective monarchy and the failure of a single dominant dynasty to emerge. Second, the preoccupation of successive emperors with matters outside the German lands, especially in Italy, and the fact that some had courts on the periphery of the German lands, especially in the east, further reinforced the elective principle and progressively empowered the princes. In order to secure money and manpower for their wars, or simply to establish some kind of power base north of the Alps, successive emperors gave away more and more privileges. Consequently, in generation after generation, royal officials were able to establish themselves as hereditary lords in the feudal nexus. By 1400, in fact, virtually all the regalia and meaningful rights of sovereignty had been lost.

The position of the German princes had strengthened progressively since the reign of Frederick Barbarossa (1152–90). By the early thirteenth century, significant privileges had been granted and confirmed in widely accepted laws such as the *statutum in favorem principum* of 1231–2, which recognized the jurisdiction of the princes over their subjects.[1] Furthermore, the conflict between emperor and papacy in the investiture controversy resulted in the emperor giving up any political and legal rights over the Church. The Concordat of Worms 1122 recognized the free election of bishops and abbots by chapters and monastic communities. The transformation of a formal royal investiture, in which the king handed over crozier and ring into an act of enfeoffment, brought the Church into the feudal system of the Reich. The implications of this compromise were subsequently elaborated. In 1220 the monarchy gave up any claim to ecclesiastical lands on the death of a bishop or abbot, and these dignitaries were recognized as princes of the empire (*confoederatio cum principibus ecclesiasticis*).[2]

In a parallel process, the Imperial and Free Cities also evolved as a distinct corporate group, though their evolution into a constitutional entity in the Reich was slower than that of the secular and ecclesiastical princes.[3] During the thirteenth century Imperial Cities were promoted by the emperor for fiscal reasons. Initially administered by a royal steward, they increasingly gained independence as city councils assumed stewardship, as well as duties of administration and justice. The Free Cities were those such as Augsburg, Cologne, and Strassburg, originally subject to the authority of a bishop.[4] By the late fifteenth century, the distinction between Imperial and Free Cities had almost disappeared, with many including both terms in their title, and some seventy cities were included in this Estate of the Reich (*Reichsstand*). Their corporate identity was strengthened by the formation of leagues such as the Rhenish League of 1254, or the later Swabian League of 1488. From 1471 there were also increasingly regular meetings of representatives of all the Free and Imperial Cities, and from 1489 they formed a distinct college or chamber in the Reichstag, though until 1648 only had a consultative role (*votum consultativum*), rather than an active vote.[5]

The steady evolution of the Imperial Estates (*Reichsstände*) was accompanied by a more erratic development of institutional structures. The most important was the emergence in the thirteenth century of a clearly defined group of Electors from the group of secular and ecclesiastical princes.[6] This group was composed of the Archchancellor and the two Vice-Archchancellors (the Archbishops of Mainz, Trier, and Cologne), and the secular incumbents of the (albeit purely honorary in the early modern period) major imperial court offices (high steward, marshall, treasurer, cup-bearer): the Count Palatine, the Duke of Saxony, the Margrave of Brandenburg, and (after some dispute with the Dukes of Bavaria in 1257–89) the Kings of Bohemia. Their role as Electors was perpetuated and reinforced by the fact that no strong ruling dynasty emerged and by the conflict between emperors and papacy. The fact that they themselves contributed to the chaotic conditions in the

---

[1] Conrad, *Rechtsgeschichte*, i, 428.
[2] Conrad, *Rechtsgeschichte*, i, 387–91, 429.
[3] Leuschner, *Deutschland*, 185–96; Conrad, *Rechtsgeschichte*, i, 440–61.
[4] Magdeburg is sometimes included in this category, but its freedom was never formally recognized: Köbler, *Lexikon*, 402–3.
[5] Schmidt, *Städtetag*, 1–18.
[6] Conrad, *Rechtsgeschichte*, i, 306–14, and ii, 94–6.

thirteenth century by double elections and the periodic support by some of their number for 'anti-kings' merely enhanced their position further.[7] They became, in fact, more than just Electors: they developed into a council of regency, with aspirations to guide and, in important ways, constrain the freedom of the monarchs.[8]

The final confirmation of the Electors' status came with the Golden Bull of 1356, which illustrates perfectly the complexity of many imperial decrees or concessions.[9] Often viewed as a triumph of the princes, it was in fact initiated by Charles IV as an attempt to secure the continued tenure of the imperial throne for his own successors by confirming the composition of an electoral body favourable to him and by granting its members privileges. The concession of the Bull failed to achieve the establishment of the Luxemburg dynasty. It did, however, both formalize the electoral procedure and the role of the Electors in the empire generally. As well as specifying in detail the procedure for an election and the principle of majority decision, it confirmed the role of the Electors as advisers to the emperor and envisaged regular annual meetings of the Electors for this purpose. In addition, the Counts Palatine and Dukes of Saxony were designated *Reichsvikare*, imperial vicars or administrators in the monarch's absence or during an interregnum. At the same time, the Bull laid down that the lands of an Elector should be indivisible and, in the case of secular Electors, subject to primogeniture.[10]

The regular annual meetings of Electors envisaged by the Golden Bull to discuss issues of internal peace and imperial reform did not in fact take place. However, these provisions of the Bull served to reinforce the oligarchic nature of the Reich: sharing power meant sharing responsibility. In particular, the Bull seemed to imply the recognition that the periodic gatherings of princes (Hoftage, later Reichstage) did not fulfil these functions adequately. Indeed, until the late fifteenth century, these gatherings were both irregular and of varying composition. Only selected princes were invited to discuss current issues, with the result that many of those who did not attend either ignored or blatantly refused to recognize resulting decisions or decrees.[11]

Similar uncertainties and obstacles seem to have attended efforts to develop other central institutions in the thirteenth and fourteenth centuries. A royal chancery existed more or less continuously from the reign of Rudolf of Habsburg (1273–91), but its actions, beyond merely issuing royal confirmations in return for relatively small amounts of money, were rarely significant. Equally, royal courts of justice such as the Hofgericht at Rottweil near Stuttgart seem to have been only intermittently effective. The continued existence of such institutions undoubtedly fostered a tradition of legally trained officialdom, but as instruments of government they

---

[7] Leuschner, *Deutschland*, 109–10.
[8] Schubert, 'Stellung'; Cohn, 'Electors'.
[9] The most recent surveys are in Hohensee et al., *Goldene Bulle*.
[10] Conrad, *Rechtsgeschichte*, i, 311.
[11] Isenmann, 'Kaiser', 192–203; Moraw, *Reich*, 178–9; Moraw 'Entstehung'.

remained lame.[12] Symptomatic of the absence of royal authority was the emergence of organizations such as the freelance courts in Westphalia, the so-called Veme or Feme. This secretive organization flourished between about 1300 and 1450 and imposed a kind of rough and ready justice, sometimes in areas far outside their native Westphalia, in the absence of any effective royal authority. The 'Feme counts' were essentially self-appointed, though they enjoyed the protection of the Archbishop of Cologne and the occasional approval of the emperor. They were able to operate because their justice was backed up by the kind of enforcement that imperial institutions lacked.[13]

The fact that no central government emerged did not, however, mean that the sense of the Reich as a polity was lost or that the Reich withered away to become a mere idea, as traditional historians often argued. Indeed, by 1600, a new structure had clearly developed. This gave a clearer definition both to the relationship between emperor and Reich and to the broad nature and purpose of the Reich itself. Though much of it developed during the course of the sixteenth century itself, the new system was fundamentally the result of the reform movement that emerged in the early fifteenth century and bore fruit in the reforming Reichstag of Worms in 1495 and Augsburg in 1500. Historians have disagreed in recent decades over the origins of these reforms. Some argue that they represented a failed attempt to create for the first time a genuine imperial state. Others see them as an attempt to return to the past, regardless of whether that was an idealized past that corresponded little to reality. Some now question the notion of continuous reform traditions in the fifteenth century. Indeed, Peter Moraw has argued that the very term 'reform' should be abandoned, since it disguises the state of flux and the openness of potential outcomes that characterized the process.[14]

This would seem to be an excessive response to the uncertainties inherent in a process that many contemporaries clearly understood as one of reform. The practical meaning of the term evolved over the course of the fifteenth century. The implementation of practical initiatives was sporadic and shaped at every juncture by new variations on old problems. The ultimate outcome in 1495–1500 was not a decisive conclusion, but rather a series of compromises that were not necessarily intended as permanent solutions. There is, however, a continuity of theme and content to the reforming ideas which remains fundamental to any understanding of the early modern Reich.

The vision of a wide-ranging reform and renewal arose out of a number of factors, both internal and external, which, from the late fourteenth century, exacerbated the endemic instability of the Reich. The first was internal disorder and conflict. The dramatic depopulation that followed the Black Death in some areas (up to 40–50 per cent in Hessen and Silesia) had economic ramifications which generated severe social tensions. The fact that towns prospered did nothing

---

[12] Du Boulay, *Germany*, 76–83.
[13] Du Boulay, 'Law enforcement'.
[14] Moraw, *Reich*, 416–21; Boockmann, *Stauferzeit*, 348–53; Leuschner, *Deutschland*, 201–19; Angermeier, *Reichsreform 1410–1555*, 13–30.

to ameliorate conditions elsewhere. Indeed, it led to new friction between princes and towns. Large parts of the German lands were rendered insecure by the regular, sporadic feuds and armed conflicts escalating to minor wars. The only law that seemed to count in many areas was the *Faustrecht*—the law of the fist. Such conditions scarcely improved when prosperity began to return after about 1450, since a new threat then arose, particularly in western areas, of roaming mercenary armies made redundant by the end of the Hundred Years War in 1453.

There were a variety of regional responses to this insecurity. Leagues of princes, knights, or towns were formed sporadically to combat the disorder that posed an existential threat to many small territories and towns and impeded trade and commerce generally. Some of these received support from emperors perennially ambitious to exploit any opportunity to establish a basis for support within the Reich. Few, however, were effective for any length of time. Even those that survived, such as the Swabian League of 1488, which endured until 1534, could not hope to solve the wider problem. The failure of the Swabian League in this regard is all the more significant for the fact that its foundation was actively supported by Frederick III in an attempt to contain Bavarian ambitions by uniting the south-western cities with the imperial crown. While periodically it acted to great effect, notably in dispossessing Duke Ulrich of Württemberg in 1519 and in mobilizing against the rebellious peasantry in 1525, the alliance between the League and the crown was largely an uneasy one. Despite strenuous efforts, Maximilian I was unable to build upon it effectively. The subsequent efforts of Charles V to do so were undermined by the inability of the League to survive the religious divisions that opened up in the 1520s and which ultimately destroyed it in 1534. Again and again, therefore, the question arose of how to promote a general peace or *Landfriede* within the Reich.

Instability and turmoil within the Reich were exacerbated by a number of external threats to its integrity. The most significant were the Hussite Wars of 1419–36 and the threat posed by the Turkish Empire after the fall of Constantinople in 1453. Both challenges generated ideas and plans for crusades to defend the Reich against heathen invasion. Both ultimately contributed to the emergence of the common cause between emperor and Estates, stimulating both to seek ways of organizing, and above all paying for, concerted action. After the 1470s, the growing conflict between the Habsburgs and Burgundy/France added a further dimension of external threat. Indeed, the reforms of the Reichstag of 1495 crystallized around the issue of the extent to which the Imperial Estates were willing to participate in a conflict which many regarded as a matter for the Habsburg dynasty, rather than the 'German nation'. In that sense, reform as a response to imperial requests for money contributed to the emergence of a distinct 'national' identity of the Reich.

The first serious, wide-ranging proposals for imperial reform arose in the context of the Church Councils of Constance (1414–18) and Basle (1431–7). The main aim of the Council of Constance was to overcome the schism in the Church, to deal with the Hussite heretics, and to promote the cause of Church reform generally. Yet these issues were clearly linked with the problem of the reform of the Reich in the mind of Emperor Sigismund, the guiding force behind the council and the person responsible for it being held on German soil. He was a ruler acutely aware of the insecurity of his empire and ambitious to find some lasting solution.

The nature of Sigismund's ambitions to reassert imperial claims on a broad basis is perhaps symbolically revealed in his introduction, in 1422, of the double-headed eagle of Byzantium as the imperial symbol.[15] Reform proposals made at Constance in 1417 by the Palatinate lawyer Job Vener, seem to have inspired the implementation of the *Reichsmatrikel* of 1422, which specified the number of armed men each Imperial Estate should provide for a crusade against the Hussites.[16] At the Reichstag of Frankfurt am Main in 1427, the first general war tax was introduced (*Gemeiner Pfennig*). These taxes were more significant as precedents than as sources of revenue: there was no treasury and only a single treasurer.[17] Above all, they must be seen as part of an attempt by Sigismund to establish imperial government on a secure footing. Other measures included attempts to ally himself with leagues of cities and knights, to align himself with a short-lived reform-minded league of Electors in 1424, and bribes made to nobles such as the Zollern Burgrave of Nuremberg (enfeoffed with Brandenburg in 1417) and the Wettin Margrave of Meissen (enfeoffed with the Duchy of Saxony in 1423).

Sigismund's initiatives of the 1420s produced no lasting solution. The idea of reform, however, was reiterated in the context of the Council of Basle by Nicholas of Cusa. His *De concordantia catholica* ('On Universal Harmony') of 1433–4 once more elaborated plans for the parallel reform of Roman Church and German Reich. Fundamental to his scheme for the Reich was the institution of annual diets and the promotion of general peace. Nicholas's proposals were formulated in the context of the Church Council, and had little impact after its end in 1437.[18] The link between Church reform and imperial reform surfaced again in the anonymous *Reformatio Sigismundi* ('Reformation of the Emperor Sigismund') of 1439, which demanded change for the sake of simple folk as well as princes. But already in the 1430s the wider question of the universal Christian Church was gradually diminishing in significance compared with the cause of imperial reform. More and more, specifically German issues became exclusive: internal peace, effective administration, a viable revenue system, stable coinage, and the effective organization of a military force for the defence of the Reich.

Repeatedly, proposals by Electors and princes on the one hand, and the Emperors Sigismund and then Frederick III on the other, came to nothing. A general public peace of 1442 (*Landfriedensordnung*) failed to hold. Proposals by the Elector of Trier (1453–4) or by the king of Bohemia (1464) to create a central executive power both failed.[19] A military tax voted at the 'Christian Diet' ('Christentag') of

---

[15] Hye, 'Doppeladler', 73–83.

[16] The term *Matrikel* means literally a register or list of names. The list was never accurate, and included some who never attended the Reichstag and omitted others who did attend. Its revision also proved problematic so that it never became wholly accurate. Nonetheless, it serves as a rough and ready guide to the German Estates.

[17] Conrad, *Rechtsgeschichte*, i, 376–7; Isenmann, 'Reichsfinanzen'; Rowan, 'Imperial Taxes'.

[18] Boockmann, *Stauferzeit*, 350–2.

[19] Isenmann, 'Kaiser', 151–5.

Regensburg in 1471 in response to Frederick III's appeal for a crusade against the Turks failed to galvanize the Reich once the Reichstag had dissolved, still less to launch a general crusade. Time and again, proposals were quashed, agreements rendered ineffective by the tension between emperor and princes, and by disagreements between reforming Electors and princes and their sceptical peers.

Nonetheless, the Reichstag of 1471 marked a change in attitude. For one thing, it brought Frederick III back into the Reich, from where he had been absent since 1444.[20] It also concentrated his mind on the idea of a marriage between his son Maximilian and the daughter and heir of Charles of Burgundy, discussed in 1473 and finally achieved in 1477. This further reinforced the emperor's interest in western affairs, and laid the foundations for the conflict with France that was to dominate the politics of the 1490s. At a time when the imperial position was under threat in the east through the ascendancy of Matthias Corvinus in Hungary, the creation of a new power base in the west was of particular importance. Equally significant, however, was the fact that this western involvement rapidly generated new problems. Between the first negotiations with Charles the Bold in Trier in 1473 and Maximilian's marriage with Mary of Burgundy in 1477, Charles himself generated a war crisis when he laid siege to Neuss (on the Rhine north of Cologne) in 1475. His death shortly before the marriage in 1477, during a campaign against the Swiss cantons, brought the Burgundian inheritance into the hands of the Habsburg dynasty. His intervention in the Reich also contributed decisively to the renewal of ideas of reform.

For both the Habsburgs and the Imperial Estates, the events of the 1470s underlined the need to reorganize the military capability of the Reich. Maximilian's marriage immediately plunged him into conflict, first with France over Artois and the Duchy of Burgundy and then with the provinces of the Low Countries. At the same time, he became involved in further conflict with Matthias Corvinus in the east. The reconquest of Vienna in 1490, after its loss in 1485, and of the Erblande thereafter raised the prospect once more of re-establishing a power base in the south-east. The inheritance of the Tyrol and the Vorlande in 1489 and the Peace of Pressburg, which in 1491 secured the right to inherit the land of Corvinus's Jagiellonian successors in Hungary, completed this process. Then in 1495 the French attack on Italy, where Maximilian's interests were enhanced by the claims of his second wife, Bianca Maria Sforza of Milan, created a new front. Maximilian's response was twofold. First, he planned an alliance with Spain by means of the marriage of his children Philipp and Margarethe to the infantas Juana and Juan. Second, he turned to the Reich for military assistance.

From the point of view of the Imperial Estates, these developments generated rather different imperatives.[21] On the one hand, they were willing to concur in the election of Maximilian as King of the Romans and therefore as successor to his father in 1486. That then led logically to Maximilian's succession as sole ruler in 1493, though he only became emperor in 1508. On the other hand, the Estates

---

[20] Koller, *Friedrich III*. 168–97.
[21] Schröcker, *Deutsche Nation*, 31–95; Isenmann, 'Kaiser', 167–84.

gradually developed a distinct agenda based on their experiences in the 1470s. The threat of the Turks in the early 1470s and Charles the Bold's attack on Neuss in 1475 had underlined the need to find a means of protecting the Reich effectively from external attack. This clearly required money, which in turn required reform and reorganization of the system. However, it did not necessarily entail a complete identification with what were increasingly perceived to be the largely dynastic interests of the Habsburgs. The repeated requests for money now made by Frederick III and especially Maximilian sharpened their awareness of the issues. The Estates now reacted increasingly both to external threats and to Habsburg responses to those threats.

The reforms thus had two driving forces: on the one hand the emperors, on the other the Reichstag.[22] Indeed, it was during this period that the Reichstag for the first time gained a sense of its identity as a constitutional organ of a specifically German Reich; the very fact that the term 'Reichstag' now took over from the original term 'Hoftag' reflected the growing independence of that body from the imperial court and the person of the king.[23] The gatherings retained many of their old functions as meetings of the emperor's vassals at which fiefdoms were renewed or granted, and as extended family reunions at which marriages were negotiated or celebrated.[24] Yet the political-constitutional dimension came increasingly to the fore.

The man who coordinated the efforts of the Estates was the Archbishop of Mainz, Berthold von Henneberg. In 1486 he gained control of the imperial chancellery in return for his support of Maximilian's election as King of the Romans. With that he was able to transform the operation of the Reichstag. For example, it now began to conduct its business in curias or colleges: the College of Electors, the College of Princes, and, from 1489, a third College of Imperial Cities. A complex procedure developed of advance consultations, proposals, and discussions, both within the colleges and between the Reichstag as a whole and the emperor, along with counterproposals, votes, and formal decisions (*Reichsschluss*), which then were promulgated at the end of a Reichstag in an imperial decree (*Reichsabschied*) and immediately became law.[25]

The formalization of procedure, which remained valid until the end of the Reich in 1806, was the essential precondition for the reforms achieved at the Reichstag of Worms (1495) and Augsburg (1500). At Worms, the princes were unwilling to accede to Maximilian's request for money to finance a campaign against the French in Italy. They regarded this as primarily a dynastic matter. Yet both sides recognized the need for reform. There was, for example, ready agreement on the publication of a 'perpetual public peace' (*Ewiger Landfriede*), which outlawed feuds. On the question of an imperial court of justice, Henneberg and the Estates were able to ensure that the Reichskammergericht (Imperial Chamber Court) was set

---

[22] Angermeier, *Reichsreform 1410–1555*, 150–64.
[23] Isenmann, 'Kaiser', 185–94.
[24] Stollberg-Rilinger, *Verfassungsgeschichte*, 23–91; Neuhaus, 'Wandlungen'.
[25] Schubert, *Reichstage*, 34–56; Rabe, *Geschichte*, 118–20.

up independently of the royal court. While the emperor had the right to appoint the presiding judge of the court (the *Kammerrichter*), the Estates gained the right to nominate the ordinary judges, of whom half were to be trained lawyers (non-noble doctors of canon and Roman laws) and half nobles. Above all, the extent to which the court assumed functions that were previously royal prerogatives became clear in the definition of its remit: to maintain the public peace and to adjudicate in disputes between the emperor's vassals.[26]

The early history of the court was characterized by disputes between emperor and Estates over the rights of appointment; in 1498 Maximilian attempted to diminish the court's influence by establishing a rival royal court (the Reichshofrat, or royal aulic council).[27] But the Reichskammergericht was at first able to maintain its position as the prime institutional court of the Reich. Furthermore, by stipulating that local or regional laws would only be regarded as valid in so far as they did not conflict with Roman law, the Reichskammergericht promoted the more widespread reception of Roman law, which rapidly became the basis for the legal system of the Reich as a whole, as well as providing a model for the territories and cities. Within a few decades, a legal training was a prerequisite even for the noble judges, which lent the court as a whole a sense of solidarity and a uniformity of outlook that further bolstered its independent position.

Two further measures agreed in 1495 served in different ways to give definition to the Reich. First, discussion of how the public peace was to be implemented resulted in a compromise formula, the so-called *Handhabung des Friedens und Rechts* (administration of peace and justice). This reminded the emperor of his duties with regard to the Reich and in particular of his obligation to call a Reichstag annually. In itself this formula perhaps merely seemed to state the obvious. Yet it represented a significant success for the Estates. They asserted their position by putting it forward, and their constitutional position as, collectively, partners if not equals of the emperor was enshrined in the diet. Above all, it paved the way for the more formal agreements between emperor and Estates that, from 1519, were negotiated before imperial elections: the *Wahlkapitulation* or election agreement, which elaborated the promises made by an emperor-elect. The effect of this formula for the 'implementation of peace and law' was therefore to define the limits of imperial power and to specify its functions within the Reich: the emperor's position was to be more that of a referee in the legal system than that of a sovereign ruler.

The decisions that were reached concerning taxation also helped determine the kind of polity the Reich would become. The attempt to introduce a general tax, the *Gemeiner Pfennig*, to finance both the Reichskammergericht and the imperial army, illustrated the limitations of the Reich. Designed as a mixture of income, wealth and poll tax, and agreed for four years in the first instance, the tax proved unworkable. The very principle of such a tax, agreed at the Reichstag by princes and lords, conflicted in many instances with the right of their own local Estates to participate in an agreement on taxes. Some major princes even regarded the very

---

[26] Smend, *Reichskammergericht*, 23–67; Press, *Reichskammergericht*.
[27] Gschließer, *Reichshofrat*, 1–3. See also pp. 364–5.

idea of raising a tax on behalf of the Reich as demeaning to their position. Everywhere, the task of collecting the money proved difficult in view of the inadequate data for the assessment of liability, the lack of tax-collecting agencies, and the incompetence of the parochial organizations of the Church. Relatively few princes and magistrates, including Maximilian himself in his own lands, in fact made much effort to collect the tax, and it was abandoned.

Further negotiations in 1507 resulted in two forms of imperial taxation based on a revision of the traditional *Matrikel*, a list of all Imperial Estates (i.e. entities represented in the Reichstag), together with an assessment of what proportion of a general levy each might contribute.[28] The so-called *Kammerzieler* for the support of the Reichskammergericht became a regular tax.[29] No such solution was found for military expenditure. These costs continued to be covered by specific levies, negotiated afresh in respect of each threat to the Reich, and calculated on the traditional basis. The *Matrikel* were used to calculate the equivalent cost of a quota of armed men for periods of one month (the so-called *Römermonate*, or 'Roman months' which referred to the medieval origins of the levy to support campaigns in Italy). The implications of the procedure for the government of the territories will be examined in relation to levies for the Turkish campaigns of the 1570s and 1580s.[30] The significance of this outcome for the constitutional structure of the Reich was, however, clear much earlier.

Even before the long-term implications of the agreements of 1495 became evident, it was apparent that the immediate problems had not been solved. Maximilian still needed the military support of the Reich. Above all, while an imperial court of law had been established, there was no mechanism for enforcing its decisions. Public peace remained a hopeless ideal as long as there was no way of policing it. Yet the question of executive powers once more raised the whole question of the balance between emperor and Estates.

In 1495, Maximilian had successfully resisted the creation of anything like a central executive. By 1500, his need for military assistance was such that he was obliged to acquiesce in the proposal for a Reichsregiment (central imperial government). This was to be a council of twenty members, including the seven Electors and others appointed by the Estates presided over by the emperor or his representative.[31] Though it was promptly established in Nuremberg, the council soon failed. It had no income and no real power. The emperor resented it from the start as a limitation of his powers and turned radically against it when Henneberg began to enter into talks with representatives from France.[32] Even the Imperial Estates failed to support their own creation, many of them seeing it as a potential threat to their own position. It was dissolved in 1502 and never revived in the same form: the Reichsregiment of 1521–31 was more of a council of regency in the

---

[28] See note 16 above.
[29] Conrad, *Rechtsgeschichte*, ii, 135–6. The name referred to the fact that it was to be levied by certain dates (*zielen* = to aim), i.e. the Frankfurt autumn and Lent fairs.
[30] See pp. 409, 515.
[31] Angermeier, 'Reichsregimenter'.
[32] Baron, 'Imperial reform', 300.

absence of Charles V. Indeed, when it was moved from Nuremberg to Esslingen in 1524 (near the court at Stuttgart, which was under Habsburg control after the dispossession of Duke Ulrich of Württemberg in 1519 until he was reinstated in 1534), the second Reichsregiment became for all the world to see, and hence to distrust more than ever, an instrument of Habsburg policy, rather than the central executive envisaged by Henneberg and the reformers.[33]

More indicative again of the idiosyncratic system of checks and balances that was the constitutional legacy of the German Middle Ages was the mechanism introduced in 1500 for the regional administration of imperial justice and organization of military support. The institution of six Kreise, or regional associations of territories, was based on an idea that dated back to 1383 and was originally intended as a way of electing the six representatives of the Estates in the Reichsregiment.[34] But once that body failed, the Kreise were all that remained. In 1507, the Kreise were made responsible for the nomination of the assessors at the Reichkammergericht. In 1512, their number was increased to include the lands of those who were formerly directly represented in the Reichsregiment. These were the lands of the Habsburgs themselves (in the Austrian and Burgundian Kreise) and those of the Electors (the ecclesiastical Electors in the Kurrheinischer Kreis or 'electoral Kreis of the Rhine'; the inclusion of Saxony and Brandenburg led to the division of the Saxon Kreis into Lower and Upper Saxon regions).

What may at first sight appear to be yet another saga of disintegration was in fact quite the opposite. By steady degrees, the Kreise developed regular internal, formalized constitutional arrangements and administrations. The *Reichsexekutionsordnung* (law regulating the implementation of justice in the Reich) agreed in 1555 was a particularly important milestone in this process. Each Kreis was headed jointly by a *Direktor* (the senior ecclesiastical prince) and a *kreisausschreibender Fürst* (a prominent secular prince who was also the military commander for the Kreise) who oversaw the chancellery, and summoned the Kreistag or Kreis assembly, modelled on the Reichstag, and presided over it. As they evolved over time, these Kreise exercised executive and integrative functions that were crucial to the Reich. They organized military contingents and saw to it that the *Matrikel* taxes raised by their members flowed to the emperor. They were charged with the implementation of imperial decrees and with maintaining peace within the region, either by mediating in disputes or by direct military intervention. Later, they came to be responsible for roads, prisons, and workhouses, for combating beggars and robber bands, and for maintaining the purity of the coinage.

Not all of these functions were implemented immediately: military organization and maintenance of the public peace were fundamental initially; the rest came later. Nor did the Kreise by any means always function in the regular manner that might be suggested by a schematic summary of their structure and duties. Some indeed never really functioned at all; and in the long term the most effective Kreise were those in Swabia and Franconia, regions characterized by extreme territorial

---

[33] See pp. 161–3.   [34] Conrad, *Rechtsgeschichte*, ii, 101–5; Dotzauer, *Reichskreise*, 23–79.

fragmentation and the absence of one or more dominant territorial princes. Furthermore, some Kreise were periodically paralysed by disputes over prerogatives, precedence, and procedure similar to those that occasionally lamed the Reichstag, as well as virtually every other institution of the Reich.

The very existence of the Kreise, however, provided an important infrastructure of regional networks in the Reich, a relatively formal set of associations. They aided communication both between their individual members and between the regions and the emperor. They added a further complex consultative machinery to that of the Reichstag, in which participation went hand in hand with the right to be consulted and the right to veto measures deemed contrary to the interests of individual Estates. They contributed to the emergence and acceptance of what might be described as the 'legal culture' of the Reich: the norms and conventions on which its legal system was founded. Not least, the institution of Kreise created a new elite group of princes within the Reich, the *kreisausschreibende Fürsten*, who joined the Electors as a group without whose consent and cooperation the emperor, and indeed the Reich itself, could not function.[35]

Many of the implications of the negotiations of 1495 and 1500 became clear only gradually. A number of the detailed arrangements for the functioning of the Reichskammergericht or the Kreise were evolved during the course of the Reichstag meetings between 1500 and the early 1520s. The wider significance of the outcome of the negotiations as a whole emerged over a much longer period as the system responded to the challenge of the Reformation and the need to find a legal-political formula to overcome religious division in the 1550s. It was only in the later sixteenth century that, following further changes and adjustments, legal and political commentators began to construct a historical narrative of the genesis of the modern Reich in the reforming diets of 1495 and 1500.[36] Nonetheless, some fundamental positions crystallized around 1500, and were even evident at the time. However, in order not to overestimate the degree of clarity achieved around 1500 it is perhaps worth setting out the main features of the situation in that year.

The reform movement, which had its origins in schemes for the parallel reform of Roman Church and Roman Reich, ended by becoming focused more exclusively on the German Reich. The idea of Church reform had not died. Indeed, Henneberg himself was very much a successor of Nicholas of Cusa. He maintained a fervent belief in the unity of Church and Reich, and consequently in the need for a new concordat and the remedy of abuses in the Church as part and parcel of the reform of the Reich.[37]

Maximilian too, though in a rather different way, aspired to maintain the union of Roman Church and Roman Reich. His political dispute with the papacy resulted in him being the first emperor not crowned by the pope in Rome and this obliged him to assume the title *Erwählter Römischer Kaiser* (Elected Roman Emperor). He did not, however, abandon his inherited claims to dominion in Rome and

[35] Schmidt, 'Deutschland', 13; Conrad, *Rechtsgeschichte*, ii, 101–5; Dotzauer, *Reichskreise*, 579–82.
[36] Stolleis, *Öffentliches Recht*, i, 48, 72–3.
[37] *NDB*, ii, 156–7; *ADB*, ii, 524–9.

protectorate over the Church. In 1511, he even toyed with the idea of having himself elected as pope. However, the Estates as a whole increasingly equated the Reich with the 'German nation', that is, the Reich north of the Alps. They, too, held on to the idea of Church reform: from 1456 the *Gravamina nationis Germanicae*, a catalogue of German grievances against the Roman Church, were reiterated and extended at every diet. They are examined in greater detail later in the discussion of the origins of the Reformation.[38] Their significance in the present context, however, is that they provide further evidence for the focus of the Estates on the Reich of the 'German nation'.

For the main issue here was the political one of the emperor's authority and power in the Reich. That in turn underlines a significant divergence in views of the Reich and its *raison d'être* between emperor and Estates. Both were bound together in a symbiotic relationship. Both shared common interests, especially in the need to defend the Reich against the Turks and other eventual enemies. Yet while there was agreement and solidarity on the Turkish question, emperor and Estates differed on the definition of other enemies.

Maximilian's view of the Reich was shaped by his dynastic inheritance. He inherited from his father a grand vision of the resurgence of imperial power based both on the complex of Habsburg lands and inheritance possibilities in the east (from the Adriatic up through Austria to Bohemia and Silesia and including Hungary) and on a similar complex in the west (from the Sundgau up through the Franche Comté to the Low Countries). This imperial vision still included Italy, and the traditional relationship between Reich and papacy, both as a religious ideological symbol and as a sphere of political influence. Frederick III had laid the foundations but, beyond simply surviving as monarch for fifty-three years, had done little to construct a reality out of the vision. His later reputation as the 'arch-sleeping cap of the Holy Roman Empire' (*'des Hl. Röm. Reiches Erzschlafmütze'*) is unjust.[39] Yet the contrast with his son and heir could hardly be more striking.[40] From the 1480s onwards Maximilian strove tirelessly to assert his rights and realize every ounce of potential on all fronts. The result, inevitably, was perennial military conflict: against France, against Venice, and even against the papacy, in addition to protracted struggles in Bohemia and Hungary, and with the Turks.

The whole enterprise was accompanied at every stage by brilliant propaganda. Leading humanists such as Conrad Celtis were enlisted to extol the glory of the Habsburg dynasty.[41] Yet the urgent need for money and military support brought conflict with the core of that empire, the German Reich. If Frederick III and Maximilian I elaborated an ideology of empire, the Imperial Estates in the German lands had, since the 1470s at the latest, developed their own distinct perspective. They viewed Habsburg dynastic ambitions with reserve, if not outright suspicion. Above all, they developed a view of the Reich as a defensive alliance.[42] In that

---

[38] See pp. 86–8, 113, 169, 172, 177–8.   [39] Koller, *Friedrich III.*, 20–32.
[40] Boockmann, *Staufer*, 326–4; Leuschner, *Deutschland*, 209–16; *NDB*, v, 486.
[41] Benecke, *Maximilian I*, 178.
[42] Isenmann, 'Kaiser', 163–7.

view, Italy or Habsburg entanglements with Burgundy and France were purely dynastic concerns, rather than matters for the 'German' Reich. Hence they denied Maximilian the full extent of the help that he requested against France in the 1490s and refused point blank to support him in his conflict with Venice between 1509 and 1517. As a result, Maximilian was increasingly forced to rely on his own resources. The reform and reorganization of his Austrian territories was forced upon him by his inability to mobilize the Reich in his service. The resources that Maximilian could not raise as emperor, he was obliged to find as *Landesherr* or territorial prince. The long-term implications were profound. The dualism of Austrian lands or *Hausmacht* and the German empire created a perpetual tension between Austria and 'Germany'.

That still left the Turks, of course, and that element of the conflict with Burgundy/France which potentially threatened the western areas of the Reich. This could not have been foreseen in 1500, however. Indeed, the threat posed by the Turks and Burgundy/France then created a perfectly viable community of interests. Maximilian still needed the support of the Estates, however limited and accompanied by whatever conditions. The Estates for their part still needed the emperor. No other German prince could supply his role.

Both emperor and Estates were therefore equally interested in the military regeneration of the Reich. The argument revolved fundamentally around the question of whose authority would be asserted in the process. In the event, neither side won. The emperor failed to push through an imperial right to tax and failed at the same time to transform the Reich into a monarchy in any meaningful sense. The Estates, for their part, failed to achieve a government in the form of the Reichsregiment, which would formally limit the emperor's powers and establish their own dominion. Henneberg and his allies failed entirely in their attempts to pursue a Reich foreign policy independently of the emperor. Symbolic of that failure was that Henneberg was obliged in 1503 to hand back the seal of the Reich which he had held as Imperial Archchancellor. Significantly, too, Henneberg had also been unable to rally the German princes. Collectively they mistrusted a strong corporate regime composed of members they themselves nominated, as much as they mistrusted the ambitions of a strong emperor.

What remained in the stalemate between emperor and Estates was a series of principles on which the imperial constitution rested until the end: the cooperative decision-making process of the Reichstag with its implicit system of checks and balances; the idea of the Reich as a defensive alliance of the Estates against external aggression; and the Reich as a *Rechts- und Friedensordnung*, a legal system for the maintenance of public peace. These were the minimal principles to which the princes and magistrates of the Reich reverted again and again in the next few centuries. These were the core principles on which all subsequent agreements, treaties, and institutions were founded. Those which conformed to them prospered; those which did not soon atrophied. They were, moreover, principles whose implications bound the Habsburg emperors as much as they did princes and magistrates: no attempt to break out of them was successful before Napoleon forced the dissolution of the Reich in 1806.

This notion of a polity based on fundamental principles over three centuries must, however, be qualified in two ways. First, the Reich was not a static entity. The institutional and legal framework evolved progressively throughout the period. In particular, it gained new contours in the Peace of Augsburg 1555 and the Peace of Westphalia in 1648. Those agreements were consciously formulated on the basis of the principles established in 1495, yet their eventual emergence could not be taken for granted from the perspective of around 1500. Second, even in the form that it then assumed, the imperial system did not function uniformly over the whole extent of the German lands. By no means all the Imperial Estates, for example, participated in the Reichstag. Not every vassal of the emperor, even in the German lands, participated in the emerging political system from the start. In the period around 1500 what might be described as the political nation was largely confined to the south, to the old Hohenstaufen core territories south of the Main and the Saale, to the areas between Alsace in the west and the Austrian duchies in the east, where the Habsburgs had extended their territories and around them, their clientele. The areas to the north, especially the north-west, only gradually became integrated during the course of the late sixteenth century. It was only after 1648 that one could speak of a Reich that functioned from the Alps to the North Sea and the Baltic.[43]

[43] Schmidt, 'Integration'.

3

Fragmented Territories

The reforms of 1495 and 1500 in a sense saved the Reich from disintegration, while at the same time revealing the limits of its integration. The construction of a central government, whether under the control of the emperor or of the Estates, was thwarted by powerful centrifugal tendencies. Nationalist historians of the nineteenth and early twentieth centuries characterized this process as the triumph of the princes, the emergence of the territorial state which hindered the consolidation of the nation state in the fifteenth and sixteenth centuries. This view distorts the reality of the Reich and underestimates the integrative potential inherent in its system. It also distorts the reality of the territories and overestimates the degree of concentration they had achieved by about 1500.

While it is possible to speak of progressive stabilization in some territories during the later fifteenth century, it is difficult to speak in any meaningful sense of a generalized process of 'state-building' or 'state formation'. If it is convenient to think of the Reich as a kind of federation, it is also misleading and technically inaccurate. Nor were the territories that belonged to the Reich a collection of closed or coherent units. For one thing they were not sovereign, and *Landeshoheit* or *Landesherrschaft* was subject to the higher authority of the emperor and the Reich.[1] Even considered as in some way subordinate entities, however, they were far from being states in the making. On the other hand, in responding to the same problems of lawlessness and insecurity that motivated the reform of the Reich, some at least of the territories achieved, by about 1500, a greater concentration of authority and power.

Something of the complexity of the territorial arrangements within the Reich was indicated earlier in the discussion of the frontier areas. An understanding of them is crucial to any understanding of early modern German history. Yet the extraordinary variety of different circumstances and constellations that prevailed across the German lands makes it difficult even to present a broad overview.[2] Indeed, the picture was subject to such constant flux and change that even the most detailed maps can only account for the situation in a given year, and are rarely able to reproduce in any meaningful visual way the mosaic of splintered territories and overlapping jurisdictions that prevailed over large areas. The fact that

[1] Conrad, *Rechtsgeschichte*, ii, 231–5.
[2] Wagner, 'Grenzen', 243–6. The most comprehensive surveys are Köbler, *Lexikon* and Sante (ed.), *Geschichte*. The latter volume, also known as the *Territorien-Ploetz*, provides a good comprehensive survey. Another broad, but less comprehensive, survey may be found in the first five volumes of Braunfels, *Kunst*: the emphasis is on architecture and art, but the scope is much broader.

primogeniture laws gained currency only gradually from the late fifteenth century adds to the problem. The history of many territories is consequently a history of perpetual partition, reunion, and further partition as the fertility of the dynasty is reflected in the division or concentration of its lands.[3] A close view of many areas would have revealed something akin to a mass of amoebae, constantly changing shape through inheritance, marriage, land purchase, sale or, more remarkably still, through the widespread practice of pawning land or jurisdictions, a device used by all from the emperor downwards, either to raise money or to extend influence, depending on which side of the deal one found oneself.[4]

The sheer number of quasi-independent units renders even a simple enumeration quite problematic. However, a rough approximation of numbers, size, and variety of conditions is essential. For only a sense of the variety of its constituent parts will provide an accurate perspective on both the degree of 'state formation' that characterized a minority of territories and the role that the Reich played as a polity that protected all of them.

The prime subordinate units of the Reich were clearly those defined as Imperial Estates: those whose lords or representatives were entitled to a seat and a vote in the Reichstag. Their numbers fluctuated over the fifteenth and sixteenth centuries, even after a supposedly definitive list was drawn up in 1521.[5] Some disappeared as dynasties died out. Others were added as they were elevated by the emperor, whose prerogative this remained until the end of the Reich. For the late fifteenth century the following rough numbers emerge. At the top of the list stood the seven Electors. In addition, there were some twenty-five major secular principalities, together with roughly ninety archbishoprics, bishoprics, and abbeys. The latter were of lesser status than the bishoprics and more or less on the level of the next gradation of higher nobility, the group of approximately one hundred counts.

The final category comprised the Free and Imperial Cities, some sixty-five by 1500. Their number also fluctuated like that of other Imperial Estates. Their main problems were debt or the hostility of neighbouring principalities, which steadily eroded their numbers until the Peace of Westphalia finally stabilized their situation, in legal terms at least, in 1648. At all stages, they varied immensely in size and significance, both economic and political. In the late fifteenth century, the scale stretched from Cologne, the largest with some 30,000 inhabitants, via Lübeck, Danzig, Hamburg, Strassburg, Ulm, and Nuremberg with over 20,000, to small cities the size of Dinkelsbühl in Franconia with well under 5,000 inhabitants, and many others with a good deal less than that; some had only a few hundred inhabitants and were scarcely more than villages.[6]

The number of units that were either Imperial Estates or, like the Imperial Cities towards the end of the fifteenth century, became Imperial Estates, fluctuates, but it

---

[3] Fichtner, *Protestantism*, 1–6.
[4] Krause, 'Pfandherrschaften', 515–24; Cohn, *Government*, 43–9, 62–5, 69–73.
[5] The 1521 list omitted some who were included later, often after protracted legal arguments; others were apparently included by mistake. The uncertainty reflected the difficulty of defining membership on the basis of an often erratic record of attendance at the Reichstag. See p. 30 (fn 16).
[6] Gerteis, *Städte*, 52–6; Amann, 'Stadt'; Mauersberg, *Städte*, 75–9.

is at least capable of being roughly calculated. That cannot be said of the lordships and other units which retained a degree of freedom from their more powerful neighbours but which were not Imperial Estates. Individually, they were perhaps of little significance. Their existence is, however, important in two ways. First their survival, like that of the Imperial Cities and Imperial Counts, illustrates the limitations of the process of territorial consolidation by the more significant secular and ecclesiastical princes. These were the groups, moreover, which, along with the Imperial Cities and the Imperial Counts, provided natural potential allies for the emperors in the fifteenth and sixteenth centuries in their struggle to frustrate the complete 'territorialization' of the Reich.[7] Ultimately, too, their survival underlines the effectiveness of the Reich as a peace-keeping system governed by law, though it is significant that these individually powerless entities had endured even the unstable and, by comparison, lawless period of the fifteenth century. Second, their concentration in a broad swathe of territory arching from the south-west, through Swabia and Franconia, and up into Hessen and Thuringia gave this part of the map of the Reich an entirely different complexion to the relatively solid blocks of territory characteristic of the Lower Rhine, the north, and north-east, or Bavaria and the Austrian duchies.

The most important of these groups, which enjoyed *Reichsunmittelbarkeit* but not *Reichsstandschaft*, were the Imperial Knights; they were nobles of the Reich subject only to the emperor but had no representation in the Reichstag.[8] Originally members of the lower nobility who remained outside the larger territorial unit, they were concentrated in Swabia, Franconia, and the Upper and Middle Rhine regions. Until the sixteenth century, they survived by periodically forming leagues, associations, and knightly societies: the Society of the Donkey in the Kraichgau, for example, or the Society of St George's Shield (*Sankt Jörgenschild*) in the Upper Swabian Allgäu. It was only after 1500, however, that wider regional associations emerged in Swabia, Franconia, and the Rhineland, and not until 1577 that these were incorporated into a joint association, the *Corpus liberae et immediate imperii nobilitatis*. These developments, in turn, were part of a wider process. The transformation of the knights from a traditional military knighthood into an independent nobility of service in the Reich proceeded gradually through the late fifteenth and sixteenth centuries.[9] The pressures that drove the process and the factors that shaped it in the Reformation period will be examined in detail below.[10] The significant point in the present context is simply the survival of these small Estates outside of any larger territorial unit, indeed their ability to leave such larger units during the course of the sixteenth century.

Special forms abounded in this relatively heterogeneous group. The institution of the *Ganerbschaft*, or community of noble heirs, was one of the

----

[7] Schmidt, 'Politische Bedeutung'.

[8] Conrad, *Rechtsgeschichte*, ii, 202–6; Press, *Reichsritterschaft*; Neuhaus, *Reich*, 36–7.

[9] The Swabian knights only finally left the Württemberg *Landtage* in the 1520s; the Franconian knights left the *Landtage* of Würzburg, Bamberg, and Brandenburg-Ansbach between 1540 and 1579; those of the Rhine region departed the Trier *Landtag* in 1577.

[10] See pp. 210–19.

most remarkable.[11] In the so-called 'noble republic' of Friedberg in Hessen, for example, twelve noble families shared a single castle (though they lived in separate residences within it). Under the constitution for the castle developed between 1337 and 1498, the network of knightly families with rights in the castle elected a *Burggraf* (burgrave), two *Baumeister*, and twelve *Regimentsburgmannen*, to represent the community, maintain its buildings and govern its affairs. During the fifteenth century, they gained control over the Imperial City of Friedberg at their gates (when the emperor pawned it), acquired a share in the noble *Ganerbschaft* of Staden (in Hessen), and purchased the nearby County of Kaichen in the Wetterau. The status of their community was reflected in the fact that their *Burggraf* acted as leader of the Wetterau knights from 1492 until 1729 and as *Hauptmann* (military commander) of the Middle Rhine knights from 1536 to 1764.[12] The Friedberg 'noble republic' was unusual in that it was sustained by a large number of families and its organization was formalized by a constitution. Other inheritance communities such as the castle of Staden or the Burg Eltz on the Moselle operated more straightforwardly and they were limited to smaller groups.[13] In the case of Burg Eltz, this took the form of an association of several branches of one family in what amounted to a family entail.

The survival as independent entities of Imperial Cities, Imperial Counts, and Imperial Knights is to a large extent explained by the fact that they had some economic (in the case of cities) or political (in all cases) function within the Reich. Until the mid-sixteenth century, in particular, they were regarded as potential partners in repeated imperial attempts to establish networks of influence and power in the south and west. The cities declined in number, as unfavourable economic conditions left many vulnerable to pressure from powerful territorial neighbours. The counts and knights, by contrast, successfully organized themselves into regional interest and self-defence groups, while their persistence in the practise of partible inheritances ensured that numbers remained high even though the unit size threatened to dwindle to insignificance. Even in the 1790s, for example, there were still perhaps as many as 1,700 Imperial Knights' 'territories'.

It is much more difficult to explain the survival, free of territorial overlords, of peasant communities without political function and with few, if any means of self-defence. In the north, such areas succumbed to systematic 'territorialization' relatively early. The tribal communities of Frisia, with their sworn council and seal of communal government inscribed *Universitas Frisonum*, gradually fell victim first to warring chieftains, then to the domineering tom Brok line (*c*.1350–1464), and finally to the rule of the Cirksena dynasty of counts (1464–1744).[14] A similar 'peasant republic' or oligarchy of regents in Dithmarschen on the right bank of the mouth of the Elbe survived until 1559, when it was incorporated into the

[11] Conrad, *Rechtsgeschichte*, i, 415–16. The term derives from the fact that a group of heirs received an inheritance in their collective hands: *zur gesamten Hand*.

[12] Köbler, *Lexikon*, 197–8; Sante, *Hessen*, 145–8.

[13] Köbler, *Lexikon*, 167, 678.

[14] Sante (ed.), *Geschichte*, 406–10; Schmidt, *Ostfriesland*; Schindling and Ziegler, *Territorien*, iii, 162–80.

Duchy of Holstein.[15] Better organized in terms of government than the Swiss communes and easily their match in wealth, Dithmarschen failed because it lacked a natural centre. Unlike the Netherlands provinces, also, it lacked contiguous natural allies along the Frisian coastal belt. Its isolated position in the north-west, for so long a natural advantage, ultimately proved its downfall in the face of the relentless hostility of the kings of Denmark and in the absence of effective imperial power in the area in the early sixteenth century.

In the south and west and in Alsace, by contrast, much smaller communities could survive. Here, a collection of so-called *Reichsdörfer* (imperial villages) formed the most minuscule and least significant independent entities of the Reich. Formerly parts of the medieval Hohenstaufen royal demesne, their inhabitants remained free men. The emperor was their only overlord, though they were not regarded as an Estate of the Reich and were not represented in the Reichstag. Originally there were some 120 in number, but relatively few survived into the early modern period; by 1803 there were only five.[16] Yet the history of these communities in Gochsheim and Sennfeld near Schweinfurt, the Free Men of the Leutkircher Heide in the Allgäu near Ravensburg, Soden in the Taunus, and Sulzbach near Frankfurt, is more than just an antiquarian curiosity. In each case the communities struggled successfully over several centuries against the implications of pawn contracts and disputes with neighbouring 'protective powers' over higher and lower jurisdictions to achieve, entirely without force of arms, recognition of their free status. Their very survival was testimony to the progressive 'juridification' of the Reich from the early sixteenth century.

The continued existence of well over a thousand smaller territories in the Reich places arguments about the 'rise of the territorial state' in perspective. There were undoubtedly larger territories that emerged and stabilized during the fifteenth and sixteenth centuries. Their growth was determined above all by the regional need to respond to the problem of public order, before they then took on a momentum of their own as instruments of power in the hands of ambitious princes. The largest blocks emerged, perhaps not surprisingly, in the north and north-east, where fifteenth-century emperors sought to extend their power and pacify the land through clients such as the Zollern Margraves of Brandenburg or the Wettin Dukes of Saxony.

Elsewhere, other powerful territorial blocks also emerged by a process of evolution. They were not closed territories but rather, in the first instance, feudal networks secondary and similar to the Reich itself: agglomerations of lordship rights only very gradually formed into principalities under anything like uniform administration. At close quarters, these apparently solid blocks of land dissolved at their peripheries into a mass of overlapping and often shared jurisdictions. The process of rounding off the boundaries, by means of sales and purchases, by pawn

---

[15] Stoob, *Dithmarschen*, 7–16, 407–12; Urban, *Dithmarschen*, 60–143; Krüger, *Verfassung*.
[16] Neuhaus, *Reich*, 38; Conrad, *Rechtsgeschichte*, ii, 205. See also the relevant entries in Köbler, *Lexikon*.

deals, by land exchanges, and not infrequently by acquisition by brute and illegal force, extended throughout the early modern period.

Equally often, the evolution of such a territorial unit was then sharply arrested, sometimes for a generation or two, sometimes in perpetuity, by partition on the death of an overlord with more than one son. The Margravate of Baden, for example, though a potentially significant territory constructed on the inheritance of the powerful Zähringer, was handicapped throughout the early modern period by repeated partitions.[17] The Wettin dynasty in Saxony might have become even more powerful had it not partitioned its lands in 1485 between an Ernestine electorate and an Albertine duchy. This was the first of numerous partitions which, by the seventeenth century, made Thuringia into the classic region of German *Kleinstaaterei*, with no less than twenty-seven courts and administrations in the combined Ernestine and Albertine lines.[18] By contrast, the emergence of Bavaria as a powerful territory in the early modern period was founded on the reunion of the duchies of Inner and Outer Bavaria after the extinction of the Landshut line of the Wittelsbachs in 1503, after which the Munich heirs introduced a primogeniture law in 1506. Even here, however, the next few decades were characterized by a bitter dispute between the brothers Wilhelm IV and Ludwig X over the interpretation of the law, which only gained clarification and acceptance in the second half of the century.[19]

The vagaries of inheritance conventions and family politics were not the only obstacles to the stabilization and consolidation of a territory. Just as the emperors could not rule against their noble Estates, so most princes could not govern against their own territorial Estates: nobles subject to them as feudal overlords (*landsässiger Adel*), towns, and in some parts even peasants.[20] An imperial law of 1231 obliged the princes to seek the consent of their nobles to any new laws or to changes of any kind. In the fifteenth century, as major princes tackled the task of creating public order, this more often than not meant seeking consent for new financial burdens. The first step towards a uniform government was therefore generally the translation of subordinate Estates into Estates-General.

This was rarely a smooth process, and in some cases, such as the Palatinate in the fifteenth century or Württemberg and others in the sixteenth century, it led to a decisive break between princes and lower nobility—counts or knights— who asserted their *Reichsunmittelbarkeit* or vassalship of the emperor himself. The remaining Landtag then consisted exclusively of clergy and towns. In Saxony, Bohemia, and the eastern Austrian Erblande, by contrast, bicameral organizations of counts or lords in a Herrenkurie and of knights in a Ritterkurie developed; in Brandenburg, bishops joined counts and lords in an 'upper' chamber, while knights and towns formed a 'lower' chamber. In some larger episcopal territories

---

[17] Press, 'Badische Markgrafen', 20–1.
[18] Klein, 'Staatsbildung?', 96, 100.
[19] *HBayG*, ii, 297–302.
[20] For the following see: Carsten, *Princes*; Press, 'Formen'; Press, 'Steuern'; Press, 'Herrschaft'; Rabe, *Geschichte*, 128–31.

the cathedral chapters assumed the role played by the Estates elsewhere, while in the lands of the Swabian prelates (imperial abbeys and the like) peasant communities formed the Landschaft with similar functions.[21]

The variety of forms of Estates—some with real political power, others functioning purely as tax generators or guarantors of princely debts; some developing quite elaborate administrations, others remaining ad hoc gatherings—reflected the variety among the territories themselves. Everywhere, however, their broad function was the same. Their *raison d'être* was the increasing need of their lords for money to finance self-defence and administration. From the 1490s the growing number of levies agreed by the Reichstag reinforced the need for Estates. It also enhanced their bargaining power, to a degree that became problematical in many territories after 1550.[22] This, in turn, underlined a second function of the Estates. They were moderators of princely rule, guarantors of stability and continuity during debt crises or minorities, or during shorter periods of partition when the Estates often persisted as a consolidated body while rule was divided between two or three male heirs.[23] Although they were rarely able to maintain unity in the face of long-term fragmentation of a ruling dynasty into several lines (the Mecklenburg Estates, which preserved their unity from 1523 until 1918, were unique), they did in many instances prevent such divisions and help bring about an inheritance settlement that preserved the integrity of the territory.

It is tempting to follow F. L. Carsten and use the more familiar terms 'parliaments' or 'diets' rather than Estates, to describe these institutions.[24] Yet this distorts the reality. They were the institutional expression of a corporate society, tied to the ruler, just as the ruler was tied to them.[25] They were institutions that mediated between competing interests. In practice, they aimed at consensus rather than conflict, and while they enjoyed greater power over policy than, say, the English Parliament, they never transcended their role to challenge their lords.

The significance of the Estates generally is underlined by the fact that even princes who enjoyed rich regalian revenues relied upon them or their equivalents. The Rhineland Electors of the Palatinate, Mainz, and Cologne profited immensely from river tolls. The Saxon Electors enjoyed highly profitable mineral rights. The rulers of Bavaria, the Austrian duchies, and Brunswick-Lüneburg derived considerable income from salt. They were thus better placed than the Dukes of Mecklenburg, with more land than some of them, but also more marginal land. Yet all of them relied increasingly, like Mecklenburg, on loans and taxes.

Much of this money went to pay for military expenses or imperial levies. Much, however, also went towards building up or intensifying administrations. The process by which early modern territorial administrations emerged from the medieval noble court was protracted and uneven. But by 1500 several territories had followed the example set by Cologne in 1469 in establishing a permanent princely council responsible for advising the ruler and overseeing major aspects of

---

[21] Quarthal, 'Krummstab'.   [22] Press, *Kriege*, 113–15; Schulze, *Geschichte*, 205–8.
[23] Carsten, *Princes*, 426–8.   [24] Carsten, *Princes*, v–vi.
[25] Press, *Kriege*, 113; Oestreich, 'Verfassungsgeschichte', 400–3; Krüger, *Verfassung*, 1–10.

government. Parallel to that process was a growing professionalization of administration with the employment of legally trained officials (*gelehrte Räte*). This, in turn, promoted interest in the foundation or reform of universities such as Tübingen, founded in 1477 by Duke Eberhard the Bearded, or Heidelberg, reformed in 1452 by Friedrich I.[26]

Increasingly, professionalization at the centre was accompanied by growing penetration downwards and across into parallel institutions such as the Church. By 1500, territories such as the Palatinate, Württemberg, Trier, and parts of Brandenburg were all more or less rigorously organized into administrative districts (Ämter) with a hierarchy of officials—some local nobles and notables, others paid 'experts'—connecting the localities with the centre. At the same time, such territories aspired, long before the Reformation, to increase their influence over the Church. They sought to arrogate for themselves the right of appointment to benefices (east of the Elbe even the right to nominate bishops). They struggled to impose limits on ecclesiastical courts and gain at least some control on church finances. Taxation of the clergy and, in some areas, the transformation of ecclesiastical tithes into a secular tax, the demand for a share of revenue from indulgences, or even the employment of indulgence revenue to pay for bridges or roads, were accompanied by a growing hostility to espiscopal or papal levies.[27]

By 1500, even the largest and most advanced territories were far from being closed territorial states. Their control over their often scattered lands was incomplete and many princes relied on feudal networks that extended over areas they never came to dominate. While they had undoubtedly created the framework for public peace in some of their own territories, many princes still spent vast sums on ceaseless military activity, defending themselves against aggression, pursuing feuds against neighbours on whose lands or jurisdictions they had designs, or simply asserting their claims against brothers or cousins. To that extent, the Reich was still characterized by an extreme degree of instability and insecurity which had begun to recede in England, France, Spain, and even Italy.[28] Despite this, and partly in response to the financial necessities imposed by these conditions, the territories had also developed infrastructures and instruments of government and corporative participation that bore favourable comparison with any elsewhere.[29]

At the same time there were signs of a changing perception of the functions of government. The traditional concern with 'peace and law' (*Friede und Recht*) was complemented by a preoccupation with notions of the 'common good'. Interpreted by legally trained officials through the conceptual language of Roman law, this led, soon after 1500, to the formulation of extensive territorial legislation: sumptuary laws and measures that aimed at the relief of the poor.[30] Increasingly, governments aspired not only to maintain good order but also to enhance the moral welfare of

---

[26] Other universities founded at this time included Greifswald (1456), Freiburg (1457), Ingolstadt (1472), Trier (1473), Mainz (1476), Wittenberg (1502), Breslau (1505), and Frankfurt an der Oder (1506). See Conrad, *Rechtsgeschichte*, i, 276.
[27] Rabe, *Geschichte*, 139–40.   [28] Cohn, *Government*, 248.
[29] Cohn, *Government*, 247–50.   [30] Rabe, *Geschichte*, 133.

their subjects, a combination that was encapsulated in the term *Polizei*. By the early sixteenth century, the promotion of good order or *Polizei* and the regulations and statutes generated by it, increasingly consolidated into comprehensive codes (*Polizeiordnungen*), had come to be seen as one of the key tasks of government.[31]

The development of *Polizei* and the new government interventionism, or at least interventionist aspirations, which the concept of *Polizei* entailed, would have been unthinkable without the administrative structures developed before 1500. It was also the product of changed circumstances in the period after 1500. One important precondition was the degree of relative stability that gradually unfolded in the Reich as a whole in the wake of the general peace of 1495. A second was the need to respond to the challenges posed by the Reformation movement.

The situation in the territories around 1500 in some ways parallels that in the Reich itself. In retrospect it might appear that a decisive watershed had been passed and that the major territories were by then irrevocably set on a path of 'state formation'. Thus, many have linked these developments with the outcome of the reform discussions of 1495 and 1500 and concluded that the decades around 1500 mark the triumph of the princes over the empty shell of the Reich. This both underestimates the Reich and overstates the position of the territories. For one thing, significant parts of the south and west were splintered territorially and characterized by the survival of Imperial Cities, Imperial Counts, and Imperial Knights. Even in areas of greater concentration, in princely territories, the power of the princes was significantly limited. Internally, power was limited by the Estates, and by the rights of subjects (particularly nobles but increasingly also others), based on the imperial law of 1231, which required princes to gain consent for innovations and, more generally, on the widespread currency of the principle *quod omnes tangit, ab omnibus approbari debet* (what concerns all must be agreed by all). Externally, power was limited by the princes' subordination to the emperor.

The definition in theory of this position only became clear later when German lawyers and theorists pondered the applicability of Bodin's theory of the sovereign state to German conditions (Bodin's *Les Six livres de la République*, or 'Six Books of the Commonwealth' of 1576 were first translated into German in 1592). Long before then, however, the limitations of princely power were explicit in the terms used to describe it. In the fifteenth century, *Landesherrschaft* described not a blanket power or authority but the cumulation of jurisdictional and prerogative rights. Most of them derived from various forms of allegiance and regalia granted by the emperor.[32] The concentration of these rights into a more uniform governmental power (albeit matched by a similar concentration of the rights of subjects in *Landstände*) was reflected in the increasing use of the term *landesfürstliche Obrigkeit* (princely authority or government). This expressed a degree of higher authority implicit in the wide-ranging legislative initiatives of the period after 1500,

---

[31] Scribner, 'Police', 104–6; Stolleis, *Öffentliches Recht*, i, 367–70; Maier, *Staats- und Verwaltungslehre*, 92–105.
[32] Cohn, *Government*, 120–3; Conrad, *Rechtsgeschichte*, i, 427–32.

and was later rendered as *Landeshoheit*.[33] The evolution of the terminology was not consistent, nor was there general agreement at all times on any distinctions between the various terms. The question of whether Imperial Knights, who unquestionably enjoyed *Landesherrschaft*, also had *Landeshoheit* was disputed in early modern discussions, as it is today.[34] One key point, however, was undisputed: even the grandest territorial prince did not enjoy sovereignty. All remained limited by their feudal obligations to the emperor and to the Reich, in other words subject to imperial law as formulated at the Reichstag. The fact that the powers accumulated in the sixteenth and seventeenth centuries increasingly seemed to belie that formal situation did nothing to change it, in theory or in practice, or even to generate explicit challenges to it until the second half of the eighteenth century.

[33] Conrad, *Rechtsgeschichte*, ii, 231–5; Oestreich, 'Verfassungsgeschichte', 394–9.
[34] Conrad, *Rechtsgeschichte*, ii, 203–4.

4

The Reich and the German Nation

If one combines the picture presented of the Reich with that presented of the territories around 1500, an impression might emerge of an inchoate and incoherent mass which could scarcely be described as a unity. The system appeared to have no centre and no unifying force. The authority of the imperial dynasty was insecure and, by many judgements, simply absent in large parts of the north. What authority it had, radiated not from the centre but from the south-eastern periphery. Moreover, the Reich had no core province or territory, no gravitational centre comparable, for example, with the province of Holland in the United Netherlands. Nor did it apparently have a close ideological bond such as that which united the Swiss cantons, first as a separate union within the Reich and ultimately as a separate state after 1648. The fragmentation of its territorial arrangements was mirrored by the variety of economic landscapes. From the Alps to the Baltic, from west of the Rhine across to the areas of Slav settlement in the east, there seems little basis for any community of interests. With a total population of some 16 million around 1500 (excluding imperial Italy, but including roughly 2 million in the Netherlands, about 2 million in the Bohemian lands, and about 600,000 in Switzerland), the Reich included roughly one-quarter of the population of Europe as a whole.[1] To what extent can one speak of a meaningful community of interests or even of unity? How did contemporaries perceive 'Germany'?

Clearly, some areas had developed their own distinct identity by 1500 or were about to do so. For that reason the Swiss cantons and the Netherlands must be excluded from any account of the Reich's early modern history, or at the very least marginalized. Bohemia is perhaps another special case, though it remained integrated and came to play a certain role once more in the later history of the Reich. In large parts of the area that remained within the Reich, one should not underestimate the degree of integration afforded by noble family networks and by clientele and patronage systems based on territorial courts, as well as on the imperial court. In the Wetterau, for example, intermarriage between the counts of the region and exchanges of land through condominium agreements and 'inheritance agreements' (*Erbeinungen* or *Erbverbrüderungen*) created a web of alliances and a sense of corporate group identity that ultimately translated into the emergence of what has been described as a 'corporative' or 'quasi-territorial' state.[2] Similarly, courts such as those of the Palatinate and Württemberg maintained clientele

---

[1] Rabe, *Geschichte*, 42–3.   [2] Schmidt, *Grafenverein*, 1–5, 113–59.

networks which extended far outside their own territories and attracted otherwise independent nobles and educated *Bürger* from Imperial Cities to the court. In ecclesiastical territories, the court was complemented by the cathedral chapters as agencies whereby outlying nobles were integrated. And more than all of these, the imperial court itself maintained a clientele network that extended westwards across virtually the whole of the southern Reich.[3]

The significance of these essentially feudal networks has led some historians to question whether a 'national' approach to the history of the Reich is justified.[4] On the other hand there is considerable evidence to suggest that a 'national' dimension became increasingly important around 1500. Indeed, it is striking that terms such as 'German nation' or 'German language' gained a new currency at this time in the context of a new preoccupation with the German past and with the question of the identity of the Germans.

There is little agreement among historians on how this phenomenon should be interpreted. Few now accept the view of traditional historians, who saw the patriotic effusions of certain humanists as evidence of the gradual emergence of the German nation, which was then promptly thwarted by political events.[5] Similarly, modern scholars who describe such sentiments as 'compensatory' nationalism are equally guilty of judging late medieval conditions by the yardstick of nineteenth- and twentieth-century circumstances.[6] Indeed, that recognition leads others to deny that anything like nationalism existed before the modern period.

However, it seems clear that even in the Middle Ages there was such a thing as national consciousness. During the fifteenth century the term 'natio', originally denoting subgroups within corporations like the Church or Church Councils, a university or a merchant community, came to assume a broader meaning in relation to a wider linguistic or cultural community. Of course, there was a world of difference between medieval and early modern national consciousness on the one hand and later nationalism on the other. For the most part, the social range of such ideas was far more limited, though there is evidence that they existed in popular mythology and propaganda. Their political implications were certainly less far-reaching. Above all, these implications did not extend to anything like a demand for a nation state.

Another major problem is the fact that the terms themselves are extremely vague. *Deutsche Nation*, for example, did not translate easily into a precise geographical area, if only because the Reich was a feudal nexus (*Personenverband*) rather than a territorial state. Despite this, however, some lines of development become clear. They build on the foundations of two key medieval traditions: first, the belief that the Germans possessed an individual and distinctive language; second, the conviction that they were the heirs to the Roman Empire in a continuous constitutional tradition.[7]

---

[3] Press, 'Patronat', 20–8. [4] Press, 'Patronat', 36.
[5] Stauber, 'Nationalismus'. [6] For example, Reinhardt, 'Primat', 91.
[7] Moraw, 'Voraussetzungen', 101–2; Thomas, 'Identitätsproblem', 155.

The first of these traditions, concerning language, presents a particularly fascinating problem, partly because of the importance attached by scholars, from Herder and Jakob Grimm in the eighteenth and nineteenth centuries onwards, to language as a key element in the formation of collective, ethnic, and national identities. According to Rüdiger Schnell, there is evidence that from the ninth to the sixteenth centuries, despite awareness of the strong regional differences that divided Germans, there was a persistent conviction that there was a single German language. In fact, this conviction is apparently contradicted by the philological evidence. Quite apart from the persistence within the Reich of various non-German-speaking linguistic groups, a standard German language only emerged in the second half of the sixteenth century. The argument for any standardization before then is tenuous.[8]

If there was a widespread standard then it was the spoken and written form of Low German based on Lübeck that had evolved and spread with the rise of the Hanseatic League. By 1500, this extended across the northern parts from Emden in the west to Riga, Dorpat, and Reval on the eastern Baltic coast.[9] The situation in Upper and Middle Germany was far more complex. These areas have been more central to philological study because of the fact that modern German ultimately emerged from an amalgam of the dialects and forms used in them. Many assumptions concerning the evolution of this amalgam are also based on the view that Martin Luther was in effect the progenitor of modern German. Much significance is accorded to Luther's reflection (c.1532, recorded in his table talk) that he had no 'particular German language' but that he used the 'common German' that could be 'understood by both high and low Germans'. He spoke, he said, 'according to the Saxon chancellery, which is followed by all dukes and princes of Germany; for all cities and princely courts write according to the Saxon chancellery of our Elector. The Emperor Maximilian and Elector Frederick have drawn all the German languages in the Roman Empire together into a single language.'[10]

Luther's conclusion is perhaps premature. Indeed, the impact of his own writings in the north was aided by the fact that they were translated into Low German.[11] His comments do, however, indicate some of the forces that may have promoted a limited degree of standardization before the 1520s. The commercial language of western Upper Germany (*das gemeine Deutsch*) seems to have been predominant as the language of commerce in the south. That, in turn, shared much in common with the written forms developed in the imperial chancellery and vigorously promoted by Emperor Maximilian's chancellor Niclas Ziegler, who saw to it that imperial documents were increasingly characterized by a uniform orthography, whether they were produced in Innsbruck or the Netherlands.[12] If the Imperial chancellery exerted influence from the south-east, it seems clear that the Meissen (Saxon) chancellery radiated a similar influence in Middle Germany further north. There were, of course, political links between the two chancelleries and so it is

[8] Schnell, 'Literatur', 298.   [9] Wiesinger, 'Sprachausformung', 339–40.
[10] Wells, *German*, 141, 198, 455.   [11] Wiesinger, 'Sprachausformung', 339.
[12] König, *Atlas*, 95.

difficult to define precise or exclusive realms of influence. It was, however, the Meissen style that prevailed in Mainz, and which became the style of the *Reichsabschiede* or proclamations of imperial laws. It was the Meissen style, too, that soon after 1500 was gradually adopted by chancelleries further north, starting with Brandenburg, and which thus contributed significantly to the long-term decline of Low German as a written language of administration.[13]

There is little consensus on the pace of these changes, or on the relative significance that should be attached to the various linguistic forms that contributed to them. It is, however, clear that the whole process was at a very early stage by 1500. The influence of printing, invented around 1450, had scarcely become apparent. The ultimate demise of Low German as the dominant language of the northern Reich, though foreshadowed by the decline of the Hanseatic League after 1450, could not be taken for granted before about 1550 (and, of course, it survived in places like Hamburg into the eighteenth century). Apart from anything else, the real standard language for scholars, administrators, and the like around 1500 was still Latin rather than any form of German.[14] Even for those humanists who sang the praises of the vernacular, Latin remained dominant. Significantly, the first attempt at a history of German literature—Johannes Trithemius's *De viris illustribus Germaniae* of 1495—listed some three hundred authors, but only one who wrote in German: Otfried von Weissenburg in the ninth century.[15]

The gulf between the reality of linguistic diversity and the perception of a single language is rendered less paradoxical if considered in relation to the second medieval tradition: the awareness of a continuous constitutional tradition in an empire descended from Rome. The basis for this perception is more apparent and founded in political reality. Yet while the ideas of a *translatio imperii* and of continuity were a leitmotif of the medieval period as a whole, they gained new dimensions in the second half of the fifteenth century. A new political context provided a framework in which humanist writers elaborated a plethora of variations on received ideas. These drew on 'pre-political' ideas of origins, language, and customs, and on what we might describe as ideas of ethnic identity. They remained, however, fundamentally linked with perceptions of the essential functions of the Holy Roman Empire. They were not manifestations of early nationalism looking forward to a future nation state, but reflections of the contemporary state of affairs.

The nature of the new momentum in imperial politics from the 1470s has already been indicated in the discussion of the imperial constitution. The emergence of a Turkish threat in the east and of a Burgundian/French threat in the west generated the rhetoric of German national self-defence that introduced a new vocabulary into the language of imperial politics. That which belonged to the 'German nation', also frequently simply defined as those areas in which the 'German tongue' was spoken, needed to be defended by the community of the Reich. At the same time, resistance to Habsburg ambitions in Italy defined another

---

[13] König, *Atlas*, 93; Wells, *German*, 136–7, 141, 198; Coupe, *Reader*, xiii–xviii.
[14] Wells, *German*, 133–4, 141–2; Lutz, *Ringen*, 79; Schnell, 'Literatur', 298–300, 307.
[15] Schnell, 'Literatur', 308.

distinction between what was German on the one hand and 'Welsch' (Latin or Italian) on the other. Maximilian insisted on the community of interests between the German and 'Welsch' nations. The German Estates assembled at the Reichstag responded by emphasizing exclusively the interests of the 'German nation'.[16]

There was nothing inherently nationalist in such exchanges. What was at stake was not a 'nation' in any nineteenth-century sense of the term, but real questions of money, defence, and power.[17] The propaganda significance of the language used is illustrated by the fact that in 1474 even the city of Bern could appeal to its Swiss neighbours to rise up against the Burgundian aggressor in the name of the 'teutsche Nation' and to defend that nation against the 'Türk im Occident'. The language of its appeal, with its equation of Charles the Bold and Mehmet II, mimicked that of the Emperor Frederick III when he appealed to the Swiss in 1455 to defend the 'German Nation' against the Turks.[18] Equally, there was nothing nationalist, or even 'multinationalist', about Maximilian's use of appeals to his nations in the 1490s. His autobiographical writings reveal that nation, Reich, and even Christianity—the terms that dominated his public political utterances—were all secondary to his own person, stylized in the heroic figures of 'Weisskunig' (the 'White King') and the wise, heroic crusading knight Theuerdank.[19]

In the literary imagination of Emperor Maximilian the language of political propaganda clearly coincides with the discussion of the nation in literary and mythological terms by the German humanists. They, too, drew on medieval and populist traditions. Indeed, the myth of the sleeping Reich, of the Emperor Barbarossa, of an imperial saviour who would rescue the Germans, continued to feature in populist prophetic writings through to the Reformation period.[20] It was, however, the humanist writers from the 1480s onwards who framed these perennial eschatologies in a new discourse. Their writings were, moreover, closely linked both with the growing political discussion of the need to defend the Reich and to reform it, and then with the imperial ambitions of Maximilian himself. The need to defend the Reich fostered a new need to define its enemies, to elaborate the national and moral boundaries between the Germans and their foes. At the same time, the growing perception of the need to reform the Reich in the late fifteenth century also fostered a desire to define its essential character and potential.

Finally, the emerging discussion of these themes was harnessed by Maximilian I in a sustained attempt to mobilize the pens of the educated as he was trying to mobilize the military resources of the Reich. The transformation of the institution of imperial poet laureate (*poeta laureatus caesareus*) is indicative of the new mood. The changes began in the later years of the reign of Frederick III. The traditional coronation ceremony for poets laureate, with its general injunction that the laureate should glorify emperor and Reich, had been used only intermittently, and then

---

[16] Schröcker, *Nation*, 118–19.   [17] Schröcker, *Nation*, 141.
[18] Sieber-Lehmann, 'Teutsche Nation'.
[19] Schröcker, *Nation*, 143–4; Benecke, *Maximilian I*, 7–30; Silver, *Maximilian, passim* analyses the iconography and its projection and dissemination.
[20] Borchardt, *Antiquity*, 199–297.

largely in Italy. With the coronation of Conrad Celtis, the first German laureate, in 1487, this rather vaguely defined office took on a new political significance.

Celtis himself was instrumental in founding the Vienna academy of poets and mathematicians in 1501. He became its first *laureae custos et collator* and received from Maximilian the right to crown suitably qualified poets. In Maximilian, his vivid literary patriotism and ambition found a kindred spirit. Between them Maximilian and Celtis crowned more laureates than in any previous period; by the time of his death in 1519 Maximilian had been responsible for the coronation of no less than thirty-seven poets. The aim was to create a legion of literary propagandists for the Reich, who would use their influence and connections to create a humanist clientele network.[21] Their political function was underlined by the obligation to perform a laudatory verse oration at the opening of a Reichstag. In this way the laureates, together with other ceremonial officials with literary functions such as the imperial heralds, helped enhance the sense of the unity and solidarity of the Reichstag.[22]

Of course, a few hundred humanists do not make a nation. It is difficult to know how far down the social scale either humanist notions or the political concerns of the Reichstag really reached. There is, however, much evidence to suggest that some elements of both at least overlapped with, perhaps even shaped, social movements and expressions of opinion at the popular level. The Bundschuh (literally 'tied boot', the symbol of protesting peasants in Alsace and the southwest) uprisings of 1493, 1502, 1513, and 1517 all generated demands for reform of the Reich and defence against France, among other more local and material demands. The astrological fantasies of Johannes Lichtenberger (especially his popular *Prognosticatio in latino* of 1488, reprinted no less than twenty-nine times between 1492 and 1530) warned that the Turks would take Cologne if the Reich were not reformed.[23] Similarly, the anonymous 'Upper Rhine Revolutionary' combined humanist mythology with millenarian eschatology in 1509, when he wrote of the Brotherhood of the Yellow Cross that would assist a new Emperor Frederick (who would be born in Alsace) in establishing a new thousand-year empire as the prelude to the Golden Age.[24] Finally, there is evidence that strong popular feelings were aroused over the imperial election of 1519. The English envoy Richard Pace, for example, among others, reported that there would be a revolution of the people if the French king were elected in favour of the 'German' Charles (a multilingual Habsburg with Burgundian, German, and Spanish antecedents, whose 'nationality' is in fact almost impossible to determine).[25]

These themes will recur in the context of the Reformation and the Peasants' War. Their significance here lies in the way that they illustrate the wider ramifications of what might otherwise be seen as a discussion conducted at a high level of

---

[21] Mertens, 'poeta laureatus', 155–7; Flood, *Poets laureate*, i, lxxxviii–ciii, On humanism, see 106–16.
[22] Schubert, *Reichstage*, 174–89.
[23] Lutz, *Ringen*, 92; Killy, *Lexikon*, vii, 266–7; *ADB*, xviii, 538–42.
[24] Borchardt, *Antiquity*, 116–19.
[25] Schmidt, 'Reichs-Staat', 23–4.

learned abstraction by a minority. In their repeated insistence on the need for reform of the Church as well as the Reich, these more radical manifestations of popular views also underline one final point about the new humanist discourse of the nation.

The overall tendency of German humanist writing was to introduce a new variation on the traditional notion of the *translatio imperii*.[26] In a very short time, the differing interpretation came to reflect the divide between Protestants and Catholics, though the divergence clearly pre-dated the Reformation. The old view of the Reich as a universal Christian empire still prevailed in the writings of humanists such as Johannes Cochlaeus. When he declared 'Teutschlandt uber alle Welt', he was referring to the 'German' Reich as the centre of this world empire. His words were later misinterpreted as an assertion of German superiority and, in the equally misunderstood formulation 'Deutschland, Deutschland über alles' by the nineteenth-century writer Hoffmann von Fallersleben, became the hymn of militant German nationalism.[27] Yet Cochlaeus himself, like other humanist 'traditionalists', was merely reflecting the centrality of 'Germany' to the contemporary Reich.[28]

The anti-Italianism of other humanist writers frequently translated into a more strident anti-Romanism. Their assertion of the 'indigenous' character of the Germans and their 'discovery' of Trojan or pre-Trojan origins, both gave the Germans a new and independent status and, for some, justified the rejection of modern Rome in the shape of the papacy. Hutten, for example, found further inspiration in the rediscovery and publication in 1515 of the early books of Tacitus's *Annals*, which contained the history of the victory of Arminius (Hermann the Cherusker) over the Romans under Quintilius Varus in the Teutoburg Forest in AD 9.[29] It is true that the German literary mythology of Arminius only really developed fully in the seventeenth and eighteenth centuries, and it developed into something approaching a cult in the nineteenth century. Yet the origins of the myth in the early sixteenth century form yet another source of the idea of a German nation at the start of the early modern period.[30] For writers like Hutten and Jakob Wimpfeling the logical conclusion from several decades of humanist research was to demand liberation from the yoke of Rome. This tendency has been aptly described as a 'partial nationalization' of the idea of the Reich. The *translatio* was now understood as the process whereby the services of the Germans to Christianity had been rewarded with custodianship of the Roman Empire.

Like so much of the constitutional precedent, the political language and 'national' self-definition of the period around 1500 was but the prelude. Just as the constitutional system evolved and unfolded over the next century, so too did the thinking about its historical origins. It was not until 1643 that Hermann Conring finally contradicted the tradition of Roman origins and formulated the theory of the

---

[26] Garber, 'Nationalismus', 24–5.
[27] Hoffmann von Fallersleben, of course, was a political liberal appealing to Germans to value Germany above their regional homelands (Prussia, Bavaria, etc.): Schlink, *Hoffmann*, 45–69.
[28] Bagchi, 'Nationalism', 52; Schmidt, 'Reichs-Staat', 22–3.
[29] Roloff, '*Arminius*'.
[30] Kuehnemund, *Arminius*, 1–19; Dorner, *Mythos*, 131–2.

specifically German genesis of the Reich.[31] The humanists, however, laid the foundations. And in doing so they reinforced a sense of community, of shared political and constitutional traditions, that bound the German lands together and made the Reich into a whole. Its frontiers were fluid. Its interior was fragmented. Its constitutional system did not yet fully embrace all parts of the north-west other than in the purely formal, and in practice sometimes tenuous, sense of the feudal bonds between imperial overlord and princely or noble vassal. Yet the essential elements, which created a full community of German lands rather than a German nation state in the early modern period, all began to coalesce in the late fifteenth century. Paradoxically, the next crucial stage in the realization of that community was a challenge that in some senses divided it: the German Reformation.

---

[31] Willoweit, 'Conring', 141–3; see p. 461.

II

THE REFORM OF THE REICH AND THE CHURCH, *c*.1490–1519

5

The Reformation Era in German History

The history of the Reich in the first half of the sixteenth century is so dominated by the religious movement associated with the name of Martin Luther that the period is often thought about and written about almost exclusively in terms of the Reformation. This is not wholly unjust. The Peace of Augsburg of 1555, which provided the first comprehensive statement of the imperial constitution after the reforms of 1495 and 1500 and the electoral capitulation of Charles V in 1521, was both a political settlement and a religious peace. In its reformulation of the relationship between emperor and Reich, and in its definition of the legal rights of the Imperial Estates, the peace reflected the outcome of developments since the early years of the century. Since the 1520s, moreover, the religious issue increasingly dominated both imperial politics and the preoccupations of princes and ruling magistrates. Indeed, at one time or another, the new religious teachings profoundly affected virtually every stratum of German society: in pursuit of the new or in passionate defence of the old, or in struggling to come to terms with or contain the actions of others.

The key question is why religious conflict did not either lead to the triumph of one side over the other or divide the Reich and paralyse and destroy it. The fragmented territorial structure of the Reich promoted the spread and regional establishment of the Reformation. That, in turn, meant that religious conflict occurred earlier there than elsewhere. The same structure and system, however, turned out to provide mechanisms, not matched in the later experience of other European states, for dealing with the conflict and ultimately for institutionalizing the differences that caused it. Indeed, arguably, the spread of the Reformation averted what might otherwise have been a dramatic confrontation between the emperor and the Reich in the 1520s. The ways in which the Reich and its members responded to the threat of conflict remained shaped by its flexible structures. The military confrontations initiated by either side proved unable to break the bonds that loosely united them all. The outcome in 1555 was a compromise: it reflected both the unity and the diversity that had now also received a religious face.

The Reformation undoubtedly unleashed much that was new, but its implications for the development of German history are best understood if it is regarded as a catalysing force within a broader political and social framework. The new religious teachings did not develop in a vacuum. At every level, from the parish to the highest institutions of the Reich, from the peasants to the princes and the emperor, the ideas of Luther and others like him played into debates and problems that often had little direct link with the issues of belief and religion as such.

Awareness of the innumerable ramifications of the Reformation has long shaped perceptions of it as a defining moment in German history. Two broad themes stand out in much of the historical writing since the early nineteenth century. One concerns the supposed effect of the Reformation on the development of the German nation. The other concerns the link between the Reformation and the potential transformation of German society in the early sixteenth century. Though these two themes appear to be distinct from, if not at odds with, each other, they share a structural similarity and a common assumption about the 1520s as a juncture of vital significance for German history as a whole.

In its modern form, the national theme was formulated by Leopold von Ranke in the 1840s.[1] He argued that the Reformation marked the culmination of a national movement that had the potential to create a German nation state. It was undermined, he argued, by Charles V's refusal to support the cause of Church reform. The emperor's failure to understand the strength of the demand for reform and his unwillingness to confront the papacy doomed the Lutheran cause to the path of sectarianism. This, in turn, reinforced the particularist tendencies inherent in German history. The German national religious movement was, according to Ranke, thwarted by foreign powers, headed by the Habsburg Emperor and the pope in Rome.

Ranke's view, though subject to innumerable permutations, has proved extraordinarily durable. Protestant historians who identified with the Prussian Reich after 1871 readily saw the relevance to their own day of a movement that struggled against Rome and foreign powers to assert the German national interest. If Catholic historians rejected such ideas, they too concurred in Ranke's judgement, though for different reasons. For them the unity of the nation, and with it the unity of Christianity, was destroyed by Luther and his disciples.[2]

If much of the mainstream of German historiography was fascinated by the potential of the nation in the early sixteenth century, the Marxist tradition was preoccupied with the potential for revolutionary transformation in this period. Again, the story was one of an opportunity missed. From Marx and Engels onwards, writers in this tradition regarded the social upheavals that culminated in the Peasants' War of 1525 as fundamentally more important than the figure of Luther or the religious movement that he inspired.[3] Indeed, according to Marx and Engels, Luther played a crucial role in the collapse of what might otherwise have developed into a root and branch revolution destroying the feudal world in Germany at the end of the medieval period. Instead, his early engagement in a bourgeois anti-feudal assault on the clerical and political structures of feudal society was rapidly overlaid by an uncompromising hostility to the revolutionary forces of the rural and urban lower classes, whose aspirations were expressed by radical theologians such as

---

[1] Dickens and Tonkin, *Reformation*, 167–75; Dickens, *Ranke*; Schmidt, 'Reichs-Staat', 25.
[2] Dickens and Tonkin, *Reformation*, 179–84.
[3] Dickens and Tonkin, *Reformation* 234–46.

Thomas Müntzer. Thus while it could be argued that in the long term the early Reformation contributed to the transition from feudalism to capitalism, the ultimate effect of Luther's actions was to reinforce the feudal regime in Germany.[4] By siding with the princes against the peasants and acting as the 'lackey ('Tellerlecker' or, literally, 'plate-licker') of absolute monarchy', Luther allegedly helped perpetuate the status quo in the German lands. The feudal social structure survived; it was locked into a territorially fragmented Reich, but it was all the stronger for the crushing defeat of the popular movement and the ensuing establishment of state churches.

While the image of Luther was considerably revised in a more positive vein by successive groups of scholars in the German Democratic Republic between 1949 and 1989, the general problem identified by Marx and Engels remained fundamental to the Marxist vision.[5] The general crisis of society, which Marxist historians identified in the early sixteenth century, failed to generate a general emancipation or breakthrough of progressive social forces. Furthermore, the triumph of the princes over the common man in 1525 had profound long-term consequences. The failure of any strong centralizing force to emerge truncated the development of the bourgeoisie and in any case meant that for the foreseeable future there was no unified target for any renewed movement of progressive forces from below.

Common to both historiographical traditions is a view of Protestantism as a progressive, nation-building force. Its failure to realize that potential in Germany in the 1520s is variously explained in terms of the obstructive machinations of Rome or of the triumph of the old feudal order of the princes. Each of these narratives also revolved around an essentially monolithic view of the historical phenomena they embraced: a single Reformation, a single nation conceived as the forerunner or foundation of the nation state, or a single social movement.

Research over the past fifty or so years has fractured many of these once relatively clear lines. The effect on Reformation studies has been particularly striking. The traditional exclusive focus on Luther, for example, has given way to the recognition of a whole series of contemporaneous critics of the old Church. Particularly significant was the reform movement that originated with Ulrich Zwingli in Zurich, which survived in the longer term, though Lutheranism remained the overwhelmingly predominant Protestant faith in the Reich. Scholars now view the Reformation generally as a complex amalgam of parallel movements: of clerical reformers, of the lower nobility, of the peasantry, of the Free Cities and towns, and of the ruling princes. An immense concentration of research on the local and regional contexts of the various movements has resulted in further differentiation. As a result, phenomena such as the Peasants' War or the 'urban Reformation' often seem to disintegrate into a conflicting mass of particular local and regional histories. Furthermore, focus on the economic, social, and political issues involved in varying combinations in these

[4] Dorpalen, *German history*, 123–9.
[5] Dorpalen, *German history*, 99–123; Wohlfeil, 'Reformation'; Dähn, 'Luther'; Müller, 'Moment', 207–17; Walinski-Kiehl, 'History'; Vogler, 'Konzept'.

parallel and overlapping Reformations has at times tended to distance them from the religious issues that were their core.

Attempts to reunite the economic, social, and political with the religious and to restore some measure of unity to the Reformation remain controversial. Peter Blickle's suggestion that the concept of 'communalism' provides the key to under-standing the experience of both rural and urban areas is a case in point.[6] In his view, the 1520s marked a crucial stage in the development of the German communes. Originally formed in the fourteenth century as local instruments of self-government in response to the lack of imperial or territorial government, the communes found themselves under increasing threat with the intensification of territorial regimes from the late fifteenth century. In a period of crisis, they seized upon a theology centered on a biblically justified community of believers, which appeared to legitimate their rights and freedoms. The 'revolution' of 1525, which, Blickle has argued, mobilized the 'common man' in both country and town, aspired above all to assert the communal principle, now elevated to the status of a divine principle. The failure of this clear challenge to all higher authority in the feudal order, ended the Reformation as a movement from below, inaugurated the 'Reformation of the princes', and, more generally and in the longer term, led to the eclipse of the communes in large parts of the German lands.

These wider implications are considered in the appropriate contexts later. Here, it is important to note that this attempt at a unified explanation of the Reformation movement has three points of weakness. First, the 'communal Reformation' may well describe important aspects of the experience of the south-western and western German lands, but it cannot be applied to much of central and northern Germany. Second, many have doubted the posited link between the rural and the urban experience, some insisting that a tradition of urban republicanism manifest partic-ularly in northern cities and towns was quite distinct from the communalism of the south-western peasantry.[7] Third, the general relevance of communalism seems to be at least partly undermined by the fact that not all communes, even in the Swiss Confederation, which plays a major role in Blickle's argument, embraced the Protestant creed which supposedly lent divine sanction to their very existence as self-governing communities.[8]

Parallel to the diversification of Reformation studies, research on the Reich over the past forty years has produced a range of insights and questions which have superseded the old debate about the potential for the emergence of a nation state in the 1520s. The Reich emerged from the reforms of 1495 and 1500 as a polity in which the emperor and the Estates coexisted, but also competed, in uneasy equilibrium.[9] The question that dominated the next decades, however, was not whether a nation state would emerge, but whether the equilibrium would be maintained and institutionalized. The exploration of this issue stimulated the

---

[6] Blickle, *Revolution* and Blickle, *Gemeindereformation*.
[7] Schilling, 'Republikanismus'.
[8] Scott, 'Common people' and 'Communal Reformation'.
[9] See pp. 31–9.

American historian Thomas Brady to investigate two particularly significant problems. First, he examined the history of south German cities to show, on the one hand, why they resisted the temptation to 'turn Swiss' and, on the other, why their option for a Protestant existence in the Reich failed to rebound to the advantage of the emperor.[10] Second, he pursued the question of why, when the Protestant territories and cities did finally unite in the late 1520s and early 1530s, they prevented Charles V from creating a centralized state in Germany and then did not create a new state themselves.[11]

The crucial factor was the response of both emperor and Estates to the Reformation movement. However one defines the Reformation—as 'communal', single, or multiple—it undoubtedly represented an unprecedented wide-scale challenge from below or at least from outside the Reich's established ruling elites. Though it was essentially a religious movement, the Reformation rapidly gained a social and political meaning for an extraordinary variety of groups. The crisis in the Church enabled these groups to voice their grievances vociferously across the Reich.

By the mid-1520s it came to seem like a seismic eruption that urgently needed to be contained. This containment took place primarily at the local or regional level, but also had profound implications at the imperial level. On the one hand, princes and magistrates moved to tame the movement by institutionalizing it in territorial or city churches, a process in which Church reform formed a crucial phase in the longer-term evolution of the systems of territorial and urban government. On the other hand, the balance of emperor and Reich needed to adjust to a situation in which significant parts of the Reich were at odds with its laws. Remarkably, the imperial system continued to function throughout. Despite friction, argument, and, from time to time, armed conflict, the solidarity of the Estates asserted itself over and above the confessional divide.

The complexity and interaction of the various elements of the story make it difficult to present the history of this period as a straightforward narrative. Many of the important phenomena and developments are interconnected. Yet all have their own independent internal history. The emphasis in what follows is primarily on the period as an era in German history, rather than on a rounded account of the Reformation. Yet the eruption of the Reformation into the history of the Reich and its territories and cities is clearly of fundamental importance and it dictates the order of the following narrative.

The starting point is an account of the reign of Maximilian I. The focus then changes to the origins of the discontent that preceded the Reformation and without which its explosive early phase cannot be understood. Then we examine Luther's personal spiritual and theological path to rebellion and consider the wider implications of his theology. Part III starts with a consideration of the first decade of the reign of Charles V. This was the period in which Luther's ideas developed into a full reform programme, with political implications for both the Reich and its

---

[10] Brady, *Turning Swiss*.   [11] Brady, *Sturm*.

territories. At the same time, other reformers emerged and their distinctive religious, social, and political views gained a wider significance and greater active potential by virtue of their loose association with the cause symbolized by Luther himself. The following chapters on the reception of the Reformation—by the Imperial Knights, by the peasantry, and by the cities—examine the impact of reforming ideas. Part IV begins with an account of the establishment of Protestantism in some territories and the persistence of Catholicism in others. The process of reform and non-reform continued through the 1530s and 1540s. In many areas, however, and particularly in those areas which embraced the Reformation relatively early, a decisive juncture was reached in the mid-1520s. By this point at the latest, the Reformation had come to pose a series of major problems for the imperial system as a whole. Part IV thus concludes with an account of the development of the imperial system under the impact of the religious transformation effected in many of its constituent parts. The Peace of Augsburg in 1555 represented the outcome of the political conflicts of the preceding decades. Managing that peace posed new challenges, which are examined in Part V.

6

The Reich under Maximilian I

At the end of September 1518, the 59-year-old Emperor Maximilian I visited his principal residence Innsbruck for the last time. He came from the Reichstag at Augsburg where, despite vast expenditure, he had failed to persuade the Electors to accept his grandson, Charles of Spain, as his imperial heir. In Innsbruck this disappointment was followed by humiliation. His principal officials there threatened to resign unless they were paid forthwith. The innkeepers of the town refused even to give shelter to his retinue on account of the 24,000 gulden they were owed from previous visits. Angered yet powerless, with his retinue literally left standing on the streets, the Emperor had no option but to move on, eastwards via Salzburg into Austria, where finally he took up residence at the modest castle of Wels on 10 December. Already sick when he left Augsburg, his health steadily deteriorated; in Wels, he sank into weeks of agonizing decline until finally, having willed his grandsons Charles and Ferdinand as joint heirs to his hereditary lands, he died on 11 January 1519. Only gradually did it become clear that Maximilian's debts in Innsbruck were but the tip of the iceberg. He died owing some 6 million gulden.[1]

It is tempting to view this pathos-laden denouement as evidence of the failure of Maximilian's self-proclaimed imperial mission. The contrast between his self-projection as the 'last knight', the universal monarch, master, and saviour of Christendom, and the apparently chaotic state of his affairs on his death is stark. It is further underlined by the widespread unrest in the Reich that accompanied his later years and by the rebellions in the Austrian hereditary lands following his death. Many commentators have seen this state of affairs as the inevitable result of a hopelessly overambitious monarch given to fantasy and the restless pursuit of an impossible dream.[2] Indeed, some have concluded that there was simply no link between vision and reality, merely a series of chaotic campaigns conducted haphazardly, with no real sense of ultimate purpose. Above all, it has been suggested that Maximilian's treatment of the German lands in particular was essentially exploitative: the Reich provided him with his title; the only other thing he wanted from it was money to pursue his ambitions elsewhere. According to this view, once the German princes made clear their reluctance to pay, he had no further use for them.

---

[1] Wiesflecker, *Maximilian*, 376–81, 386.
[2] Wiesflecker, *Maximilian*, 11–16; Wiesflecker-Friedhuber, *Quellen*, 5–27; Angermeier, 'Wormser Reichstag 1495', 1–3.

In fact, such judgements fail to do justice to the underlying coherence of his policies. His reign was indeed characterized by an extraordinary variety of initiatives pursued, often simultaneously, on virtually every front: in Burgundy and the Netherlands, in the conflict with France and the alliance with Spain, in Italy, in Hungary, and in his plans for a crusade against the Turks. Most of these initiatives, certainly the most spectacular ones, were directed at areas that lay outside the Reich. Yet the Reich was an essential and integral part of the system he sought to establish. Two concerns, each inherited from his father Frederick III, were pre-eminent: the problem of the Habsburg territorial base and the aim to explore the full implications in Europe of the claims implicit in the imperial title.

The need to create a viable territorial base of hereditary lands from which to establish his rule over the Reich was Maximilian's first priority. His father had spent years on the south-eastern periphery. He was absent from the Reich for twenty-seven years between 1444 and 1471 and towards the end of his reign was driven out of Vienna by Matthias Corvinus.[3] Maximilian sought consistently to remedy the underlying weakness stemming from the peripheral and vulnerable position of the Habsburgs' Austrian hereditary lands. He consolidated the Austrian territories, enlarged by the inheritance of the Tyrol in 1490, and he sought to protect them against Hungarian, Polish, and Turkish threats.[4] His administrative reorganization and concerted fiscal exploitation of the Erblande provided many German princes with a model for the intensification of territorial government.

His dealings with the Jagiellon kings in Hungary and Poland illustrated perfectly his fundamentally dynastic approach to politics.[5] Ladislas II's second marriage to Anne de Foix in 1502 threatened Maximilian's rights to succession in Hungary and Bohemia that had been laid down in the Treaty of Pressburg in 1491, a threat reinforced by the birth of a daughter, Anna, in 1503, and a son, Louis, in 1506. With the tempting promise of military assistance against the Turks, Maximilian was able to negotiate a double marriage contract between the Hungarian heirs and his own granddaughter and grandson (Maria and Ferdinand). The continuing refusal of the Hungarian magnates to acquiesce in a Habsburg succession and the marriage of John Zápolya's sister with King Sigismund of Poland (Ladislas's younger brother) in 1512 led to a renewed crisis. Once again, Maximilian made resolute efforts to prevail. The support of Poland for the Hungarian Estates was undermined by an alliance concluded with Sigismund's enemy, Vasily III, Grand Prince of Moscow, in 1514. This immediately facilitated the renewal of the marriage contracts, and the Habsburg succession in Hungary and in Vienna (1515). In return, Sigismund was ceded overlordship over the lands of the Teutonic Knights.

The policy with regard to the Austrian lands was built on a long tradition. Maximilian's possession of the Burgundian inheritance, which came to him by marriage to Mary of Burgundy, added a wholly new dimension to imperial

---

[3] Koller, *Friedrich III.*, 214–17.
[4] Wiesflecker-Friedhuber, *Quellen*, 4–5; Press, 'Erblande', 53–6.
[5] Pamlényi, *Hungary*, 113–18; Wiesflecker, *Maximilian*, 125–33, 148–9, 187–92; Wiesflecker-Friedhuber, *Quellen*, 18–20; Kohler, *Expansion*, 269–74.

politics.[6] It is true he ruled them only from 1482 until 1494 as regent for his son Philip the Fair. Furthermore, the latter's inclinations towards France thereafter asserted an aspiration to independence from the emperor's grand imperial schemes that was only temporarily abated by the regency of Maximilian's daughter Margaret during the minority of Philip's heir, Charles. Nonetheless, it is clear that, in effect, Maximilian treated these territories in the north-west as a second complex of hereditary lands.

Like the Austrian territories, the Burgundian inheritance was not formally part of the Reich in the sense of being represented at the Reichstag. Indeed, these territories had their own representative body in an Estates-General formed in 1477. Yet Maximilian manifestly regarded them, like the Austrian hereditary lands, as parts of the Reich whose direct access to the monarch obviated the necessity for representation via the Reichstag. Furthermore, each complex secured for the emperor the possibility of a presence in the Reich. In the case of the Austrian lands, the inheritance of the Tyrol brought with it a scatter of territories across the south of the Reich: the Vorlande consisting of the Sundgau, the Breisgau with Freiburg, and several Swabian towns, counties, and overlordships.[7] In the case of the Burgundian lands, the Habsburg presence was less clearly defined, particularly in view of the continuing failure to subjugate Guelders.[8] Yet the proximity of the Burgundian territories to the Reich (some of them were, by tradition, subject to the emperor as feudal overlord) created a Habsburg-dominated frontier girdle that stretched up from the Sundgau in northern Alsace and arched upwards via the Netherlands towards Frisia. At the same time, the court at Brussels came to act as a powerful focus for a network of clients that extended into the North German Plain and the Lower Rhineland down as far as the lands of the Wetterau counts (among them the house of Nassau, forebears of William of Orange) north of the Main.[9] Potentially at least, Maximilian's hold on the Reich was thus greater than that of any predecessor, which makes the resistance of the princes to his reform proposals and to his requests for money and military aid wholly understandable.

The consolidation of two blocks of hereditary lands potentially reinforced Maximilian's position as German king. Yet that position was also inextricably linked with the universal aspirations and prerogatives that came with his imperial title. There were two dimensions to this. On the one hand, there was the preoccupation with Italy.[10] This was not the blind obsession, still less fatal weakness, that German nationalist scholars sometimes diagnosed in an emperor who allegedly pursued the revival of an Italian empire at the expense of the Germans. In fact, Italy was fundamentally important, not only for reasons of territorial aggrandisement but also because of the need to be crowned in Rome.[11] Maximilian struggled in vain to achieve this true legitimation of his rule. And while he conceded his failure with his

[6] Rabe, *Geschichte*, 181–2; Wiesflecker, *Maximilian*, 61–5, 355–7; Kohler, *Expansion*, 327–33.
[7] Press, 'Vorderösterreich'; Quarthal, 'Vorderösterreich'.
[8] Israel, *Dutch Republic 1476–1806*, 58–64.
[9] Press, 'Niederlande', 322–5; Schmidt, 'Integration', 6–8.
[10] Kohler, *Expansion*, 334–41.
[11] Wiesflecker, *Maximilian*, 365–9.

proclamation as 'elected Roman Emperor' in Trent in 1508, that did not stop him pursuing the traditional link with Rome. Indeed, in 1511 his exasperation with Julius II's repeated treachery led him to think of contriving his own election as pope.[12] This would have enabled him to pursue the reform of the Church and, at last, to secure control over the papal state, a vital counter in his enduring conflict with Venice and in the jockeying for position on the Italian peninsula with France. Like so many of Maximilian's plans, however, this one too came to nothing, and a new alliance with Rome was forged in the same year. His campaign against Venice, which was, after all, the greater enemy, could only have been undermined by an act of usurpation that might have generated a Christian league against him.

The desire for a coronation in Rome was linked to a second factor that seems to have been equally important in Maximilian's mind: the desire, indeed the duty, to lead a crusade of Christendom against the Turks. Coronation by the pope would have been an essential precondition for such a crusade, just as control over the wealth of northern Italy would have been one of its surest foundations. Of course, an offensive against the Turks also promised clear benefits for the security of the Austrian hereditary lands. And the idea of dominion over Italy was undoubtedly fed by historical memories of the Hohenstaufen emperors a few centuries previously. Yet all these factors were in a fundamental sense subsidiary to the desire to give substance to the claim to be ruler of Christendom. At the same time, the claim to be supreme heir to the Roman Empire would be strengthened by victory over the power that had only relatively recently destroyed the last vestiges of the eastern empire in Constantinople in 1453. Unlike his predecessors as Holy Roman Emperors, Maximilian really would have been the sole 'Roman' Emperor.[13]

Preparations for a crusade against the Ottomans began in 1493 in the wake of yet another Turkish onslaught on Carniola, Styria, and Carinthia. The original aim was to forge a union of all Christian states, though it soon became clear that Venice would refuse to join and Charles VIII of France undermined all hopes of unity by launching an attack on Naples in 1494. Despite this, Maximilian persisted and hoped to use the Reichstag of Worms in 1495 to gain the support of the German Estates and to persuade the king of France to cooperate.[14] In the event, neither aim was successful. Maximilian was obliged to construct a military frontier in the south-east using the Order of the Knights of St George, the Austrian equivalent of the Teutonic Order and the Knights of St John.

In fact, for the next decade-and-a-half, Maximilian found himself relegated to the sidelines in the matter of a Christian crusade against the Turks.[15] It is true that the pressure was removed by the three-year truce concluded between Ladislas II of Hungary and Sultan Bayezid II. However, the fact that this agreement was mediated by the king of France indicated Charles VIII's own aspirations to lead

[12] Wiesflecker-Friedhuber, *Quellen*, 15.
[13] Wiesflecker, *Maximilian*, 370–1.
[14] Angermeier, 'Wormser Reichstag 1495', 11–13.
[15] See Kohler, *Expansion*, 264–8.

Christendom and to inherit the crown of the eastern Roman Empire. An Austrian truce with the Sultan in 1497 brought further security, and Maximilian could take some satisfaction in the Turkish assault on Venice between 1499 and 1503. Yet the idea of a grand crusade retained its fascination. It resurfaced in even more grandiose form at Maximilian's final Reichstag at Augsburg in 1518. The united Christian armies led by the Holy Roman Emperor, in league with the Grand Prince of Moscow and the Shah of Persia, would rescue both Constantinople and Jerusalem, then destroy not only the Ottoman Empire but also the Barbary states in North Africa and Egypt.[16]

Arguably, Maximilian's strategic vision was never particularly realistic after 1495. The Reichstag of Worms failed to forge the great Christian union. On the contrary, it placed a seal on the antagonism between the emperor and the French monarchy and forged the union of Austria with Spain. There was fuel enough in the history of the previous decades to account for this conflict. French ambitions had been thwarted in Burgundy. Maximilian's own aspirations to consolidate his Burgundian inheritance with the addition of Brittany were undermined in 1492 when Charles VIII broke his contract to marry Maximilian's daughter Margaret, only to 'steal' his second wife, Anne of Brittany, with whom he had entered into a contract in 1490. Though the marriage had not yet been consummated, which enabled the pope to annul it without qualms, this was a humiliating farce.[17] Maximilian's subsequent marriage to Bianca Maria Sforza, niece of Duke Ludovico Sforza of Milan, on 16 March 1494, was followed in August by the march of a French army through Milan, Florence, and Rome to attack Naples.

Maximilian did not immediately abandon all hope of an accommodation with France. At Worms in 1495, he engaged in speculative negotiations with Duke René II of Lorraine for a restoration of the Anjou dynasty in Naples, which might have been acceptable to Charles VIII and thus still have secured French cooperation in a crusade. Similarly, Maximilian explored the possibility of supporting the English pretender Perkin Warbeck on the grounds that the fall of Henry VII would lead to the collapse of the Anglo-French alliance and leave Charles VIII isolated and predisposed to a rapprochement with the Reich.[18] Ultimately, however, the only reliable alliance that emerged was the one offered by Ferdinand of Aragon, who was anxious to preserve his hold on the crown of Naples. The most public and spectacular symbol of the new alliance was the double wedding contract between his children, the Archduke Philip of Burgundy and the Archduchess Margaret, on the one hand, and the Infanta Juana and the Infante Juan on the other.

The Spanish alliance bore fruit in the inheritance of Philip the Fair's son, Charles, in 1515 and thus ultimately transformed the fortunes of the Habsburg dynasty. Paradoxically, it also effectively doomed Maximilian's operations in Italy to failure. His initial grand idea was never realized. The plan for a rapid campaign in Italy followed by an invasion of Provence (claimed since it was part of the old Kingdom

[16] Wiesflecker, *Maximilian*, 193–4.
[17] Wiesflecker, *Maximilian*, 73–7.
[18] Angermeier, 'Wormser Reichstag 1495', 9.

of Burgundy, the *Regnum Arelatense*) as the prelude to an Austrian, Netherlands, and Spanish assault on Paris was hopelessly overambitious.[19]

The two decades after 1495 were characterized by almost ceaseless military conflict south of the Alps. Alliances changed with bewildering frequency as Charles VIII and his successors, Louis XII and Francis I, struggled sometimes against and sometimes in league with the emperor to establish a balance of power on the peninsula.

In the final analysis, however, Maximilian himself, for all the resources he perennially poured into them, was not among the major beneficiaries of these struggles. Indeed, Maximilian's last Italian expedition in 1515 ended in complete humiliation. His troops were easily routed by the French, and the emperor was forced to flee to the Tyrol, his departure accompanied by the taunts of his own mercenaries that he was but a 'straw king'.[20] Minor additions to the southern Tyrol and a share of the County of Gorizia (Görz) could not disguise the fact that France (with Milan) and Spain (with Naples and Sicily) held the balance of power. The Reich, like Maximilian's ally, Milan, was among the losers and the Treaty of Brussels in December 1516 represented a triumph, albeit temporary, for France.[21]

The sheer range of Maximilian's activities on virtually every periphery of the Reich inevitably raises the question of the role that he envisaged for the German kingdom. Leopold von Ranke and others in the nineteenth century often sharply criticized an exploitative attitude to the German lands and regretted the lack of attention to German affairs, which they believed damaged the development of the German nation.[22]

Such judgements are clearly anachronistic. However, it seems there was indeed a clear difference between the emperor's treatment of the German lands and his dealings with their neighbours. It is striking, for example, that while Maximilian at one time or another engaged in negotiations concerning dynastic unions with most ruling houses in Europe (including France on several occasions), he stolidly refused to contemplate any union with a single German dynasty. At the same time, he repeatedly ensured that German princes who tried to negotiate unions with royal houses outside the Reich were frustrated. Without doubt he operated a two-tier system, in which the German noble families were apparently regarded as junior.[23]

In fact, however, this merely underlines the way in which the Reich differed from other fields of interest. Throughout his reign, Maximilian's prime aim in the German kingdom was to activate his royal rights and prerogatives, and to make

---

[19] Wiesflecker, *Maximilian*, 366; Wiesflecker-Friedhuber, *Quellen*, 9.
[20] Wiesflecker-Friedhuber, *Quellen*, 18.
[21] Rabe, *Geschichte*, 180–1.
[22] Wiesflecker, *Maximilian*, 13, 369, 372.
[23] Angermeier, 'Wormser Reichstag', 11–12; Kohler, *Politik, passim*. An exception was the marriage of his sister Kunigunde to Albrecht IV of Bavaria, though this took place in 1487 and, apparently, without the approval of her father, Emperor Frederick III: ADB, i, 234. Since the union was at least partly designed to strengthen Bavarian claims on the Tyrol, it exacerbated tensions between the Habsburgs and the Wittelsbachs. An important feature of his dynastic policy was the role Maximilian played in engineering marriages between families who belonged to his clientele, either through feudal ties or as court and administrative officials.

the traditional system of the kingdom function effectively by translating the old feudal nexus into a more viable community of interests. More actively than any predecessor, he sought to exploit the advantages of a rule exercised from the periphery: to intervene decisively as arbitrator and peacemaker without becoming embroiled in the internal divisions of the Reich, where the fact that he was not encumbered by family ties became a positive advantage. His efforts in the German lands are characterized by the same periodic intensity and persistence as his endeavours in other regions. Equally, his success here was as mixed as it was elsewhere. However, the reactions of the German Estates both to his German policies and to their perception of Maximilian's plans for their role in the wider empire strengthened the solidarity of the Reich and reinforced its sense of representing German 'national' interests.

The most obvious link between Maximilian's policies in the Reich and his wider imperial schemes was the continual dialogue over the provision of money and troops. From the writ he issued on 24 November 1494 summoning his first Reichstag at Worms to his final Reichstag at Augsburg in 1518, pleas for financial and military assistance were a constant theme. Time and again, the emperor appealed to the German Estates for support in his grand design for a crusade against the Turks, and in the Italian campaigns that would secure his anointing and coronation by the pope as a prelude to the crusade. From the outset these negotiations became entwined with the wider discussion of imperial reform. The issues of the emperor's right to tax and to raise an imperial army (and the discussion of whether the Reich should finance a standing army) were of paramount importance in the protracted debate over the balance of power between the emperor and the Imperial Estates.

Maximilian's persistent attempts to argue that the Estates should provide money and manpower for the defence of the Reich were met with an equally stubborn reluctance to oblige. In his propaganda, Maximilian repeatedly emphasized the centrality of 'Germany' and the Germans to his system: the Germans had been entrusted with the empire because of their brave fighting spirit.[24] It was thus their duty, in his view, to provide the material and military foundation for his campaigns. The German Estates, by contrast, took a narrower view of their patriotic duty. Increasingly they distinguished between the interests of the Reich of the 'German nation' and the wider 'universal' Reich. Thus they could see some justification in providing limited assistance for an offensive against the Turks, since they in fact threatened the German 'nation', but they refused repeatedly to contemplate support for any campaign against the French in Italy.[25]

In reality, even the limited concession of a duty to safeguard the Reich against the Turks yielded little in terms of either money or men. The traditional criticism that Maximilian pursued his universal imperial dream on the strength of German resources is without foundation. At Worms in 1495, for example, Maximilian asked for 4 million gulden over four years. Only 250,000 gulden was granted, and

[24] Wiesflecker-Friedhuber, *Quellen*, 27.
[25] Schmidt, 'Integration', 3–4.

even that was never paid in full.[26] Throughout his reign, Maximilian drew only the equivalent of 50,000 gulden per annum from the Reich. This pales into insignificance when compared with the revenue of between 500,000 gulden and 1 million gulden per annum that he drew from his Austrian territories, or the 1 million gulden he received from his uncle-in-law, the Duke of Milan, between 1494 and 1500.[27] Even the annual tax paid by the Jews of the hereditary lands and the Reich was higher than the amount ever paid by the German Estates. By far the most significant financial instrument was the loan system that Maximilian built up on the rich mineral resources of the Tyrol. In effect, the great universal imperial project depended on the sale of monopolies to south German merchants such as the Fuggers in Augsburg, and the raising of loans from the south German Imperial Cities.[28]

Men proved even more difficult to extract from the Reich than money. Maximilian essentially brought to the Reich the formula that he had inherited in Burgundy and employed to considerable effect in the struggle for the Burgundian succession in the 1480s. A combination of knights and German mercenaries had proved crucial against the French and their Swiss mercenaries.[29] As emperor after 1493, Maximilian attempted to develop this combination further, and envisaged the formation of an imperial standing army. The only relatively successful aspect of this strategy was the integration of knights and members of the upper nobility into his forces.

Maximilian's sponsorship of the Order of St George's Shield and renewal of the Austrian Order of St George ultimately did not produce a new imperial army. Nor were these organizations effective in a military sense. The Order of St George, for example, did not provide a viable basis for the projected south-eastern military frontier in Styria, Carinthia, and Carniola, although on occasion Maximilian was able to employ individuals such as Götz von Berlichingen and Franz von Sickingen as military commanders.[30] Similarly, Albert the Brave of Saxony, Rudolf of Anhalt, and Margrave Casimir of Brandenburg were members of the upper nobility who played a significant role in a variety of campaigns. All were commanders recruited through the traditional feudal clientele network, rather than as 'modern' military professionals.

Harnessing the traditions of the German mercenaries was more problematic. The *Landsknechte* did indeed become an imperial army, with an internal discipline and organization expressed in distinctive uniforms; they easily matched the standards set by the Swiss, who were generally regarded as the most formidable fighters of the time.[31] This was undoubtedly the result of Maximilian's own personal commitment and participation. In the Italian campaigns, dressed in

[26] Wiesflecker, *Maximilian*, 264.

[27] Wiesflecker, *Maximilian*, 348–9.

[28] Wiesflecker, *Maximilian*, 350; Wiesflecker-Friedhuber, *Quellen*, 11–12; Brady, *Turning Swiss*, 80–92.

[29] Rabe, *Geschichte*, 26–8; Kurzmann, *Kriegswesen*, 63.

[30] Kurzmann, *Kriegswesen*, 34–5.

[31] Kurzmann, *Kriegswesen*, 63–71.

the distinctive slit gambeson or doublet and feather cap, he led his *Landsknechte* into battle himself, as he had done earlier in Burgundy.[32] The *Landsknechte*, however, remained mercenaries. When their wages were not paid, even commanders such as Georg von Frundsberg, who normally enjoyed their respect and unconditional loyalty, were unable to control them.[33]

The fundamental obstacle both to the military integration of the knights and nobles and to the transformation of the *Landsknechte* into something approaching a 'national' imperial army was the opposition of the Estates in the Reichstag.[34] Maximilian's proposals from 1495 onwards all more or less failed because they became enmeshed in the wider debate about constitutional reform of the Reich. The Estates repeatedly refused to contemplate an imperial tax to establish an imperial standing army composed of mercenaries, since they feared this would strengthen the emperor's position. In 1510, for example, Maximilian's proposal for a standing army of 50,000 men was simply postponed to the next Reichstag in 1512, when it was rejected outright.

The Estates also proved reluctant to grant any more than minimal assistance in terms of one-off levies of men (or their financial equivalent). They favoured the periodic levy system because it gave them greater freedom to pass on the burden of any tax to their subjects (the imperial tax made no distinction between princes and their subjects). Yet in practice they were reluctant to pay anything at all towards campaigns that many regarded as not of their 'national' concern. Even when assistance was promised, as in 1505 and 1507, the money was not in fact given in full and, frequently, what was paid arrived far too late to be of any use in the campaign for which it was intended. Without the combination of Fugger loans secured on Tyrolean silver and copper and the troops that were raised in the Tyrol and the other Austrian hereditary lands, Maximilian would not have been able to march anywhere at all.

If all that Maximilian wanted from the Reich of the 'German nation' was its money and its soldiers, he clearly failed miserably. Questions of imperial taxation and the military assistance due from the Reich to its emperor were only gradually resolved during the reign of Charles V. However, there was more to Maximilian's efforts to assert his prerogatives in the Reich than this. Indeed, it is a tribute to his success that what emerged by the end of his reign was not an oligarchy of princes but a strengthened monarchy.[35] It is true that the monarchy had less power in the Reich than some other Western European monarchs had in their kingdoms. Yet the fact that the institution had been strengthened at all has often been overlooked. Given the manifest ability of the Estates to refuse both money and manpower, this outcome also perhaps represents something of a paradox.

At the level of relations between emperor and princes at the Reichstag the weakness of the monarch seems obvious. In the debate over reform after 1495

---

[32] Wiesflecker, *Maximilian*, 338; Baumann, *Landsknechte*, 36–7.
[33] Baumann, *Landsknechte*, 117.
[34] For the following, see Kurzmann, *Kriegswesen*, 16–28.
[35] Schmidt, 'Politische Bedeutung', 186.

virtually every proposal made by Maximilian was rejected or modified into meaninglessness.[36] In 1500, the princes exploited Maximilian's failure in the Swabian War and in Italy by imposing an imperial council of regency or governing council (Reichsregiment) on him.[37] While they agreed, in theory at least, to grant money and men, they deprived him of all power in the Reich and set up their own government at Nuremberg. In this new regime, Maximilian was no more than an honorary figurehead, and the princes even demanded that he be subject to its taxation and military levies in respect of his hereditary lands. Real power, it seemed, now lay with Berthold von Henneberg, the Archbishop of Mainz, and the other Electors.

As significant as the triumph of the Estates in 1500, however, was their failure in 1502. The Nuremberg governing council proved no more successful than the emperor in collecting taxes and levying an army. Two further Imperial Cities, Basle and Schaffhausen, 'left' the Reich and joined the Swiss. The French assault on Naples continued unhindered by any imperial army. In March 1502, Maximilian was able to dissolve the council and prevail over the Electoral League formed by Henneberg at Gelnhausen.[38]

The key to Maximilian's recovery in 1502, two years after he had effectively been deposed, lay in the real foundations of imperial power in the Reich: his network of allies and clients, especially among the less powerful Estates of the Reich. More systematically than any predecessor, Maximilian exploited the potential of regional leagues and unions to extend imperial influence and to create the possibility of imperial government in the Reich.

Such leagues or unions were a characteristic response to the problems of lawlessness in the Reich from the fourteenth century onwards.[39] Typically, they were formed by regional groups for the purpose of self-defence against marauding knights exploiting the institution of the feud as a cover for simple robbery, or against powerful aggrandizing princes ambitious to annexe the lands of weaker neighbours. They were also particularly favoured by independent towns and cities for self-defence and for the protection of trade routes.

From the late fourteenth century, several attempts had been made by various emperors to coordinate the activities of such leagues, or even to create an 'imperial league' extending over the whole Reich as an instrument for the maintenance of peace, stability, and imperial authority.[40] None succeeded, but it is significant that Maximilian's first reform proposals on his election as King of the Romans in 1486 hinged on the creation of a network of regional unions. Even though Maximilian at that stage envisaged that the unions should be run by the princes, a proposal which in fact would have been tantamount to a death warrant for the minor territories and

---

[36] See pp. 31–9.
[37] Wiesflecker, *Maximilian*, 269–73; for a brief account of the Swiss, or Swabian war, see Wiesflecker, *Maximilian*, 112–21 and Brady, *Turning Swiss*, 57–72.
[38] Wiesflecker, *Maximilian*, 271–3.
[39] Moraw, 'Einungen', *passim*.
[40] Dotzauer, *Reichskreise*, 23–31.

cities, they were rejected on the grounds that the proposal infringed the authority of the territories.[41]

The discussion of the need for peace-keeping mechanisms and for regional institutions bore fruit in the publication of the 'Perpetual Public Peace' (*Ewiger Landfriede*) of 1495 and in the creation of the Kreise between 1500 and 1512.[42] While those measures only became fully effective some decades later, Maximilian secured and strengthened his own position by working with existing leagues and by seeking to establish new ones modelled on them.

The oldest of these associations was the Lower Union, first established on the Upper Rhine in 1474, the result of an accord between Duke Sigmund of Tyrol, the Bishops of Basle and Strassburg, the Free Cities of Basle, Strassburg, Colmar, and Schlettstadt (Sélestat), and Duke René II of Lorraine.[43] Modelled to some extent on the Upper Union of the Swiss confederacy, its original aim, pursued in alliance with the Upper Union, was to drive the forces of Charles the Bold out of the Sundgau, the Breisgau, and the Klettgau. Duke Sigmund appeared to be the main beneficiary of this action, since he had mortgaged the lands in question to the Burgundian in 1469, and Duke René had an obvious motive for wishing to be rid of the threat of a powerful Burgundian state. Yet the interests of the other parties, such as the cities seeking to protect their trade, were equally important. Indeed, they were crucial to the renewal in 1493 of the Lower Union by Maximilian after a seven-year intermission.

Now, however, the Lower Union served a rather different function in the Habsburg strategy. For it formed the western extension of a second Habsburg-dominated union, the Swabian League, founded in 1488. This association also served a variety of related purposes.[44] From the narrowly Habsburg point of view, its aim was to pre-empt the claims of the Bavarian dukes to the Tyrol, to whose ruler, Duke Sigmund (with forty illegitimate children but no legitimate heir), they had made considerable loans. The Habsburg succession was secured when the profligate Sigmund (who at various times had aspired to exchange the Tyrol for Milan or Burgundy) was persuaded to abdicate in favour of Maximilian. But the Bavarian threat remained. It also motivated many of the lesser Swabian Estates (among them towns, abbeys, upper nobility, and knights) to join the League for the sake of the security of their lands and commerce against Wittelsbach expansionism. A third motivating force for the League was the need of both the Habsburg Tyrol and the Swabian Estates for protection against the expansionism of the Swiss confederates, notably the League above the Lake (the Haut-Rhin confederacy) and Graubünden. Finally, this in turn was linked with a general fear of sedition in both town and country, as movements of the common man were perceived to be inspired by, if not actively provoked by, the free Swiss. The League thus also fulfilled a role as

[41] Schmidt, *Grafenverein*, 24–5.
[42] Dotzauer, *Reichskreise*, 33–9. See also pp. 35–6.
[43] Brady, *Turning Swiss*, 49–52, 55–7.
[44] Brady, *Turning Swiss*, 52–4; Bock, *Schwäbischer Bund*, 1–24; Carl, 'Schwäbischer Bund', *passim*; Wiesflecker, *Maximilian*, 253–5.

an agency for the maintenance of regional law and order in two senses: against expansionist princes and against rebellious subjects.

From the outset, the League demonstrated a vitality and effectiveness rarely achieved by imperial institutions. It soon developed a constitution and established regular consultative procedures. Supported by the immense wealth of the cities, it also rapidly demonstrated its military strength. In 1492, for example, the League mustered a force to suppress a peasant uprising in the lands of the abbey of Kempten. In the same year, it mobilized 20,000 men to persuade Albrecht IV of Bavaria to renounce formally all claims on the Tyrol and to relinquish the Imperial City of Regensburg, which he had annexed in 1486.[45] It is true that the Swabian War of 1499 (also known as the Swiss War) was a disaster for both Maximilian and the League. The gulf that had opened in the last decades between the Alemannic-speakers north and south of the Rhine was too great and the political traditions of the Swiss confederations were too entrenched, and defended by formidable military strength, for the League to bring the Swiss back into the Reich.[46] Nonetheless, despite its defeat, the League was renewed in 1500, and achieved an extraordinary triumph against the Bavarians in 1504.

The Bavarian war of succession demonstrated just what the alliance of emperor and League could achieve.[47] The conflict was generated by a breach of the agreement between the two Bavarian duchies (Landshut and Munich). In 1503 Duke George the Rich of Bavaria Landshut left his lands to his daughter Elizabeth and son-in-law Count Palatine Ruprecht (son of the Elector Palatine Philip), rather than to his cousin Albrecht IV of Bavaria-Munich. Maximilian initially played the role of mediating feudal overlord in the argument between Munich and the Palatinate, granting Albrecht the right of succession on the grounds of his legal entitlement. The dispute soon escalated, however, when Ruprecht allied himself with the King of Bohemia (the Jagiellon Ladislas II) and invaded Bavarian territory to claim his inheritance. He was promptly outlawed for this breach of the peace and Maximilian mobilized the forces of the Swabian League (this time 1,200 cavalry and 12,000 infantry) against him.

The specific dispute in Bavaria was relatively swiftly resolved, helped by Ruprecht's sudden death on 20 August 1504. Yet by then it was clear that there were other issues at stake than just the Bavarian succession. Maximilian seized the opportunity to extract concessions of Bavarian territory adjoining the Tyrol from Albrecht as the price for his support. Even more important was the way that the conflict also manifested itself in western Swabia and Alsace as a struggle to reverse the southwards spread of Palatine influence. The outcome of military confrontation in both south-west and south-east was an undisputed triumph for Maximilian and the Swabian League. In addition, Maximilian made significant territorial gains in Alsace (the *Landvogtei* or Vicariate of Hagenau from the Palatinate), and in Swabia and the

---

[45] Bock, *Schwäbischer Bund*, 71.
[46] Brady, *Turning Swiss*, 58.
[47] Brady, *Turning Swiss*, 72–9.

Tyrol (both from Bavaria), while other League members such as Nuremberg and Württemberg also seized the opportunity to acquire Swabian lands from Bavaria.

Following his dismal position in 1500, Maximilian's triumph in 1504 was quite extraordinary. His ability to call again on troops and money for the purposes of mediating this regional conflict in a way that he, as emperor, had found impossible for his wider campaigns was remarkable. When he tried to behave as an imperial monarch, he was weak. When he exploited the Habsburg clientage as a feudal overlord acting neutrally to maintain the peace, however, he was strong. In this capacity, in alliance with the weaker Estates, he was able to resist the princes in a way that eluded him in the forum of imperial politics at the Reichstag. Indeed, the dynamics of this regional system were so strong that many princes were themselves forced to join the League, for example Württemberg, a notable predator of its weak neighbours, and, after 1504–5, even Bavaria, whose rivalry with the house of Habsburg had largely brought the Swabian League into being in the first place.[48]

Of course, the League developed strains and internal problems of its own. The cities in particular complained increasingly about the financial burden they were forced to carry for an emperor who they suspected was only grateful when it suited him. After about 1511–12 princes such as the Duke of Württemberg, Duke William IV of Bavaria (who succeeded Albrecht IV in 1508), and the Margraves of Brandenburg and of Baden began to turn away from the League. They became increasingly uneasy at the emperor's evident desire to use the League as an instrument of royal power. Yet, unlike the Lower Union, which disintegrated after the Swabian War of 1499, and which Maximilian subsequently failed twice to revive, the Swabian League endured. Indeed, it was so durable and successful that in 1518 Maximilian put forward to the Austrian Estates gathered at Innsbruck the idea of forging a closer union between the Austrian hereditary lands and the Habsburg clients in the south and south-west.[49] The proposed new system was to be ruled from Innsbruck, with two other provincial centres at Vienna and Ensisheim (Alsace), and its primary purpose was clear: to alleviate the crushing financial problems that weighed down on the emperor in his last years. Yet that remained entirely compatible with the traditional aims of the Swabian League: the resistance to the aggrandizing ambitions of the princes, the maintenance of peace, and the assertion of royal power.

The Austrian Estates accepted the proposals, albeit with some reluctance and suspicion. Their implementation, however, was thwarted by Maximilian's death in January 1519. It is difficult to judge what might have become of them had they been implemented. Certainly one option, as Thomas Brady has argued, could have been a South German monarchy dominated by Austria, analogous perhaps to the domination of the British monarchy by England.[50] However, it would be wrong to place too exclusive an emphasis on an implicit state-building ambition in

[48] Bock, *Schwäbischer Bund*, 93–4, 103.
[49] Brady, *Turning Swiss*, 89–92.
[50] Brady, *Turning Swiss*, 114, 224–5.

Maximilian's promotion of the Swabian League. For that would ignore the persistent attempts to establish similar leagues under imperial protection or leadership in other areas.[51] Maximilian actively promoted associations of knights and counts in Franconia and in the Wetterau. On two occasions, in varying combinations, he attempted to establish a kind of 'Frisian league' to bind the Netherlands to the Reich and to bring the north-western Reich into the imperial system.[52]

None of these associations succeeded from the point of view of imperial policy. The Frisian leagues failed because of the unwillingness of leading princes in the region, notably the Guelf Dukes of Brunswick, to become subject to Habsburg tutelage. The associations in Franconia and the Wetterau endured to become institutions for the formal representation of the rights of the weaker Estates united in them at the Reichstag, but they did not become agencies of royal government in the way that Maximilian perhaps had hoped. The key point was that they lay outside the geographical scope of the Habsburg client network and thus they had no guarantee that any benefit would accrue from declaring their loyalty to the emperor. On the contrary, such a move might have made them even more vulnerable to the ambitions of powerful expansionist neighbours such as Mainz, Hessen, Brandenburg, or Bavaria.

As with so many of the constitutional developments of the period after 1495, attempts to establish an effective system of royal government, either in south Germany or in the Reich as a whole, remained piecemeal and only intermittently effective. It is easier to speak of their potential and to speculate on what might have become of them had the circumstances been different, than to register any concrete and lasting success. The very fact that such attempts were made, however, and the fact that in at least one significant region of the Reich an imperial system functioned quite effectively is testimony to the resurgence of royal power under Maximilian. This also underlines the real significance of the Reich of the German Nation in his wider empire. It was not simply an easy source of money and men (far from it), but a real sphere of government in which aspirations to royal rule were actively and purposefully pursued. Indeed, this gave some credence to Maximilian's imperial propaganda, and it explains why that propaganda had so much positive resonance within the German Reich at every level. If the aspiration was always greater than the reality, Maximilian's government in the Reich at least demonstrated a greater vitality and power than that of any of his predecessors.

---

[51] Schmidt, *Grafenverein*, 25–6.
[52] Schmidt, 'Integration', 6–8; Israel, *Dutch Republic 1476–1806*, 29–33.

7

Reich, Papacy, and Reichskirche

Martin Luther's desire to initiate a fundamental reform of the Church and its teachings became an issue in imperial politics when he was summoned to recant his views at the Reichstag at Worms in 1521. At that point, as we shall see, Luther most self-consciously linked his concerns with other causes that had already had a long history and a considerable following in the Reich. The Reformation was not, however, the straightforward outcome of the development of the German Church over the previous century. It is difficult to identify a specific or growing crisis in either Church or society in the late fifteenth century that was commensurate with the explosive early development of the Reformation movement or its profound and lasting impact on the German lands. Attempts to identify a 'systemic' or 'general' crisis in German society during the reign of Maximilian I have been far from convincing.

What made the impact of the Reformation so intense was the fact that religious matters were so closely linked with social, economic, and political issues. This was hardly surprising in a society in which no distinction was made between religion and life. Yet the problems of the pre-Reformation era were not actually as novel as they may at first sight appear. More is known about them because the surviving source material is more plentiful. To some extent, however, that merely reflects the pronounced shift from a predominantly oral to a written culture from the fourteenth century onwards. The fact that grievances were recorded in writing and, by the late fifteenth century, in print, added an important new dimension to the previously dominant oral tradition. The emergence of a 'literature of grievance' helped to generate a growing perception of crisis. A further distortion results from the nature of the rhetoric of reform itself, for it routinely invoked nostalgic images of a vaguely defined golden age, from which the present was claimed to be a gross and dangerous deviation.

It is significant that the pre-Reformation decades seem to have been characterized by a profusion of apocalyptic thinking: an escalating sense that *something* would happen soon; that a great reformer, in some versions an 'angel prince', would emerge to set the world to rights again.[1] Many of these hopes were fixed on Emperor Maximilian. His death in 1519 and the ensuing interregnum created a vacuum that was only inadequately filled by Charles V. The interregnum seemed to create just the right conditions for intensifying a sense of expectation, for

---

[1] Strauss, 'Ideas'; Dickens, *German nation*, 8–17.

translating the sense that something would happen into a determination that something must be done. Indeed, there is evidence that during the interregnum Luther himself became widely identified as the long-awaited holy man and reformer, for a short while at least uniting aspirations for reform and renewal with more diffuse apocalyptic projections.

The distinction between perceptions and reality is essential if one is to reconcile the apparent contradictions that characterize the development of the Church in the Reich in the fifteenth century. Calls for reform had been made repeatedly, and the root and branch reform of Church and society had clearly not materialized. Yet the reiteration of complaints on that score should not be read as evidence that nothing at all had happened. On the one hand, structural problems in the Church were evident at all levels, from the papacy down to the parishes. Many of these problems were common to the Church in Europe as a whole, while others were peculiar to the German context, or at least had a more serious implication in that context. On the other hand, the period was characterized by numerous reform initiatives and revival movements driven by bishops, clergy, secular rulers, and the laity. These fell short of a fundamental reform, but they were sufficiently numerous and persistent to give the life of the Church a vigour and vitality that found expression around 1500 in vociferous criticism of abuses and in unprecedented levels of devotion and piety.

This fifteenth-century age of renewal and reform developed in the context of the unfinished work of the Councils of Constance (1414–18) and Basle (1431–49) that sought to resolve the problems generated by the Avignon papacy (1309–78) and the Great Schism (1378–1417).[2] These events had profound implications for the development of the papacy and for the position of the Church in Europe as a whole. The papacy's authority was severely damaged. The decades of 'captivity' in France had accentuated the political nature of the institution at the expense of its religious authority. These decades widened the gulf between papacy and Curia on the one hand, and the Church represented by its bishops on the other, which generated resentment against central authority in the Church similar to that harboured by Estates in monarchies and principalities. The papacy also became increasingly bureaucratized and ruthlessly imposed papal taxation, which led to a perception that the popes were milking the Church at every level, from the fees paid by new incumbents in high ecclesiastical offices to the taxes levied on the lower clergy.

The years of the schism also seriously fractured the coherence of Church teaching. The division between the obediences of Rome and Avignon opened a rift between the great theological school of Paris and the Reich. The German kings and princes remained more or less constantly loyal to Rome and they now needed to found universities in the Reich to provide for those no longer able to train in Paris: seventeen were founded between 1348 and 1502. The consequent proliferation of theological centres fostered a growing heterodoxy within the Church. By 1520 it was possible to identify no less than eight distinct schools of thought: what

---

[2] Patschovsky, 'Reformbegriff'; Leuschner, *Deutschland*, 201–9; Angermeier, *Reichsreform 1410–1555*, 63–70.

was grist to the mill of academic theologians simply fostered confusion and doubt among the laity.[3]

The schism also had important political ramifications. Secular rulers exploited the weakness of the papacy in order to secure greater control over the ecclesiastical institutions in their own lands. The establishment of national or regional churches, by a series of concordats, diminished the potential for effective papal leadership. This also contributed to the 'secularization' of the papacy as it became ever more reliant on the resources of its own Italian territories. The massive costs involved in the construction of St Peter's and the flagrantly immoral lifestyles of successive popes gave further cause for complaint among the laity. Finally, while secular rulers gained new authority over the Church, the long-term problems of the papacy also empowered the laity. Figures such as Wycliff and Hus emerged to challenge the traditional authorities and the Roman hierarchy, and to preach a renewed 'pure' Christianity based once more on the Bible and embodied in a Church composed of those chosen by God to be saved.[4] More in tune with the orthodox flow, yet also representing a highly significant new departure, were groups such as the Brethren of the Common Life: communities of laymen without vows dedicated to the pious life (the *Devotio Moderna*), which originated at Deventer and Zwolle in the 1380s.[5]

In other areas of Europe the weakness of the papacy resulted in a new accommodation between pope and monarchs, such as the Pragmatic Sanction of Bourges in 1438, which confirmed the rights of the French crown over the Gallican Church. In the Reich, the outcome was both more piecemeal and less clear. At the same time, arguments put forward to remedy the situation became part of a more general debate about reform that embraced the Reich itself as well as the Church.

Despite the problems in the Reich at the time of the schism (in 1410 three popes existed alongside no less than three German kings), the Reich came to play a key role in resolving it. German theorists such as Konrad von Gelnhausen were instrumental in developing the notion that a church council alone held the key to a solution.[6] Heinrich von Langenstein, like Konrad a scholar at the University of Paris, further proposed that such a council should address the reform of the Church generally. Their ideas found no immediate echo and both were forced to leave Paris by a French monarchy that wanted to topple the pope, rather than to reform the Church. As the political constellation changed, however, the conciliar idea resurfaced with renewed vigour. A further permutation of these arguments developed by theorists at Heidelberg, a university close to the Wittelsbach king, Ruprecht, formerly count of the Palatinate, indicated the way forward. Konrad Koler of Soest, for example, denounced the cardinals' conciliarism as a fundamental threat to the Church in Germany, which indicated a clear preference for a weak pope over a powerful oligarchy of cardinals. In his view, the right to summon a church council was the prerogative of the Roman King as future Emperor.[7]

[3] McGrath, *Origins*, 69.   [4] Cameron, *Reformation*, 74–5.
[5] Cameron, *Reformation*, 61–3.   [6] Thomas, *Geschichte*, 369.
[7] Thomas, *Geschichte*, 371–2.

Ruprecht was unable to live up to the expectations placed on him by the Heidelberg theorists. His domestic position was weak; he failed to unite the Estates, among whom the deposed King Wenzel still held considerable sway. Only the further consolidation of royal power achieved by Ruprecht's successor Sigismund brought about a breakthrough. The latter's declaration on ascending the throne that he wished to bring good order into both Church and Reich marked the beginning of protracted efforts to set both institutions to rights. Sigismund's intent was firmly buttressed by the writings of the Heidelberg school. Their elaboration of the idea of the general council as the basis for an all-embracing reform programme provided the theoretical basis for the Council of Constance, which Sigismund himself summoned and oversaw.

In the event, neither the Council of Constance nor its Basle successor brought about the root and branch renewal of either Church or Reich.[8] They did, however, result in the elaboration of an agenda. Following the council's proclamation of its own superiority over the pope in the decree *Haec Sancta Synodus* ('This Holy Synod'), the German Concordat of 1418 listed problems and suggested remedies. The agreement was limited to five years, by which time, according to the decree *Frequens* (concerning the frequency of councils), the pope would have been obliged to call a new council. Pope Martin V made his attitude clear by banning appeals to the council against the pope and by his peremptory dissolution of the council summoned to Pisa and Siena in 1423 in accordance with *Frequens*, when it tried to renew *Haec Sancta*. The renewed conflict between pope and council caused the German Church to lose much of the ground it had gained in the Concordat of 1418. As a consequence, in the prelude to the ensuing Council of Basle, the Archbishops of Mainz and Cologne instigated a series of provincial synods. The planned national synod failed to materialize, but the German 'nation' at Basle was nonetheless able to present a coherent and comprehensive agenda for reform in 1433.

Once again, proceedings were overshadowed by the tension over the fundamental issue of the supremacy of council or pope. In the interests of preserving at least some hope of practical success, Sigismund attempted to steer a neutral course, a policy continued after his death by the Electors and by his successor Albert II. In 1438 a French national synod accepted the Basle decrees and effectively withdrew from the dispute, substituting the king for both the pope and free elections in the appointments to ecclesiastical offices. The German princes, by contrast, still hoped they might negotiate a middle way. In the so-called *Mainzer Akzeptation* ('Mainz Acceptation') they undertook to accept most of the Basle reform decrees, with the notable exception of the crucial decree that effectively renewed *Haec Sancta* and the claim to conciliar superiority over the pope.[9] For eight years the position of neutrality implied in that formula held, but inevitably it was undermined by the ultimate intractability of the dispute over superiority. In the meantime, the pope was obliged to ensure that the princes abandoned the conciliar cause.

---

[8] Borgolte, *Kirche*, 28–9; Boockmann, 'Zusammenhang'; Leuschner, *Deutschland*, 205–9.
[9] Hürten, 'Akzeptation'.

The Habsburgs led the way with an agreement in 1445. Pope Eugene IV granted Frederick III the right to nominate to the six bishoprics in his own lands, as well as other concessions, including the rights over numerous lesser benefices, in return for Habsburg recognition of Eugene as the rightful pope. Two years later, the Electors reached a similar compromise in the so-called Princes' Concordat of 1447. The pope accepted the demands for recognition of the Basle decrees (with the exception of those dealing with the frequency and superiority of councils), while Austria, Bohemia, Mainz, Brandenburg, Saxony, and others swore obedience to the pope. Since Eugene subsequently cast doubt on the validity of what he had acceded to, the final conclusion was only reached under his successor Nicholas V, with the Vienna Concordat of 1448.[10]

The publication of this agreement in the form of a papal decree underlined the success of the papacy in undermining the conciliar position. The pope secured the right to collation for a significant number of German benefices in alternate (uneven) months. Episcopal elections in the ecclesiastical principalities were placed firmly in the hands of cathedral chapters, while the pope reserved the right to object to unsuitable elections. The annates (a tax on minor benefices) and the *servitium* (the first year of income for each new bishop or abbot) were confirmed as lawful papal income. Above all, the concordat explicitly took the place of the Basle decrees. All other issues were to be settled in further separate agreements with individual princes. These were concluded over the next three decades, and resulted in the rights of collation to most territorial bishoprics being placed in the hands of local rulers. This further reinforced the distinction between two kinds of ecclesiastical regime in the Reich. On the one hand, there was the Reichskirche, or Imperial Church, composed of prince-bishops and prince-abbots, elected by chapters and chantries, vassals of the emperor, yet as independent of him as the secular princes, lords, and cities. On the other hand, the ecclesiastical structures in the various principalities were, or could be, depending on the will and power of individual rulers, dominated by the relevant secular authorities.

The Vienna Concordat never gained the force of an imperial law since it was never formally promulgated by a Reichstag in a *Reichsabschied*, but it defined the relationship between the papacy and the German Church until the dissolution of the Reich in 1806. Comparisons with the French Pragmatic Sanction or with the situation in England or Spain might seem to confirm the traditional view that it represented a betrayal of 'national' interests, or at least a failure to protect them. Yet, although no German 'national church' emerged, the situation in the German lands was fundamentally similar to that elsewhere. The universal Church was replaced by a 'regionalized' Church divided according to emerging state and territorial boundaries, which in the Reich meant the realms of the Estates, rather than the Reich itself.[11]

The schism and its conciliar postscript until 1448 had further implications for the German lands. Most importantly, the whole process had generated a literature

---

[10] Meyer, 'Konkordat'.   [11] Borgolte, *Kirche*, 74–5.0

of reform that linked the renewal of the Church with that of the Reich.[12] The idea of reform, of *reformatio*, or a return to a divinely ordained original state of affairs, was not new. Indeed, it had become something of a cliché in the fourteenth century as virtually every new law was presented as a *reformatio*. In the conciliar period, however, the term gained a new relevance and once more appeared filled with a broader meaning as the key to a comprehensive renewal of human society.

Emperor Sigismund's personal interest in the combined reform of both Church and Reich, and his own apparent perception of the necessary link between the two, appears to have been crucial. The programme was elaborated by a succession of theoretical works associated with the councils at Constance and Basle. In 1417, Job Vener, formerly adviser to King Ruprecht, took up themes previously developed by writers such as Alexander von Roes and Dietrich von Niem (or Nieheim) to call for the renewal of both institutions at the council.[13]

These sentiments were echoed by Nicholas of Cusa in his *De concordantia catholica* ('On Catholic Harmony') of 1433, directed at the Council of Basle.[14] Like Vener, Nicholas of Cusa essentially reiterated the general principle without entering into a discussion of detail, but others such as Bishop Johann Schele of Lübeck (*c*.1436) and Heinrich Toke (1442) produced comprehensive lists of measures needed for the reform of papacy, German Church, and Reich.[15] While the learned treatises of Vener and his successors were clearly aimed at the emperor and the princes, and were concerned with the reform of institutions, the anonymous *Reformatio Sigismundi* ('Reformation of the Emperor Sigismund') of 1439 provides evidence of a broader appeal. It proposed, for example, the deposition of all ecclesiastical princes and the distribution of their lands to the cities and the lower nobility, and it demanded measures to protect the common man against oppression from the nobility. Fourteen manuscript editions and four printed versions between1476 and 1497 (and four more in 1520–2) amply demonstrate the enduring resonance of such ideas.[16]

After the Council of Basle, writing on reform gradually became more focused on the institutions of the Reich and on the conflicting agendas of emperor and Estates. Yet the interest in reform of the Church remained. It surfaced regularly in the more popular literature of complaint, for example in the tract of the Revolutionary of the Upper Rhine (*c*.1500–10). Above all, it became institutionalized in the so-called *Gravamina nationis Germanicae*.[17]

This catalogue of complaints of the German nation against the Church arose because the Vienna Concordat had set aside the Basle decrees. The abuses they might have addressed (excessive papal bureaucracy, burdensome papal taxes, abuse of ecclesiastical court procedures) were soon made into a political issue, not least by

---

[12] Märtl, 'Reformgedanke'; Krieger, *König*, 49–53, 114–18.
[13] Bautz, *Kirchenlexikon*, xiv, 1565–9.
[14] Bautz, *Kirchenlexikon*, vi, 889–909.
[15] Angermeier, *Reichsreform 1410–1555*, 84–9.
[16] Schulze, *Deutsche Geschichte*, 59.
[17] Gebhardt, *Gravamina*; Rublack, 'Gravamina'; 'Gravamina', in *TRE*, xiv, 131–4; Hirschi, *Wettkampf*, 143–56. For the context of the original *Gravamina*, see also Tillinghast, 'Reformation'.

the ecclesiastical princes whose revenues were affected. A first draft was formulated at the Mainz provincial synod of 1455 and discussed in the following year at an assembly of representatives of the princes (Reichsdeputationstag) in Frankfurt. In 1458 the list was extended and formally adopted by the Reichstag itself, and thereafter it featured on the agenda of virtually every Reichstag and assembly of deputies. The *Gravamina* became a kind of *idée fixe* in imperial politics and both the humanist writers and Maximilian I in his (primarily political) campaign against the papacy later exploited them for propaganda purposes. In 1518 the Estates used them to justify rejection of a request for money to finance a crusade against the Turks. The following year they were integrated into Charles V's capitulation of election in 1519, and in 1520 they found their most effective exponent in Luther, who made them the basis of his appeal to the Christian nobility.

What gave the *Gravamina* a particular edge were the allegations that Frenchmen, Italians, and Spaniards ran the Curia, and that the German lands were being milked harder than most to finance the decadent lifestyles of the popes and their minions. It is difficult to assess the validity of either claim. The preponderance of Frenchmen and Italians at the Avignon Curia was matched by a growing German presence in Rome during the schism, culminating in the pontificates of Martin V and Eugene IV. Thereafter, it seems that the German presence declined and the papal court became less attractive once the Princes' Concordat and the Vienna Concordat created regionalized churches in the Reich.[18]

Whatever the national origin of its Curial officials, the papacy certainly took care of its material well-being in ways that increasingly attracted criticism. The presentation of Curial officials to multiple benefices throughout Western Christendom was a particular bone of contention. For such individuals were rarely content with just two or three appointments. The datary and cardinal Willem van Enckenvoirt (1464–1534), for example, accumulated two bishoprics and over one hundred other benefices, including two bishoprics in twenty-six dioceses, which yielded an annual income of over 25,000 ducats. Not content with that, he was also able to provide for other members of his family in the Liège area and even sought to make some of his bounty heritable.[19] It was not surprising that anti-papal pamphleteers poured scorn on Roman 'courtesans' who cynically exploited the faithful and usurped their churches.

The question concerning fiscal exploitation is even more difficult to answer. Maximilian claimed that the pope got one hundred times more out of the Reich than he did himself.[20] It seems likely, however, that the actual amount of money that flowed from the Reich to Rome was nowhere near as great as the polemics implied, and in fact considerably less than was paid by the 'national' Church in France. Fundamentally, the papacy after the schism relied increasingly on the revenues of the papal state and less on contributions from the wider Church. Indeed, even the Protestant schisms of the sixteenth century, which might have been expected to represent a serious loss of revenue, do not seem to have made much difference to papal income as a whole.[21]

---

[18] Borgolte, *Kirche*, 90–1.   [19] Munier, 'Enckenvoirt'.   [20] Lortz, *Reformation*, i, 77.
[21] Partner, 'Financial policy', 49; Hoberg, 'Einnahmen', 83–5.

However, the perception of injustice and of exploitation clearly grew. To some extent this was based on the long-term memory of that period of particularly intense exploitation during the schism itself when the Roman pope relied almost exclusively on revenue from the Reich. Thereafter, although the papacy's own lands became increasingly important, papal reservations and other forms of taxation on benefices, together with the increasingly ruthless exploitation of indulgences after about 1450, fed a continuing campaign for reform.

The use of the term 'nation' in relation to the *Gravamina* has often been taken to demonstrate the disadvantages that accrued to 'Germany' as a result of the failure to establish a national Church, as in France or England. Even apart from the fact that France paid much more than the Estates of the Reich, the point is misplaced. For the *Gravamina* were the complaints of the 'nation' of the Estates, not the 'nation' of the people. They represented the grievances, above all, of the ecclesiastical princes who had to forgo a significant element of the rewards of their benefices. To a lesser extent, they also represented the grievances of secular princes and cities who were increasingly assuming control over the Church in their territories and who resented a tax paid to an increasingly remote and 'secularized' papacy in Rome. For rulers, both ecclesiastical and secular, the abuse of ecclesiastical courts was also a matter of real material and political concern.

The *Gravamina* became a key issue in the politics of the Reich under Maximilian, but the ecclesiastical princes drove their first formulation and their reiteration before the 1490s. While these princes seemed to speak for the nation as a whole they were, in reality, ill-placed to represent a moral challenge to a corrupt papacy. Their own situation was perceived by some to be equally problematic. For, like the papacy and unlike their counterparts in other European monarchies, the German bishops were both pastoral leaders and secular rulers. The Reichskirche was more than just the sum of the dioceses within the Reich. It was an integral part of its constitutional structure and political system. In the Concordat of Worms of 1122 the emperor had relinquished the claim to invest all bishops and abbots in the Reich with mitre and crosier in return for the right to confer the regalia on them before consecration. Consequently, the Church became a vassal of the crown and the bishops developed the same rights over their territories as their, less numerous, secular colleagues.

A map of the German Church would reveal complications similar to those in any map of the Reich as a whole, and the enumeration of bishoprics and other institutions is beset by the same kind of problems that attend the description of most aspects of the Reich. In the later medieval period, there were some fifty bishoprics north of the Alps, compared with over two hundred and fifty for the considerably smaller area of the Italian peninsula or some seventy-five for France.[22] These were organized roughly into ten provinces, each headed by an archbishop as metropolitan.

There was no formal titular head of the German Church, but by universal consent the highest-ranking cleric was the Archbishop of Mainz, an Elector and

---

[22] Moraw, *Reich*, 137.

the Imperial Archchancellor, whose province included thirteen dioceses from Halberstadt in the north to Chur in the south. The archbishops of Trier and Cologne were also Electors. However, only Cologne (albeit inferior to Trier in rank) compared with Mainz as metropolitan for five bishoprics, including Liège and Utrecht, while Trier's suffragans (Metz, Toul, and Verdun) were both less significant and outside the 'German' Reich as it crystallized in the fifteenth century. Of the other archbishoprics, only Salzburg, Hamburg-Bremen, and Magdeburg really belonged to the Reich in any meaningful sense around 1500. Those of Besançon, Gnesen, Prague, Tarentaise (metropolitan for Sitten/Sion), or the Patriarch of Aquileja (metropolitan for Trent) were more clearly marginal, even though the Archbishop of Besançon was an imperial prince until 1679 and the archbishops of Prague styled themselves as such without ever attending the Reichstag.

In view of these uncertainties, it is difficult to be precise even about the number of bishoprics in the Reich. The biographical dictionary of German bishops in the period 1448–1648 gives details for a total of sixty-two bishoprics.[23] That figure, however, includes significant numbers in non-German or peripheral areas of the Reich and its immediate vicinity. Bishoprics such as Utrecht, Lausanne or Sion, Pedena or Trieste, Pomesania or Samland in some ways distract attention from the real core of those bishoprics that were also principalities of the Reich. Even the *Reichsmatrikel* or imperial taxation register of 1521 is misleading here. In addition to the Electors of Mainz, Trier, and Cologne, fifty further bishoprics are listed, along with sixty-five abbots and provosts, fourteen abbesses, and four commanderies of the Order of Teutonic Knights.

Although a listing in the *Matrikel* implied *Reichsstandschaft*, the right to attend and vote in the Reichstag that went with active participation in the Reich in the form of payment of taxes, the true figures are considerably lower. For some of those listed did not in fact exercise independent rights and had effectively become territorial bishoprics during the fifteenth century. Thus Brandenburg, Havelberg, and Lebus were subordinate to the Elector of Brandenburg; Meissen, Merseburg, and Naumburg-Zeitz were subject to Saxony; Schwerin and Cammin were controlled by Mecklenburg and Pomerania, respectively; Samland and Pomesania were in the gift of first the Teutonic Order and then Prussia after 1525. Schleswig was listed in error, since it was subordinate to Denmark and in any case belonged to the metropolitan province of Lund.

The register of 1521 also includes four bishoprics subordinate to Salzburg (Chiemsee, Gurk, Lavant, and Seckau—the so-called *Eigenbistümer*—with Chiemsee acting as auxiliary and Lavant and Seckau as Vicars General for Styria and Carinthia, respectively), whose bishops called themselves princes without appearing as such at the Reichstag. If one further excludes the eight bishoprics that lay in the Low Countries, France, and French-speaking Switzerland (though these were reckoned to be functioning members of the Reichstag in the early

---

[23] Gatz, *Bischöfe 1448–1648*, ix.

sixteenth century), the true number of 'active' German prince-bishops lies at around forty.

In each case, the area covered by the diocese was considerably larger than the territory controlled directly by the bishop, the Hochstift.[24] The sum of these areas was substantial even so. In all, between one-sixth and one-seventh of the entire area of the Reich was in ecclesiastical hands.[25] The much greater reach of diocesan boundaries, overlapping neighbouring secular principalities and independent cities, provided numerous flashpoints for disputes over rights of collation and of taxation, the right to lay down statutes for the lower clergy, and, not least, the jurisdiction of ecclesiastical as opposed to secular courts. Disputes between bishops and Imperial Cities, where the seat of the bishopric actually lay in the city, were particularly common in the later Middle Ages and often ended with the bishop being driven out of the city. By 1500 the Prince-Bishops of Augsburg, Basle, Cologne, Constance, Speyer, Strassburg, and Worms had all been forced to take refuge in extramural residences. The later splendour of these residences, such as Bonn for Cologne or Meersburg for Constance, disguised the fact that their very existence was originally a symbol of defeat.[26]

Although the residences and governments of some bishops had been separated from their cathedrals and the authority of all bishops was uncertain beyond their own Hochstift, many still held sway over considerable territories. Salzburg, Münster, Cologne, Mainz, Trier, and Würzburg could compete with all but the largest secular principalities. Freising, Strassburg, Constance, Regensburg, Worms, and Chur were relatively small, and the last three were particularly poor, yet they were still within the middle ranks of the German territories in terms of both size and influence.

Even those ecclesiastical rulers who were intrinsically less significant sometimes played an important role in regional or even imperial politics if they became linked with some major secular territory. Thus Worms and Speyer and the Order of Teutonic Knights (whose Grand Master ruled a scatter of territories from Mergentheim in Swabia after 1527) had become virtual appanages of the Elector Palatine. The Bavarian Wittelsbachs dominated Freising and Regensburg, and in Salzburg and Passau they vied with the Habsburgs for influence over both the chapters and those whom the canons elected.[27]

The problem for many critics of the Church in Germany was that its leaders seemed to behave just like secular rulers and, all too often, exploited the potential of their ecclesiastical prerogatives and duties in order to pursue purely worldly ends. This was hardly surprising. Since the early Middle Ages, the Reichskirche had mirrored the structure of the Reich as a whole: it was an aristocratic Church. Most of the cathedral chapters which elected the bishops were composed almost

---

[24] The greater extent of dioceses as opposed to the prince-bishopric that their bishops ruled as princes is illustrated in the maps in Gatz, *Atlas*, 57–143.

[25] Moraw, *Reich*, 137.

[26] Ziegler, 'Hochstifte'.

[27] Press, 'Adel', 340.

entirely of aristocrats. In Strassburg, for example, the chapter comprised exclusively high-ranking nobles (counts and knights). In Cologne, prospective canons were obliged by a statute of 1475 to prove thirty-two noble forebears; a 1500 statute for Trier laid down sixteen noble forebears as a prerequisite for admission. Indeed, in the late fifteenth century the chapters seemed to have closed ranks generally against the scions of the new upwardly mobile, university-educated administrator class. Between 1474 and 1517, non-nobles in Basle, Augsburg, Paderborn, Münster, and Osnabrück were excluded from the chapters by statute.

In the north-west and south-east of the Reich the composition of chapters was more heterogeneous, and included peasants and burghers. In the west, however, the nobility held sway. Here the socially exclusive cathedral chapters, canonries, and abbeys truly merited the epithet 'Spitäler des deutschen Adels' (welfare institutions for the German nobility) often given to the Reichskirche as a whole. It was only after a protracted and bitter struggle that in 1500 Maximilian I persuaded the chapter of Augsburg to make an exception and to accept his protégé Matthäus Lang, later a cardinal and Archbishop of Salzburg, as provost. The exclusivity of the noble chapters was breached only rarely. Indeed, it was said that Christ himself would not have qualified to become a canon of St Alban in Mainz (a non-cathedral canonry that was far from being the most exclusive).[28]

The exclusivity of chapters that were dominated by men who were nobles first and clergy second ensured that they elected candidates of equal or, more frequently greater, rank to the highest offices. Of 166 archbishops elected in the Reich between 900 and 1500, only 4 are known to have been non-noble.[29] Of 2,074 bishops elected between the seventh and the fifteenth centuries (excluding the 31 bishops of Prague), only 115 were non-nobles, compared with 1,169 from the upper nobility (*freiadlig* or *edelfrei*, i.e. vassals of the emperor) and a further 359 from the lower nobility (vassals of a prince).[30] If a non-noble did succeed, it was almost invariably the result of wealth or of energetic royal patronage. Pious scholars such as Nicholas of Cusa, son of a Moselle boatman and later cardinal and Bishop of Brixen, were the rare exception.

The situation on the eve of the Reformation fully reflected the development over the medieval period. An analysis of thirty-eight bishoprics ruled by thirty-three prince-bishops reveals only five (Lübeck, Ratzeburg, Brandenburg, Cammin, and Chur) non-nobles. All were Germans and none fell into the category of Roman 'courtesans' that some critics alleged were in control of the German Church. Twelve were sons of princes, and four of them combined more than one bishopric. Albrecht of Brandenburg was Archbishop of both Mainz and Magdeburg and Bishop of Halberstadt, as well as the incumbent of a host of other minor benefices. Christoph of Brunswick-Wolfenbüttel combined the sees of Bremen and Verden; Erich of Brunswick-Grubenhagen occupied both Münster and Paderborn. Philipp of

---

[28] Press, 'Adel', 338.
[29] Schulte, *Adel*, 62; Schubert, *Spätmittelalter*, 253–5. The origins of a further nine are unclear.
[30] Santifaller, *Geschichte*, 132. The social origin of 421 bishops was unknown; five were 'Unfreie' (i.e. not free men); five were foreigners.

the Palatinate managed to officiate both in Naumburg and in Freising, some 400 kilometres away.[31]

As a group, the bishops were qualified for office, if at all, by their abilities as politicians and administrators, rather than by learning or piety. Examples abound of those whose pursuit of worldly goods and pleasures obviously far exceeded their interest in their pastoral functions. Ruprecht of Pfalz-Simmern never said Mass once as Bishop of Strassburg in 1440–78, and on his death it emerged that he had apparently lost the insignia of his high office, for neither mitre nor crosier could be found among his effects. Wilhelm von Honstein, elected in Strassburg in 1506, neither went to confession nor preached during his twenty-eight years as bishop.[32] It was said that Hermann von Wied of Cologne, elected in 1515, was not able to understand the Latin credentials presented by the English envoy Richard Pace when he arrived at the Reichstag in 1519 to attend the imperial election. And it is difficult to see how Magnus of Mecklenburg could have been regarded as a credible steward of the Church when he was elected bishop of Schwerin in 1516 at the age of only seven.

Even non-nobles who broke through the 'glass ceiling' of the aristocratic Church soon assumed the airs of their peers. Matthäus Lang, the son of an impoverished Augsburg patrician, had struggled to gain his first post as provost of the chapter at Augsburg in 1500. At the height of his career he held benefices in Italy, Spain, and France, as well as Germany, and allegedly enjoyed an income of some 50,000 gulden.[33] As Archbishop of Salzburg after 1519, moreover, he gave full vent to his monumental arrogance, vanity and regal hauteur, outdoing the pomp and ceremony of many of his aristocratic fellow bishops by insisting on being attended at all times by a retinue of no less than eighty persons. That at least fell into the spectrum of what was expected of an ecclesiastical potentate in the Reich. By contrast, when the pious Frederick, Count of Hohenzollern, Bishop of Augsburg (r.1486–1505), appeared at the Nuremberg Reichstag in 1487 in ecclesiastical dress he was mocked mercilessly as a 'welsche' (effete) Italian in search of a cardinal's hat.[34]

This state of affairs inevitably attracted its critics.[35] That polemical preacher and scourge of corruption in the Church, Johann Geiler of Kaisersberg (1445–1510), went so far as to claim that in over a hundred years no one had seen a German bishop carry out any priestly duty. In 1519 Berthold Pürstinger, the non-noble Bishop of Chiemsee (r.1508–26), who ultimately resigned to devote himself to monastic prayer and study, argued that his fellow bishops' neglect of their duties had brought the Church to the verge of ruin and the world to an imminent apocalypse. Such criticisms, and the realities on which they were founded, have inevitably been grist to the mills of historians in search of the causes of the Reformation. Yet things are not quite so clear-cut. Contemporary critics of the

[31] Wolgast, *Hochstift*, 22.   [32] Blickle, *Reformation*, 32.   [33] Rabe, *Geschichte*, 152.
[34] Gatz, *Bischöfe 1448–1648*, 198–200. 'Welsch' was a pejorative term that also meant anything Italian; it later came to be used more broadly to denote anything southern, including anything Spanish.
[35] For the following, see Hermelink, *Reformation*, 25, 43, 181.

hierarchy may have been vociferous but they were not numerous. Furthermore, subsequent writers have all too often measured the late medieval Church against the standards set later by the Council of Trent. The post-tridentine ideal of the bishop was one for which there were few recent historical models.

Considered in its own context, the German Church leadership was probably better, or at least less harmful to the Church, than its historical reputation might imply. For one thing, it is striking that the Reichskirche as a whole survived the Reformation. Those parts of it that ultimately became Protestant were located in the north, notably within the spheres of influence of Saxony and Brandenburg, and even these institutions were only formally converted after about 1550. The survival of the bishoprics and other ecclesiastical foundations testifies to the political, diplomatic, and military skills of their heads, if to nothing else. However secular and dissolute the lifestyle of some may have been, they showed a commitment to the institution that they represented when it was fundamentally challenged.

It is also clear that political interests and the pursuit of worldly ends as princes of the Reich did not preclude many ecclesiastical princes from an honest attempt also to fulfil their spiritual obligations. In Cologne in the later fifteenth century, the archbishops positively competed with the clergy, the city council, and the laity to improve the religious life of the community.[36] The bishops of Strassburg may not have said Mass regularly, or even at all in some cases, but they convened synods of their clergy and made repeated attempts to introduce sweeping reforms designed to improve conditions in the parishes. How effective these were is another matter, though it is significant that the lower clergy themselves energetically and success-fully resisted many of the proposed reforms. Precise information is not available, but it seems that the period 1450–1515 marked a high point in synodal activity in many bishoprics.[37]

Pastoral leadership was also enhanced in other ways. The fifteenth century saw a significant increase in the employment of auxiliary bishops and vicars general, in addition to the officials who were in charge of the legal business of the diocese.[38] By 1500 twenty-one prince-bishoprics had auxiliaries. Mainz even had two, one for its Rhineland territory and one for its Thuringian territory. Originally employed as functionaries of the bishop in order to undermine the powers of the archdeacons, who in the thirteenth century became so powerful that they threatened to usurp the bishops in some sees, the auxiliaries and the vicars general around 1500 were the pastoral agents of the bishops. While their overlords were sometimes reluctant clerics, the auxiliaries were invariably educated, non-noble, and often recruited from the monastic orders. They were thus typically good churchmen and theologians—they were also cheap, an important factor, since the bishops were responsible for paying them out of their own income.

Finally, while theologians were rare and saints unheard of among the German bishops, a significant number had pronounced humanist interests. These included Albrecht of Mainz, Magdeburg, and Halberstadt, whose cynical exploitation of

[36] Schilling, 'Reformation', 15–16.   [37] Cameron, *Reformation*, 44.
[38] Brodkorb, 'Weihbischöfe'; Wolgast, *Hochstift*, 27.

indulgences (to pay off the loans he took out to pay the pope the fees for his plurality of high offices) provoked Luther's ninety-five theses in 1517. The 'secularized' Renaissance prince-bishop was the norm. But there were enough humanist bishops to justify the more positive assessment that even the normally critical Johann Weiler once made when he wrote that 'one finds many pious leaders'.[39]

[39] Janssen, *Geschichte*, i, 629; Schindling, 'Reichskirche', 103–8; Wolgast, *Hochstift*, 26–7; Schmid, 'Humanistenbischöfe'.

8

Religious Renewal and the Laity

However much some bishops may have tried to implement elements of the reform programme developed at the Councils of Constance and Basle, there were clearly profound inadequacies in the provision of pastoral care. One fundamental problem was the sheer size of the German dioceses. Constance, for example, comprised over 1,700 parishes; Augsburg had over 1,000; even the Mainz archdeaconate of Erfurt included some 500 parishes.[1] In many dioceses the administrative problems generated by such extensive responsibilities were exacerbated by the dismantling of archdeaconates in the fourteenth and fifteenth centuries. This was a measure aimed at neutralizing the potential threat to the bishops posed by the powerful 'territorial' archdeacons, though often carried out before the system of auxiliary bishops had developed fully to take their place.[2] Furthermore, in many areas secular princes sought to 'protect' their clergy from the authority of the diocese, thus effectively undermining even the most benevolent of provincial or diocesan synodal statutes.

The role of secular rulers in coming between the lower ranks of the clergy and the noble canons and bishops indicates a further source of tension. The ordinary clergy often deeply resented the way in which debts to the Curia incurred by noble pluralists were passed down to the parishes. Just as irksome were the innumerable fines and fees imposed by bishops for all manner of things, ranging from absence from pastoral duties to the use of candles at weddings that occurred in proscribed seasons. Fiscalism characterized the approach of bishops as much as it did that of the papacy. Indeed, both bishops and popes extracted considerable income from the right to absolve the clergy as well as the laity from certain kinds of sin (including crimes against holy objects, carnal relations with a nun, sodomy, bigamy, and sorcery, to name but a few). At the same time, many in the parishes emulated some of the more worldly habits of their superiors. The cumulation of benefices operated at the local level too, while the imposition of charges for basic clerical services (christenings, weddings, last rites, and burials, etc.) and of fines for 'misbehaviour', with the threat of excommunication on failure to pay, also periodically gave rise to complaint.

The concentration of two or more benefices in one hand had inevitable implications for the level of pastoral care provided in each parish. Even more significant in its effects was the practice of incorporation, by which parishes and their income came under the control of a monastery, a cathedral chapter, or an urban hospice. Increasingly, such institutions sought to exploit their rights more intensively than noble patrons had done

---

[1] Moraw, *Reich*, 137.   [2] Maier, 'Archidiakon', 136–55.

previously. The conventual or beneficiary of the income of the parish was non-resident and often only came to read Mass on a Sunday. All other pastoral duties were carried out by vicars and chaplains, often paid no more than labourers: another discontented class of cleric, and a poorly educated front for the Church at the grass roots.

In some dioceses (for example, Constance, Strassburg, and Worms) about two-thirds of all parishes were incorporated; in Augsburg and on the Lower Rhine the figure was around 50 per cent, while in the duchy of Württemberg vicars out-numbered ordinary parish priests by five to one.[3] Unsurprisingly, this clerical 'under-class' was not only frequently criticized for its ignorance, but also despised for its assumption of the moral characteristics of the lower echelons of society generally. Complaints about clerical concubines may have been exaggerated. The fact, however, that some dioceses had recognized fees or fines payable by clerics living with a woman or on the birth of a child to such a woman indicates that such situations were prevalent.[4]

Evidence of rapacious monasteries ruthlessly exploiting incorporations and of impoverished clergy with morals no better than the most dissolute prince-bishops must, however, be placed in a broader perspective. Equally significant were the many examples of reforming or reformed communities that developed during the fifteenth century. Virtually all the religious orders experienced some kind of observant movement, and such impulses to revert to an original or stricter monastic rule were given a boost by the legatine visitation of the German lands undertaken by Nicholas of Cusa between 1450 and 1552.[5]

Two renewal movements were particularly significant. The first was the Benedictine reform that originated in Bursfelde near Göttingen. Under the guidance of Johann Dederoth (d.1439) and sponsored by the Duke of Bruns-wick, Bursfelde was transformed from a decayed shell, allegedly inhabited only by a single monk and one cow, into the centre of a network of over ninety houses in northern Germany and the Lower Rhineland down into Alsace by about 1500.[6] Similar reforming activity emanated from the Benedictine houses in Kastel in the Upper Palatinate and Melk in Austria. The second important movement was the Augustinian reform of the so-called Windesheim Congrega-tion.[7] This was the monastic equivalent of the Brethren of the Common Life, and from the early fifteenth century it spread from Cologne down into Hessen and Württemberg, ultimately embracing around a hundred houses in all. Like the Bursfelde movement, the Windesheim Congregation placed particular em-phasis on the cultivation of strict observance of monastic rules. The fact that it also emphasized that study was central to the religious life has led some to suggest that it helped prepare the way for the Reformation.

The kind of renewal represented by the Bursfelde and Windesheim congrega-tions was matched by observantine tendencies in many other religious orders.[8] They also ran parallel to lay movements that embraced similar objectives. The most important of these was the Brethren of the Common Life, which generated the

[3] Blickle, *Reformation*, 28–9.   [4] Blickle, *Reformation*, 30–1.
[5] Meuthen, *15. Jahrhundert*, 88.   [6] Du Boulay, *Germany*, 207; Heutger, *Bursfelde*.
[7] Kohl, 'Kongregation'.   [8] Meuthen, *15. Jahrhundert*, 88, 165.

Windesheim tendency. The Brethren were originally founded in Deventer around 1380 by Gert Groote and comprised a small group of clergy and laity in a single community devoted to the pursuit of a life of prayer and charity. Over the next hundred years numerous additional communities, dedicated to what became known as the *Devotio Moderna* or Modern Devotion, were established primarily in the Lower Rhineland and Westphalia. They were not monks but aimed, as Peter Dieburg of the Hildesheim community emphasized, 'to live piously in the world'.[9]

Numerous other quasi-monastic lay brotherhoods and sisterhoods proliferated after about 1450: Beguine and Beghard houses; single fraternities or brotherhoods simply devoted to communal life and prayer but also often associated with a hospice or hospital; and, finally, lay Third Order houses of the Franciscans and the Dominicans.[10] Some were intensely practical in orientation; others were more mystical, the indirect heirs of the great mystics of the fourteenth century such as Meister Eckhart and Johannes Tauler. All of them, however, in their various ways sought to practise a similar ideal. This, as set out in Thomas à Kempis's *De imitatione Christi*, the key work of the Modern Devotion, widely circulated in manuscript before it was printed in 1473, was quite simply the cultivation of the inner life by individuals who were not formally bound by conventional monastic discipline. Monks and nuns were, after all, in a sense removed from the world; the brothers and sisters lived their life of prayer within it.[11]

Although periodically suspected of heresy, these groups were fundamentally in tune with the Church of their age. They were part of the heterodox flow of late medieval Catholicism, though their forms of life and worship ran parallel to the mainstream, rather than within it. They did not explicitly challenge the Church. Even so, the emergence of such lay organizations reflected an underlying hostility to the formal ecclesiastical structures of the Church and indicated a growing desire for emancipation from an institution from which society had become estranged.[12]

Lay attitudes to the Church were ambivalent. Evidence of what appears to be growing criticism and hostility after about 1450 is balanced by an apparent intensification of the religious life of the laity in the same period. This was manifest not only in the lay brotherhoods and communities, but also in the evolution of more intense forms of popular piety: in the cults of saints and their shrines, and in pilgrimage movements and the like. Such developments make it difficult to accept the view that the Reformation grew out of an increasingly radical anticlericalism that reflected the deficiencies of the late medieval Church.

For one thing, antipapalism seems to have been strongest in precisely those areas, such as Bavaria and the Rhineland, in which the Reformation movement made least impact.[13] It is also striking that for all the criticism of virtually everyone from the pope in Rome down to the ignorant vicar in the parish, outright rejection of the Church was rare. By 1500, even the great crisis of the radical Hussite rebellion lay in the distant past. The Utraquist Church survived in Prague in uneasy coexistence

---

[9] Du Boulay, *Germany*, 211.   [10] Bailey, 'Religious poverty'.
[11] Cameron, *Reformation*, 62–3.
[12] Blickle, *Reformation*, 20; Israel, *Dutch Republic*, 41–5.
[13] Du Boulay, *Germany*, 205.

with Rome, while the Bohemian Brethren, albeit numbering some 100,000, lived a relatively enclosed existence in northern Bohemia, potential victims of persecution, and dependent on noble protection, rather than being militant aggressors.[14] Although the Brethren formally left the Roman Church in 1467, they remained in tune with some of its ideals. Even the most radical Hussite ministers who celebrated Mass 'with tin cups in barns' were in a sense practising better priesthood, rather than rejecting the notion of priesthood altogether.[15] Above all, Hussitism of any variety was essentially a limited Czech phenomenon and made little impact even in neighbouring Moravia and Silesia. In general, there was less heresy in the German lands on the eve of the Reformation than at virtually any other time previously.

Attacks on the clergy, both verbal and physical, reflected something more complex than simple rejection. Two accusations seem to have become increasingly prevalent. The first was that the clergy were exceeding their powers. The second was that their lifestyles threatened to undermine the validity of their work. The fear that the sacraments dispensed by dissolute and sinful priests were invalid was frequently voiced in the grievance literature of around 1500.[16] Both charges provide vital clues to the nature and meaning of anticlericalism and reflected a long-term transformation in the relationship between Church and society, rather than a divorce between the two.

The key to the first charge was the rejection of clerical immunity and of clerical authority in worldly affairs.[17] This was the thrust of complaints about the jurisdiction of the ecclesiastical courts, whether in Rome or on a diocesan level, as well as complaints against the employment of bans, interdicts, and excommunications by clerics.[18] The charge arose from the growing desire at all levels for a reform of the Church. Frustration at the failure of the councils increasingly prompted laymen at all levels of society to take matters into their own hands. This was no more than the logical outcome of the conciliar movement. For this had not only dented the authority of the Church, it had also endowed the laity, in the shape of secular authority, with a key role. It was, after all, the Emperor Sigismund, rather than the pope, who took the initiative in calling the Council of Constance in the first place. And while the conciliar movement itself was defeated, the papacy subsequently recognized the authority of secular powers over Church affairs in the concordats it concluded during the following decades.

In the German territories, this generated a series of initiatives by individual princes to take charge of Church affairs. To some extent this was motivated by purely political concerns and was nothing new. Rudolf von Habsburg had, for example, famously declared that he intended to be pope, archbishop, bishop, archdeacon, and dean in his own lands. Similarly, the Duke of Bavaria in 1367 denied that 'Pope, Emperor and king' had any right to dictate in his territory.[19] The legal dictum that 'The Duke of Kleve is Emperor and pope in his own lands' gained wide currency in the fifteenth century.[20]

There were several dimensions to the initiatives inspired by such notions. On the one hand, princes such as the Austrian Habsburgs, and the Electors of Brandenburg and

---

[14] Cameron, *Reformation* 71–4; Rabe, *Geschichte*, 154.   [15] Du Boulay, *Germany*, 202.
[16] Schubert, *Spätmittelalter*, 268.   [17] Du Boulay, *Germany*, 201.
[18] Cameron, *Reformation*, 27–9; Blickle, *Reformation*, 32–3.   [19] Du Boulay, *Germany*, 190–1.
[20] Moeller, *Deutschland*, 42; Hashagen, *Staat*, 550–7.

Saxony sought to establish control over the bishoprics in their sphere. These initiatives pre-dated the concordats of the 1440s, but the formal agreements placed a seal on them. Consequently, a whole series of bishoprics lost their immediate status and became *Landesbistümer* or territorial bishoprics subordinate to secular princes: Chur in the Swiss Graubünden and Gurk in Austria; Naumburg, Merseburg, and Meissen in Saxony; the Bishoprics of Brandenburg, Havelberg, and Lebus in the Electorate of Brandenburg.

The influence exerted by the Dukes of Mecklenburg over Schwerin and Ratzeburg was less formalized, but nonetheless strong. The Electors of the Palatinate failed to 'colonize' Speyer and Worms but successfully dominated them nonetheless, just as the Dukes of Bavaria strove to represent their interests in elections in Regensburg, Freising, Passau, and Salzburg.[21] The Dukes of Kleve and Jülich-Berg, by contrast, failed to remove the Church in their lands from the authority of the Archbishop of Cologne; and in Hessen the landgraves were also thwarted in their ambition to establish a bishopric subordinate to themselves. In all three territories, however, the struggle against higher ecclesiastical authority was a major preoccupation in the century before the Reformation.

Many territories also sought to gain control over the monasteries, and thus also over the parishes incorporated to them. This was a major aim even of princes like the counts and dukes of Württemberg, who eschewed any ambition to dominate the relevant diocesan authority (in this case the Bishop of Constance). To some extent this was part and parcel of the drive to undermine the standing of the ecclesiastical courts and to gain control over ecclesiastical revenues, to subject the clergy themselves to taxation. But it was also the result of the perception of a link between a well-regulated Church and a stable and prosperous territory.

Pious clergy meant pious teaching. Pious teaching meant proper instruction of the laity, and an indispensable complement of promulgated laws and regulations. Church reform promised better social discipline. For that reason, many princes promoted the observantine movements in their territories, instigating visitations, and promulgating decrees designed to improve clerical morals and practice. In Württemberg, for example, Count Eberhard not only extended his rights of patronage and tried to promote good practice in preaching. In 1477 he also established the Brothers of the Common Life in a foundation at Urach and he subsequently founded further houses, such as the one he created in 1491 at St Peter in Einsiedeln. Twelve clergy, twelve nobles, and twelve commoners under the joint governorship of an ecclesiastical provost and a noble 'administrator' were enjoined to practise the Christian communal life in a microcosm of the territory as a whole.[22]

Similar initiatives to establish rights of jurisdiction and supervision over local Church organizations were characteristic of cities in the same period. Imperial Cities such as Augsburg, Nuremberg, and Strassburg sought to extend protection over the clergy within their jurisdictions, often against the authority of the relevant bishop, and to secure the right to appoint to their own parish churches. Furthermore, they increasingly imposed guardianship, amounting in effect to close supervision, over all manner of

---

[21] Schulze, *Fürsten*, 13–45. [22] Schulze, *Fürsten*, 23–8.

clerical and charitable institutions.[23] The motives and the objectives were the same as those that drove the territorial initiatives. Increasingly, the laity desired to ensure the probity of the Church and hence the purity of the sacraments it dispensed in the conviction that this was a prerequisite for the stability and prosperity of society. This entailed a remarkable role reversal. For much of the medieval period the clergy had instructed the laity and supervised their morals. Now the laity were instructing and supervising the clergy.[24] The underlying trend was for the laity to assume control, to take responsibility for *their* Church. This fundamental shift is also evident at the level of parishes, both urban and rural. It was by no means uncommon to find communities claiming the right to appoint clergy or themselves funding, often at considerable expense, the regular provision of sermons or daily Mass.[25]

The gradual evolution of a more assertive laity who practised a more self-conscious and active faith is also reflected in many other religious phenomena of the pre-Reformation decades. Far from turning against the Church, the laity seemed both to embrace with enthusiasm much of what it offered and on occasion to extend that in forms of religious expression that ran in parallel with, but outside the formal Church.

Lay piety found expression within the Church in the boom in endowments of new Masses, which began around 1405 and did not decline until after about 1520. The same period saw an intensification of the veneration of the Eucharist, the figure of the crucified Christ, of the Virgin Mary, and of a growing number of patron saints. Indeed, the churches themselves were physically too small to accommodate the new forms of worship and this period saw an extraordinary construction boom, in new churches and alterations and extensions to existing ones, to accommodate the altars and images generated by the proliferation of cults. From Alsace and Upper Austria to Holland and the Baltic, the Late Gothic ecclesiastical building boom could scarcely keep up with the munificence of congregations, urban and rural, noble and burgher.[26] In a parallel trend, the veneration of the Eucharist and the Virgin led to the emergence of lay confraternities. The first rosary confraternity—the rosary beads themselves seem to have been invented by the Trier Carthusians after 1450—was founded in 1474 with some 5,000 members; it grew rapidly, and by 1481 it is said to have had over 100,000.[27] Corpus Christi brotherhoods enjoyed a similar popularity.

Other phenomena were more loosely tied to the mainstream of orthodox belief and worship. Pilgrimages to miraculous shrines, to worship bleeding Eucharistic hosts at Wilsnack in Brandenburg and Sternberg in Mecklenburg, to the Holy Robe first displayed in Trier in 1512, or to miraculous images of the Virgin at Grimmenthal or Regensburg (where over 100,000 pilgrims visited the shrine of a miraculous image within a year of its appearance in 1519), seem to show the laity creating their own sacred spaces.[28] The enthusiasm aroused by such shrines or by the announcement of apparitions was not always comfortable either to the Church or to the secular

[23] Cameron, *Reformation*, 59–61.   [24] Moeller, *Deutschland*, 43.
[25] Blickle, *Reformation*, 25–6; Blickle, *Gemeindereformation*, 179–83.
[26] Moeller, *Deutschland*, 37; Moeller, 'Frömmigkeit', 9–10.
[27] Schubert, *Spätmittelalter*, 275–6.
[28] Schubert, *Spätmittelalter*, 282.

authorities. It could all too easily spill over into sedition. In 1476, for example, news spread from Niklashausen in Franconia that Hans Böheim, a young drummer and piper of peasant stock, was preaching the absolution of all sins for those who devoted themselves to the Virgin Mary, while also denouncing the clergy and the nobility. He generated such excitement and unrest that the Bishop of Würzburg sent armed men to arrest him and, after a failed attempt by a militant mob to free him, he was executed.[29]

Despite differences between the attitudes of the elites and those of the mass of the population, there is a striking broad similarity between the behaviour of rich and poor. While villagers were obliged to pool their resources for the occasional Mass, nobles such as Count Werner von Zimmern in 1483 could pay for a thousand Masses to be said for their own souls in a single year.[30] Ordinary folk often travelled long distances to visit a popular shrine, whereas a ruling prince like the Elector Frederick the Wise of Saxony (r. 1486–1525) could make his own. Following a visit to Jerusalem in 1493, he spent large sums rebuilding his castle church in Wittenberg to house his collection of over 19,000 relics, which included such treasures as the body of a Holy Innocent, Mary's milk, and straw from the stable of the Nativity.[31] At roughly the same time, Albrecht of Brandenburg, Elector and Archbishop of Mainz, amassed relics that assured him no less than 39,245,120 years of absolution.[32]

Indulgences were another point of convergence between Church and laity. Though their theological foundation was debatable, the sale of indulgences was a device increasingly employed by the papacy during the fifteenth century.[33] From 1450, it was resolved that general indulgences should be sold on jubilees every twenty-five years. Numerous additional indulgences were launched, such as the special indulgence of 1506 designed to raise funds for the building of St Peter's in Rome and others that benefited specific local causes or even helped pay for the construction of roads.

At the same time, the nature of the indulgence was also developed in rather questionable ways. The 1506 indulgence represented a particularly grotesque extreme. It was promulgated in the Reich with the assistance of Albrecht of Mainz, who was granted half the yield to pay off the debts to the Fuggers and to the papacy that he had incurred in securing his elevation as archbishop. The indulgences that were sold on this occasion not only allowed the absolution to be 'cashed in' at some later date, but also permitted purchasers to effect the posthumous absolution of those already dead. This particular campaign was of profound significance for the Reformation. Yet it is important to emphasize that although a later generation would regard such practices as corrupt and theologically unsound, it is too simple to view them as evidence for the growing commercialism and degeneration of the Church. Demand was just as important as supply. Luther's objections to the indulgence cannot disguise the fact that the eagerness of the pious laity to invest in their salvation was crucial to the success of this particular form of fund-raising.

---

[29] Franz, *Bauernkrieg*, 45–52; Cameron, *Reformation*, 58. See pp. 136–7.
[30] Moeller, 'Frömmigkeit', 14.
[31] Cameron, *Reformation*, 14; Ludolphy, *Friedrich*, 355–9.
[32] Moeller, 'Frömmigkeit', 13.
[33] 'Ablaß', in *TRE*, i, 347–64, esp. 351–5.

9

Humanism in the Reich

German humanism was part of a movement of ideas that spread throughout Europe from Italy during the course of the late fourteenth and fifteenth centuries.[1] In its German inflection it combined a preoccupation with national origins and identity with new Christian ideals. There was nothing unusual in that. Humanism was essentially a method of study that aimed to read the old Greek and Latin texts in their original sense. Its motto was *Ad fontes!* This call to return to the original sources was first applied to the study of the classic academic texts, notably the prime philosophical and legal texts that were the foundation of Western thought. The philological method and the return to original meanings could equally be applied to other themes.

Almost everywhere in Europe this involved the rediscovery of national origins and national identities. To some extent, such ideas were born of competition with, or rebellion against, the 'original' Italian humanists: they rebelled against the proclamation by Italian scholars of the superiority of their own past in the ancient world. By the end of the fifteenth century, scholars in most other parts of Europe had either discovered or invented the origins of their own national communities, asserting in many cases that the origins of their own society pre-dated, and were purer and more original or indigenous than, those of the Italians.[2]

This led naturally to a degree of competition between the various national groups of humanists as they sought to eulogize the virtues of their own nation above and against those of other nations.[3] Everywhere, too, humanism fed into the academic, theological, historical, and political debates of the various European monarchies and states. In the Reich, the particular significance of humanism was that, from the mid-fifteenth century, it shaped and articulated the growing demand for the reform of Reich and Church. A variety of developments converged to form this first national intellectual constellation.

The German humanists represented a distinct subgroup of the educated laity. Though it is tempting to see them as the first exponents of a 'modern' secular philosophy, they remained within the Church. They did, however, develop a distinctive ethos that promoted a kind of piety related to, yet distinct from, that

---

[1] There are accessible overviews in Overfield, 'Germany'; Meuthen, 'Charakter'; and *TRE*, xv, 639–61.
[2] Münkler and Grünberger, 'Identität'; Münkler, Grünberger, and Mayer, *Nationenbildung*, 235–61.
[3] Hirschi, *Wettkampf*, 124–74.

of the *Devotio Moderna* and the Brethren of the Common Life. They also contributed significantly to a growth in criticism of the Church, especially in rejecting the scholasticism that they believed held a stranglehold over it, and in giving voice to an anti-Romanism that held the papacy responsible for all the ills of Church and society.

The humanists were also the product of a significant expansion of higher education during the fifteenth century. This reflected the growing needs of the developing administrations within both territories and cities for literate and qualified officials, and the consequent expansion of employment opportunities for non-nobles. In 1400, there were roughly two thousand students; by 1500, there were some twenty thousand.[4] Over roughly the same period the number of German universities increased from five (Prague, Vienna, Heidelberg, Cologne, and Erfurt) to sixteen, with the greatest concentration after 1450 in Upper Germany.[5] At the same time, many cities developed Latin schools, which served the same functions as the universities and in essence differed only in not being able to confer degrees. The Latin school at Schlettstadt, for example, easily matched the quality and the student numbers of most arts faculties after about 1450.[6]

This expanding infrastructure of higher education increasingly came under the influence of the ideals associated with the Renaissance.[7] Initially, the flow of Italian ideas into the Reich had been a trickle carried by political and trading links and by German students and scholars returning from the Italian universities. It was given a pronounced boost by the contacts between Germans and Italians fostered by the Council of Constance and the Council of Basle. Travels to or studies in Italy and contacts with Italians travelling north of the Alps remained crucial, but from about 1450 an indigenous humanism took root in various parts of the Reich.

The new educational ideals were vigorously promoted by those who pushed for curriculum reform at the universities. These initiatives were initially concentrated in the inferior arts faculties, but they spread rapidly to the superior faculties of theology and, somewhat later, medicine and law.[8] The theological faculties were particularly important: here the confrontation with scholasticism was often bitter but fruitful, and the struggle against the entrenched ecclesiastical authorities over the curriculum shaped the anticlericalism that characterized the German humanists as a whole. Outside the university context, in cities such as Augsburg and Nuremberg, rich and cultured patricians like Conrad Peutinger or Willibald Pirckheimer stood at the centre of small circles of devotees of the new thinking. By 1500 at the latest, humanist ideals were also established at some of the leading courts and their central administrations: at the Habsburg courts in Vienna and Linz, and at the courts of Mainz, Trier, and Cologne or Heidelberg, among others. Associated with the

---

[4] Schubert, *Spätmittelalter*, 286.
[5] The foundation of Heidelberg in 1386 had been preceded by Prague (1348) and Vienna (1365). Hammerstein, *Bildung*, 1–6.
[6] Schubert, *Spätmittelalter*, 285; Hammerstein, *Bildung*, 9–11.
[7] *HdtBG*, i, 39–51.
[8] Hammerstein, *Bildung*, 6–9, 13–15, 97–9, 103–4.

Habsburgs too, and also shaped by proximity to and hostility to France, was the concentration of humanist scholars and writers in the cities of Alsace.

The diverse forms of influence, geographical distribution, and institutional affiliation make it difficult to speak of German humanism as a single, coherent phenomenon. Yet the disparate scatter of individuals and groups, some with interests linked to the Church, some with literary interests, others concerned with territorial government or the reform of the Reich, comprised a wider network. They shared a consciousness, increasingly strident and self-confident, of being involved in a common project. German humanism became an increasingly dense diaspora of like-minded scholars, writers, university and Latin school teachers, and their pupils that extended across the entire Reich. Personal contacts and networks of friends and protégés held this network together. These were kept in good order by social contacts among local and regional groups, by extensive travel, and above all by correspondence. They all participated in the public forum created by the printing press; they all contributed assiduously to the avid correspondence that characterized the communicative humanist world.

The key concern of the movement was the reform of higher education and the promotion of the study of the classical liberal arts of grammar, rhetoric, poetics, history, and moral philosophy. The study of the ancient authors who had first elaborated those disciplines was fundamental, though that soon extended to the study of all ancient texts—both Latin and Greek (and later Hebrew too), pagan and Christian. The writing of elegant Latin was a core skill, as was the practice of literary forms such as the Ciceronian dialogue, in which different points of view were juxtaposed and reconciled, a literary parallel to the conversational circles and learned correspondences that characterized the social interaction of the humanists. Debate and a willingness to entertain all views were regarded as fundamental. Above all, the conviction that humanist studies could elevate and perfect the individual was a core belief.

Since humanism involved primarily method, approach, and ethos, it could give rise to innumerable different forms of intellectual and literary activity and could be devoted to any number of causes. Amidst the profusion of humanist endeavours around 1500, two broad tendencies are particularly important: Dutch Christian humanism, which spread from the north-west, and the Upper German humanism, which developed between Alsace and Vienna. The distinction is perhaps artificial. There was certainly no geographical north–south divide and there were many points of contact and overlap between the two tendencies, with many individuals moving from one sphere to the other or back and forth between them. However, there are also significant differences of emphasis.

Dutch Christian humanism grew out of the fruitful interaction between the houses and schools of the Brethren of the Common Life and the new philological studies in the 1470s and 1480s.[9] An early product of this environment was the Frisian Rudolf Agricola (*c.*1444–1485).[10] He was educated by the Brethren at

[9] Israel, *Dutch Republic 1476–1806*, 41–8.
[10] Killy, *Lexikon*, i, 634, 77; *ADB*, i, 151–6; *NDB*, i, 103–4; Laan, 'Agricola'.

Groningen. He lived in Italy for just over ten years before returning in 1479 to Groningen, where he maintained contact with figures such as Wessel Gansfort, unorthodox theologian of the Brethren, and Alexander Hegius (*c.*1433–1498), rector of the Latin school at Deventer from 1483. In 1484, Bishop Dalberg of Worms persuaded him to move to Heidelberg, where he died the following year after a trip to Italy. Agricola never held an influential position and he published little, but his *In laudem philosophiae* ('In Praise of Philosophy', 1476), an oration he delivered in Ferrara in 1475, set new standards and defined humanist aspirations.

Agricola subsequently became a role model for the humanist way of life: an independent and critical spirit, dedicated to scholarship based on philological principles, inspired by the study of classical texts, yet standing on solid Christian foundations. His inspiration and influence was pervasive among humanists of all hues. Through Hegius and the Deventer Latin school, for example, there is a link with Mutianus Rufus, influential exponent of Christian humanism and Florentine Neoplatonism, who was canon in Gotha and intellectual mentor of the humanist circle in Erfurt. From Heidelberg, Agricola's philological and literary precepts also set standards in Upper Germany.

Even more important than Agricola was Desiderius Erasmus (1466–1536), in many ways the prime exponent and embodiment of Christian humanism.[11] Erasmus, too, was a product of the Deventer Latin school, which he attended in 1477–84 and where he once heard Agricola lecture. In personal terms, his entry into the monastery of the Augustinian canons at Steyn near Gouda in 1489 (leading to his ordination in 1492) delivered him into a kind of prison from which he only escaped with difficulty after a papal dispensation in 1517. It was there, however, that he encountered a humanist circle of brothers who cultivated the study of classical languages alongside the educational mission of their order.

Extensive periods of residence in England brought contacts with Sir Thomas More and John Colet, and fostered a preoccupation with the works of the Church Fathers and with the Bible, culminating in the publication of Erasmus's edition of the Greek New Testament in 1516. A protracted stay in Italy during 1506–9 gave Erasmus experience of Turin, Padua, Bologna, Naples, Florence, and Venice, and enabled him to extend his knowledge of Greek manuscripts. His contacts with Italian Neoplatonism during this time also generated an aversion to the paganism, or secularism, cultivated by many Italian scholars and further reinforced his Christian convictions. By the time he travelled from Louvain to Basle in 1514 his reputation was already colossal.

Erasmus's voyage down the Rhine was like a triumphant imperial progress. It was punctuated by meetings with Johannes Reuchlin (1455–1522) and Ulrich von Hutten (1488–1523), among many others, and everywhere Erasmus was celebrated as the harbinger of a new age of learning that was now beginning to dawn in Germany too.[12] He himself joked that having almost become an Englishman, he was now tempted to become a German. In fact, he returned to Louvain almost

---

[11] Killy, *Lexikon*, iii, 273–82; Hammerstein, *Bildung*, 15–16.
[12] *DBE*, iii, 135.

immediately and did not settle in Basle until 1521. However, his frequent travels down the Rhine and his friendships with scholars such as Beatus Rhenanus (1485–1547, originally of Schlettstadt, then resident in Strassburg and, from 1511 in Basle), whom he called his brother, gave him a constant presence among the German humanists.[13]

Erasmus had much in common with Agricola, but he surpassed him both in the volume of his works and in the philosophical elaboration of his aims. Agricola had employed the term 'philosophia Christi' to denote his combination of elements of the *Devotio Moderna* with the new philology.[14] When Erasmus wrote of the 'philosophia Christi' he meant the elevation of the study of letters into a Christian mission, the inner fusion of erudition and piety. True Christianity was to be found not in Church dogma or in works of external piety, but only in the Bible. The Bible alone held the key to that love and piety of the heart which distinguished the thinking Christian. The best preparation for this intellectually rigorous religious way lay in the study of the classics and of the Church Fathers, all essential foundations for a proper understanding of scripture itself. Religious knowledge gained by this route, by the thinking individual independent of the guidance of the Church, was the only true religious knowledge and the only foundation for a life in imitation of Christ. That, in turn, was envisaged as the precondition, imminently realizable in the new dawn of humanist studies, for the regeneration and reform of Christianity as a whole.

Erasmus's printed works exerted their greatest influence in the German lands only after 1517. His *Enchiridion militis christiani* ('Sword or Handbook of the Christian Knight'), first published in 1503, only became widely known following the edition published by Froben in Basle in 1518. That was also the period in which his *Moriae Encomium* ('In Praise of Folly') and the *Querela Pacis* ('Lament of Peace') gained a wider currency. In the context of the Reformation debate, Erasmus came to be seen as a pioneer who had raised many of the key issues before the event, and for that reason he ultimately became the most widely read author in German after Luther.[15] Before 1517, his influence was more narrowly focused on Latinate humanist circles, though it was nonetheless intense for that.

Erasmus secured the elevated place of humanist biblical study. He also helped develop the *Devotio Moderna*'s implicit rebuke of the corruption, worldliness, and purely external piety of the Church into a systematic, philosophically and theologically founded critique. More specifically, he articulated his general unease with the Church in an antipapalist form, once describing Rome as 'the tithe barn of the whole world' and placing his hopes in a reforming general council.[16] His mockery of scholasticism and scorn for the vain and arrogant clergy reinforced both the desire that many in the Reich had for reform and renewal of the Church and the intellectual anticlericalism of many of the German humanists. The reverberations

---

[13] Schoeck, *Erasmus*, 233–5, 283–97; Stadtwald, *Popes*, 78–92.
[14] Israel, *Dutch Republic 1476–1806*, 44.   [15] Killy, *Lexikon*, iii, 277.
[16] Stadtwald, *Popes*, 81.

of the Reuchlin affair show just how intense this had become in the Reich on the eve of the Reformation.[17]

Johannes Reuchlin's vocation was formed long before Erasmus became an intellectual presence in the Reich. Trained in the liberal arts in Pforzheim and then Freiburg, he continued his studies in Paris and Basle, before switching to jurisprudence in Orleans and Poitiers. On trips to Italy in 1482 and 1490, he had become acquainted with Pico della Mirandola and his mystical philosophy, which stimulated an interest in Hebrew and the kabbala. Contacts with the Heidelberg humanists in 1496–8 preceded a judicial appointment by the Swabian League in Tübingen from 1502 to 1513 and ultimately a chair in Greek and Hebrew at Ingolstadt in 1519.

In 1509, Reuchlin's virtually unique expertise in Hebrew embroiled him in a spectacular public scandal that became a defining moment in the self-understanding of German pre-Reformation humanism. Johannes Pfefferkorn (1469–1523), a converted Jew in Cologne, managed to provoke an imperial decree obliging the Jews to hand over all anti-Christian works, which he claimed extended to the entire canon of Jewish writing.[18] Reuchlin, the author of *De rudimentis Hebraicis* (1506), was one of those consulted by the imperial authorities, and he alone stood out by defending the value of philosophical and scientific Hebrew texts, and the Hebrew versions of scripture. There were even sections of the Talmud, he argued, that were in no way harmful to Christianity and only an ass could demand that the Hebrew commentaries on scripture should be destroyed.

The literary dispute soon escalated into a bitter clash between scholasticism and the new learning. After Pfefferkorn mobilized the Cologne theological faculty, Reuchlin denounced his academic critics in print as 'goats' and 'pigs', representatives of a decrepit and senile university, triggering a heresy trial that dragged on until 1520. Meanwhile, the war of words mobilized virtually the entire humanist network in defence of one of their own. In addition to publishing his own spirited apologia, Reuchlin brought out two volumes of letters of support from other humanists. Most significant of all, in 1515 and 1517 the anonymous *Epistolae obscurorum virorum* ('Letters of Obscure Men'), addressed to Ortwin Gratius (1475–1542), the head of the Cologne theologians (and, incidentally, also a pupil of Hegius at Deventer), launched a savage attack on the academic pretensions and moral dubiety of the scholastics.[19]

The fury of the 'obscure men' could not detract from the polemical triumph of the satirists. There is no certainty about the authors of the *Epistolae*, but it seems likely that the first volume stemmed from the pen of Crotus Rubeanus (c.1480–c.1539), one of the circle of Mutianus Rufus (1470–1526) in Erfurt, and the second from Crotus's former student friend, Ulrich von Hutten.[20] The whole

---

[17] Rummel, *Reuchlin*, 3–40; Killy, *Lexikon*, ix, 398–400; *ADB*, xxviii, 785–99; Bautz, *Kirchenlexikon*, viiii, 77–80. The fullest account of the Reuchlin affair and its theological implications is Price, *Reuchlin*,
[18] Price, *Reuchlin*, 95–112.
[19] Rummel, *Reuchlin*, 23–4.
[20] *DBE*, ii, 404–5 and v, 236–7.

affair served to unite an otherwise disparate fraternity. In particular, the letters symbolize the interaction between Christian humanism and the other dominant tendency in German humanism, the patriotic humanism that flourished in the Habsburg lands from Alsace across to Austria and in Upper Germany generally, whose leading exponents the nationalist tradition generally regarded as *the* German humanists.

To some extent, the distinction is, of course, artificial. Yet Erasmus's cosmopolitan irenicism, albeit tempered by a modest pride in northern humanity and kindness, contrasts strikingly with the stridently political and 'national' views of the leading southern humanists.[21] Where Erasmus criticized the Church, condemned purely external forms of worship, and censured the papacy in measured terms, the southern humanists excoriated Rome in torrents of bitter antipapalism. Moreover, although Agricola provided a role model for the Germans, they lacked the kind of common background provided by the Deventer Latin school for many of the Christian humanists before they embarked on university study or travelled to Italy.

The shared experiences of the southern humanists were somewhat different. They too travelled to Italy, and many stayed there for several years. Like the Christian humanists, they also reacted to that experience, and subsequently developed their ideas on the solid foundation of Christianity, a religious framework that was then further reinforced by the ideas of Erasmus and others. But they also inhabited a different political world remote from Deventer. In Alsace, Upper Germany, and Austria, humanism developed at the same time as the German Reich began to crystallize. Many of these humanists found in the Reich, which they recognized as the result of the *translatio imperii*, an institutional anchor for their own enterprise, a *translatio studii*. They came to see in Maximilian I a figurehead for the new age that was dawning. Maximilian himself, fired by heroic ambitions for his empire, was more than happy to play the role of phoenix. Equally, Maximilian sought the cooperation of the humanists for more practical reasons. Like many German princes, he was eager to harness the new learning in the service of the emerging state and the humanists were invaluable propagandists in his struggles with the papacy around 1500.[22]

It is not clear just how effective the attempt to build up a humanist clientele network was. The title of poet laureate undoubtedly became much sought after and there is evidence that some at least not only took their literary duties seriously but also worked hard at extending networks among students at their home university and friends in the humanist republic.[23] The geographical focus of this literary Reich, mirroring that of the political one, was on central and southern Germany, with a particularly intense area of activity in Alsace, the frontier area most under threat from France. Jacob Wimpfeling (1450–1528) of Schlettstadt, for example, was not a laureate, but he was a tireless propagandist for the Reich nonetheless, and resigned his academic post in Heidelberg in 1501 in disgust when the Elector seemed to be conspiring with France against the emperor. Others, like Ulrich von

---

[21] Stadtwald, *Popes*, 78–9.   [22] Stadtwald, *Popes*, 206.
[23] Mertens, 'poeta laureatus', 160–5; Flood, *Poets laureate*, i, lxxxviii–ciii. See also pp. 54–5.

Hutten, crowned in 1518, became disillusioned with Maximilian and ended up supporting the Reformation.[24] Yet Hutten's frustration with the emperor's politics did not by any means detract from his patriotism or propagandist activity in the cause of the Reich. To give two further examples, both Conrad Peutinger (1465–1547), patrician of Augsburg, and Willibald Pirckheimer (1470–1530), patrician of Nuremberg, collaborated with Maximilian in various literary political projects. Peutinger advised Maximilian on the construction of his imperial tomb at Innsbruck and was responsible for Hutten's coronation. Yet, like Pirckheimer, he himself was not a crowned laureate and, again like Pirckheimer, he participated in his native city's turn to Protestantism.

It is as difficult to speak of pro-imperial and anti-imperial camps in this context as it is to do so in the context of the debate over imperial reform during 1495–1500. A literary commitment to the Reich could manifest itself in a variety of ways without necessarily being one or the other in any straightforward sense.[25] Humanists such as Heinrich Bebel (1472–1518, from Württemberg), Jacob Wimpfeling (from Alsace), or Johannes Aventinus (1477–1534, from Bavaria) combined their patriotism with regard to the Reich with a strong sense of regional or territorial loyalty, aware at all times that the unity of the 'nation' was based on the common interests of its multiple 'lands' or 'peoples'.[26]

Whatever their differences of interest and emphasis, these writings of the humanists were all inspired by a common source. The debate in which they engaged was prompted by the rediscovery of the text of Tacitus's *Germania* around 1455. This provided for the first time the possibility of a history of the Germans that was distinct from the history of the Reich. The humanists thus placed the key medieval notion of the *translatio imperii*, the idea that the Holy Roman Empire represented a continuation of the Roman Empire, in a new perspective. It was not long before some began to dismiss the theory of Roman origins as nothing but fiction.

The history of *Germania*'s reception is complex. Though it was published for the first time in 1472, its contents had already been known north of the Alps through contacts with Italian scholars.[27] Tacitus's theme was the analysis of the reasons for the failure of the Romans under Trajan's leadership to subjugate the German provinces. His ethnographical and historical study of the Germanic tribes set their positive virtues and strengths against the incipient decadence of the culture and society of the Roman Empire. It is true that Tacitus pointed out vices as well as virtues. The virtues of the Germans—courage, loyalty, monogamy, simplicity, religiosity—shone primarily when they were at war, he wrote, and made them highly effective warriors. At other times, they slept and ate, and above all drank excessively and quarrelled bitterly among themselves. But perhaps Tacitus's most

---

[24] See pp. 56, 112–14.   [25] Rabe, *Geschichte*, 160–7.
[26] Mertens, 'poeta laureatus', 165–72.
[27] Tacitus, *Germania*, 50–66. The introduction by Gerhard Perl (pp. 50–66) gives perhaps the clearest account of the rediscovery and early printing history of the text. See also Münkler, Grünberger, and Mayer, *Nationenbildung*, 163–233 and Krebs, 'Dangerous book', 285–8.

important argument was that the Germans were an indigenous people, not migrants but originating in the lands they still inhabited, descended from the god-like figure of Tuisco, to whom the Germanic tribes allegedly attributed an earthly son Mannus, progenitor of all who followed.

The early interpretations of Tacitus's rediscovered work were contradictory. On the one hand, the first Italian humanist commentators, all more or less aligned to the Roman Curia, found evidence that the Germans were backward and illiterate by comparison with the culture of Christian Rome, which had inherited the legacy of ancient Roman culture. This theme was then reversed by Enea Silvio Piccolomini (1405–1468, Pope Pius II in 1458) in refuting the complaints of the *Gravamina Germanicae nationis* of the Frankfurt Reichstag of 1456 that the German lands were being bled dry by papal fiscal demands. Piccolomini invoked Tacitus to argue that the papacy had helped the Germans escape from their original poverty and backwardness. They were now, he argued, a prosperous and highly cultured nation. Piccolomini's predecessors had irritated German scholars by implying that the Germans were 'drunken brawlers, who smelled badly and would not master classical Latin'; he himself provided little consolation by effectively arguing that Germany was a 'cultural political colony of the Roman Curia'.[28]

The implied insults of the Italian humanists wounded the pride and fired the ambition of their German counterparts. Tacitus's text provided the themes. His assertion that the Germans were 'indigenae' and his lack of clarity and precision about their origins inspired a flood of writings over the next half-century.

Some, such as Heinrich Bebel and Conrad Celtis (1459–1508), pursued the implications of the notion that the Germans were an 'original' people.[29] If the Germans were indeed 'indigenae' and they still inhabited their original lands, then those lands must now be defended. That duty, they argued, fell to Emperor Maximilian. There were also broader implications. Celtis, for example, contradicted all previous attempts to prove the common descent of Germans and Greeks, arguing that both were descended from the far more ancient Druids. Celtis thus maintained the link between the Germans and the ancient world, preserving a *translatio imperii* which entailed no major debt or subservience to the Romans. A variation on the same theme recurs in Willibald Pirckheimer's writing; his strident assertion 'germani sunt indigenae' ('the Germans are an indigenous people') led him to reject the need to prove any link at all with either Greeks or Romans.

Such theories overlapped with the second major theme of German humanist 'historical research': the identification of the 'origo' or origin of the Germans.[30] In this context the hints contained in Tacitus were complemented by the startling and fraudulent 'discovery' by Annius of Viterbo in 1498 of the 'chaldaic' author Berosius. The consequent 'revelation' that all races were descended from Noah and his three sons, Sam, Ham, and Japhet, yielded the further insight that Tuisco was Noah's adopted son. His son, in turn, was Mannius (otherwise known as

---

[28] Münkler and Grünberger, 'Identität', 224. See also pp. 53–7.
[29] Münkler and Grünberger, 'Identität', 225–31.
[30] Münkler and Grünberger, 'Identität', 232–41.

Alemannus) the original father of the various Germanic tribes. The Germans, in other words, were both infinitely older than the Trojans and racially quite distinct from the other European peoples, who were allegedly descended from Japhet.

There was no consensus either on origins or on history. Both were the subject of heated, sometimes vitriolic, learned debate over many decades. Nor could it be said that even the crowned poet laureates in any sense followed a 'party line' dictated by the throne. Maximilian himself persisted in a more traditional imperial view than his main collaborator, Celtis.[31] He claimed descent from the Trojans. He subscribed to the view that the Franks came originally from Troy, which made them equals of the Romans and superior to the French, who were a mere offshoot or subgroup of the Franks. Finally, Maximilian wove into his own personal mythology the Roman imperial cults of Osiris and Hercules, whose antecedents he traced back to Hector of Troy. Perhaps not surprisingly, dynastic genealogy bulked larger in the emperor's mind than the origins of the Reich and its legitimacy as an empire of the 'German Nation'. Yet, around 1500, this too was all entirely in the spirit of the humanist discourse of the 'nation'.

Viewed as a whole, the learned writings of the period *c*.1480–1520 contributed in a major way to creating a sense of the unity of the German lands. They fleshed out the idea of 'nation' generated by the political propaganda of the period, with a history, a mythology, and a cultural and linguistic identity. It is significant that this generation produced the first history of Germany (by Wimpfeling in 1501), the first history of German literature (by Johannes Trithemius in 1495), and the first topographies of the German lands.[32] Indeed, it was Celtis's overriding lifelong ambition to produce a definitive historical topography, to be entitled 'Germania illustrata'. He wrote tirelessly about this project and, though it remained just a plan and he died without providing more than a foretaste of the great work, the very idea of it came to be regarded by contemporaries as a major achievement in its own right.[33] Others, more modest in their ambitions, produced real works in hard covers, such as Johann Cochlaeus, whose *Brevis Germaniae Descriptio* ('Brief Description of Germany', 1512) provided a popular account of 'Germania' as the lands where the German language was spoken.[34]

The role of these individuals in Maximilian's imperial enterprise and as exponents of an early German 'national' identity has already been considered.[35] Here, the way their interests were shaped by the context of the Reich is relevant. The point is illustrated by the figure of Conrad Celtis, often styled the 'archhumanist'.[36] Celtis had been taught by Agricola in Heidelberg in 1484–5, travelled to Rome and other Italian cities in 1486–7, and was crowned the first German imperial laureate in 1487. Inspired by the Roman academy, his grand scheme for a galaxy of humanist academies in the Reich led him to found literary sodalities in Heidelberg, Augsburg, Regensburg, Olmütz, Cracow, Vienna, and Prague, and even a Sodalitas Baltica in

[31] Garber, 'Nationalismus', 28.   [32] Moraw, 'Voraussetzungen', 101.
[33] Strauss, *Germany*, 22–5.   [34] Schmidt, *Geschichte*, 49–50.   [35] See pp. 37–8.
[36] *ADB*, iv, 82–8; *NDB*, iii, 181–3; Killy, *Lexikon*, ii, 395–400.

Lübeck (which failed).[37] These efforts to create a literary infrastructure for the Reich were the natural complement to his tireless efforts to construct a medieval German literary canon, to sing the praises of German letters, and to proclaim the new era of reform he envisaged for the Reich. And reform meant renewal in the widest sense: the renewal of society and religion, as well as the renewal of imperial institutions.

The imperial patriotism of Celtis thus embraced the notion of reform of the Church. For all his vituperation against Rome, he did not reject the Roman Church or preach some pagan Nordic or Germanic rebellion against it. He envisaged that the Church would continue to exist, albeit a reformed Church. Indeed, his whole thinking was based on presuppositions similar to those that inspired Erasmus. A commitment to the new studies was fundamental. Yet these were to be firmly translated on to Christian German soil. They were to serve as a means of achieving the proper measure of true virtue and of arriving at the perception of objective truth. That truth was embodied in the laws of nature, in which God himself was the highest creative power. The individual who is capable of achieving this highest level of knowledge and insight thus models himself on the image of Christ and he thereby realizes mankind's most noble vocation.[38]

The same kind of basic philosophy combined with an even more trenchant antipapalism suffused the work of Ulrich von Hutten, often regarded as Celtis's successor.[39] The son of a Franconian knight, one of an extensive clan with numerous castles and considerable lands north-west of Würzburg, Hutten was sent to the Abbey of Fulda in 1499 at the age of eleven. His family intended him for a career in the Reichskirche, starting with the 'local' foundation to which the lower nobility of the region presented their sons. In 1503, he went to Erfurt to complete the two years of study necessary to proceed with his vocation as a monk. Instead of returning to Fulda, however, he embarked on an extended academic tour with his friend Johann Jäger (the humanist Crotus Rubeanus).

In 1512, Hutten travelled to Italy, where his father apparently hoped he would complete a law degree in Pavia and Bologna. Once more he frustrated his father's plans: when his money ran out he enlisted with Maximilian's army in northern Italy. In 1514, he returned to Germany and entered the service of Albrecht of Brandenburg, the Elector Archbishop of Mainz, who financed a second trip to Italy in the hope that Hutten might complete his legal studies. Shortly before he left he became involved in the controversy surrounding the publication of the first volume of *Epistolae virorum obscurorum*, which apparently inspired him to pen the second volume during his next period in Italy.

Though the influence of Celtis was profound, Hutten was more than just his literary heir. He played a crucial role in elaborating the mythical figure of Arminius or Hermann following the rediscovery in 1509 of Tacitus's *Annales*, which gave the first historical account of the victory of the Germans over the Romans in AD 9.[40] Hutten's noble origins and his early experiences in the Church also fostered a

[37] *ADB*, iv, 84–6; Spitz, *Celtis*, 45–62.   [38] Killy, *Lexikon*, ii, 397.
[39] Vogler, 'Ulrich von Hutten'; Gräter, *Hutten*; Killy, *Lexikon*, vi, 27–30.
[40] Münkler, Grünberger, and Mayer, *Nationenbildung*, 263–71.

sharper focus on the political implications of humanist criticism of the Church. His encounter with Erasmus in August 1514, the beginning of a friendship that lasted for some five years, was a further defining moment.[41]

Hutten was fired with enthusiasm for Erasmus's critique of the Church and its scholastic theologians and for the promise of a general reform. His second stay in Italy was also crucial. Once more he failed to gain his academic legal qualification, though his coronation as poet laureate on his return carried with it the status of a doctorate, which finally qualified him for appointment as a learned councillor ('gelehrter Hofrat') in Mainz. Rather than pursue legal studies, he now immersed himself in humanist learning and in writing. It had been crucial that in Bologna, just before his return, he had read Lorenzo Valla's critical edition of the forged Donation of Constantine, which exposed as fraudulent the popes' claim to have received from Emperor Constantine authority over the Western Empire. For Hutten this was a key experience. Valla's text reinforced his disapproval of the dissolute lifestyle of Julius II and it provided a legal justification for his consequent denial of the pope's right to grant or deny absolution from sin. Hutten returned to Mainz in the summer of 1517 already imbued with a mission to liberate the Germans from the Roman yoke.

The first salvo in this campaign soon followed, with the publication of a German edition of Valla's work, which Hutten provocatively dedicated to Leo X. This, in turn, formed the prelude to his participation, as councillor of the Elector Archbishop of Mainz, in the Augsburg Reichstag in July–September 1518. Hutten was not the only humanist present, but few were more active than he in agitating on the second great issue of the meeting after the question of the imperial succession: the pope's request for money to finance a crusade against the Turks.

In response, the Estates confronted the Papal Legate, Thomas Cajetan, with a new version of their *Gravamina* based on the compilation made in 1510 by the Nuremberg humanist, patrician, and city magistrate, Willibald Pirckheimer. Hutten was commissioned by his archbishop to write an oration urging the Estates to support the emperor and the pope in their opposition to the Turks. Unable to repress his by now almost pathological anti-Romanism, Hutten laced his advocacy of the crusade with caustic remarks about the greed of the papacy and the injustice of its exploitation of the Germans. His oration, which cunningly combined the positions of both the pope and the German Estates, was published too late to have any effect on the deliberations.[42] Yet the Reichstag and Hutten's literary activity during it marked a new phase in his career as a political activist and as a truly national figure in the Reich.

The following year he left the archbishop's service. After another military interlude as part of the Swabian League campaign against Ulrich of Württemberg, Hutten attempted to gain a position at the Brussels court of Charles V's brother Ferdinand, whom he hoped to enlist in the cause of Church reform, along with the new young emperor himself. In August 1520, having failed to gain preferment in Brussels, he

[41] Honemann, 'Erasmus', 68–9.   [42] Kalkoff, *Hutten*, 60–2.

sought refuge from prosecution by the Church authorities in the Ebernburg, the castle of the powerful *condottiere* Franz von Sickingen. It was there that Hutten began to write extensively in German for the first time, producing a flood of pamphlets during the winter of 1520–1. His subject matter was now also influenced by the fact that he had come to see Luther as a serious ally in his quest for Church and imperial reform.

In 1518, Hutten had dismissed Luther's campaign against indulgences as a mere squabble among querulous factions of monks. That changed when Luther himself, following his disputation with Johannes Eck in Leipzig in July 1519, linked his theological precepts with the principles of the patriotic-ecclesiastical reform movement.[43] From Luther's point of view, it was an alliance of convenience. The Church authorities, it is true, seemed to perceive a unity of purpose between Luther and Hutten, inserting the latter's name into the papal bull *Exsurge Domine* ('Arise, O Lord') of 15 June 1520.[44] Even before Hutten's early death in August 1523, however, the fundamental difference between their aims became apparent. Hutten was one of the last of the Maximilianean reformers, rather than a serious new Lutheran.

The wider significance of Luther's alignment with Hutten, as well as Hutten's involvement with Sickingen in the Reformation cause, is considered later in the context of the Knights' War.[45] However, the very nature of its hesitant inception is symbolic of the complexity of the relationship between humanism generally and the Reformation movement. The two ran parallel for a number of years, but they did not become identical.

Virtually without exception, the German humanists were proponents of Church reform. The majority of them were also supporters of imperial reform, or at least saw the revival of German letters as being linked with the renewal of the Reich, as well as of society generally. For some two decades before the Reformation the writings of the humanists had contributed to the growing criticism of the Church. They helped generate an increasing clamour for change and raised expectations. From Basle and Freiburg to Rostock and Greifswald, humanist circles flourished and propagated the message to the educated: to students, to officials, and to pastors. The fundamental tenet of humanist methodology, the return to original texts expressed in the slogan *Ad fontes!*, reinforces the impression that humanism prepared the ground for the Reformation. The humanist library of original texts also included ancient pagan texts that had no place in the new theology, yet Luther's work was unthinkable without the new editions of scripture and the Church Fathers.

Myriad influences do not, however, make a straightforward causal connection between humanism and the Reformation. Humanism undoubtedly brought about a fundamental transformation of the intellectual culture of the Reich. It did so, however, in ways that shaped later reformed Catholicism as much as emerging Protestantism. Its aims and ethos were not secular, but deeply Christian and fundamentally wedded to the traditional Church. Humanism aimed at the reform

---

[43] Schmidt, 'Hutten'.   [44] Burger, 'Huttens Erfahrungen', 45.   [45] See pp. 215–17.

of the old Church, not at its destruction. Like the popular piety of which the humanists so much disapproved, humanism was part of the rich ferment that characterized the late medieval Church.

Hence many humanists who contributed to the theological and political/ patriotic debate before 1517 did not support the Reformation cause thereafter. Men such as Reuchlin and Wimpfeling opposed it from the start. Mutianus Rufus had some sympathy with Luther's arguments, but shied away when they became embedded in a mass movement. For others, a protracted period of ambivalence preceded a final split. Erasmus, for example, went to great lengths to distance himself from the upheavals associated with the Lutheran cause before finally, and publicly, breaking with Luther in 1524–5. The cause of that split was itself deeply symbolic: a conflict between Luther's pessimistic view of sinful man and the profound moral optimism of humanism.[46] This tension between the older humanists and the Reformation cause is, however, balanced by the fact that the younger generation of humanists, represented above all by Reuchlin's great-nephew Philip Melanchthon, appointed professor of Greek at Wittenberg at the age of twenty-one in 1518, came to form its backbone.[47]

Humanism proved a more independently enduring force than many of the other lay movements of the late fifteenth century. Indeed, if Lutheranism had not integrated the intellectual and educational elite, simultaneously absorbing its educational ideals, it would surely not have survived. In some ways, it is more accurate to say that Lutheranism, like Catholicism slightly later, was obliged to accommodate humanism as much as humanism had to adapt to the emerging religious reform movement. The political crusading spirit of the period around 1500 rapidly diminished after 1517, however. The humanist core—the educational reform movement—prevailed in the new world of religious division as it had done in the old world of the late medieval Church. Humanist ideals proved compatible with and shaped the new confessional agendas, just as they had the old cause of Church and imperial reform. The ideal of a unified Christianity survived as one that transcended and sought to overcome the confessional divide.

Above all, however, the first generation of humanists had developed a patriotic rhetoric that firmly identified the nation with the Reich. Contrary to the long-held view that humanism expired after the generation of 1500, it persisted in a number of senses after the 1520s.[48] Its educational ideals shaped the development of both Protestant and Catholic culture into the seventeenth century. Its national discourse also remained fundamental to the political culture of the Reich.[49] The rhetoric of the nation was first mobilized by Maximilian I and Charles V, and then briefly taken up in the attempted mobilization of the nation against Rome in 1520–1. Thereafter, it rapidly became the rhetorical core of the ideological resistance to

[46] Schoeck, *Erasmus*, 298–308. See also pp. 147, 206–8.
[47] Moeller, 'Humanisten', 55–6.
[48] Overfield, 'Germany', 115; Meuthen, 'Charakter', 224–7.
[49] Schmidt, *Vaterlandsliebe*, 125–33.

the emperors in Germany.[50] Humanism thus created the patriotic language that persisted in the Reich until 1806: in the constitutional struggles of the 1540s and the Thirty Years War, in the conflicts with the Turks and the French in the sixteenth and seventeenth centuries, in the political struggle over the Fürstenbund in the 1780s, in the German reaction to the French Revolution and the French onslaught on the Reich in the 1790s.[51]

---

[50] Hirschi, *Wettkampf,* 389–412.   [51] Schmidt, 'Deutsche Freiheit'.

10

The 'Print Revolution' and the Public Sphere

The impact of German humanism and the way it shaped the pre-Reformation intellectual climate of the German lands is unthinkable without the new medium of print. The humanists were the first intellectuals who communicated both with each other and with the world around them by means of the printed word. They were not, however, the first to use print as such. Indeed, even before the explosion of humanist publications, the new medium had begun to make an impact in a wide variety of ways.

There is no doubt as to the long-term significance of the 'print revolution'. The printing press proved to be a uniquely potent and enduring 'agent of change'.[1] What was its impact around 1500, however, and to what extent can it be regarded as one of the 'causes' of the Reformation? In 1542 the historian Johannes Sleidan wrote in praise of printing as a divine gift that had 'opened German eyes' to enable them to accomplish a 'special mission'.[2] The reality was more complex. Print played a role, in fact, in all the pre-Reformation developments mentioned above. Despite the crucial role of pamphlets and printed literature in the early stages of the Reformation, the medium cannot therefore be identified as something in itself subversive of the old order.

The invention and spread of printing preceded the high tide of humanism. Indeed, since its invention by Johannes Gensfleisch, called Gutenberg, patrician of Mainz, sometime before 1450, the 'black art' had swept across Europe.[3] In the German lands alone the number of cities or towns with printing presses increased from three in 1460 (Mainz, Bamberg, and Strassburg) to sixty-two in 1500, with a total between them of some two hundred presses. By then printing had become a labour- and capital-intensive industry with at least one workshop in Basle employing about thirty craftsmen.

Before 1500 the bulk of print production was devoted to books, some 80 per cent in Latin, and largely religious in content. This included, for example, about one hundred editions of the vulgate and fifty-nine editions of Thomas à Kempis's *Imitatio Christi*.[4] Indeed, the Church was perhaps the most important factor in the early development of printing. As the Bishop of Würzburg, Rudolf von Scherenberg, explained, the printing of liturgical works was essential to 'revive and bring order' to prayers and Mass books that had 'fallen into disorder and

---

[1] Eisenstein, *Press, passim.*   [2] Eisenstein, *Press*, 305.
[3] Schubert, *Spätmittelalter*, 186–90.   [4] Schubert, *Spätmittelalter*, 188.

disrepair'.[5] Printing thus played a crucial role in the reform movement at every level, from the production of new regulations for the clergy to new prayer and instruction books for the laity.[6] It was with good reason that Jakob Wimpfeling compared printers to missionaries and described books as the heralds of the Gospels.[7]

The new lay movements also generated their own literature and created demand for printed material generally. The *Devotio Moderna*, for example, promoted literacy through its schools and communities, and cultivated the practice of both private and group reading.[8] Early printers clearly followed the example of Johann Mentelin (*c.* 1410–1478) of Strassburg, who in 1466 published the first German version of the Bible and who speculated on the interest of prosperous laymen in reading and, above all, acquiring books.[9] This was a market in which printers first competed with, and then supplanted copying workshops like that of Diebold Lauber of Hagenau (*c.*1427–1468). His workshop employed at least five scribes and fifteen draughtsmen and produced for stock as well as commission over seventy works, both secular and religious, among them a German Bible of which over eight hundred copies have survived.[10]

It is not always easy to differentiate between Church and lay literature, but the expansion of material in the vernacular is a significant indicator of growing lay demand. Between 1466 and 1522 no less than twenty-two complete editions of the Bible were published in German, most of them in Upper Germany, some richly illustrated, like the 1483 translation by Anton Koberger with its 100 woodcuts taken from Low German publications. The same period saw the publication of 131 missals and 62 editions of the Psalter.[11]

If printing had the potential to foster heresy or at least promote the emancipation of the individual from the Church, it could also work in the Church's favour. In 1499 one anonymous Cologne chronicler seemed to predict future developments when he claimed that the invention of printing enabled 'each man himself to read about or hear someone read about the path to salvation'. But this statement was embedded in praise for the invention of printing as a device given to man by God to save him from the idleness and ignorance of the priests: an example of God providing for his flock, rather than an observation of the flock deserting the Church.[12] Similarly, a slightly earlier Low German writer argued that it was a sin if people did not try to learn to read for they thereby wilfully denied themselves access to the knowledge of salvation that had been made available in books.[13] Print, in other words, added a further dimension to what was already on offer within the Church; it was not necessarily an alternative that rendered the Church redundant.

The Church seemed aware of the potential threat posed by a medium over which it had no direct control. In 1485, Archbishop Berthold von Henneberg

---

[5] Schubert, *Spätmittelalter*, 188.   [6] Giesecke, *Buchdruck*, 147.
[7] Schubert, *Spätmittelalter*, 189.   [8] Schubert, *Spätmittelalter*, 271.
[9] Schubert, *Spätmittelalter*, 271.   [10] *DBE*, vi, 264; *ABD*, xviii, 22–5.
[11] Schubert, *Spätmittelalter*, 271–2.
[12] Giesecke, *Buchdruck*, 160; for a slightly different interpretation, see Schilling, 'Reformation', 33.
[13] Giesecke, *Buchdruck*, 161.

of Mainz issued a mandate which, among other things, objected to the misuses of printing and the issue of liturgcal books in German. In 1501, Alexander VI reissued Innocent VIII's 1487 general decree demanding that all printers submit their work to the ecclesiastical authorities for approval, specifically the German archdioceses of Cologne, Mainz, Trier, and Magdeburg.[14] Such anxieties were, however, not exactly new. The activities of the serial copyists who had previously supplied German Bibles, plenariums, and missals had provoked similar misgivings. According to one complaint, they 'turned the treasure of the clergy into the plaything of the layman'.[15] There is little evidence that reading promoted heresy or heterodoxy before the Reformation.

From about 1490–1500, various other genres and forms of printed material gained currency. The growth of non-religious subject matter reflected the fruits of the first decades of humanist scholarship. At around the same time, pamphlets and broadsheets were increasingly used for propaganda purposes. Previously, only sporadically generated by conflicts between princes and cities, such propaganda instruments now became regular vehicles of political expression. To a large extent this was the result of the humanists' espousal of the cause of imperial reform, one of the many ways in which the humanists north of the Alps consciously sought to reach beyond the audience of other literati and patrons addressed by their Italian counterparts.[16]

The leading centre for production of such material was the royal chancellery in its efforts to gain the support of the German Estates for Maximilian's policies, though Maximilianean propaganda was also produced throughout Upper Germany.[17] Other princes soon imitated the emperor's example, while both imperial and territorial officials found use for print as a medium for the publication of laws and mandates, mint regulations, and a whole variety of other documents from grants of a fief to provisions against the watering down of wine.[18] The use of German as the language of government and legislation reinforced the sense of a common German polity in the Reich, as did the persistence at all levels of the Gothic type ('Fraktur') which Maximilian first commissioned for his own writings in 1508.[19]

The Reuchlin controversy after 1510 saw pamphlets being used for the first time in an essentially academic controversy, albeit one with extensive ramifications. The use of pamphlets enabled a more rapid response, but it also facilitated communication with a wider audience; indeed, it made possible the enlistment of that audience in the struggle against the forces of reaction. Ridicule, satire, and

---

[14] Hirsch, *Printing*, 88–9.   [15] Schubert, *Spätmittelalter*, 271.
[16] Hirsch, *Printing*, 137–8.   [17] Hirsch, *Printing*, 100–1; Walz, *Literatur*, 66.
[18] Hirsch, *Printing*, 101–2.
[19] Fichtenau, *Lehrbücher*; Kapr, *Fraktur*, 24–36; there is an informative survey at http:// www.typolexikon.de/f/fraktur.html (accessed 4 May 2011). Luther favoured a wider font known as 'Schwabacher', and his works continued to be printed in this, Maximilian's 'Fraktur' came to predominate. German printers used 'antiqua' fonts only for works (and words) in foreign languages. The rejection of 'antiqua' or 'Italian' was a conscious assertion of German identity and of German pride in the invention of printing.

often downright personal abuse were all weapons that Reuchlin and his supporters used with deadly virtuosity to undermine the dignity and moral authority of the 'obscure men' who dominated the ecclesiastical and academic hierarchy.[20]

The use and dissemination of printed material in the German lands was considerably wider than in other parts of Europe.[21] What is not clear is how far this could be said to have affected society as a whole before the Reformation. Sebastian Brandt complained in 1494 that the number of books was already excessive and that many did not deserve to be published at all.[22] Yet the extent of the 'print revolution' was limited in these early decades. Books were expensive and even scholarly libraries rarely exceeded a hundred works.[23] Pamphlets and broadsheets were, of course, cheaper, but their reach was still limited by the fact that only a minority could read them.

Even in the largest cities, literacy rates probably did not much exceed 20 per cent, while in the Reich as a whole the rate was probably around 5 per cent.[24] The core of the 'reading public' in the Reich as a whole was formed by the clergy, by a long way the largest literate group in society. Indeed, many of the others cannot really be included in the 'reading public' in any meaningful sense; they had 'practical literacy', necessitated by a trade or profession, rather than reading ability in the sense of being able to read books. The only media that touched them and the great majority who could not read at all—those who listened and looked—were woodcuts and illustrated broadsheets. Since the late fourteenth century, the transformations of popular piety had generated a mass market in such things as tokens sold at shrines and other pious images. That market persisted through the early decades of printing and interacted with it, for printers frequently used woodcut illustrations for their books and pamphlets. By the early sixteenth century, the hybridization of woodcuts with print resulted in illustrated broadsheets with short explanatory texts that formed a new lower, and more socially inclusive, level in the print world.[25]

Together with popular media such as the woodcut, the medium of print formed an infrastructure that, potentially at least, provided a system of communication which embraced the whole of society.[26] Furthermore, the popularizing developments since the 1490s, driven by the humanists among others, also created at least a rudimentary form of public sphere within which issues such as the future of the Reich and the reform of the Church were extensively discussed.

The issues at the core of those discussions reverberated increasingly widely, transmitted in one way or another to non-readers as well, for example by the clergy, by being read out loud, or by the images sold by the woodcut trade. The explosion of printed material during the early years of the Reformation showed just how extensive that infrastructure had become. Between 1518 and 1524 the output of the German presses increased at least sixfold, with the overwhelming bulk of material printed relating directly to the religious debate.[27] The total number of pamphlets alone was

---

[20] Walz, *Literatur*, 66–7.   [21] Hirsch, *Printing*, 100–3 and *passim*.
[22] Rabe, *Geschichte*, 168.   [23] Schulze, *Deutsche Geschichte*, 123.
[24] Scribner, *Simple folk*, 2.   [25] Scribner, *Simple folk*, 5–6; Dickens, *German nation*, 105–6.
[26] Giesecke, *Buchdruck*, 391.   [27] Dickens, *German nation*, 106.

some three thousand, many with print runs of a thousand or more, making a total of around three million pamphlets in circulation during these six years.[28] For the first time, pamphlets and popular material became more important than academic or scholarly theological works. Indeed, this explosion was so dramatic that, as Friedrich Kapp pointed out over a hundred years ago, there is a strong case for abandoning the year 1500 as the end of the age of incunabula in favour of 1520.[29]

Printing did not cause the Reformation. In the years after 1517–18 the printers were responding to demand and not dictating the public agenda. Yet they were able to do that because the foundations of an industrial and commercial infrastructure and of a popular market already existed. In various ways printing had played a vital role over the previous fifty years. It had helped create a public sphere in the Reich that was actively concerned with its reform. It had helped produce and disseminate an extensive patriotic literature that reinforced a sense of identification among an educated and aristocratic elite with a German nation that formed the basis of the Reich. It had reinforced the key trend of a growing self-consciousness and self-reliance in religious matters among the laity. It had been instrumental in sharpening the awareness of many clergy to the issue of reform. It had provided a forum and a vehicle of communication for the German humanists, who sought to mobilize society in the cause of its own renewal. If Sebastian Brandt could open his *Ship of Fools* (1494) with the exclamation that now the 'whole country is filled with Holy Scripture', that was not the least achievement of the early printing trade.[30]

One final and partially related development also came to be of enormous significance for the Reich: the establishment of a regular postal service by Maximilian I. Initially, this was simply a device to enhance communication between the Austrian duchies and Brussels.[31] In 1490, Maximilian hired a North Italian postal expert by the name of Tassis to establish a courier service between his two sets of hereditary lands, organized and paid for by Brussels. In 1505, his son, Philip the Fair (1478–1506), entered into the first postal contract with Franz von Taxis. By the time of the second contract concluded by Charles of Spain and Burgundy in 1516, the service was opened to private customers. From then on the service developed steadily both in extent and in speed, with a regular 'ordinary', publicly advertised service from 1534.

While it is not possible to speak of an imperial postal service covering almost all areas of the Reich until after the 1560s, the initial links, first between Innsbruck and Brussels and then across much of Upper Germany, marked an important breakthrough. Within a short time, it seems, private individuals were making use of the service, which created a new medium of communication and defined the emerging contexts of political and cultural discourse.[32]

---

[28] Walz, *Literatur*, 65.
[29] Kapp, *Buchhandel*, 262–3; Schulze, *Deutsche Geschichte*, 122–3.
[30] Ozment, *Reformation*, 16.
[31] Behringer, *Zeichen*, 58–63, 66–76, 99–101, 127–8.
[32] Behringer, *Zeichen*, 101–10. See also pp. 370–1.

11

Economic Landscapes, Communities, and their Grievances

Most humanists envisaged a renewal of society brought about by the spread of new learning. What gave many of their proposals a sense of urgency was the perception that the world was out of joint and the fear that failure to change would result in violent upheaval and possibly the end of all society. At the fringes of the humanist movement more radical voices, drawing on the traditions of popular writing about reform, astrology, and millenarian prophecy, gave expression to such fears in graphic form. Around 1500, for example, the anonymous writer known as the Revolutionary of the Upper Rhine denounced the ills of contemporary society and outlined a vision of a powerful emperor aided by a secret brotherhood that would purge the world of all sinners. These included the clergy and all those who exploited the poor, but also Emperor Maximilian who had allegedly failed in his vocation. After a bloodbath lasting several years, the avenging army of the brotherhood would establish a just and egalitarian society in which a new emperor would personally protect the rights of the common man.[1]

To what extent did such fraught visions reflect real economic and social problems in society at large? Little is known for certain about the Revolutionary. He was clearly an educated man with legal training. He was probably born in 1438 and seems to have lived in Alsace. It seems likely that he was an imperial official, possibly Mathias Wurm of Geudertheim. He had once held high hopes that Maximilian would construct a new imperial order founded on the Habsburg lands of the south-east and the south-west. By the time he wrote his *buchli der hundert capiteln mit vierzig statuten* ('Book of a Hundred Chapters with Forty Statutes'), however, he had clearly become disillusioned and his writing is consequently a sour indictment of the recently missed opportunity as much as it is in any sense a call to arms or a plan for the future. Moreover, there is no evidence that the Revolutionary wielded the slightest influence. His book was never published and is only known from a single manuscript source.

Yet embedded in his combination of humanist imperial nationalism and popular millenarianism is a catalogue of many of the discontents of his time: grievances of the common man against exploitation both by secular and ecclesiastical landlords

---

[1] Lauterbach, 'Revolutionär'.

and by rich urban financiers and manufacturers.[2] It is difficult to generalize for the Reich as a whole. The variety of landscapes and conditions between the Alps and the Baltic, between the Rhine and the Oder, is too great to allow the outrage of one Alsatian author to stand as a description of the problems of 'Germany'. Neither can his work be taken to reflect the inception of a general crisis in German society around 1500. The problems he described were undoubtedly real, and they played a significant role in the upheavals of the early Reformation years. They were, however, highly specific to particular regions, especially the south-western territories in which the author lived. They form part, moreover, of a complex picture characterized rather by growth and expansion than by crisis and decline.

The period after 1450 saw the progressive reversal of the demographic effects of the great plague epidemic of the mid-fourteenth century. This, together with secondary crises in subsequent decades, had decimated the population of Europe. Between one-third and one-half of the population of the German lands perished and the total population declined from roughly 11 million to about 7 million. At the same time, the number of settlements also decreased sharply from about 170,000 to some 130,000, with the result that much of the land that had been cultivated in the high Middle Ages was abandoned and returned to scrub or forest.[3] This devastating demographic crisis affected both rural and urban areas, but it had rather differing economic implications for each. In the agrarian sector, a lack of manpower and a prolonged slump in demand resulted in a long-term depression and, in many areas, a flight from the land to the towns and cities, which further exacerbated the effects of the crisis. For many other cities and towns, by contrast, once the immediate effects of the great plague had passed, the fifteenth century generally was a period of prosperity and growth, with high wages paid by expanding crafts and industries.

The renewed growth of the population after 1450, particularly noticeable after about 1470–80, marked the beginning of a recovery to the level of 1350 by about 1530 and vigorous growth rates continued for some decades thereafter. Estimates of the total population of the Reich are difficult, owing to a lack of accurate sources and the difficulty of defining the area to be considered. A calculation based on the frontiers of Germany in 1914 gives a total of 9 million for 1500. Another estimate based on different frontiers gives 11.5–12 million for the same year (plus 2 million each for the Netherlands and Bohemia, and some 600,000 for Switzerland).[4]

What is not in doubt, however, is the fact of overall growth. The increase was generally greater in the west, particularly the south-west, than in the east. In the Zurich area, for example, a population growth rate of 2.4 per cent per annum has been calculated for the period 1497–1529.[5] For Upper Swabia and the Lake Constance region as a whole, a rate of about 1–1.5 per cent per annum seems to have been normal from the 1470s into the early sixteenth century. In Saxony and

[2] Cohn, *Pursuit*, 119–26; Borchardt, *Antiquity*, 116–19.
[3] The calculation is based on the German frontiers of 1937: Wiese and Zils, *Kulturgeographie*, 68.
[4] Pfister, 'Population', 40; Rabe, *Geschichte*, 42; Schulze, *Deutsche Geschichte*, 23–4.
[5] Schulze, *Deutsche Geschichte*, 13.

the Habsburg lands, by contrast, the rate was lower at about 0.5–1 per cent per annum, though a study of three districts in eastern Thuringia reveals growth of 1.33 per cent per annum in the years 1496–1542.[6]

The impact of population growth was most acute in the towns and cities that had been able to absorb, indeed to encourage, unlimited immigration in the aftermath of the plague. By about 1500 many of them were beginning to experience what felt like acute overcrowding. Even in many rural areas complaints about overpopulation became common. The *Chronicle of the Counts of Zimmern*, written about 1550, claimed that the population of Swabia had increased so rapidly in recent times that the land had never been more intensively cultivated than at the present.[7] Somewhat earlier, Ulrich von Hutten had even suggested that a crusade against the Turks might solve the problem of overpopulation by decimating the swelling ranks of young men in town and country.[8]

This general expansion of population did not, however, accompany a simple mirror reversal of the trends of the previous hundred years. The period of contraction had seen the evolution of significant new patterns of land use and rural activity that now prevailed.[9] Most of the deserted settlements were not revived; when the renewed growth of population led to the cultivation of new land, the increased numbers tended to be concentrated in existing villages and in towns and cities. Significant tracts of abandoned land that had reverted to scrub or woodland were transformed into commercially exploited forests.

In other areas, previously cultivated land was devoted to stock rearing or dairy farming to meet the growing demand for food by the prosperous urban centres. The demand of these centres for wine also accounted for a pronounced expansion of viticulture in the later fifteenth century.[10] The greatest concentration of vineyards occurred in the south and west in Alsace, the Neckar valley, the Lower Main, the Moselle region, and the Middle Rhine from Speyer down to Koblenz. By 1500, however, vines were also cultivated in infinitely more marginal areas such as Holstein, Mecklenburg, Brandenburg, and East Prussia, as well as in Lusatia, Saxony, and Thuringia. In the most marginal regions, these activities ceased within a century, especially as beer gradually advanced to become the staple beverage, particularly in the north. Around 1500, the extraordinary expansion of viticulture, along with the growing significance of stock rearing and dairy farming, exemplifies the increased market orientation of much agricultural activity in the German lands.

The emergence of major industrial sectors also changed both the landscape and patterns of working in many areas. The marked growth of the textile industry during the fifteenth century generated a range of activities.[11] Steadily increasing demand for a growing diversity of products stimulated the cultivation of industrial crops for cloth and dyes and promoted sheep farming to supply wool, by far the

[6] Endres, 'Ursachen', 219–20.   [7] Pfister, 'Population', 41.
[8] Schulze, *Deutsche Geschichte*, 25.
[9] Rösener, *Agrarwirtschaft*, 31–6; Scott, *Society*, 72–112.
[10] Scott, *Society*, 86–9.   [11] Scott, *Society*, 97–101; Mathis, *Wirtschaft*, 22–5, 86–9.

most significant raw material for textile production. As demand rose and as merchants sought to circumvent the restrictive practices (especially limits on production) and high wage rates of the monopolistic urban guilds, manufacturing increasingly moved into the villages.

In the so-called *Verlag* system, an urban entrepreneur would use his capital to provide raw materials and then market the product manufactured by part-time peasant weavers in their own homes. This form of protoindustrialization, which remained by far the most important kind of industrial activity until the nineteenth century, had an immense impact on many regions from Swabia and the Lake Constance area to Thuringia or the Lower Rhineland and Westphalia.

The textile industry thus added a further element of diversification to the rural economy, absorbing labour and generating income (particularly significant in areas where peasant holdings were progressively diminishing in size by being subdivided). It also increased the links between town and country, particularly in the south and west in areas characterized by a proliferation of small towns often scarcely distinguishable from large villages, with less than a thousand inhabitants and sometimes as few as two or three hundred.[12] This, in turn, rendered rural areas vulnerable to 'urban' commercial crises: two slumps in demand for barracan, a coarsely woven fabric of wool, silk, and goat's hair, before and after 1500, for example, generated mass unemployment in Upper Swabia. Increasingly, rural discontent, particularly among landless wage labourers, was thus directed as much against money-grabbing urbanites as against oppressive feudal lords.

More dramatic in some ways, because driven by substantial capital investment and technological innovation, was the expansion of the mining industry during this period.[13] The invention of liquation, whereby silver was extracted from copper by means of adding lead, revolutionized the traditional silver and copper mining activities of central Germany and the Tyrol. At the same time, improvements in mining techniques, in particular new water-pumping systems, also led to an expansion of iron ore mining in the Siegerland north of Frankfurt am Main, in the Harz, and in Thuringia.

Three aspects of the rapidly developing mining sector are of particular significance. First, mining required a substantial workforce: in the Saxony Erzgebirge region mining towns such as Schneeberg or Annaberg employed workforces of between three and four thousand each; in Schwaz in the Tyrol over ten thousand were employed in mining, with some seven thousand concentrated in the Falkenstein mines alone. Such concentrations of labour not only generated demand for food and other domestic products, but also saw the evolution of early forms of labour organization, strikes, and the threat of uprisings to achieve improved pay and conditions.

---

[12] Schilling, *Stadt*, 8.
[13] Scott, *Society*, 101–7; Mathis, *Wirtschaft*, 23–5, 35–9, 57–61, 82–5; Schubert, *Spätmittelalter*, 185–6; Braunstein, 'Innovations'; the essays in *Bergbaureviere* provide a comprehensive survey of the mining industry in the Reich.

Second, increased mining activity stimulated a whole host of secondary manufacturing industries, largely, though not exclusively, in urban contexts. The technique of liquation, for example, was invented in Nuremberg after about 1450 and reinforced that city's position as a leading centre of metal working and precision industry such as instrument and clock making. Third, the relatively large sums of money required to develop the industry came from outside the mining regions. The main investors were urban merchants such as the Fuggers and Welsers of Augsburg, who were the main financiers of the industry in the Tyrol and Hungary in the first case and in Thuringia in the second. Their major partners, however, were the local princes, such as Maximilian in the Tyrol and the Counts of Mansfeld in the eastern Harz, the Saxon Electors in the Erzgebirge, and other nobles. As their need for money grew, so princes became more interested in exploiting their mineral rights, as well as the woodlands and watercourses that were essential for the exploitation of those rights and the initial processing of the resulting ores.

Like the textile industry, mining, though of necessity located away from the towns and cities, was crucially dependent on them. For the cities generated capital and commercial expertise as well as a significant element of the demand for manufactured goods. Of course, not all cities or towns can be viewed in this light. Estimates of the number of cities in the Reich vary from between two and four thousand, depending on definitions, and the date and area of survey. Whatever the total number, it is clear that the great majority of these were extremely small. One estimate suggests that about 67 per cent of all towns were really comparable to large rural communes or *Ackerbürgerstädte* (literally, peasant burgher towns) in which the majority of inhabitants were either fully engaged in agricultural pursuits or were guildsmen with part-time agricultural interests.[14] Only about 5 per cent of towns had populations of over 5,000 and a small minority (roughly thirty or 1.5 per cent) had more than 10,000.

Two groups of cities were particularly significant for trade, both within and beyond the Reich, and for generating the capital required for the development of industries such as textiles and mining. In the north, the Hanseatic League consisted of roughly ninety cities dominating the North Sea and Baltic reaches, but also extending inland down to Cologne, Brunswick, and Magdeburg.[15] Its speciality was the northern east–west trade, though by 1500 links with the Iberian Peninsula had been developed, as well as interests in textiles and mining in Cologne and Brunswick. In the fifteenth century the League had successfully made war on Denmark, the Netherlands, and England.

After 1500, however, the promotion of the interests of the Netherlands by Maximilian and Charles V inaugurated a long decline relative to the economic, and above all commercial, growth of the Low Countries and England. In addition to its commercial and military functions the Hanseatic League was also a money market. It was characterized by small trading firms of between two and four

---

[14] Brady, 'Institutions', 274.
[15] Scott, *Society*, 25–6, 121–6; Mathis, *Wirtschaft*, 71–5; Schubert, *Spätmittelalter*, 147–52.

partners, often formed for short periods of time or for specific transactions. But their activities were based on investments made by a wide variety of individuals including noblemen, clergy, and even guildsmen and harbour workers. The capital generated often provided the basis for *Verlag* or manufacturing output over wide areas, or for investment in shares, known as *Kuxen*, in mining enterprises established by princes and lords.

Even more significant was the second important network of cities in southern Germany.[16] Led by Augsburg and Nuremberg, but encompassing cities from Strassburg across to the Habsburgs' Austrian lands, this network was not formally constituted like the Hanseatic League. However, the interests of the cities were represented through the Swabian League, through direct financial links with the Habsburgs, as well as through participation in the Reichstag, which the northern Hanseatic Cities did not enjoy to the same extent. Its commercial reach was formidable. It controlled both the north–south trade (including the Levant via Venice) and the Hungarian and Polish trade, and dominated the French and the growing Iberian trade. In the period prior to the emergence of the North Sea–Atlantic economy, the south German cities represented the commercial heart of Europe and accumulated fabulous wealth.

The operation of firms in southern Germany differed significantly from the operation of those in the north. They were larger and formed on a more lasting basis. The Great Trading Company of Ravensburg, for example, founded in 1380, with 121 partners at its peak, still had 38 partners in 1497 and enjoyed a monopoly of the textile industry in its region and a major share, varying between 50 per cent and 70 per cent, of the textile trade with Barcelona.[17] The south German firms developed established networks of factors and agents in the places they traded with. Earlier and more intensively than the Hanseatic merchants these firms employed double-entry bookkeeping, kept sophisticated inventories and records of balances, and used bills of exchange—in other words, all the latest Italian commercial innovations deployed in a more dynamic context than existed south of the Alps.

To a greater extent than their Hanseatic counterparts, the south German merchants also became involved in manufacturing and active in the money market as bankers. Above all, their approach to all of these activities was characterized by a drive to establish monopolies. Indeed, the whole point of large firms with more partners, greater capital, larger agent networks, and the like was to eliminate competition. The Fugger family of Augsburg, for example, was descended from a part-time peasant weaver who moved into the city from the Lechfeld just to the south in the mid-fourteenth century.[18] By 1500, they had established a virtual monopoly of the silver and copper mines, as well as of the mint, in the Tyrol. The succession of Maximilian as Duke of Tyrol in 1490 and then as emperor in 1493 laid the foundations of a lasting alliance with the Habsburgs. This brought rewards internationally, with access to the Hungarian mines and to the Iberian trade

[16] Scott, *Society*, 126–32; Mathis, *Wirtschaft*, 31–3, 58–60, 92–3.
[17] *HbDSWG*, 351; Brady, 'Institutions', 271.
[18] Häberlein, *Die Fugger*, 17–68.

(including a pepper monopoly in Portugal and, somewhat later, sheep runs in northern Spain). Nothing underlined the symbiosis of new mercantile capital with political power in south Germany so much as the fact that Jakob Fugger, the only German merchant to be ennobled as an Imperial Count in 1514, effectively financed the election of Charles V in 1519.[19]

However progressive and 'capitalist' the activities of the south German trading houses might seem, they had much in common with those of the guilds; their activities were only possible within limits set by privileges granted by a political authority; in their case, the emperor.[20] On the other hand, the sheer scale and success of their activities made them obvious targets of complaints. Those whose trades and crafts faltered, those at the bottom end of the scale who felt themselves to be victims of the changing times, those among the lower nobility whose incomes were severely hit by the consequences of the long agrarian depression, were quick to identify the merchant princes of Augsburg as the authors of their problems. They were the backbone of the anti-monopoly protest movement that arose in the 1490s and reached a peak in the decade or so after 1512.[21]

Despite achieving a decree banning monopolies at the Trier Reichstag in 1512, the movement failed to achieve any concrete results. Neither Maximilian I nor Charles V could afford to punish those who kept them afloat financially. Yet partly because it was frustrated and protracted, the campaign assumed a wider significance. It united in loose coalition, among others, the smaller Swabian Imperial Cities, the merchants of Lübeck (incensed because the Fuggers tried to enter the Baltic trade), nobles, clergy, guildsmen, and peasants. It was the first truly national and imperial cause before the Reformation.

The campaign against monopolies also linked the discontents of the commercial, manufacturing, and craft worlds with the problems of the Church. For Fugger was banker to the popes and ecclesiastical dignitaries like the Elector Archbishop of Mainz, as well as to the emperor. Moreover, the money-lending activity with which he pleased these various masters was subject to severe theological strictures which condemned usury, unjust profits, and bills of exchange. Fugger might try to promote theologians such as Johannes Eck, who argued for the permissibility of interest rates on investments of up to 5 per cent, and commissioned the beneficiaries of his Augsburg almshouses (the 'Fuggerei') to pray for his soul,[22] but none of that assuaged the outrage of his many critics—Luther among them—who saw him as an emblem for many of the ills of the Reich.

The economic expansion of the German lands after about 1450 thus involved structural changes in various sectors. Those changes created losers as well as winners. The problems thrown up are placed in sharper focus when considered in relation to the social and legal frameworks specific to the various regions. Complaints about the monopolies may have been heard across the whole Reich,

[19] Köbler, *Lexikon*, 201; Häberlein, 'Fugger'.
[20] Schmidt, 'Frühkapitalismus', 91–113.
[21] *HbDSWG*, 486–90; Schmidt, *Städtetag*, 423–40.
[22] *HbDSWG*, 487.

but actual unrest only occurred in certain regions and certain kinds of contexts. Peasant unrest, for example, was most likely to occur in the south and south-west, in Franconia and Thuringia. The incidence of unrest in cities was more evenly distributed throughout the Reich. Both the rural and the urban environments therefore require closer examination. This will both delineate vital elements of the socio-economic context of the crisis of the 1520s and illuminate fundamental structures of German society generally.

Perhaps as much as 85 per cent of the population of the Reich lived on the land. The conditions in which they lived differed widely, however, particularly in respect of the legal constitution of rural life. Virtually none were wholly free. Truly free men existed only in isolated pockets such as Dithmarschen on the North Sea coast, north of the Elbe, or the Leutkircher Heide in Swabia and in parts of Westphalia, Lower Saxony, and Bavaria, where, however, they rarely formed more than 4–8 per cent of the peasantry.

The overwhelming majority of peasants lived in varying forms and degrees of servitude. Their condition was neither uniform nor static.[23] On the one hand, the slow process of the dissolution of the manorial system, begun in the thirteenth century, resulted in an extreme variety of regional and local circumstances, matched by a rich profusion of terminology. A system of direct estate management by nobles or ecclesiastical lords gave way to a system of peasant leaseholders subject to jurisdictional rights exercised by the former estate owners. The unfolding of this process was shaped by the degree to which the nobility remained independent or was mediatized and integrated into the emerging territorial principalities. On the other hand, long-term trends in agricultural production, as well as the demographic crisis and the fifteenth-century depression, had a crucial influence on the structures that evolved to replace the manorial system by the end of the Middle Ages. One of the most important features of these structures was the evolution of new forms of control by the nobility over the land and its population.

It is customary to divide the Reich broadly into two areas characterized by fundamentally different rural constitutions. The lands east of the Elbe and north of the Saale saw the emergence of a system of noble estates known as *Gutsherrschaft*, in which land was managed directly by the nobility and in which the peasantry was tied to the land in a condition tantamount to serfdom. Similar forms of landownership and direct noble estate management, though not any kind of serfdom or the harsher classic attributes of East Elbian *Gutsherrschaft*, also evolved in Holstein and in parts of Bavaria.[24] In most of the western and southern Reich, however, the decline of the manorial system gave way to a system of feudal landlordship or *Grundherrschaft*. Here, to widely varying degrees, the nobility claimed feudal dues and exercised rights of jurisdiction, and the peasantry enjoyed varying degrees of security of tenure over their land.

The system of *Gutsherrschaft* originated in the fourteenth century and only achieved its final form in the eighteenth century.[25] Its essential elements were,

[23] Scott, *Society*, 153–7.   [24] Scott, 'Landscapes', 11; Scott, *Society*, 188–97.
[25] Schubert, *Spätmittelalter*, 79–82; Scott, 'Landscapes', 9–11.

however, more or less in place by the end of the Middle Ages. Several factors combined to bring this about. Initially, the success of the nobility in the lands of recent colonization in gaining judicial rights, in addition to economic rights, was crucial. This gave them a more complete control over their estates and relative autonomy from any higher jurisdiction on the part of the territorial prince. In the original period of colonization, the twelfth and thirteenth centuries, relatively small noble estates coexisted with independent peasant holdings. Then in the later fourteenth and fifteenth centuries the depletion of the rural population provided the opportunity to enlarge the noble estates. Deserted land was progressively incorporated while, at the same time, efforts were made to stem the flight from the land into the cities by restricting the peasants' freedom of movement.

For much of the later Middle Ages the prime motive for these developments seems to have been simply the extension of lordship and control over land and people, an assertion, in other words, of classic noble prerogatives. Then, with the recovery of agricultural prices, especially for cereals, in the late fifteenth century and their persistent rise in the sixteenth century, economic factors became equally important. The large northern and eastern estates were ideally suited to the intensive cultivation of cereals for the north-western urban markets. The fact that in many areas up to three-quarters of the crop could be marketed gave direct noble estate management using direct labour a new economic rationale.[26] It was this which turned tied labourers into serfs during the sixteenth and seventeenth centuries and which led to the forcible enserfment of many non-estate peasants (*Bauernlegen*) into the eighteenth century.

The pace at which *Gutsherrschaft* developed and the intensity of its eventual form varied. Its classic, and ultimately most brutal, manifestation probably occurred in Holstein, Mecklenburg, and Pomerania. Less acute but nonetheless severe versions developed in parts of Brandenburg and in the Prussian lands of the Teutonic Knights. In Silesia, Lusatia, and Bohemia, *Gutsherrschaft* developed largely after 1550, even then leaving significant numbers of peasants outside the system. In Saxony, different political conditions hampered the development of *Gutsherrschaften*, though some did ultimately form. Where the system did develop, it reinforced the basic political alliance and social structure that had given rise to it in the first place. These areas developed in the grip of a powerful alliance of princes and nobles. For the peasantry at large that meant subjugation to the sole authority of a lord.

The German forms of serfdom were not comparable with what developed over roughly the same period in Russia and Poland. They were limited by the social and welfare obligations of noble patriarchal traditions and they were mitigated by the fact that in the larger territories ruling princes frequently undertook steps to ensure that peasants were protected from excessive exploitation (*Bauernschutz*).[27] Nonetheless, this system had profound implications for the development of village society.

---

[26] Scott, 'Landscapes', 10.   [27] Rabe, *Geschichte*, 99.

Despite the harshness of conditions and the brutality with which the peasant class was often treated, these regions remained relatively free from unrest and were not affected by the Peasants' War. Strong communal organizations did not develop because the conditions of colonial settlement did not require it. The original peasant settlers were not tied into the kind of complex field rotation systems that necessitated communal collaboration and hence limited self-government in the western areas of older settlement. Then, as the *Gutsherrschaften* expanded, the villages were subsumed within them. The village became an agency of the noble estate owner, its headman more or less literally his appointee. The commune thus never developed as a vehicle of collective resistance to the lords.

Conditions west of the Elbe in the areas of older settlement were very different. In these lands, for the most part, the decline of the medieval manorial system had given way to a system of peasant cultivation or *Grundherrschaft*. Furthermore, during the period of population decline and price stagnation the peasants had been able to improve their position. Manorial rights were translated into ground rents and feudal dues, many payable in money. Above all, the peasants were progressively able to improve their tenure on their land, gaining hereditary rights, though it stopped short of becoming their property.

This western area was characterized by no less than five systems of peasant landholding, each of which may be further differentiated in myriad regional and local variations.[28] It is, however, perhaps more meaningfully subdivided into two types of area. In one, representing a swathe of territories from Schleswig in the north-west to Bavaria in the south-east, relatively large peasant holdings predominated, their size preserved by a tradition of impartible inheritance, which at the same time generated a relatively large underclass of landless labourers. In the other, represented by much of the south-west, but also parts of Lower Franconia, much smaller peasant holdings were the norm, the result of a tradition of partible inheritance.

To some extent, the difference between partible and impartible inheritance reflected the degree to which the peasantry had escaped the control of their lords: for the nobility, impartible inheritance was a better guarantee of regular ground rents, while the peasantry naturally preferred the principle of division of goods.[29] Throughout the western regions, however, the attempts by the nobility in the fifteenth century to claw back or to extend feudal rights, or even to reintroduce forms of serfdom, generated major frictions. These were most acute in the areas that were later to become the centres of the Peasants' War: Alsace and the Upper Rhine, the Middle Rhine, Upper Swabia and Württemberg, Franconia, Thuringia, and the Alpine lands across to the Tyrol. Other parts, by contrast, such as the Lower Rhine, Westphalia, the north-west, or Bavaria were not affected, even though some of the same problems occurred there as elsewhere.

---

[28] Rösener, *Agrarwirtschaft*, 36–9, and Holenstein, *Bauern*, 30–4, give up-to-date surveys of the classification first worked out in Lütge, *Agrarverfassung*, 188–200.

[29] Schubert, *Spätmittelalter*, 74.

The causes of discontent and unrest were various and there is no common denominator, even among the regions that saw the worst of the violence in 1525. In areas of partible inheritance, the effect of renewed population growth after about 1470 was to increase the number of smallholdings and to inflate the number of landless rural labourers. At the same time, growing numbers of smallholders were unable to profit from the market opportunities that benefited peasants with large farms in the late fifteenth century. In many parts, this tended to open up a new gulf between rich and poor in the villages. However, even in areas such as Alsace, where the size of peasant holdings was not significantly diminished, production for the market, for example of wine or of foodstuffs, was not consistently profitable.

An alternation of bumper harvests and harvest failures around 1500 generated considerable hardship and peasant indebtedness to prosperous townspeople, ecclesiastical corporations, and Jews—all significant targets of peasant unrest in the period.[30] Similarly, areas that specialized in crops for the textile industry such as madder and flax (Upper Rhine, Swabia, and Lake Constance) or woad (Thuringia) suffered both harvest fluctuations and the cycles of the textile market, which also affected the growing numbers of part-time weavers and the like.[31] Naturally, agricultural and craft or industrial crises also hit hard at the landless underclass, which comprised up to 50 per cent of the entire rural population in some parts of Württemberg, Swabia, Franconia, Thuringia, and Saxony.[32]

Particular difficulties arose in regions where political authority was fragmented or where the process of territorialization was incomplete. The south-west of the Reich and Franconia, for example, both areas where the nobility remained free, were characterized by a complex patchwork of jurisdictions. A peasant could therefore be subject to a variety of overlords: to a prince as a subject and taxpayer, to a noble as feudal landlord, to a monastery as serf or villein, and to the court of a count in matters of jurisdiction.[33] The Lower Austrian village in which no less than twenty-seven feudal lords had rights represented the extreme, but multiple and overlapping jurisdictions, each with material implications for the peasantry, were common.[34] In the late fifteenth century, many of those agencies increased their demands or sought to exploit their rights in novel ways. Consequently, the pressures on the peasantry became increasingly burdensome.

The most obvious burden comprised the fees and duties that a peasant was obliged to render. Ground rents and the form in which they were paid (money or in kind) varied between lordships, even between holdings. They could account for anything between 20 per cent and 40 per cent of the gross yield of a farm. In addition, tithes were payable to the Church: both the 'large tithe' on grain and the 'small tithe' on vegetables. Labour services also survived in most areas. In much of the south-west this was limited to a few days a year. Throughout Middle and eastern Germany and in Lower Austria, however, where nobles and monasteries managed their own estates, the drive to increase labour services to one or two days a

[30] Buszello, 'Oberrheinlande', 83.   [31] Endres, 'Ursachen', 224.
[32] Endres, 'Ursachen', 222.   [33] Endres, 'Ursachen', 219.   [34] *HbDSWG*, 373.

week provoked acute resentment.[35] Additional occasional dues such as enfeoffment fees were also payable on the death of both a peasant or of a lord.

Much of Thuringia, Franconia, and Swabia first saw the introduction of this 'inheritance tax' during the fifteenth century. Normally it comprised between 5 per cent and 15 per cent of the value of a holding, though in some Swabian territories the so-called *Todfallabgabe* or *Handlohn* (*laudemium*) was generally assessed at 50 per cent.[36] Even the older practice of demanding the best head of cattle as a fee for the transfer of a holding (*Besthaupt*) was particularly hard on the smaller peasants, who may only have had two or three animals in the first place.[37] In some parts of the south-west, there is evidence that landlords were shortening leases to increase the revenue from transfer fees, or even retaining reverted holdings for addition to their directly managed estates.

It is not easy to say which groups of peasants were most affected by fees and dues. Conditions varied between localities: the charges that hit larger peasant hold-ings severely in one lordship burdened middling and smaller holdings in the next.[38] One thing that seems to have affected smaller holdings and the landless more than most was the drive to restrict communal rights over woods, lakes, and streams. Wood cutting and gathering, hunting, and common grazing were all diminished as industrial demand for wood encouraged more systematic commercial forest management. Many landlords sought to close forests to protect their own hunting; some also obliged peasants to undertake labour service as beaters, which was particularly bitter, as the battue was normally held at harvest time and simultaneously destroyed some of the crop the peasant was prevented from harvest-ing. Similarly, noble and ecclesiastical landlords restricted access to streams and lakes and extended artificial pond systems to benefit from the highly profitable fish trade, in which demand was kept high by the fact that the Church ordained fasting (i.e. abstention from meat) for nearly one-third of the entire year.[39] In Thuringia and Franconia, demand from the textile industry led to a massive expansion of large-scale princely, noble, and ecclesiastical sheep grazing. This required peasant labour services, blighted much peasant land, and restricted peasant use of common lands.[40]

For the most part, the system of *Grundherrschaft* in the later fifteenth century was characterized by intensification and commercialization. This was driven partly by the renewed profitability of agriculture under the impact of population growth, and partly by industrial and craft diversification. In some cases, there was a need to prevent peasants leaving the land in search of better opportunities in the flourishing urban textile industry. The inflated cost of noble lifestyles, the rising money cost of tournaments and similar activities, also played a part.

In many instances, these factors combined with political ambitions: a desire to extend control over land and people in the interests of establishing rights of govern-ment or overlordship (*Herrschaft*), a quality of authority more refined than the simple

[35] Endres, 'Ursachen', 233–4.   [36] Blickle, *Revolution*, 48–50.

[37] Rabe, *Geschichte*, 95.   [38] Endres, 'Ursachen', 227.

[39] Blickle, *Revolution*, 58–65; Endres, 'Ursachen', 231.   [40] Endres, 'Ursachen', 232–3.

control of a noble over his estate.[41] Attempts in some areas to re-establish a form of serfdom in the context of *Grundherrschaft* are a prime example of this. Many of the monastic foundations of the Allgäu in eastern Swabia, among some other lordships throughout the south-west, pursued a systematic, and brutally ruthless policy of 're-enserfment' during the fifteenth century. The Prince-Abbots of Kempten, for example, were notorious for imposing bans on freedom of movement or on marriages outside the community of their own serfs, and for their enforcement of the principle that children of a marriage between individuals of unequal status would assume the lesser status, the so-called 'Allgäu custom' of the 'lesser hand'. Similar strictures were applied by lordships in the Lake Constance and Black Forest areas, as well as parts of Alsace.

The main aim of such initiatives was to create a closed territory out of scattered estates. This gave rise not only to regional agreements between lords for the return of escaped serfs, but also to the formal exchange of land and people. Some of these contracts involved more than a thousand peasants at a time.[42] Even so, this was not comparable with the forms of serfdom that developed east of the Elbe in that the peasants were not tied to the noble estate as such.

The south-west German *Leibeigenschaft* essentially involved the translation into legal form of the obligations implicit in feudal dues and labour services by overlords whose territories were too small to establish political-legal authority in the more conventional ways. By means of the sale or exchange of land, monastic foundations such as Kempten, Weingarten, Schussenried, also some Imperial Knights and Counts, and even some Imperial Cities, created islands in which all serfs were subservient to a single authority. In the course of this 'rationalization' of the smaller territories, the peasants not only suffered heavier burdens but, as individuals and as members of communes, they also lost the relative freedom of local action that had resulted from the proliferation of competing jurisdictions. They could no longer play one authority off against another or exploit the favour of one lord against the harshness of his competitor.[43]

Even outside these lands of the so-called 'petrified serfdom', the peasantry suffered a variety of additional strains under the *Grundherrschaft* system. In the fragmented central and south-western areas of the Reich, regional instability and lawlessness often had devastating consequences. In the county of Leiningen, west of Heidelberg, there were no less than twenty-eight wars and feuds between 1452 and 1524, which resulted in the destruction of some five hundred villages. The war of succession between Bavaria and the Palatinate in 1504–5 laid waste to hundreds of communities.[44]

Where fragmentation and lawlessness gave way to consolidation and territorial control by a ruling prince, the peasantry again experienced new forms of authority in material terms. Newly consolidated territories required money to pay for their courts and administrations, and much of this was raised in direct and indirect

---

[41] Blickle, *Leibeigenschaft*, 53–74.
[42] Franz, *Bauernkrieg*, 10–14; Blickle, *Revolution*, 76.
[43] Blickle, *Revolution*, 77.   [44] Laube, 'Revolution', 35–6.

taxes.[45] Similarly, other financial burdens carried by the ruling princes were rapidly passed on to their subjects: for example, the so-called 'consecration taxes' (*Weihsteuer*) in ecclesiastical territories to defray the cost to the bishop or prince-abbot of his election, and the new imperial taxes after 1495. All of these were translated into new burdens on the peasantry and levied upon them by a more intrusive and insistent administrative machine.[46] The early bureaucracies of the German territories may have been inefficient by modern standards, but they seemed like a veritable Leviathan to the peasant who confronted them for the first time.

One feature that was common throughout the area of *Grundherrschaft* in the period following the dissolution of the manorial system was the development of the peasant commune.[47] This arose from the complexity of the field rotation systems that prevailed in the western Reich and from the need for agreement on the use and maintenance of commons and common facilities. Its evolution was, however, also evidence of the degree of relative freedom achieved by the peasantry, certainly compared with the areas east of the Elbe. In the west, the village assembly came to assume organizational, representative, and in many cases also limited jurisdictional functions. Even so, the village headman (the *Schultheiss, Amman,* or *Vogt* in the south; the *Schulze* or *Bauermeister* in the north and east; the *Heimbürger* in central regions) was generally appointed by the local lord; or his election was dependent on the approval of the local lord.[48]

The village community was far from being a homogeneous body that represented the solidarity of the peasantry against their lords.[49] For one thing, the commune itself was divided internally between the prosperous, the middling, and the landless. The fact that the head of the community was an appointee underlines the degree of cooperation that came about on a day-to-day basis between peasantry and feudal lords. Landlords, after all, could only lose from poor relations with their tenants which might, for example, result in poor quality goods paid in kind. Peasants had every interest in negotiating reasonable access to the lord's mill or in ensuring that the lord's village court regulated the maintenance of paths or the rotation and fertilization of fields in a satisfactory manner.

If disputes occurred or relations broke down it was in the interests of both landlord and community to settle them promptly. If that proved impossible, the peasantry was far from helpless. Passive resistance was perhaps the most damaging and disruptive form of action, with potentially dangerous long-term consequences for landlords because it undermined authority and feudal rights.[50] Active rebellion was also possible, and it was an option to which peasants seem to have resorted with increasing frequency during the fifteenth century.

[45] Endres, 'Ursachen', 239–45.
[46] Körner, 'Steuern'.
[47] Schubert, *Spätmittelalter*, 86–93; Scott, *Society*, 48–55; Blickle, *Gemeindereformation*, 13–204.
[48] These terms, and their numerous equivalents, may be found in Haberkern and Wallach, *Hilfs-wörterbuch*.
[49] Scott, *Society*, 176–82.
[50] Schubert, *Spätmittelalter*, 83.

Territorial fragmentation and the extreme variety of local conditions prevented the outbreak of any major 'national' rebellion similar to the French *jacquerie* of 1358 or the English Peasants' Revolt of 1381. However, some parts of the Reich experienced a greater intensity of local or regional rebellion than anywhere else in Western Europe.[51] The least stable areas were those in the south, where communal organizations were most advanced, for example from Alsace across to Styria and from Württemberg down to the Swiss cantons. Relatively few uprisings occurred in the north-west, where rural communes were less developed, or in the regions east of the Elbe. Equally, the Bavarian duchies, where village rights were relatively weak, remained fairly quiet, even though they were surrounded by areas where unrest was endemic.[52]

The majority of uprisings were protests against the intensification and commercialization of the *Grundherrschaft*. They were especially protracted and intense in territories such as Kempten, where the abbots also exploited the remnants of the system of servitude to advance the consolidation of a coherent territorial domain. Here, continuing discontent erupted periodically throughout the fifteenth and early sixteenth centuries. Similar conflicts, for example between the Abbots of St Gallen and the peasants of Appenzell or between the city of Zurich and its rural domains, marked the development of the Swiss cantons in the same period.[53] In Salzburg and in the Austrian territories, but also in Württemberg and Baden, the main objects of discontent were the manifestations of the development of the territorial state itself: changes in currency, administrative intervention, and novel forms of direct and indirect taxation.[54] As it was said in Carniola in 1515, it was the actions of the rulers that 'gave teeth' to their peasants.[55] In other territories, especially the ecclesiastical territories, excessive taxation was simply the logical consequence of hopeless debts; this was the case in the Prince-Bishopric of Würzburg, where widespread resentment fed the spectacular demonstrations that accompanied the appearance of Hans Böheim, the Piper of Niklashausen, in 1476.[56]

The majority of these uprisings were relatively small-scale, though large enough to count as local wars in the context of the small territories in which they occurred. They rarely ended in the triumph of the peasantry. Sooner or later the authorities were invariably able to defeat the peasant forces, often with help from neighbouring lordships or from regional organizations such as the Swabian League. However, compromise was probably as common an outcome as failure, which represented at least a degree of success. And sometimes a ruler, such as the Abbot of Ochsenhausen in Upper Swabia in 1502, was forced to make concessions to his peasants even after the Swabian League had crushed their uprising.[57] Whatever the outcome of

---

[51] Schubert, *Spätmittelalter*, 93.
[52] Blickle, *Unruhen*, 12–25; Franz, *Bauernkrieg*, 1–79. But for some contrary evidence, see Blickle, 'Konflikte'.
[53] Franz, *Bauernkrieg*, 3–9; Blickle, *Unruhen*, 15–17.
[54] Franz, *Bauernkrieg*, 30–41.
[55] Cited in Schubert, *Spätmittelalter*, 96, though with an inaccurate date of 1513.
[56] See pp. 100, 137; Franz, *Bauernkrieg*, 45–52.
[57] Laube, 'Revolution', 56.

individual disputes, serious uprisings were sufficiently frequent and intense as to generate a growing fear of the peasantry. Each served as a warning to a whole region, and in much of the south-west the expression 'becoming Swiss' became a code for peasant freedom and opposition to feudal authority that struck fear into landlords as it occasionally inspired their inflamed underlings.[58]

The majority of these fifteenth-century disturbances focused on a single issue or on a single lord or ruler. Even when the cause was more generalized, as in the Niklashausen disturbances of 1476, where Böheim's 'visions' led him to proclaim an elaborate programme of religious and social reform, the uproar was soon over. When Böheim was executed, the pilgrims, reportedly more than thirty thousand, simply dispersed. The memory of the events lived on in folk memory, but nothing concrete had been achieved and there was no revolutionary postscript or successor movement.

After the 1470s, however, this pattern of irregular, localized, single-issue disturbances gave way to instances of a different kind and quality of activity. From about 1500 uprisings of a more regional, rather than purely local, nature, with wider political, social, and religious objectives, characterized also by a shift from a demand for the restoration of the 'good old law' to the institution of 'godly law', formed a prelude to the explosion of 1525.

Swiss peasants seem to have been the pioneers.[59] In the so-called *Saubannerzug* ('march under the flag of the boar') of 1477, some 1,700 young men from Uri, Schwyz, Unterwalden, and Zug marched on Geneva, which had failed to pay a tribute agreed in 1475 when Swiss forces spared the city from plunder in the Burgundian war. The aim of these 'men of the just life', as they were called in contemporary chronicles, was to claim the money forcibly and to punish all the corrupt Berne patricians who had connived at the delay in payment. Here a force drawn from several localities gathered to fight a battle of principle, to assert the will of the communes over the recalcitrant authorities. The perceived seriousness of the threat is underlined by the fact that it united the fractious city and rural states of the Confederacy in a rare demonstration of solidarity in the Compact of Stans in 1481, which committed them collectively to the suppression of all illegal assemblies of subjects.[60]

A similar pattern characterized the Bundschuh uprisings in the south-west of the Reich between 1493 and 1517, and the Armer Konrad (Poor Conrad) uprising in Württemberg of 1514, together with associated disturbances in Baden and Alsace. The *Bundschuh* or peasants' laced boot had periodically occurred as a symbol of protest and resistance since the early fifteenth century.[61] In 1493, it became the emblem for a conspiratorial union of the urban and rural malcontents of Schlettstadt north of Strassburg, coordinated by Jakob Hanser, *Schultheiss* (headman) of the Imperial Village of Blienschweiler.

---

[58] Schubert, *Spätmittelalter*, 68–9, 95; Brady, *Turning Swiss*, 28–42.
[59] Blickle, *Unruhen*, 22–3.
[60] Brady, *Turning Swiss*, 32–3.
[61] Schubert, *Spätmittelalter*, 96; Blickle, *Unruhen*, 23–4; Franz, *Bauernkrieg*, 53–79.

Their complaints were wide-ranging: misrule by the bishops of Strassburg, exploitation of peasants by monastic institutions and Jewish moneylenders, unfavourable comparisons of the welfare of peasants in villages belonging to the bishop as opposed to those who were subject directly to the emperor, restriction of traditional hunting and fishing rights, and so on. The conspiracy was discovered before a general call to arms could be issued, but the revolutionary symbol and the catalogue of complaints surfaced again in Speyer in 1502. Now, however, and again in the Bundschuh revolt of 1513 in Lehen (Breisgau) and 1517 on either side of the Rhine east of Strassburg, all under the leadership of Joss Fritz, the various complaints were combined into something approaching an integrated revolutionary programme demanding the institution of 'godly law'. In 1513, the conspirators resolved that they 'no longer wished to owe obedience to any lord other than the Emperor and the Pope' and would 'kill any who opposed their design'.[62]

The Bundschuh uprisings were linked by an evolving programme of reform and by the leadership of Joss Fritz. They were, however, irregular in occurrence and did not constitute a single continuous movement. Nonetheless, the reiteration of the *Bundschuh* symbol throughout the south-western region over a period of twenty years generated an awareness of discontent and a growing expectation, in the minds of both rulers and many peasant communities, of an imminent major upheaval. Indeed, the schemes of Fritz and his co-conspirators assumed a wider significance in the light of a wave of unrelated disturbances: uprisings in the County of Pfirt in the Alsatian Jura in 1511; in the Swiss Confederacy in 1513–15; in Hungary in 1514; in Carniola, Styria, and Carinthia in 1515; in Württemberg (the Armer Konrad or Poor Conrad uprising), Baden, and Alsace in 1514.[63]

Many of these campaigns were conducted in the name of the 'good old law', and were characterized by demands for a restoration of rights subverted by corrupt or 'modernizing' rulers. Poor Conrad, for example, was a protest of peasants and poor townspeople led by Peter Gais of Remstal against new taxes imposed by the tyrannical Duke Ulrich of Württemberg to clear the debts he inherited from his saintly predecessor, Eberhard the Bearded. Peter Gais and his compatriots aimed simply to resist this new and unjust taxation rather than to reform the world.

Despite their limited and specific aims, however, Duke Ulrich's aggrieved subjects in Remstal, like other insurgents of the period, contributed to a more general sense of ferment and of instability in the south of the Reich during the reign of Maximilian I. It seems clear that more than just chronological sequence links this unrest with the religious movement after 1517. The growing frequency of appeals to 'godly law' and the appearance of revolutionary programmes, some printed as broadsheets or illustrated as woodcuts, in which Church reform featured alongside other aspirations, at the very least fostered a receptivity for key issues that emerged from Luther's early writings. Joss Fritz was not a forerunner of the Reformation, no more than he was a throwback to Jan Hus. But his activities made many

---

[62] Blickle, *Unruhen*, 24.   [63] Laube, 'Revolution', 88–9; Franz, *Bauernkrieg*, 19–41.

communities only too liable to see in Luther—wrongly as it turned out—a man who supported their cause.

Rural discontent often embraced significant elements of the urban population. Particularly in the smaller towns, especially the *Ackerbürgerstädte*, and in those embedded in areas of intensive rural industry, the community of interests among those at the bottom of the social scale was strong. The mining towns of the Erzgebirge, such as Freiberg and Schneeberg, with their organized workforces, formed another discrete category, with increasingly frequent strikes from about 1450.[64] Aside from this, however, there was also a tradition of significant urban discontent in many of the larger Imperial Cities of the Reich and in the larger territorial towns such as Magdeburg, Brunswick, Mainz, or Vienna.

The distinction between Imperial Cities and territorial towns is not as significant around 1500 as the degree of autonomy a commune enjoyed and the degree of internal differentiation.[65] The more independent a city or town was of any princely authority, the more likely its magistrates were to be regarded as a ruling authority or government and to be objects of periodic criticism or hostility. The most frequently cited list of such disturbances records 210 serious rebellions in 105 cities between 1350 and 1550, many of them periodic eruptions in festering disputes spanning decades or even a century.[66] Given the very large number of cities and towns in the Reich (as many as four thousand, according to some estimates), it is difficult to assess the significance of this finding. On the other hand, the actual incidence of urban conflicts is likely to have been much higher: the apparently growing frequency of such disturbances in the late fifteenth century at least partly reflects the greater availability of chronicles and other written records. The current evidence, however, suggests that here too there was a particular concentration of disturbances before the Reformation, with nineteen cities experiencing uprisings between 1509 and 1514 alone, and then another marked increase, linked with the Reformation, between 1521 and 1525.[67]

Urban conflicts displayed the same kind of variety as rural conflicts, though there are fundamental differences between city and countryside. Most rural conflicts focused on the demand for the restoration of either an idealized 'old law' or an equally idealized 'godly law'. Urban conflicts were generally the expression of tension between competing social groups, or disputes over constitutional issues that arose out of specific problems. They tended to occur in the large towns and cities and they were invariably concluded by compromise. Despite the extreme variety of local conditions, some broad themes emerge.

There were two forms of urban government.[68] A patrician elite, in some cases an aristocracy, either in fact or by virtue of intermarriage with the nobility of the surrounding region, dominated one. The other was dominated by craft guilds or trade associations, which nominated or elected members of the ruling city council.

---

[64] Laube, 'Revolution', 64–6.   [65] Schilling, *Stadt*, 39–40.
[66] Maschke, 'Stadt', 75–6, 95.
[67] Schubert, *Spätmittelalter*, 131; Blickle, *Unruhen*, 25.
[68] Blickle, *Reformation*, 82–5; Schilling, *Stadt*, 48–9.

In fact, relatively few cities conformed straightforwardly to either model and most urban communes were characterized by a mixture of the two. In patrician communes, the guilds perennially claimed the right to participation; while in communes dominated by guilds, the ruling council inevitably tended to be made up from a small circle of wealthier families, since they were the only ones who could afford to devote their time to public affairs.

Despite the variations, all urban communes were characterized by a similar ethos and throughout the Reich they developed elements of what has been called 'Christian republicanism' during the medieval period.[69] This stood for a set of core values upon which the urban polity was founded. The key to them was a concept of freedom that related to the community of citizens as a whole rather than to the individual. The autonomy of the community, its freedom from any external control, and its right to self-determination were fundamental.

Internally, the urban polity was founded on four paramount principles. First, all citizens enjoyed the same basic rights and freedoms, in particular the protection of person and property from arbitrary intervention. Second, all citizens carried equal obligations in terms of taxation, contribution to communal works such as the construction and maintenance of town walls, or service in the town's defence or government and administration. Third, the community as the collectivity of sworn citizens had the right to participate in decisions concerning policy, not only in administrative matters but also in questions of war and peace, taxation, changes in the constitution, and religion. Fourth, while almost all towns were governed by oligarchies, they were generally founded on the principle of openness, on the assumption that, periodically, new groups would enter the elite and that no one group or clique or individual would achieve permanent control.

Of course, the reality often contradicted the ideal. These were not modern democratic societies but rather examples of that 'neo-Roman theory of free states' that inspired other strands of republican thinking throughout the West generally in the early modern period.[70] In the German towns republican traditions were constructed on medieval corporate foundations. In practice, oligarchic government frequently confounded the republican ideal. Indeed, the growing prominence of trained lawyers and the tendency to apply 'modern' principles of Roman law to urban administration reinforced the oligarchic tendencies of urban magistracies in the second half of the fifteenth century.[71]

If the main attractions of Roman law were its comprehensive scope and its capacity to bolster the claims of secular over ecclesiastical authority, it also encouraged magistrates to think of their fellow citizens as subjects over whom they ruled. Yet the language of Roman law that made this possible may have been helpful in promoting the claims to autonomy of the commune as a whole. Both Imperial Cities clinging to independent status in a Reich increasingly dominated by princes and territorial towns determined to maintain rights independently of a prince found it convenient to cast themselves in the role of a 'sovereign law-making

---

[69] Schilling, *Aufbruch*, 170–1.   [70] Skinner, *Liberty*, 11, 17–36.
[71] Strauss, *Law*, 56–95; Stolleis, *Öffentliches Recht*, i, 66–7.

princeps'.[72] Internally, however, such affectations, which by the seventeenth century led some Imperial City councils to style themselves 'by the grace of God', provoked resentment as subversions of the very principles upon which the polity was founded.

The urban commune was generally characterized by a more distinct social structure than its rural counterpart.[73] In most cities at least four readily identifiable groups stood out. At the top of the scale a small and relatively tight-knit cluster of patrician families dominated positions of political power. Many of them, particularly in southern cities, were involved in long-distance trade; many also developed aristo-cratic tendencies and some eventually moved from the cities onto rural estates. The aristocratization of patrician families was perhaps most pronounced in places such as Nuremberg and Augsburg, which developed close links with the imperial regime in the later fifteenth century and whose leading families embraced humanist learning and artistic patronage. Patriciates everywhere, however, were socially exclusive and reluctant to admit outsiders, though some paid a heavy price for their exclusivity: in Basle, Hildesheim, and Münster, for example, they simply died out.[74]

Second, in many cities, particularly in the north, the later Middle Ages saw the emergence of groups of successful non-patrician merchants. Excluded from the ruling elite, many of these groups, sometimes formally constituted in associations or corporations, became increasingly vociferous in their demands for participation and in their representation of the 'community'. Third, in the majority of cities the craft guilds, normally representing two-thirds of the urban population, formed the main counterbalance to the political elite. The guilds themselves were often divided by major hierarchical differences, the hierarchy of guilds in each city determined by the prominence of particular trades and occupations in the local economy.[75] Finally, below the guilds, whose members were full citizens, were the labourers, servants, and the like, who normally comprised about a quarter of the population, though this was subject to wide variations, as in the new mining towns where the labouring class formed the majority.[76]

If the fifteenth century was a golden age for German towns and cities, it was also an age of their political turmoil. Most problems arose when either non-patrician merchant groups or, more frequently, guilds challenged the authority of the ruling class. The specific trigger of unrest was generally an economic crisis, a change in the currency, or the imposition of new taxation. In the late fifteenth and early sixteenth centuries, as the emperor made increasing demands on the Imperial Cities at a time when they required costly new fortifications to protect against new artillery weap-ons, taxation was a key issue. Between 1509 and 1514, for example, the so-called *Ungeld* or indirect consumption tax was the main bone of contention in most disturbances.

---

[72] J. W. Allen, quoted by Strauss, *Law*, 64.
[73] Scott, *Society*, 34–48.
[74] Rabe, *Geschichte*, 88; Du Boulay, *Germany*, 141–5.
[75] Blickle, *Unruhen*, 11–12.
[76] Rabe, *Geschichte*, 89–90; Maschke, 'Stadt', *passim*.

Discontent among the urban poor, who were hardest hit by such taxes, prompted the guilds to accuse the councils of mismanagement and corruption and to demand public scrutiny of financial affairs and guild participation in their future management. Such campaigns often extended to demands for participation in the management of those 'communal' goods that were in ecclesiastical hands and for lay control over the parishes and the appointment of clergy.[77] The fact that the clergy were exempt from taxation because they did not swear the oath of citizenship, though they enjoyed the protection of the city and exerted considerable influence over it through the ecclesiastical courts, further encouraged both magistrates and their opponents to seek to extend lay control.

The urban movement has been interpreted in various ways.[78] On the one hand, it has been identified as a parallel movement to the communal movement in the countryside, which culminated in a 'communal' Reformation and then, after a few heady years, fell victim to the 'princes' Reformation' (Fürstenreformation). On the other hand, some have seen it as the emergence of a distinctive urban republican tradition, similar to that which emerged elsewhere in Europe, yet was doomed to failure in the Reich in the long-term struggle against the regime of the princes. The perspectives differ largely on the question of whether a republican tradition survived the 1520s. More significant is perhaps the scholarly agreement that the constitutional struggles of the urban communes also embraced the problems of the local Church and that they thus fed into, or came to run parallel with, the Reformation. The very language of reforming theologians—above all, the key term *Gemeinde* or community—seemed to use the same vocabulary as the language of urban politics. The fact that the vocabulary had different meanings in each context provides one of the major themes of the Reformation movement and its reverberations in the society and politics of the Reich.

In notes made at the time of the Peasants' War in 1525, Michael Eisenhart reflected that 'If Luther had not written a single book then Germany would have remained peaceful.'[79] What seemed self-evident to a (Catholic) contemporary such as Eisenhart has been challenged implicitly by the many historians who have argued that German society was in the grip of a fundamental crisis around 1500 or even on the verge of an early bourgeois revolution.

The reign of Maximilian I saw recovery and growth but also growing tension. This created both winners and losers. Overall, there was no objective reason to expect a revolutionary explosion in the Reich. The political uncertainty that attended the imperial succession issue in 1518–19 seemed to focus hopes for reform that embraced the Reich, the Church, and society as a whole, but it was the Luther affair that triggered the crisis that unfolded after 1517. The subsequent spread of Luther's ideas and their interpretation, in many cases misinterpretation or over-interpretation, by a wide variety of groups with the most diverse concerns and interests, set the German territories collectively in motion in a way that no cause had ever done before.

---

[77] Blickle, *Gemeindereformation*, 179–83; Rabe, *Geschichte*, 198.
[78] Schilling, *Stadt*, 89–92.
[79] Maurer, *Prediger*, 24; Baumann, *Quellen*, 621, 635–6.

12

Martin Luther and the 'Luther Affair', 1517–1519

Later Protestant tradition memorialized 31 October 1517 as the day on which the Reformation started. Luther's supposed posting, by means of nailing them to the door of the castle church in Wittenberg, of his ninety-five theses protesting against the sale of indulgences was held to have unleashed the German uprising against Rome. In fact, it is unlikely that such an event ever took place. The contents of the theses became known with astonishing speed to a wider public in the Reich during November 1517, but it seems clear that Luther himself was not responsible.

Nor did the act of writing the theses and sending them to the Archbishop of Mainz on 31 October represent the first defiant act of a premeditated rebellion. On the contrary, it was the extraordinarily fierce reaction of the Church authorities that turned Luther into a heretic over the next two years. By the summer of 1519, it brought him to a point he would have considered inconceivable in 1517: in his disputation with Eck in Leipzig he publicly defended some of the ideas of the fifteenth-century Bohemian heretic Jan Hus and declared that even councils of the Church could err. That public denial of the authority of the Church was followed by ever more radical acts of defiance. The most spectacular was at Wittenberg on 10 December 1520, when Luther publicly incinerated the papal bull *Exsurge Domine*, by which the pope had declared Luther's writings heretical and demanded that he recant.

The demonization of Luther by the Church set in motion two crucial processes. First, Luther himself developed more systematically and articulated more explicitly the basic tenets of his theology that had developed in the years before 1517 but that only thereafter began to appear as a forthright alternative to the old faith. Indeed, it seems likely that it was only now that Luther consciously made his great discovery, that 'Reformation breakthrough' to the doctrine of justification by faith alone that resolved his long-standing personal crisis and provided the basis for his later theology. Second, his position attracted vigorous support from a variety of sources. By the time Luther was outlawed by the Edict of Worms in May 1521 he had already become a charismatic figure with a mass following.

There was little in Luther's background or development before 1517 that made such an outcome inevitable or even likely.[1] He was born into an upwardly mobile family on 10 October 1483 in Eisleben in the County of Mansfeld. His father was

---

[1] The most authoritative account is still Brecht, *Luther*, i. Leppin, *Luther* is an excellent recent account.

of peasant stock. As the eldest son, he was barred from a farming career by the regional law of entail by which the youngest son inherited. After a humble start as a labourer in the local copper and silver mines, and aided by marriage to the daughter of an established Eisleben burgher family, he advanced to become a moderately successful entrepreneur in the copper smelting business. Even at the height of the Mansfeld copper boom, the livelihood of a smelter master who held smelters on leases from the Counts of Mansfeld was relatively insecure and dependent on the capital and marketing skills of the great trading companies. Despite its vicissitudes, however, it ultimately ensured a degree of prosperity and status sufficient to secure contacts among the lawyers and officials of the local towns, in Mansfeld and in neighbouring Saxony. It also fuelled aspirations for the education of his eldest son in preparation for a legal career.

Little is known about Luther's early education in Mansfeld, Magdeburg, and Eisenach. In Magdeburg, however, he apparently lodged with a community of the Brethren of the Common Life; in Eisenach he lived with a family notable for its piety and its patronage of the local Franciscan monastery. Although his schooling was unexceptional, it certainly seems to have prepared him adequately for entry to the University of Erfurt, in the Thuringian territory of the Elector of Mainz, in 1501 at the age of eighteen. At the fifth oldest German university in one of the larger German cities with a population of about 20,000, Luther devoted four years to the liberal arts in preparation for higher legal studies. Though humanist studies were already establishing themselves at Erfurt at this time, Luther seems to have had little or no contact with them. His studies were entirely dominated by the more traditional scholastic mainstream, particularly in the form of the exposition of the nominalism of William of Occam (*c.*1285–*c.*1349). This provided a rigorous training in logic and argument and in nominalist teaching, which was also the foundation of the so-called *via moderna* in both philosophy and theology and represented a radical challenge to the old certainties of realism.

The conflict between the two systems at root reflected a difference over epistemology and language. The realists believed that words or concepts related directly to the things that they signified. Furthermore, all concepts have a universal validity or reality that is knowable by man. Hence the reality of God, truth, or justice may be known to man, in knowledge that has been gathered by the Church and her theologians, and that may be taught by them with some certainty. As Richard Marius has commented, 'Nominalism was the deconstructionism of its day.'[2] Occam and his disciples denied the independent existence of concepts, arguing that words referred only to specific things and that nothing could be known for certain about things that were not specific and directly experienced by us. The point of this was to emphasize that God could not possibly be bound by any universal ideas but that He is free and all-powerful. Fundamentally, He is also mysterious to man. What we know of God is what God chooses to reveal to us. Our reason can only help us gather together knowledge generated by our specific

[2] Marius, *Luther*, 35.

experiences. It may also suggest to us that God exists, though we cannot deduce the existence of God from the study of His creation. For knowledge about the ultimate truths concerning God, or issues such as the status of our souls after death, we are dependent on revelation and faith.

If nominalist teaching trained Luther in logic and argument, it also enlisted his mind in a system of anxiety and doubt. For inherent in Occam's thinking was the possibility that God was unpredictable or that what we think of as our knowledge of Him might be wrong.[3] That gave scope for intense personal anxiety and ultimately placed the Church in a potentially vulnerable position. Emphasis on revelation implied reliance on the accuracy of the transmission and interpretation of revelation by the Church. Occam held that the teachings of the Church were infallible, but many after him had challenged the idea that Rome represented the true Church. Rome had survived the challenges of Wycliff and Hus, but it remained vulnerable to the accusation that its increasingly worldly hierarchy did not represent the living succession of the faithful. Equally important was the question of interpretation. Medieval theology provided a spectrum of almost infinite variety and by 1500 humanist textual criticism offered another route to the understanding of the Bible that was, potentially at least, independent of any official Church guidance.[4]

Though there is no evidence that any of this played a conscious role in Luther's intellectual development at this stage, elements of Occamist philosophy provided the framework for his later thinking. That, however, only began to unfold some time after the completion of his Masters examination, when a dramatic conversion experience took him away from the higher study in law that his parents had planned for him and into the monastic life. On his way from Erfurt to Mansfeld on 2 July 1505, a thunderstorm broke around him and he was overcome by an intense fear of death. Immediately, he vowed to become a monk if St Anne would help him. From that point on he regarded himself as committed to the monastic life, and shortly afterwards he entered the monastery of the Observant Augustinians at Erfurt.

Luther completed his noviciate within a year and in April 1507 he was ordained and began his theological studies. From here his career developed in three ways. In each he benefited from the patronage of his powerful mentor, Johannes von Staupitz, provincial of the Saxon province of the Augustinians and Vicar General of the German Congregation, and founder, with Frederick the Wise, of the new University of Wittenberg in 1502 and its first professor of theology.[5] First, in his theological studies Luther moved steadily through the degrees until he received his doctorate (exceptionally rapidly, owing again to Staupitz's patronage) in Wittenberg in 1512, whereupon he succeeded Staupitz as professor of theology, a post that he held for the rest of his life. Second, as a monk, Luther advanced to become sub-prior of the Wittenberg Augustinian house in 1512 and district vicar for ten monasteries in Meissen and Thuringia. Third, from 1513 he also undertook regular pastoral

---

[3] Ozment, *Age of reform*, 61–2.   [4] McGrath, *Origins*, 12–31.
[5] Leppin, *Luther*, 72–89.

duties as preacher both at the Augustinian monastery and at the Wittenberg city church.[6]

These were years of professional success within what might be described as the progressive and reform-orientated realm of the German Church. There is no evidence of rebellion or dissatisfaction. Even a visit to Rome in 1510 in connection with a jurisdictional dispute among the Saxon Augustinians made no significant impact on Luther's views. His lectures and early writings reveal him to have been acutely aware of the vices of the Church and a severe critic of abuses, particularly in the upper echelons of the hierarchy.[7] But his views were entirely typical of reforming clerics at the time, and it is significant that simultaneously he sharply condemned the arrogance of those such as the Hussites who had abandoned the 'evil Christians'. Luther, by contrast, was a 'critic who had a passion for the church'.[8]

However, these years were also characterized by recurring personal crises that he referred to as 'Anfechtungen' (trials or torments) and by the development through his academic lectures of a distinctive theology that represented, at least partly, an enduring effort to overcome his own inner turmoil. The intense anxiety and fear of death that generated his conversion experience in 1505 continually frustrated his efforts to settle into the monastic routine. However much he applied himself and strove to live up to the monastic ideals, he remained beset by temptations and by a sense of inadequacy and futility. There was nothing that he could do to redeem himself. No amount of penance could eradicate his sin; even the thought of having made a full confession incurred the sin of pride.[9]

Luther's fear of God's judgement and of damnation was correspondingly great. The solutions offered to these problems by his mentor Staupitz, and by the academic theology dominant at Wittenberg, were essentially those of the *via moderna*, reflecting Staupitz's experiences with the disciples of Gabriel Biel and the Brethren of the Common Life at Tübingen between 1497 and 1500. On the one hand, the doctrine of predestination taught that, though God was unknown and mysterious, some were saved while others were damned. God's apparent arbitrariness, and the fact that His choices were not communicated to us, caused suffering to the righteous but the only remedy for that was faith. On the other hand, human beings had a limited capacity to redeem themselves by good works.[10]

The lectures on the Psalms and the Letters of St Paul that Luther delivered between 1513 and 1517 were an extended engagement with these questions, and they generated a striking alternative. Drawing on St Augustine's view of the inherent sinfulness of man, Luther denied that man could redeem himself by good works. Man can only become righteous by accepting God's judgement, and by self-abasement and lowly humility before God. Like Christ on the Cross, man can only be saved after he has been destroyed. At that point, he is both righteous and a sinner, utterly dependent on the salvation that can only come from outside.

[6] Brecht, *Luther*, i, 150–5.   [7] Brecht, *Luther*, i, 144–50.
[8] Brecht, *Luther*, i, 146.   [9] Marius, *Luther*, 59.
[10] Leppin, *Luther*, 75–8.

Although these ideas developed in a dialogue with scholastic theology, Luther's reading, at this time, of the fourteenth-century mystic Johann Tauler confirmed for him the significance of faith, the immediate relationship between God and man without any intermediate agency. Indeed, Luther claimed to have recognized his own ideas in the writings of the earlier mystics.[11]

The development of this theology of humility spawned doubts about the value of the monastic life, criticism of conventional piety and of the ceremonial that surrounded the sacraments, and finally accusations that scholastic theologians were poisoning the minds of Christians with doctrines that gave false consolation and hope. In 1516, Luther launched a public attack in a university disputation on most of the doctrines of the *via moderna*, in other words precisely the doctrine that he was employed to teach. The following year, just before the indulgences controversy began, he published a devastating critique of scholastic theology that hinged on the contradiction between St Paul's pessimism about human potential and Aristotle's optimism about man's moral capability.

The same problem came to dominate Luther's attitude to humanism. He was quick to use Erasmus's edition of the Greek New Testament and other works of humanist scholarship. However, his use of these texts also served to clarify for him his disagreement with Erasmus's conclusions on many issues. Above all, Luther rejected the whole ethos of humanist studies. For one thing, he disliked the scornful tone adopted by the authors of the *Epistolae obscurorum virorum*; Luther's criticism of the Church was formulated from within its hierarchy. But there was also a more fundamental problem. At root Luther disapproved of humanism for the same reason that he opposed scholasticism. In his eyes, both were guilty of Pelagianism, the optimistic view that man had the capacity to redeem himself.[12] Luther's public disagreement with Erasmus over this matter, publicized in an exchange of pamphlets, only occurred in 1524–5. The denial he made then of free will was, however, based on views developed ten years earlier, which meant that any initial alliance between Reformation and humanism could never be more than superficial.[13]

Luther's forthright anti-scholastic views brought him notoriety, larger student audiences than those of the scholastic professors, and a growing following among his colleagues. They did not make him a heretic. The essential elements of Reformation theology were present by 1517, but they did not yet form a new theology that conflicted with the Church. Indeed, Luther himself only realized the full significance of his own ideas somewhat later. In 1517, as he recalled later, he was still 'the maddest of papists, submerged in papal doctrines'.[14]

Even the criticism of indulgences was initially formulated in an entirely unexceptionable fashion. The issue presented itself to Luther as a pastoral problem. Some of his Wittenberg parishioners were travelling across the border into the nearby territory of the Archbishop of Mainz to buy the indulgences being promoted by the Dominican preacher Johann Tetzel. When they returned with their letters and asked Luther for absolution of their sins without any penance or

---

[11] Leppin, *Luther*, 85–8.   [12] Brecht, *Luther*, i, 162–5.
[13] Lohse, *Luther*, 72–8.   [14] Marius, *Luther*, 147.

undertaking to mend their ways, he found himself confronted with a practical illustration of one of the key problems that had dogged his conscience over the last years.

The indulgence in question was unusual only in scale and sensitive by virtue of its timing.[15] It was proclaimed in 1515 following a deal between Pope Leo X and Albrecht of Brandenburg who, at the age of twenty-four, had acquired the Archbishopric of Mainz in addition to the see of Magdeburg and the administratorship of Halberstadt. The pope aspired to complete the construction of the basilica of St Peter; the archbishop needed to pay off the debts he had incurred in securing his elections and by the papal dispensation to waive the canon law that required bishops to be over the age of thirty.

The mercenary nature of the agreement reached was underlined by the fact that the principal preacher of the indulgence, the Dominican Johann Tetzel, was accompanied everywhere by a Fugger clerk, who recorded the takings and immediately allocated them under the various headings. Even so, the full extent of the complex and dubious financial arrangements made to raise the money in advance through the Fugger banking operation and to pay it off using the Fuggers again as a clearing institution were not widely known at the time, even to Luther. What was more evident, and crucial in generating the scandal, was a degree of regional political sensitivity: Electoral Saxon hostility to the advancement of a prince of Brandenburg on its own borders led Frederick the Wise to ban sale of the indulgence in his own territory. Such was the attraction of a papal indulgence, however, that his subjects, including many from Wittenberg, travelled eagerly a few miles to Zerbst and Jüterborg to buy their salvation.

Tetzel's activities intensified misgivings that Luther had nursed for some time about the whole notion of indulgences that promised remission of sins in return for payment. Previously, he had written against the abuse of such practices and had called on the bishops to take action. Now, on 31 October 1517, he turned once again to his superiors, to Albrecht of Mainz and to his own bishop, Hieronymus Schultz of Brandenburg, warning that people were being led astray in the belief that they could buy their salvation. Either then or very soon after, he also sent them, and some of his associates, ninety-five theses in which he set out his concerns and elaborated on their theological implications.

Whether the theses were also nailed to the door of the castle church at Wittenberg, as Protestant tradition maintained into the twentieth century, is now open to doubt. There is no evidence that Luther himself sought public confrontation, or even public debate, at this stage. It is unclear just how the theses found their way into print in December 1517, and hence to a wider audience in the following months. The fact that they did, however, illustrates how the medium of print transformed a clerical dispute that might have played itself out in a local disciplinary procedure into a major issue that soon plunged both the Church and the Reich into a profound crisis.

---

[15] Rabe, *Geschichte*, 212–13; Brecht, *Luther*, i, 178–83. See also p. 101.

The ninety-five theses and the reaction to them marked a turning point in Luther's own development. The theses themselves were formulated within the framework of the traditional Church. Luther argued that the pope himself would surely be distressed by the false doctrine that was being disseminated in his name. At the same time, however, he asserted that the pope's authority was limited. He only had power to remit the penalties that he himself, or canon law, had imposed. He had no authority to grant the forgiveness that is properly God's. Still less did the pope or any cleric have authority over the dead, or the power to absolve the sins of those in purgatory. Similarly, the treasure of the Church was not a reservoir of grace to be dispensed by clerics, but the 'holy gospel of the glory and grace of God' to which all had access.

Nor did the wealth of the Church lie in temporal goods; on the contrary, it was the Church of the poor. The pope had no need of the money of ordinary Christians; his own enormous wealth could easily finance the construction of St Peter's. Fundamentally, the life of the Christian was a life of continual repentance, in which the penalty of sin remains constant until the end. The ultimate goal lay in heaven, but the call to the imitation of Christ takes man through all manner of penalties, death, and hell. Confession is allowed a role, for God does not forgive those who do not submit to their priests as vicars. Indulgences, however, and with them much of the elaborate penitential system of the Church, are placed in doubt.

Luther later claimed plausibly that he had not initially wished to attack either indulgences (as opposed to their misuse) or the pope. There was much in the theses that was provocative and even moderately heretical (for example, the idea of the Church as a Church of the poor or the challenge to the authority of the pope). Yet these statements might not have come to assume such significance if they had not been given unprecedented publicity. By the end of December, the theses were circulating widely throughout the Reich in various printed editions. There was growing support for Luther's arguments and, perhaps even more, a mounting curiosity about how the Church would respond to his challenge. The two bishops to whom Luther originally wrote moved cautiously. The indulgence preacher Teztel and the Dominican Order, by contrast, launched an almost immediate offensive. Luther was denounced as a heretic no better than Wycliffe and Hus. In January 1518, the first complaint was made to Rome, which provoked a warning to Luther from the Curia via his own Order in February.

This furious reaction, particularly the Dominican tactic of placing him in the same bracket as Wycliffe and Hus, forced Luther to clarify his ideas. His aim throughout was to prove his orthodoxy. The result was the basis for a new theology. Luther later described the moment of his discovery of the righteousness of God as a dramatic breakthrough experienced in his study in the tower of the Wittenberg monastery.

Luther's failure to provide a date for this experience has generated huge scholarly debate and elaborate arguments for points as early as 1508 and as late as 1520. A date before 1517 would conform to the picture of a lonely monk undergoing a crisis of conscience that ultimately forced him into public and, initially at least, single-handed confrontation with Rome. That would, however, make it difficult to understand why his Wittenberg lectures before 1517 so persistently understated issues that were later to become the core of his theology. Much of that was implicit in the lectures or was being developed in them. It was only the furious rejection by Tetzel and his colleagues of the ideas presented in the ninety-five theses and his stigmatization as a heretic that led Luther to elaborate a clearer view of what he saw as the truth of the Gospels. In fact, this was most probably a gradual process rather than the dramatic moment that Luther later described.[16]

Luther's key insight developed in the spring or summer of 1518 but matured over the following year, and for the first time it gave coherent sense to all of his unease and dissatisfaction with Church practice. It hinged upon the interpretation of Romans 1:17 concerning the righteousness of God. Ever since he had entered the monastery he had been troubled by a sense of his own inadequacy, by the thought that even the most diligent devotion to monastic discipline would not propitiate a God whom he could not help but see as relentlessly vengeful.

Now Luther saw that the 'righteousness of God' meant something quite different. This was not God's tendency to active judgement and condemnation, but God's unconditional gift, the 'passive righteousness of God', by which the righteous live through faith. Man is not, in other words, punished by an inscrutable deity for his sins as they are committed; as a sinner he is made righteous by a merciful and loving God. His life is a simultaneous process of repentance and automatic progressive forgiveness by God that is completed on death. Man is therefore justified by his faith, rather than by his actions. Faith and grace are inextricably linked and access to them is by means of the word of the gospel: *sola gratia, sola fide, solus Christus* and *sola scriptura* (solely by grace, faith, Christ, and scripture) are the terms that represent the essence of Luther's newly emerging understanding.[17]

Further dimensions were added or elaborated over the next two years as Luther was pressed to recant his views. In April 1518, at the Heidelberg chapter of his Order, Luther expounded his theology of the Cross in opposition to the scholastic 'theology of glory': the true theology of Christ's suffering as opposed to the superficial theology that saw God's works reflected in the actions of men. In October 1518, Luther was interrogated by Cardinal Cajetan in Augsburg. Once more he explicitly denied the authority of the pope and appealed to a general council, and at the same time he elaborated a view of the Church as a community of redeemed Christians, which, as Cajetan saw immediately, effectively meant a 'new Church'.

In July 1519, Luther engaged in a public disputation in Leipzig with the Ingolstadt theologian Johannes Eck, along with Tetzel, the main early public critic of the ninety-five theses. Now he denied the infallible authority of both the pope and the general council of the Church. Repeatedly, Luther was confronted with accusations of heresy and comparisons to Hus. Repeatedly he denied heresy, refused to recant, and rejected the comparison to Hus. Significantly, however, he refused to condemn all the teachings of the Bohemian heretic: like his own beliefs,

---

[16] Lohse, *Luther*, 157–60; Cameron, *Reformation*, 169–73.
[17] Blickle, *Reformation*, 41.

he argued, some of what Hus preached was based on scripture and therefore could not rightfully be condemned by the Church, and the Council of Constance had erred in doing so.

There were several reasons why the Church authorities were so slow to deal with Luther. It was difficult to differentiate Luther's supposed heresies from the teachings of the late medieval Church. Luther also enjoyed considerable support and protection. From the outset his own Order, particularly Staupitz, its head, stood by him. When summoned to Rome to answer the charges levelled in the heresy investigation in August 1518, Luther was protected by his ruler Frederick the Wise. The Elector did not share Luther's views; his piety expressed itself in precisely the kind of externalized display and veneration of relics that Luther rejected. Nor did the Elector ever speak with Luther: they saw each other only once at the Reichstag at Worms in 1521. On the other hand, the Elector's private secretary, Georg Spalatin, was a sympathizer and reinforced the Elector's resolve to assert his traditional rights over the Church in his territory and to deny the right of the Curia to try the case of one of his subjects.

The Elector's assertion of his jurisdictional rights over those of the Curia assumed a particular significance in the special circumstances that prevailed in the summer of 1518. All parties were anticipating the death of Emperor Maximilian. The papacy needed the cooperation of the Elector of Saxony, since it aimed to avert the succession of Charles of Spain and Burgundy to the imperial throne. It was therefore unwilling to alienate a powerful member of the electoral body, especially as the papacy believed the Elector might be a credible candidate himself. The Elector's support was also crucial if the Augsburg Reichstag was to be persuaded to grant the request made jointly by emperor and pope for a tax to support a crusade against the Turks.

Cardinal Cajetan's attempt to persuade Luther to recant at least some of his views was part of this campaign. In the autumn of 1518, the papal chamberlain, Karl von Miltitz, pursued a similar mission when he was despatched from Rome to Saxony to convey the news that the pope wished to confer upon the Elector the Golden Rose, the highest honour available for a layman.[18] Like Cajetan, Miltitz failed to make any impression on Luther. And while the prospect of being awarded the Golden Rose seemed to excite the Elector, and the delay before it was finally delivered in September 1519 increasingly irritated him, it did nothing to deflect him from his steadfast protection of his subject from the judicial process of the Church.

The failure of all informal attempts to induce Luther to recant led to the resumption of formal proceedings against him in Rome, which now ran steadily towards a logical conclusion. In June 1520, the papal bull *Exsurge Domine* was published, which threatened excommunication if he did not retract his heretical teachings within sixty days. Luther's defiant incineration of the bull, together with the books of canon law and other works, at Wittenberg on 10 December then

[18] Brecht, *Luther*, i, 265–73; Ludolphy, *Friedrich*, 411–13.

provoked a further bull on 3 January 1521 (*Decet Romanum Pontificem*, 'It Pleases the Roman Pontiff'), by which Luther was formally excommunicated. Condemned with him were Ulrich von Hutten, Willibald Pirckheimer, and Lazarus Spengler, all known for their approval of Luther's antipapal views. In condemning the group, the papacy made the question of Luther's views into a national issue. The failure of Luther's own superiors to deal with him meant that he now became a political problem for the emperor and the Reich. His personal spiritual odyssey was about to spawn a movement that shook the Reich to its foundations.

III

CHARLES V AND THE CHALLENGE OF THE REFORMATION IN THE 1520s

13

The Reich during the First Decade
of Charles V

Maximilian I's death in January 1519 before the election of his grandson Charles of Spain as his imperial successor created an interregnum characterized by uncertainty and instability. This was underlined in the minds of contemporaries by a growing sense of crisis in many areas of the Reich, especially the south and west. On his election in July 1519, Charles V inherited his grandfather's lands but, as Duke of Burgundy and King of Spain, he brought different perspectives to their management and powerful advisers deeply imbued with a new imperial vision.

Within a few years, however, the eruption of powerful religious and social forces radically challenged Charles's aim of developing further Maximilian's German system. The Reformation emerged from below, yet the ways in which the system came to terms with it soon had profound implications for the constitutional structure of the Reich. Problems outside the German Reich then diverted Charles's attention away from it for more than a decade. By the 1540s, when Charles attempted once more to establish a strong imperial government in the Reich, the religious movement had changed the situation in such a way as to make the opposition of both Protestant and Catholic princes an insuperable obstacle.

From the outset, the history of the Reich and development of the Reformation were so closely linked that it is quite artificial and unhistorical to attempt to separate the two. Any other approach to their analysis would, however, result in a narrative of impossible density and complexity. For that reason, an account of Charles V's policies in the Reich in the 1520s, with a primary focus on matters other than the religious issue, will first illuminate the continuities with the reign of Maximilian. Then the attempts of the crown and the Reichstag to deal with the 'Luther affair' are examined, as well as the nature of the religious movement that soon triggered an uncontrollable series of seismic upheavals in the Reich that culminated in the Peasants' War of 1525. For the next thirty years, German rulers struggled to re-establish equilibrium both in their own territories and in the Reich. The outcome was the Peace of Augsburg in 1555.

It is as difficult to be precise about the nature of Charles V's understanding of his empire, of his policies towards its many different parts, and his attitude towards the German Reich in particular, as it is in the case of his grandfather Maximilian. 'Empire' is the key word that seems to link the reigns of both rulers, and the empire of each confronted similar strategic problems. Yet in reality, the 'empire' of Charles

V was significantly different from that of his predecessor. There was, of course, a strong dynastic continuity of approach in relation to specific parts of the empire, but Charles V's new priorities led him to respond differently to the problems that emerged, particularly in the German Reich.

While Maximilian's perspective was shaped primarily by the Austrian hereditary lands, Charles's perspective was fundamentally western and Burgundian.[1] Indeed, in the first instance, as Maximilian sought to settle his affairs, Charles proved a most reluctant potential successor. In Brussels, as a minor, he had come under the strong influence of the high aristocratic pro-French party, particularly through his tutor and, from 1515, chief minister Guillaume de Croy, Lord of Chièvres. When he came of age in 1515, he demonstrated his independence of his grandfather's policies by adopting a conciliatory attitude towards France.[2] In the Treaty of Noyons, Charles conceded to Francis I the prospect of an inheritance in Naples in return, first, for security in his own prospects in Spain and, second, the abandonment by France of its support for the Duke of Guelders, which might finally bring the Netherlands under Habsburg control. In 1516, when Charles inherited the Spanish crown on the death of his maternal grandfather, Ferdinand of Aragon, another set of interests and advisers added further arguments against his succession to the imperial crown.

However, Charles strenuously resisted Maximilian's suggestion, supported by his aunt Margaret, the former regent in Burgundy and the Netherlands, that his brother Ferdinand might be invested with a kingdom in Austria.[3] Another consideration, which gradually strengthened Charles's interest in the imperial crown and then turned it into a burning ambition, was the fear that it would fall into the hands of France if he persisted in resisting his grandfather's wishes. Also crucial in bringing about a change of attitude was the growing influence over Charles of the Piedmontese nobleman Mercurio Arborio di Gattinara, who became his Grand Chancellor in 1518. Indeed, Gattinara seems to have been instrumental in persuading the young Burgundian King of Spain of the advantages to be gained from uniting his vast and far-flung inheritance with the imperial crown.[4]

Once the decision had been made that Charles would pursue the election, the campaign was fought with determination. Maximilian's attempt to achieve the election at the Augsburg Reichstag in 1518 was unsuccessful.[5] Five of the Electors were persuaded, but Trier remained obdurate and Frederick the Wise of Saxony was unconvinced. Trier was clearly in the pocket of the King of France, whose ambitions to acquire the imperial crown himself rapidly became blatantly clear. Saxony remained genuinely uncommitted, though also influenced by the opposition of the pope to Charles's succession.

---

[1] An excellent concise survey is Koenigsberger, 'Empire'. Kohler, *Quellen*, 1–26, and Lutz, 'Perspektiven' are also illuminating.
[2] Wiesflecker, *Maximilian*, 184.
[3] Press, 'Schwaben', 27; Brady, *Turning Swiss*, 89.
[4] Headley, 'Germany, the empire and *monarchia*'.
[5] Wiesflecker, *Maximilian*, 194–7; Rabe, *Geschichte*, 195–6.

Leo X was crucial in holding up matters in 1518 with his objection that Maximilian's failure to be crowned by the pope, and hence, formally, his failure to advance beyond being King of the Romans, made an election technically illegal, since it would result in two Kings of the Romans. His deeper motive for this obstruction was the anxiety that Charles, as King of both Spain and Naples, would pose an unprecedented threat to Rome and the Papal State. Equally, Leo X also feared that the election of Francis I, who was Duke of Milan as well as King of France, might lead to the establishment of a strong Valois empire in northern Italy. However, Leo X's attempts to prompt a campaign in favour of Frederick the Wise came to nothing, not least because Frederick refused to contemplate a position he had neither the resources nor the power to maintain. The emergence of Henry VIII of England as a candidate was, while more than an idle rumour, hardly a serious proposition, except perhaps in the unlikely event of the simultaneous collapse of the houses of Habsburg and Valois.

Maximilian I's death in January 1519 concentrated minds and injected urgency into the Electors' deliberations.[6] At the same time, the interregnum boosted the hopes of the King of France. His motives were mixed. It was clear that the election of Charles opened up the prospect of an unprecedented Habsburg encirclement of France: in the Netherlands, in Spain, and in the Reich. Thus, Francis I's attempts to exploit inner-German conflicts in Württemberg and in Hildesheim (in concert with the anti-Habsburg Duke Charles of Guelders) in the spring of 1519 were more than just reckless adventures.[7] If he had established at least a foothold in the Reich, he might have hoped to avert Habsburg dominance. On the other hand, the king's interest in the imperial crown was a logical extension of his own royal ideology and aspiration to lead Christendom as the 'most Christian king'. In that sense, the competition between Valois and Habsburg in 1519 was one between two rival dynasties with remarkably similar ambitions of European domination.[8]

For the Habsburg camp and its supporters in the Reich, the King of France represented a potentially destabilizing force. His support for Duke Ulrich of Württemberg and his involvement in the Hildesheim episcopal feud were clear evidence of this. The Württemberg crisis resulted from a clearly illegal action by Duke Ulrich.[9] The Duke was already under a ban and deprived of the right to govern for six years for the murder in 1515 of Hans von Hutten (whom he suspected of having an affair with his wife, Sabine of Bavaria, who was also a niece of Maximilian I). On 28 January 1518, he annexed the Imperial City of Reutlingen. The forces of the Swabian League under Austrian and Bavarian leadership promptly drove him out of his lands for this blatant breach of the peace and the Habsburg advisers cunningly exposed the machinations of the Duke's French royal patron. This campaign had major implications for Charles V's early years as Holy Roman Emperor.

---

[6] Fuchs, 'Zeitalter', 40–3.
[7] Fuchs, 'Zeitalter', 42; Stanelle, *Stiftsfehde*, 1–3.
[8] Bonney, *States*, 79–130.
[9] Rabe, *Geschichte*, 220–1; Brady, *Turning Swiss*, 94–7; Press, 'Herzog Ulrich'.

Equally significant, however, in 1519 was Francis I's attempt to manipulate the dispute between Bishop Johann IV of Hildesheim and the nobility of his northern bishopric.[10] Acting in collaboration with the Duke of Guelders, he supported the bishop in his unlawful attempts to claim back property that had been mortgaged to the nobles of his territory. This was a dispute with much broader implications, since it divided the various Guelf dynasties, with Duke Heinrich of Brunswick-Lüneburg reinforced by French and Guelders subsidies on the side of the bishop, and his pro-Habsburg cousins in Calenberg and Wolfenbüttel supporting the nobility. The bishop, largely financed by France and the Duke of Guelders, won an overwhelming military victory at the Battle of Soltau on 28 June 1519, the day of Charles's election.

From the outset, this first and most violent phase of the dispute was enough to unsettle the entire north west of the Reich. Yet the victory came too late to help Francis I become emperor. Indeed, the whole affair played into the hands of Habsburg officials seeking to expose the machinations of Francis I and to make clear the threat that they posed to peace and stability within the Reich. Both the bishop and Duke Heinrich were outlawed, and by 1523 the bishop was forced to restore the property he had seized from the nobility and to relinquish much of his stem territory to Calenberg and Wolfenbüttel. In the end, this attempt to destabilize imperial authority ended with its effective assertion.

The protracted electoral process and particularly the intensification of the competition between Charles and Francis I after January 1519 made the imperial election an unusually public affair. In an unprecedented way, it aroused widespread public interest.[11] Many nobles in the Reich actively lobbied the Electors, and their constantly changing views were anxiously monitored and reported by the agents and officials of all parties involved. Indeed, interest in the election also extended beyond even the princes, cities, and nobles of the Reich. According to some observers, the contested election even moved the common man in many areas. This cannot be substantiated, and such reports may well have been written up as diplomatic propaganda. However, the fact of public concern would also reflect the efforts made by the Habsburg camp to steer their candidate's claims to a successful conclusion.

The Habsburg cause had to work against the anxieties prevalent in the minds of some that, as Duke of Burgundy and King of Spain and Naples, Charles represented a potential threat to the delicate balance of power between emperor and Estates in the German Reich. Others feared that the Reich would be drawn into the traditional antagonism between France and Spain. Those who had been reluctant to be drawn into Maximilian's Italian wars were now equally reluctant to embrace the prospect of becoming embroiled in a struggle between Habsburg and Valois for northern Italy and Naples.

Three factors were successfully mobilized in favour of Charles. The first was quite simply the traditional loyalty to the Habsburg dynasty as German kings,

[10] Stanelle, *Stiftsfehde*, 1–3.
[11] Laubach, 'Wahlpropaganda'; Schmidt, *Geschichte*, 52–4; Hirschi, *Wettkampf*, 389–99.

mediators, and peacemakers in the German lands. Second, Charles was made to fit
the requirement generated by the propaganda campaign that the new emperor must
be a German prince. It was easy to counter the outrageous arguments made in
support of Francis I's German qualifications—the original brotherhood of the
Frankish and Germanic peoples and the alleged origins of the French royal dynasty
in Frankfurt—with the more convincing Habsburg claims.[12] As a Burgundian and
French native-speaker, Charles's prospects might not have seemed good in this
respect. It could, however, at least be claimed convincingly of him that he stemmed
from 'the most noble German blood'. As the Archbishop of Mainz, Albrecht of
Brandenburg, argued persuasively, if no German Elector or prince could be found,
then Charles was the next best thing.[13]

The third and ultimately decisive factor was money. As well as playing up the fear
of Habsburg domination in the Rhineland and the promise of a French royal
princess to the heir of the Elector of Brandenburg, the French campaign relied
heavily on bribery. The Habsburg camp simply outbid them. The expenditure of
over 850,000 gulden, roughly two-thirds of it backed by solid Fugger guarantees,
was enough to overcome all qualms and arguments. Consequently, after one final
attempt by the pope to promote the candidature of Frederick of Saxony failed
(Leo promised him recognition even if he only secured two votes), Charles was
elected unanimously at Frankfurt am Main on 28 June 1519. With good reason,
Jakob Fugger of Augsburg later wrote to Charles V that 'it is well known and
obvious to all that your Majesty would not have acquired the Roman crown
without my help'.[14]

In some senses, the German Reich played a subsidiary role in Charles V's system.
Clearly, Burgundy, the Netherlands, and Spain came first; the strategic priorities
were the west and the Mediterranean. The chief influence on the young emperor
was his chancellor Gattinara. In his vision of a universal monarchy based on Roman
law and the Christian faith, the German Reich merely supplied the title that would
unite the various realms and give a historical and theological legitimacy to the
monarch.[15] For Gattinara, and hence for Charles at the outset, Italy was the real
heart of the empire. Even more than Maximilian, Charles initially focused on
driving the French out of Italy and restricting the pope once more to his purely
pastoral functions. This prime ambition was linked to further aims that made
conflict with France inevitable: to regain the original Duchy of Burgundy lost to
France in 1477, to free Flanders and Artois of French feudal overlordship, and to
restore the imperial fiefdom of Provence and the former Aragonese fiefdom of
Languedoc.[16]

The grand design seems quite clear: the creation of a Spanish–Italian realm
linked with Burgundy and the Netherlands in the north. However, the political
traditions of the various territories imposed their own limitations and dictated

[12] Moeller, *Deutschland*, 69.   [13] Schmidt, 'Deutschland', 23.
[14] Moeller, *Deutschland*, 71.
[15] For the following, see Headley, 'Germany, the empire and *monarchia*' and 'Habsburg World Empire'.
[16] Rabe, *Geschichte*, 224; Kohler, *Expansion*, 352–62.

policies that necessarily severely constrained the systematic pursuit of any ideal. Charles did not even speak German when he was elected, and he knew little about the German lands. Gattinara did not know much more. First Burgundians, then Castilians dominated the Council of State, the central body set up to coordinate Charles's government of his realms, and it never included a German.[17] The Imperial Court Chancellery included a number of German officials, yet that too was dominated initially by the Piedmontese Gattinara and then by the Castilian administrator Alfonso de Valdés.

After the death of Gattinara in 1530, no successor was appointed as Grand Chancellor, and the Imperial Chancellery, to a greater degree even than before, was politically dependent on the emperor's Burgundian officials in all but purely technical matters. The impression of Charles's relative ignorance of, and consequent neglect of, the Reich appears compounded by the fact that he was absent from it continuously between 1522 and 1530, and again from 1532 until 1540.

Yet it would be wrong to conclude from all this, as some have done, that Charles had no interest in the Reich and that he failed to realize the significance of the Reformation movement and its implications for imperial government until it was too late. It is true that the emperor's return to the Reich in 1540 was the prelude to a protracted struggle to reassert royal authority in a system fundamentally transformed since the mid-1520s by the religious division. That phase, however, stood in marked contrast to the first years of Charles's reign. In these early years, elements of continuity with the previous reign were more prominent at a time when the Reformation had scarcely taken hold. Even at the Reichstag of Worms in 1521, the forum at which Luther made his first public appearance, and which promulgated the ban that formally branded him a heretic and an outlaw, questions of the general reform of the Reich in fact played a more significant role. In the first years of his reign, as much as later in the 1540s, Charles tried hard to establish an effective royal power in the Reich.

Even before Charles set foot in Germany for his coronation at Aachen in October 1520, the electoral capitulation (*Wahlkapitulation*) that the Electors negotiated as a precondition of his election established the framework for these early efforts. Though such treaties or agreements were common in episcopal elections, the formal document drawn up in 1519 represented an innovation in the Reich.[18] It also set a lasting precedent, for all subsequent emperors were obliged to subscribe to such a document. In 1519, the motive for the agreement was the anxiety felt by the Electors at the prospect of a strong monarch. They believed it was essential to summarize the constitutional position as it had developed over the last few decades, naturally with a strong bias towards the interests of the Electors.

The most important clauses of the agreement sought to tie royal prerogatives to the consent of the Electors and Estates, and to minimize the possibility of non-German influence on the Reich. The emperor was obliged to confirm the rights of

---

[17] Headley, 'Germany, the empire and *monarchia*', 22–3.

[18] Conrad, *Rechtsgeschichte*, ii, 71; Rabe, *Geschichte*, 223–4; Angermeier, *Reichsreform und Reformation*, 24–5; Kleinheyer, *Wahlkapitulationen*, 45–69.

the Electors, especially in relation to imperial elections and the vicariate to be exercised by the Palatinate and Saxony during interregnums and imperial absences. Similarly, he promised to respect the rights and dignities of all princes, counts, lords, and other Estates, and to abide by and enforce the terms of the Perpetual Peace. Foreign treaties and alliances were to be dependent on the consent of the Electors, as was the eventual mortgaging of any imperial excises and indirect taxes. The emperor promised to live in Germany and to appoint only Germans to his administration. He further undertook to permit only Latin or German as administrative languages, to promise that he would never convene meetings of the Reichstag outside the Reich, and to guarantee that he would not deploy foreign troops on German soil.

Another measure designed to safeguard the rights of the Estates against the arbitrary rule of a strong 'foreign' monarch stipulated that no subject of the Reich was to be put on trial abroad, nor be subject to an imperial ban without a full prior hearing and due trial. At the same time, the emperor committed himself to various specific reforms: for example, to negotiate with Rome for a reduction in the taxes payable by Germans, and to take steps to curb the activities of the powerful monopoly trading companies. Finally, the emperor promised to establish a new imperial governing council (Reichsregiment), similar to the one that existed between 1500 and 1502, in which both emperor and Estates would work together to remedy the defects in the Reich's constitution.

Much that the electoral capitulation stipulated was unrealistic and much of it was subsequently circumvented or ignored. Indeed, other factors soon intervened to complicate what might otherwise have been another episode in the struggle between emperor and Estates. The Habsburg acquisition of Württemberg, the complexity and ambivalence of the regency arrangements for Charles's brother Ferdinand, the consequent unsteadiness of the new governing council, and the continuing activity of the Swabian League, all conspired to frustrate any early ambitions for a decisive monarchy in the Reich.

Even as the imperial election and negotiations over the election agreement were taking place, events in Württemberg were contributing to a transformation of the imperial position.[19] Once the Swabian League had ousted Duke Ulrich, upon whom an imperial ban had been imposed following his annexation of the Imperial City of Reutlingen, the question of what to do with his lands naturally arose.[20] Charles's German and Netherlandish advisers, foremost among them Maximilian van Bergen, a leading member of the imperial party at the Burgundian court, immediately saw an opportunity to reinforce and reinvigorate the Habsburg system in the south.

The deal that Bergen negotiated showed his desire to pursue the plans formulated a few years earlier by Maximilian I. In return for paying the military costs of the Swabian League's members, the initial idea of a joint Habsburg-Bavarian trusteeship in the name of Duke Ulrich's heir was set aside and the Habsburgs

---

[19] Brady, *Turning Swiss*, 103–15.   [20] See pp. 29, 157 above.

gained exclusive control of Württemberg. Bergen had generated a sense of urgency in the mind of Charles and his close advisers by emphasizing the inherent instability of the area and by conjuring up the prospect that it would 'turn Swiss'. That might even precipitate, he suggested, a more general crisis of the monarchy in south Germany and could result in the triumph of the Imperial Cities. Equally important, however, was the traditional reliance of the emperors on the capital resources of the south German Imperial Cities. They had been crucial in Charles's election, and they soon became even more significant to the emperor's financial system when the Fugger credit facilities were extended to include mortgages on the revenues from the Spanish military orders in 1524.[21]

In the short term, the acquisition of Württemberg provided a major boost for the royal position in the Reich. The establishment of the governing council, demanded by the Estates, yet shaped by the emperor's interests, reflected this.[22] The Estates had envisaged a permanent central council of state that primarily represented their own interests. What in fact emerged following the Reichstag of Worms in 1521 was a council of regency, headed by a regent appointed by Charles and charged with the management of affairs during the emperor's absence. More important than anything else perhaps, this undermined any justification for the continuation of the imperial vicariates of the Palatinate and Electoral Saxony after the election and nullified any historical claims to a vicariate *absente rege*: that the vicars should act as regents during the monarch's absence from his kingdom.[23]

The composition of the council was a compromise. The emperor appointed his brother Ferdinand as regent and four councillors; the Electors appointed one councillor each, as did, collectively, the bishops, the princes, the prelates, and counts; the Imperial Cities appointed two, and the six original Kreise appointed one each. The potential of the council, however, was undermined by the stipulation that the tenure of all non-royal and non-Electoral appointees should be limited to four months and that one Elector should be in attendance, in three-month cycles, at all times. Furthermore, the competence of the council was limited by the fact that the emperor retained sole authority in all matters concerning foreign affairs and concerning the investiture and removal of fiefdoms. Indeed, Charles persisted in sending his own envoys to the Reichstag with instructions that often conflicted with the proposals sent to it by the council. More often than not, also, the councillors were appointed late, and the Electors soon tired of their duty to attend. Finance also proved a problem when the Estates failed to send in the money for the council's upkeep. In 1523, Ferdinand, as regent, was obliged to assume the costs of the council personally and in 1524 he was unable to resist the demand that all the councillors be replaced. At the same time, the Elector Palatine renewed his claims to exercise the imperial vicariate *absente rege*.[24]

---

[21] Kellenbenz, 'Erwägungen', 43–6.
[22] Angermeier, *Reichsreform und Reformation*, 27–36.
[23] Hermkes, *Reichsvikariat*, 1–12, 18–23, 27–46.
[24] Rabe, *Geschichte*, 245.

Ferdinand's response to this challenge and to the forthright expression of the Estates' dissatisfaction with the council, which they themselves had originally proposed, was to move it from Nuremberg to the Imperial City of Esslingen near Stuttgart in the middle of Württemberg. Yet the move away from the Reichstag to a location surrounded by Habsburg-controlled territory, with even more limited competence, finally revealed the council for what it was: no more and no less than an instrument of Habsburg government. A second move to Speyer in 1526 did nothing to change this and it survived as a relatively meaningless institution until its dissolution on Charles V's return to the Reich in 1530.[25]

One of the major obstacles to the effectiveness of the governing council, and to any attempt to build on the successful acquisition of Württemberg, was the profoundly ambivalent relationship between Charles and his brother Ferdinand.[26] Government by regency was the norm in Charles's empire, and he frequently employed members of his own family in these positions. Yet making such an appointment in the Reich was a particularly sensitive matter. For one thing, the appointment of a regent in the Reich inevitably raised the question of the succession and of a possible election as King of the Romans. More so than in many of Charles's other lands, the delicate constitutional balance between emperor and Estates in the Reich made a disloyal alliance between regent and Estates more than just an occasional nightmare. Concerning Ferdinand, the problem was that, as designated co-heir in his grandfather's will, he clearly had expectations that were greater than those that the average candidate for a regentship might have.

The sensitivity of the situation had already been underlined by Charles's vehement rejection of any suggestion that Ferdinand be given an Austrian kingdom. After 1519, the actual concession of an inheritance was slow, and gave the appearance of being granted somewhat grudgingly.[27] The principle was agreed in 1520, but it was only in April 1521 that Charles announced at Worms that he was transferring to Ferdinand all rights to the five Austrian duchies. Then, in February 1522, an agreement reached at Brussels gave him the Tyrol, the Swabian Vorlande, including Alsace, together with Württemberg. Ferdinand's position was not helped by the fact that it was also agreed to keep this latter transfer secret, leaving him, in public at least, simply as Charles's temporary governor and regent. This subterfuge was abandoned after three years, but minor tensions continued to deny Ferdinand security.

The emperor constantly delayed acting on his promise to secure Ferdinand's election as King of the Romans and after 1524 he repeatedly refused to invest Ferdinand with the Duchy of Milan. This might have strengthened Ferdinand's claims to succession to the imperial crown, since the fiefdom of Milan technically belonged to the Reich. For Charles, however, its significance lay in its potential to enhance the Spanish position in Italy, and his reluctance to transfer Milan to Ferdinand reflected his espousal of Gattinara's Ghibelline vision at the expense of the traditions of the Reich.

---

[25] Roll, *Reichsregiment, passim*; Angermeier, 'Reichsregimenter'.
[26] Laubach, 'Nachfolge'.
[27] Press, 'Schwaben', 27; Laubach, 'Nachfolge', 2–15.

These problems foreshadowed the eventual open struggle between the two brothers over the German inheritance in the 1550s that led to the partition of the Habsburg lands on Charles's abdication. In the 1520s, they had less dramatic but nonetheless fundamental implications. Ferdinand was able first to pacify the Austrian duchies and then to embark on a vigorous programme of reform, culminating in the establishment of a centralized administration in 1527. Their significance was enhanced by his inheritance of Bohemia and parts of Hungary in 1526 (though this, in turn, intensified the degree to which he was obliged to carry the burden of defending both his territories and the Reich as a whole against the Turks).

With growing control over his expanding hereditary lands, Ferdinand's position generally became more secure. Yet the extreme uncertainty of the early years allowed Duke Wilhelm of Bavaria to develop serious ambitions to become King of the Romans, ambitions that Pope Clement VII supported in 1526.[28] At about the same time, both Wilhelm and his brother and co-regent Ludwig contemplated another challenge to the Habsburgs in the form of an attempt to secure the election of one of them to the Bohemian throne. Simultaneously, the brothers maintained speculative conspiratorial links with Ferdinand's Hungarian rival John Zápolya, Voivode of Transylvania.[29] In these circumstances, Ferdinand was neither able to establish himself as an independent force in the Reich nor to function as an effective regent for his brother.[30]

The increasingly problematic position of the Swabian League, the central pillar of Maximilian's system for over two decades, further complicated the task of imperial government in the 1520s. The conquest of Württemberg in 1519 was the League's greatest triumph and this, together with an awareness of the League's past role in imperial policy, undoubtedly led Charles to press forcefully for its renewal in 1522.[31] As a force for law and order, the League continued to demonstrate its effectiveness, suppressing with considerable brutality both the Sickingen feud and Knights' War in 1522–3 and assisting in the suppression of the Peasants' War in 1525. Yet these years of apparently unrivalled success were also years of progressive decline. The League suffered from being associated so completely with the Habsburgs over the Württemberg affair. Among other things, this aroused the latent hostility of Bavaria, which soon began to distance itself from the League and to espouse the claims in Württemberg of Duke Ulrich's son, Christopher, a nephew of the Bavarian dukes.

The decision by the Reichstag of Worms in 1521 to revive the Reichskammergericht and to entrust the execution of its judgments to the Kreise threatened to render the Swabian League redundant, since the Reichstag itself now increasingly aspired to act as peacekeeper in the Reich.[32] At the same time, the League undermined its own reputation for loyalty and probity by displaying a dangerous tendency to act independently of, if not in opposition to, the regent and the governing council. Finally, precisely because the League was so effective in maintaining law and order, it came to

[28] Kohler, *Opposition*, 116–18.   [29] Press, 'Schwaben', 30.
[30] Kohler, *Opposition*, 109.   [31] Bock, *Schwäbischer Bund*, 161–3.
[32] Press, 'Reformation', 208–9.

be perceived as, and in fact was, an anti-Reformation force and hence was soon deeply distrusted by those who sympathized with the new teaching.[33]

Within a few years of Charles's accession, the Habsburg system in the Reich was far from secure. Though the acquisition of Württemberg gave it greater potential than ever before, it did not prove possible to exploit the opportunity successfully. Both the reform of the Reich envisaged in the electoral agreement and the regular business of imperial government were frustrated between 1521 and 1524. Renewed discussion about taxation at Worms in 1521 ended in victory for the Estates.[34] They also finally rejected the Common Penny (to be levied centrally on all, including the princes) in favour of the so-called *Matrikularbeiträge*.[35] These were periodic levies to be raised by the Estates in units, either fractions or multiples thereof, known as *Römermonate* or Roman Months, the notional cost of a contingent of troops raised to assist the emperor in his march to his coronation in Rome. No system could have been better designed to accommodate the Estates' habitual reluctance to pay any sum of money to their monarch, especially when help was urgently needed.

The combination of the Estates' continuing opposition to any hint of royal centralization, and the ability of dissidents to exploit the ambivalent relationship between emperor and regent, effectively undermined all of the governing council's major initiatives. Its attempt to revive the Common Penny proposal was frustrated when the cities and the clergy, who would have been taxed more heavily than the princes, appealed to the emperor, who then switched from supporting the proposal to rejecting it at the third Nuremberg Reichstag of 1524. Its efforts to raise money for the defence of the Reich against the growing Turkish threat by means of the *Matrikel* were no more successful either.[36] In 1522, the Estates agreed that the grant made in 1521 for the emperor's journey to Rome (which had not in fact taken place) might be used on the eastern front, but only once it became clear how much would be forthcoming from Hungary. Owing to the chaos that prevailed in Hungarian affairs, that information did not emerge, and so the money was not raised until 1529 (the grant made in 1530 was only paid out in 1542).

Other major reform proposals suffered the same fate as the taxation plan. A scheme for an imperial frontier tax (a combined 4 per cent import and export duty to be levied on all non-subsistence goods) failed in 1524, when the emperor once more gave way to the protests of the Imperial Cities.[37] Similarly, a proposal to limit the size of capital and the activities of the south German commercial houses (demonized as monopolies in popular literature and political discussion since the early years of the century), accepted in 1522–3, failed after an urban delegation petitioned the emperor in Valladolid in August 1523.[38] Charles ordered

[33] Bock, *Schwäbischer Bund*, 199–200.
[34] Rabe, *Geschichte*, 246–8; Schmid, 'Reichssteuern'.
[35] Schmid, 'Reichssteuern', 163–73; Isenmann, 'Reichsfinanzen', 195–8. Schmid, *Gemeiner Pfennig* gives a comprehensive account of this tax.
[36] Angermeier, *Reichsreform 1410–1555*, 237–40.
[37] Rabe, *Geschichte*, 248.
[38] Rabe, *Geschichte*, 248–50; Brady, *Turning Swiss*, 127–50; Blaich, *Reichsmonopolgesetzgebung, passim*.

the legal proceedings begun against Fuggers and others to be halted. He then thwarted the reform in 1525 with a decree that redefined the issue to exclude all ore and metal trading, which effectively reprieved all of the large companies that the campaign had always targeted.

The frontier tax and the anti-monopoly initiatives both failed because of the emperor's tendency to overrule his regent, Ferdinand, especially in matters where the interests of his own urban creditors were at stake. The more neutral issue of currency reform failed for other reasons.[39] Here the sheer complexity of the problem doomed any effort to standardize the numerous regional and local coinage systems in the Reich. The task of persuading the princes to mint more small change, of which there was an acute shortage in many areas, rather than the larger denomination coins that were more profitable for the princes to produce, was equally hopeless.

A mixture of ambition and uncertainty thus characterized Habsburg policy in the Reich in the early years of Charles V's reign. As usual, imperial ambition had the effect of provoking the suspicion and opposition of the Estates. The uncertainty of imperial policy, particularly the lack of synchronization between emperor and regent, further enhanced the significance of the Reichstag during the emperor's absence in the 1520s. Since there was no other effective agency of government, the Reichstag assumed a more pivotal role than ever before, asserting both the traditional solidarity and community of interests of the Estates and the interests of the Reich as a whole.[40] When the Estates rejected the governing council in 1524, they rejected the possibility of any higher intervention in or regulation of their affairs, whether by the emperor or by any other ruling authority. Simultaneously, they made the Reichstag their exclusive representative organ. From the point of view of the crown, the move of the governing council to Esslingen made it into a mere appendage of royal government. In the longer term, the failure of this instrument of joint rule strengthened the desire of the crown to reform the Reich by establishing a strong monarchy, which became the enduring theme of Charles V's policies after 1540. In the short term, however, during the period of the emperor's absence the Reichstag was strengthened at the expense of the crown.

The growing significance of the religious issue during the early 1520s also fostered this development. Its overwhelming importance was not immediately clear when it first became an issue in imperial politics with the confrontation of Charles V and Martin Luther at the Reichstag of Worms in 1521. Yet the growing acceptance of the new teaching soon posed a number of fundamental challenges to the existing order. At the level of the Reichstag and imperial politics, the Reformation called into question the traditional religious unity of the Reich and the emperor's traditional religious function of exercising a secular vicariate over the Church. The Reformation also required action in a way that few other issues had

---

[39] Rabe, *Geschichte*, 250–2; Conrad, *Rechtsgeschichte*, ii, 151–4; North, 'Münzpolitik'; Schefold, 'Wirtschaft'; Blaich, *Wirtschaftspolitik*, 14–19.
[40] Press, 'Reformation', 206–8; Angermeier, *Reichsreform und Reformation*, 53–5.

done previously; the refusal to grant money or the failure to agree on other reform measures did not after all fundamentally question the coherence of the system. The religious issue, by contrast, repeatedly impinged upon the key principle of the implementation and enforcement of decisions taken at the level of 'emperor and Reich'.

Increasingly, the religious issue raised the question of the degree to which dissent, 'protest', and 'protestants' could or should be tolerated or accommodated within the system without compromising its traditions of unity. In other ways, and especially at the territorial level, the religious movement also called into question the legitimacy of the entire political and social fabric. The fact that in some areas questioning gave way to a violent assault on the existing order soon led many to see the Reformation as the harbinger of nothing less than a cataclysmic general revolution. That development started with Luther's emergence onto the national stage after 1517.

14

Luther and Imperial Politics, 1517–1526

The failure of Cajetan and Miltitz to deal with Luther meant that his case remained unresolved as the Reich entered that crucial phase in imperial politics following the death of Maximilian I in January 1519.[1] A period of intrigue and uncertainty lasted until the election of Charles V on 28 June 1519, but in effect the interregnum lasted for another fifteen months until the new emperor's coronation at Aachen on 27 October 1520 and the opening of his first Reichstag at Worms on 27 January 1521. The uncertainty fostered apprehension, but also hope that the youthful Charles might succeed where the aged Maximilian had failed. Imperial reform, Church reform, reform of society—all had their protagonists at varying levels of society.

In this context, humanist propagandists of reform, foremost among them being Ulrich von Hutten, began to see the political relevance of the Luther affair. Hutten, who in 1518 had dismissed the controversy over indulgences as a trivial squabble between rival factions of monks, increasingly saw Luther as a hero in the struggle of the Germans for freedom from the tyranny of Rome. In January 1520, he sent Luther a message offering the military support of Franz von Sickingen.[2] In June, he wrote to Luther again declaring his solidarity in the struggle against Rome, a letter that was subsequently printed twice. In the autumn, Hutten published his *Clag und Vormanung gegen den übermäßigen unchristlichen Gewalt des Bapsts zu Rom, und den ungeistlichē geistlichen* ('Admonition and Warning against the Excessive, Unchristian Power of the Pope at Rome, and of the Unpriestly Priests'), his first vernacular verse pamphlet. Hutten's discovery of Luther as the new Arminius, destined to lead the Germans in rebellion against the tyranny, was an essential precondition for Luther's national standing in 1520 and 1521.[3]

Later events clearly exposed the gulf that in fact existed between Luther and Hutten and the many others who believed they had found an ally and declared their solidarity in 1519 and 1520. However, there is every sign that Luther clearly perceived the potential of this feverish and volatile political atmosphere. During the second half of 1520, he addressed himself specifically to the major political issues of the day.

The three so-called 'Reformation tracts' of 1520 contain the first relatively rounded accounts of Luther's ideas.[4] They were not a definitive statement. The contours of his theology and its myriad implications unfolded piecemeal. Much

---

[1] See pp. 79–80.   [2] See pp. 210–19.   [3] Schmidt, *Geschichte*, 59–60.
[4] For the following, see Brecht, *Luther*, i, 349–88.

became clearer in his prodigious productivity during the period of his trial, which resulted in over 150 titles in print by the end of 1522. These alone dealt with an extraordinary range of issues, from aspects of economic policy to the functions of prayer and the nature of good works. However, Luther only fully developed many of his most important views, above all the teachings on authority and the role of the state, in response to situations that arose in subsequent years. This has sometimes given rise to the impression that Luther's views lacked coherence or were simply haphazardly reactive.

In fact, Luther's development shows a remarkable consistency throughout. He neither sought confrontation with the Church nor secession from it. The criticism of indulgences was based on ideas evolved over the previous ten years. The violent reaction to that criticism produced a clarification of its underlying theological principles. Even after his excommunication, Luther continued to preach a reform of the Church based on theological principles that he had conceived within it. Only the rejection by the Church of that call, together with its immense, but unforeseen and certainly unintended, impact on society, led to the demand for the establishment of a new institution. Luther's responses throughout were consistent with the ideas that he had been developing since his early days as a professor in Wittenberg. Even so, the three tracts of 1520 presented a relatively clear and comprehensive general outline. They delineated Luther's understanding of his position, in political as well as in theological terms, on the eve of his excommunication and they provided the conceptual framework for the formulation of later responses.

In June 1520, Luther published his *An den Christlichen Adel deutscher Nation: von des Christelichen stands besserunng* ('Address to the Christian Nobility of the German Nation Concerning the Reform of the Christian Estate'). In it, he dramatically linked the specific problems in which he had become embroiled with the broader political issues embodied in the *Gravamina* of the German Estates. He appealed to the emperor and to the German nobility 'to do their Christian duty and defend the church against the Pope and see to it that a general council was summoned to reform the church and the Christian estate'.[5] In doing so, he gave the traditional *Gravamina* a theological foundation they had not previously had. Arguing that all the baptized were priests, he rejected the medieval notion of the superiority of the clerical over the worldly estate and gave laymen (as *sacerdotes*) the right to act when the clergy failed—in this case because Rome steadfastly resisted reform.

Though the appeal was made to the emperor and nobility, Luther's language was ambiguous, for his lyrical passages on the exploitation of the German people by Rome also clearly appealed to a 'nation' that embraced more than just the nobility. *An den Christlichen Adel* combined every conceivable variety of reform in a plea for the reformation of society, the restoration of true godly order, after the liberation from the tyranny of Rome.[6]

[5] Marius, *Luther*, 237.   [6] Schmidt, *Geschichte*, 56–8.

The pamphlet furthermore demonstrates both Luther's appreciation of the public sphere represented by the Estates of the Reich and his awareness of and sensitivity to the political situation of the Reich in the early 1520s. It also linked Luther's own theological ideas with wider German traditions: demands for a general council to deliberate on a wholesale reform of the Church, and criticism of the papacy and of the Church hierarchy beneath it at virtually every level down to that of the parochial clergy.

Four months later Luther presented an even more radical statement of his theology in *De Captivitate Bablyonica Ecclesiae* ('Of the Babylonian Captivity of the Church'). As Luther himself claimed, the tract contained nothing that he had not either said or implied before. Yet in expressing his thoughts on the sacraments and the need for a reform of theology in the light of Scripture, he made any collaboration with Rome all but impossible. Previous rather vague talk of Roman tyranny now turned into the accusation that the popes as rulers of a pagan 'Babylon', Antichrists no less, had held the Church in thrall to false doctrine. He dismissed four sacraments (confirmation, marriage, ordination, and extreme unction) as being without any scriptural foundation. He expressed doubts about penance. Even more provocative was his redefinition of the Eucharist. Here, according to Luther, the Roman Church had wilfully deceived the people. It had denied them the chalice; it had elaborated the theology of transubstantiation to encourage the idolatrous worship of bread and wine manipulated by priests; it had glorified the Mass as a real sacrifice offered by the priests, attendance at which was a good work in itself.

All of this had deflected the Church away from God, from the true Eucharist founded in Scripture: an act of faith made in memory of Christ and in the confidence of the remission of sins. Unlike many later reformers, Luther retained the idea of the real bodily presence of Christ in the Eucharist, albeit maintaining the parallel existence of bread and wine with body and blood, rather than a magical transubstantiation. Nevertheless, he transformed the sacrament from a miracle orchestrated by the priest before an audience into an act of faith performed by each individual member of the congregation.

Finally, in November 1520, in *Von der Freiheit eines Christenmenschen* ('Of the Freedom of a Christian'), Luther addressed the question of how the Christian, unable to earn merit through good works, could nonetheless lead a Christian life. The Christian, Luther declared, was both free and unfree. His freedom was a freedom from 'clerical tyranny . . . and the ecclesiastical prison', for man is justified by his faith alone.[7] Yet the same love of God that is man's grateful response to the gift of salvation is also a bond that constrains his behaviour in a positive way. Freedom from the necessity to perform good works to secure salvation liberated man to perform good works for their own sake in the imitation of Christ.

This new 'bondage' in faith did not of itself guarantee good conduct in life, but it opened up the possibility at least of sustained discipline if the spirit that conquered

---

[7] Brecht, *Luther*, i, 408.

the wilful body were nourished by the Word as recorded in Scripture. Confounding critics who claimed that he preached spiritual discipline combined with loose living, Luther argued that belief and faith formed the foundations for all ordered life in society. The precise implications of this argument for government, both political and ecclesiastical, were not clear at this stage. For now, in the context of his increasingly bitter dispute with the Church authorities, it sufficed for Luther to reiterate his view of the priesthood of all believers: that invisible Church known only to God, from which the Church in Rome had parted company many centuries ago.

The writings of 1520 did not represent Luther's last word on any specific issue. He did not intend them to proclaim a final rejection of Rome, but they were sufficiently forthright and programmatic to prove crucial in the political process in which the Curia's campaign against Luther became embroiled. The ban of excommunication issued on 3 January 1521 was the logical outcome of the Roman trial and of Luther's refusal to recant, as required by the bull *Exsurge Domine* ('Arise, O Lord') on June 1520. Yet it proved difficult to enforce any measures against him. Luther's books were burned in Louvain, Liège, Cologne, and Mainz, but most rulers did nothing to comply with the judgement of Rome.[8] Frederick the Wise also persisted in his support for Luther.[9] According to usual practice, a papal ban of excommunication should have led automatically to Luther being outlawed in the Reich. By the time this issue arose in January 1521 Frederick the Wise, with the support of various other princes, was already engaged in negotiations with Charles V to have Luther heard at the Reichstag that the emperor had summoned to Worms.

A variety of factors combined to bring about this attempt at a German solution to the Luther affair. Perhaps the most important was that, during the prolonged absence of the emperor, Luther himself had become a kind of national hero.[10] The papal nuncio Girolamo Aleander commented repeatedly in his reports on the astonishing extent of Luther's popularity, while the English envoy Cuthbert Tunstall claimed that the Imperial Grand Chancellor Gattinara had told him that a hundred thousand Germans were prepared to sacrifice their lives for Luther. Many were convinced that any attempt to proceed against Luther would simply provoke an uprising. At the same time Frederick the Wise, along with other influential princes, was anxious to promote the cause of Church reform at the coming Reichstag.

The question of action against Luther had also come to assume constitutional significance. The *Wahlkapitulation* of 1519, after all, stipulated that no German should be tried before a foreign court, and if the Estates could not insist on that principle eighteen months after it was formulated, there was little hope that they might prevail in more weighty matters. For several reasons, it seemed logical to Charles V to concur in the proposal to hear Luther at the Reichstag. Having, at that

[8] Fuchs, 'Zeitalter', 47; Kohnle, *Reichstag*, 45–84.
[9] Ludolphy, *Friedrich*, 383–97; Kohnle, *Reichstag*, 22–44.
[10] Joachimsen, *Reformation*, 86; Schmidt, *Geschichte*, 60.

time, to deal with the rebellion of the Comuneros in Spain, he had no desire to risk an uprising in Germany too. He also needed the support of Frederick the Wise for the political reforms, specifically the institution of a Reichsregiment, envisaged for the Reichstag meeting. Several of his advisers were strong proponents of some kind of council to initiate reform of the Church; some advocated a national council, while others pursued Erasmus's suggestion that Charles V, Henry VIII, and Louis of Hungary should constitute an impartial tribunal to pass judgement on Luther. Finally, there was every prospect that a delay in complying with the papacy's wishes concerning Luther might prove a useful way of exerting pressure on the pope to support the emperor in his conflict with France in Italy. The papacy naturally strongly opposed any suggestion of a Church council and the nuncio argued strenuously, both before and then at the Reichstag on 13 February, in favour of Luther's immediate proscription.

The emperor's delay in acting on the papal ban of excommunication encouraged those who hoped that the new reign would inaugurate a new era of reform and raised hopes for the Reichstag in Worms. What emerged was much less dramatic, though still of immense significance. Negotiations over what should be done with regard to Luther continued feverishly while the Reichstag was sitting. This included, though it was not originally on the agenda, the compilation of a new list of 104 '*Gravamina* of the German Nation' by a small committee of the Estates.[11] The Reichstag reached no conclusion on this matter, which meant in effect that it remained on the agenda for all subsequent sessions until 1530.

The Luther issue was kept separate from the *Gravamina* discussion, but the compromise eventually agreed was a radical departure from tradition. The Estates refused to contemplate any of the imperial proposals for any kind of ban on Luther or his works before he had been given a hearing. Some princes were evidently hopeful that if Luther could be persuaded to recant at least some of his more problematic views, the cause of Church reform in the Reich might still be saved. The emperor and his advisers, on the other hand, were determined to prevent Luther appearing as the spokesman for any kind of Estates-dominated imperial reform party. They succeeded in preventing any discussion or disputation, but were obliged to concede a 'hearing', an opportunity to ask Luther whether he did in fact subscribe to the heretical views imputed to him, in order to secure the continuing cooperation of the Estates. Luther's safety was to be guaranteed by a letter of safe conduct from the emperor.

The compromise was not entirely satisfactory to any party. However, the fact that emperor and Estates were discussing the matter at all, and that they were planning a political solution negotiated within the institutions of the Reich, represented a move away from the medieval view of the Reich as the worldly counterpart to the spiritual authority of the papacy.[12] Both sides proceeded implicitly on the assumption that together they, and not the pope, would decide how the problems of the Church in Germany would be resolved.

---

[11] *TRE*, xiv, 132.
[12] Joachimsen, *Reformation*, 106.

Luther's journey to Worms, begun on 2 April and accompanied by the imperial herald, turned into a triumphal progress. Everywhere crowds turned out to see him, and thronged to the sermons that he delivered en route. The hearing itself on 17 and 18 April was something of an anticlimax.[13] In the presence of the emperor and the leading Estates, Luther was asked to confirm that he was the author of the writings stacked on a table in front of him and to state whether he still stood by what he had written. After the titles of the books were read out, Luther agreed he was their author. In answer to the second question, he asked for time to think.

The following day Luther returned to deliver his considered answer. He divided his writings into three categories. The first comprised works on matters of faith and morals, which even his adversaries accepted as useful: to renounce them would be to renounce Christianity itself. The second category comprised works that dealt with the papacy and the evils of the Church: since these dealt with the tyranny that the Church had imposed on the faithful, especially in Germany, it would be sinful to renounce these too. The third category comprised polemical writings directed against his critics, and here Luther conceded that, on occasion, he might have been too harsh. Yet what he had written had been in the name of religion and he declared himself willing to withdraw anything that might be proved wrong by Scripture. When pressed once more to give a simple and unequivocal answer, Luther bluntly stated that he would not recant unless he were proved wrong by Scripture for his conscience was 'captive to the Word of God'. The later printed version of his words added the statement 'Here I stand; I can do no other.'[14]

According to the agreement reached between emperor and Estates, the outcome was now logical: Luther had failed to recant and would be outlawed. The declaration that Charles V made to the Reichstag on 19 April left no doubt about his own position. He stressed his descent from the most Christian Emperors of the German Nation, the Catholic Kings of Spain, the Archdukes of Austria and the Dukes of Burgundy. He declared himself 'perpetual defender of the Catholic faith, of sacred ceremonies, law, decrees and the sacred customs that promote the glory of God, the increase of faith and the salvation of souls'.[15] Rejecting Luther's implication that Christendom had erred for over a thousand years, Charles pronounced himself determined to uphold tradition, especially what 'my predecessors ordained at the Council of Constance and others'. He regretted having delayed so long and declared that he was now determined to act decisively. Luther would be given three weeks' safe passage in accordance with the original agreement concerning his hearing; then he would be treated as a heretic.

Even now, the Estates persuaded the emperor to permit one last attempt by a small commission to find a compromise.[16] Significantly, even princes such as Duke Georg of Saxony (r. 1500–1539), who were strongly opposed to Luther's teachings, supported this initiative. The idea was to question Luther about his individual opinions, in the hope that it might be possible to prevail upon him to recant at least

---

[13] Kohnle, *Reichstag*, 90–5.
[14] Brecht, *Luther*, i, 460; Marius, *Luther*, 294.
[15] Seibt, *Karl V*, 68–76.   [16] Kohnle, *Reichstag*, 96–9.

some of them. Under pressure perhaps from rumours of a popular uprising and of an army of four hundred knights who had sworn to protect Luther, these princes were also anxious to rescue their campaign of grievances against the Church and proposals for national Church reform from the stigma of heresy.[17]

These hearings too, conducted in private, soon reached an impasse. Luther was only prepared to accept decisions of the Reichstag or of future Church councils if they were in accordance with the Word of God. Even then he refused to contemplate making such decisions binding on the Church since, like Jan Hus, he viewed the Church as nothing more or less than the community of those chosen by God for salvation. Luther's uncompromising stance at this point ruptured the essentially political alliance between him and the proponents of the *Gravamina*, making it highly unlikely that Luther's teachings would become the basis for a general reform of the Church in the Reich.[18]

The failure of these further talks finally left the emperor with only one option: to proscribe Luther. The threat of popular unrest once more delayed an immediate decision, but an edict was issued against him on 25 May.[19] It declared Luther a heretic, threatened dire sanctions against anyone who sheltered or assisted him, and banned the reading or distribution of any of his writings. Luther himself was to be detained at the earliest possible opportunity and handed over to the imperial authorities.

From the outset, the execution of the edict was problematic. Frederick the Wise requested and, more surprisingly, but indicative of Charles V's continuing need for the support of a powerful Elector, was granted exemption from having to execute the edict in his own Ernestine Saxon lands.[20] Many other territories simply ignored the edict or failed to publish it at all. Outside the Habsburg territories, only Bavaria, Albertine Saxony, and Brunswick took any action; only in the Netherlands, where Charles V himself was the direct overlord, were the Lutherans systematically persecuted.[21] The political debate over the execution of the Edict of Worms, however, formed a key theme of the negotiations over the religious question at the Reichstag throughout the 1520s; indeed, technically, the edict remained the legal basis for all imperial policy on the religious question until 1555.[22]

From the outset, however, the Edict of Worms was a dead letter. Even before it was published, Frederick the Wise ensured that Luther was spared. On 4 May 1521, on his journey back from Worms, Luther was abducted by the Elector's agents and taken to the Wartburg castle near Eisenach. Rumours that he had been murdered caused alarm throughout the Reich—evidence again to justify the attitude of those princes and magistrates who hesitated to take action against him for fear of a popular backlash. In fact, Luther was simply withdrawn from circulation for ten months. Indeed, the Wartburg 'exile' proved a crucial period for the development of Luther's theology. It resulted in a stream of works that

[17] Brecht, *Luther*, i, 463–4.
[18] Joachimsen, *Reformation*, 112; Fuchs, 'Zeitalter', 51; Schmidt, *Geschichte*, 62–4.
[19] Kohnle, *Reichstag*, 99–104.   [20] Brecht, *Luther*, i, 474, 476.
[21] Israel, *Dutch Republic*, 79–84.   [22] Moeller, *Deutschland*, 126.

elaborated his thinking—on the Psalms, on the Magnificat, on sermons, on the sacraments, on monastic vows, among many other subjects—as well as his seminal translation of the New Testament into German.

The conclusion of the Worms Reichstag, and Luther's absence and enforced return to devotional and theological writing, occasioned a hiatus. Luther was bitterly disappointed by the failure of his appeal to the emperor and the Estates and he now turned away from the notion of a general reform born of a German national uprising against Rome. He had no interest in mobilizing a popular movement. Indeed, the threat posed to the kind of orderly reform that he desired by just such a movement now led him to concentrate on the individual princes and magistracies as the agents of change. He followed subsequent events at the Reichstag from a distance, but showed no interest in intervening or playing an active role.[23] When he did comment on imperial politics, it was to point out the contradictions that the Estates generated in their attempts to reach an agreement acceptable to all.

These efforts now revolved around the legal and political problems posed by the existence of an imperial ban against Luther. The most common reason given by princes and magistrates for not executing the ban was that to do so would simply lead to an uprising of the common man.[24] This was quite plausible, considering the public excitement generated by Luther's journey to Worms. Though the princes differed in their attitude to the new preaching, none could be described as converts to the Lutheran cause before about 1524–5.[25] However, almost all agreed that the only way forward was to proceed to a reform of the Church based on the *Gravamina*. This line was also taken by the Imperial Cities, whose position was particularly delicate, since they were both more immediately threatened by popular unrest and more politically dependent on the emperor, not least against intervention by neighbouring princes and lords.[26] At first, the proposal was for a general council of the Church; soon this was superseded by the idea of a national council, at least as a first step. In the political situation that unfolded after 1521, these ideas posed fundamental constitutional problems. Their resolution over the next five years, albeit partial, held immense constitutional significance for the Reich and its territories.

The emperor continued to insist on the execution of the Edict of Worms. However, Charles left the Reich immediately after Worms and did not return for nearly ten years. Other problems, such as the conflict with France and the Turkish threat, assumed a higher priority for him during that time. From a distance, however, he intervened to frustrate the proposal for any kind of council—either free and general or national—for Church reform. Yet Charles's absence also gave relative freedom to those who wanted such a reform. Even the Reichsregiment he had agreed to establish under Ferdinand's regency seemed at first to be a move in that

[23] Bornkamm, *Luther*, 295–316.
[24] Blickle, *Reformation*, 152; Wolgast, 'Territorialfürsten', 413–15.
[25] Wolgast, 'Territorialfürsten', 424.
[26] Brady, *Turning Swiss*, 166–83; Schmidt, *Städtetag*, 478–90.

direction.[27] Influential councillors such as Johann von Schwarzenberg, delegate of the Bishop of Bamberg, and Hans von Planitz, delegate of the Elector of Saxony, tried to ensure that the Reichsregiment remained an agency of the Estates and argued vigorously for caution and leniency in the religious question. Their advocacy led the Reichsregiment to concur in the decision of the Estates to call a German national council at Speyer for November 1524. Significantly, however, without prior consultation, Charles forbade this.[28]

In the absence of the emperor, and at a time when the new Reichsregiment was essentially an agency of the Estates, the Reichstag assumed a decisive role.[29] The religious issue posed a variety of challenges. It raised the problem of the extent of imperial power, implicit in the question of whether the Estates were obliged to execute the Edict of Worms. It also raised questions about the relationship of the Estates to each other: whether the ecclesiastical Estates should be supported against the growing threat of secularization or whether it was legitimate for staunchly Catholic princes to take action against those who appeared to favour reform. Above all, it raised the question of how the Estates should react in the face of what seemed to be a growing threat from below.

Despite the growing dissension in religious matters, the Reichstag acted according to traditional procedures. It asserted the solidarity of the Estates. Its prime concern was the defence of their rights against all threats. It sought consensus and agreements to which all could subscribe. Equally important in relation to the religious question, this assembly of secular and ecclesiastical Estates, for a time, came to act almost as a national Church council. It reached its decisions after interminable complex negotiations. They often appeared confused and obfuscatory. Yet they achieved their objective, and in doing so reinforced the German polity.

At first, the majority seemed inclined to leave matters unresolved. Indeed, at the first Nuremberg Reichstag of March–April 1522 the religious issue was ignored.[30] The Estates believed that the best way forward was to wait for a general or national council to resolve the matter. Until the *Gravamina* were settled and the Church was reformed, there could be no question of proceeding against Lutheran preachers. Even staunch Catholics like Duke Georg of Saxony took this view. In January 1522, he had persuaded the Reichsregiment to issue a decree banning all abuses in worship. The decree concluded, however, with a plea that all preachers should enjoin their congregations to remain loyal to the 'Christian customs of the Church' until the Reichstag, or a Christian gathering, or a council could undertake 'explanation, consideration and determination'.[31]

This general attitude was reinforced by the new Pope Hadrian VI's apparent commitment to reform. He despatched his legate Francesco Chieregati to the second Nuremberg Reichstag (17 November 1522–9 February 1523) to make a

[27] Joachimsen, *Reformation*, 120–1; Lutz, *Ringen*, 220.
[28] Borth, *Luthersache*, 158; Rabe, *Geschichte*, 254.
[29] Press, 'Reformation und der deutsche Reichstag', 206–7.
[30] Kohnle, *Reichstag*, 113–15
[31] Wolgast, 'Territorialfürsten', 415.

speech acknowledging the failings of the Church, in particular the sins of the Curia, and promising that the pope would undertake reform.[32]

At the same time, Chieregati demanded the execution of the Edict of Worms. The Estates responded evasively. They declared only that all preachers should 'preach the Gospel as interpreted by the writings approved by the holy Christian Church', though it was not specified which particular writings were to be regarded as authoritative.[33] In addition, the Estates demanded the opening of a free Christian council on German soil within a year. Meanwhile, Luther and his followers were to publish nothing new; clerical marriages would be banned; and monks and nuns prevented from leaving their monasteries and convents.

The Pope's death in September 1523 put paid to his reforming initiatives. At the third Nuremberg Reichstag of January–April 1524, his successor Clement VII and the new legate Lorenzo Campeggio soon reverted to the previous hard line.[34] Feelings had hardened in Germany as well. When Campeggio gave his benediction to the crowd in Augsburg, he was mocked and jeered. When he arrived at Nuremberg he was advised to enter the city in secret; then, on Maundy Thursday, he was obliged to witness the spectacle of a crowd of some three thousand, including the emperor's sister Isabella, Queen of Denmark, taking communion under both kinds.[35] Now, in addition to a free council, the Estates also demanded a national council to be convened at Speyer in November 1524 as an interim measure. The Edict of Worms was renewed, but pending the resolution of the religious question each Estate was enjoined to execute the edict 'as far as possible'. The decision taken in February 1523 was evasive for, among other things, it effectively allowed princes or magistrates to protect their Lutheran preachers against attempts by bishops to exercise discipline in their dioceses as well as their territories.

The position reached in April 1524 was even more at odds with the Edict of Worms and the will of both the emperor and the papacy. Luther for one was perplexed at what he saw as the absurdity of simultaneously reiterating the ban on his writings and calling for a national council.[36] The apparent muddle reflected, however, the approach of the councillors and delegates who dominated both Reichstag and Regiment at this time since, in the absence of the emperor, many princes chose not to attend in person. These were legally trained officials, such as Schwarzenberg and Planitz, imbued with a determination to do business, and to keep the imperial system working at all costs.[37]

There is every reason to believe that the view of Schwarzenberg and Planitz genuinely represented those of the Estates generally. However, events after the close of the Reichstag in April 1524 revealed how fissured the *Gravamina* movement was in political terms. The most active preparations for the Speyer national council were those undertaken by the Imperial Cities. The urban diet, many of its members

[32] Kohnle, *Reichstag*, 116–27.   [33] Wolgast, 'Territorialfürsten', 415–16.

[34] Kohnle, *Reichstag*, 204–46.

[35] Ranke, *Geschichte*, 303. Communion under both kinds (*sub utraque specie*) means the reception of the Eucharist under the species or appearance of both bread and wine.

[36] Bornkamm, *Luther*, 310–11.

[37] Roll, *Reichsregiment*, 329–30.

under acute pressure from popular reformation movements, met in Speyer in July 1524 to reiterate the impossibility of enforcing the Edict of Worms and the need for a general reform.[38] At the same time, however, the position of the cities was delicate with regard to both the Reichsregiment and the emperor. They felt threatened by the proposals formulated by the Reichsregiment in discussion with the noble Estates about the measures the Reichstag should take against the great trading firms and for an imperial customs duty.

In appealing to the emperor against these measures in 1523, the cities had secured his support against the promise of considerable loans to be made by them to support the various imperial campaigns. The religious issue, however, had been left unresolved. Thus, the cities' preparations for the national council were fraught. On the one hand, they argued among themselves over the possible political implications of openly disobeying the emperor, on whose goodwill they depended. On the other hand, those such as Nuremberg, Strassburg, and Ulm, in which strong reformation movements were gathering pace, urged the need to find a way of convincing the emperor that obeying his will would lead to an uprising of the common man and their ruin.

Even the apparent unanimity of the cities, however, barely covered a growing rift between those who were inclined to reform and those who remained loyal to the Catholic Church. When Nuremberg and Ulm forced through a distinctly pro-Lutheran resolution at the urban diet at Ulm in December 1524, a significant number of cities dissented.[39] Once this had happened, the whole discussion of a national reform council became redundant. For a while, the solidarity of the Imperial Cities as a corporate body seemed threatened. This was averted only because the continuing need to pursue common interests and to protect their freedom soon led them to eliminate religion as an issue from their deliberations.[40] Like other central institutions of the Reich, the cities ultimately avoided conflicts over faith by tacitly agreeing only to deal with the legal and political problems thrown up by the religious divide.

The proposal for a national council also met with problems on other fronts. Despite the opposition of Charles V, Ferdinand had given his approval, partly it seems because he initially hoped to turn the council into a formal Reichstag, which he might then ask for military assistance against the Turks.[41] The gathering opposition to the Reichsregiment as an institution undermined Ferdinand's apparent departure on an independent course. The cities opposed it bitterly, and Charles and his advisers viewed it with increasing suspicion. The Reichsregiment now faced the withdrawal of the support of the very Estates on whose behalf it had initially set out to govern, some arguing that its failure to implement the Edict of Worms demonstrated its inability to govern, others arguing that it aspired to govern too much.

[38] Brady, *Turning Swiss*, 133–50; Schmidt, *Städtetag*, 476–86.
[39] Schmidt, *Städtetag*, 487–90.
[40] Schmidt, *Städtetag*, 478, 490–522.
[41] Borth, *Luthersache*, 159.

Things came to a head at Nuremberg in January 1524, prompting the removal of the Reichsregiment to Esslingen in Habsburg Württemberg.[42] Once the putative national government had been reduced to little more than an agency of his own rather insecure regency, Ferdinand's room for manoeuvre was distinctly limited. Above all, his interest in exploring the possibility of turning the planned council into a Reichstag dwindled as it became clear that he would not succeed. Hence it was hardly surprising to find him cooperating with Campeggio in forming a new Catholic league at a conference in Regensburg in June 1524 that Dukes Wilhelm and Ludwig of Bavaria and the representatives of twelve south German bishops also attended.[43]

The papacy was determined to pre-empt the planned national council. Equally important were papal anxieties about the apparent ambitions of the Wittelsbachs in both Bavaria and the Palatinate to establish control both over the churches in their own territories and over neighbouring bishoprics.[44] The Regensburg conference furthermore reflected the anxieties of all its participants about the growing threat of the popular reform movement. Yet it also revealed a split within the ranks of those who remained steadfast in their loyalty to the Catholic Church. The Wittelsbachs were not the only secular princes who had begun to combat the new preaching by taking the Church in their territories in hand. The bishops later accused Ferdinand himself of having abused his position as ruler of the Austrian Erblande to assert his authority over the Church there more ruthlessly than any Lutheran had done.[45] Yet these initiatives, which had the tacit support of the papacy, left the German bishops struggling to contain the new preaching and attempting to fend off the threat posed to their diocesan rights by the secular princes.[46]

The Regensburg meeting ended with an agreement on mutual assistance in the execution of the Edict of Worms.[47] Furthermore, it specified that the writings of Sts Ambrose, Augustine, Cyprian, Chrysostom, Gregory, and Jerome should be the norm for all Christian teaching, and it issued a ban on the subjects of any of its participants studying at Wittenberg. For the rest, however, what was agreed was a painfully negotiated compromise of secular and ecclesiastical interests. The bishops conceded part of their incomes to the rulers of Bavaria and Austria. As a quid pro quo, the ecclesiastical reforms agreed were limited to a redefinition of the duties of the clergy, which reflected traditional Catholic reform agendas but did little to meet the criticisms of the reforming preachers.

The Regensburg gathering was significant in that it represented the first occurrence of a defensive league defined by confessional allegiance, though its effectiveness soon waned when the Bavarians turned against the Habsburgs in 1525. Most immediately, though, it cast doubt on the potential of any national

---

[42] See pp. 34–5, 162–3, 175–6.
[43] Winkler, 'Regensburger Konvent', 417.
[44] Winkler, 'Regensburger Konvent', 417.
[45] Angermeier, *Reichsreform 1410–1555*, 262. On Ferdinand's religious policies as a ruler, see Chisholm, 'Religionspolitik', 552–8.
[46] Angermeier, *Reichsreform 1410–1555*, 261–3; Borth, *Luthersache*, 163–4.
[47] Borth, *Luthersache*, 165.

council initiative. It also helped focus the minds of the bishops generally, who, at a conference at Aschaffenburg in October 1524, set about drawing up their own *Gravamina* against the secular princes.[48]

In the event, Charles V's outright rejection of the Reichstag's resolution undermined all these plans for a national Church council. On 15 July 1524, his Edict of Burgos expressly forbade it. Furthermore, Charles also reneged on his previous exemption of the Elector of Saxony from executing the Edict of Worms and ordered him, along with all other German Estates, to comply forthwith.[49] When news of this edict reached Germany in September, it finally became clear that a general settlement was now impossible.

Leopold von Ranke identified this as the point at which the German nation split in two. He blamed the emperor and the papacy for an act of 'foreign intervention' that crippled Germany for centuries. This view presupposes both that the national council might have succeeded in bringing about a reform of the Church in the Reich had Charles not intervened and that Germany was in fact divided as a result.[50] Neither assumption is valid. A national council would have been inconceivable without at least the active support and participation of Ferdinand. Furthermore, such a gathering would only have served to bring into the open the differences among the Estates over the question of what kind of reform might be required. Equally, it is not clear that Charles's intervention in fact divided the 'nation'. Luther himself had undermined the groundswell in favour of a 'national' reform that had accompanied his appearance at Worms in 1521 by declining to recant any of his views. He even refused to concede that some of them were erroneous in the interests of maintaining an alliance with the *Gravamina* movement.[51]

In fact, the antipapal and anticlerical patriotism focused on the *Gravamina* in 1520 and 1521 had subsided greatly by 1524. The broad alignment of many rulers and significant sections of the population behind the *Gravamina* campaign had given way to a new constellation. Princes and urban magistrates were now preoccupied with the threat posed by the mounting popular enthusiasm for reform. For most of them, the real issue was not faith but political and social order. This concern became paramount when the Estates faced the reality of a revolution in 1525. However, conventional responses no longer seemed to promise an effective remedy. Opinions differed over the ultimate causes of unrest (an unreformed Church or seditious preaching), as well as over both the legality of Charles's insistence on the Edict of Worms and the practicality of its execution. This increasingly threatened to undermine the traditional law and order functions of the Swabian League, since these issues prevented its council from agreeing on any form of action.[52]

---

[48] Angermeier, *Reichsreform 1410–1555*, 261.
[49] Borth, *Luthersache*, 151; Brady, *Turning Swiss*, 178.
[50] Ranke, *Geschichte*, 305–20; Joachimsen, *Reformation*, 122–3.
[51] Schmidt, 'Luther', 64–75.
[52] Bock, *Schwäbischer Bund*, 199–202.

The Regensburg conference of 1524 had demonstrated just how difficult it was to achieve the consensus required for an effective self-defence league. In 1525, the Swabian League acted against the peasants, but, after its victory, the differences between its members surfaced rapidly. Immediately, alternative forms emerged. In July 1525, Duke Georg of Saxony, together with Electors Joachim of Brandenburg and Albert of Mainz, and Dukes Erich and Heinrich of Brunswick, formed a short-lived Catholic league at Dessau. The following year at Torgau, Philip of Hessen (r. 1518–1567) and Elector Johann of Saxony (r. 1525–1532), both by now converts to Lutheranism, formed a defensive alliance. They aimed to combat popular uprising and any attempt to enforce the Edict of Worms in their territories, and they were soon joined by others, notably the Saxon clientage in north Germany.

Of course, the new alliances also reflected the fact that some princes had by now openly converted and embarked upon a systematic reform of the ecclesiastical system in their territories. When Philip of Hessen and Elector Johann of Saxony arrived at Speyer in 1526, their retinues wore the same kind of uniform with armbands inscribed with the words 'God's Word endures in eternity'.[53] Yet even now, the Estates continued to search for a formula upon which all could agree. Indeed, the shock of the events of 1525 reinforced the solidarity of the princes. Consequently, in Speyer in June 1526, the Estates resumed the discussion started at Nuremberg in April 1524. Even the bishops agreed that the return to the old practises demanded by the emperor was not feasible. Accordingly, a committee of princes, which included a number of bishops, deliberated on interim measures that might ease the situation until a general and definitive reform became possible.

The list of measures the committee proposed included clerical marriage, the lay chalice, readings in German from the Gospels and Epistles during Mass, and a German translation of the Bible. These talks collapsed, however, when Ferdinand produced an instruction from his brother forbidding any innovations, emphasizing that emperor and pope alone had the right to call a council to deliberate on such matters.[54] Once again, the Estates resolved to send a deputation to Spain to explain the difficulties of the German situation and to urge Charles to call a free general council or a national council within eighteen months. Concerning the Edict of Worms, the Reichstag now agreed that until the council met, each Estate should regulate religious matters as the laws of the Reich and the Word of God allowed.

The aim was to prevent further innovations while allowing any changes already made to stand, pending a definitive ruling by a council. The effect was altogether more dramatic. The laws of the Reich were disputed. The Word of God could be interpreted in many different ways. It was not long before the Lutheran Estates cited the 1526 Speyer mandate as justification for their local reformations. The planned deputation to Spain never took place; both Charles and Ferdinand were more preoccupied with France and the Turks, respectively than with initiating a council that they did not really want anyway. By the time Charles returned to the

---

[53] Rabe, *Geschichte*, 318; Kohnle, *Reichstag*, 257–66.
[54] Kohnle, *Reichstag*, 260–8.

Reich in 1530, he faced new realities, against which he schemed relentlessly, but ultimately fruitlessly, for the rest of his reign. This temporary expedient of 1526 thus soon gained the status of a fundamental law. It became the foundation for the German territorial Church system, in which power over religion resided in the prince or magistrate. Emperor and Reich ceased to have any competence in religious matters.

What motivated almost all princes and magistrates to opt for caution and delay, but also to participate in the search for compromise, was fear. Luther's dramatic appearance at Worms had given him a greater prominence than ever before. It was now that the Reformation movement began to develop in earnest. Moreover, from now on the debates at the Reichstag and the reactions of rulers locally were influenced by the threat of an uprising of the common man.[55] The decisions reached in the Reich and in the territories were fundamentally a response to the seemingly uncontrollable spread of the new teaching and the way that it gave new energy and direction to old campaigns and causes in both town and country. The movement's myriad local and regional manifestations erupted simultaneously throughout the Reich from the Alps to the Baltic. Its scope, intensity, and thrust far exceeded anything Luther had ever envisaged. Indeed, it soon developed characteristics that he found himself obliged to disown and condemn.

[55] Blickle, *Reformation*, 153–6.

15

Luther and the German Reform Movement

The years between 1517 and 1521 saw the emergence of a popular reform movement that left virtually no locality of the Reich untouched. Every twist of Luther's fate attracted a new and wider audience. Every stage of his prosecution by the Church gave his ideas greater publicity and helped undermine the standing of the authorities. The hearing before Charles V at Worms and Luther's defiance with impunity of the highest authority in the Reich gave further encouragement to those who demanded reform.

Luther was clearly central to the movement. No other figure achieved his truly national prominence or acquired anything like the charismatic standing that he developed in 1520 and 1521. Almost from the outset, however, the movement was characterized by a degree of variety or pluriformity that reflected differing interpretations of the new teachings and the variety of social, political, and geographical contexts in which they were received. Luther himself placed all his hopes in the community: the community of believers that constituted the only true Church and which would recognize and live by the Christian doctrines that were perfectly clear in the Bible.[1]

Confidence that the Word would prevail gave the early movement much of its momentum. Inevitably, however, it also soon gave rise to conflicting understandings of what the Word might mean and what living by it might entail, in terms of both Church reform and more fundamental changes in social and political structures. In some ways, the potential for variety was inherent in the movement from the outset, but Luther's absence from the public stage while at Wartburg castle in 1521–2 gave particular encouragement to the emergence and consolidation of centripetal tendencies.

Luther's first adherents were those predominantly young colleagues such as Andreas Karlstadt (1486–1541) and students who were enthused by his assault on Aristotle and scholasticism in 1516 and 1517. Within a short time, he had established himself as the most charismatic of the Wittenberg professors and his first practical initiative was the reform of his own university.[2] Aided by the Elector's secretary, Spalatin, and by Karlstadt, Luther brought about a fundamental change in the study of the liberal arts.[3] A key step was the establishment in August 1518 of a chair in Greek, to which Reuchlin's twenty-one-year-old great-nephew Philip Melanchthon (1497–1560), then at Tübingen, was appointed. A chair in Hebrew

---

[1] Marius, *Luther*, 271. [2] Brecht, *Luther*, i, 275–82. [3] Leppin, *Luther*, 104–6.

soon followed and the university thus became a centre for Bible-centred theology and humanist philological study.

As Luther's reputation spread outside Saxony, Wittenberg gained in popularity. By 1519, it was said that the number of students was rising like a flood, and many were apparently being turned away. Perhaps even more than Luther, Melanchthon—later given the byname of *praeceptor Germaniae*, teacher of Germany—was responsible for making Wittenberg the main university of the early Reformation movement. In 1521, his *Loci communes rerum theologicarum* ('Common Places or Principles of Theology') provided the first systematic account of Luther's theology and laid the humanist foundations of Protestant academic study.[4]

The reform of the university in 1518 would not have been possible without the support of leading members of the Elector's administration. Indeed, both legally trained and aristocratic councillors played a key role in supporting the Elector's protection of Luther and in promoting his cause after 1520. Georg Spalatin (1484–1545), the Elector's private secretary from 1512, was typical of the kind of modernizing educated official whose advocacy of Luther was crucial to his survival.[5] The existence of a network of favourably inclined officials, strengthened by academic appointments made in the various Wittenberg faculties, provided continuity of support and a vehicle for the implementation of reforms culminating in the establishment of the new Lutheran Church structure.

The ultimate decision to protect Luther and to take no action to stem the spread of his teachings was a political one taken by the Elector himself. Frederick the Wise, however, who was pious in an old-fashioned way, remained personally loyal to the Catholic Church. The first Lutheran Elector was his brother Johann the Constant, tutored as a young man by Spalatin, who became Elector in 1525. Until that point, the Electorate's leading officials, simultaneously embracing the new teaching and pursuing the governmental aims that had initiated greater secular control over the Church in the late fifteenth century, advanced the Lutheran cause. Indeed, Luther rapidly became a kind of 'spiritual mentor' to these groups.[6]

To some extent, the situation in Electoral Saxony was exceptional. A similar body of officialdom in neighbouring ducal Saxony made no impact in view of the vehement opposition to Luther of Duke Georg. However, similar groups in the adjacent County of Mansfeld apparently played a key role in inclining the counts to the new teaching. Even in the territories of the Electorate of Mainz, leading advisers of Archbishop Albrecht, most of them legally trained councillors (*gelehrte Räte*) with humanist leanings, ensured the ineffective implementation of the Edict of Worms and hence the spread of Luther's teachings.[7] Albrecht himself contributed to this. In part, he feared the consequences of repression. He also apparently aspired, though never acted, to transform his lands into a secular fief, just as his kinsman Albrecht of Brandenburg-Ansbach was in the process of transforming the

[4] Ozment, *Age of reform*, 311–14; Brecht, *Luther*, i, 275–82.
[5] Stievermann, 'Vorraussetzungen'.
[6] Selge, 'Kräfte', 220.
[7] Stievermann, 'Voraussetzungen', 166–8.

lands of the Teutonic Order of Knights into the Duchy of Prussia. The genuine sympathy of his leading officials for the Lutheran cause was nevertheless instrumental in shaping the archbishop's moderate policies.

Linked with this regional constituency of academics and officials were the many humanists in other parts of the Reich who, initially at least, rallied to Luther's cause. In Nuremberg, for example, a series of sermons preached by Johannes Staupitz in 1516 inspired the establishment of a humanist sodality that included the patrician Willibald Pirckheimer, Albrecht Dürer, the city council lawyer Christoph Scheurl, and Lazarus Spengler, secretary to the city council. Continuing contacts with Staupitz led this group to an early reception of Luther's theology. After meetings with Luther himself on his way to and from Augsburg in 1518, they became enthusiastic 'Martinians'.[8]

Some, like Pirckheimer and Scheurl, ultimately remained loyal to the old Church. However, the initial enthusiasm of leading humanists, and their identification of the new religious teachings with their own aspirations for reform and renewal were crucial in the early stages of the Reformation. The same was true in numerous Imperial Cities in the south and the south-west. Nowhere did the enthusiasm of Christian humanist groups actually bring about the breakthrough of the Reformation. Almost everywhere, however, humanist groups were electrified by Luther's trial in Rome and his hearing at Worms, which they identified as a trial and hearing of all reforming ideals, including their own.

The clergy was even more directly influential in disseminating the new teachings. The evangelical movement was above all a preaching movement. From the outset, Luther received protection from Staupitz and strong support from many of his younger Augustinian colleagues, and young clergy were among the first converts to the cause. Among the audience at Luther's disputation in Heidelberg in April 1518 was Martin Bucer, a young Dominican with strong humanist leanings, who eagerly discussed Luther's ideas with his friends Martin Frecht and Johannes Brenz.[9] The three later became reformers (of Strassburg, Ulm, and Württemberg, respectively).[10] After Worms, Augustinians formed the nucleus of a whole army of reforming preachers.

Luther's criticism of monastic vows in the autumn of 1521 led many simply to leave their monasteries.[11] The next year a chapter of the Augustinian Order in the Reich formally released its members from their vows; Staupitz's successor, Wenzeslaus Linck, openly supported Luther's teachings, and he himself soon left in order to marry. By about 1560, 69 out of 160 German Augustinian houses had ceased to exist.[12] Similar tendencies soon became clear among the Carmelites, Franciscans, and Dominicans.[13] The process of the partial dissolution of the monasteries was slow and complex, influenced by numerous local religious, political, and economic factors.

---

[8] Dickens, *German Nation*, 138–9.   [9] Leppin, *Luther*, 133–4.
[10] Brecht, *Luther*, i, 216.   [11] Lohse, *Luther*, 61.
[12] *TRE*, iv, 728–39, at 734.
[13] Ziegler, 'Klosterauflösung'.

However, the initial flurry of individual departures and dissolutions provided vital personnel for the new movement and underlined its vitality.

As important as the former inhabitants of the monasteries were the incumbents of the preacherships established in so many urban parishes in the late fifteenth century. There is no reliable statistical data to illustrate the role played by these preachers. Some undoubtedly remained loyal to Catholicism, just as some former monks simply disappeared into the flow of civil existence. Yet without the sheer number of 'local' reformers who emerged throughout the Reich, predominantly in the towns and Imperial Cities, in the early 1520s, the new teachings would never have gained the ground that they did so rapidly and, in many cases, held so permanently. A considerable number of these preachers achieved the status of reformer, however vaguely that term is defined: crucial agents in the reform of a town or territory, or theological authorities in tune with Luther but with views formed independently and shaped rather differently. Many hundreds more were simply ordinary preachers, propagators of the ideas they heard as students or read in the burgeoning literature of theological reform.

This broad group who preached the new teaching, together with the spectrum of humanist-influenced lawyers and officials in territorial and especially urban administrations, also included many of the authors of the flood of pamphlets associated with the Reformation. It is difficult to give precise figures, but it seems clear that the overwhelming majority of the over 10,000 pamphlets published in the Reich between 1500 and 1530 appeared between 1517 and 1527.[14] From 1517 to 1518 alone, there was a 530 per cent increase in the number of pamphlets published, and the number rose sharply in each subsequent year, and in 1524 some 2,400 appeared. The flood only subsided after the end of the Peasants' War in 1525, and there was a marked slump in production after 1527, when more government-led reform took the initiative away from the popular Reformation movement. Overwhelmingly, the pamphleteers were on the side of Luther and the new teachings: the Catholic response in the 1520s, typified by writers such as Johannes Eck, Hieronymous Emser, and Konrad Koch (Wimpina), was 'inadequate not merely in quantity but in popular appeal'.[15]

The most popular pamphlets commonly went through ten or even twenty editions. Assuming an average printing of 1,000 copies per edition, it has been estimated that between 1520 and 1526 alone some eleven million copies of roughly 1,100 pamphlets were printed. Most of the printed material appeared in Upper Germany, in the towns and cities of the south and south-west. Almost all dealt with theological or ecclesiastical subjects; only about 2 per cent of material printed in German concerned non-theological matters. The impact of the printed word was further enhanced by the vivid illustration of many pamphlets and by the simultaneous appearance during these years of many thousands of flysheets and single-sheet woodcuts.

---

[14] Köhler, 'Meinungsprofil'; Blickle, *Reformation*, 69–73. See also pp. 117–21.
[15] Dickens, *German Nation*, 121; Walz, *Literatur*, 106–11.

Luther himself was by far the most popular author.[16] By the end of 1520, 81 works by him had appeared in 653 editions. Initially, his reputation rested on his skill as a writer of devotional tracts. His real popularity as an author, however, began with his emergence onto the political stage in 1520. The 4,000 copies of the first edition (in itself an unusually large number) of the *An den Christlichen Adel deutscher Nation* were sold out within two weeks, and fifteen further printings followed in 1520 alone.[17] By the time the Edict of Worms was promulgated, over 500,000 copies—perhaps as many as 700,000—of works by Luther existed. No sixteenth-century government had the ability to destroy or suppress such a volume of print.

From then on the sale of Luther's writings, both of individual works and of collections, continued steadily, as did his production of new works, in both pamphlet and book form. From 1522, the phenomenal success of his translation of the New Testament and partial translation of the Old Testament overtook the sale of individual works for some years. By the end of 1525, these translations had gone through 22 authorized translations and at least 110 full or partial reprints in High German and a further 13 in Low German.[18] Luther was the first best-selling author in German history. In purely quantitative terms, his literary achievement was never matched in the early modern period.

Calculations based on hypothetical edition sizes and literacy rates, or on the presumed number of pamphlets or Luther Bibles that existed per family or group of families, may not be particularly useful. However, the statistical dimensions of the printing boom associated with the Reformation do underline the extent to which the issues that Luther raised had penetrated German society by about 1520–1. Books generally targeted the literate minority, foremost among them the educated priests in the urban centres, but the mass production of pamphlets and Bibles points to new and wider audiences.[19]

The new, cheap Bibles were aimed at the *Gemeinde*, the community or priesthood of believers, the self-reliant laymen who had no need of a priest to guide them to the Word or to translate its meaning for their daily lives. In the fourteenth century, private Bible reading had been confined to a small, wealthy, and educated elite of laymen; by the later fifteenth century, Bible reading was much more widespread: by no means universally practised by the mass, but cultivated by a growing number, often in family and other small groups.[20]

Pamphlets and woodcut flysheets targeted an audience loosely defined as the *Gemeiner Mann* or common man. The notion that he was the best judge of the Word of God was a key theme in the polemics of the early Reformation. Honesty, integrity, sense, and judgement were characteristics routinely imputed to the common man, presented in one of the most popular early pamphlets as Karsthans

---

[16] Moeller, *Deutschland*, 62–3; Walz, *Literatur*, 74–85.
[17] Brecht, *Luther*, i, 376; Walz, *Literatur*, 65.
[18] Moeller, *Deutschland*, 89–90; Walz, *Literatur*, 24–6.
[19] Scribner, *Simple folk, passim*.
[20] Schubert, *Spätmittelalter*, 270–2, 284–8.

('Jack Hoe').[21] Many pamphlets written by the reformers and their literary confederates addressed this idealized figure.

Analysis of a significant sample of pamphlets published between 1520 and 1526 reveals that the most frequently discussed matter was the scriptural principle: the recovery of the pure Word of God, which implied a return to the old truth and nourished hopes of a fundamental renewal.[22] The second most discussed topic was Luther's doctrine of justification and the theology of salvation, with issues covering the whole range of criticisms of the Catholic Church, including the implications for the sacraments, with veneration of the saints, images, and the like, in third place. Amidst all the variations of emphasis and interpretation, the catalogue of what might be described as core 'Reformation values' remained relatively clear: emancipation from the demands of late medieval Church practice, especially in relation to penance; God's exclusive power over salvation without the agency of pope or priests; Scripture as the source of all norms and the repudiation of merely human tradition; the futility of works in relation to justification; the foundations of the 'true' Church in the community; and the priesthood of all believers.[23]

It is not known how much of the theological detail was understood beyond the limited circles of the clergy or the educated urban elites.[24] Even a nobleman such as Götz von Berlichingen (1480–1562), who played an active role in both the Knights' War and the Peasants' War, did not once mention the Reformation in his autobiography.[25] At every level, there was often considerable confusion about what the new teaching was or should be: hardly surprising in view of the fact that an agreed system of dogma did not emerge for some time and was still debated in the later decades of the century. Even so crucial a subject as the Eucharist generated 'the sharpest and most bitter disagreements between reformers who on many other topics were basically at one'.[26] The confusion at the level of the common man in both town and country was often far greater, extending to complete ignorance beyond a vague, and often misinterpreted, awareness of slogans such as 'godly law' or 'Christian freedom'.

The Reformation movement originated among the educated preachers, academics, and urban administrators. Yet just as the new teachings rapidly generated interest lower down the urban social scale, with a correspondingly greater emphasis on their perceived social dimension, so the preaching movement resonated in the surrounding rural areas. The agitation that mounted between the publication of the bull *Exsurge Domine* in June 1520 and Luther's appearance at Worms in April 1521 affected rural areas as well as many urban communes.[27] A preacher such as Diepold Beringer, the so-called Peasant of Wöhrd (he was a former monk), allegedly

---

[21] Dickens, *German Nation*, 118–19; Walz, *Literatur*, 72.
[22] Köhler, 'Meinungsprofil', 259; Moeller, *Deutschland*, 89.
[23] Hamm, 'Einheit', 75–83; Dickens, *German Nation*, 132–3. Excellent introductions in English to Reformation theology are Cameron, *Reformation*, 111–67, and McGrath, *Thought*.
[24] Scribner, *Reformation*, 25–34; Dickens, *German Nation*, 128–34.
[25] Ulmschneider, *Berlichingen*, 224; Press, 'Berlichingen'.
[26] Cameron, *Reformation*, 161.
[27] Wolgast, 'Territorialfürsten', 413.

attracted audiences of many thousands, including many from the countryside, when he preached in Nuremberg and Kitzingen in 1524.[28]

Some have argued that the pamphlets that idealized the common man were simply reflecting the fact of a rural evangelical following. Similarly, the manifestos produced prior to and during the Peasants' War contained references to 'godly law' and other evangelical principles. Many of these, however, were written by educated city dwellers and thus perhaps do not really reflect a genuine mass reception of evangelical ideas in the rural areas.[29] It is difficult to gauge the precise degree of interest in and understanding of evangelical ideas among the peasantry, though there is evidence that peasant communities too sometimes demanded new preachers or were enthused by the appearance of one in their area.[30] Until 1525 at least, it is safe to conclude, the Reformation movement also had a significant rural dimension, even if only in that the expression of rural issues in evangelical language contributed substantially to the explosion of the Peasants' War.

Much depended on whose teaching was being preached, by whom, and at what point. While no other figure approached the heroic 'national' status that Luther achieved, there were numerous other reformers and major propagandists of reform. Many simply interpreted Luther's ideas or developed them in ways that rapidly diverged from Luther. Others developed their own ideas in parallel to Luther, becoming part of the broad evangelical mainstream of the early 1520s, yet often maintaining a distinct and separate identity. Some were distinguished by idiosyncratic theological beliefs alone; the ideas of others entailed, either implicitly or explicitly, programmes of radical social and political change, and were eventually challenged, persecuted, and suppressed for that reason. The early Reformation reflected and fostered the variety of reforming impulses within the late medieval Catholic Church.

---

[28] Scribner, *Reformation*, 30; Rublack, 'Kitzingen', 58–63.

[29] Blickle, *Reformation*, 111–14, summarises his argument for the existence of a popular evangelical movement in both town and country. Reservations are expressed by Scribner, *Reformation*, 30–2, and Cameron, *Reformation*, 208–9.

[30] For a detailed study of this phenomenon in Alsace, see Conrad, *Reformation, passim*.

16

Alternative Reformations and the Dominance of Lutheranism

The ultimate emergence of Lutheranism as the dominant Protestant creed has tended to obscure the extreme variety of non-Lutheran alternatives that existed in the early years.[1] Many examples appear later in the narrative. Three, however, stand out as particularly important: the interpretation of Luther's ideas by Johann Eberlin in the early 1520s; the Zwinglian Reformation in Switzerland and south Germany; and the radical notions of reform found in Wittenberg from 1521 onwards, soon primarily associated with Thomas Müntzer. Finally, Luther's quarrel with Erasmus, symptomatic of his wider rift with humanism, helps clarify the reasons for the predominance of Lutheranism in the Reich.

Johann Eberlin von Günzburg in Württemberg (c.1465–1533) was one of the most popular and prolific of the evangelical pamphleteers after 1521.[2] His education and training at Basle was strongly influenced by Erasmian Christian humanism. As a Franciscan friar, he established himself as a popular preacher at Tübingen, Ulm, and Freiburg. Luther's *An den Christlichen Adel deutscher Nation* brought about a decisive reorientation. Eberlin left his Order and in 1521 he published his own programme for the reform and regeneration of Church and society, his *15 Bundesgenossen* ('Fifteen Confederates').

The work supposedly represented the opinions of fifteen men who had formed a league devoted to reforming the world in order to prevent a revolution. It presented a vision far more comprehensive and precise than anything Luther had ever elaborated, yet it was firmly based on Luther's ideas. In Eberlin's sketch of the ideal society, given the name Wolfaria (land where all are prosperous), the community became the foundation for both Church and government. Parishes with at least five hundred souls would elect their own pastors; of every twenty pastors, one would act as bishop, meeting monthly with the pastors and annually with his fellow bishops. The same village or parish communities were to form districts, then townships and, finally, territories with representative councils at each level, with nobles elected chairmen of districts and townships and princes elected chairmen of territories, all presided over by a king elected by the princes from among their number.

---

[1] Schilling, 'Alternatives'.
[2] For the following, see Heger, *Günzburg*; Peters, *Günzburg*; Ozment, *Reformation*, 91–108; Wolgast, 'Neuordnung'.

Eberlin's outline was radical, and it promised considerable social and material benefits to the common man. Yet his whole thinking was fundamentally moderate and conservative. The *15 Bundesgenossen* essentially summarized all the pre-Reformation grievances of the *Gravamina* and the kind of imperial reform programme contained in the *Reformatio Sigismundi*. Other proposals, such as the suppression of monopolies, the restriction of imports, or the prohibition of any restrictions on rights of the nobility over wood, game, wild fowl, and fish, indicated the extent to which he associated religious renewal with the redress of social and economic grievances. The first section of the work addressed Charles V as he opened the Reichstag at Worms and urged that the Emperor ally himself with Luther and Ulrich von Hutten. Above all, Eberlin repeatedly emphasized his outright opposition to any form of violent action. In religious terms, too, his programme was strict. The faithful were to be liberated from the tyrannical demands of the old penitential system only to become subject to a new, in many ways much harsher, ecclesiastical discipline. Life in Wolfaria, for example, would include mandatory attendance at three services on all feast days, as well as strict adherence to a godly moral code that, among other things, envisaged the death penalty for adulterers.

Eberlin was a convert to the self-consciously political Luther of 1520, who deliberately linked his theological concerns with the movement for imperial reform. While Luther himself moved away from this position after he refused to cooperate with the Estates in April 1521, Eberlin remained consistent. In a string of twenty-two pamphlets and, in a translation in 1526 of Tacitus's *Germania*, Eberlin continued to promote his general patriotic reform. In his work as the reformer of the County of Wertheim between 1525 and 1530, however, such wide-ranging ideals took second place to the more mundane task of establishing a reformed Church system in the territory.

After his conversion, Eberlin's theology was fundamentally Lutheran. Others, however, developed dogmatic systems and programmes of reform independently of Luther and to some extent competed with his teachings. The most important of these was the Zurich Reformation of Ulrich Zwingli, which gained adherents across the whole of the southern Reich.

Luther's ideas developed out of a deep personal crisis. Zwingli's Reformation, by contrast, reflected more worldly concerns.[3] He was born in the Toggenburg area in 1484. The world he grew up in was characterized by perennial conflicts between the population and their overlords, the abbots of St Gallen, rulers of one of those monastic territories that pursued a relentless policy of refeudalization in the late fifteenth century. Early education at schools with humanist leanings in Weesen, Berne, and Basle was followed by study at the universities of Vienna and Basle, where he was trained in the liberal arts in the tradition of the *via antiqua*, particularly the works of Albertus Magnus, Aquinas, and Duns Scotus. His academic career ended early with an MA and without any period of actual theological study.

---

[3] For a good short introduction, see Gordon, *Reformation*, 46–85.

Following Zwingli's appointment as pastor in Glarus in 1506, two developments were decisive. First, he devoted himself to intensive private study of the Church Fathers, of the works of Duns Scotus, and of the Bible. Through friends from his student days, he also cultivated contacts with members of the Basle humanist circles. Through them he became a disciple of Erasmus, whom he met in 1515 or 1516, and a firm believer in the exclusive validity of the Bible as a source of Christian doctrine. Second, he became involved in Swiss politics because of his contacts with the powerful Cardinal Schinner, Bishop of Sion and of Novara, papal legate, and leader of the anti-French party in Switzerland, through whose offices Zwingli received a significant papal stipend. Initially, he supported Schinner's attempts to raise mercenaries for the anti-French alliance of the pope and emperor rather than for France, and in 1513 (possibly also in 1512) and 1515 he himself accompanied the men of his area into the field.

The disastrous defeat of the Swiss mercenaries at Marignano in September 1515 led the Confederacy, with the exception to Zurich, back into alliance with France. Once the French party regained the upper hand, however, Zwingli's continuing loyalty to the pope rendered his position in Glarus untenable. Consequently, he moved first to a position as stipendiary priest in Einsiedeln in Schywz and then, in January 1519, he was appointed to a similar position by the canons at the main church, the Grossmünster, in Zurich. Zurich's resolute opposition to any alliance with France (in 1521 it refused to accede to the agreement that gave Francis I the right to raise troops in the Confederacy) made it an ideal political home for Zwingli. At the same time, however, he moved away from the anti-French human-ist nationalism he had shared with Schinner. Where he had once extolled Swiss mercenaries as soldiers of Christ, he now embraced a patriotism that opposed the whole mercenary system in the Swiss Confederacy as well as the associated pension system that corrupted its political class.[4] Indeed, after Schinner raised a force in Zurich in 1521, he found himself denounced by his erstwhile protégé Zwingli as a rapacious wolf whose pockets were full of papal ducats and whose red coat was stained with blood.[5]

Exactly when Zwingli became a reformer is still disputed. Zwingli himself dated his 'conversion' to 1516, the year in which he met Erasmus and in which he read the latter's translation of the New Testament. Others have argued that the decisive turn came in 1519. On his appointment at the Zurich Grossmünster, he broke with tradition by deciding to preach systematically through St Matthew's Gospel. Then in the autumn he was deeply affected by the experience of a severe plague, which wiped out about a quarter of the city's population.[6]

Most likely, however, Zwingli's transformation was a gradual process: inspired by Erasmus, shaped by his new duties in Zurich and by his early experiences there. From the outset, he seems to have been aware of the Luther controversy, but he understood Luther's writings, especially the tracts of 1520, to be in tune with the

[4] The pensions were essentially bribes paid by various governments in return for permission to raise mercenary forces in the cantons. Locher, *Reformation*, 25–6, 175–7.

[5] *ADB*, xxxiii, 734.   [6] Stephens, *Zwingli*, 17.

Erasmian movement and broadly in support of the theological position that he himself had developed independently. At the same time, however, there were signs that Zwingli was moving away from both the Erasmian position he had occupied since 1516 and Rome. In 1520, he relinquished his papal pension of fifty gulden a year and it was then that he began to preach more controversially, challenging the veneration of the saints, conventional views of purgatory and, most radical of all, tithes.

His new style of preaching clearly enjoyed the support of the majority of the canons and of the city's ruling council, which issued a mandate early in 1520 encouraging evangelical preaching in the city and its territory.[7] Relations with the Church authorities, particularly the Bishop of Constance, remained stable, if only because Rome had good reason to urge the bishop to exercise caution in intervening in the affairs of a city that had been such a staunch political ally. Matters only came to a head in March 1522, when Zwingli openly supported a breach of the Church's laws on Lenten fasting. He was present in the home of the printer Christoph Froschbauer when smoked sausages were consumed in a provocative demonstration of Christian freedom against the laws of the Church.

Zwingli had refrained from participating, but subsequently refused to condemn what had happened. His provocative defence of Froschbauer, arguing that he could find nothing in Scripture against his action, led to a direct confrontation with the bishop. A petition to the bishop to allow clerical marriage further heightened the tension, as did a public disputation with the Franciscan Francis Lambert of Avignon over the intercession of the saints. The publication of Zwingli's *Apologetus Archeteles* ('The First and Last Word'), a robust response to the bishop's protests, which denied the authority of both Church councils and the pope, caused an open rift.

Evangelical preaching turned into practical reform in 1523. In January, the Zurich city council organized a public disputation between Zwingli and the bishop's vicar general. In front of an audience of six hundred, Zwingli carried the day with a vigorous defence of his ideas in sixty-seven theses founded on Scripture. The council decided that Zwingli should continue his preaching in the city and that all other pastors should similarly preach according to Scripture. Over the next two years the ecclesiastical regime in Zurich was fundamentally transformed. Zwingli inspired the process, and it gained momentum from a second public disputation in October 1523. Direct action on the part of the laity in iconoclastic outbursts and the like, and approved by the ruling council, were also crucial. Soon the monasteries had been dissolved, clerical marriage sanctioned, images removed from churches, the Mass abolished, a court for the regulation of marriage established, and regulations issued for the general policing of public morals. The institution of the *Prophezei* in 1525 and of the synod in 1528, respectively a Bible seminar for the instruction of the clergy and an institution for their regulation and policing, completed the imposition of proper discipline on the Church.[8]

---

[7] Locher, *Reformation*, 94–5.   [8] Gäbler, *Zwingli*, 92–3, 116–18.

The distinctive feature of Zwingli's practical Christianity was its radical Biblicism and theocentricity. More than Luther, Zwingli made what he saw as the living Word of God in Scripture the measure of all things and the only valid source of law. Their most fundamental disagreement in theological terms was over the Eucharist. Luther retained a sense of the Eucharist as a real sacrifice and interpreted Christ's words at the Last Supper, 'This is my body', to mean that the sacrament in some way contained the substance of Christ's body and blood. Zwingli, by contrast, claimed that the bread and wine were merely symbolic. Hence Luther came to espouse a 'German Mass', while Zwingli abolished the Mass and replaced it with a purely commemorative service. The sacramentarian controversy divided the evangelical movement bitterly after 1525, and it remained unresolved even after the Marburg Colloquy with Luther in 1529.

Zwingli's essentially literal (and more 'humanist') understanding of Scripture meant that faith and belief implied more than just an inner search for salvation. From the outset, Zwingli espoused a commitment to the fundamental reform of social and political life fired by optimism about what it might be possible to achieve.[9] Much earlier and more systematically than Luther, Zwingli moved away from the pure communal principle of democratic decisions taken in the parishes to an equation of state and ecclesiastical authority in a theocratic system that dealt harshly with its opponents. Godly authority had a duty to protect the pious and punish the godless. Zwingli pursued conservatives who clung to the pension system that Zwingli came to oppose, and radical Anabaptists who sought to propagate an even purer Biblicism, with uncompromising zeal.[10] The fact that the simple equation of law and gospel also led Zwingli to allow the possibility of active resistance to ungodly authority did little to soften the harsh realities that attended the realization of his ideals.

The inherent optimism of Zwingli's ideas seems to account for their widespread popularity. They were also ideally suited to relatively small urban communes such as Zurich, with a population of probably just under six thousand. While their popular appeal should not be underestimated, they proved particularly attractive to magistrates, who found themselves cast in the role of agents of God. It was, after all, logical for the reformer of Zurich to opt for an aristocratic republic as the best form of government. And if Zwingli sought to encourage the ruling 'aristocracy' by allowing the possibility of resistance to ungodly rule on the part of those who had elected the magistrates in the first place, that too was merely a theoretical reflection of the relationship in fact between citizenry and council.[11] Soon, similar ideas also began to make an impact in other Swiss cities and in Upper Germany. Martin Bucer and Wolfgang Capito in Strassburg and Johannes Oecolampadius in Basle formulated related programmes of theological and practical reform. The distinction between Zwinglian and Lutheran was, however, rarely wholly clear: Bucer, for example, was not alone in combining aspects of both in developing his own theological programme, and Strassburg was far from unusual in the eclectic nature of its Protestantism before 1536.[12]

[9] Blickle, *Reformation*, 52.   [10] Fuchs, 'Zeitalter', 83.
[11] Stephens, *Zwingli*, 126–32.   [12] Abray, *People's Reformation*, 33–41.

It is more difficult to assess the impact of Zwingli's ideas on rural areas. Through Christoph Schappeler, the reformer of Memmingen after 1523, Zwingli's views on the right to rebel against unchristian authority also seem to have influenced the political thinking of the rebellious peasantry in 1525.[13] Yet that did not mean that Zwinglianism preached liberation for all, as became clear in the relations between the city of Zurich and its surrounding subject territories.

Zwingli preached against tithes because they had no basis in Scripture. At the same time, however, he censured peasants who refused to pay them, arguing that tithes were based on human agreements that could not legally be broken. Consequently, those religious radicals in the city who criticized Zwingli's insufficient rigour in the application of Scripture to rituals such as baptism found their hostility to the reformer shared by the peasants, who even after the reform were still burdened with payments to the Grossmünster and the urban ecclesiastical foundations.[14] Once it was clear that freedom for the rural parishes simply led to chaos and the establishment of Anabaptist communities, Zwingli had no qualms about urging the imposition of the firm hand of magisterial government. At crucial points like these, where authority was challenged, it became clear that human righteousness took precedence over divine righteousness.[15] Zwingli's essentially humanist vision of peaceful and harmonious community found its greatest resonance in the urban context, particularly in the Upper German Imperial Cities where humanism had flourished since the late fifteenth century.

More mundane political considerations also reinforced such elective affinities. Unlike Luther, Zwingli was also a relentless politician. To some extent, this role was forced on him by the labyrinthine intrigues that attended virtually any move made by any canton in the Swiss Confederacy. Nevertheless, Zwingli was also a determined proselytizer who passionately believed that the Word must be spread, if necessary by force. Zurich's progress towards a reformed Church system immediately aroused the opposition of the majority of the cantons. However, their attempt to warn Zurich off any innovation in religion merely strengthened Zwingli's resolve and in 1525 Zurich refused to renew the oath of confederation because it was sworn by the saints as well as by God.[16] This led to an open split between the Catholic League of the Five Cantons (which joined with Ferdinand of Austria in a Christian Union in 1529) and those that, at varying speeds, followed Zurich's example, notably the cities of St Gallen, Schaffhausen, Basle, and Berne. A Christian Federation formed between Zurich and Constance in 1527 to defend the Reformation was soon joined by the other evangelical cantons. The Swiss Confederacy was thus soon lamed by its division into two hostile unions, each holding separate diets (Tagsatzungen) and each trying to enforce its religious policy on the territories they ruled in common (the Gemeine Herrschaften or lesser lordships).

---

[13] Blickle, *Reformation*, 116–17.
[14] Gäbler, *Zwingli*, 87–90, 112–14; Blickle, *Reformation*, 162; Potter, *Zwingli*, 198–203.
[15] Stephens, *Zwingli*, 135.
[16] Blickle, *Reformation*, 163–4.

Open war was narrowly avoided in 1529 by the first Peace of Kappel, which attempted to defuse matters by reaffirming the autonomy of the cantons in religious matters and by placing all decisions concerning religion in the Gemeine Herrschaften in the hands of their parish communities. The agreement was undermined largely by Zwingli's restless engagement with the cause of reform. In the eastern territories of Thurgau and the Imperial Abbey of St Gallen, he imposed the Reformation by force.[17] At the same time, he cast about for potential foreign alliances with Philip of Hessen, with the King of France, with the Venetian Republic, and not least with Strassburg, Constance, Ulm, and the other reformed Imperial Cities of the south-western Reich.[18] The plan for a grand alliance against the 'tyrant' Charles V and the forces of Habsburg and Catholicism came to nothing. In the event, the final confrontation was a purely Swiss one, in which the superior forces of the Catholic cantons routed the Protestants near Kappel on 1 October 1531. Zwingli himself perished on the battlefield. Zurich was forced to accept the reversal of the reforms that it had imposed on Thurgau and St Gallen and the cancellation of its Protestant alliances.[19]

Zwingli's death heralded the end of the Reformed movement in the south-western cities.[20] Increasingly, they now turned northwards to the Lutheran areas for support, and this eventually brought about doctrinal compromises, even on the key issue of the sacraments. To what extent did this also mark the demise of a distinctive republican ideology that might have formed the basis for an alternative 'bourgeois Germany' carved out of both the Reich and the Swiss Confederacy?

It is never easy to assess the viability of lost utopias, but this one rests on assumptions about both politics and religion that are dubious.[21] If the Reformation alienated the cities from the emperor, and thus put paid to any Habsburg schemes for a south German state based on an alliance of crown and cities, the Imperial Cities still retained a fundamental loyalty to the Reich. At the very least, they offered a better defence against the common man than did the Swiss Confederacy, where the common man actually held sway in the rural cantons. Participation by Imperial Cities in Zwingli's Christian Federation did not necessarily imply a desire to secede from the Reich. Zwingli might have informed the Bishop of Constance that the Swiss were not to be included among the Germans, but the Swiss Confederacy still formally belonged to the Reich, and the frontier between the two was not clear in the early sixteenth century.[22]

Moreover, assumptions about the republican vitality of Zwinglianism rest on comparisons with a supposedly conservative Lutheranism that may be unsound. Zwingli's attitude to rural discontents in the Zurich territory is little different

---

[17] The holder of the office of prince-abbot of St Gallen remained a prince of the Reich until 1798; the town of St Gallen itself had become independent of the abbey in 1457, and in 1521 the residence of the prince-abbot was moved to Rorschach: Köbler, *Lexikon*, 609.
[18] Gäbler, *Zwingli*, 126–7; Blickle, *Reformation*, 165; Brady, *Turning Swiss*, 202–6.
[19] Gäbler, *Zwingli*, 132–5.
[20] Brady, *Turning Swiss*, 206. See also pp. 240–51.
[21] Brady, *Turning Swiss*, 322–30; Brady, *Sturm*, 371–82.
[22] Gäbler, *Zwingli*, 15.

from Luther's attitude to the rebellious peasantry. Zwingli preached obedience to Christian authority as much as Luther did.[23] The political vitality and political participation that characterized Zwinglianism in the urban context in the early 1520s was later matched by similar republican tendencies in Lutheran cities in the northern Reich in the late 1520s and 1530s.[24] While the key issue of the Eucharist divided the Lutherans and the Reformed, they agreed on much else. The fact that Zwingli implied an active right of resistance where Luther merely conceded its inevitability in certain circumstances has assumed an importance for many modern commentators that it did not have originally.[25] Arguably, Zwingli's limitation of the right to resist to those who had elected the ruler in the first place imposed more of a restriction than Luther's uprising of an indignant people. Above all, however, and more important than theoretical nuances, the context was more crucial than the theology.

The fundamental harmony between the ideas of Luther and Zwingli is further emphasized when they are considered alongside the more radical visions developed in Wittenberg and by Thomas Müntzer. Luther's period of absence while at Wartburg castle permitted the emergence of a variety of more radical spiritualist and Biblicist teachings. Quietists, spiritualists, mysticists, Anabaptists, as well as activists whom Lutherans described simply as 'fanatics', all sought to pursue their differing programmes for reform during the early years of the Reformation.[26]

Like Zwingli's Anabaptist critics, many of these individuals were impatient at the slow pace of change. Others were individual eccentrics or minor prophets whose idiosyncratic personal theologies gained fleeting prominence in the wave of popular enthusiasm generated by Luther's cause in 1520 and 1521. Some were 'inspired' laymen, most were literate ex-clergy. Almost all of them espoused a more radical doctrine of the Eucharist than Luther did, and rejected infant baptism in favour of the baptism of the adult believer (hence 'Anabaptism', meaning rebaptism for most). Some were uncompromisingly literal in their interpretation of Scripture, while others, especially the spiritualists, were vague and subjective. They invariably tended to favour austere and simple church rituals and rejected sacred images. They generally challenged the very idea of a church as an institution, and favoured lay communities without pastors. Some of them—a small minority—preached the violent enforcement of reforms extending to the transformation of society.

Many of these individuals and small sectarian movements soon failed and disappeared without trace. Prophets of both violence and peace generally attracted persecution rapidly by the secular society they so often disdained. Many sects also failed because they were incapable of agreement among themselves. Even groups of no more than two or three individuals often sacrificed solidarity to the pursuit of divergent truths. From their ranks, however, emerged some who were to have a more enduring impact. By virtue of their very proliferation in the early years, and of the threat they

---

[23] Stephens, *Zwingli*, 134.
[24] Schilling, 'Alternatives', 115–16; Blickle, *Reformation*, 100–1.
[25] Ozment, *Reformation*, 131–8; Gäbler, *Zwingli*, 71–2.
[26] Schilling, 'Alternatives', 100–9; see also Cameron, *Reformation*, 319.

seemed to pose to law and order, they also brought about a significant clarification and elaboration of Luther's own ideas.

Radical and direct action was a feature of the early Reformation ever since Luther himself participated in the public incineration of the papal bull against him along with the books of canon law at Wittenberg on 10 December 1520. The first explosion of Reformation anticlericalism occurred in Erfurt in June 1521.[27] The exclusion from Mass of two canons who had participated in the jubilant reception given by the university to Luther on his way to Worms in April led to a bitter public row between the university and the church authorities. Violence against individual clergy came to a head on 2 June, when peasants refused to pay customs dues and market fees to the town's overlord, the Archbishop of Mainz. Demonstrations against church processions followed, including the Corpus Christi procession on 6 June. On 12 June church property, including the homes of the canons and the consistory court, was attacked and wrecked. At this point, the city council stepped in and forced the clergy to accept a number of humiliating conditions that reduced their economic hold over the citizenry and the peasants of the surrounding villages. Shortly thereafter, permission was given to four priests of known Lutheran sympathies to preach in the city. Over the next few years, the Church in Erfurt was systematically reorganized on Lutheran lines.

The violence that characterized the inception of the Erfurt Reformation (in this case connived at and used by the city council to diminish the economic power of the clergy and the city's overlord, the Archbishop of Mainz) also occurred elsewhere. This wave of anticlericalism and, in some cases, iconoclasm shaped events in Wittenberg too, while the outcome there, in turn, gave direction to the process of reform in Erfurt and other places after the initial wave of violence.

The situation in Wittenberg once Luther had disappeared into Wartburg castle in June 1521 was confused. Two disciples, Luther's colleague Andreas Bodenstein von Karlstadt and his fellow Augustinian Gabriel Zwilling, pressed for immediate action. Melanchthon too seemed to be in favour of prompt change and set an example by communicating in both kinds with his students in the collegiate church on 29 September. Thereupon Karlstadt and Zwilling pressed urgently for a formal revision of the liturgy and Karlstadt preached a radically revised Mass at Christmas, which he subsequently repeated twice before large congregations. As the Augustinians gradually abandoned their monastery, finally formally disbanding altogether in January, and as priests, including Karlstadt, began to marry in public, iconoclastic riots and demonstrations further destabilized the town. The arrival in late December 1521 of the 'Zwickau prophets', three laymen with wild spiritualist teachings (in particular, a rejection of infant baptism) and millenarian visions, added a further dimension of uncertainty.

Under immense pressure, and in the face of the express disapproval of the Elector, the town council found itself obliged to accept a whole range of reforms,

---

[27] Dickens, *German Nation*, 169–74; Cameron, *Reformation*, 214–15; Scribner, 'Civic Unity', 195–7.

culminating in a new church ordinance on 24 January 1522.[28] This embodied all the popular demands, as well as the reform proposals discussed by Zwilling and Karlstadt over the last few months. The Mass was reformed, begging was abolished, and a common chest funded by confraternities and mass foundations was established to support the poor; the monasteries were formally closed and the council inventorized their property.

By the time Luther was called back from the Wartburg on 6 March to restore good order, the worst was long over.[29] His Invocavit sermons, delivered daily from 9 to 16 March, preached restraint and caution to an audience whose passions had already subsided and who were willing to accept the partial abrogation by Luther of the innovations introduced by Karlstadt. The latter's departure for Orlamünde in 1523 (he was driven out of there in 1524 and eventually died as a professor in Basle in 1541) simply underlined Luther's re-establishment of control over the Wittenberg Reformation. Not long afterwards, Luther once more proclaimed his complete rejection of Karlstadt's radicalism in his pamphlet *Widder die hymelischen propheten, von den bildern und Sacrament* ('Against the Heavenly Prophets in the Matter of Images and Sacraments', 1524–5), which reiterated his condemnation of iconoclasm and the arguments in favour of the Eucharist.[30]

As Luther's pamphlet made clear, Karlstadt was his real adversary, rather than the 'Zwickau prophets'. Before their arrival in Wittenberg, however, they had already played a significant role in the spiritual development of Thomas Müntzer as pastor in Zwickau. Müntzer was born around 1490, the son of a master craftsman in Stollberg in the Harz. After studies in Leipzig (1506) and Frankfurt an der Oder (1512), he became a priest and held posts in Halle, in Frohse near Halberstadt, and in Brunswick, where he developed close ties with a group of pious laymen inspired by the *Devotio Moderna*.[31]

Luther's protest against the Roman Church prompted Müntzer's first 'conversion'. He left his post and joined Luther in Wittenberg, participated with him in the Leipzig disputation against Eck in 1519, and became notorious for a savage polemical attack on the Franciscans in Jüterborg, which provoked a defence 'contra Luteranos'—the first recorded usage of the term.[32] On Luther's recommendation, Müntzer was appointed to a temporary post in Zwickau in 1520. Here again, his fiery sermons soon attracted attention and raised fears of unrest, though that did not prevent the city council from appointing him to a permanent position in St Catherine's Church when Johannes Sylvius Egranus, an evangelical with humanist inclinations, returned to St Mary's.

Müntzer's translation to a new parish brought him into contact with a poorer congregation of weavers and other small craftsmen, and at the same time led to a growing opposition to Egranus's preaching. While the latter advocated Erasmian

---

[28] Scribner, 'Reformation as a Social Movement', 49.

[29] Edwards, *False Brethren*, 17–33.

[30] A second instalment of the pamphlet appeared as *Das ander tail wider die himlischen Propheten vom Sacrament*.

[31] Scott, *Müntzer*, 7.

[32] Williams, *Radical Reformation*, 122–3.

ideals of piety, peace, and gradual change, Müntzer spoke of the fulfilment of God's will in a new community of the elect and called for the immediate rejection of all tradition.[33] Müntzer's loyalty to Luther at this stage was not in doubt, but, in his antagonism to the humanism of Egranus, he was already developing his own distinctive ideas. Alongside Luther's teaching on Scripture and justification, Müntzer emphasized a theology of the spirit and of the Cross.

This drift away from Luther's teaching, at first barely perceptible, was further encouraged by Müntzer's encounters with the 'Zwickau prophets'. In moving to a poorer parish, he moved to a congregation of craftsmen and artisans, with whom Nikolaus Storch and his acolytes, Thomas Drechsel and Marcus Stübner, had recently gained great influence. Storch, whose proto-Anabaptist views apparently developed through contacts with the Bohemian Taborites, had made a great impression with florid visions and displays of biblical erudition, and he had formed a network of conventicles independently of the parish.[34] He also made an impression on Müntzer, who praised him publicly in a sermon as 'elevated above all priests, the only one who understands the Bible and who is knowledgeable in the spirit'.

Before his relationship with Storch could develop further, Müntzer was obliged to leave the town on 15 April. At first he went to Prague, where he attempted to convert the Bohemian Brethren to a radical Spiritualist Reformation programme, though his efforts there failed when it became clear that he was much more radical than even the most rabid Taborite. After a period of wandering in Saxony and Thuringia, he was offered a post in Allstedt, an exclave of Electoral Saxony surrounded by lands of the County of Mansfeld and the Duchy of Saxony. Here he set about implementing his own brand of reformation. In 1523, he published a German liturgy, followed by a *Deutsche Evangelische Messe* ('German Evangelical Mass') in 1524. He also formed a secretive 'league of the elect', who were to be the executors of 'the eternal covenant of God'.[35]

The nature of this covenant soon became clearer. Müntzer now openly distanced himself from Luther's teaching: he no longer regarded the Bible as the highest authority since, he declared, it merely proved the faith of those who wrote it. The path to true faith lay through neither humanist study nor Luther's exegesis. Even if a man had eaten a hundred thousand Bibles, Müntzer later declared, his soul would still be a thousand miles from God.[36] He himself stressed the inner rebirth that the elect must undergo, the knowledge of spiritual misery and the agony of despair, the experience of inner crucifixion by which man becomes a brother of Christ and which precedes his justification in the Holy Spirit.

Before long, the practical implications of this theology became clear. In March 1524 an arson attack took place on a chapel belonging to the Cistercian abbey of Naundorf. Müntzer had witnessed the attack, which was apparently inspired by his sermons and which may have been orchestrated by members of his Christian

[33] Van Dülmen, *Reformation*, 85.
[34] Van Dülmen, *Reformation*, 87–8; Williams, *Radical Reformation*, 123–5.
[35] Williams, *Radical Reformation*, 128.
[36] Blickle, *Reformation*.

League. The authorities felt obliged to act on the complaints that they were now receiving from outside the Electorate.[37] Müntzer was thereupon invited to explain himself in front of the Elector of Saxony's brother, Duke Johann and the Duke's son, Johann Friedrich, on 13 July 1524. Far from attempting to moderate or disguise his views, Müntzer took the opportunity to try to convert the princes and to persuade them that they might be predestined to lead their people into an apocalyptic 'fifth kingdom'. They should seize the opportunity to become protectors of the revolutionary saints and executors of God's wrath against the godless. If they did not, then they would prove themselves to be among the godless, to be deprived of their sword of government and killed: 'the godless', he declared, 'have no right to live'.[38]

Not surprisingly, Müntzer's sermon to the Dukes failed to persuade.[39] Faced by mounting evidence of a growing hostility to his views, on the part of both the Saxon authorities and neighbouring Catholic princes, Müntzer felt himself called to launch a second, and this time public, Christian League. After a fiery sermon on 24 July, several hundred Allstedters as well as miners from the nearby Mansfeld lands joined up to the League. The authorities once more summoned Müntzer. In a renewed appeal to the Elector, he delivered a savage denunciation of Luther, whom he suspected of orchestrating a campaign against him. The second appeal was no more successful than the first.

Rather than accept a series of strictures designed to muzzle him and to dissolve his League, Müntzer left Allstedt at the beginning of August 1524 for the Imperial City of Mühlhausen in Thuringia. Here he entered a community already convulsed by the radical preacher Heinrich Pfeiffer. Müntzer's embroilment in this situation led to his expulsion after only seven weeks. In the months of wandering that followed, he made contact with radicals in many south-western towns and cities and encountered discontented peasants in many areas. By the time he resurfaced in the spring of 1525, he was ready to form a new 'Eternal League of God' and to combine his cause with that of the peasants and the common man everywhere.[40] The Peasants' War was both the culmination of his career and its great tragedy.

The foundation of the second Christian League in July 1524 and Müntzer's subsequent departure from Allstedt marked a crucial turning point. Müntzer gave up all hope of converting the princes and turned bitterly against them. Indeed, he came to see worldly government, specifically the Electorate of Saxony, as nothing other than the instrument of Satan. The princes, he believed, had substituted their own rule for that of God and were conspiring with the godless Bible scholars to frustrate the triumph of truth.[41] It was thus logical that he also turned against Luther.

---

[37] Scott, *Müntzer*, 65–6.

[38] Scott, *Müntzer*, 70–6; Brecht, *Luther*, ii, 153.

[39] It was subsequently published as *Außlegung des andern unterschyds Danielis, deß propheten, gepredigt auffm Schlos zu Alstet vor den tetigen, thewren herzcogen und vorstehern zu Sachssen durch Thomam Muntzer, diener des wordt gottes. Alstedt MDXXIIII.*

[40] Scott, *Müntzer*, 115–16.

[41] Rabe, *Geschichte*, 277.

Müntzer's erstwhile teacher and mentor now became 'Brother Hog' or 'Brother Pussyfoot', a shameless lackey of the princes who at Worms had filled the mouths of German nobility with honey.[42] The rift between the two men now finally became insurmountable. Luther for his part clearly identified the main bone of contention in his *Ein brieff an die Fürsten zu Sachsen von dem auffrürischen geyst* ('Letter to the Princes of Saxony Concerning the Rebellious Spirit') of July 1524.[43] Differences of doctrine might in due course be resolved, but violence would not be permitted to bring about or hasten the progress of the Word. At the same time, however, Luther gave the lie to Müntzer's accusations against him: his clear advice to the princes was that they should not attempt to suppress the Allstedt teachings; the truth would ultimately triumph unaided.[44]

Müntzer's commitment to violence against both sacred objects and people in the cause of godliness raises the question of whether he was a revolutionary and, if so, of what kind. Fundamentally, Müntzer was indifferent to the prospects of social or political change. His revolution was but the prelude to the Kingdom of God, which would render all human institutions redundant. Until then, he was prepared to envisage a variety of what would effectively be transitional arrangements. These would be based on the fundamental equality of all Christians. Yet, rather like Johann Eberlin, Müntzer did not rule out a role for the (Christian) nobility. The league of the elect did not necessarily discriminate against the privileged.[45]

For Müntzer, it was axiomatic that divine election was the precondition and qualification for revolutionary action. The only true sign of election was the sense of tranquillity or inner union with God ('Gelassenheit'): that alone could justify the step to action and that alone would make even a minority triumph over the majority. In one of the last letters he wrote before his execution on 27 May 1525, he pinpointed this as the reason for the peasants' defeat: they had pursued their own selfish ends, rather than the cause of bringing 'justice to the Christian people'.[46] What became clear in 1525, however, was the fundamental difference between Müntzer's radical theology and the aspirations of the rebellious peasants. While they wanted to change the world, he looked forward to its end.

Luther's time at Wartburg, as well as the relentless hostility of loyal Catholics such as Duke Georg of Saxony, challenged him to clarify his views. At the same time, the violence that often accompanied the implementation of reform exposed the underlying tension between Luther's teaching and humanist ideals. This came to a head in 1525 in a bitter exchange of pamphlets between Luther and Erasmus on the subject of free will. Luther's stance in that controversy, like his attitude to Müntzer, was shaped fundamentally by the political ethics he had developed in 1522.

[42] Blickle, *Reformation*, 64–5; Williams, *Radical Reformation*, 133–4.
[43] Brecht, *Luther*, ii 151–2.
[44] Brecht, *Luther*, 152.
[45] Williams, *Radical Reformation*, 133; Scott, *Müntzer*, 171.
[46] Scott, *Müntzer*, 168; Blickle, *Reformation*, 63–4.

What prompted these reflections was not rebellion but the question of obedience. Catholic princes, among them Duke Georg of Albertine Saxony and the Duke of Bavaria, were demanding the prohibition of Luther's New Testament and other writings.[47] The question was whether they should be obeyed, which Luther addressed in December 1522, at the request of Duke Johann of Electoral Saxony, in his *Von welltlicher uberkeytt wie weytt man yhr gehorsam schuldig sey* ('Temporal Authority: To What Extent it Should be Obeyed'). In this work, he elaborated the notion that there were two kingdoms and two corresponding forms of government. The Kingdom of God is composed of Christians, and God alone rules it through the Word and the sacraments. True Christians have no need of the sword or of the law, for the Holy Spirit guides them and their actions are generated entirely by love and the willingness to suffer. The kingdom of the world, by contrast, was instituted for the unbelievers, to check evil and to ensure good order. The entire worldly order—the state, society, the family—is thus an institution created by God to counter sin. It is governed on His behalf by worldly authority. The ruler is the mask or *larva* of God, the mask identifying him as God's lieutenant.

The two realms are linked, of course. The Christian belongs to both and the Christian prince will seek to use his powers in a godly way and promote truth as well as maintain order. However, the spiritual kingdom contains no authority that can hold sway over the earthly kingdom, while even the highest authority in the earthly kingdom can have no power over the spiritual kingdom. No prince therefore has the right to force his subjects' consciences. Temporal laws apply to men's lives and property, but not to their souls.[48] Worldly government clearly has no authority in the invisible Church of all Christians. The visible Church, by contrast, ecclesiastical institutions and the like, clearly belong to this world and are thus subject to the temporal powers. The old question concerning the relationship between Church and state is thus resolved in favour of the state in so far as temporal matters are concerned, and in favour of the community of Christians, the invisible Church comprising the priesthood of all believers, in matters of faith.

Two crucial questions remain. The first concerns subjects. If all authority is divine in origin, then it follows that subjects must obey it. No one has the right to resist authority. On the other hand, the individual's duty to God overrides that to all others. Thus if a ruler takes off his mask and behaves in an ungodly manner; the individual cannot be obliged to do wrong. Yet while he may refuse to accede to ungodly commands, he may not rebel: he must simply endure whatever penalties his refusal to comply may incur. The second question concerns rulers and the extent to which they themselves are bound or constrained. Clearly, they cannot simply be subject to the same laws as all other Christians. In so far as a Christian participates in government he may, and indeed often must, deviate from the strict commandments of the Sermon on the Mount. The duty of worldly authority to punish the wicked may conflict with the Christian duty to love one's neighbour, but truly Christian princes might resolve the tension between these two duties.

---

[47] Lohse, *Luther*, 64–5. See also Skinner, *Foundations*, ii, 12–19; Brecht, *Luther*, ii, 115–19.
[48] Brecht, *Luther*, ii, 117.

If they allowed prayer to guide them, and avoided reliance on councillors (especially lawyers) and sycophants at court, they might fulfil their primary obligation to protect their subjects and maintain both peace and the (godly) law.

The answer to the specific question that prompted Luther's thoughts in 1522 is clear. No true Christian could feel himself obliged to comply with the ungodly dictates of a repressive Catholic prince. Yet that did not justify rebellion if one happened to be a subject of that prince, merely passive resistance and acceptance of the consequences. Resistance was permissible only against the ungodly demands of governments other than one's own: the subjects of the Ernestine Elector of Saxony had no obligation to heed the demands of the Albertine Duke of Saxony, for example, or those of any other Catholic prince.

By comparison with Zwingli, Luther gave infinitely greater power to the temporal sword. Indeed, in 1526 Luther was to boast of his accomplishment in describing and 'praising' the 'temporal sword and temporal government' more clearly than anyone 'since the time of the Apostles'.[49] Many commentators, however, have taken a negative view of this achievement. Some argue that Luther effectively gave the princes unbridled power, or even that he liberated the political realm to make its own laws.[50] Furthermore, the links between the two realms—the state's duty to protect the Christian faith, the preacher's duty to support the temporal sword—are held to have sanctified the state.[51] This, in turn, is said to have given the state an idiosyncratic autonomous standing in the German tradition, to have freed it from moral laws, and to have made it the object of unthinking obedience, even veneration, on the part of its subjects.

If the German state did indeed assume some of these characteristics in the nineteenth and twentieth centuries, and if it then used or abused its authority to employ the Church in its own power-political interests, that was far from what Luther had in mind in the 1520s. His boast in 1526 pointed clearly to his belief that 'the New Testament and especially the injunctions of St Paul' represented 'the final authority on all fundamental questions about the proper conduct of social and political life'.[52] He also shared with St Paul the expectation of the imminent end of the world, which rendered the question of the change or improvement of worldly institutions secondary.

Preparation for the end required the reform of man's soul, not the reform of state and society.[53] Furthermore, Luther's view of God as Creator and Preserver of all things also reinforced the notion of the temporal world as given and divinely ordained.

For Luther, God is the active force in history: He thus determines the rise and fall of polities, just as He creates human beings and determines the purpose of their lives. Human beings are merely the agents of God's will who carry out his plan; they

---

[49] Brecht, *Luther*, ii, 119.
[50] Lohse, *Luther*, 192–3; Krieger, *Idea of freedom*, 8–19.
[51] Blickle, *Reformation*, 49.
[52] Skinner, *Foundations*, ii, 19.
[53] Blickle, *Reformation*, 48; Lohse, *Luther*, 196.

are, after all, simply the masks (*larvae*) that God assumes or behind which He hides, and with which He does things that he can and would do anyway.[54] Consequently, the three kinds of authority that inhabit the world of the Christian (fathers, priests, and princes, with their corresponding duties or vocations of work, preaching, and government) are created or ordained by God. To overturn any one of these would be to endanger all of them.[55]

This underlying disinclination to social or political change was conditioned by Luther's experience of Electoral Saxony. His mental model of a prince was Frederick the Wise of Saxony, whose protection of Luther, a subject whose views he did not share, exemplifies the ideals that Luther sketched out in his essay of 1522. It is true that his view of the territorial state was old-fashioned in that he warned against the legal councillors who had already become indispensable agents of the new bureaucratic regimes of the late fifteenth century. However, his view of the prince as the protector of his subjects and as the guarantor of peace and the law was not remote from reality.[56] At no stage did Luther envisage the 'emancipation' of authority from all restraints. The Christian prince was constrained at all times by the Word of God mediated through prayer and the teaching of his ministers.

Luther's pronouncements on authority and obedience in 1522 must also be seen in relation to other issues that preoccupied him at the time. As a subject, the individual was to be obedient, but as a Christian and member of the invisible Church he was fully enfranchised. In September 1522 the representatives of the town of Leisnig (between Dresden and Leipzig) consulted Luther about the appointment of a pastor to a benefice that had formerly come under the patronage of the abbot of the Cistercian monastery of Buch.

Luther's advice *That a Christian Assembly or Congregation Has the Right and Power to Judge All Teaching and to Call, Appoint and Dismiss Teachers, Established and Proven by Scripture* was a forthright endorsement of the rights of the community.[57] Bishops, chapters, and monasteries were incapable of judging true faith, or at least they had failed to do so. The Christian community, the local priesthood of all believers, must therefore act, guided solely by the Word of God in Scripture. Accordingly, Luther encouraged the Leisnigers to appoint their own pastors. Subsequently, he also advised them on the best way of reforming worship to ensure the restoration of preaching the Word of God and encouraged them to incorporate all ecclesiastical property (including income from endowments and bequests) into a 'common chest' (*gemeiner Kasten*). This was to be administered by representatives of the community, and it would pay for the clergy, schoolteachers, and the upkeep of buildings, as well as support orphans, the old and infirm, and the occasional indigent stranger. Luther only urged moderation in the case of monasteries: he hoped that their remaining occupants would be treated with

---

[54] Lohse, *Luther*, 175.
[55] Schorn-Schütte, 'Drei-Stände-Lehre', 439.
[56] Lohse, *Luther*, 197.
[57] Brecht, *Luther*, ii, 69–71. The original title is: *Das eyn Christliche versamlung odder gemeyne, recht und macht habe, alle lere tzu urteylen, und lerer zu beruffen, eyn und abzusetzen, Grund vnd ursach aus der schrifft* (Wittenberg, 1523).

Christian love and supported for as long as necessary before the incomes from their foundations were credited to the common chest.

In the event, Luther's model of community management was not implemented, and the city council ended up in control of the chest. Similarly, the establishment of a more permanent reformed church order radically curtailed the principle of congregational election. Yet Luther's proposals are significant in a number of ways. They reflect the extent to which he himself realized how crucial the community and demand from below had been in launching the reform process and in securing its success. They were hugely influential in encouraging other communities to introduce similar changes. They are also indispensable to a proper understanding of Luther's attitude to authority in the early 1520s. For the real purpose of the temporal sword was quite simply to protect and foster these godly, self-regulating communities of active Christians.

These ideas underwent significant moderation in the light of the events of the Peasants' War, just as later political situations led Luther to justify active rebellion against unjust rulers (Charles V) or godless tyrants (the Ottoman Emperor). The attitudes of 1522 and 1523 were shaped by an earlier context: the problems posed by Karlstadt and Müntzer, by the attempts of some princes to enforce the Edict of Worms, and by the dynamism of the early evangelical movement driven significantly by popular demand for the new teaching.

Luther's final rift with humanism in 1524–5 was also the logical outcome of his development since 1517. His controversy with Erasmus over free will reflected an underlying tension between them that had existed from the outset. Though they shared an interest in literal exegesis of the Bible, a hatred of scholasticism, and a critical attitude to clerical abuses, they differed fundamentally in their views of human nature. Even in his reading of Erasmus's Greek New Testament in 1516, Luther became aware that Erasmus seemed to view Jesus as a 'high ethical example rather than a redeeming sacrifice for the sins of mankind'.[58] Equally, Erasmus retained a belief in the efficacy of good works, at least as a major contributory factor to salvation, a 'second cause'. He feared that Luther's doctrine of the unconditional salvation of man by God, whereby good works were quite irrelevant, simply released man from any sense of moral responsibility. At root, Erasmus believed that man really was capable of improvement by his own efforts; that he had the ability to choose to embrace or reject God's grace. Luther, by contrast, believed man was inherently sinful and could be saved only by God.

At first, a common interest in Church reform disguised this fundamental difference in outlook. Many humanists were able to commit themselves enthusiastically to Luther's cause, but Erasmus's attitude, always somewhat reserved and less than wholly enthusiastic, soon began to cool. He was uncomfortable with the growing popular dimension of the evangelical movement. He feared the barbarizing effects of violence and was alarmed at the thought that Luther's rebellion would generate hostility to all humanist studies. In the last resort, he was

---

[58] Ozment, *Age of Reform*, 292.

unwilling to contemplate any step that moved away from the reform of the old Church towards the establishment of a new one. His ambivalence intensified as the atmosphere in the Netherlands deteriorated. Finally, when Catholic hostility to Luther's ideas turned into open persecution of Luther's followers, Erasmus departed for Basle.[59]

On the surface, Erasmus remained neutral. He both ignored those who urged him to support Luther, and refused to condemn him publicly. Privately, however, he blamed Luther for the violence and for the growing schism in the Church. Yet he resisted appeals from friends, Pope Hadrian VI, and even Henry VIII, to make a public stand. In reply to all entreaties he repeatedly suggested ways to mediate in the conflict between Luther and the Church. It is not clear why he changed his mind in the summer of 1523, but the result pleased neither Luther nor his radical Catholic critics.

Erasmus's *De libero arbitrio diatribe seu collation* ('Diatribe or Discourse Concerning Free Will'), published in September 1524, confronted the key issue that Luther had debated with the scholastic theologians in 1517 and reaffirmed concisely in his defence against Leo X's bull *Exsurge Domine* in 1520.[60] This was the proposition that 'free will is really a fiction . . . because it is in no man's power to plan any evil or good'.[61] Erasmus declared that his primary concern was that the godly person should do good. The question of predetermination was best left unasked, he argued. The truth was not always useful and ecclesiastical errors, such as the notion of requiring a sinner to render satisfaction, were acceptable if they were conducive to a higher end.

Where Luther had argued from the Bible with Wycliffe and against the Council of Constance, Erasmus argued from the Bible with the saints, martyrs, and councils. Where Luther argued that man's original sinful nature, determined by God, rendered him helplessly dependent on God's mercy, Erasmus asserted that man was still free to turn to God. If Luther was right, Erasmus argued, man no longer had any incentive even to aspire to behave well: God creates man and helps him along his way, but he also progresses through his own efforts. According to Erasmus, man is predestined in two ways.

Erasmus did not actually condemn Luther, and many Catholics were disappointed that he maintained his criticism of the Church and reiterated his belief that it was in need of reform. In particular, he warned that good works had been overvalued by the Church in the past. However, Luther's response in the form of the work *De Servo Arbitrio* ('The Bondage of the Will') published in December 1525 was an unequivocal restatement of the essence of his theology.[62] Erasmus was dismissed as a sceptic who sneered at religion, a superficial scholar who would hide the truth for the sake of keeping the peace. Above all, Luther categorically excluded any possibility of freedom of choice in anything related to man's moral and religious nature. Contrary to what Aristotle and Ockham had taught, virtue could not be acquired and righteous works alone could not make a man

---

[59] Israel, *Dutch Republic 1476–1806*, 48–51.   [60] Brecht, *Luther*, ii, 220–4.
[61] Ozment, *Age of Reform*, 294.   [62] Brecht, *Luther*, ii, 235; Schoeck, *Erasmus*, 298–309.

righteous.[63] Man was essentially evil, and he was ruled by the devil until liberated by the superior power of the Holy Spirit. Even supposing he was strong enough to resist all temptations and weaknesses of the flesh, Luther taught, man himself could never hope to please God with his works. Man's only hope lay in God's supreme and unconditional mercy.

The apparent contrast between the conciliatory, undogmatic, forward-looking Erasmus and the austere, pessimistic Luther is somewhat misleading. In his pessimistic view of human nature, Luther was no more extreme than many other leading reformers. Zwingli, for example, also denied free will and the idea that human merit might lead to salvation.[64] Despite his humanist roots and reforming optimism, Zwingli, too, taught that salvation was solely dependent upon election. His only difference with Luther on this score was that he believed that God was knowable, while Luther held that He was hidden.[65] The dispute isolated Erasmus, rather than Luther.[66] In publishing his *Diatribe*, Erasmus finally broke with Luther and henceforth regarded Luther's reform as schismatic: 'this stupid and pernicious tragedy' with its 'odious dissensions'.[67] Yet, during the last ten years of his life, his irenic views found little favour in the Catholic world either.[68]

Nor did the open rejection of the evangelical reform by Erasmus and others disrupt the symbiosis between humanism and evangelical religion. The influence of humanist scholarship remained fundamental. Melanchthon's 'belief in the close connection between the humanities, sacred studies, and true piety' became part of the legacy of the Reformation.[69] At the same time, largely under Melanchthon's influence, the humanities became infused with elements of the scholastic tradition. As Melanchthon worked to systematize evangelical theology and to provide for its effective teaching in the universities and schools, he even rediscovered Aristotle, whose pernicious influence on theology Luther had denounced in his Latin disputation against scholastic theology in 1517.[70]

The dispute over free will was a scholarly one conducted in Latin. Its immediate impact was limited. However, it reflected an important dimension of the emerging social and political theory of evangelical religion. The problems thrown up by early attempts to implement a reformation of society also influenced this process. In differing ways, the 'wars' pursued, first, by sections of the lower nobility of the Reich and, second, by peasants illustrate the linkage between religious ideas and social and political grievances. Both movements failed, but each resulted in significant adjustments to the political system of the Reich. Each therefore demonstrated the capacity of the Reich to respond to, and ultimately to contain, potentially revolutionary social forces.

[63] Ozment, *Age of Reform*, 300.
[64] Stephens, *Zwingli*, 47–52; Gäbler, *Zwingli*, 69, 82, 131.
[65] Gäbler, *Zwingli*, 131.   [66] Potter, *Zwingli*, 294.
[67] Phillips, *Erasmus*, 110.   [68] Halkin, *Erasmus*, 251.
[69] Ozment, *Age of Reform*, 314.   [70] Hammerstein, *Bildung*, 17–20, 87–8.

17

The Knights' War, 1522–1523

Luther's *An den Christlichen Adel deutscher Nation* was aimed primarily at the emperor and princes, the upper nobility. Its greatest impact, however, was possibly among sections of the lower nobility. The Imperial Knights' uprising of 1522–3 was an attempt to bring about a reform of Church and society that was clearly inspired by the 'Luther affair' and its aspirations were expressed in terms derived from Luther's writings. Many of the leaders of the movement were undoubtedly genuine converts to the Lutheran cause: Franz von Sickingen's castle, the Ebern-burg near Karlsruhe was the third place after Wittenberg and Nuremberg to see the introduction of an evangelical service order.[1]

However, there was also much more at issue than just religious reform and, arguably, by the time of the uprising, the aims of its leaders had little in common with anything that Luther himself had envisaged. The movement as a whole had complex roots in the transformation of the position of the lesser nobility since the mid-fifteenth century. It gained momentum from the aspirations and schemes that accompanied the brief convergence of Luther's defence of his evangelical teaching and the cause of imperial reform between the death of Maximilian I in 1519 and the Reichstag of Worms in 1521.

The traditional view of the uprising as the heroic, but ultimately futile, last stand of a doomed feudal class derives substantially from the portrait painted of it by Ulrich von Hutten. In a letter to the Nuremberg patrician and humanist Willibald Pirckheimer in October 1518, Hutten contrasted the 'comfortable, placid, easy-going lives' of rich townspeople with the hard lives of the lesser nobility.[2] They spend their days 'in the fields, in the woods, and in fortified strongholds'. Their lands, as far as they have any left, are leased out to 'a few starveling peasants who barely manage to scratch a living' from them. These paupers are their sole source of income. Their castles are uncomfortable, cramped, noisy, and reek of dogs and excrement. Their lives are disrupted by endless discord: among their retainers, with rival nobles, and with thieves and highway robbers of all kinds. The insecurity of independent existence drove many into service with powerful princes, but even that did not necessarily solve all their problems. Obligation to a prince often, in turn, brought the enmity of that prince's rivals and his clients.

---

[1] Schilling, *Aufbruch*, 133.   [2] Strauss, *Manifestations*, 192–5.

Hutten's lament was not a picture drawn directly from life, neither his own nor that of Franz von Sickingen, the leader of the uprising of 1522–3. Nonetheless, it reinforces the impression of a crisis within significant sections of the lesser nobility around 1500. In a number of ways, these nobles faced a process of adaptation, readjustment, and reorientation that challenged the traditional assumptions and the self-image of the German knighthood. First, they were in many areas the victims of the process of territorialization and the establishment of the government of the princes. Second, their traditional military role was changing, in some ways diminishing, because of developments in the conduct of war. Third, many of them were also adversely affected by the economic developments of the late fifteenth century. Terms such as decline, disintegration, and extinction are perhaps misleading. The nobility after all outlived the Reich. However, their functions were changing markedly and the failure of the knights' uprising was crucial in accelerating that transformation.

The situation of the lower nobility in the Reich generally around 1500 was so fluid that it is difficult to differentiate clearly between an independent class of Imperial Knights (*Reichsritter*) and those who had become subservient to a prince (*landsässiger Adel*).[3] Indeed, it was only from the 1540s that the term *Reichsritter*, denoting a knight who owed loyalty directly and exclusively to the emperor and the Reich rather than to a prince, became meaningful.

Around 1500, things were still in flux. In many areas of north Germany, in Saxony, Bavaria, and the Habsburg lands, the princes had integrated the lesser nobility. Subjugation to a prince, to increasingly interventionist administrations, and to legal codes formulated by academically trained non-nobles based on the newly revived Roman law, all threatened the independence of the free nobility. They found their rights of jurisdiction over their lands challenged by new territorial courts, their hunting and fishing rights curtailed by the overriding claims of their princes; and they found themselves subjected to taxation, both on behalf of the territory and, through the territory, on behalf of the Reich.

At the same time, the knights' former privileged access to service with the princes was also threatened. The new territorial administrations required officials with academic legal training and increasingly the non-noble councillor occupied the kind of pre-eminent position in government once reserved exclusively for the nobility. Of course, many nobles also became councillors and more nobles than non-nobles occupied positions such as that of *Amtmann* or bailiff, which they held in addition to the ownership of their own Estates. Some were also beginning to respond to the demand for academically trained officials by attending universities themselves. However, the fact that many nobles thus participated in the 'modernization' of the territorial administrations did not diminish the resentment of non-noble competition and the perception of the 'modernizing' administration as a threat to noble values.

---

[3] Press, 'Führungsgruppen', 32–44.

Even where the nobility had not actually been integrated into the territory of a prince, many of the same pressures applied. In Franconia, Swabia, and on the Upper and Middle Rhine—in the regions that were close to the spheres of medieval imperial power—the process of territorialization was less advanced than in the north and east. Here too, however, free knights found themselves overshadowed by powerful neighbouring princes, competing with them for rights over local courts, hunting or simply for land. Even a 'free' knight was rarely wholly without ties. Many held at least some land from neighbouring princes as fiefs; their 'property' was composed of the same patchwork of lands and rights as that of the princes themselves. For many, this relationship of limited liegedom expressed itself in service in a prince's territory, often in serial periods of service to several princes, whether as *Amtmann* or higher central official, in the imperial court, or in military service.

Even if these knights were fundamentally free of subservience to a prince, they could also feel the pressure or threat of 'government' from the Reich. The Perpetual Peace of 1495 sought to eradicate the feuds that had been the customary law of German knighthood, and the institution of an imperial court of justice to mediate all future disputes was another example of the growing power of the non-noble lawyer in German society.[4]

Relations with the Reich were problematic in another respect too. One of the ways in which the free nobles had sought to defend their common interests and to formulate a code of conduct for dealings between them had been to form leagues and associations, and a privilege granted by Emperor Sigismund in 1422 recognized them as legitimate associations within the Reich. The most important was the League of St George's Shield in Swabia.[5] Its prime aim was the self-defence of its members, but the point of the imperial decree was to bind it, and other similar associations, to the emperor. That was only partially achieved in 1488 when the League of St George became one of the mainstays of the Swabian League. Further development of this relationship between emperor and knights was, however, arrested by the issue of taxation—ironically, precisely during the reign of the 'last knight', Maximilian I.[6]

On the introduction of the Common Penny in 1495, the free knights refused to pay. In subsequent years, Maximilian failed either to subject the knights to any kind of imperial tax or to forge a new general order or association of knights. Although the relationship between emperor and knights, as well as their precise role and status in the Reich, was unclear on Maximilian's death, the repeated attempts to engage the knights did have some positive results. They resulted in a framework which allowed the knights to retain their independence. They also kept alive the possibility, attractive to both the emperor and the knights, of a special relationship between crown and sword. While these beginnings ultimately bore fruit in the emergence of a formal incorporation of

[4] Strauss, *Law*, 56–95.
[5] Du Boulay, *Germany*, 74–6; Endres, *Adel*, 9. See p. 42.
[6] Press, 'Kaiser und Reichsritterschaft', 165–6; Paravicini, *Kultur*, 108–12; Bock, *Schwäbischer Bund*, 3–4.

knights from the 1540s. Around 1500, however, many were more preoccupied by the threat of taxation than by the promise of imperial patronage.

Changes in the conduct of warfare limited one important conventional function of the knight. The introduction of artillery during the fifteenth century under-mined the key role of the knight in medieval warfare.[7] The last battle fought with knights alone was the Battle of Soltau in June 1519, at the climax of the Hildesheim conflict.[8] Equally important, the military success of the Swiss foot soldiers in the fourteenth and fifteenth centuries encouraged many rulers to turn to mercenaries rather than rely on the traditional forces of knights on horseback. Some nobles were able to make careers as mercenary commanders or even, like Franz von Sickingen, as military entrepreneurs with their own forces, but this precarious path often led to disaster. Mercenaries had to be paid in peace as well as in war, and royal employers such as Charles V were at best reluctant to pay their bills, particularly if the outcome of a campaign was not to their satisfaction.[9]

Economic difficulties compounded these problems in many cases. Knights were as vulnerable to fluctuations and movements in the rural economy as the peasants that worked their land and provided much of their income. Some adapted success-fully to new economic conditions: they became entrepreneurs in mining and other rural industries, or large-scale livestock grazers and traders, or used their buying power and their barns to engage in speculation with agricultural products such as grain.[10] Others, however, perhaps the majority in many areas of Franconia and Swabia, were hard pressed. Their noble privileges brought them nothing but greater burdens as they struggled to find money for weapons and suits of armour and all the other accoutrements of a knight.[11] Knights were constantly reminded of the prosperity of the Imperial Cities and their patricians. Like the peasantry, the knights loathed the 'monopolists' who controlled rural industries and the money markets. They also resented the fact that representatives of this same class were competing with them for jobs in territorial and imperial administrations. The rich merchant and the non-noble official trained in Roman law were the twin bogeys of the old noble elite.

In the Reichskirche, the knights still enjoyed a near monopoly in many cathedral chapters and considerable opportunities of preferment to higher ecclesiastical, especially episcopal, benefices. There was no sign of any crisis here. Indeed, one of the perceived problems of the German Church was the domination of its upper echelons by noblemen. This link between noble family networks and the higher ecclesiastical benefices of the Reichskirche also inevitably rendered the position of the nobility with regard to the Reformation ambivalent at least.

Indeed, as the campaign for reform gradually turned into the creation of a new Church order, many knights found themselves in a difficult position. For

[7] Parker, *Revolution*, 7–10; Howard, *War*, 13–14, 30–1.   [8] See pp. 157–8.
[9] Schmidt, 'Hutten', 23–4; Blickle, *Reformation*, 77–8; Baumann, *Landsknechte*, 86–91; Redlich, *Enterpriser*, i, 3–141.
[10] Schmidt, 'Hutten', 26, 28; Endres, 'Grundlagen'; Müller, 'Lage'; Endres, *Lebensformen*, 13–17.
[11] Endres, *Lebensformen*, 18–21.

secularization logically meant the disappearance of the very institution on which their families depended for jobs and status, and which gave them their only chance of promotion to the highest ranks of the princes of the Reich.[12] The Reichskirche remained a bastion of noble privilege, but in its reduced form after the Reformation it could no longer accommodate all the sons of the free nobility. Nor did the survival of one realm of privilege compensate the class of knights as a whole for the erosion of its status and the perceived threat from the cities and their educated elites.

The knights responded to these pressures in a variety of ways. The most obvious reaction was the closure of ranks and the enforcement of noble exclusivity. In the late fifteenth century, many cathedral chapters introduced strict regulations governing qualifications for membership requiring proof of noble ancestry. There was a defiant revival of jousting tournaments, especially the so-called 'Four Lands' tournaments, between 1479 and 1487. Groups of knights from the four traditional tournament regions (Franconia, Swabia, Middle and Upper Rhine, and Bavaria) organized them; they were strictly limited to knights (to the exclusion of princes as well as patricians) and each attracted several hundred participants.[13] Such demonstrations of the identity and corporate exclusivity of knighthood were specific to the southern Reich; nothing similar occurred in the north, or indeed anywhere else in Europe in the fifteenth century.

While jousts embodied the symbolic demonstration of knightly virtues and prowess, some asserted their rights in a more violent manner. The feud was not an invention of the fifteenth century, but it was then that the 'robber baron' (*Raubritter*) became a factor in those parts of the Reich where the nobility remained free of domination by the princes.[14] For many, this was a traditional way of pursuing justice, but noble freebooters such as Thomas von Absberg and Götz von Berlichingen made a career out of highway robbery and brigandry. They maintained networks of spies in Imperial Cities such as Nuremberg and at staging posts along trade and freight routes.[15]

The formalities of the feud were often no more than a shallow excuse for raids on rich townsfolk and their property. In some areas such as southern Westphalia, accusations against noble robbers gave a misleading impression: they were frequently levelled at nobles who collected taxes and excises on behalf of princes, acting as bailiffs and the like.[16] Yet the inspiration for such unjustified complaints was the relentless life of lawless crime lived by those free knights who terrorized whole regions for years on end. Attempts by the Reichstag to stamp out this feuding activity in 1486 and 1495 failed, and in some ways merely served to draw attention to it. Efforts by the Swabian League to enforce the peace against the likes of Thomas von Absberg merely provoked him to launch a feuding war against the league. In 1522–3, even the seat of imperial government, the Reichsregiment in Nuremberg, was all but under siege, so infested with robbers were its approach roads.

---

[12] Schindling, 'Reichskirche', 100; Press, 'Adel', 337–8; Hitchcock, *Revolt*, 14–15.
[13] Paravicini, *Kultur*, 93–102. [14] Du Boulay, *Germany*, 71–4.
[15] Press, 'Berlichingen', 340–1. [16] Görner, *Raubritter*, 221–3.

More enduring, perhaps not least because they did not involve the financial outlay of a joust or the vicissitudes of a feud, were the leagues and associations of the knights themselves. They served a variety of purposes. On one level, they aspired to protect the collective interests of their members against the princes and the commercially aggressive Imperial Cities. At the same time, they were part of that more general trend, characteristic of the fifteenth century, towards unions and leagues that aimed to stabilize regions of the Reich, if not the Reich as a whole. In yet another sense, they were devoted to protecting their members against each other: their fundamental aim was to impose a degree of self-discipline on the knightly estate, and their articles of association were often more explicit on the subject of relations between members than on anything else.

Typical of such small associations was the union of heirs of the lordship and castle of Rothenberg. In 1478, forty-six Franconian knights, most of them court officials of the Margrave of Brandenburg, had purchased the lordship from the Mosbach line of the Palatinate.[17] Their aim was to establish a power base outside the spheres of the Margrave or of the Bishop of Würzburg and the city of Nuremberg and some clearly regarded the lordship simply as a base for raiding activities, particularly against Nuremberg's trade routes. The main aim of the community as a whole, however, was defensive rather than aggressive. The only thing the co-heirs agreed on consistently was that permission should never be given to an individual to conduct a feud from the castle stronghold.

The formation of a number of such associations in 1522 is generally taken to be the prelude to the rebellion of 1522–3. Leagues were established in Swabia and the Wetterau, and in August 1522 some six hundred Rhineland knights met in Landau to form a 'fraternal association' for a period of six years under the leadership of Franz von Sickingen. The articles of association proclaimed that the league aimed to maintain law and order in the Reich, above all to prevent the violent behaviour of individual knights. A similar league, formed at Schweinfurt the following spring, also sought to maintain solidarity among the Franconian knights and espoused the same general principles.[18]

The proliferation of leagues testifies to the widespread dissatisfaction among the knights in many regions of the Reich in the last years of Maximilian and the first years of Charles V. However, the fact that the leagues conformed to the established pattern of such regional associations makes it difficult to present their grievances as the inception of a campaign with revolutionary, or even reforming, potential. There was a widespread fear of what a general mobilization of the knights might achieve, but the knights found it impossible to engage in meaningful supra-regional cooperation.[19]

While the new religious teaching inspired some prominent individuals, it did not galvanize the class as a whole. Some individual knights, particularly in the Kraichgau, were among the early converts to the evangelical cause; but in regions such as Franconia, the knights remained largely unaffected by the new teaching.

[17] Zmora, *State*, 137–8; Hitchcock, *Revolt*, 13–14; Köbler, *Lexikon*, 581.
[18] Hitchcock, *Revolt*, 16–18.　　　[19] Hitchcock, *Revolt*, 15, 18, 30–1.

Indeed, overall, the free knights were not necessarily more open to the Reformation than their counterparts in the large territories were. The nobility of the Habsburg Erblande and Styria, for example, were more uniformly predisposed to Lutheranism in the early 1520s than the free knights of any region in the Reich.[20] The fact that the lesser nobles in the Swabian Habsburg Vorlande remained Catholic indicates the role played by relations between princes and territorial Estates in the confessional choices made by these nobles.[21] However, the enthusiasm of the Upper Lusatian nobility for the evangelical teaching provides an example of another group existing at a similar distance from its Habsburg overlord taking the opposite course.[22]

What appeared to unite many knights in 1522–3 was the enthusiasm of a small group of prominent individuals for reform of both Reich and Church. The movement owed everything to the dynamism and ambition of two prominent figures, Ulrich von Hutten and, above all, Franz von Sickingen, the leader of the revolt. Neither was a typical representative of his class.

Hutten's path to rebellion started with a patriotic humanist enthusiasm for the liberation of Germany from the Roman yoke. After his emergence as a national literary figure in the crusade against Reuchlin's 'obscure' antagonists, he attached great hopes to the election of Charles V.[23] Shortly afterwards, he saw the potential for national renewal in supporting Luther against the Church hierarchy, at the same time still hoping that the new emperor would also throw his weight behind the reformers. After the Edict of Worms, Hutten turned away from Charles V and began to distance himself from Luther too. Increasingly, his hopes now rested on Franz von Sickingen. They had met during the Swabian League's campaign against Duke Ulrich of Württemberg in 1519. In 1520, Hutten had moved to Sickingen's fortress, the Ebernburg. By the summer of 1521 he began to place Sickingen above Luther as leader of what he envisaged as a war against all priests.

The man whom Hutten so idolized conformed to few of the stereotypes of knightly existence that figured in Hutten's propaganda. Franz von Sickingen owned an extensive scatter of lordships and castles, as well as two towns, in the Kraichgau and the south-west of the Reich.[24] Endowed with a larger territorial base than most of his class, Sickingen also managed his estates and exploited mineral rights over iron ore and mercury deposits with an intensity characteristic of many of the principalities.[25] His early conversion to the evangelical cause and his systematic reformation of his lands were to some extent simply a logical extension of the 'territorialization' of his holdings.

Like other knights, however, Sickingen was tied into the networks of various princely overlords from whom he held fiefs. His family had links with the courts of the Palatinate, Worms, and episcopal Strassburg, as well as the imperial court, and Sickingen

[20] Moeller, *Deutschland*, 81; Schindling and Ziegler, *Territorien*, i, 106–7, 122–4.
[21] Schindling and Ziegler, *Territorien*, v, 263–8.
[22] Schindling and Ziegler, *Territorien*, vi, 98–102.
[23] See pp. 106–9, 167 above.
[24] For the following, see Scholzen, *Sickingen*; Meyer, 'Sickingen'; Birtsch, 'Sickingen'.
[25] Bechtoldt, 'Aspekte'; Scholzen, *Sickingen*, 37–49.

himself started out as an administrator or bailiff for the Palatinate. In 1515, for reasons that are not entirely clear, he launched on a series of feuds against the city of Worms, the Duke of Lorraine, the cities of Metz and Frankfurt am Main, and the Landgrave of Hessen. At the same time, he used his growing resources and extensive networks of clients and relatives to set himself up as an independent military entrepreneur. Outlawed in the Reich, he used his campaign against Lorraine to gain first a substantial annual stipend from the Duke and then an appointment with the King of France, followed by an alliance with the emperor's German enemy, the Duke of Württemberg. That, in turn, persuaded Maximilian to lift the ban on him and take him into imperial service, so that the feuds against Metz, Hessen, and Frankfurt were in a sense conducted under imperial protection.

On Maximilian I's death, Sickingen negotiated again with the King of France, but he remained loyal to the Habsburgs and supported the election of Charles V and the imperial campaign against Württemberg, from which he gained a small amount of territory. This short-term gain was soon to be outweighed by the price that he paid for his loyalty to the imperial crown. It earned him the hostility of his former patrons in the Palatinate, and the lack of a significant concentrated territorial base of his own meant that he was vulnerable to attack by the princes who dominated the regions which embraced his scattered lands. Above all, Charles V did not value his loyalty as much as Maximilian had done. When a campaign that Sickingen launched against the French at his own expense foundered, Charles simply failed to pay and he then defaulted on a substantial loan that Sickingen had advanced for the coronation.[26]

At first, Sickingen's discovery of the evangelical cause following his encounter with Hutten in the Württemberg campaign of 1519 seemed to compensate for the lesser degree of imperial protection he enjoyed from Charles V. Although previously he had cultivated the conventional piety of his predecessors, and had invested large sums in the refoundation of the convent of Trumbach, he now became a crusading reformer. He declared a feud against the Dominicans and transformed his stronghold, the Ebernburg, into a 'haven of righteousness'. He offered Luther his support and was host to both Bucer and Oecolampadius, later respectively reformers of Strassburg and Basle, and others, with whose assistance he introduced a German Mass with communion in both kinds and a reformed Church order on his estates.

In some ways, Sickingen was thus a precursor of the princes who later combined secular with religious interests in 'confessionalizing' their territories.[27] However, new political and military campaigns soon overshadowed this 'state-building' enterprise. Like Hutten, Sickingen viewed the reform of the Church as integral to the renewal of the Reich and he envisaged the knights playing a leading role in that process. While Hutten agitated to declare a general war on all priests, Sickingen sought to exploit the potential of the general discontent among the nobility. Shortly after the formation of the Landau League on 13 August 1522, he declared a feud against the Elector-Archbishop of Trier, Richard von Greiffenklau.

---

[26] Scholzen, *Sickingen*, 188–97.   [27] Press, 'Sickingen', 328.

The pretext for this campaign was essentially a personal quarrel over an unpaid ransom in respect of two of the Elector's subjects.[28] In addition, Sickingen alleged that Greiffenklau had acted against both God and the emperor, which was a plausible allegation in view of Greiffenklau's overbearing behaviour as prince and his support for the French candidacy for the imperial crown in 1519. Sickingen's real motives are unclear. On the one hand, he declared that he wished to 'create an opening for the new gospel' in the Middle Rhine and the Moselle regions. On the other hand, he may have held ambitions to become prince of a secularized Electorate of Trier. The fact that the Elector of Mainz appears to have supported him in this suggests that he was not primarily motivated by the idea of a crusade against the Reichskirche or against clerics per se.[29]

If the declaration of the feud on 27 August 1522 was intended as the signal for a general uprising, it soon failed, perhaps not least because Sickingen's ambition to become a prince was so transparent. Despite the tacit support of Mainz, Sickingen's initiative foundered. The knights of the various regions failed to unite. Those in Cologne and Jülich were threatened with the loss of their fiefs; Philip of Hessen held up a south-bound Brunswick group led by the Saxon Nickel von Minkwitz. More crucially, despite an eight-day siege, Sickingen's own force of 1,500 horse and 5,000 infantry was unable to take Trier. Greiffenklau not only stood firm but also immediately allied himself with the Landgrave of Hessen and the Elector of the Palatinate to launch a counter-offensive. In addition to pursuing their own campaign, they also encouraged the action of the Swabian League, which mobilized an army under Georg Truchsess von Waldburg against the associations of Franconian and Swabian knights. Initially at least, this initiative had nothing to do with the Sickingen affair for it was the League's response to the murder of one of its members, the count of Oettingen, by Thomas von Absberg.[30] Once the counter-offensive against Sickingen took off, however, the League's show of force in Franconia turned into a more general threat against all rebels.

A fragmented and inchoate noble opposition was easily defeated and potential rebels intimidated during the spring of 1523. In April 1523, Sickingen himself was cornered in his fortress Burg Nanstein in the Landstuhl. Its walls were destroyed by heavy artillery fire and Sickingen was mortally wounded. All his lands and castles fell into the hands of his enemies, the castles of some thirty allies were destroyed, and the Elector of Mainz, who had tacitly supported the campaign against Trier, was obliged to pay 25,000 gulden in compensation.[31] Sickingen's co-agitator Hutten had already fled after the failure of the siege of Trier and, after several failed attempts to find a safe haven, he succumbed to a long-standing syphilitic illness on the island of Ufenau in Lake Zurich on 29 August 1523.

The princes' decisive actions against the various elements of noble discontent in 1522–3 marked an undoubted triumph of the territorial princes over the 'free'

[28] Rendenbach, *Fehde*, 57. See also Scholzen, *Sickingen*, 198–233.
[29] Press, 'Sickingen', 329; Blickle, *Reformation*, 79.
[30] Carl, 'Landfriedenseinung', 486.
[31] Scholzen, *Sickingen*, 272–89.

nobility and the defeat of the national reform ideals espoused by Hutten and Sickingen. The role played by the imperial government in this process is often neglected, though it was crucial in ensuring the survival of the knights. The Nuremberg Reichsregiment or central administration clearly lacked the military power either to control the unruly element among the knights or to counter the rebellion of 1522–3. In this respect, it was entirely dependent on the Swabian League and the princes. That did not mean, however, that it meekly followed their lead. Having outlawed Sickingen in October 1522, the Reichsregiment did all that it could to protect Sickingen's allies from the wrath of their opponents and, moreover, did nothing in the spring of 1523 to throw the weight and resources of the Reich as a whole into the campaign against Sickingen. Even in this crisis, the old affinity between crown and knights asserted itself.[32]

The failure of the knights' revolt did not thus signify the absolute end of the free nobility, but merely an important milestone in its development. The feuds and lawless behaviour that generated the mythology of the *Raubritter* persisted for some decades. In Franconia, for example, the Absberg and Rosenberg families periodically held both higher nobles and Imperial Cities to ransom over several decades in their efforts to force the return of properties confiscated in 1523.[33] As late as the 1560s, the efforts of another Imperial Knight, Wilhelm von Grumbach, to secure his rights threatened the stability of the Reich.[34] In many minds, however, the experience of 1522–3, reinforced by the trauma of the Peasants' War in 1525, brought about a genuine change of outlook and behaviour.

Increasingly, defensive noble leagues gave way to attempts to construct a secure position within the Reich. They failed to achieve representation in the Reichstag, but developed a new direct relationship with the crown. The first step towards the formation of a corporative organization of Imperial Knights was their agreement to pay a tax to defend the Reich against the Turks. It was called a *subsidium charitativum*, a voluntary subsidy, but that could not disguise the fact that the knights now agreed to pay the kind of tax they had refused under Maximilian.[35] Although the subsidy agreed by the Swabian knights in 1529 was not in fact paid, both the Swabians and the Franconians agreed another in 1532.

When a new Common Penny was introduced in 1542, the knights generally asserted their independence of the princes by agreeing to pay King Ferdinand directly, through regional associations or cantons. These organizations soon assumed a more general representative function. They were provided with statutes and gained recognition as constitutional organs of the Reich, separate from the Kreise that were dominated by the princes. For the emperor, there were obvious advantages to a source of money independent of the Reichstag. From the emperor's point of view, it was also important that the knights constituted a service nobility that could be employed for both military and civil purposes. Their family networks enjoyed control over the chapters of many of the major ecclesiastical principalities,

---

[32] Grabner, *Reichsregiment*, 76–7.
[33] Carl, 'Landfriedenseinung', 491–2; Press, 'Rosenberg'.
[34] See pp. 389–94.   [35] Zmora, *State*, 141–2.

as well as considerable influence in the many secular principalities in which they served as office holders in the most diverse fields of court and administration. For the knights, subservience to the emperor and agreement to his tax demands meant continuing freedom and protection from the princes.[36]

The confessional development of the knights reflects their underlying political interests. The prominent early noble conversions to the evangelical cause did not set a trend. While genuine religious conviction undoubtedly played a part, the actions of Sickingen and others, such as the noble pamphleteer Hartmut von Cronberg, can only be understood in the context of the expectations of political reform that characterized the years 1519–21. Similarly, the perception that the knights posed a real threat to the stability of the Reich can only be understood in the context of the fear of unrest that also characterized those years. Thereafter, however, the confessional choices made by the free nobility were shaped by other factors.

From the 1530s, the knights tended to follow the lead of the emperor or of the princes from whom they held their fiefs. In Habsburg-dominated Upper Swabia, the knights tended to remain Catholic. In the ambit of the Protestant courts of Heidelberg, Stuttgart, Darmstadt, and Ansbach, many knights switched to Lutheranism. In those areas where ecclesiastical princes were the main liege lords, many among the free nobility were obliged by family interest to remain loyal to the old Church. If they had abandoned it they would have cut themselves off from the cathedral chapters and from the whole system of benefices connected with them. This consideration was so strong that many knights who became Lutherans still sent their younger sons to serve as Catholic clerics. Equally, the emperor's interest in the knights was sufficiently strong to allow the evolution of the Order of Teutonic Knights and the Order of St John as biconfessional institutions.[37] The knights as a whole remained fundamentally loyal to the imperial constitution. Their organizations were thus among the first to ignore the religious divide for the sake of unity, while after 1555 they were united in opposing Calvinism on the grounds that it was not recognized by the Peace of Augsburg.[38]

Viewed in the long-term perspective of the evolution of the free nobility, the events of the early 1520s show a group seizing the opportunity presented by the slogans of the evangelical movement. Hutten was a pagan humanist and Sickingen was a sincere convert to Lutheranism. Both, however, equated the rhetoric of Christian freedom with the political aspirations of their class in the Reich. Though they claimed to speak for the 'nation' or the Reich as a whole, their interests were actually purely sectional. At no stage did they attempt to make common cause with any other group, least of all with the 'servant rabble of the Bundschuh', as Sickingen described the peasantry.[39] Indeed, two years later, when the common man gave voice to his own concerns in the language of the Gospels, most knights joined the princes to restore law and order.

[36] Le Gates, 'Knights'; Press, *Entstehung, passim*; Rabe, *Geschichte*, 389–91.
[37] Press, 'Adel', 356–7; Schindling, 'Reichskirche', 101–2.
[38] Press, 'Adel', 363, 365. See also pp. 315–16.   [39] Blickle, *Reformation*, 81.

18

The Peasants' War, 1525

By comparison with the knights' rebellion, the Peasants' War has always seemed an altogether more profound and cataclysmic event. Leopold von Ranke judged it the 'greatest natural occurrence' or 'act of God' in the life of the 'German state'. Karl Marx deemed it the 'most radical fact of German history', while Friedrich Engels saw in it the 'most dramatic attempt at a revolution ever perpetrated by the German people'.[1] At its height, as many as 300,000 peasants may have been under arms. According to one estimate for Württemberg, some 60–70 per cent of all men capable of bearing arms joined the rebels.[2] The series of uprisings stretched from Alsace in the west across to the Tyrol and Salzburg in the east, and from the Swiss Alps in the south to the heart of Thuringia in the north. Perhaps as many as 100,000 were killed before peace was restored, and the trauma of the Peasants' War profoundly affected both the course of the Reformation and the practice of government in the German territories.

Despite its far greater scale, extent, and impact, however, the rebellion of the peasants in 1525 has some things in common with the knights' uprising that preceded it. The peasants' movement, too, was not just a single event but rather a series of local and regional uprisings. It had no one cause, but represented the eruption of diverse local and regional discontents. What lent the uprisings a coherence and unity, sometimes more apparent than real, was the formulation of those discontents in a series of articles with which peasants from diverse regions could identify. These, in turn, loosely inspired a number of visions of a future in which all grievances had been redressed and the world set to godly rights. However, the apparent unity of the movement soon collapsed. In the spring of 1525, the authorities in many areas were so intimidated by the peasant forces that they showed a willingness to negotiate. Just a few months later, however, the peasant armies collapsed one by one under the onslaught of the superior forces of the princes.

While the knights' rebellion was limited to a relatively small number from a single class, that of the peasants seemed to represent a broader front. Not only was their rebellion more widespread geographically, it was also socially more diverse. In many areas, the ranks of the peasants were augmented by their discontented urban counterparts. Indeed, the uprisings that spread north from Frankfurt into West-phalia and the Lower Rhineland in the spring of 1525 were in the first instance

---

[1] Schulze, *Deutsche Geschichte*, 89.   [2] Schulze, *Deutsche Geschichte*, 99.

urban affairs, which in turn sometimes resonated in the surrounding countryside.[3] However, only in the regions of greatest unrest was there a real link between rural and urban discontent, and it is significant that many of these regions were dotted with small towns and Imperial Cities. The fact that between 1522 and 1524 the Reformation had been introduced in many of these towns, often following considerable public turmoil, may account for the dissemination of Reformation ideas into the surrounding areas. In Thuringia, the Tyrol, Salzburg, and Styria, by contrast, the peasant ranks were joined not so much by poor townsfolk as by miners.[4]

The attitude of those higher up the social scale was almost invariably negative. Those Imperial City magistrates (as in Rothenburg or Heilbronn) who apparently supported the peasants' cause did so largely under pressure from below. Among the nobility generally, there were few serious converts. For the rest, most city magistracies tried to appear neutral, in so far as they were not themselves, as feudal overlords over rural territory, the target of rebellious peasants.[5] The treaty by which the archbishopric of Mainz allied itself with the peasants in May 1525 was purely the result of the Elector's temporary military weakness, and it was nullified the following month by the defeat of the peasants.

Apart from renegade mavericks, like the Franconian knight Florian Geyer or Götz von Berlichingen from the Odenwald, most of the small number of nobles who declared in favour of the peasants did so under duress. The more active participation of Geyer and Berlichingen does not represent any real continuity between the knights' uprising and the Peasants' War, though it may indicate a degree of lingering resentment and restlessness among some knights in the years immediately after 1523. Another group of non-peasant leaders is represented by officials such as Friedrich Weygandt, Wendel Hipler, and Michael Gaismair, all of them literate and at one time or another employed in territorial administrations, who emerged in 1525 with ambitious schemes for the reform of the Reich.

The fact that the movement in 1525 involved much of the urban as well as the rural population has led some, notably the Swiss historian Peter Blickle, to argue that what erupted in 1525 is more properly described as the 'revolution of the common man'.[6] This is justified in two particular ways. First, most contemporary sources employed the general term 'common man' rather than 'peasant' and in doing so they meant to include all subjects, rather than just those in rural areas. Second, the term conveys the fundamental opposition to authority that ran through the movement in all its manifestations, whether rural or urban. At the same time, however, it remains true, first, that the peasantry formed the core of the movement and, second, that, while general opposition produced a variety of specific suggestions for a new order of things, these proposals never attracted mass support.

The origins of the rebellion reflected the diversity of its regional spread. It began in areas of the Reich characterized by extreme territorial fragmentation, and initially it was particularly intense where lordship was in the hands of minor ecclesiastical

[3] Rabe, *Geschichte*, 292–3. [4] Blickle, *Revolution*, 188–91.
[5] Blickle, *Revolution*, 165–88. [6] Blickle, *Bauernkrieg*, 41–6.

rulers. Thus the Black Forest and Upper Swabia were early centres of unrest, while Bavaria, the Bohemian lands, and Saxony remained relatively quiet. In the final wave of rebellion, however, this pattern is confounded by the disturbances in Salzburg and the Habsburg lands. The diverse spectrum of grievances that generated the rebellion has been discussed above.[7] The crucial question here is why the general explosion occurred in 1524–5. All the various causes had been developing for several decades.

The Bundschuh conspirators in the Upper Rhineland in the spring and summer of 1517 knew nothing of Luther or the Reformation. Within a very short time, however, the kinds of grievances and programme they propagated were rendered all the more potent by the rhetoric of religious reform and the key tenets of the new teaching. The hitherto vague notion of godly or divine law that could be justified by the Bible received a radical definition, once that law was derived directly from the Gospels.[8]

Several factors combined in the early 1520s to bring matters to a head. The general sense of unrest and of anticipated change that characterized the last years of Maximilian and the early years of Charles V was fundamental. A vague expectation that something would soon happen became focused on the year 1524. In February of that year, all the planets were due to meet in the sign of Pisces, and since 1499 astrologers had been predicting that a great flood would engulf the world. As the momentous juncture approached, popular astrologers modified their view, since a flood would have violated God's promise to Noah, but they remained convinced that some great disaster would occur. In 1523, no less than fifty printed works were devoted to predicting the nature of this disaster, including some that foretold a general uprising of the peasantry. It is hardly surprising that one group of peasant rebels in Alsace later justified their behaviour by declaring they were merely acting in accordance with God's will as inscribed in the stars.[9]

Religion aggravated the uncertainty and restlessness that many claimed to read in the stars. By 1523, the evangelical preaching movement had spread across the whole Reich. Despite attempts in some territories to enforce the Edict of Worms, the new teachings spread relentlessly, first to the urban centres, and from there into the villages. It is difficult to say exactly how the message was understood. On the one hand, the intricacies of theology cannot have had much meaning for the average 'common man'. On the other hand, some key terms and demands would have resonated with the experiences of village life.

The influence of Luther on these popular movements is often judged to have been limited.[10] It is true that he later expressed a harsh view of the peasants' rebellion. Yet, before then, his advocacy of the communal election of pastors played a key role in justifying the demands that many communes made for control over their churches and clergy. Similarly, his criticisms of the old Church reinforced the anticlerical animus of those who refused to pay tithes and who rebelled against

---

[7] See pp. 122–42.   [8] Franz, *Bauernkrieg*, 89.
[9] Franz, *Bauernkrieg*, 92.   [10] Blickle, *Reformation*, 116–17.

ecclesiastical lords. Criticism of ecclesiastical authority, both doctrinal and seigneurial, led easily to the criticism of all authority.

It is easier to identify Zwingli's influence. His teaching that the Gospels should
be the yardstick for the reform of the polity and of society provided a framework for
the formulation of virtually any catalogue of grievances.[11] Furthermore, the initial
core areas of the uprising lay within the ambit of the Zurich Reformation. Many of
the leading preachers and exponents of the new teaching in Upper Germany and
Swabia were Zwingli's disciples. It would be wrong, however, to ascribe all activism
to the influence of Zwingli and all reaction to that of Luther. In many cases, both
reformers were equally influential. The Memmingen preacher Christopher Schappeler, who played a key role in the formulation of the Twelve Articles and who
wrote the introduction to them that justified the peasants' demands by reference to
the Bible, was a friend of Zwingli but also strongly influenced by Luther. Furthermore, Zwingli no more condoned the rebellion of the peasants than did Luther or
Melanchthon.[12]

As important as the religious networks was an older political network of regions
and localities in which the idea of 'turning Swiss' had been a recurrent theme
running through rebellions and periods of unrest over the previous fifty years.[13] In
1525, peasants north and south of Lake Constance rallied to the same cause.
Among those to the north, in Swabia, the Black Forest, Alsace, and Württemberg,
catchphrases such as 'to be good Swiss and to maintain solidarity' conveyed an
ambition that all understood.[14] The dynamism of the movement in the south-
western Reich owed much to the inspiration of the Swiss and they, in turn, inspired
and reinforced the movement further north in Franconia and Thuringia.

The rebellion began as a series of uncoordinated and localized protests with a
variety of causes and objectives. In 1523, evangelical preaching seems to have
prompted a refusal to pay tithes in the bishoprics of Bamberg and Speyer. Further
localized tithe strikes followed throughout Upper Germany in 1524, some accompanied by refusal to render even ordinary feudal dues, others accompanied by
demands for the right of the community to choose its own pastor. At the end of
May 1524, the inhabitants of the town of Forchheim near Nuremberg rebelled
against their alleged exploitation by the Bishop of Bamberg, or rather his provost,
their actual overlord. Their demands included not only the freedom to fish and
hunt, but also the abolition of the 'consecration taxes' (levied four times during
1501–22), the curtailment of the jurisdiction of the ecclesiastical courts in civil
matters, and the reduction of the tithe to one-thirtieth of the yield on grain only.
The unrest, apparently inflamed by the sermons of several pastors, was quickly put
down when the bishop sent a force to occupy the town.[15]

The unrest that erupted in the Thurgau in July 1524 was more directly related to
the evangelical issue, arising out of mass gatherings at evangelical (Zwinglian)
sermons and culminating in the destruction of the Carthusian monastery

---

[11] Blickle, *Reformation*, 116–17; Blickle, *Revolution*, 237–44.
[12] Blickle, *Reformation*, 116–17.   [13] Brady, *Turning Swiss*, 34–42.
[14] Blickle, *Bauernkrieg*, 51.   [15] Franz, *Bauernkrieg*, 94–6.

of Ittingen.[16] The authorities there continued to be concerned by sporadic outbursts of unrest over the following months, their anxieties intensified by the fact that the communities of the southern Black Forest were also disturbed by peasant protests from the end of May. Here, unrest in May 1524 near Staufen and among the Hauenstein peasants of the Abbot of St Blasien was followed at the end of June by the outbreak of a protracted dispute in the County of Stühlingen.

The Stühlingen dispute was precipitated by the unreasonable requirement by the Countess of Lupfen at the height of the harvest that her Stühlingen peasants collect snail shells on which she might wind her wool. This outrageous demand prompted an outpouring of grievances built up over many years. These were catalogued in no less than sixty-two complaints, which first served as the unifying cause of the peasant force that was formed, then served as the basis for negotiations with the lords and the Swabian League, and were finally sent to the Reichskammergericht for adjudication. The Stühlingen dispute differed from previous disturbances in that the peasants organized themselves formally into a troop or union (*Haufen*), with a flag, elected sergeants, and a commander, Hans Müller of Bulgenbach, a former mercenary with military experience from campaigns in France. It was Müller who led the Stühlingen peasants to the nearby town of Waldshut, where the evangelical preacher Balthasar Hubmaier had become the teacher of opposition to the town's Habsburg overlords. Soon the peasants in most of the fragmented territories of the region, in which every two or three villages belonged to a different jurisdiction, were either organized in rebellion or at least in dispute with their lords.

The general disorder seemed so great that the authorities did not dare intervene, particularly since vital Habsburg resources were currently tied up in the conflict with France in Italy. The position seemed all the more dangerous for the fact that outside forces were becoming involved. A troop of Zurich volunteers moved to support the Waldshut rebels. Even more ominously, the outlawed Duke Ulrich of Württemberg, an old ally of the King of France, seemed determined to use the peasant unrest to regain control of his territory from the Habsburg administration. With the help of French money, Duke Ulrich took up residence in the Hohentwiel fortress near Singen in the Hegau. He then declared himself for the evangelical cause, announced that he would dissolve all monasteries in his lands and use the income to liberate the peasants from their feudal obligations, and issued appeals to the Hegau peasant leaders signed 'Utz Bur' (Ulrich the farmer).

Folk memory still bitterly recalled Duke Ulrich's savage repression of the Poor Conrad uprising in 1514. The peasants were not taken in by his apparent change of heart, but they profited from his agitation nonetheless. Negotiation seemed the only solution, which resulted in a series of agreements whereby the peasants agreed to disband in return for a serious and fair legal hearing of their grievances. The truce did not last long. When it became clear that the peasants had been duped, unrest broke out again, followed by the capitulation of the authorities in another round of agreements.

---

[16] Franz, *Bauernkrieg*, 96–7.

By the end of the year, things were generally quiet once more, with the peasantry having more or less achieved their ends. They remained peaceful for as long as the lords seemed to be living up to their agreement to legal adjudication. They were not, for example, willing to participate in Duke Ulrich's attempt at the end of February 1525 to march with an army of Swiss mercenaries on his former residence of Stuttgart. However, the Duke's campaign collapsed once Swiss mercenaries were hurriedly called home after the defeat of France (with heavy Swiss losses) at the Battle of Pavia, and the way was opened for a counter-offensive against the peasants by the troops of the Swabian League under Georg Truchsess von Waldburg.

The unrest in Stühlingen and the neighbouring areas of the Klettgau, the Baar, the Hegau, and the Breisgau, essentially consisted of a discrete series of protests. They threatened violence, but acts such as the plundering of the monastery of St Trudpert south of Freiburg in December 1524 were rare. They were also primarily protests against the feudal seigneurial regime, demanding the restoration of the 'old laws' that had been usurped by the lords.

Only after some months, during the course of November and December, did the peasants begin to justify their protests with reference to the Gospels.[17] That and the fact that the cycle of protest ended before Christmas, has led some to exclude them from the 'revolution of 1525'.[18] However, there were important connections. The 1524 disturbances sent profound reverberations into the surrounding regions, notably Swabia to the east, where the next series of uprisings originated. It also seems certain that Thomas Müntzer spent time in the Klettgau and Hegau areas at the end of 1524. He exercised no influence on events there, but his contacts with the peasant leaders and the local evangelical preachers, including Balthasar Hubmaier, seem to have convinced him that their unrest was the prelude to the violent end of the world. This was a seminal insight that he took back to Mühlhausen in February 1525 and that shaped his strategy in the bloody Thuringian uprising in the following months.[19]

The second phase of unrest produced more concentrated forms of action and a programme that went beyond simple lists of local grievances. The regional focus lay in Upper Swabia, another region of great territorial fragmentation, with a number of prominent monastic foundations, and with a long tradition of conflict between peasants and lords. First stirrings of unrest in Baltringen in December 1524 led quickly to the formation of troops from various parts of the surrounding region. By February, peasant troops had been mustered in the lands of the Abbey of Kempten (the *Allgäu Haufen*), in Baltringen near Ulm, and in Rappertsweiler on the northern shore of Lake Constance (the *Seehaufen*), along with two smaller troops in Lower Swabia and Leipheim. More than 40,000 men were mobilized. What distinguished these troops from the Black Forest groups of the previous year was that they aspired to a stronger form of union. The Allgäu troop was the first to turn itself into a 'Christian union' devoted to the pursuit of justice according to divine law as laid down in the Bible. A union of the three main Swabian troops soon

---

[17] Franz, *Bauernkrieg*, 109.   [18] Blickle, *Revolution*, 23.   [19] Scott, *Müntzer*, 140–1.

followed; at the beginning of March 1525, fifty of their representatives met at Memmingen to agree on a constitution and a common programme.

The choice of Memmingen was dictated by more than just geography. The small Imperial City had just prevailed in a bitter conflict with the Bishop of Augsburg over the introduction of the new teachings.[20] Faced with popular guild pressure, but also partly out of genuine conviction, the magistrates had supported the evangelical reformer Christoph Schappeler against the bishop's attempt to ban him. By the end of 1524, the city had become more or less wholly reformed in a process led by Schappeler's sermons and enthusiastically supported by the guilds and the peasants of the villages subservient to the city, who had ceased to pay their tithes in 1524. Though the magistrates acted under duress, their relatively graceful hearing of the grievances of their own peasants gained them the reputation of being favourably inclined to the peasants' cause generally. Hence the leader of the Baltringen peasants felt emboldened to enter the city and ask for the assistance of one of the leading lay activists, the furrier Sebastian Lotzer, as 'military secretary'. As a result, the numerous local lists of peasant grievances were distilled into a single document and firmly linked with the evangelical cause.

The religious framework of the Twelve Articles was influenced as much by Luther as by Zwingli.[21] They began by declaring the right of all communities to elect and to dismiss their own pastor, and by limiting tithes for the support of the clergy to a tax on grain and similar crops. Serfdom was to be abolished, for Christ's sacrifice had rendered all men free. At the same time, the peasants would subject themselves obediently to lawful authority. All must have the right to hunt and fish and to gather wood in the common forests. Labour services must be moderated in accordance with God's Word, with custom and the original legal terms of tenure and with the value of the land held by the peasant. Customary law should bind the courts in limiting punishments, which allegedly had become arbitrary and harsh with the application of new legal codes (i.e. Roman law). Common fields and meadows that had been alienated must be returned to the communities. The death dues or tolls should be abolished, since they burdened the heirs and often led to their expropriation. Finally, the document declared that if any article could be shown to be contrary to the Word of God it would be withdrawn, just as more would be added if further points emerged from the Gospels.[22]

Most of the specific points contained in the Twelve Articles were not particularly new, yet this collation was radical and given a new edge by its justification in terms of the Bible. The peasants declared that they had no wish to resort to violence, that the Gospels taught peace, love, unity, and patience, yet their demands were rendered absolute by the insistence that rural life be regulated according to the Word of God. The demand that serfdom be abolished in effect meant the abolition of all local authority, for in the areas of extreme territorial fragmentation the bond of serfdom had become one of the main instruments of lordship and government. The simple and direct formulation of the articles accounts for the document's

---

[20] Williams, *Radical Reformation*, 151–3; Blickle, *Reformation* 90–5.
[21] Blickle, *Revolution*, 34.   [22] Blickle, *Revolution*, 25–6.

popular appeal. Within two months, the Twelve Articles had been reprinted twenty-five times, with a total perhaps 25,000 copies.[23] It became the most important tract of the peasants' movement, the manifesto of their complaints, the document by which oaths were sworn and allegiances declared.

While the Twelve Articles galvanized the peasant alliance, they also intimidated the opposition. Although the forces of the Swabian League under the command of Georg Truchsess von Waldburg achieved some initial success against the Baltringen and Leipheim troops, they were unable to prevail over the 12,000 men of the Lake Constance force or *Seehaufen*. The result was the Treaty of Weingarten, concluded on Easter Monday, 17 April 1525. The peasants were offered a tribunal to adjudicate on their grievances. Meanwhile they agreed to disband and renew their oaths of fealty to their lords. Most of the peasants of the *Seehaufen* did indeed comply with the terms of the treaty. The Baltringen troop had been all but destroyed by the Swabian League's army, but the core of the Allgäu troop, together with remnants of the Baltringen troop and radical elements from the *Seehaufen*, resolved to continue in defiance. It then linked up with renewed discontent to the west in the Black Forest region, with a new ferment in Alsace, and with the first outbreak of violence to the north in Franconia, Württemberg, the Rheingau and, finally, in Thuringia.

The centre of this new wave of disobedience was the more violent Franconian uprising, which flared up just as the Treaty of Weingarten brought peace to Upper Swabia. The Upper Swabian peasants had sought a peaceful accommodation with the lords; the Franconian troops of the Taubertal and the Odenwald declared war on them. When the Odenwald-Neckartal troop captured the fortress of Weinsberg on 16 April they promptly massacred its custodian Count Ludwig von Helfenstein and his noble colleagues.[24]

This act of outright brutality was exceptional; for the most part, the Odenwald peasants, led by Götz von Berlichingen and the Hohenlohe administrative official Wendel Hipler, were content to demand that nobles swear by the Twelve Articles. Only the Taubertal troop, led by the renegade knight Florian Geyer, retained a more fundamental commitment to destroy the castles and monasteries. For a short time, the Franconian movement seemed poised to achieve fundamental political reform. Berlichingen's tactic of persuading (albeit with thinly veiled threats) nobles, towns, and cities to affiliate to the cause was apparently successful. With the help of the Amorbach Declaration, a watered down version of the Twelve Articles, he even managed to force the Elector of Mainz to accede to the peasants' union and accept the Twelve Articles. Further uprisings in Frankfurt, Bamberg, and Würzburg, and northwards up into Thuringia, as well as in the Swiss cantons to the south, seemed to demonstrate the continuing dynamism of the movement. At the same time, Hipler formulated plans in Heilbronn for a kind of parliament of the peasants and for a general 'reformation', possibly in the form of Friedrich Weygandt's ideas for a systematic reform of the Reich.[25]

---

[23] Blickle, *Revolution*, 23–4.   [24] Franz, *Bauernkrieg*, 191–2.
[25] Blickle, *Revolution*, 206–7; Buszello, 'Legitimation', 319–21.

The Thuringian uprising soon came to assume an explicitly millenarian character, but its underlying grievances were the same as those of the peasants generally.[26] From mid-April, a wave of acts of violence against castles and monasteries swept the region. As in other areas, some independent nobles were obliged to join the Christian League, which seemed preferable to them than seeking the protection of the Duke of Saxony. The Mansfeld miners, however, remained peaceful, bribed by the Count of Mansfeld's tactical offer of a new higher rate of pay. The plans of Heinrich Pfeiffer and Thomas Müntzer added a new dimension to this relatively inchoate rural movement.[27] In February and March, they had successfully led a campaign against the Mühlhausen city council, replacing it with an 'Eternal Council' favourable to their own radical religious programme. Following this, they were ready to pursue their crusade outside the city. Müntzer in particular was determined that the mistakes made in other places should not be repeated. In his appeal to the people of Allstedt at the end of April, he urged them to rally now for the final struggle. They should avoid seductive treaties and false counsel. There could be no talk of God while the tyrants still ruled. The new covenant must rise up to destroy them.[28]

In the event, both the Heilbronn 'parliament' and Müntzer's new covenant were overtaken by the swift recovery of the authorities. On 12 May, Georg Truchsess von Waldburg defeated the Württemberg peasants at Böblingen; ten days later the Duke of Lorraine crushed the Alsace peasants at Zabern. On 15 May, Philip of Hessen and the Duke of Saxony combined forces to defeat Müntzer and the Thuringian peasants at Frankenhausen. Over 5,000 peasants were slaughtered and 600 were taken prisoner; Müntzer himself was captured after the battle, handed over to the Count of Mansfeld, tortured, and beheaded at Mühlhausen on 27 May.

By mid-July, order had been more or less restored throughout the Reich. Only in the Habsburg lands did a final wave of insurgency linger on. Starting in the Tyrol in May 1525, under the leadership of the Bishop of Brixen's secretary and tax collector Michael Gaismair, it spread south to Trent and north to Innsbruck.[29] A 'diet' convened by peasants and townsfolk in Merano at the end of May drew up sixty-four articles. When Archduke Ferdinand moved to undermine it by summoning a formal diet to Innsbruck, the number of articles grew to ninety-six. The movement soon foundered under its own internal contradictions, however, as the coalition of discontents expanded to embrace miners and rural and urban day labourers, in addition to propertied peasants. The publication of a remedy to the popular grievances in the form of a 'Territorial Constitution for the County of Tyrol' temporarily undermined the opposition.

[26] Scott, *Müntzer*, 149–58; Endres, 'Thüringen', 164–9.
[27] Scott, *Müntzer*, 172–5.
[28] Williams, *Radical Reformation*, 163–5.
[29] Macek, *Gaismair*; Bischoff-Urack, *Gaismair*; Bücking, *Gaismair*; Buszello, 'Legitimation', 317–19; Klaassen, *Gaismair*, 1–56.

Gaismair's subsequent escape from captivity and his return with a new, more radical draft collection of laws for the territory (*Landesordnung*) in the following spring failed to renew the Tyrolean rebellion and in July 1526 he was forced to flee to Venice.[30] Despite all his efforts, the contemporaneous uprisings in the Tyrol, Salzburg, Brixen, Trent, Graubünden, and Chur failed to unite into an Alpine revolution. Like the troubles in other parts of the Reich, the Austrian and Swiss uprisings never ultimately transcended their localized roots. Unlike many of the other leaders, though, Gaismair seemed at first to escape retribution. After a year in Venetian service he was able to retire to his estates near Padua, where he continued to work on schemes for an anti-Habsburg alliance of Swiss and German Protestants, until his murder in 1532, apparently by Spanish assassins in the pay of the Habsburg authorities.

The scale and extent of the unrest that swept across the southern and central areas of the Reich between 1524 and 1526 took the authorities everywhere by surprise. For a while, the rebellions seemed so overwhelming that there was little point in resisting them. In every theatre, though, once nerves had been recovered and resources marshalled, the peasants were defeated. The speed with which this was achieved raises questions about the aims of the rebels, their organization and tactics, and finally the question of the impact of their rebellion on German society.

The fundamental aim that united most of the rebels was the redress of social and economic grievances. An analysis of 54 lists of complaints from Upper Swabia containing some 550 separate points reveals the discontent of rural society at the time.[31] Ninety per cent of all complaints concerned serfdom and 70 per cent of all communities demanded its complete abolition; 81 per cent of all complaints related to communal rights over hunting, fishing, wood gathering, and use of common land; 83 per cent related to the material burdens imposed by the *Grundherrschaft* system. Finally, 67 per cent of protests were against seigneurial abuse of the courts and legal process. Demands for the abolition or reduction of tithes figured in over 40 per cent of the petitions, while demands for the right to elect pastors figured in only 13 per cent of the petitions. The Reformation issues, in other words, were added during the discussions that led to the production of the Twelve Articles: after the formation of the peasant troops, and as the troops began to formulate a regional union and a general programme. The role of the military secretaries was crucial, for they were townsmen, in some cases clerics, who introduced the peasant movement to the evangelical issues that had so recently caused turmoil in their own communities.

From the outset, the peasant troops impressed contemporaries by their order and discipline. A flag, pipers and drummers, a field ordinance, and elected officials and commanders were all in place by the time the Stühlingen peasants marched to Waldshut at the end of August. These early troops drew on a variety of traditions. They harked back to the traditions of peasant movements such as the Bundschuh (though that symbol appeared only in the Black Forest in 1525). They also drew on

---

[30] Klaassen, *Gaismair*, 56–70, 73-1-2.   [31] Blickle, *Revolution*, 32–8.

the militia traditions which made it a duty for men to defend their homeland, to provide themselves with pikes, short swords, and leather jerkins, and to respond to periodic territorial musters.[32] Above all, they used the organizational forms of the mercenary armies, in which the peasants' commanders had gained military experience and in whose main recruiting grounds the rebellions of 1524 and the spring of 1525 erupted.[33]

In the spring of 1525, however, another important dimension was added. The formation of Christian leagues or unions seemed to presage the emergence of new constitutional forms. Just how far these really went beyond the military coordination of the various troops is debatable. Owing to their short-lived nature, it is difficult to assess whether a viable political organization would have emerged, still less whether a new constitutional system could have been established. The frequent use of the term 'Landschaft' in conjunction with 'Christian union' indicates at least some level of aspiration to political organization. In contemporary usage, the term could refer either to a territorial diet and the Estates entitled to sit in it or to the inhabitants of a region generally. For the peasants in 1525, it generally meant something broader: the entire population of a region organized in a Christian union, often explicitly including any clergy and nobles willing to swear on the Twelve Articles. The communities provided the men for the *Haufen* or troop; the *Haufen*, in turn, elected both its own officers and representatives for the Landschaft.

Two main forms of political organization were envisaged. In areas dominated by a single territorial government (for example in Baden, Württemberg, Bamberg, Würzburg, Salzburg, and the Tyrol), the Landschaft was a kind of diet that governed in conjunction with or (as in Salzburg, Baden, and Württemberg) instead of the current ruling prince. In areas such as Upper Swabia and Alsace, dominated by a multiplicity of fragmented lordships, the Landschaft or Christian union was envisaged as a confederation founded on an oath of brotherhood and loyalty after the Swiss fashion. Both political forms made the community the basis of political society and each made the Word of God the sole yardstick of law and rightful authority.[34] However, the explicit appeal to the Gospels was most frequently made in areas of greater territorial fragmentation. In the larger territories, the demand for a true Landschaft could often, and just as easily, be formulated in terms of a return to the 'old law' (i.e. a supposedly original state of affairs that had accorded with the Word of God).[35]

For all their novelty, the political or constitutional plans that emerged from the militant peasant movement were not implemented systematically. The early defeat of the movement is one reason for this. Another is its inherent moderation and conservatism. The peasants lost no opportunity to reiterate their undying loyalty to the emperor. Their organizational plans did not fundamentally challenge the existing territorial arrangements, though they had a radical view of the legitimate

---

[32] Hoyer, 'Arms'.
[33] Baumann, *Landsknechte*, 29–47, 62–71, 92–130; Möller, *Regiment*, 25, 183.
[34] Blickle, *Bauernkrieg*, 94.　　　[35] Buszello, 'Legitimation', 288.

exercise of power within them. The aim was not to eliminate the lords and princes but, for the most part, to ensure that if they continued to rule they did so in accordance with the laws of God. Many lived in the hope that the old authorities might yet become 'Christian' and rule their subjects in a 'brotherly' fashion.[36] Once they secured agreement to an independent adjudication of those grievances, the peasant forces invariably agreed to desist from further action, or even to disband.

It was only when that inclination had repeatedly been cynically exploited that a degree of real radicalism began to take hold, by which time it was almost too late anyway. Although Thomas Müntzer had decided even before the Peasants' War that princes and magistrates must be destroyed, others came to that conclusion only when the first waves of violence had failed to achieve any redress of their grievances.

Perhaps the most radical pamphlet produced in 1525, *An die Versammlung gemeiner Bauernschaft* ('To the Assembly of Common Peasantry'), was written as the peasant forces were on the verge of defeat and published in Nuremberg just a few days after the battles at Böblingen, Zabern (Saverne), and Frankenhausen.[37] The author, probably someone involved with the Memmingen organization of the Swabian Christian union, had clearly lost all hope of a satisfactory agreement with the authorities. That led him to assert, on historical and biblical grounds, that it was the right and duty of the common man to depose ungodly rulers. For the sake of future generations, all tyrants should be swept away and replaced by a modified version of the Swiss Confederation: free communities of peasants living side by side with feudal lords and urban communes, without ruling princes, but under the emperor as the feudal overlord of all. The argument that ungodly rulers must be deposed also featured in Balthasar Hubmaier's constitutional draft of May 1525, though he went on to suggest that new rulers, not necessarily all nobles, should then be elected.[38]

It is striking that even these radical schemes did not abandon the idea of the Reich as the overall framework for the polity of the future. Just how much that reflected a genuine loyalty to emperor or Reich is unclear. The only plan for imperial reform produced in 1525 was that of Friedrich Weygandt, regional bailiff of Mainz at Miltenberg.[39] His ideas for a more integrated monarchy with a comprehensive judicial system and a standardized coinage drew heavily on the imperial reform tradition, but he cannot be regarded as part of the peasant movement. He never joined the peasants himself and his plans were communicated only to Wendel Hipler, leader of the Neckartal-Odenwald troop. Neither the peasant *Haufen* nor their leaders showed much interest in anything like a unified and centralized national state. The peasant troops of Alsace, for example, frequently stated that they wished to be subservient only to the emperor, yet only one of their twenty flags bore the symbol of the imperial eagle.[40] For most groups, the idea of

---

[36] Buszello, 'Legitimation', 315–16.
[37] Hoyer, 'Rights'; Blickle, *Bauernkrieg*, 98–101; Buszello, 'Legitimation', 316.
[38] Buszello, 'Legitimation', 317; Blickle, *Revolution*, 226–8.
[39] Buszello, 'State', 118–19; Buszello, 'Legitimation', 320–1.
[40] Blickle, *Revolution*, 204; Buszello, 'Legitimation', 319.

staying in the Reich simply reflected geographical reality. For the Thuringians, Franconians, and Swabians, joining the Swiss was simply not a feasible option geographically. By contrast, both the Hegau and the Sundgau peasants, direct neighbours of the Swiss, offered to place themselves under the protection of the Confederation, which would have meant leaving the Reich.[41]

Michael Gaismair's second plan for a Tyrolean constitution contained one of the most radical reform programmes of all.[42] His first constitution of May 1525 envisaged the abolition of feudal dues, of all ecclesiastical foundations and monasteries, and the restriction of nobles to the ownership of a single estate and their integration into the communes. The state itself would become essentially a collection of largely autonomous communes under the prince, financed by revenue derived from half of the tithe. The failure of the first uprising turned the reformer into a revolutionary. When he returned to the Tyrol to organize a new uprising in the spring of 1526, he brought with him the draft outlines of an entirely new society founded on the pure Word of God and the common good. The prince was no longer mentioned. All Estates were to be dissolved; all castles, fortresses, and even city walls were to be razed. All men were to be equal. Feudal dues would be abolished and the tithe used only to pay for the clergy and support the poor. The government in Brixen would comprise members elected from all parts of the land. Godly rule would be ensured by the presence in the government of three theologians from the theological high school, the sole university in this future republic.

Gaismair's plans came no closer to fruition than Müntzer's vision of the bloody prelude to the triumph of the elect over all tyrants and oppressors. The defeat of the peasant armies rendered them irrelevant. The reasons for the collapse of the peasant movements must be sought at various levels.

In military terms, the peasants were ultimately no match for the Swabian League, the Duke of Lorraine, Philip of Hessen, and their allies. The peasant armies were often sizeable: some 20,000 men faced Georg Truchsess von Waldburg at Weingarten and some 18,000 were amassed in Zabern. Many of their members had military or militia experience, and they had leaders of ability and charisma such as Hans Müller of Bulgenbach in the Black Forest, Florian Geyer in Franconia, Erasmus Gerber in Alsace, and Michael Gaismair in the Tyrol. However, they had almost no horsemen and very few firearms. None of the centres of rebel organization, such as Memmingen and Heilbronn, was really suitable as a capital, or even capable of being fortified effectively. The willingness of the peasants to negotiate and their espousal of essentially defensive aims were obstacles to success.

The threat posed by the insurgents seemed all the greater in the spring of 1525 for the handicap under which the Swabian League laboured while the German mercenaries were tied up in Italy.[43] In January 1525, there was a dearth of mercenaries for hire in the southern Reich. Just weeks after the battle of Pavia on 24 April, the market was flooded again, and Georg Truchsess von Waldburg was able

[41] Buszello, 'Legitimation', 317.
[42] Blickle, *Revolution*, 223–6; Buszello, 'Legitimation', 317–18; Hoyer, 'Landesordnung'.
[43] Baumann, *Landsknechte*, 189–93.

to use the money contributed by Swabian League members, notably Bavaria, and loaned by the Fuggers to hire a substantial force. Some mercenaries joined the peasant troops and Waldburg initially experienced difficulty in persuading those whom he hired to fight against peasants, but in the end the forces of the League, of Lorraine, and of Hessen—better equipped, better financed, and better directed—prevailed. By the summer of 1525 at the latest, the power vacuum created by the Habsburgs' campaign against France in Italy had been filled.

It is difficult to assess the significance of the role of Luther and other religious reformers in 1525. The peasants' appeal to the Gospels was clearly inspired by evangelical preaching. On the one hand, the view that Zwingli was a more important influence than Luther appears justified by the fact that Zwingli's theology envisaged the application of the Word of God in a reform of the world, while Luther did not.[44] That may well account for the engagement of many south German reformers in the peasant cause. On the other hand, the Upper Swabian peasants clearly also drew on Luther's ideas. His name appeared in the list of some twenty reformed preachers from whom the Swabian peasants sought instruction in divine justice and to whose judgement they declared themselves willing to submit. Another pamphlet produced at about the same time as the Twelve Articles suggested that Luther should arbitrate the peasant grievances together with Melanchthon or Johannes Bugenhagen.[45]

Zwingli himself did not write about the uprisings in the Reich, since they only affected Zurich and its territory peripherally. Luther's response thus assumed enormous significance. In the first instance, Luther's views were not much different from those of other leading reformers.[46] When Luther was sent a copy of the Twelve Articles, he responded with *Ermanunge zum frid, auff die zwölff Artickel der Bawrschafft in Schwaben* ('Admonition to Peace, on the Twelve Articles of the Peasants in Swabia') at the end of April. He aimed to encourage a negotiated solution, for violence would merely destroy both kingdoms 'and there will be neither worldly government nor Word of God'.[47] To the princes and lords he declared that they themselves were to blame for the distress of the peasantry. To the peasants he insisted that they had no right to take matters into their own hands.

Luther's initially sympathetic attitude to the peasants and his desire for a peaceful outcome also led him to salute the Treaty of Weingarten concluded between the Upper Swabian peasants and Georg Truchsess von Waldburg on 17 April, the text of which he published with an enthusiastic preface. The outbreak of further violence in Franconia and Thuringia, and especially the involvement of Thomas Müntzer in the latter case, created a new situation. It was this that led him to add a new postscript to the third Wittenberg edition of the *Ermanunge*, which was soon published independently as *Wider die mordischen vnd reubischen Rotten*

[44] Blickle, *Revolution*, 237–44.
[45] Bornkamm, *Luther*, 362–3.
[46] Cameron, *Reformation*, 208. For the following, see Brecht, *Luther*, ii, 174–87, and Kolb, 'Theologians'; Gäbler, *Zwingli*, 87–8; Locher, *Reformation*, 231.
[47] Ozment, *Age of reform*, 280.

der Pawren ('Against the Robbing and Murdering Hordes of Peasants'). He now accused the peasants of a breach of faith, unlawful rebellion, and abuse of the Gospels. Along with a vicious condemnation of Müntzer, 'the arch-devil of Mühl-hausen', Luther encouraged the authorities to take an uncompromising stance: if the rebels persisted in refusing talks they must be killed 'like mad dogs'.

By the time Luther's denunciation was published, the peasant armies had already suffered their first reverses. Its twenty-one editions thus served not to enjoin the peasants to peace but apparently to justify harsh repression. That was clearly not Luther's intention, and he soon found he was defending himself both against the accusation that his teachings were partly responsible for the rebellions and against the reproach that his denunciation of the peasants had been unneces-sarily savage. Equally, those who put down the rebellion—foremost among them the Catholic Dukes of Bavaria in the Swabian League, the Duke of Lorraine, and Duke Georg of Saxony—had no need of Luther's encouragement to move against the peasants.

'The blood that has been shed this year 1525', noted Zwingli's friend, colleague, and fellow opponent of Anabaptism, Johannes Stumpf, would be enough to 'drown . . . all tyrants.'[48] In a similar vein, Albrecht Dürer sketched a proposal in his 'Instruction in Mensuration of Lines and of Whole Bodies' for an ironic monument to the defeat of the peasants. It depicted a column constructed with rural artefacts and agricultural implements on a base of agricultural produce and topped by the figure of a peasant hunched in sorrow, like the suffering Christ, with a sword plunged into his back.[49] Judgements like these have often set the tone for negative assessments of the effects of the Peasants' War. In the Marxist tradition, it represented the high point of Germany's failed early bourgeois revolution and its failure ushered in an enduring feudal and patrician reaction. In the classic interpre-tation by Günther Franz, first published in 1933 and still an invaluable source of information, the Peasants' War was a failed political revolution, a tragedy that led to the departure of the German peasant from the political stage for three centuries.[50] Recent interpretations, however, have increasingly produced a more differentiated picture, and have emphasized the ways in which the trauma of 1525 shaped the behaviour of both rulers and ruled in subsequent decades.[51]

There can be little doubt about the harshness with which the authorities destroyed the peasant armies. Some 75,000 peasants perished in these confronta-tions. In some localities, as many as 10–15 per cent of the male population capable of bearing arms perished within a few brutal weeks.[52] The ringleaders of the rebellion were pursued mercilessly over the following months and years. The commanders were summarily executed; other activists were imprisoned or obliged to subscribe to new oaths of allegiance to their lords, foreswearing all further seditious activity.[53] Similarly, in many areas, the peasants faced heavy demands for compensation both from the Swabian League for the costs it incurred in

[48] Blickle, *Bauernkrieg*, 104.   [49] Blickle, *Revolution*, 275.
[50] Franz, *Bauernkrieg*, 299.   [51] Gabel and Schulze, 'Folgen'.
[52] Franz, *Bauernkrieg*, 299.   [53] Gabel and Schulze, 'Folgen', 334–5.

maintaining its forces and from the various lords and princes whose property they had damaged or destroyed.[54] In Thuringia, some villages had to mortgage their common lands to pay the penalty they incurred from the uprising.[55] The Elector of Saxony was still demanding such payments as late as 1540, and the Imperial City of Mühlhausen only regained its independence in 1548, until which point Saxony and Hessen alternated as overlords and extracted significant payments.[56]

The peasants were defeated decisively, but they did achieve some of their objectives. The princes showed themselves acutely aware of the causes of the unrest and inclined to take measures to prevent its repetition. Even as the last peasant armies were being crushed, preparations were being made to discuss the issue at a meeting of the Reichstag planned for Augsburg in September 1525. In the first instance, this meant military precautions, but the discussion ultimately widened to a consideration of the peasants' grievances.[57]

When the Reichstag finally met in Speyer in June 1526, it discussed a wide-ranging catalogue of recommendations designed to alleviate the burden on the peasantry. One suggestion was to end the payment of annates to Rome, especially the 'consecration taxes' that weighed so heavily in the episcopal territories. Another was that laymen should no longer be subject to ecclesiastical courts, and recommended that the quality of the local clergy be improved. Other recommendations included the abolition of recently introduced petty tithes, death taxes, and labour services, the return of common fields, woods and streams, and the right to protect fields against wild animals.

All Estates were urged to hold themselves in military readiness in the event of a new rebellion. Nevertheless, rulers were enjoined to treat their subjects in such a way as could be reconciled with their consciences, with 'divine and natural law' and with 'fairness'. Above all, the report insisted that all should have free access to the courts in the event of future grievances: disputes between peasants and nobles who were subject to a prince were to go before territorial courts; disputes between peasants and immediate lords were to go to the Reichskammergericht or the Reichsregiment. The enunciation of the principle of conflict resolution by judicial process in relation to arguments over compensation payments both recognized the validity of peasant grievances and created a new framework for the future.

What emerged at the Reichstag reflected the strategy of repression, compromise, and concession pursued in fact by numerous princes, lords, and magistrates. In many areas, the conclusion of formal treaties that either mitigated or abolished the more objectionable aspects of feudal subservience marked the end of the hostilities.[58] These treaties were remarkable, since many minor rulers had bitter memories of being driven out in 1525, of the pillaging and destruction of their castles and residences, or of being forced to subscribe to the peasants' cause. In general, the peasant's tenure of his land was improved and assumed the quality and legal status of ownership, and his personal freedom was secured legally. The peasants of Georg Truchsess von

[54] Gabel and Schulze, 'Folgen', 330–4.   [55] Endres, 'Thüringen', 175–6.
[56] Vogler, 'Reformation', 190; Köbler, *Lexikon*, 439.   [57] Vogler, 'Bauernkrieg', 186–91.
[58] Blickle, *Revolution*, 254–65; Gabel and Schulze, 'Folgen', 336–7.

Waldburg, for example, secured the redress of most of their grievances in the spring of 1526. Likewise, the subjects of the Abbey of Kempten, who had a long and bitter history of resentment against exploitation, achieved the removal of all the most objectionable features of personal serfdom in the Treaty of Memmingen, which remained the contractual basis for relations between the abbey and its subjects until secularization in 1803. In a similar spirit, the Imperial Cities of Nuremberg, Basle, and Memmingen moved swiftly to improve conditions for the peasants in their subservient territories.[59]

Similar outcomes also emerged in some of the larger territories.[60] In the Tyrol, the *Landesordnung* of 1526 made significant concessions to the peasantry, including improved rights of ownership, abolition of certain labour services, and deregulation of hunting and fishing. In Salzburg, a *Landesordnung* of November 1526 introduced a variety of reforms and gave the peasantry the right to pursue claims in the courts. In both Hessen and Mainz, there was consideration of peasant grievances when the repression ended and far-reaching reforms were introduced. An important aspect of this process was the extension of greater control over the nobility, over the urban magistrates, and over village communes.[61]

The conclusion of a formal treaty and the concession of improvements could also be accompanied by formal or informal changes in constitutional arrangements which allowed the peasantry to play a role in territorial government.[62] In territories such as the Tyrol, Salzburg, and Baden peasant representatives from the various districts or bailiwicks joined the Landtag or territorial Estates on a regular basis for the first time. In some smaller territories that contained no nobles or town to constitute a Landtag, the years immediately after 1525 saw the formal institution of representative bodies of the peasants or Landschaften. This kind of body was typical of the monastic lordships of Upper Swabia and parts of Bavaria. They watched over the agreements reached in 1525 and were quick to complain about innovations; their consent was crucial in matters of taxation, legislation, and territorial defence, and they were sometimes able to negotiate improvements in conditions in return for their cooperation in these matters.

What was the long-term significance of these developments?[63] The precise role played by the Landschaft or peasant representatives differed according to the size and nature of the territory, its individual history, and distinctive institutional forms. As the memory of 1525 began to recede a little, so some rulers were inclined to take a loftier view of their subjects and adopt a more robust approach to their complaints. Some Landschaften were extremely short-lived, appearing in times of crisis but then folding: the Kempten Landschaft ceased to function as early as 1527 and it was not revived until 1667. While classic tricameral Estates (often dominated by

---

[59] Blickle, *Revolution*, 265.
[60] Blickle, *Revolution*, 265–71; Gabel and Schulze, 'Folgen', 337–8.
[61] Press, 'Bauernkrieg', 126–7.
[62] Blickle, *Landschaften, passim*; Holenstein, *Bauern*, 101–3.
[63] Press, 'Herrschaft', 201–14.

the nobility) could act as a powerful 'parliamentary' check on a ruling prince, the peasant Landschaft was no match in the end for the determined efforts of an abbot or a count with legally trained advisers.

Yet allowing the participation of subjects in government could also be a way of securing dominion over a territory. In the first instance, the pressure for such involvement often came from below, but many rulers soon saw the advantage of ruling with rather than against their peasants.[64] Some seem to have encouraged the engagement of peasant representatives to ensure that their subjects paid taxes, took on government debts, and defended the territory.

The Peasants' War created a new framework for relations between rulers and peasants. The profound trauma of those events generated an enduring fear on the part of rulers and lords of a renewed outbreak of violence.[65] Even a relatively minor uprising in September 1525 in Samland in the Duchy of Prussia, which had no real connection with the Peasants' War, was immediately interpreted as evidence of continuing unrest and promptly put down.[66] The fear of further unrest encouraged vigilance and the maintenance of a high state of alert, as the Reichstag enjoined in 1526, and the criminalization of peasant resistance.[67] It also, however, generated in many a new sensitivity to the causes of peasant discontent and an awareness of the need to prevent the emergence of new grievances.

The peasants were aware of their ability to strike terror in the minds of their superiors; since actual violence invariably ended in failure, the threat of violence was often the peasants' most effective weapon. Furthermore, the Reichstag resolutions of 1526 also pointed to a potentially more rewarding way forward: the recourse to legal action, which increasingly became established as a right. Almost immediately after 1525, peasant communities in many of the areas affected by the rebellions began to seek redress for their grievances by means of legal action, rather than direct action.[68] Terms such as 'juridification' (*Verrechtlichung*) and 'conflict resolution mechanisms' might give the misleading impression of a greater degree of rationality and 'modernity' than in fact developed in German rural society after 1525.[69] Yet the Peasants' War clearly shaped an emerging political culture defined by legal process and accommodation that many eighteenth-century commentators believed to be a distinctive characteristic of the Reich.[70]

The degree of political activity of the peasantry in some areas after 1525 and the continuous history of peasant rebellion in the early modern Reich also contradict the view put forward by Günther Franz that the German peasant became an apathetic beast of burden until the nineteenth century.[71] Peasant resistance after 1525 may not have been inspired by the kind of utopian visions of a new republican society that surfaced during the Peasants' War. It was, however, perennially fired by a sense of deep injustice at the imposition of even trivial new

---

[64] Press, 'Herrschaft', 207, 209.   [65] Schulze, *Widerstand*, 49–50.
[66] Wunder, 'Bauernaufstand', 160–1; Franz, *Bauernkrieg*, 276–9.
[67] Schulze, *Widerstand*, 73–6; Blickle, *Unruhen*, 65–7.
[68] Gabel and Schulze, 'Folgen', 341–7.
[69] Schulze, *Widerstand*, 76–85; Holenstein, *Bauern*, 103–12; Blickle, *Unruhen*, 78–80.
[70] Gabel and Schulze, 'Folgen', 340.   [71] Franz, *Bauernkrieg*, 299.

demands and it was often fuelled by the dream of a life of 'Swiss' freedom without lords.[72]

The Peasants' War also had serious implications for the future of the religious reform movement. The Speyer Reichstag deliberations of 1526 made it clear that the princes saw a link between the rebellion of the common man and the evangelical movement. The determination to prevent further outbursts and to remove the main causes of the peasants' grievances by means of reform was accompanied by the desire to establish a firmer control over the religious movement. Luther himself, along with other leading reformers, encouraged this trend by abandoning some of the key communal principles of the early 1520s, most notably the right of communities to elect their own pastors.[73] At the same time, the heterodox nature of the early evangelical movement increasingly gave way to a differentiation between a dominant Lutheran tendency and a minority dissenting non-Lutheran tendency.[74]

The experience of 1525 led to the marginalization of radical groups and demonization of rebels and dissenters as reincarnations of Thomas Müntzer. In future, Anabaptists and others like the radical spiritualist Caspar von Schwenckfeld (c.1489–1561), who turned away from the Lutheran mainstream, would be regarded as the enemies of harmony, peace, and good order. The Anabaptists, whose attitudes were shaped by the defeat of the movements of 1525 and who gained some support in the aftermath, were singled out as a particular threat. They were never more than a minority, growing from forty-three communities to some five hundred communities, with perhaps around ten thousand members by 1529.[75] Yet they were anathema to both secular and Church authorities, for they refused to participate in state and society. They became radical separatists and turned away from society in their bitter disappointment at defeat in 1525.

The most ferocious persecutors of the Anabaptists were the Habsburgs, the Dukes of Bavaria, and other members of the Swabian League, but in 1529 all Estates, regardless of their religious allegiance, joined in formally outlawing them, making the profession of their heresy in the Reich a capital offence.[76] The death of Zwingli in 1531, which within a few years drove his south German disciples into the Lutheran camp, made the clear differentiation of 'heretics' and the imposition of state-sanctioned orthodoxy much easier. A final uprising in Münster in 1533–5 once more demonstrated the explosive revolutionary potential of radical apocalyptic Christianity, but also the futility of its pursuit in the Reich.[77] By the late 1530s the various Anabaptist groups had been largely relegated to rural areas on the periphery, or pushed into the Low Countries or Moravia.

The marginalization of radicals and dissenters and the move towards greater control of the religious movement have often been viewed as heralding the end of the 'people's Reformation' or of the 'evangelical social movements' that began in the early 1520s.[78] What took over now, though in some places it had already

---

[72] Schulze, *Deutsche Geschichte*, 284–5; Schulze, *Widerstand*, 121–3.
[73] Blickle, *Reformation*, 156.   [74] Schilling, 'Alternatives'.   [75] Blickle, *Reformation*, 132.
[76] Stayer, 'Anabaptists', 129–30.   [77] Cameron, *Reformation*, 324–5. See also pp. 246–8.
[78] Scribner, 'Movements', 93; Po-chia Hsia, 'People's Reformation'; Brady, 'Peoples' religions'.

started, was the 'princes' Reformation' or the 'Lutheran Reformation': a shift from spontaneity to control from above, from potential revitalization and reorientation of both Church and society from below to the reassertion of ruling power from above, from democratic-republican activism to a kind of authoritarian control.

The significance of the turning point has often been laboured, and the nature of the alternatives overdrawn, because of the assumed implications for the longer-term development of German history. Marxists viewed the events of 1525 as the failure of the early bourgeois revolution. Others have interpreted them as the defeat of a communal reform movement that might, if followed through to its logical conclusion, have resulted in an alternative political and social order, as well as an alternative Church order.[79] Each argument seeks to explain a truncation in the development of German society. In each case, it is said that the price of failure was the triumph of the princes and the feudal social order and the elimination of all progressive and democratic-republican forces in German history.

Thomas Brady's variation on this theme also sees the eruption of the common man in 1525 as a crucial turning point.[80] The challenge posed to the ruling elites of the Imperial Cities of Upper Germany obliged them to take control of religious reform. In becoming masters of the Reformation, however, they became estranged from the emperor, a rift that the emperor's preoccupation with non-German affairs and his brother Ferdinand's preoccupation with Bohemia and Hungary exacerbated. This combination of circumstances in the mid-1520s finally put paid to any hopes of the construction of a southern centralized Habsburg monarchy based at least partly on the alliance between crown and cities for which Maximilian I had earlier forged the foundations. An important corollary of these developments was the cementing of political particularism in the Reich. In Brady's view, the governing styles of both increasingly 'aristocratic' patrician elites and territorial princes were shaped by the trauma of 1525 and by the consequent need to maintain control.

---

[79] Scribner, 'Communities', 292–4; Scribner, *Reformation*, 37–42; Blickle, *Reformation*, 176–9.
[80] Brady, 'Common Man', 152.

19

Reformation in the Cities

The evangelical movement in the towns and cities cannot simply be seen as being parallel to what developed in the rural areas before 1525. For one thing, the evangelical movement was in the first instance an urban movement. It was in the towns and cities that reformed ideas were first received, discussed, and transmitted by intellectuals, whether educated clerics or lay humanists, or even just a teacher at the local Latin school. It was here that printers first disseminated evangelical principles to a wider audience.

These communities, among them the episcopal cities, with their high concentration of churches and monastic institutions, were also those in which the confrontation with the ecclesiastical hierarchy was at its most direct. In many cases, that confrontation had already occurred in the late fifteenth century as magistrates strove to gain control over clerical appointments and charitable institutions, and to establish freedom from ecclesiastical courts or episcopal control. Similarly, the pious investments made by rich citizens or guilds in altars, chapels, endowed Masses, or preacherships enhanced communal control over the Church. Indeed, in some urban communes the Reformation merely completed a process begun long before, and substantially completed before 1517.

The generalized use of the term 'community' as a slogan in the early 1520s cannot disguise the fact that there was a world of difference between the commune of the village and the larger commune of the town or city. Even in the smallest towns, the *Ackerbürgerstädte* populated largely by people who made their living on the land, the legal status of the inhabitants and the ethos in which they shared as members of an urban commune distinguished them clearly from the peasant. The latter was subject to a lord. The former was free and, in theory at least, an equal member of his community.

The urban movement also embraced a much wider geographical range and extended over a longer period. In the early 1520s, at a time when the majority of princes remained neutral or prevaricated, the breakthrough of Protestantism in some Imperial Cities was significant for the ultimate breakthrough of Protestantism in the Reich as a whole. The series of urban reformations then continued undiminished in the late 1520s and 1530s. The religious reforms of the Hanseatic Cities of the north were as significant as those in the Imperial Cities of the south-west. The reformations in these northern towns and cities, distant from the old imperial heartlands and with often only tenuous connections with the Reich at this stage, were scarcely affected either by the events of the Peasants' War or, indeed, by the subsequent upheavals of the Schmalkaldic War.[1] The incidence of popular urban reformation movements for several decades after 1525 indicates the continuing attraction of and potential for evangelical reform long after the debacle of the Peasants' War.

After the dramatic reforms of the early 1520s, the reformation process was often extremely protracted. The Imperial City of Wimpfen, for example, experienced a vigorous evangelical movement in the early 1520s, followed by a Catholic reaction after 1525.[2] In the late 1540s, the Protestant minority was virtually eliminated after the imposition of Charles V's Interim.[3] Thereafter, the Protestants fought back and gained a majority in the city council in the mid-1560s, which marked the beginnings of a Lutheran Reformation, culminating in the abolition of Catholic worship in 1589.

The extreme variety of urban reformations has generated a variety of competing explanatory models. Some stress the primacy of religious factors, though there is disagreement over whether the Reformation represented a 'sacralization' of the ideal community or the 'desacralization' or emancipation of the community from the Church.[4] Others have stressed the primacy of social, economic, and political factors and have viewed the reformation process as an internal power struggle within the community.

Much depended on the status and size of the town or city. The group of some sixty-five Imperial Cities, concentrated in the south of the Reich, was particularly susceptible to evangelical reform movements.[5] All but fourteen of them became Lutheran and only five small Swabian and Alsatian Imperial Cities remained wholly untouched by the Reformation. The Hanseatic Cities formed another group within the wider spectrum of northern towns, where autonomy or partial autonomy in the sense of self-government and independence was more or less the norm. The Reformation movements here were no less energetic than those in the Imperial Cities of the south.

This once again raises questions about possible differences between Luther and Zwingli. The significance of the division between a Zwinglian-reformed south and a Lutheran north appears diminished by the observation of similar evangelical movements in each sphere. Indeed, even in the south, the evangelical movement was Lutheran before it was Zwinglian. Once Zwingli's influence began to spread after 1523, many urban reformations such as at Nuremberg proceeded under the influence of the ideas of both major reformers. Only the controversy over the Eucharist seemed to create a clear division, which endured until the Zwinglian reformed cities returned to the Lutheran fold following Zwingli's death in 1531.

There is evidence that in some cities Luther's ideas appealed to the more prosperous elite, while Zwingli's teaching was more attractive to the middle- and

---

[1] See pp. 317–24.
[2] Schmidt, *Konfessionalisierung*, 5–6; Schindling and Ziegler, *Territorien*, v, 208–9.
[3] See pp. 323–4. [4] Schilling, *Stadt*, 94–5.
[5] Moeller, *Reichsstadt, passim*.

lower-status groups.[6] Reasons given for this include Zwingli's much clearer and more emphatic break with Catholic ritual and, above all, his emphasis on a reform of society as well as of the Church and his more rationalist—that is, less complex— understanding of the Eucharist. Some have suggested that Zwingli's rationalist view of the Eucharist appealed to intellectuals, while Luther's sacral interpretation of the Lord's Supper appealed to the communalism of the guilds.[7]

Most contemporaries, however, probably did not make the distinctions that have so preoccupied modern scholars. Even before Zwingli's emergence as a reformer, the popular evangelical movement of the 'common man' understood Luther in what one might term a 'Zwinglian' sense.[8] The abstraction of Luther's doctrine of the two kingdoms was beyond the minds of any but the educated. For the 'common man', it was obvious that the Gospels represented laws that must govern the world. Popular theology in the early urban reformation was communal theol- ogy. In the north, of course, Luther's ideas were predominant throughout and Zwingli played no part at all.[9]

The nature and outcome of an urban reformation movement was also often determined by the external situation of the city and by its internal organization. Imperial Cities may have been free, but their policies were often inhibited by factors such as dependence upon the goodwill of the emperor or the presence of an imperial institution, such as the Hofgericht at Rottweil. In Cologne, for example, one of the factors that set the city council against the evangelical movement as early as 1520 was the need to safeguard the vital trade routes along the Rhine to the Netherlands and hence to maintain good relations with Charles V.[10] Another factor was the desire to secure the support of the papal legate against the claims over the city of the Elector-Archbishop. In other cathedral towns, evangelical movements could be manifestations of rebellion against episcopal overlords, though none of these in fact succeeded.[11]

Elsewhere in the Reich, especially north of the Main, evangelical movements prevailed in many territorial towns independently of, or even against, the ruling prince. Similarly, many Imperial Cities existed in a perpetual state of tension. Powerful territorial neighbours were perennially eager to undermine their indepen- dence, a long-term struggle in which the Reformation upheavals generated new potential for conflict and armed intervention. Mühlhausen in Thuringia, for example, the centre of Thomas Müntzer's last stand in 1525, effectively lost its Imperial City status for several decades after 1525. It was subjected to the annually alternating overlordship of Saxony and Hessen until 1548.[12]

There is no typical urban Reformation.[13] The urban communes of the Reich embraced huge variety in terms of size, constitution, economic and social condi- tions, external circumstances, and both legal and actual status. These determined

---

[6] Hamm, *Bürgertum*, 138.   [7] Schilling, 'Alternatives', 118.
[8] Hamm, *Bürgertum*, 136–7; Moeller, *Reichsstadt*, 87–94; Schmidt, *Reichsstädte*, 335–6.
[9] Hamm, *Bürgertum*, 139.   [10] Scribner, 'Cologne'.
[11] Rublack, *Gescheiterte Reformation*.   [12] Köbler, *Lexikon*, 439–40.
[13] For the following, see Cameron, *Reformation*, 210–63; Dickens, *German Nation*, 135–99; Blickle, *Reformation*, 81–105; Brady, 'Godly city'.

the timing and pace of the reformation process in each commune, the nature of the social groups involved, and the political issues with which the religious movement became entwined. The immense scholarly activity devoted to exploring this variety over the last few decades, however, has revealed some common features of the urban experience.

The republican ideal yielded guiding principles, expressed in terms such as 'the common good', peace, order, unity, and justice, that influenced the approach to government of many magistrates and urban officials, particularly those trained in Roman law, whose influence grew so markedly in the later fifteenth century. Moreover, at times of internal crisis, when groups protested against mismanagement, corruption or elitism, these same principles provided an ideology of protest and a series of arguments for a return to the constitutional status quo.[14] In this urban context, the term *Gemeinde* could thus stand for a variety of causes and positions, from the ideal of equality to which protesters wished to return, to the order that magistrates sought to re-establish. These notions played a key role in shaping both the thrust of the urban evangelical movement and the way in which communities came to terms with it.

Almost invariably, things were set in motion by the reception and discussion of evangelical ideas among one or more elite groups. In some of the larger Imperial Cities such as Nuremberg or Strassburg, groups of humanists took the lead. In others, individual clergy were more influential. In some smaller towns without humanists, universities or prestigious clerics, the schoolteachers, and simple preachers represented the intellectual vanguard of the new teaching. Gradually, the dissemination of evangelical ideas by preaching and the print media fuelled a more popular movement. Associated with it was often a variety of forms of direct action: assaults on Church property and personnel, the profanation of sacred places and objects, public ridicule of the Church in carnivals, and the like. Evangelical preachers invariably attracted considerable audiences. Along with pamphlets and broadsheets, sermons also generated an appetite for action. The evangelical message thus gave a new and specific meaning to that general expectation of change that suffused much of German society around 1500. Demand for the new teaching quickly translated into demand for a thorough reform of the local church system. Once the dictum of the sole authority of the Scriptures was established as the new holy writ, the notion that Scripture should govern society as well as the Church was quick to follow.

Popular pressure for change also frequently became linked with a variety of other issues: the political and social discontents and aspirations of the 'common man', as well as his religious ideals. The demand for preaching of the true gospel, for the communal appointment of preachers, and the right of the community to determine correct doctrine and to maintain simple churches, frequently led to other more worldly demands.

---

[14] Friedeburg, 'Kommunalismus', 72; Scribner, 'Communities', 311–14.

The assertion of the rights of the community in religious matters could lead to the reassertion of those rights in political matters. In towns dominated by patriciates or by strongly oligarchic magistracies, a popular evangelical movement could become associated with a drive to reassert the core values of the urban polity as a whole. In the Hanseatic Cities of the north, notably Hamburg and Lübeck, this kind of movement was typically associated with the formation of 'citizen committees' that pushed for participation in all areas of urban government and administration.[15] In Hamburg, these 'committees' were organized on parochial lines, following a local precedent set in a major crisis in relations between magistrates and citizenry in 1410.[16] A similar pattern of events, though with guilds fulfilling the role of the 'committees', can be discerned in the oligarchic towns of Franconia and northern Swabia, where merchants and guilds excluded from the ruling elite linked the demand for evangelical reform with the demand for political participation. By contrast, in many Upper Swabian towns, where guilds were influential in the ruling councils, or even dominated them, the translation of the popular demand for evangelical reform into law proceeded more smoothly.

Even where social and economic conflicts seem to have been absent, the emergence of a vigorous popular movement often posed serious problems of order and threatened the stability and equilibrium of the polity. The response of magistrates to these issues was therefore crucial. In perhaps the majority of cases, councils initially prevaricated and attempted to steer a neutral course. This was particularly characteristic of the Upper German Imperial Cities in the early 1520s, as the Reichstag failed to agree on the execution of the Edict of Worms and while the expectation of a national Church council was high. At the same time, other considerations dictated action that was more positive. Attempts by bishops to ban evangelical preachers revived long-standing frictions over ecclesiastical jurisdiction, leading many city councils to reassert their rights by protecting 'their' clergy, in addition to appointing new ones in response to popular demand. Equally, councils were anxious to prevent radical preachers, often itinerants or mavericks, from stirring up discontent. Even before 1525, this was a prime objective; after 1525, it became an overwhelming imperative.

The device of the 'preaching mandate' or 'Scripture mandate' was ideally suited to maintaining both neutrality and control.[17] All preachers within a town's jurisdiction were ordered to preach according to Scripture, or to preach only what was consistent with Scripture or the Word of God. That enabled a council to defend itself against criticism from outside, to assert its rights over the town's churches, to prevent feuds among the clergy, and to warn off those preachers suspected of stirring up unrest. At the same time, however, councils effectively made themselves arbiters of what should be taught from the pulpits. In some cases, this resulted in the council turning for guidance to an influential local preacher, who then became the town's reformer. In Hamburg and other places in north Germany, Johannes

---

[15] Schilling, 'Hanseatic Cities'.
[16] Blickle, *Reformation*, 104.
[17] Cameron, *Reformation*, 235–8.

Bugenhagen (1485–1558), who supplied a number of urban Church ordinances, played this role. Almost every Imperial City in Upper Germany had its own 'reformer'.

Another way of determining which interpretation of the gospel, which dogma, should prevail in the town was for a council to stage a public disputation or debate. The outcome of most of these was rarely in doubt. Typically, the audience consisted of the council and representatives of the community, such as guild nominees. In some cases, referendums in which all citizens or all guild members participated took the decision on doctrine.[18] Finally, the council itself invariably took the formal decision concerning reform, thus asserting or reasserting its mastery over the polity. This does not preclude the influence of profound religious conviction or a genuine belief in the ideals of unity and harmony, the maintenance of which was so often proclaimed as the objective of 'wholesome' or 'beneficial' reform of the Church in a town or city. In the majority of cases, however, fears of unrest and ambitions to maintain the position of an oligarchy also played an important role. Taking the initiative also meant that councils could avert the threat of what might be described as a 'new papacy' even more tyrannical that the old one, whereby the town really was transformed into a godly republic ruled by dogmatic and fanatical preachers.[19]

Support for the new teaching by elite groups was crucial at two points: when it first began to take root and when the city council made the decision in favour of reform. Between those two points, popular enthusiasm generated a demand for change. That often spilled over into wider political issues, and, even where it did not happen, popular enthusiasm could threaten the stability and unity of the polity. In Nuremberg, for example, reform was introduced from above by magistrates who remained firmly in control at all times—a classic 'magisterial Reformation' carried out by an elite in which humanist and evangelical elements had been influential from the outset.[20] Yet even here, the crucial turning point came in 1524, when the city council raised a force of seven hundred men in response to the unrest generated among the guild craftsmen by the arrival in the city of a delegation of peasants from the city's outlying territory. Negotiations with the guild masters and the execution of several ringleaders subdued the unrest, but the perceived threat of violence turned a policy of restrained support for the evangelical cause into an active desire to establish clarity in religious matters. A disputation between evangelical and traditional preachers in March 1525 led to a formal decision by the city council in favour of the evangelicals. Once the council had banned traditional preachers, it embarked on the systematic reform of the city's churches and ecclesiastical institutions.

Where radical regimes actually managed to establish themselves, they soon failed. In the Imperial and Hanseatic City of Lübeck, for example, mounting popular pressure from non-patrician merchants and guild groups during the 1520s, organized in a citizens' committee from 1528, resulted in the introduction of

---

[18] Blickle, *Reformation*, 105.   [19] Brady, 'Godly city', 187.
[20] Blickle, *Reformation*, 87–90; Strauss, *Nuremberg*, 154–86; Vogler, 'Nuremberg'.

a reformed Church order formulated by Johannes Bugenhagen in 1531.[21] Unusually, however, the opposition did not simply subside after the reform.

Under the leadership of Jürgen Wullenwever (1492–1537), the popular movement continued to agitate against the patrician council.[22] Finally, in 1533, a coup established Wullenwever as *Bürgermeister*, presiding over a new council composed of non-patrician merchants and guild masters. His undoing was his overambitious foreign policy, which aspired to assert Lübeck's primacy in the Baltic over Denmark and the Netherlands. By 1535, this aim had manifestly failed and the city was unable to resist a decree from the Reichskammergericht ordering the restoration of the patrician constitution. Two years later, Wullenwever, by now *Amtmann* or bailiff in Bergedorf, was captured by the Archbishop of Bremen. He was handed over to the Archbishop's brother, the Catholic Heinrich of Brunswick-Wolfenbüttel, who promptly tried him and executed him as a robber of church property, rebel, and putative Anabaptist.[23]

Wullenwever was certainly a rebel and, from a Catholic point of view, a 'church-robber', but he was not an Anabaptist. The charge almost certainly sprang up because of events in Münster in 1534–5. Here, a radical social and political opposition to the bishop combined with apocalyptic Anabaptism in an explosion of violence that was cited even a century later as a warning of what could happen if lawful authority was removed.[24] A long-running conflict between the bishop and the town over evangelical preaching culminated in the expulsion of all Catholic priests in 1532, a move that the bishop was forced to accept in a treaty the following year.[25] Soon, however, the most prominent evangelical preacher, Bernhard Rothmann (*c*.1495–*c*.1535), fell under the influence of radical sectarians and began to denounce child baptism. The Lutheran town council's attempt to silence Rothmann merely led him and his adherents to make common cause with the radical Anabaptist groups that had become established in the Lower Rhineland and the northern Low Countries.

These successors to the radical outcasts from Switzerland and Upper Germany after 1525 were a mixture of quietists and activists, among whom the apocalyptic visionary and furrier Melchior Hofmann (*c*.1495–1543) had become a dominating influence.[26] Hofmann confidently predicted that the end of the world was due in 1534 and declared that Strassburg, where he settled in 1530 and was promptly imprisoned, would be the New Jerusalem. His disciples down the Rhine took a broader and more radical view. Hofmann himself meekly submitted to worldly authority, which he vainly hoped would heed his prophecy, but many Melchiorites, as his devotees were known, thought in terms of a new world order before the end of all order. While Hofmann languished in his Strassburg prison cell, his disciples variously identified Amsterdam, Münster, London, and Groningen, in

[21] Rabe, *Geschichte*, 339–41.
[22] Korell, *Wullenwever, passim*; Schindling and Ziegler, *Territorien*, vi, 118–22.
[23] Korrel, *Wullenwever*, 114.   [24] Friedeburg, 'Wegscheide', 561–2.
[25] Schindling and Ziegler, *Territorien*, iii, 108–20.
[26] Clasen, *Anabaptists*, and Clasen, *Anabaptism*.

addition to Strassburg, as 'possible sites for the descent of the heavenly Jerusalem'.[27] When the Leiden Melchiorite leader Jan Beukelsz (?1509–1537) visited Münster in the autumn of 1533, he found Rothmann openly denying the scriptural basis for infant baptism. Beukelsz's announcement of this news in Holland prompted many Dutch Anabaptists to flock to Münster during the winter. Foremost among them was Jan Matthijs, the prophet of Harlem, who presumed to declare that Hofmann had erred concerning both the timing and the location of the New Jerusalem.[28]

Preparations made by the bishop to take action against the Anabaptists, and possibly then the Lutherans too, merely inflamed the situation further. In the council elections of February 1534, Rothmann's supporter Bernhard Knipperdolling (*c.*1495–1536) was elected *Bürgermeister* and Melchiorite officials took all seats on the council. For six weeks the real ruler of the town was Jan Matthijs, whose campaign to exterminate the godless was only ended by his own death in a suicidal attempt to break through the bishop's siege. The twenty-five-year-old Jan Beukelsz immediately took his place, and the last days began in earnest. The council was dissolved on the grounds that it had been elected by mere humans.[29] Declaring himself the voice of the Lord, Beukelsz appointed twelve elders and instituted a radical godly order. Some two thousand who refused to repent were expelled, a community of goods was declared, and polygamy was made standard, which helped solve the problem of the imbalance in the population between five thousand women and two thousand men.

Finally, in September, Beukelsz had himself anointed and crowned by Jan Dusentschuer, the 'limping prophet', at an extraordinary mass banquet in the main square attended by the entire populace. This was the first of numerous spectacular public displays of the new 'kingdom', rendered even more theatrical by the previous training of many leading Melchiorites in the morality plays staged by the Dutch Chambers of Rhetoric. His attempt to rally the Anabaptists of the entire north-west of the Reich by sending out twenty-seven apostles failed to unleash the kind of *levée en masse* that he hoped would save his kingdom from the ungodly forces of the princes that were ranged against him.

By June 1535, Beukelsz's remaining depleted, hungry, and illness-plagued 'subjects' surrendered to the bishop who, aided by both Catholic and Protestant princes, re-entered the city. Beukelsz and his two main lieutenants were summarily tried, tortured, executed, and their corpses hung in iron cages from the spire of St Lambert's Church as a warning to all future rebels. Any remaining Anabaptists were driven from the city.[30] In the course of the brutal revenge that followed Beukelsz's fall, the Lutherans too became victims as the city elite embraced Catholicism

---

[27] Williams, *Radical Reformation*, 539.

[28] Israel, *Dutch Republic 1476–1806*, 87; Williams, *Radical Reformation*, 561.

[29] Williams, *Radical Reformation*, 567.

[30] Most of the remaining Anabaptists migrated to the Netherlands, where the most successful leader was Menno Simons (1496–1561). His followers, known as Mennonites, were periodically subject to persecution. Some remained in the northern Netherlands; others settled in England or north-west Germany. An Anabaptist tradition also survived in Switzerland and Alsace, with ramifications in south-

as the best protection against sedition.[31] Even the twenty leading Lutherans, who had opposed the radicals, were disenfranchised on their return and were prohibited from openly professing their beliefs; only after 1555 were other Lutherans once more permitted to reside, though still not to worship openly, in the city.[32]

Münster was a disaster. Princes of all religious persuasions united to crush the rebels and their defeat spelled the end of the Münster Reformation. Only the bishop's lack of money enabled the burghers to regain their civic liberties in 1541, and the city's aspirations to independence from the bishop only revived again after 1585.[33] Though exceptional, the case of Münster serves to underline the profound impact of the urban reform movement generally. The Imperial Cities may not have become godly cities, but the transformation they underwent was profound even so.[34] In the eighteenth century, the Reformation came to be commemorated in many Imperial Cities as a kind of rebirth: the religious transformation of the early sixteenth century marked the formation of their modern identity.[35]

Communal control over the Church, gradually extended since the fifteenth century, was now finally established. The old tension between ecclesiastical and civic jurisdictions was resolved in favour of the secular authorities, who now assumed full responsibility for a city's church institutions. The clergy, once a class apart, became citizens, effectively joining the educated urban elite. Clerical discipline and church discipline generally, the enforcement of morals among the laity too, remained contentious issues and were only gradually institutionalized.[36] Many cities subsequently faced claims by their clergy to be above or outside the law, in some way privileged with freedom of speech and a mission to keep secular authority on the godly path. In fact, however, the legal position of the clergy was no different to that of other citizens or 'subjects' of a council.

Communal control over the Church also significantly widened the sphere of urban government.[37] The abolition of the Mass was but the most public symbolic act in a reorganization of the religious life of the community that affected many different areas. The removal of images and altars and all the accoutrements of Catholic worship that were now considered idolatrous and superfluous to the pure worship of God physically transformed urban churches. The cluttered churches of the Middle Ages were replaced by simpler and more open interiors suitable for the sermons and communal song that were the main characteristics of the new worship.[38] The urban landscape was transformed by the dissolution of convents and monasteries. Church property, especially that of the religious foundations, was taken into secular control and its uses reassessed. Some still provided the upkeep of churches and the pay of pastors. 'Common chests' were created to fund poor relief and hospitals. Schools, too, were maintained from these funds, and many towns

---

west Germany. Various small groups, including the Amish and the Schwarzenau Brethren, migrated to America in the late seventeenth and early eighteenth centuries. See Driedger, *Heretics*, 9–15.

[31] Po-chia Hsia, *Society*, 8–9.   [32] Po-chia Hsia, *Society*, 199.
[33] Po-chia Hsia, *Society*, 18; Köbler, *Lexikon*, 442–3.   [34] Brady, 'Godly city'.
[35] Whaley, *Toleration*, 186–203; François, *Grenze*, 153–63.   [36] Cameron, *Reformation*, 260.
[37] For the following, see Cameron, *Reformation*, 246–61.   [38] Rabe, *Geschichte*, 266–8.

gradually increased both the number and type of schools, from the elementary level to the Gymnasium, the latter often providing an education similar to many universities.[39]

Communal control did not necessarily mean control by the 'common man'. The citizens' committees or guild movements that so often forced the issue of reform rarely maintained their influence after the introduction of the crucial changes. Hamburg was exceptional in institutionalizing the committees on a permanent basis: they endured into the nineteenth century as representative organs of the Bürgerschaft, responsible both for parish administration and for political negotiation with the council.[40] Even here, however, the old elites soon re-established their control and learned to manage the new representative bodies.

In most other places, the organizations and the influence they achieved in the Reformation years disappeared again as the old structures of government were re-established. Indeed, generally, the Reformation further enhanced the position and power of magistrates in the Imperial Cities. In 1548, this tendency was dramatically reinforced in the thirty or so Swabian Imperial Cities, when Charles V reasserted his imperial rights over the cities by eliminating the guilds from government (he held them responsible for the Reformation) and by imposing strictly patrician regimes upon them.[41]

The general resurgence of oligarchies did not wholly extinguish the forces that had erupted with such vigour during the Reformation. Just as the rebellious instincts of the German peasant did not perish with the defeat of 1525, so the 'common man' in the cities retained his capacity to challenge the magistrates.[42] In most Imperial Cities, the late medieval dualism of council and community remained characteristic until the eighteenth century.[43] Almost all continued to experience periodic frictions, sometimes with extreme violence, over issues such as taxation, financial management, and the extent to which the council remained representative of the burghers.

At the same time, the following decades saw an increasing differentiation between the Imperial Cities and the territorial towns. The Imperial Cities maintained their independence. Despite the religious divide among them and despite the friction between some of those that turned Protestant and the emperor, the Imperial Cities also maintained their corporative solidarity. They were able to promote their collective interests in the Reich and managed to establish their representation at the Reichstag, finally achieving a full vote in 1648. While Charles V was able to influence the constitutions of many of them, he was unable to impose his Interim religious settlement.

The traditional view that the Imperial Cities entered a long period of decline after about 1550 is no longer accepted.[44] Of course, the relative decline of the

---

[39] Hammerstein, *Bildung*, 30–3. [40] Whaley, *Toleration*, 14–22.
[41] Naujoks, *Karl V*, 35–42, 47–9, 67–8, 169–74, 335–9; Naujoks, *Obrigkeitsgedanke*, 118–53; see also pp. 325, 534–5.
[42] Gerteis, *Städte*, 65–71, 81–4; Schilling, *Stadt*, 87–93.
[43] Friedrichs, 'Town revolts'; Blickle, *Unruhen*, 41–5.
[44] Schilling, *Stadt*, 20–8.

Mediterranean economy in relation to the increasingly dynamic Atlantic–North Sea system dented the prosperity of all but the largest of the Upper German Imperial Cities. For a relatively brief period, new northward links developed via Frankfurt, Cologne, and Aachen to Antwerp. The economic fate of the majority of Upper German Imperial Cities, especially the smaller ones, was finally sealed, however, when Amsterdam eclipsed Antwerp following the Revolt of the Nether- lands. For the rest, the picture is mixed. The Lower Rhine centres of Cologne and Aachen managed to maintain relatively high levels of activity until the end of the seventeenth century. When they ultimately declined, new centres such as Hamburg gradually emerged.[45]

The free status of the Imperial Cities remained a significant asset. Cities such as Hamburg and Bremen struggled hard over many decades to achieve that status; many others failed to do so.[46] This reflects the differing fortunes of the territorial towns and the other free or autonomous towns following the Refor- mation.[47] Internally, very many of them experienced the same kind of Refor- mation turbulence and post-Reformation resurgence of oligarchy as the Imperial Cities. Yet their relationship with their territorial prince complicated their situation. While some maintained their medieval autonomy throughout the early modern period, the general trend, evident in some cases from the early sixteenth century, was for the subjugation of the territorial towns and their integration into the territories. Frequently, conflicts between councils and guilds, starting with the Reformation crisis itself, provided the pretext for princely intervention. Consequently, many city councils ultimately became agencies of princely government.

There were, of course, exceptions. In small or weak territories it did often prove possible to maintain a strong degree of urban autonomy, and some towns were able to maintain their autonomy into the nineteenth century. Lemgo, for example, fought successfully to survive as a free Lutheran enclave within the Calvinist County of Lippe.[48] Emden and Rostock were other examples of successful urban resistance to territorial rulers in the sixteenth and seventeenth centuries.[49] In general the grant to rulers, by the Peace of Augsburg in 1555, of the right to determine the religion of their territories, made such resistance increasingly diffi- cult.[50] Equally crucial was the effect of the economic pressure that resulted from the eclipse of the Mediterranean trade by the North Sea economy and the disruption that accompanied the Thirty Years War.[51]

It is doubtful whether the Reformation as such determined the long-term fate of either the Imperial Cities or the territorial towns. It saw the culmination of some fifteenth-century trends, such as communal control over the Church. It also perhaps accelerated other broad tendencies, such as the establishment of oligarchies or, in the case of territorial towns, the erosion of communal autonomy and integration into

[45] Lindberg, 'Hamburg', 647–9.   [46] Schilling, *Stadt*, 41.   [47] Merz, 'Landstädte'.
[48] Schilling, *Konfessionskonflikt.*   [49] Schilling, 'Bürgerkämpfe'; Schultz, *Auseinandersetzungen.*
[50] Schilling, *Stadt*, 41–9.   [51] Merz, 'Landstädte', 129.

the territory. Economics, rather than religion, ultimately determined the fate of both Imperial Cities and territorial towns.

The Reformation was, however, the last period in which the cities of the Reich led the way in major changes that affected the system as a whole. In the early 1520s, the cautiously pro-evangelical policies pursued by Nuremberg gave institutional support to the wider popular movement and ensured its survival. By the late 1520s, the territorial princes had taken over that role. It was the 'princes' Reformation' that ultimately mastered and institutionalized the forces unleashed by the evangelical movement.

IV

MASTERING THE REFORMATION
*c.*1526–1555

20

The Emergence of Protestant Territories

The establishment of the Reformation in many German territories lacked the drama of the urban movements but it was every bit as complicated. It started later and proceeded more slowly. As late as 1540, the majority of territories still adhered to the old religion.[1] Before 1530, only two major principalities—Electoral Saxony and Hessen, both in 1526—formally adopted the new teaching, along with three lesser territories (Lüneburg, Brandenburg-Ansbach, and Anhalt). During the 1530s, a succession of mainly northern territories followed suit. Then, during the 1550s and 1560s, a large number made the change. Most of the north-eastern prince-bishoprics were secularized. The Habsburg lands, Bavaria, Lorraine, and Jülich-Kleve-Berg were left as the sole adherents of the old faith, together with the mass of independent ecclesiastical territories, some Imperial Cities, Imperial Counts, and Imperial Knights. For the princes, the step from pre-Reformation ambitions to curb the powers of the ecclesiastical regime to assuming full responsibility for dogma and worship was a major watershed and not taken lightly.

There was no headlong rush to gain control of the Church or to plunder its lands.[2] In most cases, the decision by a prince to adopt the new religion was preceded by its widespread acceptance by many of his subjects, or at least by the effective breakdown of the old Church order at all levels down to the parishes. The 'official' princely Reformation thus frequently followed localized urban Reformations in the towns, the spread of an evangelical movement into rural areas, and the adoption of the new teaching by significant elements of the nobility and by the bureaucratic elite.

Non-religious factors also played a significant role. Geographical location and regional power structures, the relationship of a prince or count with the emperor, and family networks, all impinged on the attitude towards the religious issue.[3] Fundamental loyalty to the emperor as a symbol of the Reich gave almost all princes pause for thought. Fundamental loyalty to the system and a reluctance to render oneself guilty of transgressing its laws engendered reluctance to ride roughshod even over the diocesan rights of powerful prince-bishops. The Reformation in Hessen and Ernestine Saxony, for example, proceeded more rapidly only after the archbishop of Mainz agreed in the Treaty of Hitzkirchen in 1528 to renounce such rights in both territories, concluding a wrangle of several

---

[1] Schmidt, *Konfessionalisierung*, 9–10.
[2] The most balanced discussion of this issue in English is Cohn, 'Church property'. See also Ehmer, 'Kirchengutsfrage'.
[3] Press, 'Territorialstruktur'.

decades' duration over ecclesiastical jurisdiction.[4] The extent of a dynasty's reliance on ecclesiastical preferments to guarantee primogeniture, or at least reduce the number of potential heirs, was also a crucial factor. The policies of Brandenburg (whose Elector was the brother of Albrecht of Mainz, Magdeburg, and Halberstadt), the Bavarian and Palatinate Wittelsbachs, the Margrave of Ansbach and of the house of Brunswick were all influenced by this consideration in the 1520s.

Equally, most princes had to be aware of the vested interests of their own territorial nobility. Ecclesiastical institutions such as monasteries and canonries fulfilled valuable functions in providing for younger sons and unmarried daughters. It was for good reason, and on the basis of his own experiences, that Philip of Hessen advised Duke Christian of Holstein in 1530 to give at least some former monasteries and ecclesiastical property to the nobles 'who gain the most benefit from them'. By the same token, he advised, one should avoid imposing too great a burden of taxation on the common man and turn some monasteries into 'common hospitals, to maintain and feed the poor folk of the land'.[5]

With the exception of Philip of Hessen, converted by Melanchthon in 1524, no German prince opted for the Reformation before 1526.[6] By far the most active princes were those opposed to the new teaching. Some, like Wilhelm IV of Bavaria or Duke Georg of Saxony, were energetic proponents of Church reform, convinced that a resolution of the *Gravamina* would undermine the evangelical movement. Others, like the Elector Joachim I of Brandenburg and Heinrich the Younger of Brunswick-Wolfenbüttel, simply followed the logic of the Edict of Worms and pursued a policy of outright repression. Even so, the former could not prevent some of his nobles from protecting evangelical preachers, and the latter failed to halt the reformation of the town of Brunswick.

More numerous were those princes who maintained a neutral stance, who remained personally loyal to the old religion but who took no action against evangelical teaching in their territories as long as law and order were not threatened. The Elector of Saxony, Frederick the Wise, was the most prominent member of this group. On the one hand, he remained loyal to the old Church to his death in 1525 and enthusiastically added to his vast collection of over 19,000 relics, which he displayed in public for the last time in Wittenberg in 1522–3. On the other hand, his policy of non-intervention and non-coercion in fact led to him protecting Luther and thus promoting the evangelical cause generally. The position of Electoral Saxony was resolved on the succession of his pro-evangelical brother, Duke Johann, in 1526. By 1528, the relics had all been melted down and the reform of the Church was well under way.[7]

---

[4] Wolgast, 'Territorialfürsten', 432; Schindling and Ziegler, *Territorien*, iv, 75–6, 259–60, 265–6. The occasion of the treaty was the resolution of the 'Pack controversy': see pp. 295–6.

[5] Haug-Moritz, 'Konfessionsdissens', 143; Cohn, 'Church property', 167, 173–4.

[6] See the excellent survey in Wolgast, 'Territorialfürsten'.

[7] Ludolphy, *Friedrich*, 355–9; Schindling and Ziegler, *Territorien*, iv, 17–18.

In Brandenburg-Kulmbach, Margrave Casimir also pursued an essentially political course. After the Nuremberg Reichstag of 1524 he summoned his Estates to draw up a list of grievances for the planned Speyer national council. The Estates could not agree and, after the repression of the peasant unrest in 1525, the margrave, though now once more loyal to the Catholic cause, attempted to steer a diplomatic middle course by issuing a Church ordinance to which both loyalists and reformers could subscribe. At the same time, he placed the administration of Church property in the hands of his own officials and suspended the tax exemption of the clergy. However, his subsequent absence in Hungary fighting on behalf of Ferdinand meant he was unable to prevent a significant Catholic reaction supported by his brother Friedrich, the cathedral provost of Würzburg. Only when another brother, the Lutheran convert Georg, succeeded in 1527 did an energetic reform policy bring about a decisive change.[8] In other territories, such as Baden, Jülich-Kleve-Berg, the Palatinate, and Mecklenburg, the confessional situation remained unclear for many decades.

In the first instance, however, connivance and temporization seemed a logical stance in view of the lack of clarity at the Reichstag. As long as there was the expectation of a national Church council, of some kind of general reform of the Church that took account of the *Gravamina* and other grievances, princes could follow this line without fear of being accused of illegality or of disloyalty to the emperor. Even those who were known to be pro-Lutheran did not go much further than this before 1526. Rulers such as Philip of Hessen, Ernst of Brunswick-Lüneburg or the Counts of Anhalt and Mansfeld may have employed evangelical court preachers and councillors, but their only serious intervention in Church affairs before 1526 was the inventorization of monastic property. Philip of Hessen was not the only prince whose decision to melt down monstrances and other ecclesiastical treasures was determined largely by the need to meet the costs he incurred as a member of the Swabian League in dealing with the knights and peasants.[9]

The exception to the general tendency of the early 1520s was the Prussian territory of the Teutonic Order of Knights, which was secularized and reformed with remarkable speed in 1525.[10] The situation here was unique. For one thing, while the Order owned a scatter of minor properties in the Reich, its major territory of Prussia was not part of the Reich at all, but, since 1466, a fief of both the papacy and the Kingdom of Poland. Furthermore, it was quite unlike any of the Reich's ecclesiastical territories, since it was ruled by an organization of ordained knights under a Grand Master.

The secularization of the Teutonic Order in Prussia was driven as much by secular concerns as by religious considerations. The Order became increasingly anachronistic as a ruling noble corporation. The arrogance and exploitative policies of its knights aroused the perpetual hostility of the indigenous Prussian nobility, the

---

[8] Schindling and Ziegler, *Territorien*, i, 14–16; Wolgast, 'Territorialfürsten', 427.
[9] Schindling and Ziegler, *Territorien*, iv, 263.
[10] Boockmann, *Ostpreußen*, 227–43; Hubatsch, 'Voraussetzungen'. See also pp. 22–3, 185–6.

settler peasantry, and the urban patricians. The main source of these frictions was originally the Order's need for money to fight against the Poles.[11] That battle was lost in 1466 and the Treaty of Thorn partitioned the Prussian lands, leaving only East Prussia in the Order's hands under Polish overlordship. Soon, the desire to escape from Polish subjugation and to assert the Order's immediate status (subject only to the emperor) in the Reich led to the election of two German princes— Friedrich of Saxony in 1498 and Albrecht of Brandenburg-Ansbach in 1511—as Grand Masters. Each was encouraged by the apparent willingness of Maximilian I to support a rebellion against the Polish crown and the secession of the Order to the Reich. Each contributed to the creeping secularization of the Order in Prussia by imposing taxes not only on the local estates but now on the knights themselves as well.

Maximilian, however, proved as fickle in this as in so many other issues. When it suited him to offer a sop to the Poles to secure Hungary against the pretensions of the Polish crown in 1515, he simply abandoned the Order. Consequently, the Grand Master was once more obliged to render the oath of loyalty to King Sigismund, as required by the Peace of Thorn. Grand Master Albrecht turned first to Moscow, then to Denmark and other German princes for assistance, before deciding to launch an attack on the Poles with the aid of 80,000 gulden supplied by the German Master from the Order's lands in the Reich. That money and the mercenaries it bought to supplement the forces of the Order made the fight far from hopeless. Nevertheless, the disparity in size between the Prussian territory and the Polish kingdom (a population of some two hundred thousand pitted against roughly three million) led to an early deadlock and the conclusion of a four-year truce in 1521.[12] Just as Grand Master Friedrich had done in 1507, Albrecht returned to the Reich to rally more support, though he seems also to have considered the idea of an alternative career as a mercenary commander himself. That was averted when the introduction of the new teaching transformed the situation of Prussia.

Like many Imperial Knights, the Knights of the Teutonic Order were early enthusiasts for the evangelical cause, while Albrecht himself encountered leading supporters of Luther, such as Andreas Osiander, when he resided in Nuremberg after 1521. The Order as a whole was profoundly affected by the antipapal movement of the pre-Reformation years. In Prussia, moreover, Georg von Polentz, Bishop of Samland and regent in Albrecht's absence, and his colleague Erhard von Queiss, Bishop of Pomesania vigorously promoted the new teaching. When in 1523 Albrecht secretly approached Luther for advice on the future of the Order in view of its rapidly diminishing membership, Luther was unequivocal.[13] The knights should 'lay aside their false chastity and assume the true chastity of wedlock' and become an order of truly Christian knights. With that very public advice, and

[11] Burleigh, *Prussian society*, 94, 170.
[12] Boockmann, *Ostpreußen*, 231.
[13] Bornkamm, *Luther*, 317–36.

with the despatch of Johannes Briesmann and Johann Amandus as Lutheran preachers to Königsberg, the Reformation of Prussia proceeded in earnest.

In view of the continuing reluctance of either Charles V or the German princes to support the Order against Poland, Albrecht was obliged to negotiate with King Sigismund (who was, incidentally, his maternal uncle). Now, however, in order to avoid the Order's physical integration into the Polish kingdom, Albrecht offered to become a fief of Sigismund exclusively. The claim to papal fiefdom, which in 1466 had seemed to guarantee the Prussian knights a semi-autonomous existence, was now dropped. Albrecht became hereditary Duke of Prussia, swore an oath of fealty to Sigismund, and took a Danish princess as his wife. The remaining knights were endowed with lands formerly held by the Order and became ducal feoffees alongside the indigenous nobility. The two bishops immediately relinquished their territorial rights to the new duchy and, in return, were confirmed as Lutheran bishops. The process of Church reform became systematic with a visitation begun in 1526, an initiative that proceeded hand in hand with the establishment of a secular territorial government.

Later Prussian nationalist historians endowed these events—little short of a *coup d'état* on the part of Albrecht—with a heroic aura.[14] They saw here the origins of modern Prussia, the beginnings of Prussia's Protestant mission of German national leadership. However, the election of a Hohenzollern as Grand Master in 1511 came about quite by chance, and Albrecht was in any case a member of the junior margravial line of Ansbach, rather than a scion of Electoral Brandenburg. Furthermore, Albrecht's translation to a dukedom would not have been possible without the acquiescence of the Polish crown, in whose interests it was to isolate Prussia simultaneously from the Order, from the Reich, and from the papacy. The fact that Albrecht was Sigismund's nephew further added to the convenience of the arrangement. For, at that stage, it was not inevitable that the senior Hohenzollern line of Electoral Brandenburg rather than the Jagiellon dynasty would inherit the duchy (which it did in 1618–19).[15]

Perhaps more significant in 1525 was the fact that, distracted by the Peasants' War that destroyed its fortress at Horneck on the Neckar, the Teutonic Order failed to avert the loss of its Prussian lands. Walther von Cronberg, appointed German Master (*Deutschmeister*) or administrator of the Order's lands in the Reich in 1527, struggled to reconfigure the remaining scattered territories in the Reich from his base in Mergentheim in Swabia. He became an immediate prince of the Reich in 1529 and the following year he assumed the title of Grand and German Master (formally, *Administrator des Hochmeistertums in Preußen und Deutschmeister*, abbreviated after 1598 to *Hoch- und Deutschmeister*) when Charles V invested him with Prussia at the Augsburg Reichstag. Yet his claim to the Prussian lands was never realized and, though his fragmented territory ('Ordensstaat') generated ample

---

[14] Boockmann, *Ostpreußen*, 238.
[15] That was largely the result of the acquiescence of the Ansbach and Brandenburg guardians of Albrecht's mentally disturbed heir Albrecht Friedrich in the Lublin Union of 1569, which eliminated the autonomous rights of West Prussia.

income for its noble corporation, the Order never again played a significant role in the Reich, other than as a periodic sinecure for various Habsburgs from the late sixteenth century and as a frontier force against the Turks.

The Prussian Reformation unfolded outside the Reich and its example of an episcopal reform was not emulated. For most rulers in the Reich, events were precipitated by the Peasants' War. The 'communal Reformation' posed a profound threat to law and order. The chaos that followed its eruption in many areas left ecclesiastical institutions crippled by lack of funds and lack of personnel. The decision of the Speyer Reichstag in 1526 created a new framework in which firm action was now justifiable in terms of imperial law. All that was required was a viable formula.

The first significant attempt at an ordered territorial reform from above proved short-lived. Shortly after the Speyer Reichstag, Philip of Hessen convened a synod at Homberg to discuss a plan for a Reformation drawn up for him by the French Franciscan Franz Lambert of Avignon (1487–1530).[16] Lambert had been trained at Wittenberg, and his draft reflected both the communitarian ideals that Luther himself had espoused in the early 1520s and the influence of Swiss and Upper German urban practice. The *Reformatio ecclesiarum Hassiae*, promulgated, significantly, by the synod and not by the ruling price, envisaged a new Church structure constructed from the bottom up. There was to be an annual synod at which pastors (described in the document as 'episcopi') were to be joined by lay representatives from each parish. Parishes were to be permitted to elect their own pastors and obliged to pay them as well. Monasteries were forbidden to recruit novices and, as they became vacant after the deaths of their current incumbents, they were to be used as schools.

The educational programme envisaged by the *Reformatio* bore immediate fruit in the foundation of the University of Marburg in 1527 and continued to shape Hessian policy in this area for years to come. The ecclesiastical constitutional model as such, however, was never realized. As early as January 1527, Luther advised Philip that it was too early to embark upon such a wide-ranging scheme of reform (or 'pile of laws', as he described it) and cautioned him to undertake only what was necessary for the maintenance of domestic peace and good order in the Church.[17]

Many scholars have viewed Luther's attitude to the Hessen proposal as the reflection of his horror at the events of 1525. Of course, the Peasants' War influenced his thinking. Like ruling princes and their officials almost everywhere, Luther perceived the need for practical measures to restore a lasting stability to be more urgent than ever. Much, he believed, depended on the princes themselves, on their willingness to pass the kind of measures needed to redress the grievances of the common man. However, that also included attention to the common man's complaints concerning ecclesiastical matters.

At the same time, the situation of the Church itself demanded action. The Peasants' War had once more underlined the threat posed by radical evangelical preachers. The financial demands imposed by the suppression of the peasants

---

[16] Schindling and Ziegler, *Territorien*, v, 262.
[17] Lohse, *Luther*, 180–3; Leppin, *Luther*, 265–8.

increased the temptation for governments to draw on the resources of the Church to finance purely secular aims. Moreover, by the time peace was restored, it was clear that many congregations had no clergy at all and were genuinely confused as to which teaching they should follow. A twofold practical problem now confronted Luther as a churchman: how to obtain ordained preachers and ensure that the right kind of teaching prevailed in the congregations; and how to ensure that the wealth of the Church remained dedicated to its essential religious, educational, and social ends.

Luther's ideas on these matters, as on so much else, developed reactively. In the early 1520s, he was concerned that monks and nuns should be provided for adequately after the foundations in which they lived were dissolved. At the same time, he encouraged urban magistrates and ruling princes to defend the new teaching and to make provision for clergy who would sustain it. On Church property generally, he held that all endowments should continue to be used for their original purposes. A little later, when it became apparent that Saxon ecclesiastical revenues were being alienated by unscrupulous laymen, he opined that the cessation of papal authority meant that the property of the Church passed to the Elector, who might use for general purposes any money not required for the clergy, schools, or charity. Later, after the Augsburg Reichstag demanded the restoration of the monasteries in 1530, this view informed the principle that the prince was entitled to any excess income as a reward for his efforts on behalf of the gospel.[18]

The broader ecclesiological and legal framework within which these views unfolded also evolved. Fundamentally, Luther had no desire to create a new Church—hence his caution with regard to root and branch reform proposals such as that put forward by Philip of Hessen.[19] While he clearly rejected the papal Church, Luther held on, at least in principle, to the idea of an episcopal Church. Indeed, he later actively supported the appointment of Lutheran bishops in Naumburg-Zeitz (1542) and Merseburg (1545).[20] In the 1520s, however, there were in practice no bishops willing to heed Luther's injunctions to relinquish their political powers and to become reformed bishops. Consequently, he increasingly regarded the episcopal office as vacant and argued that the ruling princes thus had a right and a Christian duty to exercise supervisory powers over the Church. Luther only used the term 'Notbischof' (literally, 'emergency bishop') to describe this function in 1539. The sense of it, however, was already implicit in his writing in the mid-1520s.[21] Luther did not simply abdicate all responsibility to the secular powers: the prince had a Christian duty to commission a visitation; it was a duty

---

[18] Cohn, 'Church property', 163–4.   [19] Lohse, *Luther*, 180–3.

[20] Both were re-Catholicized in 1546 following the defeat of Electoral Saxony at the end of the Schmalkaldic War, but were then subsequently integrated into Saxony. The Lutheran Bishopric of Cammin in 1544–56 was essentially a pawn of the Dukes of Pomerania, who turned it into a secundogeniture thereafter. The only Lutheran bishopric that survived in the long term was Lübeck, though after 1586 that too was effectively a dynastic territory of the house of Holstein-Gottorp. Wolgast, *Hochstift*, 208–18, 237–53, 273.

[21] Trüdinger, *Briefe*, 71, 79.

of government to protect such a visitation from attack and to promote its successful completion.

These duties were elaborated by Luther's younger colleague Philipp Melanchthon. He too was deeply affected by the experience of 1525. Like Luther, who railed against the 'mob' who were 'foolish' and 'crazed', Melanchthon now thought of Herr Omnes ('Mr Everyman') not as the noble common man but as stupid, mad, and wild. He was also much more rigorous than Luther in thinking through the implications of the new need for control. Virtually every aspect of the ecclesiastical, educational, and governmental programme of Lutheran Protestantism bears the unmistakable stamp of Melanchthon's learned and systematic mind.

For all Luther's castigation of the rebellious peasants, he still clung to his belief in the evangelical renewal of society as the collective renewal of its individual members, and remained wary of any attempt to prescribe a uniform catalogue of belief and dogma. Melanchthon, by contrast, turned sharply away from the idealism of the early 1520s. He now insisted on the need for education 'so that young people may be raised to be peaceful and decent', for the revival of academic studies in order to supply teachers, and for the active engagement of government in the creation of a Christian society.[22] The epithet *Praeceptor Germaniae* (teacher of Germany) accorded to Melanchthon during his own lifetime refers specifically to his work in setting the agenda for secondary school and university reform.[23] His contribution, however, was far wider and much deeper than that. Luther remained an inspirational leader, but in practical terms he was increasingly marginalized from 1530 to his death in 1546.[24] Nevertheless, what emerged from the mid-1520s might just as well be described as Melanchthonian Protestantism as Lutheran Protestantism.

The new course took shape when in 1525, Luther urged the Elector of Saxony to undertake a personal visitation to inspect Church property and to ensure the proper payment of the clergy. In 1526, after the Reichstag of Speyer, he once again requested a formal visitation, this time to consist of four officials, two experts in revenues and two who were knowledgeable in 'teaching and people'.[25] The following year, the Elector issued an instruction for a visitation commission, which, however, proved inadequate in its detail and was criticized by both reformers and Catholic loyalists because it seemed to arrogate spiritual authority to secular government.

Finally, in 1528 a definitive visitation order written by Melanchthon was published. Luther's preface made it clear that he had turned to the secular powers to commission a visitation only because the bishops had abdicated their responsibilities. He appealed to the Elector as divinely ordained ruler that he might, out of Christian love and for the sake of God, appoint visitors to promote the Gospels and to aid and protect the poor Christians of the land. In contrast to the Elector's

22 Strauss, *House of learning*, 6; Strauss, *Law*, 222–31.
23 Hammerstein, *Bildung*, 29–31, 87–8.
24 Leppin, *Luther*, 277–339.
25 Trüdinger, *Briefe*, 68–70. See also Leppin, *Luther*, 267–76.

instruction of 1527, Luther's preface explicitly preserved the authority of theologians in religious matters.

The visitation itself, which began in October 1528, confirmed many of Luther's worst fears. 'The situation of the churches is extremely desolate,' he wrote to Spalatin, '. . . the peasants learn nothing, know nothing, pray nothing, and do nothing, except abuse their freedom. They do not take communion; it is as if they had shed all religion.'[26] The situation concerning those clergy who remained was scarcely more encouraging. Many were still loyal Catholics; others were simply confused, or had developed idiosyncratic teachings and forms of worship in the absence of any formal guidance. Almost everywhere, clerical incomes had shrunk alarmingly with the non-payment and lapse of tithes and the like. Many church buildings and charitable foundations were deteriorating rapidly.

The visitation process, which lasted until 1531, recorded these conditions but also gradually began to remedy them. The change was not immediate. Yet the visitation provided a basic framework for the instruction of the clergy in proper teaching and forms of worship. It also laid the foundations for the proper inventorying and use of Church property, and shaped the procedures for training, induction, and ordination—formal ordination only took place from 1535—and installation of new clergy.[27]

Above all, the visitation, as an essentially bureaucratic process, determined the overall structure of the new Church order. Visitations carried out consecutively in the various administrative districts of the Saxon Electorate left superintendents in charge to conduct the episcopal supervisory functions on a continuing basis. In time, central bodies were established to coordinate the work of the superintendents. Church property was now administered by agencies of territorial government, and the old legal functions of the ecclesiastical courts now passed to secular territorial courts.

Most of these changes proceeded on an ad hoc basis in specific areas or territories in response to particular problems or visitation reports. The framework was set by Luther's growing tendency after 1525 to counsel respect for the law and, above all, by Melanchthon's unequivocal espousal of Roman law as 'God's gift to humanity, to Germany in particular'.[28] The crisis of 1525 led both reformers and rulers to fuse the needs of the two realms, to perceive a link between 'police' and the 'common good' that only an executive power (*Obrigkeit*) could forge.[29] That the fusion of the two kingdoms or swords also led to confusion was only inevitable, but it did not necessarily lead to secular papacies or to abjectly submissive churchmen.

In general, Lutheran territories did not develop meaningful intermediate Church authorities or even any central institutional leadership, either in the form of a consistory or a 'general superintendent', until after 1555.[30] Even the widespread promulgation of new ecclesiastical statutes (*Kirchenordnungen*) brought no real supra-territorial uniformity, and some two-thirds of all such sixteenth-century statutes were in any case promulgated between 1550 and 1600.[31]

---

[26] Trüdinger, *Briefe*, 75.   [27] Karant-Nunn, *Pastors*, 38–52, 56–60.
[28] Strauss, *Law*, 212–14, 224–8.   [29] Strauss, *Law*, 136–7.
[30] Schmidt, *Konfessionalisierung*, 14–19.   [31] Schmidt, *Konfessionalisierung*, 20.

The outcome could not yet be described as a new 'Lutheran Church'. In imperial law, the Church remained a single entity until 1648, and, for much of the sixteenth century at least, most people regarded any arrangements made as temporary, pending either the restoration or the establishment of the 'true' Church. However, most of the arrangements made in the territories that adopted the new teaching after 1526–7 ultimately determined the long-term structure and character of German Lutheran Protestantism.

Almost everywhere, the first step was the visitation followed by the promulgation of a *Kirchenordnung*. In much of the Baltic coastal region, including the major Hanseatic Cities, the model followed was the statute formulated for Brunswick by Johannes Bugenhagen in 1528. Elsewhere, the Wittenberg statute was extremely influential, as was the Brandenburg–Nuremberg statute of 1533.[32] Implicit in both the visitation and the *Kirchenordnung* was the aspiration to promote a standard set of teachings based on the Gospels, an aspiration that was also served by the formulation of 'confessions' such as the Augsburg Confession of 1530. The need to achieve standard forms of worship to replace the colourful variety that had developed in the early 1520s was equally important. In the Lutheran sphere, this was rendered easier by the fact that the German Mass had much in common with the old Latin Mass. The offertory was abolished, and intercessions to the saints were omitted; the sermon became the focal point of the service, communion under both kinds was permitted, and singing by the congregation assumed a central role. Yet, despite the major theological implications of Luther's reforms, particularly in respect of the Eucharist, many ordinary folk saw little fundamental difference between his Mass and the old one.

Teaching and worship were, of course, dependent on reliable and educated pastors. Most ecclesiastical statutes made secure financial provision for the clergy, which could take the form of a realization of Luther's ideas for a 'common chest' that amalgamated some or all Church benefices and endowments for a given town or area.[33] In some territories, efforts were made to re-establish traditional offerings for the clergy (*Opferpfennig*, and many other local or regional terms) and surplice fees (*Stolgebühren*), though this often met with popular resistance and accusations that the old papal fiscal regime was being restored.[34]

Such arrangements were generally most effective in urban areas. The situation in the countryside was complicated by the fact that ruling princes who had appropriated monastic property to finance Church administration, education, or state government generally, were reluctant to part with it again to support the rural clergy.[35] All too frequently, rural pastors continued to live in relative deprivation, dependent on the irregular provision of goods in kind and fees that were only given grudgingly by their parishioners. Here, the Lutheran pastor as paid official of the state, a theological civil servant, with a regular income based on parochial contributions and surplice fees, did not become established until late in the century.

---

[32] Schmidt, *Konfessionalisierung*, 19–20. [33] Karant-Nunn, *Pastors*, 42–3.
[34] Karant-Nunn, *Pastors*, 43. [35] Rabe, *Geschichte*, 371–2.

The provision of proper education for pastors proved more difficult. The ignorance revealed by many of the visitations could not easily be remedied. A pastor without an income was more easily helped than one who did not know the Ten Commandments. While some of the most ignorant clergy were dismissed, many others with rudimentary and inadequate knowledge were allowed to stay. The scarcity of qualified personnel was simply too acute to permit a systematic purge.

The supply of newly trained pastors remained inadequate for decades. The numbers trained at Wittenberg were minute in relation to the numbers required, and even university training was no absolute guarantee of good ministry. The Electoral Saxon visitations of the 1530s and 1540s revealed appalling ignorance among the lower clergy. In this respect, the new clergy were in some ways very like the old, who had in effect been required only to know just a little more than most of their parishioners.[36] Indeed, the existence of Wittenberg and the early foundation of a Protestant university at Marburg in 1527, expressly designed to supply officials and clergy, may give the false impression of a lively pace of change. Even by the time Luther died in 1546, the situation in the vicinity of Wittenberg still gave rise to serious concern.[37] Elsewhere, things were often much worse and only began to improve from the 1580s.[38]

The efforts made to educate the clergy, though initially not successful, emphasize how rapidly Luther and Melanchthon had moved away from the ideal of the priesthood of all believers. From the mid-1520s, Melanchthon's programme of combining humanist *eruditio* with evangelical *pietas* gave a new impetus to the cause of educational reform.[39] To a greater or lesser degree, this had been integral to the cause of Church reform from the outset.[40] Now it became a prime concern, while the pre-Reformation competition between secular and ecclesiastical sponsorship was firmly resolved in favour of the secular authorities. Most *Kirchenordnungen*, especially those written by Johannes Bugenhagen in north Germany, emphasized the need to make good provision for education. Urgent attention was devoted to the restoration and promotion of the Latin schools. These had suffered in the early Reformation years, following the dissolution of the monastic foundations that supported them.

Recruitment of pastors was also hit by a reaction against traditional learning by radical preachers, such as Andreas Karlstadt, who rejected Latin as the language of the papacy, and who propagated a German liturgy and a life-orientated exposition of the Gospels.[41] Erasmus observed in 1528 that wherever Lutheranism prevailed, academic study declined, and as late as 1557, Melanchthon wondered whether he and his co-religionists were responsible for what he perceived as the impending collapse of higher learning.[42] In fact, however, the need of both government and

---

[36] Karant-Nunn, *Pastors*, 20.   [37] Karant-Nunn, *Pastors*, 74.
[38] Schmidt, *Konfessionalisierung*, 21.   [39] *HdtBG*, i, 165.
[40] Smolinsky, 'Kirchenreform', 35–43; *HdtBG*, i, 68–70, 165–8. An excellent general discussion of the issues is Strauss, *House of learning*, 1–28, 176–202.
[41] Smolinsky, 'Kirchenreform', 43.
[42] *HdtBG*, i, 258.

Church for trained officials, highlighted in the first visitations of the late 1520s, soon reversed the trend. New Latin schools were established in many independent cities and territorial towns from the late 1520s, and higher colleges were founded, such as the Gymnasium at Strassburg in 1539 (the Gymnasium Illustre) and Bugenhagen's Gymnasia at Hamburg (1529), Lübeck (1531), and Schleswig (1542).[43]

Despite the recognition of a pressing need, progress was relatively slow, even in the provision of education for the gifted. Schools were often the first to suffer from temporary financial crises or political reversals, such as the Interim of 1548, which temporarily re-Catholicized much of south and Middle Germany.[44] It was not until the 1540s that Albertine Saxony was able to establish the elite schools at Pforta, Grimma, and Meissen.[45] In many other areas, such institutions only emerged after the Peace of Augsburg (1555) had created the legal foundation for lasting statutory regulation of both Church and school systems.[46] In Württemberg, for example, the establishment of secondary schools followed the *Schulordnung* of 1559 that led to the reform of the Stuttgart Pädagogium, the foundation of a similar school in Tübingen, and the institution of a series of 'monastery schools'. The latter were essentially seminary schools, based in former monastic foundations and intended to train those who would then qualify as ministers at the Tübingen theology faculty.[47]

In theory, these secondary schools were part of a comprehensive structure of education, with 'particular schools' or 'German' schools below them and universities above them. In practice, however, the lower school system suffered from comparative neglect until the later decades of the century.[48] For one thing, Luther and his immediate circle were deeply ambivalent about the very idea of more general education for all. They held the growth of vernacular education responsible for the crisis in higher studies in the 1520s, and the experiences with sectarians in the same period generated anxieties about the usefulness of literacy that led to independent reading of the Bible and other texts.[49] Many 'German' schools were closed in order to focus resources on the Latin schools. For a long time, the majority of lower or 'German' schools tended therefore to be private enterprises, run by inferior teachers who were rewarded much more modestly than their high-status Latin school colleagues.

Only in the cities and larger towns, notably Nuremberg and the Hanseatic Cities, did a significant stock of licensed pre-Reformation German schools survive and grow steadily during the first half of the sixteenth century.[50] Educational provision in the rural areas was sparse and rudimentary, and made little real difference to either the literacy or the religious knowledge of the rural population. The widespread revival and growth of the lower schools only came in the second half of the century. Then the secular authorities began to appreciate the values of general literacy and elementary education and they responded to demand from

---

[43] *HdtBG*, i, 292–8; Brady, *Sturm*, 116–25.   [44] See pp. 323–4.
[45] *HdtBG*, i, 307–8.   [46] *HdtBG*, i, 283.
[47] *HdtBG*, i, 68–70, 305–7.   [48] Schmidt, *Konfessionalisierung*, 23.
[49] Strauss, *House of learning*, 194.   [50] *HdtBG*, i, 377–8.

below to provide training in literacy and numeracy, which came to be regarded by all social groups as the essential life skills.[51]

The regulation of provision for poor relief was a further integral element of the implementation of evangelical reform statutes. In this respect, the Reformation brought about the widespread acceptance of new attitudes that had been developing since the fifteenth century.[52] Major urban centres such as Nuremberg and Strassburg had led the way in emulating French and English laws to curb begging. 'Foreign' (i.e. non-indigenous) beggars were banned and brass badges were provided for those inhabitants who had proved their need and were permitted to beg. Similar measures had been introduced by many other cities by the end of the century, and attempts were made at the Reichstag at Lindau (1497), Freiburg (1498), and Augsburg (1500) to formulate legislation for the Reich as a whole.

The reformers resolved the contradiction between this new harsh attitude and the prevailing teaching of the Church, whose doctrine of purgatory continued to encourage lay benefactors to remember the poor in their wills, in favour of a robust regime for the management of the poor. Their denial of salvation by good works undermined the whole rationale of benefactions 'ad pias causas'. Furthermore, the reformers' new attitude to work led them to regard begging as a form of idleness. The able-bodied were to be forced back to regular (Christian) work. Only the deserving poor, a small minority, were entitled to Christian charity. Moreover, since the traditional charitable donations and benefactions had all but ceased, they were to receive assistance from the 'common chest', or from specially instituted 'poor chests' funded by former monastic property and an amalgamation of the many surviving medieval endowments. The new evangelical teaching therefore provided full theological sanction for harsh official attitudes to the poor and, implicitly, a call for government interventionism in the management of poverty.

Once more, Nuremberg led the way with a new alms statute in 1522. This declared the plight of the needy to be a prime concern, but defined begging as incompatible with true Christian religion. A commission of ten honourable citizens headed by two magistrates was established to examine the problem of the poor, to help the able-bodied secure work, and to distribute appropriate relief to those in genuine need. Begging was to be restricted to those licensed before the new statute came into force. Measures to prevent the need for begging included a guarantee of fair prices for craft products and interest-free loans to craftsmen who fell into difficulty.

Variations on such provisions were adopted by many other cities and towns. Shortly afterwards, the new approach was further reinforced by the influential tract *De subventione pauperum* ('Concerning Assistance to the Poor', 1526) by the Spanish humanist Juan Luis Vives (based at Bruges), which reflected the reformers' views, was soon translated into German, and rapidly became established as the standard text on the subject for decades to come.

---

[51] Strauss, *House of learning*, 20–4, 194; *HdtBG*, i, 377–9. See also pp. 504–6.

[52] For the following, see: *HdtBG*, i, 425–31; Jütte, 'Poverty', 390–3, 395–400; Jütte, *Poverty*, 105–10; Fehler, *Poor relief*, 4–44, 71–108. See also p. 546.

In this area too, however, a new approach did not necessary mean a new solution. The frequent reiteration of vagrancy statutes indicates that the problems persisted even in the best-regulated cities. In the rural areas, of course, the new thinking made little or no impact. The only real control on vagrancy was the anger of the community; the only remedy for poverty was the kind of charity that was supposed to be a thing of the past. In both town and country, the problems of poverty remained unresolved. Equally, there is little evidence of any particular crisis of vagrancy at this time. When a problem did emerge and vagrancy became an increasing threat in the second half of the century, the ideas of the Reformation period were quickly revealed as inadequate and were superseded by a much more interventionist and coercive approach.[53]

The long-term implications of these various developments for the character of territorial government and the Church in Protestant Germany remain in dispute. Four issues are particularly important: whether the Reformation effectively created an 'absolutist' state in Germany; whether the secular powers plundered the Church for their own ends; whether Lutheran Protestantism was at this point a conservative or even an authoritarian creed; and whether the attempted Christian reform of society was in any sense successful.

First, the Reformation undoubtedly enhanced the power of many princes but it did not create anything like an absolutist state system in Germany. Although at first the princes were required to act as 'emergency bishops' and were formally only ever endowed with the prerogatives of a *summus episcopus*, their role in practice soon assumed dimensions that alarmed many clergy. The temptation to combine and confuse the 'two kingdoms' was simply too great. The sheer range and scope of the tasks to be undertaken required the kind of authority and resources that only a ruler could command. In almost all of the major areas of activity, the opportunity to realize fifteenth-century ambitions to assert secular power over ecclesiastical power was irresistible. At the same time, the desire to maximize the potential of the new situation to meet the new political and military demands of the present was understandable.

The Reformation provided new opportunities, yet it was also just one phase in a longer evolutionary process. Furthermore, much of what was traditionally held to be characteristic of the development of Lutheran territories, including the extension of secular control over the Church, can also be observed in those who remained loyal to the old Church. Indeed, the most 'modern' territorial governments of the day were probably the Austrian duchies and Bavaria, with reformed institutions established well before their leading Protestant counterparts such as Hessen, Ernestine Saxony, or Württemberg.[54] Throughout the Reich, all territorial governments went through similar processes of extending their administrations. Everywhere, lawyers took over and promoted Roman law over local or regional law.

Such similarities between Protestant and Catholic territories must at least relativize many of the assumptions traditionally made about the Lutheran state.

---

[53] Bog, *Oberdeutschland*, 65–6. See also pp. 546–7.　　　[54] See pp. 486–91.

Even in territories where Lutheranism did bring about a decisive change, the similarities with developments in Catholic territories remain striking. It is true that Lutheranism abandoned the celibate ideal, abolished the sacramental quality of marriage, made parental consent mandatory, introduced divorce, and made marriage into an institution registered and policed by the state. Yet the underlying aims of Protestant reformers were little different from those of the Catholic reformers. They wanted 'better and increased legal enforcement of traditional Church teachings' to regularize and stabilize the family unit.[55] They aspired to restore traditional paternal authority and to transfer the model of the family to the state, with rulers and pastors being endowed with paternalistic authority. They sought to substitute official ceremonies and formal registration procedures for the anarchy of local customs. They also shared the experience of frustration once it became clear that their reforms had failed to make the desired impact on the people at large.

Nonetheless, the impact of the Reformation in the Protestant territories cannot be underestimated. In Württemberg, impressive legal and administrative reforms under Eberhard the Bearded in the 1490s, notably the *Landesordnung* or territorial statute of 1495, were complemented by a programme of fiscal and administrative modernization under Habsburg rule from 1520 to 1534. The reconquest of the duchy by the outlawed Duke Ulrich led to the immediate introduction of the Reformation with the appointment of two reformers (a Lutheran and a Zwinglian in recognition of Zwingli's support for Ulrich's cause) and the publication of the Stuttgart Formula of Concord on 2 August 1534. This was followed by a *Kirchenordnung*, marriage and chest statutes all published in 1536. These measures were themselves the prelude to an even more comprehensive reformation inaugurated by Ulrich's son Christoph after 1550.[56] Both the *Kirchenordnung* of 1536 and its successor of 1559 emphasized the secular ruler's responsibility for ecclesiastical matters and his duty to police Christian behaviour. The pastors had the right to dissuade sinners who wished to take communion. It was, however, the task of the officials (*Amtleute*) to prosecute blasphemy, cursing, drinking, gambling, prostitution, and other sins that might bring the wrath of God upon the duchy.[57]

First, the Protestant territories certainly gained considerable additional powers as a result of their new responsibilities for religious worship, for schools, welfare institutions, and the like. Many territorial Estates were significantly weakened by the disappearance from their gatherings of the prelates, who had often played a particularly influential role because of their links with the wider Church, with bishops and metropolitans, and with religious orders. These contacts could bring pressure to bear from outside the territory or could lobby the emperor to intervene in a domestic dispute, and their disappearance rendered the Protestant territories more 'closed'.[58]

[55] Harrington, *Marriage*, 273–8 (the quotation appears at p. 274).
[56] Schindling and Ziegler, *Territorien*, v, 170–8; Schmidt, *Konfessionalisierung*, 15–20.
[57] Schmidt, *Konfessionalisierung*, 20.
[58] Blickle, *Reformation*, 158.

Second, the Reformation undeniably provided the temptation to plunder the wealth of the Church. While much church property was used appropriately, much was also alienated. The secularization and sequestration of church property generated significant new revenues. In Hessen, Ernestine and Albertine Saxony, and Württemberg, for example, significant amounts of church property and income were diverted into military expenditure or simply used to pay off the ruler's debts from time to time.[59] Duke Ulrich of Württemberg even ordered the gold paint to be scraped off paintings in 1538, sold houses of the clergy in towns, and openly appropriated the annual surpluses generated by the ecclesiastical revenues administered by his lay officials. These abuses were bitterly criticized by theologians, both Protestant and Catholic, and they were only appeased by Ulrich's son Christoph after 1550, with the institution of a Common Church Fund (*Gemeiner Kirchenkasten*). Even so, he too continued to use the surplus of that fund to reduce his debts, together with most of the income from a second fund, the *Depositum*, which received the income of the fourteen large monasteries in his duchy.[60]

Third, it is difficult to see Lutheranism as either conservative or authoritarian at this stage. The extension of the powers of governments was accompanied by a new definition of the role of their rulers. The model of the family was extended to the polity, and rulers were endowed with paternal authority, and with the same divine sanction as natural fathers. Implicit in this was the Christian duty of subjects to obey their *Landesvater* and the denial of any right to active resistance. On the other hand, the absolute powers that might seem implicit in these Lutheran notions of authority were tempered in important ways. Princes were bound by Christian laws and, like anyone else, would be punished for transgressing them. Furthermore, it is striking that almost all princes employed at least one clerical reformer to formulate the aims and objectives of a territorial reformation. All *Kirchenordnungen* were written by clerics, although lay officials, especially those who were legally trained, may have participated. The role of the original reformers was subsequently perpetuated in definitions of the preacher's role that, as Bugenhagen put it, gave him a duty of 'alert service in the worldly government'.[61] If there was no right to resistance, there was certainly a right, even a duty, to challenge a prince who pursued ungodly policies.

Nor was the population at large merely a passive victim of repressive regimes that aspired to supervise and control. The reform process undoubtedly marked the end of that sense of expectation and promise of emancipation that fired both sectarians and the 'common man' in the early 1520s. On the one hand, those who had hoped for radical emancipation, for the institution of government by the Word of God, were bitterly frustrated. On the other hand, both the religious and the secular reforms of the years after 1525 can be regarded, at least in part, as a response to the popular demands of the preceding years. It is too extreme to see the governmental reforms as the 'continuation of the Peasants' War by other means', yet they were clearly shaped by an awareness of the lessons of 1525.[62]

---

[59] For Hessen, see Stöhr, *Verwendung* and Friedrich, *Territorialfürst*.
[60] Cohn, 'Church property', 170–1.   [61] Schmidt, *Konfessionalisierung*, 59.
[62] Schmidt, *Konfessionalisierung*, 90–1; Blickle, *Reformation*, 153–5.

The authority of centralizing governments remained limited in two important ways. On the one hand, territorial Estates may have been weakened by the removal of prelates' benches, but they remained a continuing presence, fighting vociferously to preserve traditional rights, privileges, and freedoms, still able to exert considerable and effective pressure because of their key role in providing princes with money.[63] By no means all Estates, however, included peasants, or anything but virtual representation of the 'common man', who after all generally paid the taxes demanded by the Estates. On the other hand, even at the communal level, compliance with legal statutes or religious norms could not be taken for granted.

Fourth, if compliance was irregular, should the Reformation be judged a success or a failure? Judgements vary on the degree to which the Reformation made a real impact on the beliefs or behaviour of the laity at large during the first decade of the sixteenth century. The idea that it made almost no impact at all is undoubtedly rather extreme.[64] The fact that by the 1540s reformers like Melanchthon, or even Luther himself, believed that they had failed says more about their high expectations and standards than about conditions on the ground.[65] Similarly, later calls for a new Reformation reflect the religious aspirations of a new generation of idealists, rather than the omissions of their predecessors. After all, such revivals or awakenings have been an enduring feature of the history of Protestantism.

It took time for the changes to become established. The new religious norms had no more immediate impact at the grass-roots level than the other dictates of territorial government. Both were largely dependent, like the governments themselves, on consent. In areas such as Baden, Catholics and Protestants lived side by side for a long time, sharing churches and services, largely ignorant of the differences that divided their theologians. However, there is evidence that in Imperial Cities, the Hanseatic Cities, and the territorial towns of north Germany and Westphalia, a strong confessional awareness had developed by the 1540s.[66] Other areas saw the development of mixed forms of religion, or simply confusion such as that revealed by the Lippe visitation of 1549, which found pastors still saying the breviary, fasting, and believing in anything between three and seven sacraments.[67] Old superstitions and forms of magical religious practices undoubtedly survived, only to be 'discovered' by visitations as evidence of the new depravity of society. Cursing, premarital sex, and unchristian marital behaviour continued unabated. What was new was the idea that one might change this by legislating and policing.

---

[63] Strauss, *Law*, 240–71.   [64] Strauss, *House of learning*, 299.
[65] Strauss, 'Success'.   [66] Schmidt, *Konfessionalisierung*, 104–5.
[67] Schmidt, *Konfessionalisierung*, 62. See also pp. 499–511.

21

The Persistence of Catholicism

Many, of course, remained loyal Catholics. Until about 1530, the Catholic princes predominated, but by 1555 only a handful of major secular territories remained loyal, alongside the prince-bishoprics, a few Imperial Cities (notably Cologne), some Imperial Counts, Imperial Knights, and lesser nobles. Their history between 1517 and 1555 is often neglected by comparison with the attention devoted to the progress of the evangelical cause. This relative neglect has, however, tended to obscure important points about the development of the German territories and of the Reich as a whole.

Following Ranke, much German historical writing of the nineteenth and twentieth centuries tended to emphasize the ways in which the resistance to the Reformation by the Habsburgs, the Bavarian Wittelsbachs, and the German bishops divided the nation.[1] A further implication was that this had doomed their lands to relative backwardness compared with the supposedly more progressive Protestant territories. In so far as these areas, secular or ecclesiastical, merited investigation, it was largely as agencies of the Counter-Reformation, which focused attention on the decades after 1555. This tendency has been reinforced more recently by a growth of interest in the phenomenon of 'confessionalization': the definition of confessions or systems of dogma and the establishment by governments of new Church structures that took place in the second half of the century.

Continuing loyalty did not mean that nothing changed. For one thing, most of the Catholic territories went through the same 'modernization' process as those that became Protestant. The Habsburg lands under Maximilian I and then Ferdinand provided a model of progressive administration and reforming government. 'Reactionary' princes such as Heinrich the Younger of Brunswick-Wolfenbüttel (d. 1568) or Joachim I of Brandenburg (d. 1535) were among the leading exponents of the new approach to territorial government, with administrative reforms and the introduction of Roman law. The same is true of 'neutrals' such as Johann III of Jülich-Kleve-Berg (d. 1539) and Ludwig V of the Palatinate (d. 1544). Nor did the ecclesiastical territories lag behind in this respect. Spirituality and theological expertise may not have been the forte of the German prelates of this era, but legal knowledge and administrative expertise were found as commonly among their ranks as among the ranks of the secular rulers.[2]

---

[1] Ranke, *Geschichte*, 305–20.
[2] Wolgast, *Hochstift*, 26–7; Schindling 'Reichskirche', 89–91. See also pp. 88–94.

Some of these territories continued to pursue traditional policies aimed at creating territorial churches with no less vigour than the Protestants. Others were prompted by the new situation the Reformation created to embark on such policies for the first time. In general, the challenge of the evangelical movement generated the need for firm godly government, and the need for secular authorities to intervene where the ecclesiastical authorities seemed helpless. As Duke Georg of Saxony reasoned, God would seek revenge against those who failed to act and therefore one must always keep God and justice in one's sights and not fear the 'Martinians'.[3]

At the same time, however, the Reformation also created new parameters for such activities. Ambitions to secularize and annexe bishoprics, for example, became taboo once such actions became a characteristic of Protestant politics. Thus Bavaria had to abandon any aspiration to gain control of Eichstätt or Salzburg.[4] Charles V's secularization of Utrecht in 1528—he effectively 'bought' the temporal rights from the bishop, Heinrich of Bavaria, and then claimed the territory for himself and his successors in perpetuity, to the extreme displeasure of the papacy—remained an isolated case. Even Charles V felt constrained by the negative reaction of the papacy and some princes to the Utrecht transaction from taking up a similar offer from the Archbishop of Bremen, who indicated in 1533 that he would be willing to sell his temporals to Burgundy.[5]

Other aspects of traditional religious policy were also affected. Monastic reform ceased to be a meaningful issue at a time when, even in the Catholic areas, monastic houses were emptying and novices could no longer be recruited. Many initiatives conceived before the Reformation, such as plans for educational reform or visitations, were stalled by the fact that so many hopes were pinned on a general Church council that would resolve all the outstanding issues and bring about fundamental changes in Church practice.[6] In the short term, the failure of both emperor and papacy to agree on this issue for so long, justified repeated interventions in ecclesiastical affairs by the secular Catholic princes. This further reinforced the similarity between Catholic and Protestant Church management and led to a slide towards a late Reformation in some previously loyal but neutral territories between the 1540s and 1560s. Ultimately, therefore, the delay in resolving the wider position of the Catholic Church blighted many attempts to maintain the faith. By the time the decrees of the Council of Trent were published in 1564, many territories were already lost or beyond full recovery.

The enduring adherence of the emperor and his brother Ferdinand to the Catholic Church was crucial to the survival of German Catholicism and of the Reichskirche in particular.[7] Though Charles V was absent from the Reich for much of the 1520s and 1530s, his position as emperor continued to command allegiance.

---

[3] Wolgast, 'Territorialfürsten', 420.
[4] Schindling and Ziegler, *Territorien*, vii, 75; Press, 'Territorialstruktur', 259.
[5] Wolgast, *Hochstift*, 80–2, 123–4. Temporals were the lands and rights a prince-bishop enjoyed as a ruler, as opposed to his spirituals, the powers he exercised as a bishop.
[6] Schindling and Ziegler, *Territorien*, vii, 75.
[7] Schindling, 'Reichskirche', 94–6; Press, 'Territorialstruktur', 257–9.

At the same time, Charles exerted a new authority in the west and north-west of the Reich by virtue of his rule in the Netherlands.[8] That was a decisive factor in the loyalism of the Dukes of Jülich-Kleve-Berg, the Imperial City of Cologne, the ecclesiastical Electorates of Cologne and Trier, and secular Electorate of the Palatinate. This new imperial clientele network also extended across to Brunswick-Wolfenbüttel, where Duke Heinrich the Younger resolutely defied the evangelical movement in his lands until his death in 1568.[9] The emperor's political presence in the north-west also reinforced the loyalism of the Elector Joachim of Brandenburg and Duke Georg of Albertine Saxony.

While Charles exerted influence from the north-west, Ferdinand managed the traditional Habsburg networks in the south and in Middle Germany. Although the Imperial Cities were 'lost' relatively quickly, religious developments there did not carry over to the surrounding areas. Thus the traditional clientele of Imperial Counts, Imperial Knights, and sundry ecclesiastical rulers in Swabia, remained loyal both to the crown and to the Church. Between 1520 and 1534 this network, held together by the scatter of territories from the Sundgau and Alsace across Swabia to the Vorarlberg that made up Further Austria (Vorderösterreich), was strengthened by the Habsburg occupation of Württemberg. Ferdinand's role as King of Bohemia was also significant: Joachim of Brandenburg held Bohemian fiefs, while Georg of Saxony, a grandson of the Hussite king George Podiebrad, had inherited from his mother Sidonia a deep distrust of Hussitism and any form of heresy.[10]

In the west, the link between the two Habsburg systems via the Palatinate and the Rhineland bishoprics was reinforced by the staunch Catholic loyalties of both the Habsburg Franche-Comté and the Duchy of Lorraine. Throughout the Reich, the two systems were also interlaced by the prince-bishoprics. It is true the bishops were unable to provide much active support for the emperor. Yet their assertion of their rights as imperial princes did much to demonstrate the continuing need for the legal framework provided by emperor and Reich. The archbishops and bishops were Habsburg clients that the emperor could not afford to neglect.[11]

The one territory that does not fit easily into this picture is Bavaria. Besides the Habsburgs, the Wittelsbach dukes were the most important bastions of Catholicism in the Reich. Yet they combined an unswerving loyalty to the old Church with a deeply ambivalent attitude to the Habsburgs. Maximilian had, it is true, supported the Bavarians in their struggle against the Palatinate over the right to succession in Lower Bavaria in 1503–6. Yet gratitude for that could not hide for long the fact that Bavarian ambitions were thwarted on three sides by Habsburg territory. The tensions were exacerbated by the Habsburgs' occupation of Württemberg during 1520–34, a period in which Bavaria pursued a variety of hostile

[8] Press, 'Territorialstruktur', 259.
[9] Schindling and Ziegler, *Territorien*, iii, 24–36.
[10] Schindling and Ziegler, *Territorien*, ii, 12, 39–40.
[11] Press, 'Territorialstruktur', 257.

initiatives, including an attempt to thwart the election of Ferdinand as King of the Romans.

The restitution of Duke Ulrich to his duchy in 1534 removed the most obvious bone of contention between Habsburgs and Wittelsbachs, even though it involved the immediate lurch of Württemberg into the opposing religious camp. Thereafter, Bavaria remained more firmly, if often uneasily, allied to the imperial cause. Overall, it seems fair to conclude that Bavaria's primary loyalty was to the papacy (from which it gained considerable rewards in return) and to the emperor as an institution, rather than as a Habsburg.[12]

Within this spectrum of territories that remained loyal, there was a variety of responses to the evangelical challenge. They fall roughly into three categories. First, some rulers pursued reactionary or neutral policies in the 1520s and early 1530s, but then later turned to Protestantism, particularly after 1552–5, when the ruler's right to change religious allegiances was sanctioned by imperial law. Most of these princes acted within a framework defined by loyalty to the emperor and the traditions of the Reich. Second, the Habsburg and Bavarian territories remained Catholic in the long term, albeit in the case of the Austrian lands only after a long struggle against Protestantism in the second half of the century. Third, the ecclesiastical rulers comprise a discrete category.

The first group embraced a variety of territories in which rulers with different personal religious inclinations pursued broadly similar policies. In Jülich-Kleve-Berg, Johann III and Wilhelm V (r. 1539–1592) espoused broadly Erasmian views and promoted the cause of ecclesiastical reform.[13] They were constantly monitored by the Habsburg government in Brussels, and Wilhelm's helplessness vis-à-vis the emperor was graphically underlined when in 1543 Charles V forcibly seized the Duchy of Guelders that Wilhelm had inherited in 1538. In an attempt to forestall such action, Wilhelm had sought an alliance with France and made overtures to join the Schmalkaldic League. The latter baulked at open defiance of the emperor in such an area of known strategic significance to Charles as the Netherlands. On this occasion, France proved no military match for the emperor, who was determined to defend the core of his Burgundian inheritance and was temporarily supported by an alliance with England, which seized Boulogne.[14]

Charles's assertion of his presumed rights in Guelders had obvious territorial and strategic motives relating to his position both as ruler of the Netherlands and as Holy Roman Emperor. It also had a religious dimension. The ecclesiastical statute published by Duke Johann III in 1532 (and republished in 1567) represented a genuine attempt to promote an Erasmian-humanist reform of the Catholic Church. Yet in Charles's eyes, it brought the dukes dangerously close to a Protestant Reformation. Like other neutrals, the dukes also employed Protestant officials, which in the long term led to the establishment of a Protestant presence in their territories. In the early 1540s, Jülich became unreliable because of its

---

[12] Schindling and Ziegler, *Territorien*, i, 59–61.
[13] Schindling and Ziegler, *Territorien*, iii, 90–5.
[14] Rabe, *Geschichte*, 310–12; Schmidt, *Geschichte*, 83–4, 86; Joachimsen, *Reformation*, 237, 239.

ecclesiastical policies, the employment practices of its court and administration, and because of the apparent willingness of Duke Wilhelm to become little short of a vassal of the King of France. All this seemed to threaten both the emperor's access to the Reich and his vision of the role that a north-western Burgundian Habsburg power base might play in the Reich.

In the Palatinate, the Electors Ludwig V (r. 1508–44) and Friedrich II (r. 1544–56) were personally more indifferent to religion. They remained fundamentally loyal to the emperor and committed to the old Church as a guarantor of political stability and social peace.[15] However, here more than in Jülich, the proliferation of Protestants in the territorial administration led to the creeping conversion of the Palatinate, which made the rapid Reformation immediately implemented by the Elector Ottheinrich (r. 1556–59) both inevitable and smooth. In Brandenburg, the repressive response of the Elector Joachim I (r. 1499–35) gave way to an equally neutral regime under Joachim II (r. 1535–71), who published an ecclesiastical statute in 1540 and permitted clerical marriage and communion under both kinds.[16] The shift from initial reaction to long-term reform that prepared the way for a turn to Protestantism was also characteristic of Heinrich the Younger of Brunswick-Wolfenbüttel (r. 1514–68). He had to accept that major towns such as Brunswick and Goslar turned Protestant, but he persisted in efforts to improve the Church by means of visitations.[17] It is difficult to avoid the conclusion that the last decades of his rule were essentially a long prelude to the swift Protestant reform introduced by his successor Duke Julius (r. 1568–89).

Even a more straightforward and militant, traditional orthodox Catholic attitude on the part of Duke Georg of Albertine Saxony (r. 1500–39) generated a similar outcome rather earlier.[18] While he actively pursued the rigid enforcement of the Edict of Worms, Duke Georg was one of the most outspoken proponents of a Church council. When his pleas went unheeded, he set about addressing what he saw as the main cause of the present crisis: the decline of clerical morals. He encouraged episcopal visitations aimed at the ethical improvement of the clergy, promoted the maintenance of monastic discipline, and encouraged both his officials and his senior clergy to ensure good order in secular and ecclesiastical affairs and to respect the boundaries between the two spheres.

Unusually among the German princes, Duke Georg engaged in theological polemic against Luther on several occasions and even published some of his own pamphlets on theological issues. More than any of his contemporaries, he also exploited the new print media; his prosecution of those who wrote or published Lutheran tracts was matched by an equally energetic promotion of Catholic polemics. Leipzig and Dresden became the leading centres for the printing of such literature, much of it in German. At the same time, Duke Georg promoted Catholicism in ways that were more conventional. In 1523, for example, he secured

[15] Schindling and Ziegler, *Territorien*, v, 16–18.
[16] Schindling and Ziegler, *Territorien*, ii, 42–3.
[17] Schindling and Ziegler, *Territorien*, iii, 24–7.
[18] Schindling and Ziegler, *Territorien*, ii, 11–17.

the canonization of Bishop Benno of Meissen (1066–1106), a campaign he started long before the Reformation but which now provided his duchy with a 'territorial saint', and the elevation of the saint's bones on 16 June 1524 was exploited with ostentatious anti-Reformation zeal.[19]

Though ridiculed in pamphlets and woodcuts as a craven idolator, Duke Georg in fact came to develop a more flexible attitude in the face of the deepening religious divide, which extended so far as his acquiescing in attempts at conciliation and compromise. He had corresponded regularly with Erasmus from 1517, when he tried to tempt him to his university at Leipzig, until 1531, and he had been one of those who urged Erasmus to take a public stance against Luther, which he did with the work *De libero arbitrio* in 1524.[20] In 1530, Duke Georg sought, albeit in vain, to play a mediatory role at the Augsburg Reichstag.

In his own lands, Duke Georg's stance, buttressed by the prosperity generated by mining and trade, commanded the loyalty of significant elements of both the nobility and the educated. However, it proved impossible to isolate his territory from the influence of Protestant Electoral Saxony. There was no simple frontier: the partition of Saxony between the Ernestine and Albertine lines in 1485 had deliberately created a complex of intermeshing enclaves, condominiums, and joint administrations of mining enterprises.[21] The introduction of the German Mass in Ernestine Saxony in 1525 attracted growing numbers of Albertine subjects to worship there and a corresponding tendency to refuse *communio sub una* at home.[22] By about 1530, it was clear that repression alone could not halt the gradual spread of Lutheranism, and the duke's leading councillors began to fear for the prosperity of Leipzig and the duchy generally.

While Duke Georg himself remained true to traditional Catholicism, he had no choice but to allow free rein to the powerful Erasmian group led by Georg von Carlowitz (*c.*1471–1550) that emerged at his court in the early 1530s.[23] In 1534 and 1539, this group attempted to initiate discussions between Catholic and Protestant theologians at Leipzig. Finally, in 1538, they drafted an Erasmian-humanist ecclesiastical statute, which would have permitted both clerical marriage and communion under both kinds. The theological discussions failed because it proved impossible to agree on the basis on which they should be conducted, with the Protestants insisting on the Augsburg Confession and the Catholics proposing the model of the early Church Fathers.[24] The ecclesiastical statute was never published.

The ultimate failure of Duke Georg's efforts to keep his lands Catholic was inevitable even as the reform statute was formulated. His eldest son and heir died in 1537. His second son was mentally impaired and also died in February 1539, just

---

[19] *TRE*, xii, 386.

[20] *TRE*, xii, 387. See pp. 206–8.

[21] Schindling and Ziegler, *Territorien*, ii, 9–10; Wartenberg, 'Erasmianismus', 11–12.

[22] *Communio sub una* was the traditional form of communion, where the priest took both bread and wine where the congregation took only bread.

[23] Wartenberg, 'Erasmianismus', 7–9.

[24] Schindling and Ziegler, *Territorien*, ii, 16–17.

before his father, and only four weeks after his marriage to Elisabeth von Mansfeld, arranged in a desperate bid to produce a male heir.[25] This meant that the succession of Duke Georg's brother Heinrich became inevitable. The latter's marriage to Catherine of Mecklenburg related him to the Protestant Saxon Elector Johann the Constant (d. 1532). The combination of his wife's enthusiastic avowal of the evangelical cause and the growing influence of his Wittenberg kinsman led him to undertake the Protestant reform of his Freiberg and Wolkenstein estates in 1536–7. Duke Georg's efforts to safeguard his lands, supported, it seems, by significant elements of the Saxon nobility, by making the emperor heir to some of his patrimony came to nothing.

When Duke Heinrich succeeded his brother Georg in April 1539, he immediately initiated a Protestant visitation and a commission to draw up a new liturgical order. On 25 May, Luther himself preached in Leipzig. Soon afterwards, a second visitation laid the foundations for a territorial Church and set in motion, irreversibly, the Protestant reform of all ecclesiastical and educational institutions, which was completed under his son Duke Moritz in the years after 1541. After a short period of disgrace, Duke Georg's Erasmian councillor Carlowitz resumed a leading role under Duke Moritz, developed Lutheran sympathies, and presided over the establishment of Protestant schools funded by formerly monastic property.

The rapid turn of events in Saxony after the death of Duke Georg illustrates in exemplary fashion the problems that confronted many of the territories that attempted to remain Catholic. Success or failure was almost exclusively dependent on continuity in the ruling house. As the evangelical cause made more and more converts among the higher nobility in the late 1520s and 1530s, not least among its female echelons, so the likelihood of such continuity diminished. In Saxony, even the existence of widespread support for Catholicism among the territorial nobility posed no obstacle to a change of heart in the ruling house. In Brandenburg, the Protestant cause was strengthened by the fact that Elector Joachim II's brother, Margrave Johann von Küstrin, introduced a Protestant reform in the Neumark, in Crossen, and in Cottbus in 1540.[26] In other territories, the spread of Protestantism among the nobility and the growing influence of Protestant officials in court and administration made an eventual Protestant reform look like the logical outcome of a gradual but steady process of transition.

Ultimately, any hope for a resolution of the religious conflict was undermined by imperial politics. Religious neutrality or the attempt to steer a middle way was invariably linked with loyalty to the emperor. That, in turn, made the early Catholic reformers pioneers of what became imperial policy in the late 1530s and 1540s: the attempt by Charles V to regain the initiative by constructing an imperial league and by formulating an 'interim' settlement of the religious issue.[27] That, of course, involved more than just the politics of conciliation, for Charles V's fundamental aim was the establishment of a monarchical regime in the Reich. The

[25] Wartenberg, 'Erasmianismus', 10; Midelfort, *Mad princes*, 53–5.
[26] Schindling and Ziegler, *Territorien*, ii, 44–5. See also pp. 513–14.
[27] See pp. 304–24.

inevitable resistance to that also doomed any thought of a unifying religious settlement. With the idea of religious unity impracticable, all that remained was the recognition of the division and its enshrinement in imperial law in the Peace of Augsburg in 1555.

There was also, however, another fundamental problem inherent in the Catholic Erasmian-humanist reform programmes of the 1530s. Like the Protestant reform statutes, they were passed by princely fiat, or, in the case of the unpublished Saxon edict, at least envisaged as such. While such governmental initiatives seemed justifiable in view of the inactivity of the Church authorities, however, they were contrary to the hierarchical ethos of the Church. Indeed, any programme based on the Erasmian programme of Church reform by secular government, open-ended religious disputations between theologians of all sides, mutual toleration, and sidelining of the pope, was bound to provoke the opposition of both the German hierarchy and Rome. Finally, the publication of the Tridentine decrees in 1564 put an end to any hope for an Erasmian reform of the Catholic Church.

In view of the political problems and the theological obstacles to Erasmian Catholic reform, it is hardly surprising that many of the territories governed by Catholic loyalists before 1540 had turned to Protestantism by 1555. The rest followed shortly afterwards, generally after the death of an older prince such as Heinrich the Younger of Brunswick-Wolfenbüttel, who ruled from 1514 to 1568. The main exception is Jülich-Kleve-Berg. Catholicism remained officially dominant here in the undertow of the Habsburg court at Brussels and under the constant threat from the Duke of Alba's Spanish troops. However, many towns and nobles had embraced Protestantism in the 1540s and 1550s, while the Netherlands rebellion fostered the growth of Protestant groups after 1566. At the same time, the territorial government became less and less effective after Wilhelm V succumbed to a debilitating illness in 1566, a situation not improved by the serious mental illness of his son and heir Johann Wilhelm, who finally succeeded his father in 1592.[28]

The generally precarious nature of the Catholic reform programmes in some territories makes the successful—and long-term—assertion of Catholicism in Bavaria even more remarkable. The motives of the ruling Dukes Wilhelm IV (d. 1550) and Ludwig X (d. 1545) are not entirely clear. Their loyalty to the emperor was suspect before 1535. Their personal piety seems not to have been strong, and their attitude was well summed up by Wilhelm's admission in 1543 that he was a huntsman at heart, who all his life had wanted only to live in peace and to pursue his pleasures.[29] On the other hand, both dukes inherited and felt bound by strong territorial traditions: loyalty to the Reich as an institution for which their dynasty had once provided rulers; collaboration with Rome in the management of fifteenth-century reform of the Church in their lands; and support for their university at Ingolstadt.[30]

From the outset, Bavaria combined vocal opposition to Luther, firm repression of any evangelical tendencies at home, and the vigorous pursuit of Church reform

[28] Midelfort, *Mad princes*, 94–124; Schindling and Ziegler, *Territorien*, iii, 98–101; see also pp. 423–7.
[29] Wolgast, 'Territorialfürsten', 421.
[30] Schindling and Ziegler, *Territorien*, i, 57–9.

in collaboration with Rome. The Ingolstadt theologian Johannes Eck (1486–1543) rapidly emerged as one of Luther's most prominent Catholic antagonists. The Bavarian dukes were among the first to publish the Edict of Worms and to embark on an uncompromising policy of enforcement, including, uniquely among German princes, executions of heretics in 1523, something otherwise only undertaken by Charles V in the Netherlands.[31] Simultaneously, they forced the Archbishop of Salzburg to convene a reform synod and commissioned their Chancellor Leonhard von Eck (1480–1550) to negotiate special privileges with Rome to help them reform the Bavarian Church and to form a German alliance against the evangelical movement.[32]

The privileges negotiated with Rome in 1523–4, including the right to one-fifth of all clerical income in Bavaria, the right to conduct visitations of monasteries, and jurisdiction over the clergy, were enduring and were followed by further reforms over the next decades. By contrast, the league formed with Salzburg and Austria at Regensburg in the summer of 1524 proved short-lived. It was undermined by the animosity that developed between the Habsburgs and the Wittelsbachs over Württemberg and the question of the imperial succession. Only in 1534 did relations with the Habsburgs return to normal.

Even then, however, a renewed alliance with the Habsburgs, though it made possible the reassertion of traditional Wittelsbach allegiance to emperor and Reich, did not imply an uncritical allegiance to Charles V. The crux of Bavarian policy was loyalty to both Reich and papacy as institutions. Unlike other German princes, the Bavarian Wittelsbach dukes had no truck with notions of Erasmian reform. When Charles V experimented with compromise and conciliation in the late 1530s and 1540s, they resolutely opposed him. While this stance necessarily limited the extent to which they could aspire to gain control over the Church in their lands, it also rendered them less exposed to the kind of drift towards Protestantism evident elsewhere, and less vulnerable to the vicissitudes and ultimate failure of Charles V's German policy. This idiosyncratic Bavarian policy of papal loyalism provided a more successful basis than any Erasmian clique for a government-directed reform process also supported by the hierarchy. The early successes of those reforms from the 1550s, in turn, enabled Bavaria to survive the opposition of the noble, Protestant-inclining 'chalice movement' of the 1550s and 1560s more successfully than the Habsburgs did in Austria and Bohemia.[33]

By 1555, the network of secular Catholic states had shrunk dramatically to comprise essentially the Habsburg territories in the north-west and in the south, Bavaria, Franche-Comté, Lorraine, and Jülich-Kleve-Berg. It was all the more surprising, then, that the Reichskirche remained intact. Only Utrecht had been lost, and that, ironically, to Charles V in 1528.[34] The ecclesiastical princes, after all, represented some of the most unacceptable features of the Church that the

[31] Wolgast, 'Territorialfürsten', 422.
[32] Schindling and Ziegler, *Territorien*, i, 59–60.
[33] Schindling and Ziegler, *Territorien*, i, 62–4. See also pp. 448–56.
[34] Wolgast, *Hochstift*, 80–2.

evangelical movement wished to reform. The Reformation brought to the fore a plethora of secularization plans and rekindled the ambitions of many secular princes to annexe their episcopal neighbours.[35] Many ecclesiastical princes lost some of their diocesan rights and concentrated now on preserving their territorial rights.[36] Even so, there was never an alliance of bishops to defend these or other prerogatives.

The behaviour of the leading ecclesiastical dignitaries could not be described as either valiant or militant. Contemporary observers were scathing. Johannes Eck informed Hadrian VI in 1523 that the German bishops were either all 'neutrals, who if they do not promote the movement, do not impede anything' or 'good, but pusillanimous'.[37] Little had apparently changed by 1539, when Leonhard von Eck declared to Wilhelm IV of Bavaria that the 'bishops are all asleep' and that, incredibly, they wished to be seen as 'pious, just and without fault, as if they had not muddied any water'.[38] Even though the situation of the pre-Reformation Church may not have been as bleak as many contemporaries and subsequent historians painted it, the survival of the ecclesiastical territories is striking.

The evangelical movement made little impact in much of the west and south.[39] In the dioceses of Verdun, Toul, and Trent there was virtually no evangelical movement at all. The Prince-Bishoprics of Trier, Liège, Eichstätt, Brixen, Freising, Regensburg, and Passau were also largely untouched by any disturbance. In Westphalia, the Rhineland generally, and the Main region, evangelical movements had only a limited impact. Similarly, the great ecclesiastical foundations of the south—Salem, Kempten, Ochsenhausen, Ottobeuren, Schussenried, Weingarten, and the rest—all survived.

In other areas, however, the evangelical movement brought about fundamental changes. Archbishop Albrecht of Mainz was obliged to accept the Reformation of his Thuringian exclave of Erfurt.[40] Similarly, he could not prevent the almost total victory of the evangelical movement in his Magdeburg and Halberstadt lands. Indeed, north of the line formed by the lands of Münster, Osnabrück, Hildesheim, Paderborn, Mainz, Fulda, Würzburg, and Bamberg, virtually all ecclesiastical territories became Protestant in all but name by 1555.[41]

As in the case of the secular territories, the crucial factor was the decision by the ruling prince. In fact, only one prince-bishop out of roughly a hundred in the period 1517–55, Hermann von Wied of Cologne, seems to have developed serious Protestant sympathies and only three out of one hundred and twenty suffragans (in Basle, Speyer, and Würzburg).[42] The latter is perhaps more surprising, since the majority of suffragans were non-nobles and precisely the kind of educated people who, in general, were attracted to the evangelical cause.

Almost everywhere, the cathedral chapter provided a secure anchor for Catholicism. The chapters, after all, represented powerful vested interests—family, social

---

[35] Wolgast, *Hochstift*, 57–79. [36] Wolgast, *Hochstift*, 191–2.
[37] Wolgast, *Hochstift*, 189. [38] Wolgast, *Hochstift*, 190.
[39] Schindling, 'Reichskirche', 84–6. [40] Wolgast, *Hochstift*, 192.
[41] Schindling, 'Reichskirche', 85. [42] Wolgast, *Hochstift*, 99–100.

and political networks—for example, of Imperial Knights whose future both as individuals and as a caste or corporation depended on loyalty to both Church and emperor.[43] On the one hand, some chapters saw some of their number embrace the evangelical cause; others admitted new members with evangelical leanings. On the other hand, no chapter saw the evolution of a Protestant majority before 1555, and many responded much more energetically than their prince-bishops did to the challenge posed by the evangelical movement.

The vociferous collective defence of rights and privileges was only to be expected of these corporate-collegiate bodies, whose very existence depended on the strict nurture of even the most trivial legal precedent. In a sense, cathedral chapters functioned in the same way as specially privileged Estates: in the absence of a hereditary ruling dynasty, they could plausibly claim to act as guardians of the territorial interest. Increasingly, many of them used the device of the electoral capitulation, a complex agreement which a newly elected prince-bishop was required to sign, to ensure that both the political and religious status quo was maintained.[44]

Consequently, the prince-bishops had much less freedom to choose than their secular counterparts. What Grandmaster Albrecht achieved in Prussia in 1525— the secularization of a major ecclesiastical territory—could not easily be emulated in the Reich proper. Almost no one even attempted to follow his example. The obstacles became clear when the Elector-Archbishop Hermann von Wied of Cologne set about attempting a Protestant reform of his territories in 1542.[45]

As a result of a combination of political factors, strong religious traditions, and the influence of a major theological faculty at the university, the Imperial City of Cologne had effectively suppressed the evangelical movement in the 1520s.[46] Furthermore, from 1515 to 1535 Wied ruled as a perfectly orthodox prelate, consistently loyal to both Rome and the emperor. His own personal conversion to the evangelical cause developed during the course of discussions of the formulation of new statutes for the Cologne provincial council in 1536, and by 1542 he had recruited Martin Bucer to assist in the systematic introduction of the Reformation. He met with opposition from clergy, chapter, and Estates, who immediately appealed to Charles V for support. The distraction of the Schmalkaldic War in the south left the situation in the balance for several years. Once Charles had secured victory there, however, he turned to deal with the archbishop: his commissioners executed the pope's ban of excommunication and declared Wied's forfeiture of the temporals (lands and rights as a ruler) by virtue of his loss of the spirituals (powers he exercised as a bishop). Adolf von Schaumburg, coadjutor since 1533, and a staunch opponent of Wied's reforms from the outset, was then immediately elected archbishop and signed a capitulation in which he pledged to maintain the Catholic faith in his lands. Wied himself died a declared Protestant in 1552.

Hermann von Wied simply wanted to reform rather than to secularize his territory: he envisaged it continuing as a Protestant elective archbishopric. Even that, however, was too radical a change for either his chapter or the emperor to

---

[43] Schindling, 'Reichskirche', 100–3.   [44] Wolgast, *Hochstift*, 187.
[45] Wolgast, *Hochstift*, 91–9, 136–7.   [46] Scribner, 'Cologne', *passim*.

contemplate. Cologne, as an Electorate and a major Rhineland territory of key strategic interest to Charles V, was arguably a special case. Even elsewhere, however, for example in the north-east and where a strong evangelical movement had taken hold, the formal situation remained unchanged before 1555. The minor Middle German and northern bishoprics—Samland, Pomesania, Cammin, Brandenburg, Havelberg, Lebus, Schwerin, Meissen, Merseburg, and Naumburg—can hardly be counted here, as they were already all but 'territorial bishoprics' in the fifteenth century.[47] The nearest that any Protestant prince got to capturing a neighbouring benefice that was a classic institution of the Reichskirche was to secure a succession of elections for Catholic members of his own dynasty, as did the Brandenburg Hohenzollerns in Magdeburg.[48] 'Dynastic successions' and arrangements limiting the freedom of chapters to choose only those nominated by a neighbouring prince ('gebundene Wahl') paved the way for later secularizations, but the completion of such moves depended on the very different legal framework in the Reich after 1555.

Catholic Germany was not backward: much of it developed in similar ways to Protestant Germany at the same time. However, by the 1540s there was growing evidence of a need for a more fundamental reform in both ecclesiastical and secular territories. Visitations revealed inadequacies and shortages at every level. The spread of the evangelical movement and its establishment in both urban and rural areas was unmistakable in many regions. Schools and universities were in decline.[49]

Finally, by the end of the 1540s, it became increasingly clear that the idea of a purely German reform, whether pursued by Erasmian princes and councillors or by the emperor, was simply an illusion. In some ways, it is striking that the complaints from Catholic territories echo those from the Protestant territories, where in the 1540s reformers began to lament that they had failed to change the world. In other respects, however, the crisis was more profound in the Catholic territories. Protestantism, after all, was still exerting a profound popular attraction, at the expense always of the old faith. Catholicism, too, was acutely aware of its dependence on the emperor and the vicissitudes of his ambitions in the Reich, both religious and secular. The dilemmas inherent in this situation were only resolved by the Peace of Augsburg in 1555. That peace was, however, itself the product of a complex development within the Reich since the Reichstag of Speyer in 1526.

---

[47] Wolgast, *Hochstift*, 197–253.   [48] Wolgast, *Hochstift*, 130–2.   [49] *HdtBG*, i, 312–13.

22

Charles V, Ferdinand, and the Reich in Europe

The apparently inexorable advance of Protestantism in the Reich and its permanent establishment in one major territory after another in the decades after 1526 has sometimes been taken as evidence of a steady process of the disintegration of German unity. In fact, however, the complex negotiations and periodic armed conflicts of this period ultimately enhanced the solidarity of the German Estates. The central institutions of the Reich emerged strengthened. The nature of the German monarchy itself was defined in a way that was subsequently only success-fully challenged by Napoleon. Charles V, apparently infinitely more powerful than any of his predecessors, was no more successful than Maximilian was in imposing his will on the Reich. Indeed, he failed largely because of the vast extent of his varied realms and the many, often contradictory, commitments they entailed. His defeat paved the way for a new and enduring constitutional settlement that gave final shape to the early modern Reich.

The religious issue was fundamental throughout. It was clearly divisive, but ultimately more important was the way in which the commitment to its resolution served to sustain unity. The appeal to a future Church council, variously envisaged as a general council or as a German national council, in the light of which any agreement reached would be provisional, became a constant refrain in German politics. Sometimes it barely disguised cynical opportunism and the relentless pursuit of secularization and extension of control over the local Church.

Yet though it was a rhetorical device, the appeal at least allowed compromises to be reached at the imperial level and 'final' confrontations to be avoided. The avoidance of finality, sometimes admittedly testimony to the chronic spirit of procrastination that undoubtedly suffused German political life, also enabled that life to continue. Hence, even as irreconcilable religious differences seemed to bring the system to the brink of collapse, essential legislation was agreed, joint enterprises were engaged in to preserve the domestic peace, and initiatives were launched to defend the Reich from external threat. Not least, when the threat to the Reich seemed to come from the emperor himself in the 1540s, even profound religious differences counted for little in the common struggle to preserve German freedom.

At every stage, these German negotiations and struggles were shaped both by the inner-dynastic concerns of the Habsburgs and by the ramifications of their non-German interests. The relationship between Charles and his brother Ferdinand remained superficially harmonious. Charles worked hard against considerable opposition to achieve Ferdinand's election as King of the Romans in January 1531. Ferdinand worked hard to promote his brother's interests in the Reich and to implement his policies. Yet they developed a different experience of the Reich. Ferdinand, the junior brother, was constantly present in the Reich and, in time, he grew into the role and mentality of a German prince. Charles had all the advantages of the charisma, the authority, and the almost magical mobilizing power of the imperial crown. However, for the first two decades of his reign his periods of residence in the Reich were brief (1520–1, 1530–2, 1541), and his direct experience and knowledge of German politics was consequently limited. This significantly handicapped his efforts to impose his will during his ten years of residence after 1543.

Furthermore, the brothers approached imperial politics from different geographical perspectives: Charles from the Low Countries, Ferdinand from Austria. This gradually generated differences in their perceptions of priorities and in their perceptions of how to reach a settlement in Germany. Ferdinand became the beneficiary of Charles's failure. Until then, the brothers generally rowed in the same general direction, but as time went on, rarely simultaneously or in a co-ordinated manner. Both, of course, remained loyal to what they perceived as the interests of the dynasty. Communication and understanding on German affairs was also eased by the fact that Charles benefited from the advice of Ferdinand's high chancellor from the late 1520s until his death in 1539, Cardinal Bernardo Clesio, Bishop of Trent.[1] Yet each brother was obliged to pursue a German policy in the context of a distinctly different, albeit often overlapping, set of non-German coordinates. In each case, that meant grappling with the major new factor in early sixteenth-century European politics: the emergence of the Turkish threat.

The most immediately pressing problems for the Reich were those that ensued from Ferdinand's inheritance of the Bohemian and Hungarian crowns in 1526.[2] This, in turn, resulted directly from the assault launched against Hungary in 1521 by the Ottomans. Suleiman the Magnificent's successful capture of Belgrade inaugurated a relentless succession of campaigns that periodically threatened the whole region up to and including Vienna over the next few decades. In the campaign of 1526, the Turks swept up into the heart of Hungary and comprehensively defeated the poorly armed and incompetently led army of Lewis II at Mohács in August. Lewis's death activated the agreement by the Vienna Congress of 1515, which, in the event of his dying childless, provided for the succession of his brother-in-law, Ferdinand. Yet neither in Bohemia nor in Hungary was the succession straightforward.

In Bohemia, the Estates insisted on their right of free election and only agreed to elect Ferdinand in October 1526, after numerous bribes had been paid and their electoral rights had been confirmed. His coronation in February 1527 brought Bohemia back into the Reich, though Ferdinand's authority there was limited by

---

[1] Rabe, *Geschichte*, 329. In the German literature, Clesio is generally referred to as Bernhard von Cles.
[2] Kohler, *Ferdinand I.*, 157–72.

the concessions he had been obliged to make to secure his election.[3] Matters in Hungary were more complicated. While the Bohemians had toyed with a variety of rather implausible Bavarian, Saxon, and Polish counter-candidates, in Hungary a strong national candidate emerged in the person of John Zápolya, Voivode of Transylvania, who also enjoyed the support of his father-in-law, the King of Poland.

Bribes, legal arguments, promises, and threats failed to prevent the election and coronation of Zápolya at Stuhlweissenburg (Székesfehérvár) in November 1526, which then left Ferdinand in the position of counter-claimant. However, he was able, at huge cost in pledges of long-term financial support to his widowed sister-in-law, the dowager Queen Mary, and bribes to her circle of magnate supporters, to secure his own coronation in the following month. Then, brushing aside Zápolya's offers for negotiation (that would leave Zápolya as king married to Maria, with Ferdinand as their heir), Ferdinand resolved to secure his crown by military conquest.

This fateful decision had two important consequences. First, it exposed Ferdinand's own lack of funds to pursue such an enterprise unaided. Charles prevaricated, then promised help, but sent too little too late. The Bohemians, in any case newly fortified by the privileges Ferdinand had just granted them, hesitated to lend assistance that would merely enhance the power of their new king. The German princes, having refused to support Lewis against the Turks in 1524 and 1526, now declined to contribute to what they saw as a purely Habsburg military campaign in Hungary. Second, Zápolya himself was driven into the arms of the Turks, who in January 1528 formally placed him under their protection in an alliance against Ferdinand. The following year, Suleiman's effort to establish Zápolya led to his forces laying siege to Vienna.[4]

The Turks withdrew after two weeks, before Ferdinand's forces had arrived. Suleiman had reached his limits at the gates of Vienna. Neither then nor in subsequent crises, notably another attempted onslaught that stopped just short of Vienna at Güns (Kőszeg) in 1532, was the city under real or lasting military threat. However, the eastern front remained active, and a source of perceived danger, for decades to come.[5] Short periods of truce intervened, and in 1538 Ferdinand and Zápolya reached agreement whereby each recognized the other as lawful King of Hungary, with Ferdinand to be the (as yet) childless Zápolya's heir.

All truces lasted only so long as it took Suleiman to gather forces for a new northern offensive, and the agreement of 1538 was undermined by the birth of a son just days before Zápolya's death in 1540.[6] Johann Sigismund became the immediate heir to his father's position, his considerable Magyar following, and his Turkish protectorate. The decisive campaigns were those of 1541 and 1543; a

---

[3] Its status within the Reich remained distinct: it was not subject to the legislation of 'Kaiser und Reich' and it did not belong to a Kreis; the Bohemian king, though an Elector, did not participate in the normal business of the College of Electors.

[4] Fichtner, *Ferdinand I*, 79–80, 83–5, 91–2.

[5] Kohler, *Ferdinand I.*, 207–24.

[6] Fichtner, *Ferdinand I*, 121–6.

five-year truce in 1547 gave way to further skirmishes until the agreement was renewed in 1562, though the threat was only really laid to rest with Suleiman's death in 1566. As early as 1541, the ultimate outcome was essentially clear. Hungary was divided between an independent Transylvanian principality east of the Theiss (Tisza), a large Turkish bloc on the Middle Danube, and a Habsburg frontier-belt kingdom in the north and west that paid an annual tribute to the Porte of 30,000 ducats.[7]

Ferdinand's long struggle to establish his rights in his extended hereditary lands had profound implications both for his relations with Charles and for his position with regard to the Reich. He repeatedly turned to his brother for assistance, yet Charles did his best to dissuade him from military action, and when he did promise support, it was invariably insufficient and, if actually rendered, delivered too late to be of much use. The German Estates were no more reliable. In the 1520s, the Reichstag proved reluctant to offer any help. Ferdinand made repeated representations, but the German Estates invariably declined to act, on the grounds that there was no threat to the Reich.

That reluctance was reinforced by the exasperation that many felt at the lack of any progress towards a Church council to discuss the German *Gravamina* and reform of the Church. Luther went so far as to declare that true Christians should not dream of complying with the Habsburg call to arms: for the Turk was a scourge of God and to resist the Turk was to resist God. More pragmatically, most of the German Estates—whatever their religious inclinations—saw no reason to support Ferdinand in what they saw as a dynastic and non-German concern. Some also quite cynically calculated that a Habsburg victory in Hungary would merely result in a stronger ruler able to pursue a hard line on the religious question in the Reich.[8]

The Reichstag only agreed to send 24,000 men when Ferdinand finally promised in August 1526 to convene a council within eighteen months and to permit each to rule according to his conscience until then. The process of negotiating this, however, took so long that the Reichstag adjourned only four days before the Battle of Mohács, which rendered the promised military assistance redundant. The siege of Vienna in 1529, a direct assault on the Reich, brought about a change of heart. Even though the religious crisis was now far more acute, the Estates as a whole agreed to send men to defend German territory. Once more, however, the abrupt end of the siege meant that these forces were not called upon, and once again the Estates flatly refused to allow them to be used on Hungarian soil.

From then on, the Turkish threat, and Ferdinand's regular appeals to the Reichstag, became a constant theme in German politics and a powerful bargaining tool for the Protestants and other political opponents of the Habsburgs. In fact, some princes freely contributed much more than the *Matrikel* required. In practice, however, the length of time it took to establish that there was indeed a threat, and the protracted political negotiations over the concessions to be granted in return for aid, generally meant that the forces of the Reich arrived too late to make any

---

[7] Winkelbauer, *Ständefreiheit*, i, 130.
[8] Fischer-Galati, *Imperialism*, 10–37.

difference. Prompt action might have helped Ferdinand inflict a decisive blow against the Turks in 1529 and again in 1542. On the latter occasion, the Estates consented to mobilize the military assistance agreed as long ago as 1530, but by the time the Reich's *oberster Feldhauptmann* (first commanding officer) had notified the individual Estates of this through the communication mechanisms of the Imperial Kreise, Suleiman had long since withdrawn his forces.[9] The obvious solutions of maintaining a standing force or of providing regular grants of money were, of course, out of the question, as they might be too easily employed to bolster the house of Habsburg, rather than just defend the Reich.

However ambivalent their support and however inadequate their assistance, Ferdinand remained dependent on both his brother and the German Estates. His income from his own lands did not permit him to act alone. The Bohemian crown came encumbered with substantial debts and mortgaged revenues, while the Bohemian diet proved just as penny-pinching as the German Reichstag when it came to negotiating extraordinary grants. The Venetian ambassador, who reported in 1543 that the only regular revenues left to the King of Bohemia were the tolls at the gates of Prague, was not exaggerating much.[10] The limited Hungarian territories Ferdinand ultimately came to control brought valuable mineral deposits and mines into his possession, but much of the royal patrimony had been given away in the process of securing his election, and the Hungarian Estates were far from keen on paying for their own defence.

The main burden fell on Ferdinand's Austrian lands, which were subject to increasingly heavy taxation during the 1520s, while seizure of Church property carried out under the banner of Church reform also made a significant contribution. All efforts to rationalize his financial situation, however, to consolidate his revenues, or even to summon general meetings of the Estates from all his territories, failed to produce the money he would have required in order to pursue his military campaigns in Hungary to a successful conclusion. Little wonder, then, that he repeatedly asked his brother to enfeoff him with Milan in the 1520s and to allow him to make it a 'German principality'. The dream of Milan was revived in 1538, when it seemed that Charles might include it as part of the dowry for one of Ferdinand's daughters in a projected, though never realized, marriage to the Duke of Orleans.[11]

However, Ferdinand was able to forge at least a rudimentary union between his Austrian duchies and his two kingdoms.[12] All attempts to construct a centralized administrative system failed, but the various lands at least enjoyed a legal status in common. Ferdinand was, for example, careful to maintain the legal exemption of Bohemia from imperial jurisdiction by not exercising the rights of the King of Bohemia as an Imperial Elector. This gave Bohemia and its associated territories of Silesia, Upper and Lower Lusatia, and Moravia, the same privileged status within

---

[9] Schmid, 'Reichssteuern', 194.   [10] Fichtner, *Ferdinand I*, 72.
[11] Fichtner, *Ferdinand I*, 36–7, 64, 161; Aretin, *Das Reich*, 101–3.
[12] Evans, *Making*, 146; Winkelbauer, *Ständefreiheit*, i, 196–8; Pamlényi, *Hungary*, 130; Fichtner, *Ferdinand I*, 66–78.

the Reich as the Austrian duchies. That, in turn, set their ruler apart from the other princes and reinforced his superior status. Above all, however, although Ferdinand's new lands did not bring great wealth, their sheer extent along the eastern periphery of the Reich was of immense political importance.

Bohemia and Silesia brought Ferdinand into direct contact with Saxony and Brandenburg, and their feudal networks furnished him with influence deep into Middle Germany and the north. For all his problems with his various Estates and with the Turks, his enlarged Erblande left Ferdinand in a strong position in imperial politics, albeit handicapped in ways that made him seem less threatening to the German Estates. Both his strength and his weakness were crucial factors in the evolution of his position in the Reich and his ultimate emergence as its natural overlord.

As long as Charles remained emperor, however, nothing much could be achieved in the Reich without his agreement and cooperation. Moreover, until the mid-1540s the emperor's problems outside the Reich prevented any serious engagement with German issues. In over two decades, he spent just four years in the Reich, leaving its affairs in a kind of limbo. Other problems were more pressing. Charles's first priority was the security of his Spanish, Netherlands, and Italian territories, and his approach to the politics of the Reich was shaped above all by what he referred to as his 'nidere erblande' (lower hereditary lands), the Netherlands and the Franche-Comté.[13]

The most persistent issue that he faced was the vigorous pursuit by Francis I of French claims to Milan and Naples, while Charles's own claims to Burgundy remained a continuing bone of contention.[14] For much of the period between 1520 and 1529, then again in 1536–8 and 1542–4, Valois and Habsburg were at war. Milan, claimed by the house of Valois yet also a fiefdom of the Holy Roman Empire, was the main focus of much of this hostility, since its possession held the key to Naples (for Francis) or to dominion over southern France and the possibility of regaining Burgundy (for Charles). For all of Francis's fierce ambition and determination, he was unable to defeat Charles. He was, however, able to mount a number of serious challenges that tied Charles's forces down for protracted periods.

Charles himself seemed curiously reluctant to capitalize on his victories. In 1525, his forces inflicted a devastating blow on the French at Pavia, and Francis was taken captive. The Peace of Madrid obliged him to drop all claim to Naples and cede both Milan and Burgundy to Charles. Yet no sooner was Francis free than he renounced the agreement and entered into a new anti-Habsburg league with Venice, Florence, and the papacy. In 1527, Rome fell to the Spanish troops, while in 1528, the Genoese commander Andrea Doria defected to the Habsburg side. By 1529, Charles had once more gained the upper hand, yet concluded a peace that allowed the Sforzas to return to Milan, and which imposed no other penalty on Francis than

---

[13] Press, 'Bundespläne', 77.

[14] For the following, see Tracy, *Charles V*, 39–49, 114–32; Kohler, *Reich*, 8–10, 69–73; Kohler, *Expansion*, 352–71.

the loss of his overlordship over Flanders and Artois. The Peace of Cambrai, concluded in August 1529, paved the way for Charles's coronation by the pope at Bologna in 1530, but it did not solve the problem of the French threat. The death of Francesco Sforza in November 1535 led to a new French onslaught on Milan, challenging Charles's decision that the fiefdom of Milan should revert to the imperial crown.

The hostilities were both hugely costly on both sides and inconclusive. The outcome was a ten-year truce mediated by the pope at Nice in June 1538. Subsequent negotiations, including a meeting of the two monarchs at Aigues-Mortes in August, revolved around complex plans for dynastic union. The Duke of Orleans, the French king's younger son, would marry one of Ferdinand's daughters and receive the fiefdom of Milan. Charles's son, Philip, was to marry the French king's youngest daughter, while his own eldest daughter Maria was to marry Ferdinand's son Maximilian and rule in the Netherlands, in return for which Ferdinand would renounce any claim to Naples. Yet, ultimately, Charles could not contemplate the possibility of losing control of Milan, and when he proposed a marriage of the Duke of Orleans to Maria, with a dowry consisting of the Netherlands and the Franche-Comté, together with a marriage gift of Burgundy for Francis, the French king rebelled.

The decision to invest Philip with Milan in October 1540 ended any hope of a lasting peace. Two years later hostilities resumed. This time, though the ultimate prize was Milan, the struggle was largely carried out and ultimately decided in the north, with Henry VIII in alliance with Charles, and Francis seeking assistance from the Duke of Guelders and the German Protestants. Now again, however, the French offensives failed to achieve a decisive breakthrough and, equally, Charles refrained from terms that did any more than restore the status quo. Renewed thoughts of a dynastic union, again with the possibility of investing the Duke of Orleans with Milan, were scuppered by the latter's sudden death. The Peace of Crépy (18 September 1544) finally laid to rest Francis's ambitions outside France. His rights to Burgundy were confirmed, and he retained Savoy, which he had occupied in 1536. In return, he was obliged to recognize Charles's rights to Flanders, Artois, Milan, and Naples, and to acquiesce in Charles's acquisition of Guelders.

At the same time, the secret clauses appended to the treaty point to the many ramifications of the enduring conflict with France.[15] Francis agreed to support the emperor in a campaign against the Turks, in an initiative to reform the Church, and in action against the German Protestants. He also agreed to assist the Duke of Savoy against the city of Geneva, from where Calvin's radical teachings threatened to permeate both France and the Netherlands.

In terms of Charles's wider concerns, the most crucial of these secret clauses was the one that concerned the Turks. For, just as Ferdinand was haunted by the Ottoman offensives in Hungary, Charles was tormented by the extension of their

---

[15] Schilling, *Aufbruch*, 222–3.

power in the Mediterranean.[16] The Turkish acquisition of Egypt in 1517 opened the way to the extension of Turkish protectorate over the North African kingdoms that Spain had failed to bring under its control in the early years of the century.

What started as a local Western Mediterranean problem soon became a more serious threat as the Moorish rulers of Algiers enlisted the help of the powerful pirate brothers Barbarossa, who in turn took control of Algiers and acknowledged themselves vassals of the Sultan. Appointed Pasha and Grand Admiral of the Turkish fleet in 1532, Khair ad-Din Barbarossa, previously simply a menace to the coastal settlements of Spain and Italy, launched a full-scale assault on southern Italy in 1534 and then conquered Spain's Moorish ally in Tunis.[17] A Spanish counter-attack the following year—made into a triumphant crusade, no less, by imperial propaganda—restored the status quo, now reinforced by a significant Spanish garrison in the fortress of La Goletta. Khair ad-Din's escape, however, led to continuing insecurity in the region. Despite an alliance with Venice and the papacy, Charles's navy was defeated comprehensively at Prevesa in September 1538. In 1540, his fleet was all but destroyed off Crete. The following year, an attempt to take Algiers failed miserably and merely provoked a revenge attack by Khair ad-Din on Reggio di Calabria and Nice in 1543.

The maritime threat was serious enough in itself. It rendered Spain, Naples, and Sicily, as well as all the Spanish enclaves and islands on the North African coast, permanently insecure. The raids of 1543 also, however, brought out into the open a further dimension of the problem. Having all but destroyed the city of Nice, which was saved only by the timely approach of Doria's fleet, Khair ad-Din wintered in the port of Toulon, which the French had vacated for that purpose.[18] This marked the culmination of French efforts to exploit the Habsburg–Ottoman conflict to their advantage. Since the 1520s, they had sought trade agreements of various kinds, stopping short of a formal treaty, with the Porte and in 1528 they had formally supported Zápolya after he accepted the Turkish protectorate.[19] A successful collaboration between the French crown and the Porte in the Mediterranean might have threatened the very basis of Charles's *monarchia* in Europe.

In fact, the disaster that seemed to loom in the early 1540s never materialized. The Ottoman victory at Prevesa in 1538 had tilted the balance of maritime power firmly towards the east; and even subsequent Habsburg victories such as Lepanto in 1571 failed to redress that. Yet the Ottomans, too, ultimately found the limits of their range in the Western Mediterranean. They failed to capitalize on the sack of Nice and withdrew eastwards again, soon to be more concerned with securing their Central Hungarian Vilayets (sub-provinces) and with the resumption of their war with Persia. Equally, the French derived little advantage from their gesture at

---

[16] Tracy, *Charles V*, 133–82, 311–14.

[17] Kohler, *Expansion*, 363–7.

[18] Khair ad-Din had wanted to attack Spain, but Francis suggested Nice as a target less likely to provoke an immediate Habsburg response; it was the last remaining outpost of Charles III of Savoy. Clot, *Suleiman*, 144–50.

[19] Goffman, *Ottoman Empire*, 110–11; Clot, *Suleiman*, 129–44; Williams, 'Conflict'; Hochedlinger, 'Freundschaft'.

Toulon in 1543. The full exposure of their relations with the infidel, the implications graphically underlined by horrific stories of Christian slaves being sold openly on the Toulon markets, brought them nothing but opprobrium. Crucially for Francis's ambitions further north, the German Protestant princes were also alienated. In 1535, they had rebuffed an offer of French support because of the commercial treaty with the Porte. Now, again, in the mid-1540s they shrank back from an alliance with a traitor to the common cause of Christendom.

The general security of his scattered territories and the establishment of (Spanish) Habsburg dominion over Italy were paramount in Charles's politics. Both took precedence over any sense of obligation to support Ferdinand in Hungary or indeed over any ambition to preserve the wider traditional rights of the Reich itself. Dominion over Italy was achieved in flagrant disregard of the Italian prerogatives of the Reich, which Charles was technically obliged to defend in his capacity as Reichsvikar of the *Regnum Italicum*.[20] Similar security considerations and the formal recognition of French overlordship over the Duchy of Burgundy in 1544 in effect extinguished any last thought of restoring the old Burgundian kingdom. Equally, acquiescence in the French occupation of Savoy until 1559 also in effect abandoned Reich territory, not to mention the rights of an important and loyal prince of the Reich, to the French crown. These sacrifices were all part of the price the emperor was willing to pay for the stability he had achieved by the mid-1540s, and which enabled him to contemplate dealing with the German situation.

There was, however, one further obstacle. Dealing with Germany meant dealing with the issue of reform and that was impossible without the cooperation of the papacy. Clement VII (d. 1534) was essentially little interested in Church reform. He was much more concerned with promoting the interests of his Medici relatives, which led him into repeated alliances with France. The collapse of the first French challenge in Italy in 1525, the sack of Rome by Spanish troops in 1527, and, finally, the defection of Andrea Doria from the French to the imperial cause in 1528 led Clement to change sides himself.

Following Charles's promise to restore the Medici in Florence and to cede Ravenna, Cervia, Modena, and Reggio to the papacy, Clement made his peace with the emperor in 1529. The following year in Bologna, he crowned Charles King of Italy and Holy Roman Emperor in the presence of his Italian vassals.[21] Yet the new imperial–papal entente did not endure. Charles restored the Medici, who now became subject to Spain, but he reneged on his other promises; consequently, Clement was soon busy planning the marriage of his great-niece, Catherine de Medici, to the French king's younger son. Talks with Charles in 1532 about plans for an Italian league also produced, at Charles's insistence, the announcement of an imminent Church council, but nothing came of the idea. To the end of his life, Clement proved resistant to any firm commitment to a reform council, encouraged variously by England and above all France, neither of which wanted a council dominated by the emperor.

---

[20] Aretin, *Das Reich*, 101–5.   [21] Aretin, *Das Reich*, 101.

Clement's successor, Paul III (1534–49, Alessandro Farnese) pursued a resolutely neutral policy, which contributed infinitely more to the security of the Papal States. He mediated personally between Habsburg and Valois at Aigues-Mortes in 1538, and then again in 1541 and 1543.[22] He was also committed to reform and persuaded by many of the conciliatory ideas of the influential *spirituali* reform group around Cardinal Gasparo Contarini.[23] In 1536, he issued a call for a council in Mantua in May 1537. For the first time also, something approaching a Catholic reform manifesto was now published in the form of the *Consilium de emendanda ecclesia*, though the document refrained from touching on doctrinal issues, which its authors believed would be the proper business of the council.[24]

Yet even a determined pope was unable to advance the cause far at this stage. Charles and Ferdinand remained ambivalent, since the council was not to be held in a place that the German Estates would recognize as imperial territory (it belonged to the Italian rather than the German *regnum*). The German Protestants rejected the proposal on the grounds that they did not regard the council as 'free' (i.e. free of the pope). Crucially, moreover, the King of France boycotted the council, since it bespoke an alliance, or at least an understanding, between emperor and pope that was unwelcome in the context of a renewed assault by France on northern Italy in 1536. The French demand that the council be held in France was unacceptable to both emperor and pope, and it wrecked the Mantua plan.[25] A last-ditch attempt to convene the council in Vicenza failed miserably: no one turned up.

The threat by the German Catholics to proceed to a national council if no general council was convened led to yet another initiative. This time, the pope acceded to the emperor's request for a location (just) within the German Reich at Trent. Again, however, the outright refusal of the French to cooperate, which left Paul III fearing a French schism if he proceeded, brought matters to a standstill and the ten bishops who had assembled by the summer of 1543 were sent home.[26] In the summer of 1544, the Reichstag once more placed the papacy under pressure by resolving to pursue its own 'friendly conciliation' of the religious division. The crucial change that now finally resulted in the opening of a general council of the Church in December 1545 was the King of France's agreement at Crépy in September 1544 no longer to obstruct the emperor and the pope from convening it.

In the meantime, however, a significant change had taken place in Rome. The *spirituali*, Catholic evangelicals whose ideas of ecclesiastical and doctrinal reform had been dominant in the later 1530s, fell out of favour. Contarini, as papal legate to the Reichstag, had failed to persuade the German Estates, either Catholic or Protestant, at Regensburg in 1541. Yet the fact that in the process of trying he had appeared to move towards the Lutheran position in his emphasis on the supremacy of faith over grace and merit aroused the hostility of the conservative *zelanti* faction

[22] Lutz, 'Italien', 879–80.
[23] Bonney, *States*, 58–9; Fenlon, *Heresy*, 32–3; Mullett, *Catholic Reformation*, 33–8.
[24] Fenlon, *Heresy*, 42–3.
[25] Mullett, *Catholic Reformation*, 36. See also p. 311.
[26] Rabe, *Geschichte*, 316.

led by Gian Pietro Caraffa (later Paul IV). The cause of conciliation was further weakened by the death of the influential Spanish humanist Juan de Valdés, spiritual mentor of the Italian 'evangelicals', in July 1541. His Roman disciples transferred to Viterbo later that year, just before Paul III openly switched allegiance to the conservatives and re-established the Inquisition under Caraffa in July 1542.[27] The following month Contarini himself died.

Fearing that as few as forty leading evangelicals in key ecclesiastical posts might effect the alignment of the Italian states with the German Protestant princes, the conservatives waged a determined campaign against the disciples of Contarini and Valdes. It is true that the *spirituali* were represented among the three legates charged with preparing and coordinating the Council of Trent by Cardinal Pole, who may even have been chosen to convey a positive message to the German Protestants. Yet the whole atmosphere in Rome and the Italian Church generally was turning decisively against what one critic described as Pole's 'modern and insane doctrine'.[28]

The opening of the Council of Trent was a personal triumph for the emperor. He had worked towards this end consistently since 1529. By the time the dignitaries of the Church finally assembled at Trent, however, they could not conceivably have fulfilled the expectations invested in the idea of a free and general council in the German debate since the 1520s.

That was not yet clear in 1545. More important was the fact that by 1544, for the first time in over ten years, the emperor was free to devote himself to German politics. Both Mediterranean and Hungarian fronts were relatively quiet. The conflict with France seemed settled: decisive victories had been achieved both in Italy and in Guelders in the north-west of the Reich. The papacy had ceased to be an enemy, even if it had not exactly become an ally. After two decades of intransigence, France had ceased to be an obstacle to a general council of the Church.

Yet the political situation in Germany had changed fundamentally since the emperor had last been in residence. Significant progress had been made towards a German national solution to the religious conflict. In the emperor's absence during the 1520s, the Reichstag had gained in profile and power. Moreover, it had also established a series of precedents, in the form of compromises and understandings on the religious issue, which the emperor ultimately found himself unable to set aside.

---

[27] Fenlon, *Heresy*, 69–74.   [28] Fenlon, *Heresy*, 33, 116–17, 209.

23

The Establishment of Protestantism, 1526–1530

The agreement concluded in 1526 at the Reichstag of Speyer to allow all rulers to execute the Edict of Worms as they saw fit, as far as they could reconcile their policies with their duties to God and the emperor, was intended as a temporary expedient. Princes and magistrates everywhere wished to avert the danger of further peasant unrest. Few really believed that either a general council of the Church or a national council was imminent. The emperor's continuing absence and Ferdinand's problems in Bohemia and Hungary also made security and stability within the Reich the first priority. A deliberately vague formula, a striking example of the technique of dissimulation that soon came to characterize all negotiations on the religious issue, was the only way of arriving at a norm for the Reich on which all could agree.[1]

Some princes, like Philip of Hessen and the Elector of Saxony, rapidly took the temporary expedient as a sanction in imperial law for the reformation of their territories. The ambitious Landgrave Philip of Hessen emerged as the main organizer and agitator on the side of the reformers.[2] He sought to safeguard his own position from eventual imperial sanctions by pursuing agreements and understandings with other rulers. Partly in collaboration and partly in parallel with Bavaria and Electoral Saxony, he conspired against the emperor's plans to have Ferdinand elected King of the Romans.[3]

The loose but determined anti-Habsburg league continued to strengthen through contacts with France and England. After 1526, this threw up a variety of rival aspirants to the crown: a Bavarian, a Saxon, even Philip of Hessen himself, who entertained vague plans for the reformation of the German nation as a whole and a constitutional reform of the Reich.[4] At the same time, Philip continued to build networks designed to defend those who had undertaken religious reforms from action by those who remained loyal Catholics and hard-line advocates of the execution of the Edict of Worms.

Just how febrile the atmosphere became was illustrated by Philip's reaction to the discovery in January 1528 of papers that apparently revealed the formation at Breslau in May 1527 of a secret league of Catholic princes devoted to rooting out all

---

[1] Schneider, *Ius reformandi*, 94–5.
[2] Press, 'Landgraf Philipp'.
[3] Kohler, *Antihabsburgische Politik*, 109; Laubach, 'Nachfolge', 15–33; Sicken, 'Ferdinand I.', 55–7.
[4] Angermeier, *Reichsreform 1410-1555*, 268.

'heresy'. The papers were soon exposed as a forgery perpetrated by the Duke of Saxony's Vice-Chancellor Otto von Pack.[5] Philip, however, immediately formed a defensive league with the Elector of Saxony, entered into negotiations with France, Johann Zápolya, and Strassburg, and then launched preventive military action against Mainz and Würzburg, even though Luther, Bugenhagen, and Melanchthon all cautioned restraint. A full-scale war was averted when Pack's fraud was revealed at the end of May. The hostilities were not concluded, however, before Philip had obliged both bishops to compensate him for the expenses he had incurred in attacking them, and Mainz to concede its diocesan rights and ecclesiastical jurisdiction over Hessian territory in the Treaty of Hitzkirchen.[6] Typically, Philip did not waste the opportunity to combine personal gain with the pursuit of the wider political-constitutional objective and the defence of the religious principle.

Charles V was not slow to respond. In a call issued on 30 November 1528 for a second Reichstag at Speyer, he referred to 'misunderstandings, from which unrest, ill-doing, violent and aggressive actions' had ensued.[7] The proposition put by Ferdinand to the assembled representatives on 15 March 1529 made it clear that 'misunderstandings' referred to the wilful interpretation by some of the recess of the Speyer Reichstag of 1526. The only remedy, Ferdinand insisted, was to revert to an unequivocal policy of enforcement of the Edict of Worms until such time as a general council of the Church resolved the religious issues. The loyal Catholic majority broadly supported the imperial line. Furthermore, they determined that in territories where changes had already taken place, and where such changes might not be reversed without provoking unrest, rulers were to avoid any further changes 'as far as humanly possible'. Meanwhile, such rulers should ensure that no one was hindered from celebrating the traditional religious services in their lands. In addition, no Catholic ruler should feel obliged to tolerate Lutherans in his territory. Zwinglians and Anabaptists were not to be tolerated anywhere.[8]

In theory, the words 'as far as humanly possible' again allowed both sides to subscribe to the maintenance of the public peace while believing that right was on their side. The reformers continued to claim rights over religion; the loyalists simply held back from enforcing the law of the Reich.[9] Nevertheless, both Saxony and Hessen argued strenuously against a decision they regarded as deeply prejudicial to their position. They tried to reiterate the principle they saw as implicit in the 1526 recess, namely that each ruler had both a duty and a right to act according to his own conscience. They objected absolutely to the unilateral abrogation of a law of the Reich by the regent. They rejected the notion that they could be obliged by a majority vote. On 22 April, they brought to the Reichstag a formal 'Protestation' or appeal to the emperor and the council. It was signed by five princes (Elector Johann of Saxony, Landgrave Philip of Hessen, Margrave Georg of Brandenburg-Ansbach,

---

[5] Dülfer, *Packsche Händel*, 56–63, 73. Pack's motive seems to have been largely financial.
[6] See pp. 255–6.
[7] Schneider, *Ius reformandi*, 95–9; Kohnle, *Reichstag*, 365–75.
[8] Blicke, *Reformation*, 159.
[9] Schneider, *Ius reformandi*, 99.

Duke Ernst of Brunswick-Lüneburg, and Prince Wolfgang of Anhalt) and by the representatives of fourteen reformed Imperial Cities.

The 'Protestation' henceforth gave the reformers the name Protestants. In long-term historical memory, the original act of protest was generally celebrated as a blow struck for freedom of conscience. Yet in fact, the only consciences that were invoked by the protesters in 1529 were those of the rulers. They claimed for themselves the *ius reformandi*, the right to impose a reform of religious practice on their lands; from their subjects they required passive obedience, whatever their consciences might tell them. The political and constitutional implications of the 'Protestation' were more significant. Even before the Reichstag ended, plans were being forged for a defensive alliance among the Protestants. Philip of Hessen was the prime mover again, and he now went far beyond a simple defence of the new status quo in the Protestant territories.

On the one hand, the landgrave and his advisers began to develop a radical new constitutional theory that justified the right of Protestants to resist the emperor.[10] He argued that all territorial sovereigns exercised jurisdictional powers that were ultimately ordained by God, and that all rulers had the legal right to defend themselves against violations of the treaties they had entered into with others. Applied to the Reich, that meant that princes could resist the emperor if he 'forgot . . . the most important reason why he was elected'. An emperor who failed to respect the collective decisions of his Estates, who sought to annul the decision of 1526, was clearly an unjust ruler. He aimed, Philip declared, to defend the honour of God and ensure 'salvation and grace of our souls', though he also conceded that 'our own temporal affairs are entwined in this'.[11]

On the other hand, Philip now also sought to realize ambitious plans for a grand alliance against the Habsburgs.[12] Contacts were made with France and Venice, with Denmark and with the Swiss reformers, in particular Zwingli, himself at that time embroiled in conflict with the Catholic cantons over the militant expansionist evangelicalism of Zurich. Above all, Philip sought to promote a more secure union between the Lutherans and the south German Zwinglians, against whom the Reichstag had discriminated more harshly than against the Lutherans. However, a meeting of leading theologians organized at Marburg in October 1529, including Luther and Zwingli in person, failed to reconcile the conflicting theological views. The key issue of the Eucharist—the real or the assumed presence of Christ in the communion—proved an insuperable obstacle.

After Zwingli departed, a further attempt at Schwabach to reach agreement at least with the south German cities, whose magistrates and preachers stood midway between Luther and Zwingli on so many issues of dogma and Church organization, also failed. Even their antipathy to the social radicalism of Zwinglianism and their sympathy for the firm and ordered rule of the Lutheran princes failed to motivate them to contemplate a religious compromise. The gulf between the two parties was

[10] Skinner, *Foundations*, ii, 195–6; Kohnle, *Reichstag*, 376–80; Friedeburg, *Self-defence*, 56–7.
[11] Angermeier, *Reichsreform 1410–1555*, 268–9.
[12] Brady, *Sturm*, 71, 75.

only overcome in 1536, after Zwingli's death (1531) deprived the south Germans of any lingering notions that they might gain useful assistance from their Swiss neighbours and co-religionists.[13]

At this stage, few really agreed with Philip of Hessen's radical ideas. Luther and the other theologians cautioned against resistance, and Luther for one still believed that Charles might yet call the council that he had so long promised. Furthermore, Luther advised that the Elector of Saxony, Philip was mistaken in believing that the emperor was no more than one sovereign among others in the Reich. The emperor was the 'lord' and governmental superior of the princes, and even if he were to act unjustly, neither the princes nor anyone else had the right to resist him.[14] Thus, notwithstanding their protest, the Protestants agreed to support Ferdinand against the Turks. The abrupt end of the Turkish siege of Vienna rendered the Reich's forces superfluous even before they had arrived. Both Catholic and Protestant Estates then concurred in refusing to contemplate any further military assistance to Ferdinand in Hungary. Religious differences meant little when it came to asserting the common interests of the princes in the Reich against Habsburg imperialism and expansionism.[15]

Neither Charles nor Ferdinand was under any illusion about the dangers of the situation in Germany. Hence, immediately after the Turkish threat had receded and the Peace of Cambrai had, however temporarily, neutralized the French threat, Charles summoned another Reichstag to Augsburg for June 1530. Now, moreover, strengthened by his success against France and his prestige further enhanced by his coronation by the pope in Bologna, Charles returned to the Reich for the first time in ten years. His announcement that he intended to restore peace and listen to all parties aroused expectations.[16]

However, the suspicion that Charles intended to impose his own solution on the German problem aroused anxiety and determination to resist any absolute monarchical remedy. The Protestants were apprehensive from the outset. However, even the Catholics rejected Charles's aspiration to resolve at the Reichstag all the religious issues that the papacy, in refusing to convene a general council, had failed to address. What they now saw as clearly as the Protestants was a monarch who no longer respected the traditional division between secular and spiritual authority and who arrogated to himself quasi-papal powers.[17] Some were also rightly suspicious of a monarch who had just secularized the see of Utrecht and who had persuaded the pope to grant ecclesiastical revenues to Ferdinand, who himself was accused by the ecclesiastical princes of having exploited the Church more than the Lutherans.[18]

---

[13] Brady, *Sturm*, 65–7, 80; Rabe, *Geschichte*, 348–50. The conflict between Lutherans and Zwinglians over the reformation of Württemberg in 1534 was another powerful motive for a rapprochement between the two tendencies, or rather for the south Germans to capitulate by accepting the Lutheran teaching on the Eucharist.

[14] Skinner, *Foundations*, ii, 196–7.

[15] Schmidt, *Geschichte*, 76.

[16] Rabe, *Geschichte*, 263.

[17] Angermeier, *Reichsreform 1410–1555*, 276; Luttenberger, 'Kirchenadvokatie', 193–4.

[18] Angermeier, *Reichsreform 1410–1555*, 262; Chisholm, 'Religionspolitik', 552–8.

The personal presence of the emperor immediately created a new atmosphere. For one thing, negotiations over a wide range of legislation were resumed and brought to fruition.[19] The *Reichspolizeiordnung*, a wide-ranging series of measures including sumptuary laws and regulations concerning begging and the Jews, which the Reichsregiment had failed repeatedly to secure agreement on, was now passed. The ban on monopolies was extended and intensified. Negotiations over regulation of the currency led both to a *Reichsmünzordnung* and to the commissioning of a convention composed of representatives of the Kreise to discuss the coinage further. Discussions over a uniform legal criminal code based on the principles of Roman law, another project that the Reichsregiment had failed to bring to fruition, were also revived.

With the emperor himself in residence, the opposition of some of the major territories to what they saw as an attempted abrogation of their rights by a centralizing monarch, ceased. By 1532, consequently, the code—the *Consititutio Criminalis Carolina*, the first such supra-regional code in Europe—was ready to be published, albeit with a 'clausula salvatoria' that allowed old territorial legislation to stand in so far as it was 'well-established, just and proper'.[20] Significant military assistance was agreed against the Turks. Finally, both the Reichskammergericht and the Reichsregiment were renewed, though the latter was abolished the following year, while the former immediately became embroiled in the religious conflict and was denounced by the Protestants as a mere tool of the Catholic majority.

Of course, much of this legislation was completely ineffective. The *Carolina*, however, laid down a set of Roman law norms in criminal procedure that remained valid throughout most of the Reich until the introduction of the Enlightenment legal codes of the eighteenth century. It is true that the *Reichsabschied*, the legal enactment of all agreements reached, was finalized after the departure of the Protestants and they subsequently refused to accept some of the measures (for example, taxes for the Turkish campaign) on the grounds that they had not voted for them. Yet, in a sense, the fact that issues were negotiated at all and that agreements were reached is significant in itself.

Despite religious divisions, all Estates were participating in the conduct of the normal business of the Reich. It is true this new round of reform, like previous initiatives, did not result in the creation of any lasting institutional structures, but it reinforced the evolving federal and multilayered structure of the Reich nonetheless. The tendency in much of what was agreed was to devolve responsibility for enforcement and implementation. Decisions of the Reichskammergericht relating to the public peace or the detailed resolution of matters relating to currency, rates of imperial taxation, or military levies, were delegated to the individual Estates or to the Kreise.

The most important issue was the religious question.[21] Charles certainly made good his promise to listen. The Protestants were asked to explain their beliefs, and

---

[19] Angermeier, *Reichsreform 1410–1555*, 271–2; Neuhaus, 'Augsburger Reichstag', 192–209.
[20] Conrad, *Rechtsgeschichte*, ii 406–13; Duchhardt, *Verfassungsgeschichte*, 87–8. The first French code was published in 1539.
[21] Kohnle, *Reichstag*, 381–94.

on 25 June they submitted the *Confessio Augustana* compiled by Melanchthon and others.[22] The Imperial Cities of Strassburg, Constance, Memmingen, and Lindau, which espoused a Zwinglian view of the Eucharist, submitted an alternative Protestant view, the *Confessio Tetrapolitana*, two weeks later. Catholic theologians, among them Johannes Eck, the staunch loyalist and antagonist of all reformers, were commissioned to examine the submissions and respond.

Charles rejected the first draft that theologians produced as excessively lengthy and polemical, and after much discussion a shortened and moderated *Confutatio* was presented to the Estates on 3 August. Just as the Catholics rejected the *Confessio*, so the Protestants now rejected the *Confutatio* and all dialogue on doctrinal issues finally ceased when Charles refused to accept a further response to the Catholic theologians by Melanchthon. However much goodwill there may have been on both sides, it was scarcely conceivable that Catholics and Protestants could have reached agreement on theological issues in the absence of a Church council and at a time when the Protestants did not even agree among themselves.

Once theological conciliation had failed, the only question for the emperor and the Catholic majority was the permissibility and extent of a political toleration of the Protestants until a general Church council was convened.[23] Given that Charles still insisted on the validity of the Edict of Worms, the outlook for a mutually acceptable compromise was poor. On 14 November, the Hessian and Saxon representatives departed. The following week, Charles terminated the proceedings and, with the votes of the Catholic majority, promulgated a series of peremptory measures. The validity of the Edict of Worms was reaffirmed; all innovations in religion were prohibited; Catholic services were to be permitted throughout the Reich; and all alienated Church property was to be returned immediately. Furthermore, any breach of these laws was to be regarded as a breach of the public peace, with penalty of proscription and prosecution at the Reichskammergericht. The blow against the Protestants was only softened by the fact that they were given a period of grace until 15 April 1531 to decide whether or not to comply.

The Protestants immediately began to organize their opposition. At the Reichstag, the Nuremberg representative rehearsed the arguments in favour of renewing the status quo of 1526, but now added constitutional points to the conventional reasoning on grounds of theology and the necessity of employing emergency powers. The Reich, they declared, was a 'confederation', from which it followed that each Estate had duties and rights but from which it emphatically did not 'follow that each must believe what his Imperial Majesty wishes them to believe'.[24] Outside the Reichstag, Philip of Hessen and his advisers elaborated the constitutional arguments into a full-blown theory of resistance. Since the emperor was elected (by the Electors), they reasoned, the Estates ruled jointly with him and he was

---

[22] Luther was still an outlaw under the terms of the Edict of Worms at this stage, and thus unable to attend the Reichstag, though he gave advice—and warnings against too conciliatory an attitude—from Coburg castle.
[23] Schneider, *Ius reformandi*, 99–104.
[24] Schneider, *Ius reformandi*, 100.

therefore 'no *monarcha*' or sovereign ruler in a conventional sense. As a mere *primus inter pares* he could not, therefore, require unconditional obedience to his will, especially if that contravened the laws of the Reich agreed at the Reichstag.[25]

At the same time, Saxon jurists justified resistance by means of private law theory, arguing that a ruler who behaved unjustly forfeited his office and became a private individual, whose illegal use of force thus might rightfully be resisted.[26] Since the emperor had no jurisdiction in matters of faith, it followed that it was lawful to resist him in this matter. By October 1530, Luther, Melanchthon, and the other leading theologians were now willing to declare themselves persuaded by the arguments of the lawyers. Where they had previously been reluctant, they now set about expounding the theological ramifications of resistance to an unjust monarch, while taking care to distinguish the rights of rulers and magistrates from those of ordinary human beings.[27]

From the point of view of the religious and political unity of the Reich, these were serious developments. In terms of Habsburg dynastic interests, however, another issue, negotiated in parallel with the Augsburg Reichstag, was even more fundamental: the election of Ferdinand as King of the Romans and Charles V's heir in the Reich. The emperor regarded this as imperative in view of the religious crisis, the Turkish threat, and the all too obvious problems of the Reichsregiment. The only solution was to appoint someone who might truly represent him in the Reich and enjoy at least some of his monarchical authority.[28] The proposal ran into immediate opposition. The Electors disputed the emperor's right to nominate a successor during his own lifetime (*vivente imperatore*); the Golden Bull gave them the right to a 'free election'. Finally, most of the Electors agreed to a compromise whereby Charles reaffirmed their independent electoral rights while Ferdinand remained the only candidate.

The Elector of Saxony, however, remained implacable, and the constitutional precepts developed in the context of the religious issue now began to reverberate here, too. The Golden Bull only covered the eventuality of *vacante imperio*, a vacancy after an emperor's death; no election could take place *vivente imperatore* without the 'consent of the other princes and Estates of the Reich'. Furthermore, the emperor should live up to his electoral promises and reside in the Reich; any breach of those promises must again be discussed by all.[29]

In the event, the election went ahead on 5 January 1531, with Saxony formally exempted by the emperor from having to vote. On the one hand, this represented a triumph for the monarchy.[30] The election set a deliberate precedent to ensure that

---

[25] Schmidt, *Geschichte*, 78.

[26] Skinner, *Foundations*, ii, 197–9; Friedeburg, *Self-defence*, 62.

[27] Skinner, *Foundations*, ii, 200–6; Friedeburg, *Self-defence*, 63–5.

[28] Kohler, *Antihabsburgische Politik*, 171.

[29] Kohler, *Antihabsburgische Politik*, 173–4. The Saxon arguments concerning the inadmissibility of elections during an emperor's lifetime were, of course, contradicted by the precedents during the reigns of Charles IV and Friedrich III; other legal objections put forward by the Saxon party proved equally spurious.

[30] Neuhaus, 'Augsburger Reichstag', 198–9.

the crown remained in one dynasty; it established what was tantamount to a hereditary monarchy in the Reich and effectively undermined the Estates' claims to co-rulership. On the other hand, it also fundamentally reinforced the solidarity of the Estates against the monarchy.

On 6 January, the Electors concluded a ten-year treaty of protection with King Ferdinand.[31] However, the Saxon abstention now enabled the Elector to become the focus of a movement that opposed recognition of the election. Philip of Hessen inevitably again emerged as one of the leading agitators, along with Duke Wilhelm IV of Bavaria, himself a frustrated aspirant to the crown. By October 1531, a broad cross-confessional anti-Habsburg league had been formed at Saalfeld dedicated to overturning the election, defending each other from Habsburg aggression, and to enlisting French and English support for their cause. If not life-threatening to the Habsburg position, this opposition was to have important repercussions for any attempt to deal with the religious issue.

The emperor never acted on his threat to take direct action against Protestant rulers who refused to comply with the Augsburg stipulations by April 1531. The need for money and for assistance against the Turks once again took precedence. Furthermore, Charles was an Erasmian at heart and, like Erasmus, he tended to avoid violent confrontation where possible and placed a faith in negotiation and the healing effects of the passage of time that sometimes bordered on the delusional. While Ferdinand advocated a hard line against the Zwinglians in October 1531, following their defeat, and the death of Zwingli himself at Kappel, Charles shrank back for fear of provoking France and of then aggravating the situation in Italy.

Nonetheless, while the threat of military action receded for the present, the menace of legal action through the Reichskammergericht remained. Even before the Augsburg Reichstag convened, the court had received numerous cases. Now there was little the judges could do but to rule against the Protestants in every instance. Ferdinand and his officials had already ensured that this would not be an intolerable burden on their consciences. The purge of all Protestant judges during the late 1520s left the court, by 1530–1, with the reputation of being no more than the 'Emperor's Reichskammergericht' anyway.[32] The decision to instrumentalize the Reichskammergericht in this way marked a significant turning point in constitutional terms. From the reform movement of the 1490s the court had stood for the ideal of an institutional core of the Reich independent of the emperor. Now the election of Ferdinand marked the beginning of an attempt to create a standing monarchical government in the Reich, with the court as an agency of the crown and the Catholic majority in their dispute with the Protestant minority.[33] This marked the beginning of the perpetual wrangling between Catholics and Protestants over representation in, and the competence of, institutions.

In fact, the idea that the court pursued a vindictive 'legal war' against the Protestants is far-fetched.[34] The judges did not allow themselves to become agents

[31] Kohler, *Antihabsburgische Politik*, 183–202.
[32] Angermeier, *Reichsreform 1410–1555*, 293; Smend, *Reichskammergericht*, 128–31, 140.
[33] Smend, *Reichskammergericht*, 140–1.
[34] Brady, *Sturm*, 164–5; Ruthmann, 'Religionsprozesse', 232–5; Schneider, *Ius reformandi*, 104–7.

of the crown or of the Catholic majority. Yet in cases brought before them in which secular authorities were charged with alienation of Church property and income, they could only judge according to the prevailing law of the Reich. In contentious cases, the judges invariably stopped short of proscription, and they declined to adjudicate on most ecclesiastical matters, which they left to the territorial authorities. However, the possibility that such a war might be waged was used by Philip of Hessen and others as an argument for the need to mobilize a Protestant league. Furthermore, the all too obvious fact that the process of reformation (especially reformation from above) had involved acts that were illegal under the law of the Reich led Protestants to claim that their actions were justified by the higher laws of God. Consequently, they challenged the validity both of the court and the merely human law it was charged to enforce.

Bad news from Hungary and the declaration by the Protestant princes and cities that they could not send military assistance as long as they were being threatened with proscription led to further negotiations on the religious issue during the next Reichstag, which met at Regensburg early in 1532.[35] The Protestants demanded religious freedom and the cessation of all legal cases against them. After lengthy discussions held at Schweinfurt outside and parallel to the Reichstag, Charles conceded the Truce of Nuremberg in July 1532.[36] He was now prepared to recognize the status quo until such time as matters were decided by a general Church council, which he determined would be called within six months to meet within a year. Meanwhile all restitution suits before the Reichskammergericht would be suspended. The Protestants agreed to send military aid against the Turks.

Luther greeted the Truce of Nuremberg as nothing less than a divine affirmation of the Reformation. The truce was a clear move away from the regime of the Edict of Worms. It recognized for the first time that the Reich was a system which contained two religions. In this sense, it was the first step towards the peace settlements of Augsburg 1555 and Westphalia 1648.[37] At the time, however, it was far from clear where the Truce might lead. The fact that Charles wished the suspension of the court cases to remain a secret scarcely inspired confidence. Consequently, in the absence of any formal instruction from the emperor, the court more or less continued with its work. It refused to regard cases involving secularizations or abrogation of ecclesiastical jurisdictions as religious, and simply treated them as breaches of the public peace.[38] The chimera of a 'legal war' remained an ever-present threat.

[35] Brady, *Sturm*, 80–2; Rabe, *Geschichte*, 330–2; Schneider, *Ius reformandi*, 108–14.
[36] Kohnle, *Reichstag*, 401–6.
[37] Brady, *Sturm*, 82.
[38] Schmidt, 'Schmalkaldischer Bund', 12.

24

The Schmalkaldic League, its Counterparts, and the Politics of the Reich, 1530–1541

In one way or another, both real and imagined, the threat to the Protestants after the Augsburg Reichstag was sufficient to justify the formation of a defensive league. Plans formulated in 1529 to create such a league had already been discussed while the Reichstag was still in session. The theologians' acceptance of the arguments for lawful resistance to the emperor helped overcome previous qualms. The first members, who joined at a secret meeting in Schmalkalden in December 1530, were the Elector of Saxony, Landgrave Philip of Hessen, Ernst of Brunswick-Lüneburg, the Counts of Anhalt-Bernburg and Mansfeld, and the cities of Magdeburg and Bremen.

At the end of February 1531, formal articles of association were drawn up and more cities now joined, notably Strassburg and others in the south-west, but also Lübeck. Philip of Hessen and some in Strassburg and Constance once more considered an alliance with Zwingli and the Swiss Protestants and it was resolved at the outset to approach the kings of France, England, Poland, Navarre, Denmark, Sweden, and 'other potentates'.[1] Most significant of all over the next few years was the growth of the north German membership. By 1535 Brunswick, Goslar, Einbeck, and Göttingen had all joined, as well as Esslingen in the south-west, and in 1536 six further princes and five cities (Augsburg, Frankfurt am Main, Kempten, Hamburg, and Hanover) were admitted.

The League never embraced all Protestant princes and cities; it did, however, combine more elements of north and south than any previous league had ever done.[2] Though imperial propagandists portrayed the League as a secessionist tendency, it is not clear whether it ever really posed a serious threat to either the Reich or its monarchy. Admittedly, it 'exhibited occasional statelike tendencies' and it developed a formal constitution, a system of regular diets, to agree, among other things, taxes and levies for the league's forces under the alternating command of Saxony and Hessen.[3] Yet these arrangements were made strictly for the purpose of defending the League's members from discrimination in the Reich on grounds of

---

[1] Angermeier, *Reichsreform 1410–1555*, 277.
[2] Brady, *Sturm*, 143.
[3] Brady, *Sturm*, 142.

their religion. Many members from the north of the Reich, traditionally distant from emperor and Reich and because of that not so much under threat anyway, frequently failed to pay their dues in full, or did so only grudgingly.

Philip of Hessen's early plans for the formation of an international alliance did not materialize. Zwingli's death at Kappel in October 1531 put paid to the Swiss connection. Indeed, within a few years, south German Zwinglianism was extinct and the leading southern theologians accepted the Wittenberg Concord in 1536. This enhanced the League's unity, but drew a permanent line between the Germans and the Swiss, who refused to accept Wittenberg's authority. Overtures to France and England, pursued sporadically throughout the 1530s and early 1540s, had even less impact. Indeed, they brought only suspicion of disloyalty and sedition on the League's membership as a whole.[4]

In reality, the League had limited aims. From the outset, it was made clear that the League was not directed against 'his Imperial majesty, our most gracious lord'. It aimed 'solely to preserve Christian truth and peace in the holy Reich and German nation' and 'to defend and afford protection for ourselves and our subjects and our dependants' from unjust attack.[5] The possibility of such an attack existed because of the threat of proscription and enforcement action following eventual unfavourable judgements in the Reichskammergericht. The League's entire military infrastructure—its constitution envisaged a force of 2,000 horse and 10,000 foot—was justified by this threat. For most of the time, however, the struggle was legal and political, rather than military. Indeed, the majority shrank back from the kind of aggressive and adventurous militancy that characterized Philip of Hessen's scheming, and both Saxony and the south German Imperial Cities constantly sought to avoid a direct confrontation with the Habsburgs.

Even in the legal struggle against the Reichskammergericht, the League's members insisted on their strictly limited objectives. In 1534, Philip of Hessen argued forcefully for a general recusation of the whole court on all matters, not just religious issues, but it was resolved only to declare the presiding judge and the majority of the associate judges incompetent in religious matters because of their alleged partisanship. A second proposal for a general recusation in 1538 was averted by the renewed suspension of controversial cases under the Truce of Frankfurt in 1539.[6]

Yet the fundamental problem remained. Catholics and Protestants took a different view of the law, so it was difficult to define exactly what counted as matters concerning religion. Sometimes the claims were little more than outrageous opportunism, a pseudo-legal cover for theft. Where they were genuine, however, they touched on one of the most controversial and fundamental issues of the time. Even the Protestants did not agree among themselves how Church property should be dealt with. The Imperial Cities tended to insist that taking such property into civic ownership was justified if it continued to be used for charitable purposes.

---

[4] Brady, *Sturm*, 88–9, 150–61.
[5] Fabian, *Entstehung*, 352. See also Haug-Moritz, *Schmalkaldischer Bund*, 70–8, 95–8.
[6] Brady, *Sturm*, 206–10.

Some princes had no qualms about simply adding it to their exchequers.[7] Ultimately, a general recusation really was the only solution to the Protestant grievances, and this was achieved in 1543, when the court was suspended for five years.

It might seem puzzling that it should have taken so long to arrive at that point. The generally hesitant, in some ways quite illogical, attitude to the court reflects, however, important characteristics of the League. Loyalty to the Reich and its institutions was fundamental, even if the Protestants believed that the Reich was out of kilter and that its laws needed reform. Membership of the League did not necessarily supersede dynastic traditions or territorial interests. The Electors of Saxony had always been loyalists in the Reich and the role of rebel, even if divinely sanctioned and against an unjust monarch, did not come easily. Similarly, refusing to grant assistance against the Turks might place Saxony at risk if Hungary, Bohemia, and the Austrian hereditary lands fell.[8]

Fundamentally, the League's members wanted nothing more than to perpetuate the status quo of 1526. It was a union of Protestants, yet it never moved to develop a common Protestant Church ordinance. Significantly, the two territories that did develop such a thing—the Imperial City of Nuremberg and the Margravate of Brandenburg-Ansbach, which issued a common ecclesiastical constitution in 1533—never became members.[9] The League as a whole played strictly according to the rules of 1526 and declined, for example, to admit the Protestants of Metz in 1542 on the grounds that the city magistrates were Catholics. It was strictly a union of Protestant Estates, an alliance of princes, lords, and magistrates, not a community of evangelical Christians.[10]

The League's pusillanimous attitude to the Reichskammergericht also reflected a deep fissure that ran through it. At every stage, the princes ensured that they would be the dominant members. While Philip of Hessen saw city magistrates as allies, particularly if they were in thrall to martial preachers like Zwingli, the Elector of Saxony was frankly scathing about them. The Imperial Cities had good reason for fearing that they would simply be forced to pay for the 'German liberty' of the princes for no return. Like the other lesser Estates in the Reich, they needed the Reichskammergericht to protect themselves against the aggressive expansionism of their territorial neighbours. After the Swabian League began to falter in the late 1520s, the south-west German cities sorely missed the security it had once provided. Nothing underlined that more starkly than the war that Duke Ulrich of Württemberg pursued against Esslingen after 1538. Both were members of the Schmalkaldic League, and Esslingen's struggle for survival involved launching a case at the Reichskammergericht against the tyrannical duke.[11] The 'preservation of Christian truth and peace' clearly had its limits, and the Reichskammergericht had its uses.

For all its limitations, however, the very existence of the League provided a framework for the steady advance of Protestantism in the Reich for fifteen years. It

[7] Brady, *Sturm*, 172.   [8] Schmidt, 'Schmalkaldischer Bund', 14.
[9] Brady, *Sturm*, 170.   [10] Brady, *Sturm*, 174.
[11] Schmidt, *Städtetag*, 213–24.

never aspired to replace the Reich. Yet it played such an important role that Charles V came to believe that the only way he might secure his rule in Germany was by means of its destruction.

From the start, the Schmalkaldic League was affiliated to an extensive constellation of anti-Habsburg groupings. Their human common denominator was Philip of Hessen. His Middle German lands made him a natural focal point. His dynastic and strategic interests extended in all directions, north as well as south, to the Rhine and beyond, as well as to the Elbe and the east. The various anti-Habsburg alliances also cut across confessional lines. The Saalfeld League of Catholic and Protestant opponents to Ferdinand's election ran directly parallel to the Schmalkaldic League for a while.[12] In the same year, France too sought to mobilize the courts of Saxony, Bavaria, and Hessen with promises of support for the defence of the 'libertés germaniques'.[13] In the Treaty of Scheyern of May 1532, France, Bavaria, Hessen, and Saxony agreed to push for the restitution of the Dukes of Württemberg so as to end Habsburg rule in that key territory of the south-west.

Fearing a conspiracy between Hessen and Bavaria, but also opposed to the Swabian League and to the growth of Habsburg authority, the Catholic Electors of Mainz, Trier, and the Palatinate joined a Rhenish League with Hessen in November 1532.[14] This was essentially a passive union that combined a variety of political and confessional interests. Yet it proved solid enough to be an obstacle to Charles V's attempts to rebuild his power base in the Reich from the mid-1530s. In one form or another it existed until 1552, kept going by the mutual interest of its members (joined by Würzburg in 1533) in regional security. Another defensive alliance Philip concluded with the Bishop of Münster in 1533 combined regional security considerations with a similar anti-Habsburg twist, for Philip was convinced that the emperor firmly intended to add Guelders and Münster to his recent acquisition of Utrecht.[15] Landgrave Philip spun webs of quite extraordinary complexity. He sought to provide for all eventualities and to safeguard every front. No Estate of the Reich was too insignificant to overlook as a potential ally; any potential opponent of Habsburg ambitions was a worthy alliance partner.

Leagues and alliances were one thing; direct action, let alone war, against the Habsburgs was quite another. Saxony, for example, regarded the Saalfeld League purely and simply as a demonstration of German liberty against emperor and king. The whole point of the Treaty of Scheyern was to prepare the ground for war. Yet both the Elector Johann and his successor from August 1532, Johann Friedrich, vacillated, preferring to pursue protracted negotiations with Ferdinand over the recognition of his election in return for political and religious concessions. Saxony's hesitations also influenced the Schmalkaldic League, among whose members only Strassburg supported a more active line.[16]

Consequently, the initiative shifted more and more to Hessen and Bavaria. Their most immediate target was the Habsburg-dominated Swabian League and the Habsburg regime in Württemberg. Even so, their joint action was based on a

---

[12] See p. 302.   [13] Lauchs, *Bayern*, 27.   [14] Eymelt, *Einung*, 131–6.
[15] Angermeier, *Reichsreform 1410-1555*, 287; Lauchs, *Bayern*, 29.   [16] Brady, *Sturm*, 83–4.

misapprehension. The Bavarians supported the restitution of Duke Christoph, the son of the deposed Duke Ulrich. Unlike his father, he had remained a Catholic, brought up in captivity at the court of Charles V, from where he had escaped in 1530 to join his uncles, Duke Wilhelm IV and Duke Ludwig X of Bavaria. For the Bavarians, promoting his cause meant striking a blow against the Habsburgs, enhancing their own regional power by removing the western half of the Habsburg 'clamp' on their own lands, while not compromising their religious principles. Philip of Hessen aimed to restore the Protestant Duke Ulrich in order to strengthen the Protestant cause generally. Initially, however, he pretended to support Duke Christoph for the sake of the Bavarian alliance.

They took their campaign first to the Swabian League, a majority of whose members agreed in 1533 that Württemberg should be restored to Duke Christoph. When Ferdinand refused to accept their decision, the League disintegrated. The members of the Rhenish League of 1532 resolved not to continue their membership. The Protestant members were hesitant because they feared the League's forces might soon be used against them. In the circumstances, the wily Bavarian Chancellor Leonhard von Eck was easily able to sabotage the negotiations among the League's remaining members over its renewal. The Swabian League was finally dissolved in February 1534, but the end had been clear for many months before then. What was also clear was that without the Swabian League, Württemberg was defenceless. Philip of Hessen met with the King of France at Bar-le-Duc in January 1534 and secured substantial financial aid for a military campaign. By April, he had a force of 20,000 foot and 4,000 horsemen, which invaded and occupied the duchy in the following month. With only 9,000 foot and 400 horsemen on his side, Ferdinand was forced to concede defeat after a minor confrontation at Lauffen.

When the Bavarians heard about the Bar-le-Duc meeting, they realized they had been duped: they wanted nothing to do with the restoration of a Protestant duke. On the contrary, they now feared that they themselves might become the victims of Habsburg revenge.[17] In panic, they distanced themselves from the whole enterprise. Even before the battle at Lauffen, they had launched into negotiations with the Elector Palatine and his brother, the Counts of Pfalz-Neuburg, the Bishop of Bamberg, and the Margraves of Brandenburg for an Eichstätt League against eventual Austrian aggression. Simultaneously, they hurriedly stepped up their secret negotiations with Charles V over what he might give them in return for recognition of Ferdinand's election, negotiations which they had quietly pursued throughout the period of their conspiracy with Hessen against him.[18]

All talk of Habsburg counter-offensives or of further Hessian aggression—the King of France had envisaged a continuation of the military action into Bohemia—was ended with the conclusion of the Peace of Kaaden mediated by the Electors of Mainz and Saxony in June 1534.[19] Ferdinand recognized the restoration of Duke Ulrich in Württemberg and his right to introduce the new religion there. In the Reich generally, the Truce of Nuremberg was reaffirmed, though Anabaptists and

[17] Lauchs, *Bayern*, 29–30.   [18] Kohler, *Antihabsburgische Politik*, 318–9.
[19] Kohler, *Antihabsburgische Politik*, 350–73; Lauchs, *Bayern*, 30–3.

all sectarians were explicitly excluded from it; all cases against (Lutheran) Protestants in the Reichskammergericht were to be suspended. The loss of Württemberg was softened a little by the fact that it was granted to Duke Ulrich as a hereditary *arrière*-fief of Austria, rather than as a fief of the Reich.[20] The duke also agreed to recognize Ferdinand as lawful King of the Romans.

Above all, on the conclusion of the peace terms, the Elector of Saxony now also formally recognized Ferdinand's election after three-and-a-half years of opposition. The Bavarians also agreed on principle, but took the opportunity to negotiate the promise of a marriage between the six-year-old Bavarian heir and one of Ferdinand's daughters, with the remote possibility of succession in Austria under certain circumstances, in the Peace of Linz on 11 September 1534. Philip of Hessen's concurrence was implicit in that of the Elector of Saxony; the members of the Schmalkaldic League and others now followed Saxony.

While the Peace of Linz was being negotiated, Charles V wrote to Ferdinand that to reach agreement with Bavaria on a dynastic union and on religious policy might pave the way for the 'pacification de la Germanie'.[21] It did not achieve that. Together with the Peace of Kaaden, however, it led to a major reconfiguration of German politics. The loss of Württemberg was less of a blow than Ferdinand had feared; Hungary was a far greater priority for him. He also needed to secure recognition of his kingship in the Reich, for this would enable him to rebuild a position in the Reich and to gain the support of the German Estates against Zápolya.

Yet the loss of Württemberg and particularly the demise of the Swabian League simultaneously removed the twin foundations of both Charles's and Ferdinand's German policy to date and strengthened the Schmalkaldic League. A new loyalist approach therefore became imperative. The first initiative to construct a new loyalist league came from Ferdinand, who summoned a meeting of south and Middle German Estates to Donauwörth in January 1535.[22] The resulting Nine-Year or Imperial League was a pale shadow of the Swabian League it was designed to replace. It consisted largely of the membership of the Eichstätt League plus the two Habsburg brothers and the Bishops of Salzburg and Augsburg.

At first, the Nine-Year League was a league of princes: the plethora of Imperial Cities, prelates, Imperial Counts, and Imperial Knights—the traditional Habsburg clientage of the southern Reich—was excluded at the insistence of the Brandenburg and Palatine princes. Both Ferdinand and Bavaria had wished to include at least the cities because they would lend weight, and above all money, to the League, though they intended to make sure that the Imperial Cities did not carry the same weight in votes as the princes. The majority, however, prevailed in maintaining the exclusivity of the League. The main objection put forward was the religious situation of

[20] The Dukes of Württemberg were obliged to accept this lesser status (*Reichsafterlehen*) until 1599, when they became fiefs of the Reich (*Reichslehen*) once more. As holders of an Austrian *Reichsafterlehen*, they did not have a seat or vote in the Reichstag. See: Press, 'Epochenjahr'.
[21] Kohler, *Antihabsburgische Politik*, 372.
[22] Lauchs, *Bayern*, 44–63; Endres, 'Kayserliche Bund'.

the cities, but the real objection to their membership was that as League members they could no longer be targets for the princes' territorial expansionism.

A number of cities were in fact admitted over the next year or so, including Protestant cities admitted on the same terms as Brandenburg-Ansbach.[23] Yet the cities remained second-class members of the League, while the other minor Estates were never admitted. Consequently, the new League failed in any sense to replace the Swabian League. It did not even cement the alliance between Austria and Bavaria, which had been one of Leonhard von Eck's main ambitions. Once it was clear that Ferdinand had no intention of accepting the hard line against Protestants that the Bavarians favoured, they all but reverted to the hostility and suspicion of Austria that had characterized their attitude to the Habsburgs before 1534. That only really changed in 1546. Meanwhile, the Nine-Year League existed for the duration in little more than name.

At the same time, problems in other parts of the Reich and the continuing Turkish menace in Hungary made it essential to try and achieve a broader cooperation of both Catholic and Protestant Estates. Since the convocation of a Reichstag would only have revived the religious controversy, which might create a potentially fatal breach, it was decided to operate at the level of assemblies of the Kreise (Reichskreisversammlungen or Reichskreistage).[24] Representatives of forty Estates met at Coblenz in December 1534, and similar meetings followed in Worms during 1535. Of the forty representatives who had attended at Coblenz, thirty-eight were Catholics, but the following April one hundred and forty-five attended, representing all parts of the Reich and both confessions. These were explicitly not formal Reichstag meetings. They did, however, serve the purpose of organizing a successful biconfessional assault on the Anabaptists at Münster in 1535.[25] Religious differences between Catholic and (Lutheran) Protestant princes and magistrates counted for nothing when confronted with the spectre of social revolution. These gatherings, as well as the one that followed in 1537, also agreed military aid against the Turks, though by 1539 renewed religious tensions made such an agreement impossible.

It is difficult to differentiate clearly between the policies of the emperor and those of the king. Ferdinand continually sought to maintain links with all the German Estates and to pursue the agenda of essential peace-keeping and defence issues through informal gatherings. The emperor for his part appeared to steer a rather different and by no means consistent course. Yet they shared many common assumptions, common interests, and, during the 1530s, a common adviser in Cardinal Bernardo Clesio, Ferdinand's High Chancellor and Bishop of Trent (d. 1539). Church reform, in particular through the convocation of a general council, also remained high on the emperor's agenda, and he shared Ferdinand's

---

[23] Lauchs, *Bayern*, 59.
[24] Neuhaus, *Repräsentationsformen*, esp. 38–9, 46–60, 73–5, 144–85. Neuhaus suggests that each of the three 1535 gatherings was a 'Reichstag . . . without *de jure* recognition', which may simply reflect the seriousness with which those who attended took the resolutions reached on Münster.
[25] See pp. 238, 247–8.

desire for a religious settlement in Germany. By the later 1530s, it was also clear to both brothers that such a settlement might only be achieved at the price of further religious compromise.

However, Charles was absent from the Reich again between 1532 and 1541. His conflict with the Ottomans in the Mediterranean and with France took precedence over Germany and the Turkish threat in Hungary, and the initiatives he launched in Germany from a distance enjoyed mixed fortunes.

Charles V's first move was a disaster.[26] The Schmalkaldeners' negotiations with France, England, and Denmark, and their growing numbers in the Reich, led to fears that an international coalition might undermine the emperor's authority. In October 1536, Charles V commissioned Reichsvizekanzler Matthias Held to enlist support for an 'imperial league' in the Reich. Held's instructions were cautious and rather vague. However, after the Protestants rejected an invitation in 1537 to participate in the Council of Mantua, called by Pope Paul III in an attempt to settle the religious divisions by answering the Protestant call for a general Church council, Held set out on a militant and uncompromising mission to establish an aggressively anti-Protestant league.[27] This was established in June 1538, with the rulers of Mainz, Salzburg, Bavaria, ducal Saxony, Calenberg, and Brunswick as members, in addition to Charles and Ferdinand. Its formal declared aim was defensive, but word of Held's aggressive intentions soon spread.

Though joined for a period of ten years, this so-called Christian League was a dead letter within months. Ferdinand and his advisers looked on with horror as Held threatened to undo every agreement reached with the Protestants so far. Charles V himself was so ambivalent about Held's activities that he only ratified the League on 20 March 1539, partly to scotch rumours circulated in Germany by Queen Mary of Hungary, his stadtholder in the Netherlands, that he did not support it at all.[28] The Protestants for their part reacted sharply to what they perceived as a threat of war. The emperor's conclusion of a ten-year truce with France at Nice just seven days after the League was formed merely heightened their fears. Philip of Hessen, further alarmed by the Reichskammergericht's proscription of the city of Minden on 9 October 1538, was convinced that a war was imminent.[29]

On the Catholic side, the atmosphere of general uncertainty once more activated the full repertoire of Bavarian diplomatic duplicity.[30] They sent delegations to Vienna and Spain urging Charles to return to the Reich to preside over a Reichstag in person, to resolve the religious issues, to take energetic action against the Protestants, and then, finally, to lead a crusade against the Turks. Simultaneously, they opened secret talks within the Reich to avert the prospect of a religious war,

[26] Lauchs, *Bayern*, 104–35.
[27] Mullett, *Catholic Reformation*, 36. See also p. 293.
[28] Lauchs, *Bayern*, 141–2.
[29] Brady, *Sturm*, 200–7; Schindling and Ziegler, *Territorien*, vii, 116–17. The town of Minden had embraced the new teaching in 1529–30 and joined the Schmalkaldic League in 1536. These developments were energetically opposed by the Bishop of Minden, who resided at Petershagen, since Minden was not a free city and remained legally a town under his jurisdiction.
[30] Lauchs, *Bayern*, 139–48.

and also to guard against the consequences of Charles possibly returning from Spain to impose his will in Germany. The situation seemed so fraught with danger for all German princes that the Bavarian Chancellor Leonhard von Eck now actively encouraged talks between his ducal masters and the Elector of Saxony. Both feared that a war between Catholics and Protestants might simply enhance imperial power at the expense of the princes: reason enough for Bavaria to revert to the idea of a new anti-Habsburg league.

It was less easy to establish a rapport with the more militantly anti-Catholic Philip of Hessen. He was, however, soon won over when Eck managed to contrive 'proof' that the real instigator of Catholic aggression was Duke Heinrich of Brunswick-Wolfenbüttel, a territorial rival of both Hessen and Electoral Saxony. Philip was in any case more than willing to believe in Eck's story of the emperor's ambition to ride roughshod over the 'liberties' of all German princes and to rule them like slaves. Correspondence and talks between Bavaria and Hessen persisted until the spring of 1541; they remained divided on religious issues, but they agreed absolutely on the need to defend German liberty against the imposition of an imperial *monarchia*.

Making Brunswick-Wolfenbüttel into the scapegoat gave the current crisis a further dimension, as those involved were well aware. In a letter to Duke Wilhelm IV on 22 October 1530, Eck had remarked that the emperor had 'Guelders more firmly in his head than all Turks, faith and the welfare of the German nation'.[31] Indeed, for Charles the question of the succession to Duke Charles of Guelders after June 1538 was of more immediate consequence than the fate of the Christian League. The Guelders Estates immediately recognized the succession of Wilhelm of Jülich-Kleve-Berg, who attempted to reinforce his position by allying himself with the King of France. This was anathema to Charles, who sought to claim the fief for himself, since he had forced the late Duke Charles to recognize his own overlordship over Guelders in his capacity as Duke of Brabant. In the event of a military confrontation, he might naturally have called on assistance from other north German Catholic princes, among them Duke Heinrich of Brunswick-Wolfenbüttel.

Philip of Hessen might have been expected to view the succession of Wilhelm of Jülich-Kleve-Berg favourably, since he was an opponent of Habsburg ambitions and a prince who was known to be at least tolerant of Protestants.[32] The landgrave's confessional loyalties were, however, once more subordinate to his territorial interests. Jülich-Kleve was the most substantial secular principality in the north-west. Duke Wilhelm had married a niece of the King of France; his sister Sibylla was married to the Elector of Saxony, and his sister Anne to the King of England. If Jülich-Kleve turned Protestant and then entered an alliance with the Elector of Saxony, Philip's own influence in northern and Lower Germany would be diminished. Equally, a dynastic link between Jülich and Saxony might outweigh the old Hessen–Saxony hereditary compact (*Erbeinung*). On the other hand, if Charles V took Guelders and Jülich-Kleve, then he would almost certainly be able to extend

---

[31] Lauchs, *Bayern*, 137.
[32] For the following, see Schmidt, *Geschichte*, 83–4; Brady, *Sturm*, 254–7.

his control to the neighbouring bishoprics: Münster, Osnabrück, Paderborn, and through them to Cologne and Trier as well.

In the event, personal blackmail cemented a cynical community of interests between Philip and the emperor.[33] Although married since 1523 to the daughter of Duke Georg of Saxony, Philip became infatuated with a seventeen-year-old Saxon noblewoman, Margarethe von der Saale (1522–1566), with whom he entered into a bigamous marriage in March 1540. Philip had ceased to take communion as early as 1525 because of his chronic unfaithfulness and had already consulted Luther about the question of bigamy in 1526.[34] Luther had expressed doubts about the issue then, not being convinced by Philip's citation of polygamous Old Testament patriarchs. In his infatuation now, Philip was determined to take action. Martin Bucer was persuaded to approve when faced with the argument that Philip might otherwise ally himself with the emperor. Luther and Melanchthon were presented with a hypothetical case and advised that a secret dispensation might be possible in the event of a confession.

Within weeks, however, the news leaked out. Luther now immediately distanced himself from the advice he had given in confidence and joined other leading theologians in condemning Philip. Even Philip's closest Protestant allies refused to support him. The whole situation was fraught with danger, for bigamy was a capital crime under imperial law (the *Carolina* of 1532) and no one wished to be seen protecting a criminal. Philip was obliged to throw himself on the emperor's mercy. In a secret treaty signed at Regensburg in June 1541, the emperor promised Philip his favour, friendship, and forgiveness for his crime; he also undertook not to incite anyone to take action against Hessen. Philip for his part promised not to ally himself with the King of France or any other foreign ruler, and to prevent the admission of the Duke of Jülich-Kleve into the Schmalkaldic League.

The most immediate victim of this whole affair was Duke Heinrich of Brunswick-Wolfenbüttel. Both Hessen and Saxony had been planning an attack on him for some time, since he was threatening the Protestant towns of Brunswick and Goslar.[35] They had been held back by the reluctance of the other Schmalkaldic League members, especially the Imperial Cities, to become involved in a costly and dangerous conflict. The emperor's guarantee of Philip of Hessen's security now effectively gave him a free hand to act. By July 1542, Duke Heinrich was in exile in Landshut and the forces of the Schmalkaldic League occupied his lands.

The formation of the Catholic League and the territorial problems of the northwest might seem to portend a steady drift towards an all-out religious war. Yet imperial policy also simultaneously pursued a different path. At this stage, Charles seemed to believe, like Ferdinand, that he might achieve the pacification of Germany without resort to arms. What made that a reasonable aspiration was the existence within the Reich of a sizeable neutral party. Its leaders were the Electors of

---

[33] Buchholz, 'Landgraf' and Merkel, 'Bigamie'.
[34] He reasoned, both then and in 1539, that he was driven by his nature to be unfaithful to his wife, and that seeking a second marriage was the only truly moral course of action.
[35] Rabe, *Geschichte*, 385.

the Palatinate and of Brandenburg but it also included other influential princes—
even the Dukes of Jülich, who were in so many other ways at odds with the
Habsburgs—and Imperial Cities such as Nuremberg, Augsburg, and Frankfurt.
The Elector of Mainz and the majority of the ecclesiastical princes were also an
influential neutral force, for their threatened position gave them a powerful
incentive to seek a political compromise in the Reich.[36] At one time or another,
the neutral party more or less included all but the hard line on either side of the
confessional divide. Indeed, when it came to issues that concerned the German
Estates, particularly the princes, even Hessen and Bavaria could find common
ground.

Finally, the emperor's leading advisers themselves must be included among the
forces who sought compromise in the Reich, though they, of course, sought to
establish common ground that was amenable to imperial authority. Both Charles's
Chancellor, Nicholas Perrenot de Granvelle, a Burgundian, and his Vice-Chancellor Jean de Naves, a Luxemberger, spoke the language of Erasmian humanism and,
like Charles himself, shared Erasmus's predilection for negotiation over conflict.
Moreover, they were sensitive to the relative weakness of the imperial position in
Germany during a period (1533–42) when they gave priority to the Turkish threat
in the Mediterranean. They were acutely aware, too, of Ferdinand's vulnerability
under renewed pressure from the Turks in Hungary in 1538.

A combination of factors thus made them amenable to the Elector of Brandenburg's
suggestion early in 1538 that an attempt be made to resolve the religious dispute
by peaceful negotiation and to establish a genuine peace and to restore political
security.[37] The emperor's most trusted diplomatic representative, the exiled Archbishop of Lund, Johann von Weeze, was immediately appointed imperial commissary with
powers to negotiate a provisional settlement.[38]

The first fruit of this initiative was the Truce of Frankfurt concluded with the
Schmalkaldic League in April 1539. In order to facilitate a dialogue, all Protestants
of the Augsburg Confession were to be guaranteed peace for fifteen months
(Anabaptists and 'sectarians' were naturally excluded again). The 1532 Truce of
Nuremberg was reconfirmed and all cases against the Protestants at the Reichskammergericht suspended. All parties agreed to attend talks on the religious issue
to be held at Nuremberg in August 1539, to which neither the pope nor his
representative would be invited. The Protestants agreed to provide financial aid for
a campaign against the Turks, which, however, failed to materialize.

---

[36] Albrecht of Mainz joined the hard-line Catholic group only after he was forced out of his
archbishopric of Magdeburg (he left Halle, his favourite residence, in 1541) and the failure of the
Regensburg Colloquy (1541). After his death in 1545 his successor, Sebastian von Heusenstamm, once
more made Mainz into a leading neutral territory.

[37] Lauchs, *Bayern*, 136.

[38] Weeze (1489–1548), originally from Zevenaar in Guelderland, was appointed Archbishop of
Lund at the insistence of King Christian II in 1522, but was obliged to accompany the king into exile
the following year. He held the office of Imperial Orator and undertook numerous diplomatic missions
for the emperor. In 1537, he became administrator of the Abbey of Waldsassen in Upper Palatinate
(the so-called Stiftsland); in 1538 he was elected Bishop of Constance. See Knott, 'Weeze'; Asche and
Schindling, *Dänemark*, 257–60.

Opposition from the Catholic party, notably Bavaria, and from Rome, delayed the talks until the following summer.[39] The colloquies were intense and theologians on both sides displayed remarkable goodwill. Nor did they lack prominent sponsorship: Ferdinand presided at Hagenau in 1540, Granvelle at Worms in 1540, and Charles himself at Regensburg in 1541. Yet they could reach no agreement on the essential doctrinal issues, especially on the Eucharist. Some have argued that the failure of the colloquies marks the true start of religious schism in Germany, but this underestimates the magnitude and depth of the developments of the previous two decades.[40] Even at the colloquies themselves, the pacific Melanchthon was confronted by the implacable Johann Fabri, Bishop of Vienna, and constantly aware of the disapproval and suspicion of Luther (not himself a participant).

The real result of the colloquies was not religious, but political. They reactivated the political debate in the Reich, made a new Reichstag essential, and brought Charles back into the Reich in 1541 to preside over it. Indeed, after an intermission of some ten years, the Reichstag now met annually until 1546, in session for no less than half the time between April 1541 and August 1545.[41] Although during the 1530s Charles and Ferdinand had positively avoided calling a Reichstag, both now had powerful reasons for convening the German Estates. Charles needed money and troops from the Reich against the threat posed by France in Guelders; Ferdinand still faced the Turks in Hungary. In 1542, at Speyer, the Estates voted to provide troops for Ferdinand; in 1544, again at Speyer, they voted to support Charles against France. In return, the Protestants got an extension of the religious truce, the suspension of the Reichskammergericht in 1543, and a reform of the tax system that moderated the matricular system (in particular the assessments of individual Estates). After a levy was agreed in the emergency of 1542, the princes also, in 1544, achieved the final abolition of the Common Penny, a direct property tax on all imperial subjects, including the princes.

At the same time, Charles and Ferdinand once more paid attention to the traditional Habsburg clientage. Since the demise of the Swabian League in 1534 the minor Estates, traditionally the mainstay of the League and of Habsburg influence in the core areas of Upper and Middle Germany, had been neglected. Now the brothers responded to the reinvigoration of the urban diets during the early 1540s by addressing the main grievance of the Imperial Cities: the erosion by the princes of their rights to participate in the Reichstag. In return for urban consent to taxation, the cities' rights were confirmed in 1544. The situation of the Imperial Knights, who were equally vulnerable after the demise of the Swabian League, was also addressed. In 1542, the Reichstag, in which they were not represented, resolved that they too should be obliged to contribute to the Turkish campaign.[42] Seeing an opportunity to enhance his own standing, Ferdinand offered

[39] Lauchs, *Bayern*, 151–6; Brady, *Sturm*, 210–19, 223–5.
[40] Ziegler, 'Religion'; Winkler, 'Religionsgespräch'.
[41] For the following, see Brady, *Sturm*, 225–37; Schmidt, *Städtetag*, 382–403.
[42] Press, *Reichsritterschaft, passim*; Press, 'Bundespläne', 70.

to mediate between them and the emperor. This re-established their traditional allegiance to the emperor as their immediate overlord. Against recognition of their immediate status and the promise of imperial protection against the princes, the Imperial Knights began to form their own corporate organizations for the administration of their tax contributions and the defence of their rights generally.

Despite the failure of the religious colloquies, Habsburg efforts to achieve political equilibrium in the Reich in the early 1540s appeared to result in significant success. Certainly, they rallied the Estates against the French and the Turks, and this contributed a little at least to Charles's victories over Guelders in 1543 and France in 1544, and to the conclusion of a truce with the Turks in 1545. With the emperor strengthened and the Reichstag firmly back at the centre of the political stage, many leading neutrals felt optimistic that, one way or another, a political compromise might yet be possible on the religious issue. As late as 1546, the Elector of Brandenburg was still putting forward ambitious plans for Church reform in the Reich and for the restoration of peace and harmony, noting that the chances of an agreement on the religious issue would be greatest if one left 'the Bishop of Vienna and Luther at home'.[43] Even before a general council of the Church resolved the wider and more fundamental issues, the neutrals still believed that peace and stability might be restored in the Reich.

---

[43] Angermeier, *Reichsreform 1410–1555*, 290. See also, Delius, 'Religionspolitik'.

25

Charles V as 'Lord of Germany', 1541–1548

It is not clear exactly when the emperor decided to go to war against the German Protestants. Charles returned to the Reich as a peacemaker in 1541, but the political conditions on which that strategy had been based were changing even then.

Protestantism had gained significant ground. In 1539, the death of Duke Georg of Saxony led to the introduction of the new religion in a former bastion of militant Catholicism. The first hesitant steps taken by Duke Georg's sixty-six-year-old brother Duke Heinrich (1473–1541) met with significant local opposition. The accession of Duke Moritz (1521–1553) in August 1541 inaugurated a more vehement approach and brought to power one of the most remarkable German princes of the sixteenth century.[1]

Although he died at the age of thirty-two, Duke Moritz's twelve-year reign solved key problems for his dynasty and for the Reich. By 1547, his collaboration with Charles V, first against the Turks, then against the French, and finally against the Schmalkaldic League, had won him the Electoral title from his Ernestine Saxon kinsmen. Denounced by fellow Protestants as the 'Judas of Meissen', he then distanced himself from the emperor and emerged as the leader of the Protestants against him in the Princes' Revolt of 1552. Though he died in battle the following year, he had by then forced Charles V to accept the idea of a religious settlement in the Reich. Perhaps more than any other prince of his generation, and certainly earlier than any other, Moritz understood the new dynamics of imperial and territorial power politics after the 1520s.

In the first instance, Duke Moritz's accession seemed to herald a new wave of militant Protestant activity. He immediately intensified the threat to the bishoprics of Naumburg and Meissen as he stoked up the old competition for control over them between the Ernestine and Albertine Saxon dynasties. In addition, Moritz effectively forced the secularization of Merseburg after 1542 and had his brother elected 'lay administrator' of the diocese on the death of the last bishop in 1544.[2] The Guelders conflict with Jülich-Kleve, though it ended with Charles's acquisition of Guelders in the Treaty of Venlo (September 1543), did not prevent the reformation of Jülich-Kleve itself. The Brunswick war of 1542 destroyed another Catholic bastion. Hermann von Wied's attempt to turn the Electorate of Cologne into a Protestant principality after 1542 generated tension throughout the Reich until his resignation in 1547.[3] Had he succeeded, he would have taken his other

---

[1] Rudersdorf, 'Moritz'.
[2] On Naumburg, Meissen, and Merseburg, see Wolgast, *Hochstift*, 237–53.
[3] See also pp. 282–3.

sees with him, thus transforming Münster, Osnabrück, Minden, and Paderborn as well. Furthermore, Brandenburg had embraced Protestantism in 1540, and after 1544 it was rumoured that the Palatinate would go the same way; even the new Elector of Mainz seemed favourably inclined to the Protestants. It seemed for a time as if the Catholic majority among the Electors might turn into a Protestant one.

These developments, however, did not directly benefit the Schmalkaldic League. Not all converts of the time joined. Duke Moritz's hatred of his cousin, the Elector of Saxony, led him to become an ally of the crown. The Elector Joachim of Brandenburg remained a leading member of the neutral party.[4] The Schmalkaldic League itself was significantly weakened. Its moral authority was severely damaged by Philip of Hessen's bigamy and by the ruthless assault on Brunswick-Wolfenbüttel by Hessen and Electoral Saxony, which also plunged the League into ruinous expenditure. When Duke Heinrich attempted to wrest control of his lands back from Hessian and Saxon occupation in 1545, the Schmalkaldic League incurred further military expenditure.[5] The League forces easily defeated and captured Duke Heinrich, but this outcome merely embroiled the Protestant aggressors in further problems.[6] The gradual weakening of the Schmalkaldic League diminished the most important obstacle to Habsburg authority in the Reich.

Ironically, also, the pope's renewed call for a general council of the Church in 1545 immediately jeopardized any further progress on a political compromise in the Reich. The Reichstag at Worms was paralysed by a dispute over the recognition of the council. The Protestants refused to recognize its authority, and insisted on the continuing validity of all the concessions made to them in the past and last reaffirmed at Speyer in 1544. Since they were given no assurances on this issue, they refused to cooperate on all others. Charles V's promise at the end of the proceedings to hold yet another religious colloquy was, however, more than just a cynical attempt to deceive the Protestants about his real intentions. Tension between the emperor and the pope was growing over the question of the management of the council, and a papal party emerged at Trent determined to ensure that it should not be dominated by an emperor who was flushed with military success. That made it reasonable to keep all options in the Reich open. However, both sides were acutely aware that all previous colloquies had failed.

By this time, a war plan was definitely in place. The emperor's successes in the Netherlands and in Guelders, against France and the Turks after 1543 inevitably encouraged thoughts of a more authoritarian approach in the Reich. A new assertive mood took hold. In July 1545 the papal nuncio reported that Granvelle had promised Charles V that he would make him 'lord of Germany' ('padron di Germania').[7]

---

[4] Angermeier, *Reichsreform 1410–1555*, 288.

[5] See p. 313.

[6] Duke Heinrich spent the next two years in Hessian captivity and was freed only when Charles V triumphed over the Schmalkaldic League.

[7] Brady, *Sturm*, 226. For the following, see Schmidt, 'Kampf um Kursachsen' and Tracy, *Charles V*, 204–28; an excellent short survey of the conflict with references to the older literature is in *TRE*, xxx, 228–31.

When the Reichstag next met at Regensburg, secret treaties were ready for signature by the pope and the Dukes of Bavaria and Albertine Saxony. Each promised the emperor money and men. The pope's reward was to be the reunification of Christendom; the dukes were vaguely promised promotion to Electorships in place of the Palatinate and Ernestine Saxony. Duke Wilhelm also secured agreement to a marriage between his son and one of Ferdinand's daughters, with limited potential rights to succession in Austria.

Duke Moritz additionally extracted permission to undertake the administration of the sees of Magdeburg and Halberstadt, which in fact contradicted all the principles Charles was committed to upholding. He also demanded immunity from eventual decrees of the Council of Trent on such matters as justification by faith, clerical marriages, and communion under both kinds. Duke Moritz's participation was particularly important because it would help avoid the impression of a religious war. It also helped persuade others such as the Margraves of Brandenburg-Küstrin and Brandenburg-Kulmbach and Duke Erich of Brunswick-Calenberg to join the imperial cause.

A month before the Regensburg Reichstag of July 1546, the emperor had informed the Protestant Estates that he had to take action against 'disobedient princes'. Then, four days before the Reichstag's final session, he outlawed Philip of Hessen and Johann Friedrich of Saxony for their breach of the public peace in the Brunswick war.[8] The sentence of outlawry against two individuals was designed to deflect attention away from any idea that this might be a religious war. However, even if the pope had not declared the campaign to be a crusade and offered indulgences to all who assisted in the elimination of heresy, few in Germany were under any illusions. The rhetoric was clear on both sides. If Charles V claimed to be fighting for the restoration of lawful Christian monarchical authority, his opponents employed the rhetoric of humanist nationalism to mobilize the nation in the defence of German liberty against the alien 'Spanish' monarchy.[9]

The south German members of the Schmalkaldic League began to mobilize immediately and their 57,000 men were potentially a serious threat. The emperor had to rely on troops from Spain, Italy, and the Netherlands, who would take time to arrive. The Electors of Mainz, Cologne, Trier, and Brandenburg remained neutral. Yet the League was slow to coordinate its efforts and to agree on engaging its forces; its commanders preferred endless manoeuvres to fighting. Consequently, they soon lost the initiative, and by November, Philip of Hessen and the Elector withdrew northwards to defend their own territories and Charles was master of Upper Germany. All the Imperial Cities except Constance immediately sued for peace, and one after another agreed to pay the emperor massive compensation. Even the aged Duke Ulrich of Württemberg agreed to pay 300,000 gulden and to apologize before the emperor on his knees, an act undertaken for him by his officials because of his gout.

---

[8] See p. 313.   [9] Schmidt, *Geschichte*, 87–9, 92–7; Hirschi, *Wettkampf*, 463–80.

The northern campaign was more difficult. Ferdinand's progress was impeded by a rebellion in Bohemia, where the Estates took the opportunity to declare their solidarity with their Saxon neighbours and refused to lend assistance to Spanish 'sodomites'.[10] By November, however, once Duke Moritz had formally been promised the Saxon Electorate, a combined Saxon and Bohemian force invaded Electoral Saxony. A difficult winter campaign gained new momentum when the emperor's troops turned north from Ulm the following March. On 24 April 1547, the Elector's troops were defeated at Mühlberg and he himself was captured. A month later, after a futile siege of Bremen, the imperial army itself suffered a serious reverse at Drakenburg on the Weser. Thereafter, the rebellious cities and territories of the north were left to their own devices for the time being. Only Magdeburg, which became a centre for militant Protestant refugees, was formally outlawed. The emperor was now more interested in making political capital out of his unprecedented display of military power.

First, Charles took his revenge on the main rebels. The Saxon Elector was condemned to death, but still refused to submit to the emperor's authority on the religious question. Consequently, in June, his Electoral title and much of his territory was transferred to Duke Moritz and the Albertine line in perpetuity. He himself remained a captive, the death sentence having been legally highly dubious anyway. Philip of Hessen, who capitulated on 19 June, placed his hopes in the offer of the Elector of Brandenburg and Duke Moritz to intercede on his behalf. Charles, however, proved ruthless and merciless. Philip appeared before the emperor to pay homage, but he too was taken into captivity. Both men were incarcerated in the Netherlands in the custody of the Duke of Alba for five years. Furthermore, against all German convention, the noblemen of their territories, along with all the nobles who had followed the other Schmalkaldic princes, were also forced to pay large sums in return for the emperor's forgiveness. The requirement to place loyalty to the emperor above loyalty to their immediate territorial overlord was new in the Reich.[11]

The punishment and humiliation during 1547 and 1548 of those who had rebelled against the emperor demonstrated time and again the sheer magnitude of his triumph. His troops controlled virtually the whole of the Reich, certainly more of it than any predecessor had done. Furthermore, in personal terms he now also seemed to enjoy a pre-eminent stature in Europe as a whole. The deaths of Luther (18 September 1546), Henry VIII (28 January 1547), and Francis I (31 March 1547) removed all his old rivals from the stage. Suleiman the Magnificent, his last remaining adversary, concluded a five-year truce in 1547 in order to pursue a campaign in Persia.

In the circumstances, it was quite reasonable to believe that Charles might finally be able to impose a *Pax Carolina* on the Reich: his own political, constitutional, and religious settlement designed to establish the authority of the

[10] Fichtner, *Ferdinand I*, 156.   [11] Schmidt, *Geschichte*, 89.

crown once and for all.[12] It soon became clear, however, that nemesis was to be the sole outcome of his triumph.

The Reichstag opened at Augsburg on 1 September 1547. There could be little doubt about the circumstances in which it met, and which gave it the epithet 'the armoured Reichstag'. The city was surrounded by Charles's Spanish troops. Nor was there any question by the time the session commenced about the main issues that it faced. The emperor's plans for a new 'imperial league' had lain before a committee of the Estates for several months beforehand. It was known also that he intended to restore the Reichskammergericht and to reach some kind of settlement of the religious question.

At the same time, however, two major obstacles also began to become clear. First, the German Estates were immediately deeply suspicious of a powerful emperor. The possibility that a real monarchy might be established in Germany helped overcome religious, dynastic, and territorial differences and reinforced the solidarity of the princes in defence of German liberty. Even Charles's recent allies now began to turn against him. The Bavarians, disappointed in any case by the fact that they had not acquired the Electorship from the Palatinate they had been promised as a reward for their neutrality, became staunch champions of the rights of all princes against the emperor. Many were incensed by Charles's harsh treatment of Philip of Hessen and Johann Friedrich of Saxony. Rumours of rebellion against 'brutal servitude' began to circulate. Soon it became clear that even at the height of his power the emperor could not simply dictate to the Germans.

Second, Charles now faced hostility within the Church—both at Trent and in Rome—that significantly diminished his chances of achieving a religious settlement in Germany. The Church council's decree on justification published in January 1547 left little room for negotiation with Protestant doctrines.[13] As the emperor's military victories unfolded, so the pope became hostile, and as early as February 1547 he withdrew his troops from Germany and refused to send any more money. In March an anti-imperial group at Trent, seizing the excuse of an outbreak of plague, insisted that the council should move to Bologna, which ruled out from the start any possibility of the German Protestants ever recognizing it as a true council. In September, relations with Rome were severely disturbed by the involvement of Charles's Milanese viceroy, Ferrante Gonzaga, in the murder of the pope's son Pier Luigi Farnese, Duke of Parma and Piacenza. The murder and Gonzaga's subsequent occupation of the strategically important territory of Piacenza led Paul III to plan an offensive league with Henri II of France against the emperor's 'tyranny' in Italy. The league failed to materialize, for Henri feared a counter-alliance between the emperor and the King of England and a potentially ruinous war on two fronts. The tension between emperor and pope over both the location and the agenda for the council remained, however, and led to its suspension in September 1549.

[12] Rabe, *Geschichte*, 407.   [13] Mullett, *Catholic Reformation*, 42–7.

At the Reichstag in Augsburg, the proposal for an 'imperial league', the most important item on the agenda as far as Charles was concerned, met with implacable opposition.[14] Charles aimed to replicate the Swabian League on a much larger scale and to use the Austrian or 'upper' hereditary lands and his own 'lower' hereditary lands in the Netherlands to impose a clamp on the Reich from the north-west and the south-east. The new league was to be valid for a period of twelve or fifteen years or longer. All Estates were to be included in it, regardless of confessional allegiance or past behaviour. In this structure, which was intended to exist in parallel to the Reich rather than replace it, all Estates would be equal and equally responsible for providing money to finance a standing army under the emperor's command for the maintenance of public peace and the defence of the realm. Clearly, this was a scheme aimed at capturing the Reich for the emperor, but it also aimed to make the Reich work as part of Charles's system in Europe generally.

The plan that Charles advanced was already more moderate than the scheme Ferdinand had put to him in November 1546 for turning the Reich into a hereditary Habsburg monarchy.[15] By January 1548, however, it was already a dead letter. Instead, Charles now pursued the more narrowly dynastic aim of securing the Habsburg hereditary lands. For the Netherlands, he demanded special status—protection against France in return for minimal contributions—within the Reich. Despite some opposition even to this proposal, he was able to force through the Treaty of Burgundy in June 1548.[16] The Burgundian lands were recognized as a separate Kreis of the Reich and, like the Austrian Kreis, exempt from the authority of imperial institutions. For the Austrian lands, Charles sought money to fortify the Hungarian frontier (a *Baugeld*) and to furnish a war chest for emergencies (a *Vorrat*). Typically, however, Charles insisted less on these measures, which would have benefited Ferdinand's sphere more than his own. Neither proposal yielded more than trivial and wholly inadequate amounts of money.

The grand scheme for an 'imperial league' was thus reduced to the pursuit of Habsburg dynastic interests. Other proposals were more successful.[17] The most important was the re-establishment of the Reichskammergericht on the emperor's terms. The crown retained the right to appoint all judges, while the Estates were to pay for the court by means of a regular biennial tax (*Kammerzieler*) based on the registers used to assess matricular taxes. At the same time, the codification of precedents and rules of procedure, in particular the elaborate appeals procedure based on the purest principles of Roman law, provided working guidelines for the court that made its operations more transparent. The court was thus re-established as an instrument of imperial justice, and fears that it might once more become an instrument of religious persecution were dispelled by the appointment of several Protestant judges.

---

[14] Press, 'Bundespläne', 77–80; Angermeier, *Reichsreform 1410–1555*, 296–7.
[15] Rabe, *Reichsbund*, 122–3.
[16] Press, 'Niederlande', 327–8; Mout, 'Niederlande', 147–55.
[17] Angermeier, *Reichsreform 1410–1555*, 301–6.

Almost as significant was the revision and renewal of the Public Peace. The original Perpetual Public Peace of 1495 had been designed to combat feuds.[18] The revised version of 1548 concentrated on war, rebellion, robbery, and usurpation of lands and titles. The emperor's own role in the maintenance of the public peace was further enhanced. The power to proscribe was extended to the emperor's Reichshofrat, giving it parity with the Reichskammergericht. Furthermore, the emperor was now given authority to pursue or absolve suspects on his own initiative, rather than simply acting in response to a petition. Traditionally, those found guilty of breaches of the peace could be excluded from their fiefs; now the penalty could be extended to their heirs as well, which made the emperor a significant potential beneficiary of misdemeanours. The power to impose fines on offenders and the grant of the unqualified right to march his troops through any territory in the Reich further strengthened the emperor's position. At the same time, the new law's enforcement provisions enlisted the Estates in the service of the crown, with penalties envisaged for those who refused to help or dragged their heels unreasonably in doing so.

Crucially, questions of religious dogma were removed from the public peace; no longer could Protestant princes and magistrates be outlawed on grounds of their religion. Church property and ecclesiastical jurisdictions remained protected, but the law now recognized the fact that much property and many rights had changed hands. The law effectively confirmed the validity of the concessions made to Protestant rulers between 1526 and 1544, and explicitly envisaged the possibility that more might change hands in the future.

The separation of questions of faith from issues of Church property was a prerequisite for the restoration of peace in the Reich. While this was a welcome departure from the imperial policy of the last few decades, it was accompanied by an altogether more ambitious attempt to settle the religious question. Pending the conclusion of the deliberations at Trent, Charles decreed an 'Interim' that made important concessions to the Protestants.[19] This code of religious practice permitted both clerical marriage and communion under both kinds. However, the Mass was reintroduced, albeit with the offertory interpreted as an act of remembrance and thanks, rather than as an act of propitiation. More remarkable still, the Interim made significant statements on matters of dogma such as justification by faith, the veneration of the saints, and the authority of Scripture. Even such details as the practice of fasting were touched upon, and justified pragmatically with the argument that if fasting ceased there would not be sufficient meat to feed the whole population.

The emperor's original aim had been to devise a formula to which both Catholics and Protestants in the Reich could subscribe. A committee of theologians that he had commissioned with the task had failed to reach agreement. The proposal he put forward, only edited and lightly amended by the theologians, represented nothing less than a new hybrid imperial religion, which he was determined to impose upon

---

[18] See pp. 35–6, 77.
[19] Rabe, 'Interimspolitik'; Angermeier, *Reichsreform 1410–1555*, 306–10.

the German Estates. The immediate objections of the Catholics led to it being restricted to the Protestants. Then the preamble was simply read out before the Reichstag as an imperial mandate, whereupon the Archbishop of Mainz duly accepted the whole code on behalf of the Estates without further discussion.

As audacious as the aspiration to resolve in a single act all the doctrinal issues of the last three decades, was the claim that the Interim decree made for the emperor's authority. It overrode the traditional separation between spiritual and temporal authority. The text still acknowledged the pope's God-given authority over all bishops and over the whole Church, but it relativized this by adding that 'the powers that he has should be used not to destroy but to uplift'.[20]

The Catholic Electors and prince-bishops rejected the Interim even before it was published, so it could never provide a unifying bond for all Germans. As a decree that applied only to the Protestant Estates, who were given just eighteen days to confirm their compliance, it was also problematic. Why should they now comply with something that could not possibly achieve its aim of bringing them back into the fold? Ultimately, the only answer was that the emperor now saw the introduction of the Interim as the crucial test of his authority, the ultimate means of disciplining the German Protestant Estates.

---

[20] Rabe, *Geschichte*, 420.

26

The Triumph of the Reich, 1548–1556

The struggle over the implementation of the Interim revealed the limits of Charles V's authority in the Reich. The Electors of the Palatinate and of Brandenburg along with the Duke of Jülich did in fact accept the decree, largely because it did not conflict with the rather transitional arrangements that prevailed in these 'neutral' territories anyway. The Elector of Saxony, by contrast, declared that he could not accept it without first consulting his Estates, which led to the publication of an amended version, the so-called 'Leipzig Interim'. Others accepted quietly, but then attempted to downplay the significance of the decree. The Imperial Counts of the Wetterau, for example, told their subjects that the decree merely meant that the emperor wished them to celebrate a number of feast days each year and to abstain from meat on Fridays and Saturdays.[1]

Others, however, resisted strenuously. Only the arrival of imperial troops forced Duke Ulrich of Württemberg to comply. The preachers and magistrates of the Upper German Imperial Cities proved so reluctant to adopt the new imperial religious code that the emperor had to threaten them with force. Even so, through-out south-west Germany many preachers chose to go into exile rather than submit to the Interim.[2] Martin Bucer, who sought refuge in Cambridge, where he died in 1551, was one of hundreds of refugees from the Interim. For good measure, the emperor now also moved to eradicate the guild elements in the constitutions of the Imperial Cities, since he and his advisers held the guilds responsible for the religious innovations and instability of the past few decades.[3] Starting with Augsburg and Ulm in 1548, all the Upper German cities had new constitutions imposed upon them that placed political power in the hands of relatively small patriciates. By 1552, the imperial commissioners had dealt with every southern Imperial City. The Interim did not ultimately endure, but the new constitutional arrangements survived in these Imperial Cities until the Reich was dissolved in 1806.

Force was effective—for a time at least—in those core areas of the Reich where imperial authority was traditionally accepted. In places such as Magdeburg and Bremen, however, the emperor's writ counted for little and they were out of range of his troops too. Far away from the traditional imperial sphere, princes such as Margrave Johann of Brandenburg-Küstrin, only recently loyal to the emperor during the Schmalkaldic War, began to nurse a bitter resentment against the naked tyranny

---

[1] Schmidt, *Grafenverein*, 246.
[2] Peters, 'Macht'.
[3] Naujoks, *Karl V*, 35–42, 47–9, 67–8, 169–74, 335–9; and Naujoks, *Obrigkeitsgedanke*, 118–53. See also pp. 534–5.

that the Interim affair exposed. By the time the Reichstag was next convened at Augsburg in July 1550, for a session that lasted until February 1551, the groundswell of rebellion was already beginning to form.

It is true that despite considerable argument, the Interim decree was renewed. Elector Moritz of Saxony was commissioned and allocated money to break the resistance of Magdeburg by force. Talks were scheduled with Bremen. The Protestant Estates even agreed to attend the Council at Trent. Yet the discussions made clear that the Interim was a failure; and when the Protestant representatives actually turned up at the Church Council that was reconvened in May 1551, they were not allowed to state their case without first having submitted to the Council's authority, so their mission proved fruitless.

At the same time, Charles's attempts during the Reichstag session to regulate the imperial succession generated further grounds for discontent.[4] That the Habsburg legacy would be divided had been likely since the Brussels Treaty of 1522, which gave Ferdinand hereditary rights over the Austrian lands. It had been equally clear that Charles's son Philip, born in 1527, would succeed in Spain, but the question of whether he would take precedence over Ferdinand or his children remained open. Ferdinand's election as Charles's heir in the Reich in 1531 seemed to emphasize the emerging division of the Habsburg patrimony into two distinct spheres. Ferdinand's proposal in 1546 that the Electors should be persuaded to agree to choose only members of the house of Habsburg seems to reflect his own concern over who would succeed him. In theory, the Electors would have had a free choice, but once Ferdinand became emperor he would have been in a good position to advance the cause of his own son Maximilian over Philip. The following year, however, rumours grew that Charles intended to displace Ferdinand in favour of Philip as the next imperial heir.

By the summer of 1550, when Charles and Ferdinand met at Augsburg to resolve the matter, relations between the two brothers were already extremely tense. This tension was also common knowledge in the Reich. Charles sought to boost Philip's cause by declaring him his heir in the Netherlands in addition to Spain (including Naples and Sicily, and the Duchy of Milan, which Philip had been given as a fief of the Reich in 1540). During 1549 and 1550, Philip travelled extensively in the Reich in an attempt to promote his cause with the German princes. His awkward and withdrawn character and lack of German language skills doomed this enterprise to failure, even though he tried to prove himself an equal of the German princes on one occasion by becoming quite helplessly drunk. Overall, the tour did nothing but reinforce the anti-Spanish prejudices of the Germans.[5]

Notwithstanding this, Charles insisted on a scheme designed to ensure that the two Habsburg blocks would not drift apart. Philip of Spain was to succeed Ferdinand in the Reich. Ferdinand's implacable opposition ruled out a proposal

---

[4] For the following, see Fichtner, *Ferdinand I*, 161–81; Rodríguez-Salgado, *Changing face*, 33–40; Rebitsch, *Fürstenaufstand*, 73–82; Laubach, 'Nachfolge', 33–50.

[5] Fichtner, *Ferdinand I*, 167. Maximilian, by contrast, was a match for even the most bibulous German princes: ibid., 244.

that Philip should now immediately be elected King of the Romans, which would have left the Reich with one emperor and two German kings. He was also able to secure agreement that his own son Maximilian would eventually succeed Philip in the Reich, for which he paid the price of conceding control in Italy to Philip as imperial vicar. The whole arrangement was cemented by intra-dynastic marriages, with each heir either married to or contracted to marry a cousin.[6]

As far as Charles was concerned, the prospect of Philip's ultimate succession in the Reich safeguarded the future of the Habsburg inheritance. Spain's superior resources also justified granting Philip Italy, the Burgundian lands, and the Netherlands, the areas most vulnerable to French aggression and thus most likely to need defending. For Ferdinand, the outlook was not so favourable, though he had no option but to accept and was consoled at least by the promise in writing (for the first time) of help against the Turks. On the other hand, his own son and heir, Maximilian, was bitter. Ferdinand had designated Maximilian heir in Bohemia and Hungary in his testament of 1543, but at that stage he also envisaged joint rule of the Austrian lands by all three of his sons.[7] In comparison with his cousin Philip, Maximilian thus seemed destined for relative poverty on the margins of Europe. This was not the future he had imagined as the son of the future Holy Roman Emperor and his uncle's regent in Spain between 1548 and 1550.

Charles wished to regulate the succession in his capacity as head of the dynasty, and the agreement he concluded on 9 March 1551 was a family compact (*Hausvertrag*). His deliberations paid scant regard, however, to the rights of the Electors in the matter of the imperial succession. Attempts to make them favourably inclined to Charles's intentions merely aroused disquiet at the fact that the very existence of such plans contradicted their rights to conduct a free election. Disquiet within the Electoral body was soon matched by indignation outside it among the princes generally. Ferdinand tried to persuade the Electors of Saxony and Brandenburg of the merits of Philip's succession, but Maximilian made contact with the malcontents. Before long, both father and son were firmly linked with the German opposition.

Concern over the succession issue added a further grievance to an already extensive list. There was widespread indignation at the continuing imprisonment of Philip of Hessen and Johann Friedrich of Saxony. Many considered the transfer of the latter's lands and Electoral title to Duke Moritz an abuse of the emperor's feudal prerogatives. The Interim was increasingly viewed as an act of arbitrary

---

[6] Maxmilian's marriage to Charles's daughter Mary in 1548 was successful and blessed with numerous children, though their near-incestuous union generated the hereditary deformity of the lower jaw that afflicted successive generations over the next centuries. Philip II eventually married Maximilian's daughter Anne of Austria, his own niece, in 1570 as his fourth wife. Second and third marriages to Mary I of England and Elizabeth of France, respectively took precedence over any sense of obligation to fulfil the commitment to the dynasty entered into in 1551.

[7] Kohler, *Ferdinand I*, 297–9. Ferdinand persuaded the Bohemian Estates to accept Maximilian as their future king in 1549. Following his election as King of the Romans in 1562, Maximilian was crowned King of Bohemia in 1562 and of Hungary in 1563. Ferdinand's final testament of 1554 provided for the partition of his Austrian territories among his three sons: Laubach, *Ferdinand I.*, 575; Fichtner, *Maximilian II*, 56–7.

tyranny. The continuing presence of Spanish troops in the Reich was a flagrant breach of the emperor's electoral capitulation of 1519. Now, for good measure, Charles also seemed bent on imposing a Spanish monarchy on Germany. Little wonder, then, that there was talk of the threat of a 'foreign Spanish servitude and monarchy' and of the suppression of 'German liberty'.[8]

It is difficult to assess just how deep this agitation ran. 'German liberty' meant the liberty of the Estates, in particular the princes. It did not originally mean the liberties of their subjects, though it gradually came to do so. The events of these years, however, inevitably made an impact on large sections of German society. The movements of Spanish and Italian troops, with their distinctive and outlandish dress, affected large areas of the Reich from the Lower Rhine to southern Germany. The invasion and occupation by these forces of the Upper German Imperial Cities and of territories such as Württemberg also brought them into direct contact with the German population. Imperial troops only withdrew from Württemberg in 1550. The forcible imposition of the Interim and the constitutional restructuring of the Imperial Cities lasted well into 1551. Even in the north, in areas traditionally remote from the political life of the Reich, the plight of Magdeburg and Bremen aroused passions for several years. Then the princes' rebellion re-ignited the arguments, which in fact endured until the peace of 1555.

In this general ferment, there was a revival of the kind of propaganda that characterized the late fifteenth-century crises and the agitation that accompanied the imperial election of 1519.[9] Propagandists on the Protestant side took up the theme of the defence of Germany against the Spanish. The current problems were presented as yet another chapter in the saga of the perpetual struggle of the Germans against the 'Welsche', that gather-all term for anything or anyone foreign, especially Latin or southern European.[10] When the Bohemian rebels declared that they would not fight alongside 'Spanish sodomites' they seem to have been expressing a common view.[11] In this particular instance, the negative image of the Spaniard also served to express the solidarity of the Czechs with the Germans, which could not normally be taken for granted.

At the same time, the patriotic images of Germania, Arminius, or the mythical Germanic king Ariovist, which had first been popularized by the humanists in the struggle against Rome around 1500, were mobilized again. 'Rome' was still a target, of course, but the real struggle now was against 'Spain'. Ironically, Charles V was now condemned for many of the same reasons as those for which Francis I was deemed an unacceptable ruler for the Reich in 1518–19. Charles was of German blood but had become a foreigner as a result of his struggle against Protestantism. He had promised on his election to defend the Germans from foreign troops, yet he had deployed them himself. In fostering the religious struggle between the

---

[8] Angermeier, *Reichsreform 1410-1555*, 310–11; Schmidt, 'Libertät'.
[9] Schmidt, *Geschichte*, 92–4; Hirschi, *Wettkampf*, 481–4.
[10] The term originally referred only to Italy and the Italians, but increasingly came to be applied more widely to anyone or anything anywhere south of the Alps.
[11] Fichtner, *Ferdinand I*, 156.

Germans, he was neglecting his duties as the leader of Christendom and forgoing the opportunity to unite the Germans and lead them in a crusade against the Turks.

The rhetoric of freedom and fatherland resounded in marching songs and was proclaimed in a flood of woodcut prints and pamphlets. At the same time, the Schmalkaldic League was sponsoring the creation of a more enduring historical record. In 1545, it had engaged Johannes Sleidan as the official historian of the League.[12] By October 1547, he had already completed the first four books of his history of the Reformation. In 1555, his monumental *Commentariorum de statu religionis et republicae, Carolo V. Caesare, libri XXVI* ('Commentaries on Religion and the State in the Reign of Emperor Charles V') appeared at Strassburg: nearly a thousand folio pages divided into twenty-five books. It culminated in a narrative of the Schmalkaldic War depicted as the German war of liberation against a monarch who had betrayed the German nation and who sought to subjugate it with the help of Spanish troops.

The imperial party and the Catholics reciprocated, of course.[13] Their pamphlets denounced the Protestants as evil and seditious heretics whose morals were as corrupt as those of the allegedly whoring, sodomizing, and robbing Spaniards. The imperial propagandists claimed that it was Charles who really represented true liberty, for it came originally from Rome, which had vanquished the barbarian German heathens. One pamphlet by Nikolaus Mammeranus of Luxemburg, printed in Cologne in 1552, elaborated the theme of freedom in a radically novel direction.[14] The German princes were accused of trying to stir up the common man against 'lawful and divinely ordained authority'. They had allied themselves with the King of France, who merely pretended to support the new religious teaching. In reality, he was a godless ally of the Turks and in his own lands he persecuted the Protestants mercilessly. His sole aim in Germany was allegedly to seduce the common man away from the emperor and to deliver him into eternal French servitude. The emperor stood as the guarantor of freedom and security; the King of France was a tyrant who deprived his subjects of all liberties and property rights: 'The subjects in France are oppressed and weighed down heavily like donkeys.'[15]

In juxtaposing French servitude with German security in property, Mammeranus touched on a theme that was to become a leitmotif of much German legal writing in the late seventeenth and eighteenth centuries. It is certainly true that security of tenure was a concern of increasingly large areas of the Reich after the Peasants' War of 1525. Yet it is unclear whether Mammeranus's views had any resonance at the time, and it is very doubtful that he made many converts to the imperial cause in 1552. His appeal to the common man was almost certainly as ineffective as the appeals that Charles V had made to the lower nobility of Hessen in

---

[12] Dickens and Tonkin, *Reformation*, 10–19; Brady, *Sturm*, 185–7.
[13] Schmidt, *Geschichte*, 97–9. See also Schmidt, ' "Teutsche Libertät" oder "Hispanische Servitut" '.
[14] *ADB*, xx, 158–9.
[15] Quoted by Schmidt, *Geschichte*, 98. The pamphlet was *Von der Anrichtung des newen Euangelij und der alten Libertet oder Freyheit Teutscher Nation* (Cologne, 1552).

1547, when trying to mobilize the 'liberty of the nobles' against the 'liberty of the princes'.[16] Catholic and pro-imperial propaganda was weakened by its fundamentally defensive nature.

Both sides attempted to mobilize wider sections of society. Thousands of communities became caught up in the struggle in one way or another. Yet this was not a civil war that involved German society as a whole. No amount of propaganda could disguise the fact that Charles V's attempt to tame the Reich had led not to a national uprising but to a rebellion of princes.

As early as February 1550, Johann von Küstrin concluded an alliance in Königsberg with Albrecht of Prussia and Johann Albrecht of Mecklenburg for the defence of Protestantism.[17] Küstrin envisaged a great northern league that would be joined by Denmark and Poland. The defence of Magdeburg was to be the league's first objective. This, in turn, threatened to pit the league against the Elector Moritz, who feared that being thwarted in his mission at the emperor's behest to subjugate Magdeburg might merely be the first step towards the loss of his recently won Electoral title and the reinstatement of his Ernestine relatives.

In the circumstances, Moritz chose to betray the emperor and place himself at the head of the opposition. In 1550, he established contact with the King of France; he then managed to thwart the muster of a force against him in the Bishopric of Verden, and finally, in May 1551, he entered into an agreement at Torgau with the signatories of the Königsberg compact. At the same time, he made overtures to Ferdinand, as King of Bohemia his most important territorial neighbour, who he insisted should never become a target of the new league. In November, he ostensibly fulfilled his obligation to the emperor by entering Magdeburg, but in fact the 'taking' of the city was entirely amicable and he secretly promised to defend its religion in return for being recognized as its hereditary lord.

By January 1552, Moritz and his confederates, now also joined by Moritz's uneasy ally, the hot-headed and violent Margrave Albrecht Alcibiades of Brandenburg-Kulmbach, had reached a formal agreement with Henri II of France at Chambord.[18] Henri promised to defend the liberties of the German Estates, while in return the princes promised Henri the vicariate over the Imperial Cities of Metz, Toul, and Verdun, and possession of Cambrai. Though they justified themselves with the argument that these were not cities of the 'German tongue', their concession was in fact a flagrant breach of the laws of the Reich.

The Chambord agreement was rapidly followed by a French invasion of Lorraine, in which Henri took the cities. In March, Elector Moritz led a Protestant army south to Augsburg and then on to Linz. The Catholic princes and Imperial Cities remained neutral; Charles was powerless and vulnerable at Innsbruck, only a short distance away from the Protestant force. Negotiations between the rebels and Ferdinand at Linz over the full range of the princes' grievances in the second half of April foundered on Charles's refusal to contemplate a permanent truce on the

[16] Press, 'Bundespläne', 101.
[17] For the following, see Tracy, *Charles V*, 229–40.
[18] Rebitsch, *Fürstenaufstand*, 135–61.

religious issue. The only outcome was an agreement to further talks at Passau at the end of May. However, Ferdinand had now firmly won the confidence of that majority of German princes who wanted a Habsburg future for the Reich but not a Spanish *monarchia*.[19]

To reinforce the rebels' protest, Moritz then immediately moved his forces deeper into Habsburg territory. The emperor himself only narrowly escaped capture by fleeing over the Brenner to Villach.[20] Albrecht Alcibiades, meanwhile, indulged in the kind of action that was most congenial to him by launching raids against Bamberg, Würzburg, and Nuremberg to extract tribute payments to finance the main force and, naturally, to enrich himself as well. Moritz arrived at Passau the undisputed champion of the rebels who had humiliated the emperor. He had also further enhanced his negotiating power by assuring Ferdinand of his loyalty and by distancing himself from the King of France. Charles, by contrast, was virtually without allies in the Reich. The former Elector (now Duke) Johann Friedrich was set free. To add to the emperor's humiliation, the delegates at Trent immediately suspended the Council as soon as they heard of Charles's ignominious flight from Innsbruck.

It soon became clear at the Passau talks that the neutral princes, including the prince-bishops, fully shared the rebels' concerns. The princes' main demand was the concession of a permanent truce on the religious issue. In addition, they demanded the diminution of Spanish influence on Germany, the release of Philip of Hessen, and the establishment of a commission composed of the Estates under Ferdinand's chairmanship to adjudicate on the many complaints against Charles's rule.[21] Even in his isolation, Charles refused to concede more than a temporary truce until the next meeting of the Reichstag and refused outright, on the grounds that it was an affront to his imperial majesty, to permit others to sit in judgement on his conduct. It was a tribute to Moritz's political sense that he threw himself into persuading the rebels to accept the treaty that was finally ratified on 15 August 1552.

The Treaty of Passau provided a breathing space, but it afforded Charles no opportunity to escape from the further talks that had been promised on the religious issue. His immediate priority was to drive the French out of Lorraine and retake the Imperial Cities there. The first obstacle was the mercenary force of Albrecht Alcibiades who had advanced across Germany to France in the hope of joint action with the King of France after the Treaty of Passau rendered him redundant to the German rebel cause. The Duke of Alba managed to intercept him and persuade him to join Charles. Despite his help, however, the siege of Metz had to be given up in January 1553, and Charles withdrew into the Netherlands. He never set foot in Germany again. And now, furthermore, as Albrecht Alcibiades marched back to extract the financial tributes from Bamberg and Würzburg that

[19] Lutz, *Christianitas*, 81–5.
[20] Rebitsch, *Fürstenaufstand*, 226–34.
[21] For the following, see the essays in Becker, *Passauer Vertrag*.

Charles V had been obliged to sanction as the price for his help in Metz, the emperor saw himself vilified as the ally of a notorious troublemaker.

The political situation in Germany was turning decisively against the emperor. A last attempt to launch an imperial league stalled at Memmingen in June 1553.[22] Meanwhile, other leagues and associations gained ground. Early in 1553 the Palatinate, Bavaria, Jülich, and Württemberg formed the Heidelberg League dedicated to preventing Philip's succession in the Reich, to carrying out the promises of the Treaty of Passau, and to promoting peace between France and the Reich. The revival of traditional mutual inheritance pacts between Brandenburg, Hessen, and the Ernestine and Albertine Saxon dynasties saw similar regional defence agreements emerge further north. Even more significant was the league based on the traditional hereditary Saxon–Bohemian compact that Elector Moritz negotiated with Ferdinand at Eger in April–May 1553. Designed to include Bavaria, its aim was to give Moritz security in Saxony and Ferdinand security in Austria and Bohemia, and to provide help for Ferdinand against the Turks.[23] Moritz had already demonstrated his goodwill by fighting for Ferdinand in Hungary in 1552; the prospects for the proposed league were therefore excellent. Once again, the regions of the Reich were drawing together against their emperor. This time, the German king was one of their leaders.[24]

The cohesiveness of this new constellation was immediately reinforced by the continuing marauding activities of Albrecht Alcibiades. Having extracted his tribute from the Franconian bishops, he now prepared to move north through Thuringia in the spring of 1553, intending to attack Brunswick and Saxony. He even boasted that he would have the Bohemian crown before he was finished.[25] The princes of the Heidelberg League were reluctant to take firm action, but Moritz was now determined to forge the peace whose foundations he had laid over the past year. Albrecht Alcibiades was defeated at a fierce battle at Sievershausen between Hanover and Brunswick. Duke Moritz, however, was killed in the fighting; Albrecht Alcibiades escaped, but his forces were comprehensively routed by Ferdinand in September and he was driven out of his territories into exile in France. To the last, Charles had refused to outlaw him.

Even now, Charles still seemed to be hopeful of success in Germany. He toyed with the idea of publicly revoking the Treaty of Passau in a further demonstration of imperial power guided by the traditions of the Reich and the righteousness of God, whose law the Passau agreement breached. He pursued a renewed campaign in Lorraine, taking Thérouanne and Hesdin but not the prize of Metz itself. In Italy too, his forces fought back against the French, achieving significant victories, though not a real breakthrough. The election of an anti-Spanish pope, Paul IV, in 1555 in any case revived the hostile Franco-papal alliance. In 1554, the possibility of altogether wider horizons opened up with the marriage of Philip II to Mary I of England.[26] Rumours of a pregnancy in 1555 fuelled hopes for a

[22] Press, 'Bundespläne', 88–9.   [23] Press, 'Bundespläne', 90.
[24] Kohler, 'Passau'.   [25] Fichtner, *Ferdinand I*, 205.
[26] Lutz, *Christianitas*, 408–9.

healthy heir who might in due course replace the sickly Don Carlos, Philip's son by his first wife, Mary of Portugal. The prospect that this heir would eventually inherit a Mediterranean–Atlantic empire made the German Reich seem almost insignificant by comparison. Mary's pregnancy turned out to be nothing more than wishful thinking and her death in November 1558 shattered the imperial grand design soon enough. By then, however, Charles himself was dead.

For the last two years of his life, Charles never once intervened in German politics. Things had come to fruition that he could never accept. Following the death of Moritz of Saxony, the German Estates pressed for the convocation of the Reichstag promised in the Treaty of Passau. From the outset, Charles insisted that the Treaty of Passau should not be regarded as the basis for negotiations. In June 1554, however, he gave Ferdinand full authority to preside over the coming Reichstag in his name, giving as his reason his 'insurmountable misgivings' over the religious issue. Perhaps even now he hoped that handing the responsibility for negotiating a settlement to Ferdinand might leave him free to disown what was concluded if circumstances improved.[27]

Ferdinand himself, at root, also aspired to bring about the reconciliation of confessional differences and hoped to secure agreement for another religious colloquy to this end. Throughout the proceedings, he spoke in terms of one religion only temporarily divided, and this was reflected in the final settlement, which, formally at least, regarded the Augsburg Confession as a deviation from the true path. However, Ferdinand also acted throughout under renewed pressure from the Turks; his willingness to compromise stemmed crucially from his desperation to secure further military aid from the Estates as soon as possible.[28]

By the time the Reichstag opened at Augsburg on 5 February 1555, however, the German princes had developed their own agenda. What they wanted was a new approach to the maintenance of the public peace and a political settlement of the religious issue. Remarkably, very few princes actually attended in person.[29] None of the Electors was present and only Duke Christoph of Württemberg and Duke Albrecht of Bavaria actually participated to any extent in the discussions. Most of the princes merely sent their representatives. The broad political strategy was decided at meetings of princes held elsewhere, such as the one between the ruling princes of Saxony, Brandenburg, and Hessen at Naumburg in March 1555. The final settlement at Augsburg, with its obscurities and ambiguities, fully reflected the fact that this was essentially an agreement between lawyers.

The religious issue was given the highest priority. The imperial proposition for a religious colloquy was pushed aside by the demand for a lasting religious peace and the permanent recognition of the rights of the Protestants. The Catholic princes, even the prince-bishops, concurred. Their position was difficult, since they always had to look to Rome. However, after the recent marauding of Margrave Albrecht Alcibiades, the ecclesiastical princes in particular wanted security above all else.

---

[27] Rabe, *Geschichte*, 445–6.   [28] Petritsch, 'Ferdinand I.'.   [29] Rabe, *Geschichte*, 447.

The general aspiration was clear, though the lawyers made heavy work of the myriad exceptions and peculiarities that characterized the territorial diversity of the Reich. In essence, the outcome reflected the legislation and agreements that had emerged since 1526.[30] The peace was valid in the Reich for Catholics and those of the Augsburg Confession; Zwinglians, Calvinists, and radicals were excluded. It was to remain in force 'perpetually' until the two confessions were reconciled and its terms were to take precedence over all other laws.

Until that point, each prince should determine the religion of his own territory; those subjects who objected were given the right to emigrate. Episcopal and ecclesiastical jurisdiction over the Protestant territories was to be suspended for the duration of the peace. Imperial Cities in which both confessions were present were to be biconfessional, though no mention was made of any *ius reformandi* of the cities generally, the implication being that urban magistrates did not enjoy the same prerogatives as territorial rulers. The Imperial Knights were explicitly included in the peace and their religious rights (i.e. freedom to follow either of the two recognized confessions) were guaranteed. In questions relating to ownership of Church property and to confessional affiliation of territories, the status quo of 1552 was deemed to be the norm.

A particularly thorny point, and one that was to generate conflict in the future, was the question of the ecclesiastical territories. Against the opposition of the Protestants, the 'ecclesiastical reservation' (*reservatum ecclesiasticum*) determined that where a bishop, prelate, or any other Catholic ecclesiastical officeholder embraced Lutheranism, the territory associated with that office should remain Catholic and in the possession of the Reichskirche. The so-called *Declaratio Ferdinandea*, which guaranteed freedom of conscience for Protestant nobles and cities in the ecclesiastical territories, both failed to appease the Protestants and inflamed the Catholics.[31] The fact that this was a declaration in Ferdinand's own name made it a private assurance rather than a law enforceable by the imperial courts, though that did not prevent Protestants from regarding it later as an integral part of the Augsburg settlement. Finally, the Estates agreed that the question of reconciling the divergent religious views should be tackled at the next session of the Reichstag, which they envisaged occurring at Regensburg in March 1556. In reality, however, few were under any illusions that the peace envisaged a much longer, and possibly permanent, division.

Once the religious peace was agreed, the Estates turned to secular, albeit related, matters. First, the standing orders concerning the Reichskammergericht were revised. It was charged to proceed on the basis of the terms of the religious peace, which deprived the emperor of the power of interpreting what was or was not a breach of the law.[32] All judicial positions were to be open to both Catholics and Protestants; a neutral oath ('by God and on the Holy Gospel') was introduced, and

---

[30]   For the following, see Schneider, *Ius Reformandi*, 152–69 and Gotthard, *Religionsfrieden*, 1–239. For the text of the settlement: Buschmann, *Kaiser*, i, 215–83.

[31]   Merz, 'Religionsfrieden'; Gotthard, *Religionsfrieden*, 264–71; Laubach, *Ferdinand I.*, 82–9.

[32]   Smend, *Reichskammergericht*, 179–80; Duchhardt, *Verfassungsgeschichte*, 96–100.

all judicial panels were to be balanced confessionally whenever possible (though strict parity was not stipulated until 1648). The wide powers formerly given to the Imperial Prosecutor (*Reichsfiskal*), a royal official, in the period of direct royal control of the court between 1530 and 1548, were now limited. Henceforth the approval of two judges charged with scrutinizing all potential cases was required before a prosecution could be undertaken. Finally, while in 1548 the emperor had reserved the right to make all appointments to the court, his personal nominees were now reduced to two, with four more judges nominated in respect of the Habsburg lands, six by the Electors, and twelve by the six remaining Kreise. The Reichstag now also reserved the right to conduct visitations of the court and to deal with any complaints arising from its proceedings.[33]

The revival of the Estates, or rather the affirmation of the pre-eminence of the princes in particular, was also evident in the terms agreed for the renewal of the public peace and its enforcement. An inter-Curial committee of the Reichstag or Deputation was established to coordinate peacekeeping and other activities arising from imperial legislation in the intervals between sessions.[34] The *Reichsexekutionsordnung* or Imperial Enforcement Ordinance also envisaged a more consistent and regular operation of the Kreise as regional peacekeeping agencies. Supra-regional problems were to be dealt with by the Kreise collectively by means of assemblies of their representatives under the lead of the Imperial Archchancellor, the Elector Archbishop of Mainz.[35] Similarly, the Kreise were now commissioned with the mustering of imperial armies under captains they themselves appointed. Above all, the idea of a standing army, broached repeatedly by Charles and Ferdinand in the reform discussions of recent decades, was implicitly rejected. The Reich was thus rendered incapable of expansionist or aggressive wars; even self-defence was only possible by means of exceptional matricular levies.

In all the measures concerning the public peace, the emphasis was on control by the Estates rather than by the emperor, whose peacekeeping functions were all but eliminated. This duty had passed to the Estates generally, but in essence to the princes, since the cities could pay but not fight. The Electors maintained their pre-eminence over the princes by depriving the emperor of the right to convene a Reichstag without their consent.[36] They also retained their right to elect the emperor and his heir. However, the bond formally established in 1547–8 between the Imperial Knights and the emperor remained undiminished, allowing the German crown to rely in future on the political loyalty and financial assistance of the lesser nobility of the Reich.[37] In this respect, the German crown was in a similar position to other monarchies in Europe at the time.

For Ferdinand, who had skilfully managed to emerge as the architect of the peace agreement, the outcome of the 1555 Reichstag was a triumph. For Charles V, it was

[33] Angermeier, *Reichsreform 1410–1555*, 322.
[34] Neuhaus, *Repräsentationsformen*, 425–31.
[35] Laubach, *Ferdinand I.*, 103–18.
[36] Angermeier, *Reichsreform 1410–1555*, 322.
[37] Duchhardt, *Verfassungsgeschichte*, 102–5; Neuhaus, *Reich*, 36–7.

a comprehensive setback. Even before the promulgation of the final decrees, he had given up any last hope of a favourable turn of events. An hour before the Reichstag concluded, Ferdinand received a letter from Charles announcing his immediate abdication. The letter was not read out at the Reichstag; the decrees were promulgated in Charles's name, and the transfer of power did not in fact take place for another year. Charles, however, lost all interest in the Reich. He did not even bother to send off an edict that he had drafted revoking anything agreed at Augsburg that might be to the detriment of the Roman Church.[38] He never again expressed a view on any German matter. The implications of his dramatic abdication for the position of the Habsburgs in Europe were immense. The universal monarchy that Charles had fought for—necessarily intermittently but with total commitment and all his formidable resources of political skill and military might—for the last three-and-a-half decades lay in ruins. The reform process begun in the late fifteenth century had ended in a monarchy fettered by German liberty.

[38] Rabe, *Geschichte*, 453.

PART V

MANAGING THE PEACE
1555–1618

27

Contours of the 'Confessional Age'

The Augsburg settlement ushered in sixty-three years of peace in the Reich. While much of Western Europe was embroiled in conflict—over religion or sovereignty, or a mixture of the two—the Reich remained largely stable. And when the German territories, too, were plunged into turmoil in 1618, it was because they had become embroiled in problems that essentially were not of their making. During the years of stability there were, of course, tensions. Germany was far from immune from the bitter confessional rivalry that characterized Europe as a whole during the second half of the century. Nor did the constitutional issues that had dominated the reigns of Maximilian I and Charles V lose any of their relevance or intensity. On occasion, political disputes generated military confrontations. Yet, repeatedly, the German Estates found common ground, enough at least to avert the threat of a major conflagration and to restore the peace temporarily. That this was possible was due to the evolving nature of the system itself, to the policies pursued by Ferdinand I and his successors, and to the attitudes of the German Estates towards both Reich and emperor.

Such a cautiously positive view of German history between 1555 and 1618 requires some historiographical explanation. Over the past two centuries, German historians have generally taken a very much bleaker view. For Ranke, this was a period in which Germany suffered the dismal consequences of the failure of the national uprising of the 1520s to unite the nation. For Treitschke, this was the 'ugliest phase of German history', a period in which the princes pursued their selfish interests through confessional strife.[1] Above all, it seemed clear to many scholars that the Reich was a hopeless and ineffective muddle and that, far from solving any problems, the Peace of Augsburg did little more than create a new framework of conflict in which confessional passions ultimately exploded in the Thirty Years War.

Such views prevailed until quite recently. They were the product of a mindset that regarded the nineteenth-century Prussian Protestant nation state as the yardstick by which all German history had to be judged and that placed the drama of German history at the centre of the European stage. Even after 1945, when the dominance of the Prussian Protestant master narrative was gradually undermined, the sense remained pervasive that Germany had already, in the later sixteenth century, been the tragic heart of Europe. The confessional divides of that era seemed to prefigure more contemporary political ideological divides. Similarly, parallels

---

[1] Gotthard, *Religionsfrieden*, 623–6.

could be drawn between early modern military conflicts and modern military disasters, with the German nation as the perennial victim.

The facts were less dramatic and less tragic, but nonetheless remarkable. Over several decades after 1555 a majority of the German Estates cooperated with the emperors to make the Augsburg settlement work. Domestic crises were resolved and, by and large, entanglement in conflicts outside the Reich was avoided. At the same time, the institutions and communicative mechanisms of the Reich were developed in new ways. Both the central and the regional institutions of the Reich gradually extended beyond the core areas that traditionally had been close to the crown. There was also a marked diversification of the social range of those inhabitants of the Reich who exercised the rights guaranteed by the imperial judicial system, not just nobles and princes but city dwellers and even peasants as well. The various elements of the system of Reich and Estates that had emerged in imperial legislation and developments in the territories since 1495 now began to mature into the form that would be codified in 1648. Indeed, this period saw the emergence for the first time of a literature describing and analysing the Reich and its laws.[2] This literature conceived the Reich as a coherent and functioning polity based on a clearly defined set of fundamental laws. Increasingly, too, this literature viewed the Reich as a German Reich, both in present identity and in origin, with only tenuous links at best to the Roman Empire.[3]

Of course, the religious divide, anchored and stabilized in imperial law after 1555, continued to generate extreme tensions. It was not long before the legal settlement was tested both by Lutheran expansionism and by the Catholic counter-offensive that gained a new intensity and purpose after the conclusion of the Council of Trent in 1563. The situation was also rendered more complex still by bitter rifts that opened up among the Lutheran Protestants themselves. One result of this was the emergence of a Calvinist-leaning German Reformed Church, whose status under the legislation of 1555 was dubious, and whose political protagonists among the German princes and upper nobility were fired by a new activism and internationalism.

Despite the apparent intensification of confessional rivalry and confessional activism in politics, however, it is open to question whether the period really deserves the epithet of a 'confessional age'. It is undeniable that the decades after 1555 saw the elaboration and institutionalization of a more clearly defined system of belief in the Lutheran Church, the emergence of a similarly clearly defined German Reformed confession, and the codification of Catholic beliefs by the Council of Trent. However, the emphasis by some German scholars on the absolute primacy of religion as a motivating factor and on the fundamental significance of a link between confessionalism and state formation simplifies a more complex reality.[4] Politics unfolded within a religious world view. Yet many

---

[2] Stolleis, *Öffentliches Recht*, i, 48, 72–3.　　[3] Schmidt, *Geschichte*, 188–9.
[4] For discussion of the ideas of Ernst Walter Zeeden, Heinz Schilling, and Wolfgang Reinhard, with all relevant references, see Ehrenpreis and Heumann, *Reformation*, 62–7 and Gotthard, *Religionsfrieden*, 501–27. See also pp. 477–9.

rulers and their advisers also seemed keen to differentiate between the need to enforce religious uniformity on their subjects and the need to embrace religious moderation in the politics of the Reich or in the relations between territories.

The confessional preoccupations of the age are striking, but efforts to forge harmony between divergent religious views at the political level, whether by promoting reconciliation and compromise or by seeking a political solution to the problem of religious division and conflict, are also a key feature of the period. This did not mean religious indifference, let alone atheism or the rejection of religion. It did not mean toleration, if by that is meant the freedom to believe anything or nothing in religious terms.[5] Nor did it mean secularization, though that may have been promoted by these attitudes in the very long term. What it did mean was a growing sense among many of the function and place of religion in different contexts. In the context of the territory or independent city, the business of government, the regulation and order of daily life, could not proceed without religious order. Indeed, religious order was perceived as part of the fabric of society. Yet the perpetual search for revenue, propelled by the growing expense of courts and government generally, was at least as important as a motivating force in politics.

The rulers of the German territories often pursued external policies that betrayed a sense of religion as but one of many elements of sound government. Indeed, one of the themes of the emerging theoretical literature on politics was the need for rulers to be flexible, to be as willing to promote as to desist from enforcing religious uniformity according to circumstance.[6] The art of dissimulation had been a key factor in the political life of the Reichstag since the religious issue first arose in the 1520s. By the end of the sixteenth century, the most advanced writings on politics, in particular the works of Justus Lipsius, numbered it among the key virtues of the prudent politician.[7]

The decades after 1555 were characterized overall by a desire for peace and a determination to ensure the survival of the Reich. Scholars have differed on the question of just how long that remained true. Some believe that the death of Maximilian II in 1576 marked a crucial turning point. Others suggest that the death in 1586 of the Elector August of Saxony (r. 1553–1586), the most influential prince of the peace party and a devoted imperial loyalist, was decisive. Still others emphasize what they suggest was a breakdown of imperial government as a result of Rudolf II's mental incapacity from about 1600, which allegedly exacerbated the growing problems that faced many imperial institutions in the first decade of the seventeenth century. Each case has its merits. Yet it is far from obvious that any of these junctures really represented a point of no return. At every stage, a substantial body of thought still subscribed to the old ideals of unity and concord and believed that peace would prevail.[8]

---

[5] Gotthard, *Religionsfrieden*, 560–78.
[6] Tuck, *Philosophy*, 31–64; Siedschlag, *Einfluß*, 34–89; Schindling, 'Konfessionalisierung', 40–2.
[7] Zagorin, *Ways of lying*, 123–4.
[8] Schulze, 'Concordia'.

That remained the case even when confessional tensions rose sharply from the later 1580s. As the growing tensions in Europe as a whole cast more ominous shadows over the German political scene, so German disputes seemed to assume a European dimension: many were inclined to see Spain, Rome, and the Jesuits on the one hand, and Calvinist revolutionaries on the other, lurking behind every issue. Yet the issues that confronted the German Estates were neither new nor intrinsically insoluble. Nothing that happened in the Reich between 1555 and 1618 made a protracted war inevitable.

28

Emperors, Imperial Officials, and Estates after the Peace of Augsburg

The abdication of Charles V in September 1556 left Germany with a very different monarchy. The formal transition was slow. Not until the spring of 1558 did the Electors meet in Frankfurt to accept Charles's abdication and proclaim Ferdinand, his presumptive heir for over twenty-five years, as emperor. They made their offer conditional upon Ferdinand accepting a new Electoral Capitulation that expressly incorporated the Peace of 1555 and obliged him as emperor to swear to uphold it. In practice, however, they merely articulated formally what had already emerged as fact.

Ferdinand had succeeded in brokering the Peace of Augsburg by virtue of the strong links he had forged with the German Estates. He now became the emperor of conciliation on the basis of those same links. His strength as a German ruler was, to an extent, born of his relative weakness compared with Charles V. Deprived of Spain, the Netherlands, and Italy (though Milan and other northern territories remained under the overlordship of the Reich), and reliant solely on the Habsburg Erblande, Bohemia, and Hungary, Ferdinand needed the support of the German Estates against the Turks and any other external aggressor. At the same time, his relative weakness meant that he was less likely to arouse serious domestic opposition than his brother had done.

In a sense, both the domestic and the strategic priorities of Ferdinand I's reign had more in common with those of Maximilian I around 1500 than with those of the reign of Charles V. Ferdinand's two main domestic aims were to maintain the religious truce and to secure the succession of his son to the German crown. Both objectives required him to work closely with the Electors and the German princes generally.

The only serious obstacle to the succession was, for a time at least, the putative heir himself. That Ferdinand's eldest son, Maximilian, was intensely hostile to Spain was to his great advantage. He was bitter that his marriage to his cousin Maria in September 1548 had brought him nothing more substantial than the—closely supervised—governorship of Spain, and he was deeply resentful at the efforts Charles V had made in 1551 to exclude him from the German succession. As a result, Maximilian enthusiastically presented himself as a German prince and lost no opportunity to represent the German cause on any issue. After his return from Spain in 1551, he struck up contact with both Catholic and Protestant princes. In particular, he cultivated the friendship of influential figures such as Duke Christoph of Württemberg, Duke Albrecht V of Bavaria, and the Elector August of Saxony, all three soon to be pillars of the status quo after 1555.

Maximilian's religious views were, however, more problematic.[1] In Vienna after 1552 he relished the heterodox atmosphere generated by the presence of Netherlands, Spanish, and Italian intellectuals of both Catholic and Protestant persuasions. Close links between court and university also fostered an unusually fertile cultural life at this time. Ferdinand had increasingly surrounded himself with moderate humanists and Italian artists, a network of progressive and, above all, irenic figures who formed the core of the new imperial court at Vienna. Maximilian went further. Under the influence of his court preacher, Johann Sebastian Pfauser, he progressively abandoned orthodox Catholic beliefs, while Kaspar von Niedruck assembled for him a substantial library of Protestant works. Equally influential was Jacob Acontius, the secretary to the Cardinal-Bishop of Trent who, like Pfauser, questioned the sacraments and espoused tolerant views. It was not long before the papacy began to fear the possibility of a Protestant succession in the Reich.

This was not just a Roman anxiety. It was also clear that such an eventuality would be unacceptable in Madrid and among the Catholic princes in the Reich. In the growing conflict between the emperor and his son, the reaction of the German Protestant courts proved decisive. In 1560, Maximilian sent his councillor, Nicholas von Warmsdorf, on a mission to those German Protestant courts that he believed to be sympathetic to his politics to ask whether they would support him in an emergency.[2] Out of deference to the emperor, but also because they feared anything that might destabilize the Reich, or possibly even lead to the disqualification of Maximilian in favour of Philip II, they declined to support him.

For the sake of his inheritance, Maximilian acquiesced in the emperor's banishment of Pfauser from Vienna and, after further negotiation, on 7 February 1562, he agreed to swear solemnly that he would not leave the Church of Rome.[3] The blow was softened by the grant of an income of 25,000 gulden a year from Pardubice in Bohemia and by the fact that Ferdinand went some way towards publicly recognizing the authenticity and strength of Maximilian's religious convictions. In October 1561, Ferdinand presented a case to the pope for a dispensation to allow Maximilian communion in both kinds, which was granted with considerable misgivings and some ill will.

Maximilian's pragmatic embrace of Catholicism was enough to secure him the succession. The Archbishop of Mainz suspected him of dissimulation; the Elector of the Palatinate opposed him in the hope that a vacancy on the imperial throne really might lead to the election of a Protestant. The majority of the Electors, however, remained loyal to Ferdinand and the principles of the peace of 1555. The Protestant Electors—Saxony, Brandenburg, and the Palatinate—tried to insist on the insertion in the electoral capitulation of a formal protest against

[1] Louthan, *Quest*, 2, 3, 41, 85–7; Rudersdorf, 'Maximilian II.', 81–4; Mout, 'Späthumanismus', 46–58.
[2] Rudersdorf, 'Maximilian II.', 84.
[3] Fichtner, *Maximilian II*, 44.

the oath of loyalty due by an elected King of the Romans to the pope and the Catholic Church. In the event, they were persuaded to acquiesce in the traditional formula, but they withdrew to the sacristy during that part of the coronation in Frankfurt, while, aptly, the papal representatives were too far away to hear what was sworn.

The abandonment of Aachen as the place of coronation was perhaps more significant. The death of the Archbishop of Cologne, to whose province the Imperial City of Aachen belonged, and who consequently would normally undertake the act of coronation, provided a fortuitous excuse to drop this medieval tradition. The new archbishop, Friedrich von Wied (r. 1562–7), participated in the election before he had been consecrated. That allowed Archchancellor Daniel Brendel von Homburg, Archbishop of Mainz to claim his right to officiate in the absence of a formally installed Archbishop of Cologne and to prevail in his suggestion that, without prejudice to future arrangements, the coronation should be undertaken immediately.[4] The high cost of proceeding to Aachen was cited as a reason, yet Aachen's staunch Catholicism and its location on the periphery of the Reich was just as significant. Frankfurt was central yet close to the Archchancellor's own territories. Furthermore, it was in a sense a city that embodied the spirit of 1555: a city with a Protestant majority, a Catholic minority, and monasteries and religious foundations, where the status quo was guaranteed by the religious peace that the Electors wished to preserve above all else.[5]

A few weeks before the German coronation in 1562, Maximilian had been crowned in Prague. A year later, he received the Hungarian crown. By then, following private assurances in writing concerning Maximilian's religious beliefs, the pope too had confirmed and approved the German election.[6]

Whatever doubts had been expressed about him in Germany, Maximilian as emperor after 1564 proved himself as loyal to the settlement of 1555 as his father. He, too, steadfastly pursued the ideal of a lasting reconciliation in the Reich and he remained a humanistically inclined admirer of Melanchthon to the last, refusing to take the sacraments on his deathbed.[7] His criticism of the papacy made him congenial to most of the German Estates, except perhaps the ecclesiastical princes. Protestants were encouraged by his rumoured sympathy for the evangelical cause, while many Catholics were willing to accept his protestations of loyalty to the old faith. Even his attitude to his Spanish relatives was modified by the prospect over many years, from the death of Don Carlos in 1568 until the birth of the future Philip III in 1578, of one of his sons succeeding Philip II in Spain.[8] Despite his frequently bitter differences with Philip II, especially over the Netherlands and Italy, Maximilian sent both of his eldest sons, Rudolf and Ernst, to be educated in Madrid between 1563 and 1571.

Yet the essential continuity with the previous reign belied a fundamental structural shift. A tripartite division of the Habsburg lands in Ferdinand I's will

---

[4] Conrad, *Rechtsgeschichte*, i, 311.   [5] Rudersdorf, 'Maximilian II.', 87.
[6] Fichtner, *Maximilian II*, 48.   [7] Fichtner, *Maximilian II*, 48–9.
[8] Lanzinner, 'Zeitalter', 52–3.

left Maximilian with Bohemia, Hungary, and Upper and Lower Austria. His brother Ferdinand inherited the Tyrol and the Vorlande (Vorarlberg and the scatter of Habsburg lands across to Alsace), while Karl received Inner Austria (Styria, Carinthia, and Carniola). Upper and Lower Austria were less populous than the territories of Inner Austria, but prosperous and significant nonetheless for their towns and powerful nobles, and they gave Maximilian control over the court centres of Linz and Vienna, respectively. In addition, of course, Maximilian had Bohemia, with its exceptional wealth and prosperity and roughly four million inhabitants, and Hungary, which lay outside the Reich. However, the new courts at Innsbruck (under Archduke Ferdinand II) and Graz (under Archduke Karl II) soon became centres of Catholic renewal, starting movements that contradicted Maximilian's own laxness and that ultimately contributed to the great confessional crisis that racked the Habsburg lands from the 1590s.

More significant in the short term, however, was the way the very existence of these new courts and administrations skewed Maximilian's imperial policy. Vienna suddenly seemed relatively isolated from the Reich and exposed to the Turkish threat. The new court at Innsbruck effectively blocked the traditional avenues of influence in the Reich via southern Germany and Swabia. These networks were now exploited by the Tyrolean line as it sought to consolidate its hold on its new domains and assumed the traditional Habsburg role of competitor with Bavaria for regional dominance.[9] Equally, the new court at Graz left Vienna cut off from the south. That reinforced the axis between Vienna and Prague that had been latent since the acquisition of the Bohemian crown in 1526, but which now formed the real basis of imperial government. Indeed, now, for the first time since the early fifteenth century, Prague, rather than Vienna, became the emperor's real point of access to the Reich.[10]

Seen in this context, the rule of Rudolf II represented a variation on the pattern set by Ferdinand I and Maximilian II, and, though not initially, a fundamental change. His education in Spain between 1563 and 1571 left him with a more positive attitude to the Spanish Habsburgs and to Catholicism in general than his father.[11] Yet on his return, he was successively elected King of Hungary in 1572, King of Bohemia, and then King of the Romans in 1575. His succession to the imperial crown in 1576 at the age of twenty-four was as smooth as that of Maximilian II. Indeed, his policies in the Reich were also little different from those of his predecessors. His formal move of the seat of government to Prague in the first years of his reign, made permanent in 1583, and sometimes seen as the first stage of a withdrawal from the world, simply played out the territorial logic implicit in Ferdinand's division of the Erblande in 1564.[12]

Rudolf II's religious beliefs undoubtedly differed significantly from those of his two predecessors. Ferdinand I and especially Maximilian II were both imbued with

[9] Press, 'Vorderösterreich', 24–6; Quarthal, 'Vorderösterreich', 41–2.
[10] Rudersdorf, 'Maximilian II.', 88–9.
[11] Evans, *Rudolf II*, 49.
[12] Evans, *Rudolf II*, 22–3.

the idea of an Erasmian compromise. However unrealistic it might seem in retrospect, they did genuinely believe that some kind of reform of the Church in the Reich could satisfy both sides and that even Rome might be brought to acquiesce in this. If both Ferdinand and Maximilian were in that sense German Christians, Rudolf was more of a Catholic.[13] That did not necessarily mean loyalty to the papacy or even to the rituals of the Church of Rome. His attitude to the papacy, as opposed to Catholicism, was hostile at the best of times and, by and large, he was downright anti-clerical in his general approach to the ecclesiastical hierarchy. His attendance at services became infrequent and after 1600 he seems not to have taken the sacraments at all. His religiosity developed in different directions under the influence of the religious diversity that prevailed in Bohemia, and he surrounded himself at his court in Prague with an eclectic mix of southern (mainly Italian) humanists, Catholic sectarians, and Western European (mainly Protestant) refugees. In general, he eschewed the dogmatic confines of both Catholicism and Protestantism, and remained committed to the idea of a universal mission, to the promotion of a kind of 'third way' that would transcend the contemporary conflict and reunite Christendom.

This makes it difficult to see Rudolf's succession in the Reich as the start of an imperial Counter-Reformation. Papal nuncios repeatedly lamented the emperor's failure to promote the Catholic cause, which they would typically interpret as the failure of imperial government and a symptom of the disintegration of the Reich.[14] Rudolf did not share the Counter-Reformation zeal of his uncles at Innsbruck and Graz. In his own lands of Upper and Lower Austria it was his brother Ernst, as governor, who sanctioned government sponsorship of the work of re-establishing Catholicism begun quite independently in 1580 by Melchior Khlesl (1552–1630) as vicar general of the Bishop of Passau (officially, vicar general of Lower Austria after 1581).[15] In Bohemia, the papal nuncios carried out their own programme of Tridentine Catholic renewal, and they were often frustrated by the emperor's obvious reluctance to take firm steps against non-Catholic individuals and groups.

Essentially, until after 1600 at least, Rudolf's policies in the Reich remained the same as those pursued by Maximilian II. Indeed, even after that he continued to employ Protestants such as the young Christian of Anhalt or Count Simon VI of Lippe as court officials and to rely on Protestants such as Zacharias Geizkofler (1560–1617) for advice on key issues.[16] Rudolf II was criticized for indecision, but that too was no more than prudent policy, for successful imperial policy after Charles V consisted precisely in not being decisive or impulsive. However, even that became difficult to sustain successfully when both the confessional tensions in the Reich and the international situation became more volatile from the late 1580s. And ultimately Rudolf's stance suffered the same fundamental limitation as that of Ferdinand and Maximilian. The pursuit of a truly *politique* line would have

---

[13] Evans, *Rudolf II*, 84–115. See also Mout, 'Späthumanismus', 58–64.
[14] Evans, *Rudolf II*, 85–6; Koller, 'Kaiserhof'.
[15] Schindling and Ziegler, *Territorien*, i, 127–9.
[16] Schmidt, *Grafenverein*, 376.

required the abandonment of the religious nature of the crown, a step that no Habsburg was willing to take.

The views of the emperors were reflected in and reinforced by other continuities. The imperial court, first at Vienna and then at Prague, was dominated by figures who in one way or another espoused conciliatory religious views. Lazarus von Schwendi, for example, was a Lutheran from Württemberg who had served with Charles V during the Schmalkaldic War and remained a staunch proponent of the Spanish imperial policy until 1552.[17] Then he converted to Catholicism and continued to serve Charles and Philip II until 1561, when he came increasingly to believe in the necessity of compromise as the foundation for Habsburg rule in both the Netherlands and Germany. Above all, and as a corollary of this, he also believed that Charles had failed to understand the strength of German patriotism, which was strong on both sides of the confessional divide. At the court of the Austrian Habsburgs until his death in 1584, Schwendi became a tireless advocate of what he termed the 'middle way'. In particular, in essays sent to Maximilian in 1574 and 1576, written in the aftermath of the St Bartholomew's Day Massacre, he argued forcefully for religious toleration and for the duty of civil authority to ensure peace and harmony.

In matters concerning architecture, building, and art, the Mantuan nobleman Jacopo Strada (1507–1588) was the key figure from 1556.[18] The Breslau physician and disciple of Melanchthon, Johannes Crato (1519–1585), also served all three post-1555 emperors and mitigated the influence of the Catholic court preachers. His was a constant voice for the spirit of moderation and he was a steady advocate for the Protestant Estates of the Reich. Perhaps even more surprising was the career of the Calvinist Dutchman Hugo Blotius (1533–1608), whose reform of the imperial library after 1575 carried out an irenic agenda that infuriated the Jesuits. The survival at the Habsburg court of a Calvinist, and one with links to the Dutch spiritualist sect the Family of Love and to Justus Lipsius and the other advocates of stoicism and dissimulation, bears strong testimony to the extraordinary character of the court in these decades.[19]

Dissimulation could, of course, simply mean the concealment of religious views. The debate that has surrounded the religion of Ferdinand I, Maximilian II, and Rudolf II perhaps reflects the degree to which they all shared the confessional ambivalence of their leading courtiers and consciously internalized their personal religious beliefs. On the other hand, the religious culture of the court translated into a political line in the Reich that was ideally suited to the maintenance of the settlement of 1555. Two further groups aided the pursuit of that end.

The office of Imperial Vice-Chancellor, created in 1559 with the formal establishment of the Imperial Chancellery, was a vital link between the emperor and the Estates.[20] The first incumbents, Georg Sigismund Seld (until 1565), Johann Ulrich

[17] Louthan, *Quest*, 23, 112–20. See also pp. 361–2.
[18] For the following, see Louthan, *Quest*, 24–105.
[19] Lipsius, of course, later became a loyal 'Spanish' Catholic.
[20] Gross, *Reichshofkanzlei*, 5–22, 97–9, 307–21.

Zasius (until 1570), Johannes Weber (until 1576), and Sigmund Vieheuser (until 1587), were all hugely experienced officials and, above all, firm believers in the status quo. Seld and Zasius, for example, were both loyal Catholics, but deeply critical of the papacy.[21] Seld fully reflected the views of Ferdinand and his circle when he insisted on the continuing validity of the decrees of the councils of Constance and Basle that gave precedence to the council (i.e. the German bishops) over the popes. Zasius bluntly dismissed Paul IV as 'old, wrong-headed, and silly'.[22] The effective management of the Imperial Chancellery by these figures ensured the dissemination of the culture of compromise among both imperial officials and the territorial princes and councillors with whom they dealt.

The latter were themselves another vital component in the constellation of 1555. An extensive network of princes sustained the peace settlement as the opposition to Charles V's 'Spanish' monarchy coalesced into a powerful coalition for peace in the Reich. For a short while, the Heidelberg League, formed in 1553 by the Palatinate, Mainz, Trier, Württemberg, Bavaria, and Jülich-Kleve-Berg, continued to provide a framework of communication.[23] Ferdinand himself joined this league, yet the attempt to establish it as a new imperial league, a replacement for the Swabian League that had foundered in the 1530s, failed. It was at root a league of the Estates whose sole aim had been the frustration of Charles V's plans for the succession of Philip II in the Reich. As such, it could not easily be transformed into an instrument of imperial government. After 1555, most of the league's members supported the new regime, but the Palatinate's development of a more activist political agenda contributed to the loss of its *raison d'être*, and in September 1556 it lapsed.[24]

Meanwhile, Ferdinand had been instrumental in forging the Landsberg League with Bavaria and Salzburg in June 1556, which he intended to be broadened into a supra-confessional league dedicated to the maintenance of peace and stability in Middle and southern Germany.[25] Bamberg, Würzburg, and Protestant Nuremberg also joined soon after. Württemberg and the Palatinate declined to follow suit, however, fearing that membership of such a league might inhibit the completion of the reformation of their lands. Though they shared similar attitudes to the Landsberg League, these two territories soon embarked on radically different paths.

The Palatinate's late Lutheran Reformation under Friedrich II (r. 1544–56) and Ottheinrich (r. 1556–59) was overtaken by the turn to Calvinism under Friedrich III (r. 1559–76), which had radical implications for the politics of the Palatinate in the Reich generally. Württemberg, by contrast, continued as a valuable ally of the crown. Indeed, Duke Christoph (r. 1550–68) soon became one of the most implacable opponents of the Palatine line. The desire to secure imperial sanction for the territorial reformation process, or at least protection from any eventual

---

[21] Ritter, *Geschichte*, i, 144–6.
[22] Ritter, *Geschichte*, i, 144.
[23] Rabe, *Geschichte*, 442–3. See p. 332.
[24] On Palatine policy, see Clasen, *Palatinate*, 1–19; Wolgast, 'Reichs- und Außenpolitik'.
[25] Endres, 'Bund'; Göttmann, 'Entstehung'; Lanzinner, 'Bund'.

intervention of the imperial courts, was a major consideration. The same was true of the perceived threat posed to Lutheran Church structures in Württemberg by events in the Palatinate, whose development after 1559 combined both mainstream Calvinism and the remaining currents of Upper German Zwinglianism. Equally, however, the Duke could not afford to take such an independent stance as the Elector Palatine. He counted as a prince of the Reich, yet Württemberg was still a fiefdom of the Habsburgs, rather than of the emperor. This anomaly, the condition on which the duchy had been restored to Duke Ulrich in 1534, ensured continuing Württemberg loyalism motivated at least partly by the hope that it might bring the reward of the full restoration of the dukes' original status as immediate imperial vassals.[26]

Even so, the Landsberg League did not simply become a Catholic league. Protestant Nuremberg remained as a member and neither Ferdinand nor any of the other members seems to have wished to lose the supra-confessional character of the association. Bavaria, it is true, attempted to exploit the League to advance its own ambitions. In the hope of securing the northern Rhineland and Westphalian bishoprics for the Wittelsbach younger sons, Duke Albrecht V proposed enlisting the Duke of Alba as a member in 1569–70. Simultaneously, he also attempted to recruit the Elector of Saxony and other Protestants in order to forestall a Protestant backlash, especially in the Palatinate. In the event, however, neither the Protestant princes nor the Catholics already in the League wished to become associated with Spanish policy.

The renewal of a more traditional network in the north of the Reich was equally significant. The key here was Electoral Saxony and the Albertine line that had acquired the Electorate from the disgraced Ernestines in 1547 and that now sought to consolidate its hold on the title.[27] In 1553, the Elector Moritz had persuaded Duke Johann Friedrich the Good to join with him in renewing the traditional mutual inheritance pact (*Erbverbrüderung*) between Brandenburg, Hessen, and the Ernestine and Albertine Saxon dynasties. This was then again renewed by his successor, Elector August I, at a meeting at Naumburg in March 1555, where an understanding on the aims to be pursued in a religious–political settlement was added to the traditional mutual undertakings on regional security.[28] Moreover, fearing a rapprochement between the Ernestine duke and Ferdinand I, August took the further significant step in 1557 of renewing the hereditary union between Saxony and the Bohemian crown. At the same time, August was also anxious to secure imperial goodwill in the face of his ambitions to complete the secularization and integration of the bishoprics of Meissen, Merseburg, and Naumburg. The alliance between Albertine Electoral Saxony and the crown remained solid until August's death in 1586. His leadership of the Protestant Estates generally was one of the most effective stabilizing forces in the Reich after 1555.

---

[26] Press, 'Epochenjahr' and Press, 'Herzog Christoph'.
[27] Schindling and Ziegler, *Territorien*, ii, 19–24 and iv, 19–22.
[28] Rabe, *Geschichte*, 448.

The existence of two parallel networks did not, of course, include all the princes who supported the new imperial regime. On the Lower Rhine, Ferdinand's son-in-law, Duke Wilhelm V of Jülich-Kleve-Berg, continued to pursue an irenic course in his own lands and actively supported both Ferdinand and Maximilian.[29] That only changed after 1567 with the onset of the duke's protracted mental illness and the growing threat to the stability of the duchy from the conflict in the neighbouring Netherlands. Soon, effective government became impossible; the spread of the Reformation slackened; Catholic councillors became more influential, and the forces of the Counter-Reformation gradually gained ground. Consequently, Jülich-Kleve-Berg ceased to play an active role in the politics of the Reich.

Other territories, not afflicted by dynastic problems and not threatened by the fallout from neighbouring conflicts, were able to steer a steady loyalist course. Thus, Holstein, Mecklenburg, and Pomerania all supported the settlement of 1555. In each case, of course, as in Electoral Saxony, loyalty to the crown conveniently dovetailed with the ambition of taking over a neighbouring bishopric. The situation regarding the house of Brunswick was more complex, with four main lines, two Protestant and two Catholic. Each laboured under insecurities that translated into a loyalist stance of greater or lesser enthusiasm. Only after 1568 did the first Protestant dukes of Brunswick-Wolfenbüttel, Julius (r. 1568–89) and Henry Julius (r. 1589–1613) become truly enthusiastic supporters of an imperial *via media*.[30]

The renewal of the association of Electors (Kurverein) in 1558 was the last, and the most enduring, of a series of partial and general associations of the Electors since the fourteenth century.[31] Like its predecessors, this one was formed during the preliminary negotiations over an imperial election and its aim was to maintain the 'pre-eminence' of the Electors in the Reich. In particular, the Electors reaffirmed the validity of the Golden Bull and of the religious peace, and resolved to act together if any one of them should be attacked or if unrest should break out in the Reich. They thereby once more openly staked their claim to active participation in the government of the Reich, a claim which Ferdinand I promptly recognized. The fact that the six non-Habsburg Electors (the Bohemian Electorate was only activated by the Habsburgs in imperial elections) were also evenly balanced between Catholic (Mainz, Trier, Cologne) and Protestant (Saxony, Brandenburg, the Palatinate) after 1555 also—quite coincidentally—seemed to reinforce their claims to represent the Reich as a whole. Despite the strains that soon arose when the Palatinate embraced the Reformed faith, the association of Electors formed yet another, highly influential, regional network which enhanced the stability of the Reich after 1555.

Another kind of association should also be mentioned in this context: a series of corporative associations of nobles and Imperial Cities that were either renewed or first formed after 1555. These reinforced existing regional networks or created new

---

[29] Schindling and Ziegler, *Territorien*, iii, 93–101.
[30] Evans, *Rudolf II*, 7; Schindling and Ziegler, *Territorien*, iii, 18–36.
[31] The immediate precursors were the 1519 association of Rhineland Electors (Palatinate, Trier, Mainz, and Cologne) and the general association of 1521. The articles of association of 1558 remained in effect until 1806. Gotthard, *Säulen*, i, 37–49.

ones and fulfilled a direct constitutional function, either by virtue of representation in the Reichstag or by virtue of some particular link with the crown. For the lesser Estates, such associations continued to be an important means of defending their rights, and their very survival, against the princes of larger territories.

The Imperial Cities, whose solidarity had been sorely tested by the religious division, emerged after 1555 with a less secure position in the Reich generally, but with a fully functioning system of communication.[32] Their association continued to meet biennially to deliberate on political and other issues, and they successfully avoided debating religious issues until the 1580s. They did not, however, regain serious political influence. The Cities' College at the Reichstag only achieved equal status in the legislative process with the Colleges of Electors and Princes in 1582 (the *votum decisivum* as opposed to the lesser *votum consultativum* they had enjoyed since 1548). The voice of the Cities was, moreover, somewhat diminished by the fact that they only had two collective votes (the Swabian bench and the Rhineland bench) and, in practice, the Colleges of Electors and Princes continued to dominate proceedings. However, both Nuremberg and Cologne became permanent members of the Reichsdeputation after 1555.[33] Attempts by the Hanseatic League to affiliate with the Imperial Cities failed and this regional association of sixty-three cities and towns atrophied as many of its smaller members fell victim to territorial expansionism. By 1614, only fourteen members remained, of which Hamburg, Lübeck, and Bremen alone ultimately retained their independence.[34]

By contrast, the associations of Imperial Counts which gradually evolved during the first half of the sixteenth century, assumed a more formal and purposeful character after 1555.[35] Comprising 143 families in 1521, this group of nobles formed a series of corporations. The Swabian and Wetterau counts each had a collective vote (*Kuriatstimme*) in the College of Princes at the Reichstag. In 1555, a representative of each was designated a permanent member of the Reichsdeputation. Until then, counts from Franconia or the Lower Rhine and Westphalia, who only gained a Reichstag vote in 1640–1 and 1653–4 respectively, were affiliated to the Swabian and Wetterau associations. Political representation by means of a collective vote did not give any of them much influence. On the other hand, it reinforced their unions, since the need to give their representative clear instructions required greater communication and internal coordination. The Swabian counts pursued a traditional policy of loyalty to the crown. The Wetterau counts aspired to a degree of independence. After 1555, their involvement with William of Orange reinforced this, as did the fact that many chose to turn from Lutheranism to the Reformed faith. That placed them in political difficulties, which made it seem imperative to appoint a directorate in 1566 and to form a common administration for 'external' affairs. By pooling their activities they were able to pursue their

---

[32] Schmidt, 'Politische Bedeutung', 191–4; Neuhaus, *Reich*, 34–6; Lanzinner, 'Zeitalter', 140.
[33] See pp. 359–60.
[34] Lanzinner, 'Zeitalter', 140–1; Schmidt, 'Städtetag, Städtehanse', 47–9.
[35] Neuhaus, *Reich*, 32–3; Schmidt, 'Politische Bedeutung', 199–202.

collective interests in the Reich more effectively and to defend individuals who came under threat from powerful neighbours.[36]

A similar development took place among the Imperial Knights.[37] They were never represented in the Reichstag and, in part, their associations developed as a result of the need to pay imperial taxes, especially the Turkish taxes, on their own account rather than have a levy imposed upon them by neighbouring princes, which would have undermined their independent status. By about 1550, the three hundred and fifty or so families were organized in fifteen local associations (Ritterorte, later Ritterkantone).[38] These, in turn, formed three regional associations in Franconia, Swabia, and the Rhineland, which from 1575 met in regular general assemblies (Generalkorrespondenztage). In 1577, they formally agreed on articles of association as the *Corpus liberae et immediatae imperii nobilitatis*, though a plan to maintain a permanent executive (*Generaldirektorium*) came to nothing.[39] Apart from organizing the payment of taxes (known as the *subsidium charitativum*, which underlined the voluntary, ad hoc, and non-permanent nature of the grants), the main aim of these organizations was to secure crown protection for the knights. Once this had been achieved beyond all doubt in privileges of 1559, 1561, and 1566, the organizational incentive atrophied. However, although incomplete, the networks remained active, promoting collective interests and a degree of uniformity of approach to the business of managing territories. The knights' links with the crown were further reinforced by the recruitment from among their ranks of civil and military imperial dignitaries and by their vested interest in the German Church and its many benefices.

It is not surprising that the prelates, abbots and abbesses, and other ecclesiastical dignitaries below the rank of bishop who held lands directly from the crown, many of them drawn from families of Imperial Counts and Knights, were loyal to it.[40] The tax register of 1521 lists eighty-three such dignitaries, mostly in Swabia and the Rhineland. The Swabian prelates had occupied a separate bench in the Swabian League, and after its demise in 1534, it was natural that they should seek to represent their interests in an equivalent manner. By 1575, they had developed a formal Swabian Imperial Prelates' College (Schwäbisches Reichsprälatenkollegium) with an elected director who exercised the prelates' collective vote at the Reichstag. The other prelates, most of them from the Rhineland, developed a similar organization and also held a collective vote in the Reichstag, though their association was less cohesive since it simply included all prelates outside Swabia.

The Abbot of Weingarten represented all the prelates in the Reichsdeputation after 1555.[41] Like the other groups of nobles, the prelates paid taxes, but the Swabian group also provided substantial financial support for the crown, including

---

[36] Schmidt, *Grafenverein*, 193–5. See also p. 80.
[37] See pp. 42–3, 210–19; Neuhaus, *Reich*, 36–7; Schmidt, 'Politische Bedeutung', 196–7; Lanzinner, 'Zeitalter', 78–9; Conrad, *Rechtsgeschichte*, ii, 202–4.
[38] The terminology was Swiss.
[39] The Lower Alsace *Ritterort* remained independent of the regional structure.
[40] Neuhaus, *Reich*, 30–1; Schmidt, 'Politische Bedeutung', 198–9.
[41] See pp. 359–60.

vast loans, credit guarantees, and lay benefices for many members of the imperial court. Indeed, the institution of lay benefices was actually invented by Charles V, whose administration imposed them upon the prelates.[42] The regional association of the Swabian prelates was also enhanced by its close collaboration with the Habsburg territories of Further Austria (the Vorlande or Vorderösterreich), which in fact led many of them to become Habsburg fiefs by the eighteenth century.[43]

The profusion of regional associations and leagues appears chaotic and haphazard. Yet it allows some general conclusions. First, it demonstrates both the continuing underlying unity of the German nobility and the Imperial Cities, and the many ways in which they were bound to the crown and to the Reich. The religious divide had clearly disrupted some traditional patterns of solidarity. By the second half of the century confessional differences had begun to make a significant impact on the marriage patterns of the upper nobility, for example, with two increasingly distinct intermarriage networks emerging in place of one. Yet while fundamental issues relating to their status and constitutional position in the Reich remained unresolved, the nobility remained united and characterized by fundamental loyalty to the crown.

Second, the various unions underline the strength of support for compromise, for the political settlement of the religious issue in the Reich. That could be linked with a particular territorial aspiration, such as the completion of a Reformation or the integration and ultimate secularization of a bishopric. Or it might be linked with the aspiration to promote junior family members into an ecclesiastical benefice or even one of the highest ecclesiastical offices, or to safeguard the immediate status of a city or a territory. Yet even if idealism and genuine belief in the system are set at an absolute minimum, the point remains that the overwhelming majority of the German Estates perceived the Reich to be of value and use.

Elector Johann Georg of Brandenburg said on his accession in 1571 that it would be better to 'support the old fragile structure of the Reich than to demolish it'.[44] At a time when other European states were being torn apart by religious conflict, even that minimal expression of support for the status quo in the Reich was a significant source of strength for the German polity.

---

[42] Dickel, *Reservatrecht*, 135–50.
[43] Schmidt, 'Politische Bedeutung', 198–9.
[44] Zeeden, 'Zeitalter', 141–2.

29

Constitutional Developments after 1555: Reichstag, Kreise, Courts, and Legislation

The settlement of 1555 also had major implications for the constitution of the Reich. Some developments reinforced the integrative effects of the leagues and associations just outlined. They also reflected the interests of the Estates in stabilizing the Reich's institutional structure, formalizing many of the arrangements often initiated ad hoc in the period before 1555. The decades after 1555 saw a new intensity of communication between the Estates and a number of key organizational initiatives. To some extent, also, developments after 1555 reflected the fact that the crown no longer saw the German Reich as one, albeit major, part of an international conglomerate of sovereignties, as Charles V had done. Ferdinand I and his successors had a new interest in the management of the German Reich for its own sake. The nature of these various initiatives and their limitations in practice provide key insights into the further consolidation of the German constitution in this period.

The Peace of Augsburg reinforced the status of the Reichstag as the key representative and decision-making body. In contrast to the intermittent pattern of meetings that characterized the reign of Charles V, Ferdinand I and his successors presided over regular meetings, with eleven sessions between 1556 and 1608. The procedures that had evolved before 1555 were now increasingly regarded as set in stone.[1] The only additional feature after 1555 was that the Reichstag always sat in three Colleges or *curia* (Electors, Princes, Imperial Cities), which deliberated and reported their opinions separately. These were then harmonized, if possible, for publication as law during the recess (*Reichsabschied*) which concluded the proceedings.

The main purpose of the sessions in the second half of the century was to generate taxes for the defence effort against the Turks. After 1576, the taxation issue fully dominated the proceedings. Initially, the Estates agreed to provide money largely to build defences; between 1593 and 1606 they financed a major war effort. The apparent willingness with which these taxes were granted was quite remarkable. Under Charles V the total raised, often with considerable difficulty and at the cost of significant political concessions, had been roughly 73.5 Roman Months.[2] Between 1556 and 1603 the Reichstag granted no less than 409

---

[1] Neuhaus, *Repräsentationsformen*, 424–5; Lanzinner, 'Zeitalter', 69.

[2] A Roman Month was the unit of account used to calculate the contribution of the Estates of the Reich to military expenditure—originally, and literally, it represented the monthly wage bill for the troops who formerly accompanied the emperor to Rome for his coronation by the pope.

Roman Months with a value of 30 million gulden, as well as a special grant in 1592 and a series of grants from the Kreise in the 1590s.[3] Furthermore, in contrast to the rather haphazard collection practices of the period before 1555, which saw some taxes granted but never actually collected, as much as 88 per cent of the money levied between 1576 and 1608 actually reached the imperial coffers.[4]

It would be wrong to suggest that this reflects a story of complete domestic harmony. The Reichstag sessions of this period were characterized by lively and frequently bitter disputes over imperial reform, general legislation, and, above all, the religious issue. As usual, many debates remained inconclusive, and the resulting decisions and legislation were ineffective. Increasingly also, the sessions were marked by the presentation and discussion of elaborate lists of complaints (*Gravamina*) by both Protestants and Catholics. The imperial tax demands themselves were far from uncontroversial. The generally high levels of yield mask the fact that the Electors and princes were the least conscientious contributors.

Confessional differences were not crucial at first. In 1594, the protest by seven Protestant Estates against a majority vote on the Turkish tax made little impact. Since the case involved only minor Estates (notably Duke Johann of Zweibrücken, who really could not afford to pay), Rudolf II simply referred the matter to the imperial prosecutor at the Reichskammergericht. It was only the Catholic Archbishop of Salzburg's complaint about the level of the proposed tax in 1598 that ignited a protracted debate about procedures that touched on key political issues.[5] He could not bring himself to pay such a tax, he complained, because a simple numerical majority could not be binding. The issue had recurred frequently since the late fifteenth century. It had been at the heart of the 'Protestation' of Speyer in 1529 and of many subsequent issues where a minority wished to resist the majority. Now it became the focus of a fundamental debate about the nature of the Reich and its legislative procedures.

The archbishop's protest was soon echoed by a group of Protestants who took issue with a decision reached by a Catholic majority in the Reichstag. They insisted they could only be bound by a majority decision in cases where the very existence of the Reich was at stake. The emperor and Catholic majority argued that the Roman law principle of 'quod omnes tangit, ab omnibus debet approbari' (what affects all must be agreed by all) had been superseded by the custom of the Reich. Underlying the debate was the sense of some Protestants that circumstances had conspired to deny their right to assent and to threaten a fundamental transformation of the polity. A Catholic majority in the Reichstag and the imperative of the Turkish threat, which objectively they had no wish to deny, seemed to tip the balance of power and the exercise of ultimate authority in favour of the emperor.[6]

---

[3] Schulze, *Türkengefahr*, 79.
[4] Schulze, *Türkengefahr*, 362–3. See also pp. 409–11.
[5] Schulze, *Türkengefahr*, 165–6. On the patriotic significance of the Turkish threat, see Schmidt, *Vaterlandsliebe*, 240–89.
[6] Schulze, *Türkengefahr*, 176.

The debate assumed a more ominous significance following the conclusion of peace with the Porte in 1606, after which the Protestants were no longer constrained by their support for the Reich against the Turks. It then contributed to the paralysis of the Reichstag in 1608 and 1613 and a solution was only found in the Peace of Westphalia, with the formal elaboration of the principles of parity and amicable settlement.[7] Yet the eruption of this problem around 1600 should not detract from the fact that the Reichstag had continued to function until then.

The fate of a rival representative body in the middle years of the century demonstrates both the advantages and limitations of the Reichstag as an institution of government. One of the most important features of the settlement of 1555 was the formal establishment of the Kreise as regional agencies with quasi-governmental functions in peacekeeping and the implementation of imperial legislation.[8] Gatherings of representatives of Kreise to coordinate peacekeeping initiatives had been held at various points since about 1530.[9] In the late 1540s, Charles V had shown an interest in the potential of such gatherings because they seemed to be more effective and, above all, more amenable than the Reichstag. The fact that they tended to sit as a single forum rather than in colleges or *Curia* precluded the possibility of particular groups, especially (and normally) the Electors and the more powerful princes, frustrating action on the grounds of their own sectional interests.

The failure of Charles's plans for an imperial league put paid to such speculations. But the Kreise retained the idea of collaborative action and their sense of themselves collectively as an alternative to the Reichstag, at least as an emergency government. This became apparent when Charles's manipulation of the Reichstag in 1548 temporarily discredited it and then the Princes' Revolt and the conundrum of the succession led the emperor to delay reconvening it. Meanwhile, however, the German Estates were faced with the continuing military threat from the Margrave Albrecht Alcibiades, and potentially from France as well. Pending a new Reichstag, a general assembly of the Kreise was convened at Frankfurt in 1554 to deliberate the restoration of law and order in the Reich.

Pre-empted in his preparation for a Reichstag, for which Charles had at last given him authority, Ferdinand was further surprised by what transpired. The Kreise wanted to improve their own military organizations and strengthen the central authorities of the Reich. The Electors rightly saw any proposal to create more effective regional and central structures as a threat to their own rights and freedom of action. Indeed, they perceived the very mode of procedure at the 'general assembly of the Kreise' as prejudicial to their prerogatives and constitutional role. At the Reichstag, they constituted their own college, and nothing could be decided without their consent. In a Kreistag, they were submerged within their respective Kreise, alongside representatives of the other much lesser Estates of a Kreis. Consequently, at their insistence, the Kreistag's law and order proposals were referred to the Reichstag at Augsburg in 1555, where they were renegotiated and any suggestion of an enhanced royal executive competence was removed.

---

[7] See pp. 625–6, 632–44.   [8] Hartmann, 'Reichstag'.   [9] Dotzauer, *Reichskreise*, 54–9.

The only other general meeting of representatives of the Kreise was prompted by the aftermath of the disorder generated in 1567 by the renegade Wilhelm von Grumbach, who, for the past decade, had posed as much of a threat to law and order as Margrave Albrecht Alcibiades had done.[10] This time, however, the initiative came from the Reichstag at Regensburg in the spring of 1567. Grumbach was in fact captured by the Elector of Saxony and executed in Gotha on 18 April; the only outstanding issue was the assessment and apportionment of the cost of the operation. Extracting money was never easy, but levying contributions retrospectively was particularly problematic, even though some feared that Grumbach's associates might still pursue his feuds. The Reichstag thus decided that the time-consuming business of agreeing the amounts of money that should be paid by the various Estates should be delegated to a meeting of the Kreise in Erfurt. In the event, arguments over the status of the meeting in relation to the Reichstag and the mode of procedure meant that the financial issue was left unresolved (though much discussed by other committees in the meantime) until the Speyer Reichstag of 1570.

The Erfurt Kreistag demonstrated the inherent weaknesses of the Kreistag as an institution. Few delegates exercised discipline in representing their Kreis rather than just their own territory, which prompted many of those who were not present to complain that their interests had been neglected. Particularly revealing at Erfurt also was the protracted wrangle over the order of precedence to be observed among the representatives of the Kreise. The Electors insisted that Kreise in which their territories lay (especially the Electoral Rhine Kreis with the four Electorates of Mainz, Trier, Cologne, and the Palatinate) should have precedence over the others, including the Austrian Kreis formed by the Habsburg Erblande. Essentially, this once again articulated the Electors' profound antipathy to such meetings generally. The very notion of representatives of the Estates meeting on equal terms as representatives of regions was incompatible with their constitutional 'pre-eminence'. At the same time, the Electors' arguments also underlined the ways in which such general assemblies of the Kreise marginalized the crown. Memories of these problems frustrated another, and final, attempt to organize such a meeting in the 1590s.[11]

The brief history of the general assembly of the Kreise places the Reichstag in perspective. Its main strength was that it provided an unrivalled forum for communication between the Estates (personal between princes, for example, and quasi-diplomatic via officials and agents) and for the representation of constitutional relations—between emperor and Estates, between Electors and princes and Imperial Cities, and so on. Its weakness, however, lay in the strength of the many vested interests that insisted on maintaining this order of precedence, which prevented it from ever evolving into a true parliament or a representative body in any modern sense. The Reichstag remained a gathering of individual Estates, or rather, by the second half of the sixteenth century, increasingly their officials or agents.

---

[10] Neuhaus, *Repräsentationsformen*, 373–422. On Grumbach, see pp. 390–4.
[11] Neuhaus, *Repräsentationsformen*, 493–517.

This had fundamental implications for what the Reichstag was able to achieve. The periodic arguments over majority voting were indicative. A decision of 1512 had decreed that what was decided by a majority at a Reichstag should be regarded as binding by those who had not attended the meeting. However, this was never accepted as a valid constitutional doctrine. On the contrary, even if it was rarely made explicit, the Reichstag generally proceeded according to, and worked best on, the older principle of 'Quod omnes tangit'. Consequently, it was capable of being effective at producing broad framework legislation such as the package of agreements reached in 1555.[12] These were so broad, and hence so vague or so lacking in detail, that all could accept them as compatible with their own specific interest. Such legislation was both protective of rights and prerogatives and broadly permissive in so far as policy within a territory was concerned. The Peace of Augsburg was thus a landmark, for it epitomized the most positive aspects of the Reichstag's legislative potential with its broad guarantee of the religious liberty of the Catholic and Lutheran Protestant Estates, and its recognition of the religious jurisdiction of those Estates with regard to their own territory.

Yet the more detailed work of specifying the application of legislation, adjudicating its applicability to specific areas or cases, and monitoring its operation, still needed to be done. Two kinds of committee undertook these tasks in the years after 1555. The first comprised specialist committees of the Kreise.[13] One series of meetings was convened to adjudicate on revisions of the levels of the monetary and military obligations of the Estates that were set out in the original assessment schedule (*Reichsmatrikel*) of 1521. So-called Moderationstage met until 1577, after which no further changes were made until the end of the Reich.[14] Other meetings (Reichsmünztage) were convened between 1549 and 1571 to prepare and work out the detailed implications of the Currency Ordinances of 1551 and 1559.[15] A third kind of meeting of Kreis representatives (Justiztage) was convened in 1557 and 1560 to determine rules of procedure for the Reichskammergericht, following the new Enforcement Ordinance of 1555, and to engage suitable staff for the court. Similar specialized regional committees continued to meet periodically until 1806, especially in the more active Rhineland and Upper German Kreise, where inter-Kreis meetings were not uncommon.[16]

A second type of general working committee was established by the Imperial Enforcement Ordinance (*Reichsexekutionsordnung*) of 1555. It specified that if in an emergency an association of five Kreise was unable to cope, the Elector of Mainz should summon a body (the Reichsdeputation) composed of sixteen members representing all the Kreise to meet at Frankfurt.[17] In 1559, the sixteen members

---

[12] Schmidt, 'Aushandeln'.

[13] Neuhaus, *Repräsentationsformen*, 317–422; Dotzauer, *Reichskreise*, 48–50.

[14] Numerous amendments were in fact made as territories changed in size following divided inheritance, ceased to exist following the extinction of a line, or (in the case of cities) loss of immediate status, or newly appeared following elevations to the princely estate.

[15] Dotzauer, *Reichskreise*, 441–9.

[16] Dotzauer, *Reichskreise*, 441–87, 585–616.

[17] Neuhaus, *Repräsentationsformen*, 423–92.

specified in the ordinance were confirmed as permanent members; four more were added in 1570. Under pressure from the Electors, it was also agreed in 1564 that the Reichsdeputation should be subject to the Reichstag except in the most acute emergency. Furthermore, the Electors were able to ensure that the work of the Reichsdeputation should be conducted in two colleges, one composed of the Electors and the other comprising the representatives of all the other Estates.

In fact, the Reichsdeputation was only convened three times (1564, 1569, and 1590) to deal with the kind of law and order crisis for which it was originally intended. Soon, however, it was employed to deal with currency and taxation issues, with the review of the Reichskammergericht, and with the Police Ordinance, for which purposes it was convened six times until 1600–1. The restraints imposed upon the Reichsdeputation ensured that it could never become an alternative to the Reichstag. Yet it acted as a valuable working adjunct to it, acceptable to the Electors by virtue of its clearly defined subordinate status and internal hierarchical structure. However, when the Reichstag later became deadlocked in the constitutional crisis after 1600, the Reichsdeputation became defunct. No meetings were convened after 1600–1, and the institution no longer had a role to play in the post-1648 polity, in which the Reichstag itself was in permanent session from 1663.

The Kreise did not form an alternative to the Reichstag, but they developed a vital subsidiary regional role after 1555. In addition to their peacekeeping duties, they were increasingly commissioned with exercising vital quasi-governmental functions at the regional level. Perhaps the most important structural point about what was specified in 1555 was that the rights of the individual Estates were guaranteed. Even if any members of a Kreis failed or refused to pay any eventual dues or levies, the authorities were not permitted to take action without a judgement by the Reichskammergericht.

Above all, the crown was not given any authority in the administration of the Kreise.[18] One of their prime functions was to implement decrees of the Reichstag or judgments of the Reichskammergericht, in both of which the crown played a role. The Kreise themselves, however, were self-governing and self-regulating institutions. Each had a pair of executive directors (*Kreisausschreibende Fürsten*, one a secular prince and one a bishop) and a military commander (*Kreishauptmann* or *Kreisoberst*, later *Kreis-Feldmarschall*). Each military commander was assisted or supported by six further princes (*zugeordnete Stände*), one of whom acted as deputy commander, all of whom met on a regular basis to deliberate on military and police matters (Zugeordnetentage or Deputationstage).[19] The internal affairs of each Kreis were regulated by an assembly of all its members (Kreistag), in which all had an equal vote regardless of territorial size or rank, though it was possible to have several votes if one held more than one qualifying territory.

Subsequent modifications of the system in 1564 and 1570 strengthened the potential for military collaboration between the Kreise and allowed the emperor some role in this. However, the self-governing character of the Kreise remained

---

[18] Dotzauer, *Reichskreise*, 58–60.   [19] Dotzauer, *Reichskreise*, 46.

sacrosanct. As usual, the translation of general principles into governing practice was a protracted matter. Repeated exhortations by the Reichstag indicate that even by the end of the century some Kreise had not yet implemented the provisions of the ordinance of 1555.[20] Others, however, such as the Bavarian Kreis, had a fully working system in place as early as 1560.[21] The traditional view that the Kreis system worked best, perhaps even only worked at all, in areas of extreme territorial fragmentation, or at the least in areas that included numerous small entities in addition to a handful of larger principalities, in particular Franconia and Swabia, is certainly no longer tenable. In the second half of the sixteenth century the development was more uniform.

Initially, this was driven by the immediate problems caused by Wilhelm von Grumbach's rebellion.[22] Yet some Kreise soon began to engage seriously in more diverse and wide-ranging responsibilities. In 1564, for example, the Franconian, Bavarian, and Swabian Kreise formed an association to institute periodic joint assay commissions and resolved in future to collaborate on currency issues.[23] The currency regulation formulated by the Reichstag of 1566, which sanctioned territorial currencies so long as their value relative to the imperial coinage was maintained, further encouraged such associations.[24] The fact that the Kreise never at any stage developed a sense of 'Kreis patriotism' is often seen as indicative of the strictly practical, mechanical, and ultimately limited, nature of the institution, but it also reflects their strong sense of themselves as subordinate regional agencies of the Reich.[25]

The original and prime function of the Kreise was military. It was thus natural that they played a key role in the plans of those who formulated ideas for a comprehensive reform of the Reich's military organization after 1555. The need for a more effective military system to meet both external threats and domestic challenges had been articulated frequently. Opposition to the establishment of a strong central authority, however, had driven a general tendency to devolve responsibility for military matters to the Kreise, and hence to the territories. The idea that the emperor might become a kind of commander-in-chief of the imperial armed forces was repeatedly mooted in the discussions after 1555, but the Estates always resisted. This notion recurred again in the comprehensive plan for the reform of the Reich and its military system put forward by Lazarus von Schwendi (1522–83) in 1570.

Since leaving the service of Charles V, Schwendi had served Maximilian with distinction as his military commander in Hungary in 1564.[26] After the conclusion of a truce with the Turks in 1568 he withdrew to his Estates in south-western Germany, from where he penned three extensive memoranda for the emperor between 1570 and 1576. As early as 1547, he had condemned the corruption involved in the recruitment of mercenaries. In 1566, he wrote to Maximilian from

[20] Dotzauer, *Reichskreise*, 46.   [21] Hartmann, *Bayerischer Reichskreis*, 312–19.
[22] See pp. 390–4.   [23] Hartmann, *Bayerischer Reichskreis*, 321.
[24] Conrad, *Rechtsgeschichte*, ii, 152.   [25] Dotzauer, *Reichskreise*, 38.
[26] See p. 348.

his winter quarters in Hungary, urging him to oblige all German nobles without exception to undertake military service and himself to take command of a German army against the Turks.[27]

In 1570, Schwendi elaborated detailed plans for military reform.[28] Drawing on his own experiences and on the ideas he had absorbed from his extensive correspondence with German and French humanists, Schwendi envisaged a nation of patriots at arms. He condemned the use of mercenaries and of foreign recruitment in Germany. The 'old Germans', he suggested, had constituted a nation in which all had been armed. The emperor should be appointed commander-in-chief, two princes should act as his lieutenants, and the officer class should be recruited from the German nobility; the army as a whole should be composed exclusively of Germans and be subject to strict military discipline. At the same time, the military infrastructure was to be improved by the construction of a well-stocked armoury at Strassburg or elsewhere. The whole system was to be paid for by means of a monthly levy on the Kreise. Such a reform would reinforce the unity of the Germans. They would be able to defend themselves from attack and to play a dominant role in Europe, capable of intervening effectively in the Netherlands, Italy, and the Baltic.

Schwendi clearly envisaged an altogether different Reich from the one that actually existed. The Reichstag rejected his main proposals out of hand. The Estates agreed to forbid foreign recruitment in the Reich without permission of the emperor, but this was wholly ineffective. They also agreed on the introduction of a code of military discipline for horsemen and infantry that was designed to replace the self-governing practices of the *Landsknechte* or German mercenary troops, on whom the Reich and most princes had hitherto relied. This only gradually made a difference, however, as the territories began to develop more regular military forces in the late sixteenth and seventeenth centuries.[29]

New developments in the imperial justice system bore fruit rather more immediately. The settlement of 1555 gave the Reichskammergericht a new governing ordinance as well as the additional responsibility of arbitrating in disputes arising from the religious settlement. An escalation in the number of new cases underlined the growing perception of the court as a reliable agency of justice. The period 1495–1550 saw some nine thousand cases brought to the court; between 1550 and 1594 over twenty thousand new cases were registered.[30] The dramatic escalation in the volume of work necessitated an increase in the number of judges from sixteen to forty-one by 1570. Even so, the backlog of five thousand cases that had accumulated by 1550 continued to grow, just as the duration of proceedings steadily extended. By the end of the century, roughly half of all new cases took between six and twenty years to settle. An analysis of cases launched between 1587 and 1589 reveals that 11 per cent lasted between twenty and fifty years, while 4 per cent lasted over a century.[31] Even when a

---

[27] *ADB*, xxxiii, 387–8.
[28] Lanzinner, 'Denkschrift'; Schmidt, *Vaterlandsliebe*, 193–240, 283–9.
[29] See pp. 492–7.
[30] Ranieri, *Recht*, 136–7.
[31] Ranieri, *Recht*, 216–17.

case was settled at Speyer, there was no guarantee that a judgment would be properly executed.

Despite perennial complaints about delays in the system and the effectiveness of its judgments, the court apparently enjoyed enormous respect. There were, for example, only seven appeals against its judgments between 1559 and 1589. Many cases were in fact settled out of court long before the judicial process was completed, and there is evidence that many disputes were settled by the mere threat of proceedings. Furthermore, the fact that a case was under consideration, possibly over decades, imposed obligations on the parties involved that stabilized and normalized relations between them while their dispute was removed from the locality to the confines of the court.[32]

Analysis of the cases brought before the court also sheds light on the changing character of the Reich. For the first time, significant numbers of cases came from western and northern areas, underlining the way in which the Reich now became an institutional reality in the areas that were traditionally 'remote from the throne'.[33] By contrast, cases from the Burgundian lands (like the Austrian Erblande and fully exempted under the Treaty of Burgundy 1548), from the Lorraine bishoprics of Metz, Toul, and Verdun (illegally ceded to France by the Protestant princes in 1551), and from the Swiss Confederation (formally part of the Reich until 1648) ceased altogether. Overall, the territorial distribution of cases within the Reich was now no longer affected so much by proximity to or distance from the crown as by the crown's frequent grants of exemption to territories and Imperial Cities from litigation up to a certain monetary value. The grant of these privileges undoubtedly inhibited complaints from certain areas, though that did not affect the greater geographical spread overall.[34] The *privilegium de non appellando* rarely granted complete exemption (though the Golden Bull had granted it to the Electors) and even where it did, complaints about denial of access to justice were not covered.

There were changes, too, in the social standing of those who brought cases. In the first half of the century the majority of litigants were urban dwellers involved in property disputes. After 1550, most of the litigants were either members of the lower nobility complaining about the abrogation of their rights by territorial princes (especially after 1575) or princes (especially ecclesiastical princes) in dispute with their peers. The pool of potential litigants was by no means socially exclusive. The court was regularly called upon to deal with suits submitted by Jews against territorial and civic authorities or against individuals over property matters.[35] In the years 1587–9, complaints by peasants against their lords (generally over taxation, the increase of feudal dues, or the abrogation of traditional rights) comprised some 3 per cent of new cases.[36] Indeed, such suits seem to have become more frequent in the 1590s, when rising social and economic pressures generated widespread peasant unrest and rebellion against increasingly grasping territorial authorities.[37]

In general, the Reichskammergericht contributed significantly to the general pacification and 'juridification' of the Reich after 1555. The cases brought to the

[32] Ruthmann, 'Religionsprozesse', 238.   [33] Ranieri, *Recht*, 175–9.
[34] Eisenhardt, *Kaiserliche privilegia*, 12–51.   [35] Battenberg, 'Juden', 322–4.
[36] Ranieri, *Recht*, 233; Troßbach, 'Reichsgerichte', 129–32.   [37] See pp. 541–59.

court reflect perfectly the strains generated by the further consolidation of territories of every size over the course of the century. To a considerable extent this was
driven by the taxes agreed at the Reichstag that were then passed on to the subjects
(often with a significant surcharge for the ruler concerned) in the form of local
taxes. What was equally new, however, was the recourse to law as a remedy for so
many grievances and the growing confidence of increasing numbers of inhabitants
of the Reich that they lived in an environment protected by a viable framework of
law. The court now dealt with issues that in the past might have been resolved by
feud or rebellion.

The most sensitive and increasingly numerous cases the court had to deal with
were those concerning religious matters. Remarkably, in view of the fact that
accusations of bias had brought all Reichskammergericht proceedings to a halt in
the 1530s, the court now managed to steer a neutral course for several decades.[38]
Although not formally required to do so by the ordinance of 1555, the judges soon
resolved that all cases concerning religious issues should be considered by confessionally balanced panels.

In so far as the settlement of 1555 had specified clear guidelines, these were
enforced rigorously in ways that were uncontroversial. However, many cases
concerned issues that were simply not clearly defined in 1555. Wisely, the judges
were reluctant to deal with what they termed *dubia*, and from 1557 they regularly
petitioned the Reichstag for a political solution. Since that did not happen, the
court inevitably found itself embroiled in increasingly vociferous disputes after
about 1580 over the terms of the religious peace. Some cases, particularly the
notorious 'Four Monasteries Case' in 1598, generated spectacular arguments that
undoubtedly contributed to the constitutional crisis of the early seventeenth
century.[39] Some of the most controversial cases were those concerning the right
of subjects under the peace settlement of 1555 to emigrate if they followed a
different faith from their ruler. In a surprising number of cases, the court supported
subjects against their rulers. For the most part, however, the court was careful to
maintain its neutrality and did not hesitate to communicate deadlocked verdicts
(*para vota*).

Some of the shortcomings of the Reichskammergericht were remedied by the
Reichshofrat or Imperial Aulic Council established in 1559.[40] This grew out of the
council that Ferdinand established for the Erblande in the 1520s, whose jurisdiction was now extended to the Reich, including Italy. Unlike the Reichskammergericht, it was a purely royal court and was composed of a mixture of up to twenty
nobles and lawyers appointed by the crown, some of them Protestants. At one level,
it functioned as a council of state, with its deliberations being passed up to the
highly select Privy Council. It was also available as a supreme court, however, with
jurisdiction similar to that of the Reichskammergericht, except that it acquired

---

[38] Ruthmann, 'Religionsprozesse', 235–8. For a more critical view of the court's performance, see
Gotthard, *Religionsfrieden*, 404–18.
[39] See pp. 414–16.
[40] Gschliesser, *Reichshofrat*, 1–12, 89–185.

exclusive authority in matters concerning enfeoffments. Its judgments were also scrutinized by the Privy Council before being submitted to the emperor, who rarely changed them.

Which of the two high courts individuals or groups decided to address depended on where they thought they would get the best result; many plaintiffs launched cases at both courts simultaneously. Some peasants seem to have believed that an appeal to the Reichshofrat would allow them to present their case to the emperor personally.[41] Others preferred the Reichshofrat simply because it was quicker than the Reichskammergericht and its cases did not normally become tied up in cumbersome and excessively time-consuming procedures. Its use of commissions, generally to gather evidence and mediate in the locality, proved a popular and effective method of conflict resolution.[42] The appointment of leading princes to head these commissions again increased the chances of a locally negotiated conclusion, while it also enabled the crown to involve princes in the government of the Reich. The constant correspondence between commissioner and Reichshofrat tended to reinforce the sense of participation in, and common ownership of, the political and legal system.

Remarkably, although the Reichshofrat was a predominantly Catholic court, it managed to achieve widespread recognition among Protestants. After about 1590 the Reichshofrat was frequently accused of confessional bias, yet, despite this, the number of cases it dealt with doubled between 1580 and 1610.[43] It also seems that from the outset the court attracted cases not just from the old core areas of the Reich but also from northern Germany, which further underlines the way the legal system acted as an integrating force.[44] The Reichshofrat was both an instrument of Habsburg government in the Reich and a supreme court. Its acceptance by the Estates is again testimony to the desire for peace and a collective affirmation of the Reich as a legal order after 1555.

Legislation for the Reich was formulated and agreed by the Reichstag but its implementation depended on the Kreise, on the individual rulers, and on the courts. The legislative activity of the Reich is often dismissed as irrelevant and ineffective, but that ignores the ways in which Reichstag legislation was essentially intended as framework legislation to be adapted to the specific circumstances of a territory or city and to be implemented locally. Even failed legislation could have the same effect. A prince might object to a law for the Reich that appeared to give the emperor the right to intervene in his territory, or that affected his prerogatives or income in some way. That did not mean, however, that he was necessarily averse to issuing just such a law himself. It is doubtful whether the legislation of the Reich was less effective than national legislation in other European states in the sixteenth century. The fate of legislation concerning the currency, various forms of economic activity, law and order, censorship, and the imperial postal service illustrates the problems and the potential of the Reichstag as a legislative body in this period.

[41] Troßbach, 'Reichsgerichte', 131–3.   [42] Ullmann, *Geschichte*, 194–7, 291–8.
[43] Lanzinner, 'Zeitalter', 76.   [44] Ullmann, *Geschichte*, 53–67.

Despite the beginnings of what might be described as a monetary policy in some of the Kreise after 1555, all attempts at 'national' regulation failed.[45] Around 1500 the German territorial and civic governments maintained some six hundred mints and three major currency systems competed in the Reich: the large silver coins of the Habsburgs and of Saxony and the gold florins favoured up and down the Rhine. On the North Sea and Baltic coasts, the old Lübeck mark and Flemish pound were also in regular use. In 1524, a Currency Ordinance had aimed to introduce a degree of order by formally establishing parity between the major gold and silver coins. It created a new Reichsguldiner, in gold and silver, with six further subsidiary silver coins down to the 'kleiner Gröschlein' at 1/84th of the gulden. An immensely complex valuation table was then compiled to harmonize the new currency with all existing local and regional currencies.

The impact of the ordinance was negligible. The Reichsguldiner had a higher silver content than the Saxon thaler and its introduction should have led the Saxons to withdraw and re-mint their coins. The Saxons refused to do this. Furthermore, in 1525, Charles V exempted himself and all his successors from any monetary legislation in the Reich, which enabled the Habsburgs too to mint lighter coins than legally required.[46] In fact, only the Palatinate and the Hohenzollern margraves in Ansbach and Bayreuth ever produced limited quantities of the new Reichsguldiner. The tension between the silver mining eastern territories and the gold favouring Rhineland remained. The Reichsguldiner failed to supplant the Saxon Thaler that was favoured in Middle and North Germany. Conferences convened in 1531 and 1549 failed to make any progress in resolving the currency chaos that was widely recognized as a severe problem.

A new Currency Ordinance in 1551 merely increased the number of different silver coins from seven to eight and introduced the Austrian kreuzer as the standard denomination. At the same time, the new ordinance seemed to recognize that law did not necessarily change practice, since it confirmed the continued existence of a pre-1524 gulden used as a transactional unit (Rechnungsgulden) at a value of 60 kreuzer, rather than the 72-kreuzer value of the silver coin.[47] All regional systems for smaller coins, and all foreign currencies commonly used in parts of the Reich, were also expressly permitted, again with a comprehensive valuation table. The lighter Saxon thaler was devalued to 68 kreuzer, which merely resulted in the Saxons not accepting the ordinance at all.[48] Only six years later, Philip II was responsible for a further complication when he introduced yet another thaler in his Burgundian lands, with complete disregard for the law of the Reich to which those lands still technically belonged.[49]

A new ordinance in 1559, which remained formally valid until 1806, represented both a final attempt at rationalization and an admission of failure. The attempt to maintain a dual currency was abandoned and the gold gulden was set at

[45] Blaich, *Wirtschaftspolitik*, 9–27; Schneider, *Währungspolitik*, 26–31.
[46] Bergerhausen, 'Reichsmünzordnung'.
[47] Blaich, *Wirtschaftspolitik*, 20–1.
[48] Schneider, *Währungspolitik*, 28.
[49] Schneider, *Währungspolitik*, 29.

a more realistic value of 72 kreuzer (a gold ducat worth 104 kreuzer derived from Venice via Hungary also came into limited circulation). The silver gulden was set at 60 kreuzer, which at least equated the coin with the unit of account (Rechnungs-gulden) that was actually used in commercial transactions in south Germany. At the same time, the attempt to suppress the thaler by banning it was also abandoned, and it was now included in the valuation table. In 1566, it was formally recognized as a reserve currency in the Reich with a value of 68 kreuzer.

In broad terms, the major currency systems now stabilized. The gold gulden gradually declined in significance, while the silver gulden and the Reichsthaler became established as the leading trade currency in the south and north, respectively. In 1571, Saxony formally recognized the Currency Ordinance, as did Burgundy, which abandoned the 'Philippsthaler' and began to mint a Burgundian Reichsthaler instead. However, in 1573, the emperor once again exempted the Habsburg lands, which subsequently developed a variety of thaler coinages of differing values. At the same time, the Reichstag increasingly recognized the futility of central regulation and in 1571, the Reichsdeputation delegated responsibility for currency matters to three associations of Kreise who were to 'correspond' on the matter.[50]

Over the very long term, this represented progress of a kind. However, it did little to solve the main problems of the German currency system after 1550. These were, first, the relatively high standards set for the (unregulated) smaller regional coins at a time when Central European silver mining was in decline and prices were rising and, second, the perpetual increase in the quantity of money regardless of the quantity of goods. None of the attempts at currency regulation, either by the Reichstag or the Kreise, really addressed this problem, which led to steady inflation from the early 1580s and a monetary disaster in 1618–20.[51] The continuing exemption of the Habsburg Burgundian Kreis from the currency legislation also undermined its impact in the Lower Rhineland and Westphalia, since these areas traded primarily with the Netherlands and preferred to use its coinage and to harmonize their own currency with that of the Netherlands rather than that of the Reich.[52]

Currency issues generated high passions and sustained activity because they involved a key regalian prerogative. Minting coins was one of the most public ways of demonstrating the rights of a ruler. It was also extremely profitable. Furthermore, at every level, from the imperial treasury down, authorities also had a vested interest in being paid taxes in sound coins. The most that could be achieved, however, was a broad framework within which, over time, a workable pattern of practice evolved.

In some ways, this was also true of the *Polizeiordnungen* (Police Ordinances), the last of which was agreed in 1577.[53] These codes were perhaps the best illustration of

---

[50] These were, first, the two Saxon Kreise; second, the Franconian, Swabian, and Bavarian Kreise; and, third, the Electoral Rhine Kreis together with the Upper Rhine and Lower Rhine-Westphalian Kreis. Schneider, *Währungspolitik*, 30.
[51] Blaich, *Wirtschaftspolitik*, 259–61. See p. 579.
[52] Bergerhausen, 'Reichsmünzordnung'.
[53] Weber, *Reichspolizeiordnungen*, 24–36.

the desire to regulate and govern that took root in the Reich and its territories in the wake of the religious upheaval.[54] From the outset, however, they were tailored to the idiosyncratic structure of the Reich. Like its forerunners, the *Polizeiordnung* of 1577 was never intended as an exclusively valid law, but as a code that the Estates might 'incorporate, diminish or moderate' in their lands, though 'not at all intensify or increase'.[55] It provided a programmatic definition of the aims shared by Estates: the promotion of the common good ('der gemeine Nutz') and good order ('gute Ordnung'). Essentially, it reiterated its predecessors of 1530 and 1548, and added further to the mass of regulations and guidelines concerning economic and social issues as diverse as blasphemy, begging, prostitution, the guardianship of children, and regulations governing apothecaries, goldsmiths, printers, and the book trade.[56]

The *Polizeiordnungen* have often been dismissed as irrelevant because their impact cannot be measured. However, they were never intended to provide legislation directly relevant to the areas of concern, but rather framework guidance for specific legislation to be formulated by each territory or city. In this sense, the *Polizeiordnung* of 1577 was a success in that it set a norm to which most of the Reich conformed in due course.[57]

Legislation that aspired to be prescriptive for the Reich as a whole invariably failed. The rather curious attempts to impose a ban on wool exports in 1548, 1566, and 1577 (and again in 1603), and on leather exports in 1577, all failed.[58] Even if it had been possible to enforce such categorical laws throughout the Reich, the economic benefit would have been doubtful, since the whole idea rested on deeply flawed assumptions. The aim was to prevent foreign craftsmen buying up German raw materials, thus protecting the excellent goods produced by German craftsmen by ensuring that they could continue to buy domestic raw materials at reasonable prices. An import ban might have been more logical, though probably just as impossible to enforce.

What is striking about the institutional and legislative developments of the decades after 1555 is the almost anarchic profusion of initiatives. Throughout, there is a real sense of a desire to establish a new order, to regulate and systematize, to overcome the instability of the previous decades. Many initiatives were thwarted because they posed a perceived threat to the status of individual Estates or of groups such as the Electors. Others were simply unworkable. Even so, the constitutional system of the Reich was now more fully articulated than ever before, with both a greater spread over a wider geographical area and a greater depth in the Kreise. The very existence of this new density and quality of constitutional structure played a key role in the stabilization of the Reich after 1555.

It is only as the logical result of this proliferation of activity that the first elements of what was to become German public law developed in this period.[59] The many

---

54 Härter, 'Policeygesetzgebung', 140.
55 Conrad, *Rechtsgeschichte*, ii, 257.
56 Conrad, *Rechtsgeschichte*, ii, 257, 362.
57 Weber, *Reichspolizeiordnungen*, 23–4, 36–43.
58 Blaich, *Wirtschaftspolitik*, 67–8, 107–8, 262.
59 Stolleis, *Öffentliches Recht*, i, 72–3, 127–8, 133–41. See also pp. 457–61.

upheavals of the decades before 1555 and the wealth of legislation passed since 1495 increasingly required experts for their interpretation, application, and management. A mass of printed literature came into being, consisting of both printed versions of the individual laws themselves and compilations and commentaries. The proliferation of cases at the Reichskammergericht, and its annual visitation or inspection by a delegation from the Reichstag, generated growing interest in the constitution.

The new legal culture also spawned an army of experts and professionals who supported a growing host of litigants at every stage, from the locality to the rarefied confines of the court at Speyer. Every court administration from Prague and Vienna down to the domanial estate office of the poorest Imperial Knight employed, either directly or indirectly, advisers in imperial law and custom. The Estates of the Reich, and growing numbers of their subjects, became increasingly aware of belonging to a distinctive polity. It was also clear that the Reich had little to do with the ancient Roman Empire. The Roman law categories that the German Estates were currently applying in their own regional and local legislation simply could not give an adequate description of the Reich as a whole. That Reich had largely been constructed since the Worms Reichstag in 1495 on the foundation laid by the elective monarchy defined by the Golden Bull of 1356.

The establishment of an Imperial Book Commission at Frankfurt in 1569 was an attempt by the crown to exercise a prerogative under the terms of the various *Polizeiordnungen* and the peace of 1555.[60] In 1521, the Edict of Worms had specified that it was the duty of princes and magistrates to control publications in their realms. Subsequent legislation in 1524 and 1529 turned this right into a duty, and in 1530 it was decided that the emperor would intervene if the princes failed in their duty. It is not clear exactly what prompted Maximilian II to ask the city council of Frankfurt to monitor books that were sold at the flourishing book fair. The issue is likely to have arisen in the context of talks preparatory to the Speyer Reichstag of 1570, which complained that the censorship laws agreed in the 1520s were not being enforced.

Neither Maximilian II nor, initially, Rudolf II showed any inclination to exploit the position for the Catholic side. In 1569, Maximilian was probably thinking first and foremost of his own library when he insisted on the emperor's right to receive free copies of all privileged publications, though he also mentioned the duty of all rulers to suppress sectarian literature that was contrary to the peace of the Reich. When the Frankfurt magistrates complained almost immediately about the burden of work that this imposed on them, Maximilian explained that he really only wanted to ensure that he received five copies of all books. Even the appointment of the first imperial commissioner in 1579 did not generate any further activity: the first commissioner, Dr Johann Vest, was so lax in the execution of his duties that by 1596 Rudolf II was moved to complain that he was not sufficiently conscientious in collecting the emperor's free copies.

---

[60] Kiesel and Münch, *Gesellschaft*, 108–11; Eisenhardt, *Aufsicht*, 6–7, 30–4, 64–72; Brauer, 'Bücherkommission', 184–90; Evans, *Making*, 289–90; Evans, *Wechel Presses*, 29–31.

Equally significant was the instruction that the Elector of Saxony gave to the municipal and university authorities at Leipzig in 1569 to monitor all books sold at the Leipzig fairs and to acquire free copies of all books for the Elector's library.[61] This was probably an attempt to prevent the war between the Gnesiolutherans and the Philippists in the neighbouring Duchy of Saxony from disrupting the peace of the Electorate, but it may also have been prompted by the discussion, in advance of the Reichstag, of the need to control the publication of religious works likely to disturb the peace. The Leipzig commission, which only later acquired that title, did not have the same status or authority as the imperial commission, but it came to fulfil a similar role and its very existence reinforced the Elector of Saxony's moral authority to intercede on behalf of Protestant booksellers at Frankfurt between 1608 and 1619.[62]

Given the haphazard operation of both institutions, one can scarcely speak of a coordinated approach across the Reich. Most censorship activities were carried out by local rulers. Yet the existence of two central institutions, at least theoretically supra-regional in their scope, demonstrated a will to inhibit the publication of works that might destabilize the religious peace. Almost inevitably, the imperial book commission was sucked into the general confessional conflict during the years after 1600; Rudolf II, in his later years, and Emperor Matthias were accused of using the book commission to promote their Catholic confessional agenda.[63] In time, however, both commissions assumed a more stable nature and more clearly defined modes of operation in the legal framework of the period after 1648, in which incendiary and seditious literature relating to religion and, in due course, to politics was proscribed. Each commission survived until 1806.

The emergence of the imperial postal service in 1596–7 resulted from the failure of the original Habsburg postal system and the growing demand of both Imperial Cities and many princes for a reliable service.[64] The Habsburg postal service based in Brussels fell into the hands of Philip II in 1555. As such, it became suspect to many German Protestant rulers as a 'Spanish post', and the second bankruptcy of the Spanish crown in 1565 induced a financial crisis that threatened to destroy it. At the Speyer Reichstag in 1570 the Estates demanded that the postal service be kept within the Reich, rather than under Spanish control, but the only outcome was the development of alternative postal systems by the leading Imperial Cities during the 1570s.

Repeated wrangles with Spain over the main Antwerp to Venice service through the Reich ultimately prompted demands for a root and branch reform of the postal service. In 1596, Rudolf II confirmed Leonhard von Taxis as the only official Postmaster General and the following year the whole Taxis postal service, originally simply a system linking the two sets of Habsburg Erblande in Austria and Burgundy, was turned by decree into the Imperial Postal System for the Reich as a whole. By 1615–16 four major routes covered most of the Reich from the Alps to the

---

[61] Goldfriedrich, *Geschichte*, i, 597–8 and ii, 158–62; Kirchhoff, 'Bücher-Commission', 60–1.
[62] Goldfriedrich, *Geschichte*, i, 619–42.
[63] Eisenhart, *Aufsicht*, 111, 113.
[64] Behringer, *Merkur*, 128–88.

Baltic and from the Rhine across to Saxony; by 1684 the service reached the greatest extent of its spread, linking most of the important cities in the Reich.[65] Thereafter, the development of territorial postal systems progressively undermined the mono- poly of the imperial system, though it survived into the nineteenth century.[66] Around 1600, however, few institutions demonstrated the progressive integration of the Reich as strikingly as its postal service.

---

[65] Behringer, *Merkur*, 215–16.   [66] Grillmeyer, *Habsburgs Diener*, 262–318, 425–46.

30

The Reich in Europe

The abdication of Charles V transformed the position of the Reich in Europe. During his rule and in the context of his grand imperial plans, the Reich had formed the heart of Europe. Now the Spanish Habsburgs became the dominant European power [1] It was Philip II who concluded the Peace of Cateau-Cambrésis with France in 1559. His pre-eminent position was further underlined by victory against the Turks at Lepanto in 1571 and by his succession to the Portuguese throne in 1581. It was Spanish policy that prevailed in the Netherlands and that dictated developments in Italy. In all of this, Philip II clearly regarded the interests of the Austrian Habsburgs and of the Reich as inferior. In 1559, he made no effort to bring about the return of the Lorraine bishoprics taken from the Reich in 1552. And it was not until after the death of his wife, Elizabeth of Valois, in 1568 that Philip acquiesced in plans formulated in Vienna since 1556 for a dynastic marriage that would link Paris and Vienna.

If the Reich became rather peripheral, relatively speaking, in power political terms, it also stood apart in another sense. The Europe that Spain dominated was increasingly a Europe polarized by religious division. The first fault-line here ran through France, which was plunged into civil war from 1562. On the one hand, this curtailed the ability of the French crown to become involved in German politics and, after the St Bartholomew's Day Massacre of Protestants in 1572, the French monarchy was for a time no longer a credible ally for German Protestant princes. On the other hand, the Huguenot leaders made repeated efforts from 1560 to gain support in the Reich. [2] Spanish and Netherlands troops in the pay of the French crown repeatedly violated imperial territory during the 1560s, and both sides in the French conflict recruited troops in the Reich, involving up to 20,000 Germans in the struggle. [3] A second fault-line soon opened up in the Netherlands after 1566, with even more direct implications for the Reich. Before long, Habsburg Spain, the house of Valois, and the papacy confronted a broad coalition of Huguenots, Dutch rebels, and the English crown.

Yet, as Europe became increasingly polarized between Catholic and Protestant fronts from the 1560s, the Reich remained relatively calm. It was once conventional to take this as evidence of the helpless nature of the German polity. [4] The Reich

---

[1] Kohler, *Reich*, 22–6; Lanzinner, 'Zeitalter', 57–8.
[2] On the Palatinate's early involvement with this conflict, see Wirsching, 'Konfessionalisierung'.
[3] Lanzinner, 'Zeitalter', 57.
[4] Kohler, *Reich*, 77–8.

apparently drifted aimlessly at the mercy of its more powerful neighbours, who gradually further eroded its territory. The Netherlands were lost, as were lands and prerogatives in Italy, as well as Livonia in the north-east, a territory of the Teutonic Knights since the fourteenth century, which became a secular duchy in 1530 and was annexed by Poland in 1561. Only the problems that those neighbours themselves grappled with during this time allegedly prevented even greater losses.

The inclusion of Livonia in this catalogue of alleged national disasters is telling. In the nineteenth and early twentieth centuries, Germany's eastern lands and the legacy of the Teutonic Knights occupied a key role in Prussian-German national mythology. Their 'loss' in the sixteenth century was thus inevitably understood as a matter of national shame. This overlooked a crucial point about the status of Livonia.[5] The Teutonic Knights were recruited from Germany, and their commanders were from German princely dynasties and they became princes of the Reich in 1526. Yet the territory never belonged to the medieval German Kingdom or *Regnum Teutonicum*, but rather to the much broader and more vaguely defined *Sacrum Imperium*. The status of Livonia is in many ways more comparable to that of northern Italy than to that of Brandenburg. Whatever nebulous connection to the Reich may have lingered was finally severed when Gotthard Kettler (1517–1587), the head of the Order, recognized the overlordship of Poland in 1561. Overall, it is thus more accurate to speak of territory not gained, rather than territory lost.

In fact, any attempt to quantify the Reich in such ways obscures important points about its development in the second half of the sixteenth century. Neither the emperors nor the Estates were purely passive agents on the European stage. If the Reich never really pursued a successful 'foreign' policy, that was partly because emperor and Estates consciously abstained from doing so. The priority for the Estates was the preservation of the stability and peace of the Reich. The interests of the Austrian Habsburgs, as usual, extended beyond the German Reich and to that extent, as usual, they were frustrated by the reluctance of the German Estates to support purely Habsburg, as opposed to German, interests. The result of the activities of both emperor and Estates in these decades was that frontiers, and hence ultimately identities, were becoming more clearly defined. The Reich reacted and responded to external challenges in ways that were entirely consistent with its internal evolution after 1555.

With the suspension of the French threat from 1559, Spain was the major new external point of reference and source of enduring tension for the emperors. In general, both Ferdinand I and Maximilian II maintained an underlying loyalty to the interests of the Habsburg dynasty as a whole. In the case of Maximilian, this was reinforced by the uncertainty surrounding the Spanish succession. The death of Philip's only son, Don Carlos, in 1568 left everything open, and even his fourth marriage, to Anne of Austria, only produced one surviving son in 1578, who eventually succeeded to the Spanish throne as Philip III in 1598. It is no wonder

---

[5] Lavery, *Challenge*, 16; Köbler, *Lexikon*, 386; Rabe, *Geschichte*, 469–72. See also pp. 22–3, 257–8.

that the philoprogenitive Austrian Habsburgs long harboured hopes of reuniting the Habsburg patrimony.

Meanwhile, Philip II survived and soon proved to be a ruthless and uncompromising monarch. Not surprisingly, tensions arose at the two points where Charles V's patrimony had been severed: Italy and the Netherlands. In Italy, Philip inherited the Spanish feudal network based on the Kingdom of Naples and Sicily.[6] For the next century-and-a-half that network existed in often uneasy competition with the papal and the imperial systems. The relationship between the Spanish and the imperial feudal systems in Italy was further aggravated by Philip's efforts to extend the position created by virtue of his enfeoffment with Milan in 1540. That had been granted to him as an imperial fief, which made him subject to the emperors in Vienna. Immediately after Charles's division of the Habsburg lands, Philip set about attempting to establish Milan as the independent centre of its own system of regional feudal satellites. In 1571, he went so far as to incite a rebellion against the Counts Caretto, rulers of the Ligurian coastal County of Finale, and to send troops from Milan to occupy it and other neighbouring territories, such as the Duchy of Piombino.[7] The immediate aim was to diminish the influence of Genoa, but the move brought bitter conflict with the emperor, who also claimed Finale as a fiefdom. The most that Maximilian was able to achieve was Philip II's recognition of his overlordship.

Philip's aggression had, however, stimulated the papacy to make efforts to assert its own feudal system. It had also encouraged the Duke of Savoy (reinstated by the Treaty of Cateau-Cambrésis after several decades of French occupation) to loosen further his links with the Reich and to create his own north-west Italian sphere of influence based on Turin.[8] Relations between the two Habsburg lines over Italian matters remained tense and were aggravated in 1578 by Spanish support for the conspiracy between the papacy and the Duke of Parma to drive the Doria-Landi princes out of Val di Tarro.[9] Open conflict broke out again in 1598 on the succession of Philip III, who abandoned his father's policy of formally recognizing imperial overlordship in favour of a renewed attempt to assert Spanish superiority.

The Italian issues were part of a larger game that had an acute bearing on the Reich. The real reason for Spain's determination to achieve her objectives in Italy lay in the Netherlands. Milan played a key role in the 'Spanish road', the troop supply line from the Mediterranean to the north.[10] Genoa, with its traditional control over much of the coastal region, was a potential obstacle that could only be bypassed by direct Spanish occupation of the Lunigiana. Imperial overlordship was a problem because, for the sake of his standing in Italy generally, the emperor felt obliged to protect his fiefholders such as the Counts Caretto. Furthermore, the Austrian Habsburgs, as Holy Roman Emperors, had an interest in the Netherlands

---

[6] Kohler, *Reich*, 79–81.
[7] Aretin, *Das Reich*, 106–8.
[8] The court of Savoy had moved to Turin from Chambéry when the French invaded in 1536: Köbler, *Lexikon*, 613.
[9] Aretin, *Das Reich*, 108.
[10] Parker, *Army of Flanders*, 60–1.

which formed the Reich's Burgundian Kreis. Maximilian's repeated efforts to mediate in the conflict there merely provoked further antagonism in Italy. Spanish policy in the Val di Tarro affair of 1578, for example, was dictated by the fact that the Duke of Parma, Alexander Farnese, happened to be Philip II's commander in the Netherlands.

The situation in the Netherlands became a major challenge to the stability of the Reich.[11] The rebellion in 1566 against the uncompromising religious policies pursued by the Spanish authorities in the Netherlands immediately excited concern in the Reich. In 1568, the Rhineland Electors, in a move coordinated by the Protestant Palatine Elector, petitioned Maximilian to intervene on the grounds that imperial laws had been violated. This, in fact, was a moot point. In 1548, the Treaty of Burgundy had recognized the overlordship of the emperor over the Netherlands. On the one hand, the Reich promised to defend them and they paid imperial taxes like the Electors at double the standard rate (treble in the case of a Turkish war). On the other hand, the Netherlands were explicitly exempted from the jurisdiction of the Reichskammergericht and from all laws agreed by emperor and Estates at the Reichstag (*Reichsschlüsse*).

Charles V's attempt to win all the advantages of the most privileged Estates for his north-western Erblande was originally conceived in the context of his vision of an alternating Spanish/Austrian succession to the imperial throne. When that did not materialize, the Treaty of Burgundy effectively facilitated the secession of the Netherlands from the Reich. In 1555, the Estates had insisted that the Reich's peacekeeping mechanisms should only be valid for those areas which participated fully in the Reich. The refusal of Charles V to accept the religious settlement of 1555 for the Netherlands thus automatically disqualified them from enjoying the benefits of unqualified membership of the Reich. It is true that the Austrian Erblande enjoyed a similar status. Yet the attitude of the German Estates to them was different. It was one thing to defend the Austrian lands against the Turks. It was quite another thing to enter into a commitment to the Netherlands at the risk of being drawn into a major conflict with France.

The grounds for imperial intervention after the Dutch revolt broke out were thus far from clear. The rigorous pursuit of a Spanish ecclesiastical policy was provocative, yet, arguably, not a transgression of imperial law. All that Maximilian could really do was offer to mediate. Philip brusquely dismissed his efforts in 1566 and 1568, and even threatened to denounce the religious concessions made in the Austrian Erblande to the papacy. Several new approaches over the next decades proved equally futile. The last effort made at the conference of Cologne in 1579 led directly to the formal deposition of Philip II by the Dutch rebels in 1580.[12]

The German Estates supported the various mediation attempts. They were equally clear, however, that they had no wish to become militarily involved. That

---

[11] Israel, *Dutch Republic 1476–1806*, 139–230 gives an excellent account of the developments from the 1540s to the 1580s; the following passages will deal only with the implications for German politics. See also Kohler, *Reich*, 81–3; Mout, 'Niederlande', 156–65; Arndt, *Niederlande, passim*.

[12] Arndt, *Niederlande*, 46–51, 55–66.

did not bespeak indifference to Dutch affairs. Alba's brutal attempts to suppress the rebellion, and in particular his execution of Egmont and Horn and other nobles in 1568, provoked shock and outrage across the confessional divide in the Reich. The fact that Egmont and Horn at least were loyal Catholics merely underlined the savagery of Alba's approach. Yet the German princes were wary of becoming embroiled in the problems of the Dutch.

From 1570, the Reichstag declined either to assist the rebels or to give in to the Duke of Alba's demand that they should be condemned.[13] When Alba complained that the Count of East Frisia had aided and abetted the rebellion of the lower nobility (the Sea Beggars), the Estates simply referred the matter to the emperor, for they feared that it might simply drag them into the Dutch conflict.[14] They agreed only to protest against the violation of Reich territory by Alba's troops, which had already affected several members of the Lower Rhine-Westphalian Kreis.

The radical polarization of Dutch politics had a number of immediate effects in Germany. Movements of foreign troops and recruitment campaigns unsettled many areas of the west and north-west. Bavaria attempted, but failed, to enlist the Duke of Alba in the Landsberg League. In addition to the Elector of the Palatinate, the Dutch rebels had more reliable and immediate allies in William of Orange's brothers, Count Johann VI of Nassau, and three other brothers. Count Johann not only had close links with the Palatinate, but he was also a major regional player as leader of the association of Wetterau counts, which linked him with the Westphalian counts and with Hessen as well. The Nassau network in the Reich was soon further reinforced by the fact that many of its members embraced the Reformed faith.[15]

Yet despite all the activities of Johann of Nassau, which extended to several military expeditions into the Netherlands, involving the loss of one brother's life in 1568 and of two more at the Battle of Mook in 1574, the Reich remained neutral. The Lower Rhine-Westphalia Kreis was incapable of making a firm decision without splitting along religious lines. Accordingly, on five occasions between 1568 and 1590 it referred matters to a conference of three Kreise. They, in turn, referred the matter on to a larger conference of five Kreise, which referred to a Deputation, which deferred to the Reichstag itself, which then finally placed the issue in the hands of the emperor personally.[16] Not once was any action taken.

Equally telling was the difference that became apparent in the approaches and attitude of William of Orange and his brother. Johann viewed an alliance with the Dutch Estates as an extension of his efforts to mobilize a coalition of the non-princely Estates in the Reich.[17] He did not dream of leaving the Reich and the system of the religious peace. William of Orange, by contrast, hoped for assistance from the Reich but did not view himself primarily as one of its princes. When the Reich failed to support his cause and the forces mobilized by his brothers proved inadequate, he began to think exclusively of the Netherlands as his 'fatherland' and

---

[13] Kohler, *Reich*, 24.   [14] Arndt, *Niederlande*, 86.   [15] See pp. 505–6.
[16] Arndt, *Niederlande*, 138.   [17] Schmidt, 'Des Prinzen Vaterland', 235–6.

to visualize France, anathema to German Protestants, as a potential ally against Spain.

William of Orange came to see a real advantage in the separation of Dutch affairs from the Reich, while the relative stability of the German situation guaranteed him at least one stable front.[18] At the same time, his marital problems also alienated much Protestant sympathy in Germany. His imprisonment of his second wife Anna, the niece of the Elector of Saxony, on grounds of adultery in 1571 enraged both the Elector and Wilhelm of Hessen, another uncle.[19] His subsequent marriage to Charlotte of Bourbon, a former nun whom he had met at Heidelberg, merely underlined his distance from the Lutheran moderates in the Reich and the extent to which he now thought in European rather than German terms.[20]

The Dutch conflict continued to reverberate in the Reich for the rest of the century and its twists and turns were followed with enormous interest in the Reich.[21] While Spanish forces involved in that conflict only actually invaded Reich territory on three occasions (in 1586–90, 1598, and 1614), a real propaganda war was fought out in the German print media over decades. Indeed, Germany became a particular source of the *leyenda negra*, the 'black legend' of Spanish perfidy. The anti-Spanish propaganda that ran through German politics in the early 1520s and 1540s was translated into a general demonization of Philip II (for both his morals and his politics) and the Spanish Inquisition, and into a deep suspicion of alleged Spanish plans for world hegemony.

Numerous German noble families became involved in the Dutch struggle at some stage or other. The German Reformed variant of Calvinism, which received crucial inspiration from the Netherlands Church and the Dutch refugees, came to have immense significance for the crisis of the Reich in the late sixteenth century. Yet the Dutch revolt also had a more benign effect on the Reich. The turmoil of the Netherlands emphasized the relative tranquillity of Germany, and the propaganda war also had the overall effect of highlighting the differences between the 'Spanish tyranny' in the Burgundian Kreis and the legal order in the rest of the Reich.[22] The German Estates as a whole, as opposed to individual noble families, particularly among the Rhineland, Westphalian, and Wetterau counts, remained neutral.

Even after the northern Netherlands provinces broke away from Spanish rule, the neighbouring German Estates were not tempted to join the rebels and break away from the Reich. Until the mid-seventeenth century the authorities in Vienna periodically feared that north-west Germany would 'turn Dutch', as some of the south-west had 'turned Swiss' around 1500.[23] Yet neither Johann VI of Nassau nor the counts of Tecklenburg and Bentheim, or Oldenburg, whose territories were directly threatened by Spanish troops, apparently ever considered such a move. They adopted Dutch models in the religious and military reform of their territories, but they opted for the Reich. These moves towards the consolidation of their hold on their territories were necessary both to raise money for imperial taxes and for

[18] Press, 'Wilhelm von Oranien'.   [19] Ritter, *Geschichte*, i, 460–2.
[20] Schmidt, 'Des Prinzen Vaterland', 236.   [21] Arndt, *Niederlande*, 213–93.
[22] Schmidt, 'Integration', 32–3. See also pp. 501–3.   [23] Schmidt, 'Integration', 33.

defence against external aggression. They also, however, ensured that around 1600 there would be no movement from below similar to the one that had accompanied the secession of the Swiss around 1500.

A similar sense of the perception of collective interests and the ability to translate that into effective policy characterizes the response of the Estates to developments in the Baltic after 1555. The origins of the Nordic Seven Years War in 1563 lay in the old struggle between Denmark, Sweden, and Lübeck for hegemony over the Baltic.[24] In 1536, Denmark and Sweden had combined to defeat Lübeck and to end her medieval predominance over the Scandinavian economies. Yet the harmony cemented by the Treaty of Brömsebro in 1541 soon dissolved into renewed rivalry. With the succession of Erik XIV in 1560, Sweden began to increase the size of its army and to negotiate an alliance with Philip of Hessen. From 1559, Frederik II of Denmark, also Duke of Holstein, sought to exploit his position as a prince of the Reich to build a new anti-Swedish coalition of princes and Hanseatic Cities.

Matters came to a head over Livonia. The Teutonic Knights had tried to reinforce their increasingly feeble grip on their territory by concluding a treaty with Poland in 1557.[25] That merely provoked an attack by Russia the following year, which drove the knights to recognize Polish overlordship in the Treaty of Vilna 1561. Both Frederick and Erik refused pleas for help from the knights. However, Frederick established a foothold in Livonia by purchasing the Sees of Kurland and Ösel and then sending his brother Magnus, whom he had installed as bishop, to conquer further territory from the Russians in 1560. Erik responded to a plea for help from the burghers of Reval by sending an army that took the city and its hinterland. In doing so, he occupied localities claimed by Magnus, which added a territorial dimension to the struggle for supremacy in the Baltic that erupted in 1563.

The flashpoint of Livonia also touched on imperial interests. While it was not part of the *Regnum Teutonicum*, Ferdinand I claimed it as part of his wider empire, and the German Estates broadly supported his claim. There was also a widespread fear that the conflict might well spill over into the Reich. The possibility of a Swedish victory raised the spectre of a new force in north Germany that, unlike the King of Denmark, was not bound by the legislation of 1555. Both Maximilian II and the Elector of Saxony made strenuous efforts to mediate and mobilized the consultative mechanisms of the Reich and its Kreise to ensure that the domestic peace was maintained. Finally, in 1570 Maximilian was able to broker the Peace of Stettin. Each side dropped claims against the other. In return for a promise of compensation from Maximilian, the Swedes ceded all their Livonian holdings except Reval to Frederick, who agreed to recognize the emperor as his overlord.[26]

The emperor's successful mediation in 1570 and his continuing involvement in managing the Baltic peace until 1576 were all part of a strategy that soon deviated from the interests of the German Estates.[27] Maximilian's proposals to the Reichstag of 1570 for combating Russian aggression against Livonia met with reserve. Nor

[24] Frost, *Northern wars*, 23–37. [25] See p. 373.
[26] Lavery, *Challenge*, 131. [27] Lavery, *Challenge*, 136–41.

did the princes demonstrate much interest in Maximilian's various embassies to Ivan IV. Similarly, subsequent Reichsdeputationstage shunned schemes for the 'recuperation' of Livonia, since the Estates rightly suspected that what Maximilian really wanted was the transformation of Livonia into another Habsburg fiefdom in the Reich. The German Estates also refused to contribute to the sum needed to compensate Sweden for its withdrawal from Livonia. As a result, the Swedes eventually declared Maximilian's claims null and void in 1577. The reality on the ground had in any case been determined by the knights' recognition of Polish overlordship in the Treaty of Vilna in 1561 and in the bloody struggles between Poland and Russia that ensued.[28]

The largely dynastic, rather than imperial, nature of Maximilian's interest was soon underlined further by Maximilian II's attempts to secure the Polish crown for Habsburg candidates in the elections of 1573 and 1575.[29] In the first election, his sons, Archdukes Ernst and Maximilian, lost to Henri of Valois. In the second election, occasioned by Henri's unexpected succession in France, the Polish Senate actually declared Maximilian II king but was then overruled by the more numerous lower house, which preferred István Báthory, Prince of Transylvania, to either the emperor or his sons Ernst and Ferdinand. The rewards of success might have been considerable. The Turks might have been crushed decisively. The Habsburgs would have had access to the Baltic, and might even have been able to push the Russians back.

Failure to win Poland was not dishonourable, however. The imperial crown depended on seven Electors; some fifty thousand electors held the key to the Polish crown. Yet again, the emperor lacked the money to press his case. Just as the German Estates saw no reason why they should help Maximilian acquire Livonia, so the Lower Austrian Estates saw no reason why they should pay to help him gain Poland.[30] A final opportunity to acquire the Polish throne after Báthory's death also ended in failure. The election of Archduke Maximilian III (the German Master of the Teutonic Knights) by the majority of Polish nobles was overturned by the superior force of arms of Sigismund III Vasa, who had been elected by a minority.[31] Again the German princes refused point blank to supply either money or troops.[32]

The significance for the Reich of these events lies in the German Estates' identification and assertion of their interests. When the peace of 1555 was threatened, they were able to act, and the mechanisms of the imperial constitution functioned effectively. When Habsburg dynastic interests took over from the duties of the emperor to the Reich, the Estates ceased to support him. Furthermore, these

---

[28] Rabe, *Geschichte*, 471–2; Mühlen, 'Livland', 154–72 and Mühlen, 'Ostbaltikum', 175–87. In the 1580s, Sweden, which retained Reval and Estonia, again entered into an alliance with Poland to drive out the Russians.

[29] Lavery, *Challenge*, 140–1; Stone, *Polish-Lithuanian state*, 116–22.

[30] Fichtner, *Maximilian II*, 205. Fichtner presents Maximilian's failure to acquire Poland as symptomatic of a more general incompetence, which fails to take account of the reasoning of either the German or the Austrian Estates.

[31] Stone, *Polish-Lithuanian state*, 131–2.

[32] Kohler, *Reich*, 27.

events defined new frontiers for the Reich. In the late fifteenth century, the Baltic coastal territories had been remote from the Reich. In the second half of the sixteenth century, Baltic affairs were discussed at the Reichstag. With regard to Livonia and Poland, the German Estates made consistently clear distinctions between what was German and what was Habsburg—much as they had once done with regard to Maximilian I's endeavours in Italy and Burgundy. The full integration of the north into the Reich was not complete until the mid-seventeenth century. In the decades after 1555, however, the process of integration advanced decisively.[33] A crucial indicator was the fact that the Estates of this region now already paid their imperial taxes at up to 90 per cent of the specified rate.[34]

Not new at all, finally, was the constant pressure exerted by the Turks. It had been established beyond all doubt before 1555 that the Turks were a threat to the German Reich, and there was no dissent from that view now. Indeed, the German princes several times accused Maximilian of neglecting his duties against the Turks. That little progress was made was due partly to the assumptions on which policy was based. While the Ottomans continued to dominate the Mediterranean, even after their defeat at Lepanto in 1572, the military threat they posed on land was by no means as great as Christian polemics and Ottoman propaganda implied. However, that threat certainly existed, and even when the sultans were preoccupied with their own eastern front in Persia, their vassals in Transylvania and the local governors of the border territories under their direct rule kept up constant pressure in border raids and limited local wars.

The Habsburgs responded in two ways. In the long term, the most effective response was the fortification of the frontier, started in the 1520s and continued by Ferdinand I throughout his life and by his successors. Some eighty fortresses were constructed before 1556. By 1593, the number had risen to 171, with combined permanent garrisons of well over 20,000 men.[35] In the short term, however, the relatively unresolved situation in Transylvania seemed to require more direct military action. The peace of 1547 had left Ferdinand with only a small strip of Hungarian territory; Transylvania was placed in the hands of John Zápolya's widow, Queen Isabella, during the minority of his son, John Sigismund. Real power lay in the hands of the Bishop of Varad, György Martinuzzi, and strenuous efforts were made to persuade him to subvert the Turkish suzerainty and transfer Transylvania to Austrian rule. Martinuzzi's double-dealing ended with his assassination in 1551, which once more left military confrontation as the only possible way forward. Repeated initiatives over the following years proved futile, however, and in 1562 an eight-year truce confirmed the Ottoman hegemony over much of Hungary and Transylvania, and furthermore obliged the emperor to pay a substantially increased annual tribute of 30,000 ducats in respect of the limited Hungarian territory he held.[36]

[33] North, 'Integration'.   [34] Jörn, 'Steuerzahlung', 388.
[35] Palffy, 'Verteidigung', 42.   [36] Lanzinner, 'Zeitalter', 60.

The truce allowed Suleiman the Magnificent to pursue his ambitions in the Mediterranean and against Persia, though in 1566 he turned his attention once more to Hungary, where border hostilities had escalated again since 1564. Both sides managed to strike serious blows and Maximilian II, aided by Lazarus von Schwendi as his commander in the field, probably gained a winning advantage when Suleiman died during the siege of Szigetvár in September 1566. Maximilian was criticized at the time and by historians since then for acting too defensively.[37] However, in truth the Austrians were no more capable of a decisive victory over the Turks than the Turks were of achieving such a thing against the Austrians.

The Austrian effort was always underfunded. Money promised by the Estates of the various Austrian territories was never sufficient, and the Habsburgs were perennially dependent on vast loans from a variety of sources.[38] Until 1566, the German princes agreed to give money only for fortifications, and were suspicious of imperial ambitions to exploit the Turkish threat in order to create a standing army. In the absence of any major wave of defections to the Austrian cause, either in Transylvania or elsewhere along the frontier, the Austrians could achieve little. The Turks too lost the will to fight after Suleiman's death.[39] Consequently, in the Peace of Adrianople in 1568 Maximilian and Selim II agreed to renew the truce for a further eight years on the same conditions.

Further renewals followed in 1577 and 1590. From 1574 Murad III concentrated on the Mediterranean, on asserting his interests against the Austrian Habsburgs in the various Polish royal elections, and on a major confrontation with Persia in 1579–90.[40] Maximilian and, after 1576, Rudolf focused on building up the frontier defences. While neither side wanted a war, the local conflict, often involving forces of up to 5,000 men, continued unabated. Eventually one such skirmish on the Croatian border led to the outbreak of the great Turkish war in 1593.[41] But for twenty-five years the Peace of Adrianople provided at least a minimum of security on the south-eastern front.

The Habsburgs' problems in Hungary after 1555 should not be underestimated. However, the significance of the situation there for the domestic development of the Reich in some ways outweighed the military threat. First, the Hungarian frontier was yet another theatre in which the German Estates, and to some extent the Austrian Estates as well, could decide to distinguish between what was of German (or Austrian) concern and what was purely Habsburg dynastic interest. Second, the propagandistic exaggeration of the Turkish threat ensured a greater willingness on the part of the German Estates to contribute more regularly than in the first half of the century to the defence of the Reich. Taxes to support the war against the Turks (*Türkensteuern*) became a regular feature of Reichstag meetings

---

[37] Fichtner, *Maximilian II*, 119–34.
[38] Pamlényi, *Hungary*, 132–3; Palffy, 'Verteidigung', 43.
[39] Sugar, *Southeastern Europe*, 187–96; Murphey, *Ottoman warfare*, 6–8.
[40] Shaw, *Ottoman Empire*, i, 175–83. In 1576, a Turkish envoy to Vienna pronounced that Poland had belonged to the Ottomans for 130 years: Iorge, *Osmanisches Reich*, iii, 268.
[41] Finkel, *Administration*, 8–11. See also pp. 382, 410, 432–3.

after 1555 and in some ways helped impose a discipline and routine on the proceedings. Negotiations over the level of contributions and how they should be spent contributed significantly to the evolution of 'emperor and Reich' as a constitutional entity.[42] This, in turn, had significant implications for the development of the German territories, as the Estates developed regular taxation systems to raise the money they agreed to pay.[43] Above all, the conjunction of the great Turkish war (1593–1606) with the beginnings of the great constitutional crisis of the Reich graphically illustrated the relationship between the Turkish threat and the domestic politics of the Reich.[44] Third, throughout the sixteenth century the Turkish threat exerted a significant mobilizing effect on the lower nobility in the Reich, binding Imperial Knights and Imperial Counts to the crown through military service often inspired by notions of a revival of old ideals of knighthood and patriotic royal service.[45]

In general, the 'foreign policy' of the Reich, and its response to the various European conflicts of the second half of the sixteenth century, confirms the impression gained from an examination of constitutional developments. The sense of the German Reich as a polity with its own distinctive collective interest was reinforced. The institutions created between 1495 and 1555 were challenged by the various threats to imperial territory and domestic peace and harmony. Their dependence on the consensus of all involved often precluded any very active response. Yet they worked in ways that ensured the survival of the system of 1555 and they provided the framework within which a succession of domestic issues were either resolved or managed relatively successfully until the onset of the great crisis of the Reich around 1600.

---

[42] Schulze, *Türkengefahr*; Rauscher, 'Kaiser und Reich'.
[43] See pp. 512–16.
[44] See pp. 432–3.
[45] Liepold, *Wieder den Erbfeind*, 310–14, 407–13. Lazarus von Schwendi himself exemplified this phenomenon.

31

Managing the Domestic Peace, 1555–*c*.1585

The need for money to defend the Reich against the Turks was the primary reason why both Ferdinand I and Maximilian II convened the Reichstag. The subventions for the anti-Turkish defences were the subject of the usual haggling and wrangling. Yet in the end significant sums of money were invariably agreed. Any attempts to make political capital out of the negotiation, to extract promises from the emperor on other matters in return for agreement to taxes, were soon undermined by the supportive attitude of Saxony and the other Estates of the eastern parts of the Reich. For, unlike the Palatinate or Württemberg, they all perceived the Turks as a real threat to themselves as well as to the Habsburgs. Two other issues that dominated the domestic politics of the Reich in the first decade after 1555 raised altogether more thorny issues: the religious peace and domestic security.

The religious issue was not resolved, but it was managed. Both Ferdinand I and Maximilian II were obliged to steer a delicate course. On the one hand, the Protestant Electors twice protested against the emperor's traditional oath of loyalty to the Church and to the pope: in 1558, on the occasion of Ferdinand's election, and in 1562, when Maximilian was elected as King of the Romans.[1] Their protest was stilled by the incorporation of the peace of 1555 into the electoral capitulation and by the fact that the papacy was accorded no formal role in the election and confirmation process. Indeed, in 1562 the Protestant Electors' protest was itself formally recorded in the capitulation.

On the other hand, both emperors were aware of the need to appease the papacy in some way, while not, of course, submitting to it. In 1558, Ferdinand and his advisers were adamant in denying Paul IV's claim to the right to confirm Charles V's abdication and Ferdinand's succession.[2] Hostility to the 'old, wrong-headed, and silly Pope', as the imperial councillor Zasius referred to him, also produced a clear strategy with regard to any council of the Church.[3] Reichsvizekanzler Seld argued that the decisions made by the Councils of Constance and Basle in the early fifteenth century were still valid for the Reich: the pope was merely an episcopal *primus inter pares* who exercised authority, not 'for himself alone' but in the name of the Church.[4] Furthermore, in many instances, Seld opined, the pope was obliged

---

[1] Ritter, *Geschichte*, i, 255.   [2] Kleinheyer, 'Abdankung', 129–33.
[3] Ritter, *Geschichte*, i, 144.   [4] Ritter, *Geschichte*, i, 144–5.

to submit to the authority of the council, and he insisted that the emperor had just as much right to summon it as the pope had.

The accession of the more conciliatory Pope Pius IV in August 1559 brought about a certain moderation of the imperial view. Ferdinand and his closest advisers were now determined as far as possible to avoid the fundamental issue of papal authority. Their essential aim, however, remained the same: to influence the Church Council, which Pius IV and those who had elected him were determined to resume, and to create a framework for a German settlement. What that meant was elaborated in the reform proposal Ferdinand I handed over in May 1562.[5] He sought reform of the Curia, education of the clergy, a reduction in the number of laws of the Church that sought to govern the consciences of the laity, and the recognition of clerical marriage and communion in both kinds. The reform of the Curia was the least of these proposals. What really mattered to Ferdinand were the measures designed to be acceptable to the German Protestants.

By the time the Council of Trent had begun to consider the emperor's views, it was probably too late for a genuinely religious solution in Germany. The emperor's efforts to pursue the reconciliation, as enjoined by the Treaty of Passau 1552, came to nothing. A German national council was impossible because Catholics and Protestants disagreed fundamentally about what such a council would, or could, represent: the Church, under the leadership of the pope, or a purely national gathering of ecclesiastical and secular Estates, with the Bible as sole authority and without the pope. Furthermore, any hopes Ferdinand might have had persuading the Protestants to recognize a council were frustrated for the time being at least by the fact that proceedings at Trent had been suspended and Paul IV was in no mood to reconvene. The only other option was to attempt a religious colloquy, to which the Regensburg Reichstag of 1556–7 duly consented.[6]

Neither side was particularly enthusiastic. Several leading Protestant princes were reluctant to enter into a process that envisaged concessions on both sides.[7] Melanchthon commented that few would engage in a colloquy in good faith, though some might console themselves with the thought that one or other of the bishops or princes might see the light. On the Catholic side, too, there were divided views. The bishops resented the implied diminution of their rights and those of the pope. Many secular princes were suspicious of the Protestants and deeply critical of, even contemptuous of, the episcopal princes, whom they held responsible for the corruption of the clergy as a whole. At the same time, however, some, like Duke Albrecht of Bavaria, were inclined to consider concessions such as clerical marriage, communion in both kinds, and the relaxation of rules governing fasting.[8]

In the event, the nine-day colloquy that opened in Worms under the chairmanship of Bishop Julius von Pflug of Naumburg on 11 September 1557 was fruitless.[9] An impressive array of theologians attended, including Melanchthon and Johannes Brenz for the Protestant side and Peter Canisius for the Catholics. None of the

[5] Ritter, *Geschichte*, i, 156–8.   [6] Bundschuh, *Religionsgespräch*, 170–247.
[7] Rabe, *Geschichte*, 530–1.   [8] Ritter, *Geschichte*, i, 135.
[9] Bundschuh, *Religionsgespräch*, 370–507.

other bishops or princes attended in person, which meant that nothing could have been decided anyway. However, that issue did not even arise, for bitter divisions soon developed within the Protestant camp between the adherents of Flacius Illyricus of Jena, the more moderate Melanchthon of Wittenberg, and the south-west German and Swiss tendencies. The failure of the Protestants to agree on exactly which articles of faith the *confessio Augustana* comprised precipitated the abrupt end of the colloquy on 20 September, when the Saxons departed in high dudgeon.

The Worms colloquy was the last of its kind, but its failure did not deter Ferdinand from pursuing the idea of reunification of the Church. In 1559, he followed with interest the efforts by the Duke of Jülich-Kleve-Berg to stage a colloquy in Düsseldorf.[10] That failed to come about owing to the illness of Georg Cassander (1513–1566), the prominent Catholic 'reform' theologian who was due to play a key role, but in 1564, Ferdinand commissioned Cassander to produce new proposals for a reconciliation of the differences between Catholics and Protestants. Maximilian II took over these schemes after Ferdinand's death, but they came to nothing when Cassander died.[11]

Much more effort went into securing the terms of the political compromise between the religious factions, and with greater result. While the Estates demonstrated an unwillingness to engage in theological discussion, they were positively eager to explore the terms of the religious peace and to secure clarifications of it that were to their own advantage. Within a very short time the details of the settlement of 1555 were being questioned. The ensuing debate became a key theme in German politics until 1648. However, while it might be tempting to trace a clear line from the settlement of 1555 to the outbreak of the Thirty Years War in 1618, it would be an oversimplification to see that conflict as pre-programmed from the outset. Until about 1570 at least, but arguably into the early 1580s, the negotiations over the terms of the religious peace must be seen as part of a more general search for stability. Only later did the confessional antagonism become embroiled in the fundamental constitutional disputes that led to war.

The first difficulties arose out of the simple need to clarify the broad principles of the Augsburg legislation. Two issues were immediately problematic. The stipulation that ecclesiastical property belonging to one or other confession before the Treaty of Passau (2 August 1552) 'or thereafter' should be recognized as legally owned by them, led both Catholics and Protestants to claim ownership of anything that they had held at any stage since 1552, in addition to everything they had held before then.[12] In practice, Protestant Estates simply ignored any Catholic calls for the restitution of property and continued to secularize ecclesiastical property and foundations in the lands under their control.

Even the secularization of bishoprics proceeded apace. Saxony gained Meissen (1559), Merseburg, and Naumburg (both 1565). The Electorate of Brandenburg incorporated the Bishoprics of Brandenburg, Havelburg, and Lebus in 1560, and a

---

[10] Schindling and Ziegler, *Territorien*, iii, 98.
[11] *ABD*, iv, 60–1; Louthan, *Quest*, 104–5, 130.
[12] Schindling, 'Passauer Vertrag'.

Hohenzollern archbishop turned Magdeburg and Halberstadt Protestant in 1561.[13] Mecklenburg took Schwerin (1553) and Ratzeburg (1575). Lübeck, Bremen, Verden, and Minden also all became Protestant and sooner or later fell under the control of neighbouring ruling houses. Innumerable complaints inevitably arose over the Church property issue, and they formed the bulk of the renewed *Gravamina* that both sides brought to the Augsburg Reichstag in 1559.[14]

The secularization of bishoprics also touched on a second issue: the question of the exemption ('Freistellung') of individuals and groups from the restrictions of the 1555 legislation. Initially, discussion of this point revolved around the legality and implications of the *reservatum ecclesiasticum*, the stipulation in §18 of the peace, that an ecclesiastical prince who converted to Catholicism must relinquish his benefice. This had not been recognized by the Protestants in 1555 and they protested against its inclusion in the legislation. The fact that they did not veto its inclusion earned them Ferdinand's informal concession of the right of Protestant knights, towns, and communities in ecclesiastical territories to retain their religion, the *Declaratio Ferdinandea*, which became a major bone of contention after 1576.[15] In the meantime, they refused to accept the *reservatum ecclesiasticum* as law, and almost immediately sought to undermine it.

From the outset, however, the meaning of exemption or 'Freistellung' was elastic.[16] It could refer to the rights of nobles in both ecclesiastical and secular territories. Equally problematic were the arguments over whether the magistrates of Imperial Cities had the duty to maintain the status quo that had prevailed in 1555, whether they might permit new religious communities to be established, and whether they had the right to change the official religion of their city. The issue was particularly important for all those Estates whose religious affairs were not settled by 1555, and especially for those rulers who embarked on religious reform after that date.[17] In the arguments of the Palatinate lawyers in 1556 and 1559, 'Freistellung' could mean the right of all subjects of all Estates to exercise either religion freely. The right to emigrate, they reasoned, surely implied the right to remain, and since the right to emigrate was not linked with the obligation to change one's beliefs, the right to remain could not be encumbered with such an obligation either.[18] Of course, this was not intended as a 'modern' argument in favour of universal religious freedom. When the Saxon representatives enquired in 1559 whether the Palatine Elector really wished to grant freedom to Catholics in his lands, the response was that this would be problematic. Essentially the demand for a general freedom was made in the belief that the Protestant cause would soon prevail generally anyway.[19]

---

[13] Magdeburg became a Brandenburg territory in 1648, and Halberstadt ultimately a Protestant secundogeniture of Brunswick-Wolfenbüttel: Wolgast, *Hochstift*, 275–6.

[14] Gotthard, *Religionsfrieden*, 355–8.

[15] Ritter, *Geschichte*, i, 83–4. See also pp. 334, 396–8.

[16] Schneider, *Ius reformandi*, 157–66; Gotthard, *Religionsfrieden*, 102–10, 331–55.

[17] Schmidt, *Grafenverein*, 259–61.

[18] Gotthard, *Reich*, 63–4.

[19] Ibid., 64; Ritter, *Geschichte*, i, 131.

The radical demands of the Palatine lawyers remained in the background initially. At the Regensburg Reichstag in 1556, the Elector Ottheinrich's envoys failed in their attempt to organize a Protestant party dedicated to the cause of religious freedom, and determined to refuse to contribute to the defence of the Reich until that was achieved. At Augsburg in 1559, a renewed initiative also came to nothing. The Protestant Estates again preferred to follow the lead of the conciliatory Elector of Saxony and they refused to link financial contributions to any political demands. Once more, they demanded the abrogation of the *reservatum ecclesiasticum*, and they registered their strong protest when the emperor again refused to oblige. Yet they took no further action, other than to present a detailed list of their specific complaints, to which the Catholics promptly responded in kind.

Faced with these complaints, and with the Protestant insistence that the Reichskammergericht was incapable of dealing with them, Ferdinand suggested the issue be referred to the Reichsdeputation planned for the following year to review the court and its procedures. That proposal fell because the Catholics refused to acquiesce in the Protestant demand that the court be suspended for the duration. Aware that any imperial decree or intervention would only be acceptable to the party that it favoured, Ferdinand finally contented himself with the advice that disputes should be resolved either by compromise or by resort to the law.

It is significant that both sides appeared willing to accept this outcome. Individual Estates continued to pursue their grievances, either by resort to the imperial courts or by direct action, often with the full support of neighbouring co-religionists. Yet at this stage neither side showed any real enthusiasm for any further large-scale action, such as a confessional league.[20] The Archbishop Elector of Trier, under pressure following the establishment of a Protestant community in the city of Trier itself, tried to enlist Ferdinand in a Catholic league. But the scheme came to nothing when it became clear that Ferdinand was simply interested in a Rhineland and Lower German equivalent of the Landsberg League. He envisaged a confessionally mixed association including both Philip II as ruler of the Netherlands and the Protestant rulers of the Palatinate, Electoral Saxony, and Hessen, with the aim of strengthening the Reich in the north-west and enhancing his own position as ruler.

The Protestant princes were unwilling to ally themselves with Catholics, yet schemes for a Protestant league also foundered. Even the persistent rumours of anti-Protestant alliances between German Catholic princes and non-German powers, which the German Protestants feared above all else, failed to galvanize a reaction. Philip of Hessen's scheme for a western German Protestant defensive league came to nothing in 1562. While the Dukes of Württemberg and Zweibrücken showed some interest, the majority of Protestant Estates took their cue from the perennially loyalist Elector of Saxony. Even the new Palatine Elector Friedrich III, otherwise every bit as militant as his predecessor and himself currently in the process of leading his territory to Calvinism, followed the Saxon line on this occasion.

The same fundamental commitment to the principles established in 1555, both the equilibrium between the confessional groups and the role of the emperor in it, was demonstrated at Maximilian II's first Reichstag at Augsburg in 1566.[21] This was perhaps all the more surprising in view of the dangerous developments in the religious issue over the preceding years. The religious conflict in France had led to contacts between the Huguenot leaders and various western German Protestant princes, who contributed to a loan and permitted troops to be recruited in their territories. Early contacts with the Netherlands Protestant leaders added another ominous dimension to what some feared were the beginnings of a broad international coalition. Then, in 1563, the Elector Friedrich published the Heidelberg Catechism and decreed the conversion of the Palatinate from Lutheranism to the Reformed faith. His particularly energetic pursuit of this new religious reform in the Upper Palatinate and with regard to the Imperial Knights among his Palatine clientele generated hostility among many Lutheran princes. Yet Maximilian's attempt to deal with this perennial opponent of the house of Habsburg failed miserably. His proposal that the Elector be excluded from the religious peace since he did not subscribe to the Augsburg Confession occasioned considerable tactical manoeuvring in advance of the Reichstag. Unscrupulous opportunists and incorrigible conspirators, such as the Dukes of Württemberg and Zweibrücken, saw the chance to undermine a powerful regional competitor. Other princes, such as the Elector of Brandenburg, simply wished to rid themselves of a troublemaker.

The Elector of Saxony, rather surprisingly, took a different view.[22] His argument that to accede to the emperor's demand would simply create a precedent that would potentially leave all Protestant Estates vulnerable to imperial aggression won over Friedrich's Lutheran critics and ensured that Protestant solidarity was maintained. The emperor received the reply that the Palatine Elector subscribed to all main articles of the Augsburg Confession and differed from his co-religionists only in his understanding of the communion. The emperor's riposte that he was troubled to see deviant views of the communion taken so lightly was countered with the argument that theologians both differed greatly on this issue and often taught in such obscure terms that ordinary folk could not understand them. Furthermore, since the Elector had expressed himself willing to engage in further talks on the matter, it would be contrary to the spirit of the Christian Church to condemn him.

The Protestants' determination to stand by the Palatinate led to the tacit approval of Calvinism in the Reich. In the long term, this had fateful consequences. It legitimized the Palatine position and thus gave scope for the further development of the Elector's ambitious and provocative policies, both in the Reich and abroad. It also opened the way for any other Estates to move towards Calvinism, thus potentially weakening the Protestant cause in the Reich by dividing it into two antagonistic camps. In the short term, however, other matters were more significant. First, the Peace of 1555 was reaffirmed, which was the prime aim of Saxon policy throughout. Second, the emperor had been denied the right to proscribe

---

[21] Rabe, *Geschichte*, 534–5; Lanzinner and Heil, 'Reichstag'.
[22] Ritter, *Geschichte*, i, 84–6.

'sects' and, furthermore, he had been thwarted in his desire to allay the suspicions of the Catholic Estates about his own personal religious loyalties by taking a strong stand against the Palatinate. Third, the fact that it was Saxony that had 'saved' the Palatinate and coordinated a successful Protestant rebuttal of the emperor reaffirmed the Elector of Saxony as the leader of the German (Lutheran) Protestant Estates and the arbiter of politics in the Reich generally for the foreseeable future.

The Reich was further stabilized in 1566 by the stalemate reached on other aspects of the religious issue. The presentation of *Gravamina* was met with the advice to take complaints to the courts. The emperor declined to contemplate any general clarification or elaboration of the peace of 1555. The fate of a specific request relating to the exemption issue that was brought forward by the Wetterau counts but adopted by the Protestant Estates as a whole is instructive.[23]

Among the decrees issued by the Council of Trent in 1563 was the stipulation that, henceforth, all canons should swear their loyalty to the Catholic faith and that all bishops should be consecrated within three months of being confirmed in their office. The Wetterau counts, by now all Protestant, rightly saw this as a threat to the traditional career options of their younger sons in cathedral chapters, specifically that of Cologne. It also threatened the political leverage in the Reich that they derived from their links with those from among their ranks who were elected to prince-bishoprics. Even before the Tridentine decrees were confirmed in the Reich, the counts attempted to create a precedent by persuading the Elector of Cologne (Friedrich von Wied was a scion of one the Wetterau dynasties) to convert to Protestantism. Even though Archbishop Friedrich himself refused to take the Tridentine oath (and was forced to resign in 1567 as a result), he declined to become involved with the Wetterau proposals.[24]

At Augsburg in 1566, the Wetterau counts consequently had no option but to fall in with the general proposition by the Protestant Estates that religious freedom should be granted to all. When that, predictably, failed, they attempted to advance a specific request that their relatives be exempted from the new duties and oaths, but their petition did not even earn a reply. In this case, too, the supporters of the 'Augsburg system' prevailed over those, like the Palatine Elector and the Wetterau counts, whose material and political interests lay in the radical revision of the status quo. For both the Elector and the counts, 1566 was a watershed. From then on, they began to turn away from the Protestant mainstream, ever more firmly towards Reformed Protestantism and to a commitment to the cause of Calvinist rebels in the Netherlands. Yet this was a very gradual slide into opposition, at first an almost imperceptible shift into another gear, the full significance of which only became apparent many decades later. For now, Saxony was able to hold together the Augsburg consensus unchallenged.

The Reichstag of 1566 concluded with a general 'loyal' and 'unswerving' reaffirmation of the 'most solemn' religious peace of 1555.[25] This left the Protestant malcontents as dissatisfied as the papacy.[26] The papal legate Commendone had

[23] Schmidt, *Grafenverein*, 259–73.   [24] Wolgast, *Hochstift*, 288–9.
[25] Heckel, *Deutschland*, 74.   [26] Heckel, *Deutschland*, 74–6.

been able to persuade the Catholic Estates to adopt the Tridentine decrees concerning articles of faith and the Mass; the rest they asked to postpone until better times. In joining the reaffirmation of the religious peace in the Reich, the German Catholics gave imperial law precedence over the Tridentine decrees. The papacy was powerless to prevent measures formulated for all Christians by a universal council of the Church becoming little more than a set of sectarian regulations in Germany.

As at all the sessions of the Reichstag after 1555, the solidarity of the Imperial Estates was bolstered in 1566 by the Turkish threat. The need to launch a new offensive against the Porte led them to agree a hitherto unprecedented levy of 48 Roman Months (over three million gulden).[27] More significant still, however, was the fact that this Reichstag saw the resolution of a major internal threat that challenged the internal stability of the Reich as fundamental as any dispute over religion had done in the first decade after 1555. The way that the Estates dealt with the rebellion of the Imperial Knight Wilhelm von Grumbach was a measure of the solidity of the Augsburg system.[28]

Like many rebels, Wilhelm von Grumbach appealed to traditional law and ancient rights to secure what he regarded as his inheritance.[29] In fact, he was acutely aware of the changing political world that he inhabited. He was sensitive to the ways in which the position of the Imperial Knights had changed during the middle decades of the century and he was willing to exploit both the legal system of the Reich and the Western European Protestant networks to promote his cause. He also had a talent for publicity and an extraordinary ability to portray himself as a poor victim being ground beneath the wheels of princely ambition. Though he has often been portrayed as a throwback to the medieval type of feuding knight, Grumbach was in fact very much in tune with the transformation of the position of the knights in the Reich since the late fifteenth century. He sought to remedy his grievances with a combination of traditional methods and an attempt to mobilize the new regional organizations of the knights to his own advantage in the name of a grand political vision.

The Grumbachs were a powerful Franconian dynasty, which had prospered by successfully negotiating a course between the competing political ambitions of the main regional powers, the Bishops of Würzburg and Bamberg, the Margraves of Brandenburg-Ansbach, and the Imperial City of Nuremberg. They had particularly close ties with Würzburg, from where they held many of their estates as fiefs; indeed, two of their dynasty had become Bishops of Würzburg and many had held canonries there.

Wilhelm von Grumbach, of the cadet line of the dynasty at Rimpar, was born in 1503. He was educated first at the Würzburg court of Lorenz von Bibra, just nine kilometres south of Rimpar, and then at the court of Brandenburg-Ansbach, possibly in yet another attempt by the family to assert its independence of

---

[27] Schulze, *Türkengefahr*, 76–7.
[28] Lanzinner and Heil, 'Reichstag', 622–3.
[29] For what follows, see Press, 'Grumbach'; Zmora, *State*, 143–5; *ADB*, x, 9–22.

Würzburg. He distinguished himself on the princes' side in the Peasants' War and fought in the decisive battle at Rothenburg ob der Tauber, in which his brother-in-law, Florian Geyer, the knight who had assumed leadership of the Franconian peasants, fell. Grumbach's Ansbach connections intensified when he became a close associate of the young Margrave Albrecht Alcibiades (b. 1522, and under the guardianship of his uncle from 1527). In 1538, he became bailiff in Cadolzburg, and two years later he supported the young margrave's successful bid to partition the dynastic patrimony, leaving his uncle Georg with Ansbach and himself with sole control over Kulmbach and Bayreuth. Crucially, Grumbach also accompanied his young patron to the court of Charles V at Ghent in 1540.

However, while Albrecht Alcibiades stayed on to gain the emperor's favour and to secure a military appointment in 1543, developments in Würzburg caused Grumbach to break off his stay. The death of Bishop Konrad von Thüngen led Grumbach to connive at the election of his kinsman and ally Canon Konrad von Bibra over the ambitious Dean, Melchior von Zobel. Grumbach promptly became seneschal of the new bishop's court and bailiff of two of the most profitable bailiwicks. His good fortune came to an end, however, with Bibra's death in 1544 and the election of Zobel. The following year, Grumbach resigned his court office, and in 1547 he left the bishop's service altogether. Relations had finally soured after Grumbach coordinated a petition to the Augsburg Reichstag designed to free the Franconian knights from all obligations to the regional powers.

The collapse of his Würzburg schemes led Grumbach to turn back to Albrecht Alcibiades, who appointed him his stadtholder in Kulmbach in 1551. Initially committed to Charles V, Grumbach followed the margrave into service with the anti-imperial league of Protestant princes; when this conflict was settled, both continued the struggle on their own accounts against the Bishops of Bamberg and Würzburg and the city of Nuremberg. This enterprise ended in disaster and cost Grumbach his lands. These were confiscated by Würzburg, which refused to relinquish them, despite a Reichskammergericht judgment in Grumbach's favour in the summer of 1555. Grumbach's challenge now began in earnest. He renewed his military contract in France and entered the service of the Elector of Brandenburg. He also took up contact with the two potentially most disruptive forces in German politics: the Elector of the Palatinate and Duke Johann Friedrich of Saxony. The latter, still bitterly resentful of being deprived of his Electoral title in 1547, became Grumbach's main patron after the death of Albrecht Alcibiades.

An attempt to kidnap Bishop Melchior von Zobel in 1558 ended in the bishop's accidental death at the hands of one of Grumbach's retainers. Frustrated in his aim of holding the bishop hostage to enforce the restitution of his properties, Grumbach now made even more ambitious plans. In collaboration with Duke Johann Friedrich, he hatched plans for French sponsorship of a mercenary army under their joint command that would restore the duke to his Electorate and place Duke Adolf of Holstein on the Danish throne. In 1562, Grumbach further raised the stakes and fuelled Johann Friedrich's ambitions by sponsoring the visions of a young peasant boy, Hans Tausendschön of Gotha, to whom angels had allegedly vouchsafed sure knowledge of the future.

Predictions of the violent deaths of the emperor and the new Bishop of Würz-burg merely further agitated those already fired up by the various conspiracies, notably the duke, Grumbach himself, and their immediate circles. More serious was the fact that Grumbach made appeals for support not only to the Franconian knights generally, but also to the Swabian knights and to the Bavarian lower nobility. The resonance of his struggle among the lower nobility in north Germany was equally significant. His friends and contacts among the German cavalry captains who had returned from mercenary service in France after the Treaty of Cateau-Cambrésis in 1559 (currently being recruited again on both sides of the French religious conflict of 1562–3) ensured publicity and sympathy for his cause. They provided at least the hope of some armed support from the north.[30]

In the event, Grumbach directed his next move against Würzburg. Following the publication of a pamphlet justifying his grievance against the bishopric, he led a small force from his new base near Coburg to capture the city in October 1563. Following the traditional rules of the feud, he forced the bishop and chapter to sign a treaty restoring all his property to him, whereupon he withdrew his force back to Duke Johann Friedrich's territory. This blatant breach of the public peace imme-diately eliminated any lingering sympathy for him on the part of the emperor, who promptly outlawed him.

The south German princes were now also galvanized by fears of a general uprising of the nobility, a new Knights' War in which the Swabian knights might join forces with their Franconian counterparts. The coordinator of the resistance was Duke Christoph of Württemberg, who had worked hard to compensate for being ruler of a territory without nobles by playing a leading role in the Swabian Kreis, which gave him an authority and influence over the Swabian knights which he now feared he might lose. Also active was Duke Albrecht V of Bavaria, who currently faced a Protestant noble insurgency. However, a meeting at Maulbronn in January 1564 failed to produce a clear line, owing to the Palatine Elector's underlying sympathy for the rebels: yet another manifestation of the Palatinate's interest in destabilizing the peace of 1555, in contrast to the strong interest of virtually all others in maintaining it.

Grumbach himself spun ever wider webs.[31] Once Ferdinand I had outlawed him, he placed his hopes in Maximilian, who came to the throne in June 1564. In May 1565 he even sent an emissary to Vienna, offering Maximilian an alliance of a league of counts and knights together with the Duke of Saxony, who was to be restored to his Electoral title. The aim, he suggested, was to oppose the alleged expansionist ambitions of the Elector August of Saxony and to establish a strength-ened hereditary monarchy in Germany.

Almost simultaneously, however, prospects for such a league evaporated. The Duke of Bavaria moved decisively to quell his Protestant opposition in the summer of 1564. In August of the same year, the majority of the Franconian knights disowned Grumbach, declaring their support for the peace of 1555. The Swabian

---

[30] Liepold, *Wider den Erbfeind*, 128–31; Press, 'Grumbach', 393.
[31] Press, 'Grumbach', 409–13.

knights also came to perceive their interests as lying in stability rather than insurgency. In 1565, the region's leading princes were able to forge a new alliance with the knights by 'exposing' the Palatine Elector's pro-noble sentiments as nothing but a cover for expansionism and a desire to promote the spread of Calvinism.

Maximilian himself had taken decisive steps against Grumbach even before the emissary arrived in Vienna. Though he had once been more sympathetic than Ferdinand to Grumbach's cause, he had established a common line with the Saxon Elector as early as November 1563. Maximilian's reaction to Grumbach's emissary is not known, but his policy in 1565 and 1566 was clear. Once Grumbach lost hope of support from Swabia, Bavaria, and Franconia, he was left with only his networks to the north and with Duke Johann Friedrich. That, however, sealed his fate, for it meant that he was bound to provoke the hostility of the Elector of Saxony, the main guarantor of the 1555 settlement.

At the Augsburg Reichstag in 1566 a new emissary from Grumbach (the notorious Albrecht von Rosenberg, whose career as an occasional imperial military commander and persistent feuder equally matched that of Grumbach) was arrested and the privileges of the Swabian knights were confirmed.[32] The Elector of Saxony was careful to guard against any possibility of the Palatine Elector taking Grumbach's side by ensuring that Maximilian's attempt to exclude the Calvinist Friedrich III from the religious peace failed. That then left him free to accept the emperor's commission to execute the decree against Grumbach and his confederates. A force of 15,000 men marched on Gotha, where the rebels were all captured on 13 April 1567. A week later, Grumbach was quartered alive in the market square; Duke Johann Friedrich, together with his wife, was committed to lifelong imprisonment at Wiener Neustadt, where he died in 1595.

Rumours of continuing conspiracies and of an imminent uprising among nobles continued for some years. Yet, with Grumbach out of the way, the threat soon subsided. The Estates rapidly agreed to pay the Elector of Saxony the 950,000 florins that the campaign had cost him. Equally significant, they also soon proved just as unanimous in rejecting any suggestion that the Grumbach affair had revealed flaws in the imperial law and order system which should be remedied by the creation of a standing army under the emperor.

For several years, Grumbach had indeed proved almost impossible to deal with and his rebellion had conjured up the possibility of French intervention, of an uprising of counts and knights assisted by the territorial nobility and the mercenary cavalry captains against the princes. While Maximilian hesitated, perhaps flattered by Grumbach's plans and references to the grand schemes of Maximilian I and Charles V, the princes did not. Each sought regional security, if possible achieved by negotiation and mediation, rather than by force. For the Elector of Saxony, however, mediation was not an option in this case. Grumbach's main sponsor, the Elector's Ernestine rival, threatened directly his position as Elector and the security

---

[32] On Rosenberg's involvement, see Press, 'Rosenberg', 376–81.

of his territory. Once he had secured the support of the Reichstag in 1566 he moved swiftly, and his victory in 1567 made the princes' rejection of Maximilian's military proposals in 1570 inevitable. Grumbach had aspired to destroy the princes. Ironically, he sealed the triumph of the territorial principle in the Reich.

The renewed affirmation of the Peace of 1555 by the Estates helped stabilize the Augsburg system, but also had major implications for the territories and cities. On the one hand, rulers at every level were free to pursue the consolidation of their hold on their lands. The implications of this in the wider framework of the development of the confessional Churches during the second half of the century will be explored below.[33] One important precondition, however, was still missing, namely the clarification of the legal situation and the question as to whether disputes about the meaning of the legislation of 1555 could be solved peacefully.

A series of developments in Catholic territories proved crucial in signalling a halt to the hitherto seemingly inexorable progress of Protestantism. Though they also generated complaints from the Protestants, their general effect was to create a more even balance of confessional forces in the Reich. Bavaria, which had broken the domestic opposition of its nobles in 1563, took the lead in 1569 with a policy of expelling those who did not subscribe to the Tridentine confession.[34] At the same time, Duke Albrecht V (r. 1550–79) began to plot strategies to secure major ecclesiastical preferment for younger sons, partly in emulation of the annexation policies of the major Protestant princes and partly to extend Bavarian power.

Albrecht's most successful project was his own son Ernst (1554–1612). In 1566, Ernst had been presented as Bishop of Freising at the age of eleven; in 1573, he was elected Bishop of Hildesheim, then a canon of Cologne in 1577, and Bishop of Liège in 1581.[35] He reached the pinnacle of his career when he became Elector and Archbishop of Cologne in 1583, though he also managed to add the Bishopric of Münster to his portfolio in 1585. While he was ordained a priest in 1577, he was never actually ordained as a bishop. Indeed, his scandalous lifestyle led to him being forced to hand over his ecclesiastical offices to his nephew, Ferdinand of Bavaria, in 1595, after which he retired to the castle of Arnsberg with his mistress.

The significance of Ernst of Bavaria's career, at least in the 1570s, was the way that its success contributed to the restoration of a balance of powers in the Reich. Duke Albrecht's ambitions for his son were part of the same power-political strategy that led him to exploit his guardianship of the young Philip II of Baden-Baden in order to inaugurate the re-Catholicization of that territory between 1569 and 1577.[36]

Since the 1520s, the Bavarians had competed with the Habsburgs for influence over the Baden dynasty, which traditionally had played a key role in the Habsburg system in south-west Germany.[37] After 1536, Duke Wilhelm IV had been thwarted

---

[33] See pp. 498–511.
[34] Schindling and Ziegler, *Territorien*, i, 62–5; Bautz, *Lexikon*, i, 359; *ADB*, ii, 246.
[35] *ADB*, vi, 250–7; *NDB*, iv, 614–15.
[36] Schindling and Ziegler, *Territorien*, v, 136–8.
[37] Press, 'Badische Markgrafen', 29–31.

in maintaining a strict Catholic policy during the minority of Margrave Philibert by the intervention of a Protestant administrator put in place by his fellow guardian the Palgrave of Palatinate-Simmern. The pusillanimous policies pursued by Philibert when he came into his inheritance in 1556 then simply further encouraged the spread and establishment of Protestantism.

The new minority that followed Philibert's death in 1569 thus presented an ideal opportunity for Albrecht to reassert Bavarian authority. The emperor was persuaded to ignore more obvious potential guardians, such as Karl II of Baden-Durlach or Philibert's own brother, Christoph II of Baden-Rodemachern, because they were Protestants. Instead, Albrecht was appointed, together with his mother, the Dowager Duchess Jakobäa (a daughter of Philip I of Baden), and Count Karl of Zollern-Sigmaringen. Albrecht was clearly the dominant guardian and seized the initiative by appointing his leading official Count Ottheinrich von Schwarzenberg as stadtholder. It was claimed that Baden had remained a Catholic territory under the legislation of 1555, since Margrave Philibert had never actually converted to Protestantism. By the time Margrave Philip took over the government himself in 1577, the old religion had been reintroduced throughout his territory, despite opposition from his subjects vigorously expressed at the Landtag.

Few other Catholic dynasts could match the Bavarian's simultaneous pursuit of a strict domestic policy, major ecclesiastical offices for younger sons, and exploitation of the potential of a guardianship as an instrument of 'foreign' policy within the Reich. Other rulers, however, also contributed to redressing the balance between Catholics and Protestants. In Fulda, the election of Prince-Abbot Balthasar von Dernbach in 1570 led to an internal power struggle that had wider implications.[38] Like some of the northern bishoprics, the Benedictine Imperial Abbey of Fulda was threatened by powerful Protestant neighbours such as Hessen and Ernestine Saxony. Indeed, its northern neighbour, the Abbey of Hersfeld, lost its independence to Hessen for all practical purposes in 1525, and over the next century gradually became a secularized Hessian territory.[39] Fulda benefited from the support of significant Catholic neighbours such as Mainz and Würzburg. However, even the abbot's elevated position as a member of the College of Princes, Archchancellor of the Empress, and Premier Abbot in the Reich, with the right to wear the mitre and ring of a bishop, could not automatically guarantee the survival of his immediate status.

The spread of Protestantism to the key towns of Fulda and Hammelburg, among the territorial nobility, and even among the capitularies themselves, created a clear crisis of authority by the 1560s. Any formal concession to the Protestants or even any thought of secularization would have delivered the territory sooner or later into the hands of a neighbouring prince. Hence, while Counter-Reformation attitudes clearly shaped Dernbach's conduct of government from the start, the dominant motive was quite simply the restoration of his authority over his territory and the guarantee of its continuing independence.

---

[38] Schindling and Ziegler, *Territorien*, iv, 139–42; Jäger, *Fulda*, 33–47, 72–5.
[39] Breul-Kunkel, *Herrschaftskrise*, 319–20.

Within a year of his election, Dernbach had summoned the Jesuits, reformed the educational system, re-established the pure Catholic liturgy according to the Tridentine decrees, and banished the concubines of his capitularies. The measures he took to re-establish his prerogatives as a territorial ruler were even more controversial. Wherever possible, he abolished privileges, demanded that the vassals of the chapter and nobility render him feudal dues, abrogated economic and political rights of the towns, and established a centralized administration run by legally trained officials whom he appointed. By 1573, the territorial Estates had united against him. With the strong support of the Landgrave of Hessen and the Elector of Saxony, they appealed to the Reichskammergericht, where the case revolved around the question of whether the *Declaratio Ferdinandea* was, first, valid at all and, second, relevant to circumstances in Fulda. Dernbach (himself supported by the Emperor, Mainz, Bavaria, and others) won judgment in his favour. The Landgrave of Hessen and the Elector of Saxony obeyed a decree from the court forbidding them to intervene.

Yet Dernbach's determination to push through his territorial reform programme merely galvanized an opposition comprising both his Catholic and his Protestant subjects. His undoing came when his domestic opponents found an ideal ally in the person of the new Bishop of Würzburg, Julius Echter von Mespelbrunn (r. 1573–1617). Mespelbrunn appealed to the capitularies because, as an ecclesiastical prince himself, he would ensure Fulda's continuing ecclesiastical status and hence he would be able to safeguard their benefices; he appealed to the knights because he promised to recognize them as Imperial Knights, which automatically safeguarded their right to freedom of worship.[40] In June 1576, Dernbach was forced to resign and hand over to the Bishop of Würzburg as administrator, who in turn was obliged to hand over to an imperial commissioner, the German Master of the Order of Teutonic Knights, the following year. Dernbach himself spent the next twenty-six years trying to win his reinstatement through the courts, which in 1602 gave him four further inglorious years as prince-abbot, during which he attempted to revive his original reform programme. Despite his problems, Dernbach ultimately succeeded in his original aim: Fulda remained Catholic.

The Elector Archbishop of Mainz's reassertion of Catholicism in his territory of the Eichsfeld reveals a similar deployment of Counter-Reformation methods with power-political intentions.[41] The Protestant sympathies of the local nobility and the Protestant majorities established in the towns of Duderstadt and Heiligenstadt threatened Mainz's rule over this strategically important north-eastern exclave that was surrounded by Protestant Hessen, Brunswick, and Saxon territory. In May 1574 Archbishop Daniel Brendel von Homburg marched into the district with two thousand men and in two months strove to restore both his political authority and the Catholic faith. This action has often been regarded as a prime example of

---

[40] Julius Echter's interest stemmed from a proposal he had floated in 1574 for the union of Fulda and Würzburg (under Würzburg control).
[41] Schindling and Ziegler, *Territorien*, iv, 83–5.

Counter-Reformation brutality, but violence and expulsions were avoided, and the territory was not in fact fully restored to Catholicism for many decades.

In the immediate aftermath of the armed visitation, the Eichsfeld nobility continued to assert their right to religious freedom under the *Declaratio Ferdinandea*, and they sought external support from Hessen and the Palatinate for their cause. Yet they received no support from the Imperial Knights of the Middle Rhine region, who played a leading role in the Electorate. Indeed, Protestants such as the powerful master of the household Hartmut (XIII) von Cronberg both supported the Eichsfeld operation and spoke out against any 'mutation or change' of the terms of the religious peace at the Worms assembly of the Rhineland knights that preceded the Reichstag at Regensburg in 1576.[42] The last thing they wanted was the kind of secularization process that had befallen the northern bishoprics, which had led to their being taken over by princes and counts, to the exclusion of lower-ranking benefice holders such as themselves. The Middle Rhine knights, both Catholic and Protestant, collectively supported the stabilization of the Electorate, which provided many of them with careers, and of the Reich, which guaranteed its existence.

All of these cases involved the reimposition of Catholicism on established Protestant communities. In each case, a recognized key principle of the 1555 settlement (the *ius reformandi*) was at odds with another presumed principle (the *Declaratio Ferdinandea*). The aggrieved parties appealed to outside powers for help but those powers, notably Saxony and Hessen, were unwilling to risk war. It is significant that the principle of *ius reformandi*, the right of rulers to determine the religious constitutions of their territories, prevailed over the presumed rights of knights, towns, and communities.

The accumulation of complaints over these matters generated a concerted attempt to establish the validity of the *Declaratio Ferdinandea* once and for all during the negotiations over the election of Archduke Rudolf as King of the Romans in 1575 and at the Reichstag in Regensburg in 1576.[43] Despite the threat that money for a Turkish levy would be withheld, both Maximilian II and the Catholic Estates remained adamant that Ferdinand's assurance had never been given formally and had no legal status. To recognize that assurance as law now would simply upset the balance created in 1555, and it would merely open the way for further amendments to the peace.

A subsequent plea by the Wetterau counts for the removal of the ban on the conversion of ecclesiastical territories failed even to get as far as the Reichstag. They complained that the extension of the ban on conversions to the holders of even the minor benefices was causing them great hardship, since it excluded their younger sons and daughters from the foundations to which they traditionally had access. Deprived of the traditional option of a celibate life, they complained, more were founding families and the counts were multiplying 'like young rabbits'.[44] Although it was also supported by knights in Franconia, Thuringia, and the Harz, both

---

[42] Jendorff, 'Kronberg', 48–9.
[43] Schneider, *Ius reformandi*, 261–3; Schmidt, *Grafenverein*, 293–96.
[44] Heckel, *Deutschland*, 84; on the resulting 'birth control' and 'family planning' among the Wetterau counts, see Schmidt, *Grafenverein*, 490–503.

Saxony and Brandenburg refused to contemplate such a major change to the Augsburg settlement. In the event, the Estates voted for a higher Turkish levy than ever before (60 Roman Months). As usual, it was the Palatinate that led the movement for change and Saxony that prevailed in favour of the Augsburg system.

The emperor's routine reply to any complaint concerning rights under the legislation of 1555 was that complainants should take their case to the courts. In fact it was at the Reichskammergericht that the system was made to function. This was not inevitable at the outset. Protestants and Catholics viewed the court and the law it upheld differently. Protestants believed that the legislation of 1555 guaranteed them both recognition and parity within the Reich; Catholics viewed the same legislation as temporary. However, a workable basis was established by the visitation of the court in 1560, which recommended that confessional parity should be observed for panels sitting in judgment on sensitive issues concerning the rights of confessions.[45]

In time, the court developed elaborate ways of dealing with stalemates (known as *paria vota*): employing whole series of confessionally balanced panels; resorting to compromises that gave something to both parties; recommending new hearings at lower courts; and instigating local arbitration processes. The fact that cases often took a long time to resolve was in itself helpful, since it provided time for a peaceful agreement between parties, or for a complaint to be abandoned. Because penalties for violent action undertaken while a case was pending were severe, this also served to maintain the peace for the duration.[46] No amount of judicial activity could of course restore the relatively uniform legal order that the Reformation had disrupted. The institutionalization of dissimulation and ambiguity in the law of the Reich, further complicated and obscured in the decades after 1555 by the sophistry of lawyers on both sides, could no doubt be seen as a recipe for open conflict at some stage. Yet the peace held because almost all had a vested interest in it.

Making the Augsburg system work was the achievement of Ferdinand I and Maximilian II. This was not interrupted by the succession of Rudolf II at the end of the Regensburg Reichstag in October 1576. The Reichskammergericht further refined its procedures following a visitation in 1583. Equally important, those cases that did become political issues during the first decade of Rudolf's reign demonstrated the continuing commitment of the Reich's major players to the 1555 settlement. The crises generated by disputes at Aachen, Magdeburg, and Cologne were indicative both of the inherent problems of the peace settlement and of the degree of commitment to it.

The Aachen controversy raised the question of the rights of Imperial Cities in religious matters.[47] The dispute was particularly sensitive because it unfolded in the west of the Reich, in close proximity to the religious disputes in France and the Netherlands, a fact of which all parties were acutely aware. In 1555, Aachen was formally regarded as Catholic. From about 1550, however, a small but vocal mixed

---

[45] Ruthmann, 'Religionsprozesse', 236–8.
[46] Ruthmann, 'Religionsprozesse', 238–40.
[47] Schneider, *Ius reformandi*, 229–31; Enderle, 'Reichsstädte', 240–3; Molitor, 'Aachen'.

Lutheran and Calvinist Protestant minority had begun to establish itself there. In 1559–60, Duke Wilhelm of Jülich-Kleve-Berg, who held several offices and jurisdictions in the city, and the emperor placed pressure on the magistrates to suppress the Protestants so as to preserve what they saw as a vital Catholic cordon between the Protestant north-east and the Netherlands. The magistrates dutifully issued a decree reserving all urban offices and entry to the city council to Catholics.

By 1574, however, the Catholics were powerless to resist the challenge posed to this exclusion by the growing Protestant community that had gained a majority in several guilds and was eager to claim places on the city council. When the Lutherans and the Reformed demanded the right to public worship in 1580, the Catholics, supported again by the Duke of Jülich, complained, and Rudolf sent in commissioners to ensure the enforcement of the exclusion statute of 1560. An appeal by the city council to the Reichskammergericht against the Duke of Jülich, failed to secure an agreed judgment. As a result, the conflict came to the Reichstag at Augsburg in 1582, where the Imperial Cities complained that their *ius reformandi*, their right as ruling magistrates under the legislation of 1555, was not being recognized. A commission headed by the Electors of Trier and Saxony in 1584 failed to produce a solution, whereupon the matter was taken to the Reichshofrat in Vienna.

What is significant about the way the Aachen controversy was handled is the restraint exercised by Rudolf. In 1581, he had ordered the external sponsors of the Catholic cause—the Duke of Jülich, the Archbishop of Liège, and the Duke of Parma—to avoid violence at all costs. He was content to stand by and see his ally the Duke of Jülich sued at the Reichskammergericht. When the matter came to the Reichstag, he concurred in a biconfessional commission. When the commission failed and the matter came to his own court in Vienna, he abstained from judgment for over ten years. Only in 1593 did his court decide in favour of the Catholics and once more order the enforcement of the decree of 1560; that judgment was only executed forcibly by the Elector of Cologne in 1598. In the 1580s, in other words, Rudolf hesitated to break the rules of the Augsburg system; in the 1590s he could act, because by then the Protestant camp had become fatally divided.[48]

In the Magdeburg controversy that also erupted at the Reichstag of 1582 the issue was the *reservatum ecclesiasticum*, the stipulation of 1555 that prohibited the secularization of prince-bishoprics.[49] The problem arose in respect of the question of whether a prince-bishopric might still be turned Lutheran without contravening the terms of the Peace of Augsburg. It was one thing to acquiesce in the secularization and annexation of territorial bishoprics by a ruler such as the Elector of Brandenburg in the 1550s and 1560s. It was quite another thing to turn a blind eye to the subversion of an independent neighbouring prince-bishopric. In a regular prince-bishopric, a candidate for episcopal office could not be granted a deed of enfeoffment unless he had previously been confirmed in his office by the pope.

[48] See pp. 406–9.
[49] Schneider, *Ius reformandi*, 220; Wolgast, *Hochstift*, 275–6, 281–3; Schindling and Ziegler, *Territorien*, ii, 80–2.

The Archbishopric of Magdeburg was already almost wholly Lutheran by 1552 but it remained formally Catholic under Archbishop Sigmund of Brandenburg (r. 1552–66) until 1561, when he declared the Augsburg Confession to be the basis of its religion, which he notified to the Reichstag in 1566. Sigmund had concealed his Lutheran sympathies in order to achieve papal and imperial confirmation. His successor, Joachim Friedrich of Brandenburg, heir to the Electorate, was openly Lutheran from the outset, and committed by his electoral capitulation to reform all the remaining religious foundations and monasteries. Since he already held the Brandenburg territorial bishoprics of Brandenburg, Havelberg, and Lebus, he was initially elected as administrator in Magdeburg, but his Lutheranism made papal and, hence, imperial confirmation out of the question. Just as he was therefore not an archbishop in the eyes of the Church, so also he was not even a prince in the eyes of the Reich.

Maximilian II refused to contemplate recognition of Joachim Friedrich, still less after his marriage to his cousin, Katharina of Küstrin, in January 1570. All that the emperor would consent to in 1569 was that letters from the court chancellery would be addressed to the cathedral chapter, with a request that the 'relevant authorities' be notified of their contents.[50] However, Maximilian categorically resisted demands by Cardinal Otto of Augsburg that Joachim Friedrich be forcibly evicted from Magdeburg. He preferred to behave as if Magdeburg and other sees like it were simply vacant, without actually taking any steps to fill the vacancy. Rudolf II similarly resisted requests by Joachim Friedrich and his father, the Elector of Brandenburg, for formal recognition. Yet the administrator was not prepared to accept his continuing exclusion from the Reichstag. In 1582, with the support of his father and of the Magdeburg chapter, he appeared at Augsburg and sent one of his councillors into the College of Princes to claim the Magdeburg seat.

The Catholic princes immediately objected. The Bavarians argued that to permit Magdeburg to take its seat would set a precedent that might precipitate the end of all prince-bishoprics and lead to the demise of the Catholic religion and of the Reich itself.[51] To admit Protestant administrators would be to give Protestants a majority in the College of Princes; if one of the spiritual Electors were to convert, there would be a majority of Protestant Electors and hence a Protestant emperor. The arguments were perhaps melodramatic and there was a feeling among some Protestants that Magdeburg was simply being victimized. The Administrators or Bishops of Bremen, Halberstadt, and Lübeck had, after all, taken their seats without controversy. What made them different was that Rudolf had granted them temporary deeds of enfeoffment pending papal confirmation. The crucial point was that these princes had not yet openly declared their Protestant loyalties.

When the dispute threatened to paralyse the Reichstag, and hence frustrate an urgently needed Turkish levy, Rudolf turned once more to the Elector of Saxony. Though August I had originally supported the Magdeburg cause, he now declared

---

[50] Wolgast, *Hochstift*, 280.   [51] Wolgast, *Hochstift*, 282–3.

that it was not worth the risk of a major conflict.[52] When talks about a temporary face-saving compromise for the current session failed, Joachim Friedrich withdrew.

The issue of the political rights of Protestant administrators or bishops was to play a major role in the more fraught constitutional struggles of the 1590s.[53] In 1582, however, the significant thing was that once again both the emperor and the leading princes shrank from an open confrontation over an issue of fundamental principle. And once again it was the Elector of Saxony, that perennial champion of the Augsburg system, who determined the outcome.

He also proved decisive in the struggle for Cologne, which was reaching a crucial stage at about the same time.[54] Schemes for the reformation and secularization of Cologne had been in the air since the early 1540s.[55] After 1555, the ecclesiastical status of the Electorate had become a bone of contention for the Wetterau and Westphalian counts, and the pivotal issue in the campaign was to abolish the *reservatum ecclesiasticum*. In the 1560s and 1580s the Electorate had also assumed a key strategic significance, located squarely between the religious conflicts in France and the Netherlands. For the Habsburgs, Cologne was not only the mainstay of Catholicism in the north-west of the Reich; it also formed a vital section of that corridor that enabled them to get troops north from the Mediterranean to the Low Countries.

The other factor that made the Electorate an apparently promising target for Protestant schemers was the manifest inadequacy of its archiepiscopal rulers. None of the incumbents in the century following the tenure of Adolf von Schaumburg (r. 1546–56) was consecrated as a bishop and none discharged any clerical duties. At the same time, however, none was a match for the cathedral chapter, which regarded itself as the Electorate's true guardian. Friedrich von Wied (r. 1562–7) refused to take the Tridentine oath, which he believed to be an unreasonable requirement of a prince of the Reich. However, he was unwilling to become involved with the political campaigns of the Wetterau counts, and in 1567 he resigned after rancorous disputes with the chapter over money and authority.

It was rumoured that Archbishop Friedrich's successor, Salentin von Isenburg (r. 1567–77), would resign almost immediately.[56] He was the last male of his line, and even on his election at the age of thirty-six he was more set on perpetuating his dynasty than on fulfilling the demands of his archiepiscopal office. Despite this, he contrived to have himself elected Bishop of Paderborn in 1574 and was straight-forwardly Catholic in his politics. The known fact that he wished to marry, however, soon prompted an approach from the Elector of the Palatinate, who offered him his daughter in marriage and his support in staying on in Cologne as administrator and reformer, as Duke Johann Friedrich had done in Magdeburg.

In the event, Salentin too shrank back from such a revolutionary step. Like his predecessor, he failed to tame the cathedral chapter, which denied him the consid-erable income from the Rhine tolls at Zons and refused to contemplate his request

---

[52] Rabe, *Geschichte*, 609.   [53] See pp. 412–14.
[54] Wolgast, *Hochstift*, 287–93; Schindling and Ziegler, *Territorien*, iii, 74–6.
[55] See pp. 282–3.   [56] *ADB*, xxx, 216–24.

for the appointment of Ernst of Bavaria as his coadjutor. When he did marry a daughter of the Count of Arenberg in 1577, he promptly resigned his ecclesiastical offices. A powerful coalition of the emperor, the pope, the King of Spain, and the Dukes of Bavaria and Jülich-Kleve-Berg had hoped to secure the election of Ernst of Bavaria before the resignation took effect. The core of the cathedral chapter, however, once more asserted its independence by narrowly electing Gebhard Truchsess von Waldburg (r. 1577–83), a move which asserted the traditional role of the counts in the Electorate against the princes of the Reich. The Protestant canons, and those who were less than enthusiastic Catholics, all voted for Waldburg, preferring a simple nobleman to the son of a powerful prince.

Initially, Archbishop Gebhard seemed ideally suited to his new position.[57] In 1578 he had himself ordained as a priest and swore the Tridentine oath before the Archbishop of Trier; in the spring of 1580 the pope consequently confirmed his election. The fact that, at about the same time, he began a liaison with a Protestant canoness, Agnes von Mansfeld, did not create a problem until 1582, when her brothers demanded that he marry her and convert to Protestantism. Unwilling to abandon either his relationship or his territory, Gebhard occupied Bonn by force in November 1582 and transferred the cathedral treasures to its fortress. In December, he renounced his Catholic faith and declared freedom of religion for his subjects; two months later he married Agnes.[58]

Gebhard was apparently supported in his plans by a number of the Wetterau counts, both inside and outside the chapter, and by Johann Casimir of Pfalz-Lautern, the younger brother of the Palatine Elector and the most militant Reformed prince in the Reich.[59] The Palatine Elector himself was also sympathetic. Though he was a Lutheran, he was fully committed to the traditional Palatine policy of forging a Protestant alliance in the Reich, and he had a far greater prospect of achieving a rapport with Brandenburg and Saxony than his Reformed predecessors had had.[60] The majority of the Cologne chapter, however, resolutely opposed the archbishop and they were backed by the papacy, by the King of Spain, the emperor, the Duke of Bavaria, and others. As early as March 1583, Gebhard was excommunicated and relieved of his offices. In April, the emperor outlawed him and in May, Duke Ernst of Bavaria was elected as his successor.

For a time Gebhard hoped to enlist the support of the Protestant Electors. His removal from office seemed to confirm the rumours that had been circulating since the 1560s that the papacy was seeking to control the College of Electors, even to remove one or other of the Protestant members in favour of a Catholic.[61] If that was true then the defence at all costs of the three existing spiritual Electorates was essential. Ludwig VI of the Palatinate reacted strongly against this presumed assault on the independence of the German Electors and saw Gebhard's marriage as an

[57] *ADB*, viii, 457–70.
[58] Schindling and Ziegler, *Territorien*, iii, 75. The media war that accompanied the following controversies is analysed by Schnurr, *Religionskonflikt*.
[59] Schindling and Ziegler, *Territorien*, iii, 75.
[60] Schindling and Ziegler, *Territorien*, v, 29.
[61] Gotthard. *Säulen*, i, 54–6.

opportunity to create a Protestant majority in the College of Electors. Johann Georg of Brandenburg was also aroused by this perceived threat to the German constitution, and even August of Saxony voiced his disquiet. Only Ludwig's death in October 1583 somewhat defused the situation. His heir, Friedrich IV, was a minor until 1592. Friedrich's guardian and the Palatine administrator during his minority was Johann Casimir, a fierce Calvinist, who once more revived the distrust between Lutheran Brandenburg and Saxony on the one hand, and the Reformed Palatinate on the other. Furthermore, he was not actually a member of the College of Electors, which gave Saxony's traditional policy of mediation a greater leeway.[62]

In the event, arguments about precedents, tactics, and the future of the College of Electors were overtaken by decisions reached on the ground. With money from the papacy, Bavaria, and a variety of prince-bishops, and Spanish troops from the Netherlands, Ernst soon overcame the 7,000 Palatinate troops at Gebhard's disposal. By January 1584 he had taken Bonn and established his authority in the Electorate.

The 'war' continued sporadically until the end of the decade, though to a large extent as a secondary front in the Netherlands struggle.[63] Gebhard's hopes were repeatedly raised by promises of support from the Dutch rebels and figures such as Adolf von Neuenaar, the stadtholder of Guelders, and the Gueldrian captain Martin Schenck von Hydegger, and by prospects of assistance from England. In 1587, Bonn fell to Dutch mercenaries and had to be liberated by Spanish forces. Only in 1589 did Gebhard and his wife withdraw from the fray. He retired to Strassburg, where he held the deanery of the cathedral and where, without any involvement on his part, a similar struggle for control of the archbishopric had begun in 1584 over the question of whether the *reservatum ecclesiasticum* applied to cathedral canons. That struggle was to erupt into a full-scale and altogether more dangerous confrontation for the Reich in the 1590s.[64]

Gebhard had effectively lost the struggle for Cologne in 1584, and it was a measure of his isolation in the Reich that in January 1585 the Electors of Brandenburg and Saxony formally recognized Ernst as the legitimate Elector of Cologne. The Palatine Elector's declaration in August 1583 that events in Cologne had brought the religious peace to an end was premature. In fact, the peace was once more reaffirmed by the determination of the Elector of Saxony not to tolerate any violation of it.[65]

---

[62] Gotthard, *Säulen*, i, 76–83; Clasen, *Palatinate*, 19–21.
[63] Lossen, *Kölnischer Krieg*, ii, 603–35.
[64] See pp. 412–14.
[65] Ritter, *Geschichte*, i, 612; Wolgast, *Hochstift*, 291–2.

32

The Consensus Falters *c.*1585–1603

From the mid-1580s the Augsburg system came under growing strain. Developments after the 'Cologne War' seemed to threaten a reconfessionalization of the Reich and its politics. The religious issue and the conflicting interpretations of the peace settlement of 1555 were clearly fundamental to the disputes that continued over the next two decades. Yet religion must be seen as the medium or vehicle of conflict, rather than the substance. For it became increasingly apparent that the real issue was the constitution of the Reich itself, in particular the question of the emperor's role and authority.

There was no single cause or trigger for the marked change in the political climate. One important factor was the stabilization of government and religious constitutions in most of the territories by the late 1580s. Once the broader confessional boundaries had been defined and enforced downwards (however incompletely or inadequately), there was less scope for ambiguity at the level of imperial politics. The subsequent establishment of schools and especially places of higher learning dedicated to elaborating one or other confession undoubtedly contributed to the intensification of theological and legal polemics.

Even the question of calendar reform became caught up in the wider religious controversy.[1] First, Rudolf II hesitated to implement Pope Gregory XIII's (eminently sensible) reform in the Reich. Then, after much of Western Europe, including the Netherlands, had already adopted the change, he issued a decree urging all German rulers to adopt the new calendar on 4 September 1583. Even though he expressly refrained from mentioning the pope in his decree, Rudolf's failure to consult the Estates led to a bitter pamphlet war and the refusal of the Protestants to recognize the new calendar.

The German Protestants reacted no differently to their counterparts in England (where the new calendar was only adopted in 1752) and other parts of Europe. Yet the German reaction had a particular edge, for the Estates objected both to the pope as author of the reform and to the abuse of temporal power implicit in its unilateral implementation in the Reich by the emperor.[2] It is open to question whether the particular problems generated by the Calendar of the Imperial Cities of Augsburg and Dinkelsbühl were the exception or proved the

---

[1] On 24 February 1582, Gregory XIII issued a bull decreeing that 4 October 1582 would be followed by 15 October, thus correcting an error inherent in the old Julian calendar which made the year 11 minutes 14 seconds too long. Grotefend, *Taschentuch*, 25–7.
[2] Vocelka, *Politische Propaganda*, 181–7.

rule.[3] The peace of 1555 had specified parity between Catholics and Protestants in each. The two neighbouring princes, the Bishop of Augsburg and the Duke of Bavaria, both introduced the new calendar during 1583 and, together with the Catholic inhabitants, placed the magistrates under intense pressure, escalating to the threat of military action. By the time the magistrates formally adopted the reform in 1591, not least because of the problems that a dual-date system threw up for merchants and bankers, the controversy had threatened the delicate constitutional arrangements established in 1555 several times.

By the mid-1580s, it seemed clear that to many there was a shift in attitude at the imperial court. The rising cost of defence against the Turks generated a fiscal crisis, or at least a sense of shortage, that led to a tendency to try and exercise royal prerogatives more rigorously and to extend them if possible. This tendency was evident in Italy from the mid-1580s and somewhat later in the Reich, where the office of Imperial Court Fiscal or Court Prosecutor was first formally instituted in 1596.[4] Furthermore, the specific problems of the Habsburgs as territorial rulers increasingly shaped the attitudes of the emperor and his court to the Reich, until in 1618 these problems provided the trigger for war.[5]

Most difficult of all to quantify or to delineate clearly, the crisis of the Augsburg system unfolded in the context of a general sense of crisis at the end of the sixteenth century.[6] Poor harvests, high grain prices, economic crisis, social instability, all generated tensions, hostilities, and suspicions. These inevitably spilled over into imperial politics as well. Decades devoted to creating stability made the shock of renewed instability all the greater. And it made the reactions to it all the more extreme as well. Deviants and witches were identified as instigators of all problems.[7] In the same way, religious adversaries vilified each other as the incarnations of evil and agents of the devil. The defence of 'German liberties' thus all too often rapidly became a struggle against a universal 'Spanish' Catholic empire and its Jesuit legions.[8] The defence of the Catholic Reich and of the prerogatives of the German monarchy became a struggle against the Western (Calvinist) legions of the same devil that threatened the faith from Turkey and the East. These polemical wars culminated in the centenary of the Reformation in 1617—the very first 'modern' centenary celebration commemorated as such—which stimulated both sides to extremes of interpretation that rendered communication, let alone consensus, all but impossible.[9]

The change in the political climate was as gradual as the shift in global weather patterns: a transition over many years, rather than a single season. One event, however, appears as a decisive watershed. The death of August I of Saxony in February 1586 removed the main champion and sheet anchor of the Augsburg

---

[3] Warmbrunn, *Konfessionen*, 359–86; Roeck, *Stadt*, i, 125–88; Dixon 'Urban order', 8–18.

[4] Obersteiner, 'Reichshoffiskalat', 96–7, 134–6.

[5] See pp. 428–37.

[6] Schulze, 'Untertanenrevolten'; Behringer et al., 'Konsequenzen'; Schilling, 'Crisis'; Clark, 'European crisis'.

[7] See pp. 550–7.

[8] Schmidt, *Vaterlandsliebe*, 321–8.

[9] Leppin, 'Antichrist'; Schönstädt, *Antichrist*, 10–13; Gotthard, *Reich*, 80–2.

system, and his death symbolized a change of generations. He stood for the generation who had experienced the turbulence of the Schmalkaldic War and the Princes' Revolt, who had participated in the peace negotiations in 1555, and who wanted more than anything else to maintain that peace. To that end, he was prepared to compromise again and again, placing stability above confessional loyalty.

August I's death also removed the personal bonds of loyalty and sense of common cause that had tied Saxony to the Habsburgs, Bavaria, and Mainz.[10] August's successor Christian I (r. 1586–91) allowed himself to be led by his chancellor, Nikolaus Krell, to support the activist policies of the Palatinate administrator, Johann Casimir. The Palatinate was thus able to assume de facto leadership of the Protestant party in the Reich, albeit a party diminished and no longer as united as it had been in August's heyday. While Saxony reverted to its previous policies during the minority of Christian II (1591–1601), the latter was not able to reassert the traditional Saxon Protestant leadership fully when he became sole ruler in 1601 against first the Palatinate and then the Brandenburg Elector.

The change in Brandenburg policies was very slow. Johann Georg of Brandenburg (r. 1571–98) only briefly followed the Palatinate's lead in 1590 and 1591. For the rest, despite his son's embroilment in the Magdeburg affair and his nephew's later involvement in the Strassburg troubles, Johann Georg remained true to a traditionalist loyalist Lutheran policy in the Reich.[11] The politics and religious orientation of Brandenburg only gradually changed under the Elector Joachim Friedrich (r. 1598–1608), whose influential Calvinist councillor, Ottheinrich von Bylandt von Rheydt of Jülich, prepared the way for the formal conversion of Elector Johann Sigismund (r. 1608–19) in 1613.

More disruptive in the short term was the underlying rift caused in the west of the Reich by the activism of successive Palatine Electors. Ludwig VI's support for Gebhard of Cologne in 1583 had destroyed the informal regional network of Rhineland Electors that had been the active core of the College of Electors in the late Middle Ages.[12] The rift had already been apparent in the 1570s. Now, the spiritual Electors distanced themselves from the Palatinate and refused even to contemplate the admission of the administrator Johann Casimir to the College. The Elector Friedrich IV was only admitted in 1601, nine years after his succession, having prevaricated for four years over an invitation to join, as did the other Electors for several years. Apart from this, the College of Electors continued to function reasonably effectively until the end of the century.[13] The Rhineland fault line perhaps presaged the breakdown of the political system of the Reich, but that was not a certainty in the 1580s and 1590s.

The polarizing effect of the French and Dutch conflicts had a more immediate and more serious impact on the Reich. Until the 1580s, German involvement in both

[10] Schindling and Ziegler, *Territorien*, ii, 27–9.
[11] Schindling and Ziegler, *Territorien*, ii, 49–50.
[12] Gotthard, *Säulen*, i, 66.
[13] Gotthard, *Säulen*, i, 79–85.

conflicts had essentially been limited to the initiatives of various Palatine Electors, military adventurers such as the Dukes of Zweibrücken and Württemberg, and supporters of the Dutch cause among the Wetterau relatives of William of Orange. The Reich itself remained neutral. Queen Elizabeth's intervention in the Netherlands in 1585 and Henri of Navarre's struggle for the French crown in 1585–9 created an altogether more threatening situation. England made strenuous efforts to muster Danish and German support for Leicester's governor-generalship.

Henri naturally also looked to the Huguenots' traditional allies—the English, the Dutch, and the German princes, notably the Palatinate—for assistance against the Duke of Guise and his main external supporter, Philip II of Spain, orchestrator of the Catholic League. It was clear to all parties that the conflicts were inextricably linked and that success in one would determine the outcome of the other. Indeed, Philip II believed that he would only prevail in the Netherlands if he could first destroy England and France.[14] The French and Dutch conflicts thus inflamed German politics, with all parties enlisting support in the Reich and many princes, in turn, increasingly viewing their own local and regional struggles refracted through the struggles abroad.

Attempts by Johann Casimir to forge an activist alliance immediately after the death of August of Saxony in 1586 came to nothing. Both the new Elector Christian and Landgrave Wilhelm IV of Hessen sympathized with his views but hesitated to step out of line. All they could agree on was an embassy to Henri III in the summer of 1588 to intercede on behalf of the Huguenots.[15] Henri let the German envoys wait for two months before agreeing to see them, only to dismiss their pleas.

Then, in 1587, Johann Casimir decided to act alone.[16] He concluded a treaty with Henri of Navarre in which he committed himself to ensuring the success of Navarre and the French Calvinists. Navarre, in turn, promised that he would not cease fighting until he was able to reimburse Johann Casimir the costs of all of his expeditions in France and the Netherlands to date. With the additional help of English and Danish money, a force of some 30,000 German and Swiss mercenaries was duly raised. However, Johann Casimir refused to lead the force himself—the role of mercenary commander was beneath the dignity of an administrator of an Electorate of the Reich—and the task proved to be beyond the inexperienced Duke Robert de Bouillon. By November, the Swiss had been persuaded to desert by the promise of better pay from Henri III; a few days later, the Duke of Guise routed the Germans at Auneau.

From 1588 onwards, however, Philip II's position steadily weakened. In August 1588, the Armada against England failed. In December 1588, Henry of Guise and his brother the cardinal were murdered, as was Henri III in August 1589. In 1591–2, finally, Alexander Farnese's assault on France failed to defeat Henri IV, and Farnese himself died at Arras on 8 December 1592. This immediately opened

---

[14] Parker, *Grand strategy*, 147–205; Elliott, *Europe divided*, 307–50.
[15] Ritter, *Geschichte*, ii, 5.
[16] Ritter, *Geschichte*, ii, 8–10; Beiderbeck, 'Heinrich IV.', Teil I, 27–32.

up new horizons for Philip's opponents. In particular, the Palatine administrator Johann Casimir envisaged himself emerging as the linchpin of an international Protestant alliance that would launch a devastating counter-offensive against the Spanish-Jesuit tyranny.

While Johann Casimir was now able to engage the interest of both Saxony and Brandenburg, the majority of the western German Estates were preoccupied with more pressing problems. The renewed conflicts in the Netherlands and in France intensified the incursions of foreign soldiers into the territory of the Reich. In the spring of 1590, the Westphalian Kreis and the Kreise of the Upper and the Lower Rhine deliberated on measures to defend themselves against Spanish troops. Since the problem seemed to threaten the Reich as a whole, they requested a Reichs-deputationstag, a conference of representatives of all Kreise and Estates. The meeting at Frankfurt in September 1590 foundered on the confessional divide. When Rudolf II and the Catholic Estates rejected proposals for action against the Spaniards as anti-Catholic, the Protestant Electors left in disgust.

Johann Casimir seized the opportunity that this impasse provided. Together with the Elector of Saxony, he invited the Protestant Estates to gather at Torgau in February 1591. There they agreed to levy a force to assist Henri IV: 9,000 infantry and 6,200 cavalry under the overall command of Christian of Anhalt, which formed the core of Henri IV's fighting force against both the Catholic League and Parma until the spring of 1592.[17] This was a breakthrough in itself: the first agreement among German Protestant princes on a joint force intended to fight on behalf of Protestants outside the Reich. Just as revolutionary was the decision to form a Protestant league in the Reich itself. The enduring underlying tensions between Lutherans and Calvinists prevented agreement on anything more than a purely defensive league, strictly limited to German issues. Yet its prime movers—Johann Casimir and Wilhelm of Hessen-Kassel—had visions of it becoming part of a broad European coalition. This might indeed have transpired, had it not been for the death of Christian I of Saxony in October 1591, of Johann Casimir in January 1592, and of Wilhelm of Hessen in September 1592. The activists had lost their leaders.

The fact that the league of 1591 came to nothing does not detract from its significance.[18] Though the death of Christian I led to a renewal of Lutheranism in Saxony and to the revival of its customary hostility to the Palatinate, the idea of such a league remained alive. After 1597, when Spanish military incursions again threatened the north-western Reich, an almost identical scenario unfolded.[19] The Kreise failed to agree on action because the Catholics would not oppose Spain. Christian of Anhalt, now the Palatine stadtholder in the Upper Palatinate, pro-posed a league to defend Protestants against what he believed to be a Spanish war of extermination against them.[20]

Once again, however, leading Protestant princes hesitated to become involved in a wider European conflict or in a strategy that presupposed a formal alliance with

[17] Ritter, *Geschichte*, ii, 53–4; Rabe, *Geschichte*, 596–7.   [18] Gotthard, '1591'.
[19] For the following, see Rabe, *Geschichte*, 598–9.   [20] Press, 'Christian'.

the Dutch and the possibility of an open war against the emperor and the ecclesiastical princes. Anhalt promptly declined to accept the leadership of the planned Protestant mercenary defence force. In the event, only a small contingent was hired, and by the time it was ready to be deployed on behalf of the Kreise the main Spanish force had withdrawn anyway. The league plans were relegated to the archives to form the blueprint later for the Protestant Union of 1608.[21]

In view of the apparently widening confessional divide, it is perhaps surprising that the Reichstag functioned well up to 1603. Indeed, the 1590s saw unprecedented amounts of money granted for the defence of the Reich against the Turks. The three sessions in 1594, 1598, and 1603 granted no less than 226 Roman Months or roughly 12 million gulden, a high proportion of which was actually paid.[22]

At one level, the explanation is simple. The threat posed by the Turks in the last decades of the century was actually far greater than fifty years earlier and more widely perceived as such. Before about 1560, only the eastern and southern territories felt the threat, and many others were simply unwilling to pay, on the grounds that it was not their problem. Now the sense of the coherence of the Reich, of belonging to it and of collective responsibility for it, was much more widespread.

At the same time, however, many Estates were more inclined to agree to levies for their own purely domestic reasons. Imperial levies that the princes could pass on to their subjects were viewed as a useful mechanism to reinforce their rights to taxation generally and a good discipline for their subjects. Imperial taxation was also taxation that did not require the permission of the territorial Estates and thus it provided a means of undermining local and regional resistance to princely authority. Indeed, many made a substantial profit on the Turkish levies.[23] In 1594, the Saxon chancellor accused some princes of raising twenty times as much as was required. That was almost certainly a wild exaggeration, but cases where double or more the amount required was levied were not uncommon and the 1590s saw a flood of complaints to the imperial courts from subjects who believed they were being overcharged.

The apparent willingness to agree the Turkish levies did not mean that the Reichstag sessions were unproblematic. Rudolf himself had become so anxious about the Reichstag that he only summoned it when it was absolutely necessary. Many of the issues relating to justice, the currency, or the tax registers that had preoccupied the Reichstag before 1555 were dealt with by subsidiary committees (Deputationen) or by the Kreise.[24] Summoning a Reichstag merely provided opportunities for those who wanted to pick away at the religious settlement. After the session of 1576 that had been initiated by Maximilian II, Rudolf II waited six years before convening his first Reichstag in 1582. His interest in doing so had been twofold: to achieve a Turkish levy and to gain support for his desire to mediate a settlement in the Netherlands that would secure the interests of the Reich there. In the event, while the levy was granted, the Netherlands issue was left

[21] Lanzinner, 'Zeitalter', 175. See pp. 422–3.   [22] Schulze, *Türkengefahr*, 360–3.
[23] Schulze, *Türkengefahr*, 255–70; Schwennicke, *Steuer*, 49–54.   [24] Schulze, *Türkengefahr*, 78.

unresolved and the session was overshadowed by the controversies over Aachen, Cologne, and Magdeburg. When the 1582 levy ran out, Rudolf attempted to convene a new Reichstag in 1586 and 1587, but he was unable to secure the agreement of the Electors following the death of August of Saxony.

The agitation of the Protestant princes in 1590–1 made a Reichstag seem most unwise. Attempts were made to have the issue of defence against the Turks delegated to the Kreise, which would have bypassed the Reichstag for good, but this failed, since the Estates were unwilling to pass up their rights or relinquish their national platform for airing their grievances. In 1593, however, the start of another Turkish war made a new Reichstag imperative. The session that opened in Regensburg on 2 June 1594 fully justified the emperor's apprehension.

The Saxons once again averted a disaster by thwarting the demand of the Palatinate that confessional grievances be placed on the main agenda. The Palatines were still smarting at the memory of being outvoted by a Catholic majority in 1582. Since then, they had agitated ceaselessly for procedural changes in the central institutions of the Reich: for parity representation in every Reichsdeputation or even for the enfranchisement of the largely Protestant Imperial Cities in the College of Princes so as to create a Protestant majority there.[25] All of these proposals failed, but it was a measure of the changed atmosphere by the early 1590s that they were now able to persuade a number of south German princes to attend a meeting at Heilbronn in March 1594 to discuss, among other issues, their tactics at the forthcoming Reichstag.[26] In the event, the majority of the Lutherans voted with the Catholics at Regensburg, and the activist strategy of challenging the majority principle—the authority of the emperor and of all institutions of the Reich did not recognize parity between the confessions—failed.

By 1598, however, another pre-session at Heilbronn resolved not to recognize any majority vote dictated at the Reichstag by the Catholic princes. Ironically, it was a Catholic prince who now helped give voice to the Protestant dissidents. The Archbishop of Salzburg had been outvoted in the Bavarian Kreis over the level of tax its members were willing to pay. Then, as director of the Kreis responsible for conveying the majority view to the Reichstag, the archbishop insisted not only on appending his own dissent but also that of the Protestants.[27] When the majority prevailed again—the procedure of the Reichstag allowed no other option—seven Protestant princes signed a formal protest against the majority procedure. Five years later, the same debate resurfaced. The activists were now even less inclined to accept a majority decision and even more determined to voice their grievances over the Catholic interpretation of the religious peace, to which the Catholics responded by demanding the restitution of all ecclesiastical property that had been secularized since 1552.

The 1603 Reichstag concluded with agreement on the largest ever Turkish levy of 86 Roman Months, some five-and-a-half million gulden.[28] At the same time,

[25] Schulze, *Deutsche Geschichte*, 179.
[26] Ritter, *Geschichte*, ii, 117–19.
[27] Schulze, *Türkengefahr*, 165–6. See also pp. 356–7.
[28] Stieve, *Politik*, ii, 613–78 provides a detailed account of the proceedings.

however, the distance between the imperial view and that of the dissidents was wider than ever before. A problem that had first surfaced in the 1520s had now become a fundamental constitutional issue. The dissidents did not reject the constitution or even the emperor. Indeed, despite their public declaration of their intention to refuse payment, all those involved in the protest, including the Elector of the Palatinate, had paid more or less in full by the time the 1603 Reichstag met. None wanted to risk being outlawed following a judgment against the defaulters by the Reichskammergericht in May 1602.[29]

Rudolf II's brother, Archduke Matthias, blamed the Protestants in 1603 for the fact that 'Germany is a divided polity and no longer a united body'. In fact, that was a polemical exaggeration. The Protestants had not turned their backs on the Reich. They simply rejected the view that the polity should be dictated to by the Catholic majority. They aimed to ensure the continuing viability of the polity by reducing to a minimum the core issues on which all had to agree.[30] Defence of the Reich proper against external attack was a duty; it was a duty that the emperor himself, they were keen to point out, had failed to discharge against Spanish incursions into the west of the Reich in 1598. The defence of Hungary was quite another matter.

In broader terms, the dissident rejection of the majority principle marked a major milestone in the progression from 1555 to 1648. The 1555 settlement limited the range of religious issues on which all had to agree. In 1648 it was agreed that in cases where the religious parties could not agree, the Reichstag should divide into two parallel sessions and agree to desist from a resolution if no amicable conclusion could be reached. The Protestant arguments of the 1590s were based on the principles of 1555, and they presaged the doctrine of 1648. In their time, however, they remained a minority view which the Catholic majority, and many Lutherans, denounced as revolutionary.

Despite the emperor's determination that the Reichstag sessions of 1594, 1597–8, and 1603 should deal exclusively with the Turkish levy, and despite the success of those negotiations, the atmosphere on each occasion was intensified by the simultaneous eruption of controversies that were confessional in origin. These first fuelled the debate on majority votes and then ultimately turned the impasse reached in 1603 into a confrontation that paralysed the Reichstag by 1608.

The immediate aim of those who convened the Heilbronn meeting in March 1594 had been to secure agreement on inviting Henri IV to invade the bishopric of Strassburg. This would have turned the key German political issue of these years into an international conflict. That did not happen, for the south German Protestant princes persisted in regarding the Strassburg affair as a Brandenburg problem, but it nonetheless both reflected the hardening of attitudes and greatly intensified the growing sense of crisis.[31]

---

[29] Schulze, *Türkengefahr*, 228–36.
[30] Schulze, *Türkengefahr*, 171–2, 178; Kratsch, *Justiz*, 181.
[31] For the following, see Wolgast, *Hochstift*, 293–7; Schindling and Ziegler, *Territorien*, v, 86–8; Beiderbeck, 'Heinrich IV.', Teil II, 1–10; Beiderbeck, *Religionskrieg*, 215–67.

The Strassburg problem arose in the mid-1580s as a direct result of the 'Cologne War' and those involved in it had the same awareness of the significance of such a conflict on the western borders of the Reich. Both France and Spain had vital strategic interests in the area, as did the Palatinate, Württemberg, Bavaria, and the Habsburgs, to say nothing of the interest of other German Estates in the future of a major bishopric on the Upper Rhine. By the 1580s, the Lutherans had taken most of the northern bishoprics; the Catholics had emphatically saved Cologne. To both sides, Strassburg thus seemed to represent a last opportunity.

The dispute began over the cathedral chapter in which ten canons were Catholic and seven Protestant. As a direct consequence of the 'Cologne War', three Protestant canons were expelled in 1583, together with the dean, the deposed Archbishop of Cologne, Gebhard Truchsess von Waldburg. The papal nuncio deprived them of their offices and they were excommunicated soon afterwards. The expellees promptly occupied the Bruderhof complex next to the cathedral, taking possession of the administration of the episcopal estates. The Catholic canons meanwhile elected Gebhard's arch-opponent in Cologne, the Suffragan Bishop Friedrich von Saxony-Lauenburg, as dean in his place. The magistrates of the Imperial City of Strassburg remained neutral, though in effect this stance aided the Protestant occupiers of the Bruderhof.

The conflict escalated from 1585, when each side recruited new canons to fill the vacancies and each side elected the scions of major noble dynasties, ignoring the Strassburg tradition of not electing sons of princes. The Catholics elected Cardinal Charles of Lorraine and two sons of the Duke of Bavaria; the Protestants elected princes from Brunswick, Denmark, Anhalt, Mansfeld, Württemberg, Holstein, and two sons of Joachim Friedrich, the Administrator of Magdeburg. Rudolf II issued several decrees ordering the Protestants to withdraw, and each side took military measures to pursue its case. In 1588, for example, the Catholic provost was captured and further key administrative buildings were occupied. The city magistrates assisted again by demolishing the Carthusian monastery by the city walls so that it could not be used as a base for an assault on the Protestants, with whom they concluded an agreement in 1591.

Matters escalated further when Bishop Johann von Manderscheid died on 2 May 1592. The Protestant canons now formally confirmed as administrator the thirteen-year-old Johann Georg of Brandenburg, whom they had secretly elected as early as 1588. The Catholic canons proceeded to elect Cardinal Charles of Lorraine, the Bishop of Metz, whose father, Duke Charles, had recently abandoned the customary neutrality of Lorraine to side with the Catholic League.[32] A brief but initially successful military initiative by the cardinal's French troops led to an early truce in February 1592.

The militant tendency was undermined by the death of Johann Casimir in January 1592, and the Protestant cause was weakened by an emerging rivalry between Brandenburg and the Duke of Württemberg, who wished to put forward

---

[32] Ritter, *Geschichte*, ii, 36–7. The fact that one of the duke's sisters was married to Wilhelm V of Bavaria gained his son's candidature further significant support.

one of his own sons as a candidate. This rivalry, in turn, soon dispelled any interest Henri IV might have had in invading Strasbourg.[33] When the administrator then attempted to sell the bishopric to the Duke of Württemberg in the Treaty of Stuttgart in 1597, the Protestant canons protested vehemently against what they saw as an infringement of their rights of election, and ended by withdrawing their support for him. The Duke of Württemberg, who took over leadership of the Protestant faction, was more interested in acquiring the Bailiwick of Oberkirch than in engaging with the wider struggle. Remarkably, after 1592 the Protestant Estates generally held back.[34] The Elector of Brandenburg petitioned the emperor for recognition of the rights of his grandson, but meekly accepted Rudolf's refusal. The Wetterau counts, traditionally well represented in the Strasbourg chapter, had learned a bitter lesson in Cologne and shrank back from another disaster.[35]

In the circumstances, the Catholics retained the upper hand, even though they did not control the entire bishopric for some time. In 1598, Rudolf agreed to enfeoff Charles of Lorraine in return for Charles taking his nephew Archduke Leopold as his coadjutor. In 1600, he struck a deal with the Duke of Württemberg and in 1604 the Treaty of Hagenau finally ended the conflict. Johann Georg of Brandenburg accepted compensation and withdrew. The eight Protestant canons were allowed to retain their incomes and the Bruderhof for fifteen years, but agreed not to undertake any further elections. Württemberg received Oberkirch as a mortgage property for thirty years. The magistrates of Strasbourg recognized Charles of Lorraine as 'universal bishop', with Leopold of Habsburg as his designated successor.[36]

The Strasbourg affair preoccupied the minds of many princes, and periodically wrought much local destruction, especially in the early 1590s, when the military actions that it generated exacerbated the impact of mercenary activity in Alsace generally. It involved the emperor and most of the leading princes, and potentially raised questions that affected the foundations of a stable order in the Reich. And yet it remained a regional conflict. In the last resort, neither France nor the Protestant Estates had the will to fight over Strasbourg. The city magistrates, for all their sympathy with the Protestant cause, were too weak financially to achieve their ultimate goal, namely to sever the remaining institutional links between the city and the bishopric.

The second major political issue of the 1590s, the continuing controversy over the political rights of the Protestant Administrator of Magdeburg and his counterparts in other bishoprics, had far wider and more serious ramifications. The original dispute over the administrator's right to attend and vote at the Reichstag was resumed in 1594, when Catholic protests once more prevented envoys from Magdeburg and Halberstadt from taking their seats in the College of Princes.[37]

---

[33] Beiderbeck, 'Heinrich IV.', Teil II, 6–7.
[34] Wolgast, *Hochstift*, 298.
[35] Schmidt, *Grafenverein*, 349–52; Wolff, 'Kapitelstreit'.
[36] The treaty was renewed for five years in 1619; the remaining Protestant canons were finally obliged to leave in 1627: Wolgast, *Hochstift*, 297. Leopold became Bishop in 1607; his successor in 1627 was a son of Ferdinand II.
[37] Wolgast, *Hochstift*, 283–5.

All that Joachim Friedrich achieved was an imperial decree which assured him of his territorial rights as the 'occupant of the see'. In both 1594 and 1597–8 the summons to the Reichstag was sent to the chapters and not to the 'occupants'. By then it seemed that the emperor had given up his determination not to enfeoff anyone in an ecclesiastical territory who had not first received papal confirmation, but attempts to reach a compromise in 1603 did not produce a satisfactory formula, and the matter remained unresolved until 1648.[38]

Meanwhile, a far more serious aspect of the affair had unfolded. The annual visitation or review commission for the Reichskammergericht was convened by the Elector of Mainz as Archchancellor but composed of princes by rotation. The commission's smooth functioning was vital, since it lent authority to the court's decisions and it played a vital role in reviewing appeals against those decisions. In 1588 it was to be Magdeburg's turn to serve on the commission but, in view of the recent events in Cologne and the worsening situation in Strassburg, the emperor decided to postpone the review. Since this postponement was then extended in subsequent years, the work of the court was seriously impeded. At a time when the caseload had escalated, the number of appeals had also increased dramatically, but since none were being reviewed, many judgements were simply not being executed. Yet the court was not completely paralysed. It continued to function throughout the 1590s and in fiscal cases, especially those relating to the non-payment of Turkish levies or complaints by subjects about overtaxation by their rulers, the court worked speedily and effectively.[39] However, the court's inability to resolve increasing numbers of cases concerning confessional disputes became a major issue.

In view of the emperor's continuing reluctance to sanction the normal visitation of the Reichskammergericht, the matter came to the Reichstag in 1594, which resolved to commission a deputation to carry out the review. That deputation, however, was uncertain about its terms of reference and the extent of its jurisdiction, and it failed to carry out more than a small proportion of the work. Subsequent efforts to commission a new deputation simply failed to secure agreement.

By 1600, however, a dispute over the resolution of four cases involving ecclesiastical property turned this impasse into a major constitutional issue. Two of the cases were long-running.[40] In 1569, the knights of Hirschhorn on the Neckar had secularized the Carmelite convent founded by their forebears in 1406. Legal proceedings were instituted after the knights ignored an order to return the property in 1571, but a lengthy series of negotiations during 1589–96 failed to bring about a resolution.[41] The Carthusian Order had first appealed to the Reichskammergericht in 1557 against the secularization of the monastery of Christgarten by the Count of Öttingen-Öttingen; only in 1599 did a final judgment order the

[38] Following a failed attempt at re-Catholicization in 1628–35, Magdeburg was ceded to Brandenburg in 1648 and came to that territory as a duchy after the death of the last administrator, August of Saxony, in 1680. See Köbler, *Lexikon*, 402–3; Schindling and Ziegler, *Territorien*, ii, 81–3.

[39] Schulze, *Türkengefahr*, 276–90.

[40] Schneider, *Ius reformandi*, 243–4; Kratsch, *Justiz*, 60–124.

[41] The convent was in fact only returned to the order in 1629, and the town of Hirschhorn was subsequently re-Catholicized once the Hirschhorn dynasty had died out: Schneider, *Ius reformandi*, 244.

count to return the property to the Carthusians and to assume the costs of the entire litigation. Two further cases were more recent in origin. The Margrave of Baden-Durlach had assumed responsibility for Baden-Baden in 1594 and thereby gained patronage, together with the Counts of Eberstein, over the Convent of Frauenalb. The desolate state of the nuns' morals led him to imprison the abbess and her sister the prioress, to order the nuns either to convert or to marry, and to reform all the parishes for which the convent was patron. The Bishop of Speyer sued (though he admitted the convent was a disgrace) and in 1598, Baden and Eberstein were fined and ordered to free the nuns and restore the convent. A fourth case involved the magistrates of Strassburg being ordered to restore the rights and property of the Dominican Convent of St Margaret in the city in 1598.

The cases in themselves were not unusual but, although they were not in fact linked, they assumed a collective political significance as the *Vierklösterstreit* (literally, the conflict of the four monasteries).[42] They stood out because the Reichskammergericht had normally tried to abstain from reaching a judgment in such cases. Their ability to reach a conclusion in these cases probably reflected the fact that they were relatively clear-cut. In particular, both the Catholic and the Protestant judges seem to have agreed that these cases did not come under the legislation of 1555, but that they should be judged according to the normal (Roman) law of the Reich.[43]

However, in the tense atmosphere of the later 1590s, many people believed that the very fact that in four cases the judges found against Protestant lords or magistrates reflected a change of policy. It appeared to indicate, first, that the court had now internalized the Catholic view of the laws of 1555, which only privileged institutions and property whose status had changed before 1552 and which logically dictated the automatic restitution of ecclesiastical property alienated since 1552 under the 'common law' (i.e. canon or Roman law) of the Reich. This stark reminder of the underlying legal system in the Reich was deeply alarming to many Protestant politicians and lawyers, who saw it as a threat to the very basis of the peace of 1555 and to the freedom it granted them. Second, in two of the cases—Hirschhorn and Christgarten—the defendants were faced with almost ruinous legal costs. Third, all four cases touched raw nerves in the Palatinate, a territory in which the reform process (and hence the alienation or secularization of ecclesiastical property) began largely after 1555, involving massive illegality according to the Catholic interpretation of the law.

Traditionally, German scholars have regarded the *Vierklösterstreit* as the cause of the paralysis of the imperial legal system that presaged the Thirty Years War. More recent research suggests that this was not so. The political controversy may have overshadowed and perhaps inhibited certain kinds of proceedings. The situation was certainly exacerbated by the fact that many high-profile cases (for example, the Aachen and Strassburg disputes) were now taken to the Reichshofrat in Prague.[44]

---

[42] Kratsch, *Justiz*; Ruthmann, *Religionsprozesse*, 553–66, 576–7.
[43] Ritter, *Geschichte*, ii, 162; Heckel, *Deutschland*, 92–3.
[44] Stolleis, *Öffentliches Recht*, i, 139–40.

Its original area of jurisdiction was in disputes between individual Estates, royal prerogatives, and enfeoffments, rather than in matters arising from legislation agreed at the Reichstag by 'emperor and Reich'. Consequently, its judgments were liable to be opposed as abuses of the royal prerogative or simply as invalid in cases concerning religion. Since this royal court was composed of judges appointed by the emperor, it was not subject to the kind of confessional parity rules that applied in the Reichskammergericht.

The decline in the Reichskammergericht's caseload, however, seems to have occurred only after about 1610, and it can at least partly be explained by the gradual acceptance of the Reichshofrat as a legitimate peacekeeping agency.[45] Finally, there is evidence that the effective cessation of the appeals procedure encouraged many potential litigants to seek a negotiated settlement before recourse to the court. Less positively, however, it also encouraged the use of violence in the early stages of disputes, since 'possession' was a key factor in determining the outcome of proceedings at the first level. On the other hand, precisely during this crucial period, the court dealt effectively with a substantial number of other cases, in particular those relating to complaints by subjects against excessive taxation or cases brought against rulers by the procurator fiscal for non-payment or late payment of monies due to the Reich.

The fact that the Palatine Elector and his officials seized on the cases of the four monasteries and made them into a cause célèbre was crucial. For it seemed that the 'corresponding party' was now determined to push the arguments its members had made at the Reichstag since 1594 one stage further.[46] The 1597–8 Reichstag commissioned the Reichsdeputation with the task of reviewing the work of the Reichskammergericht. However, that committee was dominated by a clear Catholic majority (the College of Electors was evenly balanced, but in the College of Princes and Cities ten Catholics outvoted eight Protestants).

When it became clear that Reichsdeputation would confirm the judgments, the Palatine representatives denied that it had any more competence to decide such matters than the Reichskammergericht. These were issues, they argued, that arose from the peace of 1555 and they could only be resolved by the parties to that peace, that is, by the emperor and Estates at the Reichstag. When their protest failed, the Palatine envoys, together with the Brandenburg and Brunswick-Wolfenbüttel representatives, simply left the Deputationstag in July 1601 and thereby prevented it from reaching a valid decision. At a subsequent meeting at Friedberg, furthermore, they resolved to block any further attempt at an extraordinary visitation of the court and despatched a delegation to the emperor to protest at the mere engagement of the Reichshofrat in cases concerning the religious peace. They declared their intention to resist all judgments the court handed down.[47]

The effective paralysis of the imperial justice system was clearly a matter of profound significance. Yet equally significant is the restraint that is evident in the behaviour of many princes in the face of the crisis. Saxony, as usual, refused to have

---

[45] Ruthmann, *Religionsprozesse*, 577.   [46] Schulze, *Türkengefahr*, 142.
[47] Ritter, *Geschichte*, ii, 165–6; Neuhaus, *Repräsentationsformen*, 488–9.

anything to do with the 'corresponders', as the dissident princes were known. In 1601, even Landgrave Moritz of Hessen shrank back from joining their open protest. On the other side, the Catholic members of the commission refrained from persisting with a majority vote. At the Reichstag in 1603, the 'corresponders' complained bitterly that the emperor deliberately levied exorbitant taxes and then only pursued the Protestants for payment in order to wear them down, while non-paying Catholic Estates were treated leniently.[48] In the end, though, they too voted with the majority for the Turkish levy, while the emperor's plenipotentiary, his brother Archduke Matthias, ensured that the levy was ratified by simply postponing consideration of any matters concerning the judicial system.[49] Of course, there were radicals on both sides. The Palatine Elector remained uncompromising. The young Duke Maximilian of Bavaria (r. 1598–1651) demanded that the Catholics stand firm in the expectation that the Protestants would back down. At this point, however, an alliance of the conciliatory and the pusillanimous prevailed.

---

[48] Gotthard, *Reich*, 75.   [49] Ritter, *Geschichte*, ii, 166–71.

33

Paralysis, 1603–1614

Did the Reich slide inexorably into war in the fifteen years before 1618? The old German national historiography, with its profound and pathos-laden sense of the tragedy of failed German unity, certainly thought so. The emergence after 1603 of confessional leagues seemed to resemble the drawing of battle lines and a marshalling of troops. Yet things were not so clear-cut. It was the German Reich that was at the core of the Thirty Years War. Scholars who have tried to 'internationalize' the conflict or to emphasize the primacy of the long-term struggle between the Habsburgs and France distort this simple fact which most contemporaries, who spoke of the 'Thirty Years War' as a 'German war', took for granted. When the conflict erupted in 1618, it was a conflict over the German constitution and over the confessional balance of power in Central Europe.[1]

Yet German issues cannot be held exclusively responsible for the outbreak of the war. The political confrontation in the Reich was brought to a head by specific developments in the Habsburg lands (both inside and outside the Reich) and by an inner dynastic struggle that resulted from them, which culminated in the Bohemian crisis. At the same time, developments on the wider European stage made a concerted Spanish–Austrian Habsburg offensive more likely on a variety of fronts, which soon internationalized and diversified the conflict. In 1603, the political situation in the Reich was still fluid. There were fundamental disagreements about how the present problems should be resolved, but there was a multiplicity of parties and factions, rather than just two fronts.

The Protestant activists, the Palatinate and other 'corresponders' or 'confederates', formed the most clearly defined party. Their policy was coordinated and driven by the Upper Palatinate stadtholder, Christian of Anhalt, who concluded mutual defence treaties with Württemberg, Nuremberg, Ansbach, and Kulmbach in 1607.[2] Contacts were kept open with numerous other mainly south-western territories. A variety of princes had good reason to welcome such overtures.

The other Reformed rulers were the most obvious allies. The Palatinate also appealed to many Lutherans, who felt threatened by a strict interpretation of the religious peace and the prospect of an edict of restitution. Some, such as Württemberg, also needed security against the incursions of Spanish troops. In Baden-Durlach, there was alarm at the Bavarian intervention in Baden-Baden, while Lutheran Pfalz-Neuburg, a scatter of small territories sandwiched between

---

[1] Asch, *Thirty Years War*, 3.
[2] Parker, *Thirty Years War*, 27 (the excellent discussion of the Union and the League was contributed by Simon Adams).

the Upper Palatinate and Bavaria, also sought security from Bavarian ambitions in an alignment with the policies of Christian of Anhalt in Amberg.[3] On the other hand, the Reformed Palatinate still aroused the suspicions of many Lutherans: Philipp Ludwig of Pfalz-Neuburg, for example, assuaged his suspicions of the Palatinate by concluding a separate agreement only with Württemberg and Baden-Durlach. Moreover, the Palatinate was unable at this time to supply the added attraction and reassurance of French support.

If Protestants were willing to accept Henri IV's conversion to Catholicism, albeit with some suspicion, his firm treatment of the rebellious Calvinist Duc de Bouillon, Prince of Sedan, seemed to many German rulers (including the Palatine Elector) to smack of religious persecution. The Germans were reluctant to understand that Henri needed to deal with Bouillon, since he threatened the stability of the French monarchy, and the affair cast a cloud over his relations with the German Protestants between 1602 and 1606.[4]

While the elements of a Protestant alliance slowly coalesced in the south-west, the Lutheran princes elsewhere largely retained their distance from the Palatine network. Ludwig V of Hessen-Darmstadt, for example, needed the emperor's support in an ongoing inheritance dispute with his cousin Moritz of Hessen-Kassel, who turned his territory Reformed, and thus pro-Palatine, in 1605. Other northern dynasties, such as those in Oldenburg, Holstein, Mecklenburg, and Pomerania, had experienced so many subdivisions that they had neither money nor the ability to engage in the wider affairs of the Reich. Brandenburg, under the Elector Joachim Friedrich (r. 1598–1608), by and large continued to pursue a political line that was both Lutheran and loyal to the emperor, not least in the hope of support for Brandenburg claims in Jülich-Kleve.

Above all, the Elector of Saxony maintained his position as one of the leading loyalist dynasties in the Reich, while the lands of his Ernestine relatives were by now so fragmented by multiple inheritances that in their politics they simply drifted in the Elector's wake. The apparent solidarity between Saxony and Brandenburg, however, such a dominant feature of the political scene in the sixteenth century, was beginning to weaken. One clear cause was the fact that both dynasties had claims on the Jülich-Kleve-Berg succession. The pursuit of the Brandenburg claim led Joachim Friedrich's heir, Johann Sigismund, to an alliance with Heidelberg in 1605. This resulted in a Palatinate–Netherlands–Brandenburg agreement and in vital links with the Palatine network throughout Germany and the Netherlands. It also laid the religious, intellectual, and political foundations for Johann Sigismund's conversion to Calvinism in 1613.

The Catholic Estates did not have to contend with the kind of confessional issues that bedevilled many of Christian of Anhalt's initiatives during these years. Yet confessional solidarity and commitment to the defence of the Catholic position on the religious peace did not at this stage translate into a more formal union. The threat

---

[3] Press, 'Fürst Christian'; Clasen, *Palatinate*, 21–6.
[4] Beiderbeck, 'Heinrich IV.', Teil II, 10–14; Beiderbeck, *Religionskrieg*, 301–60. Bouillon was defeated in 1606, and by 1608 had been fully restored to his duchy and to his principality of Sedan.

to the southern bishoprics and to re-Catholicization initiatives had subsided. Lack of support from the emperor thwarted the formation of a defensive league by the ecclesiastical Electors in 1603. Then, following the death of the hard-line Mainz Elector Johann Adam von Bicken (r. 1601–4), Johann Schweikhard von Kronberg (r. 1604–26) reverted to the traditional Mainz pursuit of consensus in the Reich. Bavaria had precipitated the collapse of the ailing Landsberg League in 1599, following disputes with Salzburg and Würzburg. Duke Maximilian (r. 1598–1651) fought shy of subsequent proposals for a new league with the papacy and Cologne, preferring initially to concentrate on reforming his duchy's finances and defence forces, rather than risking entanglement in international conflicts.[5]

In this context of relatively loose alliances, a compromise was not inconceivable. The Reichstag of 1603 had merely postponed the issues raised by the appeals in the cases of the four monasteries. The Deputationstag was no longer an option. In fact, it was not convened again until 1643. Nonetheless, attempts continued to be made to resolve both the particular disputes and the more general judicial problem. Zacharias Geizkofler, the imperial treasurer and chief quartermaster until 1603, and trusted adviser to both Rudolf II and Archduke Matthias, made proposals during the Reichstag that envisaged a complicated scrutiny process by a deputation with equal confessional representation. The Catholics did not wish to concede the principle, while the Protestants knew that Geizkofler (himself a Protestant) believed their case to be weak.[6]

The matter was also discussed in more general terms at the meeting of the Electors in Fulda in 1606. They all agreed that 'without justice the kingdom cannot exist', but then divided equally on the Catholic and Protestant view of the matter.[7] They did, however, conclude that six Catholic and six Protestant judges from the Reichskammergericht should attend the Reichstag to present the judgments made over the years in controversial cases. In 1607, Saxony proposed that the coming Reichstag should consider a 'renewal, confirmation and stabilisation' of the religious peace. The Saxon Elector was alarmed by the arguments put forward by Jesuit authors, who denied the validity of the religious peace. Yet the Catholics again feared that the Protestants simply wanted to ratify all Protestant acquisitions since 1552 and to extend the terms of the religious peace in their own favour. They knew only too well that most Protestants regarded their use of ecclesiastical property as an abuse protected only by the constitution of the Reich.[8]

The Regensburg Reichstag followed a peace treaty with the Turks in 1606. Although Rudolf had not yet ratified it, the Protestant Estates immediately sensed a greater degree of freedom in their dealings with the emperor since they were no longer obliged to vote for a Turkish levy. On the contrary, they believed that the greatest threat to their liberty now stemmed from the confessional situation, rather than from the Turks.

---

[5] Albrecht, *Maximilian I.*, 367–8, 386–9.
[6] Luttenberger, 'Kaisertum', 89–93.
[7] Kratsch, *Justiz*, 182; Gotthard, *Säulen*, i, 280–5.
[8] Kratsch, *Justiz*, 183–6.

Discussion of the legal issues was overshadowed by events at Donauwörth in 1606–7.[9] In contravention of the confessional parity specified in the settlement of 1555 (§ 27), the Protestant numerical majority in this Swabian Imperial City had progressively attempted to exclude Catholics first from the city council and then from citizenship. The Catholics had placed themselves under the protection of the Benedictine monks of the neighbouring Monastery of the Holy Cross, many of whom had been educated in the Jesuit seminary at Dillenburg. The monks were determined to assert the rights of the Catholics in the city, and from 1603, they insisted on flying their banners unfurled during processions, contravening a regulation that banners were to be rolled up on such occasions.

The resulting dispute prompted the monastery's patron, the Bishop of Augsburg, to appeal to the Reichshofrat, which in February 1606 threatened to impose sanctions on the city if it persisted in impeding the Catholics. Only two months later, a further procession provoked a riot, during which the banners were dragged through the mud and the congregation driven out of the city. The magistrates blamed the mob, but in September the imperial decree was simply renewed; when the magistrates appealed again, the emperor commissioned the Duke of Bavaria to ensure the rights of the Donauwörth Catholics. Just as the magistrates were about to agree to all points, the mob drove the duke's envoys from the city. The proscription was duly published and the Duke of Bavaria commissioned to enforce it. Bavarian troops occupied the city in December 1607 and began a process of forcible re-Catholicization. In 1609, the city was then distrained by Bavaria to cover the costs of the military action. In fact, Donauwörth remained Catholic and, after a long struggle, became a Bavarian territorial town for good.[10]

The Donauwörth affair scandalized Protestant opinion for several reasons. First, here was yet another example of partial justice being exercised by the Reichshofrat in Prague and being executed by the emperor. Second, Donauwörth lay in the Swabian Kreis and any decisions against the city should technically have been handed to the Kreis directorate, that is, the Duke of Württemberg. The Duke of Bavaria was not even a member of the Swabian Kreis. Third, Württemberg and other members of the Swabian Kreis were particularly alarmed by Bavaria's behaviour. On the one hand, they saw it as yet another instance of Bavarian expansionism, with Duke Maximilian behaving like his father in aspiring to replace the Habsburgs as the pre-eminent dynasty in the south-west of the Reich. On the other hand, the collaboration of Duke Maximilian with the Bishop of Augsburg, Heinrich V von Knöringen (r. 1598–1646), an uncompromising exponent of the Counter-Reformation, seemed to presage a new wave of wholesale re-Catholicization.

The news that Rudolf II's plenipotentiary at Regensburg in 1608 was to be Archduke Ferdinand of Styria, who was well known as an uncompromising advocate of re-Catholicization, generated further anxiety. He opened the session by insisting on discussion of a new Turkish levy (on the grounds that Rudolf had

---

[9] Schneider, *Ius reformandi*, 233–4; Dixon, 'Urban order', 18–24.
[10] It regained its imperial status briefly during 1705–14.

not yet ratified the 1606 treaty), to which the Protestants immediately objected that there was no need.[11] Indeed, the end of the Turkish war had removed that factor which had helped the emperors manage the Reichstag since 1576. Ferdinand further proposed that any confirmation of the religious peace should be accompanied by a restitution clause. His initially uncompromising attitude was almost enough to drive the Saxons to join the Palatinate activists and Brandenburg. The Protestants insisted once again that fair justice and judicial procedure were as essential to the Reich as the sun was to the earth and that they could not acquiesce in any form of general restitution.[12] Although Ferdinand soon softened his line so that the Saxons remained loyal to the crown once more, the activists simply left the Reichstag. Since both the Catholic and the Lutheran loyalists again desisted from passing a majority resolution, the Reichstag was simply adjourned. A subsequent meeting of the Electors at Fulda in July and August also divided on confessional lines and failed to produce any meaningful proposals.[13]

The tension was now much greater than in 1603. The emperor's ability to act was being inhibited not only by his usual indecisiveness but also by the fact that he himself was under acute pressure from the growing crisis in the Austrian territories.[14] In the circumstances, the political distance between the Reformed and many Lutherans narrowed, and what now appeared more like two confessional groups, Catholic and Protestant, began to develop.

Nine days after Ferdinand dissolved the Reichstag on 3 May 1608, the Palatinate, Württemberg, Pfalz-Neuburg, Kulmbach-Bayreuth, Ansbach-Bayreuth, and Baden-Durlach combined in a defensive league at Auhausen near Nördlingen in Ansbach.[15] The driving forces were Christian of Anhalt and Philipp Ludwig of Pfalz-Neuburg, while the Palatine Elector Friedrich IV was nominated as leader and commander of a planned force of 20,000 men. Within a year, Brandenburg, Zweibrücken, Hessen-Kassel, Saxony-Anhalt, and Öttingen, along with sixteen Imperial Cities, had also joined. According to its statutes, the aims of the Union were purely defensive; it had no other explicit agenda.[16] Indeed, few of its members shared the Palatine view that a major religious conflict was inevitable. However, this did not deter Christian of Anhalt from again forging plans for an international Protestant alliance.[17] He wanted formal links with Henri IV, James I, the Dutch Republic, and Christian IV of Denmark. He even envisaged membership for the Protestant nobility of the Austrian lands and corresponded with both Archduke Matthias and George Erasmus Tschernembl, the leader of the Upper Austrian Estates. However, little came of these ambitious plans.

A meeting of the Union at Rothenburg in 1608 rejected the idea of enlisting Henri IV and deferred consideration of all other affiliations. In general, the formulation of a

---

[11] Schulze, *Türkengefahr*, 153–4.
[12] Kratsch, *Justiz*, 182.
[13] Gotthard, *Säulen*, i, 285–9.
[14] See pp. 448–56.
[15] Wolgast, 'Reichs- und Außenpolitik', 180–2; Schmidt, 'Union'.
[16] Parker, *Thirty Years War*, 28.
[17] Wolgast, 'Reichs- und Außenpolitik', 182–6.

clear policy beyond the commitment to mutual defence was frustrated by the latent tensions between Reformed and Lutheran members and by the caution of the Imperial Cities. Their hackles were raised by the princes' refusal to give them equal votes in decisions for which they would inevitably bear the major cost. Moreover, their traditional dependence on the emperor for protection against the princes made them loath to alienate the crown by dabbling in alliances with foreign rulers.

Formally, the Union thus stood in the long tradition of regional defence or peacekeeping leagues.[18] Yet it was clear from the outset that it had more in common with the confessionally orientated Schmalkaldic League than with previous organizations such as the Swabian League. If the majority of its members were wary of Christian of Anhalt's activism and international plans, they still shared his fundamental internal aim. The Union was at root dedicated to combating the Catholic interpretation of the German constitution and, specifically, the abuse of imperial powers allegedly perpetrated in its name.

It was this clearly confessional and political aspect of the Union that helped bring plans for a Catholic equivalent to fruition. Following the Donauwörth affair and the collapse of the Reichstag, Duke Maximilian feared that Bavaria might now become a target for Protestant aggression. In March 1608, he urged Archduke Ferdinand of Styria to persuade the emperor to form a Catholic defence league.[19] The current crisis in Austria and the dynasty, however, rendered an imperial initiative impossible. Thus Maximilian was obliged to proceed to construct a league himself, largely for the protection of Bavaria, though ostensibly for the defence of Catholic (especially ecclesiastical) territories everywhere in the Reich. By July 1609, an association of Upper German Catholic Estates had been established.[20]

Soon afterwards, the Electors of Mainz, Cologne, and Trier also joined, leading to the formation of a Rhineland and an Upper German directorate under Mainz and Bavaria, respectively.[21] The name chosen was 'Defence or Protection Association'; its enemies gave it the name 'Catholic League', associating it with the earlier French–Spanish Ligue of 1585 that had been dedicated to the extirpation of Protestantism in France. And while he had urged Archduke Ferdinand to take action in 1608, Duke Maximilian was adamant that the League should not include the Habsburgs so that it did not become embroiled in their dynastic and territorial problems or become enlisted in their wider political causes. Only reluctantly did he agree in 1610 that, in return for a Spanish subsidy (possibly never paid), Philip III and Archduke Ferdinand should be designated as the League's honorary protector and vice-protector.[22]

In the short term, Maximilian was able to determine the League's development. He also insisted that the Jülich-Kleve-Berg succession question was not formally placed on its agenda. This, in turn, helped ensure that the potentially most explosive political issue of the day did not turn into a major international incident.

[18] Gotthard, 'Union und Liga', 82–93.
[20] Gotthard, 'Union und Liga', 94–112.
[22] Albrecht, *Maximilian I.*, 423–4.
[19] Albrecht, *Maximilian I.*, 409.
[21] Brendle, 'Kurmainz'.

Even so, the Jülich-Kleve crisis well reflected the heightened tension in German politics and the significance of both Union and League.

The death of the mentally disturbed and childless Johann Wilhelm of Jülich-Kleve-Berg in 1609 precipitated a situation that had been anticipated ever since his accession in 1592.[23] There was no shortage of claimants.[24] Saxony claimed entitlement to Jülich-Berg on grounds of a privilege granted by Maximilian I. More direct claims were advanced on behalf of Johann Wilhelm's four sisters and their sons under a privilege granted by Charles V. The eldest sister was married to the Duke of Prussia, also mentally disturbed, and had only a daughter, so her claim passed to her son-in-law, Elector Johann Sigismund of Brandenburg. The next two daughters married the Dukes of Pfalz-Neuburg (and produced a son, Wolfgang Wilhelm) and Pfalz-Zweibrücken. The fourth daughter married Karl von Burgau (morganatic son of Archduke Ferdinand of Tyrol), who also figured as a possible Habsburg candidate at various points. Among the most plausible claimants, and the most active in the few years preceding Johann Wilhelm's death, were the Elector of Brandenburg and Wolfgang Wilhelm of Pfalz-Neuburg. To complicate matters still further, however, in August 1608 the Reichshofrat declared all of the privileges that justified the various claims to be invalid, which meant that the emperor himself would be entitled to the territory when its ruler died.

The inheritance of one of the more prosperous German principalities would have been significant in any circumstances. Jülich-Kleve-Berg was, however, highly significant for other reasons as well. Lying on the Lower Rhine between Cologne and the Netherlands, it was of huge strategic importance both to the Spanish and to the Dutch. That, in turn, meant that its future was of interest to the emperor, to Cologne, and to France. The coincidence of the succession crisis with the conclusion of the Spanish–Dutch Twelve Years' Truce was particularly auspicious to Henri IV, who feared that this setback for Spanish power might tempt the Habsburgs to re-establish their position on the Lower Rhine. Finally, the fact that the dukes had not pursued a clear confessional policy meant that the territory included a majority of Catholics in Jülich and of Lutherans and Reformed in Kleve, Ravensberg, and Mark.[25]

When news of the Duke's death became known, the main aim of the two Lutheran claimants and of Henri IV was to prevent a Habsburg initiative. Henri IV let it be known that any intervention by Archduke Albrecht, the hereditary stadtholder in the Habsburg Netherlands, would immediately provoke French intervention. Meanwhile, he expected the claimants to reach an amicable agreement. However, both Wolfgang Wilhelm of Pfalz-Neuburg and Margrave Ernst of Brandenburg on behalf of the Elector immediately travelled to the territory to claim it for their respective dynasties. Unable to agree on which claim should take

---

[23] Schindling and Ziegler, *Territorien*, iii, 98–101; Anderson, *Verge, passim*; Midelfort, *Mad princes*, 94–124.
[24] Ollmann-Kösling, *Erbfolgestreit*, 51–9.
[25] Schindling and Ziegler, *Territorien*, iii, 98–101; Spohnholz, *Tactics* analyses the complex and fluid confessional situation in the Kleve town of Wesel.

precedence, they decided at Dortmund on 10 June 1610 that for the time being they would govern and protect the territory jointly, and henceforth both described themselves as the 'possessing princes'. The Jülich-Kleve Estates were content to accept this arrangement, for they feared nothing more than being invaded again by a Spanish army from Flanders and being placed under military rule from Brussels. The Duke of Zweibrücken also accepted the Dortmund Treaty, partly because he was confronted with a fait accompli, and partly because he was currently engaged as administrator of the Palatinate.

Neither Brandenburg nor Pfalz-Neuburg had the resources to secure their claim militarily, so both were still reliant on French protection. Henri IV continued to insist on an amicable settlement between the two and on the active participation of the Union as a precondition for his support.[26] Equally, although dependent on French support and eager to secure it, the 'possessing princes', like the Union, were in fact reluctant to trigger French intervention. They were nervous at the prospect of French troops on German soil and many feared that France would merely seize the opportunity to enlist the Union to advance French ambitions without any benefit to the German Protestants. Moreover, most members of the Union firmly adhered to the exclusively defensive and inner-German objectives of their association.

The impasse was broken by Rudolf II's surprisingly decisive intervention. He declared the actions of the 'possessing princes' illegal and the Dortmund Treaty invalid, and he despatched Archduke Leopold, Bishop of Passau and Strassburg, as imperial administrator, to govern Jülich-Kleve-Berg on his behalf until he decided on a new enfeoffment. The occupation of the fortress of Jülich on 23 July 1609 elevated the dispute to an entirely new level, for Leopold, who had successfully resolved the Strassburg controversy in 1607, was a symbol of Catholicism triumphant over Protestantism.[27]

The possibility of French intervention now became more interesting for both the 'possessing princes' and the Union. In denying the rights of the claimants, Rudolf could be said to have ignored the Reich's 'law and tradition'. At the same time, there was real anxiety that Leopold would receive military support from Brussels. Henri IV seems to have feared that a European religious war would now break out. His immediate forceful intervention would enable him to master the situation and avert any challenge to his own domestic position. His demand that the Union sever its contacts with the Huguenots underlines this concern. At the same time, however, he seems to have believed that success on the Lower Rhine could only be achieved if Spanish intervention were impeded by simultaneous campaigns in the Netherlands and northern Italy.

For many members of the Union, however, it was still precisely this wider European aspect of the developing crisis that made them reluctant to conclude an agreement with France for some months. Finally, in February 1610 the French, on the one hand, and the 'possessing princes' and the Union, on the other, agreed to

---

[26] For a detailed account of French policy in this affair, see Beiderbeck, *Religionskrieg*, 363–447.
[27] Beiderbeck, 'Heinrich IV.', Teil II, 17.

supply an equal number of troops (8,000 foot and 2,200 horse each) to evict Leopold from the Lower Rhine. The German princes promised to stand by the agreement in the face of any imperial prohibitions but to respect the rights of the Catholics of Jülich-Kleve. Crucially, they also agreed that once the initial objectives were achieved, they would help the French conquer the Spanish forces in the Netherlands.

When France and Savoy concluded a similar treaty a month later, agreeing an assault on the Spanish stronghold of Milan, the strategy seemed complete. Yet the expected war failed to materialize. The assassination of Henri IV in May 1610 meant that the crisis remained localized in the Lower Rhineland. Philip III and Archduke Albrecht decided not to endanger the Twelve Years' Truce with the Dutch Republic by intervening. A force composed of French, Dutch, English, and Union troops moved against Leopold, who surrendered his Jülich stronghold on 1 September. However, an attempt by the Union to launch a parallel assault on Strassburg was stood down once it became clear that Maximilian of Bavaria had also raised troops: both the cities and the more moderate Union members shied away from a wider and more expensive conflict.[28]

The Lower Rhine conflict was thus defused in the autumn of 1610. It took several years, however, before the Jülich-Kleve-Berg succession was finally re-solved.[29] Each of the 'possessing princes' continued to assert his position in the territory. Johann Sigismund of Brandenburg attempted to enlist the support of the Reformed, while Wolfgang Wilhelm of Pfalz-Neuburg worked on the Lutherans; both had trouble with the Catholics. The emperor tried once more to undermine both claimants by reviving the Saxon candidature with the aim of drawing loyalist Lutheran Saxony into the League, an idea that foundered on Bavarian opposition. However, Rudolf's position was by now so weak that the 'possessors' were scarcely distracted by anything that came from Prague. As Johann Sigismund became increasingly inclined towards the Reformed faith—he formally converted in 1613—so his links with the Palatinate strengthened. As a result, Pfalz-Neuburg saw itself increasingly disadvantaged, so that finally Wolfgang Wilhelm turned to Bavaria, where he married Duke Maximilian's sister and converted to Catholicism in 1613. Both conversions were clearly as much 'political' as anything else; each dynasty sought to give itself a distinct profile in the competition for the favour of the Jülich-Kleve-Berg Estates and of potential external sponsors.

In 1614, war threatened once more when the Catholic Wolfgang Wilhelm, now supported by Spanish troops, warded off an attempt by the Brandenburg heir Georg Wilhelm to evict him from Düsseldorf with Dutch help.[30] Although Spanish troops took the opportunity to restore the Catholic city council in Aachen, however, the Spaniards were ultimately no more willing than the Dutch to risk the truce for the sake of Jülich-Kleve-Berg. Consequently, in the Treaty of Xanten, it was agreed to divide the territory, giving Brandenburg rights over Kleve-Mark-

[28] Press, *Kriege*, 181–2.
[29] Ollmann-Kösling, *Erbfolgestreit*, 88–98.
[30] Israel, *Dutch Republic 1476–1806*, 407–8.

Ravensberg and Pfalz-Neuburg rights over Jülich-Berg-Ravenstein. It was envisaged that the administrations at Kleve and Düsseldorf would cooperate in a joint government of the territory. In practice, they soon set about establishing a permanent division, though the final details were not settled until 1682.

The Jülich-Kleve-Berg affair demonstrated the willingness of the German Protestants to contemplate war only as a last resort, but also their inability to fight one successfully. They lacked money and resources, and were dependent on foreign help. At the same time, they were fraught with doubts about whether foreign help was desirable. A powerful external force might well prove to be worse than a weak emperor. None really wanted to be dragged into a conflict outside the Reich. And all were unwilling to risk the stigma, and potential political disaster, of falling foul of the laws of the Reich, being branded an outlaw, and thus becoming subject to military sanctions applied by the Kreise or by powerful Estates commissioned by the Reichshofrat. Even at the height of the crisis, one of Henri IV's greatest fears had been that the German princes would negotiate with the emperor and submit to some kind of arbitration. It was his good fortune that by 1610 Rudolf II lacked the political cunning and the will to make such arbitration attractive to them.

34

Problems of the Habsburg Dynasty

On 17 July 1609, Henri IV bluntly informed Archduke Albrecht's ambassador that the emperor was no longer a force to be reckoned with, for he was not even master over his own city of Prague.[1] Henri articulated what was common knowledge throughout Europe: the Austrian Habsburgs were in deep crisis by the first decade of the seventeenth century. Time and again, crucial opportunities in German politics were missed because the emperor could not or would not act. Progressively, his own family turned against him and obliged him to relinquish his powers over his lands. In May 1611, finally, he was forced to abdicate the Bohemian crown. He died just eight months later, still emperor but without a kingdom to his name.

The roots of the Habsburg crisis lay in the different ways in which the various Austrian territories developed during the last decades of the sixteenth century, which created deep tensions between members of the dynasty. The initial problems stemmed from Ferdinand I's division of the Habsburg lands between his three sons in 1564; the later problems resulted from the fact that in 1576 Maximilian II left the lands he had inherited (Upper and Lower Austria) to one son who failed to produce an heir.[2] Fundamental throughout were the pressures placed on most of the Habsburg lands by the immediate threat of attack from the Turks and the pressures placed on all of them by costs the Habsburgs incurred during the Turkish wars. The burden of taxation led to a serious peasant war in Upper and Inner Austria during the 1590s. At the same time, financial pressures also generated conflicts with the various territorial Estates, which acquired greater leverage to defend, and indeed extend, their rights and privileges.

The situation was further exacerbated by religion. The Austrian territories had experienced the same rapid spread of Lutheranism among the nobility as territories like Bavaria.[3] Owing to the particular pressures under which they laboured, their Habsburg rulers, however, were unable to master the nobility in the same way that the Bavarians had mastered theirs in the 1560s. In Bohemia, Protestantism flowed into and alongside a rich indigenous tradition of religious dissent, but the same strengthening of the Estates ultimately resulted.[4] In Hungary, the situation was complicated by the very immediate proximity of the Turks, which made Habsburg

---

[1] Beiderbeck, 'Heinrich IV.', Teil II, 17 (note 43).
[2] An excellent survey of the history of the Erblande is found in Winkelbauer, *Ständefreiheit*, i, 30–78.
[3] Schindling and Ziegler, *Territorien*, i, 86–133 and v, 257–77; Winkelbauer, *Ständefreiheit*, ii, 39–63.
[4] Winkelbauer, *Ständefreiheit*, ii, 18–29.

rule more than usually dependent on the nobility and the Estates.[5] In many of the territories, the confessional issue was rendered more acute by the shift of many Lutherans (especially nobles) to Calvinism from the 1570s. This generated links with the Western European Calvinist networks, a sense of the wider significance of their struggle against the Habsburgs, and the adoption of similar theories and strategies of resistance.

The division of 1564 created separate territories for Emperor Ferdinand's second son Ferdinand in the Tyrol and Further Austria (the Vorlande or Vorderösterreich), and for Karl in Inner Austria (Styria, Carinthia, and Carniola). Each ruled more or less independently, though neither had a vote in the German Reichstag. The different development of these two territories illustrates the diversity that prevailed within the Habsburg complex and contributed to the tensions that surfaced later within the dynasty.

In the Tyrol, Archduke Ferdinand started with a territory where the old Church had been successful in preventing Lutheranism gaining much of a stronghold, and he pursued a strongly Catholic policy from the outset. Proximity to Bavaria provided a strong example and some protection. Collaboration with the regional Bishops of Brixen and Trent, whose own territories were embedded in the County of Tyrol, also helped promote an early Catholic counter-offensive. In Further Austria, governed by his son Cardinal Andreas of Austria from 1579, matters were more complicated owing to the wide scatter of the territories involved, the small size of many of them, and their proximity to Protestant territories. Here too, however, a consistent and successful Counter-Reformation policy gradually emerged.[6]

In Inner Austria, by contrast, Karl II inherited a set of territories in which Protestantism had established itself securely among the nobility and the governing elite from the 1520s. By the time Counter-Reformation measures were introduced, Protestants were able to claim that they had enjoyed religious freedom for some time, and they looked back on the reign of Ferdinand I as a golden age. The very immediate threat posed by the Turks made the rulers dependent on the nobility and thus obliged to tolerate religious heterodoxy. Karl initially concentrated on strengthening his government. While his marriage to the Bavarian princess Maria in 1571 affiliated him with the most powerful Catholic territory in the Reich, his Estates maintained close links with the Dukes of Württemberg. Indeed, in 1572, under pressure from the need to invest heavily in defences, the balance of power shifted in favour of the Estates. In the Pacification of Graz, Karl granted lords and knights, and their co-religionists, religious freedom until a 'general Christian and peaceful agreement' had been achieved.[7]

---

[5] Winkelbauer, *Ständefreiheit*, ii, 70–80.

[6] Cardinal Andreas of Austria was the son of Archduke Ferdinand by his secret morganatic marriage to Philippine Welser. He was Margrave of Burgau (a territory located between Augsburg and Ulm), and he was made a cardinal in 1576 as a reward for his father's stance at the Regensburg Reichstag. He became Bishop of Constance in 1588 and of Brixen in 1590 (coadjutor since 1580). As 'Gubernator' of Further Austria he was also bailiff of Alsace. *BWDG*, i, 400; Schindling and Ziegler, *Territorien*, v, 269–70.

[7] Pörtner, *Counter-Reformation*, 28; Schindling and Ziegler, *Territorien*, i, 110–11.

The confirmation and extension of these privileges in the Pacification of Bruck in 1578, however, provided the shock that initiated a sustained Catholic counter-offensive, which, however, faltered under the regency that followed Karl's death in 1590.[8] The Estates were able to prevent the Wittelsbach regency desired by the Archduke's widow. A succession of Habsburg regents (Rudolf II in 1590–2, Archduke Ernst in 1592–3, Archduke Maximilian in 1593–5) was too embroiled in legal disputes with the Estates and too keen to settle differences in view of a deteriorating situation on the Turkish front to take a strong line on religious issues.

Things changed radically in 1595, with the accession of Ferdinand II. Careful not to encroach on the rights of the nobility, Ferdinand pursued an uncompromising line against the Third Estate, culminating in the forcible re-Catholicization of Graz and other towns and many rural areas in 1598–1601. Thousands were obliged to emigrate and Protestantism was driven underground. The Estates protested passionately, not least because many nobles lost subjects to the emigration, but to no avail. Converts were rewarded with jobs and money. Protestant nobles were discriminated against and forbidden to keep preachers or even to attend Protestant services outside the territory. By 1628, they too, like the citizenry and peasantry earlier, faced the stark choice of emigration or conversion.

Ferdinand II's early success in Inner Austria had a profound effect on his attitude to the religious question in the Reich and on his policies as emperor after 1619. Indeed, it is perhaps no exaggeration to say that the Thirty Years War originated in the castle at Graz.[9] Ferdinand of Styria's attitude and example certainly contributed significantly to the crisis, which arose in the third group of Austrian territories inherited in 1564 by Emperor Ferdinand's eldest son and heir, Maximilian.

This group consisted of three distinct parts: Upper and Lower Austria, Bohemia, and Hungary. The latter two were both elective monarchies, which had elected Habsburgs since 1526. In Bohemia, Ferdinand I had been able to establish the primogeniture principle after the Battle of Mühlberg in 1547, though the monarchy remained elective and the balance of powers between crown and Estates remained disputed. In each monarchy, the elective powers of the nobility made their position even stronger than that of the Estates in Upper and Lower Austria.

In all of Maximilian's territories, strong Protestant traditions had been established in the first half of the century and firmly anchored in the rights of the Estates by the nobility. In 1565, Maximilian II had refused to agree to a demand for religious freedom for Lutherans, but in 1568 he did make concessions to lords and knights, though not to the towns, in return for a particularly high tax grant. This was in fact only implemented in Lower Austria (in 1571), but the nobility in both territories behaved as if the concession was unconditional and valid throughout. By the end of Maximilian's reign, roughly half of all parishes were in Protestant hands, while nearly all nobles in Upper Austria and about 90 per cent in Lower Austria were Lutheran.[10]

[8] Pörtner, *Counter-Reformation*, 110–11.
[9] Schindling and Ziegler, *Territorien*, i, 114.
[10] Schindling and Ziegler, *Territorien*, i, 126–7.

In Bohemia, too, Lutheranism took hold early among the nobility and from the late 1540s collaborated increasingly effectively with the Utraquists and the Bohemian Brethren as a political force.[11] In 1567, the Bohemian Estates demanded religious freedom and in 1575 the Protestants presented Maximilian with the *Confessio Bohemica*, which was modelled on the Augsburg Confession. Although Maximilian only ever approved this document verbally, the Estates henceforth claimed it as the source and justification of their religious rights. It certainly led to the further steady growth of Protestantism in Bohemia, embracing most of the nobility and the royal towns as well.

While Lutheranism asserted itself as the majority tendency in Bohemia, Calvinism developed in Moravia, particularly among the Brethren, whom Maximilian discriminated against even after 1575. In the Bohemian territory of Silesia, almost the entire nobility and most of the towns had become Lutheran by about 1560. In all, no more than 1–3 per cent of the population of the Bohemian lands was Calvinist around 1600, though that minority carried more weight and influence than its size would suggest. As a broad group, however, the Protestants had by then anchored their religious rights to their political rights, with the Bohemians at the centre of the monarchy, in general more vociferous and militant than either the Moravians or the Silesians. And while Catholics still tended to monopolize most of the major offices of state, the Protestants effectively created their own institutions to safeguard what had become, by the end of the century, in effect a state within the state.

In Hungary, Lutheranism made an early impact in the 1520s and at the end of the century predominated among the German nobility in western Hungary, in the mountains of Upper Hungary, and in the German colonies of Zips and Transylvania.[12] The Magyar nobility and the eight hundred or so Central Hungarian towns and markets, by contrast, eventually subscribed to various forms and degrees of Calvinism. While Protestants comprised 85–90 per cent of the total population by 1600, more than half of those subscribed to the Reformed Church. As elsewhere, this dramatic confessional imbalance between Catholic and Protestant was reflected in the balance of powers between Estates and crown. Further complications arose from the tripartite division of the country from 1541 between Habsburgs, Turks, and Transylvanian princes. The relatively small area controlled by the Habsburgs in the west and north (some 30 per cent of the total) was perhaps more consistently threatened militarily than any other Habsburg territory, while any opposition to the crown could readily rely on support from the Porte or Transylvania. At the same time, though Hungary lay outside the Reich, its Protestant Estates maintained contacts with their counterparts in the other Habsburg lands, with those in the Reich, and with those in Western Europe more generally. The Habsburgs simply could not afford to be heavy-handed rulers, least of all in religious matters.

On Maximilian II's death in 1576, the whole of this substantially Protestant complex of territories passed to Rudolf II. This sowed the seeds of future conflict

---

[11] Schindling and Ziegler, *Territorien*, i, 134–52; Winkelbauer, *Ständefreiheit*, ii, 18–29.
[12] Bahlcke, 'Calvinism', 77–8; Winkelbauer, *Ständefreiheit*, ii, 70–86.

within the dynasty, for in November 1582 Rudolf's four surviving younger brothers demanded both more substantial emoluments and more influence in government. Suitable positions were found for three of them. Ernst became stadtholder in Austria until 1593 and then exercised a similar function in the Netherlands until his death in 1595. Maximilian, the fourth son, became High German Master in 1590 and then regent in the Tyrol after 1602. Albrecht (VII), the youngest son, became Viceroy of Portugal in 1593 and then succeeded Ernst in the Netherlands in 1596; he married the Infanta Isabella Clara Eugenia, and through her he became ruling prince in Brussels.

Maximilian II's third son, Matthias, was more problematic.[13] He alone of all the brothers refused to sign a waiver of his rights of inheritance. For years, his career was dogged by failure. A spell as stadtholder of the Netherlands 1578–81 came to an ignominious end, with debts and loss of the confidence of the King of Spain. For the next decade he was forced to live in Linz, with no real function and no adequate income. Attempts to secure election as Bishop of Münster, Liège, and Speyer failed, as did his bid to be elected King of Poland (though his younger brother Maximilian fared even worse, ending up with two years' imprisonment). Even Matthias's fleeting ambition to be governor of Silesia or enfeoffed with the Upper Silesian Duchy of Oppeln-Ratibor was thwarted by the refusal of the Silesian Estates to have him.[14] Only in 1593 was he able to take over from Ernst as stadtholder in Austria, from which post he was almost immediately distracted by taking command of the army against the Turks in the long war that broke out in 1593. After the death of Archduke Ernst in 1595, Matthias was next in line to Rudolf. Since the emperor had failed to marry (he had been engaged to the Infanta Isabella Clara Eugenia for eighteen years) and had no legitimate male heirs, Matthias increasingly imagined himself as Rudolf's successor.

Matthias's growing political ambitions were fuelled by the sense of an urgent need for leadership in the emperor's territories from the mid-1590s. Initially, Rudolf had pursued the same kind of conciliatory policy as his father. If Protestantism had reached a high point under Maximilian, it continued to flourish under Rudolf. Rudolf's move to Prague in 1583, taking with him the imperial government, may have been prompted at least partly by his dispute with his brothers in November 1582, but his court there demonstrated the same heterodox mix as it had done in Vienna. Even the young Christian of Anhalt, later the Habsburgs' most militant German adversary, was a favourite at Prague, as he had been at Vienna since 1577.[15]

The emperor's diverse intellectual and artistic interests, which increasingly occupied his time, were broadly Christian but not confessionally partisan, as the papal nuncios lamented repeatedly.[16] Yet in a world of hardening confessional attitudes from the latter, that kind of humanist heterodoxy was increasingly at odds with the new style of government. From about 1578, Ferdinand of Tyrol and Karl II of Inner Austria provided examples of firm management and uncompromising

---

[13] Rill, *Matthias*, 9–101; Press, 'Matthias', 112–17.   [14] Bahlcke, *Regionalismus*, 221–2.
[15] Press, 'Christian'.   [16] Koller, 'Kaiserhof'.

policy in religious matters. Rudolf seemed impossibly lax and lacking in direction by comparison.

It is difficult to discern a coherent drift to Rudolf's rule in the 1580s and 1590s. In his own lands he seemed, by and large, content to maintain the course he had inherited, yet he also allowed himself to be influenced by key advisers or even by his brothers in matters concerning Upper and Lower Austria. In the Reich, he started out trying to maintain a balance, yet increasingly the Reichshofrat seemed to steer a resolutely pro-Catholic course, which led many Protestants to believe that the crown had lost its impartiality and was veering towards arbitrary rule.

In the 1590s, it seemed as if the emperor was simply losing interest in the business of government. He ceased to attend the Austrian and Hungarian diets; he last attended the Reichstag in 1594, and last opened the Bohemian diet in 1598. Then, around 1600, he seemed to purge the heads of his entire establishment in Bohemia and the imperial government. In Bohemia, a resolutely Catholic group, the so-called Spanish faction, now came to prominence. In the imperial government, previously trusted advisers such as Wolfgang Rumpf, Paul Sixt Trautson, and Jan Myllner were suddenly dismissed in favour of weak and rather ineffective figures, but with the general effect of giving prominence here also to staunchly Catholic figures.[17]

This scarcely represented a religious conversion on the part of the emperor. It had almost certainly more to do with his response to the push of the Counter-Reformation and above all to the activities of his brothers. Although Rudolf seemed to evade many of his responsibilities, and was increasingly afflicted by debilitating bouts of melancholia, he remained conscious, almost hysterically so, of his rank and status and jealous of any attempt to usurp his royal prerogatives.

This inevitably exacerbated the tension within the dynasty. Rudolf appointed first Ernst and then Matthias as stadtholders in Austria, only to watch them foster the kind of Counter-Reformation policies that had already between pursued effectively in Inner Austria. The emperor took the initiative in declaring war against the Turks in 1593 and developed a grand strategic vision of an alliance with Persia to crush them once and for all.[18] But he delegated the command of his forces to Matthias. When the Austrian peasants rebelled in 1595, reacting against the advance of the Counter-Reformation and against the heavy burden of taxation arising from the Turkish war, it was Matthias again who played a key role in restoring order and following through with the energetic promotion of Khlesl's forthright re-Catholicization measures.

None of these initiatives would have succeeded against the emperor's wishes; indeed, they have their parallels in Bohemia and the lands more directly under Rudolf's control. Yet there was a growing awareness among the protagonists of Catholic renewal, of the absence of a coherent or coordinated strategy and of energetic and systematic implementation. On the other hand, there were enough early signs of a Catholic renewal to alarm the Estates and to stiffen their resolve to

[17] Evans, *Rudolf II*, 71–2; Evans, *Making*, 58–9; Rill, *Matthias*, 96–7, 122–3.
[18] Evans, *Rudolf II*, 74–8.

resist and to formulate plans for collaboration among the Protestants of the various territories.

The emergence through all these events during the 1590s of Archduke Matthias as an ambitious and apparently successful manager and leader seems to have concentrated attention within the dynasty on the succession question and, increasingly, on Rudolf's manifest inability as a ruler. Things came to a head when Matthias appointed Bishop Khlesl as his chancellor in Upper and Lower Austria in 1599. For Khlesl, the driving force behind the 'renewal of religion' in Austria, seemed convinced, or at least pretended to be convinced, that Matthias could create order and a sense of purpose where Rudolf merely generated muddle and irresolution. It was largely Khlesl's doing that in November 1600 the archdukes met at Schottwien and resolved to formally approach Rudolf and demand that he appoint a successor.[19]

The emperor responded with sheer fury. The fact that in 1601, following discussions in Rome between the Bishop of Olmütz and the Spanish ambassador, Pope Clement VIII had also sent a personal letter to Rudolf urging him to regulate the succession merely increased the pressure. The Spanish and papal emissaries were simply denied any further audiences. By January 1603, the Spanish ambassador to Prague was writing to Philip III that Rudolf must be deposed. However, this would prove difficult, since Rudolf's madness was not so acute that he could not take charge of the situation if he really wanted to.[20]

The emperor's response was energetic but also catastrophic. A series of military victories against the Turks in 1602–3 gave him the confidence to launch a harsh series of Counter-Reformation reforms in the royal cities of Silesia and in Upper Hungary.[21] The Hungarian Estates protested vociferously, further inflamed by Rudolf's unilateral declaration at the Diet of Pressburg in April 1604 that complaints about religious matters would no longer be discussed with the Estates. Similar confessional measures and military occupation were threatened in Transylvania, which Sigmund Báthory had ceded to Rudolf in 1598 in the hope of escaping the relentless pincer pressure of marauding Turks and unpaid Habsburg soldiers. By November 1604, the various Hungarian discontents were ready to join with the Transylvanian nobleman István Bocskai in open rebellion against Habsburg rule, with the military support of the frontier hajduk mercenaries and the backing of the Turks.[22]

Rudolf's bungled attempt to assert his authority in Hungary merely fanned anxiety about his leadership. In 1605, the archdukes met again at Linz, but Matthias's subsequent mission to Prague was brusquely rebuffed.[23] However, the situation in Hungary was by now so desperate that Matthias simply resolved to deal with both Bocskai and the Turks without formal authority. That provoked Rudolf into formally appointing Matthias as his stadtholder in Hungary on 21 March, but

[19] Press, 'Matthias', 118.   [20] Rill, *Matthias*, 123.
[21] Bahlcke, *Regionalismus*, 310–12.
[22] Evans, *Making*, 97–8; Winkelbauer, *Ständefreiheit*, i, 142–7.
[23] Rill, *Matthias*, 124.

the wider questions of the succession and of Rudolf's competence to govern remained open. A further meeting of the archdukes in Vienna in April 1606, orchestrated by Khlesl, resolved that the Turkish war must end and that, in view of Rudolf's incompetence, Matthias should be declared head of the house of Habsburg.

Rudolf was forced to give Matthias the necessary authority to resolve the Hungarian crisis and end the Turkish war. In June 1606, Matthias concluded the Peace of Vienna with the Hungarians, granting them religious freedom, the separate financial administration of Hungary, and the right to elect a royal deputy. Bocskai himself was recognized as Prince of Transylvania and his solution for the hajduk question—the grant of land and exemption from feudal burdens in return for free military service—was adopted. Above all, Bocskai was now instrumental in facilitating the Peace of Zsitvatorok in November 1606, which agreed a twenty-year peace and abolished the annual tribute payable by the emperor to the Sultan in favour of a single compensation payment of 200,000 gulden.[24]

With all the archdukes behind him and with the explicit support of both Philip III of Spain and the papacy, Matthias was in a stronger position than ever before. Yet Rudolf still refused to ratify the treaties he had made. In Hungary, he contrived not to summon a diet for over six months, and the death of István Bocskai in December 1606 reopened the question of the Transylvanian succession. By October 1607, the hajduks were so alarmed by rumours that Rudolf wanted to continue hostilities against the Turks that they rebelled once more against the 'faithless, foreign papist' and demanded the installation of Gábor, the last of the Báthory line.[25] At the same time, Rudolf made his attitude to Matthias clear when he commissioned Ferdinand of Styria as his plenipotentiary at Regensburg in November 1607: an unwise move driven purely by spite, for the appointment of a notorious Counter-Reformer merely aggravated the German Estates and made any settlement of the Donauwörth issue virtually impossible.

Since renewed instability posed a serious threat to Habsburg rule anywhere in Hungary and threatened to spill over to other Habsburg lands, Matthias simply allied himself with the Hungarian Protestant Estates. At the Diet of Pressburg in February 1608, he formally concluded an agreement with the Hungarians and the leaders of the Upper and Lower Austrian Estates to defend the peace treaties of 1606 against all opponents, primarily the emperor himself. In 1604, Bocskai had failed to create a union of the Hungarian and Bohemian Estates; Rudolf's blind hatred for Matthias now generated precisely such an event between the Hungarians and the Austrians.[26] By April, Matthias had 15,000 men ready to march on Prague and the vocal support of István Illésházy and Georg Erasmus Tschernembl, leaders of the Hungarian and Austrian Estates.

---

[24] Lanzinner, 'Zeitalter', 184. The hajduks were freebooting frontiersmen who fought a perpetual guerrilla war against the Ottomans, but who were just as likely to turn against the Austrians if the opportunity arose.

[25] Báthory soon fell out with the hajduks; he was assassinated in 1613 and replaced by the Turkish-backed nobleman Gábor Bethlen. Pamlényi, *Hungary*, 151–2.

[26] Bahlcke, *Regionalismus*, 311–12, 323–4.

As Matthias prepared to cross the border into Bohemia, envoys from Spain and Rome urged him to leave Rudolf at least with Bohemia. Both the King of Spain and the pope feared that driving Rudolf out of Prague might cause the Habsburgs to lose first the Bohemian and then the imperial crown. The Moravian Estates decided to join the confederation. Like the Hungarians and the Austrians, they made it a formal condition of their oath of homage to Archduke Matthias that he recognized their religious liberty, the traditional independence of their territorial governments, and the reservation of major offices in them for natives of each territory (the so-called *Indigenatsrecht*).[27] The Bohemians, Silesians, and Lusatians, by contrast, calculated that they could extract better terms from Rudolf: they preferred a weak monarch to the prospect of a triumphant Matthias in league with the Estates.

In reality, Matthias was under as much pressure as Rudolf, even if he seemed poised to claim much of Rudolf's power. In June 1608, the emperor had no option but to recognize the Treaty of Zsitvatorok, and in the Treaty of Lieben he ceded to Matthias all of his rights over Hungary, Austria, and Moravia and the promise of the succession in Bohemia. Both brothers promised extensive religious freedom to secure the loyalty of 'their' Estates and Matthias achieved recognition only after he had formally agreed to all demands. Since the Bohemians and Silesians knew the Prague government was in the hands of Catholics, they entered a solemn alliance in June 1609 and vowed to defend their religious freedom 'to the last drop of blood'.[28] They agreed that no act of aggression should be directed at the king, 'the highest authority instituted by God', but his Catholic government was another matter. Faced with this extreme threat, Rudolf issued his Letter of Majesty on 9 July 1609, in which he guaranteed everything that the Estates demanded; the Silesians and Lusatians received similar assurances.

The emperor's attempts to extract himself from this dire situation were at first simply hopeless and then disastrous. Around 1607, he seems to have toyed with the idea of abandoning the extreme Catholic policies that had brought the crisis to a head in the first place. Offers of positions in his government to Calvinist noblemen in the Reich failed to make much impact.[29] By then, Rudolf simply lacked credibility. Even so, he continued to make overtures to the Protestant camp. He even entered negotiations with the Palatine Elector, which ended abruptly when the Elector died in September 1610. In the months before the emperor's death, rumours were still circulating that Christian of Anhalt was to be admitted to Rudolf's privy council, and even that the emperor intended to marry the Palatine Elector's widow.[30]

Around the same time, Rudolf formulated the desperate plan to deploy the troops raised by his nephew Archduke Leopold for use in the Jülich-Kleve-Berg struggle against both Matthias and the Bohemian Estates. Some mutinied on their way through Passau and looted parts of Austria and Bohemia.[31] When a contingent under Leopold's command finally entered Prague and threatened the Hradschin in February 1611, the Estates simply set up an alternative government.[32] In April 1611, they summoned a diet which formally deposed Rudolf from his Bohemian

[27] Bahlcke, *Regionalismus*, 324–42.   [28] Bahlcke, *Regionalismus*, 356.
[29] Schmidt, *Grafenverein*, 376.   [30] Rill, *Matthias*, 191, 193.
[31] See p. 426.   [32] Bahlcke, *Regionalismus*, 382–6.

throne. They then promptly made exorbitant demands of Matthias, but, in exchange for confirmation of their rights and privileges, they elected him king on 23 May 1611.

Matthias for his part, again under Khlesl's influence, had already begun to connive at reneging on what he had promised the various Estates in Hungary, Austria, and Moravia. Like Rudolf before him and like Ferdinand II after him, he set about consolidating his position by means of ennoblements and by systematically discriminating in favour of Catholics in his court appointments.[33] Laying foundations for the longer term, moreover, was made easier by the fact that his court was suddenly significantly more attractive to the ambitious nobleman, for he had taken everything Rudolf possessed except the imperial crown. More embittered than ever, Rudolf still adamantly refused to contemplate regulating the succession in the Reich. He died on 20 January 1612.

The previous month, the archdukes had already agreed that Matthias should succeed Rudolf. The Electors were equally impatient with Rudolf's prevarication and had decided to proceed to an election in May 1612, but they were undecided who they wished to choose. The ecclesiastical Electors distrusted Matthias because of his agreement with the Protestants; their preferred candidate, however, Albrecht of Brussels, was not acceptable to the Protestant Electors. At the end of the day, Matthias was the only plausible candidate. The influential Saxon councillor Kaspar von Schönberg had few illusions. Matthias 'offends the Emperor, shows no respect for the Reich, and will govern worse' than Rudolf, he wrote on 14 October.[34] Yet the Reich must have an emperor who has 'lands and people', for it still needed a bulwark against the Turks. The other archdukes had little or, as in the case of Maximilian, whom most inclined to favour, no land; they simply could not wear the imperial crown. On 13 July 1612, finally, Matthias was unanimously elected emperor. Ironically, however, the differences between the two groups of Electors prevented them from laying down conditions for his government of the Reich that were as restrictive as those that had been negotiated by the various Habsburg Estates.

---

[33] MacHardy, *War*, 66–8, 183–207.   [34] Gotthard, *Säulen*, ii, 548–9.

35

The Reich in the Reign of Emperor Matthias, 1612–1619

It is hardly surprising that internal problems of the Hapsburg dynasty left little time for a sensible policy in the Reich. The epic struggle between Rudolph and Matthias precipitated a prolonged crisis of state that several times seemed to threaten the very survival of the Habsburgs as a ruling dynasty in Central Europe. The leaders of the territorial Estates involved often imagined themselves as being at the centre of the political world, with visions of grand European alliances or the establishment of a Dutch-style republic in the east. In fact, the various confederations found concerted action almost impossible. Only the crass ineptitude of Rudolf and the craven ambition of Matthias permitted them moments of apparent glory. Still, the memory of the heroic stand they had taken was an important source of inspiration, both to them and to their correspondents in the Reich and elsewhere. In 1618, it was to encourage the Bohemians to undertake an even more breathtaking act of defiance, but also one that led to complete disaster.

Was there an alternative? Did Emperor Matthias have anything to offer once he had achieved the ambition that had consumed him for over twenty years? The new emperor lacked the intellectual profundity of his predecessor and was known to be vain and lazy. While he enjoyed the sociable life at court, his attention to the detailed business of government was intermittent. The capacity for leadership and determination he had demonstrated during the long Turkish war and in the struggle against Rudolf was little in evidence after he became emperor.

On the whole, he was happy to allow Bishop (from 1615 Cardinal) Khlesl to take the initiative, but this too was problematic. Khlesl was distrusted by many key figures in the Reich, for example the Archbishop of Mainz and Imperial Arch-chancellor Johann Schweikard von Kronberg, the Imperial Vice-Chancellor Johann Ludwig von Ulm, and the president of the Reichshofrat, Count Johann Georg von Hohenzollern-Hechingen, who despised him as a plebeian arriviste.[1] Khlesl's schemes represented perhaps the best chance for a lasting peace in the Reich, yet his background as the architect of the Catholic renewal of Upper and Lower Austria led many to suspect his motives after 1612. The very fact, however, that he was willing to negotiate with the Protestants set the Archdukes Maximilian and Ferdinand against him, which led to his downfall in 1618.

---

[1] Rill, *Matthias*, 199, 244; Johnston Gordon, 'Khlesl'; Angermeier, 'Politik'.

Finally, both the new emperor and his chancellor faced immense problems left by Rudolf. Matthias was the only viable candidate for the imperial throne because he alone had a sufficiently large territorial base on the frontier against the Turks, but he had also inherited vast debts of some five-and-a-half million gulden.[2] Above all, Matthias was in thrall to the Protestant Estates in his hereditary lands. For many Protestants in the Reich, the new emperor was acceptable because his power was balanced by an apparently overwhelming weakness. The almost impossible task Matthias and Khlesl faced was to mediate a solution to the problems of the Reich while asserting the emperor's rights as a ruler in his own lands. The fact that the nobles in his own hereditary lands effectively claimed the rights accorded only to princes in the peace of 1555 made a collision there almost inevitable.

Initially, Matthias was also attractive to many because he presented himself as a conciliator, declaring that 'unity is stronger than light' ('concordia lumine maior').[3] Even before the election was finalized, Khlesl was forging plans for 'Komposition', for the settlement of all disputed issues by means of bilateral agreements arrived at by discussion and compromise, rather than by majority votes. The idea was not new. The concept had been discussed intensively at the court of Duke Johann Friedrich of Württemberg in 1610; it had also been considered during the early deliberations of the Protestant Union, and was even mooted at the imperial court.[4] Zacharias Geizkofler, the Protestant former imperial treasurer, had been a key figure in those discussions and he played a role again now as Khlesl's tireless correspondent and adviser.[5] The novelty of Khlesl's strategy was that the idea became the central plank of imperial policy, with a view to creating a new loyalist imperial league that would replace the two existing confessional associations. Therein lay both the potential attraction of Khlesl's proposals to those who wanted to keep the peace, but also their potential to alienate those—both Protestant and Catholic—who were suspicious of Habsburg ambitions in the Reich.

This was problematic from the outset. The Reichstag summoned to Regensburg in August 1613 was presented with a series of proposals designed to break the deadlock over the Reichskammergericht.[6] A reform of the court was envisaged, as was a new commission to resolve the outstanding appeals, especially those relating to the four monasteries. Both Khlesl and Geizkofler were convinced that nothing further would be possible unless those particular disputes were settled. Even so, the prospects of securing any agreement at the Reichstag were slim: many leading princes failed to attend in person, and the instructions for both the Bavarian and Palatine representatives allowed them no room for manoeuvre.

Matters were made even more difficult by the fact that the Reichstag was also faced with a new demand for a Turkish levy. Khlesl envisaged an army of 20,000 men, to be financed jointly by the Estates of the Austrian lands and the German

---

[2] Rill, *Matthias*, 197.
[3] Rill, *Matthias*, 197.
[4] Gotthard, *Konfession*, 84–90; Angermeier, 'Politik' analyses Khlesl's plans.
[5] Luttenberger, 'Kaisertum'.
[6] Press, *Kriege*, 186–7; Rill, *Matthias*, 227–31; Ritter, *Geschichte*, ii, 378.

princes. The proposal at Regensburg was for a sum of 260 Roman Months, much more than had ever been requested before.[7] This was justified by a new crisis in Transylvania, where the Turks were supporting Bethlen Gábor's bid to oust Gabriel Báthory as ruling prince. The emperor argued that western Hungary could not be held if Turkey gained control over Transylvania and that the potential loss of Hungary was a threat both to the Habsburg hereditary and crown lands and to the Reich as a whole.

Like their Austrian counterparts, the German Estates refused to provide money for this purpose, since they did not believe the Turks really intended to attack either Austria or the Reich. The emperor was consequently obliged to negotiate with the Porte, and in 1615 the emperor and the sultan agreed to recognize Bethlen Gábor as prince of Transylvania, not subject to either of them. The following year they agreed to renew the Peace of Zsitvatorok.

The emperor's request for help merely aroused intense suspicion at Regensburg. Some were openly sceptical; others reported rumours that the emperor really wanted to use the army against the Protestants in the Reich. The Union princes were joined by others, though not Saxony, to form a so-called 'corresponding' group, which, as in 1608, put forward a list of demands as preconditions for any further discussion of any point. By October 1613, the Reichstag had reached deadlock again. The Catholic majority agreed a much-reduced Turkish levy of 30 Roman Months. The Reichstag was prorogued until 1 May 1614. The 'corresponding' Protestants again refused to recognize a majority vote. The gulf between the confessional fronts was as deep as it had ever been, and the Reichstag was not to meet again until 1640.

Yet Khlesl and Geizkofler persisted, and further initiatives were launched in the following years. A special 'conference on compromise' (Kompositionstag) was suggested, then the delegation of the matter to the Electors. Each proposal, in turn, was met by objections from both sides of the dispute, with the Protestants unwilling to run the risk of having to agree to any demands made by the Catholics and the Catholics unwilling to compromise at all. Throughout it all, Khlesl and Geizkofler continued to develop their ideas. In 1615, Geizkofler wrote that the first step must be a truce for twenty-five or, even better, fifty years.[8] The words of any agreement must be 'comprehensible, clear, stark, and obvious so that they could not give rise to any equivocation'. An impartial arbitration body should be established. All German Estates should agree to the treaty, and every new ruler or government in a territory should be required to swear by it. The other European states were to be drawn into a non-aggression treaty. Above all, the justice system in the Reich must be improved so that injured parties could speedily regain their right by means of an improved enforcement system.

Geizkofler's motives seem quite clear. This was but a continuation of the line that he had pursued since the late 1580s. It was fully in tune with the earlier thinking of imperial advisers such as Lazarus von Schwendi. Khlesl's motivation, suspect to many at the time, has prompted much scholarly disagreement. Had the

---

[7] Ritter, *Geschichte*, ii, 378.   [8] Kratsch, *Justiz*, 191.

former 'Reformer General' of Upper and Lower Austria really embraced the cause of compromise? Or was this simply dissembling of the most unprincipled kind?

If it was the latter, then the deception was remarkably skilled and sustained. Khlesl's private correspondence with Geizkofler seems to indicate a genuine meeting of minds. He was a true Catholic, he wrote on 7 June 1614, 'but because I cannot comprehend God's judgement, I would at least desire . . . that we might live together in quiet and peace politically, as we always did'. 'I live and die as a Catholic,' he wrote on 22 May 1615, 'but religion teaches me to preserve and promote peace, unity, and good understanding between Christians.' 'If the minds of men are united, confidence is established, and people more obliged to one another', then more progress would be made towards an ultimate reconciliation in one day than otherwise in many weeks.[9] Khlesl even believed that he could do business with Christian of Anhalt. On 26 September 1615, he informed Geizkofler: 'From my heart I wish to meet with Prince Christian, for as much as we disagree in religion we are linked in heart and intentions and it might still be possible to find a means of banishing the mistrust.'[10]

Khlesl's position was perhaps not as contradictory or as dissembling as some have maintained. Or rather, he was no more dissembling than any other contemporary politician who subscribed to the new principles of political prudence based on the teachings of Lipsius.[11] The lessons of history, an evaluation of the problems of the present, and the application of the yardstick of reason, all dictated a degree of pragmatic toleration. At the same time, this was not incompatible with the desire to impose a state religion within an individual territory. As an imperial politician after 1612, Khlesl was simply adopting the thinking of the 1555 peace settlement.

One of the prime aims of Khlesl's 'composition' strategy, and a precondition of its success, was to undermine the two confessional leagues. To a limited degree, he was in fact able to achieve this, though other factors also played a part, and the decline of the leagues failed to bring the political benefits Khlesl had hoped for.

The Protestant Union never developed coherence and unity of purpose. Its financial situation was weak, for many of its members, notably the Elector of Brandenburg, were as delinquent in the payment of their dues to the Union as they were in the payment of taxes to the Reich. Considerable debts had been incurred as a result of the costs of the operations associated with the Jülich-Kleve-Berg crisis. The Union's members, moreover, pulled in different directions.

Christian of Anhalt worked tirelessly to construct a complex web of international alliances. Treaties were concluded with England in 1612 and with the Dutch Republic in 1613. He also maintained links with the noble opposition leaders in Austria, Bohemia, Moravia, and Silesia, and conducted an active correspondence with agents in Vienna, Prague, Turin, and Venice. He made overtures to Gustavus Adolphus of Sweden and fuelled the latter's suspicions of a European Catholic conspiracy to oust him in favour of his cousin and rival, King Sigismund Vasa of Poland. He kept a particularly close eye on the conflict that erupted between the

---

[9] Kratsch, *Justiz*, 188–9.   [10] Kratsch, *Justiz*, 192.
[11] Stolleis, *Öffentliches Recht*, i, 96–8, 122–5.

Duke of Savoy and Spain in 1614, and on the war that broke out in 1615 between Venice and the Habsburg government in Graz.[12] Savoy and Venice cooperated in tying down Spanish troops in a conflict over Montferrat; England and the Dutch Republic sent ships into the Adriatic to prevent aid from Spanish Naples relieving the siege of Gradisca. However, the Protestant Union could not be drawn into any formal alliance with either Savoy or Venice. Once again, the German Estates shied away from any foreign war and from any conflict that did not involve the defence of the Reich.

Indeed, in the Reich, the Union had reached its limits and was showing signs of disintegrating.[13] The Saxon Elector refused to contemplate membership. Nor did either the Protestant administrators of the north German bishoprics or other ruling members of their dynasties see any advantage in joining the Union. None of them seriously feared the threat of forcible restitution to the Catholic Church. Württemberg strenuously opposed any agreement with Savoy or Venice for fear that Spanish troops might attack Mömpelgard or its other territories on the left bank of the Rhine. The Protestant Imperial Cities resisted any decisions that might land them with major costs or threaten their position within the Reich: they were all too well aware that the emperor and the imperial courts remained the guarantors of their independence. Finally, Brandenburg lost interest in the Union after it failed to defend the Hohenzollern interest in Jülich-Kleve-Berg, and it abandoned its membership in April 1617, when the Union decided not to place Brandenburg's Lower Rhine acquisitions under its formal protection.

With dwindling membership and few common interests, there was little enthusiasm for renewing the association in advance of the expiry of its initial ten-year term in 1618. Aware that the princes were dependent on their money, the cities drove a hard bargain. They demanded a veto over any military actions, a pledge that no new territorial claims would be supported, and that the Union would not engage in any eventual conflict between Spain and the Dutch. With these provisos, they agreed to extend the association until 14 May 1621.

The Union was undermined largely by the incompatibility of its members' interests, but also by the lack of a plausible domestic threat, which can at least partly be attributed to the spirit of 'composition'. The Catholic League was even more directly affected by Khlesl's conciliatory manoeuvring, since here Habsburg interests soon began to conflict with the Duke of Bavaria's original aims. Khlesl initially found a willing ally in Johann Schweikard of Mainz who, from the start, had wanted to admit the Elector of Saxony and any other moderate Protestants, to align

---

[12] The Uzkok War was provoked by the aggressive and criminal activity of the mixed-ethnic refugee communities who defended the Habsburg frontier with the Turks and who, incidentally, also posed a serious menace to Venetian shipping. The Venetian assault on Gradisca in December 1615 was essentially designed to stop the brigandy of the uzkoks, though in fact it targeted their Habsburg overlord, whose control over them was limited. The conflict was resolved by diplomacy in 1618, when Ferdinand agreed to execute or banish many of the uzkok leaders and install a permanent garrison in their stronghold at Zengg. The diversionary conflict in Montferrat was resolved in October 1617. See Parker, *Thirty Years War*, 40–3.

[13] See Parker, *Thirty Years War*, 35–8.

the League more firmly as a support for the emperor, and to admit some or all of the Habsburg archdukes. Khlesl painted a picture of an 'active association . . . founded on the religious and secular peace and the laws of the Reich' and spoke of the eventual inclusion of the imperial fiefdoms in Italy, of Spain, the Catholic Swiss cantons, the King of France, Venice, and Catholic Poland.[14]

The reality fell far short of such grandiose plans.[15] Spain and the papacy, and the reluctance of Saxony, helped Maximilian of Bavaria avoid the admission of Protestants, but in 1613 he was obliged to accept the admission of the High German Master Archduke Maximilian as ruler of the Tyrol and Further Austria. Accommodating Habsburg interests also meant reorganizing the League. The duumvirate (the Rhineland and Upper Germany) was replaced by a triumvirate, and the parts of the Upper German region that belonged to the Swabian Kreis were assigned, with the Tyrol and Further Austria, to a third directorate under Archduke Maximilian. Bavaria responded to this setback by not ratifying the new treaty and by entering into a subsidiary association (technically permitted by the League's rules) with Bamberg, Würzburg, Eichstätt, Augsburg, and Ellwangen. Almost immediately, a squabble broke out with Archduke Maximilian over the affiliation of Augsburg and Ellwangen with Bavaria since they were members of the Swabian Kreis and should thus have joined the new Habsburg directorate. When the Elector of Mainz tried to insist on a meeting of the three directors in 1616, Duke Maximilian simply resigned. The following year, he established an entirely new regional defence association with Bamberg, Würzburg, Eichstätt, and Ellwangen. The exclusion of Augsburg ensured that the Habsburgs would not object. The League itself was effectively dead, and was only revived again on the initiative of the Rhineland group in new circumstances in 1619.[16]

Duke Maximilian's departure from the League and formation of another with ostensibly identical aims might seem paradoxical. Privately, he criticized the reorganization of 1613 for the fact that the League was no longer dedicated to the defence of Catholicism. Yet the regional agreement he forged in 1617 was not explicit on this point either. The key issue was not whether Khlesl's 'composition' policy was idealistic or simply devious. The crux was whether 'composition' really did aim to overcome the confessional deadlock and create the preconditions for an enduring peace in the Reich (and whether that would involve concessions to the Protestants that the Bavarians could accept). Or was the real aim simply to promote the interests of the Habsburgs?[17] The Bavarians were not alone in suspecting that Khlesl was merely the agent of an ambitious ruling dynasty that was seeking to establish itself as a hereditary monarchy in the Reich.

Those suspicions were reinforced by the plan to establish a standing army.[18] The idea was first proposed in December 1614 by Johann Georg von Hohenzollern-Hechingen,

---

[14] Rill, *Matthias*, 233–5.
[15] For the following, see Albrecht, *Maximilian I*, 418–50.
[16] See p. 573.
[17] Albrecht, *Maximilian I*, 435–6.
[18] Rill, *Matthias*, 244; Albrecht, *Maximilian I*, 474–6.

the director of the Reichshofrat, to Archduke Albrecht in Brussels. A force of 25,000 foot and 4,000 horse would be financed by the League and supported by the Spanish army. It should be used to defend Jülich against Dutch and Brandenburg aggression, to reinforce the emperor's authority in the Reich, and to secure the election of a successor.

In 1616, the plan was taken over by Archduke Maximilian and presented by him to Emperor Matthias. The idea now was to aim the force more directly against the Protestants and to make Archduke Ferdinand of Styria (by then the heir most favoured by the Habsburg archdukes) its commander. The Bavarians objected strenuously that Archduke Maximilian's plans were contrary to German liberty and the freedom of the Electors, the Golden Bull, and the laws and constitution of the Reich in general. Before long, the scheme had been leaked to Christian of Anhalt, whose categorical opposition was predictable.

Widespread opposition across the confessional divide rapidly undermined any thoughts of an imperial standing army. Yet the whole affair was significant in two respects. First, it seems clear that it was Khlesl who betrayed the plan to Christian of Anhalt. Hohenzollern-Hechingen had been an appointee of Rudolf II, and his experiences during the struggle between Rudolf and Matthias left him with an enduring distrust and dislike of Khlesl. That extended to a profound scepticism about any notion of 'composition', a scepticism shared, by and large, by the archdukes, who increasingly favoured a hard-line approach to the dynasty's problems, both in the hereditary and crown lands and in the Reich. Second, the standing army episode exposed the link between the army plans, the deep distrust of Khlesl within the Habsburg camp, and the urgent issue of the succession to Emperor Matthias.

Under Rudolf II, the succession issue had occasioned prolonged and bitter disputes within the dynasty. Now there was an early agreement within the German line. Matthias's surviving brothers agreed to drop their claims in favour of Ferdinand of Styria, with whom Matthias was also content.[19] The claim of Philip III of Spain (a grandson of Maximilian II, who technically took precedence over nephew Ferdinand of Styria) was to be settled by negotiation with the new Spanish ambassador, Íñigo Vélez de Guevara, Count of Oñate. This duly happened in the secret treaty of March 1617, whereby Ferdinand promised to cede to Spain the Habsburg possessions in Alsace and the bailiwicks of Hagenau and Ortenau (on the right flank of the Rhine south of the Black Forest), and the Italian fiefdoms of Finale and Piombino. This paved the way for Matthias to adopt Ferdinand formally as his son.

The problem with the succession this time lay in the Habsburg lands, and above all in the Reich. Protestant activists everywhere, and many others, were alarmed by the prospect of the succession of Ferdinand of Styria, a hard-line Counter-Reformer. As far as they were concerned, there could be no agreement on the succession without a concession on the religious issues. Khlesl was also initially lukewarm about

---

[19] Rill, *Matthias*, 245–6, 257–9, 263–4.

Ferdinand, and he feared losing his newly gained position of power to a designated successor, or even being supplanted by one. First, he urged delay to see whether Matthias's late marriage in 1611 to Anne of Tyrol might yield a direct heir. Then, he insisted that the resolution of the succession issue must be linked with, or even preceded by, a successful 'composition' initiative. By the time he placed himself squarely behind Ferdinand's candidature, he had in effect seriously compromised his own position in the eyes of all the archdukes.[20]

Faced with growing pressure in favour of Ferdinand, the Protestant activist leadership in the Palatinate blocked an election and hatched an alternative plan.[21] In May 1616, an envoy was sent to Munich to enquire whether Duke Maximilian might be willing to stand for election. In view of his resignation as director of the Upper German League and his consternation over the standing army proposals, it was thought Maximilian might be persuaded to stand as the candidate of German liberty against Habsburg monarchism.

There is no evidence that Duke Maximilian—albeit not an Elector himself— ever contemplated the succession of anyone other than a Habsburg. Indeed, he went out of his way to assure Ferdinand of Styria (his brother-in-law) of his absolute commitment to his cause. Typically, however, he asked that in return Ferdinand recognize his wish to be addressed as 'Serene Highness' like the archdukes, thus affirming his position as premier duke in the Reich (senior even to Archduke Maximilian of Tyrol).[22]

Maximilian's demurral did not deter Christian of Anhalt. As late as February 1618, Elector Friedrich V visited Munich himself to press the case again for a Bavarian candidature. As Henry Wotton, then resident in Venice, commented in a letter to Sir Thomas Lake: the notion that one might elect the Duke of Bavaria to the imperial throne 'sounds like a dream' encouraged by the Elector Palatine. The German princes, Wotton believed, would never risk a civil war simply to block Ferdinand, who was indeed already the emperor 'in the seed' ('in semine').[23]

This was indeed the case. Khlesl had worked assiduously to shore up Catholic solidarity and to exploit the disunity of the Protestant opposition in the various hereditary and crown lands. He failed to mobilize the Estates of the hereditary lands against the Turks at the general diet of Linz in 1614, but he was able to avert the formation of an anti-monarchical noble confederation in Bohemia in 1615. And he had done enough to ensure that Ferdinand could be 'accepted' as King of Bohemia in 1617 and of Hungary in 1618. In August 1617, moreover, with the Bohemian crown secure, Emperor Matthias, Archduke Maximilian, and Khlesl travelled to Dresden, where they secured the agreement of Elector Johann Georg to a meeting of Electors for 1 February 1618 to elect Ferdinand as King of the Romans. This was

---

[20] Angermeier, 'Politik', 303–13.

[21] Albrecht, *Maximilian I*, 476–87; Altmann, *Reichspolitik*, 195–220.

[22] Albrecht, *Maximilian I*, 483. The title had been adopted by Duke Wilhelm V in 1591, but never formally recognized.

[23] Altmann, *Reichspolitik*, 220–1 (note 171, letter dated 1 June 1618).

delayed by the news of an insurrection in Bohemia, but the election eventually took place in August 1619, some five months after Matthias's death.

Henry Wotton was right. The German Estates did shy away from inner conflict and foreign involvement and rallied behind Ferdinand. Nonetheless, their reluctance to do so for some time was significant. The Habsburg succession strategy and the standing army proposal were enough to generate renewed anti-Habsburg feeling, almost an anti-Habsburg front, across the confessional divide. If Khlesl's manoeuvres had the effect of weakening the confessional blocks, elements of each were brought together again by concerns over the succession. The pressure to elect a Habsburg in 1615 and 1616 led many to question whether the proposed election would be genuine at all. Where was the freedom of choice? And what was the point of an election if the outcome was clear in advance?[24] Was this not yet another step along the road to a hereditary monarchy?

Yet again, however, there was no plausible alternative. Duke Maximilian and his advisers were sceptical about a Bavarian candidature. They did not believe that they could ever secure enough votes, anticipating endless problems with the Austrian and Spanish Habsburgs and the papacy in the event of success. They foresaw that a Wittelsbach emperor would be forced to compromise his religious principles and that he would be wholly dependent on the Palatine Elector and the Protestant princes. Not least, the Bavarians simply could not afford the cost of maintaining an imperial court: no German prince could match the resources commanded by a Habsburg who ruled Austria, Bohemia, and Hungary.[25] Even so, Duke Maximilian reported to his brother Ferdinand, the Elector of Cologne, in April 1618 that unless steps were taken, 'the German freedom of the Electors, princes and Estates would be ended, the succession would become hereditary, the secular princes gradually made into common territorial Estates, and the Roman Reich transformed'.[26]

The politics of the Reich were deadlocked by 1618. The fundamental issues were no nearer being resolved than they had been ten years earlier. Catholics and Protestants were still bitterly divided over the question of the restitution of ecclesiastical property and the status of the Protestant administrators of the northern bishoprics. Years of wrangling, conspiracy, rumour, and counter-rumour, had eroded the prospects for a workable compromise. All imperial institutions were either deadlocked or discredited; the imperial crown itself was no longer regarded as a neutral agency.

Running across the Catholic–Protestant divide, suspicion of the Habsburgs transcended confessional differences. Equally, deep suspicions remained between Lutherans and Calvinists, and between activists such as Christian of Anhalt and the Palatine party on the one hand, who looked to foreign powers, and the traditionalists on the other hand, who feared civil war and foreign intervention on German soil. The rhetoric of unity, peace, and justice remained strong in the

[24] Gotthard, *Säulen*, 636–40; Albrecht, *Maximilian I*, 474, 479.
[25] Altmann, *Reichspolitik*, 215–17; Albrecht, *Maximilian I*, 484–5.
[26] Albrecht, *Maximilian I*, 486–7.

correspondence and negotiations between princes, but it could not generate the will to seek a political compromise. If many thought a showdown was inevitable sooner or later, however, there was little that actually pointed in that direction in the Reich. In May 1618, however, news from Prague created a different and altogether more dangerous situation.

36

The Crisis of the Habsburg Lands

The apparent ease with which Ferdinand of Styria was adopted as Matthias's successor in Bohemia, Hungary, and the hereditary lands belied profound problems. Far from defusing the situation, Matthias's own succession in 1612 had merely inaugurated a new phase of the inner-Habsburg crisis. Khlesl's approach to the hereditary and crown lands differed from his approach to the Reich. In the Reich, compromise was the precondition for progress towards a political solution. In the hereditary and crown lands, it was a tactical necessity at the start of the difficult process of asserting the ruler's rights.

This was a problem that existed in each of the territories separately, and within each component part of the lands of the Bohemian crown. Each territory contained its own individual political constellation, which in each case was also shaped by attitudes to immediate territorial neighbours, to the question of collaboration with other territories, and to the issue of overall Habsburg rule.[1] While the political issues were most acute in Bohemia, and the potential opposition there was more radical, the problems elsewhere were also profound, not least in Hungary, where Matthias feared as early as 1613 that there was a very real threat to the rule of the Habsburg dynasty.[2]

The crux of the problem in Bohemia, mirrored with variations in the other lands, was the question of the Letter of Majesty of July 1609.[3] Rudolf had granted it to save his crown; Matthias had confirmed it to secure his. As significant as the Letter itself, with its formalization of the role of *Defensores* elected by the Estates to watch over its observance, were the associated political agreements that Matthias also confirmed on his coronation in 1611.[4] Essentially, the Estates' right of free election had been reaffirmed and the Bohemian–Silesian confederation was recognized, while the crown had promised to deal with four further demands of the Estates at a forthcoming diet. One of these aimed at establishing a confederation of all the Estates of Matthias's lands; another sought the formation of a system for the mutual and common defence of those territories. Regular regional assemblies of the Estates and the renewal of Bohemia's hereditary treaties with Saxony, Brandenburg, and Poland were also demanded. The aims of the Estates were quite clear: to gain

---

[1] For a detailed analysis, see Bahlcke, *Regionalismus*, 24–55, and for a general survey, Winkelbauer, *Ständefreiheit*, i, 29–173.

[2] Ritter, *Geschichte*, ii, 397.

[3] Pursell, *Winter King*, 43–64.

[4] The *Defensores* had been created before the Letter of Majesty was agreed: Bahlcke, *Regionalismus*, 355–6.

control over military power, to legalize institutions of noble resistance, and to give external powers a voice in Bohemian politics.[5]

For nearly three years, Matthias was able to prevaricate, but then lack of money for his campaigns in Hungary forced him to summon a general diet of the Austrian, Bohemian, and Hungarian Estates at Linz in 1614. Neither the crown nor the more radical forces among the representatives of the various Estates were able to exploit the occasion effectively. Matthias and Khlesl had hoped to unite the Estates behind a campaign to defend the Habsburg lands and the Reich against the Turks.[6] But the lack of a credible Turkish threat in 1613–14 undermined an attempt to levy taxes and impose Habsburg authority. All that resulted was a series of suggestions as to how the emperor might maintain peace with the Turks. Khlesl later complained to Ferdinand of Styria that the Estates at Linz were 'resolved to leave Transylvania to the Turks rather than to grant His Majesty something for the war'.[7]

A second general diet at Prague in 1615, however, summoned at the insistence of the Bohemians, did little more than underline the disunity of the opposition. It failed even to replicate the solidarity against the Habsburgs that had been achieved in Linz the year before. The Hungarians, disillusioned by the reluctance of the other territories to contribute to their high defence costs, failed to attend. The Moravians, Silesians, and Lusatians feared a union of Estates would simply lead to their subjugation by the Bohemians. The Austrians, led by Georg Erasmus von Tschernembl and Gotthard von Starhemberg, favoured a union with the Bohemians, but objected to their insistence on Bohemian leadership. As the moderate Moravian leader Karl Žerotín had predicted in advance of the Prague meeting, the opposition was hopelessly divided and its previous unions and confederations were now of no consequence.

The failure of the Estates to unite opposition to the crown at Prague led to general disillusionment and to the radicalization of a small minority.[8] This strengthened the position of the crown. In 1617, when the emperor urgently needed to have Ferdinand designated as his heir in Bohemia in order to fulfil the requirements of the Oñate Treaty with Spain, the Catholics were again able to outmanoeuvre the opposition relatively easily. Despite their declared opposition to Ferdinand and determination not to contemplate an election at the behest of the emperor, they allowed themselves to be manipulated into agreeing to 'accept, proclaim and crown' Ferdinand, with only two nobles (Counts Heinrich Matthias Thurn and Leonhard Colonna von Fels) openly opposing.

Ferdinand's 'acceptance' strengthened the confidence of the Catholic party and drove many Protestants to despair. Although some moderates still hoped to secure their rights by negotiation, others became convinced that their future could only be secured by an open confrontation.[9] Two underlying processes reinforced the sense

---

[5] Bahlcke, *Regionalismus*, 386.
[6] Ritter, *Geschichte*, ii, 387–92.
[7] In a letter written in May 1617: Bahlcke, *Regionalismus*, 390.
[8] Bahlcke, *Regionalismus*, 389; MacHardy, *War*, 68.
[9] MacHardy, *War*, 68.

that the survival of Protestantism was threatened acutely: the manipulation of court patronage and the growing Catholic pressure on the religious rights of Protestants.

In each territory, Matthias and Khlesl had intensified efforts to build up a Catholic party: Catholic nobles were promoted and ennoblements were used to strengthen existing networks.[10] The transfer of the court and of significant imperial institutions from Prague to Vienna at the end of 1612 was useful in undermining the Bohemian networks and laying new foundations. The Protestants were strong in Austria too, of course, but at least a confederation of Catholic prelates and nobles had been established there in February 1610. The move of the court also had the effect of distancing the ruler from the powerful Bohemian Estates. They resented their loss of access to the ruler, and were further weakened by the fact that the Moravians and Silesians welcomed the opportunity to bolster their independence from the Bohemians.

The same techniques of manipulation and discrimination were used throughout the Habsburg lands. By and large, only Catholic nobles were promoted to prestigious and lucrative offices. Ennoblements and promotions of Protestants to higher grades of nobility were severely curtailed. Those who openly opposed the Habsburgs, like Count Thurn, were penalized: Thurn was deprived of the valuable Burgraviate of Karlstein, and both he and others were threatened with execution.[11] The 'equation of merit and loyalty with Catholicism' deprived Protestant families of any prospect of advancement and threatened their position as champions of the political rights of the Estates against the Habsburgs.[12] The development of international contacts in the late sixteenth century had helped to bolster the Protestants' confidence in their future. By about 1610, however, the cumulative effect of systematic discrimination and exclusion was to deprive many of any sense of future perspective at all.

Growing political and social pressures were linked with mounting religious pressures.[13] As Protestants were all too well aware, Ferdinand of Styria, more than any other Habsburg, embodied the spirit of the aggressive re-Catholicizing Counter-Reformation. Even before Ferdinand became a dominant force as official heir to the crown, however, the signs of a determined Catholic counter-offensive were unmistakable. After all, Khlesl too advocated the imposition of (Catholic) religious uniformity in the Habsburg lands, regarding a compromise in the Reich, of whatever duration, as a precondition for success in Bohemia, Hungary, and the hereditary lands.[14] The problems that arose in Bohemia over the implementation of the Letter of Majesty were particularly acute in view of the fact that only 10–15 per

[10] MacHardy, *War*, 66–8, 183–207.
[11] Rill, *Matthias*, 295–6.
[12] MacHardy, *War*, 212–13.
[13] Evans, *Making*, 62–5.
[14] MacHardy, *War*, 47–70, 109–13.

cent of the population was Catholic.[15] They illustrate, however, in particular form the impact of the new policies everywhere, and they led directly to the crisis of 1618.

The initiative was led by Johann Lohelius, Archbishop of Prague, to whom Matthias had transferred ecclesiastical authority over the crown lands. Specifically, between 1611 and 1618 no less than 132 'royal' parishes were transferred to the archbishop.[16] Lohelius promptly started replacing retiring Protestant pastors with Catholic priests. He then further enraged the Protestants by recognizing Utraquist pastors as the equals of Catholics, on the grounds that the Council of Trent had explicitly sanctioned communion in both kinds for Bohemia. Before long, Protestant pastors were simply being driven out. A conflict over the status of Protestant churches on Church lands brought matters to a head.[17]

Protestants insisted that the Letter of Majesty gave inhabitants of crown lands freedom of religious association and public worship, and that this also applied to Church lands, since the Habsburgs had traditionally insisted that they were royal lands. The emperor now claimed that he did not own the Church but merely protected it, so that the Letter of Majesty did not apply. The town of Braunau belonged to the Benedictine monastery of Braunau (Broumov) and when Abbot Selender complained about the Protestant church there, the royal court encouraged him to close it down. Klostergrab was under the control of the Archbishop of Prague, as owner since 1580 of the Cistercian Abbey of Ossegg, though the townspeople claimed they were a free mining community and hence effectively a royal town in which the Letter of Majesty applied. Notwithstanding the townspeople's claims, Archbishop Lohelius drove out the Protestant pastor at the end of 1614 and sealed the Klostergrab church. Once again, Protestant complaints were overridden and the royal court ultimately backed the archbishop when he demolished the disputed building in 1617.[18]

The emperor's denial of his own sovereign rights over the Church was so patently perverse that it merely confirmed the Protestants' sense that the crown was engaged in systematic discrimination and aimed to destroy them. Matthias kept up the pressure. He refused to listen to complaints at the general diet in 1615; the following year, he punished the town of Neustraschitz for having driven out the Catholic priest who had been imposed on it.[19] Ferdinand behaved charmingly during the coronation celebrations, but then immediately began to threaten Thurn and other noble opponents. The Catholic secretary of the Bohemian chancellery spoke openly of plans to establish a garrison at Prague after the emperor's death. In several towns, a start was made with re-Catholicization, and Prague and Leitmeritz were obliged to grant Catholics civic rights. The crown was clearly attempting to enforce the principle of 'cuius regio, eius religio' as if the Letter of Majesty had never existed.

[15] Winkelbauer, *Ständefreiheit*, ii, 26.
[16] Parker, *Thirty Years War*, 48.
[17] MacHardy, *War*, 69; Evans, *Making*, 65–6; Press, *Kriege*, 188–92; Rill, *Matthias*, 294–5.
[18] Winkelbauer, *Ständefreiheit*, ii, 26, 121.
[19] Rill, *Matthias*, 295–6.

Indignant about these systematic breaches of the Letter of Majesty, the Protestant *Defensores* called a meeting of the Estates in March 1618. Their petition to the emperor merely provoked the threat of arrest if they dared meet again. While the representatives of the towns were intimidated by the crown's threats, the opposition of the nobles strengthened. On 18 May, the activist leadership composed an appeal to the people that was read in many churches the following Sunday. When a larger group, in effect a Protestant diet, did reassemble—they had decided in March to meet again on 21 May to consider the Emperor's response—their leaders were summoned to the royal castle (the Hradschin) to answer to the royal council. Thurn reported rumours of a planned Catholic assault on them and they requested permission to come armed.

Permission was granted, but it did nothing to allay their suspicions and, by this time, Thurn and his close associates were almost certainly determined to make their point by killing one or more of the emperor's representatives. On 23 May, their confrontation with the council was interrupted by the news that the royal judges had detained the (Protestant) city councillors of the old town. Thereupon, two imperial representatives, Vilém Slawata and Jaroslav Martinitz, and Philipp Fabricius, secretary of the Bohemian chancery (*Landtafelschreiber*), were seized and thrown out of the castle windows.

A similar demonstration had initiated the Hussite revolution in 1419. The victims had suffered terribly then. Now the emperor's envoys landed on a dung heap and escaped through the neighbouring Lobkowitz palace. One of the victims, Slawata, claimed angels had saved him; others alleged the intervention of the Virgin Mary. All three were rewarded with offices and promotion: Slawata and Martinitz, both from old Bohemian noble families, were made Imperial Counts in 1621 and Fabricius was ennobled as 'Baron von Hohenfall' (Lord High-Jump) in 1623.[20]

If divine foresight really had saved the victims of the defenestration, as many claimed, it almost immediately abandoned the Habsburgs. The following day, the Protestant diet formed a Directorium or provisional government, composed of representatives of the regions, and prepared to raise an army to defend itself. This was a blatant challenge to Habsburg authority. For each side in the conflict the stakes could not have been higher. The rebels risked execution for treason and the extinction of their dynasties. For the Habsburgs, the loss of Bohemia would have led to the loss of the imperial crown and the collapse of their dominant position in Europe.[21] Indeed, the Bohemian crisis was only the most acute manifestation of a challenge that confronted the Habsburgs in all their hereditary lands and in Hungary.

The news spread rapidly throughout Europe, and the significance of what had happened was immediately clear. For years, commentators had drawn parallels between the Bohemian opposition and the Dutch rebels several decades earlier. Indeed, in 1611 the moderate Moravian leader Karl Žerotín reckoned there were

---

[20] *ADB*, xx, 515–17; *NDB*, xvi, 302–3; Press, *Kriege*, 192.
[21] Winkelbauer, *Ständefreiheit*, i, 95–6.

'more malcontents in Prague now than years ago in the Netherlands'.[22] Immediately after the defenestration, Khlesl warned of the danger that 'Bohemia may become a Dutch government'.[23] This was now more than just a constitutional wrangle between a ruler and his noble Estates. It was a clash between conflicting visions of state and society, a revolution, rather than just a rebellion.

This helps explain the wider impact of the Bohemian crisis, but also its specific effect on the Reich. The status of the Bohemian crown in the Reich was not clearly defined. The King of Bohemia was an Elector, in some ways superior to the others in status by virtue of his royal title, but less engaged in the sense that he did not participate in the normal business of the Electors (though he participated in the core business of electing an emperor).[24] Yet in political terms, the lands of the Bohemian crown impinged on some of the Reich's key territories. The Elector of Saxony was a reliable ally of the Habsburg rulers of Bohemia for reasons of regional security as well as the Habsburg emperor's chief Protestant guarantor of stability in the Reich. The Elector of Brandenburg held fiefdoms of the Bohemian crown; indeed, in 1617 his aspiration to acquire the Bohemian fiefdom of the Duchy of Jägerndorf led him to agree to Ferdinand of Styria's succession.[25] Relations with the Elector Palatine were more complex, but equally crucial. The Upper Palatinate, which bordered Bohemia, had once been among the lands of the Bohemian crown, and in the sixteenth century it was still integrated into its feudal nexus.[26]

With Christian of Anhalt as stadtholder in the Upper Palatinate after 1595, these ancient ties assumed a new significance.[27] The line of communication between Prague, Amberg, and Heidelberg—almost straight through the centre of Germany—became an axis of opposition to Habsburg rule. It was one of the key links between the Bohemian 'malcontents' and Calvinist rebels in France and the Netherlands. And Christian's activities as a middleman, soon really the lynchpin of the whole European network, did much to foster among the Bohemian nobles, as among the nobles of the other Habsburg lands, that sense of the equivalence of their position and that of the Estates of the Reich. Where the Habsburgs and Khlesl saw a legally subordinate nobility in need of firm rule, the leaders of their Protestant Estates claimed liberties inspired by 'German freedom'.

It took another year for the Bohemian crisis to reach its climax.[28] The self-appointed provisional government in Prague tried to create a united front among the various lands of the Bohemian crown and to secure external allies. After some

[22] Bahlcke, *Regionalismus*, 386.

[23] Bahlcke, *Regionalismus*, 406; Begert, *Böhmen, passim*.

[24] Begert, *Böhmen*, 303–56, 574–86.

[25] Zeeden, 'Zeitalter', 143.

[26] Bahlcke, *Regionalismus*, 17, 19, 108; Köbler, *Lexikon*, 484–5. The Upper Palatinate was originally a Bavarian territory which fell to the Palatinate in the Wittelsbach partition of 1329. It was given to Karl IV as a pledge in 1353, but was redeemed by the Palatinate in 1373. Like other Bohemian subsidiary lands, the Upper Palatinate was part of the 'corona Bohemiae' rather than the 'Regnum Bohemiae', though Charles IV's Luxemburg dynasty was ultimately unable to secure its hold over it.

[27] Press, 'Christian'; Clasen, *Palatinate*, 23–6. See also Wolgast, 'Reichs- und Außenpolitik', 186–7.

[28] Schormann, *Krieg*, 25–8.

months of prevarication, the Silesians and Lusatians expressed their support, but the Moravians under the leadership Karl Žerotín refused to join the rebels. An appeal to the enemies of the house of Habsburg brought a predictable swift response from the Palatinate. However, all that was on offer in Heidelberg at this stage was diplomatic and moral support. The parlous financial state of the Palatinate meant that it could not afford to offer significant financial aid. Furthermore, Friedrich V was unwilling to be seen openly supporting the rebels and he was surrounded in the Union by allies who were reluctant to abandon the officially defensive purposes of their alliance. By vaguely holding out the prospect of election to the Bohemian crown, however, Christian of Anhalt was able to persuade the Duke of Savoy, a bitter opponent of Spain in northern Italy, to finance a mercenary force under the command of Count Ernst von Mansfeld.

Despite the uncertainty of their finances, the Prague Directors soon launched their first military offensive against the Habsburgs. Count Thurn moved south to engage imperial forces in minor skirmishes and, at the end of August, Mansfeld's mercenary force arrived. By the end of November 1618, he was able to take Pilsen.

The response in Vienna was uncertain at first. Military preparations were set in motion for a decisive move against the rebellion. An army of some 14,000 men was raised and the experienced Charles Bonaventure de Longueval, Count of Bucquoy from the Spanish Netherland, was appointed commander. An initial move towards southern Bohemia to confront Thurn's army, however, was frustrated by the arrival of Mansfeld and Bucquoy was obliged to turn back.

Khlesl once more urged negotiation, but it was clear that the leaders of the rebellion were determined not to accept any compromise. At the same time, Archdukes Ferdinand and Maximilian brought about a decisive change in approach in Vienna. The foundations had been laid in the secret agreement concluded in March 1617 by Ferdinand and the Spanish ambassador Count Oñate. Philip III promised to support Ferdinand's claims to succeed Matthias in Bohemia and Hungary, and to lend military support in the war against Venice. In return, Ferdinand promised to cede Alsace to Spain in due course. Alsace was not in fact available as it was currently held by the Habsburg Archdukes of Tyrol, but the undertaking was important for it promised to secure a vital part of the route northwards for Spanish troops to the Netherlands. Ferdinand also promised to confer the north Italian fiefdoms of Finale and Piombino on Philip after his election as emperor. The agreement was crucial in the Bohemian crisis of 1618. It strengthened Ferdinand's position with regard to Bohemia and Hungary. It all but committed Spain to assist with any resistance either there or in the Reich, and it paved the way for a cooperative Spanish–Austrian approach to issues of mutual interest in northern Italy.[29]

With these foundations laid, Ferdinand and Maximilian were able to move against Khlesl, whom they accused of abetting the rebels with his talk of negotiation. At the end of July 1618, Maximilian tricked Khlesl into coming to his

---

[29] Asch, *Thirty Years War*, 44; Parker, *Thirty Years War*, 37.

chambers in the Hofburg, where he was promptly arrested and then incarcerated in the fortress at Ambras in the Tyrol. On the intercession of the pope he was transferred to Rome in 1622. Five years later he was rehabilitated and returned to Vienna, where he died in 1630. His political role, however, ended with his arrest, which marked the beginning of a new hard line in imperial politics.

Matthias was powerless to prevent the removal of his main adviser; his own death in March 1619 ensured that the new course would prevail. Initially, the crisis deepened. In April, Thurn marched into Moravia and forced the Moravian Estates to join the rebellion. Faced with armed force and with the news that their treasury had been removed to Vienna by Colonel Wallenstein—the generalissimo's first notable demonstration of loyalty to the crown—even the Catholics acquiesced in the uprising. The Viennese authorities immediately returned the money to Moravia so as to avoid any possibility of claims of illegality being levelled against the crown.[30] Any hope, however, of that undermining the resistance was soon abandoned. Thurn turned his force to threaten Vienna, and the Protestant Estates of Lower Austria seized the moment to appear before Ferdinand and demand religious freedom.

A decisive victory by Bucquoy over Mansfeld in southern Bohemia seemed to bring relief, for Thurn was immediately recalled to Prague. By July, Ferdinand felt sufficiently secure to be able to proceed with the imperial election at Frankfurt. Yet the rebels persisted. On 31 July, they solemnly swore an oath on the *Confoederatio Bohemica*, by which they undertook to defend the fundamental laws of the kingdom and the rights and privileges of the Estates.[31] According to this, the monarchy was to be elective; the king was to be bound by the *Confoederatio*; Catholicism would be permitted, but some leading administrative positions would be reserved for Protestants nominated by the Estates, and the Jesuits would be expelled. Finally, the Silesians, Lusatians, and Moravians secured agreements that ensured they would not be dominated by the Bohemians. On 16 August, two further confederations were concluded with Lower and Upper Austria.[32] Then on 19 August, the Bohemians resolved to depose Ferdinand on grounds of his tyrannical behaviour.

A week later, they elected Elector Friedrich V of the Palatinate as their new king.[33] Other candidates had been considered: the Duke of Savoy, the Elector of Saxony, even Prince Bethlen Gábor of Transylvania. However, Savoy was an unreliable maverick, Saxony was too fundamentally loyal to the emperor, and the Transylvanian was essentially an exotic outsider. For all his prevarication, when the offer finally came Friedrich was the only realistic candidate. His contacts in the Reich and his family links with England, the Netherlands, and Sweden seemed to offer the prospect of international backing against the inevitable Habsburg backlash. For his part, Friedrich was encouraged by news that the Bohemians were

---

[30] Mann, *Wallenstein*, 168–73.
[31] Winkelbauer, *Ständefreiheit*, i, 94–5.
[32] MacHardy, *War*, 72, 104.
[33] Pursell, *Winter King*, 65–91; Wolgast, 'Reichs- und Außenpolitik', 186–7.

making military progress again, this time in collaboration with Bethlen Gábor in a joint advance on Vienna, which culminated in a renewed siege in November.

Ferdinand, meanwhile, was steadily strengthening his position. Friedrich V had done all he could to frustrate the election, even trying to persuade his cousin Maximilian of Bavaria to stand. When Maximilian declined, he tried to delay the election until the Bohemians had elected a new king, somehow hoping that if the vote of the Bohemian Elector were to end up in non-Habsburg hands it might be used to undermine Ferdinand's prospects. In the event, however, the Catholic Electors stood firm, and both Saxony and Brandenburg came to support Ferdinand. Even the Palatinate saw no alternative but to support the majority. Ferdinand was unanimously elected as emperor on 28 August and crowned on 9 September. The prestige and prerogatives of the imperial crown now gave him overwhelming advantages over his enemies in his hereditary lands and Bohemia. At the same time, Friedrich V was faced with the prospect of becoming a rebel against his own overlord in the Reich if he accepted the Bohemian crown. In October, the fateful decision was made and in November Friedrich was crowned in Prague.

By then Emperor Ferdinand II's plans to reassert his authority in his own lands were well advanced. For all the apparent ambiguities of Ferdinand's position in most of his territories, he held overwhelming advantages in his swift campaign against the usurper. It was the way that he then chose to use his victory that plunged the Reich into a prolonged and bloody war.

37

Imperial Public Law and the Struggle over the Imperial Constitution

The years that many historians have regarded as a time when the Reich was poised on the brink of war, also saw the development of both the theoretical basis for the constitutional settlement of 1648 and of new forms of patriotism. Key elements of the latter constitutional compromise were formulated in the discipline of imperial public law that emerged at Reformed and Lutheran universities in the decade or so before the outbreak of hostilities. It had a number of sources.

Roman law was fundamental in the sense that the imperial law that had been developed since the 1490s was based on Roman law foundations. That legislation also inspired the considerable body of writing about the Reich, which grew markedly from the 1560s. From 1501 onwards a quasi-official *Corpus Recessum Imperii*, a record of all agreements reached at the Reichstag, was published; in 1569 a handbook devoted to the procedure of the Reichstag was compiled, printed for the first time in 1612. Some commentaries on Reichstag procedures were specifically concerned with the growing political crisis in the Reich. An extensive literature was devoted to the question of whether decisions made by majority votes were binding on all. Related to this were the works that explored the principles of *concordia* and the extent to which *discordia* was both possible and permissible in the polity.[1]

The 1580s saw the appearance of numerous commentaries on virtually all of the major constitutional laws of the Reich. The Imperial Cities compiled their own six-volume historical-constitutional handbook known as the *Registratur* and maintained a central archive of all relevant documentation at Speyer.[2] Between 1607 and 1614 Melchior Goldast von Haiminsfeld (1575–1635) published a number of substantial collections of constitutional documents, albeit skewed towards the Reformed and Palatine interest, for Goldast hoped that his unsuccessful applications for employment in the Palatinate in 1606 and 1608 might yet succeed. In 1617, the Lutheran Saxony-Weimar councillor Friedrich Hortleder published a massive documentary history of the Schmalkaldic War. For a deeper background, writers such as Goldast and Hortleder turned to medieval sources. In the records of the investiture controversy (1075–1172), particularly the reign of Lothar III (r. 1125–37) and his alleged decree of 1135 ordering the use of the Justinian

---

[1] Schulze, *Deutsche Geschichte*, 178–86; Schulze, 'Konfessionsfundamentalismus'.
[2] Gross, *Empire*, 99–100.

Code in all schools and law courts, or of Emperor Ludwig the Bavarian's (r. 1314–47) conflict with the papacy, they found sources of guidance acutely relevant for the present crisis.[3]

In addition, a substantial literature developed in relation to the Reichskammergericht: tracts on procedure, collections of case notes, commentaries and interpretations. Significantly, most of this literature was the work of Reformed and Lutheran experts. Serious commentary on the Reichshofrat did not really start until after 1648. The Reichshofrat contributed significantly to the political crisis of the Reich before 1618 but it generated almost no literature that contributed to its resolution. It was the court in which the Protestants had a voice, the Reichskammergericht, which inspired largely Protestant writers to employ humanist methods of precise textual scholarship in order to promote their view of the Reich.[4]

Another source of the new public law was the only slightly older discipline of politics. This had developed from Melanchthon's reintroduction of Aristotle to the Protestant educational canon. The relocation of Aristotle's ethics and politics to the core of Protestant teaching on society and government created a new framework in which princes and magistrates were accorded an authority independent of clergy. The new certainty about authority and its reliable stewardship was, however, soon challenged by the reception of Machiavelli's ideas from the 1570s and the writings of Tacitus in the critical edition published by Lipsius in 1574. Both seemed to suggest that authority might be wholly divorced from religion. While this implication led many German writers to reject both Machiavelli and Tacitus as dangerous and ungodly, others were motivated to establish alternative rules or principles of political behaviour.

At about the same time, the French theorist Jean Bodin provided a powerful new analytical tool, while the French philosopher Peter Ramus offered a new methodology. Bodin's redefinition of royal power from a collection of prerogatives to the higher sovereign power, the source of all law and normally immune to disobedience, provided a new set of categories and measures by which to judge any polity. From Ramus, a Calvinist, first the German Reformed writers then, soon afterwards, the Lutherans gained the aspiration to produce perfect logically coherent systems of concepts. This, in effect, turned the new theme into a discipline in the true sense: formalized, precise in expression, and given external coherence by an internal logic. Above all, they aspired to treat politics as a science independent of theology.[5]

Around 1600, a number of experts gave decisive shape and direction to the discipline: Johannes Althusius at the Reformed academy at Herborn; Bartholomäus Keckermann at the Reformed Danzig Gymnasium; and Henning Arnisäus at Lutheran Helmstedt, the university of the Dukes of Brunswick-Wolfenbüttel.

---

[3] Stolleis, *Öffentliches Recht*, i, 140. The relevance of Lothar III lay in the implication that the emperor was the sole legislator and that Roman law was valid in the Reich by virtue of an imperial decree *ex plenitudine potestatis*. The exposure of the episode as a mere fable in effect implied the existence of fundamental laws of the Reich that were of non-Roman origin and to which the emperor himself was also subject. Gross, *Empire*, 84–6, 211, 268–74; Whaley, 'German nation', 315–20.

[4] Stolleis, *Öffentliches Recht*, i, 133.

[5] Skinner, *Foundations*, ii, 341–2, 350.

Their groundbreaking works spawned an extensive literature over the next decades, both academic and popular, that reflected much of the spectrum of views found in Western Europe as a whole. By 1620, every German Protestant university saw the publication of at least one systematic work on politics.[6]

The interest of the earliest exponents was generally theoretical, on the one hand, and focused on the Estates, on the other. Their motive for seeking to establish the principles and rules of the political realm was primarily in order to define the polity within which they lived, both as a system in its own right and as a part of the Reich. They did not on the whole treat the Reich as a separate subject, for it was not central to their concerns. Althusius was most concerned to work out the relationship between a territory's Estates and their ruling prince. For him, the really crucial issue was the nature of the covenant between rulers and ruled, which he insisted had to be conceived in terms of rights rather than religious duties. Arnisäus objected that Althusius had neglected the sovereign rights of princes. He sought to refute the works of all monarchomachs with a decisive rejection of any notion of popular sovereignty and a theory of monarchy understood as the historical agglomeration of prerogative powers, a mixed constitution, rather than an absolute monarchy. Keckermann also rejected popular sovereignty and was even more emphatic in his insistence upon a mixed constitution as the most just form of polity.

The main writers on politics were only interested peripherally in the Reich. It was not long, however, before Bodin's specific statements concerning the Reich became the centre of a different controversy. Particularly challenging was Bodin's categorization of the Reich as an aristocracy in which sovereignty resided exclusively in the Reichstag. This pleased neither the imperialists, who believed in a sovereign emperor, nor those princes who wanted to establish their authority independently of either emperor or Reichstag. Equally significant was Bodin's refutation of the Four Monarchies theory, which held that the Reich was the last of the four world monarchies described by the prophet Daniel, and his rejection of the idea of the *translatio imperii*. German theorists were obliged to rethink some of the most cherished myths about their imperial polity.

The task was made more urgent by the growing political crisis in the Reich. The changes in the imperial constitution since 1555, the growing tension between the confessions, and the consolidation of the governmental systems of the larger territories, threw up a range of practical legal issues that could not be solved by existing law. In the light of Bodin's challenges, the question was raised as to whether Roman law could really provide an adequate basis for describing the German polity. The term *ius publicum* seems to have originated in the disputations on subjects advertised as *ex iure publico* held at Altdorf from 1600 by Arnold Clapmarius: the law of the Reich, the law of war and alliances, the arcana of the polity, and its judicial system and administration.

The significance of the subject was underlined by the first public controversy over imperial public law, a dispute between Reformed Marburg and Lutheran

---

[6] Stolleis, *Öffentliches Recht*, i, 111–12.

Giessen, the universities of the two rival Hessen dynasties at Kassel and Darmstadt. The Marburg professor of law, Herman Vultejus, had published a commentary in 1599 which denied the validity of Roman law for the Germans. The Reich, he argued, was a monarchy only in appearance; its structure was aristocratic. The *translatio imperii* had lost its significance since Charlemagne had admitted the magistrates he had appointed into partnership with him, thus turning the empire into a feudal domain.[7] Vultejus's Lutheran counterparts at Giessen were not slow to realize the explosive potential of his subversive use of feudal arguments, similar in fact to those employed by Hotman and the French monarchomachs in the 1560s. In 1607, Gottfried Antonius retorted with the assertion that Rudolf II was a true monarch, who embodied the state and who had the right to act in the public good and yet was himself free from the power of the law (*legibus solutus*). In the course of the ensuing debate, Antonius conceded that the emperor was bound by the fundamental laws of the realm since they were in effect treaties. Yet he still held the emperor to be free of all other published laws.

The controversy was fired by a strong local rivalry. The University of Giessen only received its imperial charter in 1607. This marked the elevation of the Gymnasium Illustre established in 1605 by Lutheran refugees from Marburg, which had been founded in 1527 as the first new Lutheran university in the Reich but had become Reformed in 1605.[8] Former Marburg professors such as Antonius were not only keen to denounce their Reformed successors but also anxious to demonstrate their loyalty to the crown in order to secure the status of their new institution. However, on the eve of the Donauwörth incident, at the height of the political-constitutional crisis in the Reich, the controversy had wider implications.[9] The specific issues upon which it touched—imperial jurisdiction, regalian rights, sovereignty, the law of nations, reason of state (*ratio status*)—formed the core of what rapidly became established as a legal-political discipline distinct from both law and politics.

Though the Marburg–Giessen controversy had a sharp confessional edge, the discipline subsequently developed largely at the Lutheran universities of Altdorf, Giessen, Jena, and Strassburg. Notable contributions were also made by non-academics such as Tobias Paurmeister (1555–1616), Chancellor to Duke Heinrich Julius of Brunswick-Lüneburg, whose *De jurisdictione Imperii Romani libri duo* ('Two Books of the Law of the [Holy] Roman Empire') of 1608 was the first major work on German public law. Over the next decades, the subject took a distinctive course. The majority of its practitioners tended towards arguments that gave the Estates a key role in the Reich. They rejected any form of the four monarchies theory or of the *translatio imperii*, and denied the relevance of Roman law for the seventeenth-century Reich. Rather, they developed theories of sovereignty that distinguished the qualities of the realm or polity (*maiestas realis*) from the monarch

---

[7] Gross, *Empire*, 137–8.
[8] Schindling and Ziegler, *Territorien*, iv, 279–83. Liegnitz in Silesia was in fact the first Protestant university, but it closed in 1530.
[9] See p. 421.

(*maiestas personalis*) and, to varying degrees, they held the emperor to be subject to the realm. Dietrich Reinkingk at Giessen was the only traditional imperialist to persist in viewing the Reich as the 'fourth monarchy' according to the scheme set out in the Book of Daniel. Yet even Reinkingk taught that the emperor's immediate subjects (i.e. the princes) had a right to resist under certain circumstances, and emphasized that though the Reich was a monarchy, it was aristocratic in its administration.

The majority, however, followed Tobias Paurmeister's influential formulation of 1608, that all imperial law, decisions about war and peace, treaties, taxation, or other matters of state had been concluded jointly (*coniunctim*) by the emperor and the princes. The emperor was a prince like the others, except for his ability to confer privileges; he had no independent legislative power. This view underlined the growing perception of the difference between the law of the Reich and Roman law. By the 1640s, Hermann Conring was moved to conclude that Roman law was wholly irrelevant to the German polity and he also proved conclusively for the first time that the German Reich was not in any way descended from Rome.[10]

For all the radical nature of that conclusion, neither Conring nor his predecessors were fundamentally opposed to the Habsburgs or their rule in Germany. If Reinkingk was an isolated imperialist, then Philipp Bogislav von Chemnitz (1605–1678) was alone in his bitter polemics against the tyrannical house of Habsburg and the Electors, an opponent of anything that detracted from the sovereign rights of all the princes.[11] Most of his contemporaries remained loyal to the Habsburgs even throughout the war.[12] Some, like Benedict Carpzow, paid tribute to their achievements as emperors over two centuries. Others, such as Johannes Limnaeus, recognized that they were the only dynasty rich enough to be able to afford the cost of the imperial dignity and powerful enough to defend the Reich from its enemies.

The Catholic universities did not participate in the debate.[13] Their curriculum was constrained by the Jesuit *ratio studiorum* of 1599. The political works studied at them were largely translations of contemporary Italian authors, who rarely touched on jurisprudence and never on the *ius publicum* of the Reich. The only serious Catholic teaching on politics took place in Cologne and Mainz, where the Jesuit Adam Contzen (1571–1635) elaborated the theory of the Catholic confessional state in his *Politicorum libri decem* ('Ten Books on Politics') of 1620. Contzen was perhaps the prime exponent of Lipsianism in Catholic Germany, and after his years at Mainz (1609–23) he acted as confessor to Elector Maximilian of Bavaria, a role that involved both theological and pastoral counsel and advice on virtually every dimension of territorial government.[14]

---

[10] Gross, *Empire*, 146–54, 255–86.
[11] Schmidt, *Vaterlandsliebe*, 401–13. See pp. 621–2.
[12] Gross, *Empire*, 191, 207.
[13] Stolleis, *Öffentliches Recht*, i, 122–4; Evans, 'Culture', 23–4; Seifert, 'Bildungskanon'; Gross, *Empire*, 94–6.
[14] Powell, *Trammels*, 25–8; Stolleis, *Öffentliches Recht*, i, 122–4. Killy, *Lexikon*, ii, 457–7.

38

Irenicism and Patriotism on the Eve of the War

The early teaching on public law was confessional in that it was developed by Protestant writers, predominantly Lutherans. However, it was characterized in many cases by moderate or tolerant views in religion. Limnaeus, for example, was a devout Lutheran, but he rejected the use of force to impose uniformity in religion and he argued against the persecution of the Reformed who had been excluded from the settlement of 1555. If that was perhaps understandable from the point of view of Protestant solidarity in the face of a Catholic threat, it also reflected the broader, often irenic, perspective that also informed the development of public law. Its fundamental aim was to forge unity, or rather to restore a unity that had been lost. That did not in the first instance mean religious unity. It meant the cohesion of the Reich, whose traditions and laws the publicists sought to summarize and systematize.

It could, however, also mean religious unity in the longer term. The links between the publicists and the various religious currents of the period are not well understood. Clear statements of religious affiliation made for the purpose of securing employment frequently belied much more heterodox views.[1] The networks of friends and scholars within, as well as across, confessional groups have attracted little scholarship and are formidably difficult to reconstruct. The differences between individuals who were formally either Lutheran or Reformed are often particularly difficult to pin down. Johann Valentin Andreae, for example, was a Lutheran, yet he had close contacts with Reformed thinkers. His later correspondence with Comenius revealed that they had shared an interest in pansophical problems. Indeed, Comenius repeatedly acknowledged Andreae as one of the most important of all his sources.[2]

Andreae's role as a linchpin in the Rosicrucian network also seems to have been crucial.[3] There was never a fraternity as such. Yet Rosicrucian manifestos (the *Fama fraternitatis*, 1614, the *Confessio Fraternitatis*, 1615, and the *Chymische Hochzeit des Christiani Rosenkreutz Anno 1459*, 1616) and associated editions of Neoplatonic, hermetic, and kabbalistic works enjoyed considerable popularity among Protestant scholars throughout the Reich. Andreae himself was a native of Tübingen in

---

[1] Kordes, *Ratke*, 41.
[2] Wollgast, *Philosophie*, 276–9.
[3] For the following, see Hardtwig, *Genossenschaft*, 159–75; Wollgast, *Philosophie*, 263–345; Killy, *Lexikon*, i, 171–3; Gilly, 'Rosenkreuzer'.

Württemberg and a Lutheran, though he visited Strassburg, Heidelberg, Geneva, Paris, Padua, Venice, and Rome between 1607 and 1613. He explicitly denied authorship of the *Fama* and the *Confessio*, yet it seems that they emerged from the Tübingen circle of the chiliast, occultist, and professor of law, Tobias Hess (1558–1614), whom Andreae regarded as his mentor.

Andreae did admit to having written the *Chymische Hochzeit*, ('The Chemical Wedding'), perhaps the most important Rosicrucian manifesto. There is little doubt that contemporaries regarded him as the main exponent of the movement, if not its instigator. His aims were not specifically linked with Palatine politics. Indeed, the role of a third major figure in the Tübingen group suggests more affinity with Lutheran politics. Christoph Besold was professor of public law at Tübingen from 1610 and a friend of both Andreae and Kepler. His indecision between Lutheranism and radicalism led him back to the writings of the Church Fathers and ultimately, in 1635, to conversion to Catholicism and acceptance of a position at the Reichshofrat with the title of imperial councillor.[4]

Later, Andreae described the Rosicrucian writings as a game or *jeu d'esprit* and dissociated himself from the idea that there had ever in fact been a Rosicrucian society, but the construction of the fictitious brotherhood had a serious purpose.[5] The *Fama* told of a poor German nobleman, Christian Rosenkreuz, allegedly born in 1378. Educated at a monastery in Greek and Latin, he accompanied a 'brother' on a pilgrimage to Jerusalem. He learned Arabic, mathematics, and the sciences in Damascus, followed by the magical mysteries of microcosm and macrocosm in Fez. Returning to Europe, he found that scholars spurned his plans for the reform of higher studies, so he withdrew into a small community with a handful of disciples who immersed themselves in the secret philosophy before scattering across the continent. Two brothers remained with Rosenkreuz until his death in 1484 at the age of 106; his grave was to remain closed for 120 years. In 1604, it was opened by his successors and the brotherhood now wanted to recruit new members to promote the cause of the general Reformation 'divini et humani'. Significantly, they declared their loyalty to the evangelical religion, to the Holy Roman Empire, and to the Fourth Monarchy, an agenda that reflected their fundamentally Lutheran identity, even though they were far removed from the mainstream of Lutheran Orthodoxy.[6]

For Andreae, the moral of Christian Rosenkreuz's life and teachings, and the purpose of his brotherhood, was to expose the fraudulent alchemists and magicians who had invaded the imperial and princely courts. The truly wise would dissolve the dichotomy between faith and knowledge, would fight for Christ against the pope, and thereby bring about that general reformation that would lead to the spiritual rebirth of man and his mystical union with God.

---

[4] Brecht, 'Besold'; Stolleis, *Öffentliches Recht*, i, 121–2; Gross, *Empire*, 357–9; *ADB*, ii, 556–8.
[5] Wollgast, *Philosophie*, 305–6.
[6] The attempt by Montgomery, *Cross and crucible* (esp. 113–22) to portray Andreae as a straightforward Orthodox Lutheran fails to explain why he repeatedly ran into trouble for his views or his many prolonged contacts with numerous Reformed and other distinctly non-Orthodox figures.

Some have seen Heidelberg as a major centre for Rosicrucian ideals. Frances Yates even suggested that Andreae's chemical wedding was inspired by the marriage of the young Elector to James I's daughter, Elizabeth, in 1613. The whole idea of a Rosicrucian Order derived, she claimed, from the impression made on Andreae by the ceremonies that attended the Duke of Württemberg's investiture with the Order of the Garter in 1603.[7]

It is certainly true that Palatine politicians placed high hopes on the support from James I they believed the marriage would bring to their enterprises. Contacts with England might well have allowed for some to acquaint themselves with English writers on arcane matters, such as John Dee, and, perhaps more importantly, with the literature of English radical Protestantism.[8] Moreover, some of the magical-alchemical circle that had developed at Rudolf II's court at Prague migrated to the court of Friedrich V after the emperor's death.

The change of location gave a new and more radical impetus to the pursuit of the arcane sciences. It now became linked with Reformed notions of a new general reformation and with the political ambitions of the Palatine activists with regard to the Bohemian throne. From Heidelberg, furthermore, both the new enthusiasm for theosophical and pansophical schemes and the new political agenda spread down to Strasbourg and across to Silesia, where intellectuals could readily picture themselves in the vanguard of the new reformation under Friedrich's rule in Bohemia.

The Rosicrucian phenomenon, however, was not confined to Heidelberg, nor even perhaps primarily anchored in the Palatinate and the political ambitions of its rulers and their closest advisers. Andreae himself does not appear to have been caught up in the Palatine project. When he did turn to the task of creating a real society after 1617, he sought to secure the sponsorship of August, the future Duke of Brunswick-Wolfenbüttel.[9] The project, which he failed to realize, was essentially a modest initiative for a local religious reform, rather than an attempt to turn the world upside down. Indeed, he turned away from the Rosicrucian movement just as it blossomed across Europe during the 1620s. Andreae's significance lies in his ideals, in the great variety of ways in which they could be interpreted and combined with other interests and causes, and in his extraordinarily wide range of contacts, rather than in any specific practical or political project of his own.

For all their differences, the religious visions of figures such as Andreae, the mystics Valentin Weigel and Jakob Boehme, and the puritan or 'pre-Pietist' Johann Arndt were nourished by the same late humanist sources and by the ideals of scholarship and a return to authentic texts.[10] At the same time, they personified an edgy unease at the competing claims of theology and philosophy, and sought in their various ways to reconcile those claims: either encompassing both of them in a new pansophy or transcending the conflict by progressing to a new spiritual level. That is also true of the educational schemes of figures such as the Lutheran

---

[7] Yates, *Rosicrucian enlightenment*, 59–69, 70–102. See also Béhar, 'Opitz'.
[8] Evans, 'Culture', 23.
[9] Hardtwig, *Genossenschaft*, i, 173–5.
[10] The link between religious reform, Rosicrucianism, and proposals for the reform of language and literature is made by Béhar, 'Opitz'.

Wolfgang Ratke or the Reformed Johann Heinrich Alsted and Jan Comenius. There is the same sense of the need to respond to a period of anarchy and decline, the same sense that somehow a unifying bond could and would be found, the same universalist vision and encyclopaedic aspiration.[11]

Both the religious and the educational reform schemes were, in turn, often linked with another key theme of the publicists' writing, namely patriotism. Writers and thinkers as diverse as Goldast and Ratke belonged to a group that produced a variety of notable proposals for the reform of language around 1600. In this the Germans were no different from their counterparts elsewhere in Europe: similar movements were found in England, Italy, France, the Netherlands, and Sweden.[12] The cultivation of pure forms of language did not necessarily preclude continuing international communication in Latin or the borrowing of foreign models and examples in scholarship, art, rhetoric, or poetry. The debate about pure forms was Europe-wide and everywhere there were attempts to set the ancient rhetorical requirements of 'puritas, perspicuitas, brevitas, ornatus' (accuracy, clarity, brevity, and elegance') as standards for contemporary vernaculars. The desire to promote a purified vernacular language (for example, by avoiding words of foreign origin or by inventing German equivalents for them) could, however, have a clear political function and become associated with patriotic political causes.

Again, the Protestant, and especially the Reformed context for many such proposals is crucial. The key centres were the Palatinate and, above all, Silesia. The Reformed Palatinate was a natural focus for humanist studies and a collecting point for political ideas and scholarly approaches from France and the Netherlands.

Silesia was perhaps equally important for reasons that have much to do with the peculiarity of the territory itself, which mirrored the political and confessional complexity of the Reich as a whole. Upper and Lower Silesia had been lands of the Bohemian crown since the fourteenth century and they embraced a collection of principalities, counties, and lordships, some of which were under direct control of the crown and others merely subject to it.[13] However, royal authority was somewhat diluted by virtue of it being exercised via Bohemia, and both neighbouring German princes and the Polish crown afforded a degree of protection to those who resisted it. Hence the region had become a haven for a wide variety of sects and outsider groups that were persecuted elsewhere, for example Anabaptists and Socinians. By the late sixteenth century, Reformed princes ruled Liegnitz, Brieg, and Wohlau, though their subjects were largely Lutherans. In Silesia as a whole, the Habsburgs encouraged the Counter-Reformation tendencies, which generated considerable tension without solving the problem. The general crisis in the Habsburg lands around 1600 thus also embroiled Silesia, and many Silesian Protestants fully shared the hopes of their Bohemian counterparts for the election of Friedrich V of the Palatinate to the Bohemian throne.

---

[11] Hardtwig, *Genossenschaft*, i, 159–75; Evans, 'Culture', 21–3.
[12] Polenz, *Sprachgeschichte*, ii, 108; Jones, *Sprachhelden*, 3.
[13] Schindling and Ziegler, *Territorien*, ii, 102–38; Weber, *Schlesien*, 7–41; Eickels, *Schlesien*, 8–52; Bahlke, *Regionalismus*, 39–47, 343–60.

The fact that Silesia had no university added a further dimension. Silesian students were generally educated first at the Gymnasium at Danzig or (from 1601) Beuthen, then either elsewhere in the Reich or abroad. Significant numbers went to Leiden, but many more studied in Wittenberg and other German Protestant universities. Equally, among those who studied in Leiden, many are to be found at different stages in Heidelberg or Strassburg among the circles associated with figures such as the Palatine councillor Georg Michael Lingelsheim or Matthias Bernegger.

Martin Opitz is the most notable example. Born in Bunzlau in 1597, he studied in Beuthen, where he was a protégé of the imperial councillor Tobias Scultetus von Bregoschütz und Schwanensee, then at Frankfurt an der Oder, before proceeding to Heidelberg, where Lingelsheim employed him as a tutor, and from where he visited Bernegger in Strassburg. When Heidelberg was threatened by Spanish troops in the autumn of 1620, Opitz travelled to Leiden, where he visited the poet and scholar Daniel Heinsius before returning to Silesia in 1621.[14] While still at Beuthen, and the year after the publication of the last of the key Rosicrucian texts, he had written an appeal—in Latin—for the promotion of the German language, in which he had acknowledged Heinsius as the role model for a vernacular poet and identified Latin as the language of Catholicism and the oppression of Germany.[15] In 1624, his *Buch von der deutschen Poeterei* ('Book of German Poetics'), published in Breslau, set out his thoughts for the creation of a corpus of German poetry. Significantly, the first collection of Opitz's poems was published in Strassburg in 1624 by Julius Wilhelm Zincgref, a doctor of law also versed in philology and philosophy and a refugee from Heidelberg.[16]

The Silesian connection was cosmopolitan, Reformed (or at least sympathetic to the Reformed cause), and closely linked with Heidelberg and Strassburg. The political situation of Silesia brought its Protestant humanist networks into contact with the activist groups in Bohemia and the Reich generally, and also with the French and Dutch Calvinist movements. The general tendency to associate Protestantism with freedom was reinforced by the parallel with the Dutch struggle against the Habsburgs. For Opitz, Heinsius was an attractive role model precisely because he was a 'national' poet.

Opitz was in some respects a typical product of German late Humanism, though his particular concerns reflected only one, albeit central, strand of a much wider movement. Themes of the original humanist movement were resumed: the motifs from Tacitus's *Germania* that illuminated the early history and innate characteristics of the Germans; and the supposed legacy of the old Germanic orders of priest-poets, the Druids and the Bards. These inherited preoccupations were now extended by the study of medieval German literature and by a more intensive concern with the purity of the German language.

---

[14] *ABD*, xxiv, 370–2; Killy, *Lexikon*, viii, 504–5; Wollgast, *Philosophie*, 806–26; Kühlmann, *Opitz*, 18–37.
[15] Béhar, 'Opitz', 47.
[16] *DBE*, x, 673. See also Béhar, 'Opitz'.

In the case of writers such as Goldast, research into German medieval literature was combined with the study of legal and constitutional texts, both the early and high medieval texts on which the various theories of a *translatio imperii* hinged and texts that documented the nature of the current crisis in the Reich.[17] Goldast was the first to examine the fourteenth-century Heidelberg Manesse Codex in any scholarly detail. He especially admired the emphatic language of Walther von der Vogelweide's verse, as well as his criticism of Church and pope. The medieval manuscripts Goldast studied opened up a world of German literary achievement in the past. The Germans, he learned, had no need to fear that they were inferior or backward; their struggle against Rome long pre-dated the Reformation, and their assertion of their freedom had been a constant factor in their history.[18]

In writing on language and grammar, scholars around 1600 tended to develop the foundations set out by Johannes Clajus. His *Grammatica Germanicae linguae* ('Grammar of the German Language') of 1578 was a fundamental text for the new movement, and it was notable both for its insistence on the antiquity of German and for its designation of Luther as the second founder of the German language.[19] There were innumerable gradations of opinion among Protestant writers. Lutherans tended to emphasize the status of German as a sacred language and to regard its 'rediscovery' by Luther as a German destiny. Reformed commentators tended to place less emphasis on the providential nature of Luther's linguistic achievement. They preferred instead to emphasize the potential of the vernacular to restore unity and harmony, sometimes as a prelude to the creation of a wider harmony among all speakers of all the different vernaculars.[20]

These new preoccupations were often combined with a distinctive political slant. Promoting reform of the German language and proposing its employment as the uniform language of the Reich went hand in hand with rejecting Latin as the universal language of Catholicism and of the imperialists. Research into the origins of German was not new, but proposing that it should be used as the standard written language of the German people was. The first humanists around 1500 had written largely in Latin; they believed in a *translatio artium* as well as *translatio imperii*. Their successors around 1600, moving away from the idea of a *translatio imperii*, wanted to prove themselves in German as well as in Latin. In this, they fully reflected the late-humanist agenda of their contemporaries elsewhere in Europe.

In the context of a general turn to the vernacular, German writers were faced with the challenge of proving both the purity and the dignity of their own language. Opitz was essentially trying to bring German up to the level achieved in Latin long ago by German writers such as Celtis. Few wanted to abandon Latin entirely. Opitz himself continued to write poetry, epigrams, and almost all of his letters in Latin.[21] Scholars such as Goldast, who contributed so much to the new movement, wrote

---

[17] Mulsow, 'Gelehrte Praktiken'; Whaley, 'German nation', 315–20.
[18] Weber, 'Goldast'; Baade, *Goldast*, 19–20, 161–2.
[19] Engels, *Sprachgesellschaften*, 33–54; Wells, *German*, 220–1.
[20] Borst, *Turmbau*, iii pt. 1, 1342–76 gives an excellent account of German views, which demonstrated a greater variety than those found in other European countries at the time.
[21] Forster, 'Barockliteratur', 70–1.

virtually nothing in the vernacular. German intellectual life remained fully bilingual until at least the end of the seventeenth century; indeed, scholarship was still conducted almost exclusively in Latin.

Opitz's poetological ideals came to have enormous significance for later writers. However, at the time of their formulation their political thrust was probably more significant. Literary production was ancillary to the major objective that was being pursued in promoting German: the cultivation of a more effective language of government and administration. That was clearly the aim of Wolfgang Ratke's proposals of 1612. He proposed that old and young should learn to speak with God through reading Scripture in Hebrew, Greek, and Latin. He wanted to make German a language of learning instead of Latin. German was to be established alongside French and Italian as a language for politics and administration, and Ratke proposed that for the Reich as a whole there should be unity in language, in government, and, eventually, in religion.[22]

Ratke's ideas were probably never submitted to the Reichstag, but they found enthusiastic advocates in Christoph Helwig and Joachim Jungius, who became his collaborators for a while.[23] They also aroused interest in the Palatinate, Hessen, and Weimar before Ratke was taken up by Ludwig von Anhalt-Köthen. Attempts at an actual reform of the Köthen schools foundered on the opposition of the clergy, but Ratke's ideas were influential in the foundation of the Fruchtbringende Gesellschaft in Weimar in 1617, in which his mentor Ludwig was instrumental.[24]

Only much later was the label *Sprachgesellschaft* accorded—pejoratively—to this society and its imitators by historians of German literature. They have tended to focus on the progression from the 1617 foundation to the short-lived 1633 Strassburg Tannengesellschaft, the 1642–3 Hamburg Deutschgesinnte Genossenschaft, the 1644 Nuremberg Pegnesischer Blumenorden, and the 1658 Hamburg Elbschwanenorden. Yet none enjoyed the same significance as the first, which lasted over sixty years, with a total of 890 members, and which inspired the foundation of the others.[25] The societies have often been viewed as symptoms of national weakness: their preoccupation with language and the rediscovery of a heroic past as an early phase in the development of a *Kulturnation* or cultural nation that evolved in the absence of a political nation. However, this view ignores the differences between the first society and its successors, and the ideological context of the society. Furthermore, traditional interpretations generally overlook the fact that, initially, the preoccupation with language was only secondarily linked

---

[22] Polenz, *Sprachgeschichte*, ii, 110; Kordes, *Ratke*, 39–40.

[23] Both Helwig and Jungius seem to have had a pragmatic and economic interest in the promotion of German, rather than any political motivation; their break with Ratke in 1615 reflected their growing concern at Ratke's increasingly vehement rejection of authority of any kind. Wollgast, *Philosophie*, 423–5.

[24] Kühlmann, 'Sprachgesellschaften', 256–7.

[25] The Pegnesischer Blumenorden outlasted them all and it still exists today, though after 1700 it became essentially a Nuremberg literary and antiquarian association shorn of the wider national dimension that characterized its early development. The standard surveys are Otto, *Sprachgesellschaften* and Stoll, *Sprachgesellschaften*. Polenz, *Sprachgeschichte*, ii, 107–24 provides a concise summary of linguistic and some political aspects. Schultz, *Bestrebungen* published in 1888 is still useful.

with literary concerns. Indeed, the leading lights of the movement overall were clergymen, chancery officials, lawyers, and scholars.[26]

The foundation of the Fruchtbringende Gesellschaft by members of the Anhalt and ducal Saxon dynasties, owed much to the political-confessional ambitions of the prince primarily responsible for its foundation (and its patron from 1628 to 1650), Ludwig of Anhalt-Köthen, brother of Christian of Anhalt. Its members were predominantly aristocratic and did not at first include many who could be classified as writers; Martin Opitz who joined in 1629 as the 200th member was perhaps the first, though by then he was also both an imperial councillor and ennobled.[27] The society was modelled on the Florentine Academia della Crusca, and its prime aim was to establish best practice in administrative language. The wider purpose here was provided by the conviction that improving language was the first step to improving behaviour: 'association for the promotion of virtue' better describes the fundamental aim than 'language society', for language was seen as the foundation of virtue and morality.

In that sense the society has much in common with other noble associations of the period. One was the La noble Académie des Loyales, also known as the L'Ordre de la Palme d'Or, founded in 1617 at Amberg by the wife of Christian I of Anhalt. Formally dedicated to the promotion of foreign languages, this society also aimed to promote noble virtues among its exclusively female aristocratic membership.[28] Another was the Tugendliche Gesellschaft, founded in 1619 by Ludwig's wife, Amoena Amalia von Anhalt-Köthen, and his sister, Anna Sophia of Schwarzburg-Rudolstadt.[29] Like the Fruchtbringende Gesellschaft, both these societies comprised Reformed and Lutheran members, and the Tugendliche Gesellschaft, which existed until Anna Sophia's death in 1652, explicitly combined an interest in language and translation with the desire to help create a 'virtuous German nation' in a programme directly inspired by Wolfgang Ratke.

It also seems likely that members of both the Fruchtbringende Gesellschaft and the Tugendliche Gesellschaft were responsible for the formation of L'Academie des vrais amants, a group of enthusiasts for Honoré d'Urfé's *L'Astrée* (published 1607–27) who described themselves as 'une réunion pastorale'.[30] This again suggests that the Fruchtbringende Gesellschaft had a functional role, rather than that it expressed a frustrated cultural nationalism. Each of these groups represented different facets of the same broad phenomenon: the revival of the nobility as a cultured and educated caste around 1600. Associations for the promotion of French culture married late humanist culture and literary-linguistic expertise with the traditional chivalrous traditions of German aristocratic and court culture. The

[26] Jones, *Sprachhelden*, 5.

[27] Forster, 'Barockliteratur', 76.

[28] The twenty members comprised ten princesses, seven countesses, and three noblewomen. Wells, *German*, 267; Schultz, *Bestrebungen*, 19.

[29] Berns, 'Sozietätsbewegung', 62; Westphal, 'Frauen', 378–83; Conersmann, 'Tugendliche Gesellschaft'.

[30] Schultz, *Bestrebungen*, 19–21; Conersmann, 'Tugendliche Gesellschaft', 589.

parallel promotion of German by the Fruchtbringende both had a practical admin-istrative-governmental purpose and served a political-constitutional cause.

Ludwig von Anhalt-Köthen fell out with Ratke in 1619—Ratke was a vain ingrate who never remained friends with anyone for long—but he remained true to the ideals that they had discussed together. He ensured that the membership of the Fruchtbringende Gesellschaft remained open to both Lutherans and Reformed, which indeed reflected the Reformed and Lutheran convictions of the houses of Anhalt and ducal Saxony, respectively. In theory, Catholics were not explicitly excluded either, although only one was in fact admitted before 1652.[31] Significant-ly, however, Ludwig, though himself an adherent of the Reformed confession, baulked at the nomination of a 'true honest . . . Calvinist' by Christian II of Anhalt (r. 1630–56), responding that no one had ever yet been admitted as a Calvinist nor would anyone be admitted with that trouble-making title. The society, he affirmed, had accepted only good Christians. 'German sincerity and piety' were more important than confessional criteria. In the interests of harmony, clergymen of all confessions were routinely excluded, though a reluctant exception was made for Andreae. The society operated on egalitarian lines, though it was overwhelmingly aristocratic in composition and Ludwig reacted sharply when Philipp von Zesen tried to lay claim to the title of a prince of the poetic arts.[32]

The Fruchtbringende Gesellschaft mirrored the social realities of the courts and administrations that had created it and embodied the patriotic-religious imperial reform ideals that its creators hoped it would foster. The later societies were rather different in character. Their members were predominantly non-noble and, though they echoed the patriotic rhetoric of the Fruchtbringende Gesellschaft, they played a more 'provincial' role in urban 'fatherlands', rather than in the Reich as a whole.

What, if anything, did the Fruchtbringende Gesellschaft achieve? Leibniz later commented that the 'fruit-bringers' in fact bore precious little fruit.[33] Dainty literary exercises were no substitute for serious patriotic engagement. German would not be taken seriously until all 'disciplines and important matters' were conducted in it. Leibniz's comments echoed those of earlier critics in the 1640s, who satirized the early language purists as shrill opponents of foreign (*alamode*) linguistic influence who did nothing to promote the German fatherland that they so often elegized.[34] One meeting was devoted to discussing the best way of rendering the word *Materie* in German (discussed by eleven members in 1624; the answer was *Zeug*, i.e. 'stuff' or 'things'). At other meetings, the members debated the endless lists of German equiva-lents suggested by Philip von Zesen (1619–1689) (for example, suggesting *Jungfern-zwinger* for *Nonnenkloster*, or *Tageleuchter* for *Fenster*, or *Zeugemutter* for *Natur*).[35]

---

[31] Hardtwig, *Genossenschaft*, 210.

[32] Hardtwig, *Genossenschaft*, 207–24.

[33] Kühlmann, 'Sprachgesellschaften', 258.

[34] Schultz, *Bestrebungen*, 105–12; Jones, *Sprachhelden*, 8–9.

[35] For the 1624 meeting, see Otto, *Sprachgesellschaften*, 28. Linguistic purism and Zesen's activities are discussed by Wells, *German*, 285–97 and Polenz, *Sprachgeschichte*, ii, 107–23. The literal meaning of the new words is 'virgins' prison' (instead of 'convent'), 'day lighter' (instead of 'window'), and 'birth mother' (instead of 'nature').

These apparently pedantic preoccupations were grist to the mills of the later critics of the Sprachgesellschaften. However, such negative views reflect the perspective and experience of later generations to whom Zesen's activities appeared quaintly eccentric and amateur. By the 1660s, the study of grammar and literary history had become established as serious disciplines; alongside the major grammatical works produced by Justus Georg Schottelius (1612–1676) in the 1660s. Later reform proposals and societies also assumed different meanings in the context of the prelude to the peace of 1648 and the various schemes for the renewal of the Reich in its aftermath.[36]

The initiatives of the decades after 1600 were, however, highly significant in a variety of ways. They did indeed promote the language and establish a link between the German vernacular and the Reich. By 1646, what was available in German was so extensive that Philipp Harsdörffer compiled a guide to contemporary German writing. Significantly, those suggested as models for their mastery of German include not only Luther ('the German Cicero') but also the historian Aventin, Melchior Goldast, the chronicler of Speyer and collector of proverbs Christoph Lehmann (1570–1638), Friedrich Hortleder, and the various collections of *Reichs-abschiede*, which demonstrated the 'purity of our language' just as the Justinian *Corpus Juris* demonstrated the purest Latin.[37]

This reflected the role played by writing about language and philological research into medieval texts in the evolution of the new view of the Reich as an entity distinct from the Roman Empire. It gave this newly rediscovered German Reich a discursive reality based on German texts. As Johannes Limnaeus (1592–1663), then tutor to the son of the Chancellor of Brandenburg-Kulmbach, wrote in his influential treatise on public law in 1629: anyone who really wishes to know the Reich, its Estates, and those subject to them should put aside Bartolus and Baldus and turn instead to the *Reichsabschiede*, the imperial electoral capitulations, the Golden Bull, the decisions of the Reichskammergericht, and the 'works collected as a result of Goldast's industriousness'.[38]

More generally, the early seventeenth-century reformers took up and added to the language of patriotism that had developed progressively through the previous century. That included a basic stock of images and slogans from the period around 1500, and extended to the vocabulary of liberty developed in the long struggle of the Imperial Estates to assert their religious rights. It was enriched by the patriotic rhetoric evolved during the periodic debates on how best to defend the Reich from French aggression or from the Turks. By 1600, the term 'deutsche Nation', generally qualified by adjectives such as 'esteemed', 'dear' or beloved', had become a commonplace in German Protestant writing about the Reich.[39]

---

[36] See Volume 2, pp. 79–94.
[37] Forster, 'Harsdörffer's canon', 37–9. See also Stolleis, *Öffentliches Recht*, i, 132–3, 152–3.
[38] Stolleis, *Öffentliches Recht*, i, 152; on Limnaeus, see Gross, *Empire*, 204–25.
[39] Noël, 'Nation allemande', 333–4.

This patriotic discourse was now enriched both by the various research enter-prises of the later humanists and by its employment in arguments about the latest political-constitutional crisis of the Reich. The fact that it was essentially a Protes-tant discourse is a significant qualification. Catholic writers largely ignored the linguistic, grammatical, and poetological concerns of Opitz and his contemporaries. It is true that the Jesuit Friedrich von Spee wrote poetry in the vernacular, even before Opitz, so that 'God might also have his poets in the German language'. But his verse was not published until 1649, fourteen years after his death.[40] The mainstream of Catholic literature continued to divide, as before, into works composed in the most elegant Latin and dialect writings designed for more popular consumption. And while Catholic printers had often adopted Luther's orthography between 1550 and 1600, they tended, often under government direction, to revert to the old 'Catholic' conventions after 1600.[41] The differences were small and did not impede understanding, but the insistence on them was indicative nonetheless. They were as significant to many Catholic imperialists as adherence to traditional ideas of Latin as the special language of the Reich, or to ideas of the Reich as a sacred and universal empire, the direct successor to Rome.

The polarization between Catholic and Protestant on the eve of the Thirty Years War was undoubtedly profound. Clerical polemics of all persuasions give the impression of an unbridgeable gulf, the inevitable prelude to a bitter fight to the finish. Yet the new thinking about the Reich also created significant potential common ground.

It is characteristic of most Protestant late humanists and publicists that they were anti-Jesuit rather than anti-imperial. Goldast was clearly a fervent Protestant, but that did not prevent him from writing a work on the laws and privileges of the Kingdom of Bohemia, particularly the hereditary succession of the Habsburgs there. He also accepted the title of imperial councillor in 1627.[42] The fact that Opitz was a committed Protestant did not prevent him from entering the service of Karl Hannibal I von Dohna, the staunchly Catholic president of the imperial chamber in Silesia, in 1626, or from accepting ennoblement from Ferdinand II in 1627, or from serving the Catholic cause until 1633.[43] Throughout all these twists and turns, he remained faithful to the linguistic agenda he had set out in his youth. His erstwhile patron and headmaster Caspar Dornau, to cite another example, was typical of many of the older generation of Silesian late humanists who remained loyal to the crown until disillusioned by the brutal execution of the leaders of the Prague rebellion on 21 June 1621.[44]

---

[40] Borst, *Turmbau*, iii pt. 1, 1348; Emrich, *Literatur*, 99–106.

[41] Breuer, *Oberdeutsche Literatur*, 44–91; Breuer 'Nationalliteratur', 706–11. The main differences were that Catholic printers rejected Luther's adoption of the Meissen dialect and adhered to the conventions of Upper German speech patterns (syncope), the Upper German chancery style (apocope). The orthographical differences persisted until just after 1750, when there was a renewed confessional debate about the 'backwardness' of Catholic Germany. See also Volume 2, pp. 343–4, 477–80.

[42] Baade, *Goldast*, 43–4.

[43] Killy, *Lexikon*, viii, 505; Kühlmann, *Opitz*, 61–4.

[44] Seidel, *Späthumanismus*, 386–93.

Opportunism no doubt explains much. Equally, however, the fundamentally irenic religious attitudes of many led them to make a clear distinction between Jesuit machinations and imperial policy, between the tyrannical abuse of power and the rightful exercise of monarchical authority. They were anti-imperialist in that they opposed the imperial universal language of Latin, but they also espoused a German monarchy subject to the fundamental laws of the polity.[45] Hence, Ludwig von Anhalt-Köthen's sharp reaction when presented with a 'dear godly Calvinist', for he was keen to avoid anything that smacked of rebellion against the legal foundations of the Reich. The Reformed could still, just, by their own arguments at least, be accommodated within the Augsburg Confession. Indeed, the Palatine activist Christian of Anhalt seems to have been the exception among five surviving brothers. Another brother, August, also a member of the Fruchtbringende Gesellschaft from 1621, similarly shrank back from radical visions despite a profound interest in chemical and alchemical studies and their associated philosophies. In 1612, a Tyrolean adept attempted to enlist him as the 'Lion of Midnight', who, according to a pseudo-paracelsian manuscript that circulated from about 1600, would destroy the (Habsburg) eagle and inaugurate an era of peace, calm, and unity in the Reich, but August declined without hesitation. For, he declared, 'no general Reformation could ... be completed without bloodshed and death'.[46]

Nothing illustrates the ambivalent combination of loyalism and resistance to a perceived tyranny better than the establishment in October 1622 of a Teutscher Friedbund (German Peace League) by Wilhelm IV of Saxony-Weimar (1598–1662), one of the founders of the Fruchtbringende Gesellschaft and, ultimately, successor to Ludwig von Anhalt-Köthen as its head.[47] Educated by Friedrich Hortleder, who impressed upon him the heavy penalties inflicted by the Habsburgs on his Ernestine forebears following the Schmalkaldic War, Wilhelm joined the Protestant Union in November 1619. After the disaster in Bohemia he attempted to rally support for Protestant resistance in the face of the dire threat now posed by the Spanish forces and the Catholic League. His appeal set out his patriotic agenda: 'Love of our fatherland of the German nation' should inspire all to resist the 'cunning, deception, and tyranny of the Spaniards'. The peace league would promote a general and lasting peace, freedom of belief for all good Christians (for subjects as well as princes), good government in the Reich, just courts and swift justice, and foster honesty and prosperity in the whole of Germany. The war in Bohemia should be ended and each side should return what it had taken. Princes and Estates should gather under His Imperial Majesty Ferdinand II to deliberate on how to restore peace and

---

[45] Polenz, *Sprachgeschichte*, 109 follows many others in overemphasizing the anti-imperial dimension, without recognizing its essentially loyalist corollary.

[46] Gilly, 'Löwe' 253; *ABD*, i, 658–9.

[47] Menzel, 'Union'; Schmidt, 'Teutsche Kriege', 44–5. Wilhelm was the fifth of ten surviving sons of Duke Johann of Saxony-Weimar and his wife Dorothea Maria von Anhalt; he would have been acutely aware of how modest his prospects were by comparison with the power and prestige of Electors Christian II (r. 1591–1611) and Johann Georg I (r. 1611–56), who were his guardians when he came of age. His early political engagement represented a bid for a political role in the Reich that his inheritance could never have given him. Cf. *ADB*, xliii, 180–95.

prosperity. The emperor was to be acknowledged as sovereign, but he should be obliged to adhere to the terms of his electoral capitulation and to sever his links with the Spanish and Jesuit parties.

The league failed, and in October 1623 Duke Wilhelm was taken prisoner and only returned to Weimar from Vienna in February 1625. Ultimately, the league lacked credibility without the backing of the Elector of Saxony, resentment against whom was one of Wilhelm's motives for acting in the first place: both on account of his passivity and because he was the head of the Albertine line that had been awarded the Electoral title forfeited by the Ernestines. Yet Wilhelm denied he was a rebel: all he had wanted, he declared to the emperor, was to establish a loyalist league.[48] Though doomed to failure, his enterprise was nonetheless significant. His appeal sketched out the principles that were later embodied in the peace of 1648. They were the first attempt to translate the ideals of the Fruchtbringende Gesellschaft into political reality. They illustrate clearly the political-constitutional programme that much late humanist scholarship and the early language reform proposals were designed to promote. That programme was at the heart of the long conflict that began in 1618.

[48] Menzel, 'Union', 59.

VI

THE GERMAN TERRITORIES AND CITIES AFTER 1555

39

Problems of Interpretation

Did the Peace of Augsburg mark a turning point in the history of the German territories? Many German historians have followed Heinrich von Treitschke, who had no doubt that the rulers of the territories after 1555 were largely responsible for the dismal turn that he discerned at this time for German history as a whole. His contempt for a generation of 'Lutheran boozing and praying princes' ('lutherische Sauf- und Betefürsten') long set the tone for writing about the German territories in the second half of the sixteenth century. In their exclusive dedication to hunting and high living, Treitschke suggested, their only—albeit tragic—contribution to the development of German society was, by repressing their hapless subjects and extracting taxes from them, to lay the foundations for absolutism.[1]

That view has long since been revised, but elements of the old master narrative have proved surprisingly resilient. Bernd Moeller's influential 1977 survey of the period concluded that 1555 marked the end of the age of great men—Luther, Melanchthon, Emperor Charles V, Moritz of Saxony, Philip of Hessen, and the financier, merchant, and patron Anton Fugger of Augsburg. Those who came after them, Moeller suggested, were lesser figures: less original, less enterprising, ultimately less international in their significance. The epigones of the second half of the century, he suggested, were narrow-minded and blinded by confessional passions; they condemned German society to a hopeless provincialism.[2]

Recent interpretations have taken a more positive view and have focused on establishing the contribution made by German rulers in this period to a longer-term process of modernization, state development, and socio-cultural change. On the one hand, scholars have drawn on the concept of 'social disciplining' elaborated by Gerhard Oestreich in the 1960s to analyse the way that the enforcement of religious orthodoxy and Church discipline contributed to the emergence of 'absolutism' in the seventeenth century. On the other hand, they have elaborated Ernst Walter Zeeden's insights into the structural similarities in the approaches of the Lutheran, Calvinist, and Catholic Churches to the definition of systems of belief and the construction of institutional frameworks that linked Church and State. Heinz Schilling and Wolfgang Reinhard have combined both approaches to create

---

[1] Rudersdorf, 'Landesväter', 147–8.   [2] Moeller, *Deutschland*, 172.

two powerful paradigms: confessionalization and what they call territorial state formation.[3]

For Schilling, the process of confessionalization was a decisive motor in the construction of the early modern state. The extension of state control over the Church increased the range of its competence to include authority not only over the Church itself but also over poor relief, education and, through the regulation of marriage and family life, the daily personal lives of subjects. While the extension of state authority could easily arouse the opposition of the Estates or communities, especially urban ones, the dominant tendency in the relatively small political entities of the Reich was, according to Schilling, the inexorable concentration of power in the hands of the rulers. Indeed, he suggests that the definition of the Lutheran princes as *summus episcopus*, the heads of their Church in their territories, brought about a new sacralization of the ruler. State formation also plays a role in Wolfgang Reinhard's view of 'confessionalization', though his primary interest is the way in which the process promoted the formation of social-cultural groups defined by distinctive beliefs and norms, educational systems and internal disciplinary mechanisms, exclusive rituals, and even linguistic usage.[4]

Critics of the confessionalization paradigm have questioned many of its key assumptions.[5] Some have objected to the idea that the structural similarities between various Churches are more important than their distinct theological and cultural identities. Others reject the notion that confessionalization was always a top-down process or that, even where this was the case, it managed to achieve uniformity, let alone prove an effective mechanism for the control of society. More fundamentally, Winfried Schulze and others have objected that confessionalization is simply the wrong label for a process of modernization or rationalization of government and state structures that was really characterized by secularization.[6]

Depending on the specific case in time and place, there are probably elements of truth in each of the macro-historical theories developed in relation to the period. However, in general, neither the endeavours of rulers, nor the experience of those ruled, is neatly accommodated within such theories. The actions of rulers and the reactions of the ruled may well have had unintended long-term consequences. Yet the perceived problems, opportunities, and challenges of the political and social framework of the period are of greater significance for an understanding of those actions and reactions.

In this respect, the Peace of Augsburg was a turning point, similar to the conclusion reached by the Reichstag at Speyer in 1526. The decision then to leave

---

[3] For an overview with relevant references, see Ehrenpreis and Lotz-Heumann, *Reformation*, 62–79; Schmidt, *Konfessionalisierung*, 86–122. See also Schilling, 'Konfessionalisierung', and Schilling, *Konfessionalisierung*, 21–41. Fully reflecting the anxieties of the early twentieth century, the essays edited by Heinz Schilling in the volume *Konfessioneller Fundamentalismus* (2007), further develop the concept of confessionalization as a form of 'confessional fundamentalism'.

[4] For example, the employment of 'coded' Christian names, saints in the case of Catholics, Old Testament names in the case of Calvinists. See Reinhard, 'Zwang', *passim*.

[5] See Schmidt, 'Sozialdisziplinierung?'.

[6] Schulze, *Einführung*, 48–52; Schmidt, *Konfessionalisierung*, 91–4.

matters concerning religion in the hands of the princes and magistrates pending a resolution of theological issues for the Reich as a whole, stabilized the situation by undermining radical experiments and placing the initiative firmly in the hands of the rulers. In the same way, the Augsburg settlement also stabilized the situation by again reaffirming the authority of princes and magistrates in religious matters. It is true that this time there were qualifications and guarantees for certain groups in certain contexts, and the Imperial Cities were denied the *ius reformandi* or 'right of reformation' given to princes and lords. However, as in 1526, the specific agreement reached in 1555 placed the seal on developments that had already in fact occurred in some territories, and created a legal framework within which others were free either to implement reforms or to guard against innovation.[7]

That process was not immediate. It unfolded over several decades, with different triggers and varying intensity, pace, and success among territories large and small, secular and ecclesiastical, princely and urban. It is indicative that the slogan of the process—*cuius regio, eius religio*, 'whose realm, his religion'—was not coined by Joachim Stephani until 1586.[8] At that point, moreover, it represented a simplification of the complex terms of the 1555 settlement, in particular the rights granted to both Lutheran and Catholic individuals and groups who did not share their ruler's faith, and thus reflected a hardening of attitudes over time more than anything else.

Furthermore, many of the key developments after 1555, even ones that involved the ecclesiastical organization of a territory, often had little to do with religious belief as such. Or rather, religion was perceived as part of a structure of authority: obedient and loyal subjects were naturally subjects who shared their lord's religion, or at least did not reject it or rebel against it. It is therefore difficult to distinguish clearly and decisively between secular concerns and religious conviction.

Above all else, after 1555, rulers of territories and cities of all kinds were concerned with stability. After the upheavals of the previous decades, many wished nothing more than to consolidate their position or to begin to impose order. The Elector of Saxony himself had perhaps the most obvious vested interest in stabilization, for that was the best way of ensuring that his Ernestine cousins could not challenge the 1547 decision that gave the Electoral title to his own Albertine line. Other rulers had similar concerns. In many regions, decades of conflict and uncertainty had led to the neglect of key areas of ecclesiastical government and had allowed the development of ambivalent and fluid confessional situations. At the same time, involvement in these conflicts had incurred substantial costs and, for many, the development of new and expensive military and quasi-diplomatic activities in the Reich. That, in turn, gave a renewed urgency to issues of finance and taxation.

The measures taken to address this spectrum of problems formed part of a longer-term evolution of territorial and urban government that began in the fifteenth century. However, the success of some of the initiatives taken, or in some cases, the critical point reached by the cumulative impact of measures taken

---

[7] Gotthard, *Religionsfrieden*, 171–239.
[8] Schneider, *Ius reformandi*, 273, 309–12. See also Schulze, 'Concordia'.

piecemeal over anything up to a century, had implications for the political system of the Reich as a whole. By the 1580s, these developments contributed to the new assertiveness of many princes in the Reich, both of Estates against emperor and, increasingly in confessional blocs or parties, of Estate against Estate. They also intensified the alarm with which governments reacted to signs of renewed social tensions within the territories themselves. That often provided the trigger for further intervention and attempts at firmer regulation, while the higher courts of the Reich in Speyer and Vienna now also began to play a role in the resolution of some conflicts between rulers and ruled.

40

A Benign Environment?

Despite the emphasis traditionally placed on this period as one of crisis and confrontation, it did in fact provide an environment that was fundamentally favourable to initiatives towards stabilization and governmental consolidation. The most obvious factor was, of course, the Augsburg settlement itself, which laid down broad principles even if it also contained major ambiguities. The differing Catholic and Protestant interpretation of those principles and the problems inherent in the detail of many specific clauses only became apparent, and politically problematic, much later.[1]

More generally, the economic developments of the period were also favourable to the rulers of many territories, though the situation of the cities was less fortunate. This may seem paradoxical in view of the suffering experienced by much of the population as a whole, which cumulatively led to renewed unrest and instability in many areas by the 1580s. At the same time, however, other trends favoured landowners in significant ways.

From the point of view of the common man, conditions of life entered a period of sustained crisis from the early 1560s. The long period of relatively good harvests enjoyed during a series of 'warm' decades since about 1530 ended. Cooler conditions led to more meagre harvests and in some areas to the cessation of cultivation of more marginal land. Even though the evidence for this climatic shift is based largely on the study of Upper Germany and Switzerland, and therefore cannot necessarily be translated to the north German plain and the Baltic region, it seems clear that problems were widespread.[2] From about 1570 the incidence of harvest failure, sometimes prolonged, increased significantly. In these circumstances, disease spread more easily and had a more severe impact. Severe outbreaks of plague occurred in every decade, the worst during the five years between 1580 and 1585 and the ten years from 1593 to 1603. Between 1596 and 1600, Hessen, Nassau, Lower Saxony, Thuringia, Silesia, Pomerania, and East Prussia successively were particularly afflicted. Outbreaks of smallpox, dysentery, typhus, typhoid fever, and malaria were also regular occurrences throughout the Reich in this period.[3]

While overall population growth slowed somewhat from 0.6 per cent p.a. to 0.3 per cent p.a., it did not cease, and the population of 'Germany', using the frontiers of 1914, increased from about 12.6 million in 1550 to about 16.2 million

---

[1] Schneider, *Ius reformandi*, 173–84, 202–18; Gotthard, *Religionsfrieden*, 240–80.
[2] Scott, *Society*, 252–5.
[3] Lanzinner, 'Zeitalter', 126–7.

in 1600.[4] The effects of shortages and disease were extremely varied, both geographically and socially. The impact was greatest at the lowest levels of both rural and urban society. For many groups just above the lowest level in rural areas or small rural towns, however, the possibilities of subsistence cultivation, even though limited, mitigated the impact of general shortages and price rises. Although standards of living declined overall and life expectancy was curtailed, life was at least possible.[5] Where an acute crisis of either subsistence or disease decimated the population of a locality or region, the deficit was soon made up by a 'natural' downward adjustment of the age of marriage and a consequent greater fecundity.

In both rural and urban contexts, it was the established, independent producer who suffered least: tenant farmers with secure property rights rather than cottars and landless labourers, guild masters rather than journeymen. In both town and country, the gulf between relative prosperity and poverty tended to increase, generating social and, in some areas, political frictions.

The general effect of food shortages was to accentuate another major trend of the period: an increase in prices.[6] The most plausible explanation for this trend seems to be the sharp increase in demand for foodstuffs of all kinds, especially wheat and rye, caused by the dramatic increase in the population of Western Europe as a whole. By 1600, demand outstripped supply more than ever before. An increase in the money supply following the influx of South American silver from about 1550 may also have played a part. The trend may have been exacerbated towards the end of the century by currency manipulation: some German princes sought to extract short-term profit from their coinage by debasing the currency through the admixture of non-precious metals. However, population growth and the sheer increase in the overall demand for food drove the upward movement of prices throughout the century.

The major beneficiaries of rising food prices were those who produced for the market or who could generate a surplus. That included some prosperous farmers, especially in western parts of Schleswig and Holstein and along the Baltic coasts, but also in Württemberg and other regions. The increase in revenue from land transfer dues indicates confidence in the potential returns from agriculture, as does the steady increase in the price of land and the development of regional or local speculative financial markets dedicated to the purchase of land.[7] Above all, profits from agriculture benefited the nobility, both the territorial nobility subject to a prince, and the princes, counts, knights, and prelates themselves in so far as they themselves engaged in exploitation of patrimonial lands. In areas where *Gutsherrschaft* (manorialism or seigneurialism) was prevalent, there were ever stronger incentives to consolidate, extend, and intensify the system.[8] In other areas, the

---

[4] This excludes Switzerland and Austria. Scott, *Society*, 57; Pfister, *Bevölkerungsgeschichte*, 11–14.
[5] The standard of living measured in terms of rye declined by 30 per cent between 1500 and 1600 (in Augsburg by 50 per cent). In Upper Germany, some 20 per cent were without regular income or were undernourished. Rabe, *Geschichte*, 628.
[6] Lanzinner, 'Zeitalter', 129–30; Mathis, *Wirtschaft*, 98–100, 165–7.
[7] Lanzinner, 'Zeitalter', 130; Rabe, *Geschichte*, 622.
[8] See also pp. 129–31.

pressure on tenants often increased, as landlords sought to exploit the renewed potential for profit, and forms of land management often akin to *Gutsherrschaft* developed where none had existed previously, for example in Bavaria and various Austrian territories. Not least, the generation of healthy profits in agriculture in the second half of the century both underpinned the growing expectations that many rulers had of the benefit of regular tax regimes and reinforced the self-confidence of territorial Estates in dealing with tax demands from their rulers.

The general buoyancy of agricultural returns, even through the years of crisis, is reflected in the extraordinary building activity on the part of those who profited from it. Independent farmers in the south-west of the Reich or in Schleswig and Holstein in the north-west invested at least some of their profits in larger, more ornamented domestic buildings and better quality household equipment that reflected decorative as well as just functional concerns. Nobles and princes through-out the Reich engaged in ambitious construction programmes in the decades before the Thirty Years War. Depending on the region, the latest Italian, French, and Dutch styles were employed in the construction of castles and residences, or in the conversion of older structures according to the new taste.[9] In southern and eastern parts, the Italian style predominated. In northern parts, especially in Lower Saxony, the engagement of many nobles in military service in the French armies or in the Dutch cause was reflected in French and Dutch designs that were programmatic as well as purely decorative. Income from military service in the 1550s and 1560s combined with buoyant agricultural revenues to finance the so-called 'Weser Renaissance' of the later decades of the century. All along the Baltic coast, from Holstein via Mecklenburg and Pomerania to East Prussia, fortified houses began to replace the relatively simple half-timbered tower dwelling of the medieval period.[10]

In comparison with the prosperity of the nobility, the fortunes of the Reich's Imperial Cities and its thousands of territorial towns seemed to decline. Many historians have contrasted the rise of the territorial state with the fall of the urban commune. Recent research has revealed a rather more complex picture, though it has also underlined just how inadequate our understanding of the urban economy really is.[11] In particular, the experience of the myriad smaller centres, which formed regional and local networks in which town and country interacted and were interdependent, is far from clear. Where one such centre declined, another often prospered, and the overall economic output did not necessarily diminish.[12]

The most striking areas of growth and development were those engaged in the Baltic, North Sea, and Atlantic trades and in the supply of the expanding markets of Western Europe. If Dutch and English merchants led the way, their German competitors were not far behind. While the Hanseatic League declined, some

---

[9] Da Costa Kaufmann, *Court*, 139–59; Rabe, *Geschichte*, 621–2; Lanzinner, 'Zeitalter', 131. See also Schütte, *Schloß* and Müller, *Schloß*.

[10] *HbDSWG*, 404–5; Rieber, 'Burg'; Großmann, *Renaissance*; Lüpkes and Borggrefe, *Adel*.

[11] See the surveys in Schilling, *Stadt*; Rosseaux, *Städte*; Gerteis, *Städte*.

[12] Scott, *Society*, 113–52.

Hanseatic Cities still prospered. Hamburg emerged as the leading commercial and financial centre at this time.[13] In general, the commercial centres on the Elbe, the Weser (Bremen), and the Ems (Emden) prospered, as did Cologne before its economy was undermined by military conflict in the 1580s. Danzig, Breslau, Frankfurt am Main, and Leipzig also thrived.

The activities of non-indigenous merchant communities were often crucial. In Danzig, the English and Dutch merchants took over the business of transport and resale. In Hamburg, Dutch and Portuguese migrants joined indigenous merchants in creating fortunes in the South American trade and the money market.[14] From Hamburg down to the Lower Rhine centres of Cologne and Aachen, and to Frankfurt am Main, Dutch refugees also contributed manpower and the latest know-how to branches such as textile production.[15] The 'Weser Renaissance' of the Lower Saxon nobility had its urban equivalent in towns such as Hameln and Lemgo. In regions such as Westphalia generally, the medieval economic leaders such as Bergkammen, Hamm, Lippstadt, Schwerte, Soest, Unna, and Werl declined in significance relative to Bielefeld, Iserlohn, Altena, Lüdenscheid, and Siegen, though the region as a whole retained its prosperity.[16]

For Upper Germany the picture is more complex. The Mediterranean trade that had once been the most significant commercial sector in the Reich did not grow, and thus declined relatively if not absolutely. However, it remained highly significant until around 1600 at least. Some of the leading commercial dynasties of the first half of the century ceased to play a leading role. Some were ruined by the bankruptcies of the French and Spanish monarchies of the 1550s and 1560s, which undermined the south German capital market for good. Others, such as the Fuggers, withdrew from active trade and commerce and lived as patrician rentiers or ascended into the ranks of the nobility and acquired landed property.[17] New dynasties emerged, however, and the old commercial traditions remained strong. These cities were never wholly dependent upon the declining Italian trade and they maintained strong links with the dynamic Netherlands and American markets, with southern France, and the eastern Habsburg territories.

Relative shift rather than absolute decline characterized developments in other sectors as well. Copper and silver mining, smelting and working based on the reserves in the Alps, the Upper Palatinate, the Harz, and the Saxon-Bohemian Erzgebirge, diminished in significance after 1550.[18] Iron working, however, centred on Nuremberg, flourished as never before owing to continuing military demand led by operations against the Turks, but also to the strength of orders from France, the Netherlands, and England. Salt production flourished, along with a high demand for food generally. Regarding textiles, some branches such as Bavarian woollen cloths suffered because they were too expensive by comparison with similar

---

[13] Lindberg, 'Hamburg'.
[14] Kellenbenz, *Unternehmerkräfte, passim*.
[15] Schilling, 'Innovation'.
[16] Mathis, *Wirtschaft*, 93–4.
[17] Häberlein, *Fugger*, 17–68.
[18] Mathis, *Wirtschaft*, 23–5, 35–9.

products from Saxony or Bohemia (though the cheaper lodens that were exported to Italy were not affected).[19] Cotton and wool cloth making boomed. Fustian production at Augsburg continued to increase up to the end of the century and the trade also remained strong at Ulm and Strassburg. By 1600, Calw in Württemberg was already well established as a centre for the production of the cheaper and lighter fabrics, worsteds or sayes and serges, which were so much in demand by the new mass consumer markets.[20] Thus Upper Germany, too, responded to demand generated by the Baltic–North Sea nexus, as well as continuing to supply the more traditional markets.

Scholarly disagreements about whether a crisis was imminent or about the ultimately negative repercussions of the prevalence of tradition over innovation cannot conceal the fact of continuing prosperity through much of the second half of the century.[21] The territorial towns, which comprised most of the roughly 3,500 urban communities in the Reich in the sixteenth century, thus became another potential source of money and revenue for their overlords. The small minority of sixty-five Imperial Cities were free of that threat at least. Their magistrates, however, faced many of the same challenges as the princes and lords, and the ways in which they responded correspondingly changed the character of urban government.

[19] Mathis, *Wirtschaft*, 30–1; *HBayG*, i, 685.
[20] Scott, *Society*, 92–3.
[21] Scott, *Society*, 252–55; Mathis, *Wirtschaft*, 50–1, 93–8.

41

State Formation?

The use of the word 'state' to describe the German territories of the sixteenth century is problematic. For one thing they were not sovereign entities and their rulers were vassals of the emperor. After all, the Reich itself fulfilled many of the functions of a state on their behalf: external defence, the maintenance of domestic peace, the administration of justice, and the formulation of framework legislation on a growing range of subjects, including currency and police matters.[1] Even the larger territories, which appear on the map to encompass solid blocks of land, were not, strictly speaking, unified or integrated territorial entities. More detailed scrutiny often reveals them to be agglomerations of smaller holdings, to each of which a prince held separate title (and frequently on different terms), rights and jurisdictions, some of which bore no relation to landed property at all. These included, for example, stewardship over ecclesiastical foundations or lordship over persons.[2]

Just as the monarchies of Europe were composite monarchies, so the lands of the German nobility were in essence composite property holdings or estates.[3] What has often been viewed as a process of state formation in the German territories of the sixteenth century is, in many ways, better described as a new and more energetic approach to estate management. Most German princes still thought of their territories as patrimonies and their ruling strategy was dominated by dynastic concerns, rather than by any abstract view of a state with responsibility for economy and society.

Nothing illustrates the prevailing attitude more than the way ruling houses clung to the principle of partible inheritances.[4] The Golden Bull of 1356 had stipulated primogeniture as the rule for the seven Electoral principalities. For the rest, however, the death of a ruling prince generally meant the division of his lands among his male heirs. Even the Electorates often indulged in practices that had something of the same effect. It was only the title and the office of the Elector and his core lands that were the exclusive possession of the eldest son.[5] The creation of secundogenitures for younger sons inflated the number of small courts, while

---

[1] For the Reich as a state with functions devolved to Kreise and territories, see Schmidt, *Geschichte*. Two critiques of this view are Schilling, 'Reichs-Staat' and Reinhard, 'Staat'.

[2] Scott, *Society*, 14–15.

[3] Elliott, 'Composite monarchies'; Koenigsberger, 'Monarchies'.

[4] Fichtner, *Primogeniture*, 1–33. Neuhaus, 'Chronologie' provides a useful list of dates of German and other primogeniture ordinances.

[5] That excluded, for example, all territories acquired after the Gold Bull of 1356.

appanages could divert key resources from the main family line, and sometimes created a new court as well. Both the Palatinate and Brandenburg regularly provided for younger sons in these ways, while the Albertine period of Electoral Saxony after 1547 was characterized by rare stability because of the dynasty's adoption of a form of primogeniture in 1499 (though three junior lines were again created in 1652). Only the ecclesiastical territories remained unaffected by these practices.

At one point or another, partition affected virtually every dynasty in the Reich to some degree. The Habsburgs were no exception, with the division of Ferdinand I's lands between his three sons in 1564. Landgrave Philip of Hessen divided his lands unequally between his four legitimate sons in 1567.[6] Count Joachim Ernst of Anhalt, who had united his family's lands in 1570, left them to his eldest son Johann Georg in 1586, who, after years of negotiation, agreed a partition with his four brothers, creating no less than five Anhalt principalities in 1603.[7] The dynasty of the Ernestine Duke of Saxony, who lost the Electoral title in 1547, had divided into two distinct lines by 1600, followed by a further eleven divisions (four in Saxony-Weimar and seven in Saxony-Gotha) by 1640.[8]

The disadvantages of partition were widely recognized. Quite apart from the fragmentation of powerful properties, dynasties were often plunged into years of internal wrangling and bickering. Such complicated arrangements were also frequently extremely expensive. Some resulted in recourse to the Reichshofrat in Vienna in legal processes that could drag on over generations. Even where a partition was amicable, the creation of additional courts consumed substantial resources. Attempts were often made to mitigate the effects of partition by providing for joint administration of core property. Alternatively, a shared government might be established in which the eldest son acted as director of a ruling consortium and executed the policy wishes of the majority. The Estates of a territory generally supported such arrangements, for they invariably had to bear the costs of the partitions. They could only work, however, as long as the co-rulers agreed among themselves.

Few dynasties took the obvious step of adopting primogeniture. Paradoxically, it seems that the Protestant princes even came to support partition more strongly during the sixteenth century. Their adoption of Protestantism excluded their younger sons from careers in the Church, yet it also gave them a strong sense of the need to be fair to all of their male children. Catholic dynasties, by contrast, could still send their younger sons into the Church (however unwillingly they sometimes went), and it seems that they were generally more open to experiments designed to avoid partitions.

Both the Habsburgs and the Bavarian Wittelsbachs adopted the appanage system in the late sixteenth century and strove to ensure settlements that were reasonable in

---

[6] Köbler, *Lexikon*, 274.

[7] Schindling and Ziegler, *Territorien*, ii, 88–9. The Counts of Anhalt were the only counts in the College of Princes; they did not become dukes until 1806: Köbler, *Lexikon*, 16–17.

[8] Schindling and Ziegler, *Territorien*, iv, 9–10.

relation to the resources of the territory as a whole.[9] The sons of Ferdinand I eventually settled on their nephew Ferdinand II (of Styria) as sole heir, partly in order to forestall the possible claims of Spain, but also in a conscious move to bolster the Catholic cause in Central Europe. In Bavaria, the influence of the natural law theories of Justus Lipsius on William V (r. 1579–98) and Maximilian I (r. 1598–1651) seems to have been instrumental in shaping a perception of the primacy of the needs of the territory as a whole over the aspirations of younger sons. Both Habsburgs and Wittelsbachs, moreover, had an acute sense of the fact that the fate of Catholicism in Central Europe depended on the successful stewardship of their dynastic resources.

Despite the widespread persistence of attitudes that inhibited any transition from patrimonial to territorial government, the century-and-a-half after about 1450 saw significant moves towards intensification of administration, and a search for new ways of exercising power and of mobilizing resources. The timing, pace, and extent of the development of administrative offices differed from territory to territory, as did the terminology employed.[10] In some parts, for example the Palatinate, most of the key elements of the new administrative structure were in place from the 1450s and 1460s.[11] In general, however, it is held that the imperial reforms from the 1490s onwards, then the administrative reforms of the Habsburg territories introduced by Ferdinand I in 1527, and then later in Bavaria and Saxony, served as models that were emulated by others. For some territories, the Reformation proved to be the crucial incentive for reforms carried out in the late 1520s, 1530s, and 1540s, but for the majority the crucial decades were those between 1570 and 1630. By then, however, others had scarcely begun to embark upon any changes, or had given up, driven to the brink of financial ruin by the costs involved.

The underlying theme was the differentiation of court and administration. In the fifteenth century, the primary function of administration had been to serve the personal interests of the dynasty and to generate income for the prince and his court. The old German term 'stat', after all, really referred to the 'Hofstaat', the household or retinue of a prince centred on a court.[12] That gradually began to change as new administrative officials emerged alongside the old officials of the court. In the Palatinate, for example, the old hereditary court offices continued: the Counts of Erbach as cup-bearers, the Ritter von Hirschhorn as high stewards, the Wild- und Rheingrafen as hereditary marshals of the court.[13] Alongside them, however, the new offices of *Grosshofmeister* (grand or supreme major-domo),

---

[9] Fichtner, *Primogeniture*, 34–60.

[10] The most comprehensive survey, with details of the myriad variations across the Reich, is DVG, 279–467 (discussion of institutional structures), 468–941 (detailed accounts of most territories).

[11] Cohn, *Palatinate*, 202–46.

[12] Lanzinner, 'Zeitalter', 79.

[13] The Wild- und Rheingrafen, who had lost most of their lands in the thirteenth century, called themselves Counts of Salm when they inherited the lands of those counts from 1475, but the hereditary marshalcy of the Palatinate was associated with their original title. Press, *Calvinismus*, 31. At the end of the eighteenth century the total extent of all three counties was no more than about 220 km² with some 11,000 inhabitants. Köbler, *Lexikon*, 792–3. On the Counts of Erbach, see Press, 'Erbach'.

Kanzler (chancellor), and *Marshall* (in charge of the administration of the court) emerged as working administrative officials with increasingly clear terms of reference and specified rates of remuneration. Other major territorial courts such as the Saxon court at Dresden also experienced this growth of a new officialdom alongside a surviving cast of hereditary officers.[14]

Several key institutions featured in most territories.[15] First, a council was formed to advise the prince and to undertake essential government functions on his behalf. This generally had responsibility for both jurisdictional and administrative matters and was often regularly attended by the ruling prince himself. Second, the old institution of the chancery, composed of clerics, developed into a more specialized agency, staffed by legally trained laymen under the supervision of a chancellor, who was also a member of the council. Third, a Hofgericht or supreme court dealt with judicial matters. Fourth, responsibility for finances lay in the hands of the Kammer, or treasury: the *Kämmerer*'s original general focus on paying the bills at court extended to embrace an oversight over the whole range of a prince's income, from regalian rights and jurisdictional fees to demesne property and taxation, among other sources.

Finally, new specialist departments were added. Protestant territories, many following the example set by Württemberg in 1548–9, introduced a *Kirchenrat* (synod, church council, or consistory) to fulfil the government's new duties in respect of the Church. Bavaria established a parallel for the Catholic territories, including some ecclesiastical principalities, with the creation in 1570 of a *Geistlicher Rat* (ecclesiastical council) with responsibility for schools, the administration of ecclesiastical property, the appointment of parish priests, and the observance of decrees concerning religion. The introduction of a military council or *Hofkriegsrat* in Vienna in 1556 was emulated by Bavaria between 1583 and 1593, and then increasingly, on a permanent basis, by other territories over the next century.

Relatively little changed at the local level. The system established in most parts of the Reich by the fifteenth century, of districts or bailiwicks (Amt, pl. Ämter) under the administration of an appointed official—usually but not necessarily a noble—remained more or less unchanged in many parts until well into the nineteenth century.[16] Certainly, throughout the sixteenth century these districts remained the basic units of local administration, though asserting control over them could prove problematic. Indeed, in areas where the Ämter had been extensively mortgaged to noble families during the fifteenth century—by commercializing lordship rights, a highly popular way of raising money—reasserting control could be a struggle over many decades.[17] Indeed, when the Bishop of Hildesheim tried to regain his mortgaged districts from the nobility, they appealed successfully to neighbouring princes, themselves mortgagees, and the resulting military confrontation between

---

[14] Müller, *Fürstenhof*, 18–29 provides a useful survey.
[15] For the following, see *DVG*, 279–941.
[16] For a general survey, see *DVG*, 96–100 and *HDR*, i, col. 151–4.
[17] Schubert, *Spätmittelalter*, 202–3; Krause, 'Pfandherrschaften'.

1519 and 1523 led to the permanent loss of significant districts and to the abdication of the bishop.[18]

Even among the more established territories, there were also substantial variations. Saxony was able to regain control of many noble lordships and to retain control of most of the former ecclesiastical properties, thus extending the number of Ämter. In Brandenburg, by contrast, only thirteen of the forty to forty-five Ämter were listed in the official court register during the reign of Elector Joachim II (r. 1535–71). Many of them, along with a significant number of former monasteries, had fallen under noble or clerical control, often pledged in return for mortgages by this notoriously indebted ruler.[19]

Where the Ämter were unencumbered and more or less secure from external threat they could work reasonably well as links between the central bodies and the localities. The *Amtmann* (district governor or bailiff) was based in a castle or in a market town; he represented the ruling prince, and he liaised with the town council officials and village headmen or mayors to ensure the communication and enforcement of laws and edicts passed down by central officials.[20] He wielded power and influence, but he did not govern in any active sense; rather, he tried to ensure that the locally elected agencies executed the business of government. He was the first source of information about the localities when it was sought by central agencies and he played a key role in ensuring that taxes collected were passed on to the treasury.

Only Saxony, Bavaria, and the Habsburg territories developed an intermediate level of government. Both the Electorate and the Duchy of Saxony had organized their Ämter in Kreise by about 1550, each with its own *Oberamtmann*.[21] From a much earlier stage, each of the Habsburg territories had a *Viztum* in charge of finances, while Bavaria was divided into four *Viztumämter* or *Rentmeisterämter*, each under the supervision of a *Viztum*, with the *Rentmeister* or financial controller as the key officer.[22] Whether this intermediate level of government really contributed to greater efficiency, however, is unclear. The Elector August of Saxony was perennially beset by anxieties that he was being cheated at every level of his financial administration. Even as recipient of the largest income of any prince of the Reich, with a healthy average annual profit of 238,000 gulden by 1577–86, his revenue accounting system was far from transparent.[23]

The structure of the lower levels of administration thus remained more or less unchanged. They were simply expected to do more. This aspiration was frequently undermined by the dismal state of local government or by the tensions that were often inherent in the relationship between *Amtmänner* and local representatives.

---

[18] Stanelle, *Stiftsfehde*, 1–3. See also pp. 157–8.
[19] Oestreich, 'Verfassungsgeschichte', 88; Heinrich, 'Adel', 237 gives a figure of thirty Ämter and monasteries mortgaged to nobles in 1550.
[20] A good description of how the system worked in Württemberg is Scribner, 'Police', 106–8.
[21] Lanzinner, 'Zeitalter', 84–5.
[22] Haberkern and Wallach, *Hilfswörterbuch*, 647; Conrad, *Rechtsgeschichte*, ii, 304, 327.
[23] Schirmer, 'Finanzen', 179–83.

It was easier, by contrast, to respond to the pressures of more and more specialized government at the higher level. The collegial system that characterized the ruling council and other central bodies could be cumbersome and inflexible. The painstaking collation of opinions or votes weighted by the social rank and age of members took time and generally allowed the more senior and higher-status councillors to prevail; caution and downright inertia predominated more often than not.[24] While the number of officials proliferated at all levels and the central bodies developed more subordinate departments, real political decisions were increasingly made by the prince in consultation with a small group of trusted councillors. These privy councils (Geheime Räte) emerged in virtually all of the major territories during the course of the century, and others followed suit during the seventeenth century.[25]

---

[24] Willoweit, *Verfassungsgeschichte*, 127–8.
[25] Lanzinner, 'Zeitalter', 82–3; Press, *Kriege*, 118–19; Müller, *Fürstenhof*, 25–9.

42

Domestic Order and Defence

As with the elaboration of central administrations in the German territories, the development of legislation and financial management took place within the framework set by arrangements made in the Reich and by the example of the Habsburgs as territorial rulers [1] There were, of course, developments within some territories, especially urban communes such as Nuremberg, with its city reformation of 1479, and other Upper German Imperial Cities, which pre-dated the imperial and Habsburg initiatives.[2] The general tendencies, however, emerged from the initiatives of Maximilian I and Ferdinand I, which drew heavily on Burgundian/French traditions and made a decisive difference to the hitherto prevailing German/ Austrian conventions. Above all, they incorporated and fostered the spread of Roman law, making the period 1490–1530 a crucial phase in the practical reception of the new legal teachings in the Reich. In terms of legislation, their principle effect was on the collation or codification of territorial laws, on the systematization of legal procedures, and on the growing mass of police legislation.

By 1555, some leading territories, such as Bavaria, Brandenburg, and Württemberg, had already emulated the Habsburgs and had collated and published territorial laws and formulated codes of judicial procedure. Other territories that had developed such codes during the fifteenth century began to revise them in line with later imperial legislation. Similarly, criminal law codes were revised within the framework set by the imperial criminal code, the *Carolina* of 1532. After 1555, the process of legal reform became a key feature of the ongoing efforts to stabilize and consolidate the position of the territorial rulers. Roman law, with its clarity and authority, now seemed more attractive than ever to rulers and officials seeking to establish, at the regional and local level, the kind of rule of law that many believed had been achieved in the institutions of the Reich.

In some cases, the aim was quite simply to translate customary law into Roman law. The Palatinate, Baden, the County of Solms, and the Imperial Cities of Frankfurt am Main and Nuremberg followed the example set by Duke Christoph of Württemberg in 1555 and themselves became much copied models over the coming decades.[3] In Saxony, where the Elector commissioned the universities of

---

[1] Strauss, *Law*, 145–6.

[2] Schubert, *Spätmittelalter*, 124–30 argues that the very notion of *Obrigkeit* or government was invented by the cities in the thirteenth and fourteenth centuries.

[3] Strauss, *Law*, 87–90. For a survey of all the important initiatives, see Conrad, *Rechtsgeschichte*, ii, 363–73.

Leipzig and Wittenberg to collect and revise all existing territorial laws, the result in 1572 was a code that both introduced Roman law principles and retained those traditional laws that had been found to harmonize with them.

Whatever the variations and differences of emphasis, the same aims accompanied all of the parallel processes of legal revision. Law was to be written or printed and published; customary and local laws handed down by oral tradition were to be superseded. This also had the effect of removing jurisdiction from local courts and asserting the jurisdictional rights of the ruling prince, affecting not only village communities, but also the rights of the nobility and the communal rights of towns. The legal process was streamlined and accelerated, with greater decision-making power being given to judges. Moreover, the legal process was now increasingly placed in the hands of legally trained experts, who supplanted the untrained judges and assessors who had administered customary law at the grass roots. Finally, the codifications aimed to provide each territory with a single set of laws, though this was often only achieved at a relatively late stage. In Bavaria, for example, the legal code formulated for Upper (western) Bavaria in 1518 was simply used as the model for the legislation that followed in Lower (eastern) Bavaria. A single code valid for both Upper and Lower Bavaria did not come into effect until 1618.[4]

In much the same way, the *Reichspolizeiordnungen* of 1530, 1548, and 1577 set norms that were translated into much more detailed and extensive legislation in the territories.[5] Literally hundreds of police codes were published: a representative sample of thirty-nine Imperial Estates (including Electors, secular and ecclesiastical princes, counts, and Imperial Cities) registered ninety-eight in the period 1548–1600 alone (compared with fifty-three in the previous century-and-a-half).[6]

The police ordinances were generally extraordinarily wide-ranging in scope.[7] They sought to regulate anything from usury to public health and hygiene, market trading, fire protection, guilds and crafts, blasphemy, swearing and aggressive language or behaviour, and sumptuary laws. The unifying theme was once again the search for order. The objective, stated over and again, was to establish norms for the 'common good', the term that was most frequently invoked in justification of laws and regulations. Police legislation was not a grandiose attempt to establish an absolute state or to subject society to draconian regimentation. It was rather a response to the profound crisis in traditional society since the fifteenth century. Lawlessness, new economic activities and associated social patterns, and the disruption brought about by the Reformation, were just some of the diverse manifestations of the underlying problems that the police legislation was designed to solve. The frequent reiteration of such laws indicates that they were not much more effective than the imperial laws that inspired them. Indeed, a century later, Christian Thomasius mocked the *Polizeiordnungen* which, he claimed, were observed only by

---

[4] Conrad, *Rechtsgeschichte*, ii, 365.
[5] Härter, 'Entwicklung', 134–141.
[6] Härter, 'Entwicklung', 136.
[7] Maier, *Staats- und Verwaltungslehre*, 74–91; Conrad, *Rechtsgeschichte*, ii, 257–60.

the church doors and other objects to which they were fastened by way of public announcement.[8]

The Imperial Enforcement Ordinance (*Reichsexekutionsordnung*) of 1555 had also finally devolved responsibility for public order in the Reich to the territories; each ruler was enjoined to maintain himself in a state of readiness in the event of a threat to security. That almost immediately revealed the inadequacy of the existing defence systems in the territories. On the one hand, the old feudal military system based on knights and their retinues no longer worked; the lower nobility by and large preferred to discharge its military duties by means of monetary payments. On the other hand, reliance on mercenaries was both extremely expensive and itself perceived as a potential threat to public order. At the same time, the need for an effective military force was abundantly illustrated in the decades after 1555.

In this area, too, the Habsburgs led the way.[9] Faced with the serious threat posed by the Turks to the Habsburg territories, Lazarus von Schwendi argued forcefully for revitalizing and extending the old general obligation of subjects to lend aid in an emergency (*Landfolge*). The first elements of such a defensive organization were developed in the late fifteenth century in Styria, Carinthia, and Carniola. A comparable system was established for the Tyrol in 1518, and, under perennial Turkish threat, the Habsburgs continued to develop their inner Austrian militias throughout the century.[10] In 1572, Schwendi also played a key role in securing the agreement of the Estates in Alsace to a similar system, to be set up in response to the growing menace from France. This ensured reasonably effective regional cooperation until it was undermined by Protestant suspicion of the Catholic ruler of the Austrian Vorlande, Archduke Ferdinand II of the Tyrol, in 1586.[11]

What was novel about Schwendi's ideas was that he rejected the prevailing doubts of experts such as the Imperial Field Marshal Reinhard von Solms (1491– 1562) about the wisdom of arming the people.[12] In a series of influential essays, Schwendi propagated Machiavelli's view of the virtues of the Roman example of employing the people in defence of their fatherland. This idea also lay at the root of the defence plans developed by Johann VI of Nassau-Dillenburg (r. 1559–1606), which were largely executed and then continued by his son, Johann VII of Nassau-Siegen (r. 1607–23). The refusal of the Reichstag to grant freedom of religion to the Reformed, as demanded by the Palatinate in 1576, made the smaller Reformed territories feel increasingly insecure. Johann VI, in particular, was influenced by the experiences of his elder brother, William of Orange in the Netherlands, by the lessons of the French religious wars, and by the growing threat of instability in the north-west of the Reich generated by the turmoil in the Netherlands. From the early 1580s, he began to mobilize the forces of the Wetterau counts and within

[8] *DVG*, 397.
[9] Schulze, 'Heeresreform'; Schnitter, *Volk*, 39–49.
[10] Schulze, *Landesdefension*, 36–55.
[11] Oestreich, 'Heeresverfassung', 296–7.
[12] *ADB*, xxxiv, 584–5. Solms served both Charles V and Maximilian II.

a decade an impressive system of recruitment and military training had been established.[13]

The theoretical and philosophical foundations of the Nassau initiative also marked a significant advance on Schwendi's reflections in the 1560s and 1570s. The latter had invoked Machiavelli and ancient Rome in an attempt to breathe new life into the old obligations of subjects in times of emergency. The future Johann VII, as commander of the Wetterau forces, elaborated something more like a neo-stoical philosophy of the fatherland in his *Verteidigungsbuch* ('Book of Defence') of 1595. Drawing on the Calvinist contract theory of Theodore Beza and other works purchased by his father in the 1570s, he wrote of the mutual obligation of rulers and subjects.[14] Provided the people were treated well, one should have no fear of arming them. The people for their part had an obligation to defend their ruler and their fatherland.

In reviving a traditional form, the Nassau counts developed it further. They no longer saw the people in purely feudal terms, as subject to a noble, but appealed to the people as inhabitants of a territory or a fatherland. They took the precaution, of course, of specifying that the troops should have noble commanders; and, like Schwendi, they believed that those recruited should be well rewarded.[15] In general, the Nassau counts saw this kind of military organization as a way of strengthening the fatherland and of integrating and disciplining the population.

The Nassau model came to be widely emulated. Both Johann VI and Johann VII were tireless propagandists for their cause. Their authority was further bolstered by the fact that their militia successfully came to the aid of the Reformed cause in the Palatinate in 1592 and that it did indeed help save Nassau from being ransacked by passing Spanish forces in 1599.[16] The general insecurity of the period, which provoked the formation of numerous regional leagues to defend against foreign troops as well as the major confessional associations after 1600, led to a proliferation of similar initiatives throughout the Reich.[17] The Palatinate had already experimented with militias in the 1580s. In 1600 alone, militias were instituted in Hessen, Brunswick, Baden, Ansbach, and the Duchy of Prussia, while Saxony and Brandenburg followed in 1613.

The movement was not confined to Protestant territories. After several years of preparation and study of the Palatinate arrangements, but also of the system in Florence and elsewhere in Italy, Maximilian I of Bavaria issued a decree establishing a militia in 1600, joining other Catholic territories such as Mainz, Würzburg, and Bamberg.[18] In 1604, the imperial paymaster Zacharias Geizkofler advised the emperor that most of the princes in the Reich had instituted such home defence organizations over the last five years or so. He recommended a review of the

[13] Schmidt, *Grafenverein*, 135–47.
[14] Oestreich, *Antiker Geist*, 342–8; Schulze, 'Landesdefensionen', 145–6.
[15] Schulze, 'Landesdefensionen', 143–5.
[16] Oestreich, *Antiker Geist*, 298.
[17] Schnitter, *Volk*, 113–32, *HMG*, i, 66–100.
[18] Schulze, 'Landesdefensionen', 138; Albrecht, *Maximilian I*, 379–85; Frauenholz, *Entwicklungsgeschichte*, iii/2, 9, 37–46.

arrangements for the Austrian Erblande, with a view to updating them according to the modern system developed by Nassau and refined by Moritz of Hessen.

Theoretically, these militias represented a radical departure. They involved a relatively small percentage of the population: in Saxony, for example, some 10 per cent were enlisted (or every thirtieth man) and nowhere was there anything approaching universal conscription. However, the recruitment procedures showed evidence of an impressive degree of coordination and resource planning. Considerable care was taken to ensure that neither the rural nor the urban economy was disrupted and that the recruits were willing: in Hessen, for example, recruiters went through a series of standard questions including 'Do you want to be a soldier?'[19] The militias were also, for the most part, provided with the latest firearms. Duke Maximilian I of Bavaria was not, however, the only ruler to specify that the firearms should be kept securely in armouries since 'His Grace does not intend to leave the weapons in the hands of his subjects'.[20] Few fully shared the philosophy of the Nassau enterprise.

Particular attention was devoted to drilling the men; indeed, Johann VI coined the German term *Trillerey* in this context. Quite apart from the disciplinary virtue of drill exercises, the technical demands of the latest firearms required them: the Nassau instructions for loading and firing a musket specified no less than twenty separate actions, to be practised on the move and firing on moving targets.[21] Some rulers gave preference to urban recruits since, even at the lowest social levels, they were generally better educated and, hence, more likely to cope with the complex requirements of the system.

It is clear also that many rulers were enthused by the idea of enlisting a force for the defence of the territorial fatherland. The attitude of the nobility differed from region to region. In some territories, such as Saxony, the local nobility strenuously resisted the introduction of a militia system, since it undermined their own rights over their peasants.[22] Elsewhere, however, the nobility were as keen as anyone to have a reliable system of defence that was both cheap and, provided that troops had noble commanders, posed no threat to the social order. Indeed, only two generations after the Peasants' War, it is remarkable that any rulers at all were willing to enlist their subjects in the defence of their territories, and even, in some cases, to provide them with weapons that they were permitted to take home.[23]

Just how effective the militias were in military terms was another matter. The successes of the Nassau contingents in the 1590s were achieved in highly localized conflicts and in tactical skirmishes, rather than in serious military confrontations. The performance of the Bavarian militia troops during the 1620s was so disappointing that Maximilian I concluded that the money spent on them had been wasted. From the end of 1632, those who might have been recruited were in fact required to contribute to the cost of mercenaries, rather than actually serve themselves.[24] What worked in Nassau, a relatively small territory where the ruler was

[19] Schulze, 'Landesdefensionen', 140–1.   [20] Albrecht, *Maximilian I*, 381.
[21] Schulze, 'Landesdefensionen', 142–3.   [22] Schulze, 'Landesdefensionen', 133.
[23] Schulze, 'Landesdefensionen', 146.   [24] Albrecht, *Maximilian I*, 384–5.

effectively the only landlord, did not work so well where the ruler had to contend with the hostility of the nobility. Even in Nassau, it proved difficult to turn peasants into willing, let alone enthusiastic, soldiers.[25] Everywhere, the costs were considerable, as were the difficulties in securing suitably qualified commanders and trainers or even getting hold of enough of the most modern weapons. Given time, the system might have succeeded. The Thirty Years War, however, required more effective military responses, which necessitated a general return to reliance on mercenaries.[26]

[25] Schmidt, *Grafenverein*, 147, 153–5.
[26] Frauenholz, *Entwicklungsgeschichte*, iii/2, 31–4; Oestreich, *Antiker Geist*, 302–3; Schulze, 'Landesdefensionen', 147–8; Schnitter, *Volk*, 132–43.

43

Confessionalization?

That a concern for domestic order and defence was linked to issues of religion and ecclesiastical organization, education, and vigilance over morality would have seemed natural to anyone charged with government and administration. It was at least implicit in the terms of the Peace of Augsburg that the Estates of the Reich were free to set about restoring order in matters concerning religion and the Church. Among other things, that meant restoring the correspondence that had broadly existed before the Reformation between the religion of a ruler and that of his people. Political obedience and religious obedience were closely linked in the minds of princes and magistrates everywhere.

Of course, the Peace recognized that the pre-Reformation state of affairs had been fundamentally disrupted: the existence of two Christian confessions in the Reich was accepted for the time being. In the case of some Imperial Cities, it was also recognized that giving precedence to either would simply result in a civil war and so both Catholics and Protestants were given equal rights under imperial law. For the territories generally, however, despite the basic rights of emigration given to Catholic or Lutheran dissenting religious minorities in 1555, the rule of thumb was straightforward: rulers had the right to choose which would be the dominant faith in their territories. Ensuring the establishment and welfare of that faith was as much a part of the duty of a Christian ruler as maintaining the justice system or defending his people against attack.[1]

Ultimately, the attempt to impose religious discipline was shaped by the political circumstances of the Reich. The German territories experienced in an extreme form something that was common in much of East Central, Middle, and Western Europe: frontiers or at least boundaries that divided not only lordships and jurisdictions but also competing versions of Christianity. Seeking to affirm an official Church and its teachings was as natural as seeking to affirm the legitimacy of government authority. Yet the common political culture also shaped the articulation of church life in all territories in the Reich, regardless of confession. The Catholics of Bavaria had more in common with the Lutherans of Württemberg than they did with Catholics in Andalucia or Sicily.[2]

It was a while before many rulers exercised the powers granted to them in 1555. The situation was further complicated by the emergence of a second Protestant force in the Reich in the form of the Calvinist or German Reformed Church. This

---

[1] Simon, 'Gute Policey', 120–6, 108–10.
[2] Schindling, 'Konfessionalisierung', 20.

was not recognized by imperial law but, despite its illegality and the repeated refusal of the Reichstag to recognize it, it gained considerable ground and soon became established as a permanent political force, not least because of its espousal by the Palatine Electorate. Furthermore, before ecclesiastical discipline could be imposed, the Churches themselves needed to clarify what it was that they professed: confessionalization had to be preceded by the definition of the confession. Even in the case of the Catholic Church, characterized by a fundamental continuity of doctrine and dogma, the renewal stretched over many decades. There were several key milestones in this protracted process: the codification of Catholic dogma and ritual by the Council of Trent (1545–63), the development of the network of Jesuit seminaries in the Reich from 1552, the foundation of the Collegium Germanicum in Rome in 1562, the establishment of the system of nuncios and legates in the 1570s and 1580s, and, from the late 1590s, the establishment of a network of Capuchin monasteries.[3]

The evolution of the Protestant Churches was just as protracted and even more complex. Attempts by the Lutheran princes to agree on a single body of teaching and a uniform Church order in 1557, 1558, and 1561 failed. Divisions among Lutheran theologians after Luther's death in 1546 were exacerbated by the tensions between the two lines of the Saxon dynasty. In 1547 the Albertines, who had remained loyal to Charles V, were rewarded with both the Electoral title and the eastern half of the Ernestine lands, including the town and university of Wittenberg. While Dresden became the main residence of the new Electors, their claim to be leaders of the Protestant cause in the Reich was founded on ownership of the University of Wittenberg, where the theology faculty was dominated by Melanchthon, Luther's most authoritative heir.[4]

The defeated Ernestine dukes, for their part, set about rebuilding their power in the lands that were left to them, and soon established their own university at Jena from 1554 (chartered 1558).[5] The two Saxon universities provided institutional focal points for bitterly opposed schools of Lutheran thought that had emerged in the response to the Interim in 1548. While Melanchthon was conciliatory and judged matters concerning the external form of worship to be peripheral (*adiaphora* or matters indifferent), the so-called Gnesiolutherans ('ultra-Lutherans') roundly condemned the 'Philippists' for their willingness to accept 'popish' rituals. It is significant that one of the first appointments at Jena was the prominent Gnesiolutheran, Matthias Flacius Illyricus.

A series of theological controversies during the 1550s merely underlined the depth of the divisions among the Lutheran theologians. If Luther's key teachings were challenged they were capable of cooperation, as when Melanchthon and the Gnesiolutherans Nikolaus von Amsdorf and Flacius Illyricus joined forces with Calvin to denounce Andreas Osiander's denial of Luther's doctrine of justification by faith in an extended campaign after 1549. However, they were unable to agree among themselves. An attempt by Jakob Andreae, Chancellor of Tübingen, to

[3] Forster, *Catholic Germany*, 38–84.
[4] Ludwig, *Philippismus*, 45–77.
[5] Schindling and Ziegler, *Territorien*, iv, 19–26; Bauer, *Universität Jena*, 25–45.

broker an agreement in 1568–9 also foundered on the mutual suspicion between Wittenberg and Jena, and because neither camp was particularly sympathetic to an outsider whom they regarded as second-rate.

The situation in Jena had been slightly improved after Flacius was expelled in 1561 following his denunciation of what he saw as the extension of excessive ducal control over ecclesiastical affairs. The situation in Wittenberg was moderated after 1574, when the Elector imprisoned the leading Philippist theologian Christoph Pezel, his superintendent Johann Stössel, and two of his own close advisers for their alleged conspiracy to forge a union with the Calvinists.[6] The controversy was now finally laid to rest, for after the death of Duke Johann Wilhelm in 1573 the Elector August had also taken over the administration of Ernestine lands on behalf of his nephews until 1586, which dampened the competition between Wittenberg and Jena.

Meanwhile, Andreae and others made progress on a common declaration, and by 1577 a new confession was complete.[7] In June 1580, on the fiftieth anniversary of the Augsburg Confession, this was published at Dresden. Over the coming years, eighty-six governments and over eight thousand Lutheran theologians and pastors subscribed to the Formula of Concord, which thus became the formal repository of Lutheran doctrine for the next two-and-a-half centuries. The key to its success was its moderation and balance. Its recourse to the writings of Luther and the Augsburg Confession provided the foundation for a canonical tradition and a common history. At the same time, it drew a clear doctrinal line between the teachings of the Lutheran confession and those of both Catholicism and Calvinism.[8]

In view of the in-fighting of the decades that preceded it, the Formula of Concord was a triumph, yet the eighty-six governments that subscribed to it represented only about two-thirds of the Lutheran territories. In a near-reversal of the fronts of the 1550s, many Philippists now found it difficult to accept the compromises they believed the Formula made on the subject of rituals they regarded as 'popish'. In doing so, they aligned themselves with the Swiss Reformed tradition, mediated by the followers of Zwingli, Bucer, Bullinger, and Calvin, in rejecting all ritual and ceremonial and in denying the bodily presence of Christ in the Eucharistic bread. Many princes had less elevated motives for refusing the Formula. Philippists were influential in the south German Imperial Cities, but also in Pomerania, Holstein, Anhalt, Hessen, and Pfalz-Zweibrücken. For some of Saxony's smaller neighbours, fear of Saxon expansionism was the crucial factor. It drove the Counts of Reuss, for example, to formulate their own confession, which remained in force until the twentieth century, and which ensured that the Elector had no excuse to carry out a visitation in their territory.[9]

---

[6] Rabe, *Geschichte*, 511–12.
[7] Ludwig, *Philippismus*, 147–301.
[8] Cameron, *Reformation*, 368; Rabe, *Geschichte*, 512–13.
[9] Schmidt, *Geschichte*, 105–6; Schindling and Ziegler, *Territorien*, iv, 29–34.

While some Philippists remained non-aligned Lutherans, others became part of the emerging German Reformed tradition. The nature and name of this second German Protestant confessional movement have given rise to major scholarly debates since the late 1970s. The evident dissatisfaction of Philippists with the Lutheran mainstream has led some to argue that they embraced Calvinism in order to effect a 'second reformation'.[10]

However, the German movement as a whole never accepted the authority of Calvin, and its protagonists generally spoke of 'further reformation', rather than of a 'second reformation'.[11] They were, by and large, discontented with the results of the Lutheran reform and aimed now to reform life as well as just the Church. They shared Calvin's antipathy to images of any kind, replaced altars with communion tables, and used plain beakers for communion wine; the churches they built were really auditoriums focused on the pulpit: 'even a Lutheran shivered when he entered'.[12] The doctrine, too, was essentially Calvinist, especially the key sacramentarian dogma of the symbolic rather than the real presence of Christ in the Eucharistic bread, with the provision of ordinary bread rather than wafers for the laity at communion.

Yet there were also significant differences. The classic Calvinist presbyteries were characteristic only of the early Reformed movement constituted by refugees from the Netherlands, such as those in the Lower Rhine Duchies of Jülich-Kleve-Berg and in the County of Mark in the 1540s and 1550s. A similar movement turned the Imperial City of Bremen Calvinist in 1581.

Another special case—and the only example in the Reich of the combination of Calvinism and rebellion against authority that was so characteristic of the Netherlands, France, and Scotland—was the port town of Emden in East Frisia. There, Dutch refugees played a key role in a Calvinist rebellion against the established Church of Lutheran 'meat eaters', which also represented a rebellion of the urban commune against the ruling counts.[13] After decades of conflict culminating in a revolution in 1595, Count Edzard II finally agreed to recognize Calvinism as the sole legitimate religion in the town. Emden's communal rights were reaffirmed on the succession of Count Enno III in 1599, the first formal public legal recognition of Calvinism in the Reich by a non-reformed ruler, albeit invalid in terms of imperial law. From the start, however, the conflict was as much about communal rights as about religion. All the East Frisian Estates, the Lutheran majority as well as Calvinist Emden, assented to the Concordat of 1599, which obliged the counts to recognize the ecclesiastical rights of

---

[10] The best introductions, with copious references, to the extensive debates on this subject are Ehrenpreis and Lotz-Heumann, *Reformation*, 62–79; Schmidt, *Konfessionalisierung*, 44–54, 80–6. A good introduction in English is Po-chia Hsia, *Social discipline*, 1–9, 26–38 and Cohn, 'Princes'. Po-chia Hsia's survey is particularly useful, since it extends the perspective to 1750, while German accounts focus more or less exclusively on the sixteenth century.

[11] Greyerz, *Religion*, 110–27.

[12] Schilling, *Aufbruch*, 300.

[13] The jibe was a reference to the Lutheran belief in the real bodily presence of Christ in the Eucharist.

all communes, and which effectively transferred the *ius reformandi* from the ruling prince to them.[14]

More typically, however, the 'further reformation' of the German Reformed Church was imposed from above. The most prominent example was the Palatinate, where Friedrich III (r. 1559–76) introduced changes to the Lutheran regime established by his predecessors Friedrich II (r. 1544–56) and Ottheinrich (r. 1556–59), culminating in the publication of the Heidelberg Catechism in 1563. The straightforward unfolding of a reformed or Calvinist system was interrupted by the decision of Ludwig VI (r. 1576–83) to revert to Lutheranism, resulting in a purge of the court and the administration, and the expulsion of between five and six hundred pastors. In 1583, however, the Lutherans were themselves expelled by Johann Casimir, the administrator during the minority of Friedrich IV (1583–92). Friedrich IV (r. 1592–1610) continued in this vein, as did his successor Friedrich V (r. 1610–23), who led the Palatinate into the disaster of the Bohemian adventure, which resulted in his deposition, the temporary loss of the Electoral title, and the re-Catholicization of the Palatinate. Aside from its violent Lutheran intermezzo and its catastrophic denouement, the distinctive feature of the Palatine model was its top-down character.[15] In the classic west European Calvinist model, presbyteries were the foundation of both synodal organizations and communal claims to participation in government, if not self-government. The German Reformed churches, by contrast, were not developed in opposition to political authority and their presbyteries were consequently little more than agencies of the state Church and vehicles for visitations carried out by princely fiat.[16]

A series of territories followed the example of the Palatinate over the next five decades.[17] Many of them were smaller counties in the west of the Reich. In Westphalia there was Bentheim, Tecklenburg, and Lippe. Along the Rhine 'further reformations' took place in Neuenahr (including the Lower Rhine County of Moers), Simmern, Zweibrücken, and Baden-Durlach (temporarily in 1599). In the Wetterau, five counties, foremost among them Nassau-Dillenburg, were reformed between 1577 and 1589, followed by Hanau-Münzenberg in 1591, Anhalt in 1596, and Hessen-Kassel in 1606. Finally, between 1609 and 1616 a scatter of Silesian territories (Wohlau, Liegnitz, Brieg, Jägerndorf, and Beuthen) completed the diverse group of twenty-eight Calvinist or German Reformed territories in the Reich. In almost all of them, the characteristic democratic Calvinist church institutions were adapted to the structure of the German territorial church created by the Lutheran Reformation. The Lutheran ecclesiastical council was simply renamed consistory and superintendents became inspectors. In Nassau and three of the other Wetterau counties, the Herborn Synod of 1586 resolved to adopt the presbyterial system specified by the Middelburg Church Ordinance of 1585 as the norm for all

---

[14] Schilling, 'Reformation und Bürgerfreiheit'; Gross, *Empire*, 108; Schindling and Ziegler, *Territorien*, iii, 169–78.
[15] Cameron, *Reformation*, 370–1; Schindling and Ziegler, *Territorien*, v, 18–44.
[16] Schmidt, *Konfessionalisierung*, 47–8; Press, *Kriege*, 145.
[17] Cohn, 'Princes', 136–7 (a map) and *passim*; Schmidt, *Konfessionalisierung*, 44–5.

Western European Calvinists. Pastors were elected by presbyters, who were themselves elected by the community; and the ruler was made answerable to the synod. However, the count continued to 'control the church through his ecclesiastical council, superintendents and visitations; he also financed the church and regulated marriages'.[18]

For all the theological and cultural differences between the three confessions, the reforms carried out in their name had significant features in common. Though a religious experience on the part of a ruler was crucial in most cases, territorial ambitions were also paramount. The establishment of a territorial church went hand in hand with the aspiration to consolidate a territory geographically and to make its government more effective. Taking responsibility for the church also meant assuming responsibility for a range of related institutions. The administration of the great mass of charitable foundations—hospitals, poor houses, orphanages, and the like—meshed naturally with the social and welfare functions implied in the *Polizeiordnungen*.

Educational institutions were of greater strategic and political importance. The expansion of government functions and the consequent inflation in personnel generated an exceptional demand for educated officials. At the same time, the definition of confessions and the elaboration of theological systems required both academic theologians and academic teachers to instruct and train the clergy. While, formerly, the Imperial Cities had led the way in both higher and lower education, their role was now eclipsed by the initiatives taken by territorial rulers throughout the Reich. Between 1500 and 1618, the number of students in the Reich had nearly doubled from around 4,200 in 1500 to about 8,000, with much of the increase achieved following a sharp decline in numbers in the 1520s and 1530s.[19]

For the Catholic rulers, the problem was that only seven universities remained under their control after 1556.[20] Three of them (Mainz, Trier, and Erfurt) were all but extinct and the other four (Cologne, Vienna, Freiburg, and Ingolstadt) were in the throes of varying degrees of crisis. Indeed, despite the arrival of the Jesuits in 1551, Vienna effectively became a Protestant university under Maximilian II. The establishment of Jesuit seminaries did not begin to make a noticeable impact until the mid-1570s.

The Catholic secular and ecclesiastical territories of the Reich were not adequately provided with theological colleges and schools, the latter with Jesuit innovations such as training in physical education and drama to complement the usual academic curriculum, until the early seventeenth century. The engagement of key rulers such as the Duke of Bavaria or Archduke Karl II in inner Austria was critical, as was the pressure from the new permanent nuncios established by the papacy. However, cathedral chapters and the diocesan clergy often impeded progress, since

---

[18] Cohn, 'Princes', 158–9.

[19] Eulenburg, *Frequenz*, 76; Rosa di Simone, 'Admission', 303–4. Another sharp drop during the Thirty Years War was followed by a recovery to around 8,000 by 1700; there was a steady decline from 1735–40. The figures are unreliable in detail, since they incorporate many variables and estimates for missing data. The general pattern seems, however, to be accurate.

[20] *HdtBG*, i, 312–32; Hammerstein, *Bildung*, 35–43.

they resisted what they perceived to be papal interference with their rights. The full effect of the eleven Jesuit foundations between 1552 and 1616, the establishment of new universities at Augsburg (Dillingen 1553), Prague (Olmütz 1573), Würzburg (1575), and Graz (1586), and the elaboration of a network of secondary schools, was not evident until well into the seventeenth century.

The situation was better in the Lutheran territories, which contained eight of the universities established before the Reformation. Of those, five became Protestant during the 1530s, and between 1527 (Marburg) and 1623 (Altdorf) a further seven were newly founded.[21] Initially, the Protestant universities laboured under the significant disadvantage that they were unable to gain either imperial or papal legitimation for their degrees.[22] The older universities simply continued to operate under their medieval charters, despite doubts about the legality of doing so. In Marburg, however, doctorates were awarded without formal recognition until 1541, when Philip of Hessen finally managed to acquire an imperial charter.

When the foundation of Königsberg was discussed, advice was sought from both Melanchthon and the Leipzig humanist Joachim Camerarius, and both of them declared that teaching in theology must be free of papal or imperial sanctions.[23] In so far as a faculty merely issued certificates (*testimonia*) rather than degrees, they saw no problem. The conferral of doctorates in medicine and law was more problematic, though they could not suggest a remedy. The situation at Königsberg was complicated by the fact that the Duchy of Prussia, the secularized territory of the Teutonic Order, technically lay outside the Reich, and Charles V did not recognize Duke Albrecht as a vassal.[24] The Duke even applied to Rome, though, predictably, without success. A solution was found in 1560, when Königsberg received a charter from the King of Poland, Duke Albrecht's overlord since the Duchy of Prussia was a fiefdom of the Polish kingdom. Meanwhile, in the Reich, the precedent of the Marburg charter of 1541 led the Reichshofrat to grant new charters both to old institutions that had become Lutheran and to new foundations. After the Peace of Augsburg, this became more or less automatic.

Although the Lutheran university was essentially an adaptation of the pre-Reformation tradition, the most significant innovation emerged from Imperial Cities and small territories that could not afford such an expense. Often pre-Reformation Latin schools were reformed and expanded. In Hamburg (1529), Lübeck (1531), and Schleswig (1542), Johannes Bugenhagen established higher schools (Gymnasiums) that aimed to prepare local students for university study elsewhere, in particular to select those to whom the magistrates would award grants for further study.[25]

---

[21] The other new foundations were Königsberg (1544), Jena (1558), Helmstedt (1576), Giessen (1607), Rinteln and Strassburg (1621). The older foundations that were reformed were: Heidelberg, Leipzig, Rostock, Greifswald, Basle, Tübingen, Frankfurt an der Oder, and Wittenberg. *HdtBG*, i, 286–9.

[22] *HdtBG*, i, 290.

[23] Hammerstein, *Bildung*, 23–4; Gundermann, 'Anfänge'; Moeller, 'Königsberg'.

[24] See pp. 22–31, 257–9.

[25] *HdtBG*, i, 296.

The school established in Strassburg was perhaps the most influential of all. In the 1530s, Martin Bucer and Johann Sturm felt the need for an alternative to sending Strassburg students to Marburg or to Wittenberg. In 1538–9, Sturm opened what later became known as the Gymnasium Illustre.[26] By 1544, it was attracting some 600 students and was being widely imitated, with varying degrees of success, by other Imperial Cities and small territories.[27] The Strassburg magistrates, however, fostered grander ambitions. In 1566, they persuaded the Reichshofrat to recognize their courses as equivalent to the bachelor's degree, and confirmation of the school's status as a *semiuniversitas* soon led to the plea for a regular university charter, which was finally granted in 1621.[28]

While considerable energy was devoted to the reform or foundation of universities and to the establishment of similar institutions, the Lutheran territories also invested in secondary schooling to a greater degree than the Catholics.[29] In Augsburg, where one-quarter of the population was Catholic in 1623, there were twenty Protestant teachers but only four Catholics, to teach 1,550 Protestant schoolchildren and 240 Catholic schoolchildren.[30] Here too, however, the needs of the territorial government were paramount. Latin schools which might be expected to produce pastors and officials were, by and large, given precedence over German schools. In Württemberg and Brunswick-Wolfenbüttel, the old monastic foundations were retained and transformed into seminaries: again, the focus was on the social function of those educated; pastors were, after all, agents of government.

The German Reformed territories experienced different problems but also developed a different attitude to education to that of both Catholics and Lutherans.[31] Since they were not included in the religious peace, there could be no question of their being granted imperial or papal charters. Geneva had circumvented the King of France's denial of a charter by seeking one from the provinces of the northern Netherlands; Leiden sought to extend the validity of its degrees, granted without either imperial or papal charter, to England and France.[32] For the German territories and Imperial Cities, however, being part of the legal-constitutional system of the Reich, which they had no wish to reject even if they had been able to, posed fundamental problems. Only two universities became Reformed by virtue of the conversion of their rulers: Heidelberg in 1559 (and again in 1584) and Marburg in 1606, though both folded during the Thirty Years War. Similarly, the Gymnasium founded at Zerbst by the Count of Anhalt in 1582 became Reformed when its ruler converted in 1596. Further higher schools, more viable than many a

[26] The standard work is Schindling, *Hochschule*. See also Hammerstein, *Bildung*, 27–9; *HdtBG*, i, 293–5.

[27] Schindling and Ziegler, *Territorien*, v, 81; *HdtBG*, i, 295–8.

[28] *HdtBG*, i, 295.

[29] Schmidt, *Konfessionalisierung*, 23–4.

[30] Warmbrunn, *Zwei Konfessionen*, 293.

[31] Hammerstein, *Bildung*, 33–5; *HdtBG*, i, 298–9.

[32] Menk, *Herborn*, 105–6.

university, were founded in Steinfurt in the County of Bentheim, in Bremen, Danzig, and in Beuthen in Upper Silesia.[33]

The most successful of all the Reformed educational enterprises was the academy established at Herborn by Johann VI of Nassau-Dillingen in 1584. Though modelled on the Strassburg academy and its successors, Herborn surpassed them all. Within a short time it became established as the prototype of the European Calvinist academy, attracting students from Transylvania, Lithuania, Norway, and Scotland, as well as from all parts of the Reich.[34] Indeed, for a while, Herborn was arguably more significant internationally than any university in the Reich.

Originally founded in order to reduce the cost of educating the count's sons, Herborn had the good fortune to have been planned at a time when there was a ready supply of crypto-Calvinist exiles from the Palatinate and Saxony. It also benefited from Count Johann VI's exceptionally comprehensive vision of further reform and his inspired appointment of Johannes Piscator (1546–1625) as the first professor of philosophy.[35] Piscator had been educated at the Strassburg school and Tübingen. He had previously taught at Heidelberg and directed the Elector's Latin preparatory school, the Paedagogium. He brought to Herborn a mix of the Philippist tradition of Melanchthon and Bucer, of conventional Aristotelianism, and the new (anti-Aristotelian) principles of Ramism. In Piscator's star pupil, Johann Heinrich Alsted (1588–1638), Herborn both fulfilled its local role in educating a native son of Nassau and developed a European-wide intellectual mission, transmitted through Alsted's own student Johann Amos Comenius (1592–1670), which helped leaven the philosophical–scientific ferment of seventeenth-century England.[36]

Just as remarkable, and not confined to Nassau, was the attention given by Reformed territories to both secondary and elementary education.[37] Unlike the Catholics and the Lutherans, the Reformed churches emphasized basic universal literacy as a goal, both for religious reasons and, similar to the thinking behind the militia schemes, to create territorial patriots through education. Even so, the reality fell considerably short of the ideal. The network of schools in Nassau was impressive enough once Herborn began to supply sufficient teachers from around 1590: it extended to village schools and taught girls as well as boys. As a result, more people could read, but that did not constitute a real literacy revolution. Elementary literacy did not remove the educational barrier between town and country, and the Latin schools were still effectively restricted to the sons of officials, pastors, and skilled guild craftsmen. More significant than its effect on the Nassau peasantry was probably the role that the Nassau lower-school system played in the formation of Comenius's educational theories in the 1650s. For Comenius's ideas ultimately had a wider European impact, not least on the educational thinking of John Locke.

---

[33] Hammerstein, *Bildung*, 126.
[34] Hotson, *Alsted*, 6–7; Hammerstein, *Bildung*, 126–7.
[35] Hotson, *Alsted*, 17–20.
[36] Hotson, *Alsted*, esp.1–2, 7, 229.
[37] Menk, 'Territorialstaat', *passim*; Schmidt, *Konfessionalisierung*, 54.

Looking at the Reich as a whole, reformations, further reformations, and Catholic reforms or Counter-Reformations, are spread across the whole period between the Peace of Augsburg in 1555 and the Thirty Years War.[38] Some took place early on, others later; some were implemented swiftly, others were slow and piecemeal; some were successful, others failed either outright or partially. Those mentioned so far were, on the whole, in territories that were either already reasonably consolidated, or at least more or less under the control of a single ruler or dynasty.

Much greater problems arose where a ruler sought to impose his will on the territorial nobility or on towns, for both could claim exemption and prior rights and privileges, and assert them successfully.[39] Equally, the neighbours of powerful princes could either be carried along in their wake or driven to assert differences. Of the counties neighbouring Electoral Saxony, for example, some followed the Elector's lead, while others like Reuss went their own way with a distinctive 'local' confession and a successful transfer from Saxon to Bohemian vassalage.[40]

In the prince-bishoprics of Speyer and Worms, it was the Palatinate that posed a serious threat of annexation. In Speyer, the situation was made more dangerous by the fact that Bishop Marquard von Hattstein (r. 1560–81) was a lukewarm Catholic and was even rumoured to be a secret Schwenckfeldian. However, the noble canons in his cathedral chapter had no intention of becoming Palatine fiefs and thus losing both their political independence and their benefices, and it was they who became the backbone of an early Catholic revival.[41] In Worms, the bishops and the cathedral chapter were more united in their stand against their powerful neighbour and fought their cause on a political level with complaints at the Reichstag and in the imperial courts. The Catholic revival there, and a degree of territorial consolidation, only gained ground under Bishop Wilhelm von Effern (r. 1604–16), and the prince-bishopric only really found security when Bishop Georg Friedrich von Greiffenklau (r. 1616–29) also became Archbishop of Mainz in 1626 and was able to take Worms under a more powerful wing.[42]

Things became even more complicated, and sometimes impossible, in areas where jurisdictions overlapped or in condominiums where two, three, or even four dynasties simply could not agree.[43] Even the Habsburg rulers of the Tyrol were unable to enforce uniformity on their scattered Swabian territories in Further Austria: notably the Counties of Hohenberg and Sigmaringen, the Landgravate of Nellenburg, the Margravate of Burgau, and the Landvogtei of Upper and Lower Swabia.[44] Similarly, in the lands of many Imperial Knights, whose right to

---

[38] Schindling and Ziegler, *Territorien*, vii, 20–3.
[39] Schneider, *Ius reformandi*, 256–65.
[40] Schindling and Ziegler, *Territorien* iv, 29–34.
[41] Wolgast, *Hochstift*, 303–6; Press, 'Hochstift Speyer', 262–3.
[42] Wolgast, *Hochstift*, 320–1.
[43] Gotthard, *Religionsfrieden*, 292–316; Schneider, *Ius reformandi*, 242–56.
[44] On Burgau, see Schiersner, *Politik*, 31–163, 202–44, 433–9. On *Vorderösterreich* generally, see Schindling and Ziegler, *Territorien*, v, 256–77 and Quarthal, 'Vorderösterreich'. *Landvogtei* of Upper and Lower Swabia was a collection of seigneurial, judicial, and property rights rather than a territory as such.

ecclesiastical authority was disputed anyway, any decision on religious matters was often postponed for as long as possible, unless it was simply determined by deference to the nearest territorial prince or to the court at which a knight served.[45] It is difficult to estimate the percentage of either the geographical area or the population of the Reich that was not subjected to any form of confessionalization between 1555 and 1618. However, the wide distribution throughout the Reich of local and regional impediments to any such process, of confessional 'no man's lands', significantly qualifies the impression that has sometimes been given of a social disciplining of the entire German population.[46]

This suggests caution in reaching any secure evaluation of just how successful the confessionalization process, in all of its many variations, really was. On the one hand, the developments that unfolded after 1555, broadly speaking, did determine the confessional map in contours that remain discernible even in the twenty-first century.[47] On the other hand, the religious and cultural differences, which make much of south Germany and the Rhineland obviously Catholic and much of north Germany just as obviously Protestant, developed over a century or more. In the period between the Peace of Augsburg and the Thirty Years War, things were often confused and fluid. Until the confessional situation became clearer in the first half of the seventeenth century, many religious groups negotiated a delicate path to gain acceptance and security in what were de facto multi-confessional and pluralist communities.[48]

Some use was evidently made of the powers that the Peace of Augsburg gave rulers to impose their will in religious matters.[49] The Protestant Estates complained to the emperor in December 1570 that the religious peace was being undermined by rulers who drove out subjects because they did not share their religion. In 1582, they complained that subjects were being driven from their 'fatherlands' on grounds of religion, even though they were 'otherwise, in political things', obedient to their rulers. Apart from such complaints and the cases that came before the Reichskammergericht with some regularity, little is known about the extent or the impact of such migration.[50] The legislation itself was ambiguous, unclear as to whether it really gave subjects the right to emigrate or rulers the right to expel. Some were undoubtedly driven out. There is no distinction to be made between Catholic, Lutheran, and Reformed rulers. However, there does seem to have been some difference in the treatment of Anabaptists.[51] Eighty-four per cent of all

---

[45] Gotthard, *Religionsfrieden*, 242–3, 287–8; Schneider, *Ius reformandi*, 237–41.

[46] Schindling and Ziegler, *Territorien*, vii, 24–8.

[47] Gotthard, *Religionsfrieden*, 19–20, 282–92.

[48] Spohnholz, *Tactics* is a fascinating study of Calvinists, Lutherans, Catholics, Mennonites, and other dissenters in Wesel (Kleve).

[49] Gotthard, *Religionsfrieden*, 119, 243–5, 284–5, 345, 527–35, 551–4. For a general discussion, see also Schunka, 'Glaubensflucht' and Schäufele, 'Konsequenzen', 123–7. May, 'Zum "ius emigrandi"' contains much relevant information, though his perspective is skewed by the notion that Protestants who emigrated did so in search of adventure or better economic opportunities; neither is plausible.

[50] Ruthmann, *Reichskammergericht*, 296–310. For examples of the fairly numerous legal cases at the Reichskammergericht relating to this issue, see Ehrenpreis and Ruthmann, 'Jus emigrandi'.

[51] Schäufele, 'Konsequenzen', 127.

executions of Anabaptists between 1525 and 1618 were carried out by Catholic rulers. In territories such as Hessen, by contrast, they were imprisoned rather than executed, and, in isolated instances, such as in the town of Krefeld that belonged to the Reformed County of Moers, they were even openly tolerated.

As to how much use was made of a subject's right to leave of his or her own free will, the obligation to pay a departure tax of up to 30 per cent of an individual's total wealth surely makes it unlikely that many could, or would wish to, do so.[52] Many no doubt stayed and paid lip service to the official religion, but how effectively were they then 'confessionalized'?

Visitations, whether Catholic, Lutheran, or Reformed, often expressed shock and horror at the degree of irreligion that prevailed in the countryside. This was hardly surprising in view of the disruption that many areas had experienced since the late 1530s. Many parishes were without clergy for decades at a time. That did not necessarily mean a lack of religion, but rather it meant that often rather strange forms of demotic Christianity flourished. The Reformed visitation officials in the Upper Palatinate in the late sixteenth century were certainly startled to be informed that the people thereabouts believed in three gods, and sometimes in a goddess as well.[53]

The bewilderment and disappointment frequently experienced by visitation officials indicates that something of a gulf had opened up between the officialdom of the territorial governments and the social and cultural conditions that they experienced on their travels. Fired up with late humanist ideals of reform, further reform, or renewal, they were perhaps inevitably frustrated by what they experienced as superstitious irreligion. Indeed, the reform of churches, the very process of constructing confessions, distanced them from the very communities they were designed to serve. Church hierarchies became bureaucratized and concerned with procedure. Where churches were shaped into effective agencies of confessionalization they often suffered precisely from the fact that they were also agencies of government, little more welcome in the village than the tax collector.

Where a church had successfully defined its confession and system of belief, it had often become intellectualized and academic. For the definition of confessions took place in the theology faculties and was not easily translated into the language and concerns of the common man. Indeed, evidence from some areas, both Lutheran and Catholic, suggests that over the long term, attempted confessionalization from above was paralleled by other communities holding on to their own ideas of 'Christian community' through repeated changes in the official religion. This certainly seems to have been the case in Upper Hessen, which became Lutheran in 1576, Calvinist in 1605, and Lutheran again in 1624.[54] It was also true of the Upper Palatinate, where the official religion changed five times up to and including the reintroduction of Catholicism in 1621.[55] Studies of Catholic areas

---

[52] Gotthard, *Religionsfrieden*, 529.
[53] Press, *Kriege*, 136. For an excellent account of Lutheran visitations, see Strauss, *House of learning*, 249–99.
[54] Mayes, *Communal Christianity*, 23–204.
[55] Rabe, *Geschichte*, 562.

show that Catholic identities developed even where there was no strong government intervention. Where government intervention was persistent it was most successful when it adapted to communal traditions and forms of piety that had their origins in the late Middle Ages.[56]

In some senses, those who were most successfully confessionalized in the decades after 1555 were the new elites of the territorial governments themselves. These included 'lawyers, professors, school teachers, the clergy, city magistrates, merchants, guild masters, students, village elders, rich peasants, petty functionaries, rural artisans'.[57] For these groups, the celebration of the fiftieth anniversary of the Augsburg Confession in 1580 was probably just as significant as the specification of theological tenets in the Formula of Concord in reinforcing a sense of solidarity and of identity rooted in a common history. The celebration of the centenary of the Reformation in 1617 (the first 'modern' centenary) was similarly one of political as well as religious identity. It was a reminder of the ways in which the Reformation had not only introduced correct teaching, but also transformed the constitutional structure of territories, towns, and Imperial Cities, as well as that of the Reich itself.[58]

On occasion, though, Estates and towns could become rebels against a ruler's attempt to impose his religion on his territory.[59] The Saxon Estates successfully resisted Christian I's (r. 1586–91) attempts to introduce the Reformed confession. Likewise, the Estates of Baden-Durlach resisted the wishes of Margrave Ernst Friedrich (r. 1584–1604), and the Estates of Hessen-Kassel rejected the Reformed beliefs of their ruler Landgrave Moritz (r. 1592–1632, but abdicated 1627).[60] In 1600, Count Simon VI of Lippe (r. 1579–1613) sought to round off an ambitious programme of general reform and consolidation with a Reformed Church ordinance. But he soon found himself embroiled in a bitter struggle with his own capital city, Lemgo, whose magistrates and population refused to abandon their Lutheran beliefs, and by 1617 succeeded in forcing the count to recognize their religious autonomy.[61] Similarly, Lutheran Gütersloh held out against the Reformed Counts of Bentheim, just as Reformed Emden did against the Lutheran Counts of East Frisia.[62] Even the larger territories sometimes had to contend with fierce local or regional resistance. Despite the best efforts of Friedrich IV (r. 1583–1610), Friedrich V (r. 1610–23), and their stadtholder in Amberg, Christian of Anhalt, the Upper Palatinate remained predominantly Lutheran. And when the Elector Johann Sigismund of Brandenburg converted to Calvinism in 1613, not one of his many territories agreed to follow his religious choice.[63]

---

[56] Forster, *Catholic revival*, 1–5, 18–60.

[57] Po-chia Hsia, *Social discipline*, 143.

[58] Sandl, 'Interpretationswelten'; Leppin, 'Antichrist'; Schönstädt, *Antichrist*, 10–13; Gotthard, *Altes Reich*, 80–2.

[59] Schmidt, *Konfessionalisierung*, 99–100; Cameron, *Reformation*, 371–2.

[60] Po-chia Hsia, *Social discipline*, 35–6.

[61] Schilling, *Konfessionskonflikt*, 40–4, 152–351.

[62] Schmidt, *Konfessionalisierung*, 49.

[63] The County of Mark was, of course, already largely Reformed: Schindling and Ziegler, *Territorien*, iii, 102–3.

On the one hand, there were few places in the Reich where it could be said that the creation of a confessional identity was complete by 1618. On the other hand, the question of the relationship between political authority and religious affiliation had been posed at some point since 1555 in most areas. It was also clear overall that, while the structures of the Reich as a whole had been secularized, the construction of territorial churches was an irreversible feature of the development of its constituent parts.

44

Finance, Taxation, and Estates

The expanding functions of territorial government, rising military costs, and the inflation of court costs imposed unprecedented financial burdens. While some of the costs of establishing a territorial church were covered by the conversion of ecclesiastical property and foundations, others, such as the expense of a new university or higher school, were not. Typically, in the larger territories roughly half of all revenue was devoted to the court, to administration, and to buildings.[1] Dealing with these rising costs and struggling to cope with an ever-increasing burden of debt was itself part of the developmental process that characterized most of the larger territories in the sixteenth century. Indeed, the whole problem of finance showed up a growing distinction between larger and smaller territories of the Reich. The smallest units ended up still looking like large, noble, landed estates managed as demesnes, while others developed a full structure of territorial government similar to the systems developed by monarchies elsewhere in Europe. In particular, the sixteenth century saw a growing reliance on regular taxation. A tenfold increase in the burden of direct taxes has been estimated for the period 1500–1650, though for Bavaria the increase has been estimated at 2,200 per cent between 1480 and 1660.[2] Such substantial increases inevitably had serious political implications.

Most territories had developed a basic property tax, the 'bede' or 'datz', applied to all except the nobility and the clergy, and payable on a regular basis between one and three times a year, during the thirteenth century.[3] This was, however, generally fixed at the point of introduction and not raised subsequently. Steady inflation thus severely reduced its value in the long term. In Brandenburg by the early seventeenth century, for example, this 'Ur-Bede' or original tax comprised no more than a maximum of 3 per cent of the Elector's income.[4] In addition to this, further occasional taxes were levied for special purposes: for a war, for the dowry of a prince's eldest daughter, or, in the case of ecclesiastical territories, to pay the fees that a newly elected bishop had to send to Rome on his consecration and installation. More viable over a longer term, were various forms of excise duties, such as taxes imposed on wine and beer, and often extended to other products. Even these, however, were limited and not capable of meeting vastly increased costs.

---

[1] Lanzinner, 'Finanzen', 298.
[2] Edelmayer et al., 'Einleitung'; 13; Schulze, *Deutsche Geschichte*, 221.
[3] Schubert, *Einführung*, 203–4; Haberkern and Wallach, *Hilfswörterbuch*, i, 65.
[4] Klein, *Finanzen*, 14–15.

The most important traditional source of income was what came from demesne lands, either agricultural land or forest, directly managed by a ruler or leased out, or from rents and dues paid by peasants.[5] In addition, some territories benefited from mining metals or salt, from mints, or from toll dues. Saxony and its neighbouring counties and the Tyrol, for example, derived significant income from mining: around 1550 about half of the Saxon Elector's income came from various mineral rights and mining enterprises; in the 1520s, some three-quarters of the income of the ruler of the Tyrol derived from silver mining. Hessen, Cologne, and Kleve derived significant income from Rhine tolls, while other territories also relied on road, river, and bridge tolls: in the Austrian duchies, these accounted for roughly a quarter of total income, while in Brandenburg around 1600 they generated between 35–45 per cent of all income.

There is considerable evidence that the exploitation of demesne property and regalian rights intensified during the course of the sixteenth century. Indeed, some rulers became positively entrepreneurial. The development of *Gutsherrschaft* or demesne lordship east of the Elbe was one essentially entrepreneurial response to the need for more income and the perception of a growing profitable market for agricultural produce.[6] Equivalent initiatives designed to intensify farming or forestry operations and maximize income from them are found elsewhere in the Reich.

Some rulers not only produced for the market but also engaged in processing the produce. Regalian rights, especially mineral rights, were also exploited more intensively. The Dukes of Bavaria generally tried to get private individuals to exploit a mineral resource initially, but then attempted to take over a going concern.[7] A number of north German rulers were involved in highly commercialized agricultural production combined with trade in agricultural products and fish, and activities such as rearing livestock.[8] The Counts of Mansfeld in Thuringia were engaged in processing copper ore to extract silver, and entered into formal commercial agreements with neighbouring dynasties such as the Counts of Henneberg and Stolberg to enhance their production.[9] The Elector of Saxony was a regular investor in such enterprises, in addition to running his own substantial agricultural and mining concerns. In some cases, the pursuit of profit produced quite extraordinary results. Duke Julius of Brunswick-Wolfenbüttel (r. 1568–89) was the most successful princely entrepreneur of his generation: his factories and workshops produced everything from brass boxes to garden ornaments, chess sets, firearms, cannons, and cannon balls made of slag.[10]

Margrave Johann of Küstrin, brother of Elector Joachim II of Brandenburg, who ruled the principality of Brandenburg-Küstrin (a territory created for him as a younger son, largely comprising the Neumark and a number of neighbouring

---

[5] For the following see Klein, *Finanzen*, 12–14.
[6] Scott, *Society*, 188–93.
[7] *HBayG*, i, 1673–80.
[8] Redlich, 'Unternehmer', 20–6.
[9] Redlich, 'Unternehmer', 18–20, 21–2.
[10] Redlich, 'Unternehmer', 98–102. On the duke's mining interests, see Kraschewski, 'Organisationsstrukturen' and Kraschewski, 'Kohlenbergbau'.

lordships) between 1535 and 1571, was equally exceptional. His skill in the international money markets enabled him to increase his capital by a factor of twelve over thirty years. Even allowing for inflation, he generated a handsome profit, which made him one of those rare princes who not only died without debt but with assets of 569,108 thaler (some 780,000 gulden).[11]

A ruler who left such a substantial fortune was rare. Most left a more complicated legacy. Some managed to build up a secret treasury that was kept for use in emergencies or for exceptional expenditures and personal gifts. On his death in 1586, the Elector August of Saxony was found to have amassed the huge sum of 1.8 million gulden. Yet he also both inherited extensive debts and incurred further debt himself: in 1570, for example, the Saxon Estates took over no less than 3.1 million gulden of debt, without which his substantial legacy to his son in 1586 would have been impossible.[12] The practice of quietly diverting funds into a secret treasury seems to have been fairly common among the more powerful rulers, particularly those who played an active role in imperial politics. Yet even for those who did this, the norm was that debts were inherited, increased, and simply passed on to the next generation. The most intensive exploitation of demesne rarely generated enough to cover the rapidly rising costs of government and court.

Governments increasingly needed money, yet their demesne revenues did not always come in convenient forms. The accounts of Hessen under Landgrave Philip the Good around 1550 show that, besides money, over sixty types of goods in kind were used as the basis for calculation of income: everything from apples to goats.[13] Hessen was well administered, in that the landgrave knew exactly what he was worth. His detailed accounts provided an excellent basis for the quadripartite division of his lands on his death in 1567. His eldest son, Wilhelm IV of Hessen-Kassel, used them to compile a ruler's handbook, his 'ökonomischer Staat' (literally, household economy or accounts), that remained among the personal working papers of his descendants into the eighteenth century.[14] Philip of Hessen derived income from demesne property, from salt mining, Rhine tolls and some fifty land tolls, and from foreign subsidies (for example, from the king of France). Yet he was still continuously dependent on loans. In 1544, for example, he had to borrow the relatively small sum of 5,000 gulden in Frankfurt so that he could afford the 35,100 gulden cost of attending the Speyer Reichstag with his retinue. Throughout his rule, bailiwicks were continuously being mortgaged off and redeemed, and, despite excellent management, he left his sons a debt of 823,650 gulden.[15]

The fate of that debt is typical of the trend for the period. Philip's four sons jointly paid off 195,328 gulden and then divided a further 137,360 gulden of urgent debts between them. The rest was transferred to the Hessen Estates, which

---

[11] Redlich, 'Unternehmer', 104–8.
[12] Schirmer, 'Finanzen', 179–83; Klein, *Finanzen*, 17–18.
[13] Krüger, *Finanzstaat*, 35.
[14] Zimmermann, *Staat*, xxi–xxii.
[15] Krüger, *Finanzstaat*, 225–45.

then paid them off by means of taxes.[16] Hessen, like most other territories in the Reich, came to depend increasingly on more regular and higher taxes. Until 1529, demesne income accounted for some 90 per cent of all revenue; by 1540–9 it comprised only 59 per cent. Over the same period, the proportion of income generated by taxation rose from 10 per cent to 38 per cent.[17] Figures for the period 1550–86 for the Electorate of Saxony, by far the most prosperous of all territories with an annual income from demesne and tolls of around 500,000 gulden a year, are similar: on average, taxation made up 42 per cent of total income.[18]

Two related remedies were increasingly employed to maintain the solvency of a territory: taxation and the assumption of debt by the territorial Estates. The irregular general taxes previously levied on special occasions, such as the *Fräulein-steuer* for the dowry of a princess, became more frequent during the course of the sixteenth century. At the same time, there was a change in the way in which taxation was applied. Many rulers, including Philip of Hessen, preferred to move away from a system whereby taxes were apportioned to towns and bailiwicks. The towns certainly preferred a system of wealth taxes that spread the tax more fairly and enabled the inclusion of the nobility and their peasants.

The arguments used to justify the increasingly regular imposition of extraordinary taxes were crucially strengthened by the decision made at the Reichstag in 1530 that the levies for the Turkish wars might be passed on to a ruler's subjects.[19] Since these levies became a regular occurrence after 1555, the territorial taxes imposed to pay for them followed suit. Equally, governments saw the opportunity to use these taxes, effectively promulgated in the name of the emperor and the Reich, simultaneously to raise additional sums for other, purely territorial, purposes. In Hessen, for example, Landgrave Philip regularly levied up to triple the amount that he needed in order to pay his dues to the Reich.[20] His tax receipts increased hugely with the successful transition to a wealth tax, while the old *Landsteuer* was more or less confined to its original purpose of raising money for the dowry of princesses.[21] In Brandenburg, by contrast, the *Fräuleinsteuer* was a more or less annual tax in the early seventeenth century.[22]

Parallel to the increase in level and regularity of ordinary taxes, from about 1550 rulers such as Philip of Hessen also made substantial increases in indirect taxes. The medieval Hessen beer tax had become insignificant by the early sixteenth century, but in 1533 it was reintroduced for four years to finance new fortifications; then from 1555 it was established as a regular, and steadily increasing, excise duty.[23] Almost everywhere, however, the assessment and collection of taxes remained fairly haphazard. In Hessen, for example, assessment was effectively self-assessment by means of personal declarations under oath.[24] The actual collection of taxes was

[16] Krüger, *Finanzstaat*, 242.   [17] Krüger, *Finanzstaat*, 299–300.
[18] Schirmer, 'Finanzen', 150.   [19] Schwennicke, *Steuer*, 49–54.
[20] Krüger, *Finanzstaat*, 288–90.   [21] Krüger, *Finanzstaat*, 294.
[22] Klein, *Finanzen*, 14–15.   [23] Krüger, *Finanzstaat*, 279–84; Schwennicke, *Steuer*, 79–87.
[24] Krüger, *Finanzstaat*, 268.

often liable to be subverted by embezzlement, even where officials were paid well and regularly.

Whatever the form it took and however inefficient its collection and allocation, there is no doubt that regular taxation was a feature of almost all the German territories by the end of the sixteenth century. In this respect, too, a difference became clear between those Imperial Estates that could levy taxes and those that could not, on the grounds that they had too few subjects to do so meaningfully. While the tax-levying territories were not quite 'tax states', they had certainly progressed decisively from being 'demesne states' to being 'finance states' at the least. This was also reflected in the burgeoning literature on taxation and in the emphasis placed on taxation by the late sixteenth century writers on territorial government.

To some extent this was the result of commentaries on the case law that developed from the growing number of tax disputes that came before the Reichskammergericht.[25] Yet, by the 1580s, the new functions of the territorial governments were being described, explained, and justified by a widening range of political writers. Some continued to hold, in the tradition of Melchior von Osse (1505–1557), that government was ordained by God to fulfil limited public duties. These were primarily the preservation of internal and external security. Government, Osse believed, should at all times live off its own, and one of the most commonly cited principles was that 'parsimony is the best tax' ('parsimonia est optimum vectigal').[26]

By about the 1590s, this traditional theory of the 'demesne state' was being replaced. Influenced by the new theories of the state developed by Bodin and Lipsius, new watchwords came to dominate the literature. 'Money is the nerve of all things' ('pecunia nervus rerum') variously cited from either Ulpian or Tacitus, and 'Without taxes no state' ('sine tributis nullus status') cited by Lipsius from Tacitus in 1589, became the guiding maxims for a new generation of German writers.[27] The years around 1600 saw the publication of influential treatises on government finance by Eberhard von Weyhe (1553–1633?), Georg Obrecht (1547–1612), Jacob Bornitz (c. 1560–1625), and Christoph Besold (1577–1638). These were soon followed by the first publications devoted specifically to taxation, written by Caspar Klock (1583–1655), Matthias Giese (dates unknown), and Christoph Wintzler (dates unknown), whose collection of materials on taxation was reprinted several times in the years after its publication in 1608.[28]

The views of Bartholomäus Keckermann (1571–1608), who argued that the function of government was to promote public welfare ('publica felicitas'), were typical of the emerging consensus. This Calvinist professor at Heidelberg and then rector of the Danzig Gymnasium insisted that a subject had no right to resist as long as the commands of magistrates were not directed against God and his laws. Above

---

[25] Schwennicke, *Steuer*, 30–6, 102–10. [26] Schwennicke, *Steuer*, 25–9, 40–1.
[27] Schwennicke, *Steuer*, 118, 128–9.
[28] Schwennicke, *Steuer*, 110–17; Stolleis, *Pecunia*, 73–103, 127–44; Klein, *Finanzen*, 20–3. Nothing else is known about the lives of Giese and Wintzler.

all, the duties of subjects included the obligation to pay regular taxes, which would supplement demesne income.[29] As in so many other works of the time, the emphasis was on the relationship between the ruler's right to tax and his rights of jurisdiction generally. This was a logical extension of traditional regalian rights, but a ruler's right to impose taxes was now increasingly understood in the new idiom of Bodin's notions of state sovereignty. It was an attribute of the 'majestas' of a ruler.[30]

Increasing taxation was not, however, simply an attribute of the consolidation of princely power. All taxes had to be asked for, though the status of the request was ambivalent. The original terms 'bede' or 'precaria', after all, meant 'plea', but at the same time an old saying held that 'the requests of lords are sharp commands'.[31] In the fifteenth century, the larger territories had summoned their Estates irregularly for the purpose of raising extraordinary taxes. The Estates were summoned to the court, where they stayed as guests of the ruler. During the sixteenth century, meetings of territorial diets became more regular; they were increasingly held at locations distinct from the court, their proceedings became more formal, and they often developed their own permanent administrative structures.

There was a huge variety in the types of Estate representation. In the larger territories, the classic tricameral structure (clergy, nobles, and towns) prevailed.[32] However, in some cases the clergy disappeared as an Estate after the Reformation and remained, if at all, as a group of government functionaries. This served to strengthen the position of the nobility relative to the towns. In other cases, the nobility divided into two houses, as in some of the Habsburg territories, where titled nobles distinguished themselves from mere knights. This either resulted in the perpetuation of a tricameral system, where the clerical chamber had disappeared, or led to the evolution of a four-chamber system.[33] In those areas such as Baden, Württemberg, and the Franconian territories, in which the nobility had 'broken out' of the territorial framework in the early sixteenth century to become Imperial Knights or Imperial Counts, the Estates were generally composed of clergy, towns, and representatives of the districts or bailiwicks.

In some smaller southern territories (for example, Kempten and Berchtesgaden), as well as along the North Sea coast in Schleswig and Holstein, there were assemblies composed of peasants (Landschaften), rather than diets. Finally, some ecclesiastical territories, such as Worms, Speyer, Eichstätt, Regensburg, Freising, and Mainz, had no institutionalized Estates at all, and here the cathedral chapters would often assume responsibility for taxation and financial control. Similarly, the smallest territories of Imperial Knights and Imperial Counts did not have assemblies of Estates, though they communicated with their subjects in other, less formally institutionalized, ways. In Silesia, the territorial diet was essentially a

[29] Krüger, *Finanzstaat*, 20–3.
[30] Stolleis, *Öffentliches recht*, i, 154–86; Schwennicke, *Steuer*, 110–11.
[31] Schubert, *Spätmittelalter*, 203–4.
[32] Two excellent surveys are Lanzinner, 'Zeitalter', 89–90 and Press, 'Formen'. The most comprehensive bibliography is Krüger, *Verfassung*, 87–140.
[33] The Tyrol developed a four-chamber system because the peasantry was also represented through the representatives of the local courts.

gathering of the princes, including the Bishop of Breslau, while each constituent principality had its own local diet as well.[34]

The various types of diets and assemblies differed in their effectiveness. The most influential were those diets where the nobility was represented. During the sixteenth century, some developed an acute sense of their role and status, which was expressed in the construction of ornate meeting houses every bit as grand and as representative as the residence of the prince himself. The Mecklenburg Estates traditionally met in a field just outside the town of Sternberg; the duke held court in a tent but all negotiations took place in the open air.[35] The peasant assemblies along the North Sea coasts, by contrast, were really more concerned with dyke management and coastal defences.[36]

In general, as the terms 'Landtag' and 'Landschaft' imply, the Estates represented the territory. Indeed, in a sense they *were* the territory in that they generally included the holders of all subordinate powers and rights in the territory. They played a role in the development of most kinds of legislation. They frequently protested against the incursions of new legal codes or anything else that chipped away at corporate or communal rights, privileges, and traditions. Yet, fundamentally, they wanted law, order, and stability as much as a ruler did. Princely prerogatives and authority needed recognition as much as noble privileges or urban and communal rights. Meetings of diets routinely involved both acts of homage to the ruler and affirmations of the rights of subjects. Rulers and ruled were mutually dependent in so many ways.

As guarantors of a territory, the Estates frequently ensured its survival, for example in the face of dynastic partition, the succession of a minor, or the imprisonment of its ruler by another power in war. The key institutions of a territory, such as the law courts or the university, might be held in common by the several ruling heirs of a prince. The Estates thus effectively created and monitored a kind of dynastic entail. Similarly, a diet could become the guarantor of religious continuity, particularly in the face of plans by a ruler for a second or further reformation involving far-reaching administrative reforms.

Exactly how the relationship between rulers and their diets and assemblies should be defined has been much debated.[37] The potential for antagonism and conflict was matched by the scope for harmony and cooperation. The distinction between diet and court was blurred by the fact that most diets contained a 'court party' as well as a range of government functionaries. Early modern diets and assemblies undoubtedly form part of the long prehistory of modern parliaments, yet they were neither representative nor mandated in the senses that emerged in the nineteenth century.[38] Polarity and dualism, the terms once favoured by historians, now seem inadequate as descriptions of the complex and mutually dependent, yet ultimately, of course, hierarchical, relationship between rulers and Estates. During

---

[34] Press, *Kriege*, 112.   [35] Hamann, *Werden*, 60–1.   [36] Krüger, 'Nordelbien'.
[37] A full overview of the changing perspectives since the nineteenth century can be found in Krüger, *Verfassung*, 33–84.
[38] Carsten, *Princes*, v–vii, 423–8; Krüger, *Verfassung*, 62–5.

the sixteenth century, the key point is that diets, and to a lesser extent assemblies, contributed to the elaboration of the new structures of territorial government.

This is most clearly demonstrated in relation to taxation and finance. The evolution of the imperial tax regime and the formalization of the decision-making procedures of the Reichstag provided the framework for parallel developments in the territories. The approaches that rulers made to their Estates were lent greater authority by the fact that they had been commissioned to raise taxes in the name of 'emperor and Reich'. At the same time, diets increasingly responded to those approaches in the same way that the Reichstag responded to the requests of the emperor: with formal consultation processes, with negotiation over grievances, and with formal agreement on the duration and terms of any concession.[39] In addition to agreeing taxation from time to time, both diets and assemblies were increasingly called upon to assume the debts that rulers had accumulated. The management and servicing of these debts came to be one of their prime functions.[40]

These key financial functions of Estates often led to the creation of assemblies or Landschaften where none had existed previously, and to the continuing efforts by other rulers to establish mechanisms whereby a ruler's subjects could assume his debts.[41] The Duchy of Zweibrücken formed a Landschaft in 1579 with the express twofold purpose of facilitating taxation and its administration, and of securing the duke's considerable debts on the towns and districts. In Baden, the Landschaft was created in 1558 and took over responsibility for the margrave's debts in 1582. Perhaps the most striking example of such an enterprise was the attempt by the Palatinate to solve its chronic financial problems by establishing a Landschaft in 1603.

The purely financial nature of these initiatives was not necessarily an obstacle. Many towns and districts much preferred to shoulder or guarantee a portion of debt, sometimes against an indemnity provided by the ruler, rather than be mortgaged off to another territory, since that effectively involved a change of ruler. However, the same considerations did not always apply in the smallest territories. The attempt by the nine branches of the comital house of Solms to establish a Landschaft in 1614–18 failed. Their subjects clearly saw that the only motive was to extract more money and that the counts were not much interested in their grievances, still less in advice from their subjects on household economies. When the counts then began to disagree among themselves—some of them even refused to reveal their debts—the project was doomed.[42]

Where diets existed, their growing involvement in the process of government also changed their character.[43] As the business of government became more onerous and more complex, so a diet in plenary session ceased to be an effective decision-making body. From about 1550—in some cases significantly earlier, in others considerably later—the real work was done by committees, which sent decisions or final drafts of legislation to the full diet for formal approval. Meetings

[39] Press, 'Formen', 295; Krüger, *Verfassung*, 13–17. Koken, *Landstände* is a useful study of the Brunswick estates around 1600.
[40] Press, 'Formen', 292–4.
[41] Press, 'Formen', 294–5. The following information is taken from Press, 'Steuern'.
[42] Press, 'Landschaft'.   [43] Lange, *Landtag*, 2–6.

of diets could thereby be reduced to a day or two, which many nobles favoured owing to the expense of travel and accommodation, in addition to the cost of being away from one's estate at crucial times (the costs of urban delegates were paid by the municipalities).[44]

Committees, by contrast, sometimes came to be in permanent session. This process was often encouraged by rulers, who viewed plenary sessions of a diet as cumbersome and inefficient, and as an opportunity for troublemakers to raise difficult issues. Equally, the need for frequent diets subsided once the key precedents had been set in respect of the financial issues, namely taxation and administration of debts. Thereafter, it was generally easier to deal with a small group of 'sensible' (and often corruptible) delegates than with the ignorant and obstinate mass that seemed—to a ruler's mind—to dominate the plenary diet.[45]

Parallel to the developing central agencies of territorial government, the Estates often constructed their own administrative structures as growing responsibilities necessitated organization and personnel. Many princes were more than happy to allow the promulgation and collection of taxes to be conducted in their name by their Estates. Equally, many Estates were keen to administer the money collected or to manage debts in the belief that they were thereby exercising a degree of control over how much was spent. The territorial treasuries established by diets (Landkasten or Kreditwerke) often functioned rather like banks: they consolidated government debts, employed tax income to service loans, and offered opportunities for investment.[46] The institutions developed by the Estates thus complemented the institutions of territorial government.

The diets and assemblies made a substantial contribution to the development of the territories, yet the position was changing in the decades around 1600. In some territories, the Estates maintained their position into the seventeenth century and beyond. In other areas, their position was subtly undermined. The general incompetence of territorial diets in decision-making handed the initiative to rulers and their officials. Many diets were also internally divided between the conflicting interests of nobles and towns.

Members of a diet's standing committees and their officials formed their own corporate identity over time and were increasingly more willing to accommodate a ruler's wishes than push the cause of those whom they represented in the country. This was particularly significant in finance, where the committees were often inclined to agree direct taxes for longer periods of time or to acquiesce in indirect taxation. Where disputes did arise or where diets or assemblies voiced criticism of a ruler's expenditure, there was little that could be done. The position of peasant Estates was especially weak. In 1603, the peasant representatives of Lichtenberg-Kusel in Zweibrücken presumed to threaten to withhold taxes if their ruler incurred any new debts. Palsgrave Johann I simply imposed a fine on the committee for its impertinence and threatened its members with imprisonment if they had the temerity to make such a threat again.[47]

---

[44] Lange, *Landtag*, 20.   [45] Lange, 'Dualismus', 321.
[46] Krüger, *Verfassung*, 13; Carsten, *Princes*, 429.   [47] Press, 'Steuern', 72–3.

Above all, the position of diets and assemblies rested on their ability to generate money: for all the changes that had taken place, Landtage were at root still 'Geldtage' (money diets). The financial role that they played in the sixteenth century was made possible by the agricultural boom of the period, and many financial transactions were based on speculative assumptions about continuing high returns and inflation. For these calculations, the Thirty Years War was a disaster.

45

The Resurgence of the Courts

One of the things that diets most frequently criticized was extravagant expenditure at court. Over the course of the sixteenth century, there was a marked increase in the size and cost of courts. While a large court in 1500 would have comprised between a hundred and three hundred individuals, by 1600 the number would have been between three hundred and a thousand.[1] The rough cost of maintaining a court also doubled over the same period, with additional substantial sums paid for the construction of new residences. Most modern research has focused on developments in the period after 1648. Yet increases of these dimensions indicate that fundamental changes with major political implications also took place in the decades after 1555. Certainly, between about 1590 and 1620, a new quality of court life was discernible. Not least, the revival of courts about this time further consolidated the power of ruling princes, and the nobility was once more attracted back to the representative sphere of the ruler, which tended to isolate the diets and their institutions.

The court had, of course, always been the central location of medieval government, the nodal point of the ruler's vassalage, and the forum in which those noble vassals communicated with each other.[2] Its structure and functions, however, had been partially undermined by various factors. First, the determined efforts by some rulers to incorporate neighbouring nobles, especially knights, into their territories from the late fifteenth century, drove many to break out of both their territory and their vassalage. Second, the Reformation sometimes further deepened the rift between princes on the one hand and those who became Imperial Knights or Imperial Counts on the other. A late example of this was the abandonment of the Palatinate court at Heidelberg by the Protestant nobility when the Elector turned to Calvinism after 1559. The situation here was, moreover, aggravated by the fact that these nobles preferred to stay under the protection of the emperor than to run the risk of following the Elector into a religious option that was illegal under the law of the Reich. Third, the changes in the nature of territorial government meant that, from the late fifteenth century, university-educated non-nobles, especially those with legal training, tended to replace nobles in key political offices.

---

[1] Lanzinner, 'Zeitalter', 85. Similar figures are given by Müller, *Fürstenhof*, 30. The Bavarian court comprised about 160 people in 1508; by 1600 this had risen to 540; costs rose from 3800 gulden to 7,000 gulden over the same period. Ibid., 30–1.

[2] Stievermann, 'Courts', gives an informative account of several south German courts around 1500.

From around 1550, the position of the nobility gradually strengthened again. The situation of the Imperial Knights was increasingly stabilized by formal imperial recognition and protection (reaffirmed in 1566). The independence of the counts and prelates was further reinforced by a general acceptance of their enfranchisement in the Reichstag, albeit with two collective votes (*Kuriatstimmen*) for the counts and one for the prelates.[3] On the territorial level, the protection afforded by the emperor had the effect of relaxing the relationship between the nobility and the princes.

Many noble families now began to make good their educational deficit and thus become eligible for government service again. Service as a page at court and military training were complemented by travel, especially to Italy or the Netherlands (depending on political and confessional orientation), and by at least some element of academic study, if not actually a degree.[4] Increasingly, constitutions for ruling councils in the territories specified that parity should be maintained between nobles and non-nobles.

In the ecclesiastical territories, it was clear by the second half of the sixteenth century that the (Catholic) nobility would retain effective control of the Reichskirche. Cathedral chapters maintained, indeed often reinforced, their social exclusivity and continued to elect nobles as prince-bishops and archbishops. This ensured the survival of a range of episcopal and archiepiscopal courts and enhanced the position of the Catholic higher nobility in general within the Reich.

The controlling position of the new non-noble administrative elites was often undermined by the ambition of many of their members to join the nobility. Many rulers were only too happy to permit this. Some hoped to dilute the role of the old nobility, others were attracted by the payment of a significant fee for a new patent of nobility. The Heidelberg Elector, for example, sold patents of nobility in the Upper Palatinate for a sum amounting to a tenth of the cost of purchasing the land that the aspirants needed in order to qualify in the first place.[5]

Finally, many of the princes themselves wanted to rebuild their power base by once more establishing their court as the dominant regional centre. The first step was to re-engage the indigenous nobility of their territory. The next step was to engage neighbouring Imperial Knights and Imperial Counts, which enhanced the prestige of their court, as well as extending the reach of their influence.

Most of these developments took place at the courts of princes. They are largely associated with those territories where reforms and initiatives designed to intensify government are also found, or where a dynasty aimed to enhance its profile in the ranks of the higher nobility of the Reich. Not all rulers who could have developed a court did so. The matricular list drawn up by the Reichstag in 1521 for taxation

---

[3] The votes of the Swabian and Wetterau counts were established by 1550; the votes of the Franconian and Westphalian counts were admitted in 1641 and 1654, respectively. Schmidt, *Grafenverein*, 169. The collective vote of the prelates was formally recognized in 1575; from 1653 the prelates had two collective votes, one for the Swabians and one for those in the Rhineland: Conrad, *Rechtsgeschichte*, ii, 97–8.

[4] Hammerstein, *Bildung*, 46–7. *HdtBG*, i, 88.

[5] Press, 'Adel', 20.

purposes gives between 300 and 350 ruling families whose households might qualify to be labelled as a court. Imperial Knights and other members of the nobility were, by definition, excluded from this category, since they had no nobles subordinate to themselves. However, nearly 200 of those listed as princes were counts, and while the average size of their households also increased during the sixteenth century, relatively few developed a court as such. On the other hand, like many Imperial Knights and indeed many territorial nobles, comital dynasties participated in the building boom of the late sixteenth century. Collectively they built vast numbers of castles and fortified houses in the new Renaissance styles, frequently copying the fashions set by the emperor and the leading princes.[6]

Despite the benefit of high yields from agriculture, however, these projects also frequently saddled families with crippling debts. Finite resources and poor creditworthiness meant that most counts ran households rather than courts, and many preferred to save costs by entering into service with the emperor or some powerful prince. The house of Nassau, with its courts at Dillenburg and elsewhere, was a striking exception based on buoyant finances, excellent management skills, and a status enhanced by its association through Johann VI's elder brother, William, with the princely house of Orange. Two south German Hohenzollern comital lines (Hechingen and Sigmaringen) that were made into full principalities in 1623 were soon ruined by the costs they incurred in trying to run a court appropriate to their new status.[7]

Among the princes, the clear leaders and trendsetters were the Habsburgs, both the various archducal lines and the emperors themselves, with complex courts that reflected their multiple roles as Holy Roman Emperors, territorial princes, and kings of Bohemia.[8] After them, the only significant secular Catholic court was that of Bavaria, concentrated at Munich from 1550 after the dissolution of the Landshut court on the death of Ludwig X. Munich's grandeur derived partly from the Bavarian Wittelsbachs' claim to be senior to their relatives in the Palatinate, but also from their sense of being older than and senior to the Habsburgs.

Most of the other major court centres were Protestant. The court of the Saxon Elector at Dresden was the clear leader. Despite perennial financial difficulties, the Palatine Electors made strenuous efforts to establish Heidelberg as a competing centre; the Dukes of Württemberg were better placed financially, but ran a more modest court.[9] The fourth secular Elector in Brandenburg was also beset with severe financial problems, and the Berlin court was only seriously developed as a regional power centre after 1650. For the rest, notable courts were distributed across the Reich from Gottorp in Holstein to Güstrow and Schwerin in Mecklenburg, the Guelf (Brunswick) courts of Wolfenbüttel and Celle, Kassel for Hessen, Kulmbach for Ansbach, and Neuburg and Zweibrücken for the junior lines of the Palatine Wittelsbachs.

Among the ecclesiastical principalities, the courts of the Electors of Mainz at Mainz and Aschaffenburg were significant centres, as were the courts of the Electors

---

[6] Braunfels, *Kunst*, iii, 277–352.   [7] Press, 'Adelshöfe', 41–2.
[8] Press, 'Imperial court'.   [9] Mertens, 'Hofkultur'.

of Cologne and Trier. The courts of the Bishops of Würzburg, Bamberg, Münster, and Paderborn stood out as politically influential and opulent; those of the Bishops of Freising, Regensburg, Constance, Worms, and Speyer were relatively modest. While partitions tended to increase the number of secular courts (mostly Protestant), the number of ecclesiastical courts remained constant after 1555, except for the formal secularization of some northern prince-bishoprics that had been deprived of their independence before then anyway.

What distinguished a major court from a minor one was its regional status and its reach beyond the territory actually ruled by the prince. Money, size, and grandeur were key attributes, but power was fundamental. The Vienna court competed with Munich to attract the Swabian counts and Imperial Knights. Similarly, the Dresden court attracted the higher nobility of the Harz region and Thuringia, and actively competed with Prague for the loyalty of Bohemian vassals. The Wetterau counts traditionally attended the Cologne court, but after the disaster of the 'Cologne War' in 1582–3, which finally put paid to any prospect of secularizing the archbishopric, they transferred their loyalty to Heidelberg. Vienna (and Prague after 1583), Dresden, Heidelberg, and Munich were by far the most significant court centres throughout this period.

The religious divide altered decisively the social map of the upper nobility. Traditional court affiliations were broken, as were the traditional networks of those dynasties among which marital alliances were sought. Notwithstanding this general trend, the imperial court at Vienna and then at Prague continued to integrate Protestant nobles, including the Reformed Count Simon VI of Lippe at the court of Rudolf II.[10] At the level of imperial politics, religion did not necessarily outweigh all other considerations, though at the same time the growing gulf between the court and the Protestant nobles of Bohemia and the Austrian crown lands was at the core of the crisis that led to the Thirty Years War. Even in a regional context, power politics could prevail over religious conviction.

The Palatinate faced a particularly complex problem.[11] The combined effects of territorialization and religious policy severely weakened its regional system. First, many nobles escaped the Palatine vassalage to become Imperial Knights. Then Friedrich III's imposition of the Reformed faith drove the largely Lutheran knights away from the court, for in addition to being reluctant to risk following a faith that was illegal in the Reich, they also feared losing their independence by having the religious arrangements on their estates dictated by Heidelberg. Their departure was only partly compensated for by the arrival of 'foreign' nobles from as far away as East Prussia or Mecklenburg. The Lutheran restoration under Ludwig VI (r. 1576–83) brought the local nobility back to court, but they promptly left again when Johann Casimir reintroduced the Reformed faith in 1583. By 1592, when Johann Casimir died, the Heidelberg court was in crisis.

Part of the solution was an attempt to consolidate the Reformed Church within the territory, combined with forging new links with the international Reformed/

---

[10] Schmidt, *Grafenverein*, 376.   [11] Press, 'Zweite Reformation'.

Calvinist network. Equally important, however, for the stabilization of the territory was an explicit compromise with the regional Lutheran nobility designed to bring them back to the court permanently. The result of these seemingly contradictory initiatives was to enhance the distinctive intellectual character of the Palatine court.[12] Heidelberg's 'Calvinismus aulicus' had a unique profile: both territorial and regional, and at the same time international; Reformed and Philippist, yet inclusive of properly Calvinist and Lutheran elements; attractive to Lutheran Imperial Knights as much as to Calvinist exiles from all over Western, Northern, and Central Europe. The marriage of Friedrich V (r. 1610–23) with Elizabeth Stuart, daughter of James I, in 1613 further underlined the extent to which the Palatine Electors had succeeded, despite acute financial problems and an unpromising territorial base, in lifting themselves above the normal run of German politics. Triumph, however, all too easily translated into hubris.[13] The attempt to grasp the Bohemian throne was a profound miscalculation, and its failure rapidly engulfed the Palatinate in disaster.

Heidelberg was exceptional, but it was also characterized by many of the changes that affected most German courts after 1550. As the key medieval court offices turned into agencies of territorial government, their place at court was taken by a combination of noble ceremonial officers and purely household officials.[14] Traditional offices such as cup-bearer and high steward remained reserved for nobles and continued to play a major role in the increasingly complex ritual of the court. Nobles served as marshals or controllers (*Marschall* or *Hofmeister*, both sometimes encountered with the hierarchical preface of *Oberst-* or, in the case of the latter, *Gross-*), chamberlains and horse-mounted retainers, the latter often progressing from page (*Kammerjunge*), through the grades of *Hofjunker* and *Kammerjunker*, to gentleman-in-waiting (*Kammerherr*). They were joined by a growing body of non-noble kitchen masters, cellarers, quartermasters, keepers of the silver, huntsmen, stable masters, commanders of various kinds of guards' corps, goldsmiths, silversmiths, music masters, court jesters, and, more rarely, court poets. Many of these functionaries controlled substantial workforces, each organized hierarchically. A significant addition to the ranks of court officials was the father confessor at Catholic courts (the *Beichtvater*, invariably a Jesuit in the sixteenth century) and the court preacher or *Hofprediger* at Protestant courts.

Court ceremonial was shaped by old Burgundian traditions and by more recent Italian and Spanish ideals. The latter were introduced into the Reich by the Habsburgs, as were the Italian customs and styles, though they also reached the Reich via France.[15] Court cultures were often shaped by political and religious affiliation: Heidelberg drew on French as well as older Burgundian precedents and on ideas and customs from the Netherlands, while Dresden absorbed Burgundian

[12] Mertens, 'Hofkultur'; Wolgast 'Profil'; Zwierlein, 'Heidelberg'; Hepp, 'Heidelberg'; DaCosta Kaufman, *Court*, 209–11; Clasen, *Palatinate*, 33–46.
[13] Pursell, *Winter King*, 23–31, 65–91, 123–63.
[14] Müller, *Fürstenhof*, 19–25.
[15] DaCosta Kaufmann, *Court*, 50–73, 138–231; Müller, *Fürstenhof*, 11–16.

and Italian traditions via the imperial court at Vienna. Both Catholics and Protestants of all inclinations essentially followed the Habsburgs in formulating ceremonial protocols which regulated, often in minute detail, the daily life of the court and the procedures to be followed for annual feasts, baptisms, marriages, and deaths in the ruling family, and for coronations or accession ceremonies. Although German court life was not as highly ritualized as its enthusiastic embrace of the Burgundian tradition might suggest, this reflected both the small size of many German courts and also the lack of a clear distinction between court and government. Only from the late seventeenth century, when government functions were more clearly divorced from the court, could ritual take over.[16]

New forms blended with older traditions in varying combinations.[17] The traditional court entertainments retained a strong following. Extravagant feasts, heroic drinking contests, trials of strength that sometimes amounted to little more than drunken brawling, animal fights, musical entertainments, and masquerades could play a prominent role in daily life, punctuated only by the dedicated pursuit of hunting. Hunting, of course, had its political functions. Philip of Hessen advised his sons that hunting expeditions were a good way for a ruler to inspect his lands and an opportunity to meet many a poor supplicant who would not normally be allowed to address his ruler.[18] Friedrich II of Schleswig-Holstein-Sonderburg (r. 1559–88) used extended hunting expeditions to maintain contacts with his nobility.[19] Yet hunting was also characterized by excessive consumption. Despite the influence of new French and Italian ideals of nobility and civility, many German nobles made a cult out of being 'true German' ('echt teutsch'). They found notable role models in drunken princes such as Friedrich IV of the Palatinate (r. 1583–1610) or Christian II and Johann Georg I of Saxony (r. 1591–1611 and 1611–56, respectively).

Some older traditions were updated in the new Renaissance idiom. Tournaments and jousting matches still took place in the courtyard (like much of the entertainment of the court generally; German court entertainment moved inside during the seventeenth century). However, the traditional jousting tournament now began to embody new forms. It became more complex, with a number of exercises spread over several days: tilting at the ring, foot combat with sword and lance, the tilt on horseback, the *Kübelstechen*, where grooms or pages dressed up in padded jackets and wore barrels on their heads and tried to unhorse their opponents, and in conclusion a grand evening pageant and the joust with lances. The whole festival also reflected the increasingly hierarchical structure of the court and its articulation in complex pageants. While elements of serious noble military training remained a key part of the tournaments, their programmatic and communicative aspects were perhaps even more significant.[20] In the courts of the Protestant Union from

---

[16] Buttlar, 'Leben', 4–6.
[17] Buttlar, 'Leben'; Otto, 'Fürstenleben'. See also Voigt, *Hofleben*.
[18] Schulze, *Deustche Geschichte*, 213.
[19] Lockhart, *Frederik II*, 47, 49.
[20] Watanabe-O'Kelly, *Triumphall shews*, 13–35. The argument that the military function of tournaments is strengthened by the fact that lancers were only abolished in the British and German

Heidelberg to Stuttgart, Kassel, Jägerndorf in Silesia, and others, the tournament and its associated pageant became a vehicle for proclaiming the politico-religious identity of the participating princes and for broadcasting the agenda of the Protestant cause in the Reich.[21] Similar statements, in the service of different political agendas, were made through the same medium on the occasion of weddings and other festive events in Munich and Dresden.

Tournaments were but one feature of a widening range of court entertainment.[22] Innovations in this area among the German courts between about 1580 and 1618 included early forms of ballet and opera, often as part of elaborate masquerades or the tournament pageant. Pyrotechnic displays, fireworks, and illuminations originated in the leading Imperial Cities of Nuremberg and Augsburg in the early sixteenth century, but they became an increasingly regular feature of court entertainment after 1560. Around the same time, the first troupes of Italian professional actors toured the German courts, followed in the 1580s by the first English troupes. The contracts and the travel permits they were given enabled them to perform in non-court centres such as Frankfurt, Leipzig, Nuremberg, and Strassburg as well.

Finally, the courts and the towns in which they were located became centres of art, collecting, connoisseurship, and of learning. Developments in building styles after 1550 formed part of a longer-term transformation that started in the late fifteenth century. The new early modern style dates from the construction of the Wettin residence at Meissen, the Albrechtsburg, from 1471.[23] This was itself inspired by predominantly French models, such as Vincennes, the Louvre, and the castles of Jean de Berry. In the new *Schloss* (palace), the key characteristics of the medieval *Burg* (castle), especially the towers and gates, gained increasingly symbolic functions, representing the strength and justice of the ruler. At the same time, the quarters of the ruling prince, generally located near to the tower, became increasingly elaborate, both to accommodate the new governing functions of the early modern administration and to express the aspiration of the ruler to represent and reign over it. French and Italian styles were wrapped around traditionally conceived structures to express new meanings.

The styles and structures developed by the Wettins exercised a strong influence over neighbouring territories such as Brandenburg, Anhalt, Mansfeld, and Hessen. By the late sixteenth century at the latest, this had become the dominant style for Germany north of the Main, and if other centres such as Heidelberg or Landshut and Munich were now also influential, it was not least because they

---

armies after the First World War overlooks the fact that the 'modern' lancers (in Germany, the Ulanen) were an early eighteenth-century innovation introduced by Saxony. They were modelled on the Polish lancer troops formed in the sixteenth century and, in turn, modelled on the Ottoman troops, which accounts for the origin of the term *Ulan*. That is not to say that military and physical prowess, and equestrian skills, ceased to play a meaningful role in the training of nobles, though in the late sixteenth century such traditional knightly skills were being complemented by academic study. See also Schmidt, *Vaterlandsliebe*, 328–50.

[21] Watanabe-O'Kelly, *Triumphall shews*, 37–63.
[22] Berns, 'Festkultur', esp. 296–8.
[23] Müller, *Schloß*, 42–66.

too had adopted the original Wettin programme. Everywhere, older buildings were remodelled or partially rebuilt in the new manner, although the key traditional elements were retained. Indeed, the historically grown 'look' was considered extremely important in the early modern *Schloss*, something that traditional scholarship overlooked in trying to draw a contrast between the medieval *Burg* that was extended over time and the early modern residences that were allegedly conceived as single structures. When, for example, Duke Ulrich III of Mecklenburg set out to construct an entirely new main residence for his dynasty at Güstrow in 1558, he and his architect Franz Parr deliberately designed it to look as if it had been built long ago and merely adapted down the generations.[24] The governing style was also often extended to other official buildings. The same symbolic vocabulary that was developed in the early modern *Schloss* was applied to urban town halls in a prince's territory: as sites of princely administration, they too symbolized the presence and competence of governmental authority.[25]

After 1550, Italian architects and master builders refashioned the court centres of Vienna, Innsbruck, Prague, Dresden, and Munich, among others.[26] The Elector Ottheinrich (r. 1556–9) commissioned a Dutch master to construct a new Heidelberg residence in the Renaissance style on his accession in 1556. He thereby initiated a programmatic transformation of Heidelberg, just as he had previously transformed Neuburg on the Danube, the centre of the junior line of Pfalz-Neuburg, where he had been joint ruler from 1522 and sole ruler since 1542.[27] Both the Neuburg and the Heidelberg projects were part of a programme of (Lutheran) religious reform and of a general reinvigoration and intensification of government. In much the same way, Duke Julius of Brunswick-Wolfenbüttel (r. 1568–89) transformed his castle and surrounding town into a model Renaissance complex, including the longest street of new-style buildings in the Reich.[28] Similarly, building projects were as significant as financial reforms in the Catholic renewal programme launched at Würzburg by the ambitious Bishop Julius Echter von Mespelbrunn (r. 1573–1617).[29]

With building, went collecting. Maximilian II and Rudolf II were both avid collectors of antiquities, pictures, coins, and all manner of curiosities.[30] The *Kunst-und Wunderkammer*, or cabinet of art and marvels, was the typical embodiment of the restless eclecticism of the period. The Ernestine Saxon Elector Frederick the Wise (r. 1486–1525) had distinguished himself by amassing one of the largest ever collections of relics for the castle church of All Saints in Wittenberg. His Albertine successor August (r. 1553–86) laid the foundations in Dresden of what was to become one of the most spectacular and diverse ensembles of buildings and collections in Central Europe.[31] Almost every seriously ambitious prince of the

[24] Müller, *Schloß*, 247–50.
[25] Müller, *Schoß*, 358–76.
[26] DaCosta Kaufmann, *Court*, 139–65.
[27] Braunfels, *Kunst*, i, 302–4; Schütte, *Schloß*, 89–101; DaCosta Kaufmann, *Court*, 209–11.
[28] Braunfels, *Kunst*, i, 329–33.
[29] Braunfels, *Kunst*, ii, 282–3; Schock-Werner, *Bauten*, 17–18, 21–62, 201–15.
[30] Evans, *Rudolf II*, 162–95; DaCosta Kaufmann, *Court*, 166–203; Moran, 'Patronage', 169–75.
[31] Watanabe-O'Kelly, *Court culture*, 37–88; Braunfels, *Kunst*, i, 252–8.

period, at the very least, either established a major library or vastly expanded a previous one, often in conjunction with the foundation of a university or academy.

Alongside the cultivation of art and the formation of collections went the promotion of learning. Even though the courts, as fulcrums of feudal networks and seats of government, were confessionalized, the patronage of late humanist learning promoted intellectual and cultural ideals that tended to transcend confessional boundaries. In some cases, the university or higher academy was closely linked with the court. In others, the link was less close, geographically as well as in other senses. However, while the focus of some university faculties became narrower as they were pressed into service as agencies of government confessionalization drives, the court as a centre of humanist culture became part of a wider Central European network. In this respect, Lutheran Holstein in the far north was not far removed from re-Catholicized Bavaria in the south.[32] Justus Lipsius, for example, received invitations from both Protestant and Catholic courts.[33] What attracted rulers to Lipsius was his embodiment of the wide-ranging scholarly philosophical passions of the period. Philology was but the starting point for a wide-ranging engagement with every aspect of the ancient world, from its politics to its paganism; and the range of scholarship itself was extended by forays into science, magic, astrology, and alchemy. Rudolf II was exceptional in the range of his interests and the scale of his patronage. Yet he was also competing with his contemporaries in Saxony, Brandenburg, the Palatinate, Bavaria, and elsewhere in his pursuit of the great alchemical secret and in exploring the boundaries of human experience and the natural world.[34]

It would be wrong to imply an inherent antagonism or incompatibility between university and court. Rather, the court often complemented and extended the spectrum of learning embraced by the higher faculties. The court could also play a role in translating elements of academic culture into the political sphere. As the history of the first German language societies demonstrates, the cultural and intellectual role of the court was one that had profound significance for the evolving political culture of the Reich as a whole.[35]

---

[32] Evans, 'Rantzau', 258.   [33] Papy, 'Lipsius'.

[34] Evans, *Rudolf II*, 196–242; Moran, *Alchemical world*, 11–24, 171–6; Nummedal, *Alchemy*, 79–85; Lanzinner, 'Zeitalter', 124–5.

[35] See pp. 468–71.

46

The Imperial Cities

By comparison with the striking developments that took place in many territories after 1555, the development of German cities has often appeared to be characterized by stagnation and decline. The golden age of the cities, so most nineteenth- and early twentieth-century scholars agreed, had begun in the Middle Ages and it had reached its fruition in the Reformation era. Then the princes extinguished the spirit of urban freedom; developments in the European economy turned the German cities into backwaters, and the remaining Imperial Cities lost their political significance and entered a period of long decline.[1]

Research in the second half of the twentieth century did much to revise this view. The shift in patterns of economic activity was not as dramatic or as devastating as had often been assumed. Some cities lost their leading economic roles, but others gained in importance. Within established cities, some leading families disappeared, but others soon took their place: the membership of patriciates and commercial elites changed, but the social groupings remained and retained their place in the urban political hierarchy. If the Imperial Cities as a group seemed less innovative after 1555, that was at least partly because many of them had long ago introduced the kind of administrative and legislative reforms that many princes were now embracing with such vigour. In so far as most magistrates simply aimed to maintain the status quo, many cities came to seem conservative. Yet appearances could be deceptive. Certainly, the magistrates of Imperial Cities who ruled significant extramural territories—places such as Nuremberg, Ulm, Frankfurt, or Ravensburg, among others—proved themselves to be every bit as rigorous as any prince in the government of their territorial subjects.[2]

In a number of ways, the Peace of Augsburg created an entirely new framework for the Imperial Cities, which distinguished their history from that of the territories in important respects. Both their number and their status became more clearly defined than ever before. The matricular list of 1521 showed eighty-five Free and Imperial Cities. However, some of these had little interest in being included, since they feared it would simply mean that they would be burdened with imperial taxes. Indeed, some protested vehemently that they had been included by mistake and denied that they had ever been Imperial Cities. The Reichstag, for example, had declared Hamburg to be an Imperial City in 1510, but both the Duke of Holstein and the city itself disputed this. Hamburg only became interested in being an

---

[1] Gerteis, *Städte*, 1–12; Schilling, *Städte*, 51–6.
[2] Gmür, 'Städte'.

Imperial City, and in paying imperial taxes, much later, while the Holstein dukes (also kings of Denmark) only recognized this status in 1768.[3] Yet Hamburg, like a large number of mainly northern and north-western German towns, nonetheless laid claim to autonomous status: some were members of the Hanseatic League; others cited medieval charters and other legal privileges. In so far as they did not need the emperor's protection or saw no advantage in, or need for, the support of the Reich, they were content with the status quo: for most northern towns, the Reich held little practical meaning in the fifteenth and early sixteenth centuries.

The religious settlement of 1555 distinguished territorial towns from Imperial Cities more clearly. The decision to grant authority over religious matters to the rulers meant that they gained a powerful hold over their towns: imperial law could now be held to override local privileges. The protests of the north German Protestant towns were ignored and a proposal to include a special exclusion for the Hanseatic League failed. Over the course of the following decades, this led to the steady erosion of the position of many towns and cities.

The fate of the Hanseatic League is indicative. In 1554, its members agreed to pay a regular subscription, to submit to arbitration in cases of dispute, to provide mutual support, and to attend regular meetings. In 1557, representatives of sixty-three towns then met to agree new articles of confederation. However, the regular meetings failed to occur and the articles of confederation were renewed for the last time in 1579. By 1604, the League had only fourteen members, and among these, only Hamburg, Lübeck, and Bremen could be described as seriously active. The role that pressure from princes played in this decline is indicated by the fact that Duke Heinrich Julius of Brunswick-Wolfenbüttel (r. 1589–1613) referred to it as nothing more than an 'outlawed conspiracy and illegal assembly'.[4]

The process of territorialization did not by any means signify the extinction of civic liberties and traditions. Many towns played a key role in the politics of their territory. They contributed materially to the territorial economy, or played a vital role as administrative and court centres or as fortress towns. They also often helped shape policy as members of territorial Estates, defending their communal interests in much the same way as rural communes did. Government was as much based on dialogue as on command, and the voice of the urban communes was heard frequently. However, the only urban communes that succeeded in asserting their autonomy—places such as Emden and Lemgo—were those in territories where the ruler was weak. Other towns, such as Magdeburg, Erfurt, Brunswick, Münster, Göttingen, Lüneburg, Rostock, and Stralsund, preserved their de facto autonomy into the seventeenth century because they embodied a special economic or strategic significance, but most of them sooner or later succumbed to closer princely control. The communes that retained their traditional freedom were the exceptions among the four thousand or so territorial towns of the Reich in the early modern period.

For the Free and Imperial Cities, by contrast, Article 27 of the Peace of Augsburg laid down that wherever both Catholics and adherents of the Augsburg Confession

---

[3] Schmidt, 'Städtehanse', 31; Aretin, *Altes Reich*, i, 110.
[4] Schmidt, 'Städtehanse', 37.

lived within the city walls, the rights of each group were to be respected.[5] On the one hand, this affirmed the independent status of these cities. On the other hand, it denied their magistrates the *ius reformandi* and made violations, real or imagined, of Article 27 subject to appeal to the imperial courts, with the possibility of intervention by the emperor. At the same time, this uncertain status of the Imperial Cities was reflected in the fact that they did not enjoy the same political rights as the princes in the political system of the Reich. They were invited to attend the Reichstag and they formed their own college. However, all attempts to secure formal recognition of their vote foundered on the opposition of the princes.[6] Even the threat of withholding contributions to the counter-offensive against the Turks in 1582 merely elicited a meaningless assurance. It was only in 1648 that the full vote (*votum decisivum*) of the Imperial Cities was confirmed, though even then it was simultaneously rendered ineffective by the introduction of parity between the confessions in voting procedures, which cut across the collegiate voting system on crucial issues.

The failure to secure recognition for their Reichstag vote reflected the lesser status of the Imperial Cities compared with the princes, but it was also a consequence of their growing disunity. Before 1555, they had maintained a degree of solidarity in the pursuit of common interests by avoiding the increasingly obvious religious division in their ranks. After 1555, when the religious division was formalized in the Reich, the previous solidarity of the cities weakened. This, in turn, reinforced the differences of interest that prevailed generally among the sixty-five remaining Imperial Cities. Large cities such as Augsburg had little in common with those that were little more than provincial backwaters, or with the small Imperial Cities of Alsace that were beholden to the local Habsburg rulers and that ceased to be part of the Reich in 1648. Cities in those regions where imperial government had traditionally been active and which had old ties with the emperor had little in common with those in the more peripheral regions of the Reich, where imperial government was only gradually becoming meaningful. Many were also so small that, like many Imperial Counts or Imperial Knights, they tended to follow the lead of a neighbouring prince, who was frequently also the 'patron' of the city or exercised jurisdictional rights in it.

However, the ambivalent position of the Imperial Cities was, to some extent, the result of a pair of initiatives that Charles V started but did not complete. When King Ferdinand justified his refusal to grant the *ius reformandi* to urban magistrates by arguing that they did not constitute an independent authority between the crown and the citizenry, he was pursuing essentially the same line.[7] Paradoxically, under Ferdinand and his successors, the effect was to reinforce the position of the city councils, for the crown invariably supported them in any dispute between magistrates and citizenry.

---

[5] Pfeiffer, 'Religionsfriede', 271–8.
[6] Schmidt, 'Städtehanse', 54–5; Schmidt, 'Städte', 36–9.
[7] Isenmann, 'Reichsstadt', 62.

Charles V had attempted to capitalize on his victory in the Schmalkaldic War by launching a final attempt to forge confessional unity by formulating a compromise that he hoped would be acceptable to both Catholics and Protestants. The emperor had no means of inducing the majority of the princes to accept his Interim, but he was able to use his authority, reinforced by Spanish troops in the case of Augsburg, to impose it on the Upper German Imperial Cities. As a result, a number of hitherto Protestant cities were obliged to reintroduce Catholicism. Most were able to reassert their Protestantism in due course, though in some cases not until after 1555. Yet the whole episode gave an immediate legal basis for the Catholic minorities established—however temporarily—as a result of the emperor's initiative, and they remained under imperial protection even after the cities had largely reverted to Protestantism.

At the same time, Charles V had imposed constitutional reforms on a number of Upper German Imperial Cities, starting with Augsburg and Ulm, but then extending to twenty-five additional cities by 1552.[8] In each case, the involvement of guilds in urban government was eliminated and a strong patrician regime was established. His motive was quite clear: to punish those who had sided with the Schmalkaldic League. That consideration also provided him with his model: the Nuremberg constitution, in which the guilds had played no political role for the past two centuries.

For Nuremberg, though solidly Lutheran since 1525, had also remained consistently loyal to the crown; it had declined to join the Schmalkaldic League in 1531 and had remained neutral during the Schmalkaldic War. Memories of the restlessness of the common man during the Reformation were reinforced by the fact that Augsburg patricians blamed the city's disobedience to the crown during the war on the guild members of the city council. Consequently, Charles felt justified in summoning the three hundred councillors, rebuking them, and then dismissing them summarily. The next day, a smaller council of forty-one members drawn largely from patrician families, with only seven representatives from the wider community, was appointed. Similar actions were carried out in other Imperial Cities by an imperial commission headed by Dr Heinrich Haas, whose name inspired the punning epithet 'Hasenräte' or 'hare councils' for the new urban regimes, which saw some city councils limited to as few as twenty members.

Despite the resentment and contempt with which many of those who were ousted from office regarded their new masters, the changes were lasting. Indeed, in most cases the new constitutions prevailed until the nineteenth century. The subsequent amendments in various places were largely aimed at making the envisaged aristocratic constitution viable. In some cities, there had never been a formal patriciate. In many others, such as Esslingen, Reutlingen, Schwäbisch Hall, and Schwäbisch Gmünd, there were simply not enough patrician families to fill the council.[9]

---

[8] Naujoks, *Zunftverfassung*, 10–18.
[9] Rabe, *Rat*, 15–16, 168–73.

In these cases, the representative nature of the council now often became even more restricted. This led, for example, to the replacement of elections by co-option and to the need to recruit new patricians from the ranks of the leading commercial families. Even that, however, did not always prove easy, for the proportion of the male population eligible for full citizenship often declined to less then a fifth.[10] It also meant that city offices were frequently concentrated in the hands of members of the same family or group of families over generations. This was partly offset by the principle of rotation of offices that prevailed in most cases. Yet the suspicion that the Imperial Cities were in the hand of oligarchies was unavoidable, and often in fact true. A telling example of the new politics can be seen in Ulm, where the city clerk simplified the task of making sense of the extremely complicated electoral arrangements by preparing the list of results in advance. Post-election corrections were rarely necessary.[11]

Charles V did not live to build on the reforms that he initiated in either the religious or the political affairs of the Upper German Imperial Cities. It is difficult to say for certain which dimension was more significant, or whether the reforms were linked in his mind with other ideas for the creation of some kind of imperial league or reform of the Reich. Neither Ferdinand nor his successors pursued the original initiative, and the religious reform was soon undone in many places. This produced a variety of unusual constellations.[12] In Augsburg, Biberach, Ravensburg, and Dinkelsbühl, the patricians were mostly Catholics and these essentially Protestant cities now remained under the control of Catholic councils. In a number of other cities, such as Ulm, Kaufbeuren, Donauwörth, and Leutkirch, the Protestants continued to control the council even after the reintroduction of Catholicism, though they then had to come to terms with the ongoing existence of a substantial Catholic minority.

The majority of the Imperial Cities—roughly thirty-five—either remained or became Protestant. The general tendency among these—again a reflection of the relationship between the Imperial Cities and the emperor—was the adoption of strict Lutheran orthodoxy. The last thing they wanted was to run the risk of being branded as outlaws by association with Calvinism. Only Bremen, on the periphery of the Reich and with more in common with the territorial town of Emden than with any Imperial City to the south, adopted Calvinism. In 1618, some twenty Imperial Cities remained, or had once more become, Catholic. The rest were, to one degree or another, of mixed religion.

The problems generated by these varied forms of coexistence, and by the various late urban Reformations, ensured that at least one of Charles V's aims was realized. The very fact of his intervention had reinforced the traditional role of the emperor as supreme patron and overlord of the Imperial Cities. This was applied to the Imperial Cities generally after 1555. Indeed, Article 27 of the Augsburg settlement ensured that issues that gave rise to appeals to the emperor, and hence to imperial

---

[10] Rabe, *Geschichte*, 650.
[11] Rabe, *Geschichte*, 651.
[12] Warmbrunn, *Zwei Konfessionen*, 13–14.

intervention, arose in many Imperial Cities other than the twenty-seven that had been affected by Charles V's measures in the early 1550s.

Although Hamburg and Lübeck were too remote from imperial government to be much concerned by either the promise of imperial protection or the threat of imperial intervention—Hamburg still disputed its status at this stage anyway—almost all the other Imperial Cities were in one way or another potentially affected. Indeed, as Catholic lawyers were fond of pointing out, there was probably not a single city in which at least some ecclesiastical foundation or some remnant of ecclesiastical property did not remain in Catholic hands.[13]

Protestant Regensburg, for example, contained remnants of territory formerly held by the bishops, three independent Catholic foundations with imperial protection (St Emmeram, Niedermünster, and Obermünster), and the so-called Canons Regular of the Alte Kapelle under Bavarian patronage. Despite the fact that there were only three Protestant churches, compared with over ten Catholic churches, Regensburg counted as a Protestant city throughout.[14] Further north, the Dortmund Reformation reached its conclusion in 1570 after many decades of theological conflict and political struggle. Yet a Catholic minority, including influential patricians, remained; the Archbishop of Cologne continued to exercise his right to supervise the appointment of pastors until 1585, and his jurisdictional court was only abolished in 1589. Even then, three Catholic monasteries survived, and in 1616 the city council was obliged to accept the grant of parochial rights to the Franciscans in addition to the existing rights of the Dominicans.[15] In many Imperial Cities, the slow and late resolution, if at all, of intractable confessional issues meant that the process of confessionalization and the development of a confessional culture really only took hold in the seventeenth century. Indeed, for many it was the Peace of Westphalia that first created a secure framework within which that could occur.[16]

The case of Aachen illustrates the local complexity and regional ramifications of a confessional shift, as well as the serious implications for imperial politics.[17] On the one hand, Aachen's geographical position was more delicate than that of Dortmund, since it was closer to the Spanish-occupied Netherlands. Like Dortmund, Aachen had to contend with the jurisdictional claims of two regional neighbours—the Duke of Jülich and the Bishop of Liège (and with him, naturally, his superior, the Archbishop of Cologne). On the other hand, the proximity of Habsburg interests posed the additional threat of Spanish military intervention and generated a much closer imperial interest in the situation. The really crucial difference compared with Dortmund was confessional. The origins of the Dortmund Reformation lay in humanism and Lutheranism, and the city council steered a firmly orthodox Lutheran course. In Aachen from about 1544, the Lutherans and Calvinists were,

---

[13] Schneider, *Ius reformandi*, 283.
[14] Schindling and Ziegler, *Territorien*, vi, 33–57.
[15] Schilling, 'Dortmund', 163.
[16] Enderle, *Konfessionalisierung*, 384; Enderle, 'Reichsstädte', 259–69.
[17] Schneider, *Ius reformandi*, 229–31; Schilling, 'Bürgerkämpfe'; Schmitz, *Verfassung*; Molitor, 'Reformation'. For the similar case of Wesel, see Spohnholz, *Tactics*.

on the whole, prosperous refugees from Flanders and Artois in the southern Netherlands.

Attempts by the Catholic council to exclude the refugees from political participation merely led to appeals for help to Protestant princes. By the 1570s, some eight thousand Protestants lived alongside twelve thousand Catholics, and the personal and economic influence of many of the Protestants obliged the Catholic majority to admit them as full citizens and to allow them access to political office, including the city council. This, in turn, led to Catholic appeals to the Duke of Jülich, who complained to the emperor that his own rights of ecclesiastical jurisdiction over Aachen had been violated. The city council thereupon appealed to the Reichskammergericht against the Duke of Jülich. Finally, the Reichshofrat declared in 1593 that the city had no right under the Peace of Augsburg to change the confessional status quo, that the Calvinists had no standing anyway, and that all changes introduced in Aachen since 1560 were invalid. When the magistrates sought to resist this judgment by appealing to the emperor and all the Estates of the Reich, Rudolf II first threatened direct action and then, in 1598, outlawed the city and commissioned Archduke Albrecht, Governor General of the southern Netherlands, with the military execution of his decree.

Faced with the very real threat of a joint Spanish–Jülich occupation of Aachen, the Protestant councillors capitulated and the Archbishop of Cologne supervised the re-Catholicization of the city. The Protestants were then banned until an uprising in 1611 once more re-established a Protestant-dominated council, against which the emperor was powerless to act, since Jülich was now also in Protestant hands and therefore willing to exercise its jurisdictional rights by supporting the Aachen Protestants. Their triumph was short-lived, for in 1614 Spanish troops once more intervened and re-Catholicized the city for good.

Similar disputes, each with ramifications for the political situation in the Reich as a whole, erupted in Cologne, Strassburg, and, most spectacularly, in Donauwörth, which was re-Catholicized in 1607 and turned into a Bavarian territorial town.[18] Many other cities experienced less serious problems, which frequently resulted in appeals both to and against neighbouring powers, or to the imperial courts of law, and to the appointment of imperial commissioners to arbitrate the dispute. In many cases, too, there was at least the threat of external intervention and/or of armed resistance, as in Dortmund in 1604, when the Protestant citizenry armed to confront the imperial commissioners who had come to attempt to enforce a court decision in favour of the Catholics.[19] Such controversies occurred with increasing frequency from the late 1570s. They were both a reflection of and an aggravating factor in the growing confessional tension in the Reich generally.

Often entwined with these confessional disputes, but characteristic also of the much wider spectrum of Imperial Cities, were growing tensions between the city councils and their fellow citizens, which exploded in a variety of uprisings around

[18] Schneider, *Ius reformandi*, 231–4. On Donauwörth, see p. 421. Donauwörth regained its status as an Imperial City only briefly in 1705–14.

[19] Schilling, 'Dortmund', 163–4.

1600. In this respect, the implications of Charles V's Upper German urban constitutional reforms were mirrored by similar developments elsewhere. After the popular interventions of the Reformation decades, during which the guilds had often gained considerable ground politically, oligarchic tendencies began to manifest themselves among the educated and commercial elites.

Patricians who increasingly withdrew from active trade and commerce but nonetheless clung to political power aroused the resentment of active wealth producers, not to mention the guilds.[20] In cities such as Frankfurt, Aachen, and Hamburg, the arrival and establishment of refugees from the Netherlands disrupted the status quo.[21] The new economically dynamic settlers soon demanded enfranchisement and participation in urban government. Equally, where magistrates tolerated new communities of Calvinists or Jews, many felt threatened or displaced by the new competition. In many cases, also, the ever-widening gulf between rich and poor, between full citizens and mere inhabitants, was a further cause of growing tension.

This was exacerbated by the impact of growth. Economic problems in the 1570s and 1580s, and the impact of severe plague epidemics in the 1560s and late 1570s, made severe though temporary inroads. In general, vigorous birth rates and immigration (both from the countryside and from areas such as the Low Countries) ensured that in many cities population levels reached a peak in the late sixteenth century. The largest expansion usually occurred at the lower end of the social scale. Although a preponderance of economic migrants could promote prosperity, as at Aachen or Hamburg, it could also simply intensify glaring economic and social inequality, and differences in civil status and opportunities for political participation.[22]

Despite the extreme variety of causes of discontent and friction—economic, social, confessional, political—present in different degrees and combinations in most cases, confrontations were usually formulated in terms of a discourse that was common to virtually all the Imperial Cities. Indeed, what distinguished the conflicts of the seventeenth century from the late medieval challenges to the authority of urban magistrates was largely the fact that these were now framed in the language and arguments of academic law. Since 1555, the increasingly secure urban oligarchies had adopted the new humanist (and after 1576, Bodinian) language of sovereignty and adapted it to German Christian traditions. They spoke of themselves as authorities *deo gratia* (by the grace of God) or as *Obrigkeit* (rulers).[23] They described their polities as Roman-style republics, themselves as rulers—burgomasters as *consules*, council members as *senatores*—and their fellow citizens as subjects. Even the smallest Imperial Cities, such as Bopfingen (with just under 1,000 inhabitants in 1600) or Buchau (which only reached 750 inhabitants in

---

[20] Gerteis, *Städte*, 83.
[21] Schilling, 'Innovation', 14–30. For later controversies concerning the Jews, see pp. 547–50.
[22] Schilling, 'European crisis', 136–41.
[23] Schilling, 'European crisis', 150.

1632), adopted the formula 'Senatus populusque Bopfingensis' or 'Senatus popu-lusque Buchaviensis'.[24]

The critics of authority drew on different arguments. They would invariably insist that sovereignty lay with the citizenry and that the magistrates were merely entrusted with certain duties. The city, they often argued, was a *status mixtus*, a combination of aristocracy and democracy. Typical, in some ways, was the ex-change of views around 1600 in Hamburg, where there was no actual revolution. In 1602–3, a dispute about the oath of office for councillors led one burgomaster to claim that the citizenry had no right to resist the Senate, however 'godless, tyrannical, and miserly' it might be. In 1618, during a controversy over the council's intention to renew the residence permit of the Sephardic Jews (recent immigrants from Spain and the Netherlands), the citizenry demanded again to know whether the council believed Hamburg to be an aristocracy or a democracy. Wisely perhaps, the council refused to give a clear answer: such questions, Bürger-meister Vincent Moller replied, were simply useless scholastic puzzles; in reality, no city was either a pure aristocracy or a pure democracy.[25]

Moller was not the only magistrate to deploy this shrewd answer. It was also aired in Aachen and elsewhere, and it did not always defuse the situation.[26] In Frankfurt am Main, for example, there were longstanding grievances, not only concerning nepotism and corruption, but also the fact that the council had concealed the city's bankruptcy following the Schmalkaldic War (for which it had provided financial guarantees and on which it had also speculated). On the occasion of the election of Emperor Matthias in 1612, the citizenry of Frankfurt were required to swear an oath pledging the security of the imperial election ceremony held in the city. This was customary in return for confirmation of the city's privileges. On this occasion, however, the representatives of the citizenry took the opportunity to present an extensive catalogue of grievances to Matthias, to the Electors, and, finally, to the city council. They demanded the publication of all privileges that were due to be confirmed (in the hope of discovering some legal protection from taxation imposed by the council), the control of interest rates charged by the Jews, and the control of grain prices.

The council's refusal sparked an uprising, which resulted in a treaty mediated by imperial commissioners, including the Archbishop of Mainz, and representatives of the Landgrave of Hessen-Darmstadt and two other princes. This did not satisfy everyone, and a further uprising, led by the biscuit baker Vincenz Fettmilch, culminated in the ejection of the patricians from the council.[27] Fettmilch, however, was outlawed by the emperor, and the authority of the rebel 'popular' council was further undermined by the plundering of the ghetto and the expulsion of Jews from

---

[24] Press, *Kriege*, 75; *Deutsches Städtebuch*, iv pt. 2, 52, 334. This mimicked the official signature of the ancient Roman Republic: *Senatus Populusque Romanus* (the Senate and People of Rome).

[25] Schilling, 'Republikanismus', 117–18; Whaley, *Toleration*, 15–16.

[26] For a survey of the conflicts in Frankfurt and other cities, including a comprehensive chronological list, see Friedrichs, 'Town revolts' and Blicke, *Unruhen*, 41–5.

[27] Friedrichs, 'Politics'; Koch, 'Fettmilchaufstand'; Lustiger, 'Fettmilchaufstand'; Ulmer, *Turmoil*, 23–51.

the city. Meanwhile, both the Archbishop of Mainz and the Palatine Elector became increasingly concerned about the fate of the city's Catholic and Reformed communities respectively, and about the threat the disturbances posed to their own neighbouring territories.

By 1613, the unrest had spread to Worms, where the citizenry also drove out the Jews, and to Wetzlar, where the council was briefly overthrown and only restored when popular representatives were granted access to civic documents and oversight of the city's finances.[28] The prospect of an emerging regional crisis in which major players from both confessional blocs in the Reich were becoming involved made the need for imperial intervention more urgent. In the end, a military occupation was averted by a counter-rebellion against Fettmilch, who was then tortured by the imperial authorities and publicly executed in 1616. The old council was restored and the Jews were readmitted to the city.[29] Order was also rapidly restored in Worms and Wetzlar.

Like the disputes in Aachen, the Frankfurt troubles revolved around local issues, but they had dangerous implications for regional stability and security and, because of the involvement of confessional issues, they also contributed to the growing confessional tension in the Reich as a whole.[30] At the same time, three other aspects were significant. First, in a crisis the imperial authorities invariably sided with the magistrates, rather than the citizenry. If grievances were aired peacefully, the imperial courts could be relied upon to be sympathetic; imperial commissioners would intercede with the magistrates. That sympathy was then immediately exhausted if open rebellion broke out; imperial commissioners would threaten military intervention and the restoration of the status quo. Equally typical, second, was the fact that a lasting equilibrium, with some formal institutionalization of popular participation in the polity, was only achieved over a century later.[31]

Third, the Frankfurt conflict of 1612–16 proved to be the prelude to a long series of altercations that stretched into the eighteenth century. The dispute over the interpretation of the republican tradition in the Imperial Cities reached its highpoint before 1618. Its resolution came long afterwards. For all the serious damage wrought by the Thirty Years War, especially on the smallest Imperial Cities, the Imperial Cities generally represented yet another dimension of German political culture characterized by continuity throughout the entire early modern period.

---

[28] Friedrichs, 'Town revolts', 44–5.   [29] See also pp. 549–50.
[30] Meyn, *Bürgeraufstand*.   [31] Soliday, *Community*, 16.

47

Responding to Crises

There seems little doubt that there was an expansion in the size and activities of government in the territories and cities during the late sixteenth century. There were more agencies of government. There was more activity on the part of governments, more regulation, more intervention, and more attempts at codification and standardization, not only of law but also of belief and behaviour. It is easy to see why many historians have been attracted to the idea that this period saw a systematic attempt on the part of rulers to discipline society, or a decisive step towards the development of a rational approach to the problems of government. This has sometimes been linked with the imposition of religious discipline, while others see many of the same developments as the products of a reaction against religious conflict and the emergence of an emphatically secularized world view among many educated people.

In either case, the question arises as to how effective government initiatives really were, both in relation to their specific targets and in relation to their impact on society as a whole.[1] Did the aspiration to greater control in fact lead to greater discipline? Did the many measures associated with confessionalization result in a more uniform society that was less tolerant of marginal groups or those defined as deviants? Did the developments of the period really foster the emergence of a more rational or even secularized view of society and the functions of government? To what extent was German society after 1555 effective in dealing with periodic crises?

Answers to these questions partly depend on the assessment of the mentality of the period. There is certainly evidence to suggest that conflict and turmoil led some thinkers to withdraw into stoic philosophy, in which they found recipes for political stability. The cult of Lipsius was a prime expression of this ideology. Lipsius's editions of Tacitus and his own writings, which incorporated many of Tacitus's teachings, prepared the ground for the development of a science of politics from around 1600 that aspired to transcend religion and party.[2]

The immediate stimulus, in Germany as elsewhere, was *Della ragione di stato* (1589) by Giovanni Botero (*c.*1544–1617). Two major German works took up the theme in 1602: the *Discursus politicus de prudentia politica comparanda* ('On Acquiring Political Prudence') by the Saxon official and, from 1607, imperial procurator fiscal in Upper Lusatia and Lower Silesia, Jakob Bornitz (*c.*1560–

---

[1] For a sceptical view see Schmidt, 'Sozialdisziplinierung?'.
[2] Stolleis, *Öffentliches Recht*, i, 198–203; Stolleis, *Arcana*. For the wider context, Burke, 'Tacitism' and Muhlack, 'Tacitismus'.

*c.*1625), and the *Disputatio de iure publico* ('Disputation on Public Law') by the Altdorf professor, Arnold Clapmarius (1574–1604). Following Botero's lead, each sought to distinguish true political prudence from Machiavelli's evil and immoral pseudo-politics. Each author was inevitably accused of being a Machiavellian in disguise, and theologians in particular maintained a consistent denunciation of Machiavelli's life and works that delayed a serious engagement with his ideas in the Reich until the second half of the seventeenth century. However, Bornitz and Clapmarius succeeded in abstracting the notion of *ratio status* from its associations with Machiavelli and it became the touchstone of the new academic disciplines of politics and of public law.

Developments in scientific thinking have also been interpreted as reflections of a struggle between rationality and irrationality. Figures such as Johannes Kepler (1571–1630) or Matthias Bernegger (1582–1640), the Strassburg professor of history and translator of Galileo, sometimes look like heroes of a new rationalistic science, which also informed more sober and detached views of religion and politics. Kepler rigorously distinguished scientific truth from religious truth and insisted that Copernicus was mathematically correct even if the Church insisted that he was wrong on theological grounds.[3]

Kepler's own thinking seemed to illustrate the gradual triumph of reason over unreason. In 1596, aged twenty-four, he declared that a motivating spirit, the sun, resided at the centre of all planetary trajectories and that the planets were moved by a divine miraculous force which had insight into geometrical principles. Furthermore, each of the three higher planets expressed hatred for the others. By 1621, he was insisting that the word 'spirit' should be replaced by 'force' and that one should understand the term 'hatred' simply as a difference of position, movement, light, and colour. Throughout his career, Kepler's religious views were non-confessional: at some cost to himself and his family, he refused either to sign the Formula of Concord or to convert to Catholicism. He disapproved of the demonization of Calvinism and sympathized with the intellectual world of Reformed Christianity, yet he abstained from that Church too.[4]

However, the temptation to view developments in politics and science as emblematic of the period as a whole tends to oversimplify. It is easy to present the new ideas as outcomes of the confessional struggle, the triumph of light over dark. Yet that would be to overlook the fact that they also embodied continuities. The theorists of *ratio status* held that successful government depended on the mastery of the *arcana imperii*, the mysteries of government, accessible by those adepts who approached the subject with the right attitudes.

Kepler's astronomy may have been strictly empirical, but his astrology depended on a theory of planetary aspects and harmonies that was as esoteric as any theology. His duties as official mathematician at Graz and Linz, and as court mathematician in succession to Tycho Brahe in Prague from 1601 to 1612, involved the

---

[3] Press, *Kriege*, 316–17; *DBE*, v, 506–7; Wollgast, *Philosophie*, 221–62; Donahue, 'Astronomy', 581–4.
[4] Lanzinner, 'Kepler'.

preparation of horoscopes and almanacs or prognostications. His successful prediction in his first almanac of 1595 that there would be a harsh winter, a peasant uprising, and a Turkish invasion founded a lasting reputation in the field and guaranteed him a reliable source of income. In fact, Kepler's astrology was the foundation and motivation for his astronomy as he sought to establish a new and more certain ground for his belief in the relationship between heavenly phenomena and earthly events.[5] He understood the whole of his scientific endeavour not as an alternative to belief in God, but as a more effective way of becoming close to God.

Such interactions between rationality and irrationality should warn against assuming too great a gulf between elite and popular cultures. There were, in reality, many links between the two; the educated and the common people largely shared the same culture and system of belief.[6] Sixteenth-century medical literature combined empirical and 'modern' insights with the traditional wisdom of healers and herbalists.[7] Territorial rulers and magistrates were likely to employ soothsayers or other 'wise' people, more often than not gypsies or other travelling people, in the search for treasure or lost items, just as ordinary folk often sought their expertise against animal diseases, fires, and harvest failures.[8] Such practices were increasingly frowned upon during the sixteenth century and, towards 1600, they were denounced by the clergy and proscribed by many authorities, yet the beliefs that underlay them proved persistent. Some rulers continued to use them well into the eighteenth century in the search for precious minerals.[9] Court-based alchemists were, after all, scarcely more sophisticated than gypsy soothsayers and they often differed from popular magicians only in their scientific pretension, even though they did sometimes have a degree of real expertise.

The question of collective mentalities and popular attitudes is crucial in assessing the ways in which contemporaries perceived their environment. The period after 1555 saw substantial overall growth of population and of wealth for some groups. Many territories saw a consolidation and stabilization of conditions after the upheavals of the first half of the century, which is reflected in the building boom for castles and residences after about 1580. Yet many contemporaries actually experienced these decades as a period of uncertainty and instability. Indeed, clergy and other commentators were increasingly convinced that they were living in an age of pestilence and decay which could only be the prelude to the end of the world. The Brandenburg Lutheran pastor Daniel Schaller, for example, claimed that the world was changing physically: the light was darker, the soil less fertile, the waters less full of fish; even stones and iron were no longer as hard as they once were. He was not alone in expecting the imminent 'ruina mundi' (the downfall of the world).[10]

[5] North, *Astronomy*, 309–26.
[6] Friedeburg, *Lebenswelt*, 24–36.
[7] Schulze, *Deutsche Geschichte*, 266–7.
[8] Hippel, *Armut*, 43; Friedeburg, *Lebenswelt*, 33; Schubert, 'Mobilität'.
[9] Schubert, *Arme Leute*, 254; Fricke, *Zigeuner*, 143, 146–8, 408–24.
[10] Schulze, 'Untertanenrevolten', 300–1.

For Catholics, notably the Jesuit advisers who seemed to play an increasing role at virtually every Catholic court during these decades, the remedy was clear. Rulers must redouble their efforts to reinforce religious discipline internally and to combat the enemies of true religion wherever they appeared. The way forward was clear; all that was needed was the will to travel it.

Protestants tended to interpret their diagnosis of the ills of their time in much more eschatological terms.[11] Confident predictions of the end of the world were made for 1588, 1600, and 1604, and these unfulfilled expectations fed into the emergence of a broad stream of Protestant millenarianism in the early seventeenth century.[12] The commemoration of the first centenary of the Reformation in 1617 was both a celebration of a triumphant history and a fearful anticipation of the end. Scholars such as the highly regarded Matthias Bernegger articulated the views of many contemporaries with their doom-laden declarations of the dawn of a new age of barbarism.[13]

At about the same time, Johann Valentin Andreae (1586–1654), a friend of Bernegger, launched the first of a succession of plans for an association designed to bring about the rebirth of society as a whole. His fantastical narrative of the genesis of a Rosicrucian order attracted wide attention in the years after its publication in 1614, as did Andreae's critique of contemporary society in his *Christianopolis* some years later.[14] For many Calvinists, the millenarian moment came in the wake of their disaster at the White Mountain in 1620, the prelude to their repression in Central Europe and their dispersal into exile.[15] In the Reich, such ideas received renewed currency in the 1630s, which saw the classic combination of war, hunger, and disease visited upon wide areas.

The intensity of these later developments has to some extent overshadowed the experience of the decades after 1555.[16] Judgements about a general decline in morals among Protestant writers reflected the inevitable frustration of un-realistically high expectations about what the religious reform might have ach-ieved. Among Catholics, similar complaints were often laments about ground lost during the Reformation decades, intensified by similarly unrealistic expec-tations informed by new Tridentine ideals. Regular outbreaks of plague rein-forced the sense of a world that was weakening and failing. The periodic threat posed by the Turks also added grist to the mills of those seeking evidence of ways in which a sinful world was being punished. In the 1590s, some even asked whether the Reich as the fourth and final world monarchy (as envisaged in the Book of Daniel) was not destined to be superseded by the Ottoman Empire.[17]

---

[11] For this approach, with numerous examples, see Dixon, 'Astrology'.
[12] Schulze, 'Untertanenrevolten', 301.
[13] Kühlmann, *Gelehrtenrepublik*, 42–66.
[14] Wollgast, *Philosophie*, 282–99; Hardtwig, *Genossenschaft*, 158–75. See also pp. 462–4.
[15] Hotson, *Paradise*, 109–20, 160.
[16] Behringer, 'Krise', 148.
[17] Schulze, *Türkengefahr*, 40–6.

Some believed that the crisis of 1570 marked the beginning of a never-ending series of disasters, and until the 1620s, it provided a benchmark against which subsequent crisis years were measured.[18] This was the first really severe winter of the 'mini Ice Age'. It had been preceded in 1569 by disastrous harvest failures from Russia through Ukraine and Poland down to Bohemia. In many areas, the winter of 1570 was followed by three years of unfavourable weather conditions, accompanied by acute shortages of food and by severe outbreaks of plague and other diseases. Things only returned to normal by about 1575.

The nature of the crisis and its meaning were described and analysed in a flood of publications, which also enhanced its impact.[19] Printers seized the opportunity to republish old texts on all kinds of diseases and disasters, city physicians rushed into print with diagnostic guides; and clergymen hastened to publish their sermons explaining how and why the world was being punished. Commentaries on Ezekiel's dark prophecies of hunger and pestilence were particularly popular, as were works on dying and death, or tracts explaining just why the sun was failing and the world's energy was waning.

The divergent responses of theologians and physicians illustrate the Janus aspect of contemporary expertise.[20] Almost without exception, theologians blamed the crisis on mankind's sin. Physicians, by and large, viewed the crisis as a natural phenomenon, with little of the reference to the theological causality that had been characteristic of medical literature of the fifteenth century. The remedies the physicians suggested might have been useless or even harmful, but the best-informed practitioners were clear that the causes of sickness and disease would not be found in the metaphysical realm.

The response of politicians also reveals a dual aspect. Urban magistrates were frequently involved in elaborate operations to purchase grain and to provide for their people.[21] In 1572, the Augsburg magistrates even bought a substantial consignment of grain from the Turks. Governments shared intelligence about such operations at meetings of the Reichskreise or of the *Städtetag*, which also discussed further legislative measures to deal with the current crisis. The measures commonly proposed by the Kreise included laws banning excessive expenditure (sumptuary laws) or enforcing morality, curbs on beer brewing, the expulsion of alien beggars, and bans on grain speculation. In Franconia, the Kreis even discussed the creation of a regional customs-free market in grain and other foodstuffs, with penalties for members of the Kreis who were caught profiteering.[22] In the event, however, implementing this proved to be impossible.

The prescription of sumptuary and moral legislation as a remedy for the problems caused by harsh weather conditions indicates that the politicians' diagnoses of the causes of the crisis were similar to those found in the sermons of the clergy. The Bavarian Chancellor, Thaddäus Eck (1514/15–1574),

---

[18] Behringer, 'Krise', 54–8, 77–101. For a wider discussion of the issues, see the essays in Behringer et al., *Konsequenzen*.
[19] Behringer, 'Krise', 62–75.   [20] Behringer, 'Krise', 101–28.
[21] Behringer, 'Krise', 128–33, 151–2.   [22] Behringer, 'Krise', 133.

for example, produced a devastating report on the fiscal crisis in Bavaria in 1571.[23] Acute insights into the reasons for the current poverty of the taxpayers and for the escalating costs of the court and administration were combined with a general diagnosis of lax morals, sinfulness, and neglect of religion as the ultimate source of all contemporary woes. This was the public justification for the unprecedented mass of legislation that ensued over the next three years, covering everything from the quality of the coinage to blasphemy.

The expertise in crisis management that many governments were forced to acquire in the early 1570s informed their responses to similar problems over the coming decades. In many parts, governments intensified the kinds of initiative launched in the first half of the century and developed a more consistent approach to the problems of poor relief.[24] In Protestant areas, the Reformation had the effect of concentrating almost all institutions of poor relief in the hands of rulers and magistrates. In Catholic areas, centralization of existing institutions proved more difficult, but here, too, energetic rulers such as Julius Echter of Würzburg (r. 1573–1617) founded new institutions for the sick, the orphaned, and the poor as part of a broad programme of reform and renewal. The 'communalization' of poor relief also effectively meant its restriction to the indigenous poor. This was encouraged by imperial legislation of 1530, 1548, and 1577, which obliged all rulers to take care of their own poor. Registration of the poor now became increasingly common, as did attempts to expel those who were not native to a city or territory. Almost all governments made some effort to ensure that poor relief was not given to aliens and that those who did receive it also worked to the degree that they were able.

It is unclear just how effective any of these measures were. If estimates of 4–5 per cent (in cities up to 10 per cent or more) of the population as recipients of long-term assistance in normal times are accurate, it is clear that the inflated numbers in times of crisis made demands that the system simply could not meet.[25] However, even in times of crisis, the measures that almost all governments had in place undoubtedly brought relief to many. The deserving poor were neither demonized nor criminalized. The new workhouses modelled on the English Bridewell (1556) and the Amsterdam Correction House (1595) and Spinning House (1597) were only introduced later in the Reich, with foundations in Bremen (1609–13), Lübeck (1613), Hamburg (1614–22), and Danzig (1629). Their guiding principles informed debate and policy in the later seventeenth and eighteenth centuries.[26] They represented a significant departure from the conventions that prevailed in Germany around 1600 and their example was emulated more widely only after 1700.

In the late sixteenth century, the rigorous exclusion of non-natives from poor relief left a significant stratum of folk who had no option but to take to the road and beg. It is difficult to be precise about their number. In normal times, the travelling population might have amounted to about 3–4 per cent of the population. In times of shortage, that number was probably far higher. The excluded poor joined a broad spectrum of travelling groups, from gypsies to vagrants, from 'working' travellers

[23] Behringer, 'Krise', 137–42.
[24] Jütte, *Armenfürsorge*, 330–67; Fehler, *Poor relief*, 109–53. See also pp. 267–8.
[25] Hippel, *Armut*, 21.   [26] Jütte, *Poverty*, 171, 174–5. See also Volume 2, pp. 260–1, 507–12.

such as hawkers, itinerant craftsmen, such as knife grinders, and entertainers of all kinds, to plain criminals and bandits. The numbers in each subgroup are unknown, though some have estimated, probably too conservatively, that gypsies accounted for no more than a thousand or so in the Reich as a whole and the number of genuine professional bandits was also probably small.[27] Though they may have been few, their very existence could, however, generate acute anxiety. In a crisis, all travellers might be tarred with the same brush and come to seem part of a dark and dire threat to settled society. Numerous governments sought to banish aliens or prevent them from entering their territory. On the one hand, many edicts contained long lists of the kind of people to be excluded, while terms such as 'gypsy' (*Zigeuner*) were used indiscriminately to denote a wide range of different groups. Other edicts labelled non-native beggars and travellers as heretics or ungodly, outcasts from Christian society. On the other hand, the frequency with which such edicts were generally reiterated probably indicates how ineffective they were.

The fact of peaks of legislation against vagrants and gypsies in the 1570s and the period *c.* 1590–1605, and the animosity towards the Jews that was evident in some urban disputes after about 1580, seems to invite the conclusion that German society became more intolerant. Some historians have suggested that this was a direct result of confessionalization, which entailed the equation of the heavenly city of God with cities and states on earth.[28] This may well reflect the attitudes that prevailed in some Imperial Cities, whose walls and fortifications enclosed a limited space that lent itself easily to the projection of such theological images. Overall, however, things were less straightforward. The gypsies had been persecuted for most of the century; by the 1580s their reputation as untrustworthy criminals and spies of the Turks was already established, and in many edicts the term '*Zigeuner*' simply stood for any traveller.[29] It is by no means clear that they were more persecuted or rejected in 1600 than they had been in 1500. Where legislation attempted to formally expel them, along with all other vagrants, it often failed. Many smaller territories, such as those of counts and knights, in fact tolerated them, or at least lacked the resources or the will to deal with them.[30]

The case of the Jews, who numbered some 35,000–40,000 around 1600, is more complex still. After the expulsions of the fifteenth and early sixteenth centuries, large urban communities of Ashkenazi Jews (i.e. those originally from Germany, northern France, England, and Italy) only existed in Frankfurt am Main, Friedberg, Fulda, Worms, Speyer, Vienna, and Prague. Hamburg was another exception, with a small Sephardic community of refugees expelled from Spain and Antwerp in the 1580s.[31] Overall, the sixteenth century saw a steady growth in small town and rural Jewish communities across the Reich, with a particular concentration in the

[27] Hippel, *Armut*, 35–6, 42. Estimates of the number of gypsies are invariably based on nothing more than pure conjecture.
[28] Roeck, *Außenseiter*, 7–22.
[29] Fricke, *Zigeuner*, 34–5, 149; Härter, 'Kriminalisierung', 45–7.
[30] Häberlein, 'Minderheiten', 153–61.
[31] Battenberg, *Juden*, 11–12.

small and fragmented territories of the Middle Rhine, Franconia, and the Wetterau. Counts and knights were known to be more actively tolerant than rulers of large, closed territories, and, like the rulers of larger but fragmented and scattered territories, they were less able to take action anyway.[32] Difficulties in one locality could easily be evaded by slipping across a border into another jurisdiction. While some princes, such as Bishop Julius Echter of Würzburg (r. 1573–1617), systematically expelled the Jews and even tried to prevent them from travelling through their lands, others tolerated them to varying degrees.[33]

In general, such toleration was facilitated by the fact that Charles V had reasserted the traditional imperial protection of the Jews in the Reich at the Speyer Reichstag in 1544, and in extended form in 1548.[34] This forbade the harassment of Jews or the closure of their synagogues and explicitly permitted them to charge higher rates of interest than Christians to compensate for their generally disadvantaged position.

In practice, however, the Jewish communities were subject to the authority of the territorial rulers. The reception of Roman law in the territories from the late fifteenth century, which resulted in the formulation of territorial law edicts (*Landesordnungen*), also led to the formulation of *Judenordnungen*, which regulated the relationship between Christian and Jewish inhabitants. The views put forward by Johannes Reuchlin in 1511 proved particularly influential in this process. Though the Church regarded Jews as slaves, he argued, they were 'cives' (citizens) under Roman law, and hence should be treated as 'concives' (fellow citizens) of the Christians.[35]

The terms of settlement of the Jews were often carefully specified. Some territories attempted to regulate numbers by only permitting the eldest son to marry and settle.[36] Almost everywhere, the Jews were obliged to pay special taxes and periodic tributes or fees in return for permission to exercise certain trades. In 1530, the Reichstag had obliged all Jews in the Reich to wear a yellow badge, though this was not systematically implemented and was soon ignored completely.[37] Subsequent local legislation often tried to ensure that the Jews remained distinct from Christian society, and in some parts, especially the cities, they were confined to clearly delineated ghettos. In practice, however, Christian and Jewish society overlapped and interacted, and the boundaries between them tended to be drawn sharply only in times of crisis.

The steady growth of the Jewish communities in the Reich, particularly marked after 1550, occurred despite the fact that both Catholic and Lutheran theologians had an arsenal of anti-Semitic arguments, which they did not hesitate to deploy. Yet a combination of respect for the imperial protectorate over the Jews and cupidity ensured that most rulers took no action against them.

---

[32] Battenberg, *Juden*, 11–12.   [33] Roeck, *Außenseiter*, 32–3.
[34] Battenberg, *Zeitalter*, 188.   [35] Battenberg, *Zeitalter* 175–6. See pp. 106–8.
[36] Hippel, *Armut*, 41.
[37] The imperial privilege of 1544 conceded that this need not be worn outside a Jew's normal place of residence. Battenberg, *Zeitalter*, 188.

Two kinds of issues could upset this fragile balance. The first was essentially a political and constitutional problem. The Jewish communities periodically made efforts to coordinate their activities. In the early sixteenth century, local rabbis had begun to form loose regional associations and to appoint territorial rabbinical courts and chief rabbis. Some of them were granted imperial licences and Charles V himself had designated an imperial chief rabbi in the early 1520s, an office that existed at Worms until 1574.[38] In 1529, a general gathering of regional rabbis at Günzburg failed to create a more durable supra-regional organization, but it did designate Josel of Rosheim in Alsace as the representative of all the Jews in the Reich. The imperial authorities objected to his assumption of the title of 'ruler of all the Jews in German lands' but accepted him as the 'head of the Jews', and it was he who persuaded Charles V to issue his privilege of 1544. Josel's death in 1554 deprived the Jews of their most effective spokesman and advocate, and the end of the Worms imperial rabbinate in 1574 temporarily undermined what coordination had existed in the Reich.

A renewed attempt to establish a unified administrative body modelled on the Polish Council of the Four Lands met with fierce opposition.[39] A meeting of twenty-six community representatives at the autumn trade fair at Frankfurt in 1603 passed a series of resolutions reinforcing the jurisdiction of rabbinical courts, creating a central fund for internal communal purposes, and regulating the training of rabbis, among other things. An informer denounced the participants to the Electors of Mainz and Cologne as treasonable conspirators and they immediately initiated proceedings against the Frankfurt community in the name of the emperor. In 1603–4, Rudolf II was in no position to make a stand on behalf of the German Jews, despite the intercession of influential Jewish financiers and teachers close to his court at Prague.

The idea that the Jews really wanted to undermine the emperor's authority was, of course, fanciful, but the litigants insisted that the very act of convening an unauthorized 'synod' was a crime and that resolutions relating to the jurisdiction of rabbinical courts usurped imperial prerogatives. The charges were soon dismissed. However, the Elector of Cologne battled on until 1623 in his attempt to extract a significant fine from the Jews to cover his alleged 'substantial expenses'. What was really at stake from the outset was not so much imperial prerogatives, but rather the rights and interests of the territorial princes.

The 1603 initiative was the last attempt to create an organization of the Jews for the Reich as a whole. The future lay in the consolidation of regional Landjudenschaften, rather than in a single organization.[40] In the short term, the crisis of 1603 also contributed to the most spectacular example of the second kind of issue that could destabilize a Jewish community: the expulsion of Jews from Frankfurt during the Fettmilch uprising in 1614. The issue here was economic as well as political.[41] The Jews were accused of corrupting the coinage but also of unfairly

---

[38] Battenberg, *Zeitalter*, 190.
[39] Meyer, *German-Jewish history*, i, 87–91.
[40] Battenberg, *Zeitalter*, i, 242–5. See also Volume 2, pp. 264–6.
[41] Friedrichs, 'Politics'; Lustiger, 'Fettmilchaufstand'; Ulmer, *Turmoil*, 23–51.

competing with the guilds and charging unreasonable rates of interest. The really telling complaint, however, was the one against the city council: that it had exceeded its powers and acted against the interests of the city by tolerating Jews in the first place. Anger against Jews was unleashed in the context of a political crisis within Christian society. In this case, moreover, imperial patronage of the Jews proved effective in conjunction with the emperor's right to intervene directly in the affairs of an Imperial City. On the one hand, the affair, different to many others only in the degree of its severity and the political sensitivity of its location, reveals the latent opposition to Jews from Christian guildsmen and others on economic grounds which could easily erupt in violence against them. On the other hand, it underlines the interest that the emperor, urban magistrates, as well as many princes all had in protecting Jews from that violence and ensuring their continuing contribution to the economy and the official coffers.

Two further phenomena of the later sixteenth century document the degree to which the territories of the Reich were able to deal with some problems generated by specifically economic issues but seemed helpless in the face of others generated by social anxiety. The management of disputes between peasants and landlords falls into the first category. The witch craze falls into the second.

After a lull following the Peasants War of 1525, a new cycle of peasant unrest developed from the 1560s. Its principal causes were poor harvests and shortages, rising prices, the efforts by landlords to impose heavier feudal dues and obligations or to turn common lands and forests into domain property, and the ever-increasing burden caused by the increase in imperial taxation. Its main geographical centres were the territories of the south-west and Upper Austria, though unrest also spread to Bavaria, Salzburg, Passau, and the Tyrol, as well as Pomerania, Brandenburg, and Silesia after 1600. In Upper Austria, a major peasant uprising erupted in 1595–7 and many other disputes also culminated in violence or smouldered over years, with communal solidarity against extortionate landlords and periodic skirmishes conducted by both sides. However, the most marked feature of the new cycle of peasant unrest was the resort to law rather than to arms.[42] Before 1550, subjects brought cases against their rulers to the Reichskammergericht on about 180 occasions each year; thereafter the average rose to 438 per annum.

It is true that procedural obstacles were placed in the way of would-be peasant litigants.[43] In deference to the social status of counts, knights, prelates, and lords, the court procedure laid down in 1555 dictated that all complaints against them should be referred to an arbitration procedure and that they might only come to court if that failed. In 1594, it was decided that complaints by subjects should be referred to their rulers for a report before legal proceedings could begin. Furthermore, legal representation was expensive, as were travel and subsistence costs for the peasant delegations that journeyed to attend hearings at the Reichskammergericht at Speyer or the Reichshofrat at Vienna.

---

[42] Schulze, *Deutsche Geschichte*, 270–2, 282–92; Schmidt, *Geschichte*, 137–42.
[43] Gabel, 'Untertanen', 275–6.

Landlords invariably had the advantage, the more so the longer a case dragged on. Yet the complainants were by no means powerless. Many rulers and city magistrates were keen to avoid the embarrassment of a court case. They also feared a shaming defeat and the possibility of military intervention by neighbouring rulers to enforce a ruling of the court. Once a case had started, anyone who resorted to violence could be immediately outlawed and subjected to military action by the Kreis. In addition, a new profession of peasant advocates rapidly developed, available for hire and all too often more than keen to sell their services wherever they heard of a dispute.[44] Word spread steadily among the peasantry about what might be achieved by resort to the courts, and peasant delegations on a mission routinely exchanged information with those whom they encountered en route or met at the doors of the courts. In deliberations at the Reichstag and elsewhere, for example, about the issue of imperial taxes, the litigious character of the German peasantry was frequently invoked.

While many a landlord no doubt resented the rights acquired by his subjects, conflict resolution by means of legal process became increasingly established. In 1600, the Deputationstag decided that courts for hearing cases brought by subjects against their rulers should be established in all territories. That, in turn, had the effect of gradually diffusing the political-legal culture of the Reich to its constituent parts.[45] For all participants in the process, the Reich as a system with a distinctive political-legal culture was experienced as a reality that shaped their lives in the localities and regions.

Legal procedures also played a key role in the persecution of witches, though these persecutions were often driven by social anxiety. The phenomenon is often referred to as the 'witch craze', but this is in some respects misleading.[46] Many persecutions did involve hysterical behaviour and, judged from an (anachronistic) modern point of view, they were certainly irrational; they also involved extreme brutality and torture. Yet the decision to prosecute a witch and the legal proceedings that unfolded thereafter were deliberate calculations and they were generally based on sincere beliefs.

The problem was European-wide, but roughly half of the 40,000–50,000 individuals executed as witches between the fifteenth and the end of the eighteenth century, most between 1580 and 1660, were subjects of the Reich; there were perhaps some 20,000 victims in the area of present-day Germany.[47] What distinguished the new phase of witch persecutions after the early 1560s from those in the fifteenth and early sixteenth centuries was their broader scope and more complex legal and administrative procedures. The theological and above all legal justifications of witch trials were now much more elaborate. In 1572, Electoral Saxony was the first territory to extend the widespread legislation against casting harmful spells when it also decreed that making a pact with the devil was an offence punishable by

---

[44] Baumann, 'Advokaten'; Troßbach, 'Reichsgerichte', 129–31; Below and Breit, *Wald*, 157–9.

[45] Gabel, 'Untertanen', 276; Troßbach, 'Reichsgerichte', 129–30, 132; Gabel, 'Beobachtungen', 149, 165–6.

[46] See, for example, Roper, *Witch craze*. Roper's book is nonetheless the best general study of the phenomenon in any language.

[47] Behringer, *Hexen*, 192–4.

death.[48] In the earlier period, witches had been pursued by the Inquisition and by ecclesiastical authorities; now, witchcraft became a matter for secular government and the criminal justice system.[49]

The first persecutions occurred in 1562–3 and 1570–4, but they increased in frequency and severity from the mid-1580s. The worst campaigns, with several thousand victims, probably occurred during the 1630s, with a focus on activity in the Franconian bishoprics of Würzburg, Bamberg, and Eichstätt, and further persecutions in Mainz, Hessen, and Westphalia, which together claimed several thousand lives. There was a final wave of activity, with diminishing intensity, between 1650 and 1670. In Protestant areas, witch trials of any kind had effectively ceased by about 1700. In Catholic areas, there were periodic cases of individual trials and the last execution of a witch in the Reich took place in Kempten in 1775.[50]

Not all areas were affected, and in regions where witch hunts did take place, they did not follow any general pattern. Witch hunts were generally highly localized affairs, and even in territories that saw major persecutions, they were often confined to specific areas rather than spread evenly across the whole territory. In Bavaria, for example, the execution of witches was limited to a relatively small number of districts.[51] The great majority of trials involved small numbers of alleged witches, but in both south-western and south-eastern Germany the period 1562–1666 is distinguished by the incidence of large 'panic trials', which resulted in the execution of twenty or more persons.[52]

The Lower Rhine region, along with most of northern Germany except Mecklenburg, saw relatively little witch-hunting activity. In the south, Bavaria experienced relatively limited activity compared with the more territorially splintered south-western regions. The greatest concentration of witch trials occurred in the region bounded by Lorraine and Trier in the west, Westphalia, Minden, and Schaumburg in the north, then across to the Anhalt principalities and the Saxon duchies, and down through the bishoprics of Bamberg, Eichstätt, and Augsburg to Switzerland.

In the larger 'enclosed' territories such as Bavaria, Brunswick-Wolfenbüttel, and Electoral Saxony, persecutions tended to be more controlled, and often more limited, than in the smallest territories or in heavily fragmented areas such as the region around Trier, which saw some of the bloodiest persecutions of the early 1590s. By contrast, the Calvinist Palatinate, another fragmented territory, saw almost no trials at all. In general, there tended to be more witch trials in Catholic territories than in Lutheran territories, and there were relatively few witch persecutions in the larger Imperial Cities. Overall, women (especially single women) were more likely to be victims than men, but enough men were included to confound any interpretation of the phenomenon as a war on women.[53]

---

[48] Behringer, *Hexen*, 135.

[49] Behringer, *Hexen*, 72–9.

[50] Behringer, *Hexen*, 403–4; Roper, *Witch craze*, 15–43. The last execution of a witch in German-speaking Europe took place in the Protestant Swiss canton of Glarus in 1782.

[51] Behringer, *Persecution*, 389.

[52] Midelfort, *Witch hunting*, 72; Behringer, *Persecution*, 63.

[53] Schormann, *Hexenprozesse*, 116–22.

While Catholics were more likely to engage in the persecution of witches than Protestants, in both confessions proponents of religious renewal were likely to be the most avid prosecutors. Among the Catholic rulers of south-eastern Germany, for example, concubine-keeping opponents of reform such as the Prince-Abbots of Kempten or Bishop Johann Philipp von Gebsattel of Bamberg (r. 1598–1609) showed little interest in witches. Reformers such as the Bishops of Augsburg, Eichstätt, and Bamberg, along with secular rulers such as the Bavarian Dukes Wilhelm V (r. 1579–98) and Maximilian I (r. 1598–1651) were, by contrast, zealous persecutors of witches. In a finding that seems to contradict that apparently widespread correlation, however, it seems that in south-western Germany opposition to the persecution of witches came from preachers, who insisted that disasters were warnings from God rather than the work of the devil.[54]

The sheer variety of local and regional contexts for the numerous outbursts of witch hunting in the Reich has defied all attempts at a general explanation of the phenomenon.[55] The concentration of cases after 1580 suggests a clear link with the social anxieties generated by the shortages and tensions caused by the adverse climatic conditions. The *Malleus Maleficarum* ('The Hammer of the Evildoers'), a compendium of Church teaching on witches first published in 1486, went through thirteen editions by 1520; it was next republished in 1574, with two further editions in 1576 and 1579.[56] The 1580s saw the publication of several other major works on witchcraft, including a German translation of Bodin's influential *De magorum daemonomania* ('Of the Demon-mania of Sorcerers') of 1581. From 1589, the Trier-based suffragan bishop, Peter Binsfeld's *Tractatus de confessionibus maleficorum et sagarum* ('Tract on the Confessions of Magicians and Witches'), immediately translated into German, provided a comprehensive guide to the exposure and prosecution of witches. Ten years later, the Jesuit Martin Delrio's *Disquisitionum magicarum libri VI* ('Six Books of Investigations into Magic') summarized the whole of the previous literature and completed the ideological framework for the trials of the next decades.

While it is difficult to construct clear causal chains for witch persecutions, it seems highly likely that many were linked with confessional renewal programmes. The proscription of traditional magical practices by religious reformers made it easy to denounce individuals who continued to engage in them as witches. Preoccupation with the devil seems to have been a particularly marked feature of the reforming mindset and one that struck a chord with many in the population generally. The 1560s saw a flood of devil-books, some 100,000 individual copies; interest waned a little during the 1570s but revived again in the 1580s.[57] At the same time, heightened confessional tensions and sectarian invective easily led to accusations of devilry and sorcery. However, there are also many examples where traditional 'wise' women and men were the instigators of persecutions, all the more influential for their special insights.[58]

---

[54] Midelfort, *Witch hunting*, 193–4; Roper, *Witch craze*, 6, 18, 90, 95.

[55] A wealth of local and regional information is being compiled at http://www.historicum.net/ themen/hexenforschung/lexikon/ (accessed 4 May 2011).

[56] Behringer, 'Krise', 73.

[57] Midelfort, *Witch hunting*, 69–70.

[58] Rummel, '"Weise" Frauen'.

The role sometimes played by wise women and men underlines another feature of the persecutions. They generally involved collaboration between ordinary people and the educated elites.[59] Rudolf II himself lived in fear of being bewitched, as did Maximilian I of Bavaria, the Augsburg prince-bishop, Johann Egolf von Knöringen, and others. [60] It is not coincidental that the *Historia von D. Johan Fausten* ('The History of Dr Johann Faust') appeared in 1587. The anonymous fictional account of Faust's pact with the devil resonated deeply with the anxieties of the time and reflected both the contemporary fear of and fascination with the occult. No less than twenty-four editions had appeared by 1600 and what started as a very modest volume had by then grown to nearly seven hundred pages.[61] In terms of his gender and status, however, the fictional Faust had little in common with the average victim of a witch persecution.

More often than not, witches were ordinary folk denounced first by their neighbours or by their communities. Kepler's mother, for example, was involved in a lengthy investigation and trial in 1615–21 following accusations by her neighbours. Kepler himself became actively involved in her defence, never denying the existence of witches but exposing the accusations as idle women's gossip.[62] Many trials and wider investigations were instituted expressly at the demand of the local community; in some cases, the authorities stepped in to prevent the outbreak or spread of disorder. The prompt intervention of the authorities could often enhance the standing of a government in the eyes of its subjects. What could be a better proof of good government than to protect a community from the devil?

Witch trials could also be part of demonstrations of political independence, or assertions or claims to such independence. In the case of the Imperial Abbey of St Maximin near Trier, an extraordinarily high level of witch-hunting activity resulted from the desire of Prince-Abbot Reiner Biewer (r. 1581–1613) to reverse an imperial edict of 1570 that gave his territory to the Elector of Trier.[63] Between 1586 and 1596 about a fifth of the population of the abbey's territory (the list of those accused contained 6,300 names) became embroiled in investigations and trials that served largely to establish the abbot's jurisdictional rights; at least 400 were found guilty and burnt at the stake. All the cases were minutely documented and commentaries on them emphasized that the trials were conducted without reference to any higher court in Trier. In other words, Biewer seized the opportunity presented by the alleged presence of witches to exercise precisely those prerogatives formerly accorded to him by the emperor in order to assert his immediate status in the face of the Elector of Trier's claims to overlordship and superior jurisdiction.

---

[59] Friedeburg, *Lebenswelt*, 76–8.

[60] Behringer, *Persecutions*, 409.

[61] Behringer, *Hexen*, 183, 399; Völker, *Faust*, 181–2; Coupe, *Reader*, 215–17; Midelfort, *Witch hunting*, 70; Evans, 'Culture', 20. The book had 671 pages in 1600.

[62] Schulze, *Deutsche Geschichte*, 252–3.

[63] Voltmer, 'Superhunt?', 229–30 fn. 17, 249–51. The abbot also refused to pay the Elector any taxes, including taxes towards the Turkish wars. St Maximin finally lost its struggle to maintain its independence from Trier in 1669.

Similar considerations may well have played a role in the accusations levelled against an unusually high number of well-placed members of the urban elite in Trier, where the trial and execution of the erstwhile fanatical 'witch judge' Dietrich Flade on 19 September 1589 was among the most spectacular events. Trier had lost its immediate status around 1580, but it still disputed its demotion from Imperial City to territorial town of the Electorate of Trier. The pursuit of witches in Trier was one way in which the Elector sought to exploit his diocesan rights to seal the subjugation of the town to his temporal authority.

The distinction between the Elector's diocesan jurisdiction and his rights as a ruling prince was significant here. It seems that the territory of the Electorate itself (the lands already subject to the Elector as a temporal ruler) did not see particularly intense witch-hunting activity, even though the Elector-Archbishop Johann VII von Schönenberg (r. 1581–99) was an energetic reformer and, like his suffragan bishop, Peter Binsfeld, apparently terrified of being bewitched. On the other hand, the archbishop strongly supported Binsfeld's zealous pursuit of witches throughout his archdiocese outside the lands he ruled himself, particularly in areas over which he was trying to extend his authority. This included the town of Trier, as well as the Abbey of St Maximin and the fragmented Saar and Eifel regions, parts of Lorraine, and the greater part of the Luxemburg province of the Spanish Netherlands, all of which were characterized by frequent witch trials.[64]

The educated and the ordinary people shared a common belief in witches. Even those who opposed the trials, or at least urged caution, did not generally disagree entirely. From the outset, many trials generated intense internal debate within administrations, in which sceptics and advocates of caution struggled to restrain the impetuousness of the passionate witch hunters. In most cases, those who urged caution and restraint in the first instance objected to the methods that were used in the judicial process, in particular the almost inevitable outcome of torture yielding merely what the torturers wanted to hear.

This was the line pursued by some of the most prominent opponents of the trials. The Calvinist court physician at Düsseldorf, Johann Weyer (1516–1588), denounced the first wave of persecutions that began in 1561, publishing his *De praestigiis daemonum* ('On the Illusions of the Demons') in 1563, the source for most arguments against the persecutions over the next two centuries.[65] Significantly, he did not deny either the power of the devil or the existence of witches, but he argued that the statements made by witches were no more than delusions that the devil had placed in their ignorant minds.[66] He believed that the witches were the real victims and that the crimes they admitted to under torture were the work of the devil alone. The Jesuits Adam Tanner (1572–1632) and Friedrich von Spee (1591–1635), and the Lutheran theologian Matthäus Meyfahrt (1590–1642), also stand out as notable opponents. The circumstances of the publication of Spee's *Cautio Criminalis* ('A Book on Witch Trials') of 1631 are not fully clear. The

---

[64] On the leading role of suffragans, see Brodkorb, 'Weihbischöfe', 73, 81.
[65] Behringer, *Hexen*, 134–5.
[66] Schormann, *Hexenprozesse*, 34–5.

Jesuits did not prescribe a single view of witchcraft for their members, yet it may still be significant that the work appeared anonymously in the Hessian Lutheran university town of Rinteln, perhaps to avoid censorship. By and large, both Tanner and Spee argued for the conversion of witches rather than for their execution, and for more effective pastoral care rather than persecutions that could easily get out of hand.

Few openly questioned the entire basis of any belief in witchcraft and the devil. It seems, however, that from a relatively early stage some had practical insights into the disorder that witch trials could produce and the consequences of indiscriminate accusations, which gradually led to the end of the persecutions. Influential works such as Peter Binsfeld's 1589 *Tract* reassured those who wanted to believe that God would not permit the condemnation of anyone unjustly accused. Yet many still had doubts.

In Bavaria, for example, the first really serious wave of trials took place in the 1590s. By the end of the decade, there was a serious conflict at the heart of the government between proponents of further trials—largely Jesuits recruited from all over Europe and lawyers—and advocates of caution and moderation—generally indigenous nobles and patricians. The writings of Adam Tanner reflected the arguments of the moderates and, in turn, reinforced moderate views both in south-east Germany and elsewhere from the 1620s.[67] First, however, the witch hunters triumphed, and in 1612 Bavaria issued a comprehensive forty-page mandate against witches of all kinds.[68] Only a year later, the moderates were able to regain the initiative when it came to light that the 'witch judge' at Wemding, Gottfried Sattler, had filed false reports and had ordered arbitrary arrests and torture in order to embezzle the property of the victims. Sattler's case—he was executed after a short trial—was cited extensively, first by Tanner and then by Spee, as evidence that the judicial procedures employed in the persecution of witches were corrupt and flawed.[69] Their discussion of this case and others elsewhere, gradually undermined the hard-line witch-hunting factions.

The writings of Tanner and Spee continued to be influential well into the eighteenth century, and, after the effective end of the trials in the 1670s, new commentators such as the Amsterdam preacher Balthasar Bekker (1634–1698) and Christian Thomasius (1655–1728) began to dispute the demonological basis of the belief in witches.[70] The wide influence of works such as these ensured that henceforth, witches were more likely to be charged with casting spells or with fraud than with entering a pact with the devil. Similarly, their accusers were increasingly likely to be condemned for slander and trouble-making, rather than found leading a witch hunt.[71]

---

[67] Behringer, *Persecutions*, 322–3, 355–7.

[68] This was renewed in 1665 and 1746, and remained nominally in force until the great reform of criminal law in 1813. Behringer, *Persecutions*, 287.

[69] Behringer, *Persecutions*, 292–5.

[70] Schormann, *Hexenprozesse*, 39–40. For an example of a late witch panic and trial in Langenburg in the County of Hohenlohe in 1672, in which there was little evidence of the new thinking, see Robisheaux, *Last witch*.

[71] Midelfort, *Witch hunting*, 81–4.

The witch persecutions reveal something of the desperation that afflicted people who could find no earthly reason for their troubles. They also reveal that governments faced widespread social anxiety and its causes with much the same mindset as their subjects. They were fundamentally part of the same mental world. Governments were constantly seeking a remedy for the effects of famine and disease in legislation that aimed to enforce morality and religious observance. It was thus only logical that they should sanction the persecution of those suspected of having entered into a pact with the devil. At the same time, the witch hunts seem to underline the dependence of governments upon those whom they ruled and sought to discipline. If they had refused to investigate and punish, their authority might have been fatally undermined. Hence the best that the most enlightened critics of the trials could suggest was that every effort be made to reintegrate the erring witch into Christian society.

In some senses, the witch persecutions were an extreme case of prevailing attitudes to crime and wrongdoing generally.[72] Statistics on crime are not readily available for many areas. In Bavaria, which has been studied particularly thoroughly, it seems that between about 1560 and 1630 roughly 90 per cent of all executions were for crimes of violence (including murder) and crimes against property, morality, or religion.[73] In the first half of the century, prosecutions for crimes against morality and religion (36 per cent) exceeded prosecutions for crimes against property (25 per cent) and crimes of violence (20 per cent).[74] In most areas, the execution of witches formed a relatively small percentage of the total.[75] Of forty-eight people executed in Munich between 1574 and 1591, for example, thirty-one were punished for robbery and four each for murder and witchcraft.[76]

The fact that the years 1560–80 seem to have seen a peak in executions correlates both with the onset of the first crises and with the beginnings of the dovetailed process of governmental and Church reform that gained momentum in so many territories and cities at this time. More areas of human existence than ever came into the sights of governments eager to promote the business of reformation, the reform both of religion and society (though they rarely distinguished between the two). Blasphemy was defined as 'crimen laesae maiestatis divinae' (crime of injury to Divine majesty) and specified as a crime to be pursued by government.[77] Sexual deviance, including marital infidelity, was criminalized, as was prostitution, along with a list of other sexual crimes. Most Protestant territories had closed down their brothels by the 1540s and the Catholic territories steadily followed suit after 1555. In 1591, Cologne was one of the last to close down the brothel that the city magistrates themselves had established in the early fifteenth century in an attempt

---

[72] Good surveys are Van Dülmen, *Kultur*, ii, 246–74 and Conrad, *Rechtsgeschichte*, ii 406–35.

[73] Behringer, *Hexen*, 130.

[74] Behringer, 'Mörder', 99.

[75] Behringer, *Hexen*, 268.

[76] Behringer, 'Mörder', 95. Three Anabaptists were executed for heresy; two were executed for currency counterfeiting, one for threats of violence, one for sodomy, one for bigamy, and one for adultery.

[77] Van Dülmen, *Kultur*, ii, 247, 258, 269–74.

to control prostitution by containment and management. In Bavaria, prostitution was criminalized in 1562. Subsequently, Duke Wilhelm V (r. 1579–98) under-lined his motive for closing the Munich brothel that had been founded in 1433 by transferring the last seven whores to a convent. Not for nothing was he known as 'Wilhelm the Pious'.[78]

This process of extending the range and scope of justice unfolded unevenly from area to area.[79] Even where reform was relatively successful and regarded as exem-plary, its impact was probably haphazard and random. The translation of published laws into policy and the actual implementation of policy on the ground was an uncertain process. The degree of real control that it gave over society was fairly limited in most places.

What does seem to be clear, however, is that both the formulation of laws and their implementation, however inadequate, to a large degree reflected the interests of both the rulers and those whom they ruled. Despite periodic conflicts over principles and individual cases, law and punishment resulted from collaboration between governments, churches, Estates, and communities. Even limited law enforcement was not really possible without the cooperation of the populace. Indeed, many crimes only came to light when they were denounced to the authorities. The emphasis on sin as a cause of wrongdoing also reflects the views of both the educated and the common people: accusations of witchcraft and pacts with the devil were simply the most extreme manifestation of that.

The harsh punishment of crime also reflected that consensus. Subjects, judges, princes, and their councillors all believed that doing away with witches and evildoers would restore an ordered world in conformity with God's natural order.[80] There was no notion of improving the individual by means of correction; punishment was thus concentrated on atonement and setting as terrible an example as possible to others. The idea of punishment by means of confinement in houses of correction took root only gradually in the seventeenth century.[81] Before then, the death penalty in all its varied forms—hanging, beheading, breaking on the wheel, burning—was the only real sanction available for serious transgressions. Hence public executions were also rituals of purification and spectacles of instruction. They were events in which the public participated, not passively as spectators, but in the sense of interlocutors and hence, participants in the ritual. Executions that were not held in public had no social validity.[82]

The mixture of anxiety and repression, of desperate attempts at control and millenarian hope for renewal, gives the period before the Thirty Years War a particular intensity. In so far as the basic natural and economic causes of the anxiety and insecurity that beset much of the Reich from the 1560s onwards continued through the 1620s and 1630s, many of the problems remained unsolved. However,

[78] Behringer, 'Mörder', 100; Hippel, *Armut*, 38–9.
[79] Lanzinner, 'Zeitalter', 167–8.
[80] Lanzinner, 'Zeitalter', 171.
[81] Spierenburg, 'Confinement', 9–24.
[82] Van Dülmen, *Theater*, 147.

the long years of war intensified these problems and generated further pressures that led to the emergence of new solutions and a new approach to the problems of government. The visionaries of the years around 1600 had hopes for a general religious renewal. Frustrated by the failure of the successive moves towards Reformation in the sixteenth century, men such as Johann Valentin Andreae convinced themselves that the chaos of the age in which they lived marked the prelude to a new era. What emerged in fact fell far short of a general Reformation. However, the new constitutional settlement of the Reich that concluded the war in 1648 proved remarkably durable and conducive to the long-term security and stability of the Reich and its constituent parts.

VII

THE THIRTY YEARS WAR,
1618–1648

48

The Thirty Years War in German History

Since the nineteenth century, generations of historians have taken it as axiomatic that the Thirty Years War was the greatest disaster of German history. As Joachim Fest put it in 2004, the war was the 'Urkatastrophe' of the Germans.[1] It marked, he suggested, the origin of the German authoritarian tradition. While the princes trampled over their people, foreign powers trampled over Germany. The national cause was set back by two centuries.

Fest's comments reflect a long tradition that focuses on two themes. First, literary testimony from the writings of Grimmelshausen and others has dwelt on the catastrophic impact of the war on German society. The disastrous wars of the twentieth century led many subsequent authors, from Thomas Mann to Brecht and Grass, to draw analogies between the seventeenth-century conflict and the events of their own time. Indeed, Grimmelshausen's *Der abenteuerliche Simplicissimus Teutsch* ('The Adventurous Simplicissimus, a German'), the epic novel describing the traumatic experiences of the innocent Simplicius during the long years of conflict which led him to abandon Europe and end his life as a hermit in the South Atlantic, first really became a bestseller in the twentieth century. For the same reasons, Andreas Gryphius's poem *Tränen des Vaterlandes anno 1636* ('Tears of the Fatherland in 1636') remains perhaps the only German poem of the seventeenth century that is widely known and included in virtually all anthologies of German poetry.

Modern historical research has produced a more differentiated view. On the one hand, the war was undoubtedly disastrous for many communities in many parts of the Reich; the loss of population was massive and the trauma of the war shaped the thinking of generations afterwards. On the other hand, the long-term effect of the war on German society and economic development was perhaps not in fact as acute as the national tradition has assumed.

Second, both literary and historical-political writers have sought to establish the significance of the war and the Peace of Westphalia for the overall development of German history. Typical of the extremely negative judgements that long represented the norm was Heinrich Laube's lament in his novel *Der deutsche Krieg* ('The German War') of 1863–6. The war, he claimed, marked the end of over half a millennium during which the Germans had stood at the centre of Europe. According to Laube, the Peace of Westphalia 'poisoned the heart and soul of the German

[1] In *Die Welt*, 1 September 2004, available at http://www.welt.de/print-welt/article339631/ Mitleidlosigkeit_bis_zum_allerletzten_Punkt.html (accessed 4 May 2011).

Reich. It poisoned the Emperor; it poisoned the nation.'[2] That view long dominated the prevailing master narrative of German history and is still influential today.
Yet the commemoration of the 350th anniversary of the Peace of Westphalia in
1998 saw the formulation of much more positive views.[3] The treaty was praised as
the foundation of a durable peaceful order in Europe and as a German constitution,
even the foundation of the German *Rechtsstaat*, the civil state in which rights and
liberties are guaranteed by law.

The state of the Reich on the eve of the war does not at first sight seem conducive
to any revision of the old nationalist perspective. The international situation was
fraught, with most European powers embroiled in domestic conflict and poised to
act against external foes, both real and imagined.

In the Reich itself, conditions were as bad as they could be. Bad winters and poor
harvests over many decades had generated shortages, disease, and anxiety. Rural and
urban unrest was widespread. The persecution of witches was but the most striking
symptom of a society under huge strain. Confessional animosity was rife.[4] Catholic
and Calvinist activists confronted each other with unrestrained paranoia. For many
Calvinists, all Catholics were under the sway of the 'bloodthirsty Jesuits', whose
leaders were working in league with Madrid and Rome to construct a universal
monarchy. For many Catholics, all Protestants—even the Lutheran loyalists—were
under the sway of dangerous Calvinists, agents of the devil, aiming to extinguish the
Catholic faith and to subjugate the emperor and all the Estates to the dominion of
the Calvinist activists, the ruthless and irresponsible heirs of Machiavelli. The
confessional division, particularly the consequent taboo on marriages across the
divide, had undermined the traditional solidarity of the German upper nobility.

The whole political system of the Reich appeared paralysed. Years of weak and
pusillanimous government by Rudolf II and Matthias had undermined the authority of the crown. The imperial justice system had ground to a halt, no longer able to
make sense of the terms of the settlement of 1555. The Reichstag, too, was so
divided that there was no longer any point in convening it. The diminution of the
Turkish threat from about 1606 removed an important instrument of political
discipline from the imperial repertoire. Against both the spirit and all the traditions
of the Reich, armed leagues had formed in what many have argued was the prelude
to an inevitable civil war.

Yet the all too obvious political-confessional tensions only reveal part of the
picture. The extremists on both sides ignored the existence of a substantial body of
opinion that occupied the extensive ground between them. Of course, many of
those who formerly occupied the middle ground also in due course became
involved in the conflict. However, almost without exception they remained committed to the cause of the Reich. Indeed, even the extremists did not reject the
Reich. The accusation made by Catholic polemicists that the Calvinists aimed to

[2] Mannack, 'Streit', 702. Cramer, *Thirty Years' War* is an excellent study of the war in nineteenth-
century German memory.
[3] See the essays collected in Bussmann and Schilling, *1648*.
[4] Gotthard, *Altes Reich*, 80–2.

dissolve the Reich and to 'pervert and invert the existing order of things' was as wide of the mark as Calvinist polemics were about the threat of a Jesuitical world tyranny. They disagreed fundamentally about the interpretation of the terms of the settlement of 1555, and this was reflected in the deadlock of both the Reichs-kammergericht and the Reichstag.

This disagreement also implied a larger issue about the nature of the Reich itself. In a sense, this revolved around the role of the Reichshofrat, the court more directly controlled by the emperor and which, as the Reichskammergericht became more embroiled in confessional disagreements, was increasingly used to issue decrees that favoured Catholics. One of the things that had aggravated the political situation since the early 1580s was the not inaccurate Protestant perception that the Reichs-hofrat was being used as an agency of imperial government, rather than as a true court of justice. This, in turn, revived all the old arguments about the emperor's prerogatives and the balance of powers between emperor and Estates. Fundamen-tally, the issues around 1600 were the same as they had been in the debate about Maximilian I's reform proposals around 1500. The difference was that the confes-sional division had strengthened the imperial position by fostering an alliance between the crown and the Catholic Estates. This was the result, above all, of the determination to defend the ecclesiastical territories against Protestant subversion. But this community of interest was also limited and conditional: the Catholic Estates wanted the emperor to protect them; they did not want a powerful emperor per se.

49

What Kind of Conflict?

Historians have been divided over the scope and the nature of the Thirty Years War.[1] Some have argued that events in Germany must be seen as part of a much longer and wider struggle. The German Thirty Years War, some have suggested, was part of an eighty-year war in which the key issue was the position of the Habsburgs in Europe. The most important elements in this longer conflict were the rebellion of the Netherlands against Spanish rule from 1568 and the rivalry between Spain and France that culminated in prolonged military confrontation between 1635 and 1659.

However, contemporaries soon referred to the problems in the Reich as the 'German war'. By its conclusion, many were already referring to 'the thirty years German war', thereby both denoting its duration and distinguishing it from the Schmalkaldic War of the previous century.[2] Of course, the German war could not help but be related to other conflicts of the time. Numerous German princes, starting with the Habsburgs themselves, had relatives and interests outside the Reich, which shaped their perception of their own position and interests as the political and military situation evolved. Equally, neighbouring powers, such as the rulers of France, Poland, and Sweden, could not ignore the crisis of the Reich and built their assessment of it into their own calculations.

French hostility to continuing Habsburg domination in Europe, and the fear of being caught in a Spanish–Austrian pincer, was a key underlying factor in the first half of the seventeenth century, as it had been for much of the sixteenth. On the other hand, Louis XIII initially sympathized with Ferdinand's predicament, since for much of the 1620s, he faced a similar threat of a Dutch-style secession of the Huguenots in south-western France.[3] Once that problem was solved by the destruction of the Huguenot stronghold of La Rochelle in 1628, French policy focused more consistently on the problem of the Habsburg pincer, with Spain as much a target as the Austrian territories in the Reich. The Dutch rebellion, too, continued to reverberate in the Reich. Indeed, legally, the Dutch provinces only ceased to be part of the Reich in 1648. The imminent end of the Twelve Years' Truce concluded between Spain and the Dutch in 1609 was very much in the minds of politicians on all sides as the terminal date loomed.

---

[1] There is a good overview in Asch, *Thirty Years War*, 1–8. See also Burkhardt, *Krieg, passim.*
[2] Mortimer, 'Contemporaries'; Mueller, 'Thirty Years' War'; Schmidt, 'Teutsche Kriege', 49.
[3] Lublinskaya, *Absolutism*, 146–219; Asch, *Thirty Years War*, 77–9.

In northern Italy, hostile forces also continued to threaten the position of the Habsburgs, notably Venice and Savoy, with France always in the background and the papacy an unreliable ally.[4] Furthermore, the Italian situation assumed a new significance as the Twelve Years' Truce approached its end and in the context of the understanding reached between the Spanish and Austrian Habsburgs in the Oñate treaty in 1617.[5] Spanish troops needed to be able to reach the Tyrol, both to assist in Austria and to move from there up to the Low Countries. Austrian troops needed to be able to reach Lombardy.

The key lay in the Valtelline which ran between Lake Como and the Inn, a predominantly Catholic dependency of the staunchly Protestant canton of Graubünden (the Grisons). The savage repression of a Catholic rebellion there in 1618 served as the pretext for Habsburg intervention in 1620, which was temporarily secured at the cost of much Protestant blood. But Italy remained fraught with danger: France was poised to intervene on behalf of Graubünden and there were continuing uncertainties over the Mantuan succession, in which both France and the Habsburgs had an interest. The Spanish and Austrian Habsburgs had reached a rare level of understanding of their separate and mutual interests by 1617 and a determination to collaborate in promoting them. Had they succeeded in all their objectives, their power in Europe would have been immense. However, that did not mean that there was anything like a plan to create a Habsburg universal monarchy, as some of their enemies alleged.[6]

New potential fields of conflict had also opened up in the Baltic region. The Catholic Vasa dynasty in Poland maintained its claim to the Swedish crown. Sigismund III, the emperor's brother-in-law, had acquired the Swedish throne in 1592 but had been deposed there by his uncle, Duke Charles. The latter's son, the Lutheran Gustavus Adolphus, was ambitious both to secure his throne against any possible assault from Poland and to extend its footprint across the Baltic.[7] That, in turn, posed a challenge to Denmark.

The Danes had fought two major wars against Sweden in 1563–70 and 1611–13 in order to preserve their hegemony in Scandinavia and their supremacy over the Baltic. Following the second war, Christian IV (r. 1588–1648) had entered into a defensive alliance with the Dutch. He was also directly involved in German affairs for, as Duke of Holstein, he was himself a prince of the Reich. Christian IV was endowed with a substantial treasury, swollen with the vast profits derived from the Sound Dues and with the indemnity of one million thaler extracted from Sweden in 1613.[8] His predecessor Frederik II (r. 1559–88) had played a cautious game, acting as a Protestant *éminence grise* and building up a reputation as a power to be

---

[4] On Savoy, see Osbourne, *Dynasty*, 19–49, 143–92.
[5] Parker, *Thirty Years War*, 37–8.
[6] Asch, *Thirty Years War*, 34–46; Parker, *Thirty Years War*, 2–10.
[7] Parker, *Thirty Years War*, 62.
[8] From 1429, the Sound Dues were levied on all ships that passed through the Danish straits, ships being obliged to stop at Helsingør and dues set in 1567 at 1–2% of cargo value. The value of the Sound Dues diminished when Denmark was obliged to cede her provinces east of the Sound to Sweden in 1660; they were only abolished in 1857.

reckoned with but, wisely, never actually committing himself to any of the numerous schemes for the defence of European Protestantism put to him by French, Dutch, English, and German emissaries. Christian IV thought less about the wider situation of Western European Protestantism, but was fully alive to the pursuit of his own political, territorial, and dynastic interests in a regional theatre that he was convinced he could dominate.[9]

The fact that a large number of interlocking conflicts played into the Thirty Years War has also generated debates over what the war was actually about. The answer no doubt differs for different actors. Many did indeed see the conflict as a struggle against the Habsburgs in Europe. German Protestant propaganda frequently underlined the international implications of the German struggle against Habsburg authority by juxtaposing 'teutsche Libertet' with 'spanische Servitut', suggesting, as their predecessors had done in the 1580s, that Spain was the real enemy.[10] A variation on that theme was the assertion that the conflict was a European-wide struggle against the Jesuits and Catholicism, a struggle for the survival of Protestantism everywhere. Ferdinand II himself, from time to time, believed that he was fighting a holy war.[11] However, in his instructions to Wallenstein, Ferdinand urged his general to use the 'praetextum der Religion' as frequently as possible, just as his enemies had done to great effect.[12]

Religion was never the sole motivating force. The Protestant Union dissolved soon after the war started without fighting a single battle. Indeed, the war was not a straightforward conflict between Catholic and Protestant. The Protestants were divided and many Lutherans were just as suspicious of the Reformed or Calvinist activists as they were of the more activist Catholics.[13] The Lutheran Elector of Saxony was, for a time, one of the emperor's most important allies. Some moderate Reformed rulers had more in common with the Lutheran loyalists than they did with those who identified openly as Calvinists with their counterparts in the Netherlands and France. Some Lutherans, in turn, jibbed at the authority of the Saxon Elector and for that reason supported the Palatine Elector. Equally, not all Catholics were blindly committed to a struggle against Protestantism. Duke Maximilian of Bavaria was pursuing his own dynastic and territorial interests in supporting the emperor. Later, those same interests led him to oppose the crown.

Even the Jesuits, consistently vilified in much Protestant propaganda as a single force fanatically devoted to an exclusively religious end, were in reality quite flexible. Jesuit policy differed from region to region. Jesuit confessors and advisers were well aware of the worldly interests of their princely and royal masters; harmonizing their own spiritual concerns with those interests often meant counselling compromise rather than confrontation.[14] The advice given by the Jesuit confessors Wilhelm Lamormaini (1570–1648) and Adam Contzen in

[9] Lockhart, *Frederik II*, 316–17.
[10] Schmidt, *Universalmonarchie*, 29–50, 440–50.
[11] Bireley, 'Religious war'.
[12] Schormann, 'Krieg', 277.
[13] Gotthard, 'Wer sich salviren könd'.
[14] Bireley, *Jesuits*, 1–32, 267–75.

Vienna and Munich, respectively firmly supported the pursuit of militant Counter-Reformation. Yet their aim was not total victory but to restore the position that Catholicism had enjoyed in 1555 under the Peace of Augsburg. By the 1630s, it seemed unlikely that could be achieved and after 1635 their successors, Johann Gans (1591–after 1648) in Vienna and Johannes Vervaux (1585–1661) in Munich, advocated a more accommodating attitude and the abandonment of any idea of a providential mission. Their counterparts in France and Spain took different lines as well: in Madrid, Francisco Aguado viewed the war as an essentially secular conflict in which Spain's real enemies were the Dutch and the French, rather than the German Protestants. The Jesuit superior general, Muzio Vitelleschi (1563–1645), did not preside over a monolithic organization. Rather, he attempted to steer a course between the various regions, each with its own distinct perspectives.

The conflict was a religious one to the extent that any conflict in the Reich almost inevitably involved religion. The rights of German princes in matters of ecclesiastical jurisdiction were, after all, among their most fundamental prerogatives. Disputes over the ambiguities of the (religious) Peace of Augsburg had been at the root of the growing constitutional crisis of the Reich. In particular, questions relating to the lands of the Church had never been definitively resolved. The conflict that began in 1618 was, in that sense, an armed continuation of the political and legal conflict that had animated the Reich for decades. If at first the war was fought essentially to restore Habsburg control in Austria and Bohemia, it soon turned into a wider struggle that revolved around the question of the German bishoprics and around the question of imperial authority. Indeed, the emperor's treatment of Friedrich V itself became a key issue, since it raised important questions concerning the customs and laws of the Reich and the powers of the emperor.

Finally, in two respects the war was a rather different conflict to any previously. First, it was accompanied by more propaganda than ever before. That partly reflected the steady development of printing over the previous century. Pamphlets and flysheets became an integral part of any political discourse.[15] By the early seventeenth century, regular news sheets and the first newspapers had begun to appear. Around 1600, moreover, the formal separation of the Spanish postal service based in Brussels from the imperial service led to the establishment of an increasingly efficient *Reichspost* run by the Taxis family as a highly profitable commercial enterprise which hugely accelerated the transmission and exchange of information.[16] Furthermore, the absence of an effective central government in the Reich meant that the German system was subject neither to the Inquisition nor to the governmental constraints that limited the private use of equivalent systems in France and England into the 1620s.

The German war was the first war fought out in the context of the communications revolution that both created an appetite for news and, increasingly, began to create the news itself. The Frankfurt postmaster Johann von der Birghden, appointed in 1615 by the Generaloberpostmeister Lamoral von Taxis to direct

---

[15] Burkhardt, *Krieg*, 225–32; Schmidt, *Universalmonarchie*, 84–94; Langer, *Thirty Years War*, 235–57.
[16] Behringer, *Merkur*, 166–75. See also pp. 370–1.

the newly established Frankfurt postal station, soon extended the network to Nuremberg, Leipzig, Hamburg, and other centres, and supplied it with his own newspaper, the *Frankfurter kaiserliche Reichsoberpostamtszeitung*.[17] It was said that his reports, and—just as important—his false reports, were worth the equivalent of an army. As a Lutheran, he inevitably became suspect to the Catholic imperial authorities and he was sacked for alleged political agitation in 1626 (though immediately reinstated by the Swedish occupation of Frankfurt 1631–5).

The vicissitudes of the war eventually ruined many printers, but, initially, many profited from a printing boom. In 1618 alone, the Bohemian crisis generated over eighteen hundred pamphlets and several hundred flysheets. That level of production was not reached again, though the years 1629–33, 1635, and 1643–8 saw further peaks of propagandistic and literary activity. Two other forms of publication remained consistently important throughout. The first was the plethora of opinions commissioned by German rulers at every stage from legal and other experts at their own or other 'friendly' universities. In a period when imperial institutions did not function and there were no meetings of the Reichstag until 1640, the princes communicated their reactions by means of pamphlets and position papers known as *Denkschriften*.[18] The academics, especially the exponents of the new field of public law, were more than happy to oblige. Linked with that activity was the practice of publishing captured enemy documents that exposed alleged perfidy and illuminated the ramifications of convoluted conspiracies. For those who published them, such as Ferdinand II after the capture of the Winter King's Prague archive, the aim was clearly to claim the moral and legal high ground, but also to warn minor players, whose activities had been exposed, against any further seditious acts.[19]

The other novel feature of the German war was the way in which it came to be conducted militarily.[20] Most parties in the Reich were woefully ill-prepared for any prolonged conflict. The militias that German rulers had raised over the preceding decades proved next to useless in the struggles of the 1620s. At the same time, raising mercenary forces strained the resources of all but a small minority. By the early 1620s, even before any serious fighting, many German territories were already in financial crisis. By 1625, the sheer scale of the war already far surpassed any previous conflict, and over the next decade more than a quarter of a million troops served in the Reich.[21]

Traditional methods of raising money for military purposes often proved inadequate. Foreign subsidies became essential on both sides, but so too did ever more elaborate and onerous ways of allowing armies to live off the land as they fought. Various kinds of 'contributions' became routine. One involved simple marauding

[17] *ADB*, ii, 658–60; Behringer, *Merkur*, 382–92.
[18] Parker, *Thirty Years War*, 99.
[19] Schormann, *Krieg*, 32; Press, *Kriege*, 200.
[20] The military history of the war, with detailed accounts of all battles, is treated in Guthrie, *Battles* and Guthrie, *Later Thirty Years War*. The fullest account of the war in English, including much excellent military analysis, is Wilson, *Europe's tragedy*. See also Langer, *Thirty Years War*, 127–86.
[21] Parker, *Thirty Years War*, 186.

to provide troops with whatever they needed in the way of food, horses, and other goods. Another involved the formal designation of particular areas to support a garrison or other force, with all regular taxes and dues being dedicated to this purpose for the duration of the hostilities. An early example of this was the grant by the emperor to Duke Maximilian in 1620 of the right to occupy and tax the lands of the Upper Palatinate and Upper Austria.[22] The confiscation or temporary forfeit of 'rebel' property became one of the main instruments of imperial war financing, but simultaneously a further bone of contention between the emperor and his critics in the Reich.

This was also true of the boldest attempt to create an effective imperial force by the Bohemian commander Albrecht Wallenstein during the 1620s.[23] Wallenstein was not so much an innovator as an entrepreneur who developed the contribution system to its fullest extent. To circumvent the effects of the delayed payment of contributions, he organized a credit line through his banker Hans de Witte. The latter was a refugee from Flanders who formally became a Calvinist on settling in Prague in 1603, where he used his international contacts to build up a flourishing banking business which counted the imperial court among its clients. Despite his religion, de Witte had no truck with the Calvinist regime in Prague after 1618; he preferred to compromise his faith rather than tolerate the corruption and incompetence of the Bohemian Estates.[24]

Wallenstein's motives have been subject to much speculation. He later claimed that he merely wished to raise an army, rather than maintain his own private force on a permanent basis. A Bohemian nobleman of modest origins and a convert to Catholicism at the age of twenty, Wallenstein had served as colonel to the Moravian Estates from 1615. He had raised a modest mercenary force to fight on Ferdinand's behalf against Venice and he then fought for Ferdinand's victory in Bohemia, from which he profited by buying the lordships of Friedland and Reichenberg. That territorial base formed the core of what soon became an expanding and consolidated territory that Ferdinand elevated to a duchy in 1624. Marriage to the daughter of Count Harrach in 1623, meanwhile, had cemented Wallenstein's relationship to some of the most influential members of Ferdinand's court. His military enterprise also expanded apace as the business of raising new regiments was subcontracted to others who, in turn, subcontracted the recruitment of companies to form them. Unlike other mercenary commanders of the period, Wallenstein issued recruiting patents in his own name, rather than that of his employer.[25]

If Wallenstein's first moves revealed him to be an arriviste, supporting the emperor in order to secure his own gains, the relationship was soon reversed. The emperor came to be dependent upon him, or rather his ability to raise and sustain a substantial force of 24,000 men and to loan Ferdinand some eight million gulden. The creation of the Duchy of Friedland was the first part of his reward. In 1627, he was given the Silesian principality of Sagan and other confiscated properties. The following year, he was granted the Duchy of Mecklenburg, and a

[22] Press, *Kriege*, 208.   [23] *BWDG*, iii, 3025–31.
[24] Schormann, *Krieg*, 88.   [25] Anderson, *War*, 48–9.

secret contract of 1632 hinted that he might have the Electorate of Brandenburg if he could conquer it.

Such powers aroused envy, hostility, and alarm. Catholic princes such as the Duke of Bavaria resented being sidelined by the enterprising upstart. Even the emperor's closest advisers became alarmed at how powerful Wallenstein had become and at the signs that he might begin to operate as an independent quasi-sovereign power in the interests of his own growing state within a state, rather than in the interests of the Habsburgs. Hence Wallenstein was dismissed in June 1630 at the insistence of the Electors. In 1632, he was recalled to deal with the Swedes after Maximilian of Bavaria had lost both his territory and his military commander Jean Tserclaes de Tilly. By the end of the year, he had raised and armed 120,000 men. However, Wallenstein's failure to follow through his victory over Gustavus Adolphus at Lützen on 16 November 1632 aroused suspicions in Vienna. In February 1634, the emperor's decree depriving him of his command and ordering his imprisonment, or execution if that proved impossible, resulted in his murder.

Wallenstein was the most spectacular example of a military enterpriser. However, on the other side, admittedly on a lesser scale, Count Ernst von Mansfeld (until his death in 1626) and Duke Bernhard of Saxony-Weimar in the 1630s operated in much the same way. Such enterprises were able to flourish in the Reich after 1618 because the rules that governed its normal operations were suspended with the paralysis of its political and legal institutions. They gave hope alternately to either side that they might force a resolution. For much of the first decade or so of the war, the emperor and the Catholics had more grounds for optimism.

50

The Reconquest of Austria and Bohemia, 1618–1623

In the first phase of the conflict, Ferdinand mobilized allies and resources to restore his authority in Austria and Bohemia. The papacy sent two million gulden. Spain offered troops and Ambassador Count Iñigo Oñate encouraged Ferdinand to promise Maximilian of Bavaria compensation for any costs he incurred, considerable freedom of action, and the promise of any territory conquered by the German Catholic League, as well as the transfer of the Palatine Electoral title. The prospect of ending the precedence of the Palatine Wittelsbachs over the Bavarians was something that Maximilian could not resist. In the Treaty of Munich on 8 October 1619, Maximilian agreed to raise an army of the League against the rebels.

The following spring, at a series of meetings of the Electors and some princes at Würzburg and Mühlhausen, it proved possible to enlist further support to prevent the 'Bohemian fire' spreading into the Reich. The Catholic Electors promised that secularized Church lands would not be reclaimed, or if reclaimed then only against fair compensation, provided their owners remained loyal to the emperor. The Elector of Saxony was promised a lien on Lusatia if he would raise an army. The Bavarian demand that the Palatine Elector be outlawed was postponed until after the hostilities.

The emperor received further support from France in July, when the Duke of Angoulême brokered a truce between the forces of the Union and the League at Ulm on 3 July.[1] Louis XIII initially offered to send an army: he was sympathetic to his cousin's problems for he himself had faced the same kind of Calvinist threat. In the event, however, a complex peace plan was developed, though the next stage, a truce between the emperor and Friedrich V, failed to come about. In the meantime, the Ulm truce gave the imperial side a decisive advantage, since the League forces were able to move off towards Austria while the Union troops were tied down in the west by news of the advance of Ambrogio di Spinola's Spanish force from the Netherlands.[2]

The Prague government, by contrast, had managed to achieve very little. None of Friedrich's international contacts, which had been one of his main attractions for

[1] Parker, *Thirty Years War*, 54.
[2] Spinola (1569–1630) was Genoese by origin and a military commander in Spanish service. He played a key role in the Spanish attempts to reconquer the Netherlands in the early seventeenth century. See Israel, *Dutch Republic 1476–1806*, 387–8.

the rebels, offered any significant support. He was recognized as king by Denmark, Sweden, the Dutch Republic, and Venice, but only the Dutch gave him money.[3] His father-in-law, James I, hesitated to recognize a usurper on grounds of principle, but he was also anxious that events in Bohemia should not undermine his own efforts to seek an understanding with Spain: the Palatine activists failed to appreciate that James wanted peace with both the Dutch and the Spaniards.[4]

Friedrich's triumphal entry into Prague belied a precarious situation. Bohemian forces joined with Bethlen Gábor's troops in advancing again on Vienna in October 1619. The defeat of the Habsburg army in Hungary was a serious blow; the Spanish ambassador believed that the fate of the house of Austria hung in the balance.[5] However, Bethlen's advance was halted by the news that the King of Poland had permitted Ferdinand to recruit Cossack troops. In November, they had moved south into Upper Hungary and now threatened his own Transylvanian principality. Despite the fact that the rebel Hungarian diet elected him Prince of Hungary on 15 January 1620, Bethlen was obliged to withdraw from the conflict.

That left Friedrich without major allies and dependent on his own resources, the Bohemian and Austrian Estates, and on a handful of minor German princes, many of whom were younger sons with little or no land, let alone money, to their names. When the crisis came, Count Mansfeld's mercenary force of some 4,000 men was of little use, for it was quartered in Pilsen. In any case, Mansfeld was already negotiating a betrayal of the Bohemian cause with the imperial commander Count Bucquoy, in return for his own elevation as an Imperial Count in his own right and appointment as stadtholder of the province of Luxemburg.[6] Friedrich himself had little money: the Palatinate had been in severe financial crisis for decades. The Bohemian treasury was also unable to sustain a major conflict.[7] By early 1619, the provisional government was so short of funds that it resorted to raising loans from towns by force. By August, they owed their troops 1.8 million thaler in pay. The early months of Friedrich's Prague court had been marked by extraordinary festivities and almost boundless extravagance. It was no wonder that he was soon forced to pawn his silver plate and other valuables.

Nor did Friedrich reign over a united polity. The regional divisions between the various Estates remained strong; the *Confoederatio Bohemica* and its various affiliates had no clear centre or driving force. Almost all the regions still contained significant numbers of Catholic nobles as well as Protestants who remained cautious or fundamentally loyal to the emperor.[8] The noble activist leaders, furthermore, may have been rebels in their own cause, but they were generally strict authoritarians when it came to their peasants.[9] While humanist poets like the young Martin Opitz celebrated the new monarch's progress, there was little popular enthusiasm

[3] Schormann, *Krieg*, 30–1; MacHardy, *War*, 72–3.
[4] Pursell, *Winter King*, 53–7; Clasen, *Palatinate*, 25.
[5] Schormann, *Krieg*, 30; Parker, *Thirty Years War*, 46–50, 52.
[6] Ritter, *Geschichte*, iii, 192–3. Mansfeld was a younger son and thus not a ruling prince.
[7] Schorman, *Krieg*, 87–8; Clasen, *Palatinate*, 31–2.
[8] MacHardy, *War*, 76–88.
[9] Wilson, *Reich*, 121–2.

for his cause. Friedrich was by no means the dupe of his zealous Calvinist advisers, but he had precious little time to consolidate his position in Prague, let alone the kingdom at large.[10] The Calvinist reform of St Vitus Cathedral in Prague generated alienation and alarm in a city dominated by Lutherans and Catholics. At no stage was there any real prospect of a mass uprising to defend the liberties of Bohemia.

The end came with remarkable speed and decisiveness. The League forces under Count Tilly occupied Upper Austria at the end of July 1620. The imperial army under Bucquoy took Lower Austria. In the north, the Saxons moved into Lusatia. Tilly and Bucquoy then marched north towards Prague and engaged the Bohemian forces at the White Mountain just outside the city on 8 November. The battle lasted scarcely two hours. No preparations had been made for the defence of Prague. Indeed, the city closed its gates to prevent the entry of the routed Bohemian army and even intimated that it would deliver up the king. The following dawn, Friedrich and his court left for Breslau. After a futile attempt to organize resistance in Silesia, he fled first to Brandenburg and from there to The Hague. The reign of the 'Winter King' was over.

Friedrich's days as Elector of the Palatinate were also numbered. His rejection of an offer of leniency if he agreed to submit to the emperor's authority led directly to his being outlawed in January 1621. That made an immediate impression on most of the German Protestants. Combined with further imperial assurances, it resulted in the voluntary dissolution of the Union and the disbandment of its forces in April. Friedrich's retention of the Palatinate was now dependent on the support of three mercenary forces, each led by either a desperado or an adventurer. Mansfeld had moved west after the fiasco in Bohemia. At ruinous cost to himself, the Lutheran Margrave of Baden-Durlach raised nearly 10,000 men, not out of loyalty to the Palatinate but because his Catholic relatives had obtained a Reichshofrat judgment against him. He calculated that if the Palatinate fell he would lose everything anyway.[11] The motives of Christian of Brunswick, the Administrator of Halberstadt, are less obvious. Known as the 'mad Halberstädter', he was infatuated with Friedrich's English wife and inspired by grand ideals of chivalry. As the younger brother of the Duke of Brunswick-Wolfenbüttel and the Lutheran administrator of a bishopric whose cathedral chapter disapproved of his military adventures and excluded him as far as possible from government, he too faced disaster if the emperor triumphed.[12]

They were unable to save the Palatinate. The margrave was defeated at Wimpfen on 6 May 1622. Mansfeld was outmanoeuvred at every turn and withdrew into Alsace. Christian of Brunswick had slowly fought his way down from the north against opposition from imperial and Hessian forces, pillaging towns and ecclesiastical foundations to supply his troops. At Höchst, however, he was finally defeated by Tilly's forces on 20 June, before crossing the Main. By then, Spinola's Spanish troops occupied the Palatinate's territories on the left bank of the Rhine, while

[10] Pursell, *Winter King*, 93–116.
[11] Press, 'Badische Markgrafen', 36–8.
[12] *ADB*, iv, 677–83.

Tilly's League army occupied those on the right bank. Heidelberg fell to Tilly on 19 September; Mannheim followed shortly after. In March 1623, the Elector gave orders from The Hague to concede the last great Palatine fortress at Frankenthal.

Once Heidelberg had fallen, there was really little hope that Duke Wilhelm IV of Saxony-Weimar's appeal for a German Peace League launched just six weeks later might succeed. The idea that all should be forgiven and that the Estates of the Reich, including the Palatine Elector, should now convene with the emperor to deliberate on a permanent peace settlement that granted religious freedom to all was quite unrealistic.[13] Without a major backer, the idea lacked credibility. Quite apart from his habitual loyalism, the Elector of Saxony was currently more preoccupied with extracting compensation from Lusatia than with the plight of those nobles who had been implicated in the rebellion. Another of Duke Wilhelm's Ernestine cousins, Duke Friedrich of Saxony-Altenburg, raised a small force, but otherwise the appeal failed. The following summer, Tilly pursued Christian of Brunswick's army as it fled back northwards through Westphalia. His planned escape into the Dutch Republic was thwarted comprehensively on 6 August 1623 by Tilly's League army just short of the Dutch border at Stadtlohn. Key officers, including Duke Wilhelm of Weimar, were taken as prisoners to Vienna; Christian himself barely escaped with a few regiments but drew the consequences of his defeat by resigning the administratorship of Halberstadt in favour of Prince Frederik of Denmark.

---

[13] Menzel, 'Union', 38–40.

51

Ferdinand Victorious

The emperor's victory was comprehensive. The way he handled it turned out to be disastrous. Promises made to his allies now had to be honoured. Spain expected to be allowed to retain control of the Palatine left bank of the Rhine to guarantee the transit route for its troops north to the Netherlands. At the same time, the Spanish expected Austrian support in their military occupation of the Valtelline, which Graubünden was obliged to cede to Austria and Spain by the Treaty of Lindau in September 1622. Only six weeks later, however, the French monarchy concluded the Peace of Montpellier with the Huguenots. This treaty gave France a free hand to resume its support for the Swiss Protestants, which the emerging Richelieu (formally appointed in 1623) urgently argued held the key to the objective of undermining Habsburg hegemony.

The debt owed to Maximilian of Bavaria proved equally problematic. The promise of the Electoral title had been made in secrecy. However, the publication of clandestine correspondence by the Palatine councillor Ludwig Camerarius made it impossible to deny that a deal had been done. The papacy, moreover, urged that the transfer be formalized and demanded that the famous Heidelberg library should be given to Rome as a reward for its own support. The emperor hesitated to impose such a substantial penalty on Friedrich V. Maximilian hesitated to agree to such an expensive gift to the pope from the property of his own dynasty. Furthermore, he presented the emperor with a bill for his own costs amounting to precisely 116,000,771 gulden, 40 kreuzer, and 1 heller.[1]

In the event, the library went to Rome, though it was first taken to Munich, where each volume was supplied with an ex-libris of the new Bavarian Elector.[2] At a meeting of selected princes at Regensburg in January–February 1623, Maximilian was formally enfeoffed as Elector and the Palatinate was placed under joint Spanish and Bavarian administration.[3] Heidelberg remained in Bavarian hands until 1648, with a brief interruption in 1633–5 when it was occupied by Swedish troops. Maximilian was granted a temporary lien on the Upper Palatinate and Upper Austria to help him recover the twelve million gulden of his costs that Ferdinand

---

[1] Langer, 'Krieg', 290.
[2] Keunecke, 'Maximilian'; Kirschberger, 'Vorbereitung'. The German manuscripts alone were returned in 1816 following the Congress of Vienna; the books remain in Rome to this day. The Manesse Codex did not go to Rome. It may have been among the books that travelled with Friedrich V to Prague; it ended up in Paris, and was finally returned to Heidelberg in 1888.
[3] Gotthard, *Säulen*, i, 100–12.

recognized. In 1628, the Upper Palatinate was formally transferred to him in perpetuity in lieu of ten million gulden still owed by the emperor.

With the exception of the Landgrave of Hessen-Darmstadt, the Protestant princes who were invited to attend at Regensburg stayed away. The Electors of Saxony and Brandenburg were incensed by the fact that the emperor had secretly promised something so serious without consultation. In the event, they sent representatives to register their concerns. The Elector of Saxony formally withdrew from his alliance with the emperor, though not without confirming his lien from him on Upper Lusatia and securing one on Lower Lusatia as compensation for the costs that Saxony had incurred.[4] The Electors' objections caused the emperor to transfer the Electoral title to Maximilian personally for his own lifetime, rather than to his line in perpetuity. That, however, did little to assuage the growing resentment among Protestants at the emperor's unjust treatment of Friedrich V.

Their anger was further fuelled by the treatment meted out to the vanquished territories. In the Palatinate left of the Rhine, Spanish forces immediately began a systematic campaign of Counter-Reformation.[5] Maximilian of Bavaria did likewise in the right-bank territories and in the Upper Palatinate. The University of Heidelberg was closed and a Jesuit school was established in 1622. The Protestant publishing houses that had promoted Palatine Calvinist culture and prospered from it were forced out of business. The occupying forces worked with the Bishop of Speyer, Christoph von Soetern (from 1623 also Archbishop and Elector of Trier), to bring about a systematic Counter-Reformation, while Maximilian also relied heavily on the Jesuits and the Capuchins.

A variety of factors impeded these efforts. There were simply not enough Catholic clergy to take the place of the expelled Calvinists. More serious still were the conflicts that arose between the various authorities. As Bishop of Speyer, Soetern had been attacked by the Palatinate. Consequently, he now wanted the Palatinate to become a Catholic territory but a politically weak one. Maximilian, by contrast, had plans for a Jesuit citadel, a bastion of militant Catholicism on the Rhine, which alarmed both Soetern and the Electors of Mainz and Cologne. The Spaniards were driven by military concerns, but their need to transport troops north to the Netherlands inevitably brought them into conflict with the three ecclesiastical Electors, whose lands would be affected by such operations.

There were no such constraints on Maximilian in the Upper Palatinate.[6] The administration there was swiftly purged of all Calvinist officials and Catholic worship was systematically reintroduced. In 1626, all Reformed preachers were expelled and two years later, the Lutherans followed; many of the old Lutheran elite also left, preferring exile to enforced conversion. In contrast to the Rhineland Palatinate, the Catholic Counter-Reformation was successful here. By 1628,

---

[4] Köbler, *Lexikon*, 468, 483. The Habsburgs formally ceded the territories to Saxony in the Peace of Prague 1635.
[5] Schindling and Ziegler, *Territorien*, v, 39–42.
[6] Schmid, 'Kurfürst Maximilian'.

when Maximilian received permanent title to the territory, the Upper Palatinate was fully Catholic.

Ferdinand II proceeded in similar fashion in his own lands. The methods that had won him control in Graz were now employed more generally.[7] The re-establishment of political control was combined with systematic Counter-Reformation. In Bohemia, decisive steps were taken at every level to deal with the rebellion and with heresy. On 21 June 1621, twenty-seven ringleaders, including ten nobles and Jan Jesenský, rector of the Prague university, were executed in a public spectacle presided over by Ferdinand's stadtholder, Prince Karl von Liechtenstein. Over 1,500 other nobles were tried before a 'Confiscations Court' and some 600 lost all or part of their estates. Those who forfeited only part of their property were in effect deprived of the whole, as they simply received financial compensation for the rest.

That money, in turn, was paid out in a currency that was deliberately and systematically debased by Liechtenstein, in league with Hans de Witte and the Jewish financier Jakob Bassevi, as members of a fifteen-member consortium that, in January 1622, leased all the mints in Bohemia, Moravia, and Lower Austria for one year. The aim was both to ruin the rebels and to facilitate purchase of their property by loyal Catholics; the result was to ruin the Bohemian economy.[8] Their activities also destabilized other parts of the Reich, as other rulers quickly followed their example; for two years, a period known as the *Kipper- und Wipperzeit* (the 'see-saw era'), there was general currency instability.[9]

In Bohemia, the extinction of political opposition was quickly followed by the imposition of religious uniformity. First Calvinist and then Lutheran ministers were expelled. Religious freedom of any kind was formally abolished; the Anabaptists and other sects were expelled en masse. Next in line were the towns, whose privileges were abolished and lands confiscated. In 1627–8, the entire nobility was confronted with the choice between conversion to Catholicism or exile. At the same time, the legal and constitutional structures that had facilitated the rebellion were systematically subverted. In 1627, the *Verneuerte Landesordnung* ('Renewed Constitution') was promulgated for Bohemia; Moravia received a similar statute the following year.[10]

The new constitution effectively negated the rights of the Estates. The Bohemian crown ceased to be elective and was declared hereditary in the house of Habsburg. Catholicism was declared the sole religion, and the clergy resumed their position as the first Estate. Only Judaism was also tolerated. All state officials were henceforth obliged to swear an oath to the king. The office of Burgrave of Karlstein, the traditional custodians of the royal regalia, was suppressed.[11] Other offices became subject to royal appointment (and dismissal), while the king took from the Estates the right to grant patents of nobility. The crown's judicial powers were also

---

[7] Winkelbauer, *Ständefreiheit*, i, 73–8, 98–104.
[8] Parker, *Thirty Years War*, 80–1.
[9] Kindelberger, 'Economic crisis'.
[10] Evans, *Making*, 197–200. [11] Evans, *Making*, 198.

considerably enhanced. Finally, the German language was declared equal to Czech for all state purposes.

In total, some 150,000 left Bohemia for exile. The terms of the constitution were ameliorated somewhat in 1640 when the diet regained some powers of initiative, but the basic political-religious settlement defined the Bohemian polity into the nineteenth century. By no means all those who benefited from the sale of confiscated property were of non-Bohemian origin. However, the general effect of the changes in the 1620s, altered only slightly by the grants of land made to Italian, Irish, and French military commanders in the 1630s and 1640s, was to create a discrete caste of magnates loyal to the crown that dominated the social hierarchy.[12] Similar changes occurred in Moravia, driven by political calculation, rather than sentiment: even figures such as Karl Žerotín were not now rewarded for the loyalty they had demonstrated in the crisis of 1618–19. Žerotín was imprisoned after the rebellion, and finally went into exile after the expulsion of the Moravian Brethren in 1629.[13]

Upper and Lower Lusatia escaped such measures because they had been granted to the Elector of Saxony, who confirmed the existing religious liberties of their inhabitants. A similar situation developed in Silesia, which the Elector subjugated on behalf of the emperor.[14] In the Dresden Compact of 28 February 1621, the Elector agreed to the restoration of the status quo of 1618 in return for a fine of 300,000 gulden and formal recognition of Ferdinand II as the rightful ruler. Since Ferdinand was unwilling to cross the Elector and was in any case still distracted by the threat from Bethlen Gábor, he reluctantly acquiesced. The Silesian Counter-Reformation progressed piecemeal as the Habsburgs gradually gained control of one Silesian territory after another, first by conquest and then, more slowly, by inheritance as some of the indigenous dynasties died out. Even so, the Dukes of Brieg and Liegnitz-Wohlau, together with the city of Breslau and the Prince of Oels, were able to enter into a 'Conjunction' with Saxony, Brandenburg, and Sweden in 1633, which ultimately secured recognition of their rights in the Peace of Westphalia.

The cause of the Silesian Counter-Reformation was not helped by the fact that the new Bishop of Breslau elected in 1625, Prince Karl Ferdinand of Vasa, was only twelve years old. By the time he came of age, he had accumulated other high ecclesiastical offices, even though he was never either consecrated as a priest or anointed as a bishop. The fact that he ultimately preferred to live in Warsaw was a blessing to his see, for that at least allowed an energetic episcopal administrator and a committed suffragan to inaugurate real reforms from the mid-1630s.

In Lower and Upper Austria, two rather different processes unfolded. In Lower Austria, Ferdinand had persuaded 148 nobles, including 86 Protestants, to swear an oath of allegiance to him in 1620.[15] The Protestants were promised religious freedom. Those who refused to swear were outlawed and subjected to the same

---

[12] Evans, *Making*, 200–10.   [13] Bosl, *Böhmen*, 289.
[14] Schindling and Ziegler, *Territorien*, ii, 130–5; Evans, *Making*, 299–301.
[15] Schindling and Ziegler, *Territorien*, i, 130–1.

penalty of confiscation of property as their counterparts in Bohemia. In 1627, Ferdinand modified his promise of religious freedom to a simple guarantee of personal freedom of conscience and prohibited the nobility from housing Protestant preachers and schoolmasters in their castles on the grounds that they merely insulted Catholicism and fermented sedition.

Upper Austria experienced much the same brutal treatment as Bohemia.[16] The rebel leader, Georg Erasmus Tschernembl, fled to Württemberg as soon as Bavarian troops marched in. However, the progress of political repression and Counter-Reformation was delayed by the fact that Maximilian and Ferdinand were initially at cross purposes. Maximilian primarily wanted to extract money to pay his troops and recover his costs, and this required stability. Ferdinand wanted to punish and discipline, which endangered that stability. The extraction of 26,000 gulden per month in taxes to support the Bavarian garrison, combined with the effects of the currency debasement of 1622–3, harvest failures in 1622, 1623, and 1624, and a plague epidemic in 1625–6, created a highly volatile situation. This was further exacerbated by the execution, by the Bavarian occupation authorities under Adam von Herberstorff, of Ferdinand's edicts against heretics. In October 1624, Protestant preachers and teachers were given four weeks to leave the country; all non-nobles were ordered either to convert or to leave by Easter 1626.

The last straw was the arrival of numerous Italian missionaries sent by the Congregation for the Propagation of the Faith in Rome to remedy the lack of sufficient German clergy. When the foreigners moved into formerly Protestant parishes, the Austrian laity began to resist. In May 1626, matters came to a head in Frankenburg when a crowd of five thousand armed peasants besieged the castle, their leaders declaring they would rather die than turn 'papist'. Herberstorff's reaction was brutally uncompromising. He marched to Frankenburg with a force of 650 soldiers and one hangman, seized thirty-six men of good standing from towns and villages, and ordered them to throw dice for their lives, immediately hanging the seventeen who lost.

News of the 'Frankenburg game of dice' spread like wildfire. Before long, a mass uprising had been organized, led by Stefan Fadinger, a farmer and magistrate's assistant, and his brother-in-law, Christoph Zeller. Initially, the rebellion enjoyed considerable success, but Fadinger's death in combat in July left the movement leaderless. Nor did the peasants manage to secure any external help. A Danish envoy made contact but was able to offer little help. Rumours of a 'general tumult' in Austria and southern Bohemia led by nobles encouraged Count Mansfeld and Johann-Ernst of Saxony-Weimar to march south to join forces with Bethlen Gábor for a renewed attack on Vienna. However, the Upper Austrian nobility shied away from cooperation with the peasantry, fearing that a general peasants' war might turn against lords as well as rulers.[17] Furthermore, the authorities had been careful to give nobles fifty years to convert or leave.

---

[16] For the following, see Langer, 'Krieg', 309–12; Schindling and Ziegler, *Territorien*, i, 131–2.
[17] Press, *Kriege*, 208–9.

By late 1626, the rebellion had been broken. In January 1627, violence flared up again, but it was swiftly and brutally put down. Trials, confiscations of property, mass executions, and the quartering of twelve thousand troops in the region bludgeoned the populace into sullen submission. In 1628, the Bavarian occupation, one of the main aggravating features of the situation, was ended and Maximilian I was paid off with the grant in perpetuity of the Upper Palatinate. Upper Austria remained volatile, however, with further outbreaks of unrest in 1632 and 1635–6. Instability had delayed the implementation of the re-Catholicization process until 1631, but thereafter it proceeded inexorably, as elsewhere. Over 100,000 were forced into exile, mainly from Upper Austria.

The parallel activities in most of the key Habsburg lands, of extending political control and religious uniformity, have sometimes given the impression of a drive towards centralization and towards the consolidation of a Habsburg state distinct from the Reich. The creation of an Austrian court chancery (Erbländische Hofkanzlei), designed to be independent of the Imperial Archchancellor, the Elector of Mainz, was certainly another step towards exempting the Habsburg lands from all legislation of the Reich.[18] In effect, however, this simply formalized claims that had been made since the late fifteenth century, and the chancery was slow to develop any meaningful functions. More immediately significant was Ferdinand's reinvigoration of his court, integrating the higher nobility of Upper and Lower Austria, but also now including the magnates, of both German and indigenous origin, of Bohemia and Moravia. With the emperor's Jesuit confessors installed at its core, the court became the symbol of the new stability and religious uniformity of Ferdinand's territories.[19]

In other ways, however, Ferdinand behaved much like his predecessors. He installed a new dynastic line in the Tyrol and the Vorlande, with his brother Leopold, first as governor then, once Leopold had resigned his bishoprics of Passau and Strassburg and married Claudia de Medici, as ruling prince from 1621.[20] Once the immediate crisis had subsided, local institutions gradually began to play a role again in the areas under Ferdinand's own control, and everywhere he was willing to compromise with local nobilities, provided they embraced Catholicism and loyalty to the crown.[21]

Throughout the 1620s, furthermore, Ferdinand was engaged in a struggle to maintain his position in Hungary. Turkish support for Bethlen Gábor enabled the Transylvanian prince to launch repeated assaults on Royal Hungary and to threaten a link between the emperor's Protestant foes in the Reich and those in the east. That Bethlen failed was largely due to the Ottomans' own eastern struggle against Persia: the collapse of their campaign to retake Baghdad (lost in 1624) obliged Bethlen to conclude the Peace of Bratislava (Pressburg) with Ferdinand at the end

[18] Conrad, *Rechtsgeschichte*, ii, 78–9.
[19] Press, *Kriege*, 207; Press, 'Imperial court', 307–9; Bireley, *Religion*, 82–97.
[20] *BWDG*, ii, 1628–9; *ADB*, xviii, 398–402.
[21] Parker, *Thirty Years War*, 78; Pamlényi, *Hungary*, 154–7.

of December 1626.[22] Hostilities resumed soon enough, but so did the unreliability of Bethlen's support. His death in 1629 left matters unresolved; his successor György Rákóczi's attempts to collaborate with France and Sweden were no more successful and ended in the Treaty of Linz in 1647. Ferdinand, and his son Ferdinand III from 1637, managed to retain Royal Hungary, though it was not re-Catholicized (and then incompletely) until the 1670s.[23]

Far from being innovating, the policies pursued in the wake of the Bohemian and Austrian rebellions show Ferdinand catching up with what many German rulers had started decades earlier. He was the first Habsburg to pursue systematically the principle of *cuius regio eius religio* in his own territories. His actions against rebels were proper according to the prevailing rules of war; his religious policies were proper according to the religious settlement of 1555. Where he did depart strikingly from both previous policy and, arguably, legal propriety, was in attempting to pursue an identical policy in the Reich as a whole.

[22] Press, *Kriege*, 203.   [23] Evans, *Making*, 235–7.

52

Denmark and the War for the Reich, 1623–1629

The progress of Ferdinand's energetic repression of the rebellion reverberated throughout the Reich, generating shock and awe in equal measure. Tilly's victory over Christian of Brunswick on 6 August 1623 was decisive. Despite growing goodwill at Protestant courts, including that of James I of England, there seemed little prospect of the exiled Friedrich V ever securing any serious allies who might take up his cause in the Reich. Almost every German Protestant court and many outside the Reich as well received refugees who told terrible tales of the repression of their faith. Thousands began new lives in Hungary, Poland, Silesia, Sweden, Denmark, the Dutch Republic, and England. Others capitulated and tried to rebuild their old lives on new terms. Christian of Anhalt, once Ferdinand's most determined adversary, went first to Stade in the territory of the Protestant administrator of the bishopric of Bremen after he was outlawed in January 1621. Then he sought refuge in Stockholm and Flensburg. Ultimately, though, loyalty to his own dynasty and the desire to preserve its territories prevailed and he gratefully accepted reconciliation with the emperor mediated by his son. In June 1624, he swore an oath of loyalty to the emperor in Vienna and retired to his lands in Anhalt, playing no further part in political life.[1]

The Habsburg position continued to strengthen. French troops invaded Graubünden, including the Valtelline, in the autumn of 1624, but this was only a temporary setback. The Spanish campaign against the Netherlands seemed to progress favourably, reaching a high point in June 1625, when Spinola took the old Orange fortress stronghold of Breda. In the same year, Genoa was successfully defended from attack by France and Savoy, the Dutch were driven from Bahía in Brazil, and an English force was repelled from Cadiz. 'God is Spanish', the Count-Duke of Olivares wrote, 'and [He] fights for our nation these days.'[2]

The despatch of some eleven thousand Spanish troops to garrisons along the Rhine and the Ems and in Lippe in 1625 seemed also to strengthen the imperial position. Their purpose was to enforce a strict economic blockade of the Dutch Republic; their first effect was to provide security for the western flank of Tilly's

---

[1] Press, 'Fürst Christian I', 213–14; *ADB*, vi, 149. Stade, south of the Elbe just west of Hamburg, had a small Dutch Calvinist community from the late sixteenth century: Schindling and Ziegler, *Territorien*, iii, 52–4.

[2] Parker, *Thirty Years War*, 92.

force billeted in Westphalia and Hessen. To the east, in conditions of great secrecy, Wallenstein's new army moved into position from Bohemia to the borders of Lower Saxony. Already Duke of Friedland since 1623, Wallenstein had, in April 1625, been designated supreme commander of all imperial troops in the Reich and the Netherlands, and commissioned to raise a force of 24,000 men to reinforce Tilly. The previous year, discussions had also begun in Madrid and Vienna on how best to complement the Habsburg land forces with a maritime capacity in the North Sea and the Baltic.[3]

The two Habsburg dynasties had different aims in pursuing this strategic objective. Madrid clearly wanted both to maintain its economic blockade of the Dutch Republic and to establish a commercial network (including the German North Sea and Baltic ports of the Reich and the Kingdom of Poland) that was independent of it. Olivares was aware that Spain could no longer hope to subjugate the Dutch; he was also acutely aware of Spain's limited resources and precarious financial position. He wanted, above all, to establish a lasting peace on more favourable terms than the truce of 1609.

Ferdinand had more diverse objectives. His advisers urged him to consider supporting the Spanish project, for the whole Reich could only benefit from 'Indian [i.e. South American] treasure'. But they also wanted to ensure that ports in East Frisia and on the Elbe remained firmly under imperial control and that the anticipated revenue of one million thaler per annum from that part of the Spanish North Sea–Baltic project that was in the Reich flowed directly into Ferdinand's own coffers.[4] At the same time, the crisis of the early 1620s provided opportunities to resolve some of the key contentious issues of the last decades in favour of the Church and the crown.[5]

In 1620, at Mühlhausen, the Electors of Mainz and Cologne and the Duke of Bavaria had given an assurance on behalf of all the Catholic Estates that ecclesiastical property in the Lower Saxon and Upper Saxon Kreise would remain untouched as long as its owners remained loyal to the emperor.[6] This helped secure the loyalty of Saxony and others for the time being, even though the Catholic princes had, at the same time, explicitly reaffirmed their belief in the validity of the legislation of 1555, including the *reservatum ecclesiasticum* (the stipulation that an ecclesiastical prince who converted to Lutheranism should forfeit his bishopric). In 1620, however, they were in no position to insist on their interpretation of the Peace of Augsburg. After Tilly's decisive victory at Stadtlohn on 6 August 1623, however, with imperial troops advanced far into north-western Germany, it was possible for the emperor to contemplate various approaches to the problem of alienated ecclesiastical property. At the very least, action could be taken against those who had not remained loyal. More than that, it was now possible to envisage a full-scale

---

[3] Bireley, *Religion*, 24–5; Elliott, *Olivares*, 216–19; Lockhart, *Denmark*, 85–6.
[4] *Documenta Bohemica*, iii, 258–64: memoranda from Georg Ludwig von Schwarzenberg and Johann Ulrich von Eggenberg.
[5] Bireley, *Religion*, 25–7; *Documenta Bohemica*, iii, 264.
[6] Wolgast, *Hochstift*, 326.

restitution of ecclesiastical lands and their protection from future attack by means of the Spanish military cordon, the various imperial forces on land, and an imperial naval capability yet to be created in the North Sea and the Baltic. The installation of Habsburg candidates in such bishoprics would further enhance the authority of the crown.

All this had implications that went far beyond the future of the Reichskirche. The emperor and his advisers were extending their strategic thinking to parts of the Reich that had scarcely been touched by imperial policy before. Had they succeeded in all their objectives, they would have transformed the Reich into a very strong monarchy indeed.

Habsburg plans unfolded gradually over several years. However, the measures implemented by Ferdinand and Maximilian of Bavaria in Bohemia, Austria, and the Palatine lands by 1623 were already enough to convince some Protestant rulers that they would stop at nothing. A number of factors combined to rally a new opposition to Habsburg hegemony. The efforts of the exiled Friedrich V to gain support for his restitution received a new impetus with the emergence of his old Palatine councillor Ludwig Camerarius as the leading figure of his government in exile in 1623.[7] He reactivated contacts with all of the Protestant powers and, in particular, drew both Sweden and Denmark into discussion of a possible international alliance.

Matters were held up by the reluctance of either England or France to commit themselves to open and direct action; then there was a further delay caused by the death of James I in April 1625. Another major complication was the rivalry between Sweden and Denmark. Camerarius favoured a Swedish-led action.[8] In 1623, the plan was to invade through Poland to restore Friedrich as King of Bohemia, which also suited the Swedish king's own dynastic aim to undermine the power of his Catholic relatives in Poland. The following year, the plan was changed to a western invasion, with the more limited aim of restoring Friedrich to the Palatinate. Finally, however, Gustavus's demand for a force of fifty thousand men was deemed excessive, just as his stipulation that France must be excluded from any coalition was thought unreasonable.

The long negotiations with Sweden inevitably aroused the hostility of Denmark, which feared that Gustavus Adolphus might use success in Germany to advance the ambition that had fired him since the beginning of his reign in 1611 to extend hegemony over the Baltic generally. In response to this threat, Christian IV had already established the port of Glückstadt above Hamburg on the Elbe in 1616, in order to control the estuary and capture Hamburg's commerce. In 1621, he forced the city of Hamburg to recognize the overlordship of the Danish crown. When the prospect of Sweden spearheading a campaign to restore Friedrich V emerged, Christian did everything he could to make the allies a more reasonable offer than that of Gustavus. This he could well afford to do, for his finances were so buoyant

[7] Schubert, *Camerarius*, 189–213; Clasen, *Palatinate*, 26–30. See also p. 578.
[8] Camerarius was also Swedish envoy in the Dutch Republic in 1626–41: Schubert, *Camerarius*, 306–38; *ADB*, iii, 724–6.

that he could raise a considerable force on his own account and act unhindered by any constraints imposed by anxious Estates at home.

Christian IV also had other reasons for being concerned by the situation in the Reich. Unlike Gustavus Adolphus, Christian was a prince of the Reich and a member of the Lower Saxon Kreis. Furthermore, he had a strong dynastic interest in the bishoprics of Bremen, Verden, and Osnabrück, which lay to the south-west of his Duchy of Holstein.[9] Bremen and Verden were especially significant, since they potentially held the key to control over the Weser and Elbe estuaries. In 1621, Christian's son Frederik had become coadjutor of the Archbishopric of Bremen, in which his kinsman Johann Friedrich von Holstein-Gottorp was administrator (r. 1597–1634). In 1623, he also became Bishop of Verden in succession to Philipp Sigismund of Brunswick-Wolfenbüttel.[10] An attempt to arrange Frederik's succession in Philipp Sigismund's other Bishopric of Osnabrück was narrowly thwarted by the Catholic majority in the chapter there, who elected Cardinal Eitel Friedrich von Hohenzollern-Sigmaringen.[11] Frederik's rebuff at Osnabrück was itself a public political demonstration and a declaration of intent: the chapter elected a key adviser to both Ferdinand II and the Elector of Cologne, Ferdinand of Bavaria, the two leaders of the Catholic counter-offensive in the Reich.

Even though Christian had strong dynastic reasons to form a defensive force to protect the ecclesiastical lands held by his son, his genuine commitment to the defence of the liberties of the Lower Saxon Kreis should not be underestimated. He was quite capable of distinguishing between his wider strategic concerns as King of Denmark and his commitment as a German prince to the defence of German liberty against the emperor.[12] It is perhaps impossible to determine exactly the proportions in which competition with Sweden, concern over Spanish plans for the Baltic, dynastic interest in the Lower Saxon bishoprics, and fear of imperial intervention on behalf of the region's Catholics were mixed in Christian's mind. The combination of them all, however, predisposed him to action in 1625.

His first task was to mobilize the Lower Saxon Kreis. After much wrangling, Christian succeeded in having himself elected as commander of its forces in April 1625.[13] The representative of the Elector of Cologne (in his capacity as Bishop of Hildesheim) naturally opposed him, but many of the Protestant members of the Kreis were also hesitant, reluctant to be drawn into any conflict and reluctant to provide any money. When they did finally agree to raise a force of 10,000 foot and 3,000 horse, they immediately requested Christian to lay out the money in advance, promising to reimburse him in due course. They also insisted that the troops were only to be deployed within the Lower Saxon Kreis and only for defensive purposes. However, the commission that Christian received to restore

[9] Lockhart, *Denmark*, 74.
[10] Lockhart, *Frederik II*, 306–8.
[11] Eitel Friedrich was provost of Magdeburg, Cologne, and Strassburg, grand chamberlain of the Elector of Cologne, and a close adviser to the emperor in the negotiations at Frankfurt and Munich in 1619, for which Paul V made him a cardinal in January 1621. *ADB*, xlviii, 327–8.
[12] Lockhart, *Denmark*, 131–2.
[13] Schormann, *Krieg*, 36; Guthrie, *Battles*, 118–19.

Friedrich V to his Palatine Electorate, formally agreed at the Hague Convention in December 1625, immediately added an offensive thrust to his policies.[14] This further disquieted many of his neighbours in the Lower Saxon Kreis. The cities of Lübeck, Hamburg, and Bremen in particular viewed him as a dangerous and predatory foreigner. Indeed, even before the Hague Convention, the solidarity of the Kreis was already beginning to crumble.[15]

Hostilities began before the war really broke out, as each side hastened to secure winter quarters and supply lines. In addition to his own troops, Christian was able to enlist mercenary forces under Mansfeld and Johann Ernst of Saxony-Weimar. These, however, were no match for the array of imperial forces: Tilly was garrisoned on the borders of the Westphalian Kreis and the growing army of Wallenstein soon advanced northwards to the Elbe. Minor skirmishing in 1625 gave way to a full-scale imperial offensive in 1626, starting with an imperial victory at Dessau in April.[16] Mansfeld's subsequent attempt to escape south to link up with Bethlen Gábor I for another assault on Vienna was matched by an extraordinary 800 kilometre march by Wallenstein from Zerbst in Anhalt down to Upper Hungary. The planned assault on Vienna never materialized: Bethlen's Turkish sponsors suffered a defeat at Baghdad, so he made peace with Ferdinand instead of war. Both Mansfeld and Johann Ernst died shortly afterwards and the remnants of their army were brought back north by Danish commissars. Meanwhile, Christian himself had suffered a calamitous defeat at Lutter am Barenberge on 27 August 1626.

The denouement was protracted. Most of the members of the Lower Saxon Kreis gave up almost immediately. Christian's nephew, Friedrich Ulrich of Brunswick-Wolfenbüttel, instantly withdrew his troops and severed all ties with Denmark; the Dukes of Mecklenburg soon acquiesced in their nobles' demands for peace.[17] In 1627, Tilly and Wallenstein were easily able to pursue Christian's forces up into Holstein and Jutland.[18] The imperial forces began to divide the spoils of war and to plan the new order in north Germany. The most immediate beneficiary was Wallenstein himself: on 1 February 1628, he was formally enfeoffed with the Duchy of Mecklenburg, which his troops had occupied the previous year. His elevation as a prince of the Reich and, against all tradition, the grant of a confiscated ducal territory to an outsider rather than to a princely relative of the outlawed former owner was among the many grudges later held against both him and Ferdinand. In 1628, no one dared object.

Both major Habsburg policy objectives now also seemed to be within reach. First, in the wake of the military victory in the north, Olivares's plans for a Baltic–Iberian commercial network seemed to be realizable.[19] In addition to the Duchy of Mecklenburg, Wallenstein had been given the new titles of 'Generalissimo' of all the emperor's troops, with powers previously reserved for Ferdinand himself, and of 'General of the Oceanic and Baltic Seas'. The fleet did not yet exist, and the whole plan depended on the cooperation of the Hanseatic Cities and other ports.

---

[14] Asch, *Thirty Years War*, 80–8.   [15] Lockhart, *Denmark*, 126.
[16] Guthrie, *Battles*, 120–2.   [17] Lockhart, *Denmark*, 149.
[18] Lockhart, *Denmark*, 174–6.   [19] Elliott, *Olivares*, 332–5, 360–1.

The attempt to force the strategically important Pomeranian port of Stralsund to accept an imperial garrison in 1628 underlined the weakness of a land-based military position without control of the sea. Stralsund held out against an imperial siege by entering into a twenty-year pact with Sweden and receiving eight ships with munitions and men in return. The city thereby ultimately lost its freedom to Sweden, but Wallenstein's abandonment of the siege was the first serious rebuff of the imperial forces. His failure there emboldened Christian IV to take the nearby island of Usedom and to conduct a successful defence of Jutland and the Danish heartlands by diverting Wallenstein in a series of forays onto the Holstein and Pomeranian coasts.[20] This, in turn, enabled Christian to conclude a reasonably honourable peace with the emperor at Lübeck: he was permitted to keep all his lands in return for a promise to refrain from any further intervention in the Reich. Moreover, since Christian had been defeated only on land and retained control of his successful navy, all hopes of creating a Habsburg navy or even a North Sea–Baltic Habsburg commercial network were now illusory.

Second, military victory opened up the prospect of being able to deal with the bishoprics. They featured in a variety of proposals.[21] Maximilian of Bavaria wanted to appoint Catholic bishops and cathedral chapters immediately, though to retain all income from the bishoprics for a period of ten years to cover the costs of the war. At a conference in Brussels in the autumn of 1626, Ferdinand's envoy argued that the emperor should distribute the conquered benefices to his 'deserving ministers'. Wallenstein advised confiscating Halberstadt and Magdeburg under the laws of war and installing Ferdinand's second son, the fourteen-year-old Archduke Leopold Wilhelm. At a meeting of Electors at Mühlhausen in October and November 1627, the Catholic Electors were asked to put forward suggestions as to how the bishoprics and other ecclesiastical property taken, in their view illegally, since 1552 might be restituted.

Immediate progress was made. In Osnabrück, Franz Wilhelm von Wartenberg, a son of Maximilian I's uncle, Duke Ferdinand of Bavaria, by a morganatic marriage, was elected in succession to Eitel Friedrich von Hohenzollern-Sigmaringen in 1625 and installed in 1628 following the defeat of Christian IV.[22] Archduke Leopold Wilhelm was elected in Halberstadt in 1627 and in Magdeburg the following year.[23] These advances in the north encouraged a whole series of Catholic rulers elsewhere to pursue intensive confessionalization campaigns. The Electorates of Mainz and Cologne, the Prince-Bishoprics of Eichstätt, Bamberg, and Würzburg, and the territory of the Prince-Provost of Ellwangen in Swabia were prominent in this intense wave of Catholic renewal. In most of them, serious witch hunts now began for the first time, more intensive than any that had occurred before the war.[24]

[20] Lockhart, *Denmark*, 189–91.
[21] Wolgast, *Hochstift*, 326.
[22] Schwaiger, *Wartenberg*, 23–8, 31–43; *NDB*, v, 365; Gatz, *Bischöfe 1648 bis 1803*, 558–61.
[23] Wolgast, *Hochstift*, 327–8.
[24] See pp. 550–7.

Influential voices, including that of Maximilian of Bavaria and the emperor's own Jesuit confessor Wilhelm Larmormaini, urged Ferdinand to take a strong lead.

Apparently at the height of his power and fired by the seeming solidarity of the Catholic princes, Ferdinand saw fit to impose his own solution on the problems of the Reich. On 6 March 1629, he issued the Edict of Restitution.[25] All the ambiguities of the settlement of 1555 were resolved and the Reichskammergericht was instructed to adopt the imperial (i.e. Catholic) interpretation of the law. Imperial commissars were to oversee the return of all ecclesiastical property alienated by the Protestants since 1552. The rights of those who professed the Augsburg Confession were confirmed, but Calvinists and other sects were explicitly excluded from the religious peace. Anyone who obstructed the implementation of the edict was threatened with 'Acht und Aberacht' ('ban and double ban').[26]

The implications were breathtaking. Almost all secularized bishoprics were directly threatened. This meant not only Bremen and Magdeburg, but also Minden, Halberstadt, Lübeck, Verden, Ratzeburg, Schwerin, and Cammin, some of which had long been regarded as 'territorial' bishoprics. The status of Brandenburg, Havelberg, and Lebus in the Electorate of Brandenburg was unclear, though it was assumed the emperor would not dare touch them. The Elector of Saxony was assured that Meissen, Merseburg, and Naumburg, which his predecessors had territorialized, were safe. In practice, however, neither Saxony nor Brandenburg was conceded anything that went beyond the promise given in Mühlhausen in 1627 that no property would be reclaimed without due legal process, or beyond earlier promises that all their lands would be secure in so far as they remained loyal to the crown.

Definitely included in the edict were some five hundred monasteries in Swabia, Franconia, and Lower Saxony, as well as, potentially, any other ecclesiastical property in any Protestant territory of the Reich. Even before the edict's promulgation, Archduke Leopold embarked on the restitution of all Church property in Alsace and forced all his subjects to convert to Catholicism. Elsewhere, work began immediately after the promulgation. Within two years, five bishoprics and over a hundred monasteries were restored. Imperial commissars backed up by Wallenstein's troops took back nearly twenty monastic foundations; others were reclaimed in the Duchy of Brunswick, in Hessen, and in Nassau. These operations generated widespread resentment, especially as Protestants prepared to commemorate the centenary of the Augsburg Confession in June 1630. In some areas, there was fierce resistance. In Magdeburg, where the restitution of monasteries had begun in 1628, the inhabitants of the city rebelled against their council and then obliged Wallenstein to abandon a siege in September 1629.[27] The Protestant administrator, Christian Wilhelm of Brandenburg, returned in July 1630 to

---

[25] Frisch, *Restitutionsedikt*, 22–68 (the edict is printed, 183–94).
[26] 'Double ban' came into effect after one year and a day. The distinction between ban and double ban had been abandoned, though the formula was still used to emphasize the seriousness of an offence: Conrad, *Rechtsgeschichte*, i, 582–3 and ii, 424–5.
[27] Schindling and Ziegler, *Territorien*, ii, 81–3.

reclaim his lands from the sixteen-year-old Archduke Leopold Wilhelm. The archbishopric was finally taken by Tilly in May 1631, after a campaign that resulted in the almost total destruction of the city in a fire. His triumph was short-lived; in September 1631, most of the territory's towns were occupied by Swedish troops.

Swedish intervention in the war abruptly terminated the restitution process. Yet the foundations of Ferdinand's authority were eroded long before Gustavus Adolphus landed on the Pomeranian island of Usedom on 6 July 1630. While the emperor apparently progressed from one triumph to another, many became restless and anxious.

The Catholic Electors were deeply uneasy at Spain's North Sea–Baltic maritime plans and suspected that this might be part of a Habsburg plot to subvert German liberty.[28] At a meeting at Mühlhausen in September 1627, they had complained bitterly of the incursions of Spanish troops into their territories. The Elector of Cologne, Ferdinand of Bavaria, also Bishop of Hildesheim, Münster, Liège, and Paderborn, was particularly affected in all his territories by the Spanish embargo against the Dutch and by Spanish garrisons in the Reich. Above all, none of the Catholic Electors wanted to be dragged into the Spanish–Dutch conflict.

Maximilian of Bavaria was alarmed at rumours of a secret agreement concluded between the emperor and Wallenstein at Bruck an der Leitha in November 1626, allegedly granting Wallenstein the right to occupy the whole Reich, to bleed it dry, and then deliver it into the hands of the emperor.[29] A meeting of the League at Würzburg in February 1627 had despatched a formal note of protest to Vienna. Even the reconquest of the northern bishoprics gave rise to tension between Munich and Vienna.[30] The Wittelsbach Elector of Cologne had already established himself as a substantial regional power, with a spread of bishoprics on the Lower Rhine and in Westphalia. The emperor was consequently determined to promote his own son, Archduke Leopold Wilhelm. Maximilian, having already promoted his son, was now equally determined to advance his own kinsman Franz Wilhelm von Wartenberg. Maximilian may have been an upstart Elector, resented and distrusted by Saxony and Brandenburg in particular, but he was as sensitive as any of his colleagues to any attempt to strengthen the crown.

Growing unease among the Protestant princes was perhaps inevitable. Saxony's steadfast loyalty held through the 1620s, but was sorely tested. Brandenburg had been peripherally involved in the discussions that preceded the Hague Convention, but withdrew just before Christian IV mobilized the Lower Saxon Kreis.[31] Both Electors refused to approve the transfer of the Electoral title from the Palatinate to Bavaria, since it shifted the confessional balance decisively in favour of the Catholics, and they denied the emperor's right to grant such a thing, still less to a prince of lower status.[32] Neither attended the Mühlhausen meeting of Electors in 1627, but

[28] Kessel, *Spanien*, 52–7, 269–303; Israel, *Dutch Republic*, 204–23.
[29] Mann, *Wallenstein*, 441–50.
[30] Wolgast, *Hochstift*, 327–9.
[31] Lockhart, *Denmark*, 116–18.
[32] Gotthard, *Säulen*, i, 105–12.

both sent strongly worded protests at the activities of Wallenstein generally and at the transfer to him of the lands of the Duke of Mecklenburg.

Like many other Protestant princes, the Electors of Saxony and Bavaria were also incensed in 1627 by the Reichskammergericht's confirmation of the Reichshofrat's 1623 decision on the partition of Hessen.[33] The Lutheran Darmstadt line objected to the Reformed/Calvinist Kassel line's occupation of territories of the extinct Marburg line in 1604. First one court, then the other, decided in favour of Georg II of Darmstadt and, furthermore, required Wilhelm V of Kassel to pay one million thaler in compensation for his predecessor's illegal occupation. The two Electors again disputed the right of the emperor and his Reichshofrat to decide such matters, especially as it was clear that the Kassel line was being victimized on account of its religion. The Edict of Restitution moved both Saxony and Brandenburg to the brink of outright opposition. Georg Wilhelm of Brandenburg was particularly incensed, not least because he had received rumours from Vienna that Ferdinand was conspiring with the Polish king to re-Catholicize the Duchy of Prussia that the Elector held as a Polish fiefdom.

Even so, the two Protestant Electors hesitated to abandon their loyalist policies. Each had received considerable inducements. Saxony had been rewarded with Lusatia for its traditional loyalty and its assistance in putting down the Bohemian uprising. Brandenburg's position was complicated by the fact that its Elector (and his privy council) was Reformed and its Estates were Lutheran. As the only Calvinist Elector after the dispossession of Friedrich V, Georg Wilhelm of Brandenburg was particularly vulnerable. An early interest in the English–Dutch–Danish alliance was terminated by the refusal of the Estates to grant money for an army. Thereafter, policy was determined by the Elector's favourite, the Lower Rhineland Catholic Count Adam von Schwarzenberg. With excellent contacts in Vienna, but with a remarkably non-confessional approach, Schwarzenberg urged policies that promoted his master's dynasty, rather than his faith.[34] This meant supporting the crown in return for assurances about Magdeburg and Kleve, the promise of the emperor's support in the Brandenburg succession in Pomerania on the anticipated extinction of its ducal line, and the vague promise of the succession to Wallenstein in Mecklenburg.

The Mantuan War provided both Catholic and Protestant Electors with a reason to take action. The death of Duke Vincent II of Mantua and Montferrat without a direct male heir led to a struggle between France, which supported the claims of the Duke of Nevers, and the King of Spain, who wanted to thwart a French succession at all costs. Ferdinand was inevitably involved as overlord of the duchy and on account of the Spanish–Austrian guarantee of mutual support. Spain's acute financial difficulties, exacerbated by the Dutch capture of the American silver fleet on 8 September 1628, allowed Nevers to take possession and the long siege of Casale increased the strain still further. This the Spaniards could ill afford at a critical juncture in their conflict with the Dutch.

[33] Schindling and Ziegler, *Territorien*, iv, 283–4; Parker, *Thirty Years War*, 86.
[34] Kober, 'Favorit', 237–8.

The situation deteriorated further after the French monarchy finally crushed the Huguenots at La Rochelle in October 1628. In February 1629, Louis XIII led an army across the Alps to break the Spanish siege of Casale.[35] Austrian intervention became imperative to rescue the Spanish position in northern Italy. Two serious consequences ensued. First, war between France and both Spain and Austria was now all but inevitable. Second, the German Electors, reflecting opinions widely held among the princes generally, objected vociferously to the deployment of some 50,000 men from Wallenstein's army to Italy. The use of the institutions of the German Reich to pursue the interests of the Spanish Habsburgs seemed to prove the rumour-mongers right: the emperor wanted to undermine 'German liberty' by attempting to create in Germany the kind of monarchy that existed in France and Castile.

---

[35] Wilson, *Europe's tragedy*, 424, 440–6; Press, *Kriege*, 212–15; Parker, *Thirty Years War*, 41, 105–9; Schormann, 'Krieg', 245–9; Kampmann, *Europa*, 65–6.

53

What Kind of Reich? Sweden and the Defence of German Liberties, 1630–1635

The five years of conflict from 1630 are often labelled the 'Swedish War'. That fairly reflects the overwhelmingly important role played in these years by Gustavus Adolphus and his chancellor Oxenstierna. However, the description distracts attention from the main thrust of German politics after the Edict of Restitution: the efforts made by both Catholics and Protestants, albeit at odds with each other for much of the time, to secure the Reich, and of course their own interests, against both imperial and Swedish ambitions.

The first decisive moves against the emperor were driven by the Catholic Electors. With their concerns about Wallenstein now intensified, they also had more to bargain with. Since 1628, Ferdinand had been anxious to have his son, already King of Bohemia and Hungary, elected as King of the Romans. The issue was not even placed formally on the agenda for the meeting that was summoned by the Elector of Mainz for July 1630 at Regensburg.[1] It was demonstratively set aside throughout the nearly five months' duration of the meeting, while the Electors systematically drove home their own concerns.

Ferdinand was forced to agree that he should not in future commit the Reich to war without the express consent of the Electors. He was obliged to halt military activity in Italy and conclude peace with France in October. Above all, he was forced to dismiss Wallenstein and to transfer command of the imperial army, reduced in size by roughly three-quarters, to the League general, Tilly. Any idea that the Reich might intervene in the Dutch conflict, which Ferdinand had wished the Electors to consider, was deferred on the grounds that this was a matter that affected all Estates and should therefore be deliberated by all. The issues of the fate of the outlawed former Palatine Elector and of enforcement of the Edict of Restitution remained unresolved. No action was taken in the matter of the imperial succession.

The Regensburg Kurfürstentag carried out the agenda of the Catholic Electors, who were simultaneously meeting as leaders of the League. The two Protestant Electors did not in fact attend in person. They were less worried about Wallenstein than about the restitution issues. The intransigence of the Catholic majority on this point led each to reassess the wisdom of the loyalist policy that they had pursued

---

[1] Gotthard, *Säulen*, i, 370–8 and ii, 606–7, 713–19.

throughout the 1620s. Even in 1630, however, Johann Georg of Saxony prevaricated, while Georg Wilhelm of Brandenburg urged action. A meeting of the two men at Annaberg in April 1630 failed to produce a clear outcome; a second meeting at Zabeltitz in September resulted in Johann Georg calling a meeting of all German Protestant rulers in Leipzig in February 1631, to discuss their grievances and agree on a plan of action.[2]

An attempt by the Catholic Electors to forestall this meeting by announcing a conference of both Catholics and Protestants to review the Edict of Restitution, nearly caused Johann Georg to change his mind again. The fact, however, that the leading Saxon and Brandenburg theologians also met at Leipzig and resolved 'to show each other Christian love in the future' proved helpful to the deliberations of the rulers.[3] In April 1631, they formed a defensive league with an army of 40,000 men under the leadership of the Elector of Saxony. They demanded the rescission of the Edict of Restitution, the withdrawal of Tilly's imperial and League troops from all Protestant territories, and the cessation of levies towards their upkeep. Their general aim, they declared, was to 'uphold the basic laws, the Imperial constitution, and the German liberty of the Protestant Estates'.[4]

Ultimately, a key factor in the agreement between the two Protestant Electors had been the news of the King of Sweden's landing in Germany in July 1630. In the power vacuum that was left by the Regensburg Kurfürstentag, it seemed possible that they might form a third force between the emperor and Sweden.

Similar considerations drove Maximilian of Bavaria into an alliance with France in May 1631.[5] Following the Treaty of Bärwalde in January 1631 between France and Sweden, Maximilian now feared Swedish power as he had recently feared imperial power, particularly as the Franco-Swedish agreement resolved to restore the 'suppressed Estates of the Reich'. The secret Treaty of Fontainebleau gave him the assurances that he wanted: a mutual defence agreement for eight years, recognition by France of his Electoral title, and allowance made for his obligations towards emperor and Reich. For Richelieu, the most immediate attraction was the possibility that other Catholic princes might now also review their loyalty to the emperor. It also created a potential role for France as a mediator between Sweden and her opponents in the Reich.

All calculations prompted by the weakening of the emperor's position, however, were soon undermined by the progress of the Swedish armies. This was so swift that it also terminated the last attempt at a biconfessional discussion of the implications of the Edict of Restitution.[6] The conference proposed by the Catholic Electors to discuss the religious grievances met at Frankfurt in August 1631, with fourteen Catholic and twenty-one Protestant territories represented. Nothing had been

---

[2] Press, *Kriege*, 216–17; Gotthard, 'Luthertum', 88–90.
[3] Parker, *Thirty Years War*, 117. See also Nischan, 'Reformed Irenicisim'.
[4] Parker, *Thirty Years War*, 118. See also Nischan, 'Brandenburg's Reformed Räte'.
[5] Parker, *Thirty Years War*, 106–8.
[6] Gotthard, *Säulen*, i, 378–9.

achieved by early October, when the Catholic delegates fled to avoid falling into the hands of the advancing Swedish forces.

This could scarcely have been predicted when Gustavus Adolphus first landed on Usedom on 6 July 1630 with only 1,000 foot and 3,000 horse, and maps that did not even reach down as far as the Elbe. Nineteenth- and early twentieth-century German Protestants depicted the Swedish king variously as a heroic Protestant missionary, the champion of the German Protestant nation, the political equivalent to Luther, or a blonde Nordic Arian superman.[7] After his first military successes in the Reich, some contemporary pamphleteers even hailed him as the Lion of the North who had been predicted by an anonymous but extremely popular pre-war prophecy as the champion of true Christianity, the scourge of the house of Habsburg, and the architect of a new era of peace, calm, and unity in the Reich.[8] However, the defence of Protestantism did not figure at all in the Declaration of June 1630 that preceded the landing, and even six years later, and four years after the king's death in 1632, the Swedish chancellor Axel Oxenstierna reminded his council of state that the war had been 'not so much a matter of religion, but rather of saving the *status publicus*, wherein religion is also comprehended'.[9]

In truth, Swedish war aims evolved as the campaign succeeded beyond any initial expectations. In the first instance, it was initiated purely in the service of Swedish causes. Although Gustavus had shown interest in intervening in German politics in the early 1620s, his first concern was with the continuing claim to his crown by his Catholic relatives in Poland and with the threat posed to Sweden in the Baltic by Denmark, the latest in a long series of conflicts between Denmark and Sweden. Control of the Baltic was not necessarily an end in itself, but something that would guarantee security and generate much needed revenue. The Palatine councillor Ludwig Camerarius may have had visions in 1623 of a war to restore Friedrich to Bohemia and to install Gustavus Adolphus as Holy Roman Emperor.[10] But the Swedish king rapidly lost interest once the idea of an invasion down the Vistula to attack first Bohemia and then Austria was abandoned, and in 1625 he embarked on an independent campaign against Poland with an assault on Livonia and Polish Prussia.[11]

This enterprise was once again combined with the idea of a second stage of the struggle that would attack first Silesia and then the Austrian Erblande. Gustavus's success in establishing control of much of the eastern Baltic coastline from Danzig to Narva in 1626 inevitably alarmed the emperor both as brother-in-law of Sigismund III of Poland and in respect of his own military ambitions in north Germany. Fearing a Swedish attack on the Pomeranian coast, Wallenstein launched a campaign to expel the Swedes from Prussia in August 1626, and the following year he sent a regiment to support the Polish king. As he commented soon afterwards, to

---

[7] Cramer, 'Cult'; Kroener, 'Gustav-Adolf-Mythos'; Opgenoorth, 'Gustav Adolf'.
[8] Gilly, 'Löwe', 252–3, 263–8. See also p. 473.
[9] Parker, *Thirty Years War*, 109.
[10] Parker, *Thirty Years War*, 62, 66.
[11] Ritter, *Geschichte*, iii, 353; Roberts, *Imperial experience*, 32–5.

have ignored the Swedish threat would have been to create an enemy worse than the Turks.[12] Wallenstein's strategy, in turn, forced Gustavus Adolphus to redirect his attention from Silesia as an ultimate objective to Lower Saxony as the source of a more immediate threat. Indeed, the Spanish–Austrian plans for a North Sea–Baltic maritime league including Poland posed a threat to everything that Sweden had achieved, as well as, through the involvement of Poland, to the Swedish Vasa dynasty itself.

Gustavus Adolphus's struggle to secure his dynasty's hold on Sweden thus inevitably entailed a dual conflict with the Habsburgs: on the one hand, the Austrian Habsburgs supported his rivals, the Catholic Vasas, and, on the other hand, both Spanish and Austrian Habsburgs had designs on the Baltic, which would have boosted Polish power. Swedish propaganda in the 1620s reflected the two ways that could later be adapted to suit the needs and potential of the conflict in Germany.[13] First, the struggle with Poland was portrayed as a struggle between Protestantism and popery, which the Swedish crown had a moral-religious duty to pursue without pause. Second, the conflicts of the 1620s could be presented in the context of the national mythology that traced Swedish history from its Gothic origins. As embellished by sixteenth-century humanist scholarship, the claim that the Swedes were the oldest nation could be used to justify anything from their aspiration to pre-eminence over the rulers of the Holy Roman Empire to expeditions to Poland, Pomerania, and Mecklenburg based on the ninth-century precedent of King Berik.[14]

Moreover, the Swedish Gothic myth directly challenged the Spanish myth of Gothic origins. Both Swedes and Spaniards claimed descent from the same western Goths who had landed in Spain, and this inspired scholars in both countries around 1600 to construct myths about their supposed Gothic Spanish origins.[15] In each case, this was used to explain and justify engagement in a wider, universal conflict over religion. The religious theme was designed primarily for the ordinary folk and the Gothicist myth appealed to the educated, but some pictorial propaganda mixed the two by depicting Gothic warriors and Roman emperors together carrying the Swedish lion across the seas.[16]

Gustavus Adolphus obtained the agreement of his Estates for war against the emperor in January 1628, following Wallenstein's decisive push against Christian IV of Denmark in November 1627. Christian had asked for Swedish help, but his survival led Gustavus to postpone an intervention that would have proved an expensive distraction from his conflict with Poland and that might merely have served to strengthen his Danish former rival. Wallenstein's siege of Stralsund in the summer of 1628 presented an altogether more promising opportunity. A modest amount of Swedish assistance forced Wallenstein to back down and secured

[12] Mann, *Wallenstein*, 466.
[13] Roberts, *Imperial experience*, 69–73.
[14] Roberts, *Imperial experience*, 71–2; Roberts, *Early Vasas*, 91–2, 152–3, 201, 469; Frost, *Northern wars*, 134–5.
[15] Burkhardt, *Krieg*, 58–9.
[16] Burkhardt, *Krieg*, 58; Goetze, *Oxenstierna*, 22–8.

Gustavus an alliance with the city that firmly tied it to its Swedish liberators, who retained a strong garrison there.[17] This represented a western extension of the line of control he had recently established along the Polish Baltic, and shortly afterwards he began to think of Wismar, Wallenstein's only serious Baltic naval base further to the west, as another Swedish acquisition. However, despite a renewed resolution in January 1629 to fight against the emperor, no action was taken to initiate a major confrontation.

Gustavus's aims at this stage were still an extension of his strategy against Poland: to drive Wallenstein's troops away from the coast and to ensure that they did not return. In that sense, the *Declaration* that preceded the landing at Peenemünde in July 1630 was quite honest: it complained that the emperor had given help to Poland and that the Habsburgs' Baltic plans threatened Sweden. It also added that Gustavus wished to secure the liberty of the German princes. This, too, was designed to secure the Baltic coast by restoring the status quo of 1618 and ensuring that the reinstated Protestant Estates could not again be overwhelmed by Catholic imperialist forces. This was to be guaranteed by means of Swedish bases in Stralsund, Wismar, and elsewhere, which would remain in place until it was safe to remove them.[18]

Finally, it was French intervention that facilitated engagement in Germany. In September 1629, France mediated a six-year truce between Poland and Sweden at Altmark, which allowed Sweden to retain Livonia and the customs revenues of the Baltic ports between Danzig and Narva, while Poland was allowed to retain its claims to the Swedish throne. While this was a considerable risk for Gustavus, the strategic position he secured on the Baltic coast and, above all, the revenue he gained (equivalent to one-third of Sweden's total revenues) were invaluable.[19] The promise of future French support, which amounted to 400,000 thaler annually for five years given by the Treaty of Bärwalde in January 1631 to support a Swedish force of 36,000 men, made immediate action seem opportune.

Swedish troops landed at the ebb of imperial power. Wallenstein had been dismissed; the best troops were tied up in Italy, Poland, and the Netherlands; those that remained in the Reich were embroiled in a dispute over whether imperial troops should be merged with those of the League or whether Tilly should be commander-in-chief of two separate forces. This was just as well, for at the outset Sweden could scarcely afford a major campaign and the response to her intervention was far from enthusiastic. It proved easy to transfer to the mainland and to establish a bridgehead in Pomerania, forcing the dukes by the Treaty of Stettin (20 July 1630) into an 'eternal' alliance that obliged them to place their resources at the

---

[17] Roberts, *Essays*, 82–3.

[18] Roberts, *Essays*, 85–6.

[19] Sigismund III's successor, Ladislas IV (r. 1632–48) was distracted by a war with Russia in 1632–4, in which he failed either to regain lost territory or to assert his claim to the tsarist throne he had held between 1611 and 1619. Then in 1635, the Polish parliament pre-empted an attempt to launch a war to reclaim the Swedish throne by agreeing a twenty-six-year peace at Stuhmsdorf that allowed Sweden to retain Livonia but returned ducal Prussia and the Baltic port customs duties to Poland. See: Stone, *Polish-Lithuanian state*, 149–55; Frost, *Northern wars*, 33, 142–7.

disposal of the Swedish military and gave Sweden the right to sequester the duchy if Bogislav XIV died without an heir.[20] For the rest, only beleaguered Magdeburg and Bremen immediately allied themselves with the Swedes, along with a handful of dispossessed princes. It is a significant reflection of the king's initially limited war aims that the agreements concluded with most of them, simply covered their restitution and the payment of compensation (*satisfactio*) to Sweden. Only the territories on the Baltic coast were tied up in 'eternal' treaties designed to ensure lasting security (*assecuratio*) as well as compensation for Sweden.[21] Saxony and Brandenburg, meanwhile, met with other Protestant princes at Leipzig in February 1631 to declare their neutrality and independence.[22]

Their hope that the formation of the Leipzig League might induce Ferdinand to give ground so as to make Swedish intervention redundant was dashed by Tilly's assault on Magdeburg in May 1631.[23] Gustavus advanced too late to save Magdeburg but the massacre of much of the city's population and its subsequent destruction by fire created a new situation. News of Tilly's alleged brutality—in reality, he was probably not to blame—spread throughout Europe in newspapers, pamphlets, and broadsheets. Widespread sympathy for the Protestant cause, both internationally and in the Reich, simultaneously strengthened Gustavus's position and persuaded the Elector of Brandenburg, through whose lands the Swedes had marched to Magdeburg anyway, to join his campaign. The Elector of Saxony followed suit on 11 September, after Ferdinand ordered Tilly to launch a pre-emptive strike against his lands.

Once again, Ferdinand's attempt to impose his will by force failed, and worse was to come. On 17 September, the combined forces of Sweden and her various allies inflicted a devastating defeat on Tilly at Breitenfeld near Leipzig. This changed everything for it ended the long period of imperial military superiority. Gustavus was now in a position to make himself master of Germany and to implement the plan he had formulated in May 1631 for a German league under his leadership.[24] This took him far beyond the strategic Baltic coast considerations that had prompted his first involvement in the Reich. His chancellor Axel Oxenstierna was sceptical and wondered how the king would defend his position in the Baltic from bases on the Rhine, in Swabia, or in Bavaria.[25] Yet now the vague objectives implicit in Swedish religious and Gothicist propaganda suddenly seemed feasible:

---

[20] Roberts, *Essays*, 86–7. This conflicted with the Elector of Brandenburg's expectation that he would inherit Pomerania under the terms of the Treaty of Grimnitz of 1529, in which Brandenburg gave up its claim to overlordship over Pomerania and recognized the duchy's immediate state in return for the unequivocal right to inherit if the Pomeranian ducal line should die out. Brandenburg continued to use the Pomeranian coat of arms and titles. Bogislav XIV was declared unfit to govern following a stroke in 1633 and died childless in 1637, whereupon the Swedes established an occupation government. Miller and Taddey, *Lexikon*, 143, 483; *ADB*, iii, 56–8; Schindling and Ziegler, *Territorien*, ii, 203–4.

[21] Roberts, *Essays*, 86–92.

[22] Gotthard, 'Luthertum', 88–90.

[23] Schmidt, *Krieg*, 51–2; Wilson, *Europe's tragedy*, 468–70; Langer, 'Krieg', 301.

[24] Roberts, *Essays*, 91–2.

[25] Goetze, *Oxenstierna*, 87–90.

leadership of a triumphant Protestant league and the creation of a Swedish empire in Germany. At the same time, Swedish victory radicalized the demands of many of the German Protestant princes, which made compromise with the emperor less likely for a while.[26]

The Swedes allowed Tilly's army to escape. Part of it, under Count Pappenheim, moved to the north-west, from where it continued to pose a threat to Swedish supply lines. Tilly himself withdrew to Hessen-Kassel, and then moved south to Nördlingen to join forces with Maximilian to defend Bavaria. Gustavus's forces also divided. One group moved north to secure Mecklenburg. Another advanced towards Magdeburg and then Westphalia. The Saxon army marched through Bohemia to take Prague; a subsidiary unit took Silesia. The main Swedish force advanced through Thuringia to the Elector of Mainz's city of Erfurt, where Gustavus announced himself to the assembled councillors and representatives of the citizenry as the saviour of Protestantism. From there, he swept through Franconia and across to Frankfurt and Mainz, where he set up his winter quarters.

At Mainz, Gustavus Adolphus attempted to lay the foundations of a new order in Germany.[27] His consort, Maria Eleonora, was installed in a new court at Mainz and his chancellor, Axel Oxenstierna, was summoned. The Catholic princes and bishops fled; their territories were treated as the spoils of war. The libraries and art collections of churches, monasteries, and princes were plundered and the best books and art works were transported to Stockholm. Many of the lands themselves were granted by the new Duke of Franconia, as Gustavus styled himself, to loyal commanders such as Duke Bernhard of Weimar.

The king now attracted many more allies than before, but they were still largely drawn from among the less powerful nobles of the Reich: Franconian Imperial Knights, the minor Ernestine Saxony-Weimar princes, representatives from Imperial Cities such as Ulm and Strassburg and—yet again—those princes dispossessed during the 1620s, foremost among them the former Palatine Elector Friedrich V, who immediately travelled from The Hague to pay his compliments to the new master of Mainz. Others had to be forced into alliances with Sweden, agreements that were essential for Gustavus Adolphus to make the German territories pay for his armies. The heavy financial burdens imposed did not make for a popular regime. Nor was much progress made with the creation of a league or with the king's various schemes for the reform of imperial institutions. It was not even clear whether he wanted to become emperor, or simply a prince of the Reich, or to destroy it altogether. But for the time being, sheer superiority of arms ensured loyalty to his cause.

The imperial position was about to deteriorate further. An attempt by Tilly to drive Swedish troops out of Bamberg in March 1632, gave Gustavus Adolphus the excuse to advance on Bavaria, which the Treaty of Bärwalde had, up to now, obliged him to regard as neutral, since it was allied to France by the Treaty of Fontainebleau. Within weeks, the king's main force had reached the Bavarian

---

[26] Frisch, *Restitutionsedikt*, 160–9.   [27] Langer, 'Krieg', 301–2.

border. Tilly's army was crushed at Rain and Tilly himself was mortally wounded. On 17 May, Gustavus Adolphus and the dispossessed Friedrich V entered Munich in triumph. Maximilian's collections were plundered as Friedrich V's had been at Heidelberg ten years earlier, his cannon and other weaponry were captured, and surrounding towns and villages were pillaged; Maximilian himself fled to Salzburg and did not return to his own capital for three years.

The emperor's situation was now desperate. He could no longer rely on the League. At the same time, the ability of his Spanish relatives to help in the Reich was seriously impeded.[28] Swedish conquests on the Rhine had disrupted the 'Spanish road', and although Speyer was regained in spring 1632, the Spanish position remained fragile. Under renewed attack from the Dutch, the Spanish authorities in the Netherlands called up their troops garrisoned in the Reich, but they were unable to prevent the loss of Maastricht in August 1632. In Italy, Spanish forces were weakened by a severe outbreak of plague following the end of the Mantuan War.

In an ever-worsening situation, there seemed no alternative but to recall Wallenstein. Talks had already taken place in December 1631, when the general agreed to levy and equip a substantial new army of 70,000 men for the emperor. In April 1632, he was given far-reaching powers of command.[29] The precise terms of the agreement concluded at Göllersdorf in Lower Austria are not known, but they seem to have included the authority to sign limited peace treaties, supreme command of all the emperor's forces in the Reich, and the right either to confiscate all lands he conquered or to pardon their rulers. The emperor agreed, furthermore, that the King of Hungary (the emperor's heir and later Ferdinand III) should be excluded from active service and that the Edict of Restitution should be revoked. Any lands that Wallenstein himself might lose in the conflict would be compensated for by grants of land in Austria.

Wallenstein's tactics were cautious: he did not wish to risk the sole remaining imperial army. He moved westwards to join up with the remains of Maximilian's forces in the Upper Palatinate; then he ensconced himself at a heavily fortified castle outside Nuremberg. Meanwhile, his commanders began to push the Saxons northwards out of Bohemia and Moravia. Gustavus's attempt to besiege Wallenstein at Nuremberg merely tied him down for several months, caused him heavy losses, and denied him the crucial breakthrough that he would have needed to push through to Vienna. When Gustavus gave up the siege, Wallenstein moved north-east into Saxony and took Leipzig on 1 November. Believing the year's fighting to be over, he sent his men into winter quarters, but was then surprised by the Swedes, who had followed him north and now engaged him at Lützen. Evenly matched forces resulted in a fierce battle, with heavy losses on both sides. Seeing no prospect of success, Wallenstein withdrew and retired to Bohemia. He blamed his failure on the treachery of his officers, of whom he had seventeen summarily executed. For their part, the Swedes were unable to enjoy their victory, for Gustavus Adolphus had perished in the battle.

---

[28] Parker, *Thirty Years War*, 116–17, 119. [29] Mann, *Wallenstein*, 826–34.

Gustavus Adolphus's death, at only thirty-nine, caused widespread consternation among his allies: the last truly charismatic figure departed the scene. His successor, his daughter Christina, was only six years old. Swedish policy, both at home and in the Reich, lay in the hands of the chancellor Axel Oxenstierna. He knew Germany well, for he had studied in Rostock, Jena, and Wittenberg. He was more cautious, more politically adroit, and less impetuous than his late master. Yet, for all his self-assurance in dealing with princes and monarchs, he lacked the authority of a crown.

At the outset, France moved to limit Sweden's position. Concerned at the run of Swedish successes in the west and south, Richelieu continued to offer protection to German princes and cities: Trier already in 1631, many others in 1632 and 1633. In August 1633, French troops invaded Lorraine and occupied Nancy and other key places. By the end of 1634, France controlled a swathe of Reich territory between Basle in the south, Koblenz in the north, and Lorraine in the west, with strong garrisons in Kaiserslautern, Speyer, Philippsburg, Mannheim, and Ehrenbreitstein in Trier. At the same time, the payment of subsidies to Sweden was reduced and subject to increasingly awkward conditions.

Despite this, Oxenstierna was initially able to make more progress politically than Gustavus had done. He continued to push the dual strategy of securing the Baltic coast and creating a league of friendly princes to protect it. By April 1633, he had created the League of Heilbronn based on the Franconian, Swabian, and Electoral and Upper Rhine Kreise, which was devoted to fighting to secure the 'liberty of Germany', the restoration of the Protestant Estates, and the 'satisfaction' (i.e. compensation) of Sweden. He himself became sole director of the League.[30] He gave a clear sign of his future intentions when he restored the Palatinate and its Electoral title to the heirs of Friedrich V (who had died, aged thirty-six, only weeks after Gustavus Adolphus) under their guardian Philipp Ludwig von Simmern.[31]

Other former allies of Friedrich V and Gustavus Adolphus were richly rewarded: Lutheran Baden-Durlach was given Catholic Baden-Baden; Württemberg gained Catholic lands in Upper Swabia; the Counts of Hohenlohe won significant new lands; and the Imperial Cities were permitted to confiscate any remaining Catholic ecclesiastical property within their walls. Swedish generals and officers were also rewarded with grants of land: the Swedish Field Marshal Horn, for example, was endowed with the lands of the Teutonic Knights at Mergentheim. Oxenstierna indicated his personal ambitions by reserving for himself, as Swedish chancellor, the lands of the Elector of Mainz, the Imperial Archchancellor. He immediately set about constructing a government composed of Imperial Knights and initiated a programme of economic and administrative reform. The vast and heavily fortified Gustavsburg, situated at the confluence of the Main and the Rhine and capable of sheltering 17,000 men, was the military cornerstone of Oxenstierna's German system.

---

[30] Roberts, 'Oxenstierna', 77–81.   [31] Ritter, *Geschichte*, iii, 552.

Though he achieved much, Oxenstierna's system was fundamentally flawed in two respects. First, its financial foundations were insecure.[32] The League was committed to maintaining a substantial army at an annual cost of over ten million thaler. In addition, the allies agreed to pay the vast arrears of the various forces: some had not been paid since 1627 and it was not even possible to determine the exact total owing. French and Dutch subsidies were now paid directly into the League treasury; the members agreed to pay 2.5 million thaler annually, but that still left a substantial shortfall, which could only be met by means of direct local levies. Oxenstierna had no option but to allow his commanders a free hand and to give in to some outrageous demands. Bernhard of Weimar, joint commander-in-chief of the League's forces, was given the lands of the Bishops of Würzburg and Bamberg to fund his troops; his ambition as a landless younger son to acquire a hereditary principality of his own was met by his elevation to the Dukedom of Franconia as a vassal of the Swedish crown.[33]

Bernhard's Swedish co-commander Gustav Karlsson Horn, Count of Björnborg, gained control of much of Alsace. Significant discontent and threats of mutiny among the forces over the winter of 1632–3 led to other commanders and officers being likewise rewarded. Given sanction by Oxenstierna, many simply plundered and ruthlessly exploited the land placed at their disposal. Some not only paid off their men but made immense profits: substantial sums were sent back to Stockholm to build palaces, together with looted art treasures to furnish them.[34] Further taxes on all lands included in the alliance were agreed at the Frankfurt meeting of the League in July, but the financial problems were never fully resolved. Oxenstierna even resorted to selling ecclesiastical properties that had not yet been conquered. In 1633, for example, he sold Eichstätt and Augsburg as hereditary property to Count Brandenstein for over one million thaler, and added the Prince-Bishopric of Constance as a gift for good measure with the title of 'Prince of Constance'.[35] While Gustavus Adolphus had used the lands of the Church in moderation for purposes of political patronage, Oxenstierna was obliged to treat them primarily as a source of money.

An even more significant problem was Oxenstierna's failure to secure the full support of either Brandenburg or Saxony.[36] Neither was keen to join Oxenstierna's League at the outset. For Brandenburg, the key issue was the Pomeranian succession. Gaining Pomerania after the imminently expected death of Bogislav XIV, which the inheritance treaty of 1493 fully entitled Brandenburg to do, would have given Brandenburg access to the Oder estuary and the Baltic. Yet Pomerania also played a key role in Swedish plans and, along with Mecklenburg, it was a territory

---

[32] Parker, *Thirty Years War*, 121–2; Asch, *Thirty Years War*, 107–8; Langer, 'Heilbronner Bund', 121.
[33] He was thus not a prince of the Reich (only the emperor could have granted that dignity), and he had to agree that his dukedom would revert to the Swedish crown if he died without heirs. Langer, 'Heilbronner Bund', 120.
[34] Frost, *Northern wars*, 134.
[35] Wolgast, *Hochstift*, 337.
[36] Dickmann, *Frieden*, 74–7; Roberts, 'Oxenstierna', 75–6.

that the Swedes were determined to retain at all costs. Talk of a marriage between Georg Wilhelm's son and Queen Christina (Georg Wilhelm's sister had married Gustavus Adolphus) was not enough to reconcile the Brandenburg Elector to being thwarted in Pomerania. Distrust of Swedish intentions over Pomerania was enough to convince the Elector of Brandenburg to pursue his dynasty's usual policy of following Saxony's lead, though he expressed a strong preference for Saxony and Brandenburg brokering some kind of peace.

In Dresden, the Saxon Elector was besieged by envoys seeking to gain his ear. Oxenstierna himself visited and then sent others. Denmark sent Count Wartensleben to offer mediation—scarcely disinterested—between Dresden and Vienna. Landgrave Georg of Hessen-Darmstadt—fearful that his relative, the Reformed Landgrave Wilhelm of Hessen-Kassel, would exploit his own alliance with Sweden to regain the Marburg lands his father had lost in 1627—also agitated for negotiation with the emperor. Wallenstein sent emissaries with a variety of constantly changing schemes for peace and war. Foreign envoys of every persuasion brought counsel of every kind. The Elector of Saxony himself had dropped his alliance with Sweden in December 1632, after Gustavus Adolphus's death. He was now not inclined to resume it. Oxenstierna's plans merely aroused his anger that his traditional leadership of the German Protestants was being ignored and he was averse to any scheme that made him into an appendage of the Swedish crown.

Since the emperor's demands were initially too harsh, however, and for want of any more plausible scheme, Saxony once more agreed to a Swedish alliance in the spring of 1633. The Elector was at first enticed by the improbable idea that the Saxon heir might, with Swedish help, gain the Bohemian throne, since the Palatine pretender, Friedrich V, had died at Mainz on 29 November 1632. That ambition was soon modified to a plan to invade Silesia, which left greater room for eventual negotiation with the emperor. The new alliance with Sweden, in which Brandenburg followed suit, led nowhere as Oxenstierna and the Elector publicly traded insults.[37] Any prospect of either Saxony or Brandenburg formally joining the League disappeared entirely in July 1634, when Oxenstierna revealed the full extent of Swedish demands for compensation, which included the whole of Mecklenburg and Pomerania.[38]

Around all these diverse negotiations during the course of 1633 and early 1634, the fighting continued: in the south-west between French and Swedish forces on the one hand, and those of Spain, Austria, and the Catholic League, on the other; and in the north-west between Swedish allies and an imperial army on the Weser. Both of these conflicts, however, were peripheral; neither had the potential to be decisive. The really crucial fault line lay in the east between the forces of Sweden and its allies on the one hand, and the imperial army of Wallenstein on the other. Here, events in 1633 were largely determined by Wallenstein himself, with diplomacy more important than warfare.

---

[37] Langer, 'Heilbronner Bund', 119.   [38] Langer, 'Heilbronner Bund', 121–2.

54

Wallenstein and After

It is not known exactly what Wallenstein was trying to achieve. Personal dynastic ambitions are unlikely, for he had no male heir. Later accusations of treachery were almost certainly unfounded, yet some of his negotiations could certainly be construed as working against imperial interest. Before his reappointment he had corresponded with Gustavus Adolphus, though the emperor was unaware of this.[1] On his reappointment in April 1632, he was empowered to negotiate with Saxony, but the negotiations he entered into with France, Sweden, and even the Bohemian exiles almost certainly exceeded his brief. His main strategic aim throughout was to drive a wedge between Sweden and the Protestant Electors, and he agreed two-month-long truces with Saxony to promote that end. In October 1633, he pushed northward into Silesia and defeated a Swedish force at Steinau; he then occupied key neighbouring towns in Brandenburg and Lusatia. Yet he left Saxony untouched and withdrew to winter quarters in Bohemia. Then he made a renewed offer of peace to Dresden and Berlin.

To many around him his behaviour was incomprehensible. He explained little and often behaved with imperious arrogance and ruthless brutality. He combined great talent with extravagance, narcissistic vanity, and megalomania. In the last year or so of his life, he was also visibly ill and often appeared deluded, and he almost certainly pursued objectives that were contradictory. That was not unusual among the German princes, though few of them really accepted Wallenstein as their equal. Always an outsider, he was too versatile and restlessly inventive to be a meek servant of the crown. Yet he had no authority independent of it; his German principality, which many refused to recognize anyway, was to all intents and purposes lost almost immediately after he acquired it.

For all that could be held against him, however, Wallenstein was also capable of exceptional cunning and pragmatism. Though he spearheaded the Catholic counter-offensive in the north, he immediately assured the Protestant nobility of their religious rights when he became Duke of Mecklenburg.[2] In Friedland, as a vassal of the Bohemian crown, it was his duty to enforce Catholicism; as a prince of the Reich, it was his prerogative to exercise the *ius reformandi* in whichever way he chose. On his dismissal in 1630, he retired to his Bohemian estates without demur, but when he was re-engaged with wide-ranging powers he immediately sought a compromise with honour for the emperor. In 1628–9, he had held back from a fight

---

[1] Suvanto, *Politik*, 37–41.   [2] Mann, *Wallenstein*, 580.

to the finish with Christian IV, aware that he lacked the resources to destroy a monarch who commanded crucial maritime resources as well as a sizeable army. In 1632–3, he sought any solution, but most consistently compromise with Saxony and Brandenburg, in the face of enemies, notably Sweden and France, over whom he believed he could not possibly prevail. He had always been critical of Vienna's willingness to help promote Spanish ambitions in Italy and the Netherlands.

In Vienna, the chorus of Wallenstein's critics grew steadily. His dilatory behaviour in 1633 was presented as treachery, rather than as the necessary primacy of diplomacy over arms. There was evidence enough of rank failure for those who wanted to seize on it: the Protestants controlled much of Bavaria and the west. In Silesia, Wallenstein had not capitalized on his victory at Steinau. Then, Regensburg fell to Bernhard of Weimar in November 1633 after Wallenstein failed to come to the aid of Maximilian's garrison of two thousand men.

One by one, Wallenstein's allies deserted him and joined the faction around the Jesuit confessor Lamormaini, who were impatient for action. Their resolve was strengthened by the Spanish representative Marquis Sancho de Castañeda (and, from October 1633, by Count Oñate), stung by Wallenstein's notorious opposition to Austrian efforts to promote Spanish ambitions in Italy and the Netherlands. Now they intimated plans for sending a Spanish army under the command of the Cardinal Infante Ferdinand, but not until Wallenstein either relinquished or was deprived of his right to command all Catholic troops in the Reich.[3]

The last straw was the arrival of news at court that the generalissimo had required all his colonels to swear at Pilsen on 12 January 1634 that they would be loyal to him before all others. News of the 'Pilsen oath' prompted Ferdinand to order Wallenstein's arrest, alive or dead. The previous December, Ferdinand had secretly secured the complicity of Wallenstein's three main commanders, Johann von Aldringen, Matthias von Gallas, and Octavio Piccolomini. On 24 January, a secret meeting deprived Wallenstein of his command; even a second oath at Pilsen on 24 February could no longer secure the loyalty of most of his officers. With a small group of close associates, Wallenstein fled from Prague to Eger, towards the Saxons and the Swedes. Thereafter, his confidants Christian von Ilow, Adam Trčka, and Vilém Kinsky were murdered.

Wallenstein himself was assassinated by Walter Butler, Walter Leslie, Walter Devereux, and John Gordon, the Eger garrison commandant. Each had taken one or both of the Pilsen oaths. All those involved were rewarded with generous grants from the murdered general's vast estates.[4] Whether or not Ferdinand II had intended Wallenstein's death—the fact that he implored his Jesuits to pray for a successful outcome to the operation suggests that he did—this brutal judicial murder did nothing to enhance his own reputation in the Reich.[5] Oxenstierna was certainly not slow to point out to Brandenburg and Saxony that the whole affair simply proved how dangerous it was to deal with the emperor.[6]

---

[3] Asch, *Thirty Years War*, 108–9.   [4] Evans, *Making*, 202–3.
[5] Parker, *Thirty Years War*, 125.   [6] Suvanto, *Politik*, 185–6.

It did, however, pave the way to an important victory. Oxenstierna failed to extend his Heilbronn League in April 1634, but the Swedes and their allies still made significant progress when fighting resumed in July.[7] The Saxons pressed into Bohemia again and penetrated as far as Prague; Heilbronn forces advanced on Bavaria and took Landshut. But Ferdinand of Hungary, the emperor's son, to whom Wallenstein's command had been transferred, took Regensburg and Donau-wörth and laid siege to Nördlingen. At the start of September, the Cardinal Infante arrived with the promised Spanish army. Together, the two Ferdinands took the city and inflicted a crushing blow on Bernhard of Weimar's Protestant army: nearly half of his 25,000 men were killed and 4,000 were taken prisoner. Bernhard fled west into Alsace and Oxenstierna withdrew all garrisons south of the Main. The myth of Swedish invincibility was shattered. The Heilbronn League dissolved; Oxenstierna left Germany, and returned only briefly before leaving for good in 1636.[8] His oldest ally, Landgrave Wilhelm of Hessen-Kassel, was convinced that only France could now save the German Protestants from Habsburg tyranny. He even wanted to elect the King of France as emperor, for that alone, he believed, would secure 'German liberty'.[9]

There would be much discussion of this in the decades after the end of the war.[10] For now, however, the emperor was a Habsburg and the collapse of Swedish power made compromise with him the only option. After Nördlingen, the negotiations between Hessen-Darmstadt, Saxony, and the emperor begun at Leitmeritz in 1633 made rapid progress at the new location of Pirna. The emperor's most recent successes strengthened his hand considerably, yet it was clear to his advisers that he too had to compromise to secure a viable agreement. Finally, on 30 May 1635, the emperor and the Elector of Saxony concluded a peace at Prague.

The treaty declared the wish of its signatories to restore the 'precious German nation to its previous integrity, tranquillity, liberty, and security'.[11] It was designed to settle the major constitutional, religious, and territorial issues of the conflict. All bishoprics and other ecclesiastical properties that had been taken over by the Protestants before the Treaty of Passau in 1552 were confirmed in their current status. Any that had changed hands between 1552 and 12 November 1627 were to remain under their current rulers for forty years without any change in their religion. The Edict of Restitution was thus suspended. At the end of forty years, a commission composed equally of Catholics and Protestants would seek to reach an amicable agreement, failing which the status quo of 1627 would prevail.

Significantly, however, both the Imperial Knights and all Imperial Cities except Nuremberg, Strassburg, Ulm, and Frankfurt were excluded from this dispensation, which meant that the terms of the Edict of Restitution could still be enforced in much of Swabia and Franconia. Magdeburg was given to the Saxon Elector's second son August, who had been elected administrator, for his lifetime. He was to pay a lifelong rent to Brandenburg in recognition of its administratorship before

---

[7] Roberts, 'Oxenstierna', 83–4.   [8] Roberts, 'Oxenstierna', 85–92.
[9] Parker, *Thirty Years War*, 127.   [10] Schmidt, 'Französischer Kaiser?'.
[11] Wandruszka, *Reichspatriotismus*, 66.

1628. Archduke Leopold Wilhelm gave up any claim to Magdeburg but was confirmed as Prince-Bishop of Halberstadt.

Key institutions were to be reformed and revived, and measures were agreed to ensure the liberation of the Reich from foreign troops and the maintenance of peace and stability thereafter. It was envisaged that the membership of the Reichs-kammergericht would be evenly balanced between Catholics and Protestants, and that the Electors would consider the future membership of the Reichshofrat. The imperial army would remain in being and the Estates would provide finance for further troops to be integrated into it. Although the emperor was to have overall authority over this army, Saxony was given command over all Protestant troops and Maximilian of Bavaria was given command of forces that were, in effect, equivalent to those of the Catholic League.[12] With the exception of the association of the Electors and the traditional hereditary treaties between dynasties, all leagues and alliances were to be dissolved.

Some leading princes were rewarded and some of the dispossessed were reinstated. Saxony was confirmed in its ownership of Lusatia under the agreements of 1620 and 1623, and also acquired some territory from Magdeburg. Brandenburg was promised the succession in Pomerania. The Dukes of Mecklenburg and Lorraine were restored to their lands. The transfer of the Palatine Electoral title to Bavaria was confirmed, as was the grant of the Upper Palatinate; in return, Maximilian under-took to make a substantial contribution to the imperial army. The main gain for the Habsburgs was the exclusion of all their lands, with the exception of parts of Silesia, from any legislation that limited their *ius reformandi*: Ferdinand was prepared to accept the suspension of the Edict of Restitution in the Reich but not in his own territories.

Others were punished. The heirs of Friedrich V were deprived of their lands and Electoral title in perpetuity, though the emperor undertook to provide for them as princes if they became loyal. For the time being, they remained excluded from the general amnesty, along with all the others who had been involved in the 'Bohemian and Palatine troubles'. The Reformed Landgrave of Hessen-Kassel was dispossessed and his lands taken over by his Lutheran kinsman in Hessen-Darmstadt. The Lutheran Duke of Württemberg and the Reformed Margrave of Baden-Durlach, both key rebels throughout the 1620s, were also excluded until such time as the emperor decided to pardon them.[13] The various Ernestine Dukes of Saxony-Weimar were offered the possibility of inclusion if they submitted to the emperor's authority.[14]

Ferdinand II submitted the draft peace plan to a conference of twenty-four theologians. His own confessor, Lamormaini, together with four other Jesuits, vigorously opposed it. In the end, however, a majority of sixteen concurred with the more conciliatory view urged by Count Trauttmannsdorff, who had been the

---

[12] Asch, *Thirty Years War*, 115.
[13] The Duke of Württemberg was pardoned in 1638 and received some of his lands back; Friedrich V of Baden-Durlach was only restored in 1648: Schindling and Ziegler, *Territorien*, v, 144–5, 188–9.
[14] All did so, except Bernhard of Weimar: *ADB*, ii, 439–50.

emperor's key adviser in the various negotiations with the Elector of Saxony, Wallenstein, the King of Hungary, the representatives of the Spanish Habsburgs, and the imperial privy council.[15]

Lamormaini might complain that more had been conceded than God would allow, but in reality it was not enough. The peace plan went into extraordinary detail, but it still left key areas of potential conflict and ambiguity. It gave considerable advantages to the emperor and the Catholic cause generally; in particular, it ensured that south-western Germany, traditionally an area of strong Habsburg influence, remained dominated by Catholic princes. The Edict of Restitution was suspended but not rescinded. The problem of the legal status of the Reformed in the Reich had not been addressed: the Elector of Brandenburg was one of a small number of Calvinists included in the amnesty. Those who remained dispossessed continued to pursue their claims. The restitution of the Dukes of Mecklenburg and Pomerania (and the reinstatement of Brandenburg's claim to inherit the latter) was all very well, but the Swedes were still in possession of their lands, and no provision was made for Sweden's claims for compensation. Indeed, perhaps the major defect of the Peace was that it seemed to rest on the assumption that Swedish power had been shattered for good and that France would not intervene further. Those assumptions were soon proved to be wrong.

The Peace of Prague was a German peace and almost all the German Estates soon formally acceded to it.[16] It was accompanied by an extraordinary wave of patriotic peace propaganda proclaiming the salvation of German liberties and the restoration of the polity.[17] The supporters of the emperor and his allies naturally proclaimed the virtues of the new imperial order. More remarkable was the enthusiastic echo from those who had stood on the other side, or at least had remained lukewarm about the crown, for the last decade or so. Even the Reformed princes of Anhalt declared the treaty to be the true 'bond of German unity'. Some now also forcefully opposed military service against one's fatherland and placed peace and unity above confessional solidarity. Germans who remained in Swedish service came under pressure to quit and to serve their own nation instead, and three members of the Fruchtbringende Gesellschaft in fact resigned their Swedish commissions.[18]

It is true that the vocabulary employed to eulogize the Peace of Prague varied in significant ways. Austrian and Spanish authors spoke more often than not of the 'German nation' (united under the emperor).[19] Many princes thought primarily in terms of 'German liberty' (safe from Habsburg tyranny). These nuances evaporated in the early afterglow of the peace. Yet it was inescapable that the larger political-constitutional questions remained open. In particular, the emperor had repeatedly dismissed the suggestion made by Landgrave Georg of Hessen-Darmstadt that the

---

[15] Bireley, *Jesuits*, 162–4; *ADB*, xxxviii, 531–7.

[16] Asch, *Thirty Years War*, 114.

[17] Wandruszka, *Reichspatriotismus*, 71–81; Schmidt, *Geschichte*, 167–8; Hansen, 'Patriotismus', 36–48. See also, Schmidt, *Vaterlandsliebe*, 358–415.

[18] Schmidt, *Geschichte*, 168.

[19] Asch, *Thirty Years War*, 110–11.

Estates as a whole should meet to decide on key issues and that Sweden should be involved in any peace settlement. The agreement made on behalf of the princes that they should pay for the upkeep of an imperial army was a significant innovation, the implications of which were not lost on many of them: their traditional right to decide had been bypassed. The Catholic Electors, too, questioned the wisdom of the emperor concluding a treaty with a single prince, to which all others were expected to accede. The remedy might have been to summon the Reichstag, but this had not met since 1613 and the emperor was not keen on its resurrection.[20]

The Peace of Prague genuinely marked the beginning of a German peace movement that persisted, through various permutations, to the end of the war. Ultimately, elements of the Prague system and the sentiments that it inspired shaped the more durable settlement reached in 1648. But the years between 1635 and 1648 also represented another stage in the constitutional struggle that had been at the heart of the war from the outset.

[20] Höbelt, *Ferdinand III.*, 163–76.

55

France, Sweden, and the German Way, 1635–1648

In the same month as the Peace of Prague was signed, France formally declared war on Spain. The pretext was that Spanish troops had arrested Philip Christoph von Sötern, the Elector of Trier and France's ally since 1631; they handed him over to the emperor, who kept him imprisoned until 1645. The real focus of this struggle was Flanders, with subsidiary conflict zones in the Pyrenees, the Western Alps and northern Italy, and, finally, on the Upper and Middle Rhine and in the Argonne. The main conflict between France and Spain continued until the Peace of the Pyrenees in 1659, but the action in Germany played a significant role in the last decade of the Thirty Years War and justified French claims to participation and compensation in the German peace of 1648. In the south-west of the Reich, France inherited the remnants of the Swedish system as well as the strategic options of the Swedes.

Sweden had been defeated in 1634, but her position in Germany had not been destroyed. The conflict to date had imposed considerable strain on Swedish resources. Withdrawal to north Germany was accompanied by a growing sense that Sweden must exit the war as soon as possible. At the same time, however, there was general agreement in Stockholm that certain preconditions had to be met before peace was concluded: Sweden must be compensated for the sacrifices she had made on behalf of the German Protestants; she must be allowed to maintain control of all the Baltic ports; and some way must be found of limiting Habsburg authority in north Germany in perpetuity. For better or for worse, the Swedes believed themselves obliged to continue the fight until these conditions were met.

In some ways, things now promised to become easier for them. Thanks to the limitations of the Peace of Prague, there were still disaffected German princes, such as the dispossessed Wilhelm V of Hessen-Kassel. He was forced out of his territory but he managed to take his army with him. After his death in 1637, his widow Amalie Elisabeth continued to refuse to accede to the Peace of Prague. Following an extensive truce, she waged war independently and, with French help, achieved notable successes on behalf of her young son, later Wilhelm VI, during the 1640s.[1]

Similarly, many of the Reformed Wetterau counts lost their lands to Hessen-Darmstadt, to Mainz, to neighbouring Catholic dynasties, or to outright new-comers to whom the emperor was now able to dispense patronage, such as Prince

---

[1] *ADB*, i, 383–5.

Adelbert von Lobkowitz, the Reichsvizekanzler Count Ferdinand Sigmund Kurz, and the Elector of Brandenburg's Catholic favourite, Count Adam von Schwarzenberg.[2] In the north, the Dukes of Brunswick, resentful at the loss of their bishoprics, maintained an army until 1642. With France openly involved in the war, Sweden also had a powerful new ally. In March 1636, a French–Swedish treaty was negotiated at Wismar, though it was not ratified for three years, while Oxenstierna first cast around for the possibility of a peace mediated by the Elector of Saxony, and then tried to launch a new offensive into Brandenburg and Saxony. Finally, in March 1638, Oxenstierna saw no alternative but to ratify the treaty at Hamburg, which gave Sweden substantial financial aid for further military operations.

Oxenstierna had good reason to hesitate, for the French war effort was not initially successful. France too was short of resources. Her barely covert involvement in the conflict since the early 1620s had already consumed huge sums of money. Increases in taxation were a double-edged sword, for both before and after 1635 wide-scale unrest required costly military countermeasures. The opening campaigns were dogged by failure. A Franco-Dutch offensive in 1635 failed to achieve any of its objectives, and nothing was gained by the first interventions in Italy; the attempt by Bernhard of Saxony-Weimar and Cardinal de la Valette to invade southern Germany failed completely. On the contrary, a Spanish-imperial army invaded northern France almost as far down as Amiens in 1636 and the imperial general, Gallas very nearly managed to capture Dijon.

Only Bernhard of Weimar's second campaign brought success. Starting in 1637, he systematically mastered the whole of Alsace and in December 1638, took the key fortress and town of Breisach on the Rhine. But while Bernhard's military expertise was beyond doubt, he was an uncomfortable ally. From the outset in 1635, he had made financial demands that Richelieu found difficult to stomach and he seemed to want to maintain his independence from France.[3] He insisted at all stages on being recognized as commander-in-chief of his own troops, not subject to the authority of the French crown.

Furthermore, since the Dukedom of Franconia that Bernhard had been awarded by the Swedes had disappeared with the end of their regime in Mainz, he now demanded the Landgravate of Alsace together with Breisach (all formerly part of Habsburg Further Austria). Problematically, from Richelieu's point of view, Bernhard also demanded that he be allowed to hold this territory independently, rather than as a vassal of the French crown. The potential problem of the construction of an autonomous power in a strategically vital region was only solved by Bernhard's death from illness on 11 July 1639, aged thirty-five. He bequeathed his lands to any one of his brothers who might wish to accept them and expressed the wish that they should remain within the German Reich, and that his successor should remain loyal to Sweden. In fact, his death provided the opportunity for Richelieu to seize both his lands and his army, which was now under the command of his deputy, Johann Ludwig von Erlach.

---

[2] Schmidt, *Grafenverein*, 447.   [3] *ADB*, ii, 439–50.

Bernhard's success in south-west Germany coincided with a new impetus in the war generally. Taking Alsace cut the Spanish land route to Flanders. In October 1639, the destruction of the Spanish fleet off Dover by the Dutch Admiral Maarten Tromp severed the sea route as well.[4] The following year, the Spanish crown was shaken by two major uprisings: in the spring of 1640, the rebellion of the Catalans, whose leaders placed themselves under a French protectorate in January 1641; then, in December 1640, the rebellion of the Portuguese.[5] The first dragged on until Catalonia once more submitted to Castilian rule in 1652; the second was reinforced by resources from Brazil and led to the permanent secession of Portugal in 1668.

Ruptured supply lines and the need to divert resources elsewhere left the Spanish army in Flanders increasingly exposed and it suffered a devastating defeat at the hands of the French at Rocroi in 1643. Indeed, there was now nothing to prevent the northward expansion of France: by 1646, Dunkirk had fallen. The Dutch found the prospect of a strong and aggressive French neighbour so alarming that they immediately initiated negotiations for peace with Spain, which ultimately led to the formal end of Spain's eighty-year war against the Dutch rebels and to international recognition of the independence of the Dutch Republic in the Peace of Münster in 1648.

The Spanish Habsburgs were no longer able to come to the aid of the Austrians; Spain all but disappeared from German Protestant propaganda.[6] At the same time, despite feeling the huge strain on their own resources, both France and Sweden were able to maintain the pressure. Their treaty committed the Swedes to attack the Austrian Erblande from the north, while the French were to advance eastwards through south Germany.

Swedish forces under the brilliant commands of Johan Banér (until 1641), Lennart Torstensson (1641–5), and Karl Gustav Wrangel (from 1645) managed a series of effective operations, though none achieved a decisive victory. In 1639, Banér marched through Brandenburg and Saxony and, having defeated an imperial army, penetrated Bohemia as far as Prague. In 1641, Swedish and French troops marched on Regensburg in an attempt to threaten the Reichstag there. In 1642, Torstensson's troops marched down into Moravia and his mounted forces penetrated the vicinity of Vienna. On the approach of the imperial army, they withdrew to Saxony and then inflicted a decisive defeat on the imperialists at Breitenfeld. Sweden's freedom of movement in north Germany was now so great that, on hearing of talks about an alliance between Vienna and Copenhagen, and anxious to eliminate the Danes from any future peace conference, Stockholm declared war on Denmark in December 1643.[7] Torstensson's forces were able to achieve a relatively easy victory, which effectively ended Denmark's role as an international power.

An imperial army had been sent north to assist the Danes, but a Swedish diversionary alliance with György Rákóczi of Transylvania resulted in an attack in Hungary, though Turkey's refusal to back Rákóczi enabled Ferdinand to

---

[4] Israel, *Dutch Republic 1476–1806*, 537.   [5] Elliott, *Olivares*, 519–32, 571–99.
[6] Schmidt, *Universalmonarchie*, 443.   [7] Lockhart, *Denmark*, 257–65.

conclude the Peace of Vienna in December 1645. However, the early recall of the imperial army gave Torstensson the opportunity to decimate it near Magdeburg as it attempted to march back from Holstein to Bohemia. Imperial efforts to equip a new army were met by another Swedish invasion of Bohemia, which ended in disaster for the imperialists at Jankau, south-east of Prague, on 6 March 1645, the most devastating defeat they suffered during the whole war. Within weeks, Swedish troops took Krems on the Danube, and the Viennese authorities caught sight of mounted forces on the other side of the river. Deprived of the imperial alliance, the Elector of Saxony now had no option but to make peace with the Swedes. By the time peace negotiations started in earnest, Sweden was in a position to claim a place at the table and achieve the compensation that had become its only real war aim.

Though with greater difficulty, France too was able to achieve a favourable position in advance of the peace. Neither Richelieu's death nor that of Louis XIII brought a change of policy: Mazarin continued to push French troops through southern Germany. In 1643 and 1644, Bavarian troops under Count Franz von Mercy repulsed a French attack and regained Freiburg. In 1645, Turenne advanced again and took Mergentheim, although the Bavarians subsequently stood their ground at Alerheim near Nördlingen on 3 August 1645.

The following year, French and Swedish troops occupied Bavaria. However, a truce between Bavaria and the occupying powers brought but a temporary respite, for Bavaria's return to the imperial side only a few months later resulted in another devastation of the country. The occupation only ended when the peace was actually signed. In May 1648, Turenne and Wrangel inflicted a final defeat on Maximilian's troops at Zusmarshausen near Augsburg, which resulted in much of Bavaria being plundered again. As late as October 1648, Swedish forces under General Johann Christoph von Königsmarck besieged Prague and actually occupied the lesser town and the royal castle (Hradschin), where they looted the collections of Rudolf II.[8]

The fighting continued in Bohemia and Bavaria until the news of the peace arrived. Yet the battles of Jankau and Alerheim effectively marked the end of the war. The emperor had suffered a humiliating defeat; the Bavarians were eliminated from the conflict. Neither France nor Sweden had achieved their ultimate objective of invading the Erblande. However, they were able to inflict sufficient damage on the emperor to ensure that they could force him to make concessions to their German allies and to achieve the compensation that they each wanted.

There were no ultimately decisive battles. Yet the trend was clear in this war of position. The imperial forces were simply unable to mount a serious counter-offensive. The loss of the Spanish subsidies after 1640 crucially undermined the Austrians' ability to raise loans for further troops. When Swedish troops arrived at Vienna in 1645, all that Ferdinand could do was vow to erect a column to the Virgin Mary if she would ensure the city was spared, which his obituarists later praised as an appropriate response.[9] The extent to which the emperor's military position, and hence also his diplomatic bargaining power, was undermined is

---

[8] Frost, *Northern wars*, 134.   [9] Repgen, 'Ferdinand III', 147; Gantet, *Paix*, 232.

illustrated by the fact that of the roughly two hundred garrisons in the Reich in 1648 only 14.5 per cent were in Austrian and Bavarian hands: 42 per cent were held by Sweden, 28 per cent by France, and 13.5 per cent by their ally Hessen-Kassel.[10]

Although hostilities persisted to the last, there was a genuine desire for peace on virtually all sides. All the participants were feeling the strain of the war, which was generating serious domestic pressures. In France, there was a series of popular rebellions in 1636–43 and rising tensions exploded in a serious rebellion of the office-holding nobility in January 1648, the *Frondes*. In Sweden, many began to assert that they had ruined themselves in the conquest of others. The English Civil War from 1642 neutralized English policy in favour of the dispossessed Palatines and made many on the mainland more cautious of provoking a similar upheaval in their own lands. The desire for peace was also strong in the Reich itself and the early 1640s saw another wave of patriotic writing that gave voice to a longing to see the conflict resolved.[11]

For the German participants, the path to peace was shaped by the successive blows to imperial prestige and by the relationship between the emperor and the Imperial Estates. Throughout the last phase of the war, there was a series of peace initiatives which unfolded at different levels and involved varying combinations of actors. They were pursued at various stages by the emperor, by the Electors, and by individual princes and groups of princes. They interacted with French and Swedish initiatives throughout, but also, at one time or another, with attempts at mediation by the papacy, Denmark, and others. The most important feature of this often rather uncoordinated succession of peace moves was its link with a new version of the old struggle for power in the Reich.

At first, it appeared that the combination of emperor and Electors would determine the political future of the Reich. At a meeting of Electors at Regensburg in September 1636, they agreed without difficulty to the election of Ferdinand II's heir, already King of Bohemia and Hungary, as King of the Romans.[12] The Electors delayed confirmation of the election for several months in an effort to force Ferdinand to make peace. At the same time, they renewed the tax grant that had been contained in the Peace of Prague and considered the kind of wide-ranging agenda that would normally have been found at a Reichstag. Ferdinand II died before he could take any serious steps towards a peace. On his succession in February 1637, Ferdinand III inherited both the same commitment to seek peace and the same strategy to unite the Reich on Habsburg terms, regain military superiority, and expel foreign troops. Increasingly, however, the failure of the Prague system became evident and the emperor's willingness to make concessions grew. By 1645, Ferdinand III was eager to make peace at any price.

[10] Repgen, 'Ferdinand III', 151; Höbelt, *Ferdinand III.*, 224–64,
[11] Stein, 'Religion'; Hansen, 'Patriotismus', 149–69; Schmidt, *Geschichte*, 173–7; Meid, *Literatur*, 482–3.
[12] Wilson, *Europe's tragedy*, 585–7.

Yet both Ferdinand II and Ferdinand III were also determined that it should be they who actually made the peace. The Electors had other ideas. In the absence of the Reichstag, they increasingly regarded themselves as the governing body of the Reich. Their meetings had, in effect, taken the place of the Reichstag in the polity and they increasingly set themselves apart from the other princes. From the late 1620s, they became agitated about their status, in particular their claim to have the status and rights of kings in the Reich.[13] In 1628, an envoy of the Medici was accorded a better position than them in the imperial chapel. In due course, this led the republics of Venice and Genoa to claim equivalent status, which kept the Electors' hackles raised throughout the next decade. Their insistence that they alone should sit next to the emperor in chapel and at table was more than a simple squabble about pews and seating plans. The real issue was the Electors' 'pre-eminence', their premier status and their authority as 'pillars' of the Reich.

Another aspect of this situation was their relationship with the emperor. To what extent did the Electors have the authority to make policy on behalf of the crown? Could they force the emperor to conclude a peace against his will? Opinions differed among the Electors, but for much of the 1630s the Elector of Bavaria dominated the discussions, always playing the double role of the emperor's most stalwart ally and yet also his most staunch opponent, constantly seeking to secure the best outcome for Bavaria by dealing with both Vienna and Paris. Maximilian's motives were clear. He wanted to keep all that he had won from the defeat of the Palatinate, and he often behaved as if he did not much mind whether that was achieved with the help of the emperor or the King of France.

By 1640, the pressure being applied on Ferdinand III by the Electors was intense. At their discussions at Nuremberg, they again suggested that a special meeting should be convened to formulate a peace plan. They also proposed that representatives of the Kreise (the *kreisausschreibender Fürst*, or executive prince in each case) should be invited.[14] In itself this was not a bad idea: it might have made it easier to secure funds for any action and it might even have generated a certain patriotic momentum similar to that which had been generated in 1635. There were other implications, however, that were unacceptable both to Vienna and to the other princes. The fact that the initiative came from the Electors, who it was envisaged would also extend the invitations, sidelined the emperor. It clearly undermined his exclusive right to summon meetings of the Reich and implicitly challenged his authority to conclude peace on its behalf. At the same time, a group of princes headed by the Dukes of Brunswick protested vehemently that their rights too were being breached: decisions concerning the whole Reich could only be made by the Reich as a whole (i.e. the Imperial Estates collectively in the Reichstag).

The Electors were thus also both interested in peace for its own sake but also in the principle of who should make the peace. The convocation of a new body composed of

---

[13] Gotthard, *Säulen*, ii, 727–31. The Electors pursued their claim over several decades, and it became an issue at the peace negotiations in 1648 when, for the first time, they demanded the title of 'excellence' normally reserved for the envoys of sovereign states: Croxton and Tischer, *Peace*, 80.

[14] Gotthard, *Säulen*, i, 384–99.

themselves and the executive princes of the Kreise would have given them a leading role in the process. Indeed, it might have transformed the Reich into an oligarchy, with the Electors as the oligarchs. Faced with that prospect, the emperor and the other Imperial Estates now preferred to revert to traditional forms of political negotiation and management in the Reichstag. That, however, inevitably raised once more the question of the balance of power between the emperor and the Imperial Estates.

The emperor's insistence that the Reichstag should now be convened was based on his belief that only a peace agreed by all the Estates was likely to be durable. It was also based on the belief that the wider membership of the Kreise was still, or could again become, loyal to the crown or at least support the crown as the highest peace-making agency of the Reich.

This was not entirely wrong. After the Reichstag and other imperial institutions had become paralysed, the Kreise had remained virtually the only part of the infrastructure of the Reich that continued to operate throughout the war.[15] Some continued to carry out their economic functions, which was crucial during the period of monetary instability in the early 1620s. Some had coped with the growing confessional tensions by holding separate meetings of Catholic and Protestant members. Some had made determined, and occasionally successful, efforts to avoid being pressed into the service of the warring parties. The emperor had repeatedly turned to them for troops and money. The significance of the Kreise for the regional organization of the Reich was underlined by the fact that the Swedish occupation used the Kreis structure as the foundation for its new regime. The whole system of the Kreise was then given a new impetus by the Peace of Prague in 1635, not least by the decision to use them again to levy taxes and men.

This led to a new assertiveness in some of the Kreise. In the Lower Rhine Kreis, Wolfgang Wilhelm of Pfalz-Neuburg, ruler of Jülich since 1614, proposed to the Kreis assembly that the whole region should be declared neutral and that both imperial and Protestant troops should withdraw entirely. The plan came to nothing: too many parties had an interest in maintaining a presence in the strategically important territory of Jülich with its numerous Rhine crossings. In 1639, however, a similar initiative resulted in the Lower Saxon Kreis formally declaring its neutrality.[16]

The trend continued through the early 1640s. Both individuals and groups made separate peace agreements with the enemy most proximate to them or joined the general clamour among the Imperial Estates for a peace that would truly preserve their own rights and prerogatives. The Elector of Brandenburg's truce with Sweden in 1641 set a striking example and dealt a serious blow to the emperor's claim to represent the Reich as a whole.[17] Saxony followed suit in 1645. By 1648, the emperor's only serious German ally was Bavaria, whose Elector had also suffered a series of major defeats and who anyway perpetually vacillated between France and Austria.

The Regensburg Reichstag sat for over a year from September 1640.[18] The emperor was able to resist the demand that his army should come under the control of the Estates, but other points had to be conceded: a wide-ranging amnesty, though the Palatinate, Brunswick-Lüneburg, and Hessen-Kassel were still

---

[15] Magen, 'Reichskreise'.   [16] Parker, *Thirty Years War*, 149; Burkhardt, *Krieg*, 113.
[17] Dickmann, *Frieden*, 105–10.   [18] Dickmann, *Frieden*, 99–103.

excluded; and all ecclesiastical lands that had been in secular hands on 1 January 1627 were to remain untouched, which meant the abandonment of the Edict of Restitution and the Peace of Prague. The latter was agreed in the face of bitter opposition from the papacy, another significant departure from the principles on which the crown had operated until now.

However, implementation of this agreement was suspended until all Estates had made their peace with the emperor.[19] The Reichstag also committed the emperor to enter peace negotiations, but the demand that the princes be entitled to participate directly as well proved a step too far: they were merely to be permitted to send envoys to the negotiations. For Ferdinand still hoped that questions relating to internal matters might be kept separate from any peace negotiations with foreign powers. It proved impossible to reach agreement on every issue that was raised and, finally, all remaining issues were referred to a special conference or Deputationstag that was to convene at Frankfurt the following year.

The question of who should be entitled to participate in the negotiations was now acute. In December 1641, the emperor had instructed his representatives at Hamburg to agree with those of France and Sweden to enter into formal peace negotiations at last. His resistance to the involvement of anything other than delegations from the princes was undermined by subsequent events. Many Protestant princes continued to push for their inclusion. In particular, Landgravine Amalie Elisabeth of Hessen-Kassel, still an ally of France and Sweden, urged both foreign crowns to uphold the rights and liberties of the German princes. The French and the Swedes sent invitations to all, and soon a steady stream of princes or their representatives left Frankfurt for Münster and Osnabrück. Finally, after the defeat of his army at Jankau, Ferdinand gave in and conceded the right of all Imperial Estates to attend and participate. The Frankfurt gathering was hastily dissolved and the Reichstag itself was convened in two parallel sessions at the peace negotiations: Catholics at Münster and Protestants at Osnabrück.

In making that concession in 1645, the first great question of the peace was resolved: the emperor conceded the right of the princes to be involved in making any decisions concerning war and peace. At the start of the three-year-long peace negotiations, the balance between emperor and Imperial Estates as joint or collective holders of sovereignty over the Reich had already been restored. All of Ferdinand II's schemes for creating a German monarchy were brushed aside. Equally important, there was no more talk of an oligarchy of Electors either. As the princes had declared at Frankfurt in 1644: one should not imagine the Reich consists only of the emperor and the Electors; if that were the case, then in future they should fight (and pay for) their wars alone as well.[20] The balance between emperor and Reich that had been disrupted by the constitutional crisis of the early seventeenth century was beginning to reassert itself. As the peace negotiations were to show, however, this was not what the French and Swedish crowns necessarily had in mind when they said that they supported German liberty.

---

[19] Croxton and Tischer, *Peace*, 78–9.   [20] Burkhardt, *Krieg*, 11.

56

The Peace of Westphalia

The first communications between warring parties concerning peace took place as early as 1628–30.[1] From 1635, such contacts became increasingly intense. A papal proposal for a peace conference at Cologne in 1636 failed because the papacy would not deal with heretics, nor they with the pope's representatives. A conference at Lübeck, later moved to Hamburg, in 1638 also led nowhere. Gradually, however, the idea of concluding a general peace (*pax universalis*) that would settle the conflict between France and Spain, between Spain and the Netherlands, between the Holy Roman Emperor and France, and Sweden and their various allies in the Reich and elsewhere, gained ground, and a new attempt to agree on terms was mediated by Denmark at Hamburg in 1641.

The desire of all concerned to conclude a peace that was in their own best interests was reflected in intense wrangling over who should be admitted to the negotiations and on what terms.[2] Matters were complicated by the fact that France did not formally recognize Ferdinand III, for he had been elected King of the Romans before his father's death. Since he had therefore automatically succeeded his father as emperor he had not, according to the French, been properly elected as emperor. They insisted on referring to him as the King of Hungary and denied his right to participate in any treaty. Furthermore, France insisted that Spain should agree to the terms of the treaty before it was signed. As a result, the Hamburg treaty of December 1641 was concluded between imperial and Swedish representatives, while the imperial and French representatives merely exchanged notes of intent and the King of Denmark guaranteed that the King of Spain would agree.

The treaty did at least provide the framework for a peace conference. The need to conclude a number of agreements but also to take account of confessional sensitivities was overcome by specifying two neighbouring locations: Münster for negotiations between France and the Catholic powers, and Osnabrück for talks between Sweden and her allies, and the emperor. From the emperor's point of view, this arrangement gave hope that he might form a Catholic alliance that would counter excessive Swedish demands; at the same time, the imperial authorities hoped that the German issues might be kept away from the main negotiations. Both towns

---

[1] Repgen, 'Hauptprobleme', 401. The most comprehensive reference work in English, which also takes account of much of the German literature published following the 350th anniversary commemoration of the Peace of Westphalia in 1998, is Croxton and Tischer, *Peace*. Unless otherwise stated, the following account relies heavily on this excellent reference work.

[2] Dickmann, *Frieden*, 103–4.

were to become demilitarized zones under the control of multinational forces for the duration of the talks. The start was initially scheduled for 25 March 1642, but was in fact delayed until 11 July 1643. The so-called preliminary treaty did not include a general truce, which meant that the fighting continued until the final agreements were signed. As Prior Adam Adami, one of the hard-line Catholic envoys, put it: 'In winter, we negotiate, in summer, we fight.'[3]

Matters of procedure, especially the issue of participation, continued to play a central role through 1642–5.[4] The non-German powers began to send legations to the conference as soon as the opening date was announced. However, France and Sweden, as part of their pursuit of their own war aims, supported the claims advanced most vociferously by Hessen-Kassel and some Protestant princes that all Imperial Estates should be invited to participate. It was only on 29 August 1645, after the key military setbacks at Alerheim and Jankau, that the emperor finally sent out a general invitation which vastly expanded both the number of delegations and the range of issues to be decided. At one stage or another, some 194 diplomatic missions, some with up to 200 members, and 176 plenipotentiaries, representing 16 European countries, 140 Imperial Estates and 38 others, appeared at either Münster or Osnabrück. The cost of the conference alone has been estimated at 3.2 million thaler.[5]

Münster was the more prestigious of the two locations, since it was where the international negotiations took place and where France negotiated through the papal nuncio Fabio Chigi and the Venetian Ambassador Alvise Contarini. However, Osnabrück gained in significance once the Frankfurt Assembly of Estates (Deputationstag) was dissolved and the representatives of the Protestant princes joined those of Sweden in negotiating the key aspects of the peace that concerned the political and religious settlement in the Reich. Sweden dealt directly with the emperor, since it had eliminated its Danish mediator in the war of 1643–5. After the emperor had been obliged to invite all the German princes to participate, both conferences were accompanied by sessions of the Reichstag, divided into parallel meetings of Catholic and Protestant Estates at Münster and Osnabrück respectively, but regularly corresponding and conferring with each other.

What emerged? The talks failed to produce a peace between France and Spain: Spain calculated that the evident domestic weakness of the French crown (manifested in growing unrest from January 1648, and culminating in state bankruptcy in July and the beginning of the *Frondes* in August) made it logical to continue their war.[6] In January 1648, however, Spain and the Dutch Republic concluded a treaty ending their conflict which had polarized Europe for much of the past eighty years. By September 1646, France had reached an agreement over its claims for compensation; Sweden followed suit in February 1647. The main agreements concerning the Reich were concluded by April 1648. The following months were then

---

[3] Parker, *Thirty Years War*, 160.
[4] Dickmann, *Frieden*, 163–89.
[5] Bosbach, *Kosten*, 224.
[6] Repgen, 'Hauptprobleme', 407–8; Asch, *Thirty Years War*, 136–7.

occupied with the issue of the money to be paid to Sweden to withdraw its troops and with France's insistence that the emperor formally agree to desist from any assistance to Spain and that Lorraine be excluded from the peace. On 24 October 1648, the emperor signed treaties with France (*Instrumentum Pacis Monasteriense*) and Sweden (*Instrumentum Pacis Osnabrugense*). The clauses concerning Germany formulated for the latter were simply also included in the former. Both treaties were signed at Münster and together they make up the Peace of Westphalia.[7]

The sheer number of delegations and interests represented rendered negotiation on virtually all points protracted and exceptionally complicated. The envoys of foreign powers were often scathing about those who represented the German princes. The French envoy Count d'Avaux once remarked condescendingly that 'they are all learned doctors [of law]'. Even the imperial plenipotentiary Count Maximilian von Trauttmannsdorff, who was well used to the kind of representatives that German princes sent to the Reichstag and other similar gatherings, complained that the German princes had sent a 'crowd of tutors and schoolmasters, who create nothing but confusion'.[8] However, the lofty French aristocrat missed the point, while Trautt-mannsdorff was exasperated because the learned experts obliged him to give so much ground. The war had been caused by, and revolved around, German constitutional and legal issues. Those issues had been described and analysed by a vast body of largely Protestant experts in the years after 1600. By and large, those who were sent as representatives to Osnabrück and Münster were experts in that literature.

For the Protestants at Osnabrück, the time had come to translate those principles into law: to safeguard, in many cases to restore, the legal and dynastic rights of their masters in a general peace that resolved all the contentious issues of the last century. That meant tackling general constitutional principles as well as the terms of the religious peace in the Reich. In view of the numerous disputed changes in the status of property in the Reich before and during the war, it also meant dealing with a mass of individual cases. Since the crown had used much ecclesiastical and secular property taken during the 1620s to compensate its supporters, who had been promised reimbursement if it was ever returned to its original owners, the examination of individual cases involved not only scrutiny of the exact circumstances under which property had been transferred, but also compensation payable by the crown.[9]

Protestant attitudes to the main issues varied from loyalism to activism. The most uncompromising espoused the kind of views found in the tract *De ratione status in Imperio nostro Romano-Germanico* ('Of Reason of State in our Roman-German Empire') by Hippolithus à Lapide (in fact, Philipp Bogislav von Chemnitz).[10] Probably written around 1640 while the author was an officer in the Swedish army, and published sometime between 1640 and 1647, it was either a

[7] Online texts (originals plus translations) may be found at http://www.pax-westphalica.de (last accessed 14 April 2010). A good German version, cited in what follows, may be found in Buschmann, *Kaiser*, ii, 11–128.

[8] Dickmann, *Frieden*, 195.

[9] Croxton and Tischer, *Peace*, 78–9.

[10] Stolleis, *Öffentliches Recht*, i, 203–6; Gross, *Empire*, 235–54; Wandruszka, *Reichspatriotismus*, 81–3; Schmidt, *Vaterlandsliebe*, 404–10. See also p. 46.

belated reaction to the Peace of Prague or a rallying cry to the enemies of the Habsburgs during the peace negotiations. At all events, it was violently anti-Habsburg and argued a radical case for German liberty at the expense of imperial prerogative: applying Bodin's theory of sovereignty, Chemnitz denied the emperor was anything more than a figurehead and concluded that the Reich was a pure aristocracy. He proposed that the imperial title be transferred to another dynasty and that the prerogatives of the Habsburg emperors should revert to the Reichstag, which should meet with greater frequency. He was only slightly less scathing about the Electors, whom he held largely responsible for depriving the Imperial Estates generally of their rights and liberties.[11]

The most active group of Protestant princes comprised those, predominantly of the Reformed persuasion, who had been excluded from the Peace of Prague. Their most prominent advocate was the Landgravine Amalie Elisabeth of Hessen-Kassel, the last German ally of both France and Sweden, who was tireless in her efforts to mobilize French and Swedish support for the cause of German liberty. Others, particularly old-style Lutheran loyalists, may have generally sympathized with the rhetoric of German liberty, though they disapproved of the views of Chemnitz. Most Protestant writers condemned Chemnitz's work, not least because it denied the relevance of religion to the Reich and openly embraced the teachings of Machiavelli. Indeed, the book was banned in many parts and publicly burned by the hangman. However, the influence of the Elector of Saxony, the traditional leader of the German Protestants, was diminished after he concluded his truce with Sweden in 1645. The views of the activists were moderated only by the concessions that they gained and by suspicion of France.

The Catholic princes at Münster were also divided. Some had a strong interest in resisting the satisfaction of Protestant claims in north Germany. Three individuals, all fanatical supporters of the emperor and Spain, played a key role at first.[12] Cardinal Franz Wilhelm von Wartenberg, for example, was eager to regain Osnabrück, to which he had been elected in 1625, and the Prince-Bishoprics of Minden and Verden. He also represented the interests of his kinsman Ferdinand, Elector of Cologne. In addition to his own vote, he carried fifteen others by proxy. Adam Adami, prior of the Benedictine monastery of Murrhardt in Württemberg, was the envoy of the Prince-Abbot of Corvey, several Swabian abbeys and forty-one Swabian prelates. Johann Leuchselring represented the Catholic minority ruling elite of Augsburg and sixteen other Catholic Imperial Cities in Swabia. The bargaining power of this 'triumvirate' with its substantial block vote was, however, undermined by the progressive weakening of the emperor's military situation. As their influence waned, the majority was formed by those with a more moderate approach, often supporters of France such as the Elector of Trier and his clients. Ultimately, the Elector of Bavaria knew that he had more to gain from the preservation of German liberties than from the promotion of the interests of the Imperial Church.

---

[11] Gross, *Empire*, 247–8.   [12] Dickmann, *Frieden*, 199–201.

If there was one hero at Münster and Osnabrück, it was Count Maximilian von Trauttmannsdorff (1584–1650), who arrived in November 1645 and left in June 1647.[13] A member of the Reichshofrat since 1609 and of the imperial privy council since 1618 (its president since 1637), Trauttmannsdorff was Ferdinand III's most trusted adviser. He was never as independent an operator as Richelieu or Mazarin in France, or Olivares in Spain, but he was entrusted by Ferdinand III with a wide-ranging brief that he managed superbly. In particular, he fought to secure the interests of the Austrian Habsburgs as territorial rulers while maintaining their position as emperors. As far as possible, he ensured that the peace was made at the expense of others. They included not only the Reichskirche and those secular rulers who were deprived of property in the Reich, but also the emperor's Spanish relatives, who were furious at the decision to reach a settlement with France, in the last resort without Spain. Ferdinand III's secret instructions envisaged more concessions than Trauttmannsdorff in fact made. By the time he returned to Vienna in June 1647, handing over to Dr Isaak Volmar, he had overseen all of the major elements of the peace. It is a tribute to his skilful negotiation that the Reich emerged intact and under Habsburg leadership, and that a viable and durable peace was concluded.

The fundamental principle of the peace was 'perpetual forgetting and amnesty' ('perpetua oblivia et amnestia').[14] Everything that had occurred during the war should be forgotten and no one should be excluded from the general amnesty; all dynasties were to be restored to their lands and dignities; and no one was to be punished for their behaviour either before or during the war. Similarly, all lands and properties restored immediately might be reviewed by the imperial courts in due course and their restoration, if necessary, amended. In fact, over ten thousand amnesty cases were dealt with under the terms of the treaty, some specified in the text itself but thousands more implicit in its general provisions.[15]

The most important act of amnesty and restitution concerned the Palatinate, the rights of whose dispossessed and exiled rulers had become a *casus belli* in themselves. Though the terms were a disappointment to Karl Ludwig of the Palatinate, Friedrich V's son and heir, they were in fact a model of balance and compromise. Bavaria was allowed to keep the Palatine Electoral title in perpetuity, which confirmed Maximilian I as the premier secular Elector. He also retained the Upper Palatinate in return for formally writing off the debt owed him by the Habsburgs for his military assistance before 1623 and relinquishing any residual claim he had to income from Upper Austria; any documentation relating to such claims was to be handed over to the emperor so that it could be destroyed. A new eighth Electorate was created for Karl Ludwig and his heirs; as territory, he received the old Rhineland Palatinate, slightly reduced in size and encumbered with certain

[13] Croxton and Tischer, *Peace*, 297–9; *ADB*, xxxviii, 531–6; Dickmann, *Frieden*, 195, 243–6; Repgen, 'Ferdinand III.', 157–61; Höbelt, *Ferdinand III.*, 266–70.

[14] The most accessible text of the treaties of Münster (*Instrumentum Pacis Monasteriense* or *IPM*) and Osnabück (*Instrumentum Pacis Osnabrugense* or *IPO*) is in Buschmann, *Kaiser*, ii, 11–108. The amnesty principle appears in *IPO* Art. II.

[15] Press, *Kriege*, 261.

obligations concerning the religious rights of its inhabitants. Further clauses dealt with the restitution of Baden-Baden, Württemberg, and sixteen dynasties of counts who had forfeited their lands during the conflict. A succession of general clauses extended the amnesty to cover all fiefs lapsed or transactions conducted during the war, all Austrian subjects, and numerous other groups.

Restitution logically also implied the resolution of the legal problems that had given rise to dispossession in the first place, which meant a new religious settlement.[16] The Peace of Passau of 1552 and the Peace of Augsburg were renewed and designated as fundamental laws of the Reich, but they were not given a definitive interpretation. The *ius reformandi* of all German rulers was confirmed, and now formally extended to both Imperial Cities and Imperial Knights, but it really only remained valid in pure form in Austria, Bohemia, and those parts of Silesia under direct Habsburg control. The Habsburgs themselves were exempted from the general limitations that were now applied to other German rulers.

The official religion of territories was specified by applying a 'normal year' of 1 January 1624.[17] Thus Catholic ecclesiastical territories were henceforth safeguarded because an incumbent bishop or other office holder would immediately forfeit his benefice if he changed his religion. Where, however, a cathedral chapter was composed of both Protestants and Catholics on 1 January 1624, that balance was to be preserved in perpetuity. The only exceptions to this rule were the territories explicitly secularized by the peace in relation to the satisfaction of Swedish compensation claims. While the position of the Imperial Church in the south and west was thus secured, the diocesan rights of bishops over territories that were deemed, or now became officially, Protestant were suspended. Special regulations for the Imperial Cities of Augsburg, Dinkelsbühl, Biberach, and Ravensburg, where both Catholics and Protestants shared power before 1618, were designed to ensure that the political and religious rights of each confessional group were protected. The regulations set out for Augsburg even provided for the annual or biennial rotation of offices between Catholics and Protestants. The case of Donauwörth, whose problems had been a significant cause of the war, was left for a future Reichstag to determine.[18]

Everywhere, the same general principles were applied to the rights of individuals as members of confessional groups. All Protestant subjects of Catholic rulers and vice versa were guaranteed the rights (including the ownership of churches and monasteries and the right of presentation to benefices) that they had enjoyed on 1 January 1624. Adherents of the official religion enjoyed public rights of worship; others were to be allowed the right of private worship (*exercitium religionis privatum*) in chapels without either spires or bells. Catholics and Protestants, who

---

[16] Wolgast, 'Religionsfrieden', esp. 64–75, 86–91.

[17] *IPO* Art.V, § 2. For the Palatinate the 'normal year' was 1618 (*IPO* Art. IV, § 6) since otherwise the Protestant Electors would have returned to territory that had been re-Catholicized by 1624 (though Protestant communities later returned).

[18] The problem was that Bavaria had occupied the city in 1608 as compensation for the costs it had incurred in executing the court judgment against its Protestants. It only briefly regained its independence in 1705–14, before being confirmed in perpetuity as a Bavarian territorial town. See p. 421.

had not enjoyed rights of worship in a town or territory of any kind before 1 January 1624, were to be permitted the right of domestic worship (*exercitium religionis domesticum*): that meant prayers and education for their children in the family home and the right to attend churches and send their children to schools in a neighbouring territory. No one was to be discriminated against or excluded from commerce, trade, craft, or public burial on grounds of religion.

Those whose religion was tolerated before 1624 enjoyed the right to emigrate if they wished (*beneficium emigrandi*).[19] By contrast, rulers could require anyone whose religion had not been tolerated before 1624, or who had converted away from the official religion between 1624 and 1648, to emigrate, but had to allow them five years to do so; those who had changed their religion after 1648 were only allowed three years.[20] If a subject either decided or was obliged by his ruler to emigrate on account of his faith, he was to be permitted either to sell his property or to retain it and have it administered by others on his behalf.[21]

All of these rights applied only to Catholic and Protestant adherents of the Augsburg Confession. The Reformed Protestant or Calvinist Churches were defined as such adherents 'who call themselves reformed' and were therefore included within the Augsburg Confession. Within this group of Protestants (*protestantes*—the word only appeared in the treaty once), it was agreed that if a prince converted from one faith to the other, he would respect the rights of the prevailing official religion and content himself with appointing a court preacher of his own persuasion.[22] The same applied implicitly to any prince who converted from Protestantism to Catholicism. No other Christian sects were to be tolerated anywhere in the Reich.

To all intents and purposes, the principle of *cuius regio eius religio* had been abrogated. Some Protestants had argued that those forced to emigrate should be allowed up to fifteen years' grace and that rulers had no more right to impose religion on their subjects without consent than they had to impose taxes. For the Germans, they argued in one memorandum, are a 'free people'.[23] Yet despite its limitations, the new settlement removed the ambiguities that had undermined its predecessor. Furthermore, while all previous settlements had emphasized the temporary nature of the division between the Christian Churches, the peace now more or less assumed its permanence. At several points, the Treaty of Osnabrück emphasized the validity of specific stipulations until the 'religions are reunited by the grace of God', but it gave no brief to any human agency to bring that about.[24]

On the contrary, the religious division was now firmly anchored in the imperial constitution. The 1555 proscription of publications of any kind that denigrated or subverted the peace was renewed; rulers were enjoined to prevent their subjects, especially academic lawyers and theologians, from interpreting its terms in dubious

---

[19] *IPO* Art. V, § 30.
[20] *IPO* Art.V, § 36–7.
[21] He had, at all times, the right to return to his homeland without restriction in order to inspect or attend to business in respect of that property at any time.
[22] *IPO* Art. VII.
[23] Asch, 'Glaubensfreiheit', 113.
[24] *IPO* Art. V, §1, 14, 25, 31.

or contentious ways. Religious parity (*aequalitas exacta mutuaque*) was enshrined in imperial institutions.[25] All deputations were to contain an equal number of Catholics and Protestants.[26] At the Reichstag, matters concerning religion were to be debated by each confessional group independently (*itio in partes*), then settled in amicable negotiations (*amicabilis compositio*), or deferred if both parties failed to agree; there were to be no majority votes in such matters. The same parity should prevail among the judges and in the procedures at the Reichskammergericht and Reichshofrat; the Reichshofrat should be subject to visitations by the Elector of Mainz 'as often as is necessary' and he should bring contentious issues to the Reichstag; the Reichskammergericht was to resume its work as soon as possible.[27]

Since the issues at the core of the recent conflict had both resulted from and revolved around the question of the relationship between emperor and Estates, the peace included clauses intended to settle the argument about the nature of the polity once and for all. The impetus for this came partly from the French and Swedish desire to limit Habsburg power in the Reich. This ambition seemed to dovetail neatly with the aspirations of Protestant activists inspired by writers such as Chemnitz.

In the event, however, the Estates shied away from any radical adjustment of the status quo in the Reich. A Franco-Swedish proposal to ban imperial elections during the lifetime of an emperor (*vivente imperatore*) would have made it impossible for the Habsburgs to secure their succession. A proposal that only unanimous Reichstag decisions should become law and that all imperial decisions should be ratified by the Reichstag would have paralysed the entire system. The German princes rejected both. The French delegates concluded with regret that the Germans had an excessive love for their fatherland.[28] In reality, the German princes feared a strong France or Sweden more than they feared the normally relatively weak Habsburgs, whom they knew; they wanted a return to the balance of powers between 'emperor and Reich' that had been the basis of the German polity since the reign of Maximilian I.

For most princes, it sufficed to spell out the legal-constitutional implications of their admission to the negotiations in the first place. Their political and ecclesiastical rights over their territories were confirmed, which meant nothing more than the confirmation of the *ius territoriale* and the *ius territorii et superioritas* that had become established during the sixteenth century.[29] The princes thereby gained nothing more than was also granted to the Imperial Cities, and Imperial Knights and their rights now formally recognized in imperial law, still fell short of full sovereignty. Indeed, the Imperial Estates were not actually personal signatories to the peace treaties: a relatively small number signed on behalf of all. It was also confirmed that each Imperial Estate was entitled to a vote in the passing or interpretation of legislation, in matters of war and peace, the recruitment and quartering of troops, and the construction of fortresses in the Reich.

All of these things were in future to be decided by all the Estates at the Reichstag in free votes. At the same time, the right of the Imperial Estates to enter into

---

[25] *IPO* Art. V, §1.   [26] *IPO* Art. V, §51–2.   [27] *IPO* Art. V, §53–62.
[28] Asch, *Thirty Years War*, 138–9; Repgen, 'Hauptprobleme', 411.
[29] *IPO* Art. VIII, §1. See also *IPO* Art. IV, §17 and Art. VIII, §4.

alliances among themselves or with foreign powers was confirmed, subject to a provision prohibiting alliances directed against the emperor or the Reich.[30] This, too, was simply old custom, which Ferdinand II had sought to outlaw in the Peace of Prague, and which was now being restored. The Reichstag itself was to meet within six months of the ratification of the treaty to consider a wide range of reforms, including procedures for the election of imperial successors-designate, a perpetual imperial capitulation, the procedure for outlawing Imperial Estates, the reform of the Kreise, and imperial taxation. No attempt was made to define, let alone limit, the emperor's prerogative powers.

Where the peace made significant changes was in the compensation agreed with Sweden and France. Concessions to Sweden in particular had important implications for the Reichskirche and some north German princes, while the concessions to France created a new balance of power in the south-west. Despite the intentions of the French and Swedish negotiators, however, their gains did not seriously change the Reich.

Negotiations with Sweden were reasonably straightforward.[31] Sweden achieved her aim of establishing a permanent foothold on the southern Baltic coast. She gained Western Pomerania, including Stettin, Stralsund, and Rügen, and the Western Pomeranian entitlement to a portion of the benefices of the former Bishopric of Cammin in Eastern Pomerania, now defined as a secularized Protestant bishopric without a bishop. Furthermore, Sweden was also given the Mecklenburg port of Wismar, together with two adjoining districts and the former Archbishopric of Bremen and Hamburg, as well as the Bishopric of Verden as a secular duchy.

All of these territories were given as fiefs of the Reich. The Swedish monarch thus became a prince of the Reich, though in respect of the lands granted to Sweden the treaty also granted exemption from the jurisdiction of the two highest imperial courts (*privilegium de non appellando*—this meant that inhabitants could not appeal beyond the highest territorial court). Sweden was also granted the right to found a new university. The rights and privileges of the town of Stralsund were guaranteed specifically, as well as a more general guarantee for the Estates and subjects of the other territories as well. The question of compensation in respect of Sweden's military costs proved more difficult to resolve: twenty million thaler were initially demanded; five million thaler were finally agreed, in return for which Sweden agreed to withdraw her 60,000 or so troops (two-thirds of whom were foreign mercenaries in urgent need of pay and arrears of pay).[32]

The concessions made to Sweden necessitated compensation for a variety of principalities. In return for the loss of its rights to Western Pomerania and Rügen, Brandenburg received the bishoprics of Halberstadt and Minden and the right to inherit the archbishopric of Magdeburg after the death of the current administrator (this occurred in 1680). The relatively generous treatment of Brandenburg was partly the result of French interest in creating a counterbalance to Sweden in north Germany. Mecklenburg was compensated for the loss of Schwerin by the grant of the secularized bishoprics of Schwerin and Ratzeburg. Even Brunswick-Lüneburg was

[30] Ash, *Thirty Years War*, 141–2.   [31] *IPO* Art. X, § 1–16.
[32] *IPO* Art. XVI, §8. Dickmann, *Frieden*, 422–4.

compensated for the loss of its aspirations to various ecclesiastical benefices following the secularization of Magdeburg, Bremen-Hamburg, Halberstadt, and Ratzeburg, by being granted the right to present a bishop to Osnabrück on the death of the current Catholic incumbent, Franz Wilhelm von Wartenburg. The first Protestant prince-bishop was, in turn, to be succeeded by a Catholic and the alternation was to be maintained in perpetuity thereafter, without prejudice to the Catholic status of the bishopric or the rights over it of the Archbishop of Cologne as metropolitan.

A key feature of all the deliberations concerning Sweden was the resort to using ecclesiastical property as compensation. The emperor replaced the pope as the authority over the two Protestant Prince-Bishops of Lübeck (in the hands of Schleswig-Holstein-Gottorp since 1586) and Osnabrück; the diocesan rights of Catholic bishops in Protestant territories were suspended in perpetuity.[33] There was no real alternative, since, with the exception of the Dukes of Pomerania, all of the north German dynasties had survived the war and all needed to be accommodated alongside Sweden. Although the emperor was only giving up ecclesiastical lands that had, in reality, long since been lost, this set an important precedent for the future, for it enshrined the principle of secularization in the constitutional practice of the Reich.

The specific agreement between France and the Empire represented a compromise on both sides.[34] France aimed to undermine Habsburg hegemony in Europe, first, by dividing the Spanish and Austrian dynasties and, second, by reinforcing the autonomy of the German princes. Both Richelieu and Mazarin envisaged creating Italian and German alliances under French protection that would make it impossible for any emperor to mobilize the Reich. Under Mazarin from 1642, French policy also insisted on territorial compensation in Alsace and on gaining control of key fortresses on the Rhine.

The question of Lorraine was closely related to that of Alsace and the Rhine fortresses.[35] Lorraine had ceased to be an imperial fief in 1542, but it had remained under the protection of the Reich, though the associated Duchy of Bar, north-west of Lorraine, was a fief of the French crown. While Duke Henry II (d. 1624) had remained neutral, Duke Charles IV sided with Ferdinand II and Philip IV and, consequently, France occupied his lands in 1634 and later denied Lorraine's right to be admitted to the peace negotiations. It proved impossible to reach a formal agreement on the status of Lorraine, so the French occupation continued and Lorraine's rulers lived largely in exile at the imperial court until 1697. Meanwhile, the occupied duchy, wedged between French territory in the north-west and Alsace in the south, played a key role in rounding off the lands of the French crown.

The treaty proclaimed the desire to reinforce peace and friendship between the emperor and the King of France, and to promote general security. Since France had always claimed to be acting selflessly to uphold the liberty of the German princes, the gains that France finally achieved were technically a purchase. The king agreed to pay Archduke Ferdinand Karl of Tyrol, the ruler of further Austria, the sum of three million livres over three years and assume two-thirds of the debt of the

---

[33] Wolgast, *Hochstift*, 340–5.   [34] *IPM* Preamble and § 3–4, 69–91.
[35] Croxton and Tischer, *Peace*, 175–7; Dickmann, *Frieden*, 224–6, 478–82,

Habsburg government at Ensisheim. In return, Austria gave up the Landgravate of Upper and Lower Alsace and all its associated rights, together with the town and fortress of Breisach. Austria also relinquished the Bailiwick of Hagenau with all of its jurisdictional rights over the Decapolis, the league of ten Imperial Cities in Alsace. Furthermore, France was given the right to maintain fortresses on the right bank of the Rhine at Breisach and Philippsburg (in the territory of the Elector of Trier), with unrestricted rights of access to them by water or land; no further fortresses were to be constructed on the right bank between Basle and Philippsburg, nor was the course of the Rhine to be altered.

The bishoprics of Metz, Toul, and Verdun, under French control since 1552, were formally recognized as French possessions, though there was considerable ambiguity about whether that simply meant the territory of the prince-bishoprics or whether it meant the much wider area covered by the dioceses as such. The Alsatian Imperial Cities and other fiefs not directly controlled by the Habsburgs were to remain part of the Reich, but here again the position was unclear. Part of the problem was that the 'Landgravate of Alsace' that Austria ceded to France did not in fact exist, but was simply a legal fiction devised to appear attractive to France and to divert Mazarin from the idea that the King of France might become a prince of the Reich. In Italy, where the Peace of Cherasco was confirmed, France also gained the Piedmontese frontier fortress of Pinerolo.

On the one hand, Mazarin failed either to create a German league under French protection or to insinuate the King of France into the ranks of the German princes. On the other hand, the territorial terms agreed between France and the emperor contained considerable leeway for French intervention in the Reich in the future.

Probably the most important provision in the first instance was the prohibition of any Austrian assistance to Spain: the Burgundian Kreis was confirmed as part of the Reich, but both the emperor and the Imperial Estates, jointly and severally, were prohibited from engaging in any eventual conflicts in either the Spanish Netherlands or the Franche Comté.[36] Ferdinand III fiercely resisted this stipulation to the last and only gave in following an ultimatum by the Elector of Bavaria. An interesting implication of this clause was that the Dutch Republic, as part of the Burgundian Kreis, technically remained part of the Holy Roman Empire, though its independence was implicitly recognized by its inclusion in the list of allies of both the emperor and Sweden who acceded to the treaty.[37]

By contrast, the settlement of the territorial demands of the third 'victor', the Landgravine of Hessen-Kassel, was more modest.[38] The success that Landgravine Amalie Elisabeth had enjoyed in pursuing the cause of German liberty deserted her when it came to her territorial demands. She received the former Imperial Abbey of Hersfeld, but claims to lands from Mainz, Cologne, Paderborn, Münster, and the

---

[36] *IPM* § 3: Buschmann, *Kaiser*, ii, 109.
[37] *IPO* Art. XVII, § 10–11: Buschmann, *Kaiser*, ii, 104; Repgen, 'Hauptprobleme', 407. The emperors continued to invest the kings of Spain with feudal authority over the whole of the Low Countries into the eighteenth century: Croxton and Tischer, *Peace*, 309.
[38] Repgen, 'Hauptprobleme', 426–7. *IPO* Art. XV § 1–15: Buschmann, *Kaiser*, ii, 88–93.

Imperial Abbey of Fulda were translated into a financial settlement of 600,000 thaler, granted in return for the withdrawal of her troops. In addition, Hessen-Darmstadt agreed to hand back the Marburg inheritance that it had gained by virtue of a Reichshofrat judgement in 1623.

In the final resort, the desire of the German Estates for a restoration of the Reich prevailed. The essentially conservative approach of the Estates even manifested itself in their reluctance to assent to the formal release of the Swiss from the Reich. Only after considerable debate did they agree to a clause stating that the cantons were 'in actual possession, as it were, of full liberty and exemption from the Reich', which was a rather coy way of confirming that the Swiss had had nothing to do with the Reich since 1499.[39]

In general, once measures were agreed to remedy the past abuses of imperial power, there was no will to embark on any innovative reforms. To some extent, this was also reflected in the ready agreement of all concerned to revert to the system of tolls and customs dues that had prevailed in 1618.[40] Interestingly, both Sweden and France insisted on this, and the relevant clause of the peace was formulated without consulting the Estates. With a few minor exceptions, all the tolls, dues, and taxes that had been levied by various monarchs and princes during the war were abolished. The frontier on the Upper Rhine was completely opened to commerce. In the north, Sweden was permitted certain rights to help with military expenditure (which remained high in relation to the fiscal base in Sweden itself), but was enjoined to ensure that its tolls did not undermine commerce in Pomerania and Mecklenburg. For the rest, the old system, whereby tolls were approved by the emperor and the Electors, was confirmed.

The provisions relating to enforcement also represented a compromise between French and Swedish aims, on the one hand, and the interests of emperor and Imperial Estates, on the other. Initially, the foreign powers had intended that all participants in the conference—both the major powers and all the German Estates individually—should be obliged to uphold all clauses of the peace, by force of arms if necessary.[41] The imperial envoys saw clearly, however, that this would have undermined the imperial courts and thus deprived the emperor of his key role as the highest judicial authority. That, indeed, was the intention, as the French and Swedish envoys implicitly acknowledged when they immediately rejected a counter-proposal that the Swedish Riksdag and the French Parlements and États généraux be similarly empowered.

In the event, the emperor and the Imperial Estates were effectively defined as a single joint signatory representing the Reich (which conformed to the public law

[39] *IPO* Art. VI. See Croxton and Tischer, *Peace*, 288–9. Like the Dutch Republic, the Swiss did not formally gain sovereignty in 1648, and Swiss jurists continued to think about the cantons as parts of the Reich, albeit exempt from all obligations, until the mid-eighteenth century. From a modern perspective, however, it is probably accurate to regard 1648 as the origin de facto of Swiss sovereignty.

[40] Repgen, 'Regelungen'. Similarly, the treaty specified that in future those who marched troops through the Reich should be liable for the costs that they incurred; no levies were to be imposed on the civilian population: *IPO* Art. XVII, § 9.

[41] Asch, *Thirty Years War*, 140.

understanding of the sovereign entity of the German polity as 'Kaiser und Reich'). Each of the major signatories was made a guarantor of the treaty. Both France and Sweden thus acquired a qualified right to intervene in the Reich if the peace was contravened. However, that right was limited in practice by the provision that all disputes should be brought to the imperial courts in the first instance, and that the function of the guarantors was only to be activated if a dispute had not been solved peacefully within three years.[42]

It was clearly envisaged that all disputes would normally be settled by peaceful negotiation or by the imperial courts. The treaty was to be regarded as a permanent constitutional law of the Reich (*perpetua lex et pragmatica imperii sanctio*), along with the other fundamental laws (*leges et constitutiones fundamentales imperii*) from the Golden Bull onwards. The perpetual peace that it would inaugurate would be reinforced by strengthening the peacekeeping powers of the imperial Kreise (another revival or renewal rather than an innovation). No Imperial Estate was permitted to pursue its rights by means of force.[43] As a final guarantee of the peace, and probably more immediately significant than the role accorded to France and Sweden, a clause was inserted pre-empting any eventual protest against the treaty.[44] This was clearly directed against papal objections to the secularization of ecclesiastical property and the rescission of diocesan rights.[45]

The process of withdrawing troops and the restitution of property took several years; the last Swedish occupation forces left in 1653. Remarkably, the transition was accomplished peacefully. The Reichshofrat received 973 complaints before July 1654, but almost all were quickly resolved.[46] The transitional arrangements specified in the treaty, including the appointment of commissions to adjudicate disputes and a provision for the deferral of payment of debts incurred during the war, were by and large effective. The withdrawal of Swedish troops and the payments due to Sweden posed problems with which an implementation conference at Nuremberg grappled from May 1649 to November 1650.[47] Even when it had concluded its work, many issues remained unresolved. This was true also of the numerous questions that had been deferred to the next Reichstag. There was, however, good reason for the long run of celebrations of the peace that began with festivities at Münster on 15 and 17 May 1648 and concluded with one at Schweinfurt on the second Sunday after Trinity 1660. Between May and December 1648 alone, there were 178 commemorations in various parts of the Reich.[48]

---

[42] *IPO* Art. XVII, § 6. Aretin, *Altes Reich*, i, 26–9.

[43] *IPO* Art. XVII, § 7.

[44] *IPO* Art. XVII, § 3: Croxton and Tischer, *Peace*, 241–3.

[45] The papal mediator Fabio Chigi was technically correct in his objection to the creation of the eighth Electoral vote, since the Golden Bull specified that no change to the Electoral college was permitted without papal consent: Croxton and Tischer, *Peace*, 220.

[46] Luh, *Reich*, 15–18.

[47] Croxton and Tischer, *Peace*, 208–9.

[48] Gantet, *Paix*, 192, 213; Repgen. 'Friede', 632–7; Hansen, 'Patriotismus', 149–69.

57

The Impact of the War on German Society

In 1636, William Crowne, who accompanied the English envoy to the Electoral meeting at Regensburg, gave a graphic account of the impact of the war. Between Mainz and Frankfurt there was nothing but desolation.[1] The people of Mainz were so weak that they could not even crawl to receive the alms that were offered them. At Nuremberg, the ambassador, Thomas Howard, the Earl of Arundel, was able to purchase the legendary Pirckheimer library, including manuscripts illustrated by Dürer, for 350 thaler because its owner was desperate for money and food. Crowne was not the only traveller shocked by the utter devastation of the country and the degradation of its people, by scenes of brutality, and rumours of wanton murder and cannibalism.

Such accounts formed the folk memory of the war and they have shaped the narrative given of it by generations of historians. However, recent research has often questioned the relentlessly bleak picture painted in the past and queried the conclusions that have frequently been drawn about the implications of the war for the development of German society and culture. There have been three main areas of debate: first, the question of the intensity and extent of the actual impact of the war; second, the implications of that for the development of German society and the German economy; third, the question of the psychological and cultural impact of the war.

A major problem in approaching these questions lies in the nature of the sources. Many, like the accounts of Crowne and others, are undoubtedly honest descriptions of specific incidents or experiences. However, they are often amplified by literary or propagandistic sources that are perhaps less reliable. Johann Jakob Christoffel von Grimmelshausen, for example, was born in the Imperial City of Gelnhausen in 1621 or 1622 and thus experienced the conflict at first hand, but his presentation of it in his famous novels *Der abenteuerliche Simplicissimus Teutsch* ('The Adventurous Simplicissimus, a German', 1669) and *Trutz Simplex: Oder Ausführliche und wunderseltzame Lebensbeschreibung der Ertzbetrügerin und Land-störzerin Courasche* ('Spite Simplex, or Detailed and Miraculous Account of the Life of the Arch-Swindler and Runagate Courage', 1670), however realistic in parts, remains fiction nonetheless.[2] Tales of wanton violence, unimaginable cruelty, instances of mass infanticide and rape, of cannibalism and the violation of corpses, undoubtedly draw on real experience sometimes, yet they were also often the

---

[1] Parker, *Thirty Years War*, 146–7.　　[2] Kühlmann, 'Simplicissimus'.

product of unfounded rumours, if not literary topoi, that served to underline real suffering and distress by sensationalizing and demonizing.

Hard statistical evidence is more difficult to come by. Even overall population statistics are extremely vague.[3] German demographic historians have traditionally worked on estimates based on the assumed population within the frontiers of Germany in 1871 or 1914. More recent estimates of the population of the Reich are based on less anachronistic criteria, but they are guesswork nonetheless. According to one estimate made on the basis of calculations relating to the area defined by the frontiers of Germany in 1871, a population of some 15–17 million around 1600 declined to 10–13 million by 1650.[4] Those who work on the basis of estimates of the population of the early modern Reich suggest that the population declined from 20 million to some 16–17 million during the war.[5] If these figures are accurate, then the loss of population during the Thirty Years War was proportionally greater than in World War II.[6]

Günther Franz suggested that the total population decline was about 33 per cent, with 40 per cent in the countryside and 30 per cent in urban communities; others have suggested that the overall decline was closer to 15 per cent. The losses certainly varied between regions. The worst hit areas were Pomerania, Mecklenburg in the north-east, and Thuringia and Hessen in Middle Germany and the south-west. In the Habsburg territories, the lands of the Bohemian crown (Bohemia, Moravia, Silesia, Upper and Lower Lusatia) suffered losses of between 10 per cent and 30 per cent, while the population of the Austrian duchies remained more or less constant apart from 'normal' epidemics and the expulsions that followed the implementation of religious edicts.

Elsewhere in the Reich, Württemberg suffered particularly acutely. It is estimated that the population declined by 57 per cent between 1634 and 1655, with some districts losing as much as 77 per cent, others 31 per cent. The pre-war level was only recovered by 1750. Much of north-west Germany, by contrast, was scarcely affected by the war. Even where losses appeared to be high, a loss of population was the result of migration, often temporary, rather than death. In 1637, for example, when famine and illness afflicted the Saxon countryside, the population of Leipzig temporarily increased by a third.[7]

The case of Württemberg illuminates important aspects of the impact of the war on the civilian population. Most civilians were killed not by the fighting, but by the effects on their lives of marauding or occupying armies. Imperial troops invaded and occupied Württemberg after their defeat of the Swedes at Nördlingen. They unleashed a campaign of plunder and destruction similar to that which the French and the Swedes later visited upon areas of Bavaria. Financial ruin, starvation, and

---

[3] Pfister, *Bevölkerungsgeschichte*, 12–15, 76–9.

[4] Schmidt, *Krieg*, 91–2. The most detailed survey of population loss by region is still Franz, *Krieg*, 5–51. Franz's results are confirmed for Württemberg by Hippel, 'Bevölkerung'. See also Theibault, 'Demography' and Vasold, 'Bevölkerungsverluste'.

[5] Schormann, 'Krieg', 269.

[6] Parker, *Thirty Years War*, 192–3.

[7] Parker, *Thirty Years War*, 189.

disease were the inevitable result. In general, the years after 1634–5, in which armies jockeyed for positions that would enhance the bargaining powers of their masters in peace negotiations, probably saw more civilian deaths than the 1620s.

Indeed, in the first phase of the war, there is evidence that military commanders often sought to mitigate the impact of their activities on the civilian populations. As Wallenstein and other commanders realized, they depended on their ability to raise money by taxing the local communities: brutalized and traumatized civilians were unlikely to be able to contribute much, particularly if their property had been destroyed.[8] However, the relentless pressure imposed upon civilians by extortionate contributions was itself enough to ruin many areas. The fact that these burdens were often imposed by military forces with alien ethnic and confessional identities was frequently an aggravating feature.

In many parts, the war years saw an intensification of a pre-war pattern. Epidemics and shortages following bad winters and poor harvests were key causes of the Austrian peasants' war in 1625, though the situation was inevitably exacerbated by the taxation imposed by the Bavarian occupation and by the implementation of Ferdinand II's re-Catholicization measures.[9] In Bavaria itself, in 1633–4, peasant unrest was partly a response to the impositions of both Bavarian and Swedish troops. The Elector's response was uncompromising: once the extent of the unrest became clear and the peasants had organized themselves into armed bands, his forces moved in to crush them. His courts then imposed the usual draconian penalties on the ringleaders; however, he hesitated to quarter troops in the worst affected areas thereafter.[10]

Unrest in Alsace and the Breisgau around the same time had similar causes. The witch hunts that took place in the late 1620s and early 1630s in Cologne, Mainz, Bamberg, Eichstätt, Ellwangen, and Würzburg also replicated pre-war patterns. These events were intensified by the war in that they were all the more obviously associated with the re-Catholicization policies pursued by many rulers, especially ecclesiastical princes, in the wake of the Edict of Restitution. In some areas, the witch hunts were only halted by the arrival of the Swedes; in others, for example Cologne, correspondence between the Elector and the imperial court led to their cessation.[11]

For all the disruption and devastation undoubtedly caused, either directly or indirectly, by the conflict in many areas, it seems that recovery came remarkably quickly. In Württemberg and much of Bavaria, for example, rural production soon resumed. Indeed, if many of the pressures in German society before the war had resulted from over-population, that problem at least had now been solved. The post-war years brought new opportunities. Some commercial centres, such as Hamburg, to a lesser extent Bremen, but also Strassburg in the south-west, in

---

[8] Schormann, *Krieg*, 114–16.
[9] See pp. 579–83 above.
[10] Langer, 'Krieg', 312–13; Press, 'Soziale Folgen', 253–4.
[11] Schormann, *Hexenprozesse*, 54–6, 63–71.

fact expanded during the war years and profited from it at every level. Deserted farms soon found new owners. In towns, crafts and trades resumed again with new labour, and some crafts had in fact flourished throughout the conflict.

Major cities such as Augsburg, but also smaller centres such as Nördlingen, present a differentiated picture. The richest were most affected by contributions, military levies, and general looting and plundering. They were the ones that also suffered most as a result of the non-payment of interest on pre-war loans, or of the debasement of the currency during the *Kipper- und Wipperzeit* of the early 1620s. The poor were most affected by hunger and disease. Middling groups were often able to survive the ups and downs of the war, if only just.[12] The same pattern is broadly applicable to many rural areas as well. Many nobles, especially Imperial Counts and Imperial Knights, who had speculated on rising prices in the pre-war decades, were all but ruined by the disruption of income flows during the war and the longer-term downturn that the conflict precipitated.[13] Some families were saddled with a perpetual burden of debt until the nineteenth century.

East of the Elbe, however, the effect of the war on the same kind of problem was to strengthen the system of estate production, which further reinforced the grip of the nobility on peasants who were turned into unfree serfs. For nobles everywhere, both those subject directly to the emperor and those subject to the princes, economic pressures, intensified by the war, led to a renewed interest in service at court during the seventeenth century.

The role of the war in the overall economic development of the Reich is uncertain. Much of the pattern of seventeenth-century economic activity was already established in the sixteenth century. The war accentuated some developments such as the long-term relative decline of the Upper German Imperial Cities. However, the shift of emphasis of the European economy from the Mediterranean world to the North Sea–Atlantic world began long before the war and unfolded independently of it.

More certain is the fact that the war, and the conflicts that followed in the decades after 1648, posed new challenges both to the territorial administration and, by implication, to the regional structures of the imperial Kreise. Just as administrations sought to respond to perceived disorder in the late sixteenth century, they now sought to respond to the all too obvious consequences of the prolonged conflict. Reconstruction was often accompanied by a determination to formulate lasting solutions, in a new version of the search for order and stability that had characterized the response of German rulers to successive crises since the 1520s. In the case of the larger territories, this included the creation of standing armies which finally replaced the mercenary forces that had dominated warfare during the previous two centuries. Wallenstein and Bernhard of Weimar were not only the most successful military entrepreneurs: they were the last of their kind.

The war thus intensified or accelerated some long-term trends. Numerous cities, towns, villages, and regions suffered periodic catastrophic crises of disease, or

---

[12] Asch, *Thirty Years War*, 181–2.   [13] Press, 'Soziale Folgen', 246–7.

military occupation involving damage or even outright destruction. Yet in the end it is the sheer resilience of society and economy that impresses most. The war was a major crisis, yet communities often recovered remarkably rapidly from its worst effects. Another thing that makes assessment of the long-term effects of the Thirty Years War difficult is that within twenty years the Reich was plunged into another series of ruinous wars. It is true that the fighting in these later conflicts took place on the peripheries of the Reich, but the financial cost was, if anything, far greater.

Although measuring economic and social indicators and assessing their significance is an inexact science, it is almost impossible to assess the degree of social or cultural trauma caused by the conflict. Did the experience of war promote certain kinds of religiosity, favour the development of either sceptical or mystical philosophy, or foster the development of certain kinds of music? Claims that were often traditionally made about the role of the Thirty Years War as an intensifier of, even a cause of, German inwardness and spirituality often tell us more about the persistent myths developed by nineteenth-century nationalist historians than about seventeenth-century realities.[14] The Thirty Years War played a key role in the later construction of the birth-myth of an allegedly delayed or non-political nation.[15] In the process, however, the ambitions and neuroses of nineteenth- and early twentieth-century generations were superimposed upon it. Their pathos-laden accounts of a deprived and inadequate German past distorted a reality that was both more mundane and more momentous in its significance for the history of the Reich after 1648.

The popular and literary culture of the age certainly seems to reflect an urgent desire for peace and stability. The theme of the suffering of the German people and the oppression of the German fatherland runs through the writing of most major authors of the time. It seems unsurprising that Germany developed a dramatic tradition in this period that was preoccupied with the lives of tyrants and martyrs, with suffering and judgement, in which no drama was complete without a rehearsal of a gruesome catalogue of atrocities and horror stories. As Georg Philipp Harsdörffer defined it in his treatise of 1647–53 on German poetry, the stuff of tragedy was the 'despair of kings, princes, and lords, murders, persecution, perjury, deception, incest, battles, death, epitaphs, lamentations, and the like'.[16] At the same time, Harsdörffer, like Opitz and others, insisted that all should be true to life: the correlation between art and experience provided a rich subject matter.

It seems equally logical that such preoccupations fed into the longing for peace at the end of the war. After decades of turmoil, many communities were all too ready to celebrate the return to normality, even if in many areas the celebration preceded the fact by some considerable while.[17]

---

[14] See also Neveux, *Vie spirituelle*, ix–xlvii and *passim*.
[15] Faulenbach, *Ideologie*, 38–42; Schönemann, *Rezeption*; Mannack, 'Rezeption'; Mannack, 'Streit'; Cramer, 'War'; Cramer, *Thirty Years' War*; Smith, *Continuities*, 74–108.
[16] Brenner, 'Drama', 541.
[17] Repgen, 'Friede', 632–5; Gantet, *Paix*, 127–67.

58

The Thirty Years War and the German Polity

Assessment of the significance of the Thirty Years War for the German polity has been as controversial as the assessment of its significance for society and economy. On the one hand, the Peace of Westphalia has often been viewed positively as the origin of the balance of power in Europe: the 'Westphalian system' that allegedly brought lasting stability to the relationship between the sovereign powers of Europe. On the other hand, German historians frequently denounced the peace as a disaster for the German nation, a peace that finally undermined what was left of the Reich and delivered the Germans into the hands of foreign powers and tyrannical German princes. Germany, so it was often argued, was only rescued from this dire state by Brandenburg-Prussia's valiant assumption of responsibility for the nation's destiny. Both judgements should be overturned.

It was not the intention of those who framed the Peace of Westphalia to create a balance of power between sovereign states in Europe.[1] The idea that such a thing might be possible may have been one of the very long-term consequences of the peace. However, no one at the peace negotiations gave much thought to the emergence of a system of sovereign states that recognized no superior authority, or to a system guaranteed by three major powers in which all sovereign states enjoyed parity regardless of size. The aim at the time was to address the key problems of the recent past. From the French point of view, the main objectives were to break the power of the Spanish–Austrian Habsburg axis and to prevent the establishment of a Habsburg monarchy in the Reich.

Later commentators, such as Leibniz, Rousseau, Kant, and Schiller, eulogized the Peace of Westphalia as the first step towards a universal peace, yet their projections for the future should not be mistaken for descriptions of reality. In 1648, the French–Spanish conflict, regarded by both parties in some ways as the real struggle, remained unresolved; in the Baltic, major hostilities also continued until around 1660. It was not long, moreover, before Europe was plunged into multiple conflicts again. If there really ever was a Westphalian system, it was dead by about 1670, the victim of both French and Swedish abuse of their role as guarantors of the peace. It was another three decades before a true balance of power emerged.

---

[1] Duchhardt 'Westphalian System'; Parker, *Thirty Years War*, 192–6; Repgen, 'Friede', 639–40; Wolfrum, *Krieg*, 33–46.

Some fundamental issues were, of course, resolved in 1648. The conclusion of peace between Spain and the Dutch Republic removed a key issue from European politics. The struggle of the Dutch rebels against the Spaniards had polarized sympathizers and opponents in virtually every European country for the best part of eighty years.[2] The fact that people no longer viewed their own position refracted through the ideological–confessional polarity of the struggle in the Low Countries, contributed significantly to the diminution of the confessional element in European politics. This was perhaps also promoted by another unintended result of the events of 1648. The protest of the papacy against the Peace of Westphalia, widely circulated in May 1649, was perhaps logical from the point of view of the Curia, yet it underlined the growing irrelevance of the papacy in European politics.[3] The pope and the Church that he represented were no longer powers to be reckoned with. Indeed, this was precisely why the negotiators at Münster and Osnabrück pre-empted the papal challenge by inserting an 'anti-protest' clause into the treaty.[4] The peace was a secular peace, and had a secularizing effect, because it explicitly denied the right of ecclesiastical powers, Church councils, or the papacy to challenge it.

Speculation about the significance of the Peace of Westphalia for the development of the international system ignores the fact that it was fundamentally a German peace. Apart from general expressions of peaceful intent, the treaties say nothing about Europe as a whole, but a great deal about Germany in particular. Opinions about the significance of the peace in German history were traditionally negative. Fritz Dickmann, author of what remains the standard work on the peace, concluded in 1959 that it was a 'national disaster for the German people and for the Holy Roman Empire. . . . the beginning of the deadly sickness to which it finally succumbed'. 'The year 1648', he had no doubt, 'is one of the great catastrophic years (*Katastrophenjahre*) of our history.'[5] The Reich ceased to be a state, he argued, and all of its governmental functions were taken over by the territories that were confirmed in their sovereignty. In making this judgement, Dickmann followed the majority of German historians of the previous century-and-a-half, who argued that the peace subjected the Germans to the tyranny of French manipulation and control, and that, by establishing the sovereignty of the German princes, it set the cause of German unity back by over two centuries. The German national historiographical tradition focused on the loss of Alsace, of Switzerland, and the Netherlands, and on what was seen as the collapse of the Reich as a unified and functioning entity.

Such negative views are in striking contrast to the positive evaluation of the peace in the one-and-a-half centuries that immediately followed it. Writers up to the end of the eighteenth century had no doubt that the Peace of Westphalia was the true constitution of the Reich and that it provided the foundation and framework for its

---

[2] Parker, *Thirty Years War*, 196.
[3] Dickmann, *Frieden*, 494–6; Heckel, 'Konfessionalisierung', 672–84.
[4] *IPO* Art. XVII, § 3.
[5] Dickmann, *Frieden*, 496. This judgement remains unaltered in the 7th edition of the book published in 1998. See also Aretin, *Altes Reich*, i, 26–7.

peaceful development, the source of the liberties of its inhabitants.[6] Positive assessments of the treaties now became typical. Johann Gottfried von Meiern, for example, who in 1734–6 edited the proceedings of the peace conferences, wrote that it was 'a gift of God's grace and mercy'. Johann Jacob Schmauss, declared in 1766 that the Peace was 'the bond that preserves the peace of the German Reich and the friendship between Catholics and Protestants'.[7] Christoph Matthäus Pfaff wrote in 1742 of 'this palladium of the liberties of the German churches'.[8] Similar views are frequent in the vast contemporary literature on the law and politics of the eighteenth-century Reich. The commemoration of the first centenary of the Peace in 1748 was similarly characterized by invocation of the good that the peace had brought and of its role as the fundamental constitutional law of the Reich.[9]

The more positive judgements of modern historians, especially in the wake of the commemoration of the 350th anniversary of the peace in 1998, have taken these contemporary evaluations seriously again. It is not the case that the Reich was delivered into the hands of foreign powers. The emperor, after all, guaranteed the peace along with France and Sweden, and the terms of the guarantee were sufficiently vague as to make it virtually impossible to invoke.[10] Both the guarantee clause and the 'loss' of Alsace seemed important to historians writing in periods that were dominated by bitter Franco-German animosities, disputes over Alsace, and, after 1919, the 'Diktat' of Versailles. Equally, nationalist teleology distorted the meaning of the clauses that confirmed the rights of the Imperial Estates. The term used was *ius territoriale*, which was the nearest technical equivalent to the German *Landeshoheit* (lordship); the term *droit de souveraineté* (for which the normal equivalent was *maiestas*) which appeared in various French drafts did not appear in the treaty.[11] If the peace really was the 'Magna Carta of the German princes', then the rights it confirmed to them fell short of sovereignty.[12] They remained subject to the law of the Reich, to the jurisdiction of its courts, and ultimately to the jurisdiction of the emperor.

It turned out that some princes of the larger territories were ultimately able to exploit the potential of the rather ambiguous position enshrined in the peace. The minor princes and lesser Imperial Estates, especially the Imperial Knights and Imperial Cities, did not have the same potential, and they appreciated perhaps more than most the safeguards of the system which preserved their quasi-independent existence within the polity. Later developments were no more predictable in 1648 than the fact that the emperor would rebuild a strong position in the Reich in the later seventeenth century. The year 1648 spelled the end of any attempt to create a German monarchy. The treaty, however, left the emperor in place as partner in the

---

[6] Repgen, 'Friede', 637–41; Kremer, *Friede, passim*.

[7] Schmidt, *Geschichte*, 192.

[8] Schneider, *Ius reformandi*, 479 (fn 72).

[9] Gantet, *Paix*, 303–60; Repgen, 'Friede', 637–8; Whaley, *Toleration*, 186, 194; François, *Grenze*, 153–67.

[10] Aretin, *Altes Reich*, i, 26–9.

[11] Gotthard, *Altes Reich*, 103.

[12] Press, 'Soziale Folgen', 244.

sovereign entity 'Kaiser und Reich', as the ultimate judicial authority in the Reich, and as overlord of the imperial feudal system (*Lehnsreich*). It refrained from any precise definition of his prerogatives and powers.

In other ways, the Peace of Westphalia significantly strengthened the Austrian Habsburgs. Exempting their lands from the religious peace enabled them to consolidate their regime in Austria and Bohemia. This was the essential foundation for the revival of the emperors' authority in the Reich; without it, the Habsburgs would not have been able to play the key role they did in the defence of the Reich against both the Turks and the French in the later seventeenth century. In the very long run, it is true, the consolidation of the Habsburg monarchy after 1648 may also have laid the foundations for Austria's departure from of the Reich in favour of a purely Habsburg (Austro-Hungarian) empire. However, that could not have been predicted in 1648, and did not enter into the calculations of either the Habsburgs or their advisers for more than a century afterwards.

Although the peace was one of a series of fundamental laws concerning the Reich, it was one of the most comprehensive. It contained a new definition of an old balance of powers. Its numerous clauses concerning amnesty and restitution sought to resolve all the legal-constitutional issues of the past century. The work of defining those issues had been carried out by the (mainly Protestant) writers and commentators who created the new subject of public law. The Peace of Westphalia represented the constitutional implementation of the public law of the Reich that they had formulated. This was in essence the formalization of the system that had emerged from the debates over the reform proposals of Maximilian I around 1500, the principles of which had been at the core of virtually every subsequent political debate and crisis.

The key principles that were established in 1648 were 'German liberty' and the rule of law. German liberty, hitherto the rallying cry in times when the Imperial Estates opposed the emperor, was now firmly enshrined in the constitution.[13] The rule of law was formalized in the clauses concerning the resolution of conflicts and the maintenance of peace between the Imperial Estates. The concept of 'German liberty' was now also extended. Although for the most part the rights specified in the peace were the rights of rulers, the terms of the religious peace limited those rights and also guaranteed the rights of individuals. The principle of individual freedom of conscience, albeit limited to Catholics and Lutheran and Reformed Protestants, was established, as was the principle of the security of property: government was denied the right to impose on the former or detract from the latter. If the rights of either Imperial Estates or individuals were breached, they were given the possibility of pursuing them through the courts to secure judgments that had the force of law and could be enforced by the armed forces of the Kreise. The process of 'juridification' of the Reich that had begun in the mid-sixteenth century reached its conclusion.

---

[13] Schmidt, 'Westfälischer Friede'.

The political settlement of the religious conflict was definitive. The cases that it did not regulate explicitly or that could not be decided by applying the principle of the 'normal year' could be resolved by the courts. The application of the principle of religious parity to the courts and the law-making mechanisms of the Reich was designed to guarantee that such disputes as did arise, could no longer generate civil war. The result was a significant de-confessionalization of German politics. This did not mean that confessional disputes no longer arose, nor did it prevent political factions in the Reich from sometimes assuming a confessional character. There was an acute confessional crisis in the 1720s, and after 1740 Frederick the Great, a self-proclaimed unbeliever, was a master of confessional politics when the need arose.

Yet, fundamentally, the Reich and its laws were secularized in 1648. Above all, after the Bohemian uprising was crushed and its Calvinist vanguard scattered throughout Europe, and after the failure of Gustavus Adolphus, the millenarian tradition disappeared from mainstream German, and indeed European, politics.[14] It is true that Louis XIV's revocation of the Edict of Nantes in 1685 led to a revival of eschatological propaganda, not least by his Calvinist victims and their co-religionists throughout Europe. But it was relatively short-lived, and no longer had the true millennial thrust of earlier eschatological visions: it was functional propaganda designed to mobilize opinion by reviving old negative stereotypes. No one ever seriously imagined that Louis XIV was the saviour of mankind; nor did he ever promise to institute the Kingdom of Heaven on earth.

To all intents and purposes, this spelled the end of any notion of a universal or sacred Reich. Nonetheless, both Catholic and Protestant lawyers continued to talk in terms of such a thing. The legal titles that justified it were never relinquished or extinguished; *Reichsherkommen*, the custom of the Reich, was a powerful principle of the system and ensured that nothing was abandoned, however redundant it was in fact. Indeed, the idea of universalism perennially attracted certain German intellectuals, from Leibniz in the late seventeenth century to Schiller or the young Romantics in the later eighteenth century. Such ideas have often been taken as evidence of a continuing German longing or nostalgia for the loss of a great imperial dream, or of a continuing desire, sometimes benign, sometimes arrogant and overbearing, to reconstruct some kind of world empire. In reality, the rhetoric of universalism was more often a vehicle for the projection of ideals of human development as a whole, rather than for the advancement of the imperial aspirations of the Germans. Its starting point was a notion of Christianity conceived as an order that transcended individual states.

The political reality of the Reich was defined by the governmental functions of the Reichstag and the feudal functions of the emperor. The combination of the two also yields a definition of the geographical extent of the Reich in 1648. The feudal Reich included parts of Upper Italy and Burgundy; Switzerland and the Dutch

---

[14] Lau, *Stiefbrüder*, 202–51, 464–9 suggests that French aggression from the 1660s provoked a series of national reactions throughout Europe that drew strength from demonized images of Louis XIV as a 'secularized Antichrist': images derived from religious traditions now fuelled purely secular campaigns, which laid the foundations for new 'modern' national identities.

Republic were released from it de facto. The position of the lands of the Bohemian crown was ambivalent, perhaps more attached to the Habsburgs, rather than to the Reich. These were all extraneous to the 'Reich of the German nation', which was defined as those Estates that attended the Reichstag or, in the case of the Imperial Knights, paid imperial taxes. Around 1500, this Reich was largely focused on Upper Germany and the old core regions of the Hohenstaufen system. Around 1648, the old core areas remained central and they cultivated the cachet of particular closeness to the crown. However, the Reich now also functioned in the north as well, even though the northern war in 1655–60 soon made clear again the limits of its writ in the Baltic region. After 1648, many of those parts that had been indifferent to membership now sought recognition and participation, and all the concomitant benefits.

If the Reich had a constitution and a functioning political and legal system, was it a state? If the inhabitants of the Reich used and participated in the system and identified with it, defined themselves positively in terms of the liberties it secured for them and negatively against the enemies of the Reich, can it be described as being the 'state of the German nation'? German historians have traditionally denied this. Fritz Dickmann, for example, again echoed a long tradition when in 1959 he wrote that the Reich ceased to be a state in 1648.[15] Even many who turned their backs on the Prussian-German traditions after 1945 persisted in treating the Reich as a pre-national non-state federation. If anything, it was viewed as the precursor of a united Europe, rather than of the nation state of the nineteenth century. Indeed, the post-nation-state character of the pre-1989 Federal Republic seemed to invite the construction of a pre-national early modern past as its precursor, a path from which the nation state of the period 1871–1945 was a deviation.

The novel arguments advanced by Georg Schmidt in 1999 for viewing the Reich, which he termed the 'Reichs-Staat', as the early modern national state of the Germans provoked some fierce responses.[16] Yet the evidence he adduced in favour of his view is compelling. The Reich was not a centralized or centralizing state, but rather one in which the functions of government were devolved at various levels: emperor and Reichstag, imperial Kreise, territorial governments. As such, it had much in common with many other European monarchies of the time, which were composite monarchies, rather than consolidated centralized states. Comparisons of the Reich with the aspirations of some Western European monarchies, or with the model of what some of them became are misleading, and certainly less helpful than comparisons with the Polish-Lithuanian Commonwealth, with the Dutch Republic, or with the Swiss Federation.

Critics of such a view sometimes resorted to rather bizarre circumlocutions to avoid using the term 'state'. One described the Reich as a 'unique two-tiered system of governance'; another preferred the expression 'part-modernised Reich-system';

---

[15] Dickmann, *Frieden*, 494.
[16] Schmidt, *Geschichte*. On the controversy, see Whaley, 'Old Reich'; Schnettger, 'Reichs-verfassungsgeschichtsschreibung', 145–51. For Schmidt's response, see Schmidt, 'Frühneuzeitliches Reich'.

yet another suggested the Reich was best described as a 'segmented constitutional system' composed of some ten thousand largely autonomous 'local jurisdictions' (*lokale Herrschaften*).[17] The common denominator is the absence of characteristics that are taken to be integral to the European state: an integrated body of subjects or citizens, an integrated territory, a concentrated state authority with sovereignty, freedom of action abroad, and a monopoly of power within.[18]

It may be true that the very infrequently used term 'Reichs-Staat' does not in fact prove much. 'Staat' often simply meant 'system' in early modern German, and thus it no more necessarily meant 'state' when applied to the Reich than when applied to the territories that belonged to the Reich. It is also true that the Reich differed significantly from other neighbouring polities. One of the most fundamental differences was the fact that it was based on the imperial feudal nexus (the *Reichslehnsverband*), meaning, for example, that it retained the original medieval peace-keeping function of such systems. It lacked those features of post-medieval states that generated external expressions of military power, expansionism, or colonialism.

Yet the public law theorists who wrote about the Reich between 1648 and 1806 had no inhibitions in referring to the Reich as a state.[19] And Louis XIV, who knew what a state was if anyone did, was in no doubt. With withering disdain, he advised the Dauphin not to be impressed or intimidated by the emperors' resonant titles: 'A leur [i.e. the emperors] fair justice, on doit les regarder commes les chefs et les capitaines généraux d'une République d'Allemagne'—a state, just not a particularly powerful one, a republic rather than a true monarchy.[20]

A frequent corollary of the denial that the Reich was a state is the notion that it was a system that was incapable of further development after 1648. The peace, in other words, solved the problems of the previous century but allegedly provided no scope for tackling the challenges of the next. At first sight this seems plausible, for it reflects much-cited remarks about the incompetence and sclerotic nature of the Reich and its institutions in its final phase. Furthermore, the Peace of Westphalia was undoubtedly restorative in its intent, aiming to return the Reich to a previous condition, rather than to create something new.[21]

However, the inscription of that state in a treaty that declared itself to be a *perpetua lex et pragmatica imperii sanctio* ('perpetual law and general regulation for the Reich'), and that only six years later the Reichstag recognized as the *Fundamental-Gesetz des Hl. Reiches* ('fundamental law of the Holy Empire'), was itself an innovation.[22] Significantly, the term 'fundamental law of the Reich' appeared in a statutory document for the first time in 1636 in the electoral capitulation for Ferdinand III. In 1654, the Peace of Westphalia was designated the culmination and conclusion of a series of fundamental laws comprising the Golden Bull of 1356, the Perpetual Peace of 1495, and the Peace of Augsburg of 1555 and its

---

[17] Schilling, 'Reichs-Staat', 394; Reinhardt, 'Frühmoderne Staat'; Marquardt, *Reich*.
[18] Reinhard, 'Frühmoderner Staat', 347; Reinhard, *Staatsgewalt*, 52–5.
[19] Kremer, *Friede*, 67–79.
[20] Noël, 'Nation allemande', 327.
[21] Press, 'Krise'.
[22] Conrad, *Rechtsgeschichte*, ii, 360.

associated enforcement edict (*Exekutionsordnung*). At the same time, the peace conference left key issues open (the so-called *negotia remissa*), to be decided by a forthcoming Reichstag. The answers to those questions preoccupied the Reich for decades to come. The debate, and the whole nature of the Reich, was shaped by a series of major external challenges that ensured the continuing evolution of the polity into the early nineteenth century.

Glossary of German and Other Terms

Amicabilis compositio	See under '*Itio in partes*' below.
Amt, Ämter	District or bailiwick: the key administrative unit of a German territory.
Amtmann	Administrator of a bailiwick or district.
Aufklärung	The German Enlightenment.
Bildungsbürgertum	The educated classes.
Bürgertum	Citizenry of a town or city; town and city dwellers as a social stratum generally.
Bürgerschaft	The citizenry of a town or city formally constituted as a body with a constitutional role in the government of the commune.
Confessio (*Konfession*)	Articles of faith or a faith community that subscribed to such articles.
Confessio Augustana	The twenty-eight articles of faith submitted by the Protestant Estates to Charles V at the Augsburg Reichstag 1530; subsequently the basis of Lutheran doctrine, along with the Formula of Concord of 1576.
Confessionalization	The term given (first by German historians) to the process whereby new confessions and articles of faith and new Church structures were created in the century following the Reformation. Supported and often initiated by governments, the process involved the attempt to impose social discipline and to strengthen the institutions of government.
Corpus (pl. Corpora)	The organizations in the Reichstag of Protestants and Catholics devoted to defending the interests of each confessional group. See also under '*Itio in partes*' below.
Declaratio Ferdinandea	The assurance given privately by Ferdinand I in 1555 that Protestants in Catholic ecclesiastical territories would be permitted to exercise their religion. Its validity was contested by the Catholics.
Droit d'épave	The right of shoreline landowners to claim wares that washed up on the beach, a doctrine applied by Vienna after 1804 to claim ownership of any property or assets formerly belonging to a secularized territory that ended up under Austrian jurisdiction, even though the secularized territory itself (with all of its debts) had been allocated to another ruler.
Electoral capitulation (*Wahlkapitulation*)	Pre-election agreement between the emperor or the ecclesiastical princes and their Electors, confirming rights and privileges.

Erblande	Austrian hereditary lands: the Austrian archduchy and duchies, together with the County of Tyrol and other territories, which the Habsburgs held by inheritance, as opposed to other territories such as Bohemia and Hungary, in which they were elected.
Erbverbrüderung (*Erbeinung*)	A treaty between two territorial dynasties agreeing that each might inherit the lands of the other in the absence of a male heir.
Erste Bitte (*Ius primariarum precum*)	The right of the emperors since the thirteenth century to nominate to the first vacancy that arose following his coronation in any ecclesiastical foundation (including cathedral chapters) in the Reich.
Erzstift	See 'Hochstift' below.
Estates	In the Reich, the Estates (*Stände*) were the immediate subjects of the emperor, i.e. primarily the princes and others entitled to vote, either as individuals or as members of corporations, in the Reichstag, as well as the Imperial Knights who had no such vote. In the territories, the Estates (*Stände* or *Landschaft*) were the representatives of the nobility, towns, and other groups.
Fürstenbund	League of Princes, established 1785 (formally, Deutscher Fürstenbund).
Ganerbschaft	A noble property held in common, and often occupied collectively, by a group of noble families.
Geistlicher Rat	Administrative body in a territory with oversight over the territorial church and ecclesiastical affairs.
Generalsuperintendent	See '*Superintendent*' below.
Gravamina	A catalogue of complaints submitted to the Reichstag: originally a list of complaints about the Church, but then used more generally to denote any formal list of complaints.
Grundherrschaft	A system of landownership in which tenants rented land from their feudal overlord. Also *Grundwirtschaft*, the equivalent agricultural production system.
Gutsherrschaft	A system of landownership dominated by manorial estates which used dependent peasants (Leibeigene, see '*Leibeigenschaft*' below) and hired labour: largely found east of the Elbe. Also *Gutswirtschaft*, the equivalent agricultural production system.
Hochstift	The lands ruled by a bishop as a prince (as opposed to his diocese). In the case of an archbishop: Erzstift. In the case of a prelate: Stift.
Hofkriegsrat	Higher administrative body or council with responsibility for military affairs.
Immediacy	*Reichsunmittelbarkeit*, the status of a prince, etc. who was subject only to the emperor and not to any other intermediate authority.

Imperial Vicars	The Electors of Saxony and the Palatinate who held the powers of regency during interregnums in the Reich.
Itio in partes	Practice introduced in the Reichstag after 1648 in order to avoid votes by majority in religious matters: the Estates deliberated in two corpora, the Corpus Evangelicorum and the Corpus Catholicorum. The process of reaching such decisions was also referred to as *amicabilis compositio*.
Ius emigrandi	The right under the Peace of Augsburg and the Peace of Westphalia of subjects whose faith differed from that of their ruler to emigrate without loss of property.
Ius reformandi	Right of reformation, authority over the church in a territory.
Kammer	Treasury of a prince or city.
Kirchenordnung	Church ordinance, containing a comprehensive set of regulations governing Church administration, religious worship, and Church discipline.
Kleinstaaterei	A (pejorative) term coined in the early nineteenth century to denote the extreme territorial fragmentation of the Reich.
Kreis (Kreise)	Regional organizations of the Reich with responsibility for peacekeeping, enforcement of judgments of the Reichskammergericht and Reichshofrat, and currency regulation, among other things.
Kreisausschreibender Fürst	The presiding prince in a Kreis responsible for summoning meetings of its Estates.
Kreisoberst	Commanding officer of the armed forces of a Kreis.
Kreistag	Diets or meetings of representatives of the Estates of a Kreis.
Kuriatstimme	A collective vote in the Reichstag held, for example, by various groups of counts or minor ecclesiastical rulers, generally by region. (See also '*Virilstimme*' below.)
Landeshoheit	Territorial overlordship in the Reich; this fell short of sovereignty, since rulers in the Reich were subject to imperial law and authority.
Landschaft	A single-chamber territorial diet in which only peasants were represented. The term could also refer to the entirety of inhabitants of a territory.
Landtag	Territorial diet.
Lehen	Fief, fiefdom.
Leibeigenschaft	The condition of servitude deriving from medieval feudal law, differently articulated in the various regions but nowhere akin to the forms of serfdom found east of the Reich.
Normaljahr	The Treaty of Osnabrück (Art V § 2) set 1 January 1624 as the date by which ownership of Church property and rights of religious worship were to be judged. Any group or individual in possession of such property or rights on that date was deemed to be entitled to them after 1648.

Obrigkeit	Authority, government (of a prince or an Imperial City).
Panisbriefe (Litterae panis)	The right enjoyed by the emperors since the thirteenth century to issue individuals with letters that obliged an ecclesiastical foundation to provide them with food and sustenance (or the financial equivalent) for life.
Policey (Polizei)	Legislation designed to maintain order and to address social, economic, and moral issues. A *Policeyordnung* was a statute containing a mass of detailed provisions covering every conceivable subject.
Prinzipal-Kommissar	The emperor's permanent representative and spokesman at the Reichstag.
Privilegium de non appellando	A privilege which exempted a territory from the jurisdiction of the higher courts of the Reich, usually granted in some limited form, but enjoyed almost unreservedly by the Electors.
Reichsafterlehen	Arrière fief, a fief not immediately subject to the emperor, but to one of his feoffees.
Reichsarmee	Army of the Reich formed ad hoc by contingents from the Estates. This was distinct from the Austrian army, for which the German Estates also often provided troops.
Reichsabschied	The concluding document of the Reichstag, comprising all legislation agreed.
Reichsbarriere	The notion of a defensive barrier designed to protect the Reich against France. Primarily used in the late seventeenth and eighteenth centuries.
Reichsdeputation	Deputation or special committee of the Reichstag.
Reichserzkanzler	See under '*Reichsvizekanzler*' below.
Reichshofrat	Imperial court or aulic council established at Vienna in 1498 to deal with feudal matters and other imperial prerogatives; from 1558 also a second supreme court for the Reich.
Reichskammergericht	Imperial cameral court, established in 1495 to maintain the peace and act as a supreme appeal court.
Reichskirche	The Imperial Church, the sum of all prince-bishoprics and other immediate ecclesiastical foundations.
Reichskrieg	A war formally declared by the Reichstag. Austria and other German powers could engage in wars that were not *Reichskriege*; even the supply of troops by other territories did not, however, make such a campaign into a *Reichskrieg*.
Reichsmatrikel	List of territories used to allocate fiscal and military levies.
Reichsmoderationstag	Meeting of Estates of the Reich commissioned to revise and update the *Reichsmatrikel* (never actually achieved).
Reichsregiment	Imperial government or administration.
Reichsschluß	An imperial law passed at the Reichstag.

Reichstag	Imperial diet, assembly of the Estates presided over by the emperor.
Reichsunmittelbarkeit	See 'Immediacy' above.
Reichsvikar	See 'Imperial Vicars' above.
Reichsvizekanzler	Permanent official based in Vienna who served as deputy to the Archchancellor, the Elector of Mainz (the *Reichserzkanzler*) and liaised between him and the emperor over Reichstag business and all important political matters.
Reservatum ecclesiasticum	The stipulation of the Peace of Augsburg 1555 that an ecclesiastical prince who converted to Protestantism should forfeit his office and title, designed to ensure that no further ecclesiastical territories should fall to Protestantism.
Rheinbund	Confederation of the Rhine, 1806–13, established by Napoleon as a system of satellite states in Germany, excluding Austria and Prussia.
Romans, King of the	See '*Römischer König*' below.
Römermonat (Roman Month)	The unit of account used to calculate the contribution of the Estates of the Reich to military expenditure—originally and literally the monthly wage bill for the troops who formerly accompanied the emperor to Rome for his coronation by the pope. From the early sixteenth century until 1806 the levy was based on the matricular list of 1521. By the late eighteenth century, a *Römermonat* paid for 40,000 men.
Römischer König	King of the Romans, the designated heir of the Holy Roman Emperor.
Simultaneum	The joint use by two Christian confessions of a church or other ecclesiastical property; the parallel existence of two Christian confessions in a territory.
Städtetag	The sixteenth-century organization of the Imperial Cities; the term can also refer to the individual meetings or diets of the representatives of the cities.
Standesherr (*Standesherren*)	The term used to denote those members of the upper nobility who lost their immediate status between 1804 and 1815, and who became subjects of the new German sovereigns of the German Confederation in 1815. They only lost their special rights and privileges, which set them apart from the ordinary nobility of a state (*Landadel*), in the revolution of 1918–19.
Stift	See 'Hochstift' above.
Superintendent	The leading (supervisory) clergyman in a Lutheran territory, where the prince held the powers formally held by a bishop.
Vikar (*vicarius*)	Deputy (used in the Church and in the Reich).
Virilstimme	A single vote in the Reichstag. (See also '*Kuriatstimme*' above.)

Vordere Kreise   The 'further' or 'forward' Kreise most exposed to attack by Louis XIV: the Swabian, Franconian, upper Rhine, Electoral Rhine and lower Rhine-Westphalian, the Bavarian and the Austrian Kreise.

Vorderösterreich—Vorlande   The complex of minor Austrian territories attached to the County of Tyrol that stretched westwards across southern Germany to Alsace. Further Austria.

Wahlkapitulation   See 'Electoral Capitulation' above.

Bibliography

Abel, Wilhelm, *Geschichte der deutschen Landwirtschaft vom frühen Mittelalter bis zum 19. Jahrhundert*, 2nd edn (Stuttgart, 1967).

Abray, Lorna Jane, *The people's reformation: Magistrates, clergy and commons in Strasbourg 1500–1598* (Oxford, 1985).

Albrecht, Dieter, *Maximilian I. von Bayern 1573–1651* (Munich, 1998).

Allgemeine Deutsche Biographie, 56 vols (Munich and Leipzig, 1875–1902).

Altmann, Hugo, *Die Reichspolitik Maximilians I. von Bayern 1613–1618* (Munich, 1978).

Amann, Hektor, 'Wie groß war die mittelalterliche Stadt?', in C. Haase (ed.), *Die mittelalterliche Stadt, Band 1: Begriff, Entstehung und Ausbreitung* (Darmstadt, 1969), 408–15.

Anderson, Alison D., *On the verge of war: International relations and the Jülich-Kleve succession crises (1609–1614)* (Boston, 1999).

Anderson, M. S., *War and society in Europe of the Old Regime 1618–1789* (London, 1988).

Angermeier, Heinz, 'Die Reichsregimenter und ihre Staatsidee', *Historische Zeitschrift*, ccxi (1970), 265–315.

——, 'Der Wormser Reichstag in der politischen Konzeption König Maximilians. I', in Heinrich Lutz (ed.), *Das römisch-deutsche Reich im politischen System Karls V.* (Munich and Vienna, 1982), 1–13.

——, *Reichsreform und Reformation* (Munich, 1983).

——, *Die Reichsreform 1410–1555: Die Staatsproblematik in Deutschland zwischen Mittelalter und Gegenwart* (Munich, 1984).

——, 'Politik, Religion und Reich bei Kardinal Melchior Khlesl', *Zeitschrift der Savigny-Stiftung für Rechtsgeschichte*, Germanistische Abteilung, cxxiii (1993), 249–330.

——, 'Der Wormser Reichstag 1495: Ein europäisches Ereignis', *Historische Zeitschrift*, cclxi (1995), 739–68.

Aretin, Karl Otmar von, *Das Reich: Friedensordnung und europäisches Gleichgewicht 1648–1806* (Stuttgart, 1986).

——, *Das Alte Reich 1648–1806*, 4 vols (Stuttgart, 1993–2000).

Arndt, Johannes, *Das Heilige Römische Reich und die Niederlande 1566 bis 1648: Politisch-konfessionelle Verflechtung und Publizistik im Achtzigjährigen Krieg* (Cologne, 1998).

Asch, Roland G., *The Thirty Years War: The Holy Roman Empire and Europe, 1618–48* (Houndmills, 1997).

——, '"Denn es sind ja die Deutschen . . . ein frey Volk": Die Glaubensfreiheit als Problem der westfälischen Friedensverhandlungen', *Westfälische Zeitschrift*, cxlviii (1998), 113–37.

Asche, Matthias and Anton Schindling (eds), *Dänemark, Norwegen und Schweden im Zeitalter der Reformation und Konfessionalisierung: Nordische Königreiche und Konfession 1500 bis 1600* (Münster, 2003).

Aubin, Herman and Wolfgang Zorn (eds), *Handbuch der Deutschen Wirtschafts und Sozialgeschichte, Band 1: Von der Frühzeit bis zum Ende des 18. Jahrhunderts* (Stuttgart, 1978).

Baade, Anne A., *Melchior Goldast von Haiminsfeld: Collector, commentator, and editor* (New York, 1992).

Bagchi, D. V. N., '"Teutschland uber alle Welt": Nationalism and Catholicism in Early Reformation Germany', *Archiv für Reformationsgeschichte*, lxxxii (1991), 39–58.

Bahlcke, Joachim, *Regionalismus und Staatsintegration im Widerstreit: Die Länder der Böhmischen Krone im ersten Jahrhundert der Habsburgerherrschaft (1526–1619)* (Munich, 1994).

——, 'Calvinism and estate liberation movements in Bohemia and Hungary (1570–1620)', in Karin Maag (ed.), *The Reformation in Eastern and Central Europe* (Aldershot, 1997), 72–91.

Bailey, Michael D., 'Religious poverty, mendicancy, and reform in the late Middle Ages', *Church History*, lxxii (2003), 457–83.

Baron, Hans, 'Imperial Reform and the Habsburgs 1486–1504', *American Historical Review*, xliv (1939), 293–303.

Battenberg, J. Friedrich, *Das Europäische Zeitalter der Juden*, 2 vols (Darmstadt, 1990).

——, 'Juden vor dem Reichskammergericht', in Ingrid Scheurmann (ed.), *Frieden durch Recht: Das Reichskammergericht von 1495 bis 1806* (Mainz, 1994), 322–7.

——, *Die Juden in Deutschland vom 16. bis zum Ende des 18. Jahrhunderts* (Munich, 2001).

Bauer, Joachim, Andreas Klinger, Alexander Schmidt, and Georg Schmidt, *Die Universität Jena in der Frühen Neuzeit* (Heidelberg, 2008).

Baumann, Anette, 'Advokaten und Prokuratoren am Reichskammergericht in Speyer (1495–1690): Berufswege in der Frühen Neuzeit', *Zeitschrift der Savigny-Stiftung für Rechtsgeschichte*, Germanistische Abteilung, cxxx (2000), 550–63.

Baumann, Franz Ludwig (ed.) *Quellen zur Geschichte des Bauernkriegs aus Rothenburg an der Tauber* (Tübingen, 1878).

Baumann, Reinhard, *Landsknechte: Ihre Geschichte und Kultur vom späten Mittelalter bis zum Dreissigjährigen Krieg* (Munich, 1994).

Bautz, Friedrich Wilhelm (ed.), *Biographisch-bibliographisches Kirchenlexikon* (Hamm, 1970), available in updated form at http://www.bautz.de/bbkl/ (accessed 4 May 2011).

Bechtoldt, Hans-Joachim, 'Aspekte des Finanzwesens des Franz von Sickingen: Verträge im Kontext des Silberbergbaus in der Umgebung der Ebernburg im frühen 16. Jahrhundert', *Jahrbuch für westdeutsche Landesgeschichte*, xxxiii (2007), 175–212.

Becker, Winfried (ed.), *Der Passauer Vertrag von 1552: Politische Entstehung, reichsrechtliche Bedeutung und konfessionsgeschichtliche Bewertung* (Neustadt an der Aisch, 2003).

Begert, Alexander, *Böhmen, die böhmische Kur und das Reich vom Hochmittelalter bis zum Ende des Alten Reiches: Studien zur Kurwürde und zur staatsrechtlichen Stellung Böhmens* (Husum, 2003).

Béhar, Pierre, 'Martin Opitz: Weltanschauliche Hintergründe einer literarischen Bewegung', *Germanisch-Romanische Monatsschrift*, xxxiv (1984), 44–53.

Behringer, Wolfgang, *Hexen und Hexenprozesse in Deutschland* (Munich, 1988).

——, 'Mörder, Diebe, Ehebrecher. Verbrechen und Strafen in Kurbayern vom 16. bis 18. Jahrhundert', in Richard van Dülmen (ed.), *Verbrechen, Strafen und soziale Kontrolle: Studien zur historischen Kulturforschung III.* (Frankfurt am Main, 1990), 85–132, 287–93.

——, *Witchcraft persecution in Bavaria: Popular magic, religious zealotry and reason of state in early modern Europe* (Cambridge, 1997).

——, 'Die Krise von 1570: Ein Beitrag zur Krisengeschichte der Neuzeit', in Manfred Jakubowski-Tiessen and Hartmut Lehmann (eds), *Um Himmels Willen: Religion in Katastrophenzeiten* (Göttingen, 2003).

——, *Im Zeichen des Merkur: Reichspost und Kommunikationsrevolution in der Frühen Neuzeit* (Göttingen, 2003).

——, Hartmut Lehmann, and Christian Pfister, 'Kulturelle Konsequenzen der "Kleinen Eiszeit"? Eine Annäherung an die Thematik', in Wolfgang Behringer, Hartmut Lehmann, and Christian Pfister (eds), *Kulturelle Konsequenzen der 'Kleinen Eiszeit'* (Göttingen, 2005), 7–27.

Beiderbeck, Friedrich, 'Heinrich IV. von Frankreich und die protestantischen Reichsstände', *Francia, xx*iii/2 (1996), 1–31 and xxv/2 (1998), 1–25.

——, 'Frankreich und das Reich um 1600: Kooperation und Abgrenzung in den Beziehungen zwischen Heinrich IV. und den protestantischen Reichsfürsten', in Friedrich Beiderbeck (ed.), *Dimensionen der europäischen Außenpolitik* (Berlin, 2003), 35–59.

——, *Zwischen Religionskrieg, Reichskrise und europäischem Hegemoniekampf: Heinrich IV. von Frankreich und die protestantischen Reichsstände* (Berlin, 2005).

Below, Stefan von and Stefan Breit, *Wald. Von der Gottesgabe zum Privateigentum: Gerichtliche Konflikte zwischen Landesherren und Untertanen um den Wald in der frühen Neuzeit* (Stuttgart, 1998).

Benecke, Gerhard, *Maximilian I (1459–1519): An analytical biography* (London, 1982).

Bergbaureviere im 16. Jahrhundert. Vorträge des Historischen Kolloquiums (Clausthal-Zellerfeld, 1994).

Bergerhausen, Hans-Wolfgang, '"Exclusis Westphalen et Burgundt": Zum Kampf um die Durchsetzung der Reichsmünzordnung von 1559', *Zeitschrift für historische Forschung*, xx (1993), 189–203.

Berns, Jörg Jochen, 'Zur Tradition der deutschen Sozietätsbewegung im 17. Jahrhundert', in Martin Bircher and Ferdinand van Ingen (eds), *Sprachgesellschaften, Sozietäten, Dichtergruppen* (Hamburg, 1978), 53–73.

——, 'Die Festkultur der deutschen Höfe zwischen 1580 und 1730', *Germanisch-Romanische Monatsschrift*, 65 (1984), 295–311.

Betz, Hans Dieter et al. (eds), *Die Religion in Geschichte und Gegenwart Handwörterbuch für Theologie and Religionswissenschaft*, 9 vols (4th edn, Munich, 1998–2007).

Bireley, Robert, *Religion and politics in the age of Counterreformation: Emperor Ferdinand II, William Lamormaini, S.J., and the formation of imperial policy* (Chapel Hill, 1981).

——, 'The Thirty Years' War as Germany's religious war', in Konrad Repgen (ed.), *Krieg und Politik 1618–1648: Europäische Probleme und Perspektiven* (Munich, 1988), 85–106.

——, *The Jesuits and the Thirty Years War: Kings, courts and confessors* (Cambridge, 2003).

Birtsch, Günter, 'Franz von Sickingen 1481 bis 1523: Reichsritter aus Rheinpfalz', in Dieter Lau (ed.), *Vorzeiten: Geschichte in Rheinland-Pfalz* (Mainz, 1988), 87–104.

Bischoff-Urack, Angelika, *Michael Gaismair: Ein Beitrag zur Sozialgeschichte des Bauernrieges* (Innsbruck, 1983).

Blaich, Fritz, *Die Reichsmonopolgesetzgebung im Zeitalter Karls V.: Ihre ordnungspolitische Problematik* (Stuttgart, 1967).

——, *Die Wirtschaftspolitik des Reichstags im Heiligen Römischen Reich: Ein Beitrag zur Problemgeschichte wirtschaftlichen Gestaltens* (Stuttgart, 1970).

Blänsdorf, Agnes, 'Staat—Nation—Volk: Österreich und Deutschland; Zu Gerald Stourzhs Auseinandersetzung mit Karl Dietrich Erdmann', *Geschichte in Wissenschaft und Unterricht*, xlii (1991), 767–74.

Blickle, Peter, *Landschaften im Alten Reich: Die staatliche Funktion des gemeinen Mannes in Oberdeutschland* (Munich, 1973).

——, *Die Revolution von 1525*, 2nd edn (Munich and Vienna, 1981).

——, *Gemeindereformation: Die Menschen des 16. Jahrhunderts auf dem Weg zum Heil* (Munich, 1985).

——, 'Die Eidgenossen verlassen das Reich', in H. Duchhardt (ed.), *In Europas Mitte: Deutschland und seine Nachbarn* (Bonn, 1988), 96–100.

——, *Unruhen in der ständischen Gesellschaft 1300–1800* (Munich, 1988).

——, *Die Reformation im Reich*, 2nd edn (Stuttgart, 1992).

Blickle, Peter, *Der Bauernkrieg: Die Revolution des Gemeinen Mannes* (Munich, 1998).

——, 'Politische Landschaften in Oberschwaben: Bäuerliche und bürgerliche Repräsentation im Rahmen des frühen europäischen Parlamentarismus', in *idem* (ed.), *Landschaften und Landstände in Oberschwaben: Bäuerliche und bürgerliche Repräsentation im Rahmen des frühen europäischen Parlamentarismus* (Tübingen, 2000), 11–32.

——, *Von der Leibeigenschaft zu den Menschenrechten: Eine Geschichte der Freiheit in Deutschland* (Munich, 2003).

——, *Das Alte Europa: Vom Hochmittelalter bis zur Moderne* (Munich, 2008).

Blickle, Renate, 'Agrarische Konflikte und Eigentumsordnung in Altbayern, 1400–1800', in Winfried Schulze (ed.), *Aufstände, Revolten, Prozesse: Beiträge zu bäuerlichen Widerstandsbewegungen im frühneuzeitlichen Europa* (Stuttgart, 1983), 166–87.

Bock, Ernst, *Der Schwäbische Bund und seine Verfassungen (1488–1534): Ein Beitrag zur Geschichte der Zeit der Reichsreform*, 2nd edn (Aalen, 1968).

Bog, Ingomar, *Oberdeutschland: Das Heilige Römische Reich des 16. bis 18. Jahrhunderts in Funktion* (Idstein, 1986).

Bonney, Richard, *The European dynastic states 1494–1660* (Oxford, 1991).

Boockmann, Hartmut, *Der Deutsche Orden: Zwölf Kapitel aus seiner Geschichte* (Munich, 1981).

——, *Stauferzeit und spätes Mittelalter: Deutschland 1125–1517* (Berlin, 1987).

——, *Ostpreußen und Westpreußen*, 2nd edn (Berlin, 1993).

——, 'Über den Zusammenhang von Reichsreform und Kirchenreform', in Ivan Hlaváček (ed.), *Reform von Kirche und Reich zur Zeit der Konzilien von Konstanz (1414–1418) und Basel (1431–1449)* (Constance, 1996), 203–14.

Borchardt, Frank L., *German antiquity in Renaissance myth* (Baltimore and London, 1971).

Borgolte, Michael, *Die mittelalterliche Kirche* (Munich, 1992).

Bornkamm, Heinrich, *Luther in mid-career 1521–1530*, transl. E. Theodore Bachmann (London, 1983).

Borst, Arno, *Der Turmbau von Babel: Geschichte der Meinungen über Ursprung und Vielfalt der Sprachen und Völker*. 3 vols in 4 (Stuttgart, 1957–63).

Borth, Wilhem, *Die Luthersache (Causa Lutheri) 1517–1524: Die Anfänge der Reformation als Frage von Politik und Recht* (Lübeck and Hamburg, 1970).

Bosbach, Franz, *Die Kosten des Westfälischen Friedenskongresses: Eine strukturgeschichtliche Untersuchung* (Münster, 1984).

Bosl, Karl, *Böhmen und seine Nachbarn: Gesellschaft, Politik und Kultur in Mitteleuropa* (Munich, 1976).

——, Günther Franz, and Hanns Hubert Hofmann (eds), *Biographisches Worterbuch zu deutschen Geschichte* 3 vols (2nd edn, Munich, 1973–4).

Brady, Thomas A., *Turning Swiss: Cities and empire 1450–1550* (Cambridge, 1985).

——, 'The common man and the lost Austria in the West: A contribution to the German Problem', in E. I. Kouri and T. Scott (eds), *Politics and society in Reformation Europe: Essays for Sir Geoffrey Elton on his sixty-fifth birthday* (London, 1987), 142–57.

——, 'Peoples' religions in Reformation Europe', *The Historical Journal* xxxiv (1991), 173–82.

——, *Protestant politics: Jacob Sturm (1489–1553) and the German Reformation* (Atlantic Highlands, NJ, 1995).

——, 'Economic and social institutions', in Bob Scribner (ed.), *Germany: A new social and economic history 1450–1630* (London, 1996), 259–90.

——, 'In search of the godly city: The domestication of religion in the German Reformation', in *idem, Communities, politics and Reformation in early modern Europe* (Leiden, 1998), 169–88.

——, 'The Holy Roman Empire, 1555–1648', in *idem, Communities, politics and Reformation in early modern Europe* (Leiden, 1998), 371–406.

——, *German histories in the age of Reformations, 1400–1650* (Cambridge, 2009).

Brauer, Adalbert, 'Die kaiserliche Bücherkommission und der Niedergang Frankfurts als Buchhandelsmetropole Deutschlands', *Genealogisches Jahrbuch, ix* (1979), 185–97.

Braunfels, Wolfgang, *Die Kunst im Heiligen Römischen Reich*, 6 vols (Munich, 1979–89).

Braunstein, Philippe, 'Innovations in mining and metal production in Europe in the late Middle Ages', *The Journal of European Economic History*, xii (1983), 573–91.

Brechenmacher, Thomas, *Großdeutsche Geschichtsschreibung im neunzehnten Jahrhundert: Die erste Generation (1830–48)* (Berlin, 1996).

——, '"Österreich steht außer Deutschland, aber es gehört zu Deutschland": Aspekte der Bewertung des Faktors Österreich in der deutschen Historiographie', in Michael Gehler et al. (eds), *Ungleiche Partner: Österreich und Deutschland in ihrer gegenseitigen Wahrnehmung. Historische Analysen und Vergleiche aus dem 19. und 20. Jahrhundert* (Stuttgart, 1996), 31–53.

Brecht, Martin, *Martin Luther*, transl. James L. Schaaf, 3 vols (Philadelphia and Minneapolis, 1985–93).

——, 'Christoph Besold: Versuch und Ansätze einer Deutung', *Pietismus und Neuzeit*, xxvi (2000), 11–28.

Brendle, Franz, 'Kurmainz, Bayern und die Liga', in Albrecht Ernst and Anton Schindling (eds), *Union und Liga 1608/09: Konfessionelle Bündnisse im Reich: Weichenstellung zum Religionskrieg* (Stuttgart, 2010), 97–115.

Brenner, Peter J., 'Das Drama', in Albert Meier (ed.), *Die Literatur des 17. Jahrhunderts: Hansers Sozialgeschichte der deutschen Literatur vom 16. Jahrhundert bis zur Gegenwart Band 2* (Munich, 1999), 539–74.

Breuer, Dieter, *Oberdeutsche Literatur, 1565–1650: Deutsche Literaturgeschichte und Territorialgeschichte in frühabsolutistischer Zeit* (Munich, 1979).

——, 'Deutsche Nationalliteratur und katholischer Kulturkreis', in Dieter Borchmeyer (ed.), *Poetik und Geschichte* (Tübingen, 1989), 701–15.

Breul-Kunkel, Wolfgang, *Herrschaftskrise und Reformation: Die Reichsabteien Fulda und Hersfeld ca. 1500–1525* (Gütersloh, 2000).

Brodkorb, Clemens, 'Die Weihbischöfe im Heiligen Römischen Reich, 1448–1648', *Römische Quartalschrift für christliche Altertumskunde und Kirchengeschichte*, xcii (1997), 72–102.

Bruckmüller, Ernst and Peter Claus Hartmann, (eds), *Putzgers Historischer Weltatlas* (103rd edn, Bedin, 2001).

Bryce, James, *The Holy Roman Empire* (Oxford, 1864, 6th edn with corrections, 1906).

Buchholz, Stephan, 'Der Landgraf und sein Professor: Bigamie in Hessen', in Gerhard Köbler (ed.), *Wirkungen europäischer Rechtskultur* (Munich, 1997), 39–63.

Bücking, Jürgen, *Michael Gaismair: Reformer, Sozialrebell, Revolutionär; Seine Rolle im Tiroler 'Bauernkrieg' (1525/32)* (Stuttgart, 1978).

Bundschuh, Benno von, *Das Wormser Religionsgespräch von 1557: Unter besonderer Berücksichtigung der Kaiserlichen Religionspolitik* (Münster, 1988).

Burgdorf, Wolfgang, *Ein Weltbild verliert seine Welt: Der Untergang des Alten Reiches und die Generation 1806* (Munich, 2006).

Burger, Christoph. 'Huttens Erfahrungen mit Kirche und Frömmigkeit und seine Kritik', in Johannes Schilling and Ernst Giese (eds), *Ulrich von Hutten und seine Zeit* (Kassel, 1988), 35–60.

Burke, Peter, 'Tacitism, scepticism and reason of state', in J. H. Burns and M. Goldie (eds), *The Cambridge history of political thought 1450–1700* (Cambridge, 1996), 479–98.

Burkhardt, Johannes, *Der Dreißigjährige Krieg* (Frankfurt am Main, 1992).

Burleigh, Michael, *Prussian society and the German order: An aristocratic corporation in crisis c.1410–1466* (Cambridge, 1984).

Buschmann, Arno (ed.), *Kaiser und Reich: Verfassungsgeschichte des Heiligen Römischen Reiches Deutscher Nation vom Beginn des 12. Jahrhunderts bis zum Jahre 1806 in Dokumenten*, 2nd edn (Baden-Baden, 1994).

Bussmann, Klaus and Heinz Schilling (eds), *1648: War and peace in Europe*, 3 vols (Münster, 1998).

Buszello, Horst, 'The common man's view of the state in the German Peasant War', in Bob Scribner and Gerhard Benecke (eds), *The German Peasant War 1525: New Viewpoints* (London, 1979), 109–22.

——, 'Legitimation, Verlaufsformen und Ziele', in Rudolf Endres and Horst Buszello (eds), *Der deutsche Bauernkrieg* (Paderborn, 1984), 281 321.

——, 'Oberrheinlande', in Rudolf Endres and Horst Buszello (eds), *Der deutsche Bauernkrieg* (Paderborn, 1984), 61–96.

Buttlar, Kurt Treusch von, 'Das tägliche Leben an den deutschen Fürstenhöfen des 16. Jahrhunderts', *Zeitschrift für Kulturgeschichte*, iv (1897) 1–41.

Cameron, Euan, *The European Reformation* (Oxford, 1991).

Carl, Horst, 'Der Schwäbische Bund und das Reich: Konkurrenz und Symbiose', in Volker Press (ed.), *Alternativen zur Reichsverfassung in der Frühen Neuzeit?* (Munich, 1995), 43–63.

——, 'Landfriedenseinung und Standessolidarität: Der Schwäbische Bund und die Raubritter', in C. Roll (ed.), *Recht und Reich im Zeitalter der Reformation* (Frankfurt am Main, 1996), 471–92.

Carsten, F. L., *Princes and parliaments in Germany from the fifteenth to the eighteenth century* (Oxford, 1959).

Chisholm, M. A., 'The *Religionspolitik* of Emperor Ferdinand I (1521–1564): Tyrol and the Holy Roman Empire', *European History Quarterly*, xxxviii (2008), 551–77.

Clark, Peter, 'Introduction: the European crisis of the 1590s', in Peter Clark (ed.), *The European crisis of the 1590s: Essays in comparative history* (London, 1985), 3–22.

Clasen, Claus-Peter, *The Palatinate in European history 1555–1618*, revised edn (Oxford, 1966).

——, *Anabaptism: A social history, 1525–1618: Switzerland, Austria, Moravia, South and Central Germany* (Ithaca, NY, 1972).

——, *The Anabaptists in South and Central Germany, Switzerland and Austria: Their names, occupations, places of residence and dates of conversion: 1525–1618* (Ann Arbor, 1978).

Clot, André, *Suleiman the Magnificent: The man, his life, his epoch* (London, 1992).

Cohn, Norman, *The pursuit of the millennium: Revolutionary millenarians and mystical anarchists of the Middle Ages*, 3rd edn (London, 1970).

Cohn, H. J., 'The territorial princes in Germany's Second Reformation, 1559–1622', in Menna Prestwich (ed.), *International Calvinism 1541–1715* (Oxford, 1985), 135–65.

——, 'Church property in the German Protestant principalities', in E. I. Kouri and T. Scott (eds) *Politics and society in Reformation Europe: Essays for Sir Geoffrey Elton on his sixty-fifth birthday* (Houndmills, 1987), 158–87.

——, *The government of the Rhine Palatinate in the fifteenth century*, 2nd edn (Aldershot, 1991).

——, 'The electors and imperial rule at the end of the fifteenth century', in Björn K. V. Weiler (ed.), *Representations of power in medieval Germany 800–1500* (Turnhout, 2006), 295–318.

Conersmann, Klaus, 'Die Tugendliche Gesellschaft und ihr Verhältnis zur Fruchtbringenden Gesellschaft: Sittenzucht, Gesellschaftsidee und Akademiegedanke zwischen Renaissance und Aufklärung', *Daphnis. Zeitschrift für Mittlere Deutsche Literatur*, xvii (1988), 513–626.

Conrad, Franziska, *Reformation in der bäuerlichen Gesellschaft: Zur Rezeption reformatorischer Theologie im Elsass* (Stuttgart, 1984).

Conrad, Hermann, *Deutsche Rechtsgeschichte*, 2 vols (Karlsruhe, 1962–6).

Coupe, W. A. (ed.), *A sixteenth-century German reader* (Oxford, 1972).

Cramer, Kevin, 'The cult of Gustavus Adolphus: Protestant identity and German nationalism', in Helmut Walser Smith (ed.), *Protestants, Catholics and Jews in Germany, 1800–1914* (Oxford, 2001), 97–120.

——, *The Thirty Years' War and German memory in the nineteenth century* (Lincoln, NB, 2007).

——, 'Religious war, German war, total war: The shadow of the Thirty Years' War on German war making in the twentieth century', in Jenny Macleod (ed.), *Defeat and memory: Cultural histories of military defeat in the modern era* (Houndmills, 2008), 81–96.

Croxton, Derek and Anouschka Tischer, *The Peace of Westphalia: A historical dictionary* (Westport, CT, 2002).

DaCosta Kaufmann, Thomas, *Court, cloister and city: The art and culture of central Europe 1450–1800* (London, 1995).

Dähn, Horst, 'Martin Luther und die Reformation in der Geschichtswissenschaft der DDR', in Stefan Laube (ed.), *Lutherinszenierung und Reformationserinnerung* (Leipzig, 2002), 373–90.

Delius, Hans-Ulrich, 'Religionspolitik und kirchliche Ausgleichsbemühungen des Kurfürsten Joachim II. von Brandenburg', *Jahrbuch für Berlin-Brandenburgische Kirchengeschichte*, lii (1980), 25–87.

Derndarsky, Michael, 'Zwischen "Idee" und "Wirklichkeit". Das Alte Reich in der Sicht Heinrich von Srbiks', in Matthias Schnettger (ed.), *Imperium Romanum—Irregulare Corpus—Teutscher Reichs-Staat: Das Alte Reich im Verständnis der Zeitgenossen und der Historiographie* (Mainz, 2002), 189–205.

Deutsches Städtebuch: Handbuch städtischer Geschichte, edited by Erich Keyser, 5 vols in 11 (Stuttgart, 1939–74).

Dickel, Günther, *Das kaiserliche Reservatrecht der Panisbriefe auf Laienherrenpfründen: Eine Untersuchung zur Verfassungsgeschichte des Alten Reichs und zur kirchlichen Rechtsgeschichte nach Wiener Akten* (Aalen, 1985).

Dickens, A. G., *The German nation and Martin Luther*, 2nd edn (London, 1976).

——, *Ranke as Reformation historian* (Reading, 1980).

—— and John M. Tonkin, *The Reformation in historical thought* (Oxford, 1985).

Dickmann, Fritz, *Der Westfälische Frieden* (Münster, 1959, 7th edn 1998).

Dixon, C. Scott, 'Popular astrology and Lutheran propaganda in Reformation Germany', *History*, lxxxiv (1999), 403–18.

——, 'Urban order and religious coexistence in the German Imperial City: Augsburg and Donauwörth, 1548–1608', *Central European History*, xl (2007), 1–33.

Documenta Bohemica bellum tricennale illustrantia, ed. Josef Janáček, Josef Kočí, Gabriela Čechová, 7 vols (Prague, 1971–81).

Donahue, William, 'Astronomy', in Katharine Park and Lorraine Daston (eds), *The Cambridge history of science*, Vol. 3: *Early modern science* (Cambridge, 2006), 564–95.

Dorner, Andreas, *Politischer Mythos und symbolische Politik: Sinnstiftung durch symbolische Formen am Beispiel des Hermannsmythos* (Opladen, 1995).

Dorpalen, Andreas, *German history in Marxist perspective: The East German approach* (London, 1985).

Dotzauer, Winfried, *Die deutschen Reichskreise (1383–1806): Geschichte und Aktenedition* (Stuttgart, 1998).

Dreitzel, Horst, *Monarchiebegriffe in der Fürstengesellschaft: Semantik und Theorie der Einherrschaft in Deutschland von der Reformation bis zum Vormärz*, 2 vols (Cologne, 1991).

——, 'Samuel Pufendorf', in Helmut Holzhey, Wilhelm Schmidt-Biggemann, and Vilem Mudroch (eds), *Die Philosophie des 17. Jahrhunderts: Das Heilige Römische Reich Deutscher Nation, Nord- und Ostmittel-Europa*, 2 vols (Basle 2001), ii, 757–812.

——, 'Zehn Jahre Patria in der politischen Theorie in Deutschland: Prasch, Pufendorf, Leibniz, Becher 1662 bis 1672', in Robert von Friedeburg (ed.) *'Patria' und 'Patrioten' vor dem Patriotismus: Pflichten, Rechte, Glauben und Rekonfigurierung europäischer Gemeinwesen im 17. Jahrhundert* (Wiesbaden, 2005), 367–534.

Driedger, Michael D., *Obedient heretics: Mennonite identities in Lutheran Hamburg and Altona during the confessional age* (Aldershot, 2002).

Du Boulay, F. R. H., 'Law enforcement in medieval Germany', *History*, lxiii (1978), 345–55.

——, *Germany in the later Middle Ages* (London, 1983).

Duchhardt, Heinz, *Deutsche Verfassungsgeschichte 1495–1806* (Stuttgart, 1991).

——, '"Westphalian System": Zur Problematik einer Denkfigur', *Historische Zeitschrift*, cclix (1999), 305–15.

Dülfer, Kurt, *Die Packschen Händel: Darstellung und Quellen* (Marburg, 1958).

Eckert, Georg and Gerrit Walther, 'Die Geschichte der Frühneuzeitforschung in der Historischen Zeitschrift 1859–2009', *Historische Zeitschrift*, cclxxxix (2009), 149–97.

Edelmayer, Friedrich, Maximilian Lanzinner, and Peter Rauscher, 'Einleitung', in idem (eds), *Finanzen und Herrschaft: Materielle Grundlagen fürstlicher Politik in den habsburgischen Ländern und im Heiligen Römischen Reich im 16. Jahrhundert* (Vienna, 2003), 9–19.

Edwards, Mark U., *Luther and the false brethren* (Stanford, 1975).

Ehmer, Hermann, 'Die Kirchengutsfrage in der Reformation', *Blätter für württembergische Kirchengeschichte*, c (2004), 27–45.

Ehrenpreis, Stefan and Lotz-Heumann, Ute, *Reformation und konfessionelles Zeitalter* (Darmstadt, 2002).

—— and Ruthmann, Bernhard, 'Ius reformandi—ius emigrandi: Reichsrecht, Konfession und Ehre in Religionsstreitigkeiten des späten 16. Jahrhunderts', in Michael Weinzierl (ed.), *Individualisierung, Rationalisierung, Säkularisierung: Neue Wege der Religionsgeschichte* (Vienna, 1997), 67–95.

Eickels, Christine van, *Schlesien im böhmischen Ständestaat: Voraussetzungen und Verlauf der böhmischen Revolution von 1618 in Schlesien* (Cologne, 1994).

Eisenhardt, Ulrich, *Die kaiserliche Aufsicht über Buchdruck, Buchhandel und Presse im Heiligen Römischen Reich Deutscher Nation (1496–1806): Ein Beitrag zur Geschichte der Bücher- und Pressezensur* (Karlsruhe, 1970).

——, *Die kaiserlichen privilegia de non appellando* (Cologne, 1980).

Eisenstein, Elizabeth L., *The printing press as an agent of change*, 2 vols (Cambridge, 1979).

Elliott, J. H., *Europe Divided 1559–1598* (London, 1968).

——, *The Count-Duke of Olivares: The statesman in an age of decline* (New Haven, 1986).

——, 'A Europe of composite monarchies', *Past and Present*, cxxvii (1992), 48–71.

Emrich, Wilhelm, *Deutsche Literatur der Barockzeit* (Königstein im Taunus, 1981).

Enderle, Wilfried, 'Die katholischen Reichsstädte im Zeitalter der Reformation und der Konfessionsbildung', *Zeitschrift der Savigny-Stiftung für Rechtsgeschichte*, Kanonistische Abteilung lxxv, cvi (1989) 228–69.

——, *Konfessionsbildung und Ratsregiment in der katholischen Reichsstadt Überlingen (1500–1618) im Kontext der Reformationsgeschichte der oberschwäbischen Reichsstädte* (Stuttgart 1990).

Endres, Rudolf, *Adelige Lebensformen in Franken zur Zeit des Bauernkrieges* (Würzburg, 1974).

——, 'Die wirtschaftlichen Grundlagen des niederen Adels in der frühen Neuzeit', *Jahrbuch für fränkische Landesforschung*, xxxvi (1976), 215–37.

——, 'Der Kayserliche neunjährige Bund vom Jahr 1535 bis 1544', in Peter Blickle (ed.), *Bauer, Reich und Reformation* (Stuttgart, 1982), 85–103.

——, 'Der Landsberger Bund (1556–1598)', Pankraz Fried (ed.), *Festschrift für Andreas Kraus zum 60. Geburtstag* (Kallmünz, 1982), 197–212.

——, 'Thüringen', in Horst Buszello and Rudolf Endres (eds), *Der deutsche Bauernkrieg* (Paderborn 1984), 154–76.

——, 'Ursachen', in Horst Buszello and Rudolf Endres (eds), *Der deutsche Bauernkrieg* (Paderborn 1984), 217–53.

——, *Adel in der frühen Neuzeit* (Munich 1993).

Engels, Heinz, *Die Sprachgesellschaften des 17. Jahrhunderts* (Giessen, 1983).

Erler, Adalbert and Ekkehard Kaufmann (eds), *Handwörterbuch zur Deutschen Rechtsgeschichte* (Berlin, 1964–).

Eulenburg, Franz, *Die Frequenz der Deutschen Universitäten von ihrer Gründung bis zur Gegenwart* (Leipzig, 1904).

Evans, R. J. W., *Rudolf II and his world: A study in intellectual history, 1576–1612* (Oxford, 1973).

——, *The Wechel presses: Humanism and Calvinism in Central Europe 1572–1627* (Oxford, 1975).

——, *The making of the Habsburg monarchy 1550–1700: An interpretation* (Oxford, 1979).

——, 'Rantzau and Welser: Aspects of later German humanism', *History of European Ideas*, v (1984), 257–72.

——, 'Culture and anarchy in the Empire, 1540–1680', *Central European History*, xviii (1985), 14–30.

Eymelt, Friedrich, *Die Rheinische Einung des Jahres 1532 in der Reichs- und Landesgeschichte* (Bonn, 1967).

Fabian, Ekkehart, *Die Entstehung des Schmalkaldischen Bundes und seiner Verfassung 1524/29–1531/35*, 2nd edn (Tübingen, 1962).

Faulenbach, Bernd, *Ideologie des deutschen Weges: Die deutsche Geschichte in der Historiographie zwischen Kaiserreich und Nationalsozialismus* (Munich, 1980).

Fehler, Timothy G., *Poor relief and Protestantism: The evolution of social welfare in sixteenth-century Emden* (Aldershot, 1999).

Fellner, Fritz, 'Reichsgeschichte und Reichsidee als Problem der österreichischen Historiographie', in Wilhelm Braunder and Lothar Höbelt (eds), *Sacrum Imperium: Das Reich und Österreich 996–1806* (Vienna, 1996), 361–74.

Fenlon, Dermot, *Heresy and obedience in Tridentine Italy: Cardinal Pole and the Counter Reformation* (Cambridge, 1972).

Fichtenau, Heinrich, *Die Lehrbücher Maximilians I. und die Anfänge der Frakturschrift* (Hamburg, 1961).

Fichtner, Paula Sutter, *Ferdinand I of Austria: The politics of dynasticism in the age of Reformation* (New York, 1982).

——, *Protestantism and primogeniture in early modern Germany* (New Haven and London, 1989).

——, *Emperor Maximilian II* (New Haven, CT and London, 2001).

Finkel, Caroline, *The administration of warfare: The Ottoman military campaigns in Hungary, 1593–1606* (Vienna, 1988).

Fischer-Galati, Stephen, *Ottoman imperialism and German Protestantism 1521–1555* (Cambridge, MA, 1959).

Flood, John L., *Poets laureate in the Holy Roman Empire: A bio-bibliographical handbook*, 4 vols (Berlin and New York), 2006.

Forster, Leonard, 'Deutsche und europaische Barockliteratur', *Wolfenbutteler Beitrage*, ii (1973), 64–84.

—— 'Harsdörffer's Canon of German Baroque', in Hinrich Siefken and Alan Robinson (eds), *Erfahrung und Überlieferung* (Cardiff, 1974), 32–41.

Forster, Marc R., *Catholic revival in the age of the Baroque: Religious identity in southwest Germany, 1550–1750* (Cambridge, 2001).

——, *Catholic Germany from the Reformation to the Enlightenment* (Houndmills, 2007).

François, Étienne, *Die unsichtbare Grenze: Protestanten und Katholiken in Augsburg 1648–1806* (Sigmaringen, 1991).

Franz, Günther, *Geschichte des deutschen Bauernstandes: Vom frühen Mittelalter bis zum 19. Jahrhundert*, 2nd edn (Stuttgart, 1976).

——, *Der deutsche Bauernkrieg*, 11th edn (Darmstadt, 1977).

——, *Der Dreißigjährige Krieg und das deutsche Volk*, 4th edn (Stuttgart, 1979).

Frauenholz, Eugen von, Walter Elze, and Paul Schmidthenner, *Entwicklungsgeschichte des deutschen Heerwesens*, 3 vols (Munich, 1935–41).

Fricke, Thomas, *Zigeuner im Zeitalter des Absolutismus: Bilanz einer einseitigen Überlieferung: Eine sozialgeschichtliche Untersuchung anhand südwestdeutscher Quellen* (Pfaffenweiler, 1996).

Friedeburg, Robert von, '"Kommunalismus" und "Republikanismus" in der frühen Neuzeit: Überlegungen zur politischen Mobilisierung sozial differenzierter ländlicher Gemeinden unter agrar- und sozialgeschichtlichem Blickwinkel', *Zeitschrift für historische Forschung*, xxi (1994), 65–91.

——, 'Welche Wegscheide in die Neuzeit? Widerstandsrecht, "Gemeiner Mann" und konfessioneller Landespatriotismus zwischen "Münster" und "Magdeburg"', *Historische Zeitschrift*, cclxx (2000), 561–616.

——, *Lebenswelt und Kultur der unterständischen Schichten in der Frühen Neuzeit* (Munich, 2002).

——, *Self-defence and religious strife in early modern Europe: England and Germany, 1530–1680* (Aldershot, 2002).

Friedrich, Wolfgang, *Territorialfürst und Reichsjustiz: Recht und Politik im Kontext der hessischen Reformationsprozesse am Reichskammergericht* (Tübingen, 2008).

Friedrichs, Christopher R., 'German town revolts and the seventeenth-century crisis', *Renaissance and Modern Studies*, xxvi (1982) 27–51.

——, 'Politics or pogrom? The Fettmilch uprising in German and Jewish history', *Central European History*, xix (1986), 186–228.

Frisch, Michael, *Das Restitutionsedikt Kaiser Ferdinands II. vom 6. März 1629: Eine rechtsgeschichtliche Untersuchung* (Tübingen, 1992).

Frost, Robert I., *The northern wars: War, state and society in northeastern Europe, 1558–1721* (Harlow, 2000).

Fuchs, Walther P., 'Das Zeitalter der Reformation', in Herbert Grundmann (ed.), *Gebhardt: Handbuch der deutschen Geschichte, Band 2*, 9th edn (Stuttgart, 1970).

Gabel, Helmut, 'Beobachtungen zur territorialen Inanspruchnahme des Reichskammergerichts im Bereich des Niederrheinisch-Westfälischen Kreises', in Bernhard Diestelkamp (ed.), *Das Reichskammergericht in der deutschen Geschichte: Stand der Forschung, Forschungsperspektiven* (Cologne, 1990), 143–72.

——, '"Daß ihr künftig von aller Widersetzlichkeit, Aufruhr und Zusammenrottierung gänzlich abstehet": Deutsche Untertanen und das Reichskammergericht', in Ingrid Scheurmann (ed.), *Frieden durch Recht: Das Reichskammergericht von 1495 bis 1806* (Mainz, 1994), 273–80.

—— and Winfried Schulze, 'Folgen und Wirkungen', in Horst Buszello and Rudolf Endres (eds), *Der deutsche Bauernkrieg* (Paderborn 1984), 322–49.

Gäbler, Ulrich, *Huldrych Zwingli: Eine Einführung in sein Leben und sein Werk* (Munich, 1983).

Gantet, Claire, *La paix de Westphalie (1648): Une histoire sociale XVIIe-XVIIIe siècles* (Paris, 2001).

Garber, Jörn, 'Vom universalen zum endogenen Nationalismus: Die Idee der Nation im deutschen Spätmittelalter und in der frühen Neuzeit', in H. Scheuer (ed.), *Dichter und ihre Nation* (Frankfurt am Main, 1993), 16–37.

Gatz, Erwin, *Die Bischöfe des Heiligen Römischen Reiches 1648 bis 1803: Ein biographisches Lexikon* (Berlin, 1990).

——, *Die Bischöfe des Heiligen Römischen Reiches 1448 bis 1648: Ein biographisches Lexikon* (Berlin, 1996).

——, Rainald Becker, Clemens Brodkorb, Helmut Flachenecker, and Karsten Bremer (eds), *Atlas zur Kirche in Geschichte und Gegenwart: Heiliges Römisches Reich, deutschsprachige Länder* (Regensburg, 2009).

Gebhardt, Bruno, *Die Gravamina der deutschen Nation gegen den römischen Hof: Ein Beitrag zur Vorgeschichte der Reformation*, 2nd edn (Breslau, 1895).

Gerteis, Klaus, *Die deutschen Städte in der Frühen Neuzeit: Zur Vorgeschichte der 'bürgerlichen Welt'* (Darmstadt, 1986).

Geschichte des Pietismus, ed. Martin Brecht et al., 4 vols (Göttingen, 1993–2004).

Giesecke, Michael, *Der Buchdruck in der frühen Neuzeit: Eine historische Fallstudie über die Durchsetzung neuer Informations- und Kommunikationstechnologien* (Frankfurt am Main, 1991).

Gilly, Carlos, 'Der "Löwe von Mitternacht", Der "Adler" und der "Endchrist": Die politische, religiöse und chiliastische Publizistik in den Flugschriften, illustrierten Flugblättern und Volksliedern des Dreissigjährigen Krieges', in *Rosenkreuz als europäisches Phänomen im 17. Jahrhundert* (Amsterdam, 2002), 234–68.

——, 'Die Rosenkreuzer als europäisches Phänomen im 17. Jahrhundert und die verschlungenen Pfade der Forschung', in *Rosenkreuz als europäisches Phänomen im 17. Jahrhundert* (Amsterdam, 2002), 19–58.

Gmür, Rudolf, 'Städte als Landesherren vom 16. bis zum 18. Jahrhundert', in Karl Kroeschell (ed.), *Festschrift für Hans Thieme zu seinem 80. Geburtstag* (Sigmaringen, 1986), 177–97.

Gnant, Christoph, 'Die "Österreichische Reichsgeschichte" und ihre Sicht auf das Heilige Römische Reich', Harm Klueting (ed.), *Das Reich und seine Territorialstaaten im 17. und 18. Jahrhundert: Aspekte des Mit-, Neben- und Gegeneinander* (Münster, 2004), 11–22.

Goetze, Sigmund, *Die Politik des schwedischen Reichskanzlers Axel Oxenstierna gegenüber Kaiser und Reich* (Kiel, 1971).

Goffman, Daniel, *The Ottoman empire and early modern Europe* (Cambridge, 2002).

Goldfriedrich, Johann Adolf, *Geschichte des deutschen Buchhandels*, 5 vols (Leipzig, 1886–1923).

Gordon, Bruce, *The Swiss Reformation* (Manchester 2002).

Görner, Regina, *Raubritter: Untersuchungen zur Lage des spätmittelalterlichen Niederadels, besonders im südlichen Westfalen* (Münster, 1987).

Gotthard, Axel, *Konfession und Staatsräson: Die Außenpolitik Württembergs unter Herzog Johann Friedrich (1608–1628)* (Stuttgart, 1992).

——, 'Protestantische "Union" und Katholische "Liga": Subsidiäre Strukturelemente oder Alternativentwürfe?', in Volker Press (ed.), *Alternativen zur Reichsverfassung in der Frühen Neuzeit?* (Munich, 1995), 81–112.

——, *Säulen des Reiches: Die Kurfürsten im frühneuzeitlichen Reichsverband*, 2 vols (Husum, 1999).

——, 'Zwischen Luthertum und Calvinismus (1598–1640)', in Frank-Lothar Kroll (ed.), *Preußens Herrscher: Von den ersten Hohenzollern bis Wilhelm II.*, 2nd edn (Munich, 2000), 74–94.

——, '"Wer sich salviren könd, solts thun": Warum der deutsche Protestantismus in der Zeit der konfessionellen Polarisierung zu keiner gemeinsamen Politik fand', *Historisches Jahrbuch*, cxxi (2001), 64–96.

——, '1591: Zäsur der sächsischen und deutschen Geschichte', *Neues Archiv für sächsische Geschichte*, lxxi (2001), 275–84.

——, *Der Augsburger Religionsfrieden* (Münster, 2004).

——, *Das Alte Reich 1495–1806*, 3rd edn (Darmstadt, 2006).

Göttmann, Frank, 'Zur Entstehung des Landsberger Bundes im Kontext der Reichs-, Verfassungs-, und regionalen Territorialpolitik des 16. Jahrhunderts', *Zeitschrift für historische Forschung*, xix (1992), 415–44.

Grabner, Adolph, *Zur Geschichte des zweiten Nürnberger Reichsregiments 1521–23* (Berlin, 1903).

Gräter, Carlheinz, *Ulrich von Hutten: Ein Lebensbild* (Stuttgart, 1988).

Greyerz, Kaspar von, *Religion und Kultur: Europa 1500–1800* (Darmstadt, 2000).

Grillmeyer, Siegfried, *Habsburgs Diener in Post und Politik: Das 'Haus' Thurn und Taxis zwischen 1745 und 1867* (Mainz, 2005).

Gross, Hanns, *Empire and sovereignty: A history of the public law literature in the Holy Roman Empire, 1599–1804* (Chicago, MI, 1973).

Gross, Lothar, *Die Geschichte der deutschen Reichshofkanzlei von 1559 bis 1806* (Vienna, 1933).

Großmann, G. Ulrich, *Renaissance entlang der Weser: Kunst und Kultur in Nordwestdeutschland zwischen Reformation und Dreißigjährigem Krieg* (Cologne, 1989).

Grotefend, Hermann, *Taschenbuch der Zeitrechnung des deutschen Mittelalters und der Neuzeit*, 12th edn (Hanover, 1982).

Gschließer, Oswald von, *Der Reichshofrat: Bedeutung und Verfassung, Schicksal und Besetzung einer obersten Reichsbehörde von 1559–1806* (Vienna, 1942).

Gundermann, Iselin, 'Die Anfänge der Albertus-Universität zu Königsberg', in Hans Rothe (ed.), *Die Albertus-Universität zu Königsberg: Höhepunkte und Bedeutung; Vorträge aus Anlaß der 450. Wiederkehr ihrer Gründung* (Bonn, 1996), 23–44.

Guthrie, William P., *Battles of the Thirty Years War: From the White Mountain to Nördlingen, 1618–1635* (Westport, CT, 2002).

——, *The later Thirty Years War: From the battle of Wittstock to the Treaty of Westphalia* (Westport, CT, 2003).

Haberkern, Eugen and Jospeh Friedrich Wallach, *Hilfswörterbuch für Historiker*, 8th edn, 2 vols (Tübingen, 1995).

Häberlein, Mark, 'Konfessionelle Grenzen, religiöse Minderheiten und Herrschaftspraxis in süddeutschen Städten und Territorien in der Frühen Neuzeit', in Ronald G. Asch and Dagmar Freist (eds), *Staatsbildungrals uts Kultureller Prozess: Strukturwandel und Legitimation von Herrschaft in der Frühen Neuzeit* (Cologne, 2005), 151–90.

——, *Die Fugger: Geschichte einer Augsburger Familie (1367–1650)* (Stuttgart, 2006).

——, 'Jakob Fugger und die Kaiserwahl Karls V. 1519', in Johannes Burkhardt (ed.), *Die Fugger und das Reich: Eine neue Forschungsperspektive zum 500jährigen Jubiläum der ersten Fuggerherrschaft Kirchberg-Weißenhorn* (Augsburg, 2008), 65–81.

Halkin, Léon-E., *Erasmus. A critical biography*, transl. John Tonkin (Oxford, 1993).

Hamann, Manfred, *Das staatliche Werden Mecklenburgs* (Cologne and Graz, 1962).

Hamm, Bernd, *Bürgertum und Glaube: Konturen der städtischen Reformation* (Göttingen, 1998).

——, 'Einheit und Vielfalt der Reformation—oder was die Reformation zur Reformation machte', in Bernd Hamm, Bernd Moeller and Dorothea Wendebourg (eds), *Reformationstheorien: Eine kirchenhistorischer Disput über Einheit und Vielfalt der Reformation* (Göttingen, 1995), 57–127.

Hammerstein, Notker, 'Samuel Pufendorf', in Michael Stolleis (ed.), *Staatsdenker im 17. und 18. Jahrhundert: Reichspublizistik, Politik, Naturrecht*, 2nd edn (Frankfurt am Main, 1987), 172–96.

—— (ed.), *Handbuch der deutschen Bildungsgeschichte, Band 1: 15. bis 17. Jahrhundert* (Munich, 1996).

——, *Bildung und Wissenschaft vom 15. bis zum 17. Jahrhundert* (Munich, 2003).

—— and Ulrich Hermann (eds), *Handbuch der deutschen Bildungsgeschichte, Band 2: 18. Jahrhundert* (Munich, 2005).

Hansen, Josef, 'Patriotismus und Nationalethos in den Flugschriften und Friedensspielen des Dreißigjährigen Krieges' (Dissertation: Cologne, 1964).

Hardtwig, Wolfgang, *Genossenschaft, Sekte, Verein in Deutschland, Band 1: Vom Spätmittelalter bis zur Französischen Revolution* (Munich, 1997).

Harrington, Joel F., *Reordering marriage and society in Reformation Germany* (Cambridge, 1995).

Härter, Karl, 'Entwicklung und Funktion der Policeygesetzgebung des Heiligen Römischen Reiches Deutscher Nation im 16. Jahrhundert', *Ius commune. Zeitschrift für Europäische Rechtsgeschichte*, xx (1993), 61–141.

——, 'Kriminalisierung, Verfolgung und Überlebenspraxis der "Zigeuner" im frühneuzeitlichen Mitteleuropa', in Yaron Matras (ed.), *Sinti, Roma, Gypsies: Sprache, Geschichte, Gegenwart* (Berlin, 2003), 41–81.

Hartmann, Peter Claus, *Der Bayerische Reichskreis (1500 bis 1803): Strukturen, Geschichte und Bedeutung im Rahmen der Kreisverfassung und der allgemeinen institutionellen Entwicklung des Heiligen Römischen Reiches* (Berlin, 1997).

——, 'Der Augsburger Reichstag von 1555: Ein entscheidender Meilenstein für die Kompetenzerweiterung der Reichskreise', *Zeitschrift des Historischen Vereins für Schwaben*, xcviii (2005), 29–35.

——, 'Das Heilige Römische Reich, ein föderalistisches Staatsgebilde mit politischer, kultureller und religiöser Vielfalt', in *idem* (ed.), *Das Heilige Römische Reich und sein Ende 1806: Zäsur in der deutschen und europäischen Geschichte* (Regensburg, 2006), 11–22.

Hashagen, Justus, *Staat und Kirche vor der Reformation: Eine Untersuchung der vorreformatorischen Bedeutung des Laieneinflusses in der Kirche* (Essen, 1931).

Haug-Moritz, Gabriele, 'Reich und Konfessionsdissens im Reformationszeitalter: Über-legungen zur Reichskonfessionspolitik Landgraf Philipps des Großmütigen von Hessen', *Hessisches Jahrbuch für Landesgeschichte, xlvi* (1996), 137–60.

——, *Der Schmalkaldische Bund 1530–1541/42: Eine Studie zu den genossenschaftlichen Strukturelementen der politischen Ordnung des Heiligen Römischen Reiches Deutscher Nation* (Leinfelden-Echterdingen, 2002).

Headley, John M., 'The Habsburg world empire and the revival of Ghibellinism', *Medieval and Renaissance Studies*, vii (1975), 93–127.

——, 'Germany, the empire and *monarchia* in the thought and policy of Gattinara', in Heinrich Lutz (ed.), *Das römisch-deutsche Reich im politischen System Karls V.* (Munich, 1982), 15–33.

Heckel, Martin, *Deutschland im konfessionellen Zeitalter* (Göttingen, 1983).

——, 'Konfessionalisierung in Koexistenznöten: Zum Augsburger Religionsfrieden, Dreißigjährigen Krieg und Westfälischen Frieden in neuerer Sicht', *Historische Zeitschrift*, cclxxx (2005), 647–90.

Heger, Günther, *Johann Eberlin von Günzburg und seine Vorstellungen über eine Reform in Reich und Kirche* (Berlin, 1985).

Heinrich, Gerd, 'Der Adel in Brandenburg-Preußen', in Hellmuth Rössler (ed.), *Deutscher Adel 1555–1740* (Darmstadt, 1965), 259–314.

Hepp, Frieder, '"Der Pfaltz Haupt flecken": Heidelbergum 1600', in Peter Wolf (ed.), *Der Winterkönig Friedrich V.: Der letzte Kurfürst aus der oberen Pfalz; Amberg, Heidelberg, Prag, Den Haag* (Augsburg, 2003), 75–82.

Herbers, Klaus and Helmut Neuhaus, *Das Heilige Römische Reich: Schauplätze einer tausend-jährigen Geschichte* (Cologne, Weimar, and Vienna, 2005).

Hermelink, Heinrich, *Reformation und Gegenreformation* (Tübingen, 1911).

Hermkes, Wolfgang, *Das Reichsvikariat in Deutschland: Reichsvikare nach dem Tode des Kaisers von der Goldenen Bulle bis zum Ende des Reiches* (Karlsruhe, 1968).

Heutger, Nicolaus, *Bursfelde und seine Reformklöster*, 2nd edn (Hildesheim, 1975).

Hippel, Wolfgang von, 'Bevölkerung und Wirtschaft im Zeitalter des Dreißigjährigen Krieges: Das Beispiel Württemberg', *Zeitschrift für Historische Forschung*, iv (1978), 413–48.

——, *Armut, Unterschichten, Randgruppen in der frühen Neuzeit* (Munich, 1995).

Hirsch, Rudolf, *Printing, selling and reading 1450–1550* (Wiesbaden, 1967).

Hirschi, Caspar, *Wettkampf der Nationen: Konstruktionen einer deutschen Ehrgemeinschaft an der Wende vom Mittelalter zur Neuzeit* (Göttingen, 2005).

Hitchcock, William R., *The background to the Knights' Revolt 1522–1523* (Berkeley and Los Angeles, 1958).

Höbelt, Lothar, *Ferdinand III. (1608–1657): Friedenskaiser wider Willen* (Graz, 2008).

Hoberg, Hermann, 'Die Einnahmen der Apostolischen Kammer am Vorabend der Glau-bensspaltung', in Erwin Gatz (ed.), *Hundert Jahre Deutsches Priesterkolleg bei Campo Santo Teutonico 1876–1976* (Rome, 1977), 69–85.

Hochedlinger, Michael, 'Die französisch-osmanische "Freundschaft" 1525–1792: Element antihabsburgischer Politik, Gleichgewichtsinstrument, Prestigeunternehmung: Aufriß eines Problems', *Mitteilungen des Instituts für Österreichische Geschichtsforschung*, xii (1994), 108–64.

Hofmann, Hanns Hubert (ed.), *Quellen zum Verfassungsorganismus des Heiligen Römischen Reiches Deutscher Nation 1494–1815* (Darmstadt, 1976).

Hohensee, Ulrike et al. (eds), *Die Goldene Bulle: Politik—Wahrnehmung—Rezeption*, 2 vols (Berlin, 2009).

Holenstein, André, *Bauern zwischen Bauernkrieg und Dreissigjährigem Krieg* (Munich, 1996).

Holzhey, Helmut, Wilhelm Schmidt-Biggemann, and Vilem Mudroch (eds), *Die Philosophie des 17. Jahrhunderts: Das Heilige Römische Reich Deutscher Nation, Nord- und Ostmittel-Europa*, 2 vols (Basle 2001).

Honemann, Volker, 'Erasmus von Rotterdam und Ulrich von Hutten', in Johannes Schilling und Ernst Giese (eds), *Ulrich von Hutten und seine Zeit: Schlüchterner Vorträge zu seinem 500. Geburtstag* (Kassel, 1988), 61–86.

Hotson, Howard, *Johann Heinrich Alsted, 1588–1638: Between Renaissance, Reformation, and universal reform* (Oxford, 2000).

——, *Paradise postponed: Johann Heinrich Alsted and the birth of Calvinist millenarianism* (Dordrecht, 2000).

——, *Commonplace learning: Ramism and its German ramifications, 1543–1630* (Oxford, 2007)

Howard, Michael, *War in European history* (Oxford, 1976).

Hoyer, Siegfried, 'Arms and Military Organisation in the German Peasant War', in Bob Scribner and Gerhard Benecke (eds), *The German Peasant War 1525: New viewpoints* (London, 1979), 98–108.

——, 'The rights and duties of resistance in the *Pamphlet To the Assembly of the Common Peasantry* (1525)', in Bob Scribner and Gerhard Benecke (eds), *The German Peasant War 1525: New Viewpoints* (London, 1979), 123–43.

——, 'Die Tiroler Landesordnung des Michael Gaismair—Überlieferung und zeitgenössische Einflüsse', in Max Steinmetz (ed.), *Die frühbürgerliche Revolution in Deutschland* (Berlin, 1985), 288–302.

Hubatsch, Walther, 'Die inneren Voraussetzungen der Säkularisation des deutschen Ordensstaates in Preußen', *Archiv für Reformationsgeschichte*, xliii (1952), 145–72.

Hürten, Heinz, 'Die Mainzer Akzeptation von 1439', *Archiv für mittelrheinische Kirchengeschichte*, xi (1959), 42–75.

Hye, Franz Heinz, 'Der Doppeladler als Symbol für Kaiser und Reich', *Mitteilungen des Instituts für Österreichische Geschichtsforschung*, lxxxi (1973), 63–106.

Iorge, Nicolae, *Geschichte des Osmanischen Reiches*, 5 vols (Gotha, 1908–13).

Isenmann, Eberhard, 'Reichsfinanzen und Reichssteuern im 15. Jahrhundert', *Zeitschrift für historische Forschung*, vii (1980), 1–76, 129–218.

——, 'Kaiser, Reich und deutsche Nation am Ausgang des 15. Jahrhunderts', in Joachim Ehlers (ed.), *Ansätze und Diskontinuität deutscher Nationsbildung im Mittelalter* (Sigmaringen, 1989), 145–246.

——, 'Die Reichsstadt in der Frühen Neuzeit', in Georg Mölich (ed.), *Köln als Kommunikationszentrum: Studien zur frühneuzeitlichen Stadtgeschichte* (Cologne, 2000), 39–87.

Israel, Jonathan I., *The Dutch Republic and the Hispanic world, 1606–1661* (Oxford, 1982).

——, *The Dutch Republic: Its rise, greatness and fall, 1476–1806* (Oxford, 1995).

Jäger, Berthold, *Das geistliche Fürstentum Fulda in der Frühen Neuzeit: Landesherrschaft, Landstände und fürstliche Verwaltung; Ein Beitrag zur Verfassungs- und Verwaltungsgeschichte kleiner Territorien des Alten Reiches* (Marburg, 1986).

Janssen, Jonannes, *Geschichte des deutschen Volkes seit dem Ausgang des Mittelalters*, 5th edn, 8 vols (Freiburg im Breisgau, 1890–4).

Jedin, Hubert, Kenneth Scott Latourette, and Jochen Martin (eds), *Atlas zur kirchengeschichte: Die christlichen Kirchen in Geschichte und Gegenwart* (3rd rev. edn, Freiburg, 2004).

Jendorff, Alexander, 'Der Mainzer Hofmeister Hartmut (XIII.) von Kronberg (1517–1591): Kurfürstlicher Favorit oder Kreatur des erzstiftischen Politiksystems?', in

Michael Kaiser and Andreas Pečar (eds), *Der zweite Mann im Staat: Oberste Amtsträger und Favoriten im Umkreis der Reichsfürsten in der Frühen Neuzeit* (Berlin, 2003), 39–57.

Jeserich, Kurt G. A., Hans Pohl, and Georg Christoph von Unruh (eds). *Deutsche Verwaltungsgeschichte, Band 1: Vom Spätmittelalter bis zum Ende des Reiches* (Stuttgart, 1983).

Joachimsen, Paul, *Die Reformation als Epoche der deutschen Geschichte*, ed. Otto Schottenloher (Munich, 1951).

Johnston Gordon, Rona, 'Melchior Khlesl und der konfessionelle Hintergrund der kaiserlichen Politik im Reich nach 1610', in Friedrich Beiderbeck (ed.), *Dimensionen der europäischen Außenpolitik zur Zeit der Wende vom 16. zum 17. Jahrhundert* (Berlin, 2003), 199–222.

Jones, William Jervis, *Sprachhelden und Sprachverderber: Dokumente zur Erforschung des Fremdwortpurismus im Deutschen (1478–1750)* (Berlin, 1995).

Jorio, Marco (ed.), *Historisches Lexikon der Schweiz* (Basel, 2002–).

Jörn, Nils, 'Beobachtungen zur Steuerzahlung der Territorien des südlichen Ostseeraumes in der Frühen Neuzeit', in Nils Jörn (ed.), *Die Integration des südlichen Ostseeraumes in das Alte Reich* (Cologne, 2000), 312–91.

Jütte, Robert, *Obrigkeitliche Armenfürsorge in deutschen Reichsstädten der frühen Neuzeit: Städtisches Armenwesen in Frankfurt am Main und Köln* (Cologne, 1984).

——, *Poverty and deviance in early modern Europe* (Cambridge, 1994).

——, 'Poverty and poor relief', in Sheilagh Ogilvie (ed.), *Germany: A new social and economic history*, Vol. 2: *1630–1800* (London, 1996), 377–404.

Kalkoff, Paul, *Ulrich von Hutten und die Reformation: Eine kritische Geschichte seiner wichtigsten Lebenszeit und der Entscheidungsjahre der Reformation (1517–1523)* (Leipzig, 1920).

Kampmann, Christoph, *Europa und das Reich im Dreißigjährigen Krieg: Geschichte eines europäischen Konflikts* (Stuttgart, 2008).

Kapp, Friedrich, *Geschichte des deutschen Buchhandels bis in das siebzehnte Jahrhundert* (Leipzig, 1886).

Kapr, Albert, *Fraktur: Form und Geschichte der gebrochenen Schriften* (Mainz, 1993).

Karant-Nunn, Susan C., *Luther's pastors: The Reformation in the Ernestine countryside* (Philadelphia, PA, 1979).

Kellenbenz, Hermann, *Unternehmerkräfte im Hamburger Portugal- und Spanienhandel 1590–1625* (Hamburg, 1954).

——, 'Das Römisch-Deutsche Reich im Rahmen der wirtschafts- und finanzpolitischen Erwägungen Karls V. im Spannungsfeld imperialer und dynastischer Interessen', in Heinrich Lutz (ed.), *Das römisch-deutsche Reich im politischen System Karl. V.* (Munich and Vienna, 1982), 35–54.

Kessel, Jürgen, *Spanien und die geistlichen Kurstaaten am Rhein während der Regierungszeit der Infantin Isabella (1621–1633)* (Frankfurt am Main, 1979).

Keunecke, Hans-Otto, 'Maximilian von Bayern und die Entführung der Bibliotheca Palatina nach Rom', *Archiv für Geschichte des Buchwesens*, xix (1978), 1401–46.

Kiesel, Helmuth and Paul Münch, *Gesellschaft und Literatur im 18. Jahrhundert: Voraussetzungen und Entstehung des literarischen Markts in Deutschland* (Munich, 1977).

Killy, Walther (ed.), *Literatur-Lexikon: Autoren und Werke deutscher Sprache*, 15 vols (Gütersloh and Munich, 1988–93).

—— and Rudolph Vierhaus (eds), *Deutsche Biographische Enzyklopädie* 13 vols in 15 (Darmstadt, 1995–2003).

Kindelberger, Charles P., 'The economic crisis 1619 to 1623', *Journal of Economic History*, li (1991), 149–75.

Kirchhoff, Albrecht, 'Die kurf. sächsische Bücher-Commission in Leipzig', *Archiv für Geschichte des Deutschen Buchhandels*, ix (1884), 46–176.

Kirschberger, Timo, 'Die Vorbereitung zu Bewahrung und Sicherstellung der Bibliotheca Palatina in den Jahren 1621 bis 1623', *Bibliothek und Wissenschaft*, xlii (2009), 73–105.

Klaassen, Walter, *Michael Gaismair: Revolutionary and reformer* (Leiden, 1978).

Klein, Ernst, *Geschichte der öffentlichen Finanzen in Deutschland (1500–1870)* (Wiesbaden, 1974).

Klein, Thomas, 'Verpaßte Staatsbildung? Die Wettinischen Landesteilungen im Spätmittelalter und früher Neuzeit', in Johannes Kunisch (ed.), *Der dynastische Fürstenstaat: Zur Bedeutung der Sukzessionsordnungen für die Entstehung des frühmodernen Staates*, (Berlin, 1982), 89–114.

Kleinheyer, Gerd, *Die kaiserlichen Wahlkapitulationen: Geschichte, Wesen, Funktion* (Karlsruhe, 1968).

——, 'Die Abdankung des Kaisers', in Gerhard Köbler (ed.), *Wege europäischer Rechtsgeschichte* (Frankfurt am Main, 1987), 124–44.

Klueting, Harm, *Das Reich und Österreich 1648–1740* (Münster 1999).

Knott, Peter, '"Sonderbotschafter" Johann von Weeze: Administrator des Stiftlands von 1537–1548', in Hans Bäte (ed.), *Dachan, Wolf und Dinostein: Beiträge zur Geschichte unserer Heimat; Zwischen Fichtelgebirge und Böhmerwald* (Pressath, 1998), 180–205.

Kober, Ulrich, 'Der Favorit als "Factotum": Graf Adam von Schwarzenberg als Oberkämmerer und Direktor des Geheimen Rates unter Kurfürst Georg Wilhelm von Brandenburg', in Michael Kaiser and Andreas Pečar (eds), *Der zweite Mann im Staat: Oberste Amtsträger und Favoriten im Umkreis der Reichsfürsten in der Frühen Neuzeit* (Berlin, 2003), 231–52.

Köbler, Gerhard, *Historisches Lexikon der deutschen Länder: Die deutschen Territorien vom Mittelalter bis zur Gegenwart*, 7th edn (Munich, 2007).

Koch, Rainer, '1612–1616: Der Fettmilchaufstand: Sozialer Sprengstoff in der Bürgerschaft', *Archiv für Frankfurts Geschichte und Kunst*, lxiii (1997), 59–79.

Koenigsberger, Helmut G. (1978), 'Monarchies and parliament in early modern Europe: Dominium Regale or Dominium Politicum et Regale', *Theory and Society*, v (1978), 191–217.

——, 'The empire of Charles V in Europe', in G. R. Elton (ed.), *The new Cambridge modern history*, Vol. 2: *The Reformation 1520–1559*, 2nd edn (Cambridge, 1990), 339–76.

Kohl, Wilhelm, 'Die Windesheimer Kongregation', in Kaspar Elm (ed.), *Reformbemühungen und Observanzbestrebungen im spätmittelalterlichen Ordenswesen* (Berlin, 1989), 83–106.

Kohler, Alfred, *Antihabsburgische Politik in der Epoche Karls V.: Die reichsständische Opposition gegen die Wahl Ferdinands I. zum römischen König und gegen die Anerkennung seines Königstums (1524–1534)* (Göttingen, 1982).

——, 'Die innerdeutsche und die außerdeutsche Opposition gegen das politische System Karls V.', in Heinrich Lutz (ed.), *Das römisch-deutsche Reich im politischen System Karls V.* (Munich and Vienna, 1982), 107–27.

——, (ed.), *Quellen zur Geschichte Karls V.* (Darmstadt, 1990).

——, *Das Reich im Kampf um die Hegemonie in Europa 1521–1648* (Munich, 1990).

Kohler, Alfred, 'Die dynastische Politik Maximilians I.', in A. Kohler and F. Edelmeyer (eds), *Hispania—Austria: Die katholischen Könige, Maximilian und die Anfänge der Casa de Austria in Spanien* (Munich, 1993), 29–37.

——, *Ferdinand I. 1503–1564: Fürst, König und Kaiser* (Munich, 2003).

Kohler, Alfred, 'Von Passau nach Augsburg: Zur politischen Emanzipation Ferdinands I. in den Jahren 1552 bis 1555', in Karlheinz Blaschke (ed.), *Moritz von Sachsen: Ein Fürst der Reformationszeit zwischen Territorium und Reich* (Leipzig and Stuttgart, 2007), 42–56.

——, *Expansion und Hegemonie: Internationale Beziehungen 1450–1559* (Paderborn, 2008).

Köhler, Hans-Joachim, 'Erste Schritte zu einem Meinungsprofil der frühen Reformationszeit', in Volker Press and Dieter Stievermann (eds), *Martin Luther: Probleme seiner Zeit* (Stuttgart, 1986) 244–81.

Kohnle, Armin, *Reichstag und Reformation: Kaiserliche und ständische Religionspolitik von den Anfängen der Causa Lutheri bis zum Nürnberger Religionsfrieden* (Gütersloh, 2001).

Koken, Hermann, *Die Braunschweiger Landstände um die Wende des 16. Jahrhunderts unter den Herzögen Julius und Heinrich Julius 1568–1613 im Herzogtum Braunschweig-Wolfenbüttel* (Brunswick, 1914).

Kolb, R., 'The theologians and the peasants: Conservative evangelical reactions to the Peasants Revolt', *Archiv für Reformationsgeschichte*, lxix (1978), 103–30.

Koller, Alexander, 'Der Kaiserhof am Beginn der Regierung Rudolfs II. in den Berichten der Nuntien', in Richard Bösel (ed.), *Kaiserhof, Papsthof (16.–18. Jahrhundert)* (Vienna, 2006), 13–24.

Koller, Heinrich, *Kaiser Friedrich III.* (Darmstadt, 2005).

König, Werner, *dtv-Atlas zur deutschen Sprache* (Munich, 1978).

Kordes, Uwe, *Wolfgang Ratke (Ratichius, 1571–1635): Gesellschaft, Religiosität und Gelehrsamkeit im frühen 17. Jahrhundert* (Heidelberg, 1999).

Korell, Günter, *Jürgen Wullenwever: Sein sozial-politisches Wirken in Lübeck und der Kampf mit den erstarkenden Mächten Nordeuropas* (Weimar, 1980).

Körner, Martin, 'Steuern und Abgaben in Theorie und Praxis im Mittelalter und in der frühen Neuzeit', in Eckhart Schremmer (ed.), *Steuern, Abgaben und Dienste vom Mittelalter bis zur Gegenwart* (Stuttgart, 1994), 53–76.

Kraschewski, Hans-Joachim, 'Steinkohle als Energieträger: Herzog Julius von Braunschweig-Wolfenbüttel und der Kohlenbergbau bei Hohenbüchen am Hils in der zweiten Hälfte des 16. Jahrhunderts', *Niedersächsisches Jahrbuch für Landesgeschichte*, lxxvi (2004), 181–218.

——, 'Organisationsstrukturen der Bergbauverwaltung als Elemente des frühneuzeitlichen Territorialstaates: Das Beispiel Braunschweig-Wolfenbüttel', *Niedersächsisches Jahrbuch für Landesgeschichte*, ixxx (2008), 283–328.

Kratsch, Dietrich, *Justiz—Religion—Politik: Das Reichskammergericht und die Klosterprozesse im ausgehenden sechzehnten Jahrhundert* (Tübingen, 1990).

Krause, Gerhard and Gerhard Müller (eds), *Theologische Realenzyklopädie*, 38 vols (Berlin, 1977–2007).

Krause, Hans-Georg, 'Pfandherrschaften als Verfassungsrechtliches Problem', *Der Staat*, ix (1970), 387–404, 516–32.

Krebs, C. B., 'A dangerous book: The reception of the Germania', in A. J. Woodman (ed.), *The Cambridge companion to Tacitus* (Cambridge, 2010), 280–99.

Kremer, Bernd Mathias, *Der Westfälische Friede in der Deutung der Aufklärung: Zur Entwicklung des Verfassungsverständnisses im Hl. Röm. Reich Deutscher Nation vom Konfessionellen Zeitalter bis ins späte 18. Jahrhundert* (Tübingen. 1989).

Krieger, Karl-Friedrich, *König, Reich und Reichsreform im Spätmittelalter* (Munich, 1972).

Krieger, Leonard, *The German idea of freedom: History of a political tradition from the Reformation to 1871* (Chicago, MI, 1957).

Kroener, Bernhard R., 'Ein protestantisch-arischer "Held aus Mitternacht": Stationen des Gustav-Adolf-Mythos 1632 bis 1945', *Militärgeschichtliche Zeitschrift*, lix (2000), 5–22.

Krüger, Kersten, *Finanzstaat Hessen 1500–1567: Staatsbildung im Übergang vom Domänen-staat zum Steuerstaat* (Marburg, 1980).

——, *Die landständische Verfassung* (Munich, 2003).

——, 'Die landschaftliche Verfassung Nordelbiens in der frühen Neuzeit: Ein besonderer Typ politischer Partizipation', in *idem, Formung der frühen Moderne: Ausgewählte Aufsätze* (Münster, 2005), 199–224.

Kuehnemund, Richard, *Arminius or the rise of a national symbol in literature* (Chapel Hill, NC, 1953).

Kühlmann, Wilhelm, *Gelehrtenrepublik und Fürstenstaat: Entwicklung und Kritik des deutschen Späthumanismus in der Literatur des Barockzeitalters* (Tübingen, 1982).

——, 'Sprachgesellschaften und nationale Utopien', in Dieter Langewiesche and Georg Schmidt (eds), *Föderative Nation: Deutschlandkonzepte von der Reformation bis zum Ersten Weltkrieg* (Munich, 2000), 245–64.

——, *Martin Opitz: Deutsche Literatur und deutsche Nation* (Heidelberg, 2001).

——, 'Grimmelshausens Simplicius Simplicissimus und der Dreißigjährige Krieg: Histor-ische Signaturen und Problemgehalt eines Epochenromans', in Franz Brendle (ed.), *Religionskriege im Alten Reich und in Alteuropa* (Münster, 2006), 163–75.

Kurzmann, Gerhard, *Kaiser Maximilian I. und das Kriegswesen der österreichischen Länder und des Reiches* (Vienna, 1985).

Laan, Adrie van der, 'Rodolphus Agricola Phrisius. A life in letters', in Rudolf Suntrop (ed.), *Stadt, Kanzlei und Kultur im Übergang zur Frühen Neuzeit* (Frankfurt am Main, 2004), 107–21.

Lange, Ulrich, 'Der ständestaatliche Dualismus: Bemerkungen zu einem Problem der deutschen Verfassungsgeschichte', *Blätter für deutsche Landesgeschichte*, cxvii (1981), 311–34.

——, *Landtag und Ausschuß: Zum Problem der Handlungsfähigkeit landständischer Versamm-lungen im Zeitalter der Entstehung des frühmodernen Staates: Die welfischen Territorien als Beispiel (1500–1629)* (Hildesheim, 1986).

Langer, Herbert, *The Thirty Years War* (Poole, 1978).

——, 'Der Dreißigjähriger Krieg (1618 bis 1648)', in Adolf Laube and Günter Vogler (eds), *Deutsche Geschichte, Band 3: Die Epoche des Übergangs vom Feudalismus zum Kapitalismus von den siebziger Jahren des 15. Jahrhunderts bis 1789* (Berlin, 1983), 284–325.

——, 'Der Heilbronner Bund (1633–35)', in Volker Press (ed.), *Alternativen zur Reichs-verfassung in der Frühen Neuzeit?* (Munich, 1995), 113–22.

Langewiesche, Dieter, 'Reich, Nation und Staat in der jüngeren deutschen Geschichte', in *idem, Nation, Nationalismus, Nationalstaat in Deutschland und Europa* (Munich, 2000), 190–216.

——, 'Das Alte Reich nach seinem Ende. Die Reichsidee in der deutschen Politik des 19. und frühen 20. Jahrhunderts: Versuch einer nationalgeschichtlichen Neubewertung in welthistorischer Perspektive', in *idem, Reich, Nation, Föderation: Deutschland und Europa* (Munich, 2008), 211–34.

Lanzinner, Maximilian, 'Die Denkschrift des Lazarus von Schwendi zur Reichspolitik (1570)', in Johannes Kunisch, Klaus Luig and Peter Moraw (eds), *Neue Studien zur frühneuzeitlichen Reichsgeschichte* (Berlin, 1987), 141–85.

——, 'Der Landsberger Bund und seine Vorläufer', in Volker Press (ed.), *Alternativen zur Reichsverfassung in der Frühen Neuzeit?* (Munich, 1995), 65–79.

——, 'Konfessionelles Zeitalter 1555–1618', in Wolfgang Reinhard (ed.), *Gebhardt: Hand-buch der deutschen Geschichte, Band 10*, 10th edn (Stuttgart, 2001), 3–203.

Lanzinner, Maximilian, 'Finanzen in den habsburgischen Ländern und im Heiligen Römischen Reich am Beginn der Neuzeit', in Friedrich Edelmayer, Maximilian Lanzinner and Peter Rauscher (eds), *Finanzen und Herrschaft: Materielle Grundlagen fürstlicher Politik in den habsburgischen Ländern und im Heiligen Römischen Reich im 16. Jahrhundert* (Vienna and Munich, 2003), 291–304.

——, 'Johannes Kepler: A man without confession in the age of confessionalization?', *Central European History*, xxxvi (2003), 531–45.

—— and Dietmar Heil, 'Der Augsburger Reichstag 1566: Ergebnisse einer Edition', *Historische Zeitschrift*, cclxxiv (2002), 603–32.

Lau, Thomas, *'Stiefbrüder': Nation und Konfession in der Schweiz und in Europa (1656–1712)* (Cologne, 2008).

Laubach, Ernst, 'Wahlpropaganda im Wahlkampf um die deutsche Königswürde 1519', *Archiv für Kulturgeschichte*, liii (1971), 207–48.

——, 'Karl V., Ferdinand I. und die Nachfolge im Reich', *Mitteilungen des Österreichischen Staatsarchivs*, xxix (1976), 1–51.

——, *Ferdinand I. als Kaiser. Politik und Herrschaftsauffassung des Nachfolgers Karls V.* (Münster, 2001).

Laube, Adolf, 'Der beginnende Übergang vom Feudalismus zum Kapitalismus. Das Heranreifen der frühbürgerlichen Revolution', in Adolf Laube and Günter Vogler (eds), *Deutsche Geschichte, Band 3: Die Epoche des Übergangs vom Feudalismus zum Kapitalismsus von den siebziger Jahren des 15. Jahrhunderts bis 1789* (Berlin, 1983), 12–94.

Lauchs, Joachim, *Bayern und die deutschen Protestanten 1534–1546: Deutsche Fürstenpolitik zwischen Konfession und Libertät* (Neustadt an der Aisch, 1978).

Lauterbach, Klaus H., 'Der "Oberrheinische Revolutionär" und Mathias Wurm von Geudertheim: Neue Untersuchungen zur Verfasserfrage', *Deutsches Archiv für Erforschung des Mittelalters*, xlv (1989), 109–72.

Lavery, Jason, *Germany's northern challenge: The Holy Roman Empire and the Scandinavian struggle for the Baltic, 1563–1576* (Boston, MA and Leiden, 2002).

Le Gates, Marlene J., 'The Knights and the problems of political organisation in sixteenth-century Germany', *Central European History*, vii (1974), 99–136.

Leppin, Volker, *Martin Luther* (Darmstadt, 2006).

——, '"...das der Römische Antichrist offenbaret und das helle Liecht des Heiligen Evangelii wiederumb angezündet": Memoria und Aggression im Reformationsjubiläum 1617', in Heinz Schilling (ed.), *Konfessioneller Fundamentalismus: Religion als politischer Faktor im europäischen Mächtesystem um 1600* (Munich, 2007), 115–31.

Leuschner, Joachim, *Deutschland im späten Mittelalter* (Göttingen, 1975).

Lexikon des Mittelalters, 10 vols (Munich, 1980–99).

Liepold, Antonio, *Wider den Erbfeind christlichen Glaubens: Die Rolle des niederen Adels in den Türkenkriegen des 16. Jahrhunderts* (Frankfurt am Main, 1998).

Lindberg, Erik, 'The rise of Hamburg as a global marketplace in the seventeenth century: A comparative political economy perspective', *Comparative Studies in Society and History*, l (2008), 641–62.

Locher, Gottfried W., *Die Zwinglische Reformation im Rahmen der europäischen Kirchengeschichte* (Göttingen, 1979).

Lockhart, Paul Douglas, *Denmark in the Thirty Years' War, 1618–1648: King Christian IV and the decline of the Oldenburg state* (Selinsgrove, PA and London, 1996).

——, *Frederik II and the Protestant cause: Denmark's role in the Wars of Religion, 1559–1596* (Leiden and Boston, MA, 2004).

Lohse, Bernhard, *Martin Luther: Eine Einführung in sein Leben und sein Werk* (Munich, 1981).

Lortz, Joseph, *The Reformation in Germany*, transl. Ronald Walls, 2 vols (London, 1968).

Lossen, Max, *Der Kölnische Krieg*, 2 vols (Gotha, 1882, Munich 1887).

Louthan, Howard, *The quest for compromise: Peacemakers in Counter-Reformation Vienna* (Cambridge, 1997).

Lublinskaya, Aleksandra Dmitrievna, *French absolutism: The crucial phase 1620–1629* (Cambridge, 1968).

Ludolphy, Ingetraut, *Friedrich der Weise: Kurfürst von Sachsen 1463–1525* (Göttingen, 1984).

Ludwig, Ulrike, *Philippismus und orthodoxes Luthertum an der Universität Wittenberg: Die Rolle Jakob Andreäs im lutherischen Konfessionalisierungsprozeß Kursachsens (1576–1580)* (Münster, 2009).

Luh, Jürgen, *Unheiliges Römisches Reich: Der konfessionelle Gegensatz 1648 bis 1806* (Potsdam, 1995).

Lüpkes, Vera and Heiner Borggrefe (eds), *Adel im Weserraum um 1600* (Munich, 1996).

Lustiger, Arno, 'Der Fettmilchaufstand in Frankfurt und die Juden: Eine Neubewertung des historischen Geschehens', in Willi Jasper (ed.), *Preußens Himmel breitet seine Sterne . . . : Beiträge zur Kultur-, Politik- und Geistesgeschichte der Neuzeit* (Hildesheim, 2002), 473–82.

Lütge, Friederich, *Geschichte der deutschen Agrarverfassung vom frühen Mittelalter bis zum 19. Jahrhundert*, 2nd edn (Stuttgart, 1967).

Luttenberger, Albrecht P., 'Kirchenadvokatie und Religionsfriede: Kaiseridee und kaiserliche Reichspolitik im 16. und 17. Jahrhundert', in Rolf Gundlach and Hermann Weber (eds), *Legitimation und Funktion des Herrschers: Vom ägyptischen Pharao zum neuzeitlichen Diktator* (Stuttgart, 1992), 185–232.

——, 'Kaisertum und Ständetum im politischen Denken des Reichspfennigmeisters Zacharias Geizkofler', in Heinz Duchhardt and Matthias Schnettger (eds), *Reichsständische Libertät und habsburgisches Kaisertum* (Mainz, 1999), 81–105.

Lutz, Heinrich, *Christianitas afflicta: Europa, das Reich und die päpstliche Politik im Niedergang der Hegemonie Kaiser Karls V. (1552–1556)* (Göttingen, 1964).

——, 'Italien vom Frieden von Lodi bis zum Spanischen Erbfolgekrieg (1454–1700)', in Theoder Schieder (ed.), *Handbuch der europäischen Geschichte*, 7 vols (Stuttgart, 1968–79), iii, 851–901.

——, 'Perspektiven und Zusammenhänge', in *idem* (ed), *Das römisch-deutsche Reich im politischen System Karls V.* (Munich and Vienna, 1982), 269–82.

——, *Das Ringen um deutsche Einheit und kirchliche Erneuerung: Von Maximilian I. bis zum Westfälischen Frieden, 1490–1648* (Berlin, 1983).

Macek, Josef, *Michael Gaismair: Vergessener Held des Tiroler Bauernkrieges* (Vienna, 1988).

McGrath, Alister E., *The intellectual origins of the European Reformation* (Oxford, 1987).

——, *Reformation thought*, 3rd edn (Oxford, 1999).

MacHardy, Karin J., *War, religion and court patronage in Habsburg Austria: The social and cultural dimensions of political interaction, 1521–1622* (Houndmills, 2003).

Märtl, Claudia, 'Der Reformgedanke in den Reformschriften des 15. Jahrhunderts', in Ivan Hlaváček (ed.), *Reform von Kirche und Reich zur Zeit der Konzilien von Konstanz (1414–1418) und Basel (1431–1449)* (Constance, 1996), 91–108.

Magen, Ferdinand, 'Die Reichskreise in der Epoche des dreißigjährigen Krieges: Ein Überblick', *Zeitschrift für historische Forschung*, ix (1982) 409–60.

Maier, Hans, *Die ältere deutsche Staats- und Verwaltungslehre*, 2nd edn (Munich, 1980).

Maier, Konstantin, 'Der Archidiakon in der Reichskirche: Zur Typologie des Amtes im Spätmittelalter und in der frühen Neuzeit', *Römische Quartalschrift für christliche Altertumskunde und Kirchengeschichte*, lxxxvii (1992), 136–57.

Mann, Golo, *Wallenstein* (Frankfurt am Main, 1971).

Mannack, Eberhard, 'Die Rezeption des Dreißigjährigen Krieges und des Westfälischen Friedens in der deutschen Literatur des 18. bis 20. Jahrhunderts', in Klaus Bußmann (ed.), *1648: Krieg und Frieden in Europa* (Münster and Osnabrück, 1998), 385–91.

——, 'Der Streit der Historiker und Literaten über den Dreißigjährigen Krieg und Westfälischen Frieden', *Daphnis. Zeitschrift für Mittlere Deutsche Literatur und Kultur*, xxxi (2002), 701–12.

Marius, Richard, *Martin Luther: The Christian between God and death* (Cambridge, MA, 1999).

Marquardt, Bernd, *Das Römisch-Deutsche Reich als segmentäres Verfassungssystem (1348–1806/ 48). Versuch zu einer neuen Verfassungstheorie auf der Grundlage der Lokalen Herrschaften* (Zurich, 1999).

Maschke, Erich, 'Soziale Gruppen in der deutschen Stadt des späten Mittelalters', in Josef Fleckenstein (ed.), *Über Bürger, Stadt und städtische Literatur im Spätmittelalter* (Göttingen, 1980), 127–45.

Mathis, Franz, *Die deutsche Wirtschaft im 16. Jahrhundert* (Munich, 1992).

Mauersberg, Hans, *Wirtschafts- und Sozialgeschichte zentraleuropäischer Städte in neuerer Zeit: Dargestellt an den Beispielen von Basel, Frankfurt a. M., Hamburg, Hannover und München* (Munich, 1968).

Maurer, Justus, *Prediger im Bauernkrieg* (Stuttgart, 1979).

May, Georg, 'Zum "ius emigrandi" am Beginn des Konfessionellen Zeitalters', *Archiv für Katholisches Kirchenrecht*, clv (1986), 29–125.

Mayes, David, *Communal Christianity: The life and loss of a peasant vision in early modern Germany* (Leiden, 2004).

Meid, Volker, *Die deutsche Literatur im Zeitalter des Barock: Vom Späthumanismus zur Frühaufklärung, 1570–1740* (Munich, 2009).

Menk, Gerhard, *Die Hohe Schule Herborn in ihrer Frühzeit (1584–1660): Ein Beitrag zum Hochschulwesen des deutschen Kalvinismus im Zeitalter der Gegenreformation* (Wiesbaden 1981).

——, 'Territorialstaat und Schulwesen in der frühen Neuzeit: Eine Untersuchung zur religiösen Dynamik an den Grafschaften Nassau und Sayn', *Jahrbuch für westdeutsche Landesgeschichte*, ix (1983), 177–220.

Menzel, Karl, 'Die Union des Herzogs Wilhem IV. zu Sachsen-Weimar und seine Gefangenschaft in Neustadt (1622–1624)', *Archiv für die Sächsische Geschichte*, xi (1873), 32–80.

Merkel, Kerstin, 'Ein Fall von Bigamie: Landgraf Philipp von Hessen, seine beiden Frauen und deren drei Grabdenkmäler', in Wilhem Maier (ed.), *Grabmäler: Tendenzen der Forschung an Beispielen aus Mittelalter und früher Neuzeit* (Berlin, 2000), 103–26.

Mertens, Dieter, '"Bebelius ... patriam Sueviam ... restituit": Der poeta laureatus zwischen Reich und Territorium', *Zeitschrift für Württembergische Landesgeschichte*, xlii (1983), 145–73.

——, 'Hofkultur in Heidelberg und Stuttgart um 1600', in Notker Hammerstein (ed.), *Späthumanismus: Studien über das Ende einer kulturhistorischen Epoche* (Göttingen, 2000), 65–83.

Merz, Johannes, 'Landstädte und Reformation', in Anton Schindling and Walter Ziegler (eds), *Die Territorien des Reiches im Zeitalter der Reformation und Konfessionalisierung: Land und Konfession 1500–1650. Band 7: Bilanz—Forschungsperspektiven—Register* (Münster, 1997), 107–35.

——, 'Der Religionsfrieden, die "Declaratio Ferdinandea" und die Städte unter geistlicher Herrschaft', in Heinz Schilling (ed.), *Der Augsburger Religionsfrieden 1555* (Gütersloh, 2007), 321–40.

Meuthen, Erich, 'Charakter und Tendenzen des deutschen Humanismus' in Heinz Angermeier (ed.), *Säkulare Aspekte der Reformationszeit* (Munich and Vienna, 1983), 217–66.
——, *Das 15. Jahrhundert*, 3rd edn (Munich, 1996).
Meyer, Andreas, 'Das Wiener Konkordat von 1448: Eine erfolgreiche Reform des Spät-
mittelalters', *Quellen und Forschungen aus italienischen Archiven und Bibliotheken*, lvi
(1986), 108–52.
Meyer, Manfred, 'Sickingen, Hutten und die reichsritterschaftlichen Bewegungen in der
deutschen frühbürgerlichen Revolution', *Jahrbuch für Geschichte des Feudalismus*, vii
(1983), 215–46.
Meyer, Michael and Michael Brenner (eds), *German-Jewish history in modern times*, 4 vols
(New York, 1996–98).
Meyn, Matthias, *Die Reichsstadt Frankfurt vor dem Bürgeraufstand von 1612 bis 1614:
Struktur und Krise* (Frankfurt am Main, 1980).
Midelfort, H. C. Erik, *Witch hunting in southwestern Germany, 1562–1684: The social and
intellectual foundations* (Stanford, CA, 1972).
——, *Mad princes of Renaissance Germany* (Charlottesville, VA, 1994).
Miller, Max and Gerhard Taddey, *Handbuch der historischen Stätten Deutschlands: Baden
Württemberg*, 2nd edn (Stuttgart, 1980).
Moeller, Bernd, 'Die deutschen Humanisten und die Anfänge der Reformation', *Zeitschrift
für Kirchengeschichte*, lxx (1959), 46–61.
——, 'Frömmigkeit in Deutschland um 1500', *Archiv für Reformationsgeschichte*, vi (1965),
5–31.
——, *Deutschland im Zeitalter der Reformation* (Göttingen, 1977).
——, *Reichsstadt und Reformation*, 2nd edn (Berlin, 1987).
——, 'Die Universität Königsberg als Gründung der Reformation', in Bernhart Jähnig
(ed.), *450 Jahre Universität Königsberg: Beiträge zur Wissenschaftsgeschichte des Pre-
ußenlandes* (Marburg, 2001), 11–23.
Molitor, Hansgeorg, 'Reformation und Gegenreformation in der Reichsstadt Aachen',
Zeitschrift des Aachener Geschichtsvereins, xcviii–xcix (1992–93), 185–203.
Möller, Hans-Michael, *Das Regiment der Landsknechte: Untersuchungen zu Verfassung, Recht
und Selbstverständnis in deutschen Söldnerheeren des 16. Jahrhunderts* (Wiesbaden, 1976).
Monter, William, *Bewitched duchy: Lorraine and its dukes, 1477–1736* (Geneva, 2007).
Montgomery, John Warwick, *Cross and crucible: Johann Valentin Andreae (1586–1654);
Phoenix of the theologians*, 2 vols (The Hague, 1973).
Moran, Bruce T., *The alchemical world of the German court: Occult philosophy and chemical
medicine in the circle of Moritz of Hessen (1572–1632)* (Stuttgart, 1991).
——, 'Patronage and institutions: courts, universities, and academies in Germany, an
overview 1550–1750', in Bruce T. Moran (ed.), *Patronage and institutions: Science,
technoloy, and medicine at the European court 1500–1750* (Woodbridge, 1991), 169–83.
Moraw, Peter, 'Versuch über die Entstehung des Reichstags', in Hermann Weber (ed.),
Politische Ordnungen und soziale Kräfte im Alten Reich (Wiesbaden, 1980), 1–36.
——, *Von offener Verfassung zu gestalteter Verdichtung: Das Reich im Mittelalter 1250 bis
1490* (Berlin, 1985).
——, 'Bestehende, fehlende und heranwachsende Voraussetzungen des deutschen Natio-
nalbewußtseins im späten Mittelalter', in Joachim Ehlers (ed.), *Ansätze und Diskontinui-
tät deutscher Nationsbildung im Mittelalter* (Sigmaringen, 1989), 99–120.
——, 'Die Funktion von Einungen und Bünden im spätmittelalterlichen Reich', in Volker
Press (ed.), *Alternativen zur Reichsverfassung in der Frühen Neuzeit?* (Munich, 1995),
1–21.

Mortimer, G., 'Did contemporaries recognize a "Thirty Years War"?', *English Historical Review*, cxvi (2001), 124–36.

Moser, Johann Jakob, *Grund-Riss der heutigen Staatsverfassung des Teutschen Reiches* (Tübingen, 1754).

Mout, Nicolette, 'Die Niederlande und das Reich im 16. Jahrhundert (1512–1609)', in Volker Press (ed.), *Alternativen zur Reichsverfassung in der Frühen Neuzeit?* (Munich, 1995), 143–68.

——, ' "Dieser einzige Wiener Hof von Dir hat mehr Gelehrte als ganze Reiche Anderer": Späthumanismus am Kaiserhof in der Zeit Maximilians II. und Rudolfs II. (1564–1612)', in Notker Hammerstein (ed.), *Späthumanismus: Studien über das Ende einer kulturhistorischen Epoche* (Göttingen, 2000), 46–64.

Mueller, Günther H. S., 'The "Thirty Years' War" or fifty years of war?', *Journal of Modern History*, l (1978), 1053–6.

Muhlack, Ulrich, 'Der Tacitismus: Ein späthumanistisches Phänomen?', in Notker Hammerstein (ed.), *Späthumanismus: Studien über das Ende einer kulturhistorischen Epoche* (Göttingen, 2000), 160–82.

Mühlen, Heinz von zur, 'Livland von der Christianisierung bis zum Ende seiner Selbständigkeit (etwa 1186–1561)', in Gert von Pistohlkors (ed.), *Deutsche Geschichte im Osten: Die Baltischen Länder* (Berlin, 1994), 26–172.

——, 'Das Ostbaltikum unter Herrschaft und Einfluß der Nachbarmächte (1561–1710/1795)', in Gert von Pistohlkors (ed.), *Deutsche Geschichte im Osten: Die Baltischen Länder* (Berlin, 1994), 174–264.

Müller, K. O., 'Zur wirtschaftlichen Lage des schwäbischen Adels am Ausgang des Mittelalters', *Zeitschrift für Württembergische Landesgeschichte*, iii (1939), 285–328.

Müller, Laurenz, 'Revolutionary moment: Interpreting the Peasants War in the Third Reich and in the German Democratic Republic', *Central European History*, xl (2007), 193–218.

Müller, Matthias, *Das Schloß als Bild des Fürsten: Herrschaftliche Metaphorik in der Residenzarchitektur des Alten Reiches (1470–1618)* (Göttingen, 2004).

Müller, Rainer A., *Der Fürstenhof in der Frühen Neuzeit*, 2nd edn (Munich, 2004).

Mullett, Michael, *The Catholic Reformation* (London, 1999).

Mulsow, Martin, 'Gelehrte Praktiken politischer Kompromittierung: Melchior Goldast und Lipsius' Rede "De duplici Concordia" im Vorfeld der Entstehung der protestantischen Union', in Helmut Zedelmaier (ed.), *Die Praktiken der Gelehrsamkeit in der Frühen Neuzeit* (Tübingen, 2001), 307–47.

——, *Moderne aus dem Untergrund: Radikale Frühaufklärung in Deutschland 1680–1720* (Hamburg, 2002).

—— (ed.), *Spätrenaissance-Philosophie in Deutschland 1570–1650: Entwürfe zwischen Humanismus und Konfessionalisierung, okkulten Traditionen und Schulmetaphysik* (Tübingen, 2009).

Munier, W. A. J., 'De curiale loopbaan van Willem van Enckenvoirt vóór het pontificaat van Adriaan VI', *Archief voor de geschiedenis van de katholieke kerk in Nederland*, i (1959), 120–68.

Münkler, Herfried and Grünberger, Hans, 'Nationale Identität im Diskurs der Deutschen Humanisten', in Helmut Berding (ed.), *Nationales Bewußtsein und kollektive Identität: Studien zur Entwicklung des kollektiven Bewußtseins in der Neuzeit* (Frankfurt am Main, 1994), 211–48.

——, Hans Grünberger and Kathrin Mayer, *Nationenbildung: Die Nationalisierung Europas im Diskurs humanistischer Intellektueller; Italien und Deutschland* (Berlin, 1998).

Murphey, Rhoads, *Ottoman warfare 1500–1700* (London, 1999).

Naujoks, Eberhard, *Obrigkeitsgedanke, Zunftverfassung und Reformation: Studien zur Verfassungsgeschichte von Ulm, Eßlingen und Schwäb. Gmünd* (Stuttgart, 1958).

——— (ed.), *Kaiser Karl V. und die Zunftverfassung: Ausgewählte Aktenstücke zu den Verfassungensfragen in den oberdeutschen Reichsstädten (1547–1556)* (Stuttgart, 1985).

Neue Deutsche Biographie (Berlin, 1953–).

Neuhaus, Helmut. 'Der Augsburger Reichstag des Jahres 1530: Ein Forschungsbericht', *Zeitschrift für historische Forschung*, ix (1982), 167–211.

———, 'Chronologie erb- und thronrechtlicher Bestimmungen europäischer Fürstenhäuser und Staaten', in Johannes Kunisch (ed.), *Der dynastische Fürstenstaat: Zur Bedeutung von Sukzessionsordnungen für die Entstehung des frühmodernen Staates* (Berlin, 1982), 385–90.

———, *Reichsständische Repräsentationsformen im 16. Jahrhundert: Reichstag—Reichskreistag—Reichsdeputationstag* (Berlin, 1982).

———, 'Zwänge und Entwicklungsmöglichkeiten reichsständischer Beratungsformen in der zweiten Hälfte des 16. Jahrhunderts', *Zeitschrift für historische Forschung*, 10 (1983), 279–98.

———, 'Wandlungen der Reichstagsorganisation in der ersten Hälfte des 16. Jahrhunderts', in Johannes Kunisch, Klaus Luig and Peter Moraw (eds), *Neue Studien zur frühneuzeitlichen Reichsgeschichte* (Berlin, 1987), 113–40.

———, *Das Reich in der frühen Neuzeit* (Munich, 1997).

Neveux, Jean Baptiste, *Vie spirituelle et vie sociale entre Rhin et Baltique au XVIIe siècle: de J. Arndt à P. J. Spencer* (Paris, 1967).

Nischan, Bodo, 'Reformed Irenicism and the Leipzig Colloquy 1631', *Central European History*, ix (1976), 3–26.

———, 'Brandenburg's Reformed Räte and the Leipzig Manifesto of 1631', *Journal of Religious History*, x (1979), 365–80.

Noël, Jean-François, 'Le concept de nation allemande dans l'empire au XVIIe siècle', *XVIIe Siècle*, lxiv (1992) 325–44.

Nonn, Ulrich, 'Heiliges Römisches Reich Deutscher Nation', *Zeitschrift für historische Forschung*, ix (1982), 129–42.

North, John, *The Fontana history of astronomy and cosmology* (London 1994).

North, Michael, 'Integration im Ostseeraum und im Heiligen Römischen Reich', in Nils Jörn (ed.), *Die Integration des südlichen Ostseeraumes in das Alte Reich* (Cologne, 2000), 1–11.

———, 'Münzpolitik in der ersten Hälfte des 16. Jahrhunderts: Das Heilige Römische Reich und Sachsen im europäischen Kontext', in Bertram Schefold (ed.), *Die drei Flugschriften über den Münzstreit der sächsischen Albertiner und Ernestiner* (Düsseldorf, 2000), 82–98.

Nummedal, Tara E., *Alchemy and authority in the Holy Roman Empire* (Chicago, MI, 2007).

Obersteiner, Gernot Peter, 'Das Reichshoffiskalat 1596 bis 1806: Bausteine zu seiner Geschichte aus Wiener Archiven', in Anette Baumann, Peter Oestmann, Stephan Wendehorst, and Siegrid Westphal (eds), *Reichspersonal: Funktionsträger von Kaiser und Reich* (Cologne, 2003), 89–164.

Oestreich, Gerhard, 'Zur Heeresverfassung der deutschen Territorien von 1500 bis 1800', in *idem, Geist und Gestalt des frühmodernen Staates: Ausgewählte Aufsätze* (Berlin, 1969), 290–310.

———, 'Verfassungsgeschichte vom Ende des Mittelalters bis zum Ende des alten Reiches', in Herbert Grundmann (ed.), *Gebhardt: Handbuch der Deutschen Geschichte Band 2*, 9th edn (Stuttgart, 1970), 360–436.

———, *Antiker Geist und moderner Staat bei Justus Lipsius (1547–1606): Der Neustoizismus als politische Bewegung*, ed. Nicolette Mout (Göttingen, 1989).

Ollmann-Kösling, Heinz, *Der Erbfolgestreit um Jülich-Kleve: Ein Vorspiel zum Dreissigjährigen Krieg* (Regensburg, 1996).

Opgenoorth, Ernst, 'Gustav Adolf aus deutscher Sicht: Zu einigen neueren Biographien des Schwedenkönigs', in Michael Salewski (ed.), *Dienst für die Geschichte: Gedenkschrift für Walther Hubatsch (17. Mai 1915–29. Dezember 1984)* (Göttingen and Zurich, 1985), 41–61.

Osbourne, Toby, *Dynasty and diplomacy in the court of Savoy: political culture and the Thirty Years War* (Cambridge, 2002).

Otto, Eduard, 'Zur Geschichte des deutschen Fürstenlebens, namentlich der Hoffestlichkeiten im 16. und 17. Jahrhundert', *Zeitschrift für Kulturgeschichte*, viii (1901) 335–53.

Otto, Karl F., *Die Sprachgesellschaften des 17. Jahrhunderts* (Stuttgart, 1972).

Overfield, James, 'Germany', in Roy Porter and Mikuláš Teich (eds), *The Renaissance in national context* (Cambridge, 1992), 92–122.

Ozment, Steven E., *The Reformation in the cities: The Appeal of Protestantism to sixteenth-century Germany and Switzerland* (New Haven, CT, 1975).

——, *The age of reform 1250–1550: An intellectual and religious history of late Medieval and Reformation Europe* (New Haven, CT, 1980).

Palffy, Géza, 'Der Preis für die Verteidigung der Habsburgermonarchie: Die Kosten der Türkenabwehr in der zweiten Hälfte des 16. Jahrhunderts', in Friedrich Edelmayer, Maimilian Lanzinner and Pater Rauscher (eds), *Finanzen und Herrschaft: Materielle Grundlagen fürstlicher Politik in den habsburgischen Ländern und im Heiligen Römischen Reich im 16. Jahrhundert* (Munich, 2003), 20–44.

Pamlényi, Ervin (ed.), *A History of Hungary* (London, 1975).

Papy, Jan, 'Justus Lipsius and the German republic of letters. Latin philology as a means of intellectual exchange and influence', in Eckhard Keßler and Heinrich C. Kuhn (eds), *Germania Latina, Latinitas teutonica: Politik Wissenschaft, humanistische Kultur vom späten Mittelalter bis in unsere Zeit, Band 1,* (Groningen, 1992), 23–38.

Paravicini, Werner, *Die ritterlich-höfische Kultur des Mittelalters* (Munich, 1994).

Parker, Geoffrey, *The army of Flanders and the Spanish road 1567–1659: The logistics of Spanish victory and defeat in the Low Countries' wars* (Cambridge, 1972).

—— (ed.) *The Thirty Years' War*, 2nd edn (Houndmills, 1987).

——, *The Military Revolution: Military innovation and the rise of the West, 1500–1800* (Cambridge, 1988).

——, *The grand strategy of Philip II* (New Haven, CT and London, 1998).

Partner, Peter, 'Papal financial policy in the Renaissance and Counter-Reformation', *Past and Present*, lxxxviii (1980), 17–62.

Patschovsky, Alexander, 'Der Reformbegriff zur Zeit der Konzilien von Konstanz und Basel', in Ivan Hlaváček (ed.), *Reform von Kirche und Reich zur Zeit der Konzilien von Konstanz (1414–1418) und Basel (1431–1449)* (Constance, 1996), 7–28.

Peters, Christian, *Johann Eberlin von Günzburg ca. 1465–1533: Franziskanischer Reformer, Humanist und konservativer Reformer* (Gütersloh, 1994).

——, 'Der Macht des Kaisers widerstehen: Die süddeutschen Theologen und das Augsburger Interim', in Irene Dingel (ed.), *Politik und Bekenntnis: Die Reaktionen auf das Interim von 1548* (Leipzig, 2006), 65–81.

Petritsch, Ernst D., 'Ferdinand I., Moritz von Sachsen und die osmanische Frage', in Karlheinz Blascke (ed.), *Moritz von Sachsen: Ein Fürst der Reformationszeit zwischen Territorium und Reich* (Leipzig and Stuttgart, 2007), 57–74.

Pfeiffer, Gerhard, 'Der Augsburger Religionsfriede und die Reichsstädte', *Zeitschrift des Historischen Vereins für Schwaben*, lxi (1955), 213–322.

Pfister, Christian, *Bevölkerungsgeschichte und historische Demographie 1500–1800* (Munich, 1994).

——, 'The population of late medieval and early modern Germany', in Bob Scribner (ed.), *Germany: A new social and economic history 1450–1630* (London, 1996), 33–62.

Phillips, Margaret Mann, *Erasmus and the northern Renaissance* (Woodbridge, 1981).

Plessner, Helmuth, *Die verspätete Nation: Über die politische Verführbarkeit bürgerlichen Geistes* (Frankfurt am Main, 1974).

Po-chia Hsia, Ronald, *Society and Religion in Münster, 1535–1618* (New Haven, CT and London, 1984).

——, *Social discipline in the Reformation: Central Europe 1550–1750* (London. 1989).

——, 'People's, city, and princes' Reformation: Rivals or phases?' in Hans R. Guggisberg (ed.), *Die Reformation in Deutschland und Europa: Interpretationen und Debatten* (Gütersloh, 1993), 294-301.

Polenz, Peter von, *Deutsche Sprachgeschichte vom Spätmittelalter bis zur Gegenwart*, 3 vols, 2nd edn (Berlin, 1994–2000).

Pörtner, Regina, *The Counter-Reformation in Central Europe: Styria 1580–1630* (Oxford, 2001).

Potter, G. R. *Zwingli* (Cambridge, 1976).

Powell, Hugh, *Trammels of tradition: Aspects of German life and culture in the seventeenth century and their impact on the contemporary literature* (Tübingen, 1988).

Press, Volker, *Calvinismus und Territorialstaat: Regierung und Zentralbehörden der Kurpfalz 1559–1619* (Stuttgart, 1970).

——, *Kaiser Karl V., König Ferdinand und die Entstehung der Reichsritterschaft* (Wiesbaden, 1970).

——, 'Herrschaft, Landschaft und "Gemeiner Mann" in Oberdeutschland vom 15. bis zum frühen 19. Jahrhundert', *Zeitschrift für Geschichte des Oberrheins*, cxxiii (NF lxxxiv) (1975), 169–214.

——, 'Steuern, Kredit und Repräsentation: Zum Problem der Ständebildung ohne Adel', *Zeitschrift für historische Forschung*, ii (1975), 59–93.

——, 'Die Reichsritterschaft im Reich der frühen Neuzeit', *Nassauische Annalen*, lxxxvii (1976), 101–22.

——, 'Die Landschaft aller Grafen von Solms: Ein ständiches Experiment am Beginn des 17. Jahrhunderts', *Hessisches Jahrbuch für Landesgeschichte*, xvii (1977), 37–106.

——, 'Der deutsche Bauernkrieg als Systemkrise', *Gießener Universitätsblätter*, xi (1978), 106–27.

——, 'Adel, Reich und Reformation', in Wolfgang J. Mommsen (ed.), *Stadtbürgertum und Adel in der Reformation: Studien zur Sozialgeschichte der Reformation in England und Deutschland* (Stuttgart, 1979), 330–83.

——, 'Die Grafen von Erbach und die Anfänge des reformierten Bekenntnisses in Deutschland', in Herman Bannasch (ed.), *Aus Geschichte und ihren Hilfswissenschaften* (Marburg, 1979), 653–85.

——, 'Die Erblande und das Reich von Albrecht II. bis Karl VI. (1438–1740)', in Robert A. Kann und Friedrich Prinz (eds), *Deutschland und Österreich: Ein bilaterales Geschichtsbuch* (Vienna, 1980), 44–80.

——, 'Die Bundespläne Kaiser Karls V. und die Reichsverfassung', in Heinrich Lutz (ed.), *Das römisch-deutsche Reich im politischen System Karls V.* (Munich, 1982), 55–106.

——, 'Schwaben zwischen Bayern, Österreich und dem Reich 1486–1805', in Pankraz Fried (ed.), *Probleme der Integration Ostschwabens in den bayerischen Staat: Bayern und Wittelsbach in Ostschwaben* (Sigmaringen, 1982), 17–78.

Press, Volker, 'Formen des Ständewesens in den deutschen Territorialstaaten des 16. und 17. Jahrhunderts', in Peter Baumgart (ed.), *Ständetum und Staatsbildung in Brandenburg-Preußen* (Berlin, 1983), 280–318.

——, 'Landgraf Philipp der Großmütige von Hessen 1504–1567', in Klaus Scholder and Dieter Kleinmann (eds), *Protestantische Profile* (Königstein im Taunus, 1983), 60–77.

——, 'Wilhelm von Oranien, die deutschen Reichsstände und der niederländische Aufstand', *Bijdragen en Mededelingen van de Geschiednis der Nederlanden*, xcix (1984), 677–707.

——, 'Das Hochstift Speyer im Reich des späten Mittelalters und der frühen Neuzeit – Porträt eines geistlichen Staates', in *idem*, Eugen Reinhard, and Hansmartin Schwarzmeier (eds), *Barock am Oberrhein* (Karlsruhe, 1985), 251–90.

——, 'Die Niederlande und das Reich in der Frühen Neuzeit', in Willem Pieter Blockmans and Herman van Nuffel (eds), *État et religion aux xve et xvie siècles* (Brussels, 1986), 321–39.

——, 'Die Reformation und der deutsche Reichstag', in Horst Bartel (ed.), *Martin Luther. Leistung und Erbe* (Berlin, 1986), 202–15.

——, 'Die "Zweite Reformation" in der Kurpfalz', in Heinz Schilling (ed.), *Die reformierte Konfessionalisierung in Deutschland: Das Problem der "Zweiten Reformation"* (Gütersloh, 1986), 104–29.

——, *Das Reichskammergericht in der deutschen Geschichte* (Wetzlar, 1987).

——, 'Ein Epochenjahr der württembergischen Geschichte: Restitution und Reformation 1534', *Zeitschrift für Württembergische Landesgeschichte*, xlvii (1988), 203–34.

——, 'Führungsgruppen in der deutschen Gesellschaft im Übergang zur Neuzeit um 1500', in Hans Hubert Hofmann and Günther Franz (eds), *Deutsche Führungsschichten in der Neuzeit: Eine Zwischenbilanz* (Boppard am Rhein, 1988), 29–77.

——, 'Patronat und Klientel im Heiligen Römischen Reich', in Antoni Maczak (ed.), *Klientelsysteme im Europa der Frühen Neuzeit* (Munich, 1988), 19–46.

——, 'Soziale Folgen des Dreißigjährigen Krieges', in Winfried Schulze (ed.), *Ständische Gesellschaft und soziale Mobilität* (Munich, 1988), 239–68.

——, 'Die Territorialstruktur des Reiches und die Reformation', in Rainer Postel and Franklin Kopitzsch (eds), *Reformation und Revolution: Beiträge zum politischen Wandel und den sozialen Kräften am Beginn der Neuzeit* (Stuttgart, 1989), 239–68.

——, 'Vorderösterreich in der habsburgischen Reichspolitik des späten Mittelalters und der frühen Neuzeit', in Hans Maier and Volker Press (eds), *Vorderösterreich in der frühen Neuzeit* (Sigmaringen, 1989), 1–41.

——, 'Matthias (1612–1619)', in Anton Schindling and Walter Ziegler (eds), *Die Kaiser der Neuzeit 1519–1918* (Munich, 1990), 112–23.

——, 'The Imperial court of the Habsburgs: From Maximilian I to Ferdinand III, 1493–1657', in Ronald G. Asch and Adolf M. Birke (eds), *Princes, patronage and the nobility: The court at the beginning of the modern age c.1450–1650* (Oxford, 1991), 289–312.

——, 'Kaiser und Reichsritterschaft', in Rudolf Endres (ed.), *Adel in der Frühneuzeit: Ein regionaler Vergleich* (Cologne, 1991), 163–94.

——, *Kriege und Krisen: Deutschland 1600–1715* (Munich, 1991).

——, 'Die Krise des Dreißigjährigen Krieges und die Restauration des Westfälischen Friedens', in Monika Hagenmaier and Sabine Holtz (eds), *Krisenbewußtsein und Krisenbewältigung in der Frühen Neuzeit—Crisis in Early Modern Europe* (Frankfurt a. M., 1992), 61–72.

——, 'Deutsche Adelshöfe des 16. und beginnenden 17. Jahrhunderts', *Opera Historica. Editio Universitatis Bohemiae Meridionalis*, iii (1993), 33–46.

——, 'Die badischen Markgrafen im Reich der frühen Neuzeit', *Zeitschrift für die Geschichte des Oberrheins*, cxlii (1994), 19–57.

——, 'Herzog Christoph von Württemberg (1550–1568) als Reichsfürst', in Wolfang Schmierer (ed.), *Aus südwestdeutscher Geschichte* (Stuttgart, 1994), 367–82.

——, 'Der Reichshofrat im System des frühneuzeitlichen Reiches', in Friedrich Battenberg and Filippo Ranieri (eds), *Geschichte der Zentraljustiz in Mitteleuropa* (Cologne, 1994), 349–63.

——, 'Albrecht von Rosenberg—Reichsritter an der Schwelle der Zeiten' in *idem, Adel im Alten Reich: Gesammelte Vorträge und Aufsätze*, ed. Franz Brendle and Anton Schindling, (Tübingen, 1998), 357–82.

——, 'Franz von Sickingen: Wortführer des Adels, Vorkämpfer der Reformation und Freund Huttens', in *idem, Adel im Alten Reich: Gesammelte Vorträge und Aufsätze*, ed. Franz Brendle and Anton Schindling (Tübingen, 1998), 319–31.

——, 'Götz von Berlichingen (ca. 1480 bis 1562). Vom "Raubritter" zum Reichsritter', in *idem, Adel im Alten Reich: Gesammelte Vorträge und Aufsätze*, ed. Franz Brendle and Anton Schindling (Tübingen, 1998), 333–56.

——, 'Herzog Ulrich von Württemberg (1498–1550)', in *idem, Adel im Alten Reich: Gesammelte Vorträge und Aufsätze*, ed. Franz Brendle and Anton Schindling (Tübingen, 1998), 71–91.

——, 'Reichsgrafenstand und Reich: Zur Sozial- und Verfassungsgeschichte des deutschen Hochadels in der Frühen Neuzeit', in *idem, Adel im Alten Reich: Gesammelte Vorträge und Aufsätze*, ed. Franz Brendle and Anton Schindling (Tübingen, 1998), 113–38.

——, 'Wilhelm von Grumbach und die deutsche Adelskrise der 1560er Jahre', in *idem, Adel im Alten Reich: Gesammelte Vorträge und Aufsätze*, ed. Franz Brendle and Anton Schindling (Tübingen, 1998), 383–421.

——, 'Fürst Christian I. von Anhalt-Bernburg, Statthalter der Oberpfalz, Haupt der evangelischen Bewegungspartei vor dem Dreißigjährigen Krieg, 1580–1630', in Konrad Ackermann and Alois Schmid (eds), *Staat und Verwaltung in Bayern* (Munich, 2003), 193–216.

Price, David H., *Johannes Reuchlin and the campaign to destroy Jewish books* (Oxford, 2011).

Prietzel, Malte, *Das Heilige Römische Reich im Spätmittelalter* (Darmstadt, 2004).

Pursell, Brennan C., *The Winter King: Frederick V of the Palatinate and the coming of the Thirty Years War* (Aldershot, 2003).

Puschner, Uwe, 'Reichsromantik: Erinnerungen an das Alte Reich zwischen den Freiheitskriegen von 1813/14 und den Revolutionen von 1848/49', in Heinz Schilling (ed.), *Heiliges Römisches Reich Deutscher Nation 962 bis 1806: Altes Reich und neue Staaten 1495 bis 1806* (Dresden, 2006), 318–29.

Quarthal, Franz, 'Unterm Krummstab ist's gut leben: Prälaten, Mönche und Bauern im Zeitalter des Barock', in Peter Blickle (ed.), *Politische Kultur in Oberschwaben* (Tübingen, 1993), 269–86.

——, 'Vorderösterreich in der Geschichte Südwestdeutschlands', in Irmgard Christa Necker (ed.), *Vorderösterreich: Nur die Schwanzfeder des Kaiseradlers? Die Habsburger im deutschen Südwesten* (Ulm, 1999), 14–59.

Rabe, Horst, *Der Rat der niederschwäbischen Reichsstädte: Rechtsgeschichtliche Untersuchungen über die Ratsverfassung der Reichsstädte Niederschwabens bis zum Ausgang der Zunftbewegungen im Rahmen der oberdeutschen Reichs- und Bischofsstädte* (Cologne, 1966).

——, *Reichsbund und Interim: Die Verfassungs- und Religionspolitik Karls V. und der Reichstag von Augsburg 1547–8* (Cologne, 1971).

Rabe, Horst, *Deutsche Geschichte 1500–1600: Das Jahrhundert der Glaubensspaltung* (Munich, 1991).

——, 'Zur Interimspolitik Karls V.', in Luise Schorn-Schütte (ed.), *Das Interim 1548/50: Herrschaftskrise und Glaubenskonflikt* (Gütersloh, 2005), 127–46.

Ranieri, Filippo, *Recht und Gesellschaft im Zeitalter der Rezeption: Eine rechts- und sozialgeschichtliche Analyse der Tätigkeit des Reichskammergerichts im 16. Jahrhundert* (Cologne, 1985).

Ranke, Leopold von, *Deutsche Geschichte im Zeitalter der Reformation* (Vienna, 1934).

Rauscher, Peter, 'Kaiser und Reich: Die Reichstürkenhilfen von Ferdinand I. bis zum Beginn des "Langen Türkenkriegs" (1548–1593)', in Friedrich Edelmayer, Maximilian Lanzinner and Pater Rauscher (eds), *Finanzen und Herrschaft: Materielle Grundlagen fürstlicher Politik in den habsburgischen Ländern und im Heiligen Römischen Reich im 16. Jahrhundert* (Munich, 2003), 45–83.

Rebitsch, Robert, *Tirol, Karl V. und der Fürstenaufstand von 1552* (Hamburg, 2000).

Redlich, Fritz, 'Der deutsche fürstliche Unternehmer: Eine typische Erscheinung des 16. Jahrhunderts', *Tradition. Zeitschrift für Firmengeschichte und Unternehmerbiographie*, iii (1958), 17–32, 98–112.

——, *The German military enterpriser and his workforce: A study in European economic and social history*, 2 vols (Wiesbaden, 1964–5).

Reinhard, Wolfgang, 'Zwang zur Konfessionalisierung? Prolegomena zu einer Theorie des konfessionellen Zeitalters', *Zeitschrift für historische Forschung*, x (1983), 257–77.

——, *Geschichte der Staatsgewalt: Eine vergleichende Verfassungsgeschichte Europas von den Anfängen bis zur Gegenwart* (Munich, 1999).

——, 'Frühmoderner Staat und deutsches Monstrum: Die Entstehung des modernen Staates und das Alte Reich', *Zeitschrift für historische Forschung*, xxix (2002), 339–57.

Reinhardt, Volker, 'Der Primat der Innerlichkeit und die Probleme des Reiches: Zum deutschen Nationalgefühl der frühen Neuzeit', in Bernd Martin (ed.), *Deutschland in Europa: Ein historischer Überblick* (Munich, 1992), 88–104.

Rendenbach, Karl Hans, *Die Fehde Franz von Sickingens gegen Trier* (Berlin, 1933).

Repgen, Konrad, 'Ferdinand III. 1637–1657', in Anton Schindling and Walter Ziegler (eds), *Die Kaiser der Neuzeit 1519–1918* (Munich, 1990), 142–67.

——, 'Der Westfälische Friede: Ereignis und Erinnerung', *Historische Zeitschrift*, cclxvii (1998), 615–47.

——, 'Die zollpolitischen Regelungen der Friedensverträge von 1648 mit Frankreich und Schweden', in Franz Bosbach and Christoph Knappmann (eds), *Dreißigjähriger Krieg und Westfälischer Friede* (Munich, 1998), 677–94.

——, 'Die Hauptprobleme der Westfälischen Friedensverhandlungen von 1648 und ihre Lösungen', *Zeitschrift für bayerische Landesgeschichte*, lxii (1999), 399–438.

Rieber, Albrecht, 'Von der Burg zum Schloß', in Hellmuth Rössler (ed.), *Deutscher Adel 1430–1555* (Darmstadt, 1965), 24–38.

Rill, Bernd, *Kaiser Matthias: Bruderzwist und Glaubenskampf* (Graz, 1999).

Ritter, Moriz, *Deutsche Geschichte im Zeitalter der Gegenreformation und des Dreißigjährigen Krieges (1555–1648)*, 3 vols (Stuttgart, 1889–1908).

Roberts, Michael, *Essays in Swedish history* (London, 1967).

——, *The early Vasas: A history of Sweden 1523–1611* (Cambridge, 1968).

——, *The Swedish imperial experience 1560–1718* (Cambridge, 1979).

——, 'Oxenstierna in Germany, 1633–1636', *Scandia*, xlviii (1982), 61–105.

Robisheaux, Thomas, *The last witch of Langenburg: Murder in a German village* (New York, 2009).

Rodríguez-Salgado, M. J., *The changing face of empire: Charles V, Philip II and Habsburg authority, 1551–1559* (Cambridge, 1988).

Roeck, Bernd, *Eine Stadt in Krieg und Frieden: Studien zur Geschichte der Reichsstadt Augsburg zwischen Kalenderstreit und Parität*, 2 vols (Göttingen, 1989).

——, *Außenseiter, Randgruppen, Minderheiten: Fremde im Deutschland der frühen Neuzeit* (Göttingen, 1993).

Roloff, Hans-Gert, 'Der *Arminius* des Ulrich von Hutten', in Rainer Wiegels and Winfried Woesler (eds), *Arminius und die Varusschlacht: Geschichte—Mythos—Literatur* (Paderborn, 1995).

Roll, Christine, *Das zweite Reichsregiment 1521–1530* (Cologne, 1996).

Roper, Lyndal, *Witch craze: Terror and fantasy in baroque Germany* (London, 2004).

Rosa di Simone, Maria, 'Admission', in H. De Ridder-Symoens (ed.), *A History of the university in Europe.* Vol. 2: *Universities in early modern Europe* (Cambridge, 1996), 285–325.

Rösener, Werner, *Agrarwirtschaft, Agrarverfassung und ländliche Gesellschaft im Mittelalter* (Munich 1992).

Rosseaux, Ulrich, *Städte in der Frühen Neuzeit* (Darmstadt, 2006).

Rowan, S. W., 'Imperial taxes and German politics in the fifteenth century: an outline', *Central European History*, xiii (1980), 203–17.

Rublack, Hans-Christoph, *Gescheiterte Reformation: Frühreformatorische und protestantische Bewegungen in süd- und westdeutschen geistlichen Residenzen*, (Stuttgart, 1978).

——, 'Die Reformation in Kitzingen', in Dieter Demandt and Hans-Christoph Rublack (eds), *Stadt und Kirche in Kitzingen: Darstellung und Quellen zu Spätmittelalter und Reformation* (Stuttgart, 1978), 34–96.

——, 'Gravamina und Reformation', in Ingrid Bátori (ed.), *Städtische Gesellschaft und Reformation* (Stuttgart, 1980), 292–313.

Rudersdorf, Manfred, 'Die Generation der lutherischen Landesväter im Reich. Bausteine zu einer Typologie des deutschen Reformationsfürsten', in Anton Schindling and Walter Ziegler (eds), *Die Territorien des Reichs im Zeitalter der Reformation und Konfessionalisierung: Land und Konfession 1500–1650*, 7 vols (Münster, 1989–97), vii, 137–70.

——, 'Maximilian II. (1564–1576)', in Anton Schindling and Walter Ziegler (eds), *Die Kaiser der Neuzeit 1519–1918* (Munich, 1990), 79–97.

——, 'Moritz von Sachsen: Reformationsfürst, Kaisergegner, Anwalt der ständischen Libertät', in Winfried Müller (ed.), *Perspektiven der Reformationsforschung in Sachsen* (Dresden, 2008), 59–72.

Rummel, Erika, *The case against Johann Reuchlin: Religious and social controversy in sixteenth-century Germany* (Toronto, 2002).

Rummel, Walter, '"Weise" Frauen und "weise" Männer im Kampf gegen Hexerei: Die Widerlegung einer modernen Fabel', in Christof Dipper (ed.), *Europäische Sozialgeschichte* (Berlin, 2000), 353–76.

Ruthmann, Bernhard, 'Die Religionsprozesse als Folge der Glaubensspaltung', in Ingrid Scheurmann (ed.), *Frieden durch Recht: Das Reichskammergericht von 1495 bis 1806* (Mainz, 1994), 231–72.

——, *Die Religionsprozesse am Reichskammergericht (1555–1648): Eine Analyse anhand ausgewählter Prozesse* (Cologne, 1996).

Sandl, Marcus, 'Interpretationswelten der Zeitenwende: Protestantische Selbstbeschreibungen im 16. Jahrhundert zwischen Bibelauslegung und Reformationserinnerung', in Joachinm Eibach and Marcus Sandl (eds), *Protestantische Identität und Erinnerung: Von der Reformation bis zur Bürgerrechtsbewegung in der DDR* (Göttingen, 2003), 27–46.

Sante, Georg Wilhelm (ed.), *Geschichte der Deutschen Länder. "Territorien-Ploetz". Band 1: Die Territorien bis zum Ende des alten Reiches* (Würzburg, 1964).
—— (ed.), *Handbuch der historischen Stätten Deutschlands: Hessen*, 3rd edn (Stuttgart, 1976).
Santifaller, Leo, *Zur Geschichte des ottonisch-salischen Reichskirchensystems*, 2nd edn (Vienna, 1964).
Schäufele, Wolf-Friedrich, 'Die Konsequenzen des Westfälischen Friedens für den Umgang mit religiösen Minderheiten in Deutschland', in Günter Frank, Jörg Haustein and Albert de Lange (eds), *Asyl, Toleranz und Religionsfreiheit: Historische Erfahrungen und aktuelle Herausforderungen* (Göttingen 2000), 121–39.
Schefold, Bertram, 'Wirtschaft und Geld im Zeitalter der Reformation', in *idem* (ed.), *Die drei Flugschriften über den Münzstreit der sächsischen Albertiner und Ernestiner* (Düsseldorf, 2000), 5–57.
Schiersner, Dietmar, *Politik, Konfession und Kommunikation: Studien zur katholischen Konfessionalisierung der Markgrafschaft Burgau 1550–1650* (Berlin, 2005).
Schilling, Heinz, 'Bürgerkämpfe in Aachen zu Beginn des 17. Jahrhunderts: Konflikte im Rahmen der alteuropäischen Stadtgesellschaft oder im Umkreis der frühbürgerlichen Revolution?', *Zeitschrift für historische Forschung*, i (1974), 175–231.
——, 'Reformation und Bürgerfreiheit: Emdens Weg zur calvinistischen Stadtrepublik', in Bernd Moeller (ed.), *Stadt und Kirche im 16. Jahrhundert* (Gütersloh, 1978), 128–61.
——, *Konfessionskonflikt und Staatsbildung: Eine Fallstudie über das Verhältnis von religiösem und sozialem Wandel in der Frühneuzeit am Beispiel der Grafschaft Lippe* (Gütersloh, 1981).
——, 'Dortmund im 16. und 17. Jahrhundert: Reichsstädtische Gesellschaft, Reformation und Konfessionalisierung', in *Dortmund: 1100 Jahre Stadtgeschichte* (Dortmund, 1982), 153–201.
——, 'Innovation through migration: The settlements of Calvinistic Netherlanders in sixteenth- and seventeenth-century Central and Western Europe', *Histoire sociale—Social History*, xvi (1983), 7–33.
——, 'The Reformation in the Hanseatic cities', *The Sixteenth Century Journal*, xiv (1983), 443–56.
——, 'The European crisis of the 1590s: The situation in German towns', in Peter Clark (ed.), *The European crisis of the 1590s: Essays in comparative history* (London, 1985), 135–56.
——, *Aufbruch und Krise: Deutschland 1517–1648* (Berlin, 1988).
——, 'Gab es im späten Mittelalter und zu Beginn der Neuzeit in Deutschland einen städtischen "Republikanismus"? Zur politischen Kultur des alteuropäischen Stadtbürgertums', in Helmut Königsberger (ed.), *Republiken und Republikanismus im Europa der Frühen Neuzeit* (Munich, 1988), 101–44.
——, 'Die Konfessionalisierung im Reich: Religiöser und gesellschaftlicher Wandel in Deutschland zwischen 1555 und 1620', *Historische Zeitschrift*, ccxlvi (1988), 1–45.
——, 'Alternatives to the Lutheran Reformation and the rise of Lutheran identity', in A. C. Fix and S. C. Karant-Nunn (eds), *Germania Illustrata: Essays on early Modern Germany Presented to Gerald Strauss* (Kirksville, MO, 1992), 99–120.
——, 'Reformation—Umbruch oder Gipfelpunkt eines Temps des Réformes?', in Bernd Moeller (ed.), *Die frühe Reformation in Deutschland als Umbruch* (Gütersloh, 1998), 13–34.

——, 'Reichs-Staat und frühneuzeitliche Nation der Deutschen oder teilmodernisiertes Reichssystem: Überlegungen zu Charakter und Aktualität des Alten Reiches', *Historische Zeitschrift*, cclxxii (2001), 377–95.

——, *Die Stadt in der Frühen Neuzeit*, 2nd edn (Munich, 2004).

——, 'Das Reich als Verteidigungs- und Friedensorganisation', in *idem* (ed.), *Heiliges Römisches Reich Deutscher Nation 962 bis 1806: Altes Reich und neue Staaten 1495 bis 1806* (Dresden, 2006), 118–33.

——, *Konfessionalisierung und Staatsinteressen: Internationale Beziehungen 1559–1660* (Paderborn, 2007).

—— (ed.), *Konfessioneller Fundamentalismus: Religion als politischer Faktor im europäischen Mächtesystem um 1600* (Munich, 2007).

Schilling, Johannes, 'Hutten und Luther', in Johannes Schilling und Ernst Giese (eds), *Ulrich von Hutten und seine Zeit: Schlüchterner Vorträge zu seinem 500. Geburtstag* (Kassel, 1988), 87–115.

Schindling, Anton, *Humanistische Hochschule und freie Reichsstadt: Gymnasium und Akademie in Strassburg 1538–1621* (Wiesbaden, 1977).

——, 'Reichskirche und Reformation: Zu Glaubensspaltung und Konfessionalisierung in den geistlichen Fürstentümern des Reiches', in Johannes Kunisch, Klaus Luig and Peter Moraw (eds), *Neue Studien zur frühneuzeitlichen Reichsgeschichte* (Berlin, 1987), 81–112.

——, 'Konfessionalisierung und Grenzen von Konfessionalisierbarkeit', in Anton Schindling and Walter Ziegler (eds), *Die Territorien des Reichs im Zeitalter der Reformation und Konfessionalisierung: Land und Konfession 1500–1650*, 7 vols (Münster, 1989–97), vii, 9–44.

—— and Walter Ziegler, (eds), *Die Territorien des Reichs im Zeitalter der Reformation und Konfessionalisierung: Land und Konfession 1500–1650*, 7 vols (Münster, 1989–97).

——, 'Der Passauer Vertrag und die Kirchengüterfrage', in Winfried Becker (ed.), *Der Passauer Vertrag von 1552: Politische Entstehung, reichsrechtliche Bedeutung und konfessionsgeschichtliche Bewertung* (Neustadt an der Aisch, 2003), 105–23.

Schirmer, Uwe, 'Die Finanzen im Kurfürstentum Sachsen (1553–1586)', in Edelmayer, Friedrich and Lanzinner, Maximilian and Rauscher, Peter (eds), *Finanzen und Herrschaft: Materielle Grundlagen fürstlicher Politik in den habsburgischen Ländern und im Heiligen Römischen Reich im 16. Jahrhundert* (Vienna and Munich, 2003), 143–85.

Schlink, Roland, *Hoffmann von Fallerslebens vaterländische und gesellschaftskritische Lyrik*, (Stuttgart 1981).

Schmid, Alois, 'Humanistenbischöfe: Untersuchungen zum vortridentinischen Episkopat in Deutschland', *Römische Quartalschrift für christliche Altertumskunde und Kirchengeschichte*, lxxxvii (1992), 159–92.

——, 'Kurfürst Maximilian I. von Bayern und die Obere Pfalz', in Johannes Laschunger (ed.), *Der Winterkönig: Königlicher Glanz in Amberg* (Amberg, 2004), 116–31.

Schmid, Peter, 'Reichssteuern, Reichsfinanzen und Reichsgewalt in der ersten Hälfte des 16. Jahrhunderts', in Heinz Angermeier (ed.), *Säkulare Aspekte der Reformationszeit* (Munich, 1983), 153–99.

——, *Der gemeine Pfennig von 1495: Vorgeschichte und Entstehung, verfassungsgeschichtliche, politische und finanzielle Bedeutung* (Göttingen, 1989).

Schmidt, Alexander, 'Ein französischer Kaiser? Die Diskussion um die Nationalität des Reichsoberhauptes im 17. Jahrhundert', *Historisches Jahrbuch*, cxxiii (2003), 149–77.

Schmidt, Alexander, *Vaterlandsliebe und Religionskonflikt: Politische Diskurse im Alten Reich (1555–1648)* (Leiden, 2007).

Schmidt, Georg, *Der Städtetag in der Reichsverfassung: Eine Untersuchung zur korporativen Politik der freien und Reichsstädte in der ersten Hälfte des 16. Jahrhunderts* (Stuttgart, 1984).

——, '"Frühkapitalismus" und Zunftwesen: Monopolbestrebungen und Selbstverwaltung in der frühneuzeitlichen Wirtschaft', in Bernhard Kirchgässner (ed.), *Stadt und wirtschaftliche Selbstverwaltung* (Sigmaringen, 1987), 77–114.

——, 'Des Prinzen Vaterland? Wilhelm I. Von Oranien (1533–1584) zwischen Reich, deutscher Nation und den Niederlanden', in Ralph Melville (ed.), *Deutschland und Europa in der Neuzeit: Festschrift für Karl Otmar Fhrh. von Aretin zum 65. Geburtstag*, 2 vols (Stuttgart, 1988), i, 223–39.

——, 'Ulrich von Hutten, der Adel und das Reich um 1500', in Johannes Schilling und Ernst Giese (eds), *Ulrich von Hutten und seine Zeit: Schlüchterner Vorträge zu seinem 500. Geburtstag* (Kassel, 1988), 19–34.

——, 'Die politische Bedeutung der kleineren Reichsstände im 16. Jahrhundert', *Jahrbuch für Geschichte des Feudalismus*, xii (1989), 185–206.

——, *Der Wetterauer Grafenverein: Organisation und Politik einer Reichskorporation zwischen Reformation und Westfälischem Frieden* (Marburg, 1989).

——, 'Städtetag, Städtehanse und frühneuzeitliche Reichsverfassung', in Michael Stolleis (ed.), *Recht, Verfassung und Verwaltung in der frühneuzeitlichen Stadt* (Cologne and Vienna, 1991), 41–61.

——, 'Der Westfälische Frieden: Eine neue Ordnung für das Alte Reich?', in Reinhard Mußgnug (ed.), *Wendemarken in der deutschen Verfassungsgeschichte* (Berlin, 1993), 45–72.

——, 'Integration und Konfessionalisierung: Die Region zwischen Weser und Ems im Deutschland des 16. Jahrhunderts', *Zeitschrift für historische Forschung*, xxi (1994), 1–36.

——, 'Die Städte auf dem frühneuzeitlichen Reichstag', in Bernhard Kirchgässner and Hans-Peter Brecht (eds), *Vom Städtebund zum Zweckverband* (Sigmaringen, 1994), 29–43.

——, 'Deutschland am Beginn der Neuzeit: Reichs-Staat und Kulturnation?', in Christine Roll (ed.), *Recht und Reich im Zeitalter der Reformation* (Frankfurt am Main, 1996), 1–30.

——, 'Schmalkaldischer Bund und "Reichs-Staat"', in *Der Schmalkaldische Bund und die Stadt Schmalkalden* (Schmalkalden, 1996), 3–18.

——, 'Luther und die frühe Reformation: Ein nationales Ereignis?', in Bernd Möller (ed.), *Die frühe Reformation in Deutschland als Umbruch* (Gütersloh, 1998), 54–75.

——, 'Städtehanse und Reich im 16. und 17. Jahrhundert', in Antjektrin Graßmann (ed.), *Niedergang oder Übergang? Zur Spätzeit der Hanse im 16. und 17. Jahrhundert* (Cologne, 1998), 25–46.

——, *Geschichte des Alten Reiches: Staat und Nation in der Frühen Neuzeit 1495–1806* (Munich, 1999).

——, 'Teutsche Kriege: Nationale Deutungsmuster und integrative Wertvorstellungen im frühneuzeitlichen Reich', in Dieter Langewiesche and Georg Schmidt (eds), *Föderative Nation: Deutschlandkonzepte von der Reformation bis zum Ersten Weltkrieg* (Munich, 2000), 33–61.

——, 'Die "deutsche Freiheit" und der Westfälische Friede', in Klaus Garber (ed.), *Der Frieden: Rekonstruktion einer europäischen Vision* (Munich, 2001), 323–47.

——, 'Die frühneuzeitliche Idee "deutsche Nation": Mehrkonfessionalität und säkulare Werte', in Heinz-Gerhard Haupt and Dieter Langewiesche (eds), *Nation und Religion in der deutschen Geschichte* (Frankfurt am Main, 2001), 33–67.

——, 'Das früneuzeitliche Reich: Komplementärer Staat und föderative Nation', *Historische Zeitschrift*, cclxxiii (2001), 371–99.

——, '"Teutsche Libertät" oder "Hispanische Servitut": Deutungsstrategien im Kampf um den evangelischen Glauben und die Reichsverfassung, 1546–1552', In Luise Schorn-Schütte (ed.), *Das Interim 1548/50:. Herrschaftskrise und Glaubenskonflikt* (Gütersloh, 2005), 166–91.

——, '"Aushandeln" oder "Anordnen": Der komplementäre Reichs-Staat und seine Gesetze im 16. Jahrhundert', in Maximilian Lanzinner (ed.), *Der Reichstag 1486–1613: Kommunikation, Wahrnehmung, Öffentlichkeit* (Göttingen, 2006), 95–116.

Schmidt, Georg, 'Die Idee "deutsche Freiheit": Eine Leitvorstellung der politischen Kultur des Alten Reiches', in Georg Schmidt, Martin van Gelderen, Christopher Snigula (eds), *Kollektive Freiheitsvorstellungen im frühneuzeitlichen Europa, 1400–1850* (Frankfurt a. M., 2006), 159–89.

——, 'Der Kampf um Kursachsen, Luthertum und Reichsverfassung (1546–1553): Ein deutscher Freiheitskrieg?', in Volker Leppin (ed.), *Johann Friedrich I., der lutherische Kurfürst* (Gütersloh, 2006), 55–84.

——, 'Das Reich und die deutsche Kulturnation', in Heinz Schilling (ed.), *Heiliges Römisches Reich Deutscher Nation 962 bis 1806: Altes Reich und neue Staaten 1495 bis 1806* (Dresden, 2006).

——, *Der Dreissigjährige Krieg*, 8th edn (Munich, 2010).

——, 'Die Union und das Heilige Römische Reich deutscher Nation', in Albrecht Ernst and Anton Schindling (eds), *Union und Liga 1608/09: Konfessionelle Bündnisse im Reich: Weichenstellung zum Religionskrieg* (Stuttgart, 2010), 9–28.

Schmidt, Heinrich, *Ostfriesland im Schutze des Deiches* (Leer, 1975).

Schmidt, Heinrich Richard, *Reichsstädte, Reich und Reformation: Korporative Religionspolitik 1521–1529/30* (Stuttgart, 1986).

——, *Konfessionalisierung im 16. Jahrhundert* (Munich, 1992).

——, 'Sozialdisziplinierung? Ein Plädoyer für das Ende des Etatismus in der Konfessionalisierungsforschung', *Historische Zeitschrift*, cclxv (1997), 639–82.

Schmidt, Peer, *Spanische Universalmonarchie oder "teutsche Libertet": Das spanische Imperium in der Propaganda des Dreißigjährigen Krieges* (Stuttgart, 2001).

Schmitz, Walter, *Verfassung und Bekenntnis: Die Aachener Wirren im Spiegel der kaiserlichen Politik (1550–1616)* (Frankfurt a. M., 1983).

Schneider, Berhnard Christian, *Ius reformandi: Die Entwicklung eines Staatskirchenrechts von seinen Anfängen bis zum Ende des Alten Reiches* (Tübingen, 2001).

Schneider, Konrad, *Die Münz- und Währungspolititk des Oberrheinischen Reichskrieges im 18. Jahrhundert* (Koblenz, 1995).

Schnell, Rüdiger, 'Deutsche Literatur und deutsches Nationalbewußtsein im Spätmittelalter und Früher Neuzeit', in Joachim Ehlers (ed.), *Ansätze und Diskontinuität deutscher Nationsbildung im Mittelalter* (Sigmaringen, 1989), 247–319.

Schnettger, Matthias, 'Impero romano—Impero germanico: Italienische Perspektiven auf das Reich in der frühen Neuzeit', in Matthias Schnettger (ed.), *Imperium Romanum—Irregulare Corpus—Teutscher Reichs-Staat: Das Alte Reich im Verständnis der Zeitgenossen und der Historiographie* (Mainz, 2002), 53–75.

——, '*Principe sovrano*' oder '*Civitas imperialis*'? *Die Republik Genua und das Alte Reich in der frühen Neuzeit, 1556–1797* (Mainz, 2006).

Schnettger, Matthias, 'Von der "Kleinstaaterei" zum "komplementären Reichs-Staat". Die Reichsverfassungsgeschichtsschreibung seit dem Zweiten Weltkrieg', in Hans-Christof Kraus (ed.), *Geschichte der Politik: Alte und neue Wege* (Munich, 2007), 129–54.

Schnitter, Helmut, *Volk und Landesdefension: Volksaufgebote, Defensionswerke, Landmilizen in den deutschen Territorien vom 15. bis zum 18. Jahrhundert* (Berlin, 1977).

Schnurr, Eva-Maria, *Religionskonflikt und Öffentlichkeit: Eine Mediengeschichte des Kölner Kriegs (1582 bis 1590)* (Cologne, 2009).

Schobinger, Jean-Pierre (ed.), *Die Philosophie des 17. Jahrhunderts: Allgemeine Themen, Iberische Halbinsel, Italien*, 2 vols (Basle,1998).

Schock-Werner, Barbara, *Die Bauten im Fürstbistum Würzburg unter Julius Echter von Mespelbrunn 1573–1617: Struktur, Organisation, Finanzierung und künstlerische Bewertung* (Regensburg, 2005).

Schoeck, Richard J., 'Agricola and Erasmus. Erasmus' heritage of northern humanism', in Fokke Akkerman and Arie Johan Vanderjagt (eds), *Rodolphus Agricola Phrisius 1444–1485* (Leiden, 1988), 181–8.

——, *Erasmus of Europe: The prince of humanists, 1501–1536* (Edinburgh, 1993).

Scholzen, Reinhard, *Franz von Sickingen: Ein adeliges Leben im Spannungsfeld zwischen Städten und Territorien* (Kaiserslautern, 1996).

Schönemann, Bernd, *Zur Rezeption des Dreißigjährigen Krieges in Literatur und Schule vom Kaiserreich bis zum Nationalsozialismus* (Eichstätt, 2000).

Schönstädt, Hans-Jürgen, *Antichrist, Weltheilsgeschehen und Gottes Werkzeug: Römische Kirche, Reformation und Luther im Spiegel des Reformationsjubiläums 1617* (Wiesbaden, 1978).

Schormann, Gerhard, *Hexenprozesse in Deutschland* (Göttingen, 1981).

——, *Der Dreißigjährige Krieg* (Göttingen, 1985).

——, 'Der Dreißigjährige Krieg 1618–1648', in Wolfgang Reinhard (ed.), *Gebhardt: Handbuch der deutschen Geschichte, Band 10*, 10th edn (Stuttgart, 2001), 207–79.

Schorn-Schütte, Luise, 'Die Drei-Stände-Lehre im reformatorischen Umbruch', in Bernd Moeller (ed.), *Die frühe Reformation in Deutschland als Umbruch* (Gütersloh, 1998), 435–61.

Schröcker, Alfred, *Die Deutsche Nation: Beobachtungen zur politischen Propaganda des ausgehenden 15. Jahrhunderts* (Lübeck, 1974).

Schubert, Ernst, 'Die Stellung der Kurfürsten in der spätmittelalterlichen Reichsverfassung', *Jahrbuch für westdeutsche Landesgeschichte*, i (1975), 97–128.

——, *Arme Leute, Bettler und Gauner im Franken des 18. Jahrhunderts* (Neustadt an der Aisch, 1983).

——, 'Mobilität ohne Chance: Die Ausgrenzung des fahrenden Volkes', in Winfried Schulze (ed), *Ständische Gesellschaft und soziale Mobilität* (Munich, 1988), 113–64.

——, *Einführung in die Grundprobleme der deutschen Geschichte im Spätmittelalter* (Darmstadt, 1992).

Schubert, Friedrich Heinrich, *Die Deutschen Reichstage in der Staatslehre der Frühen Neuzeit* (Göttingen, 1966).

Schubert, Friedrich Hermann, *Ludwig Camerarius, 1573–1651: Eine Biographie* (Kallmünz, 1955).

Schulte, Alois, *Der Adel und die deutsche Kirche im Mittelalter*, 2nd edn (Stuttgart, 1922).

Schultz, Hans, *Die Bestrebungen der Sprachgesellschaften des XVII. Jahrhunderts für Reinigung der deutschen Sprache*, (Göttingen, 1888).

Schultz, Helga, *Soziale und politische Auseinandersetzungen in Rostock im 18. Jahrhundert* (Weimar, 1974).

Schulze, Manfred, *Fürsten und Reformation: Geistliche Reformpolitik weltlicher Fürsten vor der Reformation* (Tübingen, 1991).

Schulze, Winfried, *Landesdefension und Staatsbildung: Studien zum Kriegswesen des inner-österreichischen Territorialstaates, 1564–1619* (Vienna, 1973).

——, 'Die Heeresreform der Oranier', *Zeitschrift für Historische Forschung*, i (1974), 233–9.

——, 'Reichstage und Reichssteuern im späten 16. Jahrhundert', *Zeitschrift für historische Forschung*, ii (1975), 43–58.

——, *Reich und Türkengefahr im späten 16. Jahrhundert: Studien zu den politischen und gesellschaftlichen Auswirkungen einer äußeren Bedrohung* (Munich, 1978).

——, *Bäuerlicher Widerstand und feudale Herrschaft in der frühen Neuzeit* (Stuttgart, 1980).

——, 'Die deutschen Landesdefensionen im 16. und 17. Jahrhundert', in Barbara Stollberg-Rilinger (ed.), *Staatsverfassung und Heeresverfassung in der europäischen Geschichte der frühen Neuzeit* (Berlin, 1986), 129–49.

——, 'Concordia, discordia, tolerantia: Deutsche Politik im konfessionellen Zeitalter', in Johannes Kunisch, Klaus Luig and Peter Moraw (eds), *Neue Studien zur frühneuzeitlichen Reichsgeschichte* (Berlin, 1987), 43–79.

——, *Deutsche Geschichte im 16. Jahrhundert* (Frankfurt am Main, 1987).

——, *Einführung in die Neuere Geschichte* (Stuttgart, 1987).

——, *Deutsche Geschichtswissenschaft nach 1945* (Munich, 1989).

——, 'Untertanenrevolten, Hexenverfolgungen und "kleine Eiszeit": Eine Krisenzeit um 1600?', in Bernd Roeck (ed.), *Venedig und Oberdeutschland in der Renaissance: Beziehungen zwischen Kunst und Wirtschaft* (Sigmaringen, 1993), 289–309.

——, 'Konfessionsfundamentalismus in Europa um 1600: Zwischen *discordia* und *compositio*; Zur Deutung des konfessionellen Konflikts im katholischen Lager', in Heinz Schilling (ed.), *Konfessioneller Fundamentalismus: Religion als politischer Faktor im europäischen Mächtesystem um 1600* (Munich, 2007), 135–48.

Schunka, Alexander, 'Glaubensflucht als Migrationsoption: Konfessionell motivierte Migrationen in der Frühen Neuzeit', *Geschichte in Wissenschaft und Unterricht*, lvi (2005), 547–64.

Schütte, Ulrich, *Das Schloß als Wehranlage: Befestigte Schloßbauten der frühen Neuzeit im alten Reich* (Darmstadt, 1994).

Schwaiger, Georg, *Kardinal Franz Wilhelm von Wartenberg als Bischof von Regensburg (1649–1661)* (Munich, 1954).

Schwennicke, Andreas, *'Ohne Steuer kein Staat': Zur Entwicklung und politischen Funktion des Steuerrechts in den Territorien des Heiligen Römischen Reichs (1500–1800)* (Frankfurt a. M., 1996).

Scott, Tom, *Thomas Müntzer: Theology and revolution in the German Reformation* (London, 1989).

——, 'The common people in the German Reformation', *Historical Journal*, xxxiv (1991), 183–92.

——, 'The communal Reformation between town and country', in Hans R. Guggisberg (ed.), *Die Reformation in Deutschland und Europa: Interpretationen und Debatten* (Gütersloh, 1993), 175–92.

——, 'Economic landscapes', in Bob Scribner (ed.), *Germany: A new social and economic history 1450–1630* (London, 1996), 1–31.

——, *Society and economy in Germany, 1300–1600* (Houndmills, 2002).

Scribner, Robert W., 'Civic unity and the Reformation in Erfurt', *Past and Present*, lxvi (1975), 29-60.

Scribner, Robert W., 'Why was there no Reformation in Cologne?', *Bulletin of the Institute of Historical Research*, xlix (1976), 217–41.

——, 'The Reformation as a social movement', in Wolfgang J. Mommsen (ed.), *Stadtbürgertum und Adel in der Reformation: Studien zur Sozialgeschichte der Reformation in England und Deutschland* (Stuttgart, 1979), 49–79.

——, *The German Reformation* (London, 1986).

——, 'Police and the territorial state in sixteenth-century Württemberg', in E. I. Kouri and Tom Scott (eds), *Politics and society in Reformation Europe* (Houndmills, 1987), 103–20.

—— 'The Reformation movements in Germany', in G. R. Elton (ed.), *The new Cambridge modern history*, Vol. 2, 2nd edn (Cambridge, 1990), 69–93.

——, *For the sake of simple folk: Popular propaganda for the German Reformation*, 2nd edn (Oxford, 1994)

——, 'Communities and the nature of power', in *idem* (ed.), *Germany: A new social and economic history*, Vol, 1: *1450–1630* (London, 1996), 291–326.

——, *Religion and culture in Germany (1400–1800)*, ed. Lyndal Roper (Leiden, 2001).

Seibt, Ferdinand, *Karl V.: Der Kaiser und die Reformation* (Berlin, 1990).

Seidel, Robert, *Späthumanismus in Schlesien: Caspar Dornau (1577–1631): Leben und Werk* (Tübingen, 1994).

Seifert, Arno, 'Der jesuitische Bildungskanon im Lichte zeitgenössischer Kritik', *Zeitschrift für bayerische Landesgeschichte*, xlvii (1984), 43–75.

Selge, Kurt-Viktor, 'Luther und die gesellschaftlichen Kräfte seiner Zeit', in Erwin Iserloh and Gerhard Müller (eds), *Luther und die politische Welt* (Stuttgart, 1984) 219–26.

Shaw, Stanford J., *History of the Ottoman Empire and modern Turkey*, 2 vols (Cambridge, 1976–7).

Sicken, Bernhard, 'Ferdinand I. (1556–1564)', in Anton Schindling and Walter Ziegler (eds), *Die Kaiser der Neuzeit 1519–1918* (Munich, 1990), 55–77.

Sieber-Lehmann, Claudius, '"Teutsche Nation" und Eidgenossenschaft: Der Zusammenhang zwischen Türken- und Burgunderkriegen', *Historische Zeitschrift*, ccliii (1991), 561–602.

Siedschlag, Karl, *Der Einfluß der niederländisch-neustoischen Ethik in der politischen Theorie zur Zeit Sullys und Richelieus* (Berlin, 1978).

Silver, Larry, *Marketing Maximilian: The visual ideology of a Holy Roman Emperor* (Princeton, 2008).

Simon, Thomas, *'Gute Policey': Ordnungsleitbilder und Zielvorstellungen politischen Handelns in der Frühen Neuzeit* (Frankfurt am Main, 2004).

Skinner, Quentin, *The foundations of modern political thought*, 2 vols (Cambridge, 1978).

——, *Liberty before liberalism* (Cambridge, 1998).

Smend, Rudolf, *Das Reichskammergericht* (Weimar, 1911).

Smith, Helmut Walser, *The continuities of German history: Nation, religion, and race across the long nineteenth century* (Cambridge, 2008).

Smolinsky, Heribert, 'Kirchenreform als Bildungsreform im Spätmittelalter und in der frühen Neuzeit', in Harald Dickerhof (ed.), *Bildungs- und schulgeschichtliche Studien zu Spätmittelalter, Reformation und konfessionellem Zeitalter* (Wiesbaden, 1994), 35–51.

Soliday, Gerald L., *A community in conflict: Frankfurt society in the seventeenth and early eighteenth centuries* (Hanover, NH, 1974).

Spierenburg, Pieter, 'The sociogenesis of confinement and its development in early modern Europe', in *idem* (ed.), *The emergence of carceral institutions: prisons, galleys and lunatic asylums 1500–1990* (Rotterdam, 1984), 9–77.

Spindler, Max et al. (eds), *Handbuch der Bayerischen Geschichte*, 4 vols in 6 (Munich, 1967–75).

Spitz, Lewis W., *Conrad Celtis. The German arch-humanist* (Cambridge, MA, 1957).

Spohnholz, Jesse, *The tactics of toleration: A refugee community in the age of religious wars* (Newark, DE and Lanham, MD, 2011).

Stadler, Peter, 'Die Schweiz und das Reich in der Frühen Neuzeit', in Volker Press (ed.), *Alternativen zur Reichsverfassung in der Frühen Neuzeit?* (Munich, 1995), 131–41.

Stadtwald, Kurt, *Roman popes and German patriots: Antipapalism in the politics of the German humanist movement from Gregor Heimburg to Martin Luther* (Geneva, 1996).

Stanelle, Udo, *Die Hildesheimer Stiftsfehde in Berichten und Chroniken des 16. Jahrhunderts: Ein Beitrag zur niedersächsischen Geschichtsschreibung* (Hildesheim, 1982).

Stauber, Reinhard, 'Nationalismus vor dem Nationalismus? Eine Bestandsaufnahme der Forschung zu "Nation" und "Nationalismus" in der Frühen Neuzeit', *Geschichte in Wissenschaft und Unterricht*, xlvii (1996), 139–65.

Stayer, James M., 'The Anabaptists and the sects', in G. R. Elton (ed.), *The new Cambridge modern history*, vol. 2, 2nd edn (Cambridge, 1990), 118–43.

Stein, Leon, 'Religion and patriotism in German peace dramas during the Thirty Years' War', *Central European History*, iv (1971), 131–48.

Stephens, W. P., *Zwingli: An introduction to his thought* (Oxford, 1992).

Stieve, Felix, *Die Politik Baierns, 1591–1607*, 2 vols (Munich, 1878–83).

Stievermann, Dieter, 'Sozial- und verfassungsgeschichtliche Voraussetzungen Martin Luthers und der Reformation: Der landesherrliche Rat in Kursachsen, Kurmainz und Mansfeld', in Volker Press and Dieter Stievermann (eds), *Martin Luther: Probleme seiner Zeit*, (Stuttgart, 1986), 137–76.

——, 'Southern German courts around 1500', in Ronald G. Asch and Adolf M. Birke (eds), *Princes, patronage and the nobility: The court at the beginning of the modern age c.1450–1650* (Oxford, 1991), 157–72.

Stöhr, Ulrich, *Die Verwendung des 'Kleinen' Kirchengutes in der Landgrafschaft Hessen im Zeitalter der Reformation* (Kassel, 1996).

Stoll, Christoph, *Sprachgesellschaften im Deutschland des 17. Jahrhunderts: Fruchtbringende Gesellschaft, Aufrichtige Gesellschaft von der Tannen, Deutschgesinnte Genossenschaft, Hirten- und Blumenorden an der Pegnitz, Elbschwanenorden* (Munich, 1973).

Stollberg-Rilinger, Barbara, *Des Kaisers alte Kleider: Verfassungsgeschichte und Symbolsprache des Alten Reiches* (Munich, 2008).

Stolleis, Michael, *Arcana imperii und Ratio status: Bemerkungen zur politischen Theorie des frühen 17. Jahrhunderts* (Göttingen, 1980).

——, *Pecunia nervus rerum: Zur Staatsfinanzierung in der frühen Neuzeit* (Frankfurt am Main, 1983).

——, *Geschichte des öffentlichen Rechts in Deutschland*, 3 vols (Munich, 1988–99).

Stoob, Heinz, *Geschichte Dithmarschens im Regentenzeitalter* (Heide in Holstein, 1959).

Stone, Daniel, *The Polish-Lithuanian state, 1386–1795* (Seattle and London, 2001).

Strauss, Gerald, *Sixteenth-century Germany: Its topography and topographers* (Madison, 1959).

——, *Nuremberg in the sixteenth century* (Columbus, OH, 1966).

—— (ed.), *Manifestations of discontent in Germany on the eve of the Reformation* (Bloomington, IN and London, 1971).

——, 'Success and failure in the German Reformation', *Past and Present*, lxvii (1975), 30–63.

Strauss, Gerald, *Luther's house of learning: Indoctrination of the young in the German Reformation* (Baltimore, MD, 1978).

——, *Law, resistance and the state: The opposition to Roman law in Reformation Germany* (Princeton, NJ, 1986).

——, 'Ideas of *Reformatio* and *Renovatio* from the Middle Ages to the Reformation', in Thomas A. Brady, Heiko A. Oberman, James D. Tracy (eds), *Handbook of European history, 1400–1600: Late Middle Ages, Renaissance and Reformation*, 2 vols (Leiden, 1994–95), ii, 1–30.

Sugar, Peter F., *Southeastern Europe under Ottoman rule, 1354–1804* (Seattle, 1977).

Suvanto, Pekka, *Die deutsche Politik Oxenstiernas und Wallenstein* (Helsinki, 1979).

Tacitus, Cornelius, *Germania*, ed. and transl. by Gerhard Perl (Darmstadt, 1990).

Taddey, Gerhard, *Lexikon der deutschen Geschichte: Ereignisse—Insitutionen—Personen: Von den Anfängen bis zur Kapitulation 1945*, 3rd edn (Stuttgart, 1998).

Thamer, Hans-Ulrich, 'Das Heilige Römische Reich als politisches Argument im 19. und 20. Jahrhundert', in Heinz Schilling (ed.), *Heiliges Römisches Reich Deutscher Nation 962 bis 1806: Altes Reich und neue Staaten 1495 bis 1806* (Dresden, 2006), 382–95.

Theibault, John, 'The demography of the Thirty Years War re-visited: Günther Franz and his critics', *German History*, xv (1997), 1–21.

Thomas, Heinz, *Deutsche Geschichte des Spätmittelalters 1250–1500* (Stuttgart, 1983).

——, 'Das Identitätsproblem der Deutschen im Mittelalter', *Geschichte in Wissenschaft und Unterricht*, xliii (1992), 135–56.

Tillinghast, Pardon E., 'An aborted reformation: Germans and the papacy in the mid-fifteenth century', *Journal of Medieval History*, ii (1976), 57–79.

Tracy, James D., *Emperor Charles V, impresario of war: Campaign strategy, international finance, and domestic politics* (Cambridge, 2002).

Trapp, Wolfgang, *Kleines Handbuch der Maße, Zahlen, Gewichte und der Zeitrechnung*, 2nd edn (Stuttgart, 1996).

Troßbach, Werner, 'Die Reichsgerichte in der Sicht bäuerlicher Untertanen', in Bernhard Diestelkamp (ed.), *Das Reichskammergericht in der deutschen Geschichte: Stand der Forschung, Forschungsperspektiven* (Cologne, 1990), 129–42.

Trüdinger, Karl, *Luthers Briefe und Gutachten an weltliche Obrigkeiten zur Durchführung der Reformation* (Münster, 1975).

Trunz, Erich, 'Der deutsche Späthumanismus um 1600 als Standeskultur', in Richard Alewyn (ed.), *Deutsche Barockforschung* (Cologne and Berlin, 1965), 147–81.

Tuck, Richard, *Philosophy and government 1572–1651* (Cambridge, 1993).

Ullmann, Sabine, *Geschichte auf der langen Bank: Die Kommissionen des Reichshofrats unter Kaiser Maximilian II. (1564–1576)* (Mainz, 2006).

Ulmer, Rivka, *Turmoil, trauma, and triumph: The Fettmilch uprising in Frankfurt am Main (1612–1616) according to Megillas Vintz: A critical edition of the Yiddish and Hebrew text including an English translation* (New York, 2001).

Ulmschneider, Helgard, *Götz von Berlichingen: Ein adeliges Leben der deutschen Renaissance* (Sigmaringen, 1974).

Urban, William L., *Dithmarschen: A medieval peasant republic* (Lewiston, NY, 1991).

Van Dülmen, Richard, *Reformation als Revolution* (Munich, 1977).

——, *Theater des Schreckens: Gerichtspraxis und Strafrituale in der frühen Neuzeit* (Munich, 1985).

——, *Kultur und Alltag in der frühen Neuzeit*, 3 vols (Munich, 1990–4).

Vasold, Manfred, 'Die deutschen Bevölkerungsverluste während des Dreißigjährigen Krieges', *Zeitschrift für Bayerische Landesgeschichte*, lvi (1993), 147–60.

Verdenhalven, Fritz, *Alte Maße, Münzen und Gewichte aus dem deutschen Sprachgebiet* (Neustadt an der Aisch, 1968).

Vocelka, Karl, *Die politische Propaganda Kaiser Rudolfs II. (1576–1612)* (Vienna, 1981).

Vogler, Günter, 'Der deutsche Bauernkrieg und die Verhandlungen des Reichstags zu Speyer 1526', in Rudolf Vierhaus (ed.), *Herrschaftsverträge, Wahlkapitulationen, Fundamentalgesetze* (Göttingen, 1977), 173–91.

——, 'Reformation, Fürstenmacht und Volksbewegung vom Ende des Bauernkrieges bis zum Augsburger "Religionsfrieden" (1525/26 bis 1555)', in Adolf Laube and Günter Vogler (eds), *Deutsche Geschichte, Band 3: Die Epoche des Übergangs vom Feudalismus zum Kapitalismus von den siebziger Jahren des 15. Jahrhunderts bis 1789* (Berlin, 1983), 189–238.

——, 'Imperial City Nuremberg, 1524–1525: The reform movement in transition', in R. Po-chia Hsia (ed.), *The German people and the Reformation* (Ithaca, 1988), 33–49.

——, 'Ulrich von Hutten—Ritter, Reformer, Rebell?' in *Ulrich von Hutten: Mit Feder und Schwert: Katalog zur Ausstellung seines 500. Geburtstages 1988* (Frankfurt an der Oder, 1988), 7–38.

——, 'Das Konzept "deutsche frühbürgerliche Revolution". Genese—Aspekte—kritische Bilanz'. *Sitzungsberichte der Leibniz-Sozietät*, xlviii (2001), 87–117.

Voigt, Johannes, *Deutsches Hofleben im Zeitalter der Reformation* (Dresden, 1927).

Völker, Klaus, *Faust. Ein deutscher Mann: Die Geburt einer Legende und ihr Fortleben in den Köpfen* (Berlin, 1975).

Voltmer, Rita, ' "Germany's first 'superhunt'?" Rezeption und Konstruktion der so genannten Trierer Verfolgungen, 16.–21. Jahrhundert', in Katrin Moeller (ed.), *Realität und Mythos: Hexenverfolgung und Rezeptionsgeschichte* (Hamburg, 2003), 225–58.

Wagner, Helmut, 'Die innerdeutschen Grenzen', in A. Demandt (ed.), *Deutschlands Grenzen in der Geschichte*, 2nd edn (Munich, 1991), 240–84.

Walinski-Kiehl, Robert, 'Reformation history and political mythology in the German Democratic Republic, 1949–89', *European History Quarterly*, xxxiv (2004), 43–67.

Walz, Herbert, *Deutsche Literatur der Reformationszeit: Eine Einführung* (Darmstadt, 1988).

Wandruszka, Adam, *Reichspatriotismus und Reichspolitik zur Zeit des Prager Friedens von 1635* (Graz and Cologne, 1955).

Warmbrunn, Paul, *Zwei Konfessionen in einer Stadt: Das Zusammenleben von Katholiken und Protestanten in den paritätischen Reichsstädten Augsburg, Biberach, Ravensburg und Dinkelsbühl von 1548 bis 1648* (Wiesbaden, 1983).

Wartenberg, Günther, 'Zum "Erasmianismus" am Dresdener Hof Georgs des Bärtigen', *Nederlands Archief voor Kerkgeschiednis*, NS lvi (1986), 2–16.

Watanabe-O'Kelly, Helen, *Triumphall shews: Tournaments at German-speaking courts in their European context 1560–1730* (Berlin, 1992).

——, *Court Culture in Dresden: From Renaissance to Baroque* (Houndmills, 2002).

Weber, Hubert, 'Melchior Goldast von Haiminsfeld und die Anfänge der Walther-Philologie im 17. Jahrhundert. Eine Würdigung', in Robert Luff (ed.), *Mystik, Überlieferung, Naturkunde: Gegenstände und Methoden mediävistischer Forschungspraxis* (Hildesheim, 2002), 17–35.

Weber, Matthias, *Das Verhältnis Schlesiens zum Alten Reich in der frühen Neuzeit* (Cologne, 1992).

——, *Die Reichspolizeiordnungen von 1530, 1548 und 1577. Historische Einführung und Edition* (Frankfurt am Main, 2002).

Wehler, Hans-Ulrich, *Deutsche Gesellschaftsgeschichte*, 5 vols (Munich, 1987–2008).

Wells, C. J., *German: A Linguistic History to 1945* (Oxford, 1985).

Westphal, Siegrid, 'Frauen der Frühen Neuzeit und die deutsche Nation', in Dieter Langewische and Gerog Schmidt (eds), *Föderative Nation: Deutschlandkonzepte von der Reformation bis zum Ersten Weltkrieg* (Munich, 2000), 363–85.

Whaley, Joachim, *Religious toleration and social change in Hamburg 1529–1819* (Cambridge, 1985).

——, 'The Old Reich in modern memory: Recent controversies concerning the "relevance" of early modern German history', in Christian Emden and David Midgley (eds), *German literature, history and the nation* (Frankfurt a. M., 2004), 25–49.

——, '*Reich, Nation, Volk*: Early Modern Perspectives', Modern Languages Review, ci (2006), 442–55.

——, 'Religiöse Toleranz als allgemeines Menschenrecht in der Frühen Neuzeit?', in Georg Schmidt, Martin van Gelderen and Christopher Snigula (eds), *Kollektive Freiheitsvorstellungen im frühneuzeitlichen Europa, 1400–1850* (Frankfurt a. M., 2006), 397–416.

——, 'Kulturelle Toleranz—die deutsche Nation im europäischen Vergleich', in Georg Schmidt (ed.), *Die deutsche Nation im frühneuzeitlichen Europa: Politische Ordnung und kulturelle Identität?* (Munich, 2010), 201–24.

——, 'A German nation? National and confessional identities before the Thirty Years War', in R. J. W. Evans, Michael Schaich, and Peter H. Wilson (eds), *The Holy Roman Empire 1495-1806* (Oxford, 2011) 303–21.

Wiese, Bernd and Norbert Zils, *Deutsche Kulturgeographie: Werden, Wandel und Bewahrung deutscher Kulturlandschaften* (Herford, 1987)

Wiesflecker, Hermann, *Maximilian I.: Die Fundamente des habsburgischen Weltreiches* (Munich and Vienna, 1991).

Wiesflecker-Friedhuber, Inge (ed.), *Quellen zur Geschichte Maximilians I. und seiner Zeit* (Darmstadt, 1996).

Wiesinger, Peter, 'Regionale und überregionale Sprachausformung im Deutschen vom 12. bis 15. Jahrhundert unter dem Aspekt der Nationsbildung', in Joachim Ehlers (ed.), *Ansätze und Diskontinuität deutscher Nationsbildung im Mittelalter* (Sigmaringen, 1989), 321–43.

Williams, Ann, 'Mediterranean conflict', in Metin Kunt and Christine Woodhead (eds), *Suleyman the Magnificent: The Ottoman Empire in the early modern world* (London, 1995), 39–54.

Williams, G. H., *The Radical Reformation*, 3rd edn (Kirksville, MO, 1992).

Willoweit, Dietmar, 'Hermann Conring', in M. Stolleis (ed.), *Staatsdenker im 17. und 18. Jahrhundert: Reichspublizistik, Politik, Naturrecht*, 2nd edn (Frankfurt am Main, 1987), 129–47.

——, *Deutsche Verfassungsgeschichte: Vom Frankenreich bis zur Wiedervereinigung Deutschlands*, 4th edn (Munich, 2001).

Wilson, Peter H., *The Holy Roman Empire 1495–1806* (Houndmills, 1999).

——, *From Reich to revolution: German history, 1558–1806* (Houndmills, 2004).

——, *Europe's tragedy: A history of the Thirty Years War* (London, 2009).

Winkelbauer, Thomas, *Ständefreiheit und Fürstenmacht: Länder und Untertanen des Hauses Habsburg im konfessionllen Zeitalter*, 2 vols (Vienna, 2003).

Winkler, Gerhard B., 'Der Regensburger Konvent (27. Juni–7. Juli 1524) und die deutsche Glaubensspaltung', in Remigius Bäumer (ed.), *Reformatio Ecclesiae: Beiträge zu kirchlichen Reformbemühungen von der Alten Kirche bis zur Neuzeit* (Paderborn, 1980), 413–25.

——, 'Das Regensburger Religionsgespräch 1541', in Dieter Albrecht (ed.), *Regensburg, Stadt der Reichstage: Vom Mittelalter zur Neuzeit* (Regensburg, 1994), 72–87.

Wirsching, Andreas, 'Konfessionalisierung der Außenpolitik: Die Kurpfalz und der Beginn der französischen Religionskriege, 1559–1562', *Historisches Jahrbuch*, cvi (1986), 333–60.

Wohlfeil, Rainer, 'Reformation oder frühbürgerliche Reformation', in *idem* (ed.), *Reformation oder frühbürgerliche Revolution?* (Munich, 1972).

——, *Einführung in die Geschichte der deutschen Reformation* (Munich, 1982).

Wolff, Karl, 'Der Straßburger Kapitelstreit (1584–1604) und der Wetterauer Grafenverein', *Nassauische Annalen*, lxviii (1957), 127–55.

Wolfrum, Edgar, *Krieg und Frieden in der Neuzeit: Vom Westfälischen Frieden bis zum Zweiten Weltkrieg* (Darmstadt, 2003).

Wolgast, Eike, *Hochstift und Reformation: Studien zur Geschichte der Reichskirche zwischen 1517 und 1648* (Stuttgart, 1995).

——, 'Die deutschen Territorialfürsten und die frühe Reformation', in Bernd Moeller (ed.), *Die frühe Reformation in Deutschland als Umbruch* (Gütersloh, 1998), 407–34.

——, 'Die Neuordnung von Kirche und Welt in den deutschen Utopien der Frühreformation (1521–1526/27)', in Karl-Hermann Kästner, Knut Wolfgang Nörr and Klaus Schlaich (eds), *Festschrift für Martin Heckel zum siebzigsten Geburtstag* (Tübingen, 1999), 659–79.

——, 'Geistiges Profil und politische Ziele des Heidelberger Späthumanismus', in Christoph Strohm (ed.), *Späthumanismus und reformierte Konfession: Theologie, Jurisprudenz und Philosophie in Heidelberg an der Wende zum 17. Jahrhundert* (Tübingen, 2006), 1–25.

——, 'Religionsfrieden als politisches Problem der frühen Neuzeit', *Historische Zeitschrift*, cclxxxii (2006), 59–96.

——, 'Konfessionsbestimmte Faktoren der Reichs- und Außenpolitik der Kurpfalz, 1559–1620', in Heinz Schilling (ed.), *Konfessioneller Fundamentalismus: Religion als politischer Faktor im europäischen Mächtesystem um 1600* (Munich, 2007), 167–87.

Wollgast, Siegfried, *Philosophie in Deutschland zwischen Reformation und Aufklärung 1550–1650* (Berlin, 1988).

Wrede, Martin, *Das Reich und seine Feinde: Politische Feindbilder in der reichspatriotischen Publizistik zwischen Westfälischem Frieden und Siebenjährigem Krieg* (Mainz, 2004).

——, 'Der Kaiser, das Reich, die deutsche Nation—und ihre "Feinde": Natiogenese, Reichsidee und der "Durchbruch des Politischen" im Jahrhundert nach dem Westfälischen Frieden', *Historische Zeitschrift*, cclxxx (2005), 83–116.

Wunder, Heide, 'Der samländische Bauernaufstand von 1525: Entwurf für eine sozialgeschichtliche Forschungsstrategie' in Rainer Wohlfeil (ed.), *Der Bauernkrieg 1524–26: Bauernkrieg und Reformation* (Munich, 1975), 143–76.

Yates, Frances A., *The Rosicrucian enlightenment* (London, 1972).

Zagorin, Perez, *Ways of lying: Dissimulation, persecution, and conformity in early modern Europe* (Cambridge, MA, 1990).

Zeeden, Ernst Walter, 'Das Zeitalter der Glaubenskämpfe (1555–1648), in Herbert Grundmann (ed.), *Gebhardt: Handbuch der Deutschen Geschichte, Band 2,* 9th edn (Stuttgart, 1970), 119–239.

Zeydel, Edwin Hermann, *The Holy Roman Empire in German literature* (New York, 1918).

Ziegler, Walter, 'Reformation und Klosterauflösung: Ein ordensgeschichtlicher Vergleich', in Kapsar Elm (ed.), *Reformbemühungen und Observanzbestrebungen im spätmittelalterlichen Ordenswesen* (Berlin, 1989) 585–614.

——, 'Die Hochstifte des Reiches im konfessionellen Zeitalter 1520–1618', *Römische Quartalschrift*, lxxxvii (1992), 252–81.

Ziegler, Walter, 'Religion und Politik im Umfeld des Regensburger Religionsgesprächs von 1541', in Hans-Martin Barth (ed.), *Das Regensburger Religionsgespräch im Jahr 1541: Rückblick und aktuelle ökumenische Perspektiven* (Regensburg, 1992), 9–30.

Zimmermann, Ludwig (ed.), *Der Ökonomische Staat Landgraf Wilhelms IV., Band 2* (Marburg, 1934).

Zmora, Hillay, *State and nobility in early modern Germany: The knightly feud in Franconia, 1440–1567* (Cambridge 1998).

Zwierlein, Cornel A., 'Heidelberg und "der Westen" um 1600', in Christoph Strohm (ed.), *Späthumanismus und reformierte Konfession: Theologie, Jurisprudenz und Philosophie in Heidelberg an der Wende zum 17. Jahrhundert* (Tübingen, 2006), 27–92.

Index

Words marked by an asterisk may be found in the Glossary

9 780199 688821